MILITARY AIRC

MILITARY AIRCRAFT MARKINGS 2018
Howard J Curtis

Crécy Publishing Ltd

This 39th edition published by Crécy Publishing Ltd 2018

© Crécy Publishing Ltd 2018

© Photographs by Howard J Curtis (HJC)
unless otherwise credited

ISBN 9781910809204

Printed in England by Martins the Printer

Crecy Publishing Ltd
1a Ringway Trading Est
Shadowmoss Rd
Manchester
M22 5LH
Tel +44 (0)161 499 0024
www.crecy.co.uk

Front cover:
The Embraer Phenom has entered RAF
service to provide flight training for pilots
of multi-engine aircraft, taking over from
the King Air 200. The aircraft pictured was
the first to arrive, still carrying the civilian
registration (PR-PHK) used for its ferry
flight when seen at the 2017 Royal
International Air Tattoo, Fairford; it is now
ZM333 and is based with No 3 FTS at
RAF Cranwell. The fifth and final RAF
Phenom (ZM337) arrived at RAF
Cranwell on 30th January 2018.
(C) Jesus Moreno via Air Team Images

CONTENTS

This 39th annual edition of *abc Military Aircraft Markings*, follows the pattern of previous years and lists in alphabetical and numerical order the aircraft that carry a United Kingdom military registration and which are normally based, or might be seen, in the UK. It also includes airworthy and current RAF/RN/Army aircraft that are based permanently or temporarily overseas. Aircraft used as targets on MoD ranges to which access is restricted, and UK military aircraft that have been permanently grounded overseas and unlikely to return to Britain have generally been omitted.

Aircraft in UK military service which carry civil registrations are listed, as are historic aircraft wearing overseas markings which are based in the UK or likely to be seen in the UK. All aircraft carrying Irish military markings are listed in a separate section. Similarly, aircraft belonging to the armed forces or governments of foreign countries are listed, including American military aircraft based in the UK and Europe.

In the main, the registrations listed are those markings presently displayed on the aircraft. Where an aircraft carries a false registration it is quoted in *italic type*. Very often these registrations are carried by replicas, which are denoted by <R> after the type. The manufacturer and aircraft type are given, together with recent alternative, previous, secondary or civil identity shown in round brackets. The operating unit and its based location, along with any known unit and code markings, in square brackets, are given as accurately as possible. Where aircraft carry special or commemorative markings, a $ indicates this. To help identification of RN bases and landing platforms on ships, a list of tail-letter codes with their appropriate name, helicopter code number, ship pennant number and type of vessel, is included; as is a helicopter code number/ship's tail-letter code grid cross-reference.

Up-to-date code changes, for example when aircraft move between units, might not be as printed here because of subsequent events, but code lists are regularly updated and uploaded to the 'Military Aircraft Markings' web site, www.militaryaircraftmarkings.co.uk, from which monthly UK updates can also be accessed. Airframes which will not appear in the next edition because of sale, accident, etc., have their fates, where known, shown in italic type in the *locations* column.

Following the significant changes made from the 2016 edition onwards, it is now possible to include fates for all aircraft listed and so this 39th edition includes details of, for example, American aircraft going to storage at AMARG at Davis-Monthan Air Force Base. Additionally, the extra space has enabled the inclusion of previous identities and these have been further extended across the whole publication where space permits.

2017 saw continued change in UK military aviation. As regards front line aircraft, the Tornado fleet now has just over a year left in service, while the last Typhoon for the RAF entered the production line at Warton and indeed the Typhoon itself is now seeing early models being reduced to produce with a line set up at Coningsby. In early 2017 it was also decided to recode the whole Typhoon fleet using the 'last three' of the registration and this changeover is virtually complete with a fleet that now frequently has no distinctive squadron markings. The Sea King soldiers on in ASaC7 form with the Navy and unusually the HU5 variant was recalled into service, this time with HeliOperations at the former naval base at Portland. The last twelve months has seen the retirement of the Lynx HMA8 with the Royal Navy and then the Lynx AH9A with the Army, the last of the latter hanging on until January 2018. 1st April 2018 will be significant not least because it will see the centenary of the RAF (with several celebrations planned for later in the year) but also because it will see the full entry into service of the Juno and Jupiter helicopters. 2018 should also see the full entry into service of the Prefect, Texan and Phenom with other types slowly disappearing. Hopefully 2018 will also see more of the air cadet gliding fleet back into the air. For QinetiQ change is also under way, with the Alpha Jets retiring at the end of January, the Hawks due to finish in March and the Gazelles to follow some time in 2019; replacements have come in the form of the PC-21 (two aircraft), Grob 120TP (two aircraft) and four Airbus H.125s, all of which will go on the civil register.

Early 2018 saw the withdrawal of the Alpha Jet as far as European air arms go, with the final Portuguese examples being taken out of service. The Lynx still remains in French and Portuguese service while Denmark disposed of its fleet during December 2017. As far as heavier metal goes, A.400M and Airbus A330MRTT deliveries continue, providing much-needed work for the European aerospace industry. The US Air Force continues to receive the C-130J Hercules II, and hopefully in 2018 the KC-46A Pegasus will enter service. The Navy continues to increase its P-8A Poseidon fleet as the P-3 Orion joins service.

Another year has passed without a significant European air show incident and indeed with just one reported write-off of a UK military aircraft, both very pleasing statistics to report.

You can find 'MAM' on Facebook at www.facebook.com/MilitaryAircraftMarkings, on Twitter (@HJCurtisMAM) as well as on the 'MAM' web site, www.militaryaircraftmarkings.co.uk.

ACKNOWLEDGEMENTS

The compiler wishes to thank the many people who have taken the trouble to send comments, additions, deletions and other useful information since the publication of the previous edition of Military Aircraft Markings. In particular the following individuals: Phil Adkin, Hermann Böhm, Terry Bowcutt, Peter Budden, Nigel Burch, Glyn Coney, Oliver Curtis, Patrick Dirksen, Ben Dunnell, Ray Fitton, Graham Gaff, Gilmar Green, Norman Hibberd, Peter R March, Doug MacDonald, Tony McCarthy, Martin Pole, Lloyd P Robinson, Mark Ray, Mark Russell, Ben Sadler, Paul Saxby, Mark Shepherd, Kev Slade, David Thompson and John Varley.

The 2018 edition has also relied upon the printed publications and/or associated internet web-sites as follows: Aerodata Quantum+, 'Aeroplane' magazine, Airfields Yahoo! Group, 'Air Forces Monthly' magazine, BAEG Yahoo! Group, CAA G-INFO Web Site, Coningsby Aviation Site, Delta Reflex, Fighter Control, 'FlyPast' magazine, Joe Baugher's Home Page, Mildenhall and Lakenheath Movements Group (SMAS), Brian Pickering/'Military Aviation Review', Mil Spotters' Forum, NAMAR Yahoo! Group, The Official RAF Leeming Spotters' Group (Facebook), Planebase NG, RAF Leeming Yahoo! Group, RAF Shawbury Yahoo! Group, 'Scramble' magazine, Souairport Yahoo! group, South West of England Aviation Movements (Facebook), Tom McGhee/UK Serials Resource Centre, USMil Googlegroup, Mick Boulanger/Wolverhampton Aviation Group and 'Wrecks & Relics'.

Information shown is believed to be correct at 24 February 2018.

HJC February 2018

Note: The compiler will be pleased to receive comments, corrections and further information for inclusion in subsequent editions of *Military Aircraft Markings* and the monthly up-date of additions and amendments. Please send your information to Military Aircraft Markings, Crécy Publishing Ltd, 1a Ringway trading Estate, Shadowmoss Road, Manchester M22 5LH or by e-mail to admin@aviation-links.co.uk.

$	Aircraft in special markings
AAC	Army Air Corps
AACS	Airborne Air Control Squadron
AC	Air Cadets
ACCGS	Air Cadets Central Gliding School
ACCS	Airborne Command & Control Squadron
ACS	Air Control Squadron
ACW	Air Control Wing
ADF	Air Defence Force
ADSU	Apache Depth Support Unit
AEF	Air Experience Flight
AESS	Air Engineering & Survival School
AEW	Airborne Early Warning
AFB	Air Force Base
AFD	Air Fleet Department
AFRC	Air Force Reserve Command
AG	Airlift Group
AGA	Academia General del Aire (General Air Academy)
AGS	Air Ground Surveillance
AK	Alaska
AL	Alabama
AMD-BA	Avions Marcel Dassault-Breguet Aviation
AMG	Aircraft Maintenance Group
AM&SU	Aircraft Maintenance & Storage Unit
AMW	Air Mobility Wing
ANG	Air National Guard
AR	Arkansas
ARS	Air Refueling Squadron
ARW	Air Refueling Wing
AS	Airlift Squadron/Air Squadron
ATC	Air Training Corps
ATCC	Air Traffic Control Centre
AVDEF	Aviation Defence Service
Avn	Aviation
AW	AgustaWestland/Airlift Wing/Armstrong Whitworth Aircraft
AWC	Air Warfare Centre
BAC	British Aircraft Corporation
BAe	British Aerospace
BAPC	British Aviation Preservation Council
BATUK	British Army Training Unit Kenya
BATUS	British Army Training Unit Suffield
BBMF	Battle of Britain Memorial Flight
BDRF	Battle Damage Repair Flight
BDRT	Battle Damage Repair Training
Be	Beech
Bf	Bayerische Flugzeugwerke
BG	Bomber Group
BGA	British Gliding & Soaring Association
bk	black (squadron colours and markings)
bl	blue (squadron colours and markings)
Blt	Bojová letka (attack squadron)
BP	Boulton & Paul/Boulton Paul
br	brown (squadron colours and markings)
BS	Bomber Squadron
B-V	Boeing-Vertol
BW	Bomber Wing
CA	California
CAARP	Co-operative des Ateliers Air de la Région Parisienne
CAC	Commonwealth Aircraft Corporation
CACG	Command and Control Group
CAE	Centro Addestramento Equipaggi (Crew Training Centre)
CASA	Construcciones Aeronautics SA
CATS	Cassidian Aviation Training Services
CC	County Council
CC Air	Competence Centre Air
CCF	Combined Cadet Force/Canadian Car & Foundry Company

CEAM	Centre d'Expertise Aérienne Militaire (Centre of Military Air Expertise)
CEMAST	Centre of Excellence in Engineering & Manufacturing Advanced Skills Training
CEPA	Centre d'Expérimentation Pratique de l'Aéronautique Navale
CFAMI	Centre de Formation Aérienne Militaire Initiale de Salon
CFIA	Centre de Formation Interarmées NH.90
CFS	Central Flying School
CIEH	Centre d'Instruction des Equipages d'Hélicoptères
CHFMU	Commando Helicopter Force Maintenance Unit
CinC	Commander in Chief
CinCLANT	Commander in Chief Atlantic
CLV	Centrum Leteckeho Vycviku (Air Training Centre)
CMU	Central Maintenance Unit
Co	Company
CO	Colorado
COMALAT	Commandement de l'Aviation Légère de l'Armée de Terre
Comp	Composite with
CT	Connecticut
CV	Chance-Vought
D-BA	Daimler-Benz Aerospace
D-BD	Dassault-Breguet Dornier
D&G	Dumfries and Galloway
DCTT	Defence College of Technical Training
DE	Delaware
DE&S	Defence Equipment and Support
DEFTS	Defence Elementary Flying Training School
DEODS	Defence Explosives Ordnance Disposal School
Det	Detachment
DFTDC	Defence Fire Training and Development Centre
DGA	Délégation Générale de l'Armement
DH	de Havilland
DHC	de Havilland Canada
DHFS	Defence Helicopter Flying School
DMS	Defence Movements School
DS&TL	Defence Science & Technology Laboratory
DSAE	Defence School of Aeronautical Engineering
DSEME	Defence School of Electro-Mechanical Engineering
DSG	Defence Support Group
DSMarE	Defence School of Marine Engineering
Dvlt	Dopravná vrtul'niková letka (Helicopter Transport Squadron)
EA	Escadron Aérien (Air Squadron)
EAAT	Escadrille Avions de l'Armée de Terre
EAC	Ecole de l'Aviation de Chasse (Fighter Aviation School)
EALAT	Ecole de l'Aviation Légère de l'Armée de Terre
EAP	European Aircraft Project
EAT	Ecole de l'Aviation de Transport (Transport Aviation School)
EC	Escadre de Chasse (Fighter Wing)
E-CATS	EADS Cognac Aviation Training Services
ECG	Electronic Combat Group
ECM	Electronic Counter Measures
ECS	Electronic Countermeasures Squadron
EdC	Escadron de Convoyage
EDCA	Escadron de Détection et de Control Aéroportée (Airborne Detection & Control Sqn)
EE	English Electric/Escadrille Electronique
EEA	Escadron Electronique Aéroporté
EFA	Ecole Franco Allemande
EFTS	Elementary Flying Training School
EH	Escadron d'Helicoptères (Helicopter Flight)
EHADT	Escadrille Helicoptères de l'Armée de Terre
EHI	European Helicopter Industries
EKW	Eidgenössiches Konstruktionswerkstätte
el	Eskadra Lotnicza (Air Sqn)
EL	Escadre de Liaison (Liaison Wing)
elt	Eskadra Lotnictwa Taktycznego (Tactical Air Squadron)
eltr	Eskadra Lotnictwa Transportowego (Air Transport Squadron)
EMA	East Midlands Airport
EMB	Ecoles Militaires de Bourges

EMVO	Elementaire Militaire Vlieg Opleiding (Elementary Flying Training)
EoN	Elliot's of Newbury
EPAA	Ecole de Pilotage Elementaire de l'Armée de l'Air (Air Force Elementary Flying School)
EPNER	Ecole du Personnel Navigant d'Essais et de Reception
ER	Escadre de Reconnaissance (Reconnaissance Wing)
ERV	Escadron de Ravitaillement en Vol (Aerial Refuelling Squadron)
ES	Escadrille de Servitude
ESAM	Ecole Supérieur d'Application du Matériel
Esc	Escuadron (Squadron)
Esk	Eskadrile/Eskadrille (Squadron)
Esq	Esquadra (Squadron)
ET	Escadre de Transport (Transport Wing)
ETED	Escadron de Transformation des Equipages Mirage 2000D
ETO	Escadron de Transition Operationnelle (Operational Transition Squadron)
ETPS	Empire Test Pilots' School
ETR	Escadron de Transformation Rafale
ETS	Engineering Training School/Escadron de Transport Stratégique
ETTL	Escadre de Transport Tactique et Logistique (Tactical and Logistics Transport Wing)
EVAA	Ecole de Voltige de l'Armée de l'Air (French Air Force Aerobatics School)
FAA	Fleet Air Arm (UK)/Federal Aviation Administration (USA)
FACO	Final Assembly & Check Out
FBS	Flugbereitschaftstaffel (Flight Readiness Squadron)
FBW	Fly-by-wire
FC	Forskokcentralen (Flight Centre)
FE	Further Education
FETC	Fire and Emergency Training Centre
ff	Front fuselage
FG	Fighter Group
FH	Fairchild-Hiller
FI	Falkland Islands
FJWOEU	Fast Jet & Weapons Operational Evaluation Unit
FL	Florida
FLO	Forsvarets Logistikk Organisasjon (Defence Logistics Organisation)
FlSt	Fliegerstaffel (Flight Squadron)
Flt	Flight
FMA	Fabrica Militar de Aviones
FMV	Forsvarets Materielwerk (Defence Material Works)
FS	Fighter Squadron
FTS	Flying Training School
FTW	Flying Training Wing
Fw	Focke Wulf
FW	Fighter Wing/FlugWerk/Foster Wickner
FY	Fiscal Year
GA	Georgia
GAF	Government Aircraft Factory
GAL	General Aircraft Ltd
GAM	Groupe Aerien Mixte (Composite Air Group)
GAM/STAT	Groupement Aéromobile/Section Technique de l'Armée de Terre
gd	gold (squadron colours and markings)
GD	General Dynamics
GEA	Gruppo Efficienza Aeromobili (Italian AF)/Gruppo Esplorazione Aeromarittima (GdiF)
GEM	Grupo de Escuelas de Matacán (Matacán Group of Schools)
GI	Ground Instruction/Groupement d'Instruction (Instructional Group)
GMS	Glider Maintenance Section
gn	green (squadron colours and markings)
GRD	Gruppe fur Rustunggdienste (Group for Service Preparation)
GRV	Groupe de Ravitaillement en Vol (Air Refuelling Group)
GT	Grupo de Transporte (Transport Wing)
GTT	Grupo de Transporte de Tropos (Troop Carrier Wing)
gy	grey (squadron colours and markings)
HAF	Historic Aircraft Flight
HAPS	High Altitude Pseudo-Satellite
HavLLv	Hävittäjälentolaivue
HC	Helicopter Combat Support Squadron
HekoP	Helikopteripataljoona (Helicopter Battalion)
HF	Historic Flying Ltd

HI	Hawaii
HK	Helikopterikomppannia (Helicopter Company)
Hkp.Bat	Helikopter Bataljon (Helicopter Battalion)
HMA	Helicopter Maritime Attack
HMS	Her Majesty's Ship
HP	Handley-Page
HQ	Headquarters
HS	Hawker Siddeley
HSG	Hubschraubergeschwader (Helicopter Squadron)
IA	Iowa
IAF	Israeli Air Force
IAP	International Airport
IL	Illinois
IlmaStk	IlmataiStelukeskus
IN	Indiana
IntHubschr-	Internationales Hubschrauberausbildungszentrum
AusbZ	(International Helicopter Training Centre)
IOW	Isle Of Wight
IWM	Imperial War Museums
JADTEU	Joint Air Delivery Test and Evaluation Unit
JARTS	Joint Aircraft Recovery & Transportation Sqn
JFACTSU	Joint Forward Air Control Training & Standards Unit
JHC	Joint Helicopter Command
JMRC	Joint Multinational Readiness Centre
KHR	Kampfhubschrauberregiment (Combat Helicopter Regiment)
Kridlo	Wing
KS	Kansas
LA	Louisiana
lbvr	letka Bitevnich Vrtulníků (Attack Helicopter Squadron)
Letka	Squadron
LTDB	Lufttransportdienst des Bundes (Federal Air Transport Services)
LTG	Lufttransportgeschwader (Air Transport Wing)
lTHSSta	leichte Transporthubschrauberstaffel
LTO	Letalska Transportni Oddelek (Air Transport Department)
LtSt	Lufttransport Staffel
LTV	Ling-Temco-Vought
LVG	Luftwaffen Versorgungs Geschwader (Air Force Maintenance Wing)/Luft Verkehrs Gesellschaft
LZO	Letecky Zku ební Odbor (Aviation Test Department)
m	multi-coloured (squadron colours and markings)
MA	Massachusetts
MADG	Marshall Aerospace & Defence Group
MAPK	Mira Anachestisis Pantos Kerou (All Weather Interception Sqn)
MBB	Messerschmitt Bolkow-Blohm
MCAS	Marine Corps Air Station
McD	McDonnell Douglas
MD	Maryland
MDMF	Merlin Depth Maintenance Facility
Med	Medical
MFG	Marine Flieger Geschwader (Naval Air Wing)
MFSU	Merlin Depth Forward Support Unit
MH	Max Holste
MI	Maritime Interdiction/Michigan
MIB	Military Intelligence Battalion
MiG	Mikoyan — Gurevich
MMF	(European) Multinational Multi-Role Tanker Transport Fleet
MN	Minnesota
MO	Missouri
Mod	Modified
MoD	Ministry of Defence
MPSU	Multi-Platform Support Unit
MR	Maritime Reconnaissance
MRH	Multi-role Helikopters
M&RU	Marketing & Recruitment Unit
MS	Mississippi/Morane-Saulnier
MT	Montana

MTHR	Mittlerer Transporthubschrauber Regiment (Medium Transport Helicopter Regiment)
MTM	Mira Taktikis Metaforon (Tactical Transport Sqn)
NA	North American
NACDS	Naval Air Command Driving School
NAEW&CF	NATO Airborne Early Warning & Control Force
NAF	Naval Air Facility
NAS	Naval Air Squadron (UK)/Naval Air Station (US)
NATO	North Atlantic Treaty Organisation
NAWC	Naval Air Warfare Center
NAWC-AD	Naval Air Warfare Center Aircraft Division
NBC	Nuclear, Biological and Chemical
ND	North Dakota
NDMA	Norwegian Defence Material Agency
NE	North-East/Nebraska
NFH	NATO Frigate Helicopter
NH	New Hampshire
NI	Northern Ireland
NJ	New Jersey
NM	New Mexico
NV	Nevada
NY	New York
NYARC	North Yorks Aircraft Restoration Centre
OEU	Operational Evaluation Unit
OFMC	Old Flying Machine Company
OGMA	Oficinas Gerais de Material Aeronautico
OH	Ohio
OK	Oklahoma
or	orange (squadron colours and markings)
OSAC	Operational Support Airlift Command
OSBL	Oddelek Sholskih Bojni Letal (Training & Combat School)
P2MF	Puma 2 Maintenance Flight
PA	Pennsylvania
PAS	Presidential Airlift Squadron
PAT	Priority Air Transport Detachment
PBN	Pilatus Britten-Norman
PDSH	Puma Depth Support Hub
PLM	Pulk Lotnictwa Mysliwskiego (Fighter Regiment)
pr	purple (squadron colours and markings)
PR	Puerto Rico
r	red (squadron colours and markings)
R	Replica
RAeS	Royal Aeronautical Society
RAF	Royal Aircraft Factory/Royal Air Force
RAFC	Royal Air Force College
RAFM	Royal Air Force Museum
RAFGSA	Royal Air Force Gliding and Soaring Association
RE	Royal Engineers
Regt	Regiment
REME	Royal Electrical & Mechanical Engineers
rf	Rear fuselage
RFA	Royal Fleet Auxiliary
RHC	Régiment d'Helicoptères de Combat (Combat Helicopter Regiment)
RHFS	Régiment d'Helicoptères des Forces Spéciales (Special Forces Helicopter Regiment)
RI	Rhode Island
RJAF	Royal Jordanian Air Force
RM	Royal Marines
RMB	Royal Marines Base
RN	Royal Navy
RNAS	Royal Naval Air Station
RNGSA	Royal Navy Gliding and Soaring Association
RPAS	Remotely Piloted Air System
RQS	Rescue Squadron
R-R	Rolls-Royce
RS	Reid & Sigrist/Reconnaissance Squadron
RSV	Reparto Sperimentale Volo (Experimental Flight School)
RTP	Reduction To Produce

RW	Reconnaissance Wing
SA	Scottish Aviation
SAAB	Svenska Aeroplan Aktieboleg
SAAE	School of Army Aeronautical Engineering
SAC	Strategic Airlift Capability
SAL	Scottish Aviation Limited
SAR	Search and Rescue
Saro	Saunders-Roe
SARTU	Search and Rescue Training Unit
SC	South Carolina
SCW	Strategic Communications Wing
SD	South Dakota
SEPECAT	Société Européenne de Production de l'avion Ecole de Combat et d'Appui Tactique
SFDO	School of Flight Deck Operations
SHAPE	Supreme Headquarters Allied Powers Europe
si	silver (squadron colours and markings)
SKAMG	Sea King Aircraft Maintenance Group
Skv	Skvadron (Squadron)
SLK	Stíhacie Letecké Kridlo (Fighter Air Wing)
slt	stíhací letka (Fighter Squadron)
SLV	School Licht Vliegwezen (Flying School)
Sm	Smaldeel (Squadron)
SNCAN	Société Nationale de Constructions Aéronautiques du Nord
SOG	Special Operations Group
SOS	Special Operations Squadron
SoTT	School of Technical Training
SOW	Special Operations Wing
SPAD	Société Pour les Appareils Deperdussin
SPP	Strojirny Prvni Petilesky
Sqn	Squadron
Sz.D.REB	'Szentgyörgyi Deszö' Harcászati Repülö Bázis
TA	Territorial Army
TAP	Transporten Avio Polk (Air Transport Regiment)
TASF(N)	Tornado Aircraft Servicing Flight (North)
TAZLS	Technische Ausbildungs Zentrum Luftwaffe Süd (TAubZLwSüd, Technical Training Centre South)
TES	Test and Evaluation Squadron
TFC	The Fighter Collection
TGp	Test Groep
TH	Transporthelikopter
TIARA	Tornado Integrated Avionics Research Aircraft
tl	taktická tetka (Tactical Squadron)
TLG	Taktisches Luftwaffegeschwader (Air Force Tactical Squadron)
TMU	Typhoon Maintenance Unit
TN	Tennessee
Tr AB	Transport Aviation Brigade
TS	Test Squadron
ts	transportnia speciálni letka (special transport squadron)
TsAGI	Tsentral'ny Aerogidrodinamicheski Instut (Central Aero & Hydrodynamics Institute)
TsLw	Technische Schule der Luftwaffe (Luftwaffe Technical School)
TTH	Tactical Transport Helicopter
TukiLLv	Tukilentolaivue
TW	Test Wing
TX	Texas
UAS	University Air Squadron
UAV	Unmanned Air Vehicle
Überwg	Überwachungsgeschwader
UK	United Kingdom
US	United States
USAF	United States Air Force
USAFE	United States Air Forces in Europe
USAREUR	US Army Europe
USCGS	US Coast Guard Station
USEUCOM	United States European Command
USMC	United States Marine Corps
USN	United States Navy

USNWTSPM	United States Navy Test Pilots School
USW	University of South Wales
UT	Utah
VA	Virginia
VAAC	Vectored thrust Advanced Aircraft flight Control
VFW	Vereinigte Flugtechnische Werke
VGS	Volunteer Gliding Squadron
vlt	výcviková letka (training squadron)
VMGR	Marine Aerial Refuelling/Transport Squadron
VMGRT	Marine Aerial Refuelling/Transport Training Squadron
VQ	Fleet Air Reconnaissance Squadron
VR	Fleet Logistic Support Squadron
vrl	vrtulníková letka (helicopter squadron)
VS	Vickers-Supermarine
w	white (squadron colours and markings)
WA	Washington
WCM	Wildcat Contract Maintenance
Wg	Wing
WHL	Westland Helicopters Ltd
WI	Wisconsin
WLT	Weapons Loading Training
WMF	Wildcat Maintenance Facility
WR-ALC	Warner Robins Air Logistics Complex
WRS	Weather Reconnaissance Squadron
WS	Westland
WSK	Wytwornia Sprzetu Kominikacyjnego
WST	Wildcat Support Team
WTD	Wehrtechnische Dienstelle (Technical Support Unit)
WV	West Virginia
WW2	World War II
WY	Wyoming
WZM	Wildcat Maintenance
y	yellow (squadron colours and markings)
zDL	základna Dopravního Letectva (Air Transport Base)
zL	základna Letectva (Air Force Base)
zSL	základna Speciálního Letectva (Training Air Base)
zTL	základna Taktického Letectva (Tactical Air Base)
zVrL	základna Vrtulníkového Letectva (Helicopter Air Base)

A Guide to the Location of Operational Military Bases in the UK

This section is to assist the reader to locate the places in the United Kingdom where operational military aircraft (including helicopters and gliders) are based.

The alphabetical order listing gives each location in relation to its county and to its nearest classified road(s) (*by* means adjoining; *of* means close to), together with its approximate direction and mileage from the centre of a nearby major town or city. Some civil airports are included where active military units are also based, but **excluded** are MoD sites with non-operational aircraft (e.g. *gate guardians*), the bases of privately-owned civil aircraft that wear military markings and museums. For GPS users, Latitude and Longitude are also listed.

User	Base name	County/Region	Location [Lat./long.]	Distance/direction from (town)
Army	Abingdon	Oxfordshire	W by B4017, W of A34	5m SSW of Oxford [N51°41'16" W001°18'58"]
Army	Aldergrove/Belfast	Co Antrim Airport	W by A26	13m W of Belfast [N54°39'27" W006°12'578"]
RAF	Barkston Heath	Lincolnshire	W by B6404, S of A153	5m NNE of Grantham [N52°57'46" W000°33'38"]
RAF	Benson	Oxfordshire	E by A423	1m NE of Wallingford [N51°36'55" W001°05'45"]
QinetiQ/ RAF	Boscombe Down	Wiltshire	S by A303, W of A338	6m N of Salisbury [N51°09'12" W001°45'04"]
RAF	Brize Norton	Oxfordshire	W of A4095	5m SW of Witney [N51°45'00" W001°35'01"]

User	Base name	County/Region	Location [Lat./long.]	Distance/direction from (town)
Marshall	Cambridge Airport/ Teversham	Cambridgeshire	S by A1303	2m E of Cambridge [N52°12'18" E000°10'30"]
RAF	Coningsby	Lincolnshire	S of A153, W by B1192	10m NW of Boston [N53°05'35" W000°10'00"]
DCAE	Cosford	Shropshire	W of A41, N of A464	9m WNW of Wolverhampton [N52°38'25" W002°18'20"]
RAF	Cranwell	Lincolnshire	N by A17, S by B1429	5m WNW of Sleaford [N53°01'49" W000°29'00"]
RN	Culdrose	Cornwall	E by A3083	1m SE of Helston [N50°05'08" W005°15'17"]
USAF	Fairford	Gloucestershire	S of A417	9m ESE of Cirencester [N51°41'01" W001°47'24"]
Vector	Fleetlands Aerospace	Hampshire	E by A32	2m SE of Fareham [N50°50'06" W001°10'07"]
RAF	Halton	Buckinghamshire	N of A4011, S of B4544	4m ESE of Aylesbury [N51°47'28" W000°44'11"]
RAF	Kenley	Greater London	W of A22	1m W of Warlingham [N51°18'20" W000°05'37"]
RAF	Kirknewton	Lothian	E by B7031, N by A70	8m SW of Edinburgh [N55°52'32" W003°24'04"]
USAF	Lakenheath	Suffolk	W by A1065	8m W of Thetford [N52°24'33" E000°33'40"]
RAF/Army	Leconfield (Normandy Barracks)	East Riding of Yorkshire	E by A164	2m N of Beverley [N53°52'39" W000°26'08"]
RAF	Leeming	North Yorkshire	E by A1	5m SW of Northallerton [N54°17'33" W001°32'07"]
RAF	Leuchars	Fife	E of A919	7m SE of Dundee [N56°22'28" W002°51'50"]
RAF	Lossiemouth	Grampian	W of B9135, S of B9040	4m N of Elgin [N57°42'22" W003°20'20"]
RAF	Marham	Norfolk	N by A1122	6m W of Swaffham [N52°38'54" E000°33'02"]
Army	Middle Wallop	Hampshire	S by A343	6m SW of Andover [N51°08'35" W001°34'14"]
USAF	Mildenhall	Suffolk	S by A1101	9m NNE of Newmarket [N52°21'42" E000°29'12"]
RAF	Northolt	Greater London	N by A40	3m E of M40 jn 1 [N51°33'11" W000°25'06"]
RAF	Odiham	Hampshire	E of A32	2m S of M3 jn 5 [N51°14'03" W000°56'34"]
RN	Predannack	Cornwall	W by A3083	7m S of Helston [N50°00'07" W005°13'54"]
RAF	Scampton	Lincolnshire	W by A15	6m N of Lincoln [N53°18'28" W000°33'04"]
RAF	Shawbury	Shropshire	W of B5063	7m NNE of Shrewsbury [N52°47'53" W002°40'05"]
RAF	Syerston	Nottinghamshire	W by A46	5m SW of Newark [N53°01'22" W000°54'47"]
RAF	Ternhill	Shropshire	SW by A41	3m SW of Market Drayton [N52°52'24" W002°31'54"]
RAF/Army	Topcliffe	North Yorkshire	E of A167, W of A168	3m SW of Thirsk [N54°12'20" W001°22'55"]
RAF	Valley	Gwynedd	S of A5 on Anglesey	5m SE of Holyhead [N53°14'53" W004°32'06"]
RAF	Waddington	Lincolnshire	E by A607, W by A15	5m S of Lincoln [N53°09'58" W000°31'26"]
Army	Wattisham	Suffolk	N of B1078	5m SSW of Stowmarket [N52°07'38" E000°57'21"]
RAF	Woodvale	Merseyside	W by A565	5m SSW of Southport [N53°34'56" W003°03'24"]
RAF	Wittering	Cambridgeshire	W by A1, N of A47	3m S of Stamford [N52°36'52" W000°27'01"]
RN	Yeovilton	Somerset	S by B3151, S of A303	5m N of Yeovil [N51°00'30" W002°38'43"]

The Committee of Imperial Defence through its Air Committee introduced a standardised system of numbering aircraft in November 1912. The Air Department of the Admiralty was allocated the first batch 1-200 and used these to cover aircraft already in use and those on order. The Army was issued with the next block from 201-800, which included the number 304 which was given to the Cody Biplane now preserved in the Science Museum. By the outbreak of World War I, the Royal Navy was on its second batch of registrations 801-1600 and this system continued with alternating allocations between the Army and Navy until 1916 when number 10000, a Royal Flying Corps BE2C, was reached.

It was decided not to continue with five digit numbers but instead to start again from 1, prefixing RFC aircraft with the letter A and RNAS aircraft with the prefix N. The RFC allocations commenced with A1 an FE2D and before the end of the year had reached A9999 an Armstrong Whitworth FK8. The next group commenced with B1 and continued in logical sequence through the C, D, E and F prefixes. G was used on a limited basis to identify captured German aircraft, while H was the last block of wartime-ordered aircraft. To avoid confusion I was not used, so the new post-war machines were allocated registrations in the J range. A further minor change was made in the numbering system in August 1929 when it was decided to maintain four numerals after the prefix letter, thus omitting numbers 1 to 999. The new K series therefore commenced at K1000, which was allocated to an AW Atlas.

The Naval N prefix was not used in such a logical way. Blocks of numbers were allocated for specific types of aircraft such as seaplanes or flying-boats. By the late 1920s the sequence had largely been used up and a new series using the prefix S was commenced. In 1930 separate naval allocations were stopped and subsequent registrations were issued in the 'military' range which had by this time reached the K series. A further change in the pattern of allocations came in the L range. Commencing with L7272 numbers were issued in blocks with smaller blocks of registrations between not used. These were known as 'broken blocks'. As M had already been used as a suffix for Maintenance Command instructional airframes it was not used as a prefix. Although N had previously been used for naval aircraft it was used again for registrations allocated from 1937.

With the build-up to World War II, the rate of allocations quickly accelerated and the prefix R was being used when war was declared. The letters O and Q were not allotted, nor was S, which had been used up to S1865 for naval aircraft before integration into the RAF series. By 1940 the registration Z9999 had been reached, as part of a broken block, with the letters U and Y not used to avoid confusion.

The option to recommence registration allocation at A1000 was not taken up; instead it was decided to use an alphabetical two-letter prefix with three numerals running from 100 to 999. Thus, AA100 was allocated to a Blenheim IV and this two-letter, three-numeral registration system which started in 1940 continues today. The letters C, I, O, Q, U and Y were, with the exception of NC, not used. For various reasons the following letter combinations were not issued: DA, DB, DH, EA, GA to GZ, HA, HT, JE, JH, JJ, KR to KT, MR, NW, NZ, SA to SK, SV, TN, TR and VE. The first post-war registrations issued were in the VP range while the end of the WZs had been reached by the Korean War.

In January 1952 a civil servant at the then Air Ministry penned a memo to his superiors alerting them to the fact that a new military aircraft registration system would soon have to be devised. With allocations accelerating to accommodate a NATO response to the Korean War and a perceived Soviet threat building, he estimated that the end of the ZZs would quickly be reached. However, more than six decades later the allocations are only in the ZKs and at the present rate are unlikely to reach ZZ999 until the end of this century!

Military aircraft registrations are allocated by MoD Head Office and Corporate Services, where the Military Aircraft Register is maintained by the Military Aviation Authority. It should be pointed out that strictly the register places a space before the last three digits of the registration and, contrary to popular opinion, refers to them as 'registrations', not serials.

A change in policy in 2003 resulted in the use of the first 99 digits in the ZK sequence (ZK001 to ZK099), following on from ZJ999. The first of these, ZK001 to ZK004, were allocated to AgustaWestland Merlins. There is also a growing trend for 'out-of-sequence' registration numbers to be issued. At first this was to a manufacturer's prototype or development aircraft. However, following the Boeing C-17 Globemasters leased and subsequently purchased from Boeing (ZZ171-ZZ178), more allocations have been noted.

Since 2002 there has also been a new official policy concerning the use of military registration numbers on some types of UAV. 'Where a UAV is of modular construction the nationality and registration mark shall be applied to the fuselage of the vehicle or on the assembly forming the main part of the fuselage. To prevent the high usage of numbers for target drones which are eventually destroyed, a single registration mark (prefix) should be issued relating to the UAV type. The agency or service operating the target drone will be responsible for the identification of each individual UAV covered by that registration mark by adding a suffix.' This has resulted in the use of the same registration on a number of UAVs (or RPASs as they are now referred to) and drones with numbers following it - hence the appearance of ZZ420/001 etc. on Banshee drones. Aircraft using this system are denoted in the text by an asterisk (*).

A serial in *italics* denotes that it is not the genuine marking for that airframe.

Serial	Type (code/other identity)	Owner/operator, location or fate	Notes
46	VS361 Spitfire LF IX <R> (*MH486*/BAPC 206) [FT-E]	Michael Beetham Conservation Centre, RAFM Cosford	
168	Sopwith Tabloid Scout <R> (G-BFDE)	RAF Museum Reserve Collection, Stafford	
304	Cody Biplane (BAPC 62)	Science Museum, South Kensington	
471	RAF BE2a <R> (BAPC 321)	Montrose Air Station Heritage Centre	
687	RAF BE2c <R> (G-AWYI/*471*)	Privately owned, Sywell	
687	RAF BE2b <R> (BAPC 181)	RAF Museum, Hendon	
1264	Bristol Scout C <R> (G-FDHB)	Privately owned, Bicester	
2345	Vickers FB5 Gunbus <R> (G-ATVP)	RAF Museum, Hendon	
2699	RAF BE2c	IWM Duxford	
2783	RAF BE2b <R> (BAPC 332)	Boscombe Down Aviation Collection, Old Sarum	
3066	Caudron GIII (G-AETA/9203M)	RAF Museum, Hendon	
5964	DH2 <R> (BAPC 112)	Privately owned, Stretton on Dunsmore	
5964	DH2 <R> (G-BFVH)	Privately owned, Wickenby	
6232	RAF BE2c <R> (BAPC 41)	Yorkshire Air Museum, stored Elvington	
8359	Short 184 <ff>	FAA Museum, RNAS Yeovilton	
9828	Avro 504K <R> (*H1968*/BAPC 42)	Yorkshire Air Museum, stored Elvington	
9917	Sopwith Pup (G-EBKY/N5180)	The Shuttleworth Collection, Old Warden	
A126	Nieuport 11 <R> (G-CILI)	Privately owned,	
A301	Morane BB (frame)	RAF Museum Reserve Collection, Stafford	
A653	Sopwith Pup <R> (*A7317*/BAPC 179)	Privately owned, Stow Maries, Essex	
A1452	Vickers FB5 Gunbus <R>	Spitfire Spares, Taunton, Somerset	
A1742	Bristol Scout D <R> (BAPC 38)	Aerospace Bristol, Filton	
A2767	RAF BE2e-1 <R> (G-CJZP)	WW1 Aviation Heritage Trust, Stow Maries	
A2943	RAF BE2e-1 <R> (G-CJZO)	WW1 Aviation Heritage Trust, Bicester	
A3930	RAF RE8 <R> (ZK-TVC)	RAF Museum, Hendon	
A4850	RAF SE5a <R> (BAPC 176)	Bygone Times Antique Warehouse, Eccleston, Lancs	
A6526	RAF FE2b <R> (BAPC 400)	RAF Museum, Hendon	
A7288	Bristol F2b Fighter <R> (BAPC 386)	Aerospace Bristol, Filton	
A8226	Sopwith 1½ Strutter <R> (G-BIDW)	RAF Museum, Cosford	
A8274	Sopwith 1½ Strutter <R> (BAPC 413)	WW1 Aviation Heritage Trust, Stow Maries	
B595	RAF SE5a <R> (G-BUOD) [W]	Privately owned, Defford	
B619	Sopwith 1½ Strutter <R> (BAPC 468)	RAF Manston History Museum	
B1474	Henry Farman F.20 <R>	WW1 Aviation Heritage Trust, Stow Maries	
B5539	Sopwith F.1 Camel <R>	Privately owned, Booker	
B5577	Sopwith F.1 Camel <R> (*D3419*/BAPC 59) [W]	Montrose Air Station Heritage Centre	
B6401	Sopwith F.1 Camel <R> (G-AWYY/C1701)	FAA Museum, stored Cobham Hall, RNAS Yeovilton	
B7270	Sopwith F.1 Camel <R> (G-BFCZ)	Brooklands Museum, Weybridge	
C1096	Replica Plans SE5a <R> (G-ERFC)	Privately owned, Durley, Hants	
C1904	RAF SE5a <R> (G-PFAP) [Z]	Privately owned, Castle Bytham, Lincs	
C3009	Currie Wot (G-BFWD) [B]	Privately owned, Dunkeswell	
C3011	Phoenix Currie Super Wot (G-SWOT) [S]	Privately owned, Otherton, Staffs	
C3988	Sopwith 5F.1 Dolphin (BAPC 353) (comp D5329)	RAF Museum, Hendon	
C4451	Avro 504J <R> (BAPC 210)	Solent Sky, Southampton	
C4918	Bristol M1C <R> (G-BWJM)	The Shuttleworth Collection, Old Warden	
C4994	Bristol M1C <R> (G-BLWM)	RAF Museum, Cosford	
C5430	RAF SE5a <R> (G-CCXG) [V]	Privately owned, Wrexham	
C8996	RAF SE5a (G-ECAE/A2-25)	Privately owned, Milden	
C9533	RAF SE5a <R> (G-BUWE) [M]	Privately owned, Boscombe Down	
D276	RAF SE5a <R> (BAPC 208) [A]	Prince's Mead Shopping Centre, Farnborough	
D1851	Sopwith F.1 Camel <R> (G-BZSC) [X]	The Shuttleworth Collection, Old Warden	
D3540	RAF SE5a <R> (N125QB) [K]	WW1 Aviation Heritage Trust, Old Warden	
D5649	Airco DH9	IWM Duxford	
D6447	Sopwith F.1 Camel <R> (BAPC 385)	Privately owned, Knutsford, Cheshire	
D7560	Avro 504K	Science Museum, South Kensington	

Notes	Serial	Type (code/other identity)	Owner/operator, location or fate
	D8096	Bristol F2b Fighter (G-AEPH) [D]	The Shuttleworth Collection, Old Warden
E449		Avro 504K (G-EBJE/9205M)	RAF Museum, Hendon
	E2466	Bristol F2b Fighter (BAPC 165) [I]	RAF Museum, Hendon
	E2581	Bristol F2b Fighter [13]	IWM Duxford
	E2977	Avro 504K (G-EBHB)	Privately owned, Henlow
	E3273	Avro 504K (H5199/BK892/ G-ACNB/G-ADEV/3118M)	The Shuttleworth Collection, Old Warden
	E6655	Sopwith 7F.1 Snipe <R> (BAPC 348) [B]	RAF Museum, Hendon
	E8894	Airco DH9 (G-CDLI)	Aero Vintage, Duxford
F141		RAF SE5a <R> (G-SEVA) [G]	Privately owned, Boscombe Down
F235		RAF SE5a <R> (G-BMDB) [B]	Privately owned, Stow Maries, Essex
F904		RAF SE5a (G-EBIA)	The Shuttleworth Collection, Old Warden
F904		RAF SE5a <R>	South Yorkshire Aircraft Museum, Doncaster
F938		RAF SE5a (G-EBIC/9208M)	RAF Museum, Hendon
F943		RAF SE5a <R> (G-BIHF) [S]	Privately owned, White Waltham
F943		RAF SE5a <R> (G-BKDT) [S]	Yorkshire Air Museum, Elvington
	F1010	Airco DH9A [C]	RAF Museum, Hendon
F2367		Sopwith 7F.1 Snipe <R> (ZK-SNI)	WW1 Aviation Heritage Trust, Stow Maries
F3556		RAF RE8	IWM Duxford
F5447		RAF SE5a <R> (G-BKER) [N]	Privately owned, Bridge of Weir
F5459		RAF SE5a <R> (G-INNY) [Y]	Privately owned, Temple Bruer, Lincs
F5475		RAF SE5a <R> (BAPC 250)	Brooklands Museum, Weybridge
	F6314	Sopwith F.1 Camel (9206M) [B]	RAF Museum, Hendon
	F8010	RAF SE5a <R> (G-BDWJ) [Z]	Privately owned, Langport, Somerset
	F8614	Vickers FB27A Vimy IV <R> (G-AWAU)	RAF Museum, Hendon
	J7326	DH53 Humming Bird (G-EBQP)	de Havilland Aircraft Museum, London Colney
J7904		Gloster Gamecock (BAPC 259) <R>	Jet Age Museum, Gloucester
	J8067	Westland Pterodactyl 1a	Science Museum, South Kensington
J9941		Hawker Hart 2 (G-ABMR)	RAF Museum, Hendon
	K1786	Hawker Tomtit (G-AFTA)	The Shuttleworth Collection, Old Warden
	K1926	Hawker Fury I	Cambs Fighter & Bomber Society, Little Gransden
K2048		Isaacs Fury II (G-BZNW)	Privately owned, Linton-on-Ouse
K2050		Isaacs Fury II (G-ASCM)	Privately owned, Enstone
K2059		Isaacs Fury II (G-PFAR)	Privately owned, Netherthorpe
K2060		Isaacs Fury II (G-BKZM)	Privately owned stored, Limetree, Ireland
K2065		Isaacs Fury II (G-AYJY/*K2046*)	Privately owned, Henstridge
K2075		Isaacs Fury II (G-BEER)	Privately owned, Combrook, Warks
	K2227	Bristol 105 Bulldog IIA (G-ABBB)	RAF Museum, Hendon
	K2567	DH82A Tiger Moth (DE306/G-MOTH/7035M)	Privately owned, Tadlow
	K2572	DH82A Tiger Moth (NM129/G-AOZH)	Privately owned, Wanborough, Wilts
K2585		DH82A Tiger Moth II (T6818/G-ANKT)	The Shuttleworth Collection, Old Warden
K2587		DH82A Tiger Moth <R> (G-BJAP)	Privately owned, Shobdon
	K3241	Avro 621 Tutor (K3215/G-AHSA)	The Shuttleworth Collection, Old Warden
	K3661	Hawker Nimrod II (G-BURZ) [562]	Aero Vintage, Duxford
	K3731	Isaacs Fury (G-RODI)	Privately owned, Barkston Heath
	K4232	Avro 671 Rota I (SE-AZB)	RAF Museum, Hendon
	K4259	DH82A Tiger Moth (G-ANMO) [71]	Privately owned, Headcorn
K4556		Boulton & Paul Overstrand <R> (BAPC 358)	Norfolk & Suffolk Avn Museum, Flixton
K4972		Hawker Hart Trainer IIA (1764M)	RAF Museum, Cosford
	K5054	Supermarine Spitfire <R> (EN398/BAPC 190)	Privately owned, Hawkinge
	K5054	Supermarine Spitfire <R> (BAPC 214)	Tangmere Military Aviation Museum
	K5054	Supermarine Spitfire <R> (G-BRDV)	Privately owned, Kent
	K5054	Supermarine Spitfire <R> (BAPC 297)	Kent Battle of Britain Museum, Hawkinge
	K5054	Supermarine Spitfire <R>	Southampton Airport, on display
	K5409	Hawker Hind	*Currently not known*
K5414		Hawker Hind (G-AENP/BAPC 78) [XV]	The Shuttleworth Collection, Old Warden
	K5462	Hawker Hind	*Currently not known*
	K5554	Hawker Hind	*Currently not known*
	K5600	Hawker Audax I (G-BVVI/2015M)	Aero Vintage, Westfield, Sussex

Serial	Type (code/other identity)	Owner/operator, location or fate	Notes
K5673	Isaacs Fury II (G-BZAS)	Privately owned, Morpeth	
K5673	Hawker Fury I <R> (BAPC 249)	Brooklands Museum, Weybridge	
K5674	Hawker Fury I (G-CBZP)	Historic Aircraft Collection Ltd, Duxford	
K5682	Isaacs Fury II (S1579/G-BBVO) [6]	Privately owned, Felthorpe (wreck)	
K6035	Westland Wallace II (2361M)	RAF Museum Reserve Collection, Stafford	
K6618	Hawker Hind	Currently not known	
K6833	Hawker Hind	Currently not known	
K7271	Hawker Fury II <R> (BAPC 148)	Shropshire Wartime Aircraft Recovery Grp Mus, Sleap	
K7271	Isaacs Fury II <R> (G-CCKV)	Privately owned, Dunkeswell	
K7985	Gloster Gladiator I (L8032/G-AMRK)	The Shuttleworth Collection, Old Warden	
K8042	Gloster Gladiator II (8372M)	RAF Museum, Cosford	
K8203	Hawker Demon I (G-BTVE/2292M)	Demon Displays, Old Warden	
K8303	Isaacs Fury II (G-BWWN) [D]	Privately owned, RAF Henlow	
K9926	VS300 Spitfire I <R> (BAPC 217) [JH-C]	Privately owned, Newquay	
K9942	VS300 Spitfire I (8383M) [SD-D]	RAF Museum, Cosford	
K9998	VS300 Spitfire I (BAPC 431) <R> [QJ-K]	RAF Biggin Hill, on display	
L1019	VS300 Spitfire I <R> (BAPC 308) [LO-S]	Privately owned, Currie, Lothian	
L1035	VS300 Spitfire I <R> [SH-D]	Battle of Britain Bunker, Uxbridge	
L1067	VS300 Spitfire I <R> (BAPC 227) [XT-D]	Edinburgh Airport, on display	
L1592	Hawker Hurricane I [KW-Z]	Science Museum, South Kensington	
L1639	Hawker Hurricane I (BAPC 362)	Cambridge Fighter & Bomber Society, Little Gransden	
L1679	Hawker Hurricane I <R> (BAPC 241) [JX-G]	Tangmere Military Aviation Museum	
L1684	Hawker Hurricane I <R> (BAPC 219)	RAF Northolt, on display	
L2005	Hawker Hurricane I	Hawker Restorations, Milden	
L2301	VS Walrus I (G-AIZG)	FAA Museum, RNAS Yeovilton	
L2940	Blackburn Skua I	FAA Museum, RNAS Yeovilton	
L5343	Fairey Battle I	RAF Museum, Hendon	
L6739	Bristol 149 Bolingbroke IVT (G-BPIV/R3821) [YP-Q]	Blenheim(Duxford) Ltd, Duxford	
L6906	Miles M14A Magister I (G-AKKY/T9841/BAPC 44)	Museum of Berkshire Aviation, Woodley	
L7005	Boulton Paul P82 Defiant I <R> [PS-B]	Kent Battle of Britain Museum, Hawkinge	
L7181	Hawker Hind (G-CBLK)	Aero Vintage, Duxford	
L7191	Hawker Hind	Currently not known	
L7775	Vickers Wellington B Ic <ff>	Lincolnshire Avn Heritage Centre, E Kirkby	
L8756	Bristol 149 Bolingbroke IVT (RCAF 10001) [XD-E]	RAF Museum, Hendon	
N248	Supermarine S6A (S1596)	Solent Sky, Southampton	
N500	Sopwith LC-1T Triplane <R> (G-PENY/G-BWRA)	Privately owned, Yarcombe, Devon/RNAS Yeovilton	
N540	Port Victoria PV8 Eastchurch Kitten <R>	Yorkshire Air Museum, Elvington	
N546	Wright Quadruplane 1 <R> (BAPC 164)	Solent Sky, Southampton	
N1671	Boulton Paul P82 Defiant I (8370M) [EW-D]	RAF Museum, Cosford	
N1854	Fairey Fulmar II (G-AIBE)	FAA Museum, RNAS Yeovilton	
N2078	Sopwith Baby (8214/8215/BAPC 442)	FAA Museum, RNAS Yeovilton	
N2532	Hawker Hurricane I <R> (BAPC 272) [GZ-H]	Kent Battle of Britain Museum, Hawkinge	
N2980	Vickers Wellington Ia [R]	Brooklands Museum, Weybridge	
N3200	VS300 Spitfire IA (G-CFGJ) [QV]	IWM Duxford	
N3289	VS300 Spitfire I <R> (BAPC 65) [DW-K]	Kent Battle of Britain Museum, Hawkinge	
N3290	VS300 Spitfire I <R> [AI-H]	Privately owned, St Mawgan	
N3310	VS361 Spitfire IX <R> (BAPC 393) [A]	Privately owned, Abingdon	
N3313	VS300 Spitfire I <R> (MH314/BAPC 69) [KL-B]	Kent Battle of Britain Museum, Hawkinge	
N3317	VS329 Spitfire II <R> (P8140/BAPC 71) [BO-U]	Norfolk & Suffolk Avn Museum, Flixton	
N3378	Boulton Paul P82 Defiant I (wreck)	RAF Museum, Cosford	
N3549	DH82A Tiger Moth II (PG645/N3549)	Privately owned, Netherthorpe	
N3788	Miles M14A Magister I (V1075/G-AKPF)	Privately owned, Old Warden	
N4389	Fairey Albacore (N4172) [4M]	FAA Museum, stored Cobham Hall, RNAS Yeovilton	
N4877	Avro 652A Anson I (G-AMDA) [MK-V]	IWM Duxford	
N5137	DH82A Tiger Moth (N6638/G-BNDW)	Caernarfon Air World	
N5177	Sopwith 1½ Strutter (BAPC 452) <R>	Privately owned, stored Mersham, Surrey	
N5182	Sopwith Pup (G-APUP/9213M)	RAF Museum, Cosford	
N5195	Sopwith Pup (G-ABOX)	Museum of Army Flying, Middle Wallop	
N5199	Sopwith Pup <R> (G-BZND)	Privately owned, Yarcombe, Devon	
N5459	Sopwith Triplane <R> (BAPC 111)	FAA Museum, stored Cobham Hall, RNAS Yeovilton	

Notes	Serial	Type (code/other identity)	Owner/operator, location or fate
	N5518	Gloster Sea Gladiator (N5579)	FAA Museum, stored Cobham Hall, RNAS Yeovilton
	N5628	Gloster Gladiator II	RAF Museum, Cosford
	N5719	Gloster Gladiator II (G-CBHO)	Privately owned, Dursley, Glos
	N5903	Gloster Gladiator II (N2276/G-GLAD)	The Fighter Collection, Duxford
	N5912	Sopwith Triplane (8385M)	RAF Museum, Hendon
	N5914	Gloster Gladiator II (frame)	Jet Age Museum, Gloucester
	N6161	Sopwith Pup (G-ELRT)	Privately owned, Turweston
	N6290	Sopwith Triplane <R> (G-BOCK)	The Shuttleworth Collection, Old Warden
	N6377	Sopwith F.1 Camel <R> (G-BPOB/B2458)	Privately owned, Stow Maries
	N6452	Sopwith Pup <R> (G-BIAU)	FAA Museum, stored Cobham Hall, RNAS Yeovilton
	N6466	DH82A Tiger Moth (G-ANKZ)	Privately owned, Compton Abbas
	N6473	DH82A Tiger Moth (F-GTBO)	Privately owned, Orbigny, France
	N6537	DH82A Tiger Moth (G-AOHY)	Privately owned, Wickenby
	N6635	DH82A Tiger Moth (comp G-APAO & G-APAP) [25]	IWM Duxford
	N6720	DH82A Tiger Moth (G-BYTN/7014M) [VX]	Privately owned, stored Darley Moor, Derbyshire
	N6797	DH82A Tiger Moth (G-ANEH)	Privately owned, Swyncombe
	N6812	Sopwith 2F.1 Camel	IWM London, Lambeth
	N6847	DH82A Tiger Moth (G-APAL)	Privately owned, Braceborough, Lincs
	N6965	DH82A Tiger Moth (G-AJTW) [FL-J]	Privately owned, Tibenham
	N7033	Noorduyn AT-16 Harvard IIb (FX442)	Kent Battle of Britain Museum, Hawkinge
	N9191	DH82A Tiger Moth (G-ALND)	Privately owned, Pontypool
	N9192	DH82A Tiger Moth (G-DHZF) [RCO-N]	Privately owned, Sywell
	N9328	DH82A Tiger Moth (G-ALWS) [69]	Privately owned, Henstridge
	N9372	DH82A Tiger Moth (G-ANHK)	Privately owned, Oaksey Park
	N9389	DH82A Tiger Moth (G-ANJA)	Privately owned, Thruxton
	N9899	Supermarine Southampton I (fuselage)	RAF Museum, Hendon
	P1344	HP52 Hampden I (9175M) [PL-K]	Michael Beetham Conservation Centre, RAFM Cosford
	P2617	Hawker Hurricane I (8373M) [AF-F]	RAF Museum, Hendon
	P2725	Hawker Hurricane I (wreck)	IWM London, Lambeth
	P2725	Hawker Hurricane I <R> (BAPC 68) [TM-B]	Privately owned, Delabole, Cornwall
	P2793	Hawker Hurricane I <R> (BAPC 236) [SD-M]	Eden Camp Theme Park, stored Malton, North Yorkshire
	P2793	Hawker Hurricane I <R> (BAPC 399) [SD-M]	Eden Camp Theme Park, Malton, North Yorkshire
	P2902	Hawker Hurricane I (G-ROBT) [DX-R]	Privately owned, Duxford
	P2921	Hawker Hurricane I <R> (BAPC 273) [GZ-L]	Kent Battle of Britain Museum, Hawkinge
	P2921	Hawker Hurricane I <R> (BAPC 477) [GZ-L]	RAF Biggin Hill, on display
	P2921	Hawker Sea Hurricane X (AE977/G-CHTK) [GZ-L]	Privately owned, Biggin Hill
	P2954	Hawker Hurricane I <R> (BAPC 267) [WX-E]	IWM Duxford
	P2970	Hawker Hurricane I <R> (BAPC 291) [US-X]	Battle of Britain Memorial, Capel le Ferne, Kent
	P3059	Hawker Hurricane I <R> (BAPC 64) [SD-N]	Kent Battle of Britain Museum, Hawkinge
	P3175	Hawker Hurricane I (wreck)	RAF Museum Reserve Collection, Stafford
	P3179	Hawker Hurricane I <ff>	Tangmere Military Aviation Museum
	P3208	Hawker Hurricane I <R> (BAPC 63/L1592) [SD-T]	Kent Battle of Britain Museum, Hawkinge
	P3351	Hawker Hurricane IIa (DR393/F-AZXR) [K]	Privately owned, Cannes, France
	P3386	Hawker Hurricane I <R> (BAPC 218) [FT-A]	RAF Bentley Priory, on display
	P3395	Hawker Hurricane IV (KX829) [JX-B]	Thinktank, Birmingham
	P3554	Hawker Hurricane I (composite)	The Air Defence Collection, Salisbury
	P3679	Hawker Hurricane I <R> (BAPC 278) [GZ-K]	Kent Battle of Britain Museum, Hawkinge
	P3700	Hawker Hurricane XIIa (Z5140/G-HURI) [RF-E]	Historic Aircraft Collection, Duxford
	P3708	Hawker Hurricane I	Norfolk & Suffolk Avn Museum, Flixton (on rebuild)
	P3717	Hawker Hurricane I (composite) (DR348/G-HITT) [SW-P]	Privately owned, Old Warden
	P3873	Hawker Hurricane I <R> (BAPC 265) [YO-H]	Yorkshire Air Museum, Elvington
	P3873	Hawker Hurricane I <R> [YO-H]	Battle of Britain Bunker, Uxbridge
	P3901	Hawker Hurricane I <R> (BAPC 475) [RF-E]	Battle of Britain Bunker, Uxbridge
	P4139	Fairey Swordfish II (HS618) [5H]	FAA Museum, RNAS Yeovilton
	P6382	Miles M14A Hawk Trainer 3 (G-AJRS) [C]	The Shuttleworth Collection, Old Warden
	P7308	VS300 Spitfire IA (AR213/R9632/G-AIST) [XR-D]	Privately owned, Duxford
	P7350	VS329 Spitfire IIa (G-AWIJ) [QJ-G,QV-E]	RAF BBMF, Biggin Hill (servicing)
	P7370	VS329 Spitfire II <R> (BAPC 410) [ZP-A]	Battle of Britain Experience, Canterbury
	P7540	VS329 Spitfire IIa [DU-W]	Dumfries & Galloway Avn Mus, Dumfries
	P7666	VS329 Spitfire II <R> (BAPC 335) [EB-Z]	RAF High Wycombe, on display

Serial	Type (code/other identity)	Owner/operator, location or fate	Notes
P7819	VS329 Spitfire IIa (G-TCHZ)	Privately owned, Exeter	
P7923	VS329 Spitfire IIa <R> (BAPC 369) [TM-F]	Ulster Aviation Society, Long Kesh	
P7966	VS329 Spitfire II <R> [D-B]	Manx Aviation & Military Museum, Ronaldsway	
P8088	VS329 Spitfire II (G-CGRM) [NK-K]	Privately owned, Knutsford, Cheshire	
P8208	VS329 Spitfire IIb (G-RRFF)	Privately owned, Durley, Glos	
P8448	VS329 Spitfire II <R> (BAPC 225) [UM-D]	RAF Cranwell, on display	
P9374	VS300 Spitfire Ia (G-MKIA) [J]	Sold as N92SQ, May 2017	
P9398	Supermarine Aircraft Spitfire 26 (G-CEPL) [KL-B]	Privately owned, Rochester	
P9444	VS300 Spitfire Ia [RN-D]	Science Museum, South Kensington	
P9637	Supermarine Aircraft Spitfire 26 (G-RORB) [GR-B]	Privately owned, Perth	
R1914	Miles M14A Magister (G-AHUJ)	Privately owned, Rendcomb	
R4118	Hawker Hurricane I (G-HUPW) [UP-W]	Privately owned, Old Warden	
R4229	Hawker Hurricane I <R> (BAPC 334) [GN-J]	Alexandra Park, Windsor	
R4922	DH82A Tiger Moth II (G-APAO)	Privately owned, Henlow	
R4959	DH82A Tiger Moth II (G-ARAZ) [59]	Privately owned, Temple Bruer, Lincs	
R5136	DH82A Tiger Moth II (G-APAP)	Privately owned, Darley Moor, Derbyshire	
R5172	DH82A Tiger Moth II (G-AOIS) [FIJE]	Privately owned, Sywell	
R5246	DH82A Tiger Moth II (D-EDHA) [40]	Privately owned, Heringsdorf, Germany	
R5868	Avro 683 Lancaster I (7325M) [PO-S]	RAF Museum, Hendon	
R5868	Avro 683 Lancaster I <R> (BAPC 471) [PO-S] <ff>	Avro Heritage Museum, Woodford	
R6690	VS300 Spitfire I <R> (BAPC 254) [PR-A]	Yorkshire Air Museum, Elvington	
R6775	VS300 Spitfire I <R> (BAPC 299) [YT-J]	Battle of Britain Memorial, Capel le Ferne, Kent	
R6904	VS300 Spitfire I <R> [BT-K]	Privately owned, Cornwall	
R6915	VS300 Spitfire I	IWM London, Lambeth	
R9125	Westland Lysander III (8377M)[LX-L]	Michael Beetham Conservation Centre, RAFM Cosford	
R9612	VS300 Spitfire I (X4650/G-GUK) [LC]	Repainted as X4650, August 2017	
R9612	VS300 Spitfire I <R> [LC]	Privately owned, Duxford	
S1287	Fairey Flycatcher <R> (G-BEYB) [5]	FAA Museum, stored Cobham Hall, RNAS Yeovilton	
S1581	Hawker Nimrod I (G-BWWK) [573]	The Fighter Collection, Duxford	
S1595	Supermarine S6B [1]	Science Museum, South Kensington	
S1615	Isaacs Fury II (G-BMEU)	Privately owned, stored Netherthorpe	
T5298	Bristol 156 Beaufighter I (4552M) <ff>	Midland Air Museum, Coventry	
T5424	DH82A Tiger Moth II (G-AJOA)	Privately owned, Swindon	
T5854	DH82A Tiger Moth II (G-ANKK)	Privately owned, Baxterley	
T5879	DH82A Tiger Moth II (G-AXBW) [RUC-W]	Privately owned, Frensham	
T6296	DH82A Tiger Moth II (8387M)	RAF Museum, Cosford	
T6953	DH82A Tiger Moth II (G-ANNI)	Privately owned, Tisted, Hants	
T6991	DH82A Tiger Moth II (DE694/HB-UPY)	Privately owned, Lausanne, Switzerland	
T7109	DH82A Tiger Moth II (G-AOIM)	Privately owned, Bicester	
T7230	DH82A Tiger Moth II (G-AFVE)	Privately owned, Mazowiecke, Poland	
T7281	DH82A Tiger Moth II (G-ARTL)	Privately owned, Egton, nr Whitby	
T7290	DH82A Tiger Moth II (G-ANNK) [14]	Privately owned, Sywell	
T7793	DH82A Tiger Moth II (G-ANKV)	Privately owned, Wickenby	
T7794	DH82A Tiger Moth II (G-ASPV)	Privately owned, Bagby	
T7842	DH82A Tiger Moth II (G-AMTF)	Privately owned, Westfield, Surrey	
T7909	DH82A Tiger Moth II (G-ANON)	Privately owned, Sherburn-in-Elmet	
T7997	DH82A Tiger Moth II (NL750/G-AHUF)	Privately owned, Breighton	
T8191	DH82A Tiger Moth II (G-BWMK)	Privately owned, Henstridge	
T9707	Miles M14A Magister I (G-AKKR/8378M/T9708)	Museum of Army Flying, Middle Wallop	
T9738	Miles M14A Magister I (G-AKAT)	Privately owned, Breighton	
V3388	Airspeed AS10 Oxford I (G-AHTW)	IWM Duxford	
V6028	Bristol 149 Bolingbroke IVT (G-MKIV) [GB-D] <rf>	The Aircraft Restoration Co, stored Duxford	
V6555	Hawker Hurricane I (BAPC 411/P3144) <R> [DT-A]	Battle of Britain Experience, Canterbury	
V6799	Hawker Hurricane I <R> (BAPC 72/V7767) [SD-X]	Jet Age Museum, Gloucester	
V7313	Hawker Hurricane I <R> (BAPC 346) [US-F]	Privately owned, North Weald, on display	
V7350	Hawker Hurricane I <ff>	Romney Marsh Wartime Collection	
V7467	Hawker Hurricane I <R> (BAPC 378) [LE-D]	RAF High Wycombe, on display	

Notes	Serial	Type (code/other identity)	Owner/operator, location or fate
	V7467	Hawker Hurricane I <R> (BAPC 223) [ZJ-L]	Spitfire Visitor Centre, Blackpool
	V7467	Hawker Hurricane I <R> (BAPC 288) [LE-D]	Wonderland Pleasure Park, Farnsfield, Notts
	V7497	Hawker Hurricane I (G-HRLI) [SD-X]	Privately owned, Elmsett
	V9312	Westland Lysander IIIa (G-CCOM)	The Aircraft Restoration Co, Duxford
	V9367	Westland Lysander IIIa (G-AZWT) [MA-B]	The Shuttleworth Collection, Old Warden
	V9673	Westland Lysander IIIa (V9300/G-LIZY) [MA-J]	IWM Duxford
	V9723	Westland Lysander IIIa (V9546/OO-SOT) [MA-D]	SABENA Old Timers, Brussels, Belgium
	V9875	Westland Lysander IIIa <R> [MA-J]	Gateguards (UK), St Mawgan
	W1048	HP59 Halifax II (8465M) [TL-S]	RAF Museum, Hendon
	W2068	Avro 652A Anson I (9261M/VH-ASM) [68]	RAF Museum, Hendon
	W2718	VS Walrus I (G-RNLI)	Privately owned, Audley End
	W3257	Supermarine Aircraft Spitfire 26 (G-CENI) [FY-E]	Sold to New Zealand, June 2017
	W3644	VS349 Spitfire V <R> (BAPC 323) [QV-J]	Privately owned, Lake Fairhaven, Lancs
	W3850	VS349 Spitfire V <R> (BAPC 304) [PR-A]	Privately owned, Knutsford, Cheshire
	W4041	Gloster E28/39	Science Museum, South Kensington
	W4041	Gloster E28/39 <R> (BAPC 331)	Jet Age Museum, Gloucester
	W4050	DH98 Mosquito	de Havilland Aircraft Museum, London Colney
	W5856	Fairey Swordfish I (G-BMGC) [4A]	RN Historic Flight, Yeovilton
	W9385	DH87B Hornet Moth (G-ADND) [YG-L,3]	Privately owned, Oaksey Park
	X4178	VS300 Spitfire I <R> (BAPC 394) [EB-K]	IWM Duxford
	X4253	VS300 Spitfire I <R> (BAPC 326) [FY-N]	Spitfire Visitor Centre, Blackpool
	X4276	VS300 Spitfire I (G-CDGU)	Privately owned, Sandown
	X4590	VS300 Spitfire I (8384M) [PR-F]	RAF Museum, Hendon
	X4650	VS300 Spitfire I (R9612/G-CGUK) [KL-A]	Privately owned, Duxford
	X4683	Jurca MJ10 Spitfire (G-MUTS) [EB-N]	Privately owned, Fishburn
	X4859	VS300 Spitfire I <R> (BAPC 319) [PQ-N]	Grangemouth Spitfire Memorial Trust
	X7688	Bristol 156 Beaufighter I (3858M/G-DINT)	Sold to Australia, 2018
	X9407	Percival P.16A Q6 (G-AFFD)	Privately owned, Seething (on rebuild)
	Z1206	Vickers Wellington IV (fuselage)	Privately owned, Kenilworth
	Z2033	Fairey Firefly I (G-ASTL) [275/N]	FAA Museum, stored Cobham Hall, RNAS Yeovilton
	Z2315	Hawker Hurricane IIa (JU-E]	IWM Duxford
	Z2389	Hawker Hurricane IIa [XR-T]	Brooklands Museum, Weybridge
	Z3427	Hawker Hurricane IIc <R> (BAPC 205) [AV-R]	Michael Beetham Conservation Centre, RAFM Cosford
	Z5207	Hawker Hurricane IIb (G-BYDL)	Privately owned, Thruxton
	Z5252	Hawker Hurricane IIb (G-BWHA/Z5053) [GO-B]	Sold to Russia
	Z7015	Hawker Sea Hurricane Ib (G-BKTH) [7-L]	The Shuttleworth Collection, Old Warden
	Z7197	Percival P30 Proctor III (G-AKZN/8380M)	RAF Museum Reserve Collection, Stafford
	Z7258	DH89A Dragon Rapide (NR786/G-AHGD)	Privately owned, Membury (wreck)
	AB196	Supermarine Aircraft Spitfire 26 (G-CCGH)	Privately owned, Enstone
	AB910	VS349 Spitfire Vb (G-AISU) [SH-F]	RAF BBMF, Coningsby
	AD189	VS349 Spitfire Vb (G-CHVJ)	Privately owned, Raglan, Monmouthshire
	AD370	Jurca Spitfire (G-CHBW) [PJ-C]	Privately owned, Perranporth
	AD540	VS349 Spitfire Vb (wreck)	Privately owned, Launceston (on rebuild)
	AE436	HP52 Hampden I [PL-J] (parts)	Lincolnshire Avn Heritage Centre, E Kirkby
	AG244	Hawker Hurricane XII (RCAF 5487/G-CBOE)	Privately owned, Aalen, Germany
	AJ841	CCF T-6J Texan (MM53795/G-BJST/KF729)	Privately owned, Duxford
	AL246	Grumman Martlet I	FAA Museum, RNAS Yeovilton
	AP506	Cierva C30A (G-ACWM) (wreck)	The Helicopter Museum, Weston-super-Mare
	AP507	Cierva C30A (G-ACWP) [KX-P]	Science Museum, South Kensington
	AR501	VS349 Spitfire LF Vc (G-AWII/AR4474) [DU-E]	The Shuttleworth Collection, Old Warden
	AV511	EHI-101 Merlin <R> [511]	SFDO, RNAS Culdrose
	AW101	AgustaWestland AW101 Mk.510 (G-17-510)	AgustaWestland, Yeovil
	BB803	DH82A Tiger Moth (G-ADWJ) [75]	Privately owned, Henstridge
	BB807	DH82A Tiger Moth (G-ADWO)	Solent Sky, Southampton
	BD713	Hawker Hurricane IIb	Currently not known
	BE505	Hawker Hurricane IIb (RCAF 5403/G-HHII) [XP-L]	Privately owned, Elmsett
	BH238	Hawker Hurricane IIb	Airframe Assemblies, stored Sandown

Serial	Type (code/other identity)	Owner/operator, location or fate	Notes
BL614	VS349 Spitfire Vb (4354M) [ZD-F]	RAF Museum, Hendon	
BL655	VS349 Spitfire Vb (wreck)	Lincolnshire Avn Heritage Centre, East Kirkby	
BL688	VS349 Spitfire LF Vb (G-CJWO)	Privately owned, Launceston	
BL735	Supermarine Aircraft Spitfire 26 (G-HABT) [BT-A]	Privately owned, North Coates	
BL924	VS349 Spitfire Vb <R> (BAPC 242) [AZ-G]	Beale Park, Pangbourne, Berks	
BL927	Supermarine Aircraft Spitfire 26 (G-CGWI) [JH-I]	Privately owned, Perth	
BM361	VS349 Spitfire Vb <R> (BAPC 269) [XR-C]	RAF Lakenheath, on display	
BM481	VS349 Spitfire Vb <R> (BAPC 301) [YO-T]	Thornaby Aerodrome Memorial	
	(also wears PK651/RAO-B)		
BM539	VS349 Spitfire LF Vb (G-SSVB)	Privately owned, Hastings	
BM597	VS349 Spitfire LF Vb (G-MKVB/5718M) [JH-C]	Historic Aircraft Collection, Duxford	
BN230	Hawker Hurricane IIc (LF751/5466M) [FT-A]	RAF Manston, Memorial Pavilion	
BP926	VS353 Spitfire PR IV (G-PRIV)	Privately owned, Newport Pagnell	
BR601	VS361 Spitfire IX (G-CIYF) [SH-F]	Sold to the USA, 28 March 2017	
BR954	VS353 Spitfire PR IV <R> (N3194/BAPC 220) [JP-A]	Fishburn Historic Aviation Centre	
BS239	VS361 Spitfire IX <R> (BAPC 222) [5R-E]	Battle of Britain Bunker, Uxbridge	
BS410	VS361 Spitfire IXc (G-TCHI)	Privately owned, Biggin Hill	
BS435	VS361 Spitfire IX <R> (BAPC 324) [FY-F]	Privately owned, Lytham St Annes	
BW853	Hawker Hurricane XIIa (G-BRKE) (fuselage)	Currently not known	
DD931	Bristol 152 Beaufort VIII (9131M/BAPC 436) [L]	RAF Museum, Hendon	
DE208	DH82A Tiger Moth II (G-AGYU)	Privately owned, Treswell, Notts	
DE470	DH82A Tiger Moth II (G-ANMY) [16]	Privately owned, Garford, Oxon (rebuild)	
DE623	DH82A Tiger Moth II (G-ANFI)	Privately owned, Cardiff	
DE673	DH82A Tiger Moth II (G-ADNZ/6948M)	Privately owned, Tibenham	
DE971	DH82A Tiger Moth II (G-OOSY)	Privately owned, Bicester	
DE974	DH82A Tiger Moth II (G-ANZZ)	Privately owned, Clacton	
DE992	DH82A Tiger Moth II (G-AXXV)	Privately owned, Membury, Berks	
DF112	DH82A Tiger Moth II (G-ANRM)	Privately owned, Clacton/Duxford	
DF128	DH82A Tiger Moth II (G-AOJJ) [RCO-U]	Privately owned, White Waltham	
DF198	DH82A Tiger Moth II (G-BBRB)	Privately owned, stored West Wickham, Kent	
DG202	Gloster F9/40 (5758M)	RAF Museum, stored Cosford	
DG590	Miles M2H Hawk Major (G-ADMW/8379M)	Montrose Air Station Heritage Centre	
DP872	Fairey Barracuda II <ff>	FAA Museum, stored Cobham Hall, RNAS Yeovilton	
DP872	Fairey Barracuda II <rf>	FAA Museum, RNAS Yeovilton	
DV372	Avro 683 Lancaster I <ff>	IWM London, Lambeth	
DZ313	DH98 Mosquito B IV <R>	Privately owned, Little Rissington	
EB518	Airspeed AS10 Oxford V	Privately owned, Kenilworth	
EE416	Gloster Meteor F3 <ff>	Martin Baker Aircraft, Chalgrove, fire section	
EE425	Gloster Meteor F3 <ff>	Jet Age Museum, Gloucester	
EE531	Gloster Meteor F4 (7090M)	Midland Air Museum, Coventry	
EE549	Gloster Meteor F4 (7008M) [A]	Tangmere Military Aviation Museum	
EE602	VS349 Spitfire LF Vc (G-IBSY) [DV-V]	Privately owned, Biggin Hill	
EF545	VS349 Spitfire LF Vc (G-CDGY)	Aero Vintage, Rye	
EJ922	Hawker Typhoon Ib <ff>	Privately owned, Booker	
EM720	DH82A Tiger Moth II (G-AXAN)	Privately owned, Darley Moor, Derbyshire	
EM726	DH82A Tiger Moth II (G-ANDE) [FY]	Privately owned, Headcorn	
EM840	DH82A Tiger Moth II (G-ANBY)	Privately owned, Middle Wallop	
EN130	Supermarine Aircraft Spitfire 26B (G-ENAA) [FN-A]	Privately owned, Enstone	
EN179	VS361 Spitfire F IX (G-TCHO)	Privately owned, Exeter	
EN224	VS366 Spitfire F XII (G-FXII)	Privately owned, Sywell	
EN398	VS361 Spitfire F IX <R> [JE-J]	AMSS, Pyle, Bridgend	
EN398	VS361 Spitfire F IX <R> [JE-J]	RAF Coningsby, on display	
EN398	VS361 Spitfire F IX <R> (BAPC 184) [JE-J]	Northern 40s Re-enactment Group, Belper	
EN398	VS361 Spitfire F IX <R> [JE-J]	Spitfire Spares, Taunton, Somerset	
EN570	VS361 Spitfire F IX (G-CISP/LN-AOA)	Privately owned, Sandown	
EN961	Isaacs Spitfire <R> (G-CGIK) [SD-X]	Privately owned,	
EP120	VS349 Spitfire LF Vb (G-LFVB/5377M/8070M) [AE-A]	The Fighter Collection, Duxford	
EP121	VS349 Spitfire LF Vb <R> (BAPC 320) [LO-D]	Montrose Air Station Heritage Centre	
EP122	VS349 Spitfire F Vb (R9649/G-CISV) [GL-B]	To the USA, February 2018	
EV771	Fairchild UC-61 Argus <R> (BAPC 294)	Thorpe Camp Preservation Group, Lincs	

Notes	Serial	Type (code/other identity)	Owner/operator, location or fate
	EX976	NA AT-6D Harvard III (FAP 1657)	FAA Museum, RNAS Yeovilton
	FE511	Noorduyn AT-16 Harvard IIb (G-CIUW)	Privately owned, Old Warden
	FE695	Noorduyn AT-16 Harvard IIb (G-BTXI) [94]	The Fighter Collection, Duxford
	FE788	CCF Harvard IV (MM54137/G-CTKL)	Privately owned, Biggin Hill
	FE905	Noorduyn AT-16 Harvard IIb (LN-BNM)	RAF Museum, Hendon
	FE992	Noorduyn AT-16 Harvard IIb (G-BDAM)	Privately owned,
	FJ801	Boeing-Stearman PT-27 Kaydet (N62842/BAPC 375)	Norfolk & Suffolk Avn Museum, Flixton
	FJ992	Boeing-Stearman PT-17 Kaydet (OO-JEH) [44]	Privately owned, Wevelgem, Belgium
	FK338	Fairchild 24W-41 Argus I (G-AJOZ)	Yorkshire Air Museum, Elvington
	FL586	Douglas C-47B Dakota (OO-SMA) [AI-N] (fuselage)	WWII Remembrance Museum, Handcross, W Sussex
	FR886	Piper L-4J Grasshopper (G-BDMS)	Privately owned, Old Sarum
	FS628	Fairchild Argus 2 (43-14601/G-AIZE)	RAF Museum, Cosford
	FS728	Noorduyn AT-16 Harvard IIb (G-FRCP)	Privately owned, Gelnhausen, Germany
	FT118	Noorduyn AT-16 Harvard IIb (G-BZHL) [TM-13]	Privately owned, Hibaldstow
	FT323	NA AT-6D Harvard III (FAP 1513/G-CCOY)	Privately owned, Bruntingthorpe
	FT391	Noorduyn AT-16 Harvard IIb (G-AZBN)	Privately owned, White Waltham
	FX322	Noorduyn AT-16 Harvard IIb <ff>	Privately owned, Doncaster
	FX760	Curtiss P-40N Kittyhawk IV (A29-556/9150M) [GA-?]	RAF Museum, Hendon
	FZ626	Douglas Dakota III (KN566/G-AMPO) [YS-DH]	RAF Brize Norton, for display
	GZ100	AgustaWestland AW109SP Grand New (G-ZIOO)	RAF No 32(The Royal) Sqn, Northolt
	HB737	Fairchild Argus III (G-BCBH)	Privately owned, Spanhoe
	HB751	Fairchild Argus III (G-BCBL)	Privately owned, Woolsery, Devon
	HG691	DH89A Dragon Rapide (G-AIYR)	Privately owned, Clacton/Duxford
	HH268	GAL48 Hotspur II (HH379/BAPC 261) [H]	Museum of Army Flying, Middle Wallop
	HJ711	DH98 Mosquito NF II (BAPC 434) [VI-C]	Lincolnshire Avn Heritage Centre, E Kirkby
	HM580	Cierva C-30A (G-ACUU) [KX-K]	IWM Duxford
	HS503	Fairey Swordfish IV (BAPC 108)	RAF Museum Reserve Collection, Stafford
	IR206	Eurofighter Typhoon <R> (BAPC 360) [IR]	RAF M&RU, Bottesford
	IR808	B-V Chinook <R> (BAPC 361)	RAF M&RU, Bottesford
	JG241	Supermarine Aircraft Spitfire 26B (G-SMSP) [ZX-J]	Privately owned, Blackbushe
	JG668	VS359 Spitfire T8 (A58-441/G-CFGA)	Privately owned, Haverfordwest
	JG891	VS349 Spitfire F Vc (N5TF/G-LFVC) [RS-T]	Privately owned, Biggin Hill (on rebuild)
	JN768	Hawker Tempest V (4887M/G-TMPV)	Privately owned, Bentwaters
	JP843	Hawker Typhoon Ib [Y]	Privately owned, Shrewsbury
	JR505	Hawker Typhoon Ib <ff>	Midland Air Museum, Coventry
	JV482	Grumman Wildcat V	Ulster Aviation Society, Long Kesh
	JV579	Grumman FM-2 Wildcat (N4845V/G-RUMW) [F]	The Fighter Collection, Duxford
	KB889	Avro 683 Lancaster B X (G-LANC) [NA-I]	IWM Duxford
	KB976	Avro 683 Lancaster B X <ff>	Lincolnshire Avn Heritage Centre, E Kirkby
	KB976	Avro 683 Lancaster B X (G-BCOH) <rf>	South Yorkshire Aircraft Museum, Doncaster
	KD345	Goodyear FG-1D Corsair (88297/G-FGID) [130-A]	The Fighter Collection, Duxford
	KD431	CV Corsair IV [E2-M]	FAA Museum, RNAS Yeovilton
	KE209	Grumman Hellcat II	FAA Museum, RNAS Yeovilton
	KE418	Hawker Tempest <rf>	Currently not known
	KF183	Noorduyn AT-16 Harvard IIb (G-CORS) [3]	Privately owned, Duxford
	KF388	Noorduyn AT-16 Harvard IIb (composite)	Bournemouth Aviation Museum
	KF435	Noorduyn AT-16 Harvard IIb	Repainted in US marks as 5-666
	KF532	Noorduyn AT-16 Harvard IIb <ff>	Privately owned, Bruntingthorpe
	KF584	CCF T-6J Texan (G-RAIX) [RAI-X]	Privately owned, Lee-on-Solent
	KF650	Noorduyn AT-16 Harvard IIb <ff>	Sywell Aviation Museum
	KF741	Noorduyn AT-16 Harvard IIb <ff>	Privately owned, Kenilworth
	KG374	Douglas Dakota IV (KP208) [YS-DM]	Merville Barracks, Colchester, on display
	KG651	Douglas Dakota III (G-AMHJ)	Metheringham Airfield Visitor Centre, Lincs
	KH570	Titan T-51B Mustang (G-CIXK) [5J-X]	Privately owned, Sywell
	KH774	NA P-51D Mustang IV (44-73877/G-SHWN) [GA-S]	Privately owned, Goodwood
	KJ351	Airspeed AS58 Horsa II (TL659/BAPC 80) [23]	Museum of Army Flying, Middle Wallop

Serial	Type (code/other identity)	Owner/operator, location or fate	Notes
KJ994	Douglas Dakota III (F-AZTE)	Dakota et Cie, La Ferté Alais, France	
KK116	Douglas Dakota IV (G-AMPY)	Privately owned, Coventry	
KK527	Fairchild 24R Argus III (44-83184/G-RGUS)	Privately owned, Sibson	
KK995	Sikorsky Hoverfly I [E]	RAF Museum, Hendon	
KL216	Republic P-47D Thunderbolt (45-49295/9212M) [RS-L]	RAF Museum, Hendon	
KN353	Douglas Dakota IV (G-AMYJ)	Yorkshire Air Museum, Elvington	
KN645	Douglas Dakota IV (KG374/8355M)	RAF Museum, Cosford	
KN751	Consolidated Liberator C VI (IAF HE807) [F]	RAF Museum, Hendon	
KZ191	Hawker Hurricane IV (frame only)	Privately owned, East Garston, Bucks	
LA198	VS356 Spitfire F21 (7118M) [RAI-G]	Kelvingrove Art Gallery & Museum, Glasgow	
LA226	VS356 Spitfire F21 (7119M)	RAF Museum Reserve Collection, Stafford	
LA255	VS356 Spitfire F21 (6490M)	RAF Lossiemouth, preserved	
LA543	VS474 Seafire F46 <ff>	The Air Defence Collection, Salisbury	
LA546	VS474 Seafire F46 (G-CFZJ)	Privately owned, Colchester	
LA564	VS474 Seafire F46 (G-FRSX)	Kennet Aviation, North Weald	
LB264	Taylorcraft Plus D (G-AIXA)	RAF Museum, Hendon	
LB294	Taylorcraft Plus D (G-AHWJ)	Saywell Heritage Centre, Worthing	
LB312	Taylorcraft Plus D (HH982/G-AHXE)	Privately owned, Netheravon	
LB323	Taylorcraft Plus D (G-AHSD)	Privately owned, Spanhoe	
LB367	Taylorcraft Plus D (G-AHGZ)	Privately owned, Melksham	
LB375	Taylorcraft Plus D (G-AHGW)	Privately owned, Spanhoe	
LF363	Hawker Hurricane IIc [GN-F,SD-A]	RAF BBMF, Coningsby	
LF738	Hawker Hurricane IIc (5405M) [UH-A]	RAF Museum, Cosford	
LF789	DH82 Queen Bee (K3584/BAPC 186) [R2-K]	de Havilland Aircraft Museum, London Colney	
LF858	DH82 Queen Bee (G-BLUZ)	Privately owned, Henlow	
LH291	Airspeed AS51 Horsa I <R> (BAPC 279)	RAF Museum, stored Cosford	
LS326	Fairey Swordfish II (G-AJVH) [L2]	RN Historic Flight, Yeovilton	
LV907	HP59 Halifax III (HR792/BAPC 449) [NP-F] (marked NP763 [H7-N] on port side)	Yorkshire Air Museum, Elvington	
LZ551	DH100 Vampire	FAA Museum, RNAS Yeovilton	
LZ766	Percival P34 Proctor III (G-ALCK)	IWM Duxford	
LZ842	VS361 Spitfire F IX (G-CGZU) [EF-F]	Privately owned, Biggin Hill	
LZ844	VS349 Spitfire F Vc [UP-X]	Currently not known	
MA764	VS361 Spitfire F IX (G-MCDB)	Privately owned, Biggin Hill	
MD338	VS359 Spitfire LF VIII	Privately owned, Sandown	
MF628	Vickers Wellington T10 (9210M)	Michael Beetham Conservation Centre, RAFM Cosford	
MH314	VS361 Spitfire IX <R> (EN526/BAPC 221) [SZ-G]	RAF Northolt, on display	
MH415	VS361 Spitfire IX <R> (MJ751/BAPC 209) [DU-V]	The Aircraft Restoration Co, Duxford	
MH434	VS361 Spitfire LF IXb (G-ASJV) [ZD-B]	The Old Flying Machine Company, Duxford	
MJ627	VS509 Spitfire T9 (G-BMSB) [9G-P]	Privately owned, Biggin Hill	
MJ772	VS509 Spitfire T9 (G-AVAV) [NL-R]	Privately owned, Biggin Hill	
MJ832	VS361 Spitfire IX <R> (L1096/BAPC 229) [DN-Y]	RAF Digby, on display	
MK356	VS361 Spitfire LF IXe (5690M) [QJ-3]	RAF BBMF, Coningsby	
MK356	VS361 Spitfire LF IXc <R> [2I-V]	Kent Battle of Britain Museum, Hawkinge	
MK356	VS361 Spitfire LF IXc (BAPC 298) <R>	RAF Cosford, on display	
MK392	VS361 Spitfire LF IXc <R> [JE-J]	Boultbee Flight Academy, Goodwood	
MK805	VS361 Spitfire IX (BAPC 426) <R> [SH-B]	Simply Spitfire, Oulton Broad, Suffolk	
MK912	VS361 Spitfire LF IXc (G-BRRA) [SH-L]	Privately owned, Biggin Hill	
ML295	VS361 Spitfire LF IXe (NH341/G-CICK)	Privately owned, Duxford	
ML407	VS509 Spitfire T9 (G-LFIX) [OU-V]	Privately owned, Sywell	
ML411	VS361 Spitfire LF IXe (G-CBNU)	Privately owned, Ashford, Kent	
ML427	VS361 Spitfire IX (6457M) [HK-A]	Thinktank, Birmingham	
ML796	Short S25 Sunderland V [NS-F]	IWM Duxford	
ML824	Short S25 Sunderland V [NS-Z]	RAF Museum, Hendon	
MP425	Airspeed AS10 Oxford I (G-AITB) [G]	RAF Museum, Hendon	
MS902	Miles M25 Martinet TT1 (TF-SHC)	Museum of Berkshire Aviation, Woodley	
MT182	Auster J/1 Autocrat (G-AJDY)	Privately owned, Spanhoe	
MT197	Auster IV (G-ANHS)	Privately owned, Spanhoe	
MT438	Auster III (G-AREI)	Privately owned, Eggesford	

Notes	Serial	Type (code/other identity)	Owner/operator, location or fate
	MT818	VS502 Spitfire T8 (G-AIDN)	Privately owned, Biggin Hill
	MT847	VS379 Spitfire FR XIVe (6960M) [AX-H]	*To the USA, 2017*
	MT928	VS359 Spitfire HF VIIIc (D-FEUR/MV154/*AR654*) [ZX-M]	Privately owned, Bremgarten, Germany
	MV268	VS379 Spitfire FR XIVe (MV293/G-SPIT) [JE-J]	Privately owned, Duxford
	MW401	Hawker Tempest II (IAF HA604/G-PEST)	Privately owned, Wickenby
	MW763	Hawker Tempest II (IAF HA586/G-TEMT) [HF-A]	North Weald Heritage Aviation, North Weald
	MW810	Hawker Tempest II (IAF HA591) <ff>	Privately owned, Bentwaters
	NF314	GEC Phoenix (BAPC 408)	Army, Larkhill, on display
	NF370	Fairey Swordfish III [NH-L]	IWM Duxford
	NF389	Fairey Swordfish III [D]	RN Historic Flight, Yeovilton
	NH238	VS361 Spitfire LF IXe (G-MKIX) [D-A]	Privately owned, stored Greenham Common
	NH341	VS509 Spitfire T9 (G-CICK) [DB-E]	Privately owned, Headcorn
	NJ633	Auster 5D (G-AKXP)	Privately owned, Old Sarum
	NJ673	Auster 5D (G-AOCR)	Privately owned, Shenington, Oxon
	NJ689	Auster AOP5 (G-ALXZ)	Privately owned, Breighton
	NJ695	Auster AOP5 (G-AJXV)	Privately owned, Newark
	NJ719	Auster AOP5 (TW385/G-ANFU)	North-East Aircraft Museum, Usworth
	NJ728	Auster AOP5 (G-AIKE)	Privately owned, Little Gransden
	NJ889	Auster AOP3 (G-AHLK)	Privately owned, Ledbury, Herefordshire
	NL750	DH82A Tiger Moth II (T7997/G-AOBH)	Privately owned, Eaglescott
	NL985	DH82A Tiger Moth I (G-BWIK/7015M)	Privately owned, Oaksey Park
	NM138	DH82A Tiger Moth I (G-ANEW) [41]	Privately owned, Henstridge
	NM181	DH82A Tiger Moth I (G-AZGZ)	Privately owned, Rush Green
	NP294	Percival P31 Proctor IV [TB-M]	Lincolnshire Avn Heritage Centre, E Kirkby
	NV778	Hawker Tempest II (8386M)	RAF Museum, Hendon
	NS710	DH98 Mosquito TT35 (TJ118) <ff>	Victoria and Albert Museum, Knightsbridge, London
	NX534	Auster III (G-BUDL)	Privately owned, Spanhoe
	NX611	Avro 683 Lancaster B VII (G-ASXX/8375M) [DX-F,LE-H]	Lincolnshire Avn Heritage Centre, E Kirkby
	PA474	Avro 683 Lancaster B I [AR-L,VN-T]	RAF BBMF, Coningsby
	PD685	Slingsby T7 Cadet TX1 (BAPC 355)	Tettenhall Transport Heritage Centre
	PF179	HS Gnat T1 (XR571/8602M)	Privately owned, North Weald
	PG657	DH82A Tiger Moth II (G-AGPK)	Privately owned, Clacton
	PG712	DH82A Tiger Moth II (PH-CSL) [2]	Privately owned, Hilversum, The Netherlands
	PK519	VS356 Spitfire F22 [G-SPXX]	Privately owned, Newport Pagnell
	PK624	VS356 Spitfire F22 (8072M)	The Fighter Collection, Duxford
	PK664	VS356 Spitfire F22 (7759M) [V6-B]	Kennet Aviation, North Weald
	PK683	VS356 Spitfire F24 (7150M)	Solent Sky, Southampton
	PK724	VS356 Spitfire F24 (7288M)	RAF Museum, Hendon
	PL256	VS361 Spitfire IX <R> (BAPC 325) [AI-L]	Privately owned, Leicester
	PL279	VS361 Spitfire IX <R> (N3317/BAPC 268) [ZF-Z]	Privately owned, St Mawgan
	PL788	Supermarine Aircraft Spitfire 26 (G-CIEN)	Privately owned, Perth
	PL793	Supermarine Aircraft Spitfire 26 (G-CIXM)	Privately owned, Odiham
	PL904	VS365 Spitfire PR XI <R> (*EN343*/BAPC 226)	RAF Benson, on display
	PL965	VS365 Spitfire PR XI (G-MKXI) [R]	Hangar 11 Collection, North Weald
	PL983	VS365 Spitfire PR XI (G-PRXI)	Privately owned, Duxford (on rebuild)
	PM631	VS390 Spitfire PR XIX	RAF BBMF, Coningsby
	PM651	VS390 Spitfire PR XIX (7758M) [X]	RAF Museum Reserve Collection, Stafford
	PN323	HP Halifax VII <ff>	IWM Duxford
	PP566	Fairey Firefly I <rf>	Privately owned, Newton Abbott, Devon
	PP972	VS358 Seafire LF IIIc (G-BUAR) [11-5/N]	Privately owned, Sywell
	PR536	Hawker Tempest II (IAF HA457)[OQ-H]	RAF Museum, Hendon
	PS853	VS390 Spitfire PR XIX (G-RRGN) [C]	Rolls-Royce, East Midlands
	PS890	VS390 Spitfire PR XIX (F-AZJS) [UM-E]	Privately owned, Dijon, France
	PS915	VS390 Spitfire PR XIX (7548M/7711M)	RAF BBMF, Coningsby
	PT462	VS509 Spitfire T9 (G-CTIX/N462JC) [SW-A]	Privately owned, Caernarfon/Duxford
	PT462	VS361 Spitfire IX <R> (BAPC 318) [SW-A]	Privately owned, Moffat, Dumfries & Galloway
	PT879	VS361 Spitfire F IX (G-BYDE/G-PTIX)	Hangar 11 Collection, North Weald
	PV181	VS361 Spitfire HF IXc (RR232/G-BRSF) [RAB]	*Repainted as RR232, July 2017*

Serial	Type (code/other identity)	Owner/operator, location or fate	Notes
PV202	VS509 Spitfire T9 (H-98/W3632/G-CCCA) [5R-H]	Historic Flying Ltd, Duxford	
PV303	Supermarine Aircraft Spitfire 26 (G-CCJL) [ON-B]	Privately owned, Barton	
PZ460	BBC Mosquito (F-PMOZ) [NE-K]	Privately owned, Fontenay-le-Comte, France	
PZ865	Hawker Hurricane IIc (G-AMAU) [EG-S]	RAF BBMF, Coningsby	
QQ100	Agusta A109E Power Elite (G-CFVB)	MoD/AFD/QinetiQ, Boscombe Down	
QQ101	BAe RJ.100 (G-BZAY)	MoD/ETPS, Boscombe Down	
QQ102	BAe RJ.70ER (G-BVRJ)	MoD/ETPS, Boscombe Down	
QQ103	Diamond DA.42M-NG Twin Star (G-LTPA)	MoD/ETPS, Boscombe Down	
RA848	Slingsby T7 Cadet TX1 <ff>	Privately owned, Leeds	
RA854	Slingsby T7 Cadet TX1	Yorkshire Air Museum, Elvington	
RA897	Slingsby T7 Cadet TX1	Newark Air Museum, Winthorpe	
RA905	Slingsby T7 Cadet TX1 (BGA1143)	Trenchard Museum, RAF Halton	
RB142	Supermarine Aircraft Spitfire 26 (G-CEFC) [DW-B]	Privately owned, Lee-on-Solent	
RB159	VS379 Spitfire F XIV <R> [DW-D]	Privately owned, Delabole, Cornwall	
RB396	Hawker Typhoon IB (fuselage)	Privately owned, Goodwood	
RD220	Bristol 156 Beaufighter TF X	National Museum of Flight, stored E Fortune	
RD253	Bristol 156 Beaufighter TF X (7931M)	RAF Museum, Hendon	
RF398	Avro 694 Lincoln B II (8376M)	RAF Museum, Cosford	
RG333	Miles M38 Messenger IIA (G-AIEK)	Privately owned, Middle Wallop	
RG904	VS Spitfire <R> (BAPC 333) [BT-K]	RAF Museum, Cosford	
RH746	Bristol 164 Brigand TF1 (fuselage)	RAF Museum, stored Cosford	
RK838	VS349 Spitfire Vb <R> (BAPC 230/AB550) [GE-P]	Eden Camp Theme Park, Malton, North Yorkshire	
RK855	Supermarine Aircraft Spitfire 26 (G-PIXY) [FT-C]	Privately owned, Henstridge	
RL962	DH89A Dominie II (G-AHED)	RAF Museum Reserve Collection, Stafford	
RM169	Percival P31 Proctor IV (G-ANVY) [4-47]	Privately owned, Great Oakley, Essex	
RM221	Percival P31 Proctor IV (G-ANXR)	Privately owned, Headcorn	
RM689	VS379 Spitfire F XIV (G-ALGT)	Rolls-Royce, stored East Midlands Airport	
RM694	VS379 Spitfire F XIV (G-DBKL/6640M)	Privately owned, Booker	
RM927	VS379 Spitfire F XIV (G-JNMA)	Privately owned, Biggin Hill	
RN218	Isaacs Spitfire <R> (G-BBJI) [N]	Privately owned, Builth Wells	
RP001	AeroVironment Puma AE Micro UAV	MoD	
RP002	AeroVironment Wasp AE Micro UAV	MoD	
RP003	AeroVironment Shrike Mk1 Micro UAV	MoD	
RR232	VS361 Spitfire HF IXc (PV181/G-BRSF)	Privately owned, Goodwood	
RT486	Auster 5 (G-AJGJ)	RAF Manston History Museum	
RT520	Auster 5 (G-ALYB)	South Yorkshire Aircraft Museum, Doncaster	
RT610	Auster 5A-160 (G-AKWS)	Privately owned, Shobdon	
RW382	VS361 Spitfire LF XVIe (G-PBIX/7245M/8075M) [3W-P]	Privately owned, Biggin Hill	
RW386	VS361 Spitfire LF XVIe (SE-BIR/6944M) [NG-D]	Privately owned, Angelholm, Sweden	
RW388	VS361 Spitfire LF XVIe (6946M) [U4-U]	Stoke-on-Trent City Museum, Rochester (restoration)	
RX168	VS358 Seafire L IIIc (IAC 157/G-BWEM)	Privately owned, Launceston	
SE001*	Boeing Scan Eagle RM1 RPAS	QinetiQ, Cardigan Bay	
SL611	VS361 Spitfire LF XVIe (G-SAEA)	Supermarine Aero Engineering, Stoke-on-Trent	
SL674	VS361 Spitfire LF IX (8392M) [RAS-H]	RAF Museum Reserve Collection, Stafford	
SM520	VS509 Spitfire T9 (H-99/G-ILDA) [KJ-I]	Boultbee Flight Academy, Goodwood	
SM845	VS394 Spitfire FR XVIII (G-BUOS) [R]	Spitfire Ltd, Humberside	
SN280	Hawker Tempest V <ff>	South Yorkshire Aircraft Museum, Doncaster	
SR462	VS377 Spitfire F XV (UB415/G-TGVP)	Privately owned, Sandown, Isle of Wight	
SR661	Hawker Fury ISS (G-CBEL)	Privately owned, Sywell	
SX137	VS384 Seafire F XVII	FAA Museum, RNAS Yeovilton	
SX300	VS384 Seafire F XVII (G-RIPH)	Kennet Aviation, North Weald	
SX336	VS384 Seafire F XVII (G-KASX) [105/VL]	Kennet Aviation, North Weald	
TA122	DH98 Mosquito FB VI [UP-G]	de Havilland Aircraft Museum, London Colney	
TA634	DH98 Mosquito TT35 (G-AWJV) [8K-K]	de Havilland Aircraft Museum, London Colney	
TA639	DH98 Mosquito TT35 (7806M) [AZ-E]	RAF Museum, Cosford	
TA719	DH98 Mosquito TT35 (G-ASKC)	IWM Duxford	
TA805	VS361 Spitfire HF IX (G-PMNF) [FX-M]	Privately owned, Biggin Hill	

Notes	Serial	Type (code/other identity)	Owner/operator, location or fate
	TB382	VS361 Spitfire LF XVIe (X4277/MK673)	Privately owned, Sandown
	TB675	VS361 Spitfire LF XVIe (RW393/7293M) [4D-V]	RAF Museum, Hendon
	TB752	VS361 Spitfire LF XVIe (8086M) [KH-Z]	RAF Manston, Memorial Pavilion
	TB885	VS361 Spitfire LF XVIe (G-CKUE) [3W-V]	Privately owned, Biggin Hill
	TD248	VS361 Spitfire LF XVIe (G-OXVI/7246M) [CR-S]	Spitfire Ltd, Humberside
	TD248	VS361 Spitfire LF XVIe (BAPC 368) [8Q-T] (fuselage)	Norfolk & Suffolk Avn Mus'm, Flixton
	TD314	VS361 Spitfire LF IX (G-CGYJ) [FX-P]	Privately owned, Duxford
	TE184	VS361 Spitfire LF XVIe (G-MXVI/6850M) [9N-B]	Privately owned, Biggin Hill/Bremgarten, Germany
	TE311	VS361 Spitfire LF XVIe (MK178/7241M)	RAF BBMF, Coningsby
	TE462	VS361 Spitfire LF XVIe (7243M)	National Museum of Flight, E Fortune
	TE517	VS361 Spitfire LF IXe (G-JGCA) [HL-K]	Privately owned, Biggin Hill
	TE566	VS509 Spitfire T9 (VH-IXT)	Vintage Flyers, Cotswold Airport (rebuild)
	TG263	Saro SR A1 (G-12-1)	Solent Sky, Southampton
	TG511	HP67 Hastings T5 (8554M) [511]	RAF Museum, Cosford
	TG517	HP67 Hastings T5 [517]	Newark Air Museum, Winthorpe
	TG528	HP67 Hastings C1A [528,T]	IWM Duxford
	TJ118	DH98 Mosquito TT35 <ff>	*Repainted as NS710, 2017*
	TJ138	DH98 Mosquito B35 (7607M) [VO-L]	RAF Museum, Hendon
	TJ207	Auster AOP5 (NJ703/G-AKPI) [P]	Privately owned, Spanhoe
	TJ343	Auster AOP5 (G-AJXC)	Privately owned, White Waltham
	TJ518	Auster J/1 Autocrat (G-AJIH)	Privately owned, Bidford
	TJ534	Auster AOP5 (G-AKSY)	Privately owned, Dunsfold
	TJ569	Auster AOP5 (G-AKOW)	Museum of Army Flying, Middle Wallop
	TJ652	Auster AOP5 (TJ565/G-AMVD)	Privately owned, Hardwick, Norfolk
	TJ672	Auster 5D (G-ANIJ) [TS-D]	Privately owned, Netheravon
	TK718	GAL59 Hamilcar I (fuselage)	The Tank Museum, Bovington
	TK777	GAL59 Hamilcar I (fuselage)	Museum of Army Flying, Middle Wallop
	TP280	VS394 Spitfire FR XVIIIe (D-FSPT)	Hangar 10 Collection, Heringsdorf, Germany
	TP298	VS394 Spitfire FR XVIII [UM-T]	Privately owned, Sandown
	TS291	Slingsby T7 Cadet TX1 (BGA852)	Royal Scottish Mus'm of Flight, stored Granton
	TS798	Avro 685 York C1 (G-AGNV/MW100)	RAF Museum, Cosford
	TW439	Auster AOP5 (G-ANRP)	Privately owned, Breighton
	TW467	Auster AOP5 (G-ANIE)	Privately owned, Elmsett
	TW477	Auster AOP5 (OY-EFI)	Privately owned, Ringsted, Denmark
	TW501	Auster AOP5 (G-ALBJ)	Privately owned, Dunkeswell
	TW511	Auster AOP5 (G-APAF)	Privately owned, Chiseldon, Wilts
	TW519	Auster AOP5 (G-ANHX) [ROA-V]	Privately owned, Newark
	TW536	Auster AOP6 (G-BNGE/7704M)	Privately owned, Netheravon
	TW591	Auster 6A (G-ARIH)	Privately owned, Eggesford
	TW641	Beagle A61 Terrier 2 (G-ATDN)	Privately owned, Biggin Hill
	TX213	Avro 652A Anson C19 (G-AWRS)	North-East Aircraft Museum, Usworth
	TX214	Avro 652A Anson C19 (7817M)	RAF Museum, Cosford
	TX226	Avro 652A Anson C19 (7865M)	Montrose Air Station Heritage Centre
	TX235	Avro 652A Anson C19	Privately owned, stored Compton Verney
	TX310	DH89A Dragon Rapide 6 (G-AIDL)	Privately owned, Duxford
	TZ164	Isaacs Spitfire (G-ISAC) [01-A]	Privately owned, Hampstead Norreys, Berks
	VF301	DH100 Vampire F1 (7060M) [RAL-G]	Midland Air Museum, Coventry
	VF512	Auster 6A (G-ARRX) [PF-M]	Privately owned, Popham
	VF516	Beagle A61 Terrier 2 (G-ASMZ)	Privately owned, Compton Abbas
	VF519	Auster AOP6 (G-ASYN)	Privately owned, Doncaster
	VF526	Auster 6A (G-ARXU) [T]	Privately owned, Netheravon
	VF557	Auster 6A (G-ARHM) [H]	Privately owned, Headcorn
	VF560	Auster 6A (frame)	South Yorkshire Aircraft Museum, Doncaster
	VF581	Beagle A61 Terrier 1 (G-ARSL) [G]	National Museum of Scotland, Edinburgh
	VF631	Auster AOP6 (G-ASDK)	Privately owned, Hibaldstow
	VH127	Fairey Firefly TT4 [200/R]	FAA Museum, stored Cobham Hall, RNAS Yeovilton
	VL348	Avro 652A Anson C19 (G-AVVO)	Newark Air Museum, Winthorpe
	VL349	Avro 652A Anson C19 (G-AWSA) [V7-Q]	Norfolk & Suffolk Avn Museum, Flixton
	VM325	Avro 652A Anson C19	Privately owned, Carew Cheriton, Pembrokeshire
	VM360	Avro 652A Anson C19 (G-APHV)	National Museum of Flight, E Fortune
	VM657	Slingsby T8 Tutor TX2 (IGA-6)	Privately owned, stored Ashbridge, Eire

Serial	Type (code/other identity)	Owner/operator, location or fate	Notes
VM687	Slingsby T8 Tutor (BGA794)	Privately owned, Lee-on-Solent	
VM791	Slingsby Cadet TX3 (XA312/8876M)	RAF Manston History Museum	
VN485	VS356 Spitfire F24 (7326M)	IWM Duxford	
VN799	EE Canberra T4 (WJ874/G-CDSX)	Cornwall Aviation Heritage Centre, Newquay	
VP293	Avro 696 Shackleton T4 [X] <ff>	Shackleton Preservation Trust, Coventry	
VP519	Avro 652A Anson C19 (G-AVVR) <ff>	South Yorkshire Aircraft Museum, Doncaster	
VP952	DH104 Devon C2 (8820M)	RAF Museum, Cosford	
VP955	DH104 Devon C2 (G-DVON)	Privately owned, Cricklade, Wilts	
VP957	DH104 Devon C2 (8822M) <ff>	No 1137 Sqn ATC, Long Kesh	
VP967	DH104 Devon C2 (G-KOOL)	Yorkshire Air Museum, Elvington	
VP975	DH104 Devon C2 [M]	Science Museum, stored Wroughton	
VP981	DH104 Devon C2 (G-DHDV)	Aero Legends, Headcorn/Duxford	
VR137	Westland Wyvern TF1	FAA Museum, stored Cobham Hall, RNAS Yeovilton	
VR192	Percival P40 Prentice T1 (G-APIT)	Romney Marsh Wartime Collection	
VR249	Percival P40 Prentice T1 (G-APIY) [FA-EL]	Newark Air Museum, Winthorpe	
VR259	Percival P40 Prentice T1 (G-APJB) [M]	Aero Legends, Sywell	
VR930	Hawker Sea Fury FB11 (8382M) [110/Q]	RN Historic Flight, Yeovilton	
VS356	Percival P40 Prentice T1 (G-AOLU)	Privately owned, Montrose	
VS562	Avro 652A Anson T21 (8012M) <ff>	Shannon Aviation Museum, Eire	
VS610	Percival P40 Prentice T1 (G-AOKL)[K-L]	The Shuttleworth Collection, Old Warden	
VS618	Percival P40 Prentice T1 (G-AOLK)	RAF Museum Reserve Collection, Stafford	
VS623	Percival P40 Prentice T1 (G-AOKZ)[KQ-F]	Midland Air Museum, Coventry	
VT812	DH100 Vampire F3 (7200M) [N]	RAF Museum, Hendon	
VT935	Boulton Paul P111A (VT769)	Midland Air Museum, Coventry	
VT987	Auster AOP6 (G-BKXP)	Privately owned, Thruxton	
VV106	Supermarine 510 (7175M)	FAA Museum, stored Cobham Hall, RNAS Yeovilton	
VV217	DH100 Vampire FB5 (7323M)	de Havilland Aircraft Museum, stored London Colney	
VV400	EoN Olympia 2 (BGA1697)	Privately owned, Rivar Hill, Wilts	
VV401	EoN Olympia 2 (BGA1125) [99]	Privately owned, Ringmer, E Sussex	
VV901	Avro 652A Anson T21	Yorkshire Air Museum, Elvington	
VW453	Gloster Meteor T7 (8703M)	Jet Age Museum, Gloucester	
VW957	DH103 Sea Hornet NF21 <rf>	Privately owned, Chelmsford	
VW993	Beagle A61 Terrier 2 (G-ASCD)	Yorkshire Air Museum, Elvington	
VX113	Auster AOP6 (G-ARNO) [36]	Privately owned, Stow Maries, Essex	
VX185	EE Canberra B(I)8 (7631M) <ff>	National Museum of Flight, E Fortune	
VX250	DH103 Sea Hornet NF21 [48] <rf>	de Havilland Aircraft Museum, London Colney	
VX272	Hawker P.1052 (7174M)	FAA Museum, stored RNAS Yeovilton	
VX275	Slingsby T21B Sedbergh TX1 (BGA572/8884M)	RAF Museum Reserve Collection, Stafford	
VX281	Hawker Sea Fury T20S (G-RNHF) [120/VL]	Naval Aviation Ltd, RNAS Yeovilton	
VX573	Vickers Valetta C2 (8389M)	RAF Museum, stored Cosford	
VX580	Vickers Valetta C2 [580]	Norfolk & Suffolk Avn Museum, Flixton	
VX595	WS51 Dragonfly HR1	FAA Museum, RNAS Yeovilton	
VX665	Hawker Sea Fury FB11 <rf>	RN Historic Flight, at BAE Systems Brough	
VX924	Beagle A61 Terrier 2 (G-NTVE)	Privately owned, Fenland	
VX926	Auster T7 (G-ASKJ)	Privately owned, Gamlingay, Cambs	
VX927	Auster T7 (G-ASYG)	Privately owned, RAF Scampton	
VZ193	DH100 Vampire FB5 <ff>	Privately owned, Warrington	
VZ305	DH100 Vampire FB6 (J-1196/PX-K/LN-DHY) [N]	Norwegian AF Historical Sqn, Rygge, Norway	
VZ440	Gloster Meteor F8 (WA984) [X]	Tangmere Military Aviation Museum	
VZ477	Gloster Meteor F8 (7741M) <ff>	Midland Air Museum, Coventry	
VZ608	Gloster Meteor FR9	Newark Air Museum, Winthorpe	
VZ634	Gloster Meteor T7 (8657M)	Newark Air Museum, Winthorpe	
VZ638	Gloster Meteor T7 (G-JETM) [HF]	Gatwick Aviation Museum, Charlwood, Surrey	
VZ728	RS4 Desford Trainer (G-AGOS)	Privately owned, Spanhoe	
WA346	DH100 Vampire FB5	RAF Museum, stored Cosford	
WA473	VS Attacker F1 [102/J]	FAA Museum, RNAS Yeovilton	
WA576	Bristol 171 Sycamore 3 (G-ALSS/7900M)	Dumfries & Galloway Avn Mus, Dumfries	
WA577	Bristol 171 Sycamore 3 (G-ALST/7718M)	North-East Aircraft Museum, Usworth	
WA591	Gloster Meteor T7 (G-BWMF/7917M) [FMK-Q]	*Sold to the USA, March 2017*	
WA630	Gloster Meteor T7 [69] <ff>	Robertsbridge Aviation Society, Newhaven	
WA634	Gloster Meteor T7/8	RAF Museum, stored Cosford	

Notes	Serial	Type (code/other identity)	Owner/operator, location or fate
	WA638	Gloster Meteor T7(mod) (G-JWMA)	Martin-Baker Aircraft, Chalgrove
	WA662	Gloster Meteor T7	South Yorkshire Aircraft Museum, Doncaster
	WB188	Hawker Hunter F3 (7154M)	Tangmere Military Aviation Museum
	WB188	Hawker Hunter GA11 (XF300/G-BZPC)	Privately owned, Melksham, Wilts
	WB440	Fairey Firefly AS6 <ff>	Privately owned, Newton Abbott, Devon
	WB491	Avro 706 Ashton 2 (TS897/G-AJJW) <ff>	Newark Air Museum, Winthorpe
	WB549	DHC1 Chipmunk 22A (G-BAPB))	Privately owned, Turweston
	WB555	DHC1 Chipmunk T10 <ff>	Privately owned, Ellerton
	WB560	DHC1 Chipmunk T10 (comp WG403)	Privately owned, South Molton, Devon
	WB565	DHC1 Chipmunk 22 (G-PVET) [X]	Privately owned, Rendcomb
	WB569	DHC1 Chipmunk 22 (G-BYSJ)	Privately owned, Duxford
	WB571	DHC1 Chipmunk 22 (D-EOSF) [34]	Privately owned, Porta Westfalica, Germany
	WB584	DHC1 Chipmunk T10 (comp WG303/7706M)	Solway Aviation Society, stored Carlisle
	WB585	DHC1 Chipmunk 22 (G-AOSY) [28]	Privately owned, Audley End
	WB588	DHC1 Chipmunk 22 (G-AOTD) [D]	Privately owned, Old Sarum
	WB615	DHC1 Chipmunk 22 (G-BXIA) [E]	Privately owned, Blackpool
	WB624	DHC1 Chipmunk T10	Newark Air Museum, Winthorpe
	WB626	DHC1 Chipmunk T10 [19] <ff>	Trenchard Museum, RAF Halton
	WB627	DHC1 Chipmunk T10 (9248M) (fuselage) [N]	Dulwich College CCF
	WB645	DHC1 Chipmunk T10 (8218M) <rf>	Privately owned, Halton
	WB654	DHC1 Chipmunk 22 (G-BXGO) [U]	Privately owned, Finmere
	WB657	DHC1 Chipmunk T10 [908]	RN Historic Flight, Yeovilton
	WB670	DHC1 Chipmunk T10 (comp WG303)(8361M)	Privately owned, Carlisle
	WB671	DHC1 Chipmunk 22 (G-BWTG) [910]	Privately owned, Teuge, The Netherlands
	WB685	DHC1 Chipmunk T10 (comp WP969/G-ATHC)	de Havilland Aircraft Museum, London Colney
	WB685	DHC1 Chipmunk T10 <rf>	North-East Aircraft Museum, stored Usworth
	WB697	DHC1 Chipmunk 22 (G-BXCT) [95]	Privately owned, Wickenby
	WB702	DHC1 Chipmunk 22A (G-AOFE)	Privately owned, Audley End
	WB703	DHC1 Chipmunk 22A (G-ARMC)	Privately owned, Compton Abbas
	WB711	DHC1 Chipmunk 22 (G-APPM)	Privately owned, Sywell
	WB726	DHC1 Chipmunk 22A (G-AOSK) [E]	Privately owned, Turweston
	WB733	DHC1 Chipmunk T10 (comp WG422)	South Yorkshire Aircraft Museum, Doncaster
	WB922	Slingsby T21B Sedbergh TX1 (BGA4366)	Privately owned, Little Rissington
	WB924	Slingsby T21B Sedbergh TX1 (BGA3901)	Privately owned, Dunstable
	WB944	Slingsby T21B Sedbergh TX1 (BGA3160)	Privately owned, Bicester
	WB945	Slingsby T21B Sedbergh TX1 (BGA1254)	Privately owned, stored RAF Halton
	WB971	Slingsby T21B Sedbergh TX1 (BGA3324)	Privately owned, Felthorpe
	WB975	Slingsby T21B Sedbergh TX1 (BGA3288) [FJB]	Privately owned, Shipdham
	WB980	Slingsby T21B Sedbergh TX1 (BGA3290)	Privately owned, Husbands Bosworth
	WB981	Slingsby T21B Sedbergh TX1 (BGA3238)	Privately owned, Eaglescott
	WD286	DHC1 Chipmunk 22 (G-BBND)	Privately owned, Old Warden
	WD292	DHC1 Chipmunk 22 (G-BCRX)	Privately owned, White Waltham
	WD293	DHC1 Chipmunk T10 (7645M) <ff>	Privately owned, St Athan
	WD310	DHC1 Chipmunk 22 (G-BWUN) [B]	Privately owned, Deanland
	WD319	DHC1 Chipmunk 22 (OY-ATF)	Privately owned, Stauning, Denmark
	WD321	DHC1 Chipmunk 22 (G-BDCC)	Boscombe Down Aviation Collection, Old Sarum
	WD325	DHC1 Chipmunk T10 [N]	AAC, stored Middle Wallop
	WD331	DHC1 Chipmunk 22 (G-BXDH)	Privately owned, Farnborough
	WD355	DHC1 Chipmunk T10 (WD335/G-CBAJ)	Privately owned, Eastleigh
	WD363	DHC1 Chipmunk 22 (G-BCIH) [5]	Privately owned, Netheravon
	WD370	DHC1 Chipmunk T10 <ff>	No 225 Sqn ATC, Brighton
	WD373	DHC1 Chipmunk 22 (G-BXDI) [12]	Privately owned, Turweston
	WD377	DHC1 Chipmunk T10 <ff>	Wings Museum, Balcombe, W Sussex
	WD386	DHC1 Chipmunk T10 (comp WD377)	Ulster Aviation Soc, stored Upper Ballinderry, NI
	WD388	DHC1 Chipmunk 22 (D-EPAK) [68]	Quax Flieger, Hamm, Germany
	WD390	DHC1 Chipmunk 22 (G-BWNK) [68]	Privately owned, Compton Abbas
	WD413	Avro 652A Anson T21 (7881M/G-VROE)	Privately owned, Sleap
	WD615	Gloster Meteor TT20 (WD646/8189M) [R]	RAF Manston History Museum
	WD686	Gloster Meteor NF11 [S]	Boscombe Down Aviation Collection, Old Sarum
	WD790	Gloster Meteor NF11 (8743M) <ff>	North-East Aircraft Museum, Usworth

Serial	Type (code/other identity)	Owner/operator, location or fate	Notes
WD889	Fairey Firefly AS5 (comp VT809)	Privately owned, Newton Abbot, Devon	
WD935	EE Canberra B2 (8440M) <ff>	South Yorkshire Aircraft Museum, Doncaster	
WD954	EE Canberra B2 <ff>	Privately owned, St Mawgan	
WD956	EE Canberra B2 <ff>	RAF Defford Museum, Croome Park	
WE113	EE Canberra B2 <ff>	Privately owned, Tangmere	
WE122	EE Canberra TT18 [845] <ff>	Blyth Valley Aviation Collection, Walpole, Suffolk	
WE139	EE Canberra PR3 (8369M)	RAF Museum, Hendon	
WE168	EE Canberra PR3 (8049M) <ff>	Norfolk & Suffolk Avn Museum, Flixton	
WE173	EE Canberra PR3 (8740M) <ff>	Robertsbridge Aviation Society, Mayfield	
WE188	EE Canberra T4	Solway Aviation Society, Carlisle	
WE192	EE Canberra T4 <ff>	Blyth Valley Aviation Collection, Walpole, Suffolk	
WE275	DH112 Venom FB50 (J-1601/G-VIDI)	BAE Systems Hawarden, Fire Section	
WE558	Auster T7 (frame)	East Midlands Airport Aeropark	
WE569	Auster T7 (G-ASAJ)	Privately owned, Coventry	
WE570	Auster T7 (G-ASBU)	Privately owned, Stonehaven	
WE591	Auster T7 (F-AZTJ)	Privately owned, Toussus-le-Noble, France	
WE600	Auster T7 Antarctic (7602M)	RAF Museum, Cosford	
WE724	Hawker Sea Fury FB11 (VX653/G-BUCM) [062]	The Fighter Collection, Duxford	
WE982	Slingsby T30B Prefect TX1 (8781M)	RAF Museum, stored Cosford	
WE987	Slingsby T30B Prefect TX1 (BGA2517)	South Yorkshire Aircraft Museum, Doncaster	
WE990	Slingsby T30B Prefect TX1 (BGA2583)	Privately owned, Tibenham	
WE992	Slingsby T30B Prefect TX1 (BGA2692)	Privately owned, Little Rissington	
WF118	Percival P57 Sea Prince T1 (G-DACA) [569/CU]	Privately owned, St Athan	
WF122	Percival P57 Sea Prince T1 [575/CU]	Ulster Aviation Society, Long Kesh	
WF128	Percival P57 Sea Prince T1 (8611M)	Norfolk & Suffolk Avn Museum, Flixton	
WF145	Hawker Sea Hawk F1 <ff>	Privately owned, Newton Abbot, Devon	
WF219	Hawker Sea Hawk F1 <rf>	FAA Museum, stored Cobham Hall, RNAS Yeovilton	
WF225	Hawker Sea Hawk F1 [CU]	RNAS Culdrose, at main gate	
WF259	Hawker Sea Hawk F2 [171/A]	National Museum of Flight, E Fortune	
WF369	Vickers Varsity T1 [F]	Newark Air Museum, Winthorpe	
WF372	Vickers Varsity T1	Brooklands Museum, Weybridge	
WF408	Vickers Varsity T1 (8395M) <ff>	Privately owned, Ashford, Kent	
WF643	Gloster Meteor F8 [F]	Norfolk & Suffolk Avn Museum, Flixton	
WF784	Gloster Meteor T7 (7895M)	Jet Age Museum, Gloucester	
WF825	Gloster Meteor T7 (8359M) [A]	Montrose Air Station Heritage Centre	
WF877	Gloster Meteor T7 (G-BPOA)	Privately owned, stored Duxford (dismantled)	
WF911	EE Canberra B2 [CO] <ff>	Ulster Aviation Society, Long Kesh	
WF922	EE Canberra PR3	Midland Air Museum, Coventry	
WG303	DHC1 Chipmunk T10 (8208M) <ff>	Privately owned, Hooton Park	
WG308	DHC1 Chipmunk 22 (G-BYHL) [8]	Privately owned, Averham, Notts	
WG316	DHC1 Chipmunk 22 (G-BCAH)	Privately owned, Gamston	
WG319	DHC1 Chipmunk T10 <ff>	Privately owned, Blandford Forum, Dorset	
WG321	DHC1 Chipmunk 22 (G-DHCC)	Privately owned, Wevelgem, Belgium	
WG348	DHC1 Chipmunk 22 (G-BBMV)	Privately owned, Goodwood	
WG350	DHC1 Chipmunk 22 (G-BPAL)	Privately owned, Portimao, Portugal	
WG362	DHC1 Chipmunk T10 (8437M/8630M/WX643) <ff>	No 1094 Sqn ATC, Ely	
WG407	DHC1 Chipmunk 22 (G-BWMX) [67]	Privately owned, Croydon, Cambs	
WG418	DHC1 Chipmunk T10 (8209M/G-ATDY) <ff>	No 1940 Sqn ATC, Levenshulme, Gr Manchester	
WG419	DHC1 Chipmunk T10 (8206M) <ff>	Sywell Aviation Museum	
WG422	DHC1 Chipmunk 22 (8394M/G-BFAX) [16]	Privately owned, Eggesford	
WG432	DHC1 Chipmunk T10 [L]	Museum of Army Flying, Middle Wallop	
WG458	DHC1 Chipmunk 22 (N458BG) [2]	Privately owned, Breighton	
WG465	DHC1 Chipmunk 22 (G-BCEY)	Privately owned, White Waltham	
WG469	DHC1 Chipmunk 22 (G-BWJY) [72]	Privately owned, Sligo, Eire	
WG471	DHC1 Chipmunk T10 (8210M) <ff>	Currently not known	
WG472	DHC1 Chipmunk 22A (G-AOTY)	Privately owned, Bryngwyn Bach, Clwyd	
WG477	DHC1 Chipmunk T10 (8362M/G-ATDP) <ff>	RAF Scampton Heritage Centre	
WG486	DHC1 Chipmunk T10 [E]	RAF BBMF, Coningsby	
WG498	Slingsby T21B Sedbergh TX1 (BGA3245)	Privately owned, Aston Down	

Notes	Serial	Type (code/other identity)	Owner/operator, location or fate
	WG511	Avro 696 Shackleton T4 (fuselage)	Flambards Village Theme Park, Helston
	WG599	Hawker Sea Fury FB11 (G-SEAF) [161/R]	The Fighter Collection, Reno, Nevada, USA
	WG655	Hawker Sea Fury T20 (G-CHFP) [910/GN]	The Fighter Collection, Duxford
	WG719	WS51 Dragonfly HR5 (G-BRMA)	The Helicopter Museum, Weston-super-Mare
	WG724	WS51 Dragonfly HR5 [932]	North-East Aircraft Museum, Usworth
	WG751	WS51 Dragonfly HR5 [710/GJ]	World Naval Base, Chatham
	WG760	EE P1A (7755M)	RAF Museum, Cosford
	WG763	EE P1A (7816M)	Museum of Science & Industry, Manchester
	WG768	Short SB5 (8005M)	RAF Museum, Cosford
	WG774	BAC 221	Science Museum, at FAA Museum, RNAS Yeovilton
	WG777	Fairey FD2 (7986M)	RAF Museum, Cosford
	WG789	EE Canberra B2/6 <ff>	Norfolk & Suffolk Avn Museum, Flixton
	WH132	Gloster Meteor T7 (7906M) [J]	Privately owned, Hooton Park
	WH166	Gloster Meteor T7 (8052M) [A]	Privately owned, Birlingham, Worcs
	WH291	Gloster Meteor F8	Privately owned, Liverpool Airport
	WH301	Gloster Meteor F8 (7930M) [T]	RAF Museum, Hendon
	WH364	Gloster Meteor F8 (8169M)	Jet Age Museum, Gloucester
	WH453	Gloster Meteor F8	Bentwaters Cold War Air Museum
	WH646	EE Canberra T17A <ff>	Midland Air Museum, Coventry
	WH657	EE Canberra B2 <ff>	Romney Marsh Wartime Collection
	WH725	EE Canberra B2	IWM Duxford
	WH734	EE Canberra B2(mod) <ff>	Privately owned, Pershore
	WH739	EE Canberra B2 <ff>	No 2475 Sqn ATC, Ammanford, Dyfed
	WH740	EE Canberra T17 (8762M) [K]	East Midlands Airport Aeropark
	WH775	EE Canberra PR7 (8128M/8868M) <ff>	Privately owned, Welshpool
	WH779	EE Canberra PR7 <ff>	South Yorkshire Aircraft Museum, Doncaster
	WH779	EE Canberra PR7 [BP] <rf>	RAF AM&SU, stored Shawbury
	WH792	EE Canberra PR7 (WH791/8165M/8176M/8187M)	Newark Air Museum, Winthorpe
	WH798	EE Canberra PR7 (8130M) <ff>	Suffolk Aviation Heritage Centre, Foxhall Heath
	WH840	EE Canberra T4 (8350M)	Privately owned, Flixton
	WH846	EE Canberra T4	Yorkshire Air Museum, Elvington
	WH850	EE Canberra T4 <ff>	Privately owned, Marham
	WH863	EE Canberra T17 (8693M) <ff>	Newark Air Museum, Winthorpe
	WH876	EE Canberra B2(mod) <ff>	Boscombe Down Aviation Collection, Old Sarum
	WH887	EE Canberra TT18 [847] <ff>	Sywell Aviation Museum
	WH903	EE Canberra B2 <ff>	Yorkshire Air Museum, Elvington
	WH904	EE Canberra T19	Newark Air Museum, Winthorpe
	WH953	EE Canberra B6(mod) <ff>	Blyth Valley Aviation Collection, Walpole, Suffolk
	WH957	EE Canberra E15 (8869M) <ff>	Lincolnshire Avn Heritage Centre, East Kirkby
	WH960	EE Canberra B15 (8344M) <ff>	Rolls-Royce Heritage Trust, Derby
	WH964	EE Canberra E15 (8870M) <ff>	Privately owned, Lewes
	WH984	EE Canberra B15 (8101M) <ff>	City of Norwich Aviation Museum
	WH991	WS51 Dragonfly HR3	Yorkshire Helicopter Preservation Group, Elvington
	WJ231	Hawker Sea Fury FB11 (WE726) [115/O]	FAA Museum, RNAS Yeovilton
	WJ306	Slingsby T21B Sedbergh TX1 (BGA3240)	Privately owned, Weston-on-the-Green
	WJ306	Slingsby T21B Sedbergh TX1 (WB957/BGA2720)	Privately owned, Parham Park, Sussex
	WJ358	Auster AOP6 (G-ARYD)	Museum of Army Flying, Middle Wallop
	WJ368	Auster AOP6 (G-ASZX)	Privately owned, Eggesford
	WJ404	Auster AOP6 (G-ASOI)	Privately owned, Bidford-on-Avon, Warks
	WJ476	Vickers Valetta T3 <ff>	South Yorkshire Aircraft Museum, Doncaster
	WJ565	EE Canberra T17 (8871M) <ff>	South Yorkshire Aircraft Museum, Doncaster
	WJ567	EE Canberra B2 <ff>	Privately owned, Houghton, Cambs
	WJ576	EE Canberra T17 <ff>	Tettenhall Transport Heritage Centre
	WJ633	EE Canberra T17 <ff>	City of Norwich Aviation Museum
	WJ639	EE Canberra TT18 [39]	North-East Aircraft Museum, Usworth
	WJ677	EE Canberra B2 <ff>	Privately owned, Redruth
	WJ717	EE Canberra TT18 (9052M) <ff>	Currently not known
	WJ721	EE Canberra TT18 [21] <ff>	Moravvia, Kinloss
	WJ731	EE Canberra B2T [BK] <ff>	Privately owned, Golders Green
	WJ775	EE Canberra B6 (8581M) <ff>	Privately owned, stored Farnborough

Serial	Type (code/other identity)	Owner/operator, location or fate	Notes
WJ865	EE Canberra T4 <ff>	Boscombe Down Aviation Collection, Old Sarum	
WJ880	EE Canberra T4 (8491M) <ff>	Dumfries & Galloway Avn Mus, Dumfries	
WJ903	Vickers Varsity T1 <ff>	South Yorkshire Aircraft Museum, Doncaster	
WJ945	Vickers Varsity T1 (G-BEDV) [21]	Cornwall Aviation Heritage Centre, Newquay	
WJ975	EE Canberra T19 <ff>	South Yorkshire Aircraft Museum, Doncaster	
WJ992	EE Canberra T4	Bournemouth Airport (derelict)	
WK001	Thales Watchkeeper 450 RPAS (4X-USC)	Army 43 Battery Royal Artillery, Boscombe Down	
WK002	Thales Watchkeeper 450 RPAS (4X-USD)	Army	
WK003	Thales Watchkeeper 450 RPAS	Army	
WK004	Thales Watchkeeper 450 RPAS	Army	
WK005	Thales Watchkeeper 450 RPAS	Army 43 Battery Royal Artillery, Boscombe Down	
WK007	Thales Watchkeeper 450 RPAS	Army	
WK008	Thales Watchkeeper 450 RPAS	Army 47 Regt Royal Artillery, Boscombe Down	
WK009	Thales Watchkeeper 450 RPAS	Army	
WK010	Thales Watchkeeper 450 RPAS	Army 43 Battery Royal Artillery, Boscombe Down	
WK011	Thales Watchkeeper 450 RPAS	Army	
WK012	Thales Watchkeeper 450 RPAS	Army	
WK013	Thales Watchkeeper 450 RPAS	Army	
WK014	Thales Watchkeeper 450 RPAS	Army	
WK015	Thales Watchkeeper 450 RPAS	Army	
WK016	Thales Watchkeeper 450 RPAS	Army	
WK017	Thales Watchkeeper 450 RPAS	Army	
WK018	Thales Watchkeeper 450 RPAS	Army	
WK019	Thales Watchkeeper 450 RPAS	Army	
WK020	Thales Watchkeeper 450 RPAS	Army	
WK021	Thales Watchkeeper 450 RPAS	Army	
WK022	Thales Watchkeeper 450 RPAS	Army	
WK023	Thales Watchkeeper 450 RPAS	Army	
WK024	Thales Watchkeeper 450 RPAS	Army	
WK025	Thales Watchkeeper 450 RPAS	Army	
WK026	Thales Watchkeeper 450 RPAS	Army	
WK027	Thales Watchkeeper 450 RPAS	Army	
WK028	Thales Watchkeeper 450 RPAS	Army	
WK029	Thales Watchkeeper 450 RPAS	Army 43 Battery Royal Artillery, Boscombe Down	
WK030	Thales Watchkeeper 450 RPAS	Army 43 Battery Royal Artillery, Boscombe Down	
WK032	Thales Watchkeeper 450 RPAS	Army	
WK033	Thales Watchkeeper 450 RPAS	Army	
WK034	Thales Watchkeeper 450 RPAS	Army	
WK035	Thales Watchkeeper 450 RPAS	Army	
WK036	Thales Watchkeeper 450 RPAS	Army	
WK037	Thales Watchkeeper 450 RPAS	Army	
WK038	Thales Watchkeeper 450 RPAS	Army	
WK039	Thales Watchkeeper 450 RPAS	Army	
WK040	Thales Watchkeeper 450 RPAS	Army	
WK041	Thales Watchkeeper 450 RPAS	Army	
WK042	Thales Watchkeeper 450 RPAS	Crashed 3 February 2017, Cardigan Bay	
WK043	Thales Watchkeeper 450 RPAS	Crashed 24 March 2017, Cardigan Bay	
WK044	Thales Watchkeeper 450 RPAS	Army	
WK045	Thales Watchkeeper 450 RPAS	Army	
WK046	Thales Watchkeeper 450 RPAS	Army	
WK047	Thales Watchkeeper 450 RPAS	Army	
WK048	Thales Watchkeeper 450 RPAS	Army	
WK049	Thales Watchkeeper 450 RPAS	Army	
WK050	Thales Watchkeeper 450 RPAS	Army	
WK051	Thales Watchkeeper 450 RPAS	Army	
WK052	Thales Watchkeeper 450 RPAS	Army	
WK053	Thales Watchkeeper 450 RPAS	Army	
WK054	Thales Watchkeeper 450 RPAS	Army	
WK060	Thales Watchkeeper 450 RPAS	MoD/Thales, Aberporth	
WK102	EE Canberra T17 (8780M) <ff>	Privately owned, Welshpool	
WK118	EE Canberra TT18 [CQ] <ff>	Avro Heritage Museum, Woodford	

Notes	Serial	Type (code/other identity)	Owner/operator, location or fate
	WK122	EE Canberra TT18 <ff>	Privately owned, Wesham, Lancs
	WK124	EE Canberra TT18 (9093M) [CR]	Privately owned, Gilberdyke, E Yorks
	WK126	EE Canberra TT18 (N2138J) [843]	Jet Age Museum, stored Gloucester
	WK127	EE Canberra TT18 (8985M) <ff>	Privately owned, stored Handcross, W Sussex
	WK146	EE Canberra B2 <ff>	Gatwick Aviation Museum, Charlwood, Surrey
	WK163	EE Canberra B2/6 (G-BVWC/G-CTTS)	Vulcan To The Sky Trust, Doncaster Sheffield Airport
	WK198	VS Swift F4 (7428M) (fuselage)	Brooklands Museum, Weybridge
	WK275	VS Swift F4	Privately owned, Doncaster Sheffield Airport
	WK277	VS Swift FR5 (7719M) [N]	Newark Air Museum, Winthorpe
	WK281	VS Swift FR5 (7712M) [S]	Tangmere Military Aviation Museum
	WK393	DH112 Venom FB1 <ff>	Privately owned, Lavendon, Bucks
	WK436	DH112 Venom FB50 (J-1614/G-VENM)	*Sold to the USA, April 2017*
	WK512	DHC1 Chipmunk 22 (G-BXIM) [A]	Privately owned, RAF Halton
	WK514	DHC1 Chipmunk 22 (G-BBMO)	Privately owned, Wellesbourne Mountford
	WK517	DHC1 Chipmunk 22 (G-ULAS)	Privately owned, Goodwood
	WK518	DHC1 Chipmunk T10 [C]	RAF BBMF, Coningsby
	WK522	DHC1 Chipmunk 22 (G-BCOU)	Privately owned, Duxford
	WK549	DHC1 Chipmunk 22 (G-BTWF)	Privately owned, Breighton
	WK558	DHC1 Chipmunk 22A (G-ARMG) [DH]	Privately owned, Shenington, Oxon
	WK562	DHC1 Chipmunk 22 (F-AZUR) [91]	Privately owned, La Baule, France
	WK570	DHC1 Chipmunk T10 (8211M) <ff>	No 424 Sqn ATC, Solent Sky, Southampton
	WK576	DHC1 Chipmunk T10 (8357M) <ff>	Tettenhall Transport Heritage Centre
	WK577	DHC1 Chipmunk 22 (G-BCYM)	Privately owned, Oaksey Park
	WK584	DHC1 Chipmunk T10 (7556M) <ff>	No 511 Sqn ATC, Ramsey, Cambs
	WK585	DHC1 Chipmunk 22 (9265M/G-BZGA)	Privately owned, Compton Abbas
	WK586	DHC1 Chipmunk 22 (G-BXGX) [V]	Privately owned, Shoreham
	WK590	DHC1 Chipmunk 22 (G-BWVZ) [69]	Privately owned, Grimbergen, Belgium
	WK608	DHC1 Chipmunk T10 [906]	RN Historic Flight, Yeovilton
	WK609	DHC1 Chipmunk 22 (G-BXDN) [93]	Privately owned, Booker
	WK611	DHC1 Chipmunk 22 (G-ARWB)	Privately owned, Thruxton
	WK620	DHC1 Chipmunk T10 [T] (fuselage)	Privately owned, Enstone
	WK622	DHC1 Chipmunk 22 (G-BCZH)	Privately owned, Horsford
	WK624	DHC1 Chipmunk 22A (G-BWHI)	Privately owned, Blackpool
	WK626	DHC1 Chipmunk T10 (8213M) <ff>	South Yorkshire Aircraft Museum, Doncaster
	WK628	DHC1 Chipmunk 22 (G-BBMW)	Privately owned, Goodwood
	WK630	DHC1 Chipmunk 22 (G-BXDG)	Privately owned, Felthorpe
	WK633	DHC1 Chipmunk 22 (G-BXEC) [A]	Privately owned, Duxford
	WK634	DHC1 Chipmunk T10 (G-CIGE) [902]	Privately owned, Dunkeswell
	WK635	DHC1 Chipmunk 22 (G-HFRH)	Privately owned, Hawarden
	WK638	DHC1 Chipmunk 22 (G-BWJZ) (fuselage)	Privately owned, South Marston, Swindon
	WK640	DHC1 Chipmunk 22A (G-BWUV) [C]	Privately owned, Hooton Park (wreck)
	WK640	OGMA/DHC1 Chipmunk T20 (G-CERD)	Privately owned, Spanhoe
	WK642	DHC1 Chipmunk 22 (EI-AFZ) [94]	Privately owned, Kilrush, Eire
	WK654	Gloster Meteor F8 (8092M)	City of Norwich Aviation Museum
	WK800	Gloster Meteor D16 [Z]	Boscombe Down Aviation Collection, Old Sarum
	WK864	Gloster Meteor F8 (WL168/7750M) [C]	Yorkshire Air Museum, Elvington
	WK935	Gloster Meteor Prone Pilot (7869M)	RAF Museum, Cosford
	WK991	Gloster Meteor F8 (7825M)	IWM Duxford
	WL131	Gloster Meteor F8 (7751M) <ff>	South Yorkshire Aircraft Museum, Doncaster
	WL181	Gloster Meteor F8 [X]	North-East Aircraft Museum, Usworth
	WL332	Gloster Meteor T7 [888]	Privately owned, Long Marston
	WL345	Gloster Meteor T7 (comp WL360)	Privately owned, Booker
	WL349	Gloster Meteor T7	Jet Age Museum, Gloucester
	WL375	Gloster Meteor T7(mod)	Dumfries & Galloway Avn Mus, Dumfries
	WL405	Gloster Meteor T7 <ff>	Privately owned, Parbold, Lancs
	WL419	Gloster Meteor T7(mod) (G-JSMA)	Martin-Baker Aircraft, Chalgrove
	WL505	DH100 Vampire FB9 (7705M/G-FBIX)	Privately owned, Mendlesham
	WL626	Vickers Varsity T1 (G-BHDD) [P]	East Midlands Airport Aeropark
	WL627	Vickers Varsity T1 (8488M) [D] <ff>	Privately owned, Preston, E Yorkshire
	WL679	Vickers Varsity T1 (9155M)	RAF Museum, Cosford

Serial	Type (code/other identity)	Owner/operator, location or fate	Notes
WL732	BP P108 Sea Balliol T21	RAF Museum, Cosford	
WL795	Avro 696 Shackleton MR2C (8753M) [T]	Privately owned, Newquay	
WL798	Avro 696 Shackleton MR2C (8114M) <ff>	Privately owned, Elgin	
WM145	AW Meteor NF11 <ff>	Privately owned, Over Dinsdale, N Yorks	
WM167	AW Meteor NF11 (G-LOSM)	Sold to the USA, April 2017	
WM224	AW Meteor TT20 (WM311/8177M) [X]	East Midlands Airport Aeropark	
WM267	AW Meteor NF11 <ff>	City of Norwich Aviation Museum	
WM292	AW Meteor TT20 [841]	FAA Museum, stored Cobham Hall, RNAS Yeovilton	
WM366	AW Meteor NF13 (4X-FNA) (comp VZ462)	Jet Age Museum, Gloucester	
WM367	AW Meteor NF13 <ff>	East Midlands Airport Aeropark	
WM571	DH112 Sea Venom FAW21 [VL]	Solent Sky, stored Romsey	
WM729	DH113 Vampire NF10 <ff>	de Havilland Aircraft Mus'm, stored London Colney	
WM913	Hawker Sea Hawk FB5 (8162M) [456/J]	Newark Air Museum, Winthorpe	
WM961	Hawker Sea Hawk FB5 [J]	Caernarfon Air World	
WM969	Hawker Sea Hawk FB5 [10/Z]	IWM Duxford	
WN105	Hawker Sea Hawk FB3 (WF299/8164M)	Privately owned, Birlingham, Worcs	
WN108	Hawker Sea Hawk FB5 [033]	Ulster Aviation Society, Long Kesh	
WN149	BP P108 Balliol T2 [AT]	RAF Museum, stored Cosford	
WN411	Fairey Gannet AS1 (fuselage)	Privately owned, Sholing, Hants	
WN493	WS51 Dragonfly HR5	FAA Museum, RNAS Yeovilton	
WN499	WS51 Dragonfly HR5	South Yorkshire Aircraft Museum, stored Doncaster	
WN516	BP P108 Balliol T2 <ff>	Tettenhall Transport Heritage Centre	
WN534	BP P108 Balliol T2 <ff>	Tettenhall Transport Heritage Centre	
WN890	Hawker Hunter F2 <ff>	Boscombe Down Aviation Collection, Old Sarum	
WN904	Hawker Hunter F2 (7544M)	Sywell Aviation Museum	
WN907	Hawker Hunter F2 (7416M) <ff>	Robertsbridge Aviation Society, Newhaven	
WN957	Hawker Hunter F5 <ff>	Morayvia, Kinloss	
WP185	Hawker Hunter F5 (7583M)	Privately owned, Great Dunmow, Essex	
WP190	Hawker Hunter F5 (7582M/8473M/WP180) [K]	Tangmere Military Aviation Museum	
WP255	DH113 Vampire NF10 <ff>	South Yorkshire Aircraft Museum, stored Doncaster	
WP266	EoN AP.5 Primary (BAPC 423)	Privately owned, Fishburn	
WP269	EoN Eton TX1 (BGA3214)	Privately owned, Little Rissington	
WP270	EoN Eton TX1 (8598M)	Gliding Heritage Centre, Lasham	
WP308	Percival P57 Sea Prince T1 (G-GACA) [572/CU]	Gatwick Aviation Museum, Charlwood, Surrey	
WP313	Percival P57 Sea Prince T1 [568/CU]	FAA Museum, stored Cobham Hall, RNAS Yeovilton	
WP314	Percival P57 Sea Prince T1 (8634M) [573/CU]	Privately owned, Carlisle Airport	
WP321	Percival P57 Sea Prince T1 (G-BRFC) [750/CU]	Privately owned, St Athan	
WP772	DHC1 Chipmunk T10 (WK518) [4]	RAF Manston History Museum	
WP784	DHC1 Chipmunk T10 (comp WZ876) [RCY-E]	East Midlands Airport Aeropark	
WP788	DHC1 Chipmunk 22A (G-BCHL)	Privately owned, Sleap	
WP790	DHC1 Chipmunk T10 (G-BBNC) [T]	de Havilland Aircraft Museum, London Colney	
WP795	DHC1 Chipmunk 22 (G-BVZZ) [901]	Privately owned, Lee-on-Solent	
WP800	DHC1 Chipmunk 22 (G-BCXN) [2]	Privately owned, RAF Halton	
WP803	DHC1 Chipmunk 22 (G-HAPY) [G]	Privately owned, Booker	
WP805	DHC1 Chipmunk 22 (G-MAJR) [D]	Privately owned, Lee-on-Solent	
WP809	DHC1 Chipmunk 22A (G-BVTX) [78]	Privately owned, Husbands Bosworth	
WP835	DHC1 Chipmunk 22 (D-ERTY)	Privately owned, Porta Westfalica, Germany	
WP840	DHC1 Chipmunk 22 (F-AZQM) [9]	Privately owned, Reims, France	
WP844	DHC1 Chipmunk 22 (G-BWOX) [85]	Privately owned, Adriers, France	
WP848	DHC1 Chipmunk 22 (8342M/G-BFAW)	Privately owned, Old Buckenham	
WP859	DHC1 Chipmunk 22 (G-BXCP) [E] (wreck)	Privately owned, Fishburn	
WP860	DHC1 Chipmunk 22 (G-BXDA) [6]	Privately owned, Kirknewton	
WP863	DHC1 Chipmunk T10 (8360M/G-ATJI) <ff>	No 1011 Sqn ATC, Boscombe Down	
WP869	DHC1 Chipmunk T10 (8215M) <ff>	de Havilland Aircraft Museum, London Colney	
WP870	DHC1 Chipmunk 22 (G-BCOI) [12]	Privately owned, Rayne Hall Farm, Essex	
WP896	DHC1 Chipmunk 22 (G-BWVY)	Privately owned, RAF Halton	
WP901	DHC1 Chipmunk 22 (G-BWNT) [B]	Privately owned, Biggin Hill	
WP903	DHC1 Chipmunk 22 (G-BCGC)	Privately owned, Henlow	
WP912	DHC1 Chipmunk T10 (8467M)	RAF Museum, Cosford	

Notes	Serial	Type (code/other identity)	Owner/operator, location or fate
	WP921	DHC1 Chipmunk T10 (G-ATJJ) <ff>	Privately owned, Brooklands
	WP925	DHC1 Chipmunk 22 (G-BXHA) <ff>	Privately owned, Meppershall
	WP927	DHC1 Chipmunk 22 (8216M/G-ATJK) <ff>	Privately owned, St Neots, Cambs
	WP928	DHC1 Chipmunk 22 (G-BXGM) [D]	Privately owned, Goodwood
	WP929	DHC1 Chipmunk 22 (G-BXCV) [F]	Privately owned, Duxford
	WP930	DHC1 Chipmunk 22 (G-BXHF) [J]	Privately owned, Redhill
	WP962	DHC1 Chipmunk T10 (9287M) [C]	RAF Museum, Hendon
	WP964	DHC1 Chipmunk T20 (G-HDAE)	Privately owned, Wellesbourne Mountford
	WP971	DHC1 Chipmunk 22 (G-ATHD)	Privately owned, Denham
	WP973	DHC1 Chipmunk 22 (G-BCPU)	Privately owned, Turweston
	WP977	DHC1 Chipmunk 22 (G-BHRD) <ff>	Privately owned, South Molton, Devon
	WP983	DHC1 Chipmunk 22 (G-BXNN) [B]	Privately owned, Eggesford
	WP984	DHC1 Chipmunk 22 (G-BWTO) [H]	Privately owned, Little Gransden
	WR410	DH112 Venom FB50 (J-1539/G-DHUU)	Shannon Aviation Museum, Eire
	WR470	DH112 Venom FB50 (J-1542/G-DHVM)	Sold to the USA, April 2017
	WR539	DH112 Venom FB4 (8399M) <ff>	Privately owned, Cantley, Norfolk
	WR960	Avro 696 Shackleton AEW2 (8772M)	Museum of Science & Industry, Manchester
	WR963	Avro 696 Shackleton AEW2 (G-SKTN) [B-M]	Shackleton Preservation Trust, Coventry
	WR971	Avro 696 Shackleton MR3/3 (8119M) [Q] (fuselage)	Fenland & W Norfolk Aviation Museum, Wisbech
	WR974	Avro 696 Shackleton MR3/3 (8117M) [K]	Privately owned, Bruntingthorpe
	WR977	Avro 696 Shackleton MR3/3 (8186M) [B]	Newark Air Museum, Winthorpe
	WR982	Avro 696 Shackleton MR3/3 (8106M) [J]	Gatwick Aviation Museum, Charlwood, Surrey
	WR985	Avro 696 Shackleton MR3/3 (8103M) [H]	Privately owned, Long Marston
	WS103	Gloster Meteor T7 [709]	FAA Museum, stored Cobham Hall, RNAS Yeovilton
	WS692	Gloster Meteor NF12 (7605M) [C]	Newark Air Museum, Winthorpe
	WS726	Gloster Meteor NF14 (7960M) [H]	No 1855 Sqn ATC, Royton, Gr Manchester
	WS739	Gloster Meteor NF14 (7961M)	Newark Air Museum, Winthorpe
	WS760	Gloster Meteor NF14 (7964M)	East Midlands Airport Aeropark, stored
	WS776	Gloster Meteor NF14 (7716M) [K]	Bournemouth Aviation Museum
	WS788	Gloster Meteor NF14 (7967M) [Z]	Yorkshire Air Museum, Elvington
	WS792	Gloster Meteor NF14 (7965M) [K]	Brighouse Bay Caravan Park, Borgue, D&G
	WS807	Gloster Meteor NF14 (7973M) [N]	Jet Age Museum, Gloucester
	WS832	Gloster Meteor NF14 [W]	Solway Aviation Society, Carlisle
	WS838	Gloster Meteor NF14 [D]	Midland Air Museum, Coventry
	WS840	Gloster Meteor NF14 (7969M) [N] <rf>	Privately owned, Upper Ballinderry, NI
	WS843	Gloster Meteor NF14 (7937M) [J]	RAF Museum, Cosford
	WT121	Douglas Skyraider AEW1 [415/CU]	FAA Museum, stored Cobham Hall, RNAS Yeovilton
	WT205	EE Canberra B15 <ff>	RAF Manston History Museum
	WT308	EE Canberra B(I)6	RN, Predannack Fire School
	WT309	EE Canberra B(I)6 <ff>	Farnborough Air Sciences Trust, Farnborough
	WT319	EE Canberra B(I)6 <ff>	Privately owned, Lavendon, Bucks
	WT333	EE Canberra B6(mod) (G-BVXC)	Privately owned, Bruntingthorpe
	WT339	EE Canberra B(I)8 (8198M)	RAF Barkston Heath Fire Section
	WT482	EE Canberra T4 <ff>	Privately owned, Marske by the Sea, Durham
	WT486	EE Canberra T4 (8102M) <ff>	Privately owned, Newtownards
	WT507	EE Canberra PR7 (8131M/8548M) [44] <ff>	No 384 Sqn ATC, Mansfield
	WT520	EE Canberra PR7 (8094M/8184M) <ff>	Rays-Tek Surplus Ltd, Biddulph, Staffs
	WT525	EE Canberra T22 [855] <ff>	Cornwall College, Newquay Airport
	WT532	EE Canberra PR7 (8728M/8890M) <ff>	Bournemouth Aviation Museum
	WT534	EE Canberra PR7 (8549M) [43] <ff>	South Yorkshire Aircraft Museum, Doncaster
	WT536	EE Canberra PR7 (8063M) <ff>	Privately owned, Walcott, Norfolk
	WT555	Hawker Hunter F1 (7499M)	Vanguard Haulage, Greenford, London
	WT569	Hawker Hunter F1 (7491M)	No 2117 Sqn ATC, Kenfig Hill, Mid-Glamorgan
	WT612	Hawker Hunter F1 (7496M)	RAF Henlow, on display
	WT619	Hawker Hunter F1 (7525M)	RAF Museum Reserve Collection, Stafford
	WT648	Hawker Hunter F1 (7530M) <ff>	Boscombe Down Aviation Collection, Old Sarum
	WT651	Hawker Hunter F1 (7532M) [C]	Newark Air Museum, Winthorpe
	WT660	Hawker Hunter F1 (7421M) [C]	Highland Aviation Museum, Inverness
	WT680	Hawker Hunter F1 (7533M) [J]	Privately owned, Holbeach, Lincs

Serial	Type (code/other identity)	Owner/operator, location or fate	Notes
WT684	Hawker Hunter F1 (7422M) <ff>	Privately owned, Lavendon, Bucks	
WT694	Hawker Hunter F1 (7510M)	Caernarfon Air World	
WT711	Hawker Hunter GA11 [833/DD]	Lakes Lightnings, Spark Bridge, Cumbria	
WT720	Hawker Hunter F51 (RDAF E-408/8565M) [B]	Privately owned, Manmoel, Gwent	
WT722	Hawker Hunter T8C (G-BWGN) [873]	Cornwall Aviation Heritage Centre, Newquay	
WT723	Hawker Hunter PR11 (XG194/G-PRII) [692/LM]	Hunter Flight Academy, St Athan	
WT741	Hawker Hunter GA11 [791] <ff>	Privately owned, South Yorks Air Mus'm, Doncaster	
WT744	Hawker Hunter GA11 [868/VL]	Privately owned, Braunton, Devon	
WT746	Hawker Hunter F4 (XF506/7770M) [A]	Dumfries & Galloway Avn Mus, Dumfries	
WT799	Hawker Hunter T8C [879]	Blue Lagoon Diving Centre, Womersley, N Yorks	
WT804	Hawker Hunter GA11 [831/DD]	Privately owned, Todenham, Glos	
WT806	Hawker Hunter GA11	Privately owned, Bruntingthorpe	
WT859	Supermarine 544 <ff>	Boscombe Down Aviation Collection, Old Sarum	
WT867	Slingsby T31B Cadet TX3	Privately owned, Eaglescott	
WT874	Slingsby T31B Cadet TX3 (BGA1255)	Privately owned, Lasham	
WT877	Slingsby T31B Cadet TX3	Tettenhall Transport Heritage Centre	
WT905	Slingsby T31B Cadet TX3	Privately owned, Keevil	
WT908	Slingsby T31B Cadet TX3 (BGA3487)	Privately owned, Dunstable	
WT910	Slingsby T31B Cadet TX3 (BGA3953)	Privately owned, Llandegla, Denbighshire	
WT914	Slingsby T31B Cadet TX3 (BGA3194) (fuselage)	East Midlands Airport Aeropark	
WT933	Bristol 171 Sycamore 3 (G-ALSW/7709M)	Newark Air Museum, Winthorpe	
WV106	Douglas Skyraider AEW1 [427/C]	FAA Museum, stored Cobham Hall, RNAS Yeovilton	
WV198	Sikorsky S55 Whirlwind HAR21 (G-BJWY) [K]	Solway Aviation Society, Carlisle	
WV256	Hawker Hunter GA11 (WB188/G-BZPB)	Cornwall Aviation Heritage Centre, Newquay	
WV314	Hawker Hunter F51 (G-9-445/E-424) [B]	South Yorkshire Aircraft Museum, Doncaster	
WV318	Hawker Hunter T7A (9236M/G-FFOX)	Hunter Flight Academy, Cranfield	
WV322	Hawker Hunter T8C (G-BZSE/9096M) [22/VL]	Privately owned, North Weald	
WV332	Hawker Hunter F4 (7673M) <ff>	Tangmere Military Aircraft Museum	
WV381	Hawker Hunter GA11 (732) <ff>	Privately owned, Chiltern Park, Wallingford	
WV382	Hawker Hunter GA11 [830/VL]	East Midlands Airport Aeropark	
WV383	Hawker Hunter T7	Farnborough Air Sciences Trust, Farnborough	
WV396	Hawker Hunter T8C (9249M) [91]	Tacla Taid Museum, Newborough, Anglesey	
WV493	Percival P56 Provost T1 (G-BDYG/7696M) [29]	National Museum of Flight, stored E Fortune	
WV499	Percival P56 Provost T1 (G-BZRF/7698M) [P-G]	Privately owned, Westonzoyland, Somerset	
WV514	Percival P56 Provost T51 (G-BLIW) [N-C]	Privately owned, Shoreham	
WV605	Percival P56 Provost T1 [T-B]	Norfolk & Suffolk Avn Museum, Flixton	
WV606	Percival P56 Provost T1 (7622M)[P-B]	Newark Air Museum, Winthorpe	
WV679	Percival P56 Provost T1 (7615M) [O-J]	Wellesbourne Wartime Museum	
WV705	Percival P66 Pembroke C1 <ff>	Privately owned, Awbridge, Hants	
WV740	Percival P66 Pembroke C1 (G-BNPH)	Privately owned, St Athan	
WV746	Percival P66 Pembroke C1 (8938M)	RAF Museum, Cosford	
WV781	Bristol 171 Sycamore HR12 (G-ALTD/7839M) <ff>	Caernarfon Air World	
WV783	Bristol 171 Sycamore HR12 (G-ALSP/7841M)	RAF Museum, Hendon	
WV787	EE Canberra B2/8 (8799M)	Newark Air Museum, Winthorpe	
WV795	Hawker Sea Hawk FGA6 (8151M)	Privately owned, Dunsfold	
WV797	Hawker Sea Hawk FGA6 (8155M) [491/J]	Midland Air Museum, Coventry	
WV798	Hawker Sea Hawk FGA6 [026/CU]	Privately owned, Newquay	
WV838	Hawker Sea Hawk FGA4 [182] <ff>	Norfolk & Suffolk Avn Museum, Flixton	
WV856	Hawker Sea Hawk FGA6 [163]	FAA Museum, RNAS Yeovilton	
WV903	Hawker Sea Hawk FGA6 (8153M) [128] <ff>	Privately owned, Stranraer	
WV908	Hawker Sea Hawk FGA6 (8154M) [188/A]	RN Historic Flight, stored Shawbury	
WV910	Hawker Sea Hawk FGA6 <ff>	Boscombe Down Aviation Collection, Old Sarum	
WV911	Hawker Sea Hawk FGA4 [115/C]	RNAS Yeovilton, Fire Section	
WW138	DH112 Sea Venom FAW22 [227/Z]	FAA Museum, RNAS Yeovilton	
WW145	DH112 Sea Venom FAW22 [680/LM]	National Museum of Flight, E Fortune	
WW217	DH112 Sea Venom FAW22 [351]	Newark Air Museum, Winthorpe	
WW388	Percival P56 Provost T1 (7616M) [O-F]	Privately owned, Cambridge	
WW421	Percival P56 Provost T1 (WW450/G-BZRE/7689M)	Bournemouth Aviation Museum	
WW442	Percival P56 Provost T1 (7618M) [N]	East Midlands Airport Aeropark	
WW444	Percival P56 Provost T1 [D]	Privately owned, Brownhills, Staffs	

Notes	Serial	Type (code/other identity)	Owner/operator, location or fate
	WW447	Percival P56 Provost T1 [F]	Privately owned, Shoreham
	WW453	Percival P56 Provost T1 (G-TMKI) [W-S]	Privately owned, Westonzoyland, Somerset
	WW654	Hawker Hunter GA11 [834/DD]	Privately owned, Ford, W Sussex
	WW664	Hawker Hunter F4 <ff>	Privately owned, Norfolk
	WX788	DH112 Venom NF3 <ff>	South Yorkshire Aircraft Museum, stored Doncaster
	WX853	DH112 Venom NF3 (7443M)	de Havilland Aircraft Mus'm, stored London Colney
	WX905	DH112 Venom NF3 (7458M)	Newark Air Museum, Winthorpe
	WZ425	DH115 Vampire T11	Privately owned, Birlingham, Worcs
	WZ447	DH115 Vampire T55 (U-1230/PX-M/LN-DHZ)	Norwegian AF Historical Sqn, Rygge, Norway
	WZ450	DH115 Vampire T11 <ff>	Privately owned, Corscombe, Dorset
	WZ507	DH115 Vampire T11 (G-VTII) [74]	Privately owned, North Weald
	WZ515	DH115 Vampire T11 [60]	Solway Aviation Society, Carlisle
	WZ518	DH115 Vampire T11 [B]	North-East Aircraft Museum, Usworth
	WZ549	DH115 Vampire T11 (8118M) [F]	Ulster Aviation Society, Long Kesh
	WZ553	DH115 Vampire T11 (G-DHYY) <ff>	Privately owned, Stockton, Warks
	WZ557	DH115 Vampire T11	Privately owned, Over Dinsdale, N Yorks
	WZ572	DH115 Vampire T11 (8124M) [65] <ff>	Privately owned, Sholing, Hants
	WZ581	DH115 Vampire T11 <ff>	The Vampire Collection, Hemel Hempstead
	WZ584	DH115 Vampire T11 (G-BZRC) [K]	Privately owned, Binbrook
	WZ589	DH115 Vampire T11 [19]	Privately owned, Wigmore, Kent
	WZ590	DH115 Vampire T11 [49]	IWM Duxford
	WZ662	Auster AOP9 (G-BKVK)	Privately owned, Eggesford
	WZ679	Auster AOP9 (7863M/XP248/G-CIUX)	Currently not known
	WZ706	Auster AOP9 (7851M/G-BURR)	Privately owned, Eggesford
	WZ711	Auster AOP9/Beagle E3 (G-AVHT)	South Yorkshire Aircraft Museum, stored Doncaster
	WZ721	Auster AOP9	Museum of Army Flying, Middle Wallop
	WZ724	Auster AOP9 (7432M) (frame)	Museum of Army Flying, Middle Wallop
	WZ729	Auster AOP9 (G-BXON)	Crashed at Spanhoe, 18 June 2017
	WZ736	Avro 707A (7868M)	Museum of Science & Industry, Manchester
	WZ744	Avro 707C (7932M)	RAF Museum, stored Cosford
	WZ753	Slingsby T38 Grasshopper TX1	Solent Sky, Southampton
	WZ755	Slingsby T38 Grasshopper TX1 (BGA3481)	Tettenhall Transport Heritage Centre
	WZ757	Slingsby T38 Grasshopper TX1 (comp XK820)	Privately owned, Kirton-in-Lindsey, Lincs
	WZ767	Slingsby T38 Grasshopper TX1	North-East Aircraft Museum, stored Usworth
	WZ772	Slingsby T38 Grasshopper TX1	Trenchard Museum, RAF Halton
	WZ773	Slingsby T38 Grasshopper TX1	Edinburgh Academy
	WZ784	Slingsby T38 Grasshopper TX1 (comp WZ824)	Solway Aviation Society, stored Carlisle
	WZ784	Slingsby T38 Grasshopper TX1	Privately owned, stored Felixstowe
	WZ791	Slingsby T38 Grasshopper TX1 (8944M)	RAF Museum, Hendon
	WZ793	Slingsby T38 Grasshopper TX1	Privately owned, Keevil
	WZ796	Slingsby T38 Grasshopper TX1	Privately owned, stored Aston Down
	WZ798	Slingsby T38 Grasshopper TX1	Privately owned, Eaglescott
	WZ816	Slingsby T38 Grasshopper TX1 (BGA3979)	Privately owned, Redhill
	WZ818	Slingsby T38 Grasshopper TX1 (BGA4361)	Privately owned, Nympsfield
	WZ819	Slingsby T38 Grasshopper TX1 (BGA3498)	Privately owned, Halton
	WZ820	Slingsby T38 Grasshopper TX1 <ff>	Sywell Aviation Museum, stored
	WZ822	Slingsby T38 Grasshopper TX1	South Yorkshire Aircraft Museum, stored Doncaster
	WZ824	Slingsby T38 Grasshopper TX1	Privately owned, Bridge of Weir, Renfrewshire
	WZ826	Vickers Valiant B(K)1 (XD826/7872M) <ff>	Privately owned, Rayleigh, Essex
	WZ828	Slingsby T38 Grasshopper TX1 (BGA4421)	Privately owned, Little Rissington
	WZ831	Slingsby T38 Grasshopper TX1	Privately owned, stored Nympsfield, Glos
	WZ846	DHC1 Chipmunk 22 (G-BCSC/8439M)	No 2427 Sqn ATC, Biggin Hill
	WZ847	DHC1 Chipmunk 22 (G-CPMK) [F]	Privately owned, Sleap
	WZ868	DHC1 Chipmunk 22 (WG322/G-ARMF)	Privately owned, stored St Athan
	WZ869	DHC1 Chipmunk T10 (8019M) <ff>	Privately owned, Leicester
	WZ872	DHC1 Chipmunk 22 (G-BZGB) [E]	Privately owned, Blackpool
	WZ876	DHC1 Chipmunk 22 (G-BBWN) <ff>	Tangmere Military Aviation Museum
	WZ879	DHC1 Chipmunk 22 (G-BWUT) [X]	Privately owned, Duxford
	WZ882	DHC1 Chipmunk 22 (G-BXGP) [K]	Privately owned, Eaglescott

Serial	Type (code/other identity)	Owner/operator, location or fate	Notes
XA109	DH115 Sea Vampire T22	Montrose Air Station Heritage Centre	
XA127	DH115 Sea Vampire T22 <ff>	FAA Museum, RNAS Yeovilton	
XA129	DH115 Sea Vampire T22	FAA Museum, stored Cobham Hall, RNAS Yeovilton	
XA225	Slingsby T38 Grasshopper TX1	Privately owned, RAF Odiham	
XA226	Slingsby T38 Grasshopper TX1	Norfolk & Suffolk Avn Museum, Flixton	
XA228	Slingsby T38 Grasshopper TX1	National Museum of Flight, East Fortune	
XA230	Slingsby T38 Grasshopper TX1 (BGA4098)	Privately owned, Henlow	
XA231	Slingsby T38 Grasshopper TX1 (8888M)	RAF Manston History Museum	
XA240	Slingsby T38 Grasshopper TX1 (BGA4556)	Privately owned, Portmoak, Perth & Kinross	
XA241	Slingsby T38 Grasshopper TX1	Shuttleworth Collection, stored Old Warden	
XA243	Slingsby T38 Grasshopper TX1 (8886M)	Privately owned, Gransden Lodge, Cambs	
XA244	Slingsby T38 Grasshopper TX1	Privately owned, Brent Tor, Devon	
XA282	Slingsby T31B Cadet TX3	Caernarfon Air World	
XA289	Slingsby T31B Cadet TX3	Privately owned, Eaglescott	
XA290	Slingsby T31B Cadet TX3	Privately owned, Portmoak, Perth & Kinross	
XA293	Slingsby T31B Cadet TX3 <ff>	Privately owned, Breighton	
XA295	Slingsby T31B Cadet TX3 (BGA3336)	Privately owned, Eaglescott	
XA302	Slingsby T31B Cadet TX3 (BGA3786)	RAF Museum, Hendon	
XA310	Slingsby T31B Cadet TX3 (BGA4963)	Privately owned, Little Rissington	
XA459	Fairey Gannet ECM6 [E]	Privately owned, White Waltham	
XA460	Fairey Gannet ECM6 [768/BY]	Ulster Aviation Society, Long Kesh	
XA466	Fairey Gannet COD4 [777/LM]	FAA Museum, RNAS Yeovilton	
XA508	Fairey Gannet T2 [627/GN]	FAA Museum, at Midland Air Museum, Coventry	
XA564	Gloster Javelin FAW1 (7464M)	RAF Museum, Cosford	
XA634	Gloster Javelin FAW4 (7641M)	Jet Age Museum, stored Gloucester	
XA699	Gloster Javelin FAW5 (7809M)	Midland Air Museum, Coventry	
XA847	EE P1B (8371M)	Privately owned, Stowmarket, Suffolk	
XA862	WS55 Whirlwind HAR1 (G-AMJT) [704] <ff>	South Yorkshire Aircraft Museum, Doncaster	
XA864	WS55 Whirlwind HAR1	FAA Museum, stored Cobham Hall, RNAS Yeovilton	
XA870	WS55 Whirlwind HAR1 [911]	South Yorkshire Aircraft Museum, Doncaster	
XA880	DH104 Devon C2 (G-BVXR)	Privately owned, Little Rissington	
XA893	Avro 698 Vulcan B1 (8591M) <ff>	RAF Museum, stored Cosford	
XA903	Avro 698 Vulcan B1 <ff>	Privately owned, Stoneykirk, D&G	
XA917	HP80 Victor B1 (7827M) <ff>	Privately owned, Cupar, Fife	
XB259	Blackburn B101 Beverley C1 (G-AOAI)	Fort Paull Armoury	
XB261	Blackburn B101 Beverley C1 <ff>	Newark Air Museum, Winthorpe	
XB446	Grumman TBM-3 Avenger ECM6B	FAA Museum, Yeovilton	
XB480	Hiller HT1 [537]	FAA Museum, stored Cobham Hall, RNAS Yeovilton	
XB812	Canadair CL-13 Sabre F4 (9227M) [U]	RAF Museum, Cosford	
XD145	Saro SR53	RAF Museum, Cosford	
XD163	WS55 Whirlwind HAR10 (8645M) [X]	The Helicopter Museum, Weston-super-Mare	
XD165	WS55 Whirlwind HAR10 (8673M)	Caernarfon Airfield Fire Section	
XD215	VS Scimitar F1 <ff>	Privately owned, Cheltenham	
XD235	VS Scimitar F1 <ff>	Privately owned, Lavendon, Bucks	
XD317	VS Scimitar F1 [112/R]	FAA Museum, RNAS Yeovilton	
XD332	VS Scimitar F1 [194/C]	Solent Sky, stored Romsey	
XD375	DH115 Vampire T11 (7887M)	Privately owned, Elland, W Yorks	
XD377	DH115 Vampire T11 (8203M) <ff>	South Yorkshire Aircraft Museum, stored Doncaster	
XD382	DH115 Vampire T11 (comp XD534) [41]	East Midlands Airport Aeropark	
XD425	DH115 Vampire T11 <ff>	Morayvia, Kinloss	
XD434	DH115 Vampire T11 [25]	Fenland & W Norfolk Aviation Museum, Wisbech	
XD445	DH115 Vampire T11 [51]	Tettenhall Transport Heritage Centre	
XD447	DH115 Vampire T11 [50]	East Midlands Airport Aeropark	
XD452	DH115 Vampire T11 (7990M) [66] <ff>	Privately owned, Dursley, Glos	
XD459	DH115 Vampire T11 [57] <ff>	Privately owned, Hanningfield, Essex	
XD506	DH115 Vampire T11 (7983M)	Suffolk Aviation Heritage Centre, Foxhall Heath	
XD515	DH115 Vampire T11 (7998M/XM515)	RAF Museum, stored Cosford	
XD525	DH115 Vampire T11 (7882M) <ff>	Privately owned, Templepatrick, NI	
XD542	DH115 Vampire T11 (7604M) [N]	Privately owned, Patrington, E Yorks	
XD547	DH115 Vampire T11 [Z] (composite)	Privately owned, Cantley, Norfolk	

Notes	Serial	Type (code/other identity)	Owner/operator, location or fate
	XD593	DH115 Vampire T11	Newark Air Museum, Winthorpe
	XD595	DH115 Vampire T11 <ff>	Privately owned, Glentham, Lincs
	XD596	DH115 Vampire T11 (7939M)	Solent Sky, stored Timsbury, Hants
	XD599	DH115 Vampire T11 [A] <ff>	Sywell Aviation Museum
	XD616	DH115 Vampire T11 [56]	Suffolk Aviation Heritage Centre, Foxhall Heath
	XD624	DH115 Vampire T11	Privately owned, Hooton Park
	XD626	DH115 Vampire T11 [Q]	Midland Air Museum, stored Coventry
	XD674	Hunting Jet Provost T1 (7570M)	RAF Museum, Cosford
	XD693	Hunting Jet Provost T1 (XM129/G-AOBU) [Z-Q]	Kennet Aviation, North Weald
	XD816	Vickers Valiant B(K)1 <ff>	Brooklands Museum, Weybridge
	XD818	Vickers Valiant B(K)1 (7894M)	RAF Museum, Cosford
	XD857	Vickers Valiant B(K)1 <ff>	RAF Marham Aviation Heritage Centre
	XD875	Vickers Valiant B(K)1 <ff>	Morayvia, Kinloss
	XE317	Bristol 171 Sycamore HR14 (G-AMWO)	South Yorkshire Aircraft Museum, Doncaster
	XE339	Hawker Sea Hawk FGA6 (8156M) [149] <ff>	Privately owned, Glos
	XE339	Hawker Sea Hawk FGA6 (8156M) [E] <rf>	Privately owned, Booker
	XE340	Hawker Sea Hawk FGA6 [131/Z]	FAA Museum, stored Cobham Hall, RNAS Yeovilton
	XE364	Hawker Sea Hawk FGA6 (G-JETH) (comp WM983) [485/J]	Gatwick Aviation Museum, Charlwood, Surrey
	XE368	Hawker Sea Hawk FGA6 [200/J]	Privately owned, Barrow-in-Furness
	XE521	Fairey Rotodyne Y (parts)	The Helicopter Museum, Weston-super-Mare
	XE584	Hawker Hunter FGA9 <ff>	Privately owned, Hooton Park
	XE597	Hawker Hunter FGA9 (8874M) <ff>	Privately owned, Bromsgrove
	XE620	Hawker Hunter F6A (XE606/8841M) [B]	RAF Waddington, on display
	XE624	Hawker Hunter FGA9 (8875M) [G]	Privately owned, Wickenby
	XE627	Hawker Hunter F6A [T]	IWM Duxford
	XE643	Hawker Hunter FGA9 (8586M) <ff>	No 1137 Sqn ATC, Aldergrove
	XE650	Hawker Hunter FGA9 (G-9-449) <ff>	Farnborough Air Sciences Trust, Farnborough
	XE664	Hawker Hunter F4 <ff>	Jet Age Museum, Gloucester
	XE665	Hawker Hunter T8C (G-BWGM)	Privately owned, stored Cotswold Airport
	XE668	Hawker Hunter GA11 [832/DD]	Hamburger Hill Paintball, Marksbury, Somerset
	XE670	Hawker Hunter F4 (7762M/8585M) <ff>	RAF Museum, Cosford
	XE683	Hawker Hunter F51 (RDAF E-409) [G]	City of Norwich Aviation Museum
	XE685	Hawker Hunter GA11 (G-GAII) [861/VL]	RAF Scampton Heritage Centre
	XE689	Hawker Hunter GA11 (G-BWGK) <ff>	Privately owned, Cotswold Airport
	XE707	Hawker Hunter GA11 (N707XE) [865]	Bentwaters Cold War Museum
	XE786	Slingsby T31B Cadet TX3 (BGA4033)	Privately owned, Arbroath
	XE793	Slingsby T31B Cadet TX3 (8666M)	Privately owned, Tamworth
	XE797	Slingsby T31B Cadet TX3	South Yorkshire Aviation Museum, Doncaster
	XE799	Slingsby T31B Cadet TX3 (8943M) [R]	Privately owned, stored Lasham
	XE802	Slingsby T31B Cadet TX3 (BGA5283)	Privately owned, North Hill, Devon
	XE852	DH115 Vampire T11 [58]	No 2247 Sqn ATC, Hawarden
	XE855	DH115 Vampire T11 <ff>	Midland Air Museum, stored Coventry (wreck)
	XE856	DH115 Vampire T11 (G-DUSK) [V]	Bournemouth Aviation Museum
	XE864	DH115 Vampire T11(comp XD435) <ff>	Privately owned, Ingatstone, Essex
	XE872	DH115 Vampire T11 [62]	Midland Air Museum, Coventry
	XE874	DH115 Vampire T11 (8582M)	Paintball Commando, Birkin, W Yorks
	XE897	DH115 Vampire T11 (XD403)	Privately owned, Errol, Tayside
	XE921	DH115 Vampire T11 [64] <ff>	Privately owned, Stoneykirk, D&G
	XE935	DH115 Vampire T11	South Yorkshire Aircraft Museum, Doncaster
	XE946	DH115 Vampire T11 (7473M) <ff>	RAF Cranwell Aviation Heritage Centre
	XE956	DH115 Vampire T11 (G-OBLN)	De Havilland Aviation, stored Rochester
	XE979	DH115 Vampire T11 [54]	Privately owned, Cantley, Norfolk
	XE982	DH115 Vampire T11 (7564M) (fuselage)	Privately owned, Glos
	XE985	DH115 Vampire T11 (*WZ476*)	Privately owned, New Inn, Torfaen
	XF113	VS Swift F7 [19] <ff>	Boscombe Down Aviation Collection, Old Sarum
	XF114	VS Swift F7 (G-SWIF)	Solent Sky, stored Romsey
	XF314	Hawker Hunter F51 (RDAF E-412) [N]	*Repainted as XF368*
	XF321	Hawker Hunter T7 <ff>	*To Laarbruch, Germany, January 2018*
	XF321	Hawker Hunter T7 <rf>	Phoenix Aviation, Bruntingthorpe

Serial	Type (code/other identity)	Owner/operator, location or fate	Notes
XF368	Hawker Hunter F51 (RDAF E-412/XF314)	Brooklands Museum, Weybridge	
XF375	Hawker Hunter F6A (8736M/G-BUEZ) [6]	Boscombe Down Aviation Collection, Old Sarum	
XF382	Hawker Hunter F6A [15]	Midland Air Museum, Coventry	
XF383	Hawker Hunter F6 (8706M) <ff>	Gloster Aviation Club, Gloucester	
XF418	Hawker Hunter F51 (RDAF E-430)	Gatwick Aviation Museum, Charlwood, Surrey	
XF509	Hawker Hunter F6 (8708M)	Fort Paull Armoury	
XF522	Hawker Hunter F6 <ff>	Herts & Bucks ATC Wing, RAF Halton	
XF526	Hawker Hunter F6 (8679M) [78/E]	Privately owned, Birlingham, Worcs	
XF527	Hawker Hunter F6 (8680M)	RAF Halton, on display	
XF545	Percival P56 Provost T1 (7957M) [O-K]	Privately owned, Bucklebury, Berks	
XF597	Percival P56 Provost T1 (G-BKFW) [AH]	Privately owned, Brimpton, Berks	
XF603	Percival P56 Provost T1 (G-KAPW)	Shuttleworth Collection, Old Warden	
XF690	Percival P56 Provost T1 (8041M/G-MOOS)	Kennet Aviation, Yeovilton	
XF708	Avro 716 Shackleton MR3/3 [C]	IWM Duxford	
XF785	Bristol 173 (7648M/G-ALBN)	Aerospace Bristol, Filton	
XF836	Percival P56 Provost T1 (8043M/G-AWRY) [JG]	Privately owned stored, Newbury	
XF840	Percival P56 Provost T1 <ff>	Tangmere Military Aviation Museum	
XF926	Bristol 188 (8368M)	RAF Museum, Cosford	
XF940	Hawker Hunter F4 <ff>	Privately owned, Kew Stoke, Somerset	
XF994	Hawker Hunter T8C (G-CGHU) [873/VL]	Hawker Hunter Aviation, Scampton	
XF995	Hawker Hunter T8B (G-BZSF/9237M) [K]	Hawker Hunter Aviation, Scampton	
XG154	Hawker Hunter FGA9 (8863M)	RAF Museum, Hendon	
XG160	Hawker Hunter F6A (8831M/G-BWAF) [U]	Bournemouth Aviation Museum	
XG164	Hawker Hunter F6 (8681M)	Davidstow Airfield & Cornwall At War Museum	
XG168	Hawker Hunter F6A (XG172/8832M) [10]	City of Norwich Aviation Museum	
XG190	Hawker Hunter F51 (RDAF E-425) [C]	Solway Aviation Society, Carlisle	
XG193	Hawker Hunter FGA9 (XG297) (comp with WT741) <ff>	South Yorkshire Aircraft Museum, Doncaster	
XG194	Hawker Hunter FGA9 (8839M)	Wattisham Station Heritage Museum	
XG195	Hawker Hunter FGA9 <ff>	Privately owned, Lewes	
XG196	Hawker Hunter F6A (8702M) [31]	Privately owned, Bentwaters	
XG209	Hawker Hunter F6 (8709M) <ff>	Privately owned, Kingston-on-Thames	
XG210	Hawker Hunter F6	Privately owned, Beck Row, Suffolk	
XG225	Hawker Hunter F6A (8713M)	DSAE Cosford, at main gate	
XG226	Hawker Hunter F6A (8800M) <ff>	RAF Manston History Museum	
XG254	Hawker Hunter FGA9 (8881M) [A]	Norfolk & Suffolk Avn Museum, Flixton	
XG274	Hawker Hunter F6 (8710M) [71]	Privately owned, Newmarket	
XG290	Hawker Hunter F6 (8711M) <ff>	Boscombe Down Aviation Collection, Old Sarum	
XG290	Hawker Hunter T7 (comp XL578 & XL586)	To Laarbruch, Germany, January 2018	
XG297	Hawker Hunter FGA9 [Y] <ff>	South Yorkshire Aircraft Museum, Doncaster	
XG325	EE Lightning F1 <ff>	Privately owned, Norfolk	
XG329	EE Lightning F1 (8050M)	Privately owned, Flixton	
XG331	EE Lightning F1 <ff>	Privately owned, Glos	
XG337	EE Lightning F1 (8056M) [M]	RAF Museum, Cosford	
XG452	Bristol 192 Belvedere HC1 (7997M/G-BRMB)	The Helicopter Museum, Weston-super-Mare	
XG454	Bristol 192 Belvedere HC1 (8366M)	Museum of Science & Industry, Manchester	
XG462	Bristol 192 Belvedere HC1 <ff>	The Helicopter Museum, Weston-super-Mare	
XG474	Bristol 192 Belvedere HC1 (8367M) [O]	RAF Museum, Hendon	
XG502	Bristol 171 Sycamore HR14	Museum of Army Flying, Middle Wallop	
XG518	Bristol 171 Sycamore HR14 (8009M) [S-E]	Norfolk & Suffolk Avn Museum, Flixton	
XG523	Bristol 171 Sycamore HR14 <ff> [V]	Norfolk & Suffolk Avn Museum, Flixton	
XG574	WS55 Whirlwind HAR3 [752/PO]	FAA Museum, stored Cobham Hall, RNAS Yeovilton	
XG588	WS55 Whirlwind HAR3 (G-BAMH/VR-BEP)	East Midlands Airport Aeropark	
XG592	WS55 Whirlwind HAS7 [54]	Task Force Adventure Park, Cowbridge, S Glam	
XG594	WS55 Whirlwind HAS7 [517]	FAA Museum, stored Cobham Hall, RNAS Yeovilton	
XG596	WS55 Whirlwind HAS7 [66]	The Helicopter Museum, stored Weston-super-Mare	
XG629	DH112 Sea Venom FAW22	Privately owned, Stone, Staffs	
XG680	DH112 Sea Venom FAW22 [438]	North-East Aircraft Museum, Usworth	
XG692	DH112 Sea Venom FAW22 [668/LM]	Privately owned, Stockport	
XG730	DH112 Sea Venom FAW22	de Havilland Aircraft Museum, London Colney	
XG736	DH112 Sea Venom FAW22	Privately owned, East Midlands	

Notes	Serial	Type (code/other identity)	Owner/operator, location or fate
	XG737	DH112 Sea Venom FAW22 [220/Z]	East Midlands Airport Aeropark
	XG743	DH115 Sea Vampire T22 [597/LM]	Fishburn Historic Aviation Centre
	XG797	Fairey Gannet ECM6 [277]	IWM Duxford
	XG831	Fairey Gannet ECM6 [396]	Davidstow Airfield & Cornwall At War Museum
	XG882	Fairey Gannet T5 (8754M) [771/LM]	Privately owned, Errol, Tayside
	XG883	Fairey Gannet T5 [773/BY]	FAA Museum, at Museum of Berkshire Aviation, Woodley
	XG900	Short SC1	Science Museum, South Kensington
	XG905	Short SC1	Ulster Folk & Transport Mus, Holywood, Co Down
	XH131	EE Canberra PR9	Ulster Aviation Society, Long Kesh
	XH134	EE Canberra PR9 (G-OMHD)	Privately owned, stored Cotswold Airport
	XH135	EE Canberra PR9	Privately owned, Cotswold Airport
	XH136	EE Canberra PR9 (8782M) [W] <ff>	Romney Marsh Wartime Collection
	XH165	EE Canberra PR9 <ff>	Blyth Valley Aviation Collection, Walpole
	XH168	EE Canberra PR9	Scrapped
	XH169	EE Canberra PR9	RAF Marham, on display
	XH170	EE Canberra PR9 (8739M)	RAF Wyton, on display
	XH171	EE Canberra PR9 (8746M) [U]	RAF Museum, Cosford
	XH174	EE Canberra PR9 <ff>	Privately owned, Leicester
	XH175	EE Canberra PR9 <ff>	Privately owned, Bewdley, Worcs
	XH177	EE Canberra PR9 <ff>	Newark Air Museum, Winthorpe
	XH278	DH115 Vampire T11 (8595M/7866M) [42]	Yorkshire Air Museum, Elvington
	XH312	DH115 Vampire T11	Privately owned, Dodleston, Cheshire
	XH313	DH115 Vampire T11 (G-BZRD) [E]	Tangmere Military Aviation Museum
	XH318	DH115 Vampire T11 (7761M) [64]	Privately owned, Sholing, Hants
	XH328	DH115 Vampire T11 <ff>	Privately owned, Cantley, Norfolk
	XH330	DH115 Vampire T11 [73]	Privately owned, Milton Keynes
	XH537	Avro 698 Vulcan B2MRR (8749M) <ff>	Bournemouth Aviation Museum
	XH558	Avro 698 Vulcan B2 (G-VLCN)	Vulcan To The Sky Trust, Doncaster Sheffield Airport
	XH560	Avro 698 Vulcan K2 <ff>	Privately owned, Foulness
	XH563	Avro 698 Vulcan B2MRR <ff>	Privately owned, Over Dinsdale, N Yorks
	XH584	EE Canberra T4 (G-27-374) <ff>	South Yorkshire Aircraft Museum, Doncaster
	XH592	HP80 Victor B1A (8429M) <ff>	Midland Air Museum, Coventry
	XH648	HP80 Victor K1A	IWM Duxford
	XH669	HP80 Victor K2 (9092M) <ff>	Privately owned, Foulness
	XH670	HP80 Victor SR2 <ff>	Privately owned, Foulness
	XH672	HP80 Victor K2 (9242M)	RAF Museum, Cosford
	XH673	HP80 Victor K2 (8911M)	RAF Marham, on display
	XH767	Gloster Javelin FAW9 (7955M) [L]	Yorkshire Air Museum, Elvington
	XH783	Gloster Javelin FAW7 (7798M) <ff>	Privately owned, Catford
	XH837	Gloster Javelin FAW7 (8032M) <ff>	Caernarfon Air World
	XH892	Gloster Javelin FAW9R (7982M) [J]	Norfolk & Suffolk Avn Museum, Flixton
	XH897	Gloster Javelin FAW9	IWM Duxford
	XH903	Gloster Javelin FAW9 (7938M) [G]	Jet Age Museum, Gloucester
	XH992	Gloster Javelin FAW8 (7829M) [P]	Newark Air Museum, Winthorpe
	XJ314	RR Thrust Measuring Rig	Science Museum, South Kensington
	XJ380	Bristol 171 Sycamore HR14 (8628M)	Boscombe Down Aviation Collection, Old Sarum
	XJ389	Fairey Jet Gyrodyne (XD759/G-AJJP)	Museum of Berkshire Aviation, Woodley
	XJ398	WS55 Whirlwind HAR10 (XD768/G-BDBZ)	South Yorkshire Aircraft Museum, Doncaster
	XJ407	WS55 Whirlwind HAR10 (N7013H)	Privately owned, Tattershall Thorpe
	XJ435	WS55 Whirlwind HAR10 (XD804/8671M) [V]	RAF Manston History Museum, spares use
	XJ476	DH110 Sea Vixen FAW1 <ff>	Boscombe Down Aviation Collection, Old Sarum
	XJ481	DH110 Sea Vixen FAW1 [VL]	FAA Museum, stored Cobham Hall, RNAS Yeovilton
	XJ482	DH110 Sea Vixen FAW1 [713/VL]	Norfolk & Suffolk Avn Museum, Flixton
	XJ488	DH110 Sea Vixen FAW1 <ff>	Robertsbridge Aviation Society, Mayfield
	XJ494	DH110 Sea Vixen FAW2 [121/E]	Privately owned, Bruntingthorpe
	XJ560	DH110 Sea Vixen FAW2 (8142M) [243/H]	Newark Air Museum, Winthorpe
	XJ565	DH110 Sea Vixen FAW2 [127/E]	de Havilland Aircraft Museum, London Colney
	XJ571	DH110 Sea Vixen FAW2 (8140M) [242/R]	Solent Sky, Southampton
	XJ575	DH110 Sea Vixen FAW2 <ff> [SAH-13]	Wellesbourne Wartime Museum
	XJ579	DH110 Sea Vixen FAW2 <ff>	Midland Air Museum, stored Coventry

Serial	Type (code/other identity)	Owner/operator, location or fate	Notes
XJ580	DH110 Sea Vixen FAW2 [131/E]	Tangmere Military Aviation Museum	
XJ714	Hawker Hunter FR10 (comp XG226)	East Midlands Airport Aeropark	
XJ723	WS55 Whirlwind HAR10	Moravyia, Dallachy, Moray	
XJ726	WS55 Whirlwind HAR10	Caernarfon Air World	
XJ727	WS55 Whirlwind HAR10 (8661M) [L]	Privately owned, Ramsgate	
XJ729	WS55 Whirlwind HAR10 (8732M/G-BVGE)	Privately owned, Chard, Somerset	
XJ758	WS55 Whirlwind HAR10 (8464M) <ff>	Privately owned, Welshpool	
XJ772	DH115 Vampire T11 [H]	de Havilland Aircraft Museum, London Colney	
XJ823	Avro 698 Vulcan B2A	Solway Aviation Society, Carlisle	
XJ824	Avro 698 Vulcan B2A	IWM Duxford	
XJ917	Bristol 171 Sycamore HR14 [H-S]	Bristol Sycamore Group, stored Filton	
XJ918	Bristol 171 Sycamore HR14 (8190M)	RAF Museum, Cosford	
XK416	Auster AOP9 (7855M/G-AYUA)	Privately owned, Widmerpool	
XK417	Auster AOP9 (G-AVXY)	Privately owned, Messingham, Lincs	
XK418	Auster AOP9 (7976M)	93rd Bomb Group Museum, Hardwick, Norfolk	
XK421	Auster AOP9 (8365M) (frame)	Privately owned, Lincs	
XK488	Blackburn NA39 Buccaneer S1	FAA Museum, stored Cobham Hall, RNAS Yeovilton	
XK526	Blackburn NA39 Buccaneer S2 (8648M)	RAF Honington, at main gate	
XK527	Blackburn NA39 Buccaneer S2D (8818M) <ff>	Privately owned, North Wales	
XK532	Blackburn NA39 Buccaneer S2D (8867M) [632/LM]	Highland Aviation Museum, Inverness	
XK533	Blackburn NA39 Buccaneer S1 <ff>	Royal Scottish Mus'm of Flight, stored Granton	
XK590	DH115 Vampire T11 [V]	Wellesbourne Wartime Museum	
XK623	DH115 Vampire T11 (G-VAMP) [56]	Caernarfon Air World	
XK624	DH115 Vampire T11 [32]	Norfolk & Suffolk Avn Museum, Flixton	
XK625	DH115 Vampire T11 [14]	Romney Marsh Wartime Collection	
XK627	DH115 Vampire T11 <ff>	Davidstow Airfield & Cornwall At War Museum	
XK632	DH115 Vampire T11 <ff>	Privately owned, Greenford, London	
XK637	DH115 Vampire T11 [56]	Top Gun Flight Simulation Centre, Stalybridge	
XK695	DH106 Comet C2(RC) (G-AMXH/9164M) <ff>	de Havilland Aircraft Museum, London Colney	
XK699	DH106 Comet C2 (7971M) <ff>	Boscombe Down Aviation Collection, Old Sarum	
XK724	Folland Gnat F1 (7715M)	RAF Museum, stored Cosford	
XK740	Folland Gnat F1 (8396M)	Solent Sky, Southampton	
XK776	ML Utility 1	Museum of Army Flying, Middle Wallop	
XK789	Slingsby T38 Grasshopper TX1	Midland Air Museum, Coventry	
XK790	Slingsby T38 Grasshopper TX1	Privately owned, stored Husbands Bosworth	
XK819	Slingsby T38 Grasshopper TX1	Privately owned, stored Rufforth	
XK822	Slingsby T38 Grasshopper TX1	Privately owned, Partridge Green, W Sussex	
XK885	Percival P66 Pembroke C1 (8452M/N46EA)	Privately owned, St Athan	
XK895	DH104 Sea Devon C20 (G-SDEV) [19/CU]	Cornwall Aviation Heritage Centre, Newquay	
XK907	WS55 Whirlwind HAS7	Midland Air Museum, stored Coventry	
XK911	WS55 Whirlwind HAS7(mod)	Privately owned, Dagenham	
XK936	WS55 Whirlwind HAS7 [62]	IWM Duxford	
XK940	WS55 Whirlwind HAS7 (G-AYXT) [911]	The Helicopter Museum, Weston-super-Mare	
XK970	WS55 Whirlwind HAR10 (8789M)	Army, Bramley, Hants (for disposal)	
XL149	Blackburn B101 Beverley C1 (7988M) <ff>	South Yorkshire Aircraft Museum, Doncaster	
XL160	HP80 Victor K2 (8910M) <ff>	Norfolk & Suffolk Avn Museum, Flixton	
XL164	HP80 Victor K2 (9215M) <ff>	Bournemouth Aviation Museum	
XL190	HP80 Victor K2 (9216M) <ff>	RAF Manston History Museum	
XL231	HP80 Victor K2	Yorkshire Air Museum, Elvington	
XL318	Avro 698 Vulcan B2 (8733M)	RAF Museum, Hendon	
XL319	Avro 698 Vulcan B2	North-East Aircraft Museum, Usworth	
XL360	Avro 698 Vulcan B2A	Midland Air Museum, Coventry	
XL388	Avro 698 Vulcan B2 <ff>	South Yorkshire Aircraft Museum, Doncaster	
XL426	Avro 698 Vulcan B2 (G-VJET)	Vulcan Restoration Trust, Southend	
XL445	Avro 698 Vulcan K2 (8811M) <ff>	Norfolk & Suffolk Avn Museum, Flixton	
XL449	Fairey Gannet AEW3 <ff>	Privately owned, Steventon, Oxon	
XL472	Fairey Gannet AEW3 [044/R]	Hunter Flying Ltd, St Athan (spares use)	
XL497	Fairey Gannet AEW3 [041/R]	Dumfries & Galloway Avn Mus, Dumfries	
XL500	Fairey Gannet AEW3 (G-KAEW) [CU]	Privately owned, St Athan	
XL502	Fairey Gannet AEW3 (8610M/G-BMYP)	Yorkshire Air Museum, Elvington	

Notes	Serial	Type (code/other identity)	Owner/operator, location or fate
	XL503	Fairey Gannet AEW3 [070/E]	FAA Museum, stored Cobham Hall, RNAS Yeovilton
	XL563	Hawker Hunter T7 (9218M)	Farnborough Air Sciences Trust, stored Farnborough
	XL564	Hawker Hunter T7 <ff>	Privately owned, Tilehurst, Berks
	XL565	Hawker Hunter T7 (parts of WT745) [Y]	Privately owned, Bruntingthorpe
	XL568	Hawker Hunter T7A (9224M) [X]	RAF Museum, Cosford
	XL569	Hawker Hunter T7 (8833M)	East Midlands Airport Aeropark
	XL571	Hawker Hunter T7 (XL572/8834M/G-HNTR) [V]	Yorkshire Air Museum, Elvington
	XL573	Hawker Hunter T7 (G-BVGH)	Hunter Flying Ltd, St Athan
	XL580	Hawker Hunter T8M [723]	FAA Museum, stored Cobham Hall, RNAS Yeovilton
	XL586	Hawker Hunter T7 (comp XL578)	Action Park, Wickford, Essex
	XL587	Hawker Hunter T7 (8807M/G-HPUX)	Hawker Hunter Aviation, stored Scampton
	XL591	Hawker Hunter T7	Gatwick Aviation Museum, Charlwood, Surrey
	XL592	Hawker Hunter T7 (8836M) [Y]	Maidenhead Heritage Centre
	XL601	Hawker Hunter T7 (G-BZSR) [874/VL]	Classic Fighters, Brustem, Belgium
	XL602	Hawker Hunter T8M (G-BWFT)	Hunter Flying Ltd, St Athan
	XL609	Hawker Hunter T7 <ff>	Privately owned, South Molton, Devon
	XL612	Hawker Hunter T7 [2]	Sold to France, December 2017
	XL621	Hawker Hunter T7 (G-BNCX)	Privately owned, Dunsfold
	XL623	Hawker Hunter T7 (8770M)	The Planets Leisure Centre, Woking
	XL629	EE Lightning T4	MoD/QinetiQ Boscombe Down, at main gate
	XL714	DH82A Tiger Moth II (T6099/G-AOGR)	Privately owned, Boughton, Lincs
	XL736	Saro Skeeter AOP12	The Helicopter Museum stored, Weston-super-Mare
	XL738	Saro Skeeter AOP12 (XM565/7861M)	Privately owned, Storwood, Yorkshire
	XL739	Saro Skeeter AOP12	Privately owned, Forncett St Peter, Norfolk
	XL762	Saro Skeeter AOP12 (8017M)	National Museum of Flight, E Fortune
	XL763	Saro Skeeter AOP12	Privately owned, Storwood, Yorkshire
	XL764	Saro Skeeter AOP12 (7940M) [J]	Newark Air Museum, Winthorpe
	XL765	Saro Skeeter AOP12	Privately owned, Melksham, Wilts
	XL770	Saro Skeeter AOP12 (8046M)	Solent Sky, Southampton
	XL809	Saro Skeeter AOP12 (G-BLIX)	Privately owned, Wilden, Beds
	XL811	Saro Skeeter AOP12	The Helicopter Museum, Weston-super-Mare
	XL812	Saro Skeeter AOP12 (G-SARO)	AAC Historic Aircraft Flight, stored Middle Wallop
	XL813	Saro Skeeter AOP12	Museum of Army Flying, Middle Wallop
	XL814	Saro Skeeter AOP12	AAC Historic Aircraft Flight, Middle Wallop
	XL824	Bristol 171 Sycamore HR14 (8021M)	Aerospace Bristol, Filton
	XL829	Bristol 171 Sycamore HR14	The Helicopter Museum, Weston-super-Mare
	XL840	WS55 Whirlwind HAS7	Privately owned, Bawtry
	XL853	WS55 Whirlwind HAS7 [PO]	FAA Museum, stored Cobham Hall, RNAS Yeovilton
	XL875	WS55 Whirlwind HAR9	Perth Technical College
	XL929	Percival P66 Pembroke C1 (G-BNPU)	Privately owned, stored Compton Verney
	XL954	Percival P66 Pembroke C1 (9042M/N4234C/G-BXES)	Privately owned, Weston, Ireland
	XL993	SAL Twin Pioneer CC2 (8388M)	RAF Museum, Cosford
	XM135	BAC Lightning F1 [B]	IWM Duxford
	XM144	BAC Lightning F1 (8417M) <ff>	Shannon Aviation Museum, Eire
	XM169	BAC Lightning F1A (8422M) <ff>	Morayvia, Kinloss
	XM172	BAC Lightning F1A (8427M)	Lakes Lightnings, Spark Bridge, Cumbria
	XM173	BAC Lightning F1A (8414M) [A]	Privately owned, Malmesbury, Glos
	XM191	BAC Lightning F1A (7854M/8590M) <ff>	Privately owned, Thorpe Wood, N Yorks
	XM192	BAC Lightning F1A (8413M) [K]	Thorpe Camp Preservation Group, Lincs
	XM223	DH104 Devon C2 (G-BWWC) [J]	Privately owned, stored Compton Verney
	XM279	EE Canberra B(I)8 <ff>	Privately owned, Flixton
	XM300	WS58 Wessex HAS1	Privately owned, Nantgarw, Rhondda
	XM328	WS58 Wessex HAS3 [653/PO]	The Helicopter Museum, Weston-super-Mare
	XM330	WS58 Wessex HAS1	The Helicopter Museum, Weston-super-Mare
	XM350	Hunting Jet Provost T3A (9036M)	South Yorkshire Aircraft Museum, Doncaster
	XM351	Hunting Jet Provost T3 (8078M) [Y]	RAF Museum, Cosford
	XM355	Hunting Jet Provost T3 (8229M)	Newcastle Aviation Academy
	XM358	Hunting Jet Provost T3A (8987M) [53]	Privately owned, Newbridge, Powys
	XM362	Hunting Jet Provost T3 (8230M)	DSAE No 1 SoTT, Cosford
	XM365	Hunting Jet Provost T3A (G-BXBH)	Privately owned, Bruntingthorpe
	XM373	Hunting Jet Provost T3 (7726M) [2] <ff>	Yorkshire Air Museum, Elvington

Serial	Type (code/other identity)	Owner/operator, location or fate	Notes
XM383	Hunting Jet Provost T3A [90]	Newark Air Museum, Winthorpe	
XM402	Hunting Jet Provost T3 (8055AM) [18]	Fenland & W Norfolk Aviation Museum, Wisbech	
XM404	Hunting Jet Provost T3 (8055BM) <ff>	South Yorkshire Aircraft Museum, Doncaster	
XM409	Hunting Jet Provost T3 (8082M) <ff>	Air Scouts, Guernsey Airport	
XM410	Hunting Jet Provost T3 (8054AM) [B]	Privately owned, Gillingham, Kent	
XM411	Hunting Jet Provost T3 (8434M) <ff>	South Yorkshire Aircraft Museum, Doncaster	
XM412	Hunting Jet Provost T3A (9011M) [41]	Privately owned, Balado Bridge, Scotland	
XM414	Hunting Jet Provost T3A (8996M)	Ulster Aviation Society, Long Kesh	
XM417	Hunting Jet Provost T3 (8054AM) [D] <ff>	Privately owned, Bracknell	
XM419	Hunting Jet Provost T3A (8990M) [102]	Newcastle Aviation Academy	
XM424	Hunting Jet Provost T3 (G-BWDS)	Privately owned, Coventry	
XM425	Hunting Jet Provost T3A (8995M) [88]	Privately owned, Longton, Staffs	
XM463	Hunting Jet Provost T3A [38] (fuselage)	RAF Museum, Hendon	
XM468	Hunting Jet Provost T3 (8081M) <ff>	Wings Museum, Balcombe, W Sussex	
XM473	Hunting Jet Provost T3A (8974M/G-TINY)	Privately owned, Wethersfield	
XM474	Hunting Jet Provost T3 (8121M) <ff>	Privately owned, South Reddish, Stockport	
XM479	Hunting Jet Provost T3A (G-BVEZ) [U]	Privately owned, Newcastle	
XM480	Hunting Jet Provost T3 (8080M)	4x4 Car Centre, Chesterfield	
XM496	Bristol 253 Britannia C1 (EL-WXA) [496]	Britannia Preservation Society, Cotswold Airport	
XM497	Bristol 175 Britannia 312F (G-AOVF) [497]	RAF Museum, Cosford	
XM529	Saro Skeeter AOP12 (7979M/G-BDNS)	Privately owned, Handforth	
XM553	Saro Skeeter AOP12 (G-AWSV)	Yorkshire Air Museum, Elvington	
XM555	Saro Skeeter AOP12 (8027M)	North-East Aircraft Museum, Usworth	
XM557	Saro Skeeter AOP12 <ff>	The Helicopter Museum, stored Weston-super-Mare	
XM564	Saro Skeeter AOP12	The Tank Museum, stored Bovington	
XM569	Avro 698 Vulcan B2 <ff>	Jet Age Museum, Gloucester	
XM575	Avro 698 Vulcan B2A (G-BLMC)	East Midlands Airport Aeropark	
XM594	Avro 698 Vulcan B2	Newark Air Museum, Winthorpe	
XM597	Avro 698 Vulcan B2	National Museum of Flight, E Fortune	
XM598	Avro 698 Vulcan B2 (8778M)	RAF Museum, Cosford	
XM602	Avro 698 Vulcan B2 (8771M) <ff>	Avro Heritage Museum, Woodford	
XM603	Avro 698 Vulcan B2	Avro Heritage Museum, Woodford	
XM607	Avro 698 Vulcan B2 (8779M)	RAF Waddington, on display	
XM612	Avro 698 Vulcan B2	City of Norwich Aviation Museum	
XM651	Saro Skeeter AOP12 (XM561/7980M)	South Yorkshire Aircraft Museum, Doncaster	
XM652	Avro 698 Vulcan B2 <ff>	Privately owned, Welshpool	
XM655	Avro 698 Vulcan B2 (G-VULC)	Privately owned, Wellesbourne Mountford	
XM685	WS55 Whirlwind HAS7 (G-AYZJ) [513/PO]	Newark Air Museum, Winthorpe	
XM692	HS Gnat T1 <ff>	Privately owned, Dunkeswell	
XM693	HS Gnat T1 (7891M)	BAE Systems Hamble, on display	
XM697	HS Gnat T1 (G-NAAT)	Reynard Garden Centre, Carluke, S Lanarkshire	
XM708	HS Gnat T1 (8573M)	Privately owned, Lytham St Annes	
XM715	HP80 Victor K2	Cold War Jets Collection, Bruntingthorpe	
XM717	HP80 Victor K2 <ff>	RAF Museum, Hendon	
XM819	Lancashire EP9 Prospector (G-APXW)	Museum of Army Flying, Middle Wallop	
XM833	WS58 Wessex HAS3	North-East Aircraft Museum, Usworth	
XN126	WS55 Whirlwind HAR10 (8655M) [S]	Pinewood Studios, Elstree	
XN137	Hunting Jet Provost T3 <ff>	Privately owned, Little Addington, Northants	
XN156	Slingsby T21B Sedbergh TX1 (BGA3250)	Privately owned, Portmoak, Perth & Kinross	
XN157	Slingsby T21B Sedbergh TX1 (BGA3255)	Privately owned, Long Mynd	
XN185	Slingsby T21B Sedbergh TX1 (8942M/BGA4077)	Privately owned, Scampton	
XN186	Slingsby T21B Sedbergh TX1 (BGA3905) [HFG]	Privately owned, Wethersfield	
XN187	Slingsby T21B Sedbergh TX1 (BGA3903)	Privately owned, RAF Halton	
XN198	Slingsby T31B Cadet TX3	Privately owned, Bodmin	
XN238	Slingsby T31B Cadet TX3 <ff>	South Yorkshire Aircraft Museum, Doncaster	
XN239	Slingsby T31B Cadet TX3 (8889M) [G]	IWM Duxford, stored	
XN246	Slingsby T31B Cadet TX3	Solent Sky, Southampton	
XN258	WS55 Whirlwind HAR9 [589/CU]	North-East Aircraft Museum, Usworth	
XN297	WS55 Whirlwind HAR9 (XN311) [12]	Privately owned, Hull	
XN298	WS55 Whirlwind HAR9 [810/LS]	Privately owned	
XN304	WS55 Whirlwind HAS7 [WW/B]	Norfolk & Suffolk Avn Museum, Flixton	

Notes	Serial	Type (code/other identity)	Owner/operator, location or fate
	XN332	Saro P531 (G-APNV) [759]	FAA Museum, stored Cobham Hall, RNAS Yeovilton
	XN334	Saro P531	FAA Museum, stored Cobham Hall, RNAS Yeovilton
	XN344	Saro Skeeter AOP12 (8018M)	Science Museum, South Kensington
	XN345	Saro Skeeter AOP12 <ff>	The Helicopter Museum, stored Weston-super-Mare
	XN351	Saro Skeeter AOP12 (G-BKSC)	Privately owned, Norwich
	XN380	WS55 Whirlwind HAS7	RAF Manston History Museum
	XN385	WS55 Whirlwind HAS7	Battleground Paintball, Yarm, Cleveland
	XN386	WS55 Whirlwind HAR9 [435/ED]	South Yorkshire Aircraft Museum, Doncaster
	XN412	Auster AOP9	Auster 9 Group, Melton Mowbray
	XN437	Auster AOP9 (G-AXWA)	Privately owned, North Weald
	XN441	Auster AOP9 (G-BGKT)	Privately owned, Exeter
	XN458	Hunting Jet Provost T3 (8234M/*XN594*) [19]	Privately owned, Northallerton
	XN459	Hunting Jet Provost T3A (G-BWOT) [59]	Kennet Aviation, North Weald
	XN462	Hunting Jet Provost T3A [17]	FAA Museum, stored Cobham Hall, RNAS Yeovilton
	XN466	Hunting Jet Provost T3A [29] <ff>	No 184 Sqn ATC, Gr Manchester
	XN492	Hunting Jet Provost T3 (8079M) <ff>	East Midlands Airport Aeropark
	XN494	Hunting Jet Provost T3A (9012M) [43]	Privately owned, Newquay
	XN500	Hunting Jet Provost T3A	Norfolk & Suffolk Avn Museum, Flixton
	XN503	Hunting Jet Provost T3 <ff>	Boscombe Down Aviation Collection, Old Sarum
	XN511	Hunting Jet Provost T3 [12] <ff>	South Yorkshire Aircraft Museum, Doncaster
	XN549	Hunting Jet Provost T3 (8235M) <ff>	Privately owned, Warrington
	XN551	Hunting Jet Provost T3 (8984M)	Privately owned, Felton Common, Bristol
	XN554	Hunting Jet Provost T3 (8436M) [K]	Gunsmoke Paintball, Colchester, Essex
	XN573	Hunting Jet Provost T3 [E] <ff>	Newark Air Museum, Winthorpe
	XN579	Hunting Jet Provost T3A (9137M) [14]	Gunsmoke Paintball, Colchester, Essex
	XN582	Hunting Jet Provost T3A (8957M) [95,H]	Privately owned, Bruntingthorpe
	XN584	Hunting Jet Provost T3A (9014M) [E]	USW Aerospace Centre, Treforest, Glamorgan
	XN586	Hunting Jet Provost T3A (9039M) [91]	Brooklands Museum, Weybridge
	XN589	Hunting Jet Provost T3A (9143M) [46]	RAF Linton-on-Ouse, on display
	XN597	Hunting Jet Provost T3 (7984M) <ff>	Privately owned, Market Drayton, Shrops
	XN607	Hunting Jet Provost T3 <ff>	Morayvia, Kinloss
	XN623	Hunting Jet Provost T3 (XN632/8352M)	Privately owned, Birlingham, Worcs
	XN629	Hunting Jet Provost T3A (G-BVEG/G-KNOT) [49]	Suffolk Aviation Heritage Centre, Foxhall Heath
	XN634	Hunting Jet Provost T3A <ff>	Privately owned, Blackpool
	XN634	Hunting Jet Provost T3A [53] <rf>	BAE Systems Warton Fire Section
	XN637	Hunting Jet Provost T3 (G-BKOU) [03]	Privately owned, North Weald
	XN647	DH110 Sea Vixen FAW2 <ff>	Privately owned, Steventon, Oxon
	XN650	DH110 Sea Vixen FAW2 [456] <ff>	Privately owned, Norfolk
	XN651	DH110 Sea Vixen FAW2 <ff>	Privately owned, Lavendon, Bucks
	XN685	DH110 Sea Vixen FAW2 (8173M) [703/VL]	Midland Air Museum, Coventry
	XN696	DH110 Sea Vixen FAW2 [751] <ff>	North-East Aircraft Museum, Usworth
	XN714	Hunting H126	RAF Museum, Cosford
	XN726	EE Lightning F2A (8545M) <ff>	Boscombe Down Aviation Collection, Old Sarum
	XN728	EE Lightning F2A (8546M) <ff>	Privately owned, Binbrook
	XN774	EE Lightning F2A (8551M) <ff>	Privately owned, Boston
	XN776	EE Lightning F2A (8535M) [C]	National Museum of Flight, E Fortune
	XN795	EE Lightning F2A <ff>	Privately owned, Rayleigh, Essex
	XN819	AW660 Argosy C1 (8205M) <ff>	Newark Air Museum, Winthorpe
	XN923	HS Buccaneer S1 [13]	Gatwick Aviation Museum, Charlwood, Surrey
	XN928	HS Buccaneer S1 (8179M) <ff>	Privately owned, Gravesend
	XN957	HS Buccaneer S1 [630/LM]	FAA Museum, RNAS Yeovilton
	XN964	HS Buccaneer S1 [118/V]	Newark Air Museum, Winthorpe
	XN967	HS Buccaneer S1 [233] <ff>	City of Norwich Aviation Museum
	XN972	HS Buccaneer S1 (8183M/XN962) <ff>	RAF Museum, Cosford
	XN974	HS Buccaneer S2A	Yorkshire Air Museum, Elvington
	XN981	HS Buccaneer S2B (fuselage)	Privately owned, Errol
	XN983	HS Buccaneer S2B <ff>	Fenland & W Norfolk Aviation Museum, Wisbech
	XP110	WS58 Wessex HAS3 (A2636)	DSAE RNAESS, *HMS Sultan*, Gosport
	XP137	WS58 Wessex HAS3 [11/DD]	*Currently not known*
	XP142	WS58 Wessex HAS3	FAA Museum, stored Cobham Hall, RNAS Yeovilton
	XP150	WS58 Wessex HAS3 [LS]	FETC, Moreton-in-Marsh, Glos

Serial	Type (code/other identity)	Owner/operator, location or fate	Notes
XP165	WS Scout AH1	The Helicopter Museum, Weston-super-Mare	
XP190	WS Scout AH1	South Yorkshire Aircraft Museum, Doncaster	
XP191	WS Scout AH1	Privately owned, Prenton, The Wirral	
XP226	Fairey Gannet AEW3	Newark Air Museum, Winthorpe	
XP241	Auster AOP9 (G-CEHR)	Privately owned, Spanhoe	
XP242	Auster AOP9 (G-BUCI)	AAC Historic Aircraft Flight, Middle Wallop	
XP244	Auster AOP9 (7864M/M7922)	Privately owned, Stretton on Dunsmore	
XP254	Auster AOP11 (G-ASCC)	Privately owned, Cambs	
XP279	Auster AOP9 (G-BWKK)	Privately owned, stored Winchester	
XP280	Auster AOP9	Privately owned, stored Leics	
XP281	Auster AOP9	IWM Duxford	
XP282	Auster AOP9 (G-BGTC)	Privately owned, Scampton	
XP286	Auster AOP9	Privately owned, South Molton, Devon	
XP299	WS55 Whirlwind HAR10 (8726M)	RAF Museum, Hendon	
XP328	WS55 Whirlwind HAR10 (G-BKHC)	Privately owned, Tattershall Thorpe (wreck)	
XP329	WS55 Whirlwind HAR10 (8791M) [V]	Privately owned, Tattershall Thorpe (wreck)	
XP330	WS55 Whirlwind HAR10	CAA Fire School, Durham/Tees Valley	
XP344	WS55 Whirlwind HAR10 (8764M) [H723]	RAF North Luffenham Training Area	
XP345	WS55 Whirlwind HAR10 (8792M) [N]	Yorkshire Helicopter Preservation Group, Doncaster	
XP346	WS55 Whirlwind HAR10 (8793M)	Privately owned, Honeybourne, Worcs	
XP350	WS55 Whirlwind HAR10	Privately owned, Bassetts Pole, Staffs	
XP351	WS55 Whirlwind HAR10 (8672M) [Z]	*Currently not known*	
XP354	WS55 Whirlwind HAR10 (8721M)	Privately owned, Mullingar, Eire	
XP355	WS55 Whirlwind HAR10 (8463M/G-BEBC)	City of Norwich Aviation Museum	
XP360	WS55 Whirlwind HAR10 [V]	Privately owned, Bicton, nr Leominster	
XP398	WS55 Whirlwind HAR10 (8794M)	*Currently not known*	
XP404	WS55 Whirlwind HAR10 (8682M)	The Helicopter Museum, stored Weston-super-Mare	
XP411	AW660 Argosy C1 (8442M) [C]	RAF Museum, Cosford	
XP454	Slingsby T38 Grasshopper TX1	Privately owned, Sywell	
XP459	Slingsby T38 Grasshopper TX1	Privately owned, stored Nayland, Suffolk	
XP463	Slingsby T38 Grasshopper TX1 (frame)	Privately owned, Rufforth	
XP463	Slingsby T38 Grasshopper TX1 (BGA4372)	Privately owned, Lasham	
XP488	Slingsby T38 Grasshopper TX1	Privately owned, Keevil	
XP490	Slingsby T38 Grasshopper TX1 (BGA4552)	Privately owned, stored Watton	
XP492	Slingsby T38 Grasshopper TX1 (BGA3480)	*Currently not known*	
XP493	Slingsby T38 Grasshopper TX1	Privately owned, stored Aston Down	
XP494	Slingsby T38 Grasshopper TX1	Privately owned, stored Baxterley	
XP505	HS Gnat T1	Science Museum, stored Wroughton	
XP513	HS Gnat T1 (N513X)	Privately owned, North Weald	
XP516	HS Gnat T1 (8580M) [16]	Farnborough Air Sciences Trust, Farnborough	
XP540	HS Gnat T1 (8608M) [62]	Privately owned, North Weald	
XP542	HS Gnat T1 (8575M)	No 424 Sqn ATC, Southampton	
XP556	Hunting Jet Provost T4 (9027M) [B]	RAF Cranwell Aviation Heritage Centre	
XP557	Hunting Jet Provost T4 (8494M) [72]	Dumfries & Galloway Avn Mus, Dumfries	
XP558	Hunting Jet Provost T4 (8627M) <ff>	Privately owned, Stoneykirk, D&G	
XP558	Hunting Jet Provost T4 (8627M)[20] <rf>	Privately owned, Sproughton	
XP568	Hunting Jet Provost T4	East Midlands Airport Aeropark	
XP573	Hunting Jet Provost T4 (8236M) [19]	Jersey Airport Fire Section	
XP585	Hunting Jet Provost T4 (8407M) [24]	NE Wales Institute, Wrexham	
XP627	Hunting Jet Provost T4	North-East Aircraft Museum, stored Usworth	
XP629	Hunting Jet Provost T4 (9026M) [P]	Gunsmoke Paintball, Colchester, Essex	
XP640	Hunting Jet Provost T4 (8501M) [M]	Yorkshire Air Museum, Elvington	
XP642	Hunting Jet Provost T4 <ff>	Cornwall Aviation Heritage Centre, Newquay	
XP672	Hunting Jet Provost T4 (8458M/G-RAFI) [03]	Privately owned, Bruntingthorpe	
XP680	Hunting Jet Provost T4 (8460M)	FETC, Moreton-in-Marsh, Glos	
XP686	Hunting Jet Provost T4 (8401M/8502M) [G]	Gunsmoke Paintball, Colchester, Essex	
XP701	BAC Lightning F3 (8924M) <ff>	Robertsbridge Aviation Society, Mayfield	
XP703	BAC Lightning F3 <ff>	Lightning Preservation Group, Bruntingthorpe	
XP706	BAC Lightning F3 (8925M)	South Yorkshire Aircraft Museum, Doncaster	
XP743	BAC Lightning F3 <ff>	Wattisham Station Heritage Museum	
XP745	BAC Lightning F3 (8453M) <ff>	Vanguard Haulage, Greenford, London	
XP757	BAC Lightning F3 <ff>	Privately owned, Boston, Lincs	

Notes	Serial	Type (code/other identity)	Owner/operator, location or fate
	XP765	BAC Lightning F6 (XS897) [A]	Lakes Lightnings, RAF Coningsby
	XP820	DHC2 Beaver AL1 (G-CICP)	Army Historic Aircraft Flight, Middle Wallop
	XP821	DHC2 Beaver AL1 [MCO]	Museum of Army Flying, Middle Wallop
	XP822	DHC2 Beaver AL1	Museum of Army Flying, Middle Wallop
	XP831	Hawker P.1127 (8406M)	Science Museum, South Kensington
	XP841	Handley-Page HP115	FAA Museum, RNAS Yeovilton
	XP847	WS Scout AH1	Museum of Army Flying, Middle Wallop
	XP848	WS Scout AH1	Farnborough Air Sciences Trust, Farnborough
	XP849	WS Scout AH1 (XP895)	Privately owned, Woodley, Berks
	XP853	WS Scout AH1	Privately owned, Sutton, Surrey
	XP854	WS Scout AH1 (7898M/TAD 043)	Mayhem Paintball, Abridge, Essex
	XP855	WS Scout AH1	Privately owned, Arncott, Oxon
	XP883	WS Scout AH1	Currently not known
	XP883	WS Scout AH1 (XW281/G-BYNZ) [T]	Privately owned, Dungannon, NI
	XP884	WS Scout AH1	AAC, stored Middle Wallop
	XP885	WS Scout AH1	AAC Wattisham, instructional use
	XP886	WS Scout AH1	The Helicopter Museum, stored Weston-super-Mare
	XP888	WS Scout AH1	Privately owned, Sproughton
	XP890	WS Scout AH1 [G] (fuselage)	Privately owned, Ipswich
	XP899	WS Scout AH1	Boscombe Down Aviation Collection, Old Sarum
	XP900	WS Scout AH1	AAC Wattisham, instructional use
	XP902	WS Scout AH1 <ff>	South Yorkshire Aircraft Museum, Doncaster
	XP905	WS Scout AH1	Privately owned, stored Sproughton
	XP907	WS Scout AH1 (G-SROE)	Privately owned, Wattisham
	XP910	WS Scout AH1	Museum of Army Flying, Middle Wallop
	XP924	DH110 Sea Vixen D3 (G-CVIX) [134/E]	Fly Navy Heritage Trust, Yeovilton
	XP925	DH110 Sea Vixen FAW2 [752] <ff>	Privately owned, Chorley, Lancs
	XP980	Hawker P.1127	FAA Museum, RNAS Yeovilton
	XP984	Hawker P.1127	Brooklands Museum, Weybridge
	XR220	BAC TSR2 (7933M)	RAF Museum, Cosford
	XR222	BAC TSR2	IWM Duxford
	XR232	Sud Alouette AH2 (F-WEIP)	Museum of Army Flying, Middle Wallop
	XR239	Auster AOP9	Privately owned, Stretton on Dunsmore
	XR240	Auster AOP9 (G-BDFH)	Privately owned, Eggesford
	XR241	Auster AOP9 (G-AXRR)	Privately owned, Eggesford
	XR244	Auster AOP9 (G-CICR)	Army Historic Aircraft Flight, Middle Wallop
	XR246	Auster AOP9 (7862M/G-AZBU)	Privately owned, Melton Mowbray
	XR267	Auster AOP9 (G-BJXR)	Privately owned, Hucknall
	XR271	Auster AOP9	Privately owned, stored Wroughton
	XR346	Northrop Shelduck D1 (comp XW578)	Bournemouth Aviation Museum
	XR371	SC5 Belfast C1	RAF Museum, Cosford
	XR379	Sud Alouette AH2 (2-ALOU)	Privately owned, Deighton, N Yorks
	XR453	WS55 Whirlwind HAR10 (8873M) [A]	RAF Odiham, on gate
	XR458	WS55 Whirlwind HAR10 (8662M) [H]	Privately owned, Irthlingborough, Northants
	XR485	WS55 Whirlwind HAR10 [Q]	Norfolk & Suffolk Avn Museum, Flixton
	XR486	WS55 Whirlwind HCC12 (8727M/G-RWWW)	The Helicopter Museum, Weston-super-Mare
	XR498	WS58 Wessex HC2 (9342M)	RAF Cosford
	XR503	WS58 Wessex HC2	MoD DFTDC, Manston
	XR506	WS58 Wessex HC2 (9343M) [V]	Privately owned, Corley Moor, Warks
	XR516	WS58 Wessex HC2 (9319M) [V]	RAF Shawbury, on display
	XR517	WS58 Wessex HC2 [N]	Ulster Aviation Society, Long Kesh
	XR523	WS58 Wessex HC2 [M]	MoD Pembrey Sands Air Weapons Range, GI use
	XR525	WS58 Wessex HC2 [G]	RAF Museum, Cosford
	XR526	WS58 Wessex HC2 (8147M)	The Helicopter Museum, stored Weston-super-Mare
	XR528	WS58 Wessex HC2	Morayvia, Kinloss
	XR529	WS58 Wessex HC2 (9268M) [E]	RAF Aldergrove, on display
	XR534	HS Gnat T1 (8578M) [65]	Newark Air Museum, Winthorpe
	XR537	HS Gnat T1 (8642M/G-NATY)	Privately owned, North Weald
	XR538	HS Gnat T1 (8621M/G-RORI) [01]	Heritage Aircraft Trust, North Weald
	XR540	HS Gnat T1 (XP502/8576M) [2]	Privately owned, Cotswold Airport
	XR571	HS Gnat T1 (8493M)	RAF Scampton Heritage Centre

Serial	Type (code/other identity)	Owner/operator, location or fate	Notes
XR574	HS Gnat T1 (8631M) [72]	Trenchard Museum, Halton	
XR595	WS Scout AH1 (G-BWHU) [M]	Privately owned, North Weald	
XR601	WS Scout AH1	Privately owned, Sproughton	
XR627	WS Scout AH1 [X]	Privately owned, Storwood, Yorkshire	
XR628	WS Scout AH1	Privately owned, Ipswich	
XR629	WS Scout AH1 (fuselage)	Privately owned, Ipswich	
XR635	WS Scout AH1	Midland Air Museum, Coventry	
XR650	Hunting Jet Provost T4 (8459M) [28]	Boscombe Down Aviation Collection, Old Sarum	
XR654	Hunting Jet Provost T4 <ff>	Privately owned, Chester	
XR658	Hunting Jet Provost T4 (8192M)	RAF Manston History Museum	
XR662	Hunting Jet Provost T4 (8410M) [25]	Privately owned, Gilberdyke, E Yorks	
XR673	Hunting Jet Provost T4 (G-BXLO/9032M) [L]	Privately owned, Gamston	
XR681	Hunting Jet Provost T4 (8588M)	Robertsbridge Aviation Society, Mayfield	
XR700	Hunting Jet Provost T4 (8589M) <ff>	No 1137 Sqn ATC, Aldergrove	
XR713	BAC Lightning F3 (8935M) [C]	Lightning Preservation Grp, Bruntingthorpe	
	(wears XR718 on starboard side)		
XR718	BAC Lightning F6 (8932M) [DA]	Privately owned, Over Dinsdale, N Yorks	
XR724	BAC Lightning F6 (G-BTSY)	The Lightning Association, Binbrook	
XR725	BAC Lightning F6	Privately owned, Binbrook	
XR726	BAC Lightning F6 <ff>	Privately owned, Harrogate	
XR728	BAC Lightning F6 [JS]	Lightning Preservation Grp, Bruntingthorpe	
XR747	BAC Lightning F3 (8934M) [DA]	Privately owned, Peterhead	
XR751	BAC Lightning F3 <ff>	Privately owned, Thorpe Wood, N Yorks	
XR753	BAC Lightning F6 (8969M) [XI]	RAF Coningsby on display	
XR753	BAC Lightning F53 (ZF578) [A]	Tangmere Military Aviation Museum	
XR754	BAC Lightning F6 (8972M) <ff>	Privately owned, Upwood, Cambs	
XR755	BAC Lightning F6	Privately owned, Callington, Cornwall	
XR757	BAC Lightning F6 <ff>	Newark Air Museum, Winthorpe	
XR759	BAC Lightning F6 <ff>	Privately owned, Haxey, Lincs	
XR770	BAC Lightning F6 [AA]	RAF Manston History Museum	
XR771	BAC Lightning F6 [BF]	Midland Air Museum, Coventry	
XR806	BAC VC10 C1K (9285M) <ff>	RAF Brize Norton, BDRT	
XR808	BAC VC10 C1K [R] $	RAF Museum, Cosford	
XR810	BAC VC10 C1K <ff>	Privately owned, Crondall, Hants	
XR944	Wallis WA116 (G-ATTB)	Privately owned, Old Buckenham	
XR977	HS Gnat T1 (8640M)	RAF Museum, Hendon	
XR992	HS Gnat T1 (8624M/XS102/G-MOUR)	Heritage Aircraft Trust, North Weald	
XR993	HS Gnat T1 (8620M/XP534/G-BVPP)	Privately owned, Bruntingthorpe	
XS100	HS Gnat T1 (8561M) <ff>	Privately owned, London SW3	
XS100	HS Gnat T1 (8561M) <rf>	Privately owned, North Weald	
XS104	HS Gnat T1 (8604M/G-FRCE)	Privately owned, North Weald	
XS149	WS58 Wessex HAS3 [661/GL]	The Helicopter Museum, Weston-super-Mare	
XS176	Hunting Jet Provost T4 (8514M) <ff>	Privately owned, Kinloss	
XS177	Hunting Jet Provost T4 (9044M) [N]	Privately owned, Gilberdyke, E Yorks	
XS179	Hunting Jet Provost T4 (8237M) [20]	Secret Nuclear Bunker, Hack Green, Cheshire	
XS180	Hunting Jet Provost T4 (8238M/8338M) [21]	MoD JARTS, Boscombe Down	
XS181	Hunting Jet Provost T4 (9033M) <ff>	Lakes Lightnings, Spark Bridge, Cumbria	
XS183	Hunting Jet Provost T4 <ff>	Privately owned, Plymouth	
XS186	Hunting Jet Provost T4 (8408M) [M]	Metheringham Airfield Visitors Centre	
XS209	Hunting Jet Provost T4 (8409M)	Solway Aviation Society, Carlisle	
XS216	Hunting Jet Provost T4 <ff>	South Yorkshire Aircraft Museum, Doncaster	
XS218	Hunting Jet Provost T4 (8508M) <ff>	No 447 Sqn ATC, Henley-on-Thames, Berks	
XS231	BAC Jet Provost T5 (G-ATAJ)	Boscombe Down Aviation Collection, Old Sarum	
XS235	DH106 Comet 4C (G-CPDA)	Cold War Jets Collection, Bruntingthorpe	
XS238	Auster AOP9 (TAD 200)	Newark Air Museum, Winthorpe	
XS416	BAC Lightning T5	Privately owned, New York, Lincs	
XS417	BAC Lightning T5 [DZ]	Newark Air Museum, Winthorpe	
XS420	BAC Lightning T5	Lakes Lightnings, FAST, Farnborough	
XS421	BAC Lightning T5 <ff>	Privately owned, Foulness	
XS456	BAC Lightning T5 [DX]	Skegness Water Leisure Park	

Notes	Serial	Type (code/other identity)	Owner/operator, location or fate
	XS457	BAC Lightning T5 <ff>	Privately owned, Binbrook
	XS458	BAC Lightning T5 [T]	T5 Projects, Cranfield
	XS459	BAC Lightning T5 [AW]	Fenland & W Norfolk Aviation Museum, Wisbech
	XS481	WS58 Wessex HU5	South Yorkshire Aircraft Museum, Doncaster
	XS482	WS58 Wessex HU5	RAF Manston History Museum
	XS486	WS58 Wessex HU5 (9272M) [524/CU,F]	The Helicopter Museum, Weston-super-Mare
	XS488	WS58 Wessex HU5 (9056M) [F]	Privately owned, Tiptree, Essex
	XS489	WS58 Wessex HU5 [R]	Privately owned, Westerham, Kent
	XS493	WS58 Wessex HU5	Vector Aerospace, stored Fleetlands
	XS507	WS58 Wessex HU5	RAF Benson, for display
	XS508	WS58 Wessex HU5	FAA Museum, RNAS Yeovilton
	XS510	WS58 Wessex HU5 [626/PO]	No 1414 Sqn ATC, Crowborough, Sussex
	XS511	WS58 Wessex HU5 [M]	Tangmere Military Aircraft Museum
	XS513	WS58 Wessex HU5	RNAS Yeovilton Fire Section
	XS515	WS58 Wessex HU5 [N]	Army, Keogh Barracks, Aldershot, instructional use
	XS516	WS58 Wessex HU5 [Q]	Privately owned, Redruth, Cornwall
	XS520	WS58 Wessex HU5 [F]	*Currently not known*
	XS522	WS58 Wessex HU5 [ZL]	Blackball Paintball, Truro, Cornwall
	XS527	WS Wasp HAS1	FAA Museum, stored Cobham Hall, RNAS Yeovilton
	XS529	WS Wasp HAS1	Privately owned, Redruth, Cornwall
	XS539	WS Wasp HAS1 [435]	Vector Aerospace Fleetlands Apprentice School
	XS567	WS Wasp HAS1 [434/E]	IWM Duxford
	XS568	WS Wasp HAS1 (A2715) [441]	DSAE RNAESS, *HMS Sultan*, Gosport
	XS574	Northrop Shelduck D1 <R>	FAA Museum, stored Cobham Hall, RNAS Yeovilton
	XS576	DH110 Sea Vixen FAW2 [125/E]	IWM Duxford
	XS587	DH110 Sea Vixen FAW(TT)2 (8828M/G-VIXN)	Gatwick Aviation Museum, Charlwood, Surrey
	XS590	DH110 Sea Vixen FAW2 [131/E]	FAA Museum, RNAS Yeovilton
	XS639	HS Andover E3A (9241M)	RAF Museum, Cosford
	XS641	HS Andover C1PR (9198M) [fuselage]	Privately owned, Sandbach, Cheshire
	XS643	HS Andover E3A (9278M) <ff>	Privately owned, Dudley, W Mids
	XS646	HS Andover C1(mod) (fuselage)	MoD JARTS, Boscombe Down
	XS651	Slingsby T45 Swallow TX1 (BGA1211)	Privately owned, Little Rissington
	XS652	Slingsby T45 Swallow TX1 (BGA1107)	Privately owned, Chipping, Lancs
	XS674	WS58 Wessex HC2 [R]	Privately owned, Biggin Hill
	XS695	HS Kestrel FGA1 [5]	RAF Museum, Cosford
	XS709	HS125 Dominie T1 [M]	RAF Museum, Cosford
	XS710	HS125 Dominie T1 (9259M) [O]	RAF Cranwell Fire Section
	XS713	HS125 Dominie T1 [C]	RAF Shawbury Fire Section
	XS714	HS125 Dominie T1 (9246M) [P]	MoD DFTDC, Manston
	XS726	HS125 Dominie T1 (9273M) [T]	Newark Air Museum, Winthorpe
	XS727	HS125 Dominie T1 [D]	RAF Cranwell, on display
	XS731	HS125 Dominie T1 (N19XY) (fuselage)	Privately owned, Marlborough, Wilts
	XS733	HS125 Dominie T1 (9276M) [Q]	*Buried at Bramford, Suffolk, March 2016*
	XS734	HS125 Dominie T1 (9260M) [N]	Privately owned, Sproughton
	XS735	HS125 Dominie T1 (9264M) [R]	South Yorkshire Aircraft Museum, Doncaster
	XS736	HS125 Dominie T1 [S]	MoD Winterbourne Gunner, Wilts
	XS738	HS125 Dominie T1 (9274M) [U]	RN, Predannack Fire School
	XS743	Beagle B206Z	QinetiQ Apprentice Training School, Boscombe Down
	XS765	Beagle B206 Basset CC1 (G-BSET)	QinetiQ Apprentice Training School, Boscombe Down
	XS770	Beagle B206 Basset CC1 (G-HRHI)	*Currently not known*
	XS790	HS748 Andover CC2 <ff>	Boscombe Down Aviation Collection, Old Sarum
	XS791	HS748 Andover CC2 (fuselage)	Privately owned, Stock, Essex
	XS859	Slingsby T45 Swallow TX1 (BGA1136) [859]	Privately owned, stored Felthorpe
	XS863	WS58 Wessex HAS1 [304/R]	IWM Duxford
	XS865	WS58 Wessex HAS1 (A2694)	Privately owned, Ballygowan, NI
	XS885	WS58 Wessex HAS1 [512/CU]	Laser Combat, Liverpool
	XS886	WS58 Wessex HAS1 [527/CU]	Privately owned, Ditchling, E Sussex
	XS887	WS58 Wessex HAS1 [403/FI]	South Yorkshire Aircraft Museum, Doncaster
	XS888	WS58 Wessex HAS1 [521]	Guernsey Airport Fire Section
	XS898	BAC Lightning F6 <ff>	Privately owned, Lavendon, Bucks
	XS899	BAC Lightning F6 <ff>	Privately owned, Binbrook
	XS903	BAC Lightning F6 [BA]	Yorkshire Air Museum, Elvington

Serial	Type (code/other identity)	Owner/operator, location or fate	Notes
XS904	BAC Lightning F6 [BQ]	Lightning Preservation Grp, Bruntingthorpe	
XS919	BAC Lightning F6	Privately owned,	
XS921	BAC Lightning F6 <R> [BA]	BAE Systems, Samlesbury, on display	
XS922	BAC Lightning F6 (8973M) <ff>	Lakes Lightnings, Spark Bridge, Cumbria	
XS923	BAC Lightning F6 <ff>	Privately owned, Welshpool	
XS925	BAC Lightning F6 (8961M) [BA]	RAF Museum, Hendon	
XS928	BAC Lightning F6 [AD]	BAE Systems Warton, on display	
XS932	BAC Lightning F6 <ff>	Privately owned, Walcott, Lincs	
XS933	BAC Lightning F6 <ff>	Privately owned, Farnham	
XS933	BAC Lightning F53 (ZF594) [BF]	North-East Aircraft Museum, Usworth	
XS936	BAC Lightning F6	Castle Motors, Liskeard, Cornwall	
XT108	Agusta-Bell 47G-3 Sioux AH1 [U]	Museum of Army Flying, Middle Wallop	
XT123	WS Sioux AH1 (XT827) [D]	AAC Middle Wallop, at main gate	
XT131	Agusta-Bell 47G-3 Sioux AH1 (G-CICN) [B]	Army Historic Aircraft Flight, Middle Wallop	
XT140	Agusta-Bell 47G-3 Sioux AH1	Privately owned, Malmesbury	
XT150	Agusta-Bell 47G-3 Sioux AH1 (7883M) [R]	South Yorkshire Aircraft Museum, stored Doncaster	
XT151	WS Sioux AH1	Museum of Army Flying, stored Middle Wallop	
XT176	WS Sioux AH1 [U]	FAA Museum, stored Cobham Hall, RNAS Yeovilton	
XT190	WS Sioux AH1	The Helicopter Museum, Weston-super-Mare	
XT200	WS Sioux AH1 [F]	Newark Air Museum, Winthorpe	
XT208	WS Sioux AH1 (wreck)	Privately owned, Fivemiletown, Co Tyrone, NI	
XT236	WS Sioux AH1 (frame only)	South Yorkshire Aircraft Museum, stored Doncaster	
XT242	WS Sioux AH1 (composite) [12]	South Yorkshire Aircraft Museum, Doncaster	
XT257	WS58 Wessex HAS3 (8719M)	Bournemouth Aviation Museum	
XT277	HS Buccaneer S2A (8853M) <ff>	Privately owned, Welshpool	
XT280	HS Buccaneer S2A <ff>	Dumfries & Galloway Avn Mus, Dumfries	
XT284	HS Buccaneer S2A (8855M) <ff>	Privately owned, Felixstowe	
XT288	HS Buccaneer S2B (9134M)	National Museum of Flight, E Fortune	
XT420	WS Wasp HAS1 (G-CBUI) [606]	Privately owned, Thruxton	
XT427	WS Wasp HAS1 [606]	FAA Museum, stored RNAS Yeovilton	
XT431	WS Wasp HAS1 (comp XS463) [462]	Bournemouth Aviation Museum	
XT434	WS Wasp HAS1 (G-CGGK) [455]	Privately owned, Breighton	
XT435	WS Wasp HAS1 (NZ3907/G-RIMM) [430]	Privately owned, Badwell Green, Suffolk	
XT437	WS Wasp HAS1 [423]	Boscombe Down Aviation Collection, Old Sarum	
XT439	WS Wasp HAS1 [605]	Privately owned, Hemel Hempstead	
XT443	WS Wasp HAS1 [422/AU]	The Helicopter Museum, Weston-super-Mare	
XT453	WS58 Wessex HU5 (A2756) [B/PO]	DSAE, stored *HMS Sultan*, Gosport	
XT455	WS58 Wessex HU5 (A2654) [U]	Mayhem Paintball, Abridge, Essex	
XT456	WS58 Wessex HU5 (8941M) [XZ]	Belfast Airport Fire Section	
XT466	WS58 Wessex HU5 (A2617/8921M) [XV]	Privately owned, Cotswold Airport	
XT467	WS58 Wessex HU5 (8922M) [BF]	Gunsmoke Paintball, Hadleigh, Suffolk	
XT469	WS58 Wessex HU5 (8920M)	Privately owned, Clatterford, Isle of Wight	
XT472	WS58 Wessex HU5 [XC]	The Helicopter Museum, stored Weston-super-Mare	
XT480	WS58 Wessex HU5 [468/RG]	Rednal Paintball, Shropshire	
XT482	WS58 Wessex HU5 [ZM/VL]	FAA Museum, RNAS Yeovilton	
XT486	WS58 Wessex HU5 (8919M)	Dumfries & Galloway Avn Mus, Dumfries	
XT550	WS Sioux AH1 [D]	*Currently not known*	
XT575	Vickers Viscount 837 <ff>	Brooklands Museum, Weybridge	
XT581	Northrop Shelduck D1	Muckleburgh Collection, Weybourne, Norfolk	
XT583	Northrop Shelduck D1	Privately owned, stored Wroughton	
XT596	McD F-4K Phantom FG1	FAA Museum, RNAS Yeovilton	
XT597	McD F-4K Phantom FG1	Privately owned, Bentwaters	
XT601	WS58 Wessex HC2 (9277M) (composite)	RAF Odiham, BDRT	
XT604	WS58 Wessex HC2	East Midlands Airport Aeropark	
XT617	WS Scout AH1	Wattisham Station Heritage Museum	
XT621	WS Scout AH1	Defence Academy of the UK, Shrivenham	
XT623	WS Scout AH1	DSAE SAAE, Lyneham	
XT626	WS Scout AH1 (G-CIBW) [Q]	Army Historic Aircraft Flt, Middle Wallop	
XT630	WS Scout AH1 (G-BXRL) [X]	*Currently not known*	
XT631	WS Scout AH1 [D]	Privately owned, Ipswich	
XT633	WS Scout AH1	Farnborough Air Sciences Trust, Farnborough	

Notes	Serial	Type (code/other identity)	Owner/operator, location or fate
	XT634	WS Scout AH1 (G-BYRX) [T]	MoD Air Accidents Investigation Branch, Farnborough
	XT638	WS Scout AH1 [N]	AAC Middle Wallop, at main gate
	XT640	WS Scout AH1	Privately owned, Sproughton
	XT643	WS Scout AH1	Army, Thorpe Camp, East Wretham (wreck)
	XT653	Slingsby T45 Swallow TX1 (BGA3469)	Privately owned, Oakhill, Somerset
	XT672	WS58 Wessex HC2 [WE]	RAF Stafford, on display
	XT681	WS58 Wessex HC2 (9279M) [U] <ff>	Privately owned, Wallingford, Oxon
	XT761	WS58 Wessex HU5	Privately owned, Chard, Somerset
	XT762	WS58 Wessex HU5	Hamburger Hill Paintball, Marksbury, Somerset
	XT765	WS58 Wessex HU5 [J]	FAA Museum, RNAS Yeovilton
	XT765	WS58 Wessex HU5 (XT458/A2768) [P/VL]	RNAS Yeovilton, on display
	XT769	WS58 Wessex HU5 [823]	FAA Museum, RNAS Yeovilton
	XT771	WS58 Wessex HU5 [620/PO]	Privately owned, Chard, Somerset
	XT773	WS58 Wessex HU5 (9123M)	RAF Shawbury Fire Section
	XT778	WS Wasp HAS1 [430]	FAA Museum, stored Cobham Hall, RNAS Yeovilton
	XT780	WS Wasp HAS1 [636]	CEMAST, Fareham College, Lee-on-Solent
	XT787	WS Wasp HAS1 (NZ3905/G-KAXT)	Westland Wasp Historic Flt, Barton Ashes, Hants
	XT788	WS Wasp HAS1 (G-BMIR) [474]	Privately owned, Storwood, Yorkshire
	XT793	WS Wasp HAS1 (G-BZPP) [456] <ff>	Boscombe Down Aviation Collection, Old Sarum (spares use)
	XT863	McD F-4K Phantom FG1 <ff>	Privately owned, Cowes, IOW
	XT864	McD F-4K Phantom FG1 (8998M/XT684) [A]	Ulster Aviation Society, Long Kesh
	XT891	McD F-4M Phantom FGR2 (9136M)	RAF Coningsby, at main gate
	XT903	McD F-4M Phantom FGR2	RAF Museum, stored Cosford
	XT905	McD F-4M Phantom FGR2 (9286M) [P]	Privately owned, Bentwaters
	XT907	McD F-4M Phantom FGR2 (9151M) [W]	Privately owned, Bentwaters
	XT914	McD F-4M Phantom FGR2 (9269M) [Z]	Wattisham Station Heritage Museum
	XV106	BAC VC10 C1K <ff>	Avro Heritage Museum, Woodford
	XV108	BAC VC10 C1K <ff>	East Midlands Airport Aeropark
	XV109	BAC VC10 C1K <ff>	Privately owned, Bruntingthorpe
	XV118	WS Scout AH1 (9141M) <ff>	Kennet Aviation, North Weald
	XV122	WS Scout AH1 [D]	Defence Academy of the UK, Shrivenham
	XV123	WS Scout AH1	Privately owned, Bentwaters
	XV124	WS Scout AH1 [W]	Privately owned, Godstone, Surrey
	XV127	WS Scout AH1	Museum of Army Flying, Middle Wallop
	XV130	WS Scout AH1 (G-BWJW) [R]	Privately owned, stored Thruxton
	XV136	WS Scout AH1 [X]	Ulster Aviation Society, Long Kesh
	XV137	WS Scout AH1 (G-CRUM)	Privately owned, Chiseldon, Wilts
	XV137	WS Scout AH1 (XV139)	South Yorkshire Aircraft Museum, stored Doncaster
	XV138	WS Scout AH1 (G-SASM) [S]	Privately owned, Thruxton
	XV139	WS Scout AH1 (comp XP886)	South Yorkshire Aircraft Museum, Doncaster
	XV141	WS Scout AH1	REME Museum, Lyneham
	XV148	HS Nimrod MR1(mod) <ff>	Privately owned, Malmesbury
	XV161	HS Buccaneer S2B (9117M) <ff>	Dundonald Aviation Centre
	XV165	HS Buccaneer S2B <ff>	Privately owned, Ashford, Kent
	XV168	HS Buccaneer S2B [AF]	Yorkshire Air Museum, Elvington
	XV177	Lockheed C-130K Hercules C3A [177]	RAF, St Athan (wfu)
	XV188	Lockheed C-130K Hercules C3A [188]	RAF, St Athan (wfu)
	XV196	Lockheed C-130K Hercules C1 [196]	Scrapped at St Athan, 2017
	XV200	Lockheed C-130K Hercules C1 [200]	RAF, St Athan (wfu)
	XV201	Lockheed C-130K Hercules C1K <ff>	Marshalls, Cambridge
	XV202	Lockheed C-130K Hercules C3 [202]	RAF Museum, Cosford
	XV208	Lockheed C-130K Hercules W2 <ff>	Marshalls, Cambridge
	XV209	Lockheed C-130K Hercules C3A [209]	RAF, St Athan (wfu)
	XV221	Lockheed C-130K Hercules C3 <ff>	Privately owned, White Waltham
	XV226	HS Nimrod MR2 $	Cold War Jets Collection, Bruntingthorpe
	XV229	HS Nimrod MR2 [29]	MoD DFTDC, Manston
	XV231	HS Nimrod MR2 [31]	Aviation Viewing Park, Manchester
	XV232	HS Nimrod MR2 [32]	Privately owned, Coventry
	XV235	HS Nimrod MR2 [35] <ff>	Avro Heritage Museum, Woodford
	XV240	HS Nimrod MR2 [40] <ff>	Morayvia, Kinloss

Serial	Type (code/other identity)	Owner/operator, location or fate	Notes
XV241	HS Nimrod MR2 [41] <ff>	National Museum of Flight, E Fortune	
XV244	HS Nimrod MR2 [44]	Morayvia, RAF Kinloss	
XV249	HS Nimrod R1 $	RAF Museum, Cosford	
XV250	HS Nimrod MR2 [50]	Yorkshire Air Museum, Elvington	
XV252	HS Nimrod MR2 [52] <ff>	Privately owned, Cullen, Moray	
XV254	HS Nimrod MR2 [54] <ff>	Highland Aviation Museum, Inverness	
XV255	HS Nimrod MR2 [55]	City of Norwich Aviation Museum	
XV259	BAe Nimrod AEW3 <ff>	Privately owned, Wales	
XV263	BAe Nimrod AEW3P (8967M) <ff>	BAE Systems, Brough	
XV263	BAe Nimrod AEW3P (8967M) <rf>	MoD/BAE Systems, Woodford	
XV268	DHC2 Beaver AL1 (G-BVER)	Privately owned, Cumbernauld	
XV277	HS P.1127(RAF)	National Museum of Flight, E Fortune	
XV279	HS P.1127(RAF) (8566M)	Harrier Heritage Centre, RAF Wittering	
XV280	HS P.1127(RAF) <ff>	South Yorkshire Aviation Museum, Doncaster	
XV281	HS P.1127(RAF)	South Yorkshire Aviation Museum, Doncaster	
XV302	Lockheed C-130K Hercules C3 [302]	Marshalls, Cambridge, fatigue test airframe	
XV304	Lockheed C-130K Hercules C3A	RAF JADTEU, Brize Norton, instructional use	
XV328	BAC Lightning T5 <ff>	Lightning Preservation Group, Bruntingthorpe	
XV333	HS Buccaneer S2B [234/H]	FAA Museum, RNAS Yeovilton	
XV344	HS Buccaneer S2C	QinetiQ Farnborough, on display	
XV350	HS Buccaneer S2B	East Midlands Airport Aeropark	
XV352	HS Buccaneer S2B <ff>	RAF Manston History Museum	
XV359	HS Buccaneer S2B [035/R]	Privately owned, Topsham, Devon	
XV361	HS Buccaneer S2B	Ulster Aviation Society, Long Kesh	
XV370	Sikorsky SH-3D (A2682) [260]	DSAE RNAESS, *HMS Sultan*, Gosport	
XV371	WS61 Sea King HAS1(DB) [61/DD]	RN, Predannack Fire School	
XV372	WS61 Sea King HAS1	MoD Pembrey Sands Air Weapons Range, GI use	
XV383	Northrop MQM-57A/3 (fuselage)	Privately owned, Wimborne, Dorset	
XV401	McD F-4M Phantom FGR2 [I]	Privately owned, Bentwaters	
XV402	McD F-4M Phantom FGR2 <ff>	Privately owned, Kent	
XV406	McD F-4M Phantom FGR2 (9098M) [CK]	Solway Aviation Society, Carlisle	
XV408	McD F-4M Phantom FGR2 (9165M) [Z]	Tangmere Military Aviation Museum	
XV411	McD F-4M Phantom FGR2 (9103M) [L]	MoD DFTDC, Manston	
XV415	McD F-4M Phantom FGR2 (9163M) [E]	RAF Boulmer, on display	
XV424	McD F-4M Phantom FGR2 (9152M) [I]	RAF Museum, Hendon	
XV426	McD F-4M Phantom FGR2 <ff>	City of Norwich Aviation Museum	
XV426	McD F-4M Phantom FGR2 [P] <rf>	RAF Coningsby, BDRT	
XV460	McD F-4M Phantom FGR2 <ff>	Privately owned, Bentwaters	
XV474	McD F-4M Phantom FGR2 [T]	The Old Flying Machine Company, Duxford	
XV490	McD F-4M Phantom FGR2 [R] <ff>	Newark Air Museum, Winthorpe	
XV497	McD F-4M Phantom FGR2 (9295M) [D]	Privately owned, Bentwaters	
XV499	McD F-4M Phantom FGR2 <ff>	Privately owned, St Athan	
XV581	McD F-4K Phantom FG1 (9070M) <ff>	Staffordshire Wing ATC Aerospace & Technology Centre	
XV582	McD F-4K Phantom FG1 (9066M) [M]	Privately owned, RAF Cosford	
XV586	McD F-4K Phantom FG1 (9067M) [010-R]	Privately owned, RNAS Yeovilton	
XV591	McD F-4K Phantom FG1 [013] <ff>	RAF Museum, Cosford	
XV625	WS Wasp HAS1 (A2649) [471]	*Sold as N834PZ, November 2017*	
XV631	WS Wasp HAS1 (fuselage)	Farnborough Air Sciences Trust, stored Farnborough	
XV642	WS61 Sea King HAS2A (A2614) [259]	DSAE RNAESS, *HMS Sultan*, Gosport	
XV643	WS61 Sea King HAS6 [262]	DSAE No 1 SoTT, Cosford	
XV647	WS61 Sea King HU5 [28]	DSAE RNAESS, *HMS Sultan*, Gosport	
XV648	WS61 Sea King HU5 [18/CU]	Privately owned, stored Colsterworth	
XV649	WS61 Sea King ASaC7 [180]	DSAE, stored *HMS Sultan*, Gosport	
XV651	WS61 Sea King HU5	Mini Moos Farm, Edmondsley, Durham	
XV653	WS61 Sea King HAS6 (9326M) [63/CU]	DSAE No 1 SoTT, Cosford	
XV654	WS61 Sea King HAS6 [705/DD] (wreck)	RN, Predannack Fire School	
XV655	WS61 Sea King HAS6 [270/N]	DSAE RNAESS, *HMS Sultan*, Gosport	
XV656	WS61 Sea King ASaC7 [185]	RN No 849 NAS, Culdrose	
XV657	WS61 Sea King HAS5 (ZA135) [32/DD]	RN, Predannack Fire School	
XV659	WS61 Sea King HAS6 (9324M) [62/CU]	DSAE No 1 SoTT, Cosford	
XV660	WS61 Sea King HAS6 [269/N]	DSAE RNAESS, *HMS Sultan*, Gosport	
XV661	WS61 Sea King HU5 [26]	Privately owned, Colsterworth	

Notes	Serial	Type (code/other identity)	Owner/operator, location or fate
	XV663	WS61 Sea King HAS6 [18]	FAA Museum, RNAS Yeovilton
	XV664	WS61 Sea King ASaC7 [190]	DSAE, stored *HMS Sultan*, Gosport
	XV665	WS61 Sea King HAS6 [507/CU]	DSAE RNAESS, *HMS Sultan*, Gosport
	XV666	WS61 Sea King HU5	HeliOperations Ltd, Portland
	XV670	WS61 Sea King HU5 [17]	DSAE, stored *HMS Sultan*, Gosport
	XV671	WS61 Sea King ASaC7 [183/CU]	RN No 849 NAS, Culdrose
	XV672	WS61 Sea King ASaC7 [187]	DSAE, stored *HMS Sultan*, Gosport
	XV673	WS61 Sea King HU5 [827/CU]	RN Culdrose, on display
	XV674	WS61 Sea King HAS6	Privately owned, Horsham
	XV675	WS61 Sea King HAS6 [701/PW]	DSAE RNAESS, *HMS Sultan*, Gosport
	XV676	WS61 Sea King HC6 [ZE]	DSAE RNAESS, *HMS Sultan*, Gosport
	XV677	WS61 Sea King HAS6 [269]	South Yorkshire Aircraft Museum, Doncaster
	XV696	WS61 Sea King HAS6 [267/L]	SFDO, RNAS Culdrose
	XV697	WS61 Sea King ASaC7 [181/CU]	RN No 849 NAS, Culdrose
	XV699	WS61 Sea King HU5 [823/PW]	DSAE RNAESS, *HMS Sultan*, Gosport
	XV700	WS61 Sea King HC6 [ZC]	RAF St Mawgan, instructional use
	XV701	WS61 Sea King HAS6 [268/N,64]	DSAE RNAESS, *HMS Sultan*, Gosport
	XV703	WS61 Sea King HC6 [ZD]	DSAE RNAESS, *HMS Sultan*, Gosport
	XV705	WS61 Sea King HU5 [29]	Privately owned, Colsterworth, Leics
	XV706	WS61 Sea King HAS6 (9344M) [017/L]	DSAE RNAESS, *HMS Sultan*, Gosport
	XV707	WS61 Sea King ASaC7 [184]	DSAE, stored *HMS Sultan*, Gosport
	XV708	WS61 Sea King HAS6 [501/CU]	DSAE RNAESS, *HMS Sultan*, Gosport
	XV709	WS61 Sea King HAS6 (9303M)	MoD/QinetiQ, Boscombe Down
	XV711	WS61 Sea King HAS6 [15/CW]	DSAE RNAESS, *HMS Sultan*, Gosport
	XV712	WS61 Sea King HAS6 [66]	IWM Duxford
	XV713	WS61 Sea King HAS6 (A2646) [018/L]	DSAE RNAESS, *HMS Sultan*, Gosport
	XV714	WS61 Sea King ASaC7 [188]	RN No 849 NAS, Culdrose
	XV720	WS58 Wessex HC2 (A2701)	Privately owned, Culham, Oxon
	XV722	WS58 Wessex HC2 (8805M) [WH]	Privately owned, Badgers Mount, Kent
	XV724	WS58 Wessex HC2	DSAE RNAESS, *HMS Sultan*, Gosport
	XV725	WS58 Wessex HC2 [C]	MoD DFTDC, Manston
	XV726	WS58 Wessex HC2 [J]	Privately owned, Biggin Hill
	XV728	WS58 Wessex HC2 [A]	Newark Air Museum, Winthorpe
	XV731	WS58 Wessex HC2 [Y]	Privately owned, Badgers Mount, Kent
	XV732	WS58 Wessex HCC4	RAF Museum, Hendon
	XV733	WS58 Wessex HCC4	The Helicopter Museum, Weston-super-Mare
	XV741	HS Harrier GR3 (A2608)	Privately owned, Thorpe Wood, N Yorks
	XV744	HS Harrier GR3 (9167M) [3K]	Tangmere Military Aviation Museum
	XV748	HS Harrier GR3 [3D]	Yorkshire Air Museum, Elvington
	XV751	HS Harrier GR3 [AU]	Gatwick Aviation Museum, Charlwood, Surrey
	XV752	HS Harrier GR3 (9075M) [B]	South Yorkshire Aircraft Museum, Doncaster
	XV753	HS Harrier GR3 (9078M) [53/DD]	Cornwall Aviation Heritage Centre, Newquay
	XV755	HS Harrier GR3 [M]	*Sold to Australia*
	XV759	HS Harrier GR3 [O] <ff>	Privately owned, Hitchin, Herts
	XV760	HS Harrier GR3 <ff>	Solent Sky, Southampton
	XV779	HS Harrier GR3 (8931M)	Harrier Heritage Centre, RAF Wittering
	XV783	HS Harrier GR3 [83/DD]	Privately owned, Corley Moor, Warks
	XV784	HS Harrier GR3 (8909M) <ff>	Boscombe Down Aviation Collection, Old Sarum
	XV786	HS Harrier GR3 [123] <ff>	RNAS Culdrose Fire Section
	XV786	HS Harrier GR3 [S] <rf>	RN, Predannack Fire School
	XV798	HS Harrier GR1(mod) (BAPC 450)	The Helicopter Museum, Weston-super-Mare
	XV806	HS Harrier GR3 <ff>	Privately owned, Staffs
	XV808	HS Harrier GR3 (9076M/A2687) [08/DD]	Privately owned, Chetton, Shrops
	XV810	HS Harrier GR3 (9038M) [K]	Privately owned, Walcott, Lincs
	XV814	DH106 Comet 4 (G-APDF) <ff>	Privately owned, Chipping Campden
	XV863	HS Buccaneer S2B (9115M/9139M/9145M) [S]	Privately owned, Weston, Eire
	XV864	HS Buccaneer S2B (9234M)	MoD DFTDC, Manston
	XV865	HS Buccaneer S2B (9226M)	IWM Duxford
	XV867	HS Buccaneer S2B <ff>	Morayvia, Kinloss
	XW175	HS Harrier T4(VAAC)	DSAE No 1 SoTT, Cosford
	XW198	WS Puma HC1	RAF AM&SU, stored Shawbury

Serial	Type (code/other identity)	Owner/operator, location or fate	Notes
XW199	WS Puma HC2	RAF No 28 Sqn/No 33 Sqn/No 230 Sqn, Benson	
XW202	WS Puma HC1	Army, Stensall Barracks, York	
XW204	WS Puma HC2	RAF No 28 Sqn/No 33 Sqn/No 230 Sqn, Benson	
XW208	WS Puma HC1	Newark Air Museum, Winthorpe	
XW209	WS Puma HC2	RAF No 28 Sqn/No 33 Sqn/No 230 Sqn, Benson	
XW210	WS Puma HC1 (comp XW215)	RAF AM&SU, stored Shawbury	
XW212	WS Puma HC2	RAF No 28 Sqn/No 33 Sqn/No 230 Sqn, Benson	
XW213	WS Puma HC2	RAF/Airbus, Romania	
XW214	WS Puma HC2	RAF No 28 Sqn/No 33 Sqn/No 230 Sqn, Benson	
XW216	WS Puma HC2 (F-ZWDD)	RAF No 28 Sqn/No 33 Sqn/No 230 Sqn, Benson	
XW217	WS Puma HC2	RAF No 28 Sqn/No 33 Sqn/No 230 Sqn, Benson	
XW219	WS Puma HC2	RAF No 28 Sqn/No 33 Sqn/No 230 Sqn, Benson	
XW220	WS Puma HC2	RAF No 28 Sqn/No 33 Sqn/No 230 Sqn, Benson	
XW222	WS Puma HC1	Ulster Aviation Society, Long Kesh	
XW223	WS Puma HC1	RAF AM&SU, stored Shawbury	
XW224	WS Puma HC2	MoD/AFD/QinetiQ, Boscombe Down	
XW226	WS Puma HC1	RAF AM&SU, stored Shawbury	
XW231	WS Puma HC2	RAF No 28 Sqn/No 33 Sqn/No 230 Sqn, Benson	
XW232	WS Puma HC2 (F-ZWDE)	RAF/Airbus, Romania	
XW235	WS Puma HC2 (F-ZWBI)	RAF No 28 Sqn/No 33 Sqn/No 230 Sqn, Benson	
XW236	WS Puma HC1	RAF Defence Movements School, Brize Norton	
XW237	WS Puma HC2	RAF No 28 Sqn/No 33 Sqn/No 230 Sqn, Benson	
XW241	Sud SA330E Puma	Farnborough Air Sciences Trust, Farnborough	
XW264	HS Harrier T2 <ff>	Jet Age Museum, Gloucester	
XW265	HS Harrier T4A (9258M) <ff>	No 2345 Sqn ATC, RAF Leuchars	
XW267	HS Harrier T4 (9263M)	Privately owned, Bentwaters	
XW268	HS Harrier T4N	City of Norwich Aviation Museum	
XW269	HS Harrier T4 [TB]	Caernarfon Air World	
XW270	HS Harrier T4 [T]	Coventry University, instructional use	
XW276	Aérospatiale SA341 Gazelle (F-ZWRI)	Newark Air Museum, Winthorpe	
XW283	WS Scout AH1 (G-CIMX) [U]	Kennet Aviation, North Weald	
XW289	BAC Jet Provost T5A (G-BVXT/G-JPVA) [73]	Kennet Aviation, Yeovilton	
XW290	BAC Jet Provost T5A (9199M) [41,MA]	Privately owned, Bruntingthorpe	
XW293	BAC Jet Provost T5 (G-BWCS) [Z]	Privately owned, Bournemouth	
XW299	BAC Jet Provost T5A (9146M) [60,MB]	QinetiQ Apprentice Training School, Boscombe Down	
XW303	BAC Jet Provost T5A (9119M) [127]	RAF Halton	
XW304	BAC Jet Provost T5 (9172M) [MD]	Privately owned, Eye, Suffolk	
XW310	BAC Jet Provost T5 (9179M) [V,ME]	Hartlepool College of Further Education	
XW311	BAC Jet Provost T5 (9180M) [W,MF]	Privately owned, North Weald	
XW315	BAC Jet Provost T5A <ff>	Privately owned, Preston	
XW320	BAC Jet Provost T5A (9015M) [71]	DSAE No 1 SoTT, Cosford	
XW321	BAC Jet Provost T5A (9154M) [62,MH]	Privately owned, Bentwaters	
XW323	BAC Jet Provost T5A (9166M) [86]	RAF Museum, Hendon	
XW324	BAC Jet Provost T5 (G-BWSG) [U]	Privately owned, East Midlands	
XW325	BAC Jet Provost T5B (G-BWGF) [E]	Privately owned, Coventry	
XW327	BAC Jet Provost T5A (9130M) [62]	DSAE No 1 SoTT, Cosford	
XW330	BAC Jet Provost T5A (9195M) [82,MJ]	Privately owned, Knutsford, Cheshire	
XW333	BAC Jet Provost T5A (G-BVTC)	Global Aviation, Humberside	
XW353	BAC Jet Provost T5A (9090M) [3]	RAF Cranwell, on display	
XW354	BAC Jet Provost T5A (XW355/G-JPTV)	Privately owned, Gamston	
XW358	BAC Jet Provost T5A (9181M) [59,MK]	CEMAST, Fareham College, Lee-on-Solent	
XW360	BAC Jet Provost T5A (9153M) [61,ML]	Privately owned, Thorpe Wood, N Yorks	
XW363	BAC Jet Provost T5A [36]	Dumfries & Galloway Avn Mus, stored Dumfries	
XW364	BAC Jet Provost T5A (9188M) [35,MN]	RAF Halton	
XW370	BAC Jet Provost T5A (9196M) [72,MP]	Privately owned, Sproughton	
XW375	BAC Jet Provost T5A (9149M) [52]	DSAE No 1 SoTT, Cosford	
XW404	BAC Jet Provost T5A (9049M) [77]	Hartlepool FE College	
XW405	BAC Jet Provost T5A (9187M)	Hartlepool FE College, on display	
XW409	BAC Jet Provost T5A (9047M)	Privately owned, Hawarden	
XW410	BAC Jet Provost T5A (9125M) [80] <ff>	Privately owned, Norwich	
XW416	BAC Jet Provost T5A (9191M) [84,MS]	Privately owned, Bentwaters	
XW418	BAC Jet Provost T5A (9173M) [MT]	RAF Museum, Cosford	

Notes	Serial	Type (code/other identity)	Owner/operator, location or fate
	XW419	BAC Jet Provost T5A (9120M) [125]	Highland Aviation Museum, Inverness
	XW420	BAC Jet Provost T5A (9194M) [83,MU]	Privately owned, St Athan
	XW422	BAC Jet Provost T5A (G-BWEB) [3]	Privately owned, Cotswold Airport
	XW423	BAC Jet Provost T5A (G-BWUW) [14]	Deeside College, Connah's Quay, Clwyd
	XW430	BAC Jet Provost T5A (9176M) [77,MW]	Privately owned, Arncott, Oxon
	XW432	BAC Jet Provost T5A (9127M) [76,MX]	Privately owned, Thame
	XW433	BAC Jet Provost T5A (G-JPRO)	Inverness Airport, on display
	XW434	BAC Jet Provost T5A (9091M) [78,MY]	Halfpenny Green Airport, on display
	XW436	BAC Jet Provost T5A (9148M) [68]	DSAE No 1 SoTT, Cosford
	XW530	HS Buccaneer S2B [530]	Buccaneer Service Station, Elgin
	XW541	HS Buccaneer S2B (8858M) <ff>	Privately owned, Lavendon, Bucks
	XW544	HS Buccaneer S2B (8857M) [O]	The Buccaneer Aviation Group, Bruntingthorpe
	XW547	HS Buccaneer S2B (9095M/9169M) [R]	RAF Museum, Hendon
	XW550	HS Buccaneer S2B <ff>	Privately owned, Bruntingthorpe
	XW560	SEPECAT Jaguar S <ff>	Boscombe Down Aviation Collection, Old Sarum
	XW563	SEPECAT Jaguar S (XX822/8563M)	County Hall, Norwich, on display
	XW566	SEPECAT Jaguar B	Farnborough Air Sciences Trust, Farnborough
	XW612	WS Scout AH1 (G-KAXW)	Privately owned, Old Warden
	XW613	WS Scout AH1 (G-BXRS)	Privately owned, Thruxton
	XW616	WS Scout AH1	AAC Dishforth, instructional use
	XW630	HS Harrier GR3	RNAS Yeovilton, Fire Section
	XW635	Beagle D5/180 (G-AWSW)	Privately owned, Spanhoe
	XW664	HS Nimrod R1	East Midlands Airport Aeropark
	XW666	HS Nimrod R1 <ff>	South Yorkshire Aircraft Museum, Doncaster
	XW763	HS Harrier GR3 (9002M/9041M) <ff>	Privately owned, Wigston, Leics
	XW768	HS Harrier GR3 (9072M) [N]	MoD DFTDC, Manston
	XW784	Mitchell-Procter Kittiwake I (G-BBRN) [VL]	Privately owned, RNAS Yeovilton
	XW795	WS Scout AH1	Privately owned, Fivemiletown, Co Tyrone, NI
	XW796	WS Scout AH1	Gunsmoke Paintball, Colchester, Essex
	XW838	WS Lynx (TAD009)	DSAE SAAE, Lyneham
	XW839	WS Lynx	The Helicopter Museum, Weston-super-Mare
	XW844	WS Gazelle AH1	Vector Aerospace Fleetlands, preserved
	XW846	WS Gazelle AH1	AAC No 667 Sqn/7 Regt, Middle Wallop
	XW847	WS Gazelle AH1	AAC No 667 Sqn/7 Regt, Middle Wallop
	XW848	WS Gazelle AH1 [D]	Privately owned, Stapleford Tawney
	XW849	WS Gazelle AH1	Privately owned, Hurstbourne Tarrant, Hants
	XW852	WS Gazelle HCC4 (9331M)	DSAE RNAESS, HMS Sultan, Gosport
	XW855	WS Gazelle HCC4	RAF Museum, Hendon
	XW858	WS Gazelle HT3 (G-ONNE) [C]	Privately owned, Steeple Bumstead, Cambs
	XW860	WS Gazelle HT2 (TAD 021)	DSAE SAAE, Lyneham
	XW863	WS Gazelle HT2 (TAD 022)	Privately owned, Middle Wallop
	XW864	WS Gazelle HT2 [54/CU]	FAA Museum, stored Cobham Hall, RNAS Yeovilton
	XW865	WS Gazelle AH1	AAC No 667 Sqn/7 Regt, Middle Wallop
	XW870	WS Gazelle HT3 (9299M) [F]	MoD DFTDC, Manston
	XW888	WS Gazelle AH1 (TAD 017)	DSAE SAAE, Lyneham
	XW889	WS Gazelle AH1 (TAD 018)	Currently not known
	XW890	WS Gazelle HT2	RNAS Yeovilton, on display
	XW892	WS Gazelle AH1 (G-CGJX/9292M)	Privately owned, Hurstbourne Tarrant, Hants
	XW897	WS Gazelle AH1	DSAE No 1 SoTT, Cosford
	XW899	WS Gazelle AH1 [Z]	DSAE No 1 SoTT, Cosford
	XW900	WS Gazelle AH1 (TAD 900)	Army, Bramley, Hants
	XW904	WS Gazelle AH1 [H]	AAC MPSU, Middle Wallop
	XW906	WS Gazelle HT3 [J]	QinetiQ Apprentice Training School, Boscombe Down
	XW908	WS Gazelle AH1 [A]	QinetiQ, Boscombe Down (spares use)
	XW909	WS Gazelle AH1	Privately owned, Stapleford Tawney
	XW912	WS Gazelle AH1 (TAD 019)	DSAE SAAE, Lyneham
	XW913	WS Gazelle AH1	Privately owned, Stapleford Tawney
	XW917	HS Harrier GR3 (8975M)	NATS Air Traffic Control Centre, Swanwick
	XW922	HS Harrier GR3 (8885M)	MoD DFTDC, Manston
	XW923	HS Harrier GR3 (8724M) <ff>	Harrier Heritage Centre, RAF Wittering
	XW924	HS Harrier GR3 (9073M) [G]	RAF Coningsby, preserved
	XW927	HS Harrier T4 <ff>	Privately owned, South Molton, Devon

Serial	Type (code/other identity)	Owner/operator, location or fate	Notes
XW934	HS Harrier T4 [Y]	Farnborough Air Sciences Trust, Farnborough	
XW994	Northrop Chukar D1	FAA Museum, stored Cobham Hall, RNAS Yeovilton	
XW999	Northrop Chukar D1	Davidstow Airfield & Cornwall At War Museum	
XX108	SEPECAT Jaguar GR1(mod)	IWM Duxford	
XX109	SEPECAT Jaguar GR1 (8918M) [GH]	City of Norwich Aviation Museum	
XX110	SEPECAT Jaguar GR1 (8955M) [EP]	RAF Cosford, on display	
XX110	SEPECAT Jaguar GR1 <R> (BAPC 169)	DSAE No 1 SoTT, Cosford	
XX112	SEPECAT Jaguar GR3A [EA]	DSAE No 1 SoTT, Cosford	
XX115	SEPECAT Jaguar GR1 (8821M) (fuselage)	DSAE No 1 SoTT, Cosford	
XX116	SEPECAT Jaguar GR3A [EO]	MoD DFTDC, Manston	
XX117	SEPECAT Jaguar GR3A [ES]	DSAE No 1 SoTT, Cosford	
XX119	SEPECAT Jaguar GR3A (8898M) [AI]$	DSAE No 1 SoTT, Cosford	
XX121	SEPECAT Jaguar GR1 [EQ]	Privately owned, Selby, N Yorks	
XX139	SEPECAT Jaguar T4 [PT]	Privately owned, Sproughton	
XX140	SEPECAT Jaguar T2 (9008M) <ff>	Privately owned, Selby, N Yorks	
XX141	SEPECAT Jaguar T2A (9297M) [T]	DSAE No 1 SoTT, Cosford	
XX144	SEPECAT Jaguar T2A [U]	Privately owned, Sproughton	
XX145	SEPECAT Jaguar T2A	Privately owned, Bruntingthorpe	
XX146	SEPECAT Jaguar T4 [GT]	Bradwell Bay Military & Science Museum, Essex	
XX153	WS Lynx AH1 (9320M)	Museum of Army Flying, Middle Wallop	
XX154	HS Hawk T1	MoD/ETPS, Boscombe Down	
XX156	HS Hawk T1 [156]	RAF Valley, on display	
XX157	HS Hawk T1A [157/CU]	RN No 736 NAS, Culdrose	
XX158	HS Hawk T1A [158]	RAF AM&SU, stored Shawbury	
XX159	HS Hawk T1A [159]	RN No 736 NAS, Culdrose	
XX160	HS Hawk T1A [160]	RAF AM&SU, stored Shawbury	
XX161	HS Hawk T1A [161]	RN No 736 NAS, Culdrose	
XX162	HS Hawk T1	RAF Centre of Aviation Medicine, Boscombe Down	
XX165	HS Hawk T1 [165] (fuselage)	QinetiQ, Boscombe Down, spares use	
XX167	HS Hawk T1 [167]	RAF AM&SU, stored Shawbury	
XX168	HS Hawk T1 [168]	RAF AM&SU, stored Shawbury	
XX169	HS Hawk T1W [169]	RAF AM&SU, stored Shawbury	
XX170	HS Hawk T1 [CH]	RAF AM&SU, stored Shawbury	
XX171	HS Hawk T1 [171]	RAF AM&SU, stored Shawbury	
XX172	HS Hawk T1 [172] (fuselage)	QinetiQ Boscombe Down, GI use	
XX173	HS Hawk T1	RAF AM&SU, stored Shawbury	
XX174	HS Hawk T1 [174]	RAF AM&SU, stored Shawbury	
XX175	HS Hawk T1 [175]	Privately owned, St Athan	
XX176	HS Hawk T1W [176]	RAF AM&SU, stored Shawbury	
XX177	HS Hawk T1	RAF *Red Arrows*, Scampton	
XX178	HS Hawk T1W [178]	RAF AM&SU, stored Shawbury	
XX181	HS Hawk T1 [181]	RAF AM&SU, stored Shawbury	
XX184	HS Hawk T1 [CQ]	RN No 1710 NAS, Portsmouth	
XX185	HS Hawk T1 [185]	RAF AM&SU, stored Shawbury	
XX187	HS Hawk T1A [187]	RAF No 100 Sqn, Leeming	
XX188	HS Hawk T1A	RAF *Red Arrows*, Scampton	
XX189	HS Hawk T1A [189]	RN No 736 NAS, Culdrose	
XX190	HS Hawk T1A [CN]	RAF AM&SU, stored Shawbury	
XX191	HS Hawk T1A [CC]	RAF No 100 Sqn, Leeming	
XX194	HS Hawk T1A [CP]	RAF AM&SU, stored Shawbury	
XX195	HS Hawk T1W [195]	RAF AM&SU, stored Shawbury	
XX198	HS Hawk T1A [CH]	RAF No 100 Sqn, Leeming	
XX199	HS Hawk T1A [199]	RAF AM&SU, stored Shawbury	
XX200	HS Hawk T1A [CO]	RN No 736 NAS, Culdrose	
XX201	HS Hawk T1A [CQ]	RAF AM&SU, stored Shawbury	
XX202	HS Hawk T1A [CS]	RAF No 100 Sqn, Leeming	
XX203	HS Hawk T1A [CF]	RAF No 100 Sqn, Leeming	
XX204	HS Hawk T1A	RAF *Red Arrows*, Scampton	
XX205	HS Hawk T1A [CK]	RAF No 100 Sqn, Leeming	
XX217	HS Hawk T1A [217]	RAF AM&SU, stored Shawbury	
XX218	HS Hawk T1A [218]	RAF AM&SU, stored Shawbury	

Notes	Serial	Type (code/other identity)	Owner/operator, location or fate
	XX219	HS Hawk T1A	RAF *Red Arrows*, Scampton
	XX220	HS Hawk T1A [220]	RAF AM&SU, stored Shawbury
	XX221	HS Hawk T1A [CO]	RAF No 100 Sqn, Leeming
	XX222	HS Hawk T1A [CI]	RAF AM&SU, stored Shawbury
	XX223	HS Hawk T1 <ff>	*Scrapped*
	XX224	HS Hawk T1 [224]	RAF AM&SU, stored Shawbury
	XX225	HS Hawk T1 [322]	RAF AM&SU, stored Shawbury
	XX226	HS Hawk T1 [226]	Privately owned, St Athan
	XX227	HS Hawk T1 <R> (*XX226/BAPC 152*)	RAF Scampton Heritage Centre
	XX227	HS Hawk T1A	RAF Scampton (wfu)
	XX228	HS Hawk T1 [CG]	RAF AM&SU, stored Shawbury
	XX230	HS Hawk T1A [CM]	RAF AM&SU, stored Shawbury
	XX231	HS Hawk T1W [213]	RAF AM&SU, stored Shawbury
	XX232	HS Hawk T1	RAF *Red Arrows*, Scampton
	XX234	HS Hawk T1 [234]	RAF AM&SU, stored Shawbury
	XX235	HS Hawk T1 [235]	RAF AM&SU, stored Shawbury
	XX236	HS Hawk T1W [236]	RAF AM&SU, stored Shawbury
	XX237	HS Hawk T1	RAF AM&SU, stored Shawbury
	XX238	HS Hawk T1 [238]	RAF AM&SU, stored Shawbury
	XX239	HS Hawk T1W [CI]	RAF No 100 Sqn, Leeming
	XX240	HS Hawk T1 [840/CU]	RAF AM&SU, stored Shawbury
	XX242	HS Hawk T1	RAF *Red Arrows*, Scampton
	XX244	HS Hawk T1	RAF *Red Arrows*, Scampton
	XX245	HS Hawk T1	RAF *Red Arrows*, Scampton
	XX246	HS Hawk T1A [CA]	RAF No 100 Sqn, Leeming
	XX247	HS Hawk T1A [247]	RAF Woodvale, at main gate
	XX248	HS Hawk T1A [CJ]	RAF AM&SU, stored Shawbury
	XX250	HS Hawk T1W [250]	RAF AM&SU, stored Shawbury
	XX253	HS Hawk T1A	RAF Scampton, on display
	XX254	HS Hawk T1A <R>	Privately owned, Marlow, Bucks
	XX255	HS Hawk T1A [CB]	RAF No 100 Sqn, Leeming
	XX256	HS Hawk T1A [256]	RAF HSF, Valley
	XX257	HS Hawk T1A (fuselage)	*Currently not known*
	XX258	HS Hawk T1A [CE]	RAF No 100 Sqn, Leeming
	XX260	HS Hawk T1A	RAF AM&SU, stored Shawbury
	XX261	HS Hawk T1A $	RAF HSF, Valley
	XX263	HS Hawk T1A	RAF AM&SU, stored Shawbury
	XX264	HS Hawk T1A $	RAF AM&SU, stored Shawbury
	XX265	HS Hawk T1A [CP]	RAF AM&SU, stored Shawbury
	XX266	HS Hawk T1A	RAF Scampton, instructional use
	XX278	HS Hawk T1A	RAF *Red Arrows*, Scampton
	XX280	HS Hawk T1A [280]	RN No 736 NAS, Culdrose
	XX281	HS Hawk T1A	RN No 736 NAS, Culdrose
	XX283	HS Hawk T1W [283]	RAF AM&SU, stored Shawbury
	XX284	HS Hawk T1A [CN]	RAF AM&SU, stored Shawbury
	XX285	HS Hawk T1A	RN No 736 NAS, Culdrose
	XX286	HS Hawk T1A [286]	RAF AM&SU, stored Shawbury
	XX287	HS Hawk T1A [287]	RAF AM&SU, stored Shawbury
	XX289	HS Hawk T1A [CO]	RAF AM&SU, stored Shawbury
	XX290	HS Hawk T1W	Privately owned, St Athan
	XX292	HS Hawk T1	Privately owned, Bentwaters
	XX294	HS Hawk T1	RAF AM&SU, stored Shawbury
	XX295	HS Hawk T1 [295]	RAF AM&SU, stored Shawbury
	XX296	HS Hawk T1 [296]	RAF AM&SU, stored Shawbury
	XX299	HS Hawk T1W [299]	RAF AM&SU, stored Shawbury
	XX301	HS Hawk T1A $	RAF AM&SU, stored Shawbury
	XX303	HS Hawk T1A [CR]	RAF No 100 Sqn, Leeming
	XX304	HS Hawk T1A <rf>	Cardiff International Airport Fire Section
	XX306	HS Hawk T1A	RAF Scampton, on display
	XX307	HS Hawk T1 [307]	RAF AM&SU, stored Shawbury
	XX308	HS Hawk T1	RAF AM&SU, stored Shawbury
	XX308	HS Hawk T1	National Museum of Flight, E Fortune

Serial	Type (code/other identity)	Owner/operator, location or fate	Notes
XX309	HS Hawk T1	RAF AM&SU, stored Shawbury	
XX310	HS Hawk T1	RAF *Red Arrows*, Scampton	
XX311	HS Hawk T1	RAF *Red Arrows*, Scampton	
XX312	HS Hawk T1W	RAF AM&SU, stored Shawbury	
XX313	HS Hawk T1W [313]	RAF AM&SU, stored Shawbury	
XX314	HS Hawk T1W [314]	RAF AM&SU, stored Shawbury	
XX315	HS Hawk T1A [315]	RAF AM&SU, stored Shawbury	
XX316	HS Hawk T1A [849/CU]	RAF No 100 Sqn, Leeming	
XX317	HS Hawk T1A [317]	RN No 736 NAS, Culdrose	
XX318	HS Hawk T1A [CG]	RAF No 100 Sqn, Leeming	
XX319	HS Hawk T1A	RAF *Red Arrows*, Scampton	
XX320	HS Hawk T1A <ff>	RAF Scampton Heritage Centre	
XX321	HS Hawk T1A [CI]	RAF HSF, Valley	
XX322	HS Hawk T1A	RAF *Red Arrows*, Scampton	
XX323	HS Hawk T1A	RAF *Red Arrows*, Scampton	
XX324	HS Hawk T1A [324]	RN No 736 NAS, Culdrose	
XX325	HS Hawk T1	RAF *Red Arrows*, Scampton	
XX326	HS Hawk T1A	*Scrapped*	
XX327	HS Hawk T1	RAF Centre of Aviation Medicine, Boscombe Down	
XX329	HS Hawk T1A [CJ]	RN No 736 NAS, Culdrose	
XX330	HS Hawk T1A [330]	RAF AM&SU, stored Shawbury	
XX331	HS Hawk T1A [331]	RAF AM&SU, stored Shawbury	
XX332	HS Hawk T1A [CD]	RAF No 100 Sqn, Leeming	
XX335	HS Hawk T1A [335]	DSAE No 1 SoTT, Cosford	
XX337	HS Hawk T1A [CM]	RAF No 100 Sqn, Leeming	
XX338	HS Hawk T1W	RAF AM&SU, stored Shawbury	
XX339	HS Hawk T1A [CL]	RAF No 100 Sqn, Leeming	
XX341	HS Hawk T1 ASTRA	MoD/ETPS, Boscombe Down	
XX342	HS Hawk T1 [2]	MoD/ETPS, Boscombe Down	
XX343	HS Hawk T1 [3] (fuselage)	Boscombe Down Aviation Collection, Old Sarum	
XX345	HS Hawk T1A [CB]	RAF AM&SU, stored Shawbury	
XX346	HS Hawk T1A [CP]	RAF No 100 Sqn, Leeming	
XX348	HS Hawk T1A [CQ]	RAF No 100 Sqn, Leeming	
XX349	HS Hawk T1W <ff>	RAF Scampton Fire Section	
XX350	HS Hawk T1A [D] $	RAF AM&SU, stored Shawbury	
XX351	HS Hawk T1A	RAF No 71(IR) Sqn, Wittering, GI use	
XX372	WS Gazelle AH1 <ff>	Privately owned, Hurstbourne Tarrant, Hants	
XX375	WS Gazelle AH1	Privately owned,	
XX378	WS Gazelle AH1 [Q]	AAC MPSU, stored Middle Wallop	
XX379	WS Gazelle AH1 [Y]	MoD Boscombe Down, GI use	
XX380	WS Gazelle AH1 [A]	AAC Wattisham, on display	
XX381	WS Gazelle AH1	Privately owned, Welbeck	
XX383	WS Gazelle AH1 [D]	*Sold as ZU-RMU, August 2017*	
XX386	WS Gazelle AH1	Privately owned, Stapleford Tawney	
XX387	WS Gazelle AH1 (TAD 014)	Privately owned, stored Cranfield	
XX392	WS Gazelle AH1	Army, Middle Wallop, preserved	
XX394	WS Gazelle AH1 [X]	Privately owned, Stapleford Tawney	
XX396	WS Gazelle HT3 (8718M) [N]	Privately owned, Arncott, Oxon	
XX398	WS Gazelle AH1	Privately owned, Stapleford Tawney	
XX399	WS Gazelle AH1 <ff>	Privately owned, Hurstbourne Tarrant, Hants	
XX403	WS Gazelle AH1 [U]	AAC MPSU, stored Middle Wallop	
XX405	WS Gazelle AH1	AAC 7 Regiment Conversion Flt, Middle Wallop	
XX406	WS Gazelle HT3 (G-CBSH) [P]	Privately owned, Hurstbourne Tarrant, Hants	
XX411	WS Gazelle AH1 [X]	South Yorkshire Aircraft Museum, Doncaster	
XX411	WS Gazelle AH1 <rf>	FAA Museum, RNAS Yeovilton	
XX412	WS Gazelle AH1 [B]	DSAE No 1 SoTT, Cosford	
XX414	WS Gazelle AH1 [V]	Privately owned, Biggin Hill	
XX416	WS Gazelle AH1	Privately owned, Stapleford Tawney	
XX418	WS Gazelle AH1 <ff>	Privately owned, Hurstbourne Tarrant, Hants	
XX419	WS Gazelle AH1	AAC MPSU, Middle Wallop	
XX431	WS Gazelle HT2 (9300M) [43/CU]	DSAE RNAESS, *HMS Sultan*, Gosport	
XX433	WS Gazelle AH1 <ff>	Privately owned, Hurstbourne Tarrant, Hants	

Notes	Serial	Type (code/other identity)	Owner/operator, location or fate
	XX435	WS Gazelle AH1 (fuselage)	QinetiQ, Boscombe Down (spares use)
	XX436	WS Gazelle HT2 (G-ZZLE) [39/CU]	Privately owned, Hurstbourne Tarrant, Hants
	XX437	WS Gazelle AH1	Privately owned, Stapleford Tawney
	XX438	WS Gazelle AH1 [F]	Privately owned, Stapleford Tawney
	XX442	WS Gazelle AH1 [E]	AAC MPSU, stored Middle Wallop
	XX443	WS Gazelle AH1 [Y]	Army, Aldergrove, on display
	XX444	WS Gazelle AH1	Wattisham Station Heritage Museum
	XX445	WS Gazelle AH1 [T]	Privately owned, Stapleford Tawney
	XX447	WS Gazelle AH1 [D1]	AAC MPSU, stored Middle Wallop
	XX449	WS Gazelle AH1	MoD/QinetiQ, Boscombe Down
	XX450	WS Gazelle AH1 [D]	Privately owned, Hurstbourne Tarrant, Hants
	XX453	WS Gazelle AH1	MoD/QinetiQ, Boscombe Down
	XX454	WS Gazelle AH1 (TAD 023)	DSAE SAAE, Lyneham
	XX455	WS Gazelle AH1	Privately owned, Stapleford Tawney
	XX456	WS Gazelle AH1	Privately owned, Stapleford Tawney
	XX457	WS Gazelle AH1 (TAD 001)	East Midlands Airport Aeropark
	XX460	WS Gazelle AH1	AAC AM&SU, stored Shawbury
	XX462	WS Gazelle AH1 [W]	Privately owned, Stapleford Tawney
	XX466	HS Hunter T66B/T7 [830] <ff>	Privately owned, Glos
	XX467	HS Hunter T66B/T7 (XL605/G-TVII) [86]	Newark Air Museum, Winthorpe
	XX477	HP137 Jetstream T1 (G-AXXS/8462M) <ff>	South Yorkshire Aircraft Museum, Doncaster
	XX478	HP137 Jetstream T2 (G-AXXT) [564/CU]	Solihull College, Woodlands Campus
	XX479	HP137 Jetstream T2 (G-AXUR)	RN, Predannack Fire School
	XX482	SA Jetstream T1 [J]	Privately owned, Hixon, Staffs
	XX483	SA Jetstream T2 [562] <ff>	Dumfries & Galloway Avn Mus, Dumfries
	XX486	SA Jetstream T2 [567/CU]	Sold to Lithuania
	XX487	SA Jetstream T2 [568/CU]	Barry Technical College, instructional use
	XX491	SA Jetstream T1 [K]	Northbrook College, Shoreham, instructional use
	XX492	SA Jetstream T1 [A]	Newark Air Museum, Winthorpe
	XX494	SA Jetstream T1 [B]	East Midlands Airport Aeropark
	XX495	SA Jetstream T1 [C]	Bedford College, instructional use
	XX496	SA Jetstream T1 [D]	RAF Museum, Cosford
	XX499	SA Jetstream T1 [G]	Brooklands Museum, Weybridge
	XX500	SA Jetstream T1 [H]	Scrapped
	XX510	WS Lynx HAS2 [69/DD]	SFDO, RNAS Culdrose
	XX513	SA Bulldog T1 (G-KKKK) [10]	Privately owned, Bagby
	XX515	SA Bulldog T1 (G-CBBC) [4]	Privately owned, Blackbushe
	XX518	SA Bulldog T1 (G-UDOG) [S]	Privately owned, Ursel, Belgium
	XX520	SA Bulldog T1 (9288M) [A]	No 172 Sqn ATC, Haywards Heath
	XX521	SA Bulldog T1 (G-CBEH) [H]	Privately owned, Charney Bassett, Oxon
	XX522	SA Bulldog T1 (G-DAWG) [06]	Privately owned, Blackpool
	XX524	SA Bulldog T1 (G-DDOG) [04]	Privately owned, Malaga, Spain
	XX528	SA Bulldog T1 (G-BZON) [D]	Privately owned, North Weald
	XX530	SA Bulldog T1 (XX637/9197M) [F]	No 2175 Sqn ATC, RAF Kinloss
	XX534	SA Bulldog T1 (G-EDAV) [B]	Privately owned, Tollerton
	XX537	SA Bulldog T1 (G-CBCB) [C]	Privately owned, RAF Halton
	XX538	SA Bulldog T1 (G-TDOG) [O]	Privately owned, Shobdon
	XX539	SA Bulldog T1 [L]	Privately owned, Derbyshire
	XX543	SA Bulldog T1 (G-UWAS) [U]	Repainted as XX625, 2017
	XX546	SA Bulldog T1 (G-WINI) [03]	Privately owned, Conington
	XX549	SA Bulldog T1 (G-CBID) [6]	Privately owned, White Waltham
	XX550	SA Bulldog T1 (G-CBBL) [Z]	Privately owned, Abbeyshrule, Eire
	XX551	SA Bulldog T1 (G-BZDP) [E]	Privately owned, Boscombe Down
	XX554	SA Bulldog T1 (G-BZMD) [09]	Privately owned, Wellesbourne Mountford
	XX557	SA Bulldog T1	Privately owned, stored Fort Paull, Yorks
	XX561	SA Bulldog T1 (G-BZEP) [7]	Privately owned, Eggesford
	XX611	SA Bulldog T1 (G-CBDK) [7]	Privately owned, Coventry
	XX612	SA Bulldog T1 (G-BZXC) [A,03]	Ayr College, instructional use
	XX614	SA Bulldog T1 (G-GGRR) [1]	Privately owned, Cotswold Airport
	XX619	SA Bulldog T1 (G-CBBW) [T]	Privately owned, Coventry
	XX621	SA Bulldog T1 (G-CBEF) [H]	Privately owned, Leicester
	XX622	SA Bulldog T1 (G-CBGX) [B]	Privately owned, Shoreham

Serial	Type (code/other identity)	Owner/operator, location or fate	Notes
XX623	SA Bulldog T1 [M]	Privately owned, Hurstbourne Tarrant, Hants	
XX624	SA Bulldog T1 (G-KDOG) [E]	Privately owned, Hurstbourne Tarrant, Hants	
XX625	SA Bulldog T1 (XX543/G-UWAS) [U]	Privately owned, Tain	
XX625	SA120 Bulldog (G-AZHX) [45]	Not taken up	
XX626	SA Bulldog T1 (G-CDVV/9290M) [W,02]	Privately owned, Abbots Bromley, Staffs	
XX628	SA Bulldog T1 (G-CBFU) [9]	Privately owned, Faversham	
XX629	SA Bulldog T1 (G-BZXZ)	Privately owned, Wellesbourne Mountford	
XX630	SA Bulldog T1 (G-SIJW) [5]	Privately owned, Audley End	
XX631	SA Bulldog T1 (G-BZXS) [W]	Privately owned, Sligo, Eire	
XX634	SA Bulldog T1 [T]	Newark Air Museum, Winthorpe	
XX636	SA Bulldog T1 (G-CBFP) [Y]	Privately owned, Netherthorpe	
XX638	SA Bulldog T1 (G-DOGG)	Privately owned, Hurstbourne Tarrant, Hants	
XX639	SA Bulldog T1 (F-AZTF) [D]	Privately owned, La Baule, France	
XX654	SA Bulldog T1 [3]	RAF Museum, Cosford	
XX655	SA Bulldog T1 (9294M) [V] <ff>	Privately owned, Stockport	
XX656	SA Bulldog T1 [C]	Privately owned, Derbyshire	
XX658	SA Bulldog T1 (G-BZPS) [07]	Privately owned, Wellesbourne Mountford	
XX659	SA Bulldog T1 [E]	Privately owned, Derbyshire	
XX664	SA Bulldog T1 (F-AZTV) [04]	Privately owned, Pontoise, France	
XX665	SA Bulldog T1 (9289M) [V]	Privately owned, Thorpe Wood, N Yorks	
XX667	SA Bulldog T1 (G-BZFN) [16]	Privately owned, Ronaldsway, IoM	
XX668	SA Bulldog T1 (G-CBAN) [1]	Privately owned, St Athan	
XX669	SA Bulldog T1 (8997M) [B]	South Yorkshire Aircraft Museum, Doncaster	
XX687	SA Bulldog T1 [F]	Barry Technical College, Cardiff Airport	
XX690	SA Bulldog T1 [A]	Privately owned, Strathaven, S Lanarks	
XX692	SA Bulldog T1 (G-BZMH) [A]	Privately owned, Wellesbourne Mountford	
XX693	SA Bulldog T1 (G-BZML) [07]	Privately owned, Elmsett	
XX694	SA Bulldog T1 (G-CBBS) [E]	Privately owned, Newcastle	
XX695	SA Bulldog T1 (G-CBBT)	Privately owned, Perth	
XX698	SA Bulldog T1 (G-BZME) [9]	Privately owned, Sleap	
XX700	SA Bulldog T1 (G-CBEK) [17]	Privately owned, Thruxton	
XX702	SA Bulldog T1 (G-CBCR) [π]	Privately owned, Egginton	
XX704	SA122 Bulldog (G-BCUV/G-112)	Privately owned, Bournemouth	
XX705	SA Bulldog T1 [5]	Privately owned, Norfolk	
XX707	SA Bulldog T1 (G-CBDS) [4]	Privately owned, stored Caernarfon	
XX711	SA Bulldog T1 (G-CBBU) [X]	Privately owned, stored Perth	
XX720	SEPECAT Jaguar GR3A [FL]	Privately owned, Sproughton	
XX722	SEPECAT Jaguar GR1 (9252M) <ff>	Currently not known	
XX723	SEPECAT Jaguar GR3A [EU]	DSAE No 1 SoTT, Cosford	
XX724	SEPECAT Jaguar GR3A [C]	DSAE No 1 SoTT, Cosford	
XX725	SEPECAT Jaguar GR3A [KC-F,T]	DSAE No 1 SoTT, Cosford	
XX726	SEPECAT Jaguar GR1 (8947M) [EB]	DSAE No 1 SoTT, Cosford	
XX727	SEPECAT Jaguar GR1 (8951M) [ER]	DSAE No 1 SoTT, Cosford	
XX729	SEPECAT Jaguar GR3A [EL]	DSAE No 1 SoTT, Cosford	
XX734	SEPECAT Jaguar GR1 (8816M)	Boscombe Down Aviation Collection, Old Sarum	
XX736	SEPECAT Jaguar GR1 (9110M) <ff>	South Yorkshire Aircraft Museum, Doncaster	
XX738	SEPECAT Jaguar GR3A [ED]	DSAE No 1 SoTT, Cosford	
XX739	SEPECAT Jaguar GR1 (8902M) [I]	Delta Force, stored Upminster	
XX741	SEPECAT Jaguar GR1A [EJ]	Bentwaters Cold War Museum	
XX743	SEPECAT Jaguar GR1 (8949M) [EG]	DSAE No 1 SoTT, Cosford	
XX744	SEPECAT Jaguar GR1 (9251M)	Mayhem Paintball, Abridge, Essex	
XX745	SEPECAT Jaguar GR1A <ff>	No 1350 Sqn ATC, Fareham	
XX746	SEPECAT Jaguar GR1 (8895M) [S]	DSAE No 1 SoTT, Cosford	
XX747	SEPECAT Jaguar GR1 (8903M)	QinetiQ Boscombe Down, GI use	
XX748	SEPECAT Jaguar GR3A [L]	DSAE No 1 SoTT, Cosford	
XX751	SEPECAT Jaguar GR1 (8937M) [10]	Privately owned, Bentwaters	
XX752	SEPECAT Jaguar GR3A [EK]	DSAE No 1 SoTT, Cosford	
XX753	SEPECAT Jaguar GR1 (9087M) <ff>	Newark Air Museum, Winthorpe	
XX756	SEPECAT Jaguar GR1 (8899M) [W]	DSAE No 1 SoTT, Cosford	
XX761	SEPECAT Jaguar GR1 (8600M) <ff>	Boscombe Down Aviation Collection, Old Sarum	
XX763	SEPECAT Jaguar GR1 (9009M) [24]	Bournemouth Aviation Museum	
XX764	SEPECAT Jaguar GR1 (9010M)	Privately owned, Enstone	

Notes	Serial	Type (code/other identity)	Owner/operator, location or fate
	XX765	SEPECAT Jaguar ACT	RAF Museum, Cosford
	XX766	SEPECAT Jaguar GR3A [EF]	DSAE No 1 SoTT, Cosford
	XX767	SEPECAT Jaguar GR3A [Z]	DSAE No 1 SoTT, Cosford
	XX818	SEPECAT Jaguar GR1 (8945M) [DE]	DSAE No 1 SoTT, Cosford
	XX819	SEPECAT Jaguar GR1 (8923M) [CE]	DSAE No 1 SoTT, Cosford
	XX821	SEPECAT Jaguar GR1 (8896M) [P]	DSAE No 1 SoTT, Cosford
	XX824	SEPECAT Jaguar GR1 (9019M) [AD]	RAF Museum, Hendon
	XX825	SEPECAT Jaguar GR1 (9020M) [BN]	DSAE No 1 SoTT, Cosford
	XX826	SEPECAT Jaguar GR1 (9021M) [34] <ff>	Shannon Aviation Museum, Eire
	XX829	SEPECAT Jaguar T2A [GZ]	Newark Air Museum, Winthorpe
	XX830	SEPECAT Jaguar T2 <ff>	City of Norwich Aviation Museum
	XX833	SEPECAT Jaguar T2B	DSAE No 1 SoTT, Cosford
	XX835	SEPECAT Jaguar T4 [P]	DSAE No 1 SoTT, Cosford
	XX836	SEPECAT Jaguar T2A [X]	Privately owned, Sproughton
	XX837	SEPECAT Jaguar T2 (8978M) [Z]	DSAE No 1 SoTT, Cosford
	XX838	SEPECAT Jaguar T4 [FZ]	Privately owned, Bentwaters
	XX840	SEPECAT Jaguar T4 [T]	DSAE No 1 SoTT, Cosford
	XX841	SEPECAT Jaguar T4	Privately owned, Tunbridge Wells
	XX842	SEPECAT Jaguar T2A [FX]	Privately owned, Bentwaters
	XX845	SEPECAT Jaguar T4 [EV]	RN, Predannack Fire School
	XX847	SEPECAT Jaguar T4 [EZ]	DSAE No 1 SoTT, Cosford
	XX885	HS Buccaneer S2B (9225M/G-HHAA)	Hawker Hunter Aviation, Scampton
	XX888	HS Buccaneer S2B <ff>	Privately owned, Barnstaple
	XX889	HS Buccaneer S2B [T]	Privately owned, Bruntingthorpe
	XX893	HS Buccaneer S2B <ff>	Blue Sky Experiences, Methven, Perth & Kinross
	XX894	HS Buccaneer S2B [020/R]	The Buccaneer Aviation Group, Bruntingthorpe
	XX895	HS Buccaneer S2B <ff>	Privately owned, Tattershall Thorpe
	XX897	HS Buccaneer S2B(mod)	Shannon Aviation Museum, Eire
	XX899	HS Buccaneer S2B <ff>	Midland Air Museum, Coventry
	XX900	HS Buccaneer S2B [900]	Cold War Jets Collection, Bruntingthorpe
	XX901	HS Buccaneer S2B	Yorkshire Air Museum, Elvington
	XX910	WS Lynx HAS2	The Helicopter Museum, Weston-super-Mare
	XX919	BAC 1-11/402AP (PI-C1121) <ff>	Boscombe Down Aviation Collection, Old Sarum
	XX946	Panavia Tornado (P02) (8883M)	RAF Museum, stored Cosford
	XX958	SEPECAT Jaguar GR1 (9022M) [BK]	DSAE No 1 SoTT, Cosford
	XX959	SEPECAT Jaguar GR1 (8953M) [CJ]	DSAE No 1 SoTT, Cosford
	XX965	SEPECAT Jaguar GR1A (9254M) [C]	DSAE No 1 SoTT, Cosford
	XX967	SEPECAT Jaguar GR1 (9006M) [AC]	DSAE No 1 SoTT, Cosford
	XX968	SEPECAT Jaguar GR1 (9007M) [AJ]	DSAE No 1 SoTT, Cosford
	XX969	SEPECAT Jaguar GR1 (8897M) [01]	DSAE No 1 SoTT, Cosford
	XX970	SEPECAT Jaguar GR3A [EH]	DSAE No 1 SoTT, Cosford
	XX975	SEPECAT Jaguar GR1 (8905M) [07]	DSAE No 1 SoTT, Cosford
	XX976	SEPECAT Jaguar GR1 (8906M) [BD]	DSAE No 1 SoTT, Cosford
	XX977	SEPECAT Jaguar GR1 (9132M) [DL,05] <rf>	Privately owned, Sproughton
	XX979	SEPECAT Jaguar GR1A (9306M) <ff>	RAF Air Defence Radar Museum, Neatishead
	XZ103	SEPECAT Jaguar GR3A [EF]	DSAE No 1 SoTT, Cosford
	XZ104	SEPECAT Jaguar GR3A [FM]	DSAE No 1 SoTT, Cosford
	XZ106	SEPECAT Jaguar GR3A [FR]	RAF Manston History Museum
	XZ107	SEPECAT Jaguar GR3A [FH]	Privately owned, Bentwaters
	XZ109	SEPECAT Jaguar GR3A [EN]	DSAE No 1 SoTT, Cosford
	XZ112	SEPECAT Jaguar GR3A [GW]	DSAE No 1 SoTT, Cosford
	XZ113	SEPECAT Jaguar GR3 [FD,FG]	Morayvia, Kinloss
	XZ114	SEPECAT Jaguar GR3 [EO]	DSAE No 1 SoTT, Cosford
	XZ115	SEPECAT Jaguar GR3 [ER]	DSAE No 1 SoTT, Cosford
	XZ117	SEPECAT Jaguar GR3 [ES]	DSAE No 1 SoTT, Cosford
	XZ119	SEPECAT Jaguar GR1A (9266M) [FG]	National Museum of Flight, E Fortune
	XZ130	HS Harrier GR3 (9079M) [A]	Privately owned, Thorpe Wood, N Yorks
	XZ131	HS Harrier GR3 (9174M) <ff>	Privately owned, Spark Bridge, Cumbria
	XZ132	HS Harrier GR3 (9168M) [C]	Privately owned, Thorpe Wood, N Yorks
	XZ133	HS Harrier GR3 [10]	IWM Duxford
	XZ138	HS Harrier GR3 (9040M) <ff>	RAFC Cranwell, Trenchard Hall

Serial	Type (code/other identity)	Owner/operator, location or fate	Notes
XZ146	HS Harrier T4 (9281M) [S]	Harrier Heritage Centre, RAF Wittering	
XZ166	WS Lynx HAS2 <ff>	Farnborough Air Sciences Trust, stored Farnborough	
XZ170	WS Lynx AH9	DSAE SAAE, Lyneham	
XZ171	WS Lynx AH7	Army, Salisbury Plain	
XZ172	WS Lynx AH7	DSAE SAAE, Lyneham	
XZ173	WS Lynx AH7 [6] <ff>	Privately owned, Weeton, Lancs	
XZ174	WS Lynx AH7 <ff>	Defence Coll of Policing, Gosport, instructional use	
XZ175	WS Lynx AH7	Privately owned, Barby, Northants	
XZ177	Aérospatiale SA341G Gazelle (G-SFTA/XZ345) [T]	North-East Aircraft Museum, Usworth	
XZ177	WS Lynx AH7	Delta Force, Kegworth	
XZ178	WS Lynx AH7 <ff>	Bilsthorpe Paintball Park, Notts	
XZ179	WS Lynx AH7 <ff>	Privately owned, Sproughton	
XZ180	WS Lynx AH7 [C]	DSAE SAAE, Lyneham	
XZ181	WS Lynx AH1	AAC Middle Wallop Fire Section	
XZ183	WS Lynx AH7 <ff>	MoD St Athan, instructional use	
XZ184	WS Lynx AH7 [B]	AAC Middle Wallop, at main gate	
XZ187	WS Lynx AH7	DSAE SAAE, Lyneham	
XZ188	WS Lynx AH7	DSAE SAAE, Lyneham	
XZ190	WS Lynx AH7 <ff>	Army, Longmoor Camp, Hants, GI use	
XZ191	WS Lynx AH7 [R]	DSAE SAAE, Lyneham	
XZ192	WS Lynx AH7 [H]	AAC, stored St Athan	
XZ193	WS Lynx AH7 [4] <ff>	Privately owned, Weeton, Lancs	
XZ194	WS Lynx AH7 [V]	IWM Duxford	
XZ195	WS Lynx AH7 <ff>	Privately owned, Mildenhall	
XZ198	WS Lynx AH7 <ff>	Skydock, Faldingworth, Lincs	
XZ203	WS Lynx AH7 [F]	Army, Salisbury Plain	
XZ206	WS Lynx AH7 <ff>	Privately owned, Hixon, Staffs	
XZ207	WS Lynx AH7 <rf>	DSAE SAAE, Lyneham	
XZ208	WS Lynx AH7	Privately owned, Sproughton	
XZ209	WS Lynx AH7 <ff>	MoD JARTS, Boscombe Down	
XZ211	WS Lynx AH7	Bawtry Paintball Park, S Yorks	
XZ212	WS Lynx AH7 [X]	AAC Middle Wallop, GI use	
XZ213	WS Lynx AH1 (TAD 213)	Vector Aerospace Fleetlands Apprentice School	
XZ214	WS Lynx AH7 <ff>	DSAE SAAE, Lyneham	
XZ216	WS Lynx AH7 <ff>	MoD DFTDC, Manston	
XZ217	WS Lynx AH7	Privately owned, Guildford	
XZ218	WS Lynx AH7	Warfighters R6 Centre, Barby, Northants	
XZ219	WS Lynx AH7 <ff>	Army, Bramley, Hants	
XZ220	WS Lynx AH7 <ff>	Privately owned, Weeton, Lancs	
XZ222	WS Lynx AH7	DSAE SAAE, Lyneham	
XZ228	WS Lynx HAS3GMS [313]	AAC, stored Middle Wallop	
XZ229	WS Lynx HAS3GMS [360/MC]	Privately owned, Hixon, Staffs	
XZ230	WS Lynx HAS3GMS	Destroyed	
XZ232	WS Lynx HAS3GMS	Falck Nutec UK, Aberdeen, GI use	
XZ233	WS Lynx HAS3S [635] $	AAC, stored Middle Wallop	
XZ234	WS Lynx HAS3S	Privately owned, Gloucester	
XZ235	WS Lynx HAS3S(ICE) [630]	Wild Park Derbyshire, Brailsford	
XZ236	WS Lynx HMA8 [LST-1]	RN, stored St Athan	
XZ237	WS Lynx HAS3S [631]	Privately owned, Wild Park, Derbyshire	
XZ239	WS Lynx HAS3GMS [633]	Privately owned, Hixon, Staffs	
XZ245	WS Lynx HAS3GMS	Sold to Germany, February 2017	
XZ246	WS Lynx HAS3S(ICE) [434/EE]	South Yorkshire Aircraft Museum, Doncaster	
XZ248	WS Lynx HAS3S	SFDO, RNAS Culdrose	
XZ250	WS Lynx HAS3S [426/PO] $	RN, Portland, on display	
XZ252	WS Lynx HAS3S	Privately owned, Hixon, Staffs	
XZ254	WS Lynx HAS3S	Privately owned, Hixon, Staffs	
XZ255	WS Lynx HMA8SRU [454/DF]	RN, stored St Athan	
XZ257	WS Lynx HAS3S	RN Yeovilton, GI use (Wildcat ground trainer)	
XZ287	BAe Nimrod AEW3 (9140M) (fuselage)	RAF TSW, Stafford	
XZ290	WS Gazelle AH1	AAC No 665 Sqn/5 Regt, Aldergrove	
XZ292	WS Gazelle AH1	Privately owned, Stapleford Tawney	
XZ294	WS Gazelle AH1 [X]	AAC AM&SU, stored Shawbury	

Notes	Serial	Type (code/other identity)	Owner/operator, location or fate
	XZ295	WS Gazelle AH1	MoD/ETPS, Boscombe Down
	XZ296	WS Gazelle AH1 [V]	Sold as ZU-RMT, August 2017
	XZ298	WS Gazelle AH1 <ff>	AAC Middle Wallop, GI use
	XZ300	WS Gazelle AH1	Army, Bramley, Hants
	XZ303	WS Gazelle AH1	AAC MPSU, stored Middle Wallop
	XZ304	WS Gazelle AH1	Privately owned, Stapleford Tawney
	XZ305	WS Gazelle AH1 (TAD 020)	DSAE RNAESS HMS Sultan, Gosport
	XZ308	WS Gazelle AH1	QinetiQ, Boscombe Down (spares use)
	XZ311	WS Gazelle AH1 [U]	AAC MPSU, Middle Wallop
	XZ312	WS Gazelle AH1	RAF Henlow, instructional use
	XZ313	WS Gazelle AH1 <ff>	Privately owned, Shotton, Durham
	XZ314	WS Gazelle AH1 [A]	Privately owned, Stapleford Tawney
	XZ315	WS Gazelle AH1 <ff>	Privately owned, Babcary, Somerset
	XZ316	WS Gazelle AH1 [B]	DSAE SAAE, Lyneham
	XZ318	WS Gazelle AH1 (fuselage)	Tong Paintball Park, Shropshire
	XZ320	WS Gazelle AH1	AAC No 665 Sqn/5 Regt, Aldergrove
	XZ321	WS Gazelle AH1 (G-CDNS) [D]	Privately owned, Hurstbourne Tarrant, Hants
	XZ322	WS Gazelle AH1 (9283M) [N]	DSAE SAAE, Lyneham
	XZ323	WS Gazelle AH1	Currently not known
	XZ324	WS Gazelle AH1	Privately owned, Stapleford Tawney
	XZ325	WS Gazelle AH1	DSAE SAAE, Lyneham
	XZ326	WS Gazelle AH1	AAC No 667 Sqn/7 Regt, Middle Wallop
	XZ327	WS Gazelle AH1	AAC Middle Wallop (recruiting aid)
	XZ328	WS Gazelle AH1 [C]	AAC AM&SU, stored Shawbury
	XZ329	WS Gazelle AH1 (G-BZYD) [J]	Privately owned, East Garston, Bucks
	XZ330	WS Gazelle AH1 [Y]	AAC Wattisham, instructional use
	XZ331	WS Gazelle AH1 [D]	Currently not known
	XZ332	WS Gazelle AH1	DSAE SAAE, Lyneham
	XZ333	WS Gazelle AH1	DSAE SAAE, Lyneham
	XZ334	WS Gazelle AH1	AAC No 665 Sqn/5 Regt, Aldergrove
	XZ335	WS Gazelle AH1 <ff>	South Yorkshire Aviation Museum, Doncaster
	XZ337	WS Gazelle AH1 [Z]	MoD Abbey Wood, Bristol, on display
	XZ340	WS Gazelle AH1	AAC No 29 Flt, BATUS, Suffield, Canada
	XZ341	WS Gazelle AH1	AAC AM&SU, stored Shawbury
	XZ342	WS Gazelle AH1	Currently not known
	XZ343	WS Gazelle AH1	AAC AM&SU, stored Shawbury
	XZ344	WS Gazelle AH1 [Y]	Privately owned, Stapleford Tawney
	XZ345	WS Gazelle AH1 [M]	AAC No 667 Sqn/7 Regt, Middle Wallop
	XZ346	WS Gazelle AH1	AAC Middle Wallop, at main gate
	XZ356	SEPECAT Jaguar GR3A [FU]	Privately owned, Welshpool
	XZ358	SEPECAT Jaguar GR1A (9262M) [L]	DSAE No 1 SoTT, Cosford
	XZ360	SEPECAT Jaguar GR3 [FN]	Privately owned, Bentwaters
	XZ363	SEPECAT Jaguar GR1A <R> (XX824/BAPC 151) [A]	RAF M&RU, Bottesford
	XZ364	SEPECAT Jaguar GR3A <ff>	Privately owned, Tunbridge Wells
	XZ366	SEPECAT Jaguar GR3A [FC]	Privately owned, Bentwaters
	XZ367	SEPECAT Jaguar GR3 [GP]	DSAE No 1 SoTT, Cosford
	XZ368	SEPECAT Jaguar GR1 [8900M] [E]	DSAE No 1 SoTT, Cosford
	XZ369	SEPECAT Jaguar GR3A [EU]	Delta Force Paintball, Rugby
	XZ370	SEPECAT Jaguar GR1 (9004M) [JB]	DSAE No 1 SoTT, Cosford
	XZ371	SEPECAT Jaguar GR1 (8907M) [AP]	DSAE No 1 SoTT, Cosford
	XZ372	SEPECAT Jaguar GR3 [FV]	Aberdeen Airport Fire Section
	XZ374	SEPECAT Jaguar GR1 (9005M) [JC]	DSAE, stored Cosford
	XZ375	SEPECAT Jaguar GR1A (9255M) <ff>	City of Norwich Aviation Museum
	XZ377	SEPECAT Jaguar GR3A [P]	DSAE No 1 SoTT, Cosford
	XZ378	SEPECAT Jaguar GR1A [EP]	Privately owned, Topsham, Devon
	XZ382	SEPECAT Jaguar GR1 (8908M)	Cold War Jets Collection, Bruntingthorpe
	XZ383	SEPECAT Jaguar GR1 (8901M) [AF]	DSAE No 1 SoTT, Cosford
	XZ384	SEPECAT Jaguar GR1 (8954M) [BC]	DSAE No 1 SoTT, Cosford
	XZ385	SEPECAT Jaguar GR3A [FT]	Privately owned, Bentwaters
	XZ389	SEPECAT Jaguar GR1 (8946M) [BL]	DSAE No 1 SoTT, Cosford
	XZ390	SEPECAT Jaguar GR1 (9003M) [DM]	DSAE No 1 SoTT, Cosford
	XZ391	SEPECAT Jaguar GR3A [ET]	DSAE No 1 SoTT, Cosford

Serial	Type (code/other identity)	Owner/operator, location or fate	Notes
XZ392	SEPECAT Jaguar GR3A [EM]	DSAE No 1 SoTT, Cosford	
XZ394	SEPECAT Jaguar GR3	Shoreham Airport, on display	
XZ398	SEPECAT Jaguar GR3A [EQ]	DSAE No 1 SoTT, Cosford	
XZ399	SEPECAT Jaguar GR3A [EJ]	DSAE No 1 SoTT, Cosford	
XZ400	SEPECAT Jaguar GR3A [FQ]	Privately owned, Bentwaters	
XZ431	HS Buccaneer S2B (9233M) <ff>	South Yorkshire Aviation Museum, stored Doncaster	
XZ440	BAe Sea Harrier FA2 [40/DD]	SFDO, RNAS Culdrose	
XZ455	BAe Sea Harrier FA2 [001] (wreck)	Privately owned, Thorpe Wood, N Yorks	
XZ457	BAe Sea Harrier FA2 [104/VL]	Boscombe Down Aviation Collection, Old Sarum	
XZ459	BAe Sea Harrier FA2 [126]	Privately owned, Sussex	
XZ493	BAe Sea Harrier FRS1 (comp XV760) [001/N]	FAA Museum, RNAS Yeovilton	
XZ493	BAe Sea Harrier FRS1 <ff>	RN Yeovilton, Fire Section	
XZ494	BAe Sea Harrier FA2 [128]	Privately owned, Wedmore, Somerset	
XZ497	BAe Sea Harrier FA2 [126]	Privately owned, Charlwood	
XZ499	BAe Sea Harrier FA2 [003]	FAA Museum, stored Cobham Hall, RNAS Yeovilton	
XZ559	Slingsby T61F Venture T2 (G-BUEK)	Privately owned, Tibenham	
XZ570	WS61 Sea King HAS5(mod)	RN, Predannack Fire School	
XZ574	WS61 Sea King HAS6	FAA Museum, stored Cobham Hall, RNAS Yeovilton	
XZ575	WS61 Sea King HU5	Privately owned, Horsham	
XZ576	WS61 Sea King HAS6	DSAE RNAESS, HMS Sultan, Gosport	
XZ578	WS61 Sea King HU5 [30]	Privately owned, Brynrefail, Gwynedd	
XZ579	WS61 Sea King HAS6 [707/PW]	DSAE RNAESS, HMS Sultan, Gosport	
XZ580	WS61 Sea King HC6 [ZB]	DSAE RNAESS, HMS Sultan, Gosport	
XZ581	WS61 Sea King HAS6 [69/CU]	DSAE RNAESS, HMS Sultan, Gosport	
XZ585	WS61 Sea King HAR3 [A]	RAF Museum, Hendon	
XZ586	WS61 Sea King HAR3 [B]	DSAE, stored HMS Sultan, Gosport	
XZ587	WS61 Sea King HAR3 [C]	RAF St Mawgan, on display	
XZ588	WS61 Sea King HAR3 [D]	Vector Aerospace Fleetlands Apprentice School	
XZ589	WS61 Sea King HAR3 [E] $	DSAE RNAESS, HMS Sultan, Gosport	
XZ590	WS61 Sea King HAR3 [F]	DSAE, stored HMS Sultan, Gosport	
XZ591	WS61 Sea King HAR3 (fuselage)	Scrapped at Fleetlands, 2016	
XZ592	WS61 Sea King HAR3 [H]	Morayvia, Forres, Moray	
XZ594	WS61 Sea King HAR3	DSAE, stored HMS Sultan, Gosport	
XZ595	WS61 Sea King HAR3 [K]	Privately owned, Charlwood	
XZ596	WS61 Sea King HAR3	DSAE, stored HMS Sultan, Gosport	
XZ597	WS61 Sea King HAR3 [M]	Privately owned, Chard, Somerset	
XZ598	WS61 Sea King HAR3 [N]	Privately owned, Scarborough	
XZ599	WS61 Sea King HAR3 (fuselage)	Scrapped at Fleetlands, 2016	
XZ605	WS Lynx AH7	Wattisham Station Heritage Museum	
XZ606	WS Lynx AH7 [O]	Delta Force Paintball, Billericay, Essex	
XZ607	WS Lynx AH7 <ff>	MoD DFTDC, Manston	
XZ607	WS Lynx AH7 (comp XZ215)	MoD DFTDC, Manston	
XZ608	WS Lynx AH7 (fuselage)	Army Bury St Edmunds, GI use	
XZ608	WS Lynx AH7 (ZD272)[W]	Privately owned, Weeton, Lancs	
XZ609	WS Lynx AH7	Army Bury St Edmunds, GI use	
XZ611	WS Lynx AH7 <ff>	Bilsthorpe Paintball Park, Notts	
XZ612	WS Lynx AH7	Delta Force Paintball, Bovingdon	
XZ613	WS Lynx AH7 [F]	Privately owned, Belstead, Suffolk	
XZ615	WS Lynx AH7 <ff>	Currently not known	
XZ616	WS Lynx AH7	MoD/Vector Aerospace, stored Fleetlands	
XZ617	WS Lynx AH7 <ff>	DSAE SAAE, Lyneham	
XZ630	Panavia Tornado (P12) (8976M)	RAF Halton, on display	
XZ631	Panavia Tornado GR4	Yorkshire Air Museum, Elvington	
XZ642	WS Lynx AH7	DSAE SAAE, Lyneham	
XZ643	WS Lynx AH7 [C]	Privately owned, Culham, Oxon	
XZ645	WS Lynx AH7	Delta Force Paintball, Romsey, Hants	
XZ646	WS Lynx AH7 <ff>	MoD JARTS, Boscombe Down	
XZ646	WS Lynx AH7 (really XZ649)	Bristol University, instructional use	
XZ647	WS Lynx AH7 <ff>	Aberdeen Airport Fire Section	
XZ648	WS Lynx AH7 <ff>	Privately owned, Weeton, Lancs	
XZ651	WS Lynx AH7 [O]	AAC MPSU, Middle Wallop	
XZ652	WS Lynx AH7	IFTC, Durham/Tees Valley	

Notes	Serial	Type (code/other identity)	Owner/operator, location or fate
	XZ653	WS Lynx AH7	DSAE SAAE, Lyneham
	XZ654	WS Lynx AH7	Shannon Aviation Museum, Eire
	XZ655	WS Lynx AH7 [3] <ff>	Privately owned, Weeton, Lancs
	XZ661	WS Lynx AH7 [V]	Army, Bramley, Hants
	XZ663	WS Lynx AH7 <ff>	Privately owned, Hixon, Staffs
	XZ664	WS Lynx AH7	Warfighters R6 Centre, Barby, Northants
	XZ665	WS Lynx AH7	Privately owned, Barby, Northants
	XZ666	WS Lynx AH7	DSAE SAAE, Lyneham
	XZ668	WS Lynx AH7 [UN] <ff>	Privately owned, stored Cranfield
	XZ670	WS Lynx AH7 [A]	RNAS Yeovilton, on display
	XZ671	WS Lynx AH7 <ff>	Leonardo MW, Yeovil, instructional use
	XZ672	WS Lynx AH7 <ff>	AAC Middle Wallop Fire Section
	XZ673	WS Lynx AH7 [5]	Privately owned, Weeton, Lancs
	XZ674	WS Lynx AH7 [T]	RNAS Yeovilton Fire Section
	XZ675	WS Lynx AH7 [H]	Museum of Army Flying, Middle Wallop
	XZ676	WS Lynx AH7 [N]	Privately owned, Weeton, Lancs
	XZ677	WS Lynx AH7 <ff>	Army, Longmoor Camp, Hants, GI use
	XZ678	WS Lynx AH7 <ff>	Privately owned, Sproughton
	XZ679	WS Lynx AH7 [W]	DSAE SAAE, Lyneham
	XZ680	WS Lynx AH7 <ff>	Privately owned, Weeton, Lancs
	XZ689	WS Lynx HMA8SRU [314]	RN, stored St Athan
	XZ690	WS Lynx HMA8SRU [640]	Delta Force Paintball, West Glasgow
	XZ691	WS Lynx HMA8SRU [310]	RN, stored St Athan
	XZ692	WS Lynx HMA8SRU [764/SN] $	DSAE RNAESS, *HMS Sultan*, Gosport
	XZ693	WS Lynx HAS3S [311]	Wild Park Derbyshire, Brailsford
	XZ696	WS Lynx HAS3GMS [633]	Privately owned, Hixon, Staffs
	XZ697	WS Lynx HMA8SRU [313]	MoD/Vector Aerospace, Fleetlands
	XZ698	WS Lynx HMA8SRU [316]	*Rebuilt as ZD249, 2017*
	XZ699	WS Lynx HAS2	FAA Museum, RNAS Yeovilton
	XZ719	WS Lynx HMA8SRU [64]	RNAS Yeovilton Fire Section
	XZ720	WS Lynx HAS3GMS [410/GC]	FAA Museum, RNAS Yeovilton
	XZ721	WS Lynx HAS3GMS [322]	East Midlands Airport Aeropark
	XZ722	WS Lynx HMA8SRU [671]	*Sold to the US, December 2017*
	XZ723	WS Lynx HMA8SRU [672]	Delta Force Paintball, Thornbury, Glos
	XZ725	WS Lynx HMA8SRU [415/MM]	RN, stored St Athan
	XZ726	WS Lynx HMA8SRU [316]	School of Maritime Survival *HMS Raleigh*, Plymouth
	XZ727	WS Lynx HAS3S [634]	Delta Force Paintball, Romsey, Hants
	XZ728	WS Lynx HMA8 [326/AW]	RNAS Yeovilton, on display
	XZ729	WS Lynx HMA8SRU [425/DT]	RN, stored St Athan
	XZ730	WS Lynx HAS3S	Privately owned, Hixon, Staffs
	XZ731	WS Lynx HMA8SRU [311/VL]	AAC, stored Middle Wallop
	XZ732	WS Lynx HMA8SRU [315/VL]	RN, stored St Athan
	XZ735	WS Lynx HAS3GMS <ff>	Privately owned, Sproughton
	XZ736	WS Lynx HMA8SRU [815]	RN Yeovilton, GI use
	XZ791	Northrop Shelduck D1	Davidstow Airfield & Cornwall at War Museum
	XZ795	Northrop Shelduck D1	Museum of Army Flying, Middle Wallop
	XZ920	WS61 Sea King HU5 [24]	DSAE, stored *HMS Sultan*, Gosport
	XZ921	WS61 Sea King HAS6 [269/N]	Mini Moos Farm, Edmondsley, Durham
	XZ922	WS61 Sea King HC6 [ZA]	DSAE RNAESS, *HMS Sultan*, Gosport
	XZ930	WS Gazelle HT3 (A2713)	DSAE RNAESS, *HMS Sultan*, Gosport
	XZ933	WS Gazelle HT3 (*XZ936*/G-CGJZ)	Privately owned, Hurstbourne Tarrant, Hants
	XZ934	WS Gazelle HT3 (G-CBSI)	Privately owned, Hurstbourne Tarrant, Hants
	XZ935	WS Gazelle HCC4 (9332M)	DSAE SAAE, Lyneham
	XZ936	WS Gazelle HT3 [6]	MoD, stored Boscombe Down (damaged)
	XZ939	WS Gazelle HT3	MoD/ETPS, Boscombe Down
	XZ941	WS Gazelle HT3 (9301M) [B]	*Currently not known*
	XZ964	BAe Harrier GR3 [D]	Royal Engineers Museum, Chatham
	XZ966	BAe Harrier GR3 (9221M) [G]	MoD DFTDC, Manston
	XZ968	BAe Harrier GR3 (9222M) [3G]	Muckleborough Collection, Weybourne
	XZ969	BAe Harrier GR3 [69/DD]	RN, Predannack Fire School
	XZ971	BAe Harrier GR3 (9219M)	HQ DSDA, Donnington, Shropshire, on display
	XZ987	BAe Harrier GR3 (9185M) [C]	RAF Stafford, at main gate

Serial	Type (code/other identity)	Owner/operator, location or fate	Notes
XZ990	BAe Harrier GR3 <ff>	*Currently not known*	
XZ990	BAe Harrier GR3 <rf>	RAF Wittering, derelict	
XZ991	BAe Harrier GR3 (9162M) [AD]	DSAE Cosford, on display	
XZ993	BAe Harrier GR3 (9240M) <ff>	Privately owned, Welshpool	
XZ994	BAe Harrier GR3 (9170M) [U]	MoD JARTS, Boscombe Down	
XZ995	BAe Harrier GR3 (9220M/G-CBGK) [3G]	Privately owned, Dolly's Grove, Co Dublin, Eire	
XZ996	BAe Harrier GR3 [96/DD]	Privately owned, Bentwaters	
XZ997	BAe Harrier GR3 (9122M) [V]	RAF Museum, Hendon	
ZA101	BAe Hawk 100 (G-HAWK)	BAE Systems Academy for Skills & Knowledge, Samlesbury	
ZA105	WS61 Sea King HAR3 [Q]	DSAE, stored *HMS Sultan*, Gosport	
ZA110	BAe Jetstream T2 (F-BTMI) [563/CU]	Aberdeen Airport Fire Section	
ZA111	BAe Jetstream T2 (9Q-CTC) [565/CU]	RN, Predannack Fire School	
ZA126	WS61 Sea King ASaC7 [191]	RN No 849 NAS, Culdrose	
ZA127	WS61 Sea King HAS6 [509/CU]	Privately owned, Thornhill, Stirlingshire	
ZA128	WS61 Sea King HAS6 [010]	DSAE No 1 SoTT, Cosford	
ZA130	WS61 Sea King HU5 [19]	Privately owned, Charlwood	
ZA131	WS61 Sea King HAS6 [271/N]	DSAE RNAESS, *HMS Sultan*, Gosport	
ZA133	WS61 Sea King HAS6 [831/CU]	DSAE RNAESS, *HMS Sultan*, Gosport	
ZA134	WS61 Sea King HU5 [25]	DSAE, stored *HMS Sultan*, Gosport	
ZA135	WS61 Sea King HAS6	Privately owned, Woodperry, Oxon	
ZA136	WS61 Sea King HAS6 [018]	Mayhem Paintball, Abridge, Essex	
ZA137	WS61 Sea King HU5 [20]	DSAE, stored *HMS Sultan*, Gosport	
ZA144	BAe VC10 K2 (G-ARVC) <ff>	*Scrapped*	
ZA147	BAe VC10 K3 (5H-MMT) [F]	Privately owned, Bruntingthorpe	
ZA148	BAe VC10 K3 (5Y-ADA) [G]	Cornwall Aviation Heritage Centre, Newquay	
ZA150	BAe VC10 K3 (5H-MOG) [J]	Brooklands Museum, Dunsfold	
ZA166	WS61 Sea King HU5	HeliOperations Ltd, Portland	
ZA167	WS61 Sea King HU5 [22/CU]	DSAE RNAESS, *HMS Sultan*, Gosport	
ZA168	WS61 Sea King HAS6 [830/CU]	DSAE RNAESS, *HMS Sultan*, Gosport	
ZA169	WS61 Sea King HAS6 [515/CW]	DSAE No 1 SoTT, Cosford	
ZA170	WS61 Sea King HAS5	*Currently not known*	
ZA175	BAe Sea Harrier FA2	Norfolk & Suffolk Avn Museum, Flixton	
ZA176	BAe Sea Harrier FA2 [126/R]	Newark Air Museum, Winthorpe	
ZA195	BAe Sea Harrier FA2	Tangmere Military Aviation Museum	
ZA209	Short MATS-B	Museum of Army Flying, Middle Wallop	
ZA220	Short MATS-B (ZA242)	Boscombe Down Aviation Collection, Old Sarum	
ZA242	Short MATS-B (ZA220)	*Repainted as ZA220*	
ZA250	BAe Harrier T52 (G-VTOL)	Brooklands Museum, Weybridge	
ZA267	Panavia Tornado F2 (9284M)	RAF, stored Marham	
ZA291	WS61 Sea King HC4 [N]	Mini Moos Farm, Edmondsley, Durham	
ZA292	WS61 Sea King HC4 (fuselage)	*Scrapped at Fleetlands, 2016*	
ZA293	WS61 Sea King HC4 (fuselage)	*Scrapped at Fleetlands, 2016*	
ZA295	WS61 Sea King HC4	*To Pakistan, December 2017*	
ZA296	WS61 Sea King HC4 [Q]	*Dismantled at Fleetlands, 2017*	
ZA297	WS61 Sea King HC4 (fuselage)	*Scrapped at Fleetlands, 2016*	
ZA298	WS61 Sea King HC4 (G-BJNM) [Y]	FAA Museum, RNAS Yeovilton	
ZA299	WS61 Sea King HC4 [D]	*Sunk at Vobster Quay, Somerset, 23 January 2018*	
ZA312	WS61 Sea King HC4 [E]	Privately owned, Charlwood	
ZA313	WS61 Sea King HC4 [M]	Mini Moos Farm, Edmondsley, Durham	
ZA314	WS61 Sea King HC4 [WT]	DSAE, stored *HMS Sultan*, Gosport	
ZA319	Panavia Tornado GR1 (9315M)	DSDA, Arncott, Oxon, on display	
ZA320	Panavia Tornado GR1 (9314M) [TAW]	DSAE No 1 SoTT, Cosford	
ZA323	Panavia Tornado GR1 [TAZ]	DSAE No 1 SoTT, Cosford	
ZA325	Panavia Tornado GR1 <ff>	RAF Manston History Museum	
ZA325	Panavia Tornado GR1 [TAX] <rf>	RAF AM&SU, stored Shawbury	
ZA326	Panavia Tornado GR1P	Privately owned, Bruntingthorpe	
ZA327	Panavia Tornado GR1 <ff>	BAE Systems, Warton	
ZA328	Panavia Tornado GR1	BAE Systems, Samlesbury	
ZA353	Panavia Tornado GR1 [B-53]	Privately owned, Thorpe Wood, N Yorks	
ZA354	Panavia Tornado GR1	Yorkshire Air Museum, Elvington	

Notes	Serial	Type (code/other identity)	Owner/operator, location or fate
	ZA355	Panavia Tornado GR1 (9310M) [TAA]	Swansea Airport, on display
	ZA356	Panavia Tornado GR1 <ff>	RAF Tornado Maintenance School, Marham
	ZA357	Panavia Tornado GR1 [TTV]	DSAE No 1 SoTT, Cosford
	ZA359	Panavia Tornado GR1	Privately owned, Thorpe Wood, N Yorks
	ZA360	Panavia Tornado GR1 (9318M) <ff>	RAF Marham, instructional use
	ZA362	Panavia Tornado GR1 [TR]	Highland Aviation Museum, Inverness
	ZA369	Panavia Tornado GR4A [003]	RAF Leeming, RTP
	ZA370	Panavia Tornado GR4A [004]	RAF Leeming, RTP
	ZA372	Panavia Tornado GR4A [006]	Scrapped at Leeming, 2017
	ZA375	Panavia Tornado GR1 (9335M) [AJ-W]	Scrapped at Marham
	ZA398	Panavia Tornado GR4A $	RAF, St Mawgan
	ZA399	Panavia Tornado GR1 (9316M) [AJ-C]	Privately owned, Knutsford, Cheshire
	ZA406	Panavia Tornado GR4 [015]	RAF Leeming, RTP
	ZA407	Panavia Tornado GR1 (9336M) [AJ-N]	RAF Marham, on display
	ZA409	Panavia Tornado GR1 [VII]	Scrapped
	ZA411	Panavia Tornado GR1	Scrapped
	ZA447	Panavia Tornado GR4 [019]	RAF Marham (wfu)
	ZA449	Panavia Tornado GR4 [020]	RAF CMU, Marham
	ZA450	Panavia Tornado GR1 (9317M) [TH]	DSAE No 1 SoTT, Cosford
	ZA452	Panavia Tornado GR4 [021]	Midland Air Museum, Coventry
	ZA453	Panavia Tornado GR4 [022]	RAF Leeming, RTP
	ZA457	Panavia Tornado GR1 [AJ-J]	RAF Museum, Hendon
	ZA458	Panavia Tornado GR4 [024]	RAF Leeming, RTP
	ZA459	Panavia Tornado GR4 [025]	RAF, stored Marham
	ZA462	Panavia Tornado GR4 [027]	RAF Leeming, RTP
	ZA463	Panavia Tornado GR4 [028]	RAF Marham, WLT
	ZA465	Panavia Tornado GR1 [FF]	IWM Duxford
	ZA469	Panavia Tornado GR4 [029] $	RAF Marham (wfu)
	ZA472	Panavia Tornado GR4 [031]	RAF No 31 Sqn, Marham
	ZA473	Panavia Tornado GR4 [032]	RAF TASF, Marham
	ZA474	Panavia Tornado GR1 (9312M)	Scrapped
	ZA475	Panavia Tornado GR1 (9311M) [AJ-G]	RAF Lossiemouth, on display
	ZA541	Panavia Tornado GR4 [034]	Scrapped at Leeming, 2017
	ZA542	Panavia Tornado GR4 [035]	RAF No 31 Sqn, Marham
	ZA543	Panavia Tornado GR4 [036]	RAF No 31 Sqn, Marham
	ZA546	Panavia Tornado GR4 [038]	RAF No 9 Sqn, Marham
	ZA548	Panavia Tornado GR4 [040] $	RAF Leeming, RTP
	ZA549	Panavia Tornado GR4 [041]	RAF Marham (wfu)
	ZA550	Panavia Tornado GR4 [042]	RAF Leeming, RTP
	ZA551	Panavia Tornado GR4 [043]	Currently not known
	ZA553	Panavia Tornado GR4 [045]	RAF No 31 Sqn, Marham
	ZA554	Panavia Tornado GR4 [046]	RAF No 31 Sqn, Marham
	ZA556	Panavia Tornado GR4 [047]	RAF No 12 Sqn, Marham
	ZA556	Panavia Tornado GR1 <R> (ZA368/BAPC 155) [Z]	RAF M&RU, Bottesford
	ZA559	Panavia Tornado GR4 [049]	RAF Leeming, RTP
	ZA560	Panavia Tornado GR4 [EB-Q]	RAF Marham (wfu)
	ZA585	Panavia Tornado GR4 [054]	RAF No 31 Sqn, Marham
	ZA587	Panavia Tornado GR4 [055]	RAF CMU, Marham
	ZA588	Panavia Tornado GR4 [056]	RAF No 31 Sqn, Marham
	ZA591	Panavia Tornado GR4 [058]	RAF Marham (wfu)
	ZA592	Panavia Tornado GR4 [059]	Scrapped at Leeming, 2017
	ZA594	Panavia Tornado GR4 [060]	Scrapped at Leeming, 2017
	ZA597	Panavia Tornado GR4 [063]	RAF No 31 Sqn, Marham
	ZA601	Panavia Tornado GR4 [066]	RAF No 12 Sqn, Marham
	ZA602	Panavia Tornado GR4 [F] $	Scrapped at Leeming, 2017
	ZA607	Panavia Tornado GR4 [EB-X]	RAF Marham (wfu)
	ZA611	Panavia Tornado GR4 [073]	RAF Marham (wfu)
	ZA612	Panavia Tornado GR4 [074]	RAF No 31 Sqn, Marham
	ZA613	Panavia Tornado GR4 [075]	RAF CMU, Marham
	ZA614	Panavia Tornado GR4 [076]	RAF No 31 Sqn, Marham
	ZA630	Slingsby T61F Venture T2 (G-BUGL)	Privately owned, Tibenham
	ZA634	Slingsby T61F Venture T2 (G-BUHA) [C]	Privately owned, Saltby, Leics

Serial	Type (code/other identity)	Owner/operator, location or fate	Notes
ZA652	Slingsby T61F Venture T2 (G-BUDC)	Privately owned, Enstone	
ZA656	Slingsby T61F Venture T2 (G-BTWC)	Privately owned, Nympsfield	
ZA665	Slingsby T61F Venture T2 (G-BVKK)	Privately owned, Saltby, Leics	
ZA670	B-V Chinook HC4 (N37010)	RAF No 18 Sqn, Odiham	
ZA671	B-V Chinook HC4 (N37011) [AB]	RAF No 18 Sqn, Odiham	
ZA674	B-V Chinook HC4 (N37019)	MoD/Vector Aerospace, Fleetlands	
ZA675	B-V Chinook HC4 (N37020) [AE]	RAF No 28 Sqn, Benson	
ZA677	B-V Chinook HC4 (N37022) [AF]	RAF No 28 Sqn, Benson	
ZA678	B-V Chinook HC1 (N37023/9229M) [EZ] (wreck)	RAF Odiham, BDRT	
ZA679	B-V Chinook HC4 (N37025) [AG]	RAF No 28 Sqn, Benson	
ZA680	B-V Chinook HC4 (N37026) [AH]	MoD/Vector Aerospace, Fleetlands	
ZA681	B-V Chinook HC6A (N37027) [AI]	MoD/Boeing/QinetiQ, Boscombe Down (conversion)	
ZA682	B-V Chinook HC6A (N37029) [AJ]	MoD/Boeing/QinetiQ, Boscombe Down (conversion)	
ZA683	B-V Chinook HC6A (N37030) $	MoD/Boeing/QinetiQ, Boscombe Down (conversion)	
ZA684	B-V Chinook HC6A (N37031) [AL]	MoD/Boeing/QinetiQ, Boscombe Down (conversion)	
ZA704	B-V Chinook HC4 (N37033)	MoD/Vector Aerospace, Fleetlands	
ZA705	B-V Chinook HC4 (N37035) [AN]	RAF No 28 Sqn, Benson	
ZA707	B-V Chinook HC4 (N37040) [AO]	RAF No 27 Sqn, Odiham	
ZA708	B-V Chinook HC4 (N37042) [AP]	MoD/Vector Aerospace, Fleetlands	
ZA710	B-V Chinook HC4 (N37044)	RAF No 18 Sqn, Odiham	
ZA711	B-V Chinook HC4 (N37046) $	RAF No 18 Sqn, Odiham	
ZA712	B-V Chinook HC4 (N37047) [W] $	MoD/Vector Aerospace, Fleetlands	
ZA713	B-V Chinook HC4 (N37048)	RAF No 27 Sqn, Odiham	
ZA714	B-V Chinook HC4 (N37051)	RAF No 28 Sqn, Benson	
ZA717	B-V Chinook HC1 (N37056/9238M) (wreck)	Newark Air Museum, Winthorpe	
ZA718	B-V Chinook HC4 (N37058) [BN]	MoD/Vector Aerospace, Fleetlands	
ZA720	B-V Chinook HC4 (N37060)	RAF No 18 Sqn, Odiham	
ZA726	WS Gazelle AH1 [F1]	Privately owned, Stapleford Tawney	
ZA726	WS Gazelle AH1 (XW851/G-CIEY)	Privately owned, Escrick, N Yorks	
ZA728	WS Gazelle AH1 [E]	Privately owned, Stapleford Tawney	
ZA729	WS Gazelle AH1	AAC Wattisham, BDRT	
ZA730	WS Gazelle AH1 (G-FUKM) <ff>	Privately owned, Hurstbourne Tarrant, Hants	
ZA731	WS Gazelle AH1	AAC No 29 Flt, BATUS, Suffield, Canada	
ZA735	WS Gazelle AH1	DSAE SAAE, Lyneham	
ZA736	WS Gazelle AH1	AAC No 29 Flt, BATUS, Suffield, Canada	
ZA737	WS Gazelle AH1	Museum of Army Flying, Middle Wallop	
ZA766	WS Gazelle AH1	AAC No 667 Sqn/7 Regt, Middle Wallop	
ZA768	WS Gazelle AH1 [F] (wreck)	*Scrapped*	
ZA769	WS Gazelle AH1 [K]	DSAE SAAE, Lyneham	
ZA771	WS Gazelle AH1	DSAE No 1 SoTT, Cosford	
ZA772	WS Gazelle AH1	AAC No 665 Sqn/5 Regt, Aldergrove	
ZA773	WS Gazelle AH1 [F]	AAC AM&SU, stored Shawbury	
ZA774	WS Gazelle AH1	Privately owned, Babcary, Somerset	
ZA775	WS Gazelle AH1	MoD/Vector Aerospace, Fleetlands	
ZA776	WS Gazelle AH1 [F]	Privately owned, Stapleford Tawney	
ZA804	WS Gazelle HT3	Privately owned, Solstice Park, Amesbury, Wilts	
ZA935	WS Puma HC2	RAF No 28 Sqn/No 33 Sqn/No 230 Sqn, Benson	
ZA936	WS Puma HC2	RAF No 28 Sqn/No 33 Sqn/No 230 Sqn, Benson	
ZA937	WS Puma HC1	*Currently not known*	
ZA939	WS Puma HC2	RAF No 28 Sqn/No 33 Sqn/No 230 Sqn, Benson	
ZA940	WS Puma HC2 (F-ZWBZ)	RAF/Airbus, Romania	
ZA947	Douglas Dakota C3	RAF BBMF, Coningsby	
ZB116	BAE Systems Hawk Mk.165	*To Saudi Arabia as 7907, 14 June 2017*	
ZB118	BAE Systems Hawk Mk.165	*To Saudi Arabia as 7909, 5 December 2017*	
ZB119	BAE Systems Hawk Mk.165	*To Saudi Arabia as 2110, 13 November 2017*	
ZB120	BAE Systems Hawk Mk.165	*To Saudi Arabia as 2111, 14 June 2017*	
ZB121	BAE Systems Hawk Mk.165	*To Saudi Arabia as 7910, 4 September 2017*	
ZB122	BAE Systems Hawk Mk.165	*To Saudi Arabia as 7911, 13 November 2017*	
ZB123	BAE Systems Hawk Mk.166	*To RAFO as 161, 25 September 2017*	
ZB124	BAE Systems Hawk Mk.166	*To RAFO as 162, 24 July 2017*	
ZB125	BAE Systems Hawk Mk.166	*To RAFO as 163, 24 July 2017*	

BRITISH MILITARY AIRCRAFT MARKINGS

Notes	Serial	Type (code/other identity)	Owner/operator, location or fate
	ZB126	BAE Systems Hawk Mk.166	*To RAFO as 164, 25 September 2017*
	ZB127	BAE Systems Hawk Mk.166	*To RAFO as 165, 30 October 2017*
	ZB128	BAE Systems Hawk Mk.166	*To RAFO as 166, 30 October 2017*
	ZB129	BAE Systems Hawk Mk.166	*To RAFO as 167, 4 December 2017*
	ZB130	BAE Systems Hawk Mk.166	*To RAFO as 168, 4 December 2017*
	ZB500	WS Lynx 800 (G-LYNX/ZA500)	The Helicopter Museum, Weston-super-Mare
	ZB506	WS61 Sea King Mk 4X	Privately owned, Horsham
	ZB507	WS61 Sea King HC4 [F]	*Currently not known*
	ZB601	BAe Harrier T4 (fuselage)	Privately owned, Selby, N Yorks
	ZB603	BAe Harrier T8 [T03/DD]	SFDO, RNAS Culdrose
	ZB604	BAe Harrier T8 [722]	FAA Museum, stored Cobham Hall, RNAS Yeovilton
	ZB615	SEPECAT Jaguar T2A	DSAE No 1 SoTT, Cosford
	ZB625	WS Gazelle HT3	MoD/ETPS, Boscombe Down
	ZB627	WS Gazelle HT3 (G-CBSK) [A]	Privately owned, Hurstbourne Tarrant, Hants
	ZB646	WS Gazelle HT2 (G-CBGZ) [59/CU]	Privately owned, Knebworth
	ZB647	WS Gazelle HT2 (G-CBSF) [40]	Privately owned, Hurstbourne Tarrant, Hants
	ZB665	WS Gazelle AH1	AAC No 665 Sqn/5 Regt, Aldergrove
	ZB667	WS Gazelle AH1	AAC, stored Middle Wallop
	ZB668	WS Gazelle AH1 (TAD 015)	DSAE SAAE, Lyneham
	ZB669	WS Gazelle AH1	AAC No 665 Sqn/5 Regt, Aldergrove
	ZB670	WS Gazelle AH1	*Currently not known*
	ZB671	WS Gazelle AH1	AAC No 29 Flt, BATUS, Suffield, Canada
	ZB672	WS Gazelle AH1	Army Training Regiment, Winchester
	ZB673	WS Gazelle AH1 [P]	Privately owned, Stapleford Tawney
	ZB674	WS Gazelle AH1	MoD/Vector Aerospace, Fleetlands
	ZB677	WS Gazelle AH1 [5B]	MoD/QinetiQ, Boscombe Down
	ZB678	WS Gazelle AH1	AAC No 665 Sqn/5 Regt, Aldergrove
	ZB679	WS Gazelle AH1	AAC 7 Regt Conversion Flt, Middle Wallop
	ZB683	WS Gazelle AH1	AAC No 665 Sqn/5 Regt, Aldergrove
	ZB684	WS Gazelle AH1	RAF JADTEU, Brize Norton, instructional use
	ZB686	WS Gazelle AH1 <ff>	The Helicopter Museum, Weston-super-Mare
	ZB689	WS Gazelle AH1	AAC No 665 Sqn/5 Regt, Aldergrove
	ZB690	WS Gazelle AH1	MoD/Vector Aerospace, Fleetlands
	ZB691	WS Gazelle AH1 [S]	AAC 7 Regt Conversion Flt, Middle Wallop
	ZB692	WS Gazelle AH1 [Y]	AAC 7 Regt Conversion Flt, Middle Wallop
	ZB693	WS Gazelle AH1	AAC No 665 Sqn/5 Regt, Aldergrove
	ZD230	BAC Super VC10 K4 (G-ASGA) <ff>	Privately owned, Crondall, Hants
	ZD240	BAC Super VC10 K4 (G-ASGL) <ff>	Privately owned, Crondall, Hants
	ZD241	BAC Super VC10 K4 (G-ASGM) [N]	Privately owned, Bruntingthorpe
	ZD242	BAC Super VC10 K4 (G-ASGP) <ff>	JARTS, Boscombe Down
	ZD249	WS Lynx HAS3S <rf>	*Rebuilt with cabin of XZ698, 2017*
	ZD249	WS Lynx HMA8SRU (XZ698) (comp ZD249) [316]	Delta Force Paintball, Edinburgh
	ZD250	WS Lynx HAS3S [636]	RAF Henlow, instructional use
	ZD251	WS Lynx HAS3S	Privately owned, Hixon, Staffs
	ZD252	WS Lynx HMA8SRU [312/VL]	AAC, stored Middle Wallop
	ZD254	WS Lynx HAS3S [305]	DSAE AESS, HMS Sultan, Gosport
	ZD255	WS Lynx HAS3GMS [635]	Bawtry Paintball Park, S Yorks
	ZD257	WS Lynx HMA8SRU [302/VL]	AAC MPSU, Middle Wallop
	ZD258	WS Lynx HMA8SRU [365]	Privately owned, Bentwaters
	ZD259	WS Lynx HMA8SRU [474/RM]	RN, stored St Athan
	ZD260	WS Lynx HMA8SRU [313/VL]	RN, stored St Athan
	ZD261	WS Lynx HMA8SRU [314]	RN, stored St Athan
	ZD262	WS Lynx HMA8SRU [316]	AAC MPSU, Middle Wallop
	ZD263	WS Lynx HAS3S [632]	Bawtry Paintball Park, S Yorks
	ZD264	WS Lynx HAS3GMS [407] (fuselage)	Air Defence Collection, Wilts
	ZD265	WS Lynx HMA8SRU [302]	AAC Middle Wallop, GI use
	ZD266	WS Lynx HMA8SRU [673]	Bradwell Bay Military & Science Museum, Essex
	ZD267	WS Lynx HMA8 (comp XZ672) [LST-2]	RN, stored St Athan
	ZD268	WS Lynx HMA8SRU [366/YB]	RN, stored St Athan
	ZD273	WS Lynx AH7 [E]	Territorial Army, Bury St Edmunds, Suffolk
	ZD274	WS Lynx AH7 [M]	Privately owned, Sproughton

Serial	Type (code/other identity)	Owner/operator, location or fate	Notes
ZD276	WS Lynx AH7	Mayhem Paintball, Abridge, Essex	
ZD278	WS Lynx AH7 [F]	Delta Force, Liverpool	
ZD279	WS Lynx AH7 <ff>	Privately owned, Hixon, Staffs	
ZD280	WS Lynx AH7	Farnborough Air Sciences Trust, Farnborough	
ZD281	WS Lynx AH7 [K]	Privately owned, Willenhall, Staffs	
ZD283	WS Lynx AH7 <ff>	Privately owned,	
ZD284	WS Lynx AH7 [K]	Privately owned, Corley Moor, Warks	
ZD285	WS Lynx AH7	QinetiQ Apprentice Training School, Boscombe Down	
ZD318	BAe Harrier GR7A	Harrier Heritage Centre, RAF Wittering	
ZD353	BAe Harrier GR5 (fuselage)	Sold to the USA, March 2017	
ZD412	BAe Harrier GR5 (fuselage)	Privately owned, Sproughton	
ZD433	BAe Harrier GR9A [45A]	FAA Museum, RNAS Yeovilton	
ZD461	BAe Harrier GR9A [51A]	IWM London, Lambeth	
ZD462	BAe Harrier GR7 (9302M) [52]	Privately owned, Malmesbury, Glos	
ZD465	BAe Harrier GR9 [55]	DSAE AESS, HMS Sultan, Gosport	
ZD469	BAe Harrier GR7A	RAF Wittering, on display	
ZD476	WS61 Sea King HC4 [WZ]	Privately owned, Colsterworth, Leics	
ZD477	WS61 Sea King HC4 [E]	East Midlands Airport Aeropark	
ZD478	WS61 Sea King HC4 [J]	Privately owned, Hixon, Staffs	
ZD479	WS61 Sea King HC4 [WQ]	DSAE RNAESS, HMS Sultan, Gosport	
ZD480	WS61 Sea King HC4 [J]	Vector Aerospace, Fleetlands, on display	
ZD559	WS Lynx AH5X	QinetiQ Apprentice Training School, Boscombe Down	
ZD560	WS Lynx AH7	Privately owned, Hants	
ZD565	WS Lynx HMA8SRU [404/IR]	Delta Force Paintball, Cardiff	
ZD566	WS Lynx HMA8SRU [305]	Privately owned,	
ZD574	B-V Chinook HC6A (N37077) [DB]	MoD/Boeing/QinetiQ, Boscombe Down (conversion)	
ZD575	B-V Chinook HC4 (N37078) [DC]	RAF No 27 Sqn, Odiham	
ZD578	BAe Sea Harrier FA2 [000,122]	RNAS Yeovilton, at main gate	
ZD579	BAe Sea Harrier FA2 [79/DD]	SFDO, RNAS Culdrose	
ZD581	BAe Sea Harrier FA2 [124]	RN, Predannack Fire School	
ZD582	BAe Sea Harrier FA2 [002/N]	Privately owned, Banbury, Oxon	
ZD607	BAe Sea Harrier FA2	DSDA, Arncott, Oxon, preserved	
ZD610	BAe Sea Harrier FA2 [714,002/N]	Aerospace Bristol, Filton	
ZD611	BAe Sea Harrier FA2 [001]	RN, Portsmouth, preserved	
ZD612	BAe Sea Harrier FA2 [724]	Privately owned, Topsham, Devon	
ZD613	BAe Sea Harrier FA2 [127/R]	Privately owned, Cross Green, Leeds	
ZD614	BAe Sea Harrier FA2	Privately owned, Lymington, Hants	
ZD620	BAe 125 CC3	Bournemouth Aviation Museum	
ZD621	BAe 125 CC3	RAF Northolt, on display	
ZD625	WS61 Sea King HC4 [P]	Mini Moos Farm, Edmondsley, Durham	
ZD626	WS61 Sea King HC4 (fuselage)	Scrapped at Fleetlands, 2016	
ZD627	WS61 Sea King HC4 <ff>	Privately owned, Bruntingthorpe	
ZD630	WS61 Sea King HAS6 [012/L]	DSAE RNAESS, HMS Sultan, Gosport	
ZD631	WS61 Sea King HAS6 [66] (fuselage)	Privately owned, St Agnes, Cornwall	
ZD634	WS61 Sea King HAS6 [503]	DSAE AESS, HMS Sultan, Gosport	
ZD636	WS61 Sea King ASaC7 [182/CU]	DSAE, stored HMS Sultan, Gosport	
ZD637	WS61 Sea King HAS6 [700/PW]	DSAE RNAESS, HMS Sultan, Gosport	
ZD667	BAe Harrier GR3 (9201M) [U]	Bentwaters Cold War Museum	
ZD703	BAe 125 CC3	Privately owned, Shepton Mallet	
ZD704	BAe 125 CC3	MoD DFTDC, Manston	
ZD710	Panavia Tornado GR1 <ff>	Privately owned, Hawarden	
ZD711	Panavia Tornado GR4 [079]	RAF Marham (wfu)	
ZD713	Panavia Tornado GR4 [081]	RAF Leeming, RTP	
ZD715	Panavia Tornado GR4 [083]	RAF Cosford, GI use	
ZD716	Panavia Tornado GR4 [084]	RAF No 9 Sqn, Marham	
ZD739	Panavia Tornado GR4 [087]	RAF Leeming, RTP	
ZD741	Panavia Tornado GR4 [LS-F] $	RAF Leeming, RTP	
ZD742	Panavia Tornado GR4 [090]	RAF Leeming, RTP	
ZD744	Panavia Tornado GR4 [092]	RAF No 9 Sqn, Marham	
ZD792	Panavia Tornado GR4 [100]	RAF No 31 Sqn, Marham	
ZD793	Panavia Tornado GR4 [101]	DSAE No 1 SoTT, Cosford	
ZD848	Panavia Tornado GR4 [109]	RAF CMU, Marham	

Notes	Serial	Type (code/other identity)	Owner/operator, location or fate
	ZD849	Panavia Tornado GR4 [110]	RAF No 31 Sqn, Marham
	ZD851	Panavia Tornado GR4 [112]	*Scrapped at Leeming, 2017*
	ZD890	Panavia Tornado GR4 [113]	RAF Leeming, RTP
	ZD899	Panavia Tornado F2	Gr Manchester Fire & Rescue Training Centre, Bury
	ZD902	Panavia Tornado F2A(TIARA)	Privately owned, Church Fenton
	ZD906	Panavia Tornado F2 (comp ZE294) <ff>	*Scrapped*
	ZD932	Panavia Tornado F2 (comp ZE255) (9308M) (fuselage)	Privately owned, Thorpe Wood, N Yorks
	ZD936	Panavia Tornado F2 (comp ZE251) <ff>	Boscombe Down Aviation Collection, Old Sarum
	ZD938	Panavia Tornado F2 (comp ZE295) <ff>	South Yorkshire Aircraft Museum, Doncaster
	ZD939	Panavia Tornado F2 (comp ZE292) <ff>	DSAE No 1 SoTT, Cosford, instructional use
	ZD948	Lockheed TriStar KC1 (G-BFCA/N304CS)	Privately owned, Bruntingthorpe
	ZD951	Lockheed TriStar K1 (G-BFCD/N309CS) $	Privately owned, Bruntingthorpe
	ZD980	B-V Chinook HC4 (N37082) [DD]	RAF No 18 Sqn, Odiham
	ZD981	B-V Chinook HC4 (N37083)	MoD/Vector Aerospace, Fleetlands
	ZD982	B-V Chinook HC6A (N37085) [DF]	MoD/Boeing/QinetiQ, Boscombe Down (conversion)
	ZD983	B-V Chinook HC6A (N37086)	RAF No 18 Sqn, Odiham
	ZD984	B-V Chinook HC6A (N37088) [DH]	MoD/Boeing/QinetiQ, Boscombe Down (conversion)
	ZD990	BAe Harrier T8 [T90/DD]	Privately owned, St Athan
	ZD992	BAe Harrier T8 [724]	Privately owned, Knutsford, Cheshire
	ZE114	Panavia Tornado IDS (RSAF 703)	BAE Systems, Warton
	ZE119	Panavia Tornado IDS (RSAF 760)	BAE Systems, Warton
	ZE165	Panavia Tornado F3 [GE]	MoD DFTDC, Manston
	ZE168	Panavia Tornado F3 <ff>	Privately owned, Thorpe Wood, N Yorks
	ZE204	Panavia Tornado F3 [FC]	MoD DFTDC, Manston
	ZE256	Panavia Tornado F3 [DZ] (wears ZE343 on port side)	Privately owned, Thorpe Wood, N Yorks
	ZE340	Panavia Tornado F3 (ZE758/9298M) [GO]	DSAE No 1 SoTT, Cosford
	ZE342	Panavia Tornado F3 [HP]	Rolls Royce, RAF Leeming
	ZE350	McD F-4J(UK) Phantom (9080M) <ff>	*To Australia, October 2017*
	ZE352	McD F-4J(UK) Phantom (9086M) <ff>	*Currently not known*
	ZE360	McD F-4J(UK) Phantom (9095M) [O]	MoD DFTDC, Manston
	ZE368	WS61 Sea King HAR3 [R]	Mini Moos Farm, Edmondsley, Durham
	ZE369	WS61 Sea King HAR3 [S]	Privately owned, Charlwood
	ZE370	WS61 Sea King HAR3 [T]	DSAE, stored *HMS Sultan*, Gosport
	ZE375	WS Lynx AH9A	Privately owned, Bentwaters
	ZE376	WS Lynx AH9A	AAC MPSU, Middle Wallop
	ZE378	WS Lynx AH7	AAC MPSU, Middle Wallop
	ZE379	WS Lynx AH7 <ff>	QinetiQ, Boscombe Down
	ZE380	WS Lynx AH9A	AAC, stored Middle Wallop
	ZE381	WS Lynx AH7 [X]	DSAE SAAE, Lyneham
	ZE395	BAe 125 CC3	Privately owned, Dunsfold
	ZE396	BAe 125 CC3	*To the Netherlands, September 2017*
	ZE410	Agusta A109A (AE-334)	Museum of Army Flying, stored Middle Wallop
	ZE412	Agusta A109A	Army, Credenhill
	ZE413	Agusta A109A	Perth Technical College
	ZE416	Agusta A109E Power Elite (G-ESLH)	MoD/ETPS, Boscombe Down
	ZE418	WS61 Sea King ASaC7 [186]	DSAE, stored *HMS Sultan*, Gosport
	ZE420	WS61 Sea King ASaC7 [189]	RN No 849 NAS, Culdrose
	ZE422	WS61 Sea King ASaC7 [192]	RN No 849 NAS, Culdrose
	ZE425	WS61 Sea King HC4 [WR]	Mini Moos Farm, Edmondsley, Durham
	ZE426	WS61 Sea King HC4 [WX]	DSAE RNAESS, *HMS Sultan*, Gosport
	ZE427	WS61 Sea King HC4 [K]	DSAE, stored *HMS Sultan*, Gosport
	ZE428	WS61 Sea King HC4 [H]	Mini Moos Farm, Edmondsley, Durham
	ZE432	BAC 1-11/479FU (DQ-FBV) <ff>	Bournemouth Aviation Museum
	ZE449	SA330L Puma HC1 (9017M/PA-12)	Army Whittington Barracks, Lichfield, on display
	ZE477	WS Lynx 3	The Helicopter Museum, Weston-super-Mare
	ZE495	Grob G103 Viking T1 (BGA3000) [VA]	RAF/Serco GMS, Syerston
	ZE496	Grob G103 Viking T1 (BGA3001) [VB]	RAF ACCGS/No 644 VGS, Syerston
	ZE498	Grob G103 Viking T1 (BGA3003) [VC]	RAF, stored Little Rissington
	ZE499	Grob G103 Viking T1 (BGA3004) [VD]	RAF, stored Little Rissington
	ZE502	Grob G103 Viking T1 (BGA3007) [VF]	RAF ACCGS/No 644 VGS, Syerston

Serial	Type (code/other identity)	Owner/operator, location or fate	Notes
ZE503	Grob G103 Viking T1 (BGA3008) [VG]	MoD/MADG, Cambridge (spares use)	
ZE504	Grob G103 Viking T1 (BGA3009) [VH]	RAF/Serco, stored Syerston	
ZE520	Grob G103 Viking T1 (BGA3010) [VJ]	RAF/Serco GMS, Syerston	
ZE521	Grob G103 Viking T1 (BGA3011) [VK]	RAF No 622 VGS, Upavon	
ZE522	Grob G103 Viking T1 (BGA3012) [VL]	RAF, stored Little Rissington	
ZE524	Grob G103 Viking T1 (BGA3014) [VM]	RAF No 637 VGS, Little Rissington, GI use	
ZE526	Grob G103 Viking T1 (BGA3016) [VN]	RAF, stored Little Rissington	
ZE527	Grob G103 Viking T1 (BGA3017) [VP]	MoD/Southern Sailplanes, Membury	
ZE528	Grob G103 Viking T1 (BGA3018) [VQ]	RAF No 622 VGS, Upavon	
ZE529	Grob G103 Viking T1 (BGA3019) (comp ZE655) [VR]	RAF, stored Little Rissington	
ZE530	Grob G103 Viking T1 (BGA3020) [VS]	RAF, stored Little Rissington	
ZE531	Grob G103 Viking T1 (BGA3021) [VT]	RAF, stored Little Rissington	
ZE532	Grob G103 Viking T1 (BGA3022) [VU]	MoD/Southern Sailplanes, Membury	
ZE533	Grob G103 Viking T1 (BGA3023) [VV]	MoD/Southern Sailplanes, Membury	
ZE550	Grob G103 Viking T1 (BGA3025) [VX]	MoD/MADG, Cambridge (spares use)	
ZE551	Grob G103 Viking T1 (BGA3026) [VY]	RAF, stored Little Rissington	
ZE552	Grob G103 Viking T1 (BGA3027) [VZ]	RAF, stored Little Rissington	
ZE553	Grob G103 Viking T1 (BGA3028) [WA]	RAF ACCGS/No 644 VGS, Syerston	
ZE554	Grob G103 Viking T1 (BGA3029) [WB]	RAF, stored Little Rissington	
ZE555	Grob G103 Viking T1 (BGA3030) [WC]	RAF No 632 VGS, Ternhill	
ZE556	Grob G103 Viking T1 (BGA3031) <ff>	RAF/Serco, stored Syerston	
ZE557	Grob G103 Viking T1 (BGA3032) [WE]	RAF/Serco, stored Syerston	
ZE558	Grob G103 Viking T1 (BGA3033) [WF]	RAF, stored Little Rissington	
ZE559	Grob G103 Viking T1 (BGA3034) [WG]	RAF/Serco GMS, Syerston	
ZE560	Grob G103 Viking T1 (BGA3035) [WH]	MoD/Southern Sailplanes, Membury	
ZE561	Grob G103 Viking T1 (BGA3036) [WJ]	MoD/Southern Sailplanes, Membury	
ZE562	Grob G103 Viking T1 (BGA3037) [WK]	RAF, stored Little Rissington	
ZE563	Grob G103 Viking T1 (BGA3038) [WL]	RAF/Serco GMS, Syerston	
ZE564	Grob G103 Viking T1 (BGA3039) [WN]	RAF, stored Little Rissington	
ZE584	Grob G103 Viking T1 (BGA3040) [WP]	RAF/Serco GMS, Syerston	
ZE585	Grob G103 Viking T1 (BGA3041) [WQ]	RAF, stored Little Rissington	
ZE586	Grob G103 Viking T1 (BGA3042) [WR]	RAF ACCGS/No 644 VGS, Syerston	
ZE587	Grob G103 Viking T1 (BGA3043) [WS]	MoD/Southern Sailplanes, Membury	
ZE590	Grob G103 Viking T1 (BGA3046) [WT]	RAF No 622 VGS, Upavon	
ZE591	Grob G103 Viking T1 (BGA3047) [WU]	RAF, stored Little Rissington	
ZE592	Grob G103 Viking T1 (BGA3048) <ff>	RAFGSA, stored Halton	
ZE593	Grob G103 Viking T1 (BGA3049) [WW]	RAF, stored Little Rissington	
ZE594	Grob G103 Viking T1 (BGA3050) [WX]	RAF ACCGS/No 644 VGS, Syerston	
ZE595	Grob G103 Viking T1 (BGA3051) [WY]	RAF, stored Little Rissington	
ZE600	Grob G103 Viking T1 (BGA3052) [WZ]	RAF, stored Little Rissington	
ZE601	Grob G103 Viking T1 (BGA3053) [XA]	RAF ACCGS/No 644 VGS, Syerston	
ZE602	Grob G103 Viking T1 (BGA3054) [XB]	RAF/Serco GMS, Syerston	
ZE603	Grob G103 Viking T1 (BGA3055) [XC]	RAF, stored Little Rissington	
ZE604	Grob G103 Viking T1 (BGA3056) [XD]	RAF, stored Little Rissington	
ZE605	Grob G103 Viking T1 (BGA3057) [XE]	RAF No 621 VGS/No 637 VGS, Little Rissington	
ZE606	Grob G103 Viking T1 (BGA3058) [XF]	RAF/Serco GMS, Syerston	
ZE607	Grob G103 Viking T1 (BGA3059) [XG]	RAF, stored Little Rissington	
ZE608	Grob G103 Viking T1 (BGA3060) [XH]	RAF/Serco GMS, Syerston	
ZE609	Grob G103 Viking T1 (BGA3061) [XJ]	RAF/Serco GMS, Syerston	
ZE610	Grob G103 Viking T1 (BGA3062) [XK]	RAF, stored Little Rissington	
ZE611	Grob G103 Viking T1 (BGA3063) [XL]	RAF, stored Little Rissington	
ZE613	Grob G103 Viking T1 (BGA3065) [XM]	MoD/Southern Sailplanes, Membury	
ZE614	Grob G103 Viking T1 (BGA3066) [XN]	MoD/Southern Sailplanes, Membury	
ZE625	Grob G103 Viking T1 (BGA3067) [XP]	RAF No 621 VGS/No 637 VGS, Little Rissington	
ZE626	Grob G103 Viking T1 (BGA3068) [XQ]	RAF No 621 VGS/No 637 VGS, Little Rissington	
ZE627	Grob G103 Viking T1 (BGA3069) [XR]	RAF, stored Little Rissington	
ZE628	Grob G103 Viking T1 (BGA3070) [XS]	MoD/Southern Sailplanes, Membury	
ZE629	Grob G103 Viking T1 (BGA3071) [XT]	RAF/Serco GMS, Syerston	
ZE630	Grob G103 Viking T1 (BGA3072) [XU]	RAF ACCGS/No 644 VGS, Syerston	
ZE631	Grob G103 Viking T1 (BGA3073) [XV]	MoD/Southern Sailplanes, Membury	
ZE632	Grob G103 Viking T1 (BGA3074) [XW]	MoD/Southern Sailplanes, Membury	
ZE633	Grob G103 Viking T1 (BGA3075) [XX]	RAF/Serco GMS, Syerston	

Notes	Serial	Type (code/other identity)	Owner/operator, location or fate
	ZE636	Grob G103 Viking T1 (BGA3078) [XZ]	RAF, Little Rissington (mobile display aircraft)
	ZE637	Grob G103 Viking T1 (BGA3079) [YA]	RAF/Serco GMS, Syerston
	ZE650	Grob G103 Viking T1 (BGA3080) [YB]	RAF/Serco GMS, Syerston
	ZE651	Grob G103 Viking T1 (BGA3081) [YC]	RAF/Serco GMS, Syerston
	ZE652	Grob G103 Viking T1 (BGA3082) [YD]	RAF/Serco, stored Syerston
	ZE653	Grob G103 Viking T1 (BGA3083) [YE]	MoD/Southern Sailplanes, Membury
	ZE656	Grob G103 Viking T1 (BGA3086) [YH]	RAF, stored Little Rissington
	ZE657	Grob G103 Viking T1 (BGA3087) [YJ]	RAF, stored Little Rissington
	ZE658	Grob G103 Viking T1 (BGA3088) [YK]	RAF/Serco, stored Syerston
	ZE677	Grob G103 Viking T1 (BGA3090) [YM]	RAF, stored Little Rissington
	ZE678	Grob G103 Viking T1 (BGA3091) [YN]	RAF/Serco, stored Syerston
	ZE679	Grob G103 Viking T1 (BGA3092) [YP]	RAF, stored Little Rissington
	ZE680	Grob G103 Viking T1 (BGA3093) [YQ]	MoD/MADG, Cambridge
	ZE681	Grob G103 Viking T1 (BGA3094) <ff>	Privately owned, Frampton Cotterell, Glos, GI use
	ZE682	Grob G103 Viking T1 (BGA3095) [YS]	RAF ACCGS/No 644 VGS, Syerston
	ZE683	Grob G103 Viking T1 (BGA3096) [YT]	RAF, stored Little Rissington
	ZE684	Grob G103 Viking T1 (BGA3097) [YU]	RAF, stored Little Rissington
	ZE685	Grob G103 Viking T1 (BGA3098) [YV]	RAF No 632 VGS, Ternhill
	ZE686	Grob G103 Viking T1 (BGA3099) <ff>	RAF Museum, Hendon
	ZE690	BAe Sea Harrier FA2 [90/DD]	SFDO, RNAS Culdrose
	ZE691	BAe Sea Harrier FA2 [710]	Classic Autos, Winsford, Cheshire
	ZE692	BAe Sea Harrier FA2 [92/DD]	SFDO, RNAS Culdrose
	ZE694	BAe Sea Harrier FA2 [004]	Midland Air Museum, Coventry
	ZE697	BAe Sea Harrier FA2 [006]	Privately owned, Binbrook
	ZE698	BAe Sea Harrier FA2 [001]	Privately owned, Charlwood
	ZE700	BAe 146 CC2 (G-6-021) $	RAF No 32(The Royal) Sqn, Northolt
	ZE701	BAe 146 CC2 (G-6-029)	RAF No 32(The Royal) Sqn, Northolt
	ZE704	Lockheed TriStar C2 (N508PA/N507CS)	Privately owned, Bruntingthorpe
	ZE705	Lockheed TriStar C2 (N509PA/N703CS)	Privately owned, Bruntingthorpe
	ZE707	BAe 146 C3 (OO-TAZ)	RAF No 32(The Royal) Sqn, Northolt
	ZE708	BAe 146 C3 (OO-TAY)	RAF No 32(The Royal) Sqn, Northolt
	ZE760	Panavia Tornado F3 (MM7206) [AP]	RAF Coningsby, on display
	ZE887	Panavia Tornado F3 [GF] $	RAF Museum, Hendon
	ZE934	Panavia Tornado F3 [TA]	National Museum of Flight, E Fortune
	ZE936	Panavia Tornado F3 <ff>	RAF Air Defence Radar Museum, Neatishead
	ZE965	Panavia Tornado F3 <ff>	Privately owned,
	ZE966	Panavia Tornado F3 [VT]	Tornado Heritage Centre, Hawarden
	ZE967	Panavia Tornado F3 [UT]	RAF Leuchars, at main gate
	ZF115	WS61 Sea King HC4 [R,WV]	DSAE, stored HMS Sultan, Gosport
	ZF116	WS61 Sea King HC4 [WP]	Privately owned, Charlwood
	ZF117	WS61 Sea King HC4 [18]	To Pakistan as 4518, December 2017
	ZF118	WS61 Sea King HC4 [O]	School of Maritime Survival HMS Raleigh, Plymouth
	ZF119	WS61 Sea King HC4 [WY]	DSAE, stored HMS Sultan, Gosport
	ZF120	WS61 Sea King HC4 [Z]	Privately owned, Colsterworth, Leics
	ZF121	WS61 Sea King HC4 [T]	Mini Moos Farm, Edmondsley, Durham
	ZF122	WS61 Sea King HC4 [V]	Privately owned, Chard, Somerset
	ZF135	Shorts Tucano T1 [135]	RAF No 1 FTS, Linton-on-Ouse
	ZF137	Shorts Tucano T1 [137]	RAF, stored Linton-on-Ouse
	ZF139	Shorts Tucano T1 [139]	RAF No 1 FTS, Linton-on-Ouse
	ZF140	Shorts Tucano T1 [140] $	RAF No 1 FTS/72 Sqn, Linton-on-Ouse
	ZF142	Shorts Tucano T1 [142]	RAF No 1 FTS, Linton-on-Ouse
	ZF143	Shorts Tucano T1 [143]	RAF No 1 FTS, Linton-on-Ouse
	ZF144	Shorts Tucano T1 [144]	RAF No 1 FTS, Linton-on-Ouse
	ZF145	Shorts Tucano T1 [145]	RAF No 1 FTS, Linton-on-Ouse
	ZF160	Shorts Tucano T1 [160]	Privately owned, Bentwaters
	ZF163	Shorts Tucano T1 [163]	RAF AM&SU, stored Shawbury
	ZF166	Shorts Tucano T1 [166]	Privately owned, Bentwaters
	ZF167	Shorts Tucano T1 (fuselage)	Ulster Aviation Society, Long Kesh
	ZF169	Shorts Tucano T1 [169]	RAF, stored Linton-on-Ouse
	ZF170	Shorts Tucano T1 [MP-A]	RAF, stored Linton-on-Ouse
	ZF171	Shorts Tucano T1 [171]	RAF No 1 FTS, Linton-on-Ouse

Serial	Type (code/other identity)	Owner/operator, location or fate	Notes
ZF172	Shorts Tucano T1 [172]	RAF No 1 FTS, Linton-on-Ouse	
ZF202	Shorts Tucano T1 [202]	RAF Linton-on-Ouse, on display	
ZF204	Shorts Tucano T1 [204]	RAF No 1 FTS, Linton-on-Ouse	
ZF205	Shorts Tucano T1 [205]	RAF No 1 FTS/72 Sqn, Linton-on-Ouse	
ZF210	Shorts Tucano T1 [210]	RAF, stored Linton-on-Ouse	
ZF211	Shorts Tucano T1 [211]	Privately owned, Bentwaters	
ZF239	Shorts Tucano T1 [239]	RAF No 1 FTS, Linton-on-Ouse	
ZF240	Shorts Tucano T1 [240]	RAF No 1 FTS/72 Sqn, Linton-on-Ouse	
ZF243	Shorts Tucano T1 [243]	RAF No 1 FTS, Linton-on-Ouse	
ZF244	Shorts Tucano T1 [244] $	RAF No 1 FTS/72 Sqn, Linton-on-Ouse	
ZF263	Shorts Tucano T1 [263]	RAF AM&SU, stored Shawbury	
ZF264	Shorts Tucano T1 [264]	RAF No 1 FTS, Linton-on-Ouse	
ZF268	Shorts Tucano T1 [268]	RAF AM&SU, stored Shawbury	
ZF269	Shorts Tucano T1 [269]	RAF No 1 FTS, Linton-on-Ouse	
ZF286	Shorts Tucano T1 [286]	RAF AM&SU, stored Shawbury	
ZF287	Shorts Tucano T1 [287]	RAF No 1 FTS, Linton-on-Ouse	
ZF288	Shorts Tucano T1 [288]	RAF AM&SU, stored Shawbury	
ZF289	Shorts Tucano T1 [289]	RAF No 1 FTS/72 Sqn, Linton-on-Ouse	
ZF290	Shorts Tucano T1 [290]	RAF No 1 FTS, Linton-on-Ouse	
ZF291	Shorts Tucano T1 [291]	RAF No 1 FTS, Linton-on-Ouse	
ZF292	Shorts Tucano T1 [292]	RAF, stored Linton-on-Ouse	
ZF293	Shorts Tucano T1 [293]	RAF No 1 FTS/72 Sqn, Linton-on-Ouse	
ZF294	Shorts Tucano T1 [294]	RAF, stored Linton-on-Ouse	
ZF295	Shorts Tucano T1 [295] $	RAF, stored Linton-on-Ouse	
ZF315	Shorts Tucano T1 [315]	RAF No 1 FTS, Linton-on-Ouse	
ZF317	Shorts Tucano T1 [317]	RAF No 1 FTS, Linton-on-Ouse	
ZF318	Shorts Tucano T1 [318] $	RAF AM&SU, stored Shawbury	
ZF319	Shorts Tucano T1 [319]	RAF, stored Linton-on-Ouse	
ZF338	Shorts Tucano T1 [338]	RAF No 1 FTS, Linton-on-Ouse	
ZF339	Shorts Tucano T1 [339]	Dismantled at Linton-on-Ouse, November 2017	
ZF341	Shorts Tucano T1 [341]	RAF, stored Linton-on-Ouse	
ZF342	Shorts Tucano T1 [342]	RAF No 1 FTS, Linton-on-Ouse	
ZF343	Shorts Tucano T1 [343]	RAF No 1 FTS/72 Sqn, Linton-on-Ouse	
ZF347	Shorts Tucano T1 [347]	RAF No 1 FTS, Linton-on-Ouse	
ZF348	Shorts Tucano T1 [348]	RAF No 1 FTS, Linton-on-Ouse	
ZF349	Shorts Tucano T1 [349] (fuselage)	Bombardier, stored Belfast (wreck)	
ZF350	Shorts Tucano T1 [350]	RAF AM&SU, stored Shawbury	
ZF355	WS Lynx HAS3S(ICE) (XZ238) [633]	Privately owned, White Waltham	
ZF372	Shorts Tucano T1 [372]	RAF AM&SU, stored Shawbury	
ZF374	Shorts Tucano T1 [374]	RAF No 1 FTS, Linton-on-Ouse	
ZF376	Shorts Tucano T1 [376]	RAF AM&SU, stored Shawbury	
ZF377	Shorts Tucano T1 [377]	RAF No 1 FTS, Linton-on-Ouse	
ZF378	Shorts Tucano T1 [RN-S] $	RAF No 1 FTS/72 Sqn, Linton-on-Ouse	
ZF379	Shorts Tucano T1 [379]	RAF No 1 FTS, Linton-on-Ouse	
ZF380	Shorts Tucano T1 [380]	Privately owned, Bentwaters	
ZF405	Shorts Tucano T1 [405]	RAF AM&SU, stored Shawbury	
ZF406	Shorts Tucano T1 [406]	RAF, stored Linton-on-Ouse	
ZF407	Shorts Tucano T1 [407]	RAF No 1 FTS, Linton-on-Ouse	
ZF408	Shorts Tucano T1 [408]	RAF AM&SU, stored Shawbury	
ZF412	Shorts Tucano T1 [412]	Privately owned, Bentwaters	
ZF414	Shorts Tucano T1 [414]	RAF AM&SU, stored Shawbury	
ZF416	Shorts Tucano T1 [416]	RAF AM&SU, stored Shawbury	
ZF417	Shorts Tucano T1 [417]	RAF No 1 FTS, Linton-on-Ouse	
ZF418	Shorts Tucano T1 [418]	RAF AM&SU, stored Shawbury	
ZF446	Shorts Tucano T1 [446]	RAF AM&SU, stored Shawbury	
ZF448	Shorts Tucano T1 [448]	RAF, stored Linton-on-Ouse	
ZF449	Shorts Tucano T1 [449]	RAF AM&SU, stored Shawbury	
ZF485	Shorts Tucano T1 (G-BULU) [485]	RAF No 1 FTS, Linton-on-Ouse	
ZF486	Shorts Tucano T1 [486]	RAF AM&SU, stored Shawbury	
ZF487	Shorts Tucano T1 [487]	RAF AM&SU, stored Shawbury	
ZF488	Shorts Tucano T1 [488]	RAF AM&SU, stored Shawbury	
ZF489	Shorts Tucano T1 [489]	RAF No 1 FTS, Linton-on-Ouse	

Notes	Serial	Type (code/other identity)	Owner/operator, location or fate
	ZF490	Shorts Tucano T1 [490]	RAF AM&SU, stored Shawbury
	ZF491	Shorts Tucano T1 [491]	RAF No 1 FTS, Linton-on-Ouse
	ZF492	Shorts Tucano T1 [492]	RAF AM&SU, stored Shawbury
	ZF510	Shorts Tucano T1 [510]	MoD/AFD/QinetiQ, Boscombe Down
	ZF511	Shorts Tucano T1 [511]	MoD/AFD/QinetiQ, Boscombe Down
	ZF512	Shorts Tucano T1 [512]	RAF No 1 FTS/72 Sqn, Linton-on-Ouse
	ZF513	Shorts Tucano T1 [513]	RAF AM&SU, stored Shawbury
	ZF515	Shorts Tucano T1 [515]	RAF No 1 FTS, Linton-on-Ouse
	ZF516	Shorts Tucano T1 [516]	Privately owned, Bentwaters
	ZF534	BAe EAP	RAF Museum, Cosford
	ZF537	WS Lynx AH9A	AAC, stored Middle Wallop
	ZF538	WS Lynx AH9A	AAC, stored Middle Wallop
	ZF539	WS Lynx AH9A	Privately owned, Sproughton
	ZF557	WS Lynx HMA8SRU [426/PD]	AAC, stored Middle Wallop
	ZF558	WS Lynx HMA8SRU [336/WK]	AAC, stored Middle Wallop
	ZF560	WS Lynx HMA8SRU [456]	RN, stored St Athan
	ZF562	WS Lynx HMA8SRU [353/MB]	AAC, stored Middle Wallop
	ZF563	WS Lynx HMA8SRU [312/VL]	AAC, stored Middle Wallop
	ZF573	PBN 2T Islander CC2 (G-SRAY)	Sold as G-BJOH July 2017
	ZF579	BAC Lightning F53 (53-671/203)	Repainted in Saudi colours as 53-671, 2017
	ZF580	BAC Lightning F53 (53-672/204)	Cornwall Aviation Heritage Centre, St Athan (rest'n)
	ZF581	BAC Lightning F53 (53-675/206)	Bentwaters Cold War Museum
	ZF582	BAC Lightning F53 (53-676/210/207) <ff>	Bournemouth Aviation Museum
	ZF583	BAC Lightning F53 (53-681/306/210)	Solway Aviation Society, Carlisle
	ZF584	BAC Lightning F53 (53-682/307/211)	Dumfries & Galloway Avn Mus, Dumfries
	ZF587	BAC Lightning F53 (53-691/215) <ff>	Lashenden Air Warfare Museum, Headcorn
	ZF587	BAC Lightning F53 (53-691/215) <rf>	Privately owned, Stowmarket, Suffolk
	ZF588	BAC Lightning F53 (53-693/216) [L]	East Midlands Airport Aeropark
	ZF589	BAC Lightning F53 (53-700/218) <ff>	Gatwick Aviation Museum, stored Charlwood
	ZF590	BAC Lightning F53 (53-679/206/1302/220) <ff>	Privately owned, stored Bruntingthorpe
	ZF595	BAC Lightning T55 (55-714/212/1317/231) (fuselage)	Privately owned, Binbrook
	ZF596	BAC Lightning T55 (55-715/305/205/220/233) <ff>	Lakes Lightnings, Spark Bridge, Cumbria
	ZF622	Piper PA-31 Navajo Chieftain 350 (N3548Y)	QinetiQ, Boscombe Down, GI use
	ZF641	EHI-101 [PP1]	SFDO, RNAS Culdrose
	ZF649	EHI-101 Merlin (A2714) [PP5]	DSAE AESS, HMS Sultan, Gosport
	ZG101	EHI-101 (mock-up) [GB]	Currently not known
	ZG347	Northrop Chukar D2	Davidstow Airfield & Cornwall At War Museum
	ZG477	BAe Harrier GR9 $	RAF Museum, Hendon
	ZG478	BAe Harrier GR9 (fuselage)	Privately owned, Sproughton
	ZG509	BAe Harrier GR7 [80]	Privately owned, Petersfield, Hants
	ZG631	Northrop Chukar D2	Farnborough Air Sciences Trust, Farnborough
	ZG705	Panavia Tornado GR4A [118]	RAF Leeming, RTP
	ZG707	Panavia Tornado GR4A [119]	RAF Leeming, RTP
	ZG714	Panavia Tornado GR4A [124]	Scrapped at Leeming, 2017
	ZG750	Panavia Tornado GR4 [128] $	RAF Leeming, RTP
	ZG751	Panavia Tornado F3 (fuselage)	MoD JARTS, Boscombe Down
	ZG752	Panavia Tornado GR4 [129]	RAF No 31 Sqn, Marham
	ZG771	Panavia Tornado GR4 $	RAF Marham, WLT
	ZG773	Panavia Tornado GR4	Excel Centre, London (on display)
	ZG775	Panavia Tornado GR4 [134]	RAF No 31 Sqn, Marham
	ZG777	Panavia Tornado GR4 [135]	RAF Leeming, RTP
	ZG779	Panavia Tornado GR4 [136]	RAF Leeming, RTP
	ZG791	Panavia Tornado GR4 [137]	RAF CMU, Marham
	ZG816	WS61 Sea King HAS6 [014/L]	DSAE RNAESS, HMS Sultan, Gosport
	ZG817	WS61 Sea King HAS6 [702/PW]	DSAE RNAESS, HMS Sultan, Gosport
	ZG818	WS61 Sea King HAS6 [707/PW]	DSAE RNAESS, HMS Sultan, Gosport
	ZG819	WS61 Sea King HAS6 [265/N]	DSAE RNAESS, HMS Sultan, Gosport
	ZG821	WS61 Sea King HC4 [19]	To Pakistan as 4519, December 2017
	ZG822	WS61 Sea King HC4 [WS]	Privately owned, Bruntingthorpe
	ZG844	PBN 2T Islander AL1 (G-BLNE)	AAC AM&SU, stored Shawbury
	ZG845	PBN 2T Islander AL1 (G-BLNT)	AAC No 651 Sqn/5 Regt, Aldergrove

Serial	Type (code/other identity)	Owner/operator, location or fate	Notes
ZG846	PBN 2T Islander AL1 (G-BLNU)	AAC No 651 Sqn/5 Regt, Aldergrove	
ZG847	PBN 2T Islander AL1 (G-BLNV)	AAC AM&SU, stored Shawbury	
ZG848	PBN 2T Islander AL1 (G-BLNY)	AAC No 651 Sqn/5 Regt, Aldergrove	
ZG875	WS61 Sea King HAS6 [013] <ff>	Privately owned, Market Drayton, Shrops	
ZG875	WS61 Sea King HAS6 <rf>	Mayhem Paintball, Aybridge, Essex	
ZG884	WS Lynx AH9A	Privately owned, Bentwaters	
ZG885	WS Lynx AH9A	AAC, stored Middle Wallop	
ZG886	WS Lynx AH9A	Privately owned, Bentwaters	
ZG887	WS Lynx AH9A	AAC MPSU, stored Middle Wallop	
ZG888	WS Lynx AH9A	Privately owned, Sproughton	
ZG889	WS Lynx AH9A	Privately owned, Bentwaters	
ZG914	WS Lynx AH9A	AAC MPSU, Middle Wallop	
ZG915	WS Lynx AH9A	RN, Predannack Fire School	
ZG916	WS Lynx AH9A	Privately owned, Bentwaters	
ZG917	WS Lynx AH9A $	AAC, stored Middle Wallop	
ZG918	WS Lynx AH9A	AAC, stored Middle Wallop	
ZG919	WS Lynx AH9A	RN, Predannack Fire School	
ZG920	WS Lynx AH9A	AAC, stored Middle Wallop	
ZG921	WS Lynx AH9A	AAC MPSU, Middle Wallop	
ZG922	WS Lynx AH9	Privately owned, Staverton, instructional use	
ZG923	WS Lynx AH9A	AAC, stored Middle Wallop	
ZG969	Pilatus PC-9 (HB-HQE)	BAE Systems, Warton, GI use	
ZG989	PBN 2T Islander ASTOR [01]	*To G-DLRA, November 2016*	
ZG993	PBN 2T Islander AL1 (G-BOMD)	Museum of Army Flying, stored Middle Wallop	
ZG994	PBN 2T Islander AL1 (G-BPLN) (fuselage)	Britten-Norman, stored Bembridge	
ZG995	PBN 2T Defender AL1 (G-SURV)	AAC No 651 Sqn/5 Regt, Aldergrove	
ZG996	PBN 2T Defender AL1 (G-BWPR)	AAC No 651 Sqn/5 Regt, Aldergrove	
ZG997	PBN 2T Defender AL2 (G-BWPV)	AAC No 651 Sqn/5 Regt, Aldergrove	
ZG998	PBN 2T Defender AL2 (G-BWPX)	AAC No 651 Sqn/5 Regt, Aldergrove	
ZH001	PBN 2T Defender AL2 (G-CEIO)	AAC No 651 Sqn/5 Regt, Aldergrove	
ZH002	PBN 2T Defender AL2 (G-CEIP)	AAC No 651 Sqn/5 Regt, Aldergrove	
ZH003	PBN 2T Defender AL2 (G-CEIR)	AAC, Brize Norton (damaged)	
ZH004	PBN 2T Defender T3 (G-BWPO)	AAC No 651 Sqn/5 Regt, Aldergrove	
ZH005	PBN 2T Defender AL2 (G-CGVB)	AAC No 651 Sqn/5 Regt, Aldergrove	
ZH101	Boeing E-3D Sentry AEW1 [01]	RAF No 8 Sqn/No 54 Sqn, Waddington	
ZH102	Boeing E-3D Sentry AEW1 [02]	RAF No 8 Sqn/No 54 Sqn, Waddington	
ZH103	Boeing E-3D Sentry AEW1 [03]	RAF No 8 Sqn/No 54 Sqn, Waddington	
ZH104	Boeing E-3D Sentry AEW1 [04]	RAF No 8 Sqn/No 54 Sqn, Waddington	
ZH105	Boeing E-3D Sentry AEW1 [05]	RAF, stored Waddington	
ZH106	Boeing E-3D Sentry AEW1 [06]	RAF No 8 Sqn/No 54 Sqn, Waddington	
ZH107	Boeing E-3D Sentry AEW1 [07] $	RAF, stored Waddington	
ZH115	Grob G109B Vigilant T1 [TA]	RAF, stored Little Rissington	
ZH116	Grob G109B Vigilant T1 [TB]	RAF, stored Watton	
ZH117	Grob G109B Vigilant T1 [TC]	RAF, stored Little Rissington	
ZH118	Grob G109B Vigilant T1 [TD]	RAF, stored Watton	
ZH119	Grob G109B Vigilant T1 [TE]	RAF, stored Little Rissington	
ZH120	Grob G109B Vigilant T1 [TF]	RAF, stored Little Rissington	
ZH121	Grob G109B Vigilant T1 [TG]	RAF, stored Little Rissington	
ZH122	Grob G109B Vigilant T1 [TH]	RAF, stored Little Rissington	
ZH123	Grob G109B Vigilant T1 [TJ]	RAF ACCGS/No 644 VGS, Syerston	
ZH124	Grob G109B Vigilant T1 [TK]	RAF, stored Little Rissington	
ZH125	Grob G109B Vigilant T1 [TL]	RAF, stored Little Rissington	
ZH126	Grob G109B Vigilant T1 [TM]	RAF/Serco, stored Syerston	
ZH127	Grob G109B Vigilant T1 (D-KGRA) [TN]	RAF/Serco GMS, Syerston	
ZH128	Grob G109B Vigilant T1 (D-KEEC) [TP]	RAF/Serco GMS, Syerston	
ZH129	Grob G109B Vigilant T1 [TQ]	RAF/Serco GMS, Syerston	
ZH139	BAe Harrier GR7 <R> (BAPC 191/*ZD472*)	Currently not known	
ZH144	Grob G109B Vigilant T1 [TR]	Grob Aircraft, Tussenhausen, Germany (for disposal)	
ZH145	Grob G109B Vigilant T1 [TS]	RAF, stored Little Rissington	
ZH146	Grob G109B Vigilant T1 [TT]	RAF, stored Linton-on-Ouse	
ZH147	Grob G109B Vigilant T1 [TU]	RAF, stored Little Rissington	

Notes	Serial	Type (code/other identity)	Owner/operator, location or fate
	ZH148	Grob G109B Vigilant T1 [TV]	RAF/Serco GMS, Syerston
	ZH184	Grob G109B Vigilant T1 [TW]	RAF, stored Little Rissington
	ZH185	Grob G109B Vigilant T1 [TX]	RAF/Serco GMS, Syerston
	ZH186	Grob G109B Vigilant T1 [TY]	RAF ACCGS/No 644 VGS, Syerston
	ZH187	Grob G109B Vigilant T1 [TZ]	RAF, stored Little Rissington
	ZH188	Grob G109B Vigilant T1 [UA]	RAF, stored Little Rissington
	ZH189	Grob G109B Vigilant T1 [UB]	RAF, stored Little Rissington
	ZH190	Grob G109B Vigilant T1 [UC]	RAF, stored Little Rissington
	ZH191	Grob G109B Vigilant T1 [UD]	RAF, stored Abingdon
	ZH192	Grob G109B Vigilant T1 [UE]	RAF, stored Little Rissington
	ZH193	Grob G109B Vigilant T1 [UF]	RAF, stored Woodvale
	ZH194	Grob G109B Vigilant T1 [UG]	RAF, stored Little Rissington
	ZH195	Grob G109B Vigilant T1 [UH]	RAF, stored Little Rissington
	ZH196	Grob G109B Vigilant T1 [UJ]	RAF, stored Little Rissington
	ZH197	Grob G109B Vigilant T1 [UK]	RAF/Serco GMS, Syerston
	ZH200	BAe Hawk 200	Loughborough University
	ZH205	Grob G109B Vigilant T1 [UL]	RAF, stored Linton-on-Ouse
	ZH206	Grob G109B Vigilant T1 [UM]	RAF/Serco GMS, Syerston
	ZH207	Grob G109B Vigilant T1 [UN]	RAF No 645 VGS, Topcliffe
	ZH208	Grob G109B Vigilant T1 [UP]	RAF, stored Little Rissington
	ZH209	Grob G109B Vigilant T1 [UQ]	RAF, stored Little Rissington
	ZH211	Grob G109B Vigilant T1 [UR]	RAF, stored Little Rissington
	ZH247	Grob G109B Vigilant T1 [US]	RAF, stored Little Rissington
	ZH248	Grob G109B Vigilant T1 [UT]	RAF, stored Little Rissington
	ZH249	Grob G109B Vigilant T1 [UU]	RAF/Serco GMS, Syerston
	ZH257	B-V CH-47C Chinook (9217M) (fuselage)	RAF Odiham, BDRT
	ZH263	Grob G109B Vigilant T1 [UV]	RAF, stored Little Rissington
	ZH264	Grob G109B Vigilant T1 [UW]	RAF, stored Little Rissington
	ZH265	Grob G109B Vigilant T1 [UX]	RAF, stored Little Rissington
	ZH266	Grob G109B Vigilant T1 [UY]	RAF, stored Abingdon
	ZH267	Grob G109B Vigilant T1 [UZ]	RAF, stored Little Rissington
	ZH268	Grob G109B Vigilant T1 [SA]	RAF, stored Little Rissington
	ZH269	Grob G109B Vigilant T1 [SB]	RAF, stored Little Rissington
	ZH270	Grob G109B Vigilant T1 [SC]	RAF, stored Little Rissington
	ZH271	Grob G109B Vigilant T1 [SD]	RAF No 645 VGS, Topcliffe
	ZH278	Grob G109B Vigilant T1 (D-KAIS) [SF]	RAF, stored Little Rissington
	ZH279	Grob G109B Vigilant T1 (D-KNPS) [SG]	RAF, stored Little Rissington
	ZH536	PBN 2T Islander CC2A (G-BSAH)	*Sold as G-BSAH, May 2017*
	ZH537	PBN 2T Islander CC2 (G-SELX)	*Sold as G-BJEC, June 2017*
	ZH544	WS61 Sea King HAR3A [17]	*To Pakistan as 4517, December 2017*
	ZH545	WS61 Sea King HAR3A [Z]	Vector Aerospace, Fleetlands, for Pakistan (spares)
	ZH552	Panavia Tornado F3	RAF Leeming, at main gate
	ZH553	Panavia Tornado F3 [RT]	RAF, St Mawgan
	ZH588	Eurofighter Typhoon (DA2)	RAF Museum, Hendon
	ZH590	Eurofighter Typhoon (DA4)	IWM Duxford
	ZH654	BAe Harrier T10 <ff>	*Currently not known*
	ZH655	BAe Harrier T10 <ff>	Privately owned, Bentwaters
	ZH658	BAe Harrier T10/539DD (fuselage)	Privately owned, Sproughton
	ZH763	BAC 1-11/539GL (G-BGKE)	Cornwall Aviation Heritage Centre, Newquay
	ZH775	B-V Chinook HC6A (N7424J) [HB]	MoD/Boeing/QinetiQ, Boscombe Down (conversion)
	ZH776	B-V Chinook HC6A (N7424L) [HC]	RAF No 27 Sqn, Odiham
	ZH777	B-V Chinook HC6A (N7424M) $	RAF No 18 Sqn, Odiham
	ZH796	BAe Sea Harrier FA2 [001/L]	DSAE No 1 SoTT, stored Cosford
	ZH797	BAe Sea Harrier FA2 [97/DD]	SFDO, RNAS Culdrose
	ZH798	BAe Sea Harrier FA2 [98/DD]	SFDO, RNAS Culdrose
	ZH799	BAe Sea Harrier FA2 [730]	*Sold to Australia, December 2017*
	ZH800	BAe Sea Harrier FA2 (ZH801) [123]	RNAS Yeovilton, stored
	ZH801	BAe Sea Harrier FA2 (ZH800) [001]	RNAS Yeovilton, stored
	ZH802	BAe Sea Harrier FA2 [02/DD]	SFDO, RNAS Culdrose
	ZH803	BAe Sea Harrier FA2 [03/DD]	Privately owned, St Athan
	ZH804	BAe Sea Harrier FA2 [003/L]	RN, stored Culdrose
	ZH806	BAe Sea Harrier FA2 [007]	Privately owned, Bentwaters

Serial	Type (code/other identity)	Owner/operator, location or fate	Notes
ZH807	BAe Sea Harrier FA2 <ff>	Privately owned, Thorpe Wood, N Yorks	
ZH810	BAe Sea Harrier FA2 [125]	Privately owned, Sproughton	
ZH811	BAe Sea Harrier FA2 [002/L]	RN, stored Culdrose	
ZH812	BAe Sea Harrier FA2 [005/L]	Privately owned, Bentwaters	
ZH813	BAe Sea Harrier FA2 [13/DD]	SFDO, RNAS Culdrose	
ZH814	Bell 212HP AH1 (G-BGMH) [X]	AAC No 7 Flt, Brunei	
ZH815	Bell 212HP AH1 (G-BGCZ) [Y]	AAC No 7 Flt, Brunei	
ZH816	Bell 212HP AH1 (G-BGMG)	AAC, Middle Wallop	
ZH821	EHI-101 Merlin HM1	RN AM&SU, stored Shawbury	
ZH822	EHI-101 Merlin HM1	RN AM&SU, stored Shawbury	
ZH823	EHI-101 Merlin HM1	RN AM&SU, stored Shawbury	
ZH824	EHI-101 Merlin HM2 [83]	RN No 824 NAS, Culdrose	
ZH825	EHI-101 Merlin HM1 [583]	RN AM&SU, stored Shawbury	
ZH826	EHI-101 Merlin HM2 [68/CU]	MoD/AFD/QinetiQ, Boscombe Down	
ZH827	EHI-101 Merlin HM2 [10]	RN No 820 NAS, Culdrose	
ZH828	EHI-101 Merlin HM2 [88/CU]	RN No 829 NAS, Culdrose	
ZH829	EHI-101 Merlin HM2 [NL]	MoD/AFD/QinetiQ, Boscombe Down	
ZH830	EHI-101 Merlin HM1	QinetiQ, stored Boscombe Down	
ZH831	EHI-101 Merlin HM2	MoD/Leonardo MW, Yeovil (conversion)	
ZH832	EHI-101 Merlin HM2 [81]	RN No 824 NAS, Culdrose	
ZH833	EHI-101 Merlin HM2 [82]	RN MDMF, Culdrose	
ZH834	EHI-101 Merlin HM2 [87]	RN No 824 NAS, Culdrose	
ZH835	EHI-101 Merlin HM2 [13]	RN No 820 NAS, Culdrose	
ZH836	EHI-101 Merlin HM2 [80]	RN No 824 NAS, Culdrose	
ZH837	EHI-101 Merlin HM2	RN MDMF, Culdrose	
ZH838	EHI-101 Merlin HM1 [70]	QinetiQ, stored Boscombe Down	
ZH839	EHI-101 Merlin HM2 [69]	RN No 814 NAS, Culdrose	
ZH840	EHI-101 Merlin HM2 [11]	RN MDMF, Culdrose	
ZH841	EHI-101 Merlin HM2 [501]	RN No 829 NAS, Culdrose	
ZH842	EHI-101 Merlin HM2 [82]	RN No 824 NAS, Culdrose	
ZH843	EHI-101 Merlin HM2	RN No 829 NAS, Culdrose	
ZH845	EHI-101 Merlin HM2 [69]	RN MDMF, Culdrose	
ZH846	EHI-101 Merlin HM2 [12/CU]	RN No 820 NAS, Culdrose	
ZH847	EHI-101 Merlin HM2 [70]	RN No 814 NAS, Culdrose	
ZH848	EHI-101 Merlin HM1	QinetiQ, stored Boscombe Down	
ZH849	EHI-101 Merlin HM1 [67]	QinetiQ, stored Boscombe Down	
ZH850	EHI-101 Merlin HM2 [67]	RN No 814 NAS, Culdrose	
ZH851	EHI-101 Merlin HM2 [84]	RN No 824 NAS, Culdrose	
ZH852	EHI-101 Merlin HM1(mod)	QinetiQ, stored Boscombe Down	
ZH853	EHI-101 Merlin HM2 [68]	RN No 814 NAS, Culdrose	
ZH854	EHI-101 Merlin HM2 [14]	RN No 820 NAS, Culdrose	
ZH855	EHI-101 Merlin HM1 [68]	QinetiQ, stored Boscombe Down	
ZH856	EHI-101 Merlin HM2 [13]	RN MDMF, Culdrose	
ZH857	EHI-101 Merlin HM2 [86]	RN No 824 NAS, Culdrose	
ZH858	EHI-101 Merlin HM1 [17]	QinetiQ, stored Boscombe Down	
ZH860	EHI-101 Merlin HM2 [66]	RN No 820 NAS, Culdrose	
ZH861	EHI-101 Merlin HM2 [NL]	RN No 829 NAS, Culdrose	
ZH862	EHI-101 Merlin HM2 [85]	MoD/AFD/QinetiQ, Boscombe Down	
ZH863	EHI-101 Merlin HM1	RN stored, QinetiQ Boscombe Down	
ZH864	EHI-101 Merlin HM2 [85]	RN No 824 NAS, Culdrose	
ZH865	Lockheed C-130J-30 Hercules C4 (N130JA) [865]	RAF No 24 Sqn/No 30 Sqn/No 47 Sqn, Brize Norton	
ZH866	Lockheed C-130J-30 Hercules C4 (N130JE) [866] $	MoD/AFD/QinetiQ, Boscombe Down	
ZH867	Lockheed C-130J-30 Hercules C4 (N130JJ) [867]	RAF No 24 Sqn/No 30 Sqn/No 47 Sqn, Brize Norton	
ZH868	Lockheed C-130J-30 Hercules C4 (N130JN) [868]	RAF No 24 Sqn/No 30 Sqn/No 47 Sqn, Brize Norton	
ZH869	Lockheed C-130J-30 Hercules C4 (N130JV) [869]	RAF No 24 Sqn/No 30 Sqn/No 47 Sqn, Brize Norton	
ZH870	Lockheed C-130J-30 Hercules C4 (N78235) [870]	RAF No 24 Sqn/No 30 Sqn/No 47 Sqn, Brize Norton	
ZH871	Lockheed C-130J-30 Hercules C4 (N73238) [871]	RAF No 24 Sqn/No 30 Sqn/No 47 Sqn, Brize Norton	
ZH872	Lockheed C-130J-30 Hercules C4 (N4249Y) [872]	RAF No 24 Sqn/No 30 Sqn/No 47 Sqn, Brize Norton	
ZH873	Lockheed C-130J-30 Hercules C4 (N4242N) [873]	RAF No 24 Sqn/No 30 Sqn/No 47 Sqn, Brize Norton	
ZH874	Lockheed C-130J-30 Hercules C4 (N41030) [874]	RAF No 24 Sqn/No 30 Sqn/No 47 Sqn, Brize Norton	
ZH875	Lockheed C-130J-30 Hercules C4 (N4099R) [875]	RAF No 24 Sqn/No 30 Sqn/No 47 Sqn, Brize Norton	
ZH877	Lockheed C-130J-30 Hercules C4 (N4081M) [877]	RAF No 24 Sqn/No 30 Sqn/No 47 Sqn, Brize Norton	

Notes	Serial	Type (code/other identity)	Owner/operator, location or fate
	ZH878	Lockheed C-130J-30 Hercules C4 (N73232) [878]	RAF No 24 Sqn/No 30 Sqn/No 47 Sqn, Brize Norton
	ZH879	Lockheed C-130J-30 Hercules C4 (N4080M) [879]	RAF No 24 Sqn/No 30 Sqn/No 47 Sqn, Brize Norton
	ZH880	Lockheed C-130J Hercules C5 (N73238) [880]	MADG, Cambridge, for R Bahraini AF as 701
	ZH881	Lockheed C-130J Hercules C5 (N4081M) [881]	MoD/MADG, Cambridge (wfu)
	ZH882	Lockheed C-130J Hercules C5 (N4099R) [882]	RAF No 24 Sqn/No 30 Sqn/No 47 Sqn, Brize Norton
	ZH883	Lockheed C-130J Hercules C5 (N4242N) [883] $	RAF No 24 Sqn/No 30 Sqn/No 47 Sqn, Brize Norton
	ZH884	Lockheed C-130J Hercules C5 (N4187W) [884]	MoD/MADG, Cambridge (wfu)
	ZH885	Lockheed C-130J Hercules C5 (N41030) [885]	MoD/MADG, Cambridge (wfu)
	ZH886	Lockheed C-130J Hercules C5 (N73235) [886]	MADG, Cambridge, for R Bahraini AF as 702
	ZH887	Lockheed C-130J Hercules C5 (N4187W) [887]	RAF No 24 Sqn/No 30 Sqn/No 47 Sqn, Brize Norton
	ZH888	Lockheed C-130J Hercules C5 (N4187) [888]	RAF No 1312 Flt, Mount Pleasant, FI
	ZH889	Lockheed C-130J Hercules C5 (N4099R) [889]	RAF No 24 Sqn/No 30 Sqn/No 47 Sqn, Brize Norton
	ZH890	Grob G109B Vigilant T1 [SE]	RAF ACCGS/No 644 VGS, Syerston
	ZH891	B-V Chinook HC6A (N20075) [HF]	MoD/Boeing/QinetiQ, Boscombe Down (conversion)
	ZH892	B-V Chinook HC6A (N2019V) [HG]	RAF No 27 Sqn, Odiham
	ZH893	B-V Chinook HC6A (N2025L)	RAF No 27 Sqn, Odiham
	ZH894	B-V Chinook HC6A (N2026E) [HI]	RAF No 27 Sqn, Odiham
	ZH895	B-V Chinook HC6A (N2034K) [HJ]	RAF No 27 Sqn, Odiham
	ZH896	B-V Chinook HC6A (N2038G) [HK]	RAF No 27 Sqn, Odiham
	ZH897	B-V Chinook HC5 (N2045G)	MoD/Boeing/QinetiQ, Boscombe Down
	ZH898	B-V Chinook HC5 (N2057Q)	MoD/Vector Aerospace, Fleetlands (conversion)
	ZH899	B-V Chinook HC5 (N2057R)	RAF No 18 Sqn, Odiham
	ZH900	B-V Chinook HC5 (N2060H)	RAF No 27 Sqn, Odiham
	ZH901	B-V Chinook HC5 (N2060M)	RAF No 27 Sqn, Odiham
	ZH902	B-V Chinook HC5 (N2064W)	MoD/AFD/QinetiQ, Boscombe Down
	ZH903	B-V Chinook HC5 (N20671) [HR]	RAF No 27 Sqn, Odiham
	ZH904	B-V Chinook HC5 (N2083K)	MoD/AFD/QinetiQ, Boscombe Down
	ZH962	Westland Lynx Mk.21A (AH-11B) (N-4001)	Leonardo MW, Yeovil
	ZH965	Westland Lynx Mk.21A (AH-11B) (N-4004)	Leonardo MW, Yeovil (conversion)
	ZJ100	BAe Hawk 102D	BAE Systems National Training Academy, Humberside
	ZJ117	EHI-101 Merlin HC3 [A]	QinetiQ, stored Boscombe Down
	ZJ118	EHI-101 Merlin HC3i [B]	RN No 846 NAS, Yeovilton
	ZJ119	EHI-101 Merlin HC3 [C]	RN No 845 NAS, Yeovilton
	ZJ120	EHI-101 Merlin HC4 [D]	MoD/Leonardo MW, Yeovil
	ZJ121	EHI-101 Merlin HC4 [E]	MoD/Leonardo MW, Yeovil
	ZJ122	EHI-101 Merlin HC4 [F]	MoD/Leonardo MW, Yeovil
	ZJ123	EHI-101 Merlin HC3 [G]	RN No 846 NAS, Yeovilton
	ZJ124	EHI-101 Merlin HC4 [H]	MoD/Leonardo MW, Yeovil (conversion)
	ZJ125	EHI-101 Merlin HC4 [J]	MoD/Leonardo MW, Yeovil (conversion)
	ZJ126	EHI-101 Merlin HC3i [K]	RN No 846 NAS, Yeovilton
	ZJ127	EHI-101 Merlin HC4 [L]	MoD/Leonardo MW, Yeovil
	ZJ128	EHI-101 Merlin HC4 [M]	MoD/Leonardo MW, Yeovil (conversion)
	ZJ129	EHI-101 Merlin HC4 [N]	MoD/Leonardo MW, Yeovil (conversion)
	ZJ130	EHI-101 Merlin HC3i [O]	RN No 846 NAS, Yeovilton
	ZJ131	EHI-101 Merlin HC4 [P]	MoD/Leonardo MW, Yeovil (conversion)
	ZJ132	EHI-101 Merlin HC3i [Q]	RN MDMF, Culdrose
	ZJ133	EHI-101 Merlin HC3i [R]	QinetiQ, stored Boscombe Down
	ZJ134	EHI-101 Merlin HC4 [S]	MoD/Leonardo MW, Yeovil (conversion)
	ZJ135	EHI-101 Merlin HC3i [T]	RN No 846 NAS, Yeovilton
	ZJ136	EHI-101 Merlin HC3i [U]	RN No 846 NAS, Yeovilton
	ZJ137	EHI-101 Merlin HC3i [W]	RN No 846 NAS, Yeovilton
	ZJ138	EHI-101 Merlin HC3 [X]	QinetiQ, stored Boscombe Down
	ZJ164	AS365N-2 Dauphin 2 (G-BTLC)	RN/Bond Helicopters, Newquay
	ZJ165	AS365N-2 Dauphin 2 (G-NTOO)	RN/Bond Helicopters, Newquay
	ZJ166	WAH-64 Apache AH1 (N9219G)	AAC ADSU, stored Wattisham
	ZJ167	WAH-64 Apache AH1 (N3266B)	AAC ADSU, stored Wattisham
	ZJ168	WAH-64 Apache AH1 (N3123T)	AAC ADSU, stored Wattisham
	ZJ169	WAH-64 Apache AH1 (N3114H)	AAC ADSU, stored Wattisham
	ZJ170	WAH-64 Apache AH1 (N3065U)	AAC ADSU, stored Wattisham
	ZJ171	WAH-64 Apache AH1 (N3266T)	AAC ADSU, stored Wattisham
	ZJ172	WAH-64 Apache AH1	AAC ADSU, stored Wattisham

Serial	Type (code/other identity)	Owner/operator, location or fate	Notes
ZJ173	WAH-64 Apache AH1 (N3266W)	AAC ADSU, stored Wattisham	
ZJ174	WAH-64 Apache AH1	AAC ADSU, stored Wattisham	
ZJ175	WAH-64 Apache AH1 (N3218V)	AAC ADSU, stored Wattisham	
ZJ176	WAH-64 Apache AH1	AAC ADSU, stored Wattisham	
ZJ177	WAH-64 Apache AH1	DSAE (wreck)	
ZJ178	WAH-64 Apache AH1	AAC No 673 Sqn/7 Regt, Middle Wallop	
ZJ179	WAH-64 Apache AH1	AAC ADSU, Wattisham	
ZJ180	WAH-64 Apache AH1	AAC No 673 Sqn/7 Regt, Middle Wallop	
ZJ181	WAH-64 Apache AH1	AAC No 3 Regt, Wattisham	
ZJ182	WAH-64 Apache AH1	AAC No 3 Regt, Wattisham	
ZJ183	WAH-64 Apache AH1	AAC No 3 Regt, Wattisham	
ZJ184	WAH-64 Apache AH1	AAC No 3 Regt, Wattisham	
ZJ185	WAH-64 Apache AH1	AAC No 4 Regt, Wattisham	
ZJ186	WAH-64 Apache AH1	AAC No 3 Regt, Wattisham	
ZJ187	WAH-64 Apache AH1	AAC No 673 Sqn/7 Regt, Middle Wallop	
ZJ188	WAH-64 Apache AH1	AAC No 673 Sqn/7 Regt, Middle Wallop	
ZJ189	WAH-64 Apache AH1	AAC No 4 Regt, Wattisham	
ZJ190	WAH-64 Apache AH1	AAC No 3 Regt, Wattisham	
ZJ191	WAH-64 Apache AH1	AAC ADSU, stored Wattisham	
ZJ192	WAH-64 Apache AH1	AAC No 4 Regt, Wattisham	
ZJ193	WAH-64 Apache AH1	AAC No 3 Regt, Wattisham	
ZJ194	WAH-64 Apache AH1	AAC No 3 Regt, Wattisham	
ZJ195	WAH-64 Apache AH1	MoD/AFD/QinetiQ, Boscombe Down	
ZJ196	WAH-64 Apache AH1	AAC No 3 Regt, Wattisham	
ZJ197	WAH-64 Apache AH1	AAC No 4 Regt, Wattisham	
ZJ198	WAH-64 Apache AH1	AAC No 4 Regt, Wattisham	
ZJ199	WAH-64 Apache AH1	AAC No 3 Regt, Wattisham	
ZJ200	WAH-64 Apache AH1	AAC No 4 Regt, Wattisham	
ZJ202	WAH-64 Apache AH1	To Boeing, Mesa, USA, 2017	
ZJ203	WAH-64 Apache AH1	AAC No 3 Regt, Wattisham	
ZJ204	WAH-64 Apache AH1	AAC No 3 Regt, Wattisham	
ZJ205	WAH-64 Apache AH1	AAC ADSU, Wattisham	
ZJ206	WAH-64 Apache AH1	AAC ADSU, stored Wattisham	
ZJ207	WAH-64 Apache AH1	AAC No 3 Regt, Wattisham	
ZJ208	WAH-64 Apache AH1	AAC No 4 Regt, Wattisham	
ZJ209	WAH-64 Apache AH1	AAC No 673 Sqn/7 Regt, Middle Wallop	
ZJ210	WAH-64 Apache AH1	AAC No 4 Regt, Wattisham	
ZJ211	WAH-64 Apache AH1	AAC No 3 Regt, Wattisham	
ZJ212	WAH-64 Apache AH1	AAC ADSU, stored Wattisham	
ZJ213	WAH-64 Apache AH1	AAC No 3 Regt, Wattisham	
ZJ214	WAH-64 Apache AH1	AAC ADSU, stored Wattisham	
ZJ215	WAH-64 Apache AH1	AAC No 4 Regt, Wattisham	
ZJ216	WAH-64 Apache AH1	AAC No 673 Sqn/7 Regt, Middle Wallop	
ZJ217	WAH-64 Apache AH1	AAC No 673 Sqn/7 Regt, Middle Wallop	
ZJ218	WAH-64 Apache AH1	AAC No 4 Regt, Wattisham	
ZJ219	WAH-64 Apache AH1	AAC ADSU, stored Wattisham	
ZJ220	WAH-64 Apache AH1	AAC No 4 Regt, Wattisham	
ZJ221	WAH-64 Apache AH1	AAC No 3 Regt, Wattisham	
ZJ222	WAH-64 Apache AH1	AAC ADSU, Wattisham	
ZJ223	WAH-64 Apache AH1	AAC No 3 Regt, Wattisham	
ZJ224	WAH-64 Apache AH1	AAC No 4 Regt, Wattisham	
ZJ225	WAH-64 Apache AH1	AAC No 3 Regt, Wattisham	
ZJ226	WAH-64 Apache AH1	AAC No 4 Regt, Wattisham	
ZJ227	WAH-64 Apache AH1	AAC No 673 Sqn/7 Regt, Middle Wallop	
ZJ228	WAH-64 Apache AH1	AAC No 3 Regt, Wattisham	
ZJ229	WAH-64 Apache AH1	AAC No 3 Regt, Wattisham	
ZJ230	WAH-64 Apache AH1	AAC No 673 Sqn/7 Regt, Middle Wallop	
ZJ231	WAH-64 Apache AH1	AAC ADSU, Wattisham	
ZJ232	WAH-64 Apache AH1	AAC No 4 Regt, Wattisham	
ZJ233	WAH-64 Apache AH1	AAC No 3 Regt, Wattisham	
ZJ234	Bell 412EP Griffin HT1 (G-BWZR) [S]	DHFS No 60 Sqn, RAF Shawbury	
ZJ235	Bell 412EP Griffin HT1 (G-BXBF) [I]	DHFS No 60 Sqn, RAF Shawbury	

Notes	Serial	Type (code/other identity)	Owner/operator, location or fate
	ZJ236	Bell 412EP Griffin HT1 (G-BXBE) [X]	DHFS No 60 Sqn, RAF Shawbury
	ZJ237	Bell 412EP Griffin HT1 (G-BXFF) [T]	DHFS No 60 Sqn, RAF Shawbury
	ZJ238	Bell 412EP Griffin HT1 (G-BXHC) [Y]	DHFS No 60 Sqn, RAF Shawbury
	ZJ239	Bell 412EP Griffin HT1 (G-BXFH) [R]	DHFS No 202 Sqn, RAF Valley
	ZJ240	Bell 412EP Griffin HT1 (G-BXIR) [U]	DHFS No 60 Sqn, RAF Shawbury
	ZJ242	Bell 412EP Griffin HT1 (G-BXDK) [E]	DHFS No 60 Sqn, RAF Shawbury
	ZJ243	AS350BA Squirrel HT2 (G-BWZS) [43]	DHFS, RAF Shawbury
	ZJ244	AS350BA Squirrel HT2 (G-BXMD) [44]	School of Army Aviation/No 670 Sqn, Middle Wallop
	ZJ245	AS350BA Squirrel HT2 (G-BXME) [45]	School of Army Aviation/No 670 Sqn, Middle Wallop
	ZJ246	AS350BA Squirrel HT2 (G-BXMJ) [46]	School of Army Aviation/No 670 Sqn, Middle Wallop
	ZJ248	AS350BA Squirrel HT2 (G-BXNE) [48]	School of Army Aviation/No 670 Sqn, Middle Wallop
	ZJ249	AS350BA Squirrel HT2 (G-BXNJ) [49]	School of Army Aviation/No 670 Sqn, Middle Wallop
	ZJ250	AS350BA Squirrel HT2 (G-BXNY) [50]	School of Army Aviation/No 670 Sqn, Middle Wallop
	ZJ251	AS350BA Squirrel HT2 (G-BXOG) [51]	DHFS, RAF Shawbury
	ZJ252	AS350BA Squirrel HT2 (G-BXOK) [52]	School of Army Aviation/No 670 Sqn, Middle Wallop
	ZJ253	AS350BA Squirrel HT2 (G-BXPG) [53]	School of Army Aviation/No 670 Sqn, Middle Wallop
	ZJ254	AS350BA Squirrel HT2 (G-BXPJ) [54]	School of Army Aviation/No 670 Sqn, Middle Wallop
	ZJ255	AS350BB Squirrel HT1 (G-BXAG) [55]	*Sold as G-BXAG, 27 February 2018*
	ZJ256	AS350BB Squirrel HT1 (G-BXCE) [56]	*Sold as G-BXCE, 28 November 2017*
	ZJ257	AS350BB Squirrel HT1 (G-BXDJ) [57]	DHFS, RAF Shawbury
	ZJ260	AS350BB Squirrel HT1 (G-BXGB) [60]	*Sold as G-BXGB, 14 November 2017*
	ZJ261	AS350BB Squirrel HT1 (G-BXGJ) [61]	DHFS, RAF Shawbury
	ZJ262	AS350BB Squirrel HT1 (G-BXHB) [62]	*Sold as G-BXHB, 27 February 2018*
	ZJ264	AS350BB Squirrel HT1 (G-BXHW) [64]	DHFS, RAF Shawbury
	ZJ265	AS350BB Squirrel HT1 (G-BXHX) [65]	DHFS, RAF Shawbury
	ZJ266	AS350BB Squirrel HT1 (G-BXIL) [66]	*Sold as G-BXIL, 30 November 2017*
	ZJ267	AS350BB Squirrel HT1 (G-BXIP) [67]	DHFS, RAF Shawbury
	ZJ268	AS350BB Squirrel HT1 (G-BXJE) [68]	DHFS, RAF Shawbury
	ZJ269	AS350BB Squirrel HT1 (G-BXJN) [69]	*Sold as G-BXJN, 30 November 2017*
	ZJ270	AS350BB Squirrel HT1 (G-BXJR) [70]	*Sold as G-BXJR, 27 February 2018*
	ZJ271	AS350BB Squirrel HT1 (G-BXKE) [71]	DHFS, RAF Shawbury
	ZJ272	AS350BB Squirrel HT1 (G-BXKN) [72]	DHFS, RAF Shawbury
	ZJ273	AS350BB Squirrel HT1 (G-BXKP) [73]	DHFS, RAF Shawbury
	ZJ274	AS350BB Squirrel HT1 (G-BXKR) [74]	*Sold as G-BXKR, 27 February 2018*
	ZJ275	AS350BB Squirrel HT1 (G-BXLB) [75]	*Sold as G-BXLB, 20 November 2017*
	ZJ276	AS350BB Squirrel HT1 (G-BXLE) [76]	DHFS, RAF Shawbury
	ZJ277	AS350BB Squirrel HT1 (G-BXLH) [77]	DHFS, RAF Shawbury
	ZJ278	AS350BB Squirrel HT1 (G-BXMB) [78]	*Sold as G-BXMB, 27 February 2018*
	ZJ279	AS350BB Squirrel HT1 (G-BXMC) [79]	DHFS, RAF Shawbury
	ZJ280	AS350BB Squirrel HT1 (G-BXMI) [80]	DHFS, RAF Shawbury
	ZJ369	GEC Phoenix RPAS	Defence Academy of the UK, Shrivenham
	ZJ385	GEC Phoenix RPAS	Muckleburgh Collection, Weybourne, Norfolk
	ZJ392	GEC Phoenix RPAS	Privately owned, Holt Heath, Worcs
	ZJ449	GEC Phoenix RPAS	REME Museum, Lyneham
	ZJ452	GEC Phoenix RPAS	Science Museum, stored Wroughton
	ZJ469	GEC Phoenix RPAS	Army, Larkhill, on display
	ZJ493	GAF Jindivik 104AL (A92-814)	RAF Museum Reserve Collection, Stafford
	ZJ496	GAF Jindivik 104AL (A92-901)	Farnborough Air Sciences Trust, Farnborough
	ZJ515	BAE Systems Nimrod MRA4 (XV258) <ff>	Cranfield University, instructional use
	ZJ620	AgustaWestland Merlin Simulator	RN No 824 NAS, Culdrose
	ZJ621	AgustaWestland Merlin Simulator	RN No 824 NAS, Culdrose
	ZJ622	AgustaWestland Merlin Simulator	RN No 824 NAS, Culdrose
	ZJ623	AgustaWestland Merlin Simulator	RN No 824 NAS, Culdrose
	ZJ624	AgustaWestland Merlin Simulator	RN No 824 NAS, Culdrose
	ZJ625	AgustaWestland Merlin Simulator	RN No 824 NAS, Culdrose
	ZJ626	AgustaWestland Merlin Simulator	RN No 824 NAS, Culdrose
	ZJ645	D-BD Alpha Jet (98+62) [45]	MoD/QinetiQ, stored Boscombe Down
	ZJ646	D-BD Alpha Jet (98+55) [46]	MoD/QinetiQ, stored Boscombe Down
	ZJ647	D-BD Alpha Jet (98+71) [47]	MoD/QinetiQ, stored Boscombe Down
	ZJ648	D-BD Alpha Jet (98+09) [48]	MoD/QinetiQ Boscombe Down, spares use
	ZJ649	D-BD Alpha Jet (98+73) [49]	MoD/QinetiQ, stored Boscombe Down
	ZJ650	D-BD Alpha Jet (98+35)	MoD/QinetiQ, stored Boscombe Down

Serial	Type (code/other identity)	Owner/operator, location or fate	Notes
ZJ651	D-BD Alpha Jet (41+42) [51]	MoD/QinetiQ, stored Boscombe Down	
ZJ652	D-BD Alpha Jet (41+09)	MoD/QinetiQ Boscombe Down, spares use	
ZJ653	D-BD Alpha Jet (40+22)	MoD/QinetiQ Boscombe Down, spares use	
ZJ654	D-BD Alpha Jet (41+02)	MoD/QinetiQ Boscombe Down, spares use	
ZJ655	D-BD Alpha Jet (41+19)	MoD/QinetiQ Boscombe Down, spares use	
ZJ656	D-BD Alpha Jet (41+40)	MoD/QinetiQ Boscombe Down, spares use	
ZJ690	Bombardier Sentinel R1 (C-GJRG)	RAF No 5 Sqn, Waddington	
ZJ691	Bombardier Sentinel R1 (C-FZVM)	RAF No 5 Sqn, Waddington	
ZJ692	Bombardier Sentinel R1 (C-FZWW)	RAF No 5 Sqn, Waddington	
ZJ693	Bombardier Sentinel R1 (C-FZXC)	MoD/Raytheon, stored Hawarden	
ZJ694	Bombardier Sentinel R1 (C-FZYL)	RAF No 5 Sqn, Waddington	
ZJ699	Eurofighter Typhoon (PT001)	MoD/BAE Systems, Warton	
ZJ700	Eurofighter Typhoon (PS002)	MoD/BAE Systems, Warton	
ZJ703	Bell 412EP Griffin HAR2 (G-CBST) [Spades,3]	AAC, Middle Wallop	
ZJ704	Bell 412EP Griffin HAR2 (G-CBWT) [Clubs,4]	RAF No 84 Sqn, Akrotiri	
ZJ705	Bell 412EP Griffin HAR2 (G-CBXL) [Hearts,5]	MoD/AFD/QinetiQ, Boscombe Down	
ZJ706	Bell 412EP Griffin HAR2 (G-CBYR) [Diamonds,6]	RAF No 84 Sqn, Akrotiri	
ZJ707	Bell 412EP Griffin HT1 (G-CBUB) [O]	DHFS No 60 Sqn, RAF Shawbury	
ZJ708	Bell 412EP Griffin HT1 (G-CBVP) [K]	DHFS/FBS, RAF Shawbury	
ZJ765	Meteor Mirach 100/5	QinetiQ Apprentice Training School, Boscombe Down	
ZJ780	AS365N-3 Dauphin AH1 (G-CEXT)	AAC No 658 Sqn, Credenhill	
ZJ781	AS365N-3 Dauphin AH1 (G-CEXU)	AAC No 658 Sqn, Credenhill	
ZJ782	AS365N-3 Dauphin AH1 (G-CEXV)	AAC No 658 Sqn, Credenhill	
ZJ783	AS365N-3 Dauphin AH1 (G-CEXW)	AAC No 658 Sqn, Credenhill	
ZJ785	AS365N-3 Dauphin AH1 (G-CFFW)	AAC No 658 Sqn, Credenhill	
ZJ787	AS365N-3 Dauphin AH1 (G-CHNJ)	AAC No 658 Sqn, Credenhill	
ZJ800	Eurofighter Typhoon T3 [BC]	RAF No 29 Sqn, Coningsby	
ZJ801	Eurofighter Typhoon T3 [BJ]	RAF, stored Coningsby	
ZJ802	Eurofighter Typhoon T3 [802]	RAF No 3 Sqn, Coningsby	
ZJ803	Eurofighter Typhoon T3 [803]	RAF No 2 Sqn, Lossiemouth	
ZJ804	Eurofighter Typhoon T3 [804]	RAF Coningsby, RTP	
ZJ805	Eurofighter Typhoon T3 [BD]	RAF, stored Coningsby	
ZJ806	Eurofighter Typhoon T3 (fuselage)	RAF Coningsby, RTP	
ZJ807	Eurofighter Typhoon T3 [807]	RAF No 29 Sqn, Coningsby	
ZJ808	Eurofighter Typhoon T3 (fuselage)	RAF, stored Coningsby	
ZJ809	Eurofighter Typhoon T3 [809]	RAF Coningsby, RTP	
ZJ810	Eurofighter Typhoon T3 [810]	RAF No 29 Sqn, Coningsby	
ZJ811	Eurofighter Typhoon T3 [811]	RAF Coningsby, RTP	
ZJ812	Eurofighter Typhoon T3 [812]	RAF No 29 Sqn, Coningsby	
ZJ813	Eurofighter Typhoon T3 [BL]	RAF Coningsby, GI use	
ZJ814	Eurofighter Typhoon T3 [814]	RAF, stored Coningsby	
ZJ815	Eurofighter Typhoon T3 (fuselage)	RAF, stored Coningsby	
ZJ910	Eurofighter Typhoon FGR4 [DO]	RAF AM&SU, stored Shawbury	
ZJ911	Eurofighter Typhoon FGR4 [QO-Z]	RAF AM&SU, stored Shawbury	
ZJ912	Eurofighter Typhoon FGR4 [912]	RAF AM&SU, stored Shawbury	
ZJ913	Eurofighter Typhoon FGR4 [913]	RAF No 2 Sqn, Lossiemouth	
ZJ914	Eurofighter Typhoon FGR4 [914]	RAF No 29 Sqn, Coningsby	
ZJ915	Eurofighter Typhoon FGR4 [F]	RAF No 1435 Flt, Mount Pleasant, FI	
ZJ916	Eurofighter Typhoon FGR4 [S]	RAF TMF, Coningsby	
ZJ917	Eurofighter Typhoon FGR4 [917]	RAF No 3 Sqn, Coningsby	
ZJ918	Eurofighter Typhoon FGR4	RAF AM&SU, stored Shawbury	
ZJ919	Eurofighter Typhoon FGR4 [919]	RAF No 1 Sqn, Lossiemouth	
ZJ920	Eurofighter Typhoon FGR4 [920]	RAF No 29 Sqn, Coningsby	
ZJ921	Eurofighter Typhoon FGR4 [921]	RAF No 2 Sqn, Lossiemouth	
ZJ922	Eurofighter Typhoon FGR4 [QO-C]	MoD/BAE Systems, Warton	
ZJ923	Eurofighter Typhoon FGR4 [923]	RAF No 2 Sqn, Lossiemouth	
ZJ924	Eurofighter Typhoon FGR4 [924]	RAF No 29 Sqn, Coningsby	
ZJ925	Eurofighter Typhoon FGR4 [DXI] $	RAF AM&SU, stored Shawbury	
ZJ926	Eurofighter Typhoon FGR4 [H]	RAF No 1435 Flt, Mount Pleasant, FI	
ZJ927	Eurofighter Typhoon FGR4 [927]	RAF AM&SU, stored Shawbury	
ZJ928	Eurofighter Typhoon FGR4 [928]	RAF No 11 Sqn, Coningsby	
ZJ929	Eurofighter Typhoon FGR4 [929]	RAF No 3 Sqn, Coningsby	

Notes	Serial	Type (code/other identity)	Owner/operator, location or fate
	ZJ930	Eurofighter Typhoon FGR4 [930]	RAF AM&SU, stored Shawbury
	ZJ931	Eurofighter Typhoon FGR4 [931]	RAF No 2 Sqn, Lossiemouth
	ZJ932	Eurofighter Typhoon FGR4 [DB]	RAF AM&SU, stored Shawbury
	ZJ933	Eurofighter Typhoon FGR4 [C]	RAF No 1435 Flt, Mount Pleasant, FI
	ZJ934	Eurofighter Typhoon FGR4 [934]	RAF AM&SU, stored Shawbury
	ZJ935	Eurofighter Typhoon FGR4 [935]	RAF No 3 Sqn, Coningsby
	ZJ936	Eurofighter Typhoon FGR4 [QO-C]	RAF AM&SU, stored Shawbury
	ZJ937	Eurofighter Typhoon FGR4 [937]	RAF TMF, Coningsby
	ZJ938	Eurofighter Typhoon FGR4	MoD/BAE Systems, Warton
	ZJ939	Eurofighter Typhoon FGR4 [939]	RAF No 3 Sqn, Coningsby
	ZJ940	Eurofighter Typhoon FGR4 [DJ666]	RAF, stored Coningsby
	ZJ941	Eurofighter Typhoon FGR4 [D]	RAF No 1435 Flt, Mount Pleasant, FI
	ZJ942	Eurofighter Typhoon FGR4 [942]	RAF No 29 Sqn, Coningsby
	ZJ943	Eurofighter Typhoon FGR4 (fuselage)	RAF AM&SU, stored Shawbury (wreck)
	ZJ944	Eurofighter Typhoon FGR4	RAF TMF, Coningsby
	ZJ945	Eurofighter Typhoon FGR4	RAF, stored Coningsby
	ZJ946	Eurofighter Typhoon FGR4 [946]	RAF TMF, Coningsby
	ZJ947	Eurofighter Typhoon FGR4 [947]	RAF No 6 Sqn, Lossiemouth
	ZJ948	Eurofighter Typhoon FGR4	RAF, stored Coningsby
	ZJ949	Eurofighter Typhoon FGR4 [949]	RAF No 11 Sqn, Coningsby
	ZJ950	Eurofighter Typhoon FGR4 [950]	RAF TMF, Coningsby
	ZJ951	BAE Systems Advanced Hawk 120D	MoD/BAE Systems, Warton
	ZJ954	SA330H Puma HC2 (SAAF 144)	RAF No 28 Sqn/No 33 Sqn/No 230 Sqn, Benson
	ZJ955	SA330H Puma HC2 (SAAF 148) [P] $	RAF No 28 Sqn/No 33 Sqn/No 230 Sqn, Benson
	ZJ956	SA330H Puma HC2 (SAAF 172/F-ZWCC)	RAF No 28 Sqn/No 33 Sqn/No 230 Sqn, Benson
	ZJ957	SA330H Puma HC2 (SAAF 169)	RAF No 28 Sqn/No 33 Sqn/No 230 Sqn, Benson
	ZJ960	Grob G109B Vigilant T1 (D-KSMU) [SH]	RAF, stored Little Rissington
	ZJ961	Grob G109B Vigilant T1 (D-KLCW) [SJ]	RAF, stored Little Rissington
	ZJ962	Grob G109B Vigilant T1 (D-KBEU) [SK]	RAF, stored Little Rissington
	ZJ963	Grob G109B Vigilant T1 (D-KMSN) [SL]	RAF/Serco, stored Syerston
	ZJ967	Grob G109B Vigilant T1 (G-DEWS) [SM]	RAF/Serco GMS, Syerston
	ZJ968	Grob G109B Vigilant T1 (N109BT) [SN]	RAF, stored Woodvale
	ZJ969	Bell 212HP AH1 (G-BGLJ) [K]	AAC JHC/No 7 Regt, Middle Wallop
	ZJ990	EHI-101 Merlin HC3A (M-501) [AA]	RN No 845 NAS, Yeovilton
	ZJ992	EHI-101 Merlin HC3A (M-503) [AB]	RN No 845 NAS, Yeovilton
	ZJ994	EHI-101 Merlin HC3A (M-505) [AC]	RN No 845 NAS, Yeovilton
	ZJ995	EHI-101 Merlin HC3A (M-506) [AD]	RN MDMF, Culdrose
	ZJ998	EHI-101 Merlin HC3A (M-509) [AE]	RN No 845 NAS, Yeovilton
	ZK001	EHI-101 Merlin HC3A (M-511) [AF]	RN No 845 NAS, Yeovilton
	ZK005	Grob G109B Vigilant T1 (OH-797) [SP]	RAF, stored Little Rissington
	ZK010	BAE Systems Hawk T2 [A]	RAF No 4 FTS/4 Sqn, Valley
	ZK011	BAE Systems Hawk T2 [B]	RAF No 4 FTS/4 Sqn, Valley
	ZK012	BAE Systems Hawk T2 [C]	RAF No 4 FTS/4 Sqn, Valley
	ZK013	BAE Systems Hawk T2 [D]	RAF No 4 FTS/4 Sqn, Valley
	ZK014	BAE Systems Hawk T2 [E]	RAF No 4 FTS/4 Sqn, Valley
	ZK015	BAE Systems Hawk T2 [F]	RAF No 4 FTS/4 Sqn, Valley
	ZK016	BAE Systems Hawk T2 [G]	RAF HSF, stored Valley
	ZK017	BAE Systems Hawk T2 [H]	RAF HSF, Valley
	ZK018	BAE Systems Hawk T2 [I] $	RAF HSF, stored Valley
	ZK019	BAE Systems Hawk T2 [J]	RAF No 4 FTS/4 Sqn, Valley
	ZK020	BAE Systems Hawk T2 [K] $	RAF No 4 FTS/4 Sqn, Valley
	ZK021	BAE Systems Hawk T2 [L]	RAF No 4 FTS/4 Sqn, Valley
	ZK022	BAE Systems Hawk T2 [M]	RAF No 4 FTS/4 Sqn, Valley
	ZK023	BAE Systems Hawk T2 [N]	RAF No 4 FTS/4 Sqn, Valley
	ZK024	BAE Systems Hawk T2 [O]	RAF No 4 FTS/4 Sqn, Valley
	ZK025	BAE Systems Hawk T2 [P]	RAF No 4 FTS/4 Sqn, Valley
	ZK026	BAE Systems Hawk T2 [Q]	RAF No 4 FTS/4 Sqn, Valley
	ZK027	BAE Systems Hawk T2 [R]	RAF No 4 FTS/4 Sqn, Valley
	ZK028	BAE Systems Hawk T2 [S]	RAF No 4 FTS/4 Sqn, Valley
	ZK029	BAE Systems Hawk T2 [T]	RAF No 4 FTS/4 Sqn, Valley
	ZK030	BAE Systems Hawk T2 [U]	RAF No 4 FTS/4 Sqn, Valley

Serial	Type (code/other identity)	Owner/operator, location or fate	Notes
ZK031	BAE Systems Hawk T2 [V]	RAF No 4 FTS/4 Sqn, Valley	
ZK032	BAE Systems Hawk T2 [W]	RAF No 4 FTS/4 Sqn, Valley	
ZK033	BAE Systems Hawk T2 [X]	RAF HSF, stored Valley	
ZK034	BAE Systems Hawk T2 [Y]	RAF No 4 FTS/4 Sqn, Valley	
ZK035	BAE Systems Hawk T2 [Z]	RAF No 4 FTS/4 Sqn, Valley	
ZK036	BAE Systems Hawk T2 [AA]	RAF No 4 FTS/4 Sqn, Valley	
ZK037	BAE Systems Hawk T2 [AB]	RAF No 4 FTS/4 Sqn, Valley	
ZK067	Bell 212HP AH3 (G-BFER) [B]	AAC No 7 Flt, Brunei	
ZK114	M2370 RPAS	QinetiQ	
ZK150*	Lockheed Martin Desert Hawk 3 RPAS	Army 47 Regt Royal Artillery, Thorney Island	
ZK150	Lockheed Martin Desert Hawk 3 RPAS (ZK150/617)	Imperial War Museum, Lambeth	
ZK155*	Honeywell T-Hawk RPAS	Army 32 Regt Royal Artillery, Larkhill	
ZK192	AgustaWestland Super Lynx Mk.140	To Algeria as LC-32, 2017	
ZK195	AgustaWestland Super Lynx Mk.140	To Algeria as LC-35, April 2017	
ZK205	Grob G109B Vigilant T1 (D-KBRU) [SS]	RAF/Serco GMS, Syerston	
ZK210	BAE Systems Mantis RPAS	MoD/BAE Systems, Warton	
ZK300	Eurofighter Typhoon FGR4 [300]	RAF No 2 Sqn, Lossiemouth	
ZK301	Eurofighter Typhoon FGR4 [301]	RAF TMF, Coningsby	
ZK302	Eurofighter Typhoon FGR4 [302]	RAF No 3 Sqn, Coningsby	
ZK303	Eurofighter Typhoon T3 [AX]	MoD/BAE Systems, Warton	
ZK304	Eurofighter Typhoon FGR4 [304]	RAF No 3 Sqn, Coningsby	
ZK305	Eurofighter Typhoon FGR4 [305]	RAF TMF, Coningsby	
ZK306	Eurofighter Typhoon FGR4 [306]	RAF No 1 Sqn, Lossiemouth	
ZK307	Eurofighter Typhoon FGR4 [307]	RAF No 3 Sqn, Coningsby	
ZK308	Eurofighter Typhoon FGR4 [308]	RAF No 11 Sqn, Coningsby	
ZK309	Eurofighter Typhoon FGR4 [QO-P]	RAF No 3 Sqn, Coningsby	
ZK310	Eurofighter Typhoon FGR4 [310]	RAF No 3 Sqn, Coningsby	
ZK311	Eurofighter Typhoon FGR4	RAF No 11 Sqn, Coningsby	
ZK312	Eurofighter Typhoon FGR4 [312]	RAF No 11 Sqn, Coningsby	
ZK313	Eurofighter Typhoon FGR4 [313]	RAF No 3 Sqn, Coningsby	
ZK314	Eurofighter Typhoon FGR4 [314]	RAF No 6 Sqn, Lossiemouth	
ZK315	Eurofighter Typhoon FGR4 [EB-V] $	RAF AWC/FJWOEU/No 41 Sqn, Coningsby	
ZK316	Eurofighter Typhoon FGR4 [316]	RAF No 11 Sqn, Coningsby	
ZK317	Eurofighter Typhoon FGR4 [317]	RAF No 6 Sqn, Lossiemouth	
ZK318	Eurofighter Typhoon FGR4 [318]	RAF No 29 Sqn, Coningsby	
ZK319	Eurofighter Typhoon FGR4 [319]	RAF No 1 Sqn, Lossiemouth	
ZK320	Eurofighter Typhoon FGR4 [320]	RAF No 6 Sqn, Lossiemouth	
ZK321	Eurofighter Typhoon FGR4 [321]	RAF TMF, Coningsby	
ZK322	Eurofighter Typhoon FGR4 [322]	RAF TMF, Coningsby	
ZK323	Eurofighter Typhoon FGR4 [323]	RAF No 6 Sqn, Lossiemouth	
ZK324	Eurofighter Typhoon FGR4	RAF TMF, Coningsby	
ZK325	Eurofighter Typhoon FGR4 [325]	RAF No 3 Sqn, Coningsby	
ZK326	Eurofighter Typhoon FGR4 [FB]	RAF, stored Coningsby	
ZK327	Eurofighter Typhoon FGR4 [327]	RAF No 6 Sqn, Lossiemouth	
ZK328	Eurofighter Typhoon FGR4 [328]	RAF No 1 Sqn, Lossiemouth	
ZK329	Eurofighter Typhoon FGR4 [329]	RAF No 1 Sqn, Lossiemouth	
ZK330	Eurofighter Typhoon FGR4 [330]	RAF TMF, Coningsby	
ZK331	Eurofighter Typhoon FGR4 [331]	RAF No 2 Sqn, Lossiemouth	
ZK332	Eurofighter Typhoon FGR4 [332]	RAF No 3 Sqn, Coningsby	
ZK333	Eurofighter Typhoon FGR4 [333]	RAF No 6 Sqn, Lossiemouth	
ZK334	Eurofighter Typhoon FGR4 [334]	RAF No 6 Sqn, Lossiemouth	
ZK335	Eurofighter Typhoon FGR4 [335]	RAF AWC/FJWOEU/No 41 Sqn, Coningsby	
ZK336	Eurofighter Typhoon FGR4 [336]	RAF TMF, Coningsby	
ZK337	Eurofighter Typhoon FGR4 [337]	RAF No 2 Sqn, Lossiemouth	
ZK338	Eurofighter Typhoon FGR4 [338]	RAF No 3 Sqn, Coningsby	
ZK339	Eurofighter Typhoon FGR4 [EB-E]	RAF AWC/FJWOEU/No 41 Sqn, Coningsby	
ZK340	Eurofighter Typhoon FGR4 [340]	RAF No 11 Sqn, Coningsby	
ZK341	Eurofighter Typhoon FGR4 [341]	RAF No 11 Sqn, Coningsby	
ZK342	Eurofighter Typhoon FGR4 [342]	RAF No 29 Sqn, Coningsby	
ZK343	Eurofighter Typhoon FGR4	RAF No 29 Sqn, Coningsby	
ZK344	Eurofighter Typhoon FGR4 [344]	RAF No 1 Sqn, Lossiemouth	
ZK345	Eurofighter Typhoon FGR4 [345]	RAF No 3 Sqn, Coningsby	

Notes	Serial	Type (code/other identity)	Owner/operator, location or fate
	ZK346	Eurofighter Typhoon FGR4 [346]	RAF No 11 Sqn, Coningsby
	ZK347	Eurofighter Typhoon FGR4 [347]	RAF TMF, Coningsby
	ZK348	Eurofighter Typhoon FGR4 [348]	RAF No 3 Sqn, Coningsby
	ZK349	Eurofighter Typhoon FGR4 [349]	RAF No 6 Sqn, Lossiemouth
	ZK350	Eurofighter Typhoon FGR4	MoD/BAE Systems, Warton
	ZK351	Eurofighter Typhoon FGR4 [351]	RAF No 6 Sqn, Lossiemouth
	ZK352	Eurofighter Typhoon FGR4 [352]	RAF No 29 Sqn, Coningsby
	ZK353	Eurofighter Typhoon FGR4	RAF No 3 Sqn, Coningsby
	ZK354	Eurofighter Typhoon FGR4 [354]	RAF No 11 Sqn, Coningsby
	ZK355	Eurofighter Typhoon FGR4	MoD/BAE Systems, Warton
	ZK356	Eurofighter Typhoon FGR4	MoD/BAE Systems, Warton
	ZK357	Eurofighter Typhoon FGR4	RAF TMF, Coningsby
	ZK358	Eurofighter Typhoon FGR4	RAF No 3 Sqn, Coningsby
	ZK359	Eurofighter Typhoon FGR4	MoD/BAE Systems, Warton
	ZK360	Eurofighter Typhoon FGR4	RAF TMF, Coningsby
	ZK361	Eurofighter Typhoon FGR4 [361]	RAF No 11 Sqn, Coningsby
	ZK362	Eurofighter Typhoon FGR4	RAF TMF, Coningsby
	ZK363	Eurofighter Typhoon FGR4	RAF TMF, Coningsby
	ZK364	Eurofighter Typhoon FGR4	RAF No 11 Sqn, Coningsby
	ZK365	Eurofighter Typhoon FGR4 [EB-L]	RAF AWC/FJWOEU/No 41 Sqn, Coningsby
	ZK366	Eurofighter Typhoon FGR4 [366]	RAF No 11 Sqn, Coningsby
	ZK367	Eurofighter Typhoon FGR4 [EB-R]	RAF AWC/FJWOEU/No 41 Sqn, Coningsby
	ZK368	Eurofighter Typhoon FGR4 [368]	RAF No 2 Sqn, Lossiemouth
	ZK369	Eurofighter Typhoon FGR4 [369]	RAF No 2 Sqn, Lossiemouth
	ZK370	Eurofighter Typhoon FGR4	MoD/BAE Systems, Warton
	ZK371	Eurofighter Typhoon FGR4	RAF No 3 Sqn, Coningsby
	ZK372	Eurofighter Typhoon FGR4 [372]	RAF No 2 Sqn, Lossiemouth
	ZK373	Eurofighter Typhoon FGR4 [373]	RAF No 29 Sqn, Coningsby
	ZK374	Eurofighter Typhoon FGR4	MoD/BAE Systems, Warton
	ZK375	Eurofighter Typhoon FGR4	RAF TMF, Coningsby
	ZK376	Eurofighter Typhoon FGR4	RAF AWC/FJWOEU/No 41 Sqn, Coningsby
	ZK377	Eurofighter Typhoon FGR4 [377]	RAF No 3 Sqn, Coningsby
	ZK378	Eurofighter Typhoon FGR4	RAF No 1 Sqn, Lossiemouth
	ZK379	Eurofighter Typhoon T3 [379]	RAF AWC/FJWOEU/No 41 Sqn, Coningsby
	ZK380	Eurofighter Typhoon T3 [380]	RAF No 29 Sqn, Coningsby
	ZK381	Eurofighter Typhoon T3 [381]	RAF No 29 Sqn, Coningsby
	ZK382	Eurofighter Typhoon T3 [382]	RAF No 29 Sqn, Coningsby
	ZK383	Eurofighter Typhoon T3 [383]	RAF No 29 Sqn, Coningsby
	ZK424	Eurofighter Typhoon FGR4	RAF TMF, Coningsby
	ZK425	Eurofighter Typhoon FGR4	MoD/BAE Systems, Warton
	ZK426	Eurofighter Typhoon FGR4	MoD/BAE Systems, Warton
	ZK427	Eurofighter Typhoon FGR4	RAF TMF, Coningsby
	ZK428	Eurofighter Typhoon FGR4	RAF TMF, Coningsby
	ZK429	Eurofighter Typhoon FGR4	MoD/BAE Systems, Warton
	ZK430	Eurofighter Typhoon FGR4	MoD/BAE Systems, Warton
	ZK431	Eurofighter Typhoon FGR4	DE&S/BAE Systems, Warton
	ZK432	Eurofighter Typhoon FGR4	DE&S/BAE Systems, Warton
	ZK433	Eurofighter Typhoon FGR4	DE&S/BAE Systems, Warton
	ZK434	Eurofighter Typhoon FGR4	DE&S/BAE Systems, Warton
	ZK435	Eurofighter Typhoon FGR4	DE&S/BAE Systems, Warton
	ZK436	Eurofighter Typhoon FGR4	DE&S/BAE Systems, Warton
	ZK437	Eurofighter Typhoon FGR4	DE&S/BAE Systems, Warton
	ZK438	Eurofighter Typhoon FGR4	DE&S/BAE Systems, Warton
	ZK439	Eurofighter Typhoon FGR4	DE&S/BAE Systems, Warton
	ZK451	Beech King Air B200 (G-RAFK) [K]	SERCO/RAF No 3 FTS/45 Sqn, Cranwell
	ZK452	Beech King Air B200 (G-RAFL) [L]	SERCO/RAF No 3 FTS/45 Sqn, Cranwell
	ZK455	Beech King Air B200 (G-RAFO) [O]	SERCO/RAF No 3 FTS/45 Sqn, Cranwell
	ZK456	Beech King Air B200 (G-RAFP) [P]	SERCO/RAF No 3 FTS/45 Sqn, Cranwell
	ZK458	Hawker Beechcraft King Air B200GT (G-RAFD) [D]	SERCO/RAF No 3 FTS/45 Sqn, Cranwell
	ZK459	Hawker Beechcraft King Air B200GT (G-RAFX) [X]	SERCO/RAF No 3 FTS/45 Sqn, Cranwell
	ZK460	Hawker Beechcraft King Air B200GT (G-RAFU) [U] $	SERCO/RAF No 3 FTS/45 Sqn, Cranwell
	ZK531	BAe Hawk T53 (LL-5306)	Humberside Airport, on display

Serial	Type (code/other identity)	Owner/operator, location or fate	Notes
ZK532	BAe Hawk T53 (LL-5315)	MoD/BAE Systems, Warton	
ZK533	BAe Hawk T53 (LL-5317)	BAE Systems Aircraft Maintenance Academy, Humberside	
ZK534	BAe Hawk T53 (LL-5319)	Horizon Aircraft Services, St Athan	
ZK535	BAe Hawk T53 (LL-5320)	BAE Systems Aircraft Maintenance Academy, Humberside	
ZK550	Boeing Chinook HC6 (N701UK)	RAF No 7 Sqn, Odiham	
ZK551	Boeing Chinook HC6 (N702UK)	RAF No 7 Sqn, Odiham	
ZK552	Boeing Chinook HC6 (N703UK)	RAF No 7 Sqn, Odiham	
ZK553	Boeing Chinook HC6 (N700UK)	RAF No 7 Sqn, Odiham	
ZK554	Boeing Chinook HC6 (N705UK)	RAF No 7 Sqn, Odiham	
ZK555	Boeing Chinook HC6 (N706UK)	RAF No 7 Sqn, Odiham	
ZK556	Boeing Chinook HC6 (N707UK)	MoD/Vector Aerospace, Fleetlands	
ZK557	Boeing Chinook HC6 (N708UK)	RAF No 7 Sqn, Odiham	
ZK558	Boeing Chinook HC6 (N709UK)	RAF No 7 Sqn, Odiham	
ZK559	Boeing Chinook HC6 (N710UK)	RAF No 7 Sqn, Odiham	
ZK560	Boeing Chinook HC6 (N711UK)	RAF No 7 Sqn, Odiham	
ZK561	Boeing Chinook HC6 (N712UK)	RAF No 7 Sqn, Odiham	
ZK562	Boeing Chinook HC6 (N713UK)	RAF No 7 Sqn, Odiham	
ZK563	Boeing Chinook HC6 (N714UK)	RAF No 7 Sqn, Odiham	
ZK620	Eurofighter Typhoon	*To R Saudi AF as 8021, 30 March 2017*	
ZK621	Eurofighter Typhoon	*To R Saudi AF as 8022, 30 March 2017*	
ZK622	Eurofighter Typhoon	*To R Saudi AF as 8023, 6 June 2017*	
ZK623	Eurofighter Typhoon	*To R Saudi AF as 8024, 6 June 2017*	
ZK848	McD F-4F Phantom II (38+48)	For Hawker Hunter Aviation	
ZM135	Lockheed Martin F-35B Lightning II (168315/BK-1)	RAF No 17 Sqn, Edwards AFB, California	
ZM136	Lockheed Martin F-35B Lightning II (168316/BK-2)	RAF/LMTAS, Eglin AFB, Florida	
ZM137	Lockheed Martin F-35B Lightning II (168737/BK-3)	RAF/VMFAT-501, MCAS Beaufort, South Carolina	
ZM138	Lockheed Martin F-35B Lightning II (169170/BK-4)	RAF No 17 Sqn, Edwards AFB, California	
ZM139	Lockheed Martin F-35B Lightning II (169298/BK-5)	RAF/VMFAT-501, MCAS Beaufort, South Carolina	
ZM140	Lockheed Martin F-35B Lightning II (169299/BK-6)	RAF/VMFAT-501, MCAS Beaufort, South Carolina	
ZM141	Lockheed Martin F-35B Lightning II (169300/BK-7)	RAF/VMFAT-501, MCAS Beaufort, South Carolina	
ZM142	Lockheed Martin F-35B Lightning II (169301/BK-8)	RAF/VMFAT-501, MCAS Beaufort, South Carolina	
ZM143	Lockheed Martin F-35B Lightning II (169417/BK-9)	RAF/VMFAT-501, MCAS Beaufort, South Carolina	
ZM144	Lockheed Martin F-35B Lightning II (169418/BK-10)	RAF/VMFAT-501, MCAS Beaufort, South Carolina	
ZM145	Lockheed Martin F-35B Lightning II (169419/BK-11)	RAF/VMFAT-501, MCAS Beaufort, South Carolina	
ZM146	Lockheed Martin F-35B Lightning II (169420/BK-12)	RAF/VMFAT-501, MCAS Beaufort, South Carolina	
ZM147	Lockheed Martin F-35B Lightning II (169421/BK-13)	RAF/VMFAT-501, MCAS Beaufort, South Carolina	
ZM148	Lockheed Martin F-35B Lightning II (169422/BK-14)	RAF/VMFAT-501, MCAS Beaufort, South Carolina	
ZM149	Lockheed Martin F-35B Lightning II (169596/BK-15)	RAF/VMFAT-501, MCAS Beaufort, South Carolina	
ZM150	Lockheed Martin F-35B Lightning II (169597/BK-16)	LMTAS, Fort Worth, USA, for RAF/RN	
ZM151	Lockheed Martin F-35B Lightning II (169598/BK-17)	LMTAS, Fort Worth, USA, for RAF/RN	
ZM152	Lockheed Martin F-35B Lightning II (BK-18)	LMTAS, Fort Worth, USA, for RAF/RN	
ZM153	Lockheed Martin F-35B Lightning II	Reservation for RAF/RN	
ZM154	Lockheed Martin F-35B Lightning II	Reservation for RAF/RN	
ZM155	Lockheed Martin F-35B Lightning II	Reservation for RAF/RN	
ZM156	Lockheed Martin F-35B Lightning II	Reservation for RAF/RN	
ZM157	Lockheed Martin F-35B Lightning II	Reservation for RAF/RN	
ZM158	Lockheed Martin F-35B Lightning II	Reservation for RAF/RN	
ZM159	Lockheed Martin F-35B Lightning II	Reservation for RAF/RN	
ZM160	Lockheed Martin F-35B Lightning II	Reservation for RAF/RN	
ZM161	Lockheed Martin F-35B Lightning II	Reservation for RAF/RN	
ZM162	Lockheed Martin F-35B Lightning II	Reservation for RAF/RN	
ZM163	Lockheed Martin F-35B Lightning II	Reservation for RAF/RN	
ZM164	Lockheed Martin F-35B Lightning II	Reservation for RAF/RN	
ZM165	Lockheed Martin F-35B Lightning II	Reservation for RAF/RN	
ZM166	Lockheed Martin F-35B Lightning II	Reservation for RAF/RN	
ZM167	Lockheed Martin F-35B Lightning II	Reservation for RAF/RN	
ZM168	Lockheed Martin F-35B Lightning II	Reservation for RAF/RN	
ZM169	Lockheed Martin F-35B Lightning II	Reservation for RAF/RN	
ZM170	Lockheed Martin F-35B Lightning II	Reservation for RAF/RN	
ZM171	Lockheed Martin F-35B Lightning II	Reservation for RAF/RN	
ZM172	Lockheed Martin F-35B Lightning II	Reservation for RAF/RN	

Notes	Serial	Type (code/other identity)	Owner/operator, location or fate
	ZM173	Lockheed Martin F-35B Lightning II	Reservation for RAF/RN
	ZM174	Lockheed Martin F-35B Lightning II	Reservation for RAF/RN
	ZM175	Lockheed Martin F-35B Lightning II	Reservation for RAF/RN
	ZM176	Lockheed Martin F-35B Lightning II	Reservation for RAF/RN
	ZM177	Lockheed Martin F-35B Lightning II	Reservation for RAF/RN
	ZM178	Lockheed Martin F-35B Lightning II	Reservation for RAF/RN
	ZM179	Lockheed Martin F-35B Lightning II	Reservation for RAF/RN
	ZM180	Lockheed Martin F-35B Lightning II	Reservation for RAF/RN
	ZM181	Lockheed Martin F-35B Lightning II	Reservation for RAF/RN
	ZM182	Lockheed Martin F-35B Lightning II	Reservation for RAF/RN
	ZM183	Lockheed Martin F-35 Lightning II	Reservation for RAF/RN
	ZM184	Lockheed Martin F-35 Lightning II	Reservation for RAF/RN
	ZM185	Lockheed Martin F-35 Lightning II	Reservation for RAF/RN
	ZM186	Lockheed Martin F-35 Lightning II	Reservation for RAF/RN
	ZM187	Lockheed Martin F-35 Lightning II	Reservation for RAF/RN
	ZM188	Lockheed Martin F-35 Lightning II	Reservation for RAF/RN
	ZM189	Lockheed Martin F-35 Lightning II	Reservation for RAF/RN
	ZM190	Lockheed Martin F-35 Lightning II	Reservation for RAF/RN
	ZM191	Lockheed Martin F-35 Lightning II	Reservation for RAF/RN
	ZM192	Lockheed Martin F-35 Lightning II	Reservation for RAF/RN
	ZM193	Lockheed Martin F-35 Lightning II	Reservation for RAF/RN
	ZM194	Lockheed Martin F-35 Lightning II	Reservation for RAF/RN
	ZM195	Lockheed Martin F-35 Lightning II	Reservation for RAF/RN
	ZM196	Lockheed Martin F-35 Lightning II	Reservation for RAF/RN
	ZM197	Lockheed Martin F-35 Lightning II	Reservation for RAF/RN
	ZM198	Lockheed Martin F-35 Lightning II	Reservation for RAF/RN
	ZM199	Lockheed Martin F-35 Lightning II	Reservation for RAF/RN
	ZM200	Lockheed Martin F-35 Lightning II	Reservation for RAF/RN
	ZM300	Grob G120TP-A Prefect T1 (D-ETPJ/G-MFTS)	Affinity/RAF No 3 FTS, Barkston Heath
	ZM301	Grob G120TP-A Prefect T1 (D-EGUX/G-MEFT)	Affinity/RAF No 3 FTS, Barkston Heath
	ZM302	Grob G120TP-A Prefect T1 (D-ETPT/G-CJYB)	Affinity/RAF No 3 FTS, Barkston Heath
	ZM303	Grob G120TP-A Prefect T1 (G-CJYG)	Affinity/RAF No 3 FTS, Barkston Heath
	ZM304	Grob G120TP-A Prefect T1 (G-CJYH)	MoD/Grob, Germany
	ZM305	Grob G120TP-A Prefect T1 (G-CJZR)	Affinity/RAF No 3 FTS, Barkston Heath
	ZM306	Grob G120TP-A Prefect T1 (G-CJZJ)	Affinity/RAF No 3 FTS, Cranwell
	ZM307	Grob G120TP-A Prefect T1 (G-CJZI)	Affinity/RAF No 3 FTS, Barkston Heath
	ZM308	Grob G120TP-A Prefect T1 (G-CJZF)	Affinity/RAF No 3 FTS, Cranwell
	ZM309	Grob G120TP-A Prefect T1 (G-CKCO)	Affinity/RAF No 3 FTS, Barkston Heath
	ZM310	Grob G120TP-A Prefect T1 (G-CKCS)	Affinity/RAF No 3 FTS, Barkston Heath
	ZM311	Grob G120TP-A Prefect T1 (G-CKIA)	Affinity/RAF No 3 FTS, Barkston Heath
	ZM312	Grob G120TP-A Prefect T1 (G-CKIB)	Affinity/RAF No 3 FTS, Barkston Heath
	ZM313	Grob G120TP-A Prefect T1 (G-CKIC)	Affinity/RAF No 3 FTS, Barkston Heath
	ZM314	Grob G120TP-A Prefect T1 (G-CKID)	Affinity/RAF No 3 FTS, Cranwell
	ZM315	Grob G120TP-A Prefect T1 (G-CKIV)	Affinity/RAF No 3 FTS, Cranwell
	ZM316	Grob G120TP-A Prefect T1 (G-CKIW)	Affinity/RAF No 3 FTS, Cranwell
	ZM317	Grob G120TP-A Prefect T1 (G-CKLJ)	Affinity/RAF No 3 FTS, Cranwell
	ZM318	Grob G120TP-A Prefect T1 (G-CKLO)	Affinity/RAF No 3 FTS, Cranwell
	ZM319	Grob G120TP-A Prefect T1 (G-CKRP)	Affinity/RAF No 3 FTS, Cranwell
	ZM320	Grob G120TP-A Prefect T1 (G-CKRY)	Affinity/RAF No 3 FTS, Cranwell
	ZM321	Grob G120TP-A Prefect T1	For RAF
	ZM322	Grob G120TP-A Prefect T1	For RAF
	ZM323	Beechcraft T-6C Texan II (N2824B) [323]	Raytheon, Wichita, KS, for RAF
	ZM324	Beechcraft T-6C Texan II	Raytheon, Wichita, KS, for RAF
	ZM325	Beechcraft T-6C Texan II (N2843B) [325]	Affinity/RAF No 4 FTS, Valley
	ZM326	Beechcraft T-6C Texan II (N2770B) [326]	Affinity/RAF No 4 FTS, Valley
	ZM327	Beechcraft T-6C Texan II	For RAF
	ZM328	Beechcraft T-6C Texan II	For RAF
	ZM329	Beechcraft T-6C Texan II	For RAF
	ZM330	Beechcraft T-6C Texan II	For RAF
	ZM331	Beechcraft T-6C Texan II	For RAF
	ZM332	Beechcraft T-6C Texan II	For RAF
	ZM333	Embraer EMB-500 Phenom 100 (PR-PHK/G-MEPT)	Affinity/RAF No 3 FTS, Cranwell

Serial	Type (code/other identity)	Owner/operator, location or fate	Notes
ZM334	Embraer EMB-500 Phenom 100 (PR-ING/G-MEPS)	Affinity/RAF No 3 FTS, Cranwell	
ZM335	Embraer EMB-500 Phenom 100 (PR-LTE/G-CJXH)	Affinity/RAF No 3 FTS, Cranwell	
ZM336	Embraer EMB-500 Phenom 100 (PR-LTF/G-CKCU)	Affinity/RAF No 3 FTS, Cranwell	
ZM337	Embraer EMB-500 Phenom 100 (PR-LTJ/G-CKEF)	Affinity/RAF No 3 FTS, Cranwell	
ZM398	Airbus A400M Atlas Full Flight Simulator	RAF Brize Norton	
ZM399	Airbus A400M Atlas Full Flight Simulator	RAF Brize Norton	
ZM400	Airbus A400M Atlas C1 (A4M015/EC-405)	MoD/Airbus Defence & Space, Getafe	
ZM401	Airbus A400M Atlas C1 (A4M016/EC-406)	RAF No 24 Sqn/No 70 Sqn, Brize Norton	
ZM402	Airbus A400M Atlas C1 (A4M017/EC-407)	RAF No 24 Sqn/No 70 Sqn, Brize Norton	
ZM403	Airbus A400M Atlas C1 (A4M020)	RAF No 24 Sqn/No 70 Sqn, Brize Norton	
ZM404	Airbus A400M Atlas C1 (A4M021/EC-401)	RAF No 24 Sqn/No 70 Sqn, Brize Norton	
ZM405	Airbus A400M Atlas C1 (A4M024)	RAF No 24 Sqn/No 70 Sqn, Brize Norton	
ZM406	Airbus A400M Atlas C1 (A4M025/EC-405) $	RAF No 24 Sqn/No 70 Sqn, Brize Norton	
ZM407	Airbus A400M Atlas C1 (A4M026)	RAF No 24 Sqn/No 70 Sqn, Brize Norton	
ZM408	Airbus A400M Atlas C1 (A4M027)	RAF No 24 Sqn/No 70 Sqn, Brize Norton	
ZM409	Airbus A400M Atlas C1 (A4M034) $	RAF No 24 Sqn/No 70 Sqn, Brize Norton	
ZM410	Airbus A400M Atlas C1 (A4M038)	RAF No 24 Sqn/No 70 Sqn, Brize Norton	
ZM411	Airbus A400M Atlas C1 (A4M039)	RAF No 24 Sqn/No 70 Sqn, Brize Norton	
ZM412	Airbus A400M Atlas C1 (A4M042)	MoD/Airbus Defence & Space, Getafe	
ZM413	Airbus A400M Atlas C1 (A4M045)	RAF No 24 Sqn/No 70 Sqn, Brize Norton	
ZM414	Airbus A400M Atlas C1 (A4M047)	RAF No 24 Sqn/No 70 Sqn, Brize Norton	
ZM415	Airbus A400M Atlas C1 (A4M052)	RAF No 24 Sqn/No 70 Sqn, Brize Norton	
ZM416	Airbus A400M Atlas C1 (A4M058)	RAF No 24 Sqn/No 70 Sqn, Brize Norton	
ZM417	Airbus A400M Atlas C1 (A4M060)	RAF No 24 Sqn/No 70 Sqn, Brize Norton	
ZM418	Airbus A400M Atlas C1 (A4M072)	Airbus Defence & Space, Seville, for RAF	
ZM419	Airbus A400M Atlas C1 (A4M077)	Airbus Defence & Space, Seville, for RAF	
ZM420	Airbus A400M Atlas C1 (A4M095)	Airbus Defence & Space, Seville, for RAF	
ZM421	Airbus A400M Atlas C1 (A4M056)	Airbus Defence & Space, Seville, for RAF	
ZM500	Airbus H145 Jupiter HT1 (D-HADT/G-CJIV) [00]	DHFS No 202 Sqn, RAF Valley	
ZM501	Airbus H145 Jupiter HT1 (D-HADM/G-CJIZ/G-CKGE) [01]	DHFS No 202 Sqn, RAF Valley	
ZM502	Airbus H145 Jupiter HT1 (D-HADQ/G-CJRW) [02]	DHFS No 202 Sqn, RAF Valley	
ZM503	Airbus H145 Jupiter HT1	Reservation for MoD	
ZM504	Airbus H135 Juno HT1 (D-HECZ/G-CJJG) [04]	DHFS, RAF Shawbury	
ZM505	Airbus H135 Juno HT1 (D-HECV/G-CJIW) [05]	DHFS, RAF Shawbury	
ZM506	Airbus H135 Juno HT1 (D-HECW/G-CJIY) [06]	DHFS, RAF Shawbury	
ZM507	Airbus H135 Juno HT1 (D-HECX/G-CJRP) [07]	DHFS, RAF Shawbury	
ZM508	Airbus H135 Juno HT1 (D-HECD/G-CJRY) [08]	DHFS, RAF Shawbury	
ZM509	Airbus H135 Juno HT1 (D-HECB/G-CJTZ) [09]	DHFS, RAF Shawbury	
ZM510	Airbus H135 Juno HT1 (D-HECG/G-CJUA) [10]	DHFS, RAF Shawbury	
ZM511	Airbus H135 Juno HT1 (D-HECJ/G-CJUC) [11]	DHFS, RAF Shawbury	
ZM512	Airbus H135 Juno HT1 (D-HECQ/G-CJXS) [12]	DHFS, RAF Shawbury	
ZM513	Airbus H135 Juno HT1 (D-HECP/G-CJXU) [13]	DHFS, RAF Shawbury	
ZM514	Airbus H135 Juno HT1 (D-HECV/G-CJXV) [14]	DHFS, RAF Shawbury	
ZM515	Airbus H135 Juno HT1 (D-HECT/G-CJSO) [15]	DHFS, RAF Shawbury	
ZM516	Airbus H135 Juno HT1 (D-HECY/G-CJZS) [16]	DHFS, RAF Shawbury	
ZM517	Airbus H135 Juno HT1 (D-HECL/G-CJZT) [17]	DHFS, RAF Shawbury	
ZM518	Airbus H135 Juno HT1 (D-HCBA/G-CKEO) [18]	DHFS, RAF Shawbury	
ZM519	Airbus H135 Juno HT1 (D-HCBC/G-CKEU) [19]	DHFS, RAF Shawbury	
ZM520	Airbus H135 Juno HT1 (D-HCBD/G-CKEW) [20]	DHFS, RAF Shawbury	
ZM521	Airbus H135 Juno HT1 (G-CKIK) [21]	DHFS, RAF Shawbury	
ZM522	Airbus H135 Juno HT1 (D-HCKIM) [22]	DHFS, RAF Shawbury	
ZM523	Airbus H135 Juno HT1 (G-CKJW) [23]	DHFS, RAF Shawbury	
ZM524	Airbus H135 Juno HT1 (D-HECK/G-CKJU) [24]	DHFS, RAF Shawbury	
ZM525	Airbus H135 Juno HT1 (D-HECQ/G-CKJX) [25]	DHFS, RAF Shawbury	
ZM526	Airbus H135 Juno HT1 (D-HECU/G-CKOC) [26]	DHFS, RAF Shawbury	
ZM527	Airbus H135 Juno HT1 (D-HECX/G-CKOB) [27]	DHFS, RAF Shawbury	
ZM528	Airbus H135 Juno HT1 (G-CKOA) [28]	DHFS, RAF Shawbury	
ZM529	Airbus H135 Juno HT1 (D-HECW/G-CKPT) [29]	Airbus Helicopters, Kidlington	
ZM530	Airbus H135 Juno HT1 (D-HECD/G-CKRA) [30]	Airbus Helicopters, Kidlington	
ZM531	Airbus H135 Juno HT1 (G-CKSB)	Airbus Helicopters, Kidlington	
ZM532	Airbus H135 Juno HT1 (D-HECY/G-CKSA)	Airbus Helicopters, Kidlington	

Notes	Serial	Type (code/other identity)	Owner/operator, location or fate
	ZM533	Airbus H135 Juno HT1	Reservation for MoD
	ZM534	Airbus H135 Juno HT1	Reservation for MoD
	ZP801	Boeing P-8A Poseidon	For RAF
	ZP802	Boeing P-8A Poseidon	For RAF
	ZP803	Boeing P-8A Poseidon	For RAF
	ZP804	Boeing P-8A Poseidon	For RAF
	ZP805	Boeing P-8A Poseidon	For RAF
	ZP806	Boeing P-8A Poseidon	For RAF
	ZP807	Boeing P-8A Poseidon	For RAF
	ZP808	Boeing P-8A Poseidon	For RAF
	ZP809	Boeing P-8A Poseidon	For RAF
	ZP810	Boeing P-8A Poseidon	Reservation for RAF
	ZP811	Boeing P-8A Poseidon	Reservation for RAF
	ZP812	Boeing P-8A Poseidon	Reservation for RAF
	ZP813	Boeing P-8A Poseidon	Reservation for RAF
	ZP814	Boeing P-8A Poseidon	Reservation for RAF
	ZP815	Boeing P-8A Poseidon	Reservation for RAF
	ZR283	AgustaWestland AW139 (G-FBHA)	MoD/FBS, Newquay
	ZR324	Agusta A109E Power (G-EMHB)	MoD/FBS, Newquay
	ZR325	Agusta A109E Power (G-BZEI)	MoD/FBS, Newquay
	ZR339	AgustaWestland AW101 Mk.641 (ZW-4302)	Leonardo MW, Yeovil
	ZR342	AgustaWestland AW101 Mk.641 (ZW-4305)	Leonardo MW, Yeovil
	ZR346	AgustaWestland AW101 Mk.641 (ZW-4309)	Leonardo MW, Yeovil
	ZR347	AgustaWestland AW101 Mk.641 (ZW-4310)	Leonardo MW, Yeovil, for Azerbaijan as 4K-Ai010
	ZR348	AgustaWestland AW101 Mk.641 (ZW-4311)	Leonardo MW, Yeovil
	ZR349	AgustaWestland AW101 Mk.641 (ZW-4312)	Leonardo MW, Yeovil
	ZR356	AgustaWestland AW101 Mk.611 [15-05]	*To It AF as MM81868, 2017*
	ZR357	AgustaWestland AW101 Mk.611 [15-06]	*To the Italian AF as MM81869, March 2017*
	ZR401	Eurofighter Typhoon	*To RAFO as 210, 7 August 2017*
	ZR402	Eurofighter Typhoon	*To RAFO as 211, 9 October 2017*
	ZR403	Eurofighter Typhoon	*To RAFO as 212, 9 October 2017*
	ZR404	Eurofighter Typhoon	*To RAFO as 213, 20 November 2017*
	ZR405	Eurofighter Typhoon	*To RAFO as 214, 20 November 2017*
	ZR406	Eurofighter Typhoon	*To RAFO as 215, 5 February 2018*
	ZR407	Eurofighter Typhoon	*To RAFO as 216, 5 February 2018*
	ZR408	Eurofighter Typhoon	BAE Systems, for RAFO as 217
	ZR409	Eurofighter Typhoon	BAE Systems, for RAFO as 218
	ZR410	Eurofighter Typhoon T	*To RAFO as 200, 19 June 2017*
	ZR411	Eurofighter Typhoon T	*To RAFO as 201, 19 June 2017*
	ZR412	Eurofighter Typhoon T	*To RAFO as 212, 7 August 2017*
	ZS782	WS WG25 Sharpeye	The Helicopter Museum, Weston-super-Mare
	ZT800	WS Super Lynx Mk 300	Yeovil College, instructional use
	ZZ100	AgustaWestland AW101 Mk.612	Leonardo MW, Yeovil, for Norway as 0262
	ZZ101	AgustaWestland AW101 Mk.612	Leonardo MW, Yeovil, for Norway as 0264
	ZZ102	AgustaWestland AW101 Mk.612	*To Norway as 0265, 19 January 2018*
	ZZ103	AgustaWestland AW101 Mk.612	*To Norway as 0268, 17 November 2017*
	ZZ104	AgustaWestland AW101 Mk.612	Leonardo MW, Yeovil, for Norway as 0270
	ZZ105	AgustaWestland AW101 Mk.612	Leonardo MW, Yeovil, for Norway as 0273
	ZZ106	AgustaWestland AW101 Mk.612	Leonardo MW, Yeovil, for Norway as 0275
	ZZ107	AgustaWestland AW101 Mk.612	Leonardo MW, Yeovil, for Norway as 0276
	ZZ108	AgustaWestland AW101 Mk.612	Leonardo MW, Yeovil, for Norway as 0277
	ZZ109	AgustaWestland AW101 Mk.612	Leonardo MW, Yeovil, for Norway as 0278
	ZZ110	AgustaWestland AW101 Mk.612	Leonardo MW, Yeovil, for Norway as 0279
	ZZ111	AgustaWestland AW101 Mk.612	Leonardo MW, Yeovil, for Norway as 0280
	ZZ112	AgustaWestland AW101 Mk.612	Leonardo MW, Yeovil, for Norway as 0281
	ZZ113	AgustaWestland AW101 Mk.612	Leonardo MW, Yeovil, for Norway as 0282
	ZZ114	AgustaWestland AW101 Mk.612	Leonardo MW, Yeovil, for Norway as 0283

Serial	Type (code/other identity)	Owner/operator, location or fate	Notes
ZZ115	AgustaWestland AW101 Mk.612	Leonardo MW, Yeovil, for Norway as 0284	
ZZ171	Boeing C-17A Globemaster III (00-201/N171UK)	RAF No 99 Sqn, Brize Norton	
ZZ172	Boeing C-17A Globemaster III (00-202/N172UK)	RAF No 99 Sqn, Brize Norton	
ZZ173	Boeing C-17A Globemaster III (00-203/N173UK)	RAF/Boeing, San Antonio, Texas, USA	
ZZ174	Boeing C-17A Globemaster III (00-204/N174UK)	RAF No 99 Sqn, Brize Norton	
ZZ175	Boeing C-17A Globemaster III (06-0205/N9500Z)	RAF No 99 Sqn, Brize Norton	
ZZ176	Boeing C-17A Globemaster III (08-0206/N9500B) $	RAF No 99 Sqn, Brize Norton	
ZZ177	Boeing C-17A Globemaster III (09-8207/N9500B)	RAF No 99 Sqn, Brize Norton	
ZZ178	Boeing C-17A Globemaster III (12-0208/N9500N)	RAF No 99 Sqn, Brize Norton	
ZZ190	Hawker Hunter F58 (J-4066/G-HHAE)	Hawker Hunter Aviation, Scampton	
ZZ191	Hawker Hunter F58 (J-4058/G-HHAD)	Hawker Hunter Aviation, Scampton	
ZZ192	Grob G109B Vigilant T1 (D-KLVI) [SQ]	RAF, stored Little Rissington	
ZZ193	Grob G109B Vigilant T1 (D-KBLO) [SR]	RAF, stored Little Rissington	
ZZ194	Hawker Hunter F58 (J-4021/G-HHAC)	Hawker Hunter Aviation, Scampton	
ZZ201	General Atomics Reaper RPAS (07-0111)	RAF No 13 Sqn/No 39 Sqn, Creech AFB, Nevada, USA	
ZZ202	General Atomics Reaper RPAS (07-0117)	RAF No 13 Sqn/No 39 Sqn, Creech AFB, Nevada, USA	
ZZ203	General Atomics Reaper RPAS (08-0113)	RAF No 13 Sqn/No 39 Sqn, Creech AFB, Nevada, USA	
ZZ204	General Atomics Reaper RPAS (10-0157)	RAF No 13 Sqn/No 39 Sqn, Creech AFB, Nevada, USA	
ZZ205	General Atomics Reaper RPAS (10-0162)	*Crashed, August 2016*	
ZZ206	General Atomics Reaper RPAS (12-0707)	RAF No 13 Sqn/No 39 Sqn, Creech AFB, Nevada, USA	
ZZ207	General Atomics Reaper RPAS (12-0708)	RAF No 13 Sqn/No 39 Sqn, Creech AFB, Nevada, USA	
ZZ208	General Atomics Reaper RPAS (12-0709)	RAF No 13 Sqn/No 39 Sqn, Creech AFB, Nevada, USA	
ZZ209	General Atomics Reaper RPAS (12-0710)	RAF No 13 Sqn/No 39 Sqn, Creech AFB, Nevada, USA	
ZZ210	General Atomics Reaper RPAS (12-0711)	RAF No 13 Sqn/No 39 Sqn, Creech AFB, Nevada, USA	
ZZ211	General Atomics Reaper RPAS	General Atomics, for RAF	
ZZ212	General Atomics Reaper RPAS	General Atomics, for RAF	
ZZ213	General Atomics Reaper RPAS	General Atomics, for RAF	
ZZ250	BAE Systems Taranis RPAS	BAE Systems, Warton	
ZZ251	BAE Systems HERTI RPAS	BAE Systems, Warton	
ZZ252	BAE Systems HERTI RPAS	BAE Systems, Woomera, Australia	
ZZ253	BAE Systems HERTI RPAS	BAE Systems, Woomera, Australia	
ZZ254	BAE Systems HERTI RPAS	BAE Systems, Warton	
ZZ330	Airbus A330 Voyager KC2 (MRTT017/EC-337/G-VYGA)	RAF No 10 Sqn/No 101 Sqn, Brize Norton	
ZZ331	Airbus A330 Voyager KC2 (MRTT018/EC-331/G-VYGB)	RAF No 10 Sqn/No 101 Sqn, Brize Norton	
ZZ332	Airbus A330 Voyager KC3 (MRTT019/EC-330/G-VYGC)	RAF No 10 Sqn/No 101 Sqn, Brize Norton	
ZZ333	Airbus A330 Voyager KC3 (MRTT020/EC-337/G-VYGD)	RAF No 10 Sqn/No 101 Sqn, Brize Norton	
ZZ334	Airbus A330 Voyager KC3 (MRTT016/EC-335/G-VYGE)	RAF No 10 Sqn/No 101 Sqn, Brize Norton	
ZZ335	Airbus A330 Voyager KC3 (MRTT021/EC-338/G-VYGF)	RAF No 10 Sqn/No 101 Sqn, Brize Norton	
ZZ336	Airbus A330 Voyager KC3 (MRTT022/EC-333/G-VYGG)	RAF No 10 Sqn/No 101 Sqn, Brize Norton	
ZZ337	Airbus A330 Voyager KC3 (MRTT023/EC-336/G-VYGH)	RAF No 1312 Flt, Mount Pleasant, FI	
ZZ338	Airbus A330 Voyager KC3 (MRTT024/EC-331/G-VYGI)	RAF No 10 Sqn/No 101 Sqn, Brize Norton	
ZZ339	Airbus A330-243 (MRTT025/EC-333/G-VYGJ)	Airtanker Ltd, Brize Norton [flies as G-VYGJ]	
ZZ340	Airbus A330-243 (MRTT026/EC-330/G-VYGK) [flies as G-VYGK]	Airtanker Ltd/Thomas Cook Airlines, Manchester	
ZZ341	Airbus A330-243 (MRTT027/EC-336/G-VYGL) [flies as G-VYGL]	Airtanker Ltd/Eurowings, Cologne, Germany	
ZZ342	Airbus A330-243 (MRTT028/EC-332/G-VYGM) [flies as G-VYGM]	Airtanker Ltd/TUI Fly Belgium, Brussels	
ZZ343	Airbus A330 Voyager KC2 (MRTT029/EC-331/G-VYGN)	RAF No 10 Sqn/No 101 Sqn, Brize Norton	
ZZ375	AgustaWestland AW159 Wildcat HMA2	RN No 815 NAS, Yeovilton	
ZZ376	AgustaWestland AW159 Wildcat HMA2	RN No 825 NAS, Yeovilton	
ZZ377	AgustaWestland AW159 Wildcat HMA2	RN No 825 NAS, Yeovilton	

Notes	Serial	Type (code/other identity)	Owner/operator, location or fate
	ZZ378	AgustaWestland AW159 Wildcat HMA2	RN No 825 NAS, Yeovilton
	ZZ379	AgustaWestland AW159 Wildcat HMA2	RN No 815 NAS, Yeovilton
	ZZ380	AgustaWestland AW159 Wildcat HMA2	RN No 815 NAS, Yeovilton
	ZZ381	AgustaWestland AW159 Wildcat HMA2	RN No 815 NAS, Yeovilton
	ZZ382	AgustaWestland AW159 Wildcat AH1	AAC No 1 Regiment, Yeovilton
	ZZ383	AgustaWestland AW159 Wildcat AH1	AAC WCM, Yeovilton
	ZZ384	AgustaWestland AW159 Wildcat AH1	RN No 847 NAS, Yeovilton
	ZZ385	AgustaWestland AW159 Wildcat AH1	AAC No 1 Regiment, Yeovilton
	ZZ386	AgustaWestland AW159 Wildcat AH1	RN No 847 NAS, Yeovilton
	ZZ387	AgustaWestland AW159 Wildcat AH1	AAC No 1 Regiment, Yeovilton
	ZZ388	AgustaWestland AW159 Wildcat AH1	AAC WCM, Yeovilton
	ZZ389	AgustaWestland AW159 Wildcat AH1	RN No 847 NAS, Yeovilton
	ZZ390	AgustaWestland AW159 Wildcat AH1	MoD/Leonardo MW, Yeovil
	ZZ391	AgustaWestland AW159 Wildcat AH1	AAC WCM, Yeovilton
	ZZ392	AgustaWestland AW159 Wildcat AH1	AAC No 1 Regiment, Yeovilton
	ZZ393	AgustaWestland AW159 Wildcat AH1	AAC No 1 Regiment, Yeovilton
	ZZ394	AgustaWestland AW159 Wildcat AH1	RN No 847 NAS, Yeovilton
	ZZ395	AgustaWestland AW159 Wildcat AH1	RN No 847 NAS, Yeovilton
	ZZ396	AgustaWestland AW159 Wildcat HMA2	RN No 815 NAS, Yeovilton
	ZZ397	AgustaWestland AW159 Wildcat HMA2	RN No 815 NAS, Yeovilton
	ZZ398	AgustaWestland AW159 Wildcat AH1	AAC WST, stored Yeovilton
	ZZ399	AgustaWestland AW159 Wildcat AH1	AAC No 1 Regiment, Yeovilton
	ZZ400	AgustaWestland AW159 Wildcat (TI01)	Army, stored Middle Wallop
	ZZ401	AgustaWestland AW159 Wildcat (TI02)	RNAS Yeovilton, instructional use
	ZZ402	AgustaWestland AW159 Wildcat (TI03)	DSAE RNAESS, *HMS Sultan*, Gosport
	ZZ403	AgustaWestland AW159 Wildcat AH1	AAC No 1 Regiment, Yeovilton
	ZZ404	AgustaWestland AW159 Wildcat AH1	AAC No 1 Regiment, Yeovilton
	ZZ405	AgustaWestland AW159 Wildcat AH1	AAC No 1 Regiment, Yeovilton
	ZZ406	AgustaWestland AW159 Wildcat AH1	AAC WST, stored Yeovilton
	ZZ407	AgustaWestland AW159 Wildcat AH1	AAC No 1 Regiment, Yeovilton
	ZZ408	AgustaWestland AW159 Wildcat AH1	RN No 847 NAS, Yeovilton
	ZZ409	AgustaWestland AW159 Wildcat AH1	AAC WST, stored Yeovilton
	ZZ410	AgustaWestland AW159 Wildcat AH1	RN No 847 NAS, Yeovilton
	ZZ413	AgustaWestland AW159 Wildcat HMA2	RN No 815 NAS, Yeovilton
	ZZ414	AgustaWestland AW159 Wildcat HMA2	RN No 815 NAS, Yeovilton
	ZZ415	AgustaWestland AW159 Wildcat HMA2	MoD/Leonardo MW, Yeovil
	ZZ416	Hawker Beechcraft Shadow R1 (G-JENC)	RAF No 14 Sqn, Waddington
	ZZ417	Hawker Beechcraft Shadow R2 (G-NICY)	RAF No 14 Sqn, Waddington
	ZZ418	Hawker Beechcraft Shadow R1 (G-JIMG)	RAF No 14 Sqn, Waddington
	ZZ419	Hawker Beechcraft Shadow R1 (G-OTCS)	RAF No 14 Sqn, Waddington
	ZZ500	Hawker Beechcraft Avenger T1 (G-MFTA)	RN No 750 NAS, Culdrose
	ZZ501	Hawker Beechcraft Avenger T1 (G-MFTB)	RN No 750 NAS, Culdrose
	ZZ502	Hawker Beechcraft Avenger T1 (G-MFTC)	RN No 750 NAS, Culdrose
	ZZ503	Hawker Beechcraft Avenger T1 (G-MFTD)	RN No 750 NAS, Culdrose
	ZZ504	Hawker Beechcraft Shadow R1 (G-CGUM)	RAF No 14 Sqn, Waddington
	ZZ510	AgustaWestland AW159 Wildcat AH1	AAC No 1 Regiment, Yeovilton
	ZZ511	AgustaWestland AW159 Wildcat AH1	AAC WCM, Yeovilton
	ZZ512	AgustaWestland AW159 Wildcat AH1	RN No 847 NAS, Yeovilton
	ZZ513	AgustaWestland AW159 Wildcat HMA2	MoD/Leonardo MW, Yeovil
	ZZ514	AgustaWestland AW159 Wildcat HMA2	RN No 825 NAS, Yeovilton
	ZZ515	AgustaWestland AW159 Wildcat HMA2	MoD/Leonardo MW, Yeovil
	ZZ516	AgustaWestland AW159 Wildcat HMA2	RN No 815 NAS, Yeovilton
	ZZ517	AgustaWestland AW159 Wildcat HMA2	RN No 815 NAS, Yeovilton
	ZZ518	AgustaWestland AW159 Wildcat HMA2	RN No 825 NAS, Yeovilton
	ZZ519	AgustaWestland AW159 Wildcat HMA2	RN No 815 NAS, Yeovilton
	ZZ520	AgustaWestland AW159 Wildcat AH1	AAC No 1 Regiment, Yeovilton
	ZZ521	AgustaWestland AW159 Wildcat AH1	AAC No 1 Regiment, Yeovilton
	ZZ522	AgustaWestland AW159 Wildcat HMA2	RN No 825 NAS, Yeovilton
	ZZ523	AgustaWestland AW159 Wildcat AH1	AAC WCM, Yeovilton
	ZZ524	AgustaWestland AW159 Wildcat AH1	AAC No 1 Regiment, Yeovilton
	ZZ525	AgustaWestland AW159 Wildcat AH1	AAC No 1 Regiment, Yeovilton
	ZZ526	AgustaWestland AW159 Wildcat AH1	AAC No 1 Regiment, Yeovilton

Serial	Type (code/other identity)	Owner/operator, location or fate	Notes
ZZ527	AgustaWestland AW159 Wildcat AH1	MoD/Leonardo MW, Yeovil	
ZZ528	AgustaWestland AW159 Wildcat HMA2	RN No 815 NAS, Yeovilton	
ZZ529	AgustaWestland AW159 Wildcat HMA2	MoD/Leonardo MW, Yeovil	
ZZ530	AgustaWestland AW159 Wildcat HMA2	RN No 815 NAS, Yeovilton	
ZZ531	AgustaWestland AW159 Wildcat HMA2	RN No 815 NAS, Yeovilton	
ZZ532	AgustaWestland AW159 Wildcat HMA2	MoD/Leonardo MW, Yeovil	
ZZ533	AgustaWestland AW159 Wildcat HMA2	RN No 815 NAS, Yeovilton	
ZZ534	AgustaWestland AW159 Wildcat HMA2	RN No 825 NAS, Yeovilton	
ZZ535	AgustaWestland AW159 Wildcat HMA2	MoD/Leonardo MW, Yeovil	
ZZ549	AgustaWestland AW159 Mk.220	Leonardo MW, for Philippine Navy	
ZZ550	AgustaWestland AW159 Mk.220	Leonardo MW, for Philippine Navy	
ZZ664	Boeing RC-135W (64-14833) $	RAF No 51 Sqn, Waddington	
ZZ665	Boeing RC-135W (64-14838)	RAF No 51 Sqn, Waddington	
ZZ666	Boeing RC-135W (64-14830)	RAF No 51 Sqn, Waddington	

Hawk T1A XX227 is one of the few that have been constant with the Red Arrows and reports suggest that when it is shortly withdrawn from use, it will be preserved.

Typhoon FGR4 ZK334 wore the familiar triangular code 'A' of 2 Squadron at RAF Lossiemouth, except that it was being operated by 1(F) Sqn at the time. No distinguishable squadron marks were worn.

95

Notes	Serial	Type (code/other identity)	Owner/operator, location or fate
	G-BVRJ	BAe RJ.70ER	To QQ102, 20 June 2017
	G-BYUA	Grob G.115E Tutor T1	Sold to Finland, 25 September 2017
	G-BYUB	Grob G.115E Tutor T1	Babcock/No 16 Sqn/No 57 Sqn, Cranwell
	G-BYUC	Grob G.115E Tutor T1	Babcock/No 16 Sqn/No 57 Sqn, Cranwell
	G-BYUD	Grob G.115E Tutor T1	Babcock/No 16 Sqn/No 57 Sqn, Cranwell
	G-BYUE	Grob G.115E Tutor T1	Babcock/Oxford UAS, Benson
	G-BYUF	Grob G.115E Tutor T1	Babcock/Northumbrian Universities AS, Leeming
	G-BYUG	Grob G.115E Tutor T1	Sold to Finland, 24 May 2017
	G-BYUH	Grob G.115E Tutor T1	Babcock/Southampton UAS, Boscombe Down
	G-BYUI	Grob G.115E Tutor T1	Babcock/Liverpool UAS/Manchester and Salford Universities AS, Woodvale
	G-BYUJ	Grob G.115E Tutor T1	Babcock/East of Scotland UAS, Leuchars
	G-BYUK	Grob G.115E Tutor T1	Babcock/Cambridge UAS/East Midlands Universities AS/ University of London AS/No 115 Sqn, Wittering
	G-BYUL	Grob G.115E Tutor T1	Babcock/Liverpool UAS/Manchester and Salford Universities AS, Woodvale
	G-BYUM	Grob G.115E Tutor T1	Babcock/Cambridge UAS/East Midlands Universities AS/ University of London AS/No 115 Sqn, Wittering
	G-BYUN	Grob G.115E Tutor T1	Babcock/No 16 Sqn/No 57 Sqn, Cranwell
	G-BYUO	Grob G.115E Tutor T1	Babcock/No 16 Sqn/No 57 Sqn, Cranwell
	G-BYUP	Grob G.115E Tutor T1	Sold to Finland, 25 May 2017
	G-BYUR	Grob G.115E Tutor T1	Babcock/East of Scotland UAS, Leuchars
	G-BYUS	Grob G.115E Tutor T1	Babcock/No 16 Sqn/No 57 Sqn, Cranwell
	G-BYUU	Grob G.115E Tutor T1	Babcock/Cambridge UAS/East Midlands Universities AS/ University of London AS/No 115 Sqn, Wittering
	G-BYUV	Grob G.115E Tutor T1	Babcock/Bristol UAS, Boscombe Down
	G-BYUW	Grob G.115E Tutor T1	Babcock/No 16 Sqn/No 57 Sqn, Cranwell
	G-BYUX	Grob G.115E Tutor T1	Babcock/No 16 Sqn/No 57 Sqn, Cranwell
	G-BYUY	Grob G.115E Tutor T1	Babcock/Yorkshire Universities AS, Linton-on-Ouse
	G-BYUZ	Grob G.115E Tutor T1	Babcock/No 16 Sqn/No 57 Sqn, Cranwell
	G-BYVA	Grob G.115E Tutor T1	Babcock/Bristol UAS, Boscombe Down
	G-BYVB	Grob G.115E Tutor T1	Babcock/University of Wales AS, St Athan
	G-BYVC	Grob G.115E Tutor T1	Babcock/Cambridge UAS/East Midlands Universities AS/ University of London AS/No 115 Sqn, Wittering
	G-BYVD	Grob G.115E Tutor T1	Babcock/Southampton UAS, Boscombe Down
	G-BYVE	Grob G.115E Tutor T1	Babcock/Oxford UAS, Benson
	G-BYVF	Grob G.115E Tutor T1	Babcock/RN No 727 NAS, Yeovilton
	G-BYVG	Grob G.115E Tutor T1	Babcock/Cambridge UAS/East Midlands Universities AS/ University of London AS/No 115 Sqn, Wittering
	G-BYVH	Grob G.115E Tutor T1	Babcock/No 16 Sqn/No 57 Sqn, Cranwell
	G-BYVI	Grob G.115E Tutor T1	Babcock/No 16 Sqn/No 57 Sqn, Cranwell
	G-BYVJ	Grob G.115E Tutor T1	Sold to Finland, 25 September 2017
	G-BYVK	Grob G.115E Tutor T1	Babcock/RN No 727 NAS, Yeovilton
	G-BYVL	Grob G.115E Tutor T1	Babcock/University of Birmingham AS, Cosford
	G-BYVM	Grob G.115E Tutor T1	Babcock/No 16 Sqn/No 57 Sqn, Cranwell
	G-BYVO	Grob G.115E Tutor T1	Babcock/No 16 Sqn/No 57 Sqn, Cranwell
	G-BYVP	Grob G.115E Tutor T1	Babcock/Cambridge UAS/East Midlands Universities AS/ University of London AS/No 115 Sqn, Wittering
	G-BYVR	Grob G.115E Tutor T1	Babcock/Cambridge UAS/East Midlands Universities AS/ University of London AS/No 115 Sqn, Wittering
	G-BYVS	Grob G.115E Tutor T1	Sold to Finland, 24 May 2017
	G-BYVT	Grob G.115E Tutor T1	Sold to Finland, 20 November 2017
	G-BYVU	Grob G.115E Tutor T1	Babcock/No 1 EFTS/676 Sqn, Middle Wallop
	G-BYVV	Grob G.115E Tutor T1	Sold to Finland, 20 October 2017
	G-BYVW	Grob G.115E Tutor T1	Babcock/University of Wales AS, St Athan
	G-BYVX	Grob G.115E Tutor T1	Sold to Finland, 25 September 2017
	G-BYVY	Grob G.115E Tutor T1	Babcock/No 1 EFTS/676 Sqn, Middle Wallop
	G-BYVZ	Grob G.115E Tutor T1	Babcock/No 16 Sqn/No 57 Sqn, Cranwell

Serial	Type (code/other identity)	Owner/operator, location or fate	Notes
G-BYWA	Grob G.115E Tutor T1	Babcock/Yorkshire Universities AS, Linton-on-Ouse	
G-BYWB	Grob G.115E Tutor T1	Babcock/No 16 Sqn/No 57 Sqn, Cranwell	
G-BYWC	Grob G.115E Tutor T1	*Sold to Finland, 20 October 2017*	
G-BYWD	Grob G.115E Tutor T1	Babcock/University of Birmingham AS, Cosford	
G-BYWE	Grob G.115E Tutor T1	*Sold to Finland, 25 September 2017*	
G-BYWF	Grob G.115E Tutor T1	Babcock/Cambridge UAS/East Midlands Universities AS/ University of London AS/No 115 Sqn, Wittering	
G-BYWG	Grob G.115E Tutor T1	Babcock/University of Birmingham AS, Cosford	
G-BYWH	Grob G.115E Tutor T1	Babcock/Cambridge UAS/East Midlands Universities AS/ University of London AS/No 115 Sqn, Wittering	
G-BYWI	Grob G.115E Tutor T1	Babcock/No 16 Sqn/No 57 Sqn, Cranwell	
G-BYWJ	Grob G.115E Tutor T1	*Sold to Finland, 24 May 2017*	
G-BYWK	Grob G.115E Tutor T1	Babcock/Northumbrian Universities AS, Leeming	
G-BYWL	Grob G.115E Tutor T1	Babcock/Bristol UAS, Boscombe Down	
G-BYWM	Grob G.115E Tutor T1	Babcock/RN No 727 NAS, Yeovilton	
G-BYWN	Grob G.115E Tutor T1	*Sold to Finland, 20 October 2017*	
G-BYWO	Grob G.115E Tutor T1	Babcock/Cambridge UAS/East Midlands Universities AS/ University of London AS/No 115 Sqn, Wittering	
G-BYWP	Grob G.115E Tutor T1	*Sold to Finland, 25 November 2017*	
G-BYWR	Grob G.115E Tutor T1	Babcock/No 16 Sqn/No 57 Sqn, Cranwell	
G-BYWS	Grob G.115E Tutor T1	Babcock/No 16 Sqn/No 57 Sqn, Cranwell	
G-BYWT	Grob G.115E Tutor T1	*Sold to Finland, 25 September 2017*	
G-BYWU	Grob G.115E Tutor T1	Babcock/University of Birmingham AS, Cosford	
G-BYWV	Grob G.115E Tutor T1	Babcock/Yorkshire Universities AS, Linton-on-Ouse	
G-BYWW	Grob G.115E Tutor T1	Babcock/Southampton UAS, Boscombe Down	
G-BYWX	Grob G.115E Tutor T1	Babcock/Cambridge UAS/East Midlands Universities AS/ University of London AS/No 115 Sqn, Wittering	
G-BYWY	Grob G.115E Tutor T1	Babcock/No 16 Sqn/No 57 Sqn, Cranwell	
G-BYWZ	Grob G.115E Tutor T1	Babcock/Cambridge UAS/East Midlands Universities AS/ University of London AS/No 115 Sqn, Wittering	
G-BYXA	Grob G.115E Tutor T1	Babcock/University of Birmingham AS, Cosford	
G-BYXB	Grob G.115E Tutor T1	*Sold to Finland, 25 November 2017*	
G-BYXC	Grob G.115E Tutor T1	Babcock/Cambridge UAS/East Midlands Universities AS/ University of London AS/No 115 Sqn, Wittering	
G-BYXD	Grob G.115E Tutor T1	Babcock/University of Wales AS, St Athan	
G-BYXE	Grob G.115E Tutor T1	Babcock/Cambridge UAS/East Midlands Universities AS/ University of London AS/No 115 Sqn, Wittering	
G-BYXF	Grob G.115E Tutor T1	Babcock/No 1 EFTS/676 Sqn, Middle Wallop	
G-BYXG	Grob G.115E Tutor T1	Babcock/No 16 Sqn/No 57 Sqn, Cranwell	
G-BYXH	Grob G.115E Tutor T1	Babcock/Cambridge UAS/East Midlands Universities AS/ University of London AS/No 115 Sqn, Wittering	
G-BYXI	Grob G.115E Tutor T1	Babcock/No 1 EFTS/676 Sqn, Middle Wallop	
G-BYXJ	Grob G.115E Tutor T1	Babcock/Northumbrian Universities AS, Leeming	
G-BYXK	Grob G.115E Tutor T1	Babcock/RN No 727 NAS, Yeovilton	
G-BYXL	Grob G.115E Tutor T1	Babcock/East of Scotland UAS, Leuchars	
G-BYXM	Grob G.115E Tutor T1 $	Babcock/Cambridge UAS/East Midlands Universities AS/ University of London AS/No 115 Sqn, Wittering	
G-BYXN	Grob G.115E Tutor T1	*Sold to Finland, 24 May 2017*	
G-BYXO	Grob G.115E Tutor T1	Babcock/East of Scotland UAS, Leuchars	
G-BYXP	Grob G.115E Tutor T1	Babcock/Cambridge UAS/East Midlands Universities AS/ University of London AS/No 115 Sqn, Wittering	
G-BYXS	Grob G.115E Tutor T1	Babcock/RN No 727 NAS, Yeovilton	
G-BYXT	Grob G.115E Tutor T1	Babcock/Yorkshire Universities AS, Linton-on-Ouse	
G-BYXX	Grob G.115E Tutor T1	Babcock/No 16 Sqn/No 57 Sqn, Cranwell	
G-BYXY	Grob G.115E Tutor T1	*Sold to Finland, 20 November 2017*	
G-BYXZ	Grob G.115E Tutor T1	Babcock/Cambridge UAS/East Midlands Universities AS/ University of London AS/No 115 Sqn, Wittering	
G-BYYA	Grob G.115E Tutor T1	Babcock/Northumbrian Universities AS, Leeming	

Notes	Serial	Type (code/other identity)	Owner/operator, location or fate
	G-BYYB	Grob G.115E Tutor T1	Babcock/Yorkshire Universities AS, Linton-on-Ouse
	G-CEYO	AS350BB Squirrel HT3 [00]	*Sold as ZK-IDR, March 2017*
	G-CGKB	Grob G.115E Tutor T1EA	*Sold to Finland, 20 November 2017*
	G-CGKC	Grob G.115E Tutor T1EA	*Sold to Finland, 20 November 2017*
	G-CGKD	Grob G.115E Tutor T1EA	Babcock/Oxford UAS, Benson
	G-CGKE	Grob G.115E Tutor T1EA	Babcock/Universities of Glasgow & Strathclyde AS, Glasgow
	G-CGKF	Grob G.115E Tutor T1EA	*Sold to Finland, 20 October 2017*
	G-CGKG	Grob G.115E Tutor T1EA	Babcock/Oxford UAS, Benson
	G-CGKH	Grob G.115E Tutor T1EA	Babcock/Oxford UAS, Benson
	G-CGKI	Grob G.115E Tutor T1EA	*Sold to Finland, 20 October 2017*
	G-CGKJ	Grob G.115E Tutor T1EA	*Sold to Finland, 20 November 2017*
	G-CGKK	Grob G.115E Tutor T1EA	Babcock/Oxford UAS, Benson
	G-CGKL	Grob G.115E Tutor T1EA	Babcock/Oxford UAS, Benson
	G-CGKM	Grob G.115E Tutor T1EA	Babcock/Oxford UAS, Benson
	G-CGKN	Grob G.115E Tutor T1EA	Babcock/Cambridge UAS/East Midlands Universities AS/ University of London AS/No 115 Sqn, Wittering
	G-CGKO	Grob G.115E Tutor T1EA	Babcock/No 16 Sqn/No 57 Sqn, Cranwell
	G-CGKP	Grob G.115E Tutor T1EA	Babcock/Oxford UAS, Benson
	G-CGKR	Grob G.115E Tutor T1EA	Babcock/Universities of Glasgow & Strathclyde AS, Glasgow
	G-CGKS	Grob G.115E Tutor T1EA	Babcock/No 16 Sqn/No 57 Sqn, Cranwell
	G-CGKT	Grob G.115E Tutor T1EA	Babcock/No 3 FTS/45 Sqn, D Flt, Cranwell
	G-CGKU	Grob G.115E Tutor T1EA	Babcock/Universities of Glasgow & Strathclyde AS, Glasgow
	G-CGKV	Grob G.115E Tutor T1EA	*Sold to Finland, 20 November 2017*
	G-CGKW	Grob G.115E Tutor T1EA	Babcock/No 3 FTS/45 Sqn, D Flt, Cranwell
	G-CGKX	Grob G.115E Tutor T1EA	Babcock/No 16 Sqn/No 57 Sqn, Cranwell
	G-DAYP	Hawker Beechcraft Super King Air 350C	RAF No 14 Sqn, Waddington
	G-DOIT	AS350BB Squirrel HT3 [99]	*Sold as ZK-IFI, March 2017*
	G-ETPA	Pilatus PC-21 (HB-HYX)	For QinetiQ
	G-ETPB	Pilatus PC-21 (HB-HYY)	For QinetiQ
	G-ETPC	Grob G.120TP-A (D-ETQI)	QinetiQ/ETPS, MoD Boscombe Down
	G-ETPD	Grob G.120TP-A (D-ETIQ)	QinetiQ/ETPS, MoD Boscombe Down
	G-ETPE	Airbus Helicopters H.125	QinetiQ/ETPS, MoD Boscombe Down
	G-ETPF	Airbus Helicopters H.125	QinetiQ/ETPS, MoD Boscombe Down
	G-ETPG	Airbus Helicopters H.125	QinetiQ/ETPS, MoD Boscombe Down
	G-ETPH	Airbus Helicopters H.125	QinetiQ/ETPS, MoD Boscombe Down
	G-FFRA	Dassault Falcon 20DC (N902FR)	Cobham Leasing Ltd, Durham/Tees Valley
	G-FRAD	Dassault Falcon 20E (9M-BDK)	Cobham Leasing Ltd, Bournemouth
	G-FRAF	Dassault Falcon 20E (N911FR)	Cobham Leasing Ltd, Bournemouth
	G-FRAH	Dassault Falcon 20DC (N900FR)	Cobham Leasing Ltd, Durham/Tees Valley
	G-FRAI	Dassault Falcon 20E (N901FR)	Cobham Leasing Ltd, Bournemouth
	G-FRAJ	Dassault Falcon 20E (N903FR)	Cobham Leasing Ltd, Bournemouth
	G-FRAK	Dassault Falcon 20DC (N905FR)	Cobham Leasing Ltd, Bournemouth
	G-FRAL	Dassault Falcon 20DC (N904FR)	Cobham Leasing Ltd, Durham/Tees Valley
	G-FRAO	Dassault Falcon 20DC (N906FR)	*Withdrawn from use, 2017*
	G-FRAP	Dassault Falcon 20DC (N908FR)	Cobham Leasing Ltd, Bournemouth
	G-FRAR	Dassault Falcon 20DC (N909FR)	Cobham Leasing Ltd, Durham/Tees Valley
	G-FRAS	Dassault Falcon 20C (117501)	Cobham Leasing Ltd, Durham/Tees Valley
	G-FRAT	Dassault Falcon 20C (117502)	Cobham Leasing Ltd, Bournemouth
	G-FRAU	Dassault Falcon 20C (117504)	Cobham Leasing Ltd, Bournemouth
	G-FRAW	Dassault Falcon 20ECM (117507)	Cobham Leasing Ltd, Durham/Tees Valley
	G-GMAD	Hawker Beechcraft Super King Air 350C	RAF No 14 Sqn, Waddington
	G-LBSB	Hawker Beechcraft Super King Air 350C	RAF No 14 Sqn, Waddington

64M/K4972	7491M/WT569	7839M/WV781	8019M/WZ869
15M/K5600	7496M/WT612	7841M/WV783	8021M/XL824
92M/K8203	7499M/WT555	7851M/WZ706	8027M/XM555
61M/K6035	7510M/WT694	7854M/XM191	8032M/XH837
18M/H5199/(BK892)	7525M/WT619	7855M/XK416	8034M/*XL554*/ (XL703)
58M/X7688	7530M/WT648	7859M/XP283	8041M/XF690
54M/BL614	7532M/WT651	7861M/*XL738*/(XM565)	8043M/XF836
52M/T5298	7533M/WT680	7862M/XR246	8046M/XL770
87M/JN768	7544M/WN904	7863M/*XP248*	8049M/WE168
77M/EP120	7548M/PS915	7864M/XP244	8050M/XG329
05M/LF738	7556M/WK584	7865M/TX226	8052M/WH166
66M/*BN230*/(LF751)	7564M/XE982	7866M/XH278	8054AM/XM410
90M/MK356	7570M/XD674	7868M/WZ736	8054BM/XM417
18M/BM597	7582M/WP190	7869M/WK935	8055AM/XM402
58M/DG202	7583M/WP185	7872M/*WZ826*/(XD826)	8055BM/XM404
57M/ML427	7602M/WE600	7881M/WD413	8056M/XG337
90M/LA255	7605M/WS692	7882M/XD525	8057M/XR243
40M/RM694	7606M/*XF688*/ (WV562)	7883M/XT150	8063M/WT536
50M/TE184	7607M/TJ138	7887M/XD375	8070M/EP120
46M/RW388	7615M/WV679	7891M/XM693	8072M/PK624
48M/DE673	7616M/WW388	7894M/XD818	8073M/TB252
60M/MT847	7618M/WW442	7895M/WF784	8075M/RW382
08M/EE549	7622M/WV606	7898M/XP854	8078M/XM351
14M/N6720	7631M/VX185	7900M/WA576	8080M/XM480
15M/NL985	7641M/XA634	7906M/WH132	8081M/XM468
35M/*K2567*/(DE306)	7645M/WD293	7917M/WA591	8082M/XM409
60M/VF301	7648M/XF785	7930M/WH301	8086M/TB752
90M/EE531	7673M/WV332	7931M/RD253	8092M/WK654
18M/LA198	7689M/*WW421*/(WW450)	7932M/WZ744	8094M/WT520
19M/LA226	7696M/WV493	7933M/XR220	8097M/XN492
50M/PK683	7698M/WV499	7937M/WS843	8101M/WH984
54M/WB188	7704M/TW536	7938M/XH903	8102M/WT486
74M/VX272	7705M/WL505	7939M/XD596	8103M/WR985
75M/VV106	7706M/WB584	7940M/XL764	8106M/WR982
00M/VT812	7709M/WT933	7955M/XH767	8114M/WL798
41M/TE311/*(MK178)*	7711M/PS915	7957M/XF545	8117M/WR974
43M/TE462	7712M/WK281	7960M/WS726	8118M/WZ549
45M/RW382	7715M/XK724	7961M/WS739	8119M/WR971
46M/TD248	7716M/WS776	7964M/WS760	8121M/XM474
56M/TB752	7718M/WA577	7965M/WS792	8124M/WZ572
57M/TB252	7719M/WK277	7967M/WS788	8128M/WH775
79M/TB752	7726M/XM373	7969M/WS840	8130M/WH798
81M/TB252	7741M/VZ477	7971M/XK699	8131M/WT507
88M/PK724	7750M/*WK864*/(WL168)	7973M/WS807	8140M/XJ571
93M/*TB675*/(RW393)	7751M/WL131	7979M/XM529	8142M/XJ560
23M/VV217	7755M/WG760	7980M/XM561	8147M/XR526
25M/R5868	7759M/PK664	7982M/XH892	8151M/WV795
26M/VN485	7761M/XH318	7983M/XD506	8153M/WV903
62M/475081/(VP546)	7762M/XE670	7984M/XN597	8154M/WV908
16M/WN907	7764M/XH318	7986M/WG777	8155M/WV797
21M/WT660	7770M/*XF506*/(WT746)	7988M/XL149	8156M/XE339
22M/WT684	7793M/XG523	7990M/XD452	8158M/XE369
28M/WK198	7798M/XH783	7997M/XG452	8162M/WM913
32M/WZ724	7806M/TA639	7998M/*XM515*/(XD515)	8164M/*WN105*/(WF299)
38M/*18671*/(WP905)	7809M/XA699	8005M/WG768	8165M/WH791
43M/WX853	7816M/WG763	8009M/XG518	8169M/WH364
58M/WX905	7817M/TX214	8010M/XG547	8173M/XN685
64M/XA564	7825M/WK991	8012M/VS562	8176M/WH791
70M/XA553	7827M/XA917	8017M/XL762	8177M/WM224
73M/XE946	7829M/XH992	8018M/XN344	8179M/XN928

8183M/*XN972*/(XN962)	8394M/WG422	8538M/XN781	8703M/VW453	
8184M/WT520	8395M/WF408	8545M/XN726	8706M/XF383	
8186M/WR977	8396M/XK740	8546M/XN728	8708M/XF509	
8187M/WH791	8399M/WR539	8548M/WT507	8709M/XG209	
8189M/*WD615* (WD646)	8401M/XP686	8549M/WT534	8710M/XG274	
8190M/XJ918	8406M/XP831	8554M/TG511	8711M/XG290	
8192M/XR658	8407M/XP585	8561M/XS100	8713M/XG225	
8198M/WT339	8408M/XS186	8563M/*XX822*/(XW563)	8718M/XX396	
8203M/XD377	8409M/XS209	8565M/*WT720*/(E-408)	8719M/XT257	
8205M/XN819	8410M/XR662	8566M/XV279	8721M/XP354	
8206M/WG419	8413M/XM192	8573M/XM708	8724M/XW923	
8208M/WG303	8414M/XM173	8575M/XP542	8726M/XP299	
8209M/WG418	8417M/XM144	8576M/XP502	8727M/XR486	
8210M/WG471	8422M/XM169	8578M/XR534	8728M/WT532	
8211M/WK570	8427M/XM172	8581M/WJ775	8729M/WJ815	
8213M/WK626	8429M/XH592	8582M/XE874	8732M/XJ729	
8215M/WP869	8434M/XM411	8583M/BAPC 94	8733M/XL318	
8216M/WP927	8436M/XN554	8585M/XE670	8736M/XF375	
8218M/WB645	8437M/WG362	8586M/XE643	8739M/XH170	
8229M/XM355	8439M/WZ846	8588M/XR681	8740M/WE173	
8230M/XM362	8440M/WD935	8589M/XR700	8741M/XW329	
8234M/XN458	8442M/XP411	8590M/XM191	8743M/WD790	
8235M/XN549	8452M/XK885	8591M/XA813	8746M/XH171	
8236M/XP573	8453M/XP745	8595M/XH278	8749M/XH537	
8237M/XS179	8458M/XP672	8598M/WP270	8751M/XT255	
8238M/XS180	8459M/XR650	8600M/XX761	8753M/WL795	
8338M/XS180	8460M/XP680	8602M/*PF179*/(XR541)	8762M/WH740	
8342M/WP848	8462M/XX477	8604M/XS104	8764M/XP344	
8344M/WH960	8463M/XP355	8606M/XP530	8768M/A-522	
8350M/WH840	8464M/XJ758	8608M/XP540	8769M/A-528	
8352M/XN632	8465M/W1048	8610M/XL502	8770M/XL623	
8355M/KN645	8466M/L-866	8611M/WF128	8771M/XM602	
8357M/WK576	8467M/WP912	8620M/XP534	8772M/WR960	
8359M/WF825	8468M/MM5701/(BT474)	8621M/XR538	8778M/XM598	
8361M/WB670	8469M/100503	8624M/*XR991*/(XS102)	8779M/XM607	
8362M/WG477	8470M/584219	8627M/XP558	8780M/WK102	
8364M/WG464	8471M/701152	8628M/XJ380	8781M/WE982	
8365M/XK421	8472M/120227/(VN679)	8630M/WG362	8782M/XH136	
8366M/XG454	8473M/WP190	8631M/XR574	8785M/XS642	
8367M/XG474	8474M/494083	8633M/3W-17/MK732	8789M/XK970	
8368M/XF926	8475M/360043/(PJ876)	8634M/WP314	8791M/XP329	
8369M/WE139	8476M/24	8640M/XR977	8792M/XP345	
8370M/N1671	8477M/4101/(DG200)	8642M/XR537	8793M/XP346	
8371M/XA847	8478M/10639	8645M/XD163	8794M/XP398	
8372M/K8042	8479M/730301	8648M/XK526	8796M/XK943	
8373M/P2617	8481M/191614	8653M/XS120	8799M/WV787	
8375M/NX611	8482M/112372/(VK893)	8655M/XN126	8800M/XG226	
8376M/RF398	8483M/420430	8656M/XP405	8805M/XV722	
8377M/R9125	8484M/5439	8657M/VZ634	8807M/XL587	
8378M/*T9707*	8485M/997	8661M/XJ727	8810M/XJ825	
8379M/DG590	8486M/BAPC 99	8662M/XR458	8816M/XX734	
8380M/Z7197	8487M/J-1172	8666M/XE793	8818M/XK527	
8382M/VR930	8488M/WL627	8671M/XJ435	8820M/VP952	
8383M/K9942	8491M/WJ880	8672M/XP351	8821M/XX115	
8384M/X4590	8493M/XR571	8673M/XD165	8822M/VP957	
8385M/N5912	8494M/XP557	8676M/XL577	8828M/XS587	
8386M/NV778	8501M/XP640	8679M/XF526	8830M/*N-294*/(XF515)	
8387M/T6296	8502M/XP686	8680M/XF527	8831M/XG160	
8388M/XL993	8508M/XS218	8681M/XG164	8832M/*XG168*/(XG172)	
8389M/VX573	8509M/XT141	8682M/XP404	8833M/XL569	
8390M/SL542	8514M/XS176	8693M/WH863	8834M/*XL571*	
8392M/SL674	8535M/XN776	8702M/XG196	8836M/XL592	

8838M/*34037*/(429356)	8947M/XX726	9070M/XV581	9180M/XW311
8839M/XG194	8949M/XX743	9072M/XW768	9181M/XW358
8841M/XE606	8951M/XX727	9073M/XW924	9185M/XZ987
8853M/XT277	8953M/XX959	9075M/XV752	9187M/XW405
8855M/XT284	8954M/XZ384	9076M/XV808	9188M/XW364
8857M/XW544	8955M/XX110	9078M/XV753	9191M/XW416
8858M/XW541	8957M/XN582	9079M/XZ130	9194M/XW420
8863M/XG154	8961M/XS925	9080M/ZE350	9195M/XW330
8867M/XK532	8967M/XV263	9086M/ZE352	9196M/XW370
8868M/WH775	8969M/XR753	9087M/XX753	9197M/*XX530*/(XX637)
8869M/WH957	8972M/XR754	9090M/XW353	9198M/XS641
8870M/WH964	8973M/XS922	9091M/XW434	9199M/XW290
8871M/WJ565	8974M/XM473	9092M/XH669	9201M/ZD667
8873M/XR453	8975M/XW917	9093M/WK124	9203M/*3066*
8874M/XE597	8976M/XZ630	9095M/XW547	9205M/*E449*
8875M/XE624	8978M/XX837	9096M/WV322	9206M/F6314
8876M/*VM791*/(XA312)	8984M/XN551	9098M/XV406	9207M/8417/18
8880M/XF435	8985M/WK127	9103M/XV411	9208M/F938
8881M/XG254	8986M/XV261	9110M/XX736	9210M/MF628
8883M/XX946	8987M/XM358	9111M/XW421	9211M/733682
8884M/VX275	8990M/XM419	9115M/XV863	9212M/*KL216*/(45-49295)
8885M/XW922	8995M/XM425	9117M/XV161	9213M/N5182
8886M/XA243	8996M/XM414	9119M/XW303	9215M/XL164
8888M/XA231	8997M/XX669	9120M/XW419	9216M/XL190
8889M/XN239	8998M/XT864	9122M/XZ997	9217M/ZH257
8890M/WT532	9002M/XW763	9123M/XT773	9218M/XL563
8895M/XX746	9003M/XZ390	9125M/XW410	9219M/XZ971
8896M/XX821	9004M/XZ370	9127M/XW432	9221M/XZ966
8897M/XX969	9005M/XZ374	9130M/XW327	9222M/XZ968
8898M/XX119	9006M/XX967	9131M/*DD931*	9224M/XL568
8899M/XX756	9007M/XX968	9132M/XX977	9225M/XX885
8900M/XZ368	9008M/XX140	9133M/*413573*	9226M/XV865
8901M/XZ383	9009M/XX763	9134M/XT288	9227M/XB812
8902M/XX739	9010M/XX764	9136M/XT891	9229M/ZA678
8903M/XX747	9011M/XM412	9137M/XN579	9233M/XZ431
8905M/XX975	9012M/XN494	9139M/XV863	9234M/XV864
8906M/XX976	9014M/XN584	9140M/XZ287	9236M/WV318
8907M/XZ371	9015M/XW320	9141M/XV118	9237M/XF445
8908M/XZ382	9017M/ZE449	9143M/XN589	9238M/ZA717
8909M/XV784	9019M/XX824	9145M/XV863	9239M/7198/18
8910M/XL160	9020M/XX825	9146M/XW299	9241M/XS639
8911M/XH673	9021M/XX826	9148M/XW436	9242M/XH672
8918M/XX109	9022M/XX958	9149M/XW375	9246M/XS714
8919M/XT486	9026M/XP629	9150M/*FX760*	9248M/WB627
8920M/XT469	9027M/XP556	9151M/XT907	9249M/WV396
8921M/XT466	9032M/XR673	9152M/XV424	9251M/XX744
8922M/XT467	9033M/XS181	9153M/XW360	9252M/XX722
8923M/XX819	9036M/XM350	9154M/XW321	9254M/XX965
8924M/XP701	9038M/XV810	9155M/WL679	9255M/XZ375
8925M/XP706	9039M/XN586	9162M/XZ991	9257M/XX962
8931M/XV779	9040M/XZ138	9163M/XV415	9258M/XW265
8932M/XR718	9041M/XW763	9166M/XW323	9259M/XS710
8934M/XR749	9042M/XL954	9167M/XV744	9260M/XS734
8935M/XR713	9044M/XS177	9168M/XZ132	9261M/*W2068*
8937M/XX751	9047M/XW409	9169M/XW547	9262M/XZ358
8938M/WV746	9048M/XM403	9170M/XZ994	9263M/XW267
8941M/XT456	9049M/XW404	9172M/XW304	9264M/XS735
8942M/XN185	9052M/WJ717	9173M/XW418	9265M/WK585
8943M/XE799	9056M/XS488	9174M/XZ131	9266M/XZ119
8944M/WZ791	9059M/ZE360	9175M/P1344	9267M/XW269
8945M/XX818	9066M/XV582	9176M/XW430	9268M/XR529
8946M/XZ389	9067M/XV586	9179M/XW309	9269M/XT914

9270M/XZ145	9290M/XX626	9315M/ZA319	9336M/ZA407
9272M/XS486	9292M/XW892	9316M/ZA399	9337M/ZA774
9273M/XS726	9293M/XX830	9317M/ZA450	9338M/ZA325
9274M/XS338	9294M/XX655	9318M/ZA360	9339M/ZA323
9275M/XS729	9295M/XV497	9319M/XR516	9340M/XX745
9277M/XT601	9298M/ZE340	9320M/XX153	9341M/ZA357
9278M/XS643	9299M/XW870	9321M/XZ367	9342M/XR498
9279M/XT681	9300M/XX431	9322M/ZB686	9343M/XR506
9281M/XZ146	9301M/XZ941	9323M/XV643	9344M/XV706
9283M/XZ322	9302M/ZD462	9324M/XV659	
9284M/ZA267	9303M/XV709	9326M/XV653	
9285M/XR806	9306M/XX979	9328M/ZD607	
9286M/XT905	9308M/ZD932	9329M/ZD578	
9287M/WP962	9310M/ZA355	9330M/ZB684	
9288M/XX520	9311M/ZA475	9331M/XW852	
9289M/XX665	9314M/ZA320	9332M/XZ935	

Tucano T1 ZF338 wears 76(R) Sqn markings and the name 'WHIZZO'. Seen here at its Linton-on-Ouse base flying with No 1 FTS, the Tucano is another type that is scheduled for withdrawal.

Squirrel HT1 ZJ273/73 is seen here in the markings of the Defence Helicopter Flying School at RAF Shawbury. The type is in decline as it is being replaced by the Juno HT1.

eck Letters	Vessel Name and Pennant No.	Vessel Type and Unit
3	HMS *Albion* (L14)	Assault
S	RFA *Argus* (A135)	Aviation Training ship
Y	HMS *Argyll* (F231)	Type 23
K	HMS *Bulwark* (L15)	Assault
V	RFA *Black Rover* (A273)	Fleet tanker
B	RFA *Cardigan Bay* (L3009)	Landing ship
J	RNAS Culdrose (HMS *Seahawk*)	
A	HMS *Daring* (D32)	Type 45
E	HMS *Defender* (D36)	Type 45
G	RFA *Diligence* (A132)	Maintenance
M	HMS *Diamond* (D34)	Type 45
N	HMS *Dragon* (D35)	Type 45
T	HMS *Dauntless* (D33)	Type 45
U	HMS *Duncan* (D37)	Type 45
A	RFA *Fort Austin* (A386)	Support ship
E	RFA *Fort Rosalie* (A385)	Support ship
V	RFA *Fort Victoria* (A387)	Auxiliary Oiler
	HMS *Iron Duke* (F234)	Type 23
	HMS *Kent* (F78)	Type 23
A	HMS *Lancaster* (F229)	Type 23
B	RFA *Mounts Bay* (L3008)	Landing ship
M	HMS *Monmouth* (F235)	Type 23
R	HMS *Montrose* (F236)	Type 23
L	HMS *Northumberland* (F238)	Type 23
	HMS *Ocean* (L12)	Helicopter carrier
	HMS *Prince of Wales* (R09)	Aircraft carrier
	HMS *Queen Elizabeth* (R08)	Aircraft carrier
D	HMS *Portland* (F79)	Type 23
M	HMS *Richmond* (F239)	Type 23
B	HMS *St Albans* (F83)	Type 23
M	HMS *Somerset* (F82)	Type 23
U	HMS *Sutherland* (F81)	Type 23
	RNAS Yeovilton (HMS *Heron*)	
K	RFA *Wave Knight* (A389)	Fleet tanker
M	HMS *Westminster* (F237)	Type 23
B	RFA *Lyme Bay* (L3007)	Landing ship
	HMS *Protector* (A173)	Ice patrol
	RFA *Wave Ruler* (A390)	Fleet tanker

RN CODE – SQUADRON – BASE – AIRCRAFT CROSS-CHECK

eck/Base ode Numbers	Letters	Unit	Location	Aircraft Type(s)
0 — 015	CU	820 NAS	Culdrose	Merlin HM2
0 — 190	CU	849 NAS	Culdrose	Sea King ASaC7
4 — 274	CU	814 NAS	Culdrose	Merlin HM2
0 — 515	CU	829 NAS	Culdrose	Merlin HM2
0 — 588	CU	824 NAS	Culdrose	Merlin HM2

ote that only the 'last two' digits of the Code are worn by some aircraft types, especially helicopters.

This table gives brief details of the markings worn by aircraft of RAF squadrons. While this may help to identify the operator of a particular machine, it may not always give the true picture. For example, from time to time aircraft are loaned to other units while others wear squadron marks but are actually operated on a pool basis. Squadron badges are usually located on the front fuselage.

Squadron	Type(s) operated	Base(s)	Distinguishing marks & other comments
No 1(F) Sqn	Typhoon T3/FGR4	RAF Lossiemouth	Badge (on tail): A red 1 with yellow wings on a white background, flanked in red. Roundel is flanked by two white chevrons, edged in red.
No 2(AC) Sqn/ II(AC) Sqn	Typhoon T3/FGR4	RAF Lossiemouth	Badge: A wake knot on a white circular background flanked on either side by black and white triangles. Tail fin has a black stripe with white triangles and the badge repeated on it.
No 3(F) Sqn	Typhoon T3/FGR4	RAF Coningsby	Badge: A blue cockatrice on a white circular background flanked by two green bars edged with yellow. Tail fin as a green stripe edged with yellow.
No 4 Sqn	Hawk T2	RAF Valley	Badge (on nose): A yellow lightning flash on a red background with IV superimposed. Aircraft carry a yellow lightning flash on a red and black background on the tail and this is repeated in bars either side of the roundel on the fuselage. Part of No 4 FTS.
No 5(AC) Sqn/ V(AC) Sqn	Sentinel R1	RAF Waddington	Badge (on tail): A green maple leaf on a white circle over a red horizontal band.
No 6 Sqn	Typhoon T3/FGR4	RAF Lossiemouth	Badge (on tail): A red, winged can opener on a blue shield, edged in red. The roundel is flanked by a red zigzag on a blue background.
No 7 Sqn	Chinook HC6	RAF Odiham	Badge (on tail): A blue badge containing the seven stars of Ursa Major ('The Plough') in yellow.
No 8 Sqn	Sentry AEW1	RAF Waddington	Badge (on tail): A grey, sheathed, Arabian dagger. Aircraft pooled with No 54 Sqn.
No 9 Sqn/ IX Sqn	Tornado GR4/GR4A	RAF Marham	Badge: A green bat on a black circular background, flanked by yellow and green horizontal stripes. The green bat also appears on the tail, edged in yellow.
No 10 Sqn	Voyager KC2/KC3	RAF Brize Norton	No markings worn.
No 11 Sqn	Typhoon T3/FGR4	RAF Coningsby	Badge (on tail): Two eagles in flight on a white shield. The roundel is flanked by yellow and black triangles.
No 12(B) Sqn	Tornado GR4/GR4A	RAF Marham	Roundel is superimposed on a green chevron. Tail fin has a black and white horizontal stripe with the squadron badge, a fox's head on a white circle, in the middle. [To move to Coningsby and re-equip with the Typhoon.]
No 13 Sqn	Reaper	RAF Waddington	No markings worn.
No 14 Sqn	Shadow R1	RAF Waddington	No markings worn.
No 16 Sqn	Tutor T1	RAF Cranwell	No markings carried. Aircraft pooled with No 57 Sqn. Part of No 1 EFTS.

Squadron	Type(s) operated	Base(s)	Distinguishing marks & other comments
No 17 Test & Evaluation Sqn	Lightning II	Edwards AFB, USA	No markings worn
No 18(B) Sqn	Chinook HC4/ HC5/HC6A	RAF Odiham	Badge (on tail): A red winged horse on a black circle. Aircraft pooled with No 27 Sqn.
No 24 Sqn/ XXIV Sqn	Hercules C4/C5/ Atlas C1	RAF Brize Norton	No squadron markings carried. Aircraft pooled with No 30 Sqn, No 47 Sqn and No 70 Sqn.
No 27 Sqn	Chinook HC4/ HC5	RAF Odiham	Badge (on tail): A dark green elephant on a green circle, flanked by green and dark green stripes. Aircraft pooled with No 18 Sqn.
No 28 Sqn	Chinook HC4/ Puma HC2	RAF Benson	Badge: A winged horse above two white crosses on a red shield.
No 29 Sqn	Typhoon T3/FGR4	RAF Coningsby	Badge (on tail): An eagle in flight, preying on a buzzard, with three red Xs across the top. The roundel is flanked by two white bars outlined by a red line, each containing three red Xs.
No 30 Sqn	Hercules C4/C5	RAF Brize Norton	No squadron markings carried. Aircraft pooled with No 24 Sqn and No 47 Sqn.
No 31 Sqn	Tornado GR4/GR4A	RAF Marham	Badge: A gold, five-pointed star on a yellow circle flanked by yellow and green checks. The star is repeated on the tail.
No 32(The Royal) Sqn	BAe 146 CC2/146 C3/ Agusta 109	RAF Northolt	No squadron markings carried but aircraft carry a distinctive livery with a red stripe, edged in blue along the middle of the fuselage and a red tail.
No 33 Sqn	Puma HC2	RAF Benson	Badge: A stag's head.
No 39 Sqn	Predator/ Reaper	Nellis AFB Creech AFB	No markings worn
No 41 Test & Evaluation Sqn [FJWOEU]	Typhoon T3/FGR4	RAF Coningsby	Badge: A red, double armed cross on the tail with a gold crown above. White and red horizontal bars flanking the roundel on the fuselage. Aircraft are coded EB-*.
No 45 Sqn	Phenom/Super King Air 200/200GT/Tutor T1EA	RAF Cranwell	The King Airs carry a dark blue stripe on the tail superimposed with red diamonds. Part of No 3 FTS.
No 47 Sqn	Hercules C4/C5	RAF Brize Norton	No squadron markings usually carried. Aircraft pooled with No 24 Sqn and No 30 Sqn.
No 51 Sqn	RC-135W	RAF Waddington	Badge (on tail): A red goose in flight.
No 54 Sqn [ISTAR OCU]	Sentry AEW1	RAF Waddington	Based aircraft as required.
No 56 Sqn [ISTAR Test & Evaluation Sqn]	Shadow R1/ Sentry AEW1/ Sentinel R1	RAF Waddington	Based aircraft as required.
No 57 Sqn	Prefect T1/Tutor T1	RAF Cranwell	No markings carried. Aircraft pooled with No 16 Sqn. Part of No 1 EFTS.

Squadron	Type(s) operated	Base(s)	Distinguishing marks & other comments
No 60 Sqn	Griffin HT1	RAF Shawbury [DHFS]	No squadron markings usually carried.
No 70 Sqn Fixed Wing Air Mobility OCU/LXX Sqn	Atlas C1	RAF Brize Norton	No squadron markings usually carried. Aircraft pooled with No 24 Sqn.
No 72 Sqn	Tucano T1	RAF Linton-on-Ouse	Badge: A black swift in flight on a red disk, flanked by blue bars edged with red. The blue bars edged with red also flank the roundel on the fuselage; part of No 1 FTS
No 84 Sqn	Griffin HAR2	RAF Akrotiri	Badge (on tail): A scorpion on a playing card symbol (diamonds, clubs etc.). Aircraft carry a vertical light blue stripe through the roundel on the fuselage.
No 99 Sqn	Globemaster III	RAF Brize Norton	Badge (on tail): A black puma leaping.
No 100 Sqn	Hawk T1A	RAF Leeming	Badge (on tail): A skull in front of two bones crossed. Aircraft are usually coded C*. Incorporates the Joint Forward Air Control Training and Standards Unit (JFACTSU)
No 101 Sqn	Voyager KC2/KC3	RAF Brize Norton	No markings worn.
No 115 Sqn	Tutor T1	Wittering	No markings carried. Part of the CFS.
No 202 Sqn	Jupiter HT1/ Griffin HT1	RAF Valley	Badge: A mallard alighting on a white circle.
No 206 Sqn [HAT&ES]	Hercules C4/C5	RAF Brize Norton/ Boscombe Down	No squadron markings usually carried.
No 230 Sqn	Puma HC2	RAF Benson	Badge: A tiger in front of a palm tree on a black pentagon.
No 617 Sqn	Lightning II	MCAS Beaufort, USA	No markings worn
No 1310 Flt	Chinook HC4	Mount Pleasant, FI	No markings worn
No 1312 Flt	Hercules C5/ Voyager KC2/KC3	Mount Pleasant, FI	Badge (on tail): A red Maltese cross on a white circle, flanked by red and white horizontal bars.
No 1435 Flt	Typhoon FGR4	Mount Pleasant, FI	Badge (on tail): A red Maltese cross on a white circle, flanked by red and white horizontal bars.

Hawk T1A XX191/CC wears the distinctive markings of No 100 Sqn, based at RAF Leeming. The Hawk fleet underwent considerable changes with many aircraft swapping units but part of this process will ensure that the 'Red Arrows' have plenty of aircraft to continuing flying the type for some time yet.

As from 7 September 2015 all UAS flights and AEFs are commanded and managed by No 6 FTS RAF. Some UAS aircraft carry squadron badges and markings, usually on the tail. Squadron crests all consist of a white circle surrounded by a blue circle, topped with a red crown and having a yellow scroll beneath. Each differs by the motto on the scroll, the UAS name running around the blue circle & by the contents at the centre and it is the latter which are described below.

* All AEFs come under the administration of local UASs and these are listed here.

UAS	Base	Marks
Bristol UAS/ No 3 AEF	Boscombe Down	A sailing ship on water.
Cambridge UAS/ No 5 AEF	Wittering	A heraldic lion in front of a red badge. Aircraft pooled with University of London AS.
East Midlands Universities AS/ No 7 AEF	Wittering	A yellow quiver, full of arrows.
East of Scotland UAS/ No 12 AEF	RAF Leuchars	An open book in front of a white diagonal cross edged in blue.
Liverpool UAS	RAF Woodvale	A bird atop an open book, holding a branch in its beak. Aircraft pooled with Manchester and Salford Universities AS
Manchester and Salford Universities AS/ No 10 AEF	RAF Woodvale	A bird of prey with a green snake in its beak. Aircraft pooled with Liverpool UAS
Northern Ireland Universities AS/ No 14 AEF	JHFS Aldergrove	(Currently not known)
Northumbrian Universities AS/ No 11 AEF	RAF Leeming	A white cross on a blue background.
Oxford UAS/ No 6 AEF	RAF Benson	An open book in front of crossed swords.
Southampton UAS/ No 2 AEF	Boscombe Down	A red stag in front of a stone pillar.
Universities of Glasgow and Strathclyde AS/ No 4 AEF	Glasgow	A bird of prey in flight, holding a branch in its beak, in front of an upright sword.
University of Birmingham AS/ No 8 AEF	DCAE Cosford	A blue griffon with two heads.
University of London AS	Wittering	A globe superimposed over an open book. Aircraft pooled with Cambridge UAS.
University of Wales AS/ No 1 AEF	MoD St Athan	A red Welsh dragon in front of an open book, clasping a sword. Some aircraft have the dragon in front of white and green squares.
Yorkshire Universities AS/ No 9 AEF	RAF Linton-on-Ouse	An open book in front of a Yorkshire rose with leaves.

This table gives brief details of the markings worn by aircraft of FAA squadrons. Squadron badges, when worn, are usually located on the front fuselage. All FAA squadron badges comprise a crown atop a circle edged in gold braid and so the badge details below list only what appears in the circular part.

Squadron	Type(s) operated	Base(s)	Distinguishing marks & other comments
No 700X NAS	Scan Eagle RM1	RNAS Culdrose	Badge: No markings carried.
No 727 NAS	Tutor T1	RNAS Yeovilton	Badge: The head of Britannia wearing a gold helmet on a background of blue and white waves.
No 736 NAS	Hawk T1A	RNAS Culdrose & RNAS Yeovilton	A white lightning bolt on the tail.
No 750 NAS	Avenger T1	RNAS Culdrose	Badge: A Greek runner bearing a torch & sword on a background of blue and white waves.
No 814 NAS	Merlin HM2	RNAS Culdrose	Badge: A winged tiger mask on a background of dark blue and white waves.
No 815 NAS	Wildcat HMA2	RNAS Yeovilton	Badge: A winged, gold harpoon on a background of blue and white waves.
No 820 NAS	Merlin HM2	RNAS Culdrose	Badge: A flying fish on a background of blue and white waves.
No 824 NAS	Merlin HM2	RNAS Culdrose	Badge: A heron on a background of blue and white waves.
No 825 NAS	Wildcat HMA2	RNAS Yeovilton	Badge: An eagle over a Maltese cross.
No 829 NAS	Merlin HM2	RNAS Culdrose	Badge: A kingfisher hovering on a background of blue and white waves.
No 845 NAS	Merlin HC3i	RNAS Yeovilton	Badge: A dragonfly on a background of blue and white waves.
No 846 NAS	Merlin HC3/HC3A	RNAS Yeovilton	Badge: A swordsman riding a winged horse whilst attacking a serpent on a background of blue and white waves.
No 847 NAS	Wildcat AH1	RNAS Yeovilton	Badge (not currently worn): A gold sea lion on a blue background.
No 849 NAS	Sea King ASaC7	RNAS Culdrose	Badge: A winged streak of lightning with an eye in front on a background of blue and white waves.

Hawk T1 XX240/840 began 2017 in the hands of 736 NAS but ended the year at RAF Shawbury. By the end of the year 736 NAS had no aircraft wearing its code sequence with the last example, '849' (XX316), flying in full colours but now with the RAF at Leeming.

This section lists the codes worn by some UK military aircraft and, alongside, the Registration of the aircraft currently wearing this code. It should be pointed out that in some cases more than one aircraft wears the same code but the aircraft listed is the one believed to be in service with the unit concerned at the time of going to press. This list will be updated regularly and those with Internet access can download the latest version via the 'Military Aircraft Markings' Web Site, www.militaryaircraftmarkings.co.uk.

Code	Serial	Code	Serial	Code	Serial	Code	Serial
ROYAL AIR FORCE		P	ZK456	**Eurofighter Typhoon**		14	ZH854
BAE Hawk T1/T2		U	ZK460	C	ZJ935	66	ZH860
A	ZK010	X	ZK459	D	ZJ941	67	ZH850
B	ZK011			F	ZJ915	68	ZH826 & ZH853
C	ZK012	**Bell 412EP Griffin HT1**		H	ZJ926	69	ZH839
D	ZK013	E	ZJ242	S	ZJ916	70	ZH847
E	ZK014	I	ZJ235	AX	ZK303	80	ZH836
F	ZK015	K	ZJ708	EB-E	ZK339	81	ZH832
G	ZK016	O	ZJ707	EB-L	ZK365	82	ZH842
H	ZK017	R	ZJ239	EB-R	ZK367	83	ZH824
I	ZK018	S	ZJ234	EB-V	ZK315	84	ZH851
J	ZK019	T	ZJ237	QO-P	ZK309	85	ZH862 & ZH864
K	ZK020	U	ZJ240			86	ZH857
L	ZK021	X	ZJ236	**Panavia Tornado GR4**		87	ZH834
M	ZK022	Y	ZJ238	020	ZA449	501	ZH841
N	ZK023			025	ZA459	A	ZJ117
O	ZK024	**B-V Chinook**		028	ZA463	B	ZJ118
P	ZK025	W	ZA712	031	ZA472	C	ZJ119
Q	ZK026	AA	ZA670	032	ZA473	D	ZJ120
R	ZK027	AB	ZA671	035	ZA542	E	ZJ121
S	ZK028	AD	ZA674	036	ZA543	F	ZJ122
T	ZK029	AE	ZA675	038	ZA546	G	ZJ123
U	ZK030	AF	ZA677	045	ZA553	H	ZJ124
V	ZK031	AG	ZA679	046	ZA554	J	ZJ125
W	ZK032	AH	ZA680	047	ZA556	K	ZJ126
X	ZK033	AI	ZA681	054	ZA585	L	ZJ127
Y	ZK034	AJ	ZA682	055	ZA587	M	ZJ128
Z	ZK035	AL	ZA684	056	ZA588	N	ZJ129
AA	ZK036	AN	ZA705	063	ZA597	O	ZJ130
AB	ZK037	AO	ZA707	066	ZA601	P	ZJ131
CA	XX246	AP	ZA708	073	ZA611	Q	ZJ132
CB	XX255	AR	ZA710	074	ZA612	R	ZJ133
CC	XX191	AV	ZA714	075	ZA613	S	ZJ134
CD	XX332	AW	ZA720	076	ZA614	T	ZJ135
CE	XX258	BN	ZA718	084	ZD716	U	ZJ136
CF	XX203	DB	ZD574	092	ZD744	W	ZJ137
CG	XX318	DC	ZD575	100	ZD792	X	ZJ138
CH	XX198	DD	ZD980	101	ZD793	AA	ZJ990
CI	XX239	DF	ZD982	109	ZD848	AB	ZJ992
CJ	XX329	DG	ZD983	110	ZD849	AC	ZJ994
CK	XX205	DH	ZD984	129	ZG752	AD	ZJ995
CL	XX339	HB	ZH775	134	ZG775	AE	ZJ998
CM	XX337	HC	ZH776	137	ZG791	AF	ZK001
CO	XX200 & XX221	HF	ZH891				
CP	XX346	HG	ZH892	**Shorts Tucano T1**		**WS61 Sea King**	
CQ	XX348	HH	ZH893	MP-A	ZF170	181	XV697
CR	XX303	HI	ZH894	RN-S	ZF378	183	XV671
CS	XX202	HJ	ZH895			185	XV656
		HK	ZH896	**ROYAL NAVY**		188	XV714
Beech King Air 200		HR	ZH903	**EHI-101 Merlin**		189	ZE420
D	ZK458			10	ZH827	191	ZA126
K	ZK451			11	ZH840	192	ZE422
L	ZK452			12	ZH846		
O	ZK455			13	ZH835		

Code	Serial	Code	Serial	Code	Serial	Code	Serial
ARMY AIR CORPS		**WS Gazelle AH1**					
Bell 212		M	XZ345				
B	ZK067	S	ZB691				
K	ZJ969	Y	ZB692				
X	ZH814						
Y	ZH815						

Typhoon ZK365/EB-L is unusual in that it still wears colourful squadron codes and markings, in this case of No 41 (R) Test & Evaluation Squadron, based at RAF Coningsby. The lumps on the rear fuselage identify this as a Tranche 3 Typhoon, the latest version, capable of carrying conformal fuel tanks.

ZZ386 is a Wildcat AH1, seen returning to its base at Yeovilton. The fleet of AH1s are operated by 1 Regiment Army Air Corps and the Royal Marines' 847 Naval Air Squadron, although the latter still carry Army titles. A handful of 847 NAS machines supported the work after the devastation in the Caribbean and returned to Yeovilton after deployment in December 2017 unusually carrying Royal Navy stickers.

Some *historic, classic and warbird* aircraft carry the markings of overseas air arms and can be seen in the UK, mainly preserved in museums and collections or taking part in air shows.

Serial	Type (code/other identity)	Owner/operator, location or fate	Notes
AFGHANISTAN			
-	Hawker Afghan Hind (K4672/BAPC 82)	RAF Museum Reserve Collection, Stafford	
ARGENTINA			
-	Bell UH-1H Iroquois (AE-406/*998-8888*) [Z]	RAF Valley, instructional use	
0729	Beech T-34C Turbo Mentor	FAA Museum, stored Cobham Hall, RNAS Yeovilton	
0767	Aermacchi MB339AA	South Yorkshire Aircraft Museum, Doncaster	
A-515	FMA IA58 Pucará (ZD485)	RAF Museum, stored Cosford	
A-517	FMA IA58 Pucará (G-BLRP)	Privately owned, Channel Islands	
A-522	FMA IA58 Pucará (8768M)	FAA Museum, at NE Aircraft Museum, Usworth	
A-528	FMA IA58 Pucará (8769M)	Norfolk & Suffolk Avn Museum, Flixton	
A-533	FMA IA58 Pucará (ZD486) <ff>	Privately owned, Chelmsford	
A-549	FMA IA58 Pucará (ZD487)	IWM Duxford	
AE-331	Agusta A109A (ZE411)	FAA Museum, stored Cobham Hall, RNAS Yeovilton	
AE-409	Bell UH-1H Iroquois [656]	Museum of Army Flying, Middle Wallop	
AE-422	Bell UH-1H Iroquois	FAA Museum, stored Cobham Hall, RNAS Yeovilton	
AUSTRALIA			
369	Hawker Fury ISS (F-AZXL) [D]	Privately owned, Cannes, France	
A2-4	Supermarine Seagull V (VH-ALB)	RAF Museum Reserve Collection, Stafford	
A11-301	Auster J/5G (G-ARKG) [931-NW]	Privately owned, Spanhoe	
A16-199	Lockheed Hudson IIIA (G-BEOX) [SF-R]	RAF Museum, Hendon	
A17-48	DH82A Tiger Moth (G-BPHR)	Privately owned, Wanborough, Wilts	
A17-376	DH82A Tiger Moth (T6830/G-ANJI) [376]	Privately owned, Gloucester	
A19-144	Bristol 156 Beaufighter XIc (JM135/A8-324)	The Fighter Collection, Duxford	
A92-255	GAF Jindivik 102	QinetiQ Apprentice Training School, Boscombe Down	
A92-664	GAF Jindivik 103A	Boscombe Down Aviation Collection, Old Sarum	
A92-708	GAF Jindivik 103BL	Aerospace Bristol, stored Filton	
A92-908	GAF Jindivik 104AL (ZJ503)	Privately owned, Llanbedr	
N16-114	WS61 Sea King Mk.50A	Privately owned, Horsham	
N16-125	WS61 Sea King Mk.50A	Privately owned, Horsham	
N16-238	WS61 Sea King Mk.50A	Privately owned, Horsham	
N16-239	WS61 Sea King Mk.50A	Privately owned, Horsham	
N16-918	WS61 Sea King Mk.50B	Privately owned, Horsham	
WH589	Hawker Fury ISS (F-AZXJ) [115-NW]	Privately owned, Dijon, France	
AUSTRIA			
5S-TC	Short SC.7 Skyvan 3 Variant 100 (G-BEOL)	Invicta Aviation, Rotterdam, The Netherlands	
BELGIUM			
A-41	SA318C Alouette II	The Helicopter Museum, Weston-super-Mare	
FT-36	Lockheed T-33A Shooting Star	Dumfries & Galloway Avn Mus, Dumfries	
H-02	Agusta A109HO (N504TS)	Privately owned, Cotswold Airport	
H-05	Agusta A109HO (N504WG)	*Currently not known*	
H-50	Noorduyn AT-16 Harvard IIb (OO-DAF)	Privately owned, Brasschaat, Belgium	
IF-68	Hawker Hunter F6 <ff>	Privately owned, Kings Lynn	
L-44	Piper L-18C Super Cub (OO-SPQ)	Royal Aéro Para Club de Spa, Belgium	
L-47	Piper L-18C Super Cub (OO-SPG)	Aeroclub Brasschaat VZW, Brasschaat, Belgium	
OL-L49	Piper L-18C Super Cub (L-156/OO-LGB)	Aeroclub Brasschaat VZW, Brasschaat, Belgium	
V-4	SNCAN Stampe SV-4B (OO-EIR)	Antwerp Stampe Centre, Antwerp-Deurne, Belgium	
V-18	SNCAN Stampe SV-4B (OO-GWD)	Antwerp Stampe Centre, Antwerp-Deurne, Belgium	

Notes	Serial	Type (code/other identity)	Owner/operator, location or fate
	V-29	SNCAN Stampe SV-4B (OO-GWB)	Antwerp Stampe Centre, Antwerp-Deurne, Belgium
	V-66	SNCAN Stampe SV-4C (OO-GWA)	Antwerp Stampe Centre, Antwerp-Deurne, Belgium
	BRAZIL		
	1317	Embraer T-27 Tucano	Shorts, Belfast (engine test bed)
	BURKINA FASO		
	BF8431	SIAI-Marchetti SF.260 (G-NRRA) [31]	Privately owned, Lydd
	CANADA		
	-	Lockheed T-33A Shooting Star (17473)	Midland Air Museum, Coventry
	595	CCF T-6J Harvard IV (20306/G-CJWE) [310]	*Repainted in US markings as 481273, 2017*
	622	Piasecki HUP-3 Retriever (51-16622/N6699D)	The Helicopter Museum, Weston-super-Mare
	920	VS Stranraer (CF-BXO) [Q-N]	RAF Museum, Hendon
	3091	NA81 Harvard II (3019/G-CPPM)	Beech Restorations, Bruntingthorpe
	3349	NA64 Yale (G-BYNF)	Privately owned, Duxford
	5084	DH82C Tiger Moth (G-FCTK)	Privately owned, Hailsham
	9041	Bristol 149 Bolingbroke IV <ff>	Manx Aviation Museum, Ronaldsway
	9048	Bristol 149 Bolingbroke IV	Aerospace Bristol, Filton
	9893	Bristol 149 Bolingbroke IVT	Kent Battle of Britain Museum, Hawkinge
	9940	Bristol 149 Bolingbroke IVT	National Museum of Flight, E Fortune
	15252	Fairchild PT-19A Cornell (comp 15195)	RAF Museum Reserve Collection, Stafford
	16693	Auster J/1N Alpha (G-BLPG) [693]	Privately owned, Darley Moor, Derbys
	18393	Avro Canada CF-100 Canuck 4B (G-BCYK)	IWM Duxford
	18671	DHC1 Chipmunk 22 (WP905/7438M/G-BNZC) [671]	The Shuttleworth Collection, Old Warden
	20249	Noorduyn AT-16 Harvard IIb (PH-KLU) [XS-249]	Privately owned, Texel, The Netherlands
	21417	Canadair CT-133 Silver Star	Yorkshire Air Museum, Elvington
	23140	Canadair CL-13A Sabre 5 [AX] <rf>	Midland Air Museum, Coventry
	23380	Canadair CL-13B Sabre 6 <rf>	Privately owned, Haverigg
	KN448	Douglas Dakota IV <ff>	Science Museum, South Kensington
	CHILE		
	H-225	Aérospatiale SA330H Puma	Ultimate Activity, Faygate
	CHINA		
	68 r	Nanchang CJ-6A Chujiao (2751219/G-BVVG)	Privately owned, White Waltham
	61367	Nanchang CJ-6A Chujiao (4532009/G-CGHB) [37]	Privately owned, Redhill
	CZECH REPUBLIC		
	3677	Letov S-103 (MiG-15bisSB) (613677)	National Museum of Flight, E Fortune
	3794	Letov S-102 (MiG-15) (623794)	Norfolk & Suffolk Avn Museum, Flixton
		(starboard side only, painted in Polish marks as 1972 on port side)	
	9147	Mil Mi-4	The Helicopter Museum, Weston-super-Mare
	DENMARK		
	A-011	SAAB A-35XD Draken	Privately owned, Westhoughton, Lancs
	AR-107	SAAB S-35XD Draken	Newark Air Museum, Winthorpe
	E-419	Hawker Hunter F51 (G-9-441)	North-East Aircraft Museum, Usworth
	E-420	Hawker Hunter F51 (G-9-442) <ff>	Privately owned, Walton-on-Thames
	E-421	Hawker Hunter F51 (G-9-443)	Brooklands Museum, Weybridge
	E-424	Hawker Hunter F51 (G-9-445)	*Repainted as WV314*
	ET-272	Hawker Hunter T53 <ff>	Norfolk & Suffolk Avn Museum, Flixton
	K-682	Douglas C-47A Skytrain (OY-BPB)	Foreningen For Flyvende Mus, Vaerløse, Denmark
	L-866	Consolidated PBY-6A Catalina (8466M)	RAF Museum, Cosford
	P-129	DHC-1 Chipmunk 22 (OY-ATO)	Privately owned, Roskilde, Denmark
	P-139	DHC-1 Chipmunk 22 (OY-AVF)	Privately owned, Roskilde, Denmark
	R-756	Lockheed F-104G Starfighter	Midland Air Museum, Coventry
	S-881	Sikorsky S-55C	The Helicopter Museum, Weston-super-Mare

Serial	Type (code/other identity)	Owner/operator, location or fate	Notes
S-882	Sikorsky S-55C	Skirmish Paintball, Portishead	
S-886	Sikorsky S-55C	Hamburger Hill Paintball, Marksbury, Somerset	
S-887	Sikorsky S-55C	The Helicopter Museum, Weston-super-Mare	
EGYPT			
356	Heliopolis Gomhouria Mk 6	Privately owned, stored Ellerton, E Yorks	
764	Mikoyan MiG-21SPS <ff>	Privately owned, Northampton	
773	WS61 Sea King Mk.47 (WA.823)	RNAS Yeovilton Fire Section	
774	WS61 Sea King Mk.47 (WA.822)	Currently not known	
775	WS61 Sea King Mk.47 (WA.824)	Currently not known	
776	WS61 Sea King Mk.47 (WA.825) <ff>	Mayhem Paintball, Aybridge, Essex	
0446	Mikoyan MiG-21UM <ff>	Currently not known	
7907	Sukhoi Su-7 <ff>	Robertsbridge Aviation Society, Mayfield	
FINLAND			
GA-43	Gloster Gamecock II (G-CGYF)	Privately owned, Dursley, Glos	
GN-101	Folland Gnat F1 (XK741)	Midland Air Museum, Coventry	
SZ-12	Focke-Wulf Fw44J Stieglitz (D-EXWO)	Privately owned, Bienenfarm, Germany	
VI-3	Valtion Viima 2 (OO-EBL)	Privately owned, Brasschaat, Belgium	
FRANCE			
1/4513	Spad XIII <R> (G-BFYO/S3398)	American Air Museum, Duxford	
7	Nord NC854 (G-NORD)	Privately owned, English Bicknor, Glos	
37	Nord 3400 (G-ZARA) [MAB]	Privately owned, Swanton Morley	
45	Dassault Mirage IVP [BR]	Yorkshire Air Museum, Elvington	
54	SNCAN NC856A Norvigie (G-CGWR) [AOM]	Privately owned, Spanhoe	
67	SNCAN 1101 Noralpha (F-GMCY) [CY]	Privately owned, la Ferté-Alais, France	
70	Dassault Mystère IVA [8-NV]	Midland Air Museum, Coventry	
78	Nord 3202B-1 (G-BIZK)	Privately owned, Norfolk	
79	Dassault Mystère IVA [2-EG]	Norfolk & Suffolk Avn Museum, Flixton	
82	Curtiss H75-C1 Hawk (G-CCVH) [X-881]	The Fighter Collection, Duxford	
82	NA T-28D Fennec (F-AZKG)	Privately owned, Strasbourg, France	
83	Dassault Mystère IVA [8-MS]	Newark Air Museum, Winthorpe	
83	Morane-Saulnier MS733 Alcyon (F-AZKS)	Privately owned, Montlucon, France	
84	Dassault Mystère IVA [8-NF]	Scrapped at Headcorn, 26 February 2018	
85	Dassault Mystère IVA [8-MV]	Cold War Jets Collection, Bruntingthorpe	
104	MH1521M Broussard (F-GHFG) [307-FG]	Privately owned, Montceau-les-Mines, France	
105	Nord N2501F Noratlas (F-AZVM) [62-SI]	Le Noratlas de Provence, Marseilles, France	
106	MH1521M Broussard (F-GKJT) [33-JT]	Privately owned, Montceau-les-Mines, France	
108	MH1521M Broussard (F-BNEX) [50S9]	Privately owned, Lelystad, The Netherlands	
108	SO1221 Djinn (FR108) [CDL]	The Helicopter Museum, Weston-super-Mare	
121	Dassault Mystère IVA [8-MY]	City of Norwich Aviation Museum	
128	Morane-Saulnier MS733 Alcyon (F-BMMY)	Privately owned, St Cyr, France	
143	Morane-Saulnier MS733 Alcyon (G-MSAL)	Privately owned, Spanhoe	
146	Dassault Mystère IVA [8-MC]	North-East Aircraft Museum, Usworth	
154	MH1521M Broussard (F-GKRO) [315-SM]	Privately owned, Damyns Hall, Essex	
156	SNCAN Stampe SV-4B (G-NIFE)	Privately owned, Gloucester	
158	Dassault MD312 Flamant (F-AZGE) [12-XA]	Privately owned, Albert, France	
160	Dassault MD312 Flamant (F-AZDR) [V]	Privately owned, Alençon, France	
189	Dassault MD312 Flamant (F-AZVG) [G]	Ailes Anciennes de Corbas, Lyon, France	
208	MH1521C1 Broussard (G-YYYY) [IR]	Privately owned, Eggesford	
226	Dassault MD312 Flamant (F-AZES) [319-CG]	Privately owned, Montbeliard, France	
237	Dassault MD312 Flamant (F-AZFE) [319-DM]	Privately owned, Alençon, France	
255	MH1521M Broussard (G-CIGH) [5-ML]	Privately owned, Breighton	
260	Dassault MD311 Flamant (F-AZKT) [316-KT]	Privately owned, Albert, France	
261	MH1521M Broussard (F-GIBN) [30-QA]	Privately owned, Walldürn, Germany	
276	Dassault MD311 Flamant (F-AZER)	Privately owned, Alençon, France	
290	Dewoitine D27 (F-AZJD)	Les Casques de Cuir, la Ferté-Alais, France	
316	MH1521M Broussard (F-GGKR) [315-SN]	Privately owned, Lognes, France	
318	Dassault Mystère IVA [8-NY]	Dumfries & Galloway Avn Mus, Dumfries	
319	Dassault Mystère IVA [8-ND]	Rebel Air Museum, Andrewsfield	
351	Morane-Saulnier MS317 (G-MOSA) [HY22]	Privately owned, Barton	

Notes	Serial	Type (code/other identity)	Owner/operator, location or fate
	354	Morane-Saulnier MS315E-D2 (G-BZNK)	Privately owned, Wickenby
	538	Dassault Mirage IIIE [3-QH]	Yorkshire Air Museum, Elvington
	569	Fouga CM170R Magister [F-AZZP]	Privately owned, Le Havre, France
	24541	Cessna L-19E Bird Dog (G-JDOG) [BMG]	Privately owned, Cotswold Airport
	42157	NA F-100D Super Sabre [11-ML]	North-East Aircraft Museum, stored Usworth
	54419	Lockheed T-33A Shooting Star (55-4439) [WI]	North-East Aircraft Museum, Usworth
	63938	NA F-100F Super Sabre [11-EZ]	*Scrapped at Headcorn, 26 February 2018*
	125716	Douglas AD-4N Skyraider (F-AZFN) [22-DG]	Privately owned, Mélun, France
	127002	Douglas AD-4NA Skyraider (F-AZHK) [20-LN]	Privately owned, Avignon, France
	517692	NA T-28S Fennec (G-TROY) [142]	*Repainted in US marks as 17692, October 2016*
	18-5395	Piper L-18C Super Cub (52-2436/G-CUBJ) [CDG]	Privately owned, Old Warden
	C850	Salmson 2A2 <R>	Barton Aviation Heritage Society, Barton
	FR41	Piasecki H-21C	The Helicopter Museum, Weston-super-Mare
	MS824	Morane-Saulnier Type N <R> (G-AWBU)	Privately owned, Stow Maries
	N856	SNCAN NC856 (G-CDWE)	Privately owned, Wickenby
	N1977	Nieuport Scout 17/23 <R> (N1723/G-BWMJ) [8]	Privately owned, Stow Maries
	XC	Piper L-4J Grasshopper (44-80513/G-BSYO)	Privately owned, Postling, Kent

GERMANY

Notes	Serial	Type (code/other identity)	Owner/operator, location or fate
	-	Fieseler Fi103R-IV (V-1) (BAPC 91)	Lashenden Air Warfare Museum, Headcorn
	-	Fokker Dr1 Dreidekker <R> (BAPC 88)	FAA Museum, stored Cobham Hall, RNAS Yeovilton
	-	Messerschmitt Bf109 <R> (6357/BAPC 74) [6]	Kent Battle of Britain Museum, Hawkinge
	-	Messerschmitt Bf109 <R> [<-]	Battle of Britain Experience, Canterbury
	Black 1	Hispano HA 1.112M1L Buchón (C.4K-31/G-AWHE)	*Sold to Germany, 20 April 2017*
	Green 1	Messerschmitt Bf109G <R> (BAPC 240)	Yorkshire Air Museum, Elvington
	White 1	Focke-Wulf Fw190 <R> (G-WULF)	Privately owned, Halfpenny Green
	Black 2	Hispano HA 1.112M1L Buchón (C.4K-102/G-AWHK)	*Repainted as Black 8, June 2017*
	3	SNCAN 1101 Noralpha (G-BAYV) (fuselage)	Privately owned, Newquay
	Yellow 3	Messerschmitt Bf109G-10 (D-FDME)	Messerschmitt Stiftung, Manching, Germany
	Black 6	Messerschmitt Bf109G-2/Trop (10639/8478M/G-USTV)	RAF Museum, Cosford
	Red 7	Messerschmitt Bf109G-4 (D-FWME)	Messerschmitt Stiftung, Manching, Germany
	Yellow 7	Hispano HA 1.112M1L Buchón (C.4K-99/N90604)	Privately owned, Sywell
	Black 8	Hispano HA 1.112M1L Buchón (C.4K-102/G-AWHK)	Historic Flying Ltd, Duxford
	White 9	Focke-Wulf Fw190 <R> (G-CCFW)	Privately owned, Oaksey Park
	Red 11	Hispano HA 1.112K1L Buchón (C.4K-112/G-AWHC)	Privately owned, Sywell
	Yellow 12	Messerschmitt Bf109G-2(13605/G-JIMP)	Privately owned, Knutsford
	White 14	Messerschmitt Bf109 <R> (BAPC 67)	Kent Battle of Britain Museum, Hawkinge
	White 14	Messerschmitt Bf109E-4 (G-CIPB)	Privately owned, Biggin Hill
	Yellow 14	Nord 1002 (G-ETME)	Privately owned, White Waltham
	Yellow 27	Hispano HA 1.112K1L Buchón (D-FMGZ)	Air Fighter Academy, Heringsdorf, Germany
	33/15	Fokker EIII <R> (G-CHAW)	Privately owned, Membury
	87	Heinkel He111 <R> <ff>	Privately owned, East Kirkby
	105/15	Fokker EIII <R> (G-UDET)	Privately owned, Horsham
	152/17	Fokker Dr1 Dreidekker <R> (F-AZPQ)	Les Casques de Cuir, la Ferté-Alais, France
	152/17	Fokker Dr1 Dreidekker <R> (G-BVGZ)	Privately owned, Breighton
	157/18	Fokker D.VIII <R> (BAPC 239)	Norfolk & Suffolk Air Museum, Flixton
	210/16	Fokker EIII (BAPC 56)	Science Museum, South Kensington
	403/17	Fokker Dr1 Dreidekker <R> (G-CDXR)	Privately owned, Popham
	416/15	Fokker EIII <R> (G-GSAL)	Privately owned, Aston Down
	422/15	Fokker EIII <R> (G-AVJO)	Privately owned, Stow Maries
	422/15	Fokker EIII <R> (G-FOKR)	Privately owned, Eshott
	425/17	Fokker Dr1 Dreidekker <R> (BAPC 133)	Kent Battle of Britain Museum, Hawkinge
	425/17	Fokker Dr1 Dreidekker <R> (G-DREI)	Privately owned, Felthorpe
	477/17	Fokker Dr1 Dreidekker <R> (G-FOKK)	Privately owned, Sywell
	556/17	Fokker Dr1 Dreidekker <R> (G-CFHY)	Privately owned, Tibenham
	626/8	Fokker DVII <R> (N6268)	Privately owned, Booker
	764	Mikoyan MiG-21SPS <ff>	Privately owned, Norfolk
	959	Mikoyan MiG-21SPS	Midland Air Museum, Coventry
	1160	Dornier Do17Z-2	Michael Beetham Conservation Centre, Cosford
	1190	Messerschmitt Bf109E-3 [White 4]	IWM Duxford
	1480	Messerschmitt Bf109 <R> (BAPC 66) [6]	Kent Battle of Britain Museum, Hawkinge

Serial	Type (code/other identity)	Owner/operator, location or fate	Notes
801/18	Bowers Fly Baby 1A (G-BNPV)	Privately owned, Chessington	
803/18	Bowers Fly Baby 1A (G-BUYU)	Privately owned, Chessington	
983	Messerschmitt Bf109E-3 (G-EMIL)	Privately owned, Colchester	
579	Messerschmitt Bf109E-7 (G-CIPB) [14+]	Privately owned, Biggin Hill	
101	Messerschmitt Bf109E-3 (DG200/8477M) [Black 12]	RAF Museum, Hendon	
477	CASA 1.131E Jungmann (G-RETA) [GD+EG]	The Shuttleworth Collection, Old Warden	
198/18	LVG CVI (G-AANJ/9239M)	Michael Beetham Conservation Centre, Cosford	
417/18	Fokker DVII (9207M)	RAF Museum, Hendon	
2802	Antonov An-2T (D-FOFM)	Historische Flugzeuge, Grossenhain, Germany	
00143	Focke-Achgelis Fa330A-1 Bachstelze	IWM Duxford	
00502	Focke-Achgelis Fa330A-1 Bachstelze	Privately owned, Millom	
00503	Focke-Achgelis Fa330A-1 Bachstelze (8469M)	RAF Museum, Cosford	
00509	Focke-Achgelis Fa330A-1 Bachstelze	Science Museum, stored Wroughton	
00545	Focke-Achgelis Fa330A-1 Bachstelze	FAA Museum, RNAS Yeovilton	
00549	Focke-Achgelis Fa330A-1 Bachstelze	Lashenden Air Warfare Museum, Headcorn	
12372	Messerschmitt Me262A-2a (VK893/8482M) [Yellow 4]	RAF Museum, Cosford	
20227	Heinkel He162A-2 Salamander (VN679/8472M) [Red 2]	RAF Museum, Hendon	
20235	Heinkel He162A-1 Salamander (AM.68) [Yellow 6]	IWM Duxford	
91316	Messerschmitt Me163B Komet	Science Museum, South Kensington	
91454	Messerschmitt Me163B Komet <R> (BAPC 271)	The Shuttleworth Collection, Old Warden	
91461	Messerschmitt Me163B Komet (191614/8481M) [Yellow 14]	RAF Museum, Cosford	
91659	Messerschmitt Me163B Komet (8480M) [Yellow 15]	National Museum of Flight, E Fortune	
80020	Flettner Fl282/B-V20 Kolibri (frame only)	Midland Air Museum, Coventry	
60043	Junkers Ju88R-1 (PJ876/8475M) [D5+EV]	RAF Museum, Cosford	
20430	Messerschmitt Me410A-1/U2 (AM.72/8483M) [3U+CC]	RAF Museum, Cosford	
75081	Fieseler Fi156C-7 Storch (VP546/AM.101/7362M)[GM+AK]	RAF Museum, Cosford	
94083	Junkers Ju87D-3 (8474M) [RI+JK]	RAF Museum, Hendon	
02074	Heliopolis Gomhouria Mk 6 (158/G-CGEV) [CG+EV]	Privately owned, Breighton	
84219	Focke-Wulf Fw190F-8/U1 (AM.29/8470M) [Black 38]	RAF Museum, Hendon	
01152	Heinkel He111H-23 (8471M) [NT+SL]	RAF Museum, Hendon	
30301	Messerschmitt Bf110G-4 (AM.34/8479M) [D5+RL]	RAF Museum, Hendon	
33682	Focke-Wulf Fw190A-8/R7 (AM.75/9211M)	RAF Museum, Cosford	
80554	Flug Werk FW190A-8/N (D-FWMW)	Meier Motors, Bremgarten, Germany	
+1	Focke-Wulf Fw190 <R> (G-SYFW) [7334]	Privately owned, Empingham, Rutland	
0+45	Mikoyan MiG-23BN	Privately owned, Danbury, Essex	
2+35	Lockheed F-104G Starfighter	Privately owned, Bruntingthorpe	
8+08	Aero L-39ZO Albatros (142/28+04)	Pinewood Studios, Bucks	
E+RA	Fieseler Fi-156C-3 Storch (F-AZRA)	Amicale J-B Salis, la Ferté-Alais, France	
+1	Focke-Wulf Fw190 <R> (G-BSLX)	Privately owned, Norwich	
G+ED	Slepcev Storch (G-BZOB) [5447]	Privately owned, Breighton	
7+86	McD F-4F Phantom II <ff>	Privately owned,	
7+89	McD F-4F Phantom II	Hawker Hunter Aviation Ltd, Scampton (spares)	
8+89	Dornier Do28D-2 Skyservant (D-ICDY)	Privately owned, Uetersen, Germany	
0+55	MBB Bo.105M	Lufthansa Resource Technical Training, Cotswold Airport	
0+77	MBB Bo.105M	Lufthansa Resource Technical Training, Cotswold Airport	
1+00	MBB Bo.105M (D-HZYR)	The Helicopter Museum, Weston-super-Mare	
6+26	Mil Mi-24D (421)	The Helicopter Museum, Weston-super-Mare	
8+14	Sukhoi Su-22M-4	Hawker Hunter Aviation Ltd, stored Scampton	
9+18	NA OV-10B Bronco (G-ONAA)	Bronco Demo Team, Wevelgem, Belgium	
9+26	NA OV-10B Bronco (G-BZGL)	Bronco Demo Team, Wevelgem, Belgium	
Z+JU	CASA 3.52L (F-AZJU)	Amicale J-B Salis, la Ferté-Alais, France	
B+103	Canadair CL-13B Sabre 6 (1730/JB+114)	Privately owned,	
F+070	CCF T-6J Texan (G-CHYN)	Privately owned, Dunkeswell	
G+KM	Nord 1002 Pingouin (G-ASTG)	Privately owned, Peterborough	
U+CC	CASA 1.131E Jungmann (G-BUCC)	Privately owned, Sandown	
X+HI	CASA 1.131E Jungmann (E.3B-379/G-CDJU)	Privately owned, Sleap	
7343/17	Albatros DVA <R> (ZK-TVD)	RAF Museum, Hendon	
G+EB	CASA 1.131E Jungmann (E.3B-350/G-BHPL)	Privately owned, Henstridge	
M+BK	Morane-Saulnier MS505 (G-BPHZ)	Aero Vintage, Westfield, E Sussex	

Notes	Serial	Type (code/other identity)	Owner/operator, location or fate
	E37/15	Fokker EIII <R> (G-CGJF)	Privately owned, Herts
	ES+BH	Messerschmitt Bf108B-2 (D-ESBH)	Messerschmitt Stiftung, Manching, Germany
	FI+S	Morane-Saulnier MS505 (G-BIRW)	National Museum of Flight, E Fortune
	FM+BB	Messerschmitt Bf109G-6 (D-FMBB)	Messerschmitt Stiftung, Manching, Germany
	KB+GB	CASA 1.131E Jungmann (G-BHSL)	Privately owned, Oaksey Park
	LG+01	CASA 1.133L Jungmeister (ES.1-16/G-CIJV)	Privately owned, Sleap
	LG+03	Bücker Bü133C Jungmeister (G-AEZX)	Privately owned, Milden
	NJ+C11	Nord 1002 (G-ATBG)	Privately owned, Duxford
	NM+AA	CASA 1.131E Jungmann 1000 (G-BZJV)	Privately owned, Sleap
	NQ+NR	Klemm Kl35D (D-EQXD)	Quax Flieger, Paderborn, Germany
	NV+KG	Focke-Wulf Fw44J Stieglitz (D-ENAY)	Quax Flieger, Paderborn, Germany
	S4-A07	CASA 1.131E Jungmann (G-BWHP)	Privately owned, Yarcombe, Devon
	TP+WX	Heliopolis Gomhouria Mk 6 (G-TPWX)	Privately owned, Swanborough
	GHANA		
	G360	PBN 2T Islander (G-BRSR)	Privately owned, Biggin Hill
	G361	PBN 2T Islander (G-BRPB)	Privately owned, Biggin Hill
	G362	PBN 2T Islander (G-BRPC)	Privately owned, Biggin Hill
	G363	PBN 2T Islander (G-BRSV)	Privately owned, Biggin Hill
	GREECE		
	52-6541	Republic F-84F Thunderflash [541]	North-East Aircraft Museum, Usworth
	HONG KONG		
	HKG-5	SA128 Bulldog (G-BULL)	Privately owned, Cotswold Airport
	HKG-6	SA128 Bulldog (G-BPCL)	Privately owned, North Weald
	HKG-11	Slingsby T.67M Firefly 200 (G-BYRY)	Privately owned, Wellesbourne Mountford
	HKG-13	Slingsby T.67M Firefly 200 (G-BXKW)	Privately owned, St Ghislain, Belgium
	HUNGARY		
	125	Aero L-39ZO Albatros (831125/G-JMGP)	Privately owned, France
	335	Mil Mi-24D (3532461715415)	Privately owned, Dunsfold
	501	Mikoyan MiG-21PF	IWM Duxford
	503	Mikoyan MiG-21SMT (G-BRAM)	RAF Museum, Cosford
	INDIA		
	E296	Hindustan Gnat F1 (G-SLYR)	Privately owned, North Weald
	Q497	EE Canberra T4 (WE191) <ff>	Privately owned, Stoneykirk, D&G
	HA561	Hawker Tempest II (MW743)	Privately owned, stored Wickenby
	VP905	Douglas C-47B Skytrain (KN397/G-AMSV)	Privately owned, Coventry
	INDONESIA		
	LL-5313	BAe Hawk T53	BAE Systems, Brough, on display
	IRAQ		
	333	DH115 Vampire T55 <ff>	South Yorkshire Aircraft Mus'm, stored Doncaster
	ITALY		
	MM5701	Fiat CR42 (BT474/8468M) [13-95]	RAF Museum, Hendon
	MM53211	Fiat G46-1B (MM52799) [ZI-4]	Privately owned, Shipdham
	MM53692	CCF T-6G Texan	RAeS Medway Branch, Rochester
	MM53774	Fiat G59-4B (I-MRSV) [181]	Privately owned, Parma, Italy
	MM54099	NA T-6G Texan (G-BRBC) [RR-56]	Privately owned, Chigwell
	MM54532	SIAI-Marchetti SF.260AM (G-ITAF) [70-42]	Privately owned, Leicester
	MM80270	Agusta-Bell AB204B (MM80279)	London Motor Museum, Hayes
	MM80927	Agusta-Bell AB206A-1 JetRanger [CC-49]	The Helicopter Museum, Weston-super-Mare
	MM81205	Agusta A109A-2 SEM [GF-128]	The Helicopter Museum, Weston-super-Mare
	MM54-2372	Piper L-21B Super Cub	Privately owned, Foxhall Heath, Suffolk

Serial	Type (code/other identity)	Owner/operator, location or fate	Notes
JAPAN			
	Kawasaki Ki100-1B (16336/8476M/BAPC 83)	RAF Museum, Cosford	
	Mitsubishi A6M5-52 Zero (196) [CI-05] <ff>	IWM Duxford	
	Yokosuka MXY 7 Ohka II (BAPC 159)	IWM Duxford, stored	
97	Yokosuka MXY 7 Ohka II (8485M/BAPC 98)	Museum of Science & Industry, Manchester	
143	NA T-6 Texan Zero (F-AZRO)	Privately owned, St Rambert d'Albon, France	
439	Mitsubishi Ki46-III (8484M/BAPC 84)	RAF Museum, Cosford	
5-1585	Yokosuka MXY 7 Ohka II (BAPC 58)	Science Museum, at FAA Museum, RNAS Yeovilton	
13	Yokosuka MXY 7 Ohka II (8486M/BAPC 99)	RAF Museum, Cosford	
2-176	Mitsubishi A6M3-2 Zero (3685) [76]	IWM London, Lambeth	
JORDAN			
08	SA125 Bulldog (G-BDIN)	*Currently not known*	
KENYA			
15	Dornier Do28D-2 Skyservant	Privately owned, stored Hibaldstow	
17	Dornier Do28D-2 Skyservant	Privately owned, stored Hibaldstow	
MALAYSIA			
25-04	SA102 Bulldog (fuselage)	Privately owned, Cotswold Airport	
MYANMAR			
B441	VS361 Spitfire IX (ML119/G-SDNI)	Privately owned, Sandown	
THE NETHERLANDS			
6-218	Consolidated PBY-5A Catalina (2459/PH-PBY)	Neptune Association, Lelystad, The Netherlands	
74	Fokker S-11 Instructor (E-31/G-BEPV) [K]	Privately owned, Spanhoe	
79	Fokker S-11 Instructor (PH-ACG) [K]	Privately owned, Lelystad, The Netherlands	
97	Fokker S-11 Instructor (PH-GRY) [K]	KLu Historic Flt, Gilze-Rijen, The Netherlands	
04	Lockheed SP-2H Neptune [V]	RAF Museum, Cosford	
-57	DH82A Tiger Moth (PH-TYG)	KLu Historic Flt, Gilze-Rijen, The Netherlands	
-64	Noorduyn AT-16 Harvard IIb (PH-LSK)	KLu Historic Flt, Gilze-Rijen, The Netherlands	
-71	Noorduyn AT-16 Harvard IIb (PH-MLM)	KLu Historic Flt, Gilze-Rijen, The Netherlands	
-118	Noorduyn AT-16 Harvard IIb (PH-IIB)	KLu Historic Flt, Gilze-Rijen, The Netherlands	
-182	Noorduyn AT-16 Harvard IIb (PH-TBR)	KLu Historic Flt, Gilze-Rijen, The Netherlands	
-14	Fokker S-11 Instructor (PH-AFS)	Privately owned, Lelystad, The Netherlands	
-15	Fokker S-11 Instructor (G-BIYU)	Privately owned, RAF Topcliffe	
-20	Fokker S-11 Instructor (PH-GRB)	Privately owned, Gilze-Rijen, The Netherlands	
-27	Fokker S-11 Instructor (PH-HOL)	Privately owned, Lelystad, The Netherlands	
-29	Fokker S-11 Instructor (PH-HOK)	Privately owned, Lelystad, The Netherlands	
-32	Fokker S-11 Instructor (PH-HOl)	Privately owned, Gilze-Rijen, The Netherlands	
-39	Fokker S-11 Instructor (PH-HOG)	Privately owned, Lelystad, The Netherlands	
-29	Beech D18S (PH-KHV)	KLu Historic Flt, Gilze-Rijen, The Netherlands	
H424	VS361 Spitfire LF IXc (MJ271/H-53/G-IRTY)	Privately owned, Duxford	
K732	VS361 Spitfire LF IXc (8633M/PH-OUQ) [3W-17]	KLu Historic Flt, Gilze-Rijen, The Netherlands	
-202	Hawker Hunter F6 [10] <ff>	Privately owned, Stockport	
-250	Hawker Hunter F6 (G-9-185) <ff>	IWM Duxford	
-294	Hawker Hunter F6A (XF515/G-KAXF)	Stichting Hawker Hunter Foundation, Leeuwarden, The Netherlands	
-302	Hawker Hunter T7 (ET-273/G-9-431) <ff>	South Yorkshire Aircraft Museum, Doncaster	
-315	Hawker Hunter T7 (comp XM121)	Privately owned, Netherley, Aberdeenshire	
-321	Hawker Hunter T8C (G-BWGL)	Stichting Hawker Hunter Foundation, Leeuwarden, The Netherlands	
N5-149	NA B-25J Mitchell (44-29507/HD346/PH-XXV) [232511]	KLu Historic Flt, Gilze-Rijen, The Netherlands	
R-18	Auster III (PH-NGK)	KLu Historic Flt, Gilze-Rijen, The Netherlands	
R-55	Piper L-18C Super Cub (52-2466/G-BLMI)	Privately owned, Antwerp, Belgium	
R-109	Piper L-21B Super Cub (54-2337/PH-GAZ)	KLu Historic Flt, Gilze-Rijen, The Netherlands	
R-122	Piper L-21B Super Cub (54-2412/PH-PPW)	KLu Historic Flt, Gilze-Rijen, The Netherlands	
R-124	Piper L-21B Super Cub (54-2414/PH-APA)	Privately owned, Eindhoven, The Netherlands	
R-137	Piper L-21B Super Cub (54-2427/PH-PSC)	Privately owned, Gilze-Rijen, The Netherlands	
R-151	Piper L-21B Super Cub (54-2441/G-BIYR)	Privately owned, Yarcombe, Devon	

Notes	Serial	Type (code/other identity)	Owner/operator, location or fate
	R-156	Piper L-21B Super Cub (54-2446/G-ROVE)	Privately owned, Damyn's Hall
	R-167	Piper L-21B Super Cub (54-2457/G-LION)	Privately owned
R-170		Piper L-21B Super Cub (52-6222/PH-ENJ)	Privately owned, Midden Zealand, The Netherlands
	R-177	Piper L-21B Super Cub (54-2467/PH-KNR)	KLu Historic Flt, Gilze-Rijen, The Netherlands
	R-181	Piper L-21B Super Cub (54-2471/PH-GAU)	Privately owned, Gilze-Rijen, The Netherlands
	R-213	Piper L-21A Super Cub (51-15682/PH-RED)	Privately owned, Seppe, The Netherlands
R-345		Piper L-4J Grasshopper (PH-UCS)	Privately owned, Hilversum, The Netherlands
	S-9	DHC2 L-20A Beaver (55-4585/PH-DHC)	KLu Historic Flt, Gilze-Rijen, The Netherlands

NEW ZEALAND

	NZ3909	WS Wasp HAS1 (XT782/G-KANZ)	To New Zealand, 2018
	NZ5911	Bristol 170 Freighter 31M (ZK-EPG)	Aerospace Bristol, stored Filton

NORTH KOREA

	-	WSK Lim-2 (MiG-15) (01420/G-BMZF)	FAA Museum, RNAS Yeovilton

NORTH VIETNAM

	1211	WSK Lim-5 (MiG-17F) (G-MIGG)	Privately owned, North Weald

NORWAY

145		DH82A Tiger Moth II (DE248/LN-BDM)	Privately owned, Kjeller, Norway
163		Fairchild PT-19A Cornell (42-83641/LN-BIF)	Privately owned, Kjeller, Norway
171		DH82A Tiger Moth II (T6168/LN-KAY)	Privately owned, Kjeller, Norway
599		Canadair CT-133AUP Silver Star Mk.3 (133599/NX865SA)	Norwegian AF Historical Sqn, Ørland, Norway
848		Piper L-18C Super Cub (LN-ACL) [FA-N]	Privately owned, Norway
56321		SAAB S91B Safir (G-BKPY)	Newark Air Museum, Winthorpe
PX-K		DH100 Vampire FB6 (LN-DHY)	Repainted as VZ305, January 2018
PX-M		DH115 Vampire T55 (LN-DHZ)	Repainted as WZ447, January 2018

OMAN

417		BAC Strikemaster Mk.80A (G-RSAF)	Privately owned, Hawarden
425		BAC Strikemaster Mk.82A (G-SOAF)	Privately owned, Hawarden
801		Hawker Hunter T66B <ff>	Privately owned, St Athan
801		Hawker Hunter T66B <rf>	Privately owned, Hawarden
853		Hawker Hunter FR10 (XF426)	RAF Museum, stored Cosford
XF688		Percival P56 Provost T1 (WV562/7606M)	Michael Beetham Conservation Centre, Cosford
XL554		SAL Pioneer CC1 (XL703/8034M)	Michael Beetham Conservation Centre, Cosford

POLAND

05		WSK SM-2 (Mi-2) (S2-03006)	The Helicopter Museum, Weston-super-Mare
309		WSK SBLim-2A (MiG-15UTI) <ff>	R Scottish Mus'm of Flight, stored Granton
458		Mikoyan MiG-23ML (04 red/024003607)	Newark Air Museum, Winthorpe
618		Mil Mi-8P (10618)	The Helicopter Museum, Weston-super-Mare
1018		WSK-PZL Mielec TS-11 Iskra (1H-1018/G-ISKA)	Cold War Jets Collection, Bruntingthorpe
1120		WSK Lim-2 (MiG-15bis)	RAF Museum, Cosford
1706		WSK-PZL Mielec TS-11 Iskra (1H-0408)	Midland Air Museum, Coventry
1972		Letov S-102 (MiG-15) (623794)	Norfolk & Suffolk Avn Museum, Flixton
		(port side only, painted in Czech marks as 3794 on starboard side)	

PORTUGAL

1350		OGMA/DHC1 Chipmunk T20 (G-CGAO)	Privately owned, Spanhoe
1365		OGMA/DHC1 Chipmunk T20 (G-DHPM)	Privately owned, Sywell
1367		OGMA/DHC1 Chipmunk T20 (G-UANO)	Privately owned, Sherburn-in-Elmet
1372		OGMA/DHC1 Chipmunk T20 (HB-TUM)	Privately owned, Switzerland
1373		OGMA/DHC1 Chipmunk T20 (G-CBJG)	Privately owned, Winwick, Cambs
1375		OGMA/DHC1 Chipmunk T20 (F-AZJV)	Privately owned, Valenciennes, France
1377		DHC1 Chipmunk 22 (WK520/G-BARS)	Privately owned, Yeovilton
1741		CCF T-6J Texan (G-HRVD)	Privately owned, Bruntingthorpe
1747		CCF T-6J Texan (20385/G-BGPB)	The Aircraft Restoration Co, Duxford
3303		MH1521M Broussard (G-CBGL)	Privately owned, Rochester

Serial	Type (code/other identity)	Owner/operator, location or fate	Notes
QATAR			
A10	Hawker Hunter FGA78	Yorkshire Air Museum, Elvington	
A12	Hawker Hunter FGA78 <ff>	Privately owned, New Inn, Torfaen	
P30	WS Lynx Mk.28 (G-BFDV/TAD013)	DSAE SAAE, Lyneham	
P31	WS Lynx Mk.28	Vector Aerospace Fleetlands Apprentice School	
P32	WS Lynx Mk.28 (TD 016) [A]	DSAE SAAE, Lyneham	
ROMANIA			
	LET L-29 Delfin	Privately owned, Pocklington	
	LET L-29 Delfin <ff>	Privately owned, Catshill, Worcs	
	LET L-29 Delfin <rf>	Privately owned, Hinstock, Shrops	
	LET L-29 Delfin <ff>	Top Gun Flight Simulator Centre, Stalybridge	
	LET L-29 Delfin [66654]	Privately owned, Bruntingthorpe	
RUSSIA (& FORMER SOVIET UNION)			
	Mil Mi-24D (3532464505029)	Midland Air Museum, Coventry	
0 w	Yakovlev Yak-3M (0470202/G-OLEG)	Privately owned, Goodwood	
w	SPP Yak C-11 (171314/G-BZMY)	Privately owned, Booker	
1 y	Yakovlev Yak-52 (9311709/G-YKSZ)	Privately owned, White Waltham	
8 bl	Yakovlev Yak-55M (910103/RA-01274)	Privately owned, Halfpenny Green	
1 w	Yakovlev Yak-18A (1160403/G-CEIB)	Privately owned, Breighton	
w	Yakovlev Yak-3UA (0470204/D-FYGJ)	Privately owned, Bremgarten, Germany	
5 y	Yakovlev Yak-9UM (HB-RYA)	Flying Fighter Association, Bex, Switzerland	
" y	WSK SM-1 (Mi-1) (Polish AF 2007)	The Helicopter Museum, Weston-super-Mare	
7 y	Yakovlev Yak-18M (G-BMJY)	Privately owned, Membury, Bucks	
w	SPP Yak C-11 (1701139/G-OYAK)	Privately owned, Little Gransden	
0 r	Yakovlev Yak-50 (801810/G-BTZB)	Privately owned, Lee-on-Solent	
0 r	Yakovlev Yak-50 (877610/G-YAKE)	Privately owned, Henstridge	
1 y	SPP Yak C-11 (G-YCII)	Sold to Finland, June 2017	
2 r	LET L-29 Delfin (194555/ES-YLM/G-DELF)	Privately owned, St Athan	
4 r	WSK-PZL An-2R (HA_MKE)	Morayvia, Kinloss	
5 w	SPP Yak C-11 (170103/D-FYAK)	Classic Aviation Company, Hannover, Germany	
3 r	LET L-29 Delfin (591771/YL-PAF)	Privately owned, Hawarden	
8 r	WSK SBLim-2 (MiG-15UTI) (1A01004/N104CJ)	Norwegian AF Historical Sqn, Rygge, Norway	
0 r	Yakovlev Yak-50 (812003/G-YAAK)	Privately owned, Henstridge	
0 w	Lavochkin La-11	The Fighter Collection, Duxford	
1 w	Yakovlev Yak-3UA (0470203/G-CDBJ)	Privately owned, Folkestone	
1 w	Yakovlev Yak-9UM (0470403/D-FENK)	Privately owned, Magdeburg, Germany	
3 y	Bell P-39Q Airacobra (44-2911)	Privately owned, Sussex	
3 r	Mikoyan MiG-27D (83712515040)	Privately owned, Hawarden	
5 bl	Yakovlev Yak-52 (9111306/G-BVXK)	Privately owned, White Waltham	
7 w	Yakovlev Yak-3UTI-PW (9/04623/F-AZIM)	Privately owned, la Ferté-Alais, France	
" r	Yakovlev Yak-52 (9111307/G-YAKX)	Privately owned, Popham	
3 w	Polikarpov Po-2 (0094/G-BSSY)	The Shuttleworth Collection, Old Warden	
3 r	Yakovlev Yak-50 (853206/G-YAKZ)	Privately owned, Henstridge	
3 w	Yakovlev Yak-52 (899915/G-YAKH)	Privately owned, White Waltham	
5 r	Sukhoi Su-17M-3 (25102)	Privately owned, Hawarden	
6 w	LET/Yak C-11 (171101/G-KYAK)	Privately owned, North Weald	
6 r	Yakovlev Yak-52 (9111604/G-IUII)	Privately owned, St Athan	
3 bl	Yakovlev Yak-52 (877601/G-BWSV)	Privately owned, North Weald	
3 w	Yakovlev Yak-3UPW <R> (F-AZZK)	Privately owned, Lelystad, The Netherlands	
9 r	Yakovlev Yak-50 (822305/G-YAKU)	Privately owned, Henstridge	
0 gy	Yakovlev Yak-52 (9111415/G-CBRW)	Meier Motors, Bremgarten, Germany	
1 r	LET L-29 Delfin (893019/G-BZNT)	Sold as LN-RWN, 2018	
1 r	LET L-29S Delfin (491273/YL-PAG)	Privately owned, Breighton	
1 y	Yakovlev Yak-50 (812004/G-BWYK)	Privately owned, West Meon, Hants	
2 w	Yakovlev Yak C-11 (171312/G-BTZE)	Sold to Germany, February 2017	
2 w	Yakovlev Yak-52 (9612001/G-CCJK)	Privately owned, White Waltham	
2 y	Yakovlev Yak-52 (878202/G-BWVR)	Privately owned, Eshott	
4 r	Sukhoi Su-17M (69004)	Privately owned, Hawarden	
1 r	Yakovlev Yak-50 (842710/G-YAKM)	Privately owned, Henstridge	
5 r	Yakovlev Yak-52 (855905/G-YAKN)	Privately owned, Henstridge	

Notes	Serial	Type (code/other identity)	Owner/operator, location or fate
	67 r	Yakovlev Yak-52 (822013/G-CBSL)	Privately owned, Belgium
	71 r	Mikoyan MiG-27K (61912507006)	Newark Air Museum, Winthorpe
	74 w	Yakovlev Yak-52 (877404/G-OUGH) [JA-74, IV-62]	Privately owned, Swansea
	86 r	Yakovlev Yak-52 (867212/G-YAKC)	Privately owned, Henstridge
	93 w	Yakovlev Yak-50 (853001/G-JYAK) [R]	Privately owned, North Weald
	100 bl	Yakovlev Yak-52 (866904/G-YAKI)	Privately owned, Popham
	100 w	Yakovlev Yak-3M (0470107/G-CGXG)	Privately owned, Bentwaters
	139 y	Yakovlev Yak-52 (833810/G-BWOD)	Privately owned, Sywell
	526 bk	Mikoyan MiG-29 (2960725887) <ff>	Fenland & West Norfolk Aviation Museum, Wisbech
	1342	Yakovlev Yak-1 (G-BTZD)	Privately owned, Westfield, Sussex
	1870710	Ilyushin Il-2 (G-BZVW)	Privately owned, Wickenby
	1878576	Ilyushin Il-2 (G-BZVX)	Privately owned, Wickenby
	(RK858)	VS361 Spitfire LF IX (G-CGJE)	The Fighter Collection, Duxford
	(SM639)	VS361 Spitfire LF IX	Privately owned, Catfield

SAUDI ARABIA

Notes	Serial	Type (code/other identity)	Owner/operator, location or fate
	1115	BAC Strikemaster Mk.80A	Global Aviation, Humberside
	1129	BAC Strikemaster Mk.80A	Humberside Airport, on display
	1133	BAC Strikemaster Mk.80A (G-BESY)	IWM Duxford
	53-671	BAC Lightning F53 (203/ZF579)	Gatwick Aviation Museum, Charlwood
	53-686	BAC Lightning F53 (G-AWON/201/1305/223/ZF592)	City of Norwich Aviation Museum
	55-713	BAC Lightning T55 (206/1316/235/ZF598) [C]	Midland Air Museum, Coventry

SIERRA LEONE

Notes	Serial	Type (code/other identity)	Owner/operator, location or fate
	SL-01	Westland Commando Mk.2C	Privately owned, Dunsfold

SINGAPORE

Notes	Serial	Type (code/other identity)	Owner/operator, location or fate
	311	BAC Strikemaster Mk.84 (G-MXPH)	Privately owned, Leeds East
	323	BAC Strikemaster Mk.81 (N21419)	Privately owned, stored Hawarden

SOUTH AFRICA

Notes	Serial	Type (code/other identity)	Owner/operator, location or fate
	91	Westland Wasp HAS1 (pod)	Privately owned, Oaksey Park
	92	Westland Wasp HAS1 (G-BYCX)	Privately owned, Thruxton
	6130	Lockheed Ventura II (AJ469)	RAF Museum, stored Cosford
	7429	NA AT-6D Harvard III (D-FASS)	Privately owned, Aachen, Germany

SOUTH ARABIA

Notes	Serial	Type (code/other identity)	Owner/operator, location or fate
	104	BAC Jet Provost T52A (G-PROV)	Privately owned, North Weald

SOUTH VIETNAM

Notes	Serial	Type (code/other identity)	Owner/operator, location or fate
	24550	Cessna L-19E Bird Dog (G-PDOG) [GP]	Privately owned, Fenland

SPAIN

Notes	Serial	Type (code/other identity)	Owner/operator, location or fate
	B.2I-27	CASA 2.111B (He111H-16) (B.2I-103)	IWM Duxford, stored
	E.3B-143	CASA 1.131E Jungmann (G-JUNG)	Privately owned, White Waltham
	E.3B-153	CASA 1.131E Jungmann (G-BPTS) [781-75]	Privately owned, Egginton
	E.3B-350	CASA 1.131E Jungmann (G-BHPL) [05-97]	*Repainted as DG+EB, February 2018*
	E.3B-494	CASA 1.131E Jungmann (G-CDLC) [81-47]	Privately owned, Chiseldon
	E.3B-521	CASA 1.131E Jungmann [781-3]	RAF Museum Reserve Collection, Stafford
	E.3B-599	CASA 1.131E Jungmann (G-CGTX) [31]	Privately owned, Archerfield, Lothian
	E.18-2	Piper PA-31P Navajo 425 [42-71]	High Harthay Outdoor Pursuits, Huntingdon

SRI LANKA

Notes	Serial	Type (code/other identity)	Owner/operator, location or fate
	CT180	Nanchang CJ-6A Chujiao (2632016/G-BXZB)	Privately owned, White Waltham

SWEDEN

Notes	Serial	Type (code/other identity)	Owner/operator, location or fate
	-	Thulin A/Bleriot XI (SE-XMC)	Privately owned, Loberod, Sweden
	087	CFM 01 Tummelisa <R> (SE-XIL)	Privately owned, Loberod, Sweden
	2542	Fiat CR42 (G-CBLS)	The Fighter Collection, Duxford
	5033	Klemm Kl35D (SE-BPT) [78]	Privately owned, Barkaby, Sweden
	5060	Klemm Kl35D (SE-BPU) [174]	Privately owned, Barkaby, Sweden

Serial	Type (code/other identity)	Owner/operator, location or fate	Notes
05108	DH60 Moth	Privately owned, Langham	
17239	SAAB B 17A (SE-BYH) [7-J]	Flygvapenmuseum, Linköping, Sweden	
29640	SAAB J 29F [20-08]	Midland Air Museum, Coventry	
29670	SAAB J 29F (SE-DXB) [10-R]	Swedish Air Force Historic Flt, Såtenäs, Sweden	
32028	SAAB 32A Lansen (G-BMSG) <ff>	Privately owned, Willenhall, Staffs	
32542	SAAB J 32B Lansen (SE-RMD) [23]	Swedish Air Force Historic Flt, Såtenäs, Sweden	
35075	SAAB J 35A Draken [40]	Dumfries & Galloway Aviation Museum	
35515	SAAB J 35F Draken [49]	Airborne Systems, Llangeinor	
35810	SAAB Sk 35C Draken (SE-DXP) [79]	Swedish Air Force Historic Flt, Såtenäs, Sweden	
37098	SAAB AJSF 37 Viggen (SE-DXN) [52]	Swedish Air Force Historic Flt, Såtenäs, Sweden	
37918	SAAB AJSH 37 Viggen [57]	Newark Air Museum, Winthorpe	
60140	SAAB Sk 60E (SE-DXG) [140-5]	Swedish Air Force Historic Flt, Såtenäs, Sweden	
91130	SAAB S91A Safir (SE-BNN) [10-30]	Privately owned, Barkaby, Sweden	

SWITZERLAND

-	DH112 Venom FB54 (J-1758/N203DM)	Grove Technology Park, Wantage, Oxon	
A-10	CASA 1.131E Jungmann (G-BECW)	Privately owned, Rochester	
A-44	CASA 1.131E Jungmann 2000 (G-CIUE)	Privately owned, Breighton	
A-57	CASA 1.131E Jungmann (G-BECT)	Privately owned, Goodwood	
A-125	Pilatus P2-05 (G-BLKZ) (fuselage)	Privately owned, Newquay	
A-806	Pilatus P3-03 (G-BTLL)	Privately owned, Guist, Norfolk	
A-815	Pilatus P3-03 (HB-RCQ)	Privately owned, Locarno, Switzerland	
A-818	Pilatus P3-03 (HB-RCH)	Privately owned, Ambri, Switzerland	
A-829	Pilatus P3-03 (HB-RCJ)	Privately owned, Altenrhein, Switzerland	
A-873	Pilatus P3-03 (HB-RCL)	Privately owned, Locarno, Switzerland	
C-552	EKW C-3605 (G-DORN)	Privately owned, Little Gransden (dismantled)	
C-558	EKW C-3605 (G-CCYZ)	Privately owned, Wickenby	
J-143	F+W D-3801 (MS406) (HB-RCF)	Privately owned, Bex, Switzerland	
J-1008	DH100 Vampire FB6	de Havilland Aircraft Museum, London Colney	
J-1169	DH100 Vampire FB6	Privately owned, Henley-on-Thames	
J-1172	DH100 Vampire FB6 (8487M)	RAF Museum Reserve Collection, Stafford	
J-1573	DH112 Venom FB50 (G-VICI) <ff>	Privately owned, Glos	
J-1605	DH112 Venom FB50 (G-BLID)	Gatwick Aviation Museum, Charlwood, Surrey	
J-1629	DH112 Venom FB50	Privately owned, Shropshire	
J-1632	DH112 Venom FB50 (G-VNOM) <ff>	Privately owned, Cantley, Norfolk	
J-1649	DH112 Venom FB50 <ff>	Cornwall Aviation Heritage Centre, Newquay	
J-1704	DH112 Venom FB54	RAF Museum, stored Cosford	
J-1712	DH112 Venom FB54 <ff>	Sold to New Zealand, 2017	
J-1790	DH112 Venom FB54 (G-BLKA/WR410)	Historic Aviation Centre, Fishburn	
J-4015	Hawker Hunter F58 (J-4040/HB-RVS)	Privately owned, St Stephan, Switzerland	
J-4064	Hawker Hunter F58 (HB-RVQ)	Fliegermuseum Altenrhein, Switzerland	
J-4083	Hawker Hunter F58 (G-EGHH)	Sold to Canada, December 2017	
J-4086	Hawker Hunter F58 (HB-RVU)	Privately owned, Altenrhein, Switzerland	
J-4110	Hawker Hunter F58A (XF318/G-CJWL)	Hawker Hunter Aviation Ltd, Scampton	
J-4201	Hawker Hunter T68 (HB-RVR)	Amici dell'Hunter, Sion, Switzerland	
J-4205	Hawker Hunter T68 (HB-RVP)	Fliegermuseum Altenrhein, Switzerland	
J-4206	Hawker Hunter T68 (HB-RVV)	Fliegermuseum Altenrhein, Switzerland	
U-80	Bücker Bü133D Jungmeister (G-BUKK)	Privately owned, Kirdford, W Sussex	
U-95	Bücker Bü133C Jungmeister (G-BVGP)	Privately owned, Turweston	
U-99	Bücker Bü133C Jungmeister (G-AXMT)	Privately owned, Italy	
U-1215	DH115 Vampire T11 (XE998)	Solent Sky, Southampton	
U-1229	DH115 Vampire T55 (G-HATD)	Aviation Heritage Ltd, Coventry	
V-54	SE3130 Alouette II (G-BVSD)	Privately owned, Glos	

UNITED ARAB EMIRATES

DU-103	Bell 206B JetRanger II	Privately owned, Coney Park, Leeds	

USA

-	Noorduyn AT-16 Harvard IIB (KLu B-168)	American Air Museum, Duxford	
001	Ryan ST-3KR Recruit (G-BYPY)	Privately owned, Goodwood	
07	Boeing-Stearman PT-17 Kaydet (N62658)	Privately owned, Hurstbourne Tarrant, Hants	
14	Boeing-Stearman A75N-1 Kaydet (3486/G-ISDN)	Privately owned, Oaksey Park	

Notes	Serial	Type (code/other identity)	Owner/operator, location or fate
	23	Fairchild PT-23 (N49272)	Privately owned, Sleap
	26	Boeing-Stearman A75N-1 Kaydet (G-BAVO)	Privately owned, Enstone
	27	Boeing-Stearman N2S-3 Kaydet (4304/G-CJYK)	Privately owned, Enstone
	27	NA SNJ-7 Texan (90678/G-BRVG)	Privately owned, Rochester
	31	Boeing-Stearman A75N-1 Kaydet (42-16338/G-KAYD)	Privately owned, Enstone
	43	Noorduyn AT-16 Harvard IIB (43-13064/G-AZSC) [SC]	Privately owned, Goodwood
	44	Boeing-Stearman D75N-1 Kaydet (41-15852/G-RJAH)	Privately owned, Duxford
	72	NA SNJ-5 Texan (42-85897/N6972C/G-DHHF) [JF]	Privately owned, Compton Abbas
	85	WAR P-47 Thunderbolt <R> (G-BTBI)	Privately owned, Perth
	104	Boeing-Stearman PT-13D Kaydet (42-16931/N4712V) [W]	Privately owned, Hardwick, Norfolk
	107	Boeing-Stearman PT-17 Kaydet (42-16107/N62658)	Privately owned, Hurstbourne Tarrant, Hants
	112	Boeing-Stearman PT-13D Kaydet (42-17397/G-BSWC)	Privately owned, Gloucester
	131	Boeing-Stearman PT-17 Kaydet (38254/N74677)	Privately owned, Enstone
	164	Boeing-Stearman PT-13B Kaydet (41-0823/N60320)	Privately owned, Fenland
	286	Boeing-Stearman N2S-4 Kaydet (55749/N10053)	Privately owned, Streethay, Staffs
	317	Boeing-Stearman PT-18 Kaydet (41-61042/G-CIJN)	Privately owned, Goodwood
	379	Boeing-Stearman PT-13D Kaydet (42-14865/G-ILLE)	Privately owned, Hohenems, Austria
	399	Boeing-Stearman N2S-5 Kaydet (38495/N67193)	Privately owned, Gelnhausen, Germany
	441	Boeing-Stearman N2S-4 Kaydet (30010/G-BTFG)	Privately owned, Postling, Kent
	443	Boeing-Stearman E75 Kaydet (N43YP) [6018]	Privately owned, Bicester
	466	Boeing-Stearman PT-13A Kaydet (37-0089/G-PTBA)	Privately owned, Gloucester
	540	Piper L-4H Grasshopper (43-29877/G-BCNX)	Privately owned, Monewden
	560	Bell UH-1H Iroquois (73-22077/G-HUEY)	Privately owned, North Weald
	578	Boeing-Stearman N2S-5 Kaydet (N1364V)	Privately owned, North Weald
	586	Boeing-Stearman N2S-3 Kaydet (07874/N74650)	Privately owned, Seppe, The Netherlands
	628	Beech D17S (44-67761/N18V)	Privately owned, stored East Garston, Bucks
	669	Boeing-Stearman A75N-1 Kaydet (37869/G-CCXA)	Privately owned, Old Buckenham
	671	Boeing-Stearman PT-13D Kaydet (61181/G-CGPY)	Privately owned, Gloucester
	699	Boeing-Stearman N2S-3 Kaydet (38233/G-CCXB)	Privately owned, Goodwood
	716	Boeing-Stearman PT-13D Kaydet (42-17553/N1731B)	Privately owned, Compton Abbas
	718	Boeing-Stearman PT-13D Kaydet (42-17555/N5345N)	Privately owned, Tibenham
	744	Boeing-Stearman A75N-1 Kaydet (42-16532/OO-USN)	Privately owned, Wevelgem, Belgium
	805	Boeing-Stearman PT-17 Kaydet (42-17642/N3922B)	Privately owned, Tibenham
	854	Ryan PT-22 Recruit (41-20854/G-BTBH)	Privately owned, Goodwood
	855	Ryan PT-22 Recruit (41-15510/N56421)	Privately owned, Sleap
	897	Aeronca 11AC Chief (G-BJEV) [E]	Privately owned, English Bicknor, Glos
	985	Boeing-Stearman PT-13D Kaydet (42-16930/OO-OPS)	Privately owned, Brasschaat, Belgium
	1102	Boeing-Stearman N2S-5 Kaydet (43449/G-AZLE) [102]	Privately owned, Compton Abbas
	1164	Beech D18S (G-BKGL)	Privately owned,
	3072	NA T-6G Texan (49-3072/G-TEXN) [72]	Privately owned, Goodwood
	3397	Boeing-Stearman N2S-3 Kaydet (G-OBEE) [174]	Privately owned, Old Buckenham
	3403	Boeing-Stearman N2S-3 Kaydet (N75TQ) [180]	Privately owned, Tibenham
	3583	Piper L-4B Grasshopper (45-0583/G-FINT) [44-D]	Privately owned, Eggesford
	3681	Piper L-4J Grasshopper (44-80248/G-AXGP)	Privately owned, Bentwaters
	4406	Naval Aircraft Factory N3N-3 (G-ONAF) [12]	Privately owned, Sandown
	4826	Boeing-Stearman PT-17 Kaydet (42-16663/G-CJIN) [582]	Privately owned, Enstone
	6136	Boeing-Stearman A75N-1 Kaydet(42-16136/G-BRUJ) [205]	Privately owned, Liverpool
	6771	Republic F-84F Thunderstreak (BAF FU-6)	RAF Museum, stored Cosford
	7797	Aeronca L-16A Grasshopper (47-0797/G-BFAF)	Privately owned, Finmere
	8242	NA F-86A Sabre (48-0242) [FU-242]	Midland Air Museum, Coventry
	01532	Northrop F-5E Tiger II <R> (BAPC 336)	RAF Alconbury on display
	02538	Fairchild PT-19B (N33870)	Privately owned, Mendlesham, Suffolk
	07539	Boeing-Stearman N2S-3 Kaydet (N63590) [143]	Privately owned, North Weald
	14286	Lockheed T-33A Shooting Star (51-4286)	IWM, stored Duxford
	O-14419	Lockheed T-33A Shooting Star (51-4419)	Midland Air Museum, Coventry
	14863	NA AT-6D Harvard III (41-33908/G-BGOR)	Privately owned, Rednal
	15372	Piper L-18C Super Cub (51-15372/N123SA) [372-A]	Privately owned, Crowfield
	15979	Hughes OH-6A Cayuse (69-15979)	RAF Mildenhall, instructional use
	15990	Bell AH-1F Hueycobra (70-15990)	Museum of Army Flying, Middle Wallop
	16011	Hughes OH-6A Cayuse (69-16011/G-OHGA)	Privately owned, Wesham, Lancs
	16037	Piper J-3C-65 Cub (G-BSFD)	Privately owned, Sleap
	16171	NA F-86D Sabre (51-6171)	North-East Aircraft Museum, Usworth

Serial	Type (code/other identity)	Owner/operator, location or fate	Notes
16445	Bell AH-1F Hueycobra (69-16445)	Defence Academy of the UK, Shrivenham	
16506	Hughes OH-6A Cayuse (67-16506)	The Helicopter Museum, Weston-super-Mare	
16544	NA AT-6A Texan (41-16544/N13FY) [FY]	Privately owned, Hilversum, The Netherlands	
16579	Bell UH-1H Iroquois (66-16579)	The Helicopter Museum, Weston-super-Mare	
16718	Lockheed T-33A Shooting Star (51-6718)	City of Norwich Aviation Museum	
17692	NA T-28S Fennec (51-7692/G-TROY) [TL-692]	Privately owned, Duxford	
17962	Lockheed SR-71A Blackbird (61-7962)	American Air Museum, Duxford	
18263	Boeing-Stearman PT-17 Kaydet (41-8263/N38940) [822]	Privately owned, Tibenham	
19252	Lockheed T-33A Shooting Star (51-9252)	Tangmere Military Aviation Museum	
21300	Cessna O-2A Super Skymaster (67-21300/N590D)	Privately owned, Lelystad, The Netherlands	
21509	Bell UH-1H Iroquois (72-21509/G-UHIH)	Privately owned, Wesham, Lancs	
21605	Bell UH-1H Iroquois (72-21605)	American Air Museum, Duxford	
24538	Kaman HH-43F Huskie (62-4535)	Midland Air Museum, Coventry	
24568	Cessna L-19E Bird Dog (LN-WNO)	Army Aviation Norway, Kjeller, Norway	
24582	Cessna L-19E Bird Dog (G-VDOG)	Privately owned, Dundee	
28521	CCF T-6J Texan(52-8521/G-TVIJ) [TA-521]	Privately owned, Woodchurch, Kent	
28562	CCF T-6J Texan (52-8562/*20310*/G-BSBG) [TA-562]	Privately owned, Tatenhill	
30274	Piper AE-1 Cub Cruiser (N203SA)	Privately owned, Nangis, France	
30861	NA TB-25J Mitchell (44-30861/N9089Z)	Privately owned, Booker	
31145	Piper L-4B Grasshopper (43-1145/G-BBLH) [26-G]	Privately owned, Biggin Hill	
31430	Piper L-4B Grasshopper (43-1430/G-BHVV)	Privately owned, Perranporth	
31952	Aeronca O-58B Defender (G-BRPR)	Privately owned, Belchamp Water	
34037	NA TB-25N Mitchell (44-29366/N9115Z/8838M)	RAF Museum, Hendon	
34064	NA B-25J Mitchell (44-31171/N7614C) [8U]	American Air Museum, Duxford	
36922	Titan T-51 Mustang (G-CMPC) [WD-Y]	Privately owned, Benwick, Cambs	
37414	McD F-4C Phantom II (63-7414)	Midland Air Museum, stored Coventry	
39624	Wag Aero Sport Trainer (EI-GMH) [39-D]	Privately owned, Abbeyshrule, Eire	
41386	Thomas-Morse S4 Scout <R> (G-MJTD)	Privately owned, Lutterworth	
42165	NA F-100D Super Sabre (54-2165) [VM]	IWM, stored Duxford	
42196	NA F-100D Super Sabre (54-2196)	Norfolk & Suffolk Avn Museum, Flixton	
43517	Boeing-Stearman N2S-5 Kaydet (G-NZSS) [227]	Privately owned, Woodchurch, Kent	
46214	Grumman TBM-3E Avenger (69327/CF-KCG) [X-3]	IWM, Duxford	
51970	NA AT-6D Texan (41-33888/G-TXAN) [V-970]	Privately owned, Aalen, Germany	
53319	Grumman TBM-3E Avenger (HB-RDG) [19]	Privately owned, Lausanne, Switzerland	
54433	Lockheed T-33A Shooting Star (55-4433) [TR-433]	Norfolk & Suffolk Avn Museum, Flixton	
54884	Piper L-4J Grasshopper (45-4884/N61787) [57-D]	Privately owned, Sywell	
55771	Boeing-Stearman N2S-4 Kaydet (N68427) [427]	Privately owned, Bodmin	
56498	Douglas C-54Q Skymaster (N44914)	Privately owned, stored North Weald	
60312	McD F-101F Voodoo (56-0312)	Midland Air Museum, Coventry	
60344	Ryan Navion (N4956C)	Privately owned, Earls Colne	
60689	Boeing B-52D Stratofortress (56-0689)	American Air Museum, Duxford	
63319	NA F-100D Super Sabre (54-2269) [FW-319]	RAF Lakenheath, on display	
66692	Lockheed U-2CT (56-6692)	American Air Museum, Duxford	
70270	McD F-101B Voodoo (57-270) (fuselage)	Midland Air Museum, stored Coventry	
80105	Replica SE5a <R> (PH-WWI/G-CCBN) [19]	Privately owned, White Waltham	
82062	DHC U-6A Beaver (58-2062)	Midland Air Museum, Coventry	
85061	NA SNJ-5 Texan (G-CHIA) [7F]	Privately owned, White Waltham	
86690	Grumman FM-2 Wildcat (G-KINL) [F-2]	Privately owned, Duxford	
96995	CV F4U-4 Corsair (OE-EAS) [BR-37]	Flying Bulls, Salzburg, Austria	
111836	NA AT-6C Harvard IIa (41-33262/G-TSIX) [JZ-6]	Privately owned, Gamston	
111989	Cessna L-19A Bird Dog (51-11989/N33600)	Museum of Army Flying, Middle Wallop	
114700	NA T-6G Texan (51-14700/G-TOMC)	Privately owned, Netherthorpe	
115042	NA T-6G Texan (51-15042/G-BGHU) [TA-042]	Privately owned, Postling, Kent	
115227	NA T-6G Texan (51-15227/G-BKRA)	Privately owned, Gloucester	
115302	Piper L-18C Super Cub (51-15302/G-BJTP) [TP]	Privately owned, Defford	
115373	Piper L-18C Super Cub (51-15373/G-AYPM) [A-373]	Privately owned, Leicester	
115684	Piper L-21A Super Cub (51-15684/G-BKVM) [849-DC]	Privately owned, Strubby	
117415	Canadair CT-133 Silver Star (G-BYOY) [TR-415]	RAF Manston History Museum	
121714	Grumman F8F-2P Bearcat (G-RUMM) [201-B]	The Fighter Collection, Duxford	
123716	CV F4U-5NL Corsair (124541/D-FCOR) [19-WF]	Meier Motors, Bremgarten, Germany	
124143	Douglas AD-4NA Skyraider (F-AZDP) [205-RM]	Amicale J-B Salis, la Ferté-Alais, France	
124485	Boeing B-17G Flying Fortress (44-85784/G-BEDF)[DF-A]	B-17 Preservation Ltd, Duxford	

Notes	Serial	Type (code/other identity)	Owner/operator, location or fate
	124724	CV F4U-5NL Corsair (F-AZEG) [22]	Les Casques de Cuir, la Ferté-Alais, France
	126922	Douglas AD-4NA Skyraider (G-RADR) [503-H]	Kennet Aviation, North Weald
134076		NA AT-6D Texan (41-34671/F-AZSC) [TA076]	Privately owned, Yvetot, France
	138179	NA T-28A Trojan (OE-ESA) [BA]	The Flying Bulls, Salzburg, Austria
	138266	NA T-28B Trojan (HB-RCT) [266-CT]	Jet Alpine Fighter, Sion, Switzerland
	138343	NA T-28B Trojan (N343NA) [212]	Privately owned, Siegerland, Germany
	140547	NA T-28C Trojan (F-AZHN) [IF-28]	Privately owned, Toussus le Noble, France
	140566	NA T-28C Trojan (N556EB) [252]	Privately owned, la Ferté-Alais, France
	146289	NA T-28C Trojan (N99153) [2W]	Norfolk & Suffolk Avn Museum, Flixton
150225		WS58 Wessex 60 (G-AWOX) [123]	Privately owned, Lulsgate
155454		NA OV-10B Bronco (158300/99+24/F-AZKM) [26]	Privately owned, Montelimar, France
	155529	McD F-4J(UK) Phantom II (ZE359) [AJ-114]	American Air Museum, Duxford
	155848	McD F-4S Phantom II [WT-11]	National Museum of Flight, E Fortune
	159233	HS AV-8A Harrier [CG-33]	IWM North, Salford Quays
	162068	McD AV-8B Harrier II <ff>	Privately owned, Thorpe Wood, N Yorks
	162071	McD AV-8B Harrier II (fuselage)	Rolls-Royce, Filton
	162074	McD AV-8B Harrier II <ff>	Privately owned, South Molton, Devon
	162730	McD AV-8B Harrier II <ff>	Privately owned, Liverpool
	162737	McD AV-8B Harrier II (fuselage) [38]	MoD/JARTS, Boscombe Down
	162958	McD AV-8B Harrier II <ff>	QinetiQ, Farnborough
	162964	McD AV-8B Harrier II <ff>	Harrier Heritage Centre, RAF Wittering
	162964	McD AV-8B Harrier II <rf>	Privately owned, Charlwood, Surrey
	163205	McD AV-8B Harrier II (fuselage)	Privately owned, Thorpe Wood, N Yorks
	163423	McD AV-8B Harrier II <ff>	QinetiQ, Boscombe Down
	163423	McD AV-8B Harrier II <rf>	Privately owned, Sproughton
210766		Douglas C-47B Skytrain (composite) (K-1) [4U]	Wings Museum, Balcombe, W Sussex
	217786	Boeing-Stearman PT-17 Kaydet (41-8169/CF-EQS) [25]	American Air Museum, Duxford
224319		Douglas C-47D Skytrain (44-77047/G-AMSN) <ff>	Privately owned, Sussex
226413		Republic P-47D Thunderbolt (45-49192/N47DD) [ZU-N]	American Air Museum, Duxford
	234539	Fairchild PT-19B Cornell (42-34539/N50429) [63]	Privately owned, Dunkeswell
	236657	Piper L-4A Grasshopper (42-36657/G-BGSJ) [72-D]	Privately owned, Langport, Somerset
237123		Waco CG-4A Hadrian <R> (fuselage)	Yorkshire Air Museum, Elvington
	238133	Boeing B-17G Flying Fortress (44-83735/F-BDRS) [C]	American Air Museum, Duxford
	238410	Piper L-4A Grasshopper (42-38410/G-BHPK) [44-A]	Privately owned, Tibenham
241079		Waco CG-4A Hadrian <R> (BAPC 370)	RAF Museum, stored Cosford
243809		Waco CG-4A Hadrian (BAPC 185)	Museum of Army Flying, Middle Wallop
	252983	Schweizer TG-3A (42-52983/N66326)	IWM Duxford, stored
	285068	NA AT-6D Texan (42-85068/G-KAMY)	Kennet Aviation, North Weald/Yeovilton
	298177	Stinson L-5A Sentinel (42-98177/N6438C) [8-R]	Privately owned, Tibenham
	313048	NA AT-6D Texan (44-81506/G-TDJN)	Privately owned, Gloucester
	314887	Fairchild Argus III (43-14887/G-AJPI)	Privately owned, Eelde, The Netherlands
	315509	Douglas C-47A Skytrain (43-15509/G-BHUB) [W7-S]	American Air Museum, Duxford
319764		Waco CG-4A Hadrian (237123/BAPC 157) (fuselage)	Yorkshire Air Museum, Elvington
	329282	Piper J-3C-65 Cub (N46779)	Privately owned, Abbots Bromley
	329405	Piper L-4H Grasshopper (43-29405/G-BCOB) [23-A]	Privately owned, Bicester
329417		Piper L-4A Grasshopper (42-38400/G-BDHK)	Privately owned, English Bicknor, Glos
	329471	Piper L-4H Grasshopper (43-29471/G-BGXA) [44-F]	Privately owned, Martley, Worcs
	329601	Piper L-4H Grasshopper (43-29601/G-AXHR) [44-D]	Privately owned, Nayland
	329707	Piper L-4H Grasshopper (43-29707/G-BFBY) [44-S]	Privately owned, Old Buckenham
	329854	Piper L-4H Grasshopper (43-29854/G-BMKC) [44-R]	Privately owned, Biggin Hill
	329934	Piper L-4H Grasshopper (43-29934/G-BCPH) [72-B]	Privately owned, Garford, Oxon
	330238	Piper L-4H Grasshopper (43-30238/G-LIVH) [24-A]	Privately owned, Yarcombe, Devon
	330244	Piper L-4H Grasshopper (43-30244/G-CGIY) [46-C]	Privately owned, Church Fenton
	330314	Piper L-4H Grasshopper (43-30314/G-BAET)	Privately owned, Winwick, Cambs
	330372	Piper L-4H Grasshopper (43-30372/G-AISX)	Privately owned, Booker
330426		Piper L-4J Grasshopper (45-4884/N61787) [53-K]	Privately owned, Sywell
	330485	Piper L-4H Grasshopper (43-30485/G-AJES) [44-C]	Privately owned, Shifnal
	379994	Piper J-3L-65 Cub (G-BPUR) [52-J]	Privately owned, Popham
	411622	NA P-51D Mustang (44-74427/F-AZSB) [G4-C]	Privately owned, Melun, France
	411631	NA P-51D Mustang (44-73979/472218) [MX-V]	American Air Museum, Duxford
413317		NA P-51D Mustang (44-74409/N51RT) [VF-B]	RAF Museum, Hendon
413357		NA P-51D Mustang <R> [B7-R]	Privately owned, Byfleet, Surrey

124

Serial	Type (code/other identity)	Owner/operator, location or fate	Notes
413573	NA P-51D Mustang (44-73415/9133M/N6526D) [B6-V]	RAF Museum, stored Cosford	
413578	NA P-51D Mustang (44-74923/PH-JAT) [C5-W]	Privately owned, Lelystad, The Netherlands	
413704	NA P-51D Mustang (44-73149/G-BTCD) [B7-H]	Sold to Turkey, January 2018	
413926	Stewart S-51 Mustang (G-CGOI) [E2-S]	Privately owned, Benwick, Cambs	
414237	NA P-51D Mustang (44-73656/F-AZXS) [HO-W]	Privately owned, Avignon, France	
414673	Bonsall Replica Mustang (G-BDWM) [LH-I]	Privately owned, Gamston	
414907	Titan T-51 Mustang (G-DHYS) [CY-S]	Privately owned, Pershore	
433915	Consolidated PBV-1A Canso A (RCAF 11005/G-PBYA)	Privately owned, Duxford	
434602	Douglas A-26B Invader (44-34602/LN-IVA) [B]	Nordic Warbirds, Västerås, Sweden	
436021	Piper J-3C-65 Cub (G-BWEZ)	Privately owned, Archerfield, Lothian	
441968	Titan T-51 Mustang (G-FION) [VF-E]	Privately owned, Netherthorpe	
442268	Noorduyn AT-16 Harvard IIb (KF568/LN-TEX) [TA-268]	Privately owned, Kjeller, Norway	
454467	Piper L-4J Grasshopper (45-4467/G-BILI) [44-J]	Privately owned, RAF Halton	
454537	Piper L-4J Grasshopper (45-4537/G-BFDL) [04-J]	Privately owned, Shempston Farm, Lossiemouth	
461748	Boeing B-29A Superfortress (44-61748/G-BHDK) [Y]	American Air Museum, Duxford	
463209	NA P-51D Mustang <R> (BAPC 255) [WZ-S]	American Air Museum, Duxford	
472216	NA P-51D Mustang (44-72216/G-BIXL) [HO-M]	Privately owned, Goodwood	
472218	Titan T-51 Mustang (G-MUZY) [WZ-I]	Privately owned, Tibenham	
472773	NA P-51D Mustang (44-72773/D-FPSI) [QP-M]	Meier Motors, Bremgarten, Germany	
472922	NA TF-51D Mustang (44-72922/PH-VDF) [L2-W]	Privately owned, Brasschaat, Belgium	
473871	NA TF-51D Mustang (44-73871/D-FTSI) [TF-871]	Meier Motors, Bremgarten, Germany	
474008	Jurca MJ77 Gnatsum (G-PSIR) [VF-R]	Privately owned, Fishburn	
474425	NA P-51D Mustang (44-74425/PH-PSI) [OC-G]	Privately owned, Lelystad, The Netherlands	
479712	Piper L-4H Grasshopper (44-79826/G-AHIP) [8-R]	Privately owned, Coleford	
479744	Piper L-4H Grasshopper (44-79744/G-BGPD) [49-M]	Privately owned, Marsh, Bucks	
479766	Piper L-4H Grasshopper (44-79766/G-BKHG) [63-D]	Privately owned, Frogland Cross	
479781	Piper L-4H Grasshopper (44-79781/G-AISS)	Privately owned, Insch (under restoration)	
479897	Piper L-4H Grasshopper (44-79897/G-BOXJ) [JD]	Privately owned, Rochester	
480015	Piper L-4H Grasshopper (44-80015/G-AKIB) [44-M]	Privately owned, Perranporth	
480133	Piper L-4J Grasshopper (44-80133/G-BDCD) [44-B]	Privately owned, Slinfold	
480173	Piper L-4J Grasshopper (44-80609/G-RRSR) [57-H]	Privately owned, Shotteswell	
480321	Piper L-4J Grasshopper (44-80321/G-FRAN) [44-H]	Privately owned, Rayne, Essex	
480480	Piper L-4J Grasshopper (44-80480/G-BECN) [44-E]	Privately owned, Rayne, Essex	
480636	Piper L-4J Grasshopper (44-80636/G-AXHP) [58-A]	Privately owned, Spanhoe	
480723	Piper L-4J Grasshopper (44-80723/G-BFZB) [E5-J]	Privately owned, Egginton	
480752	Piper L-4J Grasshopper (44-80752/G-BCXJ) [39-E]	Privately owned, Melksham	
481273	CCF T-6J Harvard IV (20306/G-CJWE)	Privately owned, Sywell	
483868	Boeing B-17G Flying Fortress (44-83868/N5237V) [A-N]	RAF Museum, Hendon	
493209	NA T-6G Texan (49-3209/G-DDMV/41)	Privately owned, Headcorn	
779465	Hiller UH-12C (N5315V)	Privately owned, Lower Upham, Hants	
2106638	Titan T-51 Mustang (G-CIFD) [E9-R]	Privately owned, Shobdon	
2100882	Douglas C-47A Skytrain (42-100882/N473DC) [3X-P]	Privately owned, East Kirkby	
2100884	Douglas C-47A Skytrain (42-100884/N147DC) [L4-D]	Privately owned, Dunsfold	
2104590	Curtiss P-40M Kittyhawk (43-5802/G-KITT) [44]	Sold to the US, June 2017	
2105915	Curtiss P-40N Kittyhawk (42-105915/F-AZKU)	France's Flying Warbirds, Melun, France	
03-08003	B-V CH-47F Chinook [DT]	RAF Odiham, at main gate	
3-1923	Aeronca O-58B Defender (43-1923/G-BRHP)	Privately owned, Chiseldon	
5-666	Noorduyn AT-16 Harvard IIb (KF435)	Maidenhead Heritage Centre	
18-2001	Piper L-18C Super Cub (52-2401/G-BIZV)	Privately owned, Wicklow, Ireland	
22-296	Eberhardt SE5E Replica (G-BLXT)	Privately owned, Sywell	
39-139	Beech YC-43 Traveler (N295BS)	Duke of Brabant AF, Eindhoven, The Netherlands	
39-0285	Curtiss P-40B Warhawk	The Fighter Collection, stored Duxford (wreck)	
39-0287	Curtiss P-40B Warhawk	The Fighter Collection, stored Duxford (wreck)	
40-2538	Fairchild PT-19A Cornell (N33870)	Privately owned, Mendlesham	
41-8689	Boeing-Stearman PT-17D Kaydet (G-BIXN) (frame)	Privately owned, Rendcomb	
41-13357	Curtiss P-40C Warhawk (G-CIIO) [160,10AB]	The Fighter Collection, Duxford	
41-19393	Douglas A-20C Havoc (wreck)	Wings Museum, Balcombe, W Sussex	
41-33275	NA AT-6C Texan (G-BICE) [CE]	Privately owned, Great Oakley, Essex	
42-66841	Lockheed P-38H Lightning [153]	Privately owned, Bentwaters	
42-12417	Noorduyn AT-16 Harvard IIb (KLu. B-163)	Newark Air Museum, Winthorpe	
42-35870	Taylorcraft DCO-65 (G-BWLJ) [129]	Privately owned, Nayland	
42-46703	Stinson AT-19 Reliant (FK877/N69745)	Privately owned, Birmingham	

Notes	Serial	Type (code/other identity)	Owner/operator, location or fate
	42-58678	Taylorcraft DF-65 (G-BRIY) [IY]	Privately owned, Carlisle
	42-78044	Aeronca 11AC Chief (G-BRXL)	Privately owned, Andrewsfield
	42-84555	NA AT-6D Harvard III (FAP.1662/G-ELMH) [EP-H]	Privately owned, Hardwick, Norfolk
	42-93510	Douglas C-47A Skytrain [CM] <ff>	Privately owned, Kew
	43-9628	Douglas A-20G Havoc <ff>	Privately owned, Hinckley, Leics
	43-11137	Bell P-63C Kingcobra (wreck)	Wings Museum, Balcombe, W Sussex
	43-21664	Douglas A-20G Havoc (wreck)	Wings Museum, Balcombe, W Sussex
	43-29964	Piper L-4H Grasshopper (G-AKRA) [JA]	Sold to Germany, 16 May 2017
	43-35943	Beech 3N (G-BKRN) [943]	Beech Restorations, Bruntingthorpe
	43-36140	NA B-25J Mitchell <ff>	Wings Museum, Balcombe, W Sussex
	44-4315	Bell P-63C Kingcobra	Wings Museum, Balcombe, W Sussex
	44-4368	Bell P-63C Kingcobra	Privately owned, Surrey
	44-13954	NA P-51D Mustang (G-UAKE)	Mustang Restoration Co Ltd, Coventry
	44-14574	NA P-51D Mustang (fuselage)	East Essex Aviation Museum, Clacton
	44-42914	Douglas DC-4 (N31356) <ff>	Privately owned, Burtonwood
	44-51228	Consolidated B-24M Liberator [EC-493]	American Air Museum, Duxford
	44-79609	Piper L-4H Grasshopper (G-BHXY) [PR]	Privately owned, Bealbury, Cornwall
	44-79649	Piper L-4H Grasshopper (G-AIIH)	Privately owned, Stonesfield, Oxon
	44-80594	Piper L-4J Grasshopper (G-BEDJ)	Privately owned, White Waltham
	44-80647	Piper L-4J Grasshopper (D-EGAF)	Privately owned, Donauwörth, Germany
	45-5772	Piper J-5A Cub Cruiser (G-BSXT)	Privately owned, Norwich
	51-9036	Lockheed T-33A Shooting Star	Newark Air Museum, Winthorpe
	51-15319	Piper L-18C Super Cub (G-FUZZ) [A-319]	Privately owned, Elvington
	51-15555	Piper L-18C Super Cub (G-OSPS)	Privately owned, Andrewsfield
	52-8543	CCF T-6J Texan (G-BUKY) [66]	Privately owned, Dortmund, Germany
	54-005	NA F-100D Super Sabre (54-2163)	Dumfries & Galloway Avn Mus, Dumfries
	54-174	NA F-100D Super Sabre (54-2174) [SM]	Midland Air Museum, Coventry
	54-2223	NA F-100D Super Sabre	Newark Air Museum, Winthorpe
	54-2445	Piper L-21B Super Cub (G-OTAN) [A-445]	Privately owned, Hawarden
	54-2447	Piper L-21B Super Cub (G-SCUB)	Privately owned, Anwick
	55-138354	NA T-28B Trojan (138354/N1328B) [TL-354]	Privately owned, Antwerp, Belgium
	63-699	McD F-4C Phantom II (63-7699) [CG]	Midland Air Museum, Coventry
	64-17657	Douglas B-26K Counter Invader (N99218) <ff>	WWII Remembrance Museum, Handcross, W Sussex
	65-777	McD F-4C Phantom II (63-7419) [SA]	RAF Lakenheath, on display
	66-374	Helio H.295 Super Courier (G-BAGT) [EO]	Privately owned, Spanhoe
	67-120	GD F-111E Aardvark (67-0120) [UH]	American Air Museum, Duxford
	68-0060	GD F-111E Aardvark <ff>	Dumfries & Galloway Avn Mus, Dumfries
	68-8284	Sikorsky MH-53M Pave Low IV	RAF Museum, Cosford
	70-0389	GD F-111E Aardvark (68-0011) [LN]	RAF Lakenheath, on display
	72-1447	GD F-111F Aardvark <ff>	American Air Museum, Duxford
	74-0177	GD F-111F Aardvark [FN]	RAF Museum, Cosford
	76-020	McD F-15A Eagle (76-0020)	American Air Museum, Duxford
	76-124	McD F-15B Eagle (76-0124) [LN]	RAF Lakenheath, instructional use
	77-259	Fairchild A-10A Thunderbolt (77-0259) [AR]	American Air Museum, Duxford
	80-219	Fairchild GA-10A Thunderbolt (80-0219) [WR]	Bentwaters Cold War Museum
	82-23762	B-V CH-47D Chinook <ff>	RAF Odiham, instructional use
	83-24104	B-V CH-47D Chinook [BN] <ff>	RAF Museum, Hendon
	86-180	McD F-15A Eagle (74-0131) [LN] (starboard side only, painted as 86-169 on port side)	RAF Lakenheath, on display
	86-01677	B-V CH-47D Chinook	RAF, stored Odiham
	89-00159	B-V CH-47D Chinook	RAF, stored Odiham
	108-1601	Stinson 108-1 Voyager (G-CFGE) [H]	Privately owned, Spanhoe
	146-11042	Wolf W-11 Boredom Fighter (G-BMZX) [7]	Privately owned, Popham
	146-11083	Wolf W-11 Boredom Fighter (G-BNAI) [5]	Privately owned, Haverfordwest
	A3-3	NA P-51D Mustang (44-72035/G-SIJJ)	Hangar 11 Collection, North Weald
	X-17	Curtiss P-40F Warhawk (41-19841/G-CGZP)	The Fighter Collection, Duxford
	CY-D	NA TF-51D Mustang (44-84847/G-TFSI)	Privately owned, Duxford (damaged)
	CY-G	Titan T-51 Mustang (G-TSIM)	Privately owned, Shobdon
	PA50	Curtiss P-36C Hawk (38-0210/G-CIXJ)	The Fighter Collection, Duxford

Serial	Type (code/other identity)	Owner/operator, location or fate	Notes
YUGOSLAVIA			
30131	Soko P-2 Kraguj [131]	Privately owned, stored Minskip, N Yorks	
30140	Soko P-2 Kraguj (G-RADA) [140]	Privately owned, Fishburn	
30146	Soko P-2 Kraguj (G-BSXD) [146]	Privately owned, Fishburn	
30149	Soko P-2 Kraguj (G-SOKO) [149]	Privately owned, Fenland	
51109	UTVA-66 (YU-DLG)	Privately owned, Morpeth	

Yakovlev Yak-52 G-YAKH is based at White Waltham and is marked as 33 white in this unusual camouflage scheme.

146-11083 is actually part of the construction number of this delightfully named Wolf W-11 Boredom Fighter, G-BNAI, based at Haverfordwest.

Notes	Serial	Type (code/other identity)	Owner/operator, location or fate
	C7	Avro 631 Cadet (EI-AGO)	IAC Museum, Baldonnel
	34	Miles M14A Magister I (N5392)	National Museum of Ireland, Dublin
	141	Avro 652A Anson C19	IAC Museum, Baldonnel
	164	DHC1 Chipmunk T20	IAC Museum, Baldonnel
	168	DHC1 Chipmunk T20 (EI-HFA)	Irish Historic Flight, Ballyboy
	169	DHC1 Chipmunk 22 (WD305/EI-HFB)	Irish Historic Flight, Ballyboy
	170	DHC1 Chipmunk 22 (WP857/EI-HFC)	Irish Historic Flight, Ballyboy
	172	DHC1 Chipmunk T20	IAC, stored Baldonnel
	173	DHC1 Chipmunk T20	South East Aviation Enthusiasts, Dromod
	176	DH104 Dove 4 (VP-YKF)	South East Aviation Enthusiasts, Waterford
	183	Percival P56 Provost T51	IAC Museum, Baldonnel
	184	Percival P56 Provost T51	South East Aviation Enthusiasts, Dromod
	187	DH115 Vampire T55 <ff>	South East Aviation Enthusiasts, Dromod
	191	DH115 Vampire T55	IAC Museum, Baldonnel
	192	DH115 Vampire T55 <ff>	South East Aviation Enthusiasts, Dromod
	195	Sud SA316 Alouette III (F-WJDH)	IAC Museum, stored Baldonnel
	198	DH115 Vampire T11 (XE977)	National Museum of Ireland, Dublin
	199	DHC1 Chipmunk T20	IAC, stored Baldonnel
	202	Sud SA316 Alouette III	Ulster Aviation Society, Long Kesh
	203	Reims-Cessna FR172H	IAC No 104 Sqn/1 Operations Wing, Baldonnel
	205	Reims-Cessna FR172H	IAC No 104 Sqn/1 Operations Wing, Baldonnel
	206	Reims-Cessna FR172H	IAC No 104 Sqn/1 Operations Wing, Baldonnel
	207	Reims-Cessna FR172H	IAC, stored Waterford
	208	Reims-Cessna FR172H	IAC No 104 Sqn/1 Operations Wing, Baldonnel
	210	Reims-Cessna FR172H	IAC No 104 Sqn/1 Operations Wing, Baldonnel
	215	Fouga CM170R Super Magister	Dublin Institute of Technology
	216	Fouga CM170R Super Magister	IAC Museum, Baldonnel
	218	Fouga CM170R Super Magister	Shannon Aerospace, Shannon Airport
	219	Fouga CM170R Super Magister	IAC Museum, Baldonnel
	220	Fouga CM170R Super Magister	Cork University, instructional use
	221	Fouga CM170R Super Magister [3-KE]	IAC Museum, stored Baldonnel
	231	SIAI SF-260WE Warrior	IAC Museum, Baldonnel
	240	Beech Super King Air 200MR	IAC No 102 Sqn/1 Operations Wing, Baldonnel
	251	Grumman G1159C Gulfstream IV (N17584)	IAC No 102 Sqn/1 Operations Wing, Baldonnel
	252	Airtech CN.235 MPA Persuader	IAC No 101 Sqn/1 Operations Wing, Baldonnel
	253	Airtech CN.235 MPA Persuader	IAC No 101 Sqn/1 Operations Wing, Baldonnel
	254	PBN-2T Defender 4000 (G-BWPN)	IAC No 106 Sqn/1 Operations Wing, Baldonnel
	256	Eurocopter EC135T-1 (G-BZRM)	IAC No 106 Sqn/1 Operations Wing, Baldonnel
	258	Gates Learjet 45 (N5009T)	IAC No 102 Sqn/1 Operations Wing, Baldonnel
	260	Pilatus PC-9M (HB-HQS)	IAC Flying Training School, Baldonnel
	261	Pilatus PC-9M (HB-HQT)	IAC Flying Training School, Baldonnel
	262	Pilatus PC-9M (HB-HQU)	IAC Flying Training School, Baldonnel
	263	Pilatus PC-9M (HB-HQV)	IAC Flying Training School, Baldonnel
	264	Pilatus PC-9M (HB-HQW)	IAC Flying Training School, Baldonnel
	266	Pilatus PC-9M (HB-HQY)	IAC Flying Training School, Baldonnel
	267	Pilatus PC-9M (HB-HQZ)	IAC Flying Training School, Baldonnel
	269	Pilatus PC-9M (HB-HXI)	IAC Flying Training School, Baldonnel
	270	Eurocopter EC135P-2 (D-HECF)	IAC No 302 Sqn/3 Operations Wing, Baldonnel
	271	Eurocopter EC135P-2 (D-HECB)	IAC No 302 Sqn/3 Operations Wing, Baldonnel
	272	Eurocopter EC135T-2 (G-CECT)	IAC No 106 Sqn/1 Operations Wing, Baldonnel
	274	AgustaWestland AW139	IAC No 301 Sqn/3 Operations Wing, Baldonnel
	275	AgustaWestland AW139	IAC No 301 Sqn/3 Operations Wing, Baldonnel
	276	AgustaWestland AW139	IAC No 301 Sqn/3 Operations Wing, Baldonnel
	277	AgustaWestland AW139	IAC No 301 Sqn/3 Operations Wing, Baldonnel
	278	AgustaWestland AW139	IAC No 301 Sqn/3 Operations Wing, Baldonnel
	279	AgustaWestland AW139	IAC No 301 Sqn/3 Operations Wing, Baldonnel
	2..	Pilatus PC.XII/47	IAC (on order)
	2..	Pilatus PC.XII/47	IAC (on order)
	2..	Pilatus PC.XII/47	IAC (on order)

rial	Type (code/other identity)	Owner/operator, location or fate	Notes

craft included in this section include those likely to be seen visiting UK civil and military airfields on transport flights, exchange visits, ercises and for air shows. It is not a comprehensive list of *all* aircraft operated by the air arms concerned.

ALGERIA

Ministry of Defence

-VPC	Grumman G.1159C Gulfstream IVSP (1418)	Ministry of Defence, Boufarik	
-VPG	Gulfstream Aerospace Gulfstream V (617)	Ministry of Defence, Boufarik	
-VPM	Grumman G.1159C Gulfstream IVSP (1421)	Ministry of Defence, Boufarik	
-VPP	Airbus A.340-541	Ministry of Defence, Boufarik	
-VPR	Grumman G.1159C Gulfstream IVSP (1288)	Ministry of Defence, Boufarik	
-VPS	Grumman G.1159C Gulfstream IVSP (1291)	Ministry of Defence, Boufarik	

Force Aérienne Algérienne (FAA)/Al Quwwat al Jawwiya al Jaza'eriya

-WHA	Lockheed C-130H-30 Hercules (4997)	FAA 2 ETTL, Boufarik	
-WHB	Lockheed C-130H-30 Hercules (5224)	FAA 2 ETTL, Boufarik	
-WHD	Lockheed C-130H-30 Hercules (4987)	FAA 2 ETTL, Boufarik	
-WHE	Lockheed C-130H Hercules (4935)	FAA 2 ETTL, Boufarik	
-WHF	Lockheed C-130H Hercules (4934)	FAA 2 ETTL, Boufarik	
-WHI	Lockheed C-130H Hercules (4930)	FAA 2 ETTL, Boufarik	
-WHJ	Lockheed C-130H Hercules (4928)	FAA 2 ETTL, Boufarik	
-WHL	Lockheed C-130H-30 Hercules (4989)	FAA 2 ETTL, Boufarik	
-WHN	Lockheed C-130H-30 Hercules (4894)	FAA 2 ETTL, Boufarik	
-WHO	Lockheed C-130H-30 Hercules (4897)	FAA 2 ETTL, Boufarik	
-WHP	Lockheed C-130H-30 Hercules (4921)	FAA 2 ETTL, Boufarik	
-WHQ	Lockheed C-130H Hercules (4926)	FAA 2 ETTL, Boufarik	
-WHR	Lockheed C-130H Hercules (4924)	FAA 2 ETTL, Boufarik	
-WHS	Lockheed C-130H Hercules (4912)	FAA 2 ETTL, Boufarik	
-WHT	Lockheed C-130H Hercules (4911)	FAA 2 ETTL, Boufarik	
-WHY	Lockheed C-130H Hercules (4913)	FAA 2 ETTL, Boufarik	
-WHZ	Lockheed C-130H Hercules (4914)	FAA 2 ETTL, Boufarik	
-WIA	Ilyushin Il-76MD	FAA 347 ETS, Boufarik	
-WIB	Ilyushin Il-76MD	FAA 347 ETS, Boufarik	
-WIC	Ilyushin Il-76MD	FAA 347 ETS, Boufarik	
-WID	Ilyushin Il-76TD	FAA 347 ETS, Boufarik	
-WIE	Ilyushin Il-76TD	FAA 347 ETS, Boufarik	
-WIF	Ilyushin Il-78	FAA 357 ERV, Boufarik	
-WIG	Ilyushin Il-76TD	FAA 347 ETS, Boufarik	
-WIL	Ilyushin Il-78	FAA 357 ERV, Boufarik	
-WIM	Ilyushin Il-76TD	FAA 347 ETS, Boufarik	
-WIN	Ilyushin Il-78	FAA 357 ERV, Boufarik	
-WIP	Ilyushin Il-76TD	FAA 347 ETS, Boufarik	
-WIQ	Ilyushin Il-78	FAA 357 ERV, Boufarik	
-WIR	Ilyushin Il-76TD	FAA 347 ETS, Boufarik	
-WIS	Ilyushin Il-78	FAA 357 ERV, Boufarik	
-WIT	Ilyushin Il-76TD	FAA 347 ETS, Boufarik	
-WIU	Ilyushin Il-76TD	FAA 347 ETS, Boufarik	
-WIV	Ilyushin Il-76TD	FAA 347 ETS, Boufarik	

ANGOLA

?-ANG	Bombardier Global 5000	Angola Government, Luanda	

ARMENIA

1	Airbus A.319CJ-132	Armenian Government, Yerevan	

AUSTRALIA

Royal Australian Air Force (RAAF)

?-656	Lockheed AP-3C Orion	RAAF 10 Sqn/92 Wing, Edinburgh, NSW	
-657	Lockheed EAP-3C Orion	RAAF 10 Sqn/92 Wing, Edinburgh, NSW	
-658	Lockheed AP-3C Orion	*Withdrawn from use, 2016*	
?-659	Lockheed AP-3C Orion	RAAF 10 Sqn/92 Wing, Edinburgh, NSW	
-660	Lockheed EAP-3C Orion	RAAF 10 Sqn/92 Wing, Edinburgh, NSW	
-661	Lockheed AP-3C Orion	RAAF 10 Sqn/92 Wing, Edinburgh, NSW	
?-662	Lockheed AP-3C Orion	RAAF 10 Sqn/92 Wing, Edinburgh, NSW	

Notes	Serial	Type (code/other identity)	Owner/operator, location or fate
	A9-664	Lockheed AP-3C Orion $	RAAF 10 Sqn/92 Wing, Edinburgh, NSW
	A9-665	Lockheed AP-3C Orion	RAAF 10 Sqn/92 Wing, Edinburgh, NSW
	A9-751	Lockheed AP-3C Orion	*Withdrawn from use, 16 November 2017*
	A9-752	Lockheed AP-3C Orion	RAAF 1 Sqn/92 Wing, Edinburgh, NSW
	A9-753	Lockheed AP-3C Orion	*Withdrawn from use, 3 November 2017*
	A9-757	Lockheed AP-3C Orion	RAAF 10 Sqn/92 Wing, Edinburgh, NSW
	A9-759	Lockheed AP-3C Orion	RAAF 10 Sqn/92 Wing, Edinburgh, NSW
	A9-760	Lockheed AP-3C Orion	RAAF 10 Sqn/92 Wing, Edinburgh, NSW
	A30-001	Boeing E-7A Wedgetail (737-7ES)	RAAF 2 Sqn/41 Wing, Canberra, ACT
	A30-002	Boeing E-7A Wedgetail (737-7ES)	RAAF 2 Sqn/41 Wing, Canberra, ACT
	A30-003	Boeing E-7A Wedgetail (737-7ES)	RAAF 2 Sqn/41 Wing, Canberra, ACT
	A30-004	Boeing E-7A Wedgetail (737-7ES)	RAAF 2 Sqn/41 Wing, Canberra, ACT
	A30-005	Boeing E-7A Wedgetail (737-7ES)	RAAF 2 Sqn/41 Wing, Canberra, ACT
	A30-006	Boeing E-7A Wedgetail (737-7ES)	RAAF 2 Sqn/41 Wing, Canberra, ACT
	A36-001	Boeing 737-7DT	RAAF 34 Sqn/84 Wing, Canberra, ACT
	A36-002	Boeing 737-7DF	RAAF 34 Sqn/84 Wing, Canberra, ACT
	A37-001	Canadair CL.604 Challenger	RAAF 34 Sqn/84 Wing, Canberra, ACT
	A37-002	Canadair CL.604 Challenger	RAAF 34 Sqn/84 Wing, Canberra, ACT
	A37-003	Canadair CL.604 Challenger	RAAF 34 Sqn/84 Wing, Canberra, ACT
	A39-001	Airbus KC-30A (A.330-203 MRTT)	RAAF 33 Sqn/84 Wing, Amberley, Queenslan
	A39-002	Airbus KC-30A (A.330-203 MRTT)	RAAF 33 Sqn/84 Wing, Amberley, Queenslan
	A39-003	Airbus KC-30A (A.330-203 MRTT)	RAAF 33 Sqn/84 Wing, Amberley, Queenslan
	A39-004	Airbus KC-30A (A.330-203 MRTT)	RAAF 33 Sqn/84 Wing, Amberley, Queenslan
	A39-005	Airbus KC-30A (A.330-203 MRTT)	RAAF 33 Sqn/84 Wing, Amberley, Queenslan
	A39-006	Airbus KC-30A (A.330-203 MRTT) (VH-EBH)	RAAF 33 Sqn/84 Wing, Amberley, Queenslan
	A39-007	Airbus KC-30A (A.330-203 MRTT) (VH-EBI)	Airbus, Getafe (on order)
	A41-206	Boeing C-17A Globemaster III (06-0206)	RAAF 36 Sqn/86 Wing, Amberley, Queenslan
	A41-207	Boeing C-17A Globemaster III (06-0207)	RAAF 36 Sqn/86 Wing, Amberley, Queenslan
	A41-208	Boeing C-17A Globemaster III (06-0208)	RAAF 36 Sqn/86 Wing, Amberley, Queenslan
	A41-209	Boeing C-17A Globemaster III (06-0209)	RAAF 36 Sqn/86 Wing, Amberley, Queenslan
	A41-210	Boeing C-17A Globemaster III (11-0210)	RAAF 36 Sqn/86 Wing, Amberley, Queenslan
	A41-211	Boeing C-17A Globemaster III (12-0211)	RAAF 36 Sqn/86 Wing, Amberley, Queenslan
	A41-212	Boeing C-17A Globemaster III (14-0001)	RAAF 36 Sqn/86 Wing, Amberley, Queenslan
	A41-213	Boeing C-17A Globemaster III (14-0002)	RAAF 36 Sqn/86 Wing, Amberley, Queenslan
	A47-001	Boeing P-8A Poseidon (N940DS)	RAAF 11 Sqn/92 Wing, Edinburgh, NSW
	A47-002	Boeing P-8A Poseidon (N956DS)	RAAF 11 Sqn/92 Wing, Edinburgh, NSW
	A47-003	Boeing P-8A Poseidon (N959DS)	RAAF 11 Sqn/92 Wing, Edinburgh, NSW
	A47-004	Boeing P-8A Poseidon (N974DS)	RAAF 11 Sqn/92 Wing, Edinburgh, NSW
	A47-005	Boeing P-8A Poseidon (N832DS)	RAAF 11 Sqn/92 Wing, Edinburgh, NSW
	A47-006	Boeing P-8A Poseidon (N849DS)	RAAF 11 Sqn/92 Wing, Edinburgh, NSW
	A47-007	Boeing P-8A Poseidon	RAAF (on order)
	A47-008	Boeing P-8A Poseidon	RAAF (on order)
	A47-009	Boeing P-8A Poseidon	RAAF (on order)
	A47-010	Boeing P-8A Poseidon	RAAF (on order)
	A47-011	Boeing P-8A Poseidon	RAAF (on order)
	A47-012	Boeing P-8A Poseidon	RAAF (on order)
	A97-440	Lockheed C-130J-30 Hercules II	RAAF 37 Sqn/86 Wing, Richmond, NSW
	A97-441	Lockheed C-130J-30 Hercules II	RAAF 37 Sqn/86 Wing, Richmond, NSW
	A97-442	Lockheed C-130J-30 Hercules II	RAAF 37 Sqn/86 Wing, Richmond, NSW
	A97-447	Lockheed C-130J-30 Hercules II	RAAF 37 Sqn/86 Wing, Richmond, NSW
	A97-448	Lockheed C-130J-30 Hercules II	RAAF 37 Sqn/86 Wing, Richmond, NSW
	A97-449	Lockheed C-130J-30 Hercules II	RAAF 37 Sqn/86 Wing, Richmond, NSW
	A97-450	Lockheed C-130J-30 Hercules II	RAAF 37 Sqn/86 Wing, Richmond, NSW
	A97-464	Lockheed C-130J-30 Hercules II	RAAF 37 Sqn/86 Wing, Richmond, NSW
	A97-465	Lockheed C-130J-30 Hercules II	RAAF 37 Sqn/86 Wing, Richmond, NSW
	A97-466	Lockheed C-130J-30 Hercules II	RAAF 37 Sqn/86 Wing, Richmond, NSW
	A97-467	Lockheed C-130J-30 Hercules II	RAAF 37 Sqn/86 Wing, Richmond, NSW
	A97-468	Lockheed C-130J-30 Hercules II	RAAF 37 Sqn/86 Wing, Richmond, NSW

AUSTRIA
Öesterreichische Luftstreitkräfte (OL)

	3C-OA	Bell OH-58B Kiowa	OL Mehrzweckhubschrauberstaffel, Tulln

ial	Type (code/other identity)	Owner/operator, location or fate	Notes
OB	Bell OH-58B Kiowa	OL Mehrzweckhubschrauberstaffel, Tulln	
OC	Bell OH-58B Kiowa	OL Mehrzweckhubschrauberstaffel, Tulln	
OD	Bell OH-58B Kiowa	OL Mehrzweckhubschrauberstaffel, Tulln	
OE	Bell OH-58B Kiowa	OL Mehrzweckhubschrauberstaffel, Tulln	
OH	Bell OH-58B Kiowa	OL Mehrzweckhubschrauberstaffel, Tulln	
OI	Bell OH-58B Kiowa	OL Mehrzweckhubschrauberstaffel, Tulln	
OJ	Bell OH-58B Kiowa	OL Mehrzweckhubschrauberstaffel, Tulln	
OK	Bell OH-58B Kiowa $	OL Mehrzweckhubschrauberstaffel, Tulln	
OL	Bell OH-58B Kiowa	OL Mehrzweckhubschrauberstaffel, Tulln	
EB	Pilatus PC-6B/B2-H2 Turbo Porter	OL leichte Lufttransportstaffel, Tulln	
ED	Pilatus PC-6B/B2-H2 Turbo Porter	OL leichte Lufttransportstaffel, Tulln	
EE	Pilatus PC-6B/B2-H2 Turbo Porter	OL leichte Lufttransportstaffel, Tulln	
EF	Pilatus PC-6B/B2-H2 Turbo Porter	OL leichte Lufttransportstaffel, Tulln	
EG	Pilatus PC-6B/B2-H2 Turbo Porter	OL leichte Lufttransportstaffel, Tulln	
EH	Pilatus PC-6B/B2-H2 Turbo Porter	OL leichte Lufttransportstaffel, Tulln	
EL	Pilatus PC-6B/B2-H2 Turbo Porter	OL leichte Lufttransportstaffel, Tulln	
EN	Pilatus PC-6B/B2-H4 Turbo Porter $	OL leichte Lufttransportstaffel, Tulln	
FA	Pilatus PC-7 Turbo Trainer	OL Lehrabteilung Fläche, Zeltweg	
FB	Pilatus PC-7 Turbo Trainer	OL Lehrabteilung Fläche, Zeltweg	
FC	Pilatus PC-7 Turbo Trainer $	OL Lehrabteilung Fläche, Zeltweg	
FD	Pilatus PC-7 Turbo Trainer	OL Lehrabteilung Fläche, Zeltweg	
FE	Pilatus PC-7 Turbo Trainer	OL Lehrabteilung Fläche, Zeltweg	
FF	Pilatus PC-7 Turbo Trainer	OL Lehrabteilung Fläche, Zeltweg	
FG	Pilatus PC-7 Turbo Trainer $	OL Lehrabteilung Fläche, Zeltweg	
FH	Pilatus PC-7 Turbo Trainer	OL Lehrabteilung Fläche, Zeltweg	
FJ	Pilatus PC-7 Turbo Trainer	OL Lehrabteilung Fläche, Zeltweg	
FK	Pilatus PC-7 Turbo Trainer	OL Lehrabteilung Fläche, Zeltweg	
FL	Pilatus PC-7 Turbo Trainer	OL Lehrabteilung Fläche, Zeltweg	
FM	Pilatus PC-7 Turbo Trainer	OL Lehrabteilung Fläche, Zeltweg	
FO	Pilatus PC-7 Turbo Trainer	OL Lehrabteilung Fläche, Zeltweg	
HB	Agusta-Bell AB.212	OL 1 Staffel/2 Staffel ITHSSta, Linz	
HC	Agusta-Bell AB.212	OL 1 Staffel/2 Staffel ITHSSta, Linz	
HD	Agusta-Bell AB.212	OL 1 Staffel/2 Staffel ITHSSta, Linz	
HF	Agusta-Bell AB.212	OL 1 Staffel/2 Staffel ITHSSta, Linz	
HG	Agusta-Bell AB.212	OL 1 Staffel/2 Staffel ITHSSta, Linz	
HH	Agusta-Bell AB.212	OL 1 Staffel/2 Staffel ITHSSta, Linz	
HI	Agusta-Bell AB.212	OL 1 Staffel/2 Staffel ITHSSta, Linz	
HJ	Agusta-Bell AB.212	OL 1 Staffel/2 Staffel ITHSSta, Linz	
HK	Agusta-Bell AB.212	OL 1 Staffel/2 Staffel ITHSSta, Linz	
HL	Agusta-Bell AB.212	OL 1 Staffel/2 Staffel ITHSSta, Linz	
HN	Agusta-Bell AB.212	OL 1 Staffel/2 Staffel ITHSSta, Linz	
HO	Agusta-Bell AB.212	OL 1 Staffel/2 Staffel ITHSSta, Linz	
HP	Agusta-Bell AB.212	OL 1 Staffel/2 Staffel ITHSSta, Linz	
HQ	Agusta-Bell AB.212	OL 1 Staffel/2 Staffel ITHSSta, Linz	
HR	Agusta-Bell AB.212	OL 1 Staffel/2 Staffel ITHSSta, Linz	
HS	Agusta-Bell AB.212	OL 1 Staffel/2 Staffel ITHSSta, Linz	
HT	Agusta-Bell AB.212	OL 1 Staffel/2 Staffel ITHSSta, Linz	
HU	Agusta-Bell AB.212	OL 1 Staffel/2 Staffel ITHSSta, Linz	
HV	Agusta-Bell AB.212	OL 1 Staffel/2 Staffel ITHSSta, Linz	
HW	Agusta-Bell AB.212	OL 1 Staffel/2 Staffel ITHSSta, Linz	
HX	Agusta-Bell AB.212	OL 1 Staffel/2 Staffel ITHSSta, Linz	
HY	Bell 212	OL 1 Staffel/2 Staffel ITHSSta, Linz	
HZ	Agusta-Bell AB.212 $	OL 1 Staffel/2 Staffel ITHSSta, Linz	
BA	Sikorsky S-70A	OL mittlere Transporthubschrauberstaffel, Tulln	
BB	Sikorsky S-70A	OL mittlere Transporthubschrauberstaffel, Tulln	
BC	Sikorsky S-70A	OL mittlere Transporthubschrauberstaffel, Tulln	
BD	Sikorsky S-70A	OL mittlere Transporthubschrauberstaffel, Tulln	
BE	Sikorsky S-70A	OL mittlere Transporthubschrauberstaffel, Tulln	
BF	Sikorsky S-70A	OL mittlere Transporthubschrauberstaffel, Tulln	
BG	Sikorsky S-70A	OL mittlere Transporthubschrauberstaffel, Tulln	
BH	Sikorsky S-70A	OL mittlere Transporthubschrauberstaffel, Tulln	
BI	Sikorsky S-70A	OL mittlere Transporthubschrauberstaffel, Tulln	

Notes	Serial	Type (code/other identity)	Owner/operator, location or fate
	7L-WA	Eurofighter EF.2000	OL 1 Staffel/2 Staffel Überwg, Zeltweg
	7L-WB	Eurofighter EF.2000	OL 1 Staffel/2 Staffel Überwg, Zeltweg
	7L-WC	Eurofighter EF.2000 $	OL 1 Staffel/2 Staffel Überwg, Zeltweg
	7L-WD	Eurofighter EF.2000	OL 1 Staffel/2 Staffel Überwg, Zeltweg
	7L-WE	Eurofighter EF.2000	OL 1 Staffel/2 Staffel Überwg, Zeltweg
	7L-WF	Eurofighter EF.2000	OL 1 Staffel/2 Staffel Überwg, Zeltweg
	7L-WG	Eurofighter EF.2000	OL 1 Staffel/2 Staffel Überwg, Zeltweg
	7L-WH	Eurofighter EF.2000	OL 1 Staffel/2 Staffel Überwg, Zeltweg
	7L-WI	Eurofighter EF.2000	OL 1 Staffel/2 Staffel Überwg, Zeltweg
	7L-WJ	Eurofighter EF.2000	OL 1 Staffel/2 Staffel Überwg, Zeltweg
	7L-WK	Eurofighter EF.2000	OL 1 Staffel/2 Staffel Überwg, Zeltweg
	7L-WL	Eurofighter EF.2000	OL 1 Staffel/2 Staffel Überwg, Zeltweg
	7L-WM	Eurofighter EF.2000	OL 1 Staffel/2 Staffel Überwg, Zeltweg
	7L-WN	Eurofighter EF.2000	OL 1 Staffel/2 Staffel Überwg, Zeltweg
	7L-WO	Eurofighter EF.2000	OL 1 Staffel/2 Staffel Überwg, Zeltweg
	8T-CA	Lockheed C-130K Hercules	OL Lufttransportstaffel, Linz
	8T-CB	Lockheed C-130K Hercules	OL Lufttransportstaffel, Linz
	8T-CC	Lockheed C-130K Hercules	OL Lufttransportstaffel, Linz
	BA-31	SAAB 105ÖE [blue A]	OL Düsentrainerstaffel Überwg, Linz
	BE-35	SAAB 105ÖE [blue E]	OL Düsentrainerstaffel Überwg, Linz
	BF-36	SAAB 105ÖE [blue F]	OL Düsentrainerstaffel Überwg, Linz
	BG-37	SAAB 105ÖE [blue G]	OL Düsentrainerstaffel Überwg, Linz
	BI-39	SAAB 105ÖE [blue I]	OL, stored Linz
	BJ-40	SAAB 105ÖE [blue J]	OL Düsentrainerstaffel Überwg, Linz
	GD-14	SAAB 105ÖE [green D] $	OL Düsentrainerstaffel Überwg, Linz
	GG-17	SAAB 105ÖE [green G]	OL Düsentrainerstaffel Überwg, Linz
	RB-22	SAAB 105ÖE [red B]	OL Düsentrainerstaffel Überwg, Linz
	RC-23	SAAB 105ÖE [red C]	OL Düsentrainerstaffel Überwg, Linz
	RD-24	SAAB 105ÖE [red D]	OL Düsentrainerstaffel Überwg, Linz
	RE-25	SAAB 105ÖE [red E] $	OL Düsentrainerstaffel Überwg, Linz
	RF-26	SAAB 105ÖE [red F] $	OL Düsentrainerstaffel Überwg, Linz
	RG-27	SAAB 105ÖE [red G]	OL Düsentrainerstaffel Überwg, Linz
	RH-28	SAAB 105ÖE [red H]	OL Düsentrainerstaffel Überwg, Linz
	RI-29	SAAB 105ÖE [red I]	OL Düsentrainerstaffel Überwg, Linz
	RJ-30	SAAB 105ÖE [red J]	OL Düsentrainerstaffel Überwg, Linz
	YI-09	SAAB 105ÖE [yellow I]	OL Düsentrainerstaffel Überwg, Linz
	YJ-10	SAAB 105ÖE [yellow J]	OL Düsentrainerstaffel Überwg, Linz

AZERBAIJAN

	4K-AI01	Boeing 767-32LER	Azerbaijan Government, Baku
	4K-AI02	Airbus A.319-115LR	Azerbaijan Government, Baku
	4K-AI88	Gulfstream Aerospace G.650	Azerbaijan Government, Baku

BAHRAIN

	A9C-AWL	BAE RJ.100	Royal Bahraini Air Force
	A9C-BAH	Gulfstream Aerospace G.650	Bahrain Royal Flight
	A9C-BDF	BAE RJ.100	Royal Bahraini Air Force
	A9C-BG	Grumman G.1159 Gulfstream IITT	Bahrain Royal Flight
	A9C-BHR	Gulfstream Aerospace G.450	Bahrain Royal Flight
	A9C-BRF	Grumman G.1159C Gulfstream IV-SP	Bahrain Royal Flight
	A9C-BRN	Gulfstream Aerospace G.550	Bahrain Royal Flight
	A9C-HAK	Boeing 747SP-Z5	Bahrain Royal Flight
	A9C-HMH	Boeing 767-4FSER	Bahrain Royal Flight
	A9C-HMK	Boeing 747-4P8	Bahrain Royal Flight
	A9C-HWR	BAE RJ.85	Royal Bahraini Air Force
	A9C-ISA	Boeing 737-86J	Bahrain Royal Flight

BELGIUM

Force Aérienne Belge (FAB)/Belgische Luchtmacht: Composante Aérienne Belge/Belgische Luchtcomponent

	AT-01	D-BD Alpha Jet 1B+	FAB 11 Sm (1 Wg), Cazaux, France (ET 02.00
	AT-02	D-BD Alpha Jet 1B+	FAB 11 Sm (1 Wg), Cazaux, France (ET 02.00
	AT-03	D-BD Alpha Jet 1B+	FAB 11 Sm (1 Wg), Cazaux, France (ET 02.00

rial	Type (code/other identity)	Owner/operator, location or fate	Notes
-05	D-BD Alpha Jet 1B+	FAB 11 Sm (1 Wg), Cazaux, France (ET 02.008)	
-06	D-BD Alpha Jet 1B+	FAB 11 Sm (1 Wg), Cazaux, France (ET 02.008)	
-08	D-BD Alpha Jet 1B+	FAB 11 Sm (1 Wg), Cazaux, France (ET 02.008)	
-10	D-BD Alpha Jet 1B+	FAB 11 Sm (1 Wg), Cazaux, France (ET 02.008)	
-11	D-BD Alpha Jet 1B+	FAB 11 Sm (1 Wg), Cazaux, France (ET 02.008)	
-12	D-BD Alpha Jet 1B+	FAB 11 Sm (1 Wg), Cazaux, France (ET 02.008)	
-13	D-BD Alpha Jet 1B+	FAB 11 Sm (1 Wg), Cazaux, France (ET 02.008)	
-14	D-BD Alpha Jet 1B+	FAB 11 Sm (1 Wg), Cazaux, France (ET 02.008)	
-15	D-BD Alpha Jet 1B+	FAB 11 Sm (1 Wg), Cazaux, France (ET 02.008)	
-17	D-BD Alpha Jet 1B+	FAB 11 Sm (1 Wg), Cazaux, France (ET 02.008)	
-18	D-BD Alpha Jet 1B+	FAB 11 Sm (1 Wg), Cazaux, France (ET 02.008)	
-19	D-BD Alpha Jet 1B+	FAB 11 Sm (1 Wg), Cazaux, France (ET 02.008)	
-20	D-BD Alpha Jet 1B+	FAB 11 Sm (1 Wg), Cazaux, France (ET 02.008)	
-21	D-BD Alpha Jet 1B+	*Withdrawn from use, October 2016*	
-22	D-BD Alpha Jet 1B+	FAB 11 Sm (1 Wg), Cazaux, France (ET 02.008)	
-23	D-BD Alpha Jet 1B+	FAB 11 Sm (1 Wg), Cazaux, France (ET 02.008)	
-24	D-BD Alpha Jet 1B+	FAB 11 Sm (1 Wg), Cazaux, France (ET 02.008)	
-25	D-BD Alpha Jet 1B+	FAB 11 Sm (1 Wg), Cazaux, France (ET 02.008)	
-26	D-BD Alpha Jet 1B+	FAB 11 Sm (1 Wg), Cazaux, France (ET 02.008)	
-27	D-BD Alpha Jet 1B+	FAB 11 Sm (1 Wg), Cazaux, France (ET 02.008)	
-28	D-BD Alpha Jet 1B+	FAB 11 Sm (1 Wg), Cazaux, France (ET 02.008)	
-29	D-BD Alpha Jet 1B+ $	FAB 11 Sm (1 Wg), Cazaux, France (ET 02.008)	
-30	D-BD Alpha Jet 1B+	FAB 11 Sm (1 Wg), Cazaux, France (ET 02.008)	
-31	D-BD Alpha Jet 1B+	FAB 11 Sm (1 Wg), Cazaux, France (ET 02.008)	
-32	D-BD Alpha Jet 1B+ $	FAB 11 Sm (1 Wg), Cazaux, France (ET 02.008)	
-33	D-BD Alpha Jet 1B+ $	FAB 11 Sm (1 Wg), Cazaux, France (ET 02.008)	
)-01	Dassault Falcon 900B	FAB 21 Smaldeel (15 Wg), Brussels/Melsbroek	
E-01	Embraer ERJ.135LR	FAB 21 Smaldeel (15 Wg), Brussels/Melsbroek	
E-02	Embraer ERJ.135LR	FAB 21 Smaldeel (15 Wg), Brussels/Melsbroek	
E-03	Embraer ERJ.145LR $	FAB 21 Smaldeel (15 Wg), Brussels/Melsbroek	
E-04	Embraer ERJ.145LR $	FAB 21 Smaldeel (15 Wg), Brussels/Melsbroek	
H-01	Lockheed C-130H Hercules	FAB 20 Smaldeel (15 Wg), Brussels/Melsbroek	
H-03	Lockheed C-130H Hercules	FAB 20 Smaldeel (15 Wg), Brussels/Melsbroek	
H-04	Lockheed C-130H Hercules	FAB 20 Smaldeel (15 Wg), Brussels/Melsbroek	
H-05	Lockheed C-130H Hercules	FAB 20 Smaldeel (15 Wg), Brussels/Melsbroek	
H-07	Lockheed C-130H Hercules $	FAB 20 Smaldeel (15 Wg), Brussels/Melsbroek	
H-08	Lockheed C-130H Hercules	*Withdrawn from use, December 2017*	
H-09	Lockheed C-130H Hercules	FAB 20 Smaldeel (15 Wg), Brussels/Melsbroek	
H-10	Lockheed C-130H Hercules	FAB 20 Smaldeel (15 Wg), Brussels/Melsbroek	
H-11	Lockheed C-130H Hercules	FAB 20 Smaldeel (15 Wg), Brussels/Melsbroek	
H-12	Lockheed C-130H Hercules	FAB 20 Smaldeel (15 Wg), Brussels/Melsbroek	
H-13	Lockheed C-130H Hercules $	FAB 20 Smaldeel (15 Wg), Brussels/Melsbroek	
a-56	SABCA (GD) F-16A MLU Fighting Falcon	FAB 31 Sm/349 Sm/OCU (10 Wg), Kleine-Brogel	
a-57	SABCA (GD) F-16A MLU Fighting Falcon	FAB 1 Sm/350 Sm (2 Wg), Florennes	
-67	SABCA (GD) F-16A MLU Fighting Falcon	FAB 1 Sm/350 Sm (2 Wg), Florennes	
a-68	SABCA (GD) F-16A MLU Fighting Falcon $	FAB 1 Sm/350 Sm (2 Wg), Florennes	
a-69	SABCA (GD) F-16A MLU Fighting Falcon	FAB 31 Sm/349 Sm/OCU (10 Wg), Kleine-Brogel	
-70	SABCA (GD) F-16A MLU Fighting Falcon	FAB 31 Sm/349 Sm/OCU (10 Wg), Kleine-Brogel	
a-71	SABCA (GD) F-16A MLU Fighting Falcon	FAB 1 Sm/350 Sm (2 Wg), Florennes	
a-72	SABCA (GD) F-16A MLU Fighting Falcon	FAB 1 Sm/350 Sm (2 Wg), Florennes	
-77	SABCA (GD) F-16A MLU Fighting Falcon $	FAB 31 Sm/349 Sm/OCU (10 Wg), Kleine-Brogel	
a-81	SABCA (GD) F-16A MLU Fighting Falcon	FAB 31 Sm/349 Sm/OCU (10 Wg), Kleine-Brogel	
a-82	SABCA (GD) F-16A MLU Fighting Falcon	FAB 31 Sm/349 Sm/OCU (10 Wg), Kleine-Brogel	
-83	SABCA (GD) F-16A MLU Fighting Falcon	FAB 1 Sm/350 Sm (2 Wg), Florennes	
a-84	SABCA (GD) F-16A MLU Fighting Falcon $	FAB 1 Sm/350 Sm (2 Wg), Florennes	
a-86	SABCA (GD) F-16A MLU Fighting Falcon	FAB 31 Sm/349 Sm/OCU (10 Wg), Kleine-Brogel	
a-87	SABCA (GD) F-16A MLU Fighting Falcon	FAB 31 Sm/349 Sm/OCU (10 Wg), Kleine-Brogel	
-89	SABCA (GD) F-16A MLU Fighting Falcon	FAB 1 Sm/350 Sm (2 Wg), Florennes	
a-91	SABCA (GD) F-16A MLU Fighting Falcon	FAB 31 Sm/349 Sm/OCU (10 Wg), Kleine-Brogel	
a-92	SABCA (GD) F-16A MLU Fighting Falcon	FAB 1 Sm/350 Sm (2 Wg), Florennes	
a-94	SABCA (GD) F-16A MLU Fighting Falcon	FAB 31 Sm/349 Sm/OCU (10 Wg), Kleine-Brogel	
a-95	SABCA (GD) F-16A MLU Fighting Falcon	FAB 31 Sm/349 Sm/OCU (10 Wg), Kleine-Brogel	

Notes	Serial	Type (code/other identity)	Owner/operator, location or fate
	FA-97	SABCA (GD) F-16A MLU Fighting Falcon	FAB 31 Sm/349 Sm/OCU (10 Wg), Kleine-Bro
	FA-98	SABCA (GD) F-16A MLU Fighting Falcon	FAB 1 Sm/350 Sm (2 Wg), Florennes
	FA-101	SABCA (GD) F-16A MLU Fighting Falcon $	FAB 31 Sm/349 Sm/OCU (10 Wg), Kleine-Bro
	FA-102	SABCA (GD) F-16A MLU Fighting Falcon	FAB 31 Sm/349 Sm/OCU (10 Wg), Kleine-Bro
	FA-103	SABCA (GD) F-16A MLU Fighting Falcon	FAB 31 Sm/349 Sm/OCU (10 Wg), Kleine-Bro
	FA-104	SABCA (GD) F-16A MLU Fighting Falcon $	FAB 31 Sm/349 Sm/OCU (10 Wg), Kleine-Bro
	FA-106	SABCA (GD) F-16A MLU Fighting Falcon $	FAB 31 Sm/349 Sm/OCU (10 Wg), Kleine-Bro
	FA-107	SABCA (GD) F-16A MLU Fighting Falcon	FAB 31 Sm/349 Sm/OCU (10 Wg), Kleine-Bro
	FA-109	SABCA (GD) F-16A MLU Fighting Falcon	FAB 1 Sm/350 Sm (2 Wg), Florennes
	FA-110	SABCA (GD) F-16A MLU Fighting Falcon	FAB 31 Sm/349 Sm/OCU (10 Wg), Kleine-Bro
	FA-114	SABCA (GD) F-16A MLU Fighting Falcon	FAB 31 Sm/349 Sm/OCU (10 Wg), Kleine-Bro
	FA-116	SABCA (GD) F-16A MLU Fighting Falcon	FAB 1 Sm/350 Sm (2 Wg), Florennes
	FA-117	SABCA (GD) F-16A MLU Fighting Falcon	FAB 1 Sm/350 Sm (2 Wg), Florennes
	FA-118	SABCA (GD) F-16A MLU Fighting Falcon	FAB 31 Sm/349 Sm/OCU (10 Wg), Kleine-Bro
	FA-119	SABCA (GD) F-16A MLU Fighting Falcon	FAB 31 Sm/349 Sm/OCU (10 Wg), Kleine-Bro
	FA-121	SABCA (GD) F-16A MLU Fighting Falcon	FAB 1 Sm/350 Sm (2 Wg), Florennes
	FA-123	SABCA (GD) F-16A MLU Fighting Falcon	FAB 31 Sm/349 Sm/OCU (10 Wg), Kleine-Bro
	FA-124	SABCA (GD) F-16A MLU Fighting Falcon	FAB 31 Sm/349 Sm/OCU (10 Wg), Kleine-Bro
	FA-126	SABCA (GD) F-16A MLU Fighting Falcon	FAB 1 Sm/350 Sm (2 Wg), Florennes
	FA-127	SABCA (GD) F-16A MLU Fighting Falcon	FAB 1 Sm/350 Sm (2 Wg), Florennes
	FA-128	SABCA (GD) F-16A MLU Fighting Falcon	FAB 1 Sm/350 Sm (2 Wg), Florennes
	FA-129	SABCA (GD) F-16A MLU Fighting Falcon	FAB 1 Sm/350 Sm (2 Wg), Florennes
	FA-130	SABCA (GD) F-16A MLU Fighting Falcon	FAB 31 Sm/349 Sm/OCU (10 Wg), Kleine-Bro
	FA-131	SABCA (GD) F-16A MLU Fighting Falcon	FAB 31 Sm/349 Sm/OCU (10 Wg), Kleine-Bro
	FA-132	SABCA (GD) F-16A MLU Fighting Falcon $	FAB 1 Sm/350 Sm (2 Wg), Florennes
	FA-133	SABCA (GD) F-16A MLU Fighting Falcon	FAB 1 Sm/350 Sm (2 Wg), Florennes
	FA-134	SABCA (GD) F-16A MLU Fighting Falcon	FAB 31 Sm/349 Sm/OCU (10 Wg), Kleine-Bro
	FA-135	SABCA (GD) F-16A MLU Fighting Falcon $	FAB 1 Sm/350 Sm (2 Wg), Florennes
	FA-136	SABCA (GD) F-16A MLU Fighting Falcon	FAB 31 Sm/349 Sm/OCU (10 Wg), Kleine-Bro
	FB-12	SABCA (GD) F-16B MLU Fighting Falcon	FAB 1 Sm/350 Sm (2 Wg), Florennes
	FB-14	SABCA (GD) F-16B MLU Fighting Falcon	FAB 31 Sm/349 Sm/OCU (10 Wg), Kleine-Bro
	FB-15	SABCA (GD) F-16B MLU Fighting Falcon	FAB 31 Sm/349 Sm/OCU (10 Wg), Kleine-Bro
	FB-17	SABCA (GD) F-16B MLU Fighting Falcon	FAB 31 Sm/349 Sm/OCU (10 Wg), Kleine-Bro
	FB-18	SABCA (GD) F-16B MLU Fighting Falcon	FAB 31 Sm/349 Sm/OCU (10 Wg), Kleine-Bro
	FB-20	SABCA (GD) F-16B MLU Fighting Falcon	FAB 31 Sm/349 Sm/OCU (10 Wg), Kleine-Bro
	FB-21	SABCA (GD) F-16B MLU Fighting Falcon	FAB 1 Sm/350 Sm (2 Wg), Florennes
	FB-22	SABCA (GD) F-16B MLU Fighting Falcon	FAB 1 Sm/350 Sm (2 Wg), Florennes
	FB-23	SABCA (GD) F-16B MLU Fighting Falcon	FAB 31 Sm/349 Sm/OCU (10 Wg), Kleine-Bro
	FB-24	SABCA (GD) F-16B MLU Fighting Falcon $	FAB 31 Sm/349 Sm/OCU (10 Wg), Kleine-Bro
	G-01	Cessna 182Q Skylane	FAB Federal Police, Brussels/Melsbroek
	G-04	Cessna 182R Skylane	FAB Federal Police, Brussels/Melsbroek
	G-10	MDH MD.902 Explorer	FAB Federal Police, Brussels/Melsbroek
	G-11	MDH MD.902 Explorer	FAB Federal Police, Brussels/Melsbroek
	G-12	MDH MD.902 Explorer	FAB Federal Police, Brussels/Melsbroek
	G-14	MDH MD.520N	FAB Federal Police, Brussels/Melsbroek
	G-15	MDH MD.520N	FAB Federal Police, Brussels/Melsbroek
	G-16	MDH MD.902 Explorer	FAB Federal Police, Brussels/Melsbroek
	H-20	Agusta A109HA	FAB, stored Beauvechain
	H-21	Agusta A109HA	FAB 17 Smaldeel MRH (1 Wg), Beauvechain
	H-22	Agusta A109HA	FAB 17 Smaldeel MRH (1 Wg), Beauvechain
	H-24	Agusta A109HA $	FAB 17 Smaldeel MRH (1 Wg), Beauvechain
	H-25	Agusta A109HA	FAB, stored Beauvechain
	H-26	Agusta A109HA	FAB 17 Smaldeel MRH (1 Wg), Beauvechain
	H-27	Agusta A109HA	FAB 17 Smaldeel MRH (1 Wg), Beauvechain
	H-28	Agusta A109HA	FAB 17 Smaldeel MRH (1 Wg), Beauvechain
	H-29	Agusta A109HA $	FAB 17 Smaldeel MRH (1 Wg), Beauvechain
	H-30	Agusta A109HA	FAB, stored Beauvechain
	H-31	Agusta A109HA	FAB 17 Smaldeel MRH (1 Wg), Beauvechain
	H-33	Agusta A109HA	FAB, stored Beauvechain
	H-35	Agusta A109HA	FAB, stored Beauvechain
	H-36	Agusta A109HA	FAB 17 Smaldeel MRH (1 Wg), Beauvechain
	H-38	Agusta A109HA	FAB 17 Smaldeel MRH (1 Wg), Beauvechain

rial	Type (code/other identity)	Owner/operator, location or fate	Notes
39	Agusta A109HA	*Withdrawn from use 2017*	
40	Agusta A109HA	FAB, stored Beauvechain	
41	Agusta A109HA	FAB, stored Beauvechain	
42	Agusta A109HA	FAB SLV (1 Wg), Beauvechain	
44	Agusta A109HA	FAB 17 Smaldeel MRH (1 Wg), Beauvechain	
45	Agusta A109HA	FAB 17 Smaldeel MRH (1 Wg), Beauvechain	
46	Agusta A109HA	FAB 17 Smaldeel MRH (1 Wg), Beauvechain	
-01	Piper L-21B Super Cub	FAB Air Cadets, Florennes/Goetsenhoeven/Zoersel	
-02	Piper L-21B Super Cub	FAB Air Cadets, Florennes/Goetsenhoeven/Zoersel	
-03	Piper L-21B Super Cub	FAB Air Cadets, Florennes/Goetsenhoeven/Zoersel	
-05	Piper L-21B Super Cub	FAB Air Cadets, Florennes/Goetsenhoeven/Zoersel	
1	Sud SA.316B Alouette III	FAB 40 Smaldeel, Koksijde	
2	Sud SA.316B Alouette III	FAB 40 Smaldeel, Koksijde	
3	Sud SA.316B Alouette III	FAB 40 Smaldeel, Koksijde	
N-01	NH Industries NH.90-NFH	FAB 40 Smaldeel (1 Wg), Koksijde	
N-02	NH Industries NH.90-NFH	FAB 40 Smaldeel (1 Wg), Koksijde	
N-03	NH Industries NH.90-NFH	FAB 40 Smaldeel (1 Wg), Koksijde	
N-04	NH Industries NH.90-NFH	FAB 40 Smaldeel (1 Wg), Koksijde	
N-05	NH Industries NH.90-TTH	FAB 18 Smaldeel MRH (1 Wg), Beauvechain	
N-06	NH Industries NH.90-TTH	FAB 18 Smaldeel MRH (1 Wg), Beauvechain	
N-07	NH Industries NH.90-TTH	FAB 18 Smaldeel MRH (1 Wg), Beauvechain	
N-08	NH Industries NH.90-TTH	FAB 18 Smaldeel MRH (1 Wg), Beauvechain	
S-02	Westland Sea King Mk.48	FAB 40 Smaldeel (1 Wg), Koksijde	
S-04	Westland Sea King Mk.48	FAB 40 Smaldeel (1 Wg), Koksijde	
S-05	Westland Sea King Mk.48 $	FAB 40 Smaldeel (1 Wg), Koksijde	
T-02	SIAI Marchetti SF260M+	FAB 5 Smaldeel/9 Smaldeel, CC Air, Beauvechain	
T-03	SIAI Marchetti SF260M+	FAB 5 Smaldeel/9 Smaldeel, CC Air, Beauvechain	
T-04	SIAI Marchetti SF260M+	FAB 5 Smaldeel/9 Smaldeel, CC Air, Beauvechain	
T-06	SIAI Marchetti SF260M+	FAB *Red Devils*, CC Air, Beauvechain	
T-12	SIAI Marchetti SF260M+	FAB 5 Smaldeel/9 Smaldeel, CC Air, Beauvechain	
T-15	SIAI Marchetti SF260M+	FAB *Red Devils*, CC Air, Beauvechain	
T-16	SIAI Marchetti SF260M+	FAB 5 Smaldeel/9 Smaldeel, CC Air, Beauvechain	
T-17	SIAI Marchetti SF260M+	FAB 5 Smaldeel/9 Smaldeel, CC Air, Beauvechain	
T-18	SIAI Marchetti SF260M+	FAB 5 Smaldeel/9 Smaldeel, CC Air, Beauvechain	
T-19	SIAI Marchetti SF260M+	FAB 5 Smaldeel/9 Smaldeel, CC Air, Beauvechain	
T-20	SIAI Marchetti SF260M+	FAB 5 Smaldeel/9 Smaldeel, CC Air, Beauvechain	
T-22	SIAI Marchetti SF260M+	FAB *Red Devils*, CC Air, Beauvechain	
T-23	SIAI Marchetti SF260M+	FAB *Red Devils*, CC Air, Beauvechain	
T-24	SIAI Marchetti SF260M+	FAB 5 Smaldeel/9 Smaldeel, CC Air, Beauvechain	
T-25	SIAI Marchetti SF260M+	FAB 5 Smaldeel/9 Smaldeel, CC Air, Beauvechain	
T-26	SIAI Marchetti SF260M+	FAB 5 Smaldeel/9 Smaldeel, CC Air, Beauvechain	
T-27	SIAI Marchetti SF260M+	FAB *Red Devils*, CC Air, Beauvechain	
T-30	SIAI Marchetti SF260M+ $	FAB 5 Smaldeel/9 Smaldeel, CC Air, Beauvechain	
T-31	SIAI Marchetti SF260M+	FAB *Red Devils*, CC Air, Beauvechain	
T-32	SIAI Marchetti SF260M+	FAB 5 Smaldeel/9 Smaldeel, CC Air, Beauvechain	
T-34	SIAI Marchetti SF260M+	FAB *Red Devils*, CC Air, Beauvechain	
T-35	SIAI Marchetti SF260M+	FAB *Red Devils*, CC Air, Beauvechain	
T-36	SIAI Marchetti SF260M+	FAB *Red Devils*, CC Air, Beauvechain	
T-40	SIAI Marchetti SF260D	FAB 5 Smaldeel/9 Smaldeel, CC Air, Beauvechain	
T-41	SIAI Marchetti SF260D	FAB 5 Smaldeel/9 Smaldeel, CC Air, Beauvechain	
T-42	SIAI Marchetti SF260D	FAB 5 Smaldeel/9 Smaldeel, CC Air, Beauvechain	
T-43	SIAI Marchetti SF260D	FAB 5 Smaldeel/9 Smaldeel, CC Air, Beauvechain	
T-44	SIAI Marchetti SF260D	FAB 5 Smaldeel/9 Smaldeel, CC Air, Beauvechain	
T-45	SIAI Marchetti SF260D	FAB 5 Smaldeel/9 Smaldeel, CC Air, Beauvechain	
T-46	SIAI Marchetti SF260D	FAB 5 Smaldeel/9 Smaldeel, CC Air, Beauvechain	
T-47	SIAI Marchetti SF260D	FAB 5 Smaldeel/9 Smaldeel, CC Air, Beauvechain	
T-48	SIAI Marchetti SF260D	FAB 5 Smaldeel/9 Smaldeel, CC Air, Beauvechain	
S-TRJ	Airbus A.321-231	FAB 21 Smaldeel (15 Wg), Brussels/Melsbroek	

Notes	Serial	Type (code/other identity)	Owner/operator, location or fate
	BOTSWANA		
	Botswana Defence Force (BDF)		
	OK1	Bombardier Global Express	BDF VIP Sqn, Sir Seretse Kharma IAP, Gaboror
	OM-1	Lockheed C-130B Hercules	BDF Z10 Sqn, Thebephatshwa
	OM-2	Lockheed C-130B Hercules	BDF Z10 Sqn, Thebephatshwa
	OM-3	Lockheed C-130B Hercules	BDF Z10 Sqn, Thebephatshwa
	BRAZIL		
	Força Aérea Brasileira (FAB)		
	2101	Airbus A.319-133CJ (VC-1A)	FAB 1º GT Especial, 1º Esq, Brasilia
	2454	Lockheed C-130E Hercules	FAB 1º GTT, 1º Esq, Afonsos
	2459	Lockheed SC-130E Hercules	FAB 1º GTT, 1º Esq, Afonsos
	2461	Lockheed KC-130H Hercules	FAB 1º GT, 1º Esq, Galeão
	2462	Lockheed KC-130H Hercules	FAB 1º GT, 1º Esq, Galeão
	2463	Lockheed C-130H Hercules	FAB 1º GT, 1º Esq, Galeão
	2464	Lockheed C-130H Hercules	FAB 1º GT, 1º Esq, Galeão
	2465	Lockheed C-130M Hercules	FAB 1º GT, 1º Esq, Galeão
	2466	Lockheed C-130M Hercules	FAB 1º GT, 1º Esq, Galeão
	2467	Lockheed C-130H Hercules	FAB 1º GT, 1º Esq, Galeão
	2470	Lockheed C-130M Hercules	*Scrapped King George Island, Antarctica, 2017*
	2472	Lockheed C-130H Hercules	FAB 1º GT, 1º Esq, Galeão
	2473	Lockheed C-130H Hercules	FAB 1º GT, 1º Esq, Galeão
	2474	Lockheed C-130H Hercules	FAB 1º GT, 1º Esq, Galeão
	2475	Lockheed C-130H Hercules	FAB 1º GT, 1º Esq, Galeão
	2476	Lockheed C-130M Hercules	FAB 1º GTT, 1º Esq, Afonsos
	2479	Lockheed C-130M Hercules	FAB 1º GT, 1º Esq, Galeão
	2550	Embraer VC-99A Legacy	FAB 2º GT Especial, 1º Esq, Brasilia
	2560	Embraer VC-99C Legacy	FAB 2º GT Especial, 1º Esq, Brasilia
	2561	Embraer VC-99C Legacy	FAB 2º GT Especial, 1º Esq, Brasilia
	2580	Embraer VC-99B Legacy	FAB 2º GT Especial, 1º Esq, Brasilia
	2581	Embraer VC-99B Legacy	FAB 2º GT Especial, 1º Esq, Brasilia
	2582	Embraer VC-99B Legacy	FAB 2º GT Especial, 1º Esq, Brasilia
	2583	Embraer VC-99B Legacy	FAB 2º GT Especial, 1º Esq, Brasilia
	2584	Embraer VC-99B Legacy	FAB 2º GT Especial, 1º Esq, Brasilia
	2585	Embraer VC-99B Legacy	FAB 2º GT Especial, 1º Esq, Brasilia
	2586	Embraer VC-99B Legacy	FAB 2º GT Especial, 1º Esq, Brasilia
	2590	Embraer EMB.190-190IGW (VC-2)	FAB 1º GT Especial, 1º Esq, Brasilia
	2591	Embraer EMB.190-190IGW (VC-2)	FAB 1º GT Especial, 1º Esq, Brasilia
	2900	Boeing 767-31AER (C-767)	FAB 2º GT, 2º Esq, Galeão
	6700	Embraer E-99	FAB 2º Esq, 6º GAv, Anapolis
	6701	Embraer R-99A	FAB 2º Esq, 6º GAv, Anapolis
	6702	Embraer R-99A	FAB 2º Esq, 6º GAv, Anapolis
	6703	Embraer E-99	FAB 2º Esq, 6º GAv, Anapolis
	6704	Embraer R-99A	FAB 2º Esq, 6º GAv, Anapolis
	6750	Embraer R-99B	FAB 2º Esq, 6º GAv, Anapolis
	6751	Embraer R-99B	FAB 2º Esq, 6º GAv, Anapolis
	6752	Embraer R-99B	FAB 2º Esq, 6º GAv, Anapolis
	BRUNEI		
	V8-001	Airbus A.340-212 (V8-BKH)	Brunei Government, Bandar Seri Bergawan
	V8-ALI	Boeing 747-430	*Withdrawn from use, March 2017*
	V8-BKH	Boeing 747-8LQ	Brunei Government, Bandar Seri Bergawan
	V8-MHB	Boeing 767-27GER	Brunei Government, Bandar Seri Bergawan
	BULGARIA		
	Bulgarsky Voenno-Vazdushni Sily (BVVS)		
	020	Pilatus PC.XII/45	BVVS 16 TAP, Sofia/Dobroslavtzi
	055	Antonov An-30	BVVS 16 TAP, Sofia/Dobroslavtzi
	071	Aeritalia C-27J Spartan	BVVS 16 TAB, Sofia/Vrazhdebna
	072	Aeritalia C-27J Spartan	BVVS 16 TAB, Sofia/Vrazhdebna
	073	Aeritalia C-27J Spartan	BVVS 16 TAB, Sofia/Vrazhdebna

Serial	Type (code/other identity)	Owner/operator, location or fate	Notes
Bulgarian Government			
LZ-AOB	Airbus A.319-112	Bulgarian Government/BH Air, Sofia	
LZ-OOI	Dassault Falcon 2000	Bulgarian Government, Sofia	
BURKINA FASO			
XT-BFA	Boeing 727-282	Government of Burkina Faso, Ouagadougou	
CAMEROON			
TJ-AAW	Grumman G.1159A Gulfstream III	Government of Cameroon, Yaounde	
CANADA			
Royal Canadian Air Force (RCAF)			
15001	Airbus CC-150 Polaris (A.310-304) [991]	RCAF 437 Sqn (8 Wing), Trenton	
15002	Airbus CC-150 Polaris (A.310-304F) [992]	RCAF 437 Sqn (8 Wing), Trenton	
15003	Airbus CC-150 Polaris (A.310-304F) [993]	RCAF 437 Sqn (8 Wing), Trenton	
15004	Airbus CC-150 Polaris (A.310-304F) [994]	RCAF 437 Sqn (8 Wing), Trenton	
15005	Airbus CC-150 Polaris (A.310-304F) [995]	RCAF 437 Sqn (8 Wing), Trenton	
130332	Lockheed CC-130H(SAR) Hercules	RCAF 413 Sqn (14 Wing), Greenwood	
130334	Lockheed CC-130H(SAR) Hercules	RCAF 413 Sqn (14 Wing), Greenwood	
130335	Lockheed CC-130H Hercules	RCAF 426 Sqn (8 Wing), Trenton	
130336	Lockheed CC-130H Hercules	RCAF 426 Sqn (8 Wing), Trenton	
130337	Lockheed CC-130H Hercules	RCAF 426 Sqn (8 Wing), Trenton	
130338	Lockheed CC-130H(T) Hercules	RCAF 435 Sqn (17 Wing), Winnipeg	
130339	Lockheed CC-130H(T) Hercules	RCAF 435 Sqn (17 Wing), Winnipeg	
130340	Lockheed CC-130H(T) Hercules	RCAF 435 Sqn (17 Wing), Winnipeg	
130341	Lockheed CC-130H(T) Hercules	RCAF 435 Sqn (17 Wing), Winnipeg	
130343	Lockheed CC-130H-30 Hercules	RCAF 426 Sqn (8 Wing), Trenton	
130344	Lockheed CC-130H-30 Hercules	RCAF 426 Sqn (8 Wing), Trenton	
130601	Lockheed CC-130J Hercules II	RCAF 436 Sqn (8 Wing), Trenton	
130602	Lockheed CC-130J Hercules II	RCAF 436 Sqn (8 Wing), Trenton	
130603	Lockheed CC-130J Hercules II	RCAF 436 Sqn (8 Wing), Trenton	
130604	Lockheed CC-130J Hercules II	RCAF 436 Sqn (8 Wing), Trenton	
130605	Lockheed CC-130J Hercules II	RCAF 436 Sqn (8 Wing), Trenton	
130606	Lockheed CC-130J Hercules II	RCAF 436 Sqn (8 Wing), Trenton	
130607	Lockheed CC-130J Hercules II	RCAF 436 Sqn (8 Wing), Trenton	
130608	Lockheed CC-130J Hercules II	RCAF 436 Sqn (8 Wing), Trenton	
130609	Lockheed CC-130J Hercules II	RCAF 436 Sqn (8 Wing), Trenton	
130610	Lockheed CC-130J Hercules II	RCAF 436 Sqn (8 Wing), Trenton	
130611	Lockheed CC-130J Hercules II	RCAF 436 Sqn (8 Wing), Trenton	
130612	Lockheed CC-130J Hercules II	RCAF 436 Sqn (8 Wing), Trenton	
130613	Lockheed CC-130J Hercules II	RCAF 436 Sqn (8 Wing), Trenton	
130614	Lockheed CC-130J Hercules II	RCAF 436 Sqn (8 Wing), Trenton	
130615	Lockheed CC-130J Hercules II	RCAF 436 Sqn (8 Wing), Trenton	
130616	Lockheed CC-130J Hercules II	RCAF 436 Sqn (8 Wing), Trenton	
130617	Lockheed CC-130J Hercules II	RCAF 436 Sqn (8 Wing), Trenton	
140101	Lockheed CP-140M Aurora	RCAF 404 Sqn/405 Sqn (14 Wing), Greenwood	
140102	Lockheed CP-140 Aurora	RCAF 404 Sqn/405 Sqn (14 Wing), Greenwood	
140103	Lockheed CP-140M Aurora	RCAF 404 Sqn/405 Sqn (14 Wing), Greenwood	
140104	Lockheed CP-140M Aurora	RCAF 404 Sqn/405 Sqn (14 Wing), Greenwood	
140105	Lockheed CP-140M Aurora	RCAF 407 Sqn (19 Wing), Comox	
140106	Lockheed CP-140 Aurora	RCAF 404 Sqn/405 Sqn (14 Wing), Greenwood	
140107	Lockheed CP-140 Aurora	RCAF 407 Sqn (19 Wing), Comox	
140108	Lockheed CP-140M Aurora	RCAF 404 Sqn/405 Sqn (14 Wing), Greenwood	
140109	Lockheed CP-140 Aurora	RCAF 407 Sqn (19 Wing), Comox	
140110	Lockheed CP-140 Aurora	RCAF 404 Sqn/405 Sqn (14 Wing), Greenwood	
140111	Lockheed CP-140M Aurora	RCAF 404 Sqn/405 Sqn (14 Wing), Greenwood	
140112	Lockheed CP-140 Aurora	RCAF 407 Sqn (19 Wing), Comox	
140113	Lockheed CP-140 Aurora	RCAF 407 Sqn (19 Wing), Comox	
140114	Lockheed CP-140M Aurora	RCAF 404 Sqn/405 Sqn (14 Wing), Greenwood	
140115	Lockheed CP-140M Aurora	RCAF 407 Sqn (19 Wing), Comox	
140116	Lockheed CP-140 Aurora	RCAF 404 Sqn/405 Sqn (14 Wing), Greenwood	
140117	Lockheed CP-140M Aurora	RCAF 404 Sqn/405 Sqn (14 Wing), Greenwood	

Notes	Serial	Type (code/other identity)	Owner/operator, location or fate
	140118	Lockheed CP-140M Aurora	RCAF 404 Sqn/405 Sqn (14 Wing), Greenwood
	142803	de Havilland Canada CT-142	RCAF 402 Sqn (17 Wing), Winnipeg
	142804	de Havilland Canada CT-142	RCAF 402 Sqn (17 Wing), Winnipeg
	142805	de Havilland Canada CT-142	RCAF 402 Sqn (17 Wing), Winnipeg
	142806	de Havilland Canada CT-142	RCAF 402 Sqn (17 Wing), Winnipeg
	144614	Canadair CC-144B Challenger (C-GCUP)	RCAF 412 Sqn (8 Wing), Ottawa
	144615	Canadair CC-144B Challenger (C-GCUR)	RCAF 412 Sqn (8 Wing), Ottawa
	144617	Canadair CC-144C Challenger (C-GKGR)	RCAF 412 Sqn (8 Wing), Ottawa
	144618	Canadair CC-144C Challenger (C-GKGS)	RCAF 412 Sqn (8 Wing), Ottawa
	177701	Boeing CC-177 Globemaster III (07-7701/N9500B)	RCAF 429 Sqn (8 Wing), Trenton
	177702	Boeing CC-177 Globemaster III (07-7702/N9500H)	RCAF 429 Sqn (8 Wing), Trenton
	177703	Boeing CC-177 Globemaster III (07-7703/N9500N)	RCAF 429 Sqn (8 Wing), Trenton
	177704	Boeing CC-177 Globemaster III (07-7704/N9500R) $	RCAF 429 Sqn (8 Wing), Trenton
	177705	Boeing CC-177 Globemaster III (14-0004/N273ZD)	RCAF 429 Sqn (8 Wing), Trenton

CHAD

| | TT-ABD | Boeing 737-74Q | Chad Government, N'djamena |

CHILE
Fuerza Aérea de Chile (FACh)

	145	Extra EA-300L [5]	FACh *Los Halcones*, Santiago
	146	Extra EA-300L [4]	FACh *Los Halcones*, Santiago
	147	Extra EA-300L [2]	FACh *Los Halcones*, Santiago
	902	Boeing 707-351C	FACh, Grupo de Aviación 10, Santiago
	904	Boeing 707-358C	FACh, Grupo de Aviación 10, Santiago
	911	Grumman G.1159C Gulfstream IV	FACh, Grupo de Aviación 10, Santiago
	912	Grumman G.1159C Gulfstream IV	FACh, Grupo de Aviación 10, Santiago
	921	Boeing 737-58N	FACh, Grupo de Aviación 10, Santiago
	922	Boeing 737-330	FACh, Grupo de Aviación 10, Santiago
	982	Boeing KC-135E Stratotanker	FACh, Grupo de Aviación 10, Santiago
	983	Boeing KC-135E Stratotanker	FACh, Grupo de Aviación 10, Santiago
	985	Boeing 767-3Y0ER	FACh, Grupo de Aviación 10, Santiago
	990	Lockheed KC-130R Hercules	FACh, Grupo de Aviación 10, Santiago
	991	Lockheed C-130H Hercules	FACh, Grupo de Aviación 10, Santiago
	992	Lockheed KC-130R Hercules	FACh, Grupo de Aviación 10, Santiago
	995	Lockheed C-130H Hercules	FACh, Grupo de Aviación 10, Santiago
	996	Lockheed C-130H Hercules	FACh, Grupo de Aviación 10, Santiago
	999	Lockheed KC-130R Hercules	FACh, Grupo de Aviación 10, Santiago
	1304	Extra EA-300L [3]	FACh *Los Halcones*, Santiago
	1325	Extra EA-300L [1]	FACh *Los Halcones*, Santiago

COLOMBIA
Fuerza Aérea Colombiana (FAC)

| | FAC-0001 | Boeing 737-74V | FAC Escuadrón de Transporte Especial, Bogotà |

CROATIA
Hrvatske Zračne Snage (HZS)

	054	Pilatus PC-9M	HZS 93 Zakroplova Baza, Zadar
	055	Pilatus PC-9M	HZS 93 Zakroplova Baza, Zadar
	056	Pilatus PC-9M	HZS 93 Zakroplova Baza, Zadar
	057	Pilatus PC-9M	HZS 93 Zakroplova Baza, Zadar
	059	Pilatus PC-9M $	HZS 93 Zakroplova Baza, Zadar
	061	Pilatus PC-9M	HZS 93 Zakroplova Baza, Zadar
	062	Pilatus PC-9M	HZS 93 Zakroplova Baza, Zadar
	063	Pilatus PC-9M	HZS 93 Zakroplova Baza, Zadar
	064	Pilatus PC-9M	HZS 93 Zakroplova Baza, Zadar
	066	Pilatus PC-9M	HZS 93 Zakroplova Baza, Zadar
	067	Pilatus PC-9M	HZS 93 Zakroplova Baza, Zadar
	068	Pilatus PC-9M	HZS 93 Zakroplova Baza, Zadar
	069	Pilatus PC-9M	HZS 93 Zakroplova Baza, Zadar
	070	Pilatus PC-9M	HZS 93 Zakroplova Baza, Zadar

Serial	Type (code/other identity)	Owner/operator, location or fate	Notes
Croatian Government			
9A-CRO	Canadair CL.601 Challenger	Croatian Government, Zagreb	
9A-CRT	Canadair CL.601 Challenger	Croatian Government, Zagreb	
CZECH REPUBLIC			
Vzdušné Síly Armády (Czech Air Force)			
0103	Aero L-39C Albatros	Czech AF CLV, Pardubice	
0106	Aero L-39C Albatros	Czech AF CLV, Pardubice	
0107	Aero L-39C Albatros	Czech AF CLV, Pardubice	
0108	Aero L-39C Albatros	Czech AF CLV, Pardubice	
0113	Aero L-39C Albatros	Czech AF CLV, Pardubice	
0115	Aero L-39C Albatros	Czech AF CLV, Pardubice	
0260	Yakovlev Yak-40	Czech AF 241.dlt/24.zDL, Praha/Kbely	
0441	Aero L-39C Albatros	Czech AF CLV, Pardubice	
0444	Aero L-39C Albatros	Czech AF CLV, Pardubice	
0445	Aero L-39C Albatros	Czech AF CLV, Pardubice	
0452	CASA C-295M	Czech AF 242.tsl/24.zDL, Praha/Kbely	
0453	CASA C-295M	Czech AF 242.tsl/24.zDL, Praha/Kbely	
0454	CASA C-295M	Czech AF 242.tsl/24.zDL, Praha/Kbely	
0455	CASA C-295M	Czech AF 242.tsl/24.zDL, Praha/Kbely	
0458	Evektor EV-55M Outback	Evektor, Kunovice	
0731	LET L-410UVP-E Turbolet	Czech AF CLV, Pardubice	
0803	Mil Mi-17	Czech AF 243.vrl/24.zDL, Praha/Kbely	
0811	Mil Mi-17	Czech AF 243.vrl/24.zDL, Praha/Kbely	
0828	Mil Mi-17	Czech AF 243.vrl/24.zDL, Praha/Kbely	
0832	Mil Mi-17	Czech AF 243.vrl/24.zDL, Praha/Kbely	
0834	Mil Mi-17	Czech AF 243.vrl/24.zDL, Praha/Kbely	
0836	Mil Mi-17	Czech AF CLV, Pardubice	
0837	Mil Mi-17	Czech AF CLV, Pardubice	
0839	Mil Mi-17	Czech AF 243.vrl/24.zDL, Praha/Kbely	
0840	Mil Mi-17	Czech AF 243.vrl/24.zDL, Praha/Kbely	
0848	Mil Mi-17	Czech AF 243.vrl/24.zDL, Praha/Kbely	
0849	Mil Mi-17	Czech AF 243.vrl/24.zDL, Praha/Kbely	
0850	Mil Mi-17	Czech AF 243.vrl/24.zDL, Praha/Kbely	
0928	LET L-410UVP-T Turbolet	Czech AF CLV, Pardubice	
0981	Mil Mi-24V2	Czech AF 221.lbvr/22.zL, Náměšt	
1257	Yakovlev Yak-40K	Czech AF 241.dlt/24.zDL, Praha/Kbely	
1504	LET L-410UVP Turbolet	*Withdrawn from use*	
1526	LET L-410FG Turbolet	Czech AF 242.tsl/24.zDL, Praha/Kbely	
2344	Aero L-39ZA Albatros	Czech AF 213.vlt/21.zTL, Čáslav	
2415	Aero L-39ZA Albatros	Czech AF 213.vlt/21.zTL, Čáslav	
2421	Aero L-39ZA Albatros	Czech AF 213.vlt/21.zTL, Čáslav	
2433	Aero L-39ZA Albatros $	Czech AF 213.vlt/21.zTL, Čáslav	
2436	Aero L-39ZA Albatros	Czech AF 213.vlt/21.zTL, Čáslav	
2601	LET L-410UVP-E Turbolet	Czech AF 242.tsl/24.zDL, Praha/Kbely	
2602	LET L-410UVP-E Turbolet	Czech AF 242.tsl/24.zDL, Praha/Kbely	
2626	Aero L-39CW Albatros	Aero, Vodochody	
2801	Airbus A.319CJ-115X	Czech AF 241.dlt/24.zDL, Praha/Kbely	
3085	Airbus A.319CJ-115X	Czech AF 241.dlt/24.zDL, Praha/Kbely	
3361	Mil Mi-35 $	Czech AF 221.lbvr/22.zL, Náměšt	
3362	Mil Mi-35	Czech AF 221.lbvr/22.zL, Náměšt	
3365	Mil Mi-35	Czech AF 221.lbvr/22.zL, Náměšt	
3366	Mil Mi-35 $	Czech AF 221.lbvr/22.zL, Náměšt	
3367	Mil Mi-35	Czech AF 221.lbvr/22.zL, Náměšt	
3368	Mil Mi-35	Czech AF 221.lbvr/22.zL, Náměšt	
3369	Mil Mi-35	Czech AF 221.lbvr/22.zL, Náměšt	
3370	Mil Mi-35 $	Czech AF 221.lbvr/22.zL, Náměšt	
3371	Mil Mi-35	Czech AF 221.lbvr/22.zL, Náměšt	
3903	Aero L-39ZA Albatros	Czech AF 213.vlt/21.zTL, Čáslav	
5015	Aero L-39ZA Albatros	Czech AF 213.vlt/21.zTL, Čáslav	
5017	Aero L-39ZA Albatros	Czech AF 213.vlt/21.zTL, Čáslav	
5019	Aero L-39ZA Albatros	Czech AF 213.vlt/21.zTL, Čáslav	

Notes	Serial	Type (code/other identity)	Owner/operator, location or fate
	5105	Canadair CL.601-3A Challenger	Czech 241.dlt/24.zDL, Praha/Kbely
	5832	Aero L-159B ALCA	Czech AF LZO, Praha/Kbely
	6046	Aero L-159T-1 ALCA	Czech AF 213.vlt/21.zTL, Cáslav
	6047	Aero L-159T-1 ALCA	Czech AF 213.vlt/21.zTL, Cáslav
	6048	Aero L-159A ALCA	Czech AF 212.tl/21.zTL, Cáslav
	6050	Aero L-159A ALCA	Czech AF 212.tl/21.zTL, Cáslav
	6051	Aero L-159A ALCA	Czech AF 212.tl/21.zTL, Cáslav
	6052	Aero L-159A ALCA	Czech AF 212.tl/21.zTL, Cáslav
	6053	Aero L-159A ALCA (AD572/DU-C) $	Czech AF 212.tl/21.zTL, Cáslav
	6054	Aero L-159A ALCA	Czech AF 212.tl/21.zTL, Cáslav
	6057	Aero L-159A ALCA	Czech AF 212.tl/21.zTL, Cáslav
	6058	Aero L-159A ALCA	Czech AF 212.tl/21.zTL, Cáslav
	6059	Aero L-159A ALCA	Czech AF 212.tl/21.zTL, Cáslav
	6060	Aero L-159A ALCA	Czech AF 212.tl/21.zTL, Cáslav
	6062	Aero L-159A ALCA	Czech AF 212.tl/21.zTL, Cáslav
	6063	Aero L-159A ALCA	Czech AF 212.tl/21.zTL, Cáslav
	6064	Aero L-159A ALCA	Czech AF 212.tl/21.zTL, Cáslav
	6066	Aero L-159A ALCA $	Czech AF 212.tl/21.zTL, Cáslav
	6069	Aero L-159B ALCA	Czech AF 212.tl/21.zTL, Cáslav
	6070	Aero L-159A ALCA	Czech AF 212.tl/21.zTL, Cáslav
	6073	Aero L-159T-2X ALCA	Aero, Vodochody
	6075	Aero L-159T-1 ALCA	Czech AF 213.vlt/21.zTL, Cáslav
	6078	Aero L-159T-1 ALCA	Czech AF 213.vlt/21.zTL, Cáslav
	6079	Aero L-159T-1 ALCA	Czech AF 213.vlt/21.zTL, Cáslav
	7353	Mil Mi-24V $	Czech AF 221.lbvr/22.zL, Náměšt
	7354	Mil Mi-24V	Czech AF 221.lbvr/22.zL, Náměšt
	7355	Mil Mi-24V	Czech AF 221.lbvr/22.zL, Náměšt
	7356	Mil Mi-24V	Czech AF 221.lbvr/22.zL, Náměšt
	7357	Mil Mi-24V	Czech AF 221.lbvr/22.zL, Náměšt
	7360	Mil Mi-24V	Czech AF 221.lbvr/22.zL, Náměšt
	9234	SAAB JAS 39C Gripen	Czech AF 211.tl/21.zTL, Cáslav
	9235	SAAB JAS 39C Gripen $	Czech AF 211.tl/21.zTL, Cáslav
	9236	SAAB JAS 39C Gripen $	Czech AF 211.tl/21.zTL, Cáslav
	9237	SAAB JAS 39C Gripen	Czech AF 211.tl/21.zTL, Cáslav
	9238	SAAB JAS 39C Gripen	Czech AF 211.tl/21.zTL, Cáslav
	9239	SAAB JAS 39C Gripen	Czech AF 211.tl/21.zTL, Cáslav
	9240	SAAB JAS 39C Gripen $	Czech AF 211.tl/21.zTL, Cáslav
	9241	SAAB JAS 39C Gripen $	Czech AF 211.tl/21.zTL, Cáslav
	9242	SAAB JAS 39C Gripen	Czech AF 211.tl/21.zTL, Cáslav
	9243	SAAB JAS 39C Gripen	Czech AF 211.tl/21.zTL, Cáslav
	9244	SAAB JAS 39C Gripen	Czech AF 211.tl/21.zTL, Cáslav
	9245	SAAB JAS 39C Gripen	Czech AF 211.tl/21.zTL, Cáslav
	9767	Mil Mi-171Sh	Czech AF 221.lbvr & 222.vrlt/22.zVrL, Náměšt
	9774	Mil Mi-171Sh	Czech AF 221.lbvr & 222.vrlt/22.zVrL, Náměšt
	9781	Mil Mi-171Sh	Czech AF 221.lbvr & 222.vrlt/22.zVrL, Náměšt
	9799	Mil Mi-171Sh	Czech AF 221.lbvr & 222.vrlt/22.zVrL, Náměšt
	9806	Mil Mi-171Sh	Czech AF 221.lbvr & 222.vrlt/22.zVrL, Náměšt
	9813	Mil Mi-171Sh	Czech AF 221.lbvr & 222.vrlt/22.zVrL, Náměšt
	9819	SAAB JAS 39D Gripen $	Czech AF 211.tl/21.zTL, Cáslav
	9820	SAAB JAS 39D Gripen	Czech AF 211.tl/21.zTL, Cáslav
	9825	Mil Mi-171Sh	Czech AF 221.lbvr & 222.vrlt/22.zVrL, Náměšt
	9837	Mil Mi-171Sh	Czech AF 221.lbvr & 222.vrlt/22.zVrL, Náměšt
	9844	Mil Mi-171Sh	Czech AF 221.lbvr & 222.vrlt/22.zVrL, Náměšt
	9868	Mil Mi-171Sh	Czech AF 221.lbvr & 222.vrlt/22.zVrL, Náměšt
	9873	Mil Mi-171Sh	Czech AF 221.lbvr & 222.vrlt/22.zVrL, Náměšt
	9887	Mil Mi-171Sh	Czech AF 221.lbvr & 222.vrlt/22.zVrL, Náměšt
	9892	Mil Mi-171Sh	Czech AF 221.lbvr & 222.vrlt/22.zVrL, Náměšt
	9904	Mil Mi-171Sh	Czech AF 221.lbvr & 222.vrlt/22.zVrL, Náměšt
	9915	Mil Mi-171Sh	Czech AF 221.lbvr & 222.vrlt/22.zVrL, Náměšt
	9926	Mil Mi-171Sh	Czech AF 221.lbvr & 222.vrlt/22.zVrL, Náměšt
	....	CASA C-295M	Czech AF (on order)
	....	CASA C-295M	Czech AF (on order)

Serial	Type (code/other identity)	Owner/operator, location or fate	Notes
DENMARK			
Kongelige Danske Flyvevåben (KDF)			
B-536	Lockheed C-130J-30 Hercules II	KDF Eskadrille 721, Aalborg	
B-537	Lockheed C-130J-30 Hercules II	KDF Eskadrille 721, Aalborg	
B-538	Lockheed C-130J-30 Hercules II	KDF Eskadrille 721, Aalborg	
B-583	Lockheed C-130J-30 Hercules II	KDF Eskadrille 721, Aalborg	
C-080	Canadair CL.604 Challenger	KDF Eskadrille 721, Aalborg	
C-168	Canadair CL.604 Challenger $	KDF Eskadrille 721, Aalborg	
C-172	Canadair CL.604 Challenger	KDF Eskadrille 721, Aalborg	
C-215	Canadair CL.604 Challenger	KDF Eskadrille 721, Aalborg	
E-004	SABCA (GD) F-16A MLU Fighting Falcon	KDF Eskadrille 727, Skrydstrup	
E-005	SABCA (GD) F-16A MLU Fighting Falcon	KDF Eskadrille 727, Skrydstrup	
E-006	SABCA (GD) F-16A MLU Fighting Falcon	KDF Eskadrille 730, Skrydstrup	
E-007	SABCA (GD) F-16A MLU Fighting Falcon	KDF Eskadrille 727, Skrydstrup	
E-008	SABCA (GD) F-16A MLU Fighting Falcon $	KDF Eskadrille 727, Skrydstrup	
E-011	GD F-16A MLU Fighting Falcon	KDF Eskadrille 727, Skrydstrup	
E-016	SABCA (GD) F-16A MLU Fighting Falcon	KDF Eskadrille 727, Skrydstrup	
E-017	SABCA (GD) F-16A MLU Fighting Falcon	KDF Eskadrille 727, Skrydstrup	
E-018	SABCA (GD) F-16A MLU Fighting Falcon	KDF Eskadrille 730, Skrydstrup	
E-024	GD F-16A MLU Fighting Falcon	KDF Eskadrille 727, Skrydstrup	
E-074	GD F-16A MLU Fighting Falcon	KDF Eskadrille 730, Skrydstrup	
E-075	GD F-16A MLU Fighting Falcon	KDF Eskadrille 727, Skrydstrup	
E-107	GD F-16A MLU Fighting Falcon	KDF Eskadrille 727, Skrydstrup	
E-189	SABCA (GD) F-16A MLU Fighting Falcon	KDF Eskadrille 730, Skrydstrup	
E-190	SABCA (GD) F-16A MLU Fighting Falcon	KDF Eskadrille 730, Skrydstrup	
E-191	SABCA (GD) F-16A MLU Fighting Falcon	KDF Eskadrille 730, Skrydstrup	
E-194	SABCA (GD) F-16A MLU Fighting Falcon $	KDF Eskadrille 730, Skrydstrup	
E-596	SABCA (GD) F-16A MLU Fighting Falcon	KDF Eskadrille 730, Skrydstrup	
E-597	SABCA (GD) F-16A MLU Fighting Falcon	KDF Eskadrille 730, Skrydstrup	
E-598	SABCA (GD) F-16A MLU Fighting Falcon	KDF Eskadrille 727, Skrydstrup	
E-599	SABCA (GD) F-16A MLU Fighting Falcon	KDF, stored Skrydstrup	
E-600	SABCA (GD) F-16A MLU Fighting Falcon	KDF Eskadrille 730, Skrydstrup	
E-601	SABCA (GD) F-16A MLU Fighting Falcon	KDF Eskadrille 730, Skrydstrup	
E-602	SABCA (GD) F-16A MLU Fighting Falcon	KDF Eskadrille 730, Skrydstrup	
E-603	SABCA (GD) F-16A MLU Fighting Falcon	KDF Eskadrille 730, Skrydstrup	
E-604	SABCA (GD) F-16A MLU Fighting Falcon	KDF Eskadrille 727, Skrydstrup	
E-605	SABCA (GD) F-16A MLU Fighting Falcon	KDF Eskadrille 730, Skrydstrup	
E-606	SABCA (GD) F-16A MLU Fighting Falcon	KDF Eskadrille 730, Skrydstrup	
E-607	SABCA (GD) F-16A MLU Fighting Falcon	KDF Eskadrille 727, Skrydstrup	
E-608	SABCA (GD) F-16A MLU Fighting Falcon	KDF Eskadrille 727, Skrydstrup	
E-609	SABCA (GD) F-16A MLU Fighting Falcon	KDF Eskadrille 727, Skrydstrup	
E-610	SABCA (GD) F-16A MLU Fighting Falcon	KDF Eskadrille 730, Skrydstrup	
E-611	SABCA (GD) F-16A MLU Fighting Falcon	KDF Eskadrille 727, Skrydstrup	
ET-022	Fokker (GD) F-16B MLU Fighting Falcon	KDF Eskadrille 730, Skrydstrup	
ET-197	Fokker (GD) F-16B MLU Fighting Falcon	KDF Eskadrille 727, Skrydstrup	
ET-198	Fokker (GD) F-16B MLU Fighting Falcon	KDF Eskadrille 730, Skrydstrup	
ET-199	Fokker (GD) F-16B MLU Fighting Falcon	KDF Eskadrille 730, Skrydstrup	
ET-207	SABCA (GD) F-16B MLU Fighting Falcon	KDF Eskadrille 727, Skrydstrup	
ET-208	SABCA (GD) F-16B MLU Fighting Falcon	KDF Eskadrille 730, Skrydstrup	
ET-210	SABCA (GD) F-16B MLU Fighting Falcon	KDF Eskadrille 727/730, Skrydstrup	
ET-612	SABCA (GD) F-16B MLU Fighting Falcon	KDF Eskadrille 727, Skrydstrup	
ET-613	SABCA (GD) F-16B MLU Fighting Falcon	KDF Eskadrille 727, Skrydstrup	
ET-614	SABCA (GD) F-16B MLU Fighting Falcon	KDF Eskadrille 727, Skrydstrup	
ET-615	SABCA (GD) F-16B MLU Fighting Falcon	KDF Eskadrille 727, Skrydstrup	
M-502	AgustaWestland EH.101 Mk.512	KDF Eskadrille 722, Karup	
M-504	AgustaWestland EH.101 Mk.512	KDF Eskadrille 722, Karup	
M-507	AgustaWestland EH.101 Mk.512	KDF Eskadrille 722, Karup	
M-508	AgustaWestland EH.101 Mk.512	KDF Eskadrille 722, Karup	
M-510	AgustaWestland EH.101 Mk.512	KDF Eskadrille 722, Karup	
M-512	AgustaWestland EH.101 Mk.512	KDF Eskadrille 722, Karup	
M-513	AgustaWestland EH.101 Mk.512	KDF Eskadrille 722, Karup	
M-514	AgustaWestland EH.101 Mk.512	KDF Eskadrille 722, Karup	

Notes	Serial	Type (code/other identity)	Owner/operator, location or fate
	M-515	AgustaWestland EH.101 Mk.512	KDF Eskadrille 722, Karup
	M-516	AgustaWestland EH.101 Mk.512	KDF Eskadrille 722, Karup
	M-517	AgustaWestland EH.101 Mk.512	KDF Eskadrille 722, Karup
	M-518	AgustaWestland EH.101 Mk.512	KDF Eskadrille 722, Karup
	M-519	AgustaWestland EH.101 Mk.512	KDF Eskadrille 722, Karup
	M-520	AgustaWestland EH.101 Mk.512	KDF Eskadrille 722, Karup
	N-971	Sikorsky MH-60R Sea Hawk	KDF Eskadrille 723, Karup
	N-972	Sikorsky MH-60R Sea Hawk	KDF Eskadrille 723, Karup
	N-973	Sikorsky MH-60R Sea Hawk	KDF Eskadrille 723, Karup
	N-974	Sikorsky MH-60R Sea Hawk	KDF Eskadrille 723, Karup
	N-975	Sikorsky MH-60R Sea Hawk	KDF Eskadrille 723, Karup
	N-976	Sikorsky MH-60R Sea Hawk	KDF Eskadrille 723, Karup
	N-977	Sikorsky MH-60R Sea Hawk	KDF Eskadrille 723, Karup
	N-978	Sikorsky MH-60R Sea Hawk	KDF Eskadrille 723, Karup
	N-979	Sikorsky MH-60R Sea Hawk	KDF Eskadrille 723, Karup
	P-090	Aérospatiale AS.550C-2 Fennec	KDF Eskadrille 724, Karup
	P-234	Aérospatiale AS.550C-2 Fennec	KDF Eskadrille 724, Karup
	P-254	Aérospatiale AS.550C-2 Fennec	KDF Eskadrille 724, Karup
	P-275	Aérospatiale AS.550C-2 Fennec	KDF Eskadrille 724, Karup
	P-276	Aérospatiale AS.550C-2 Fennec	KDF Eskadrille 724, Karup
	P-287	Aérospatiale AS.550C-2 Fennec	KDF Eskadrille 724, Karup
	P-288	Aérospatiale AS.550C-2 Fennec	KDF Eskadrille 724, Karup
	P-319	Aérospatiale AS.550C-2 Fennec	KDF Eskadrille 724, Karup
	P-320	Aérospatiale AS.550C-2 Fennec	KDF Eskadrille 724, Karup
	P-339	Aérospatiale AS.550C-2 Fennec	KDF Eskadrille 724, Karup
	P-352	Aérospatiale AS.550C-2 Fennec	KDF Eskadrille 724, Karup
	P-369	Aérospatiale AS.550C-2 Fennec	KDF Eskadrille 724, Karup
	S-134	Westland Lynx Mk.90B	*Withdrawn from use, December 2017*
	S-142	Westland Lynx Mk.90B	*Withdrawn from use, December 2017*
	S-170	Westland Lynx Mk.90B	*Withdrawn from use, December 2017*
	S-175	Westland Lynx Mk.90B	*Withdrawn from use, December 2017*
	S-181	Westland Lynx Mk.90B	*Withdrawn from use, December 2017*
	S-191	Westland Lynx Mk.90B $	*Withdrawn from use, December 2017*
	S-256	Westland Lynx Mk.90B	*Withdrawn from use, December 2017*
	T-401	SAAB T-17 Supporter	KDF Flyveskolen, Karup
	T-402	SAAB T-17 Supporter	KDF Flyveskolen, Karup
	T-403	SAAB T-17 Supporter	KDF Flyveskolen, Karup
	T-404	SAAB T-17 Supporter	KDF Flyveskolen, Karup
	T-405	SAAB T-17 Supporter	KDF Skrydstrup Station Flight
	T-407	SAAB T-17 Supporter	KDF Eskadrille 721, Aalborg
	T-409	SAAB T-17 Supporter	KDF Aalborg Station Flight
	T-410	SAAB T-17 Supporter	KDF Skrydstrup Station Flight
	T-411	SAAB T-17 Supporter	KDF Skrydstrup Station Flight
	T-412	SAAB T-17 Supporter	KDF Flyveskolen, Karup
	T-413	SAAB T-17 Supporter	KDF Flyveskolen, Karup
	T-414	SAAB T-17 Supporter	KDF Eskadrille 721, Aalborg
	T-415	SAAB T-17 Supporter	KDF Flyveskolen, Karup
	T-417	SAAB T-17 Supporter	KDF Flyveskolen, Karup
	T-418	SAAB T-17 Supporter	KDF Skrydstrup Station Flight
	T-419	SAAB T-17 Supporter	KDF Flyveskolen, Karup
	T-420	SAAB T-17 Supporter	KDF Skrydstrup Station Flight
	T-421	SAAB T-17 Supporter	KDF Flyveskolen, Karup
	T-423	SAAB T-17 Supporter	KDF Flyveskolen, Karup
	T-425	SAAB T-17 Supporter	KDF Flyveskolen, Karup
	T-426	SAAB T-17 Supporter	KDF Flyveskolen, Karup
	T-427	SAAB T-17 Supporter	KDF Flyveskolen, Karup
	T-428	SAAB T-17 Supporter	KDF Flyveskolen, Karup
	T-429	SAAB T-17 Supporter	KDF Flyveskolen, Karup
	T-430	SAAB T-17 Supporter	KDF Skrydstrup Station Flight
	T-431	SAAB T-17 Supporter	KDF Eskadrille 721, Aalborg
	T-432	SAAB T-17 Supporter	KDF Skrydstrup Station Flight

Serial	Type (code/other identity)	Owner/operator, location or fate	Notes
ECUADOR			
Fuerza Aérea Ecuatoriana (FAE)			
FAE-051	Embraer ERJ.135 Legacy 600	FAE Escuadrón de Transporte 1114, Quito	
FAE-052	Dassault Falcon 7X	FAE Escuadrón de Transporte 1114, Quito	
EGYPT			
Al Quwwat al-Jawwiya il Misriya (Egyptian Air Force)			
1271	Lockheed C-130H Hercules (SU-BAB)	Egyptian AF 16 Sqn, Cairo West	
1273	Lockheed C-130H Hercules (SU-BAD)	Egyptian AF 16 Sqn, Cairo West	
1274	Lockheed C-130H Hercules (SU-BAE)	Egyptian AF 16 Sqn, Cairo West	
1275	Lockheed C-130H Hercules (SU-BAF)	Egyptian AF 16 Sqn, Cairo West	
1277	Lockheed C-130H Hercules (SU-BAI)	Egyptian AF 16 Sqn, Cairo West	
1278	Lockheed C-130H Hercules (SU-BAJ)	Egyptian AF 16 Sqn, Cairo West	
1279	Lockheed C-130H Hercules (SU-BAK)	Egyptian AF 16 Sqn, Cairo West	
1280	Lockheed C-130H Hercules (SU-BAL)	Egyptian AF 16 Sqn, Cairo West	
1281	Lockheed C-130H Hercules (SU-BAM)	Egyptian AF 16 Sqn, Cairo West	
1282	Lockheed C-130H Hercules (SU-BAN)	Egyptian AF 16 Sqn, Cairo West	
1283	Lockheed C-130H Hercules (SU-BAP)	Egyptian AF 16 Sqn, Cairo West	
1284	Lockheed C-130H Hercules (SU-BAQ)	Egyptian AF 16 Sqn, Cairo West	
1285	Lockheed C-130H Hercules (SU-BAR)	Egyptian AF 16 Sqn, Cairo West	
1286	Lockheed C-130H Hercules (SU-BAS)	Egyptian AF 16 Sqn, Cairo West	
1287	Lockheed C-130H Hercules (SU-BAT)	Egyptian AF 16 Sqn, Cairo West	
1288	Lockheed C-130H Hercules (SU-BAU)	Egyptian AF 16 Sqn, Cairo West	
1289	Lockheed C-130H Hercules (SU-BAV)	Egyptian AF 16 Sqn, Cairo West	
1290	Lockheed C-130H Hercules (SU-BEW)	Egyptian AF 16 Sqn, Cairo West	
1291	Lockheed C-130H Hercules (SU-BEX)	Egyptian AF 16 Sqn, Cairo West	
1292	Lockheed C-130H Hercules (SU-BEY)	Egyptian AF 16 Sqn, Cairo West	
1293	Lockheed C-130H-30 Hercules (SU-BKS)	Egyptian AF 16 Sqn, Cairo West	
1294	Lockheed C-130H-30 Hercules (SU-BKT)	Egyptian AF 16 Sqn, Cairo West	
1295	Lockheed C-130H-30 Hercules (SU-BKU)	Egyptian AF 16 Sqn, Cairo West	
1296	Lockheed C-130H Hercules (SU-BPJ)	Egyptian AF 16 Sqn, Cairo West	
1297	Lockheed C-130H Hercules (SU-BPK)	Egyptian AF 16 Sqn, Cairo West	
1298	Lockheed C-130H Hercules (SU-BPL)	Egyptian AF 16 Sqn, Cairo West	
....	Lockheed C-130J Hercules II	Egyptian AF (on order)	
....	Lockheed C-130J Hercules II	Egyptian AF (on order)	
Egyptian Government			
SU-BGV	Grumman G.1159A Gulfstream III	Egyptian AF/Government, Cairo	
SU-BNC	Grumman G.1159C Gulfstream IV	Egyptian AF/Government, Cairo	
SU-BND	Grumman G.1159C Gulfstream IV	Egyptian AF/Government, Cairo	
SU-BNO	Grumman G.1159C Gulfstream IV-SP	Egyptian AF/Government, Cairo	
SU-BNP	Grumman G.1159C Gulfstream IV-SP	Egyptian AF/Government, Cairo	
SU-BPE	Gulfstream Aerospace G.400	Egyptian AF/Government, Cairo	
SU-BPF	Gulfstream Aerospace G.400	Egyptian AF/Government, Cairo	
SU-BRF	Cessna 680 Citation Sovereign	Egyptian Government, Cairo	
SU-BRG	Cessna 680 Citation Sovereign	Egyptian Government, Cairo	
SU-BTU	Dassault Falcon 7X	Egyptian AF/Government, Cairo	
SU-BTV	Dassault Falcon 7X	Egyptian AF/Government, Cairo	
SU-GGG	Airbus A.340-211	Egyptian Government, Cairo	
ESTONIA			
Estonian Air Force			
10	Aero L-39C Albatros	Estonian AF Fixed Wing Squadron, Ämari	
11	Aero L-39C Albatros	Estonian AF Fixed Wing Squadron, Ämari	
20 y	WSK-PZL An-2T	Estonian AF Fixed Wing Squadron, Ämari	
40 y	WSK-PZL An-2T	Estonian AF Fixed Wing Squadron, Ämari	
41 y	Antonov An-2	Estonian AF Fixed Wing Squadron, Ämari	
FINLAND			
Suomen Ilmavoimat (Finnish Air Force) & Suomen Maavoimat (Finnish Army)			
CC-1	CASA C-295M	Ilmavoimat TukiLLv, Tampere/Pirkkala	
CC-2	CASA C-295M	Ilmavoimat TukiLLv, Tampere/Pirkkala	
CC-3	CASA C-295M	Ilmavoimat TukiLLv, Tampere/Pirkkala	

Notes	Serial	Type (code/other identity)	Owner/operator, location or fate
	FF-1	Fokker F.27-100 Friendship	Ilmavoimat TukiLLv, Tampere/Pirkkala
	HN-401	McDonnell Douglas F-18C Hornet	Ilmavoimat HävLLv 31, Kuopio/Rissala
	HN-402	McDonnell Douglas F-18C Hornet	Ilmavoimat HävLLv 11, Roveniemi
	HN-403	McDonnell Douglas F-18C Hornet	Ilmavoimat HävLLv 31, Kuopio/Rissala
	HN-404	McDonnell Douglas F-18C Hornet	Ilmavoimat HävLLv 31, Kuopio/Rissala
	HN-405	McDonnell Douglas F-18C Hornet	Ilmavoimat HävLLv 31, Kuopio/Rissala
	HN-406	McDonnell Douglas F-18C Hornet	Ilmavoimat HävLLv 31, Kuopio/Rissala
	HN-407	McDonnell Douglas F-18C Hornet	Ilmavoimat HävLLv 31, Kuopio/Rissala
	HN-408	McDonnell Douglas F-18C Hornet	Ilmavoimat HävLLv 31, Kuopio/Rissala
	HN-409	McDonnell Douglas F-18C Hornet	Ilmavoimat HävLLv 11, Roveniemi
	HN-410	McDonnell Douglas F-18C Hornet	Ilmavoimat IlmaStk, Tampere/Pirkkala
	HN-411	McDonnell Douglas F-18C Hornet	Ilmavoimat HävLLv 11, Roveniemi
	HN-412	McDonnell Douglas F-18C Hornet	Ilmavoimat HävLLv 31, Kuopio/Rissala
	HN-414	McDonnell Douglas F-18C Hornet	Ilmavoimat HävLLv 11, Roveniemi
	HN-415	McDonnell Douglas F-18C Hornet	Ilmavoimat HävLLv 11, Roveniemi
	HN-416	McDonnell Douglas F-18C Hornet	Ilmavoimat HävLLv 11, Roveniemi
	HN-417	McDonnell Douglas F-18C Hornet	Ilmavoimat HävLLv 31, Kuopio/Rissala
	HN-418	McDonnell Douglas F-18C Hornet	Ilmavoimat HävLLv 31, Kuopio/Rissala
	HN-419	McDonnell Douglas F-18C Hornet	Ilmavoimat HävLLv 11, Roveniemi
	HN-420	McDonnell Douglas F-18C Hornet	Ilmavoimat HävLLv 31, Kuopio/Rissala
	HN-421	McDonnell Douglas F-18C Hornet	Ilmavoimat HävLLv 11, Roveniemi
	HN-422	McDonnell Douglas F-18C Hornet	Ilmavoimat HävLLv 11, Roveniemi
	HN-423	McDonnell Douglas F-18C Hornet	Ilmavoimat HävLLv 31, Kuopio/Rissala
	HN-424	McDonnell Douglas F-18C Hornet	Ilmavoimat HävLLv 11, Roveniemi
	HN-425	McDonnell Douglas F-18C Hornet	Ilmavoimat HävLLv 31, Kuopio/Rissala
	HN-426	McDonnell Douglas F-18C Hornet	Ilmavoimat HävLLv 31, Kuopio/Rissala
	HN-427	McDonnell Douglas F-18C Hornet	Ilmavoimat HävLLv 11, Roveniemi
	HN-428	McDonnell Douglas F-18C Hornet	Ilmavoimat HävLLv 11, Roveniemi
	HN-429	McDonnell Douglas F-18C Hornet	Ilmavoimat HävLLv 11, Roveniemi
	HN-431	McDonnell Douglas F-18C Hornet	Ilmavoimat HävLLv 31, Kuopio/Rissala
	HN-432	McDonnell Douglas F-18C Hornet	Ilmavoimat HävLLv 31, Kuopio/Rissala
	HN-433	McDonnell Douglas F-18C Hornet	Ilmavoimat HävLLv 31, Kuopio/Rissala
	HN-434	McDonnell Douglas F-18C Hornet	Ilmavoimat HävLLv 31, Kuopio/Rissala
	HN-435	McDonnell Douglas F-18C Hornet	Ilmavoimat HävLLv 31, Kuopio/Rissala
	HN-436	McDonnell Douglas F-18C Hornet	Ilmavoimat HävLLv 31, Kuopio/Rissala
	HN-437	McDonnell Douglas F-18C Hornet	Ilmavoimat HävLLv 31, Kuopio/Rissala
	HN-438	McDonnell Douglas F-18C Hornet	Ilmavoimat HävLLv 11, Roveniemi
	HN-439	McDonnell Douglas F-18C Hornet	Ilmavoimat HävLLv 31, Kuopio/Rissala
	HN-440	McDonnell Douglas F-18C Hornet	Ilmavoimat HävLLv 11, Roveniemi
	HN-441	McDonnell Douglas F-18C Hornet	Ilmavoimat HävLLv 11, Roveniemi
	HN-442	McDonnell Douglas F-18C Hornet	Ilmavoimat HävLLv 11, Roveniemi
	HN-443	McDonnell Douglas F-18C Hornet	Ilmavoimat HävLLv 31, Kuopio/Rissala
	HN-444	McDonnell Douglas F-18C Hornet	Ilmavoimat HävLLv 11, Roveniemi
	HN-445	McDonnell Douglas F-18C Hornet	Ilmavoimat HävLLv 11, Roveniemi
	HN-446	McDonnell Douglas F-18C Hornet	Ilmavoimat HävLLv 11, Roveniemi
	HN-447	McDonnell Douglas F-18C Hornet	Ilmavoimat HävLLv 11, Roveniemi
	HN-448	McDonnell Douglas F-18C Hornet	Ilmavoimat HävLLv 31, Kuopio/Rissala
	HN-449	McDonnell Douglas F-18C Hornet	Ilmavoimat HävLLv 11, Roveniemi
	HN-450	McDonnell Douglas F-18C Hornet	Ilmavoimat HävLLv 11, Roveniemi
	HN-451	McDonnell Douglas F-18C Hornet	Ilmavoimat HävLLv 31, Kuopio/Rissala
	HN-452	McDonnell Douglas F-18C Hornet	Ilmavoimat HävLLv 11, Roveniemi
	HN-453	McDonnell Douglas F-18C Hornet	Ilmavoimat HävLLv 31, Kuopio/Rissala
	HN-454	McDonnell Douglas F-18C Hornet	Ilmavoimat HävLLv 11, Roveniemi
	HN-455	McDonnell Douglas F-18C Hornet	Ilmavoimat HävLLv 31, Kuopio/Rissala
	HN-456	McDonnell Douglas F-18C Hornet	Ilmavoimat HävLLv 31, Kuopio/Rissala
	HN-457	McDonnell Douglas F-18C Hornet	Ilmavoimat HävLLv 31, Kuopio/Rissala
	HN-461	McDonnell Douglas F-18D Hornet	Ilmavoimat HävLLv 31, Kuopio/Rissala
	HN-462	McDonnell Douglas F-18D Hornet	Ilmavoimat IlmaStk, Tampere/Pirkkala
	HN-463	McDonnell Douglas F-18D Hornet	Ilmavoimat HävLLv 11, Roveniemi
	HN-464	McDonnell Douglas F-18D Hornet	Ilmavoimat HävLLv 11, Roveniemi
	HN-465	McDonnell Douglas F-18D Hornet	Ilmavoimat HävLLv 31, Kuopio/Rissala
	HN-466	McDonnell Douglas F-18D Hornet	Ilmavoimat HävLLv 31, Kuopio/Rissala

Serial	Type (code/other identity)	Owner/operator, location or fate	Notes
HN-467	McDonnell Douglas F-18D Hornet	Ilmavoimat HävLLv 31, Kuopio/Rissala	
HW-307	BAe Hawk 51	Ilmavoimat HävLLv 41, Jyväskylä/Tikkakoski	
HW-320	BAe Hawk 51	Ilmavoimat, stored Halli (for upgrade)	
HW-321	BAe Hawk 51	Ilmavoimat, stored Halli (for upgrade)	
HW-327	BAe Hawk 51	Ilmavoimat HävLLv 41, Jyväskylä/Tikkakoski	
HW-330	BAe Hawk 51	Ilmavoimat, stored Halli (for upgrade)	
HW-333	BAe Hawk 51	Ilmavoimat HävLLv 41, Jyväskylä/Tikkakoski	
HW-334	BAe Hawk 51 [3]	Ilmavoimat HävLLv 41, Jyväskylä/Tikkakoski	
HW-336	BAe Hawk 51	Ilmavoimat, stored Halli (for upgrade)	
HW-338	BAe Hawk 51	Ilmavoimat HävLLv 41, Jyväskylä/Tikkakoski	
HW-339	BAe Hawk 51	Ilmavoimat, stored Halli (for upgrade)	
HW-340	BAe Hawk 51 [2]	Ilmavoimat HävLLv 41, Jyväskylä/Tikkakoski	
HW-341	BAe Hawk 51 [1]	Ilmavoimat HävLLv 41, Jyväskylä/Tikkakoski	
HW-343	BAe Hawk 51	Ilmavoimat HävLLv 41, Jyväskylä/Tikkakoski	
HW-344	BAe Hawk 51	Ilmavoimat, stored Halli (for upgrade)	
HW-345	BAe Hawk 51 [4]	Ilmavoimat HävLLv 41, Jyväskylä/Tikkakoski	
HW-348	BAe Hawk 51	Ilmavoimat, stored Halli (for upgrade)	
HW-349	BAe Hawk 51	Ilmavoimat, stored Halli (for upgrade)	
HW-350	BAe Hawk 51	Ilmavoimat, stored Halli (for upgrade)	
HW-351	BAe Hawk 51A	Ilmavoimat HävLLv 41, Jyväskylä/Tikkakoski	
HW-352	BAe Hawk 51A [7]	Ilmavoimat HävLLv 41, Jyväskylä/Tikkakoski	
HW-353	BAe Hawk 51A	Ilmavoimat HävLLv 41, Jyväskylä/Tikkakoski	
HW-354	BAe Hawk 51A	Ilmavoimat HävLLv 41, Jyväskylä/Tikkakoski	
HW-355	BAe Hawk 51A	Ilmavoimat HävLLv 41, Jyväskylä/Tikkakoski	
HW-356	BAe Hawk 51A	Ilmavoimat HävLLv 41, Jyväskylä/Tikkakoski	
HW-357	BAe Hawk 51A	Ilmavoimat HävLLv 41, Jyväskylä/Tikkakoski	
HW-360	BAe Hawk 66	Ilmavoimat HävLLv 41, Jyväskylä/Tikkakoski	
HW-361	BAe Hawk 66	Ilmavoimat HävLLv 41, Jyväskylä/Tikkakoski	
HW-362	BAe Hawk 66	Ilmavoimat HävLLv 41, Jyväskylä/Tikkakoski	
HW-363	BAe Hawk 66	Ilmavoimat HävLLv 41, Jyväskylä/Tikkakoski	
HW-364	BAe Hawk 66	Ilmavoimat HävLLv 41, Jyväskylä/Tikkakoski	
HW-365	BAe Hawk 66	Ilmavoimat HävLLv 41, Jyväskylä/Tikkakoski	
HW-366	BAe Hawk 66	Ilmavoimat HävLLv 41, Jyväskylä/Tikkakoski	
HW-367	BAe Hawk 66	Ilmavoimat HävLLv 41, Jyväskylä/Tikkakoski	
HW-368	BAe Hawk 66	Ilmavoimat HävLLv 41, Jyväskylä/Tikkakoski	
HW-370	BAe Hawk 66	Ilmavoimat HävLLv 41, Jyväskylä/Tikkakoski	
HW-371	BAe Hawk 66	Ilmavoimat HävLLv 41, Jyväskylä/Tikkakoski	
HW-373	BAe Hawk 66	Ilmavoimat HävLLv 41, Jyväskylä/Tikkakoski	
HW-374	BAe Hawk 66	Ilmavoimat HävLLv 41, Jyväskylä/Tikkakoski	
HW-375	BAe Hawk 66	Ilmavoimat HävLLv 41, Jyväskylä/Tikkakoski	
HW-376	BAe Hawk 66	Ilmavoimat HävLLv 41, Jyväskylä/Tikkakoski	
HW-377	BAe Hawk 66	Ilmavoimat HävLLv 41, Jyväskylä/Tikkakoski	
LJ-1	Gates Learjet 35A	Ilmavoimat TukiLLv (Det.), Kuopio/Rissala	
LJ-2	Gates Learjet 35A	Ilmavoimat TukiLLv, Tampere/Pirkkala	
LJ-3	Gates Learjet 35A	Ilmavoimat TukiLLv, Tampere/Pirkkala	
NH-202	NH Industries NH.90-TTH	Maavoimat 1.HK/HekoP, Utti	
NH-203	NH Industries NH.90-TTH	Maavoimat 1.HK/HekoP, Utti	
NH-204	NH Industries NH.90-TTH	Maavoimat 1.HK/HekoP, Utti	
NH-205	NH Industries NH.90-TTH	Maavoimat 1.HK/HekoP, Utti	
NH-206	NH Industries NH.90-TTH	Maavoimat 1.HK/HekoP, Utti	
NH-207	NH Industries NH.90-TTH	Maavoimat 1.HK/HekoP, Utti	
NH-208	NH Industries NH.90-TTH	Maavoimat 1.HK/HekoP, Utti	
NH-209	NH Industries NH.90-TTH	Maavoimat 1.HK/HekoP, Utti	
NH-210	NH Industries NH.90-TTH	Maavoimat 1.HK/HekoP, Utti	
NH-211	NH Industries NH.90-TTH	Maavoimat 1.HK/HekoP, Utti	
NH-212	NH Industries NH.90-TTH	Maavoimat 1.HK/HekoP, Utti	
NH-213	NH Industries NH.90-TTH	Maavoimat 1.HK/HekoP, Utti	
NH-214	NH Industries NH.90-TTH	Maavoimat 1.HK/HekoP, Utti	
NH-215	NH Industries NH.90-TTH	Maavoimat 1.HK/HekoP, Utti	
NH-216	NH Industries NH.90-TTH	Maavoimat 1.HK/HekoP, Utti	
NH-217	NH Industries NH.90-TTH	Maavoimat 1.HK/HekoP, Utti	
NH-218	NH Industries NH.90-TTH	Maavoimat 1.HK/HekoP, Utti	

Notes	Serial	Type (code/other identity)	Owner/operator, location or fate
	NH-219	NH Industries NH.90-TTH	Maavoimat 1.HK/HekoP, Utti
	NH-220	NH Industries NH.90-TTH	Maavoimat 1.HK/HekoP, Utti
	NH-221	NH Industries NH.90-TTH	Maavoimat 1.HK/HekoP, Utti
	PI-01	Pilatus PC-12/47E	Ilmavoimat TukiLLv, Tampere/Pirkkala
	PI-02	Pilatus PC-12/47E	Ilmavoimat TukiLLv, Tampere/Pirkkala
	PI-03	Pilatus PC-12/47E	Ilmavoimat TukiLLv, Tampere/Pirkkala
	PI-04	Pilatus PC-12/47E	Ilmavoimat TukiLLv, Tampere/Pirkkala
	PI-05	Pilatus PC-12/47E	Ilmavoimat TukiLLv, Tampere/Pirkkala
	PI-06	Pilatus PC-12/47E	Ilmavoimat TukiLLv, Tampere/Pirkkala

FRANCE

NB: Due to the way in which French military aircraft serials are issued, this section is sorted by type

Armée de l'Air (AA)

Notes	Serial	Type (code/other identity)	Owner/operator, location or fate
	418	Airbus A.310-304 (F-RADC)	AA ET 03.060 *Esterel*, Paris/Charles de Gaulle
	421	Airbus A.310-304 (F-RADA)	AA ET 03.060 *Esterel*, Paris/Charles de Gaulle
	422	Airbus A.310-304 (F-RADB)	AA ET 03.060 *Esterel*, Paris/Charles de Gaulle
	240	Airbus A.330-223 (F-RARF)	AA ET 00.060, Evreux
	1735	Airbus A.330-243 MRTT Phénix (F-WWCK/EC-330)	AA GRV 02.093 *Bretagne*, Istres (on order)
	1808	Airbus A.330-243 MRTT Phénix (EC-338)	AA GRV 02.093 *Bretagne*, Istres (on order)
	1...	Airbus A.330-243 MRTT Phénix	AA GRV 02.093 *Bretagne*, Istres (on order)
	1...	Airbus A.330-243 MRTT Phénix	AA GRV 02.093 *Bretagne*, Istres (on order)
	1...	Airbus A.330-243 MRTT Phénix	AA GRV 02.093 *Bretagne*, Istres (on order)
	1...	Airbus A.330-243 MRTT Phénix	AA GRV 02.093 *Bretagne*, Istres (on order)
	1...	Airbus A.330-243 MRTT Phénix	AA GRV 02.093 *Bretagne*, Istres (on order)
	1...	Airbus A.330-243 MRTT Phénix	AA GRV 02.093 *Bretagne*, Istres (on order)
	1...	Airbus A.330-243 MRTT Phénix	AA GRV 02.093 *Bretagne*, Istres (on order)
	1...	Airbus A.330-243 MRTT Phénix	AA GRV 02.093 *Bretagne*, Istres (on order)
	1...	Airbus A.330-243 MRTT Phénix	AA GRV 02.093 *Bretagne*, Istres (on order)
	1...	Airbus A.330-243 MRTT Phénix	AA GRV 02.093 *Bretagne*, Istres (on order)
	075	Airbus A.340-212 (F-RAJA)	AA ET 03.060 *Esterel*, Paris/Charles de Gaulle
	081	Airbus A.340-212 (F-RAJB)	AA ET 03.060 *Esterel*, Paris/Charles de Gaulle
	0007	Airbus Military A.400M (F-RBAA)	AA ET 01.061 *Touraine*, Orléans
	0008	Airbus Military A.400M (F-RBAB)	AA ET 01.061 *Touraine*, Orléans
	0010	Airbus Military A.400M (F-RBAC)	AA ET 01.061 *Touraine*, Orléans
	0011	Airbus Military A.400M (F-RBAD)	AA ET 01.061 *Touraine*, Orléans
	0012	Airbus Military A.400M (F-RBAE)	AA ET 01.061 *Touraine*, Orléans
	0014	Airbus Military A.400M (F-RBAF)	AA ET 01.061 *Touraine*, Orléans
	0019	Airbus Military A.400M (F-RBAG)	AA ET 01.061 *Touraine*, Orléans
	0031	Airbus Military A.400M (F-RBAH)	AA ET 01.061 *Touraine*, Orléans
	0033	Airbus Military A.400M (F-RBAI)	AA ET 01.061 *Touraine*, Orléans
	0037	Airbus Military A.400M (F-RBAJ)	AA ET 01.061 *Touraine*, Orléans
	0053	Airbus Military A.400M (F-RBAK)	AA ET 01.061 *Touraine*, Orléans
	0062	Airbus Military A.400M (F-RBAL)	AA ET 01.061 *Touraine*, Orléans
	0065	Airbus Military A.400M (F-RBAM)	AA ET 01.061 *Touraine*, Orléans
	0073	Airbus Military A.400M (F-RBAN)	AA (on order)
	0...	Airbus Military A.400M (F-RBAO)	AA (on order)
	0...	Airbus Military A.400M (F-RBAP)	AA (on order)
	0...	Airbus Military A.400M (F-RBAQ)	AA (on order)
	0...	Airbus Military A.400M (F-RBAR)	AA (on order)
	0...	Airbus Military A.400M (F-RBAS)	AA (on order)
	045	Airtech CN-235M-200 [62-IB]	AA ET 01.062 *Vercours*, Evreux
	065	Airtech CN-235M-200 [52-IC]	AA ET 00.052 *La Tontouta*, Nouméa
	066	Airtech CN-235M-200 [52-ID]	AA ET 00.052 *La Tontouta*, Nouméa
	071	Airtech CN-235M-200 [62-IE]	AA ET 01.062 *Vercours*, Evreux
	072	Airtech CN-235M-200 [62-IF]	AA ET 01.062 *Vercours*, Evreux
	105	Airtech CN-235M-200 [52-IG]	AA ET 00.052 *La Tontouta*, Nouméa
	107	Airtech CN-235M-200 [52-IH]	AA ET 00.052 *La Tontouta*, Nouméa
	111	Airtech CN-235M-200 [62-II]	AA ET 01.062 *Vercours*, Evreux
	114	Airtech CN-235M-200 [62-IJ]	AA ET 01.062 *Vercours*, Evreux
	123	Airtech CN-235M-200 [62-IM]	AA ET 01.062 *Vercours*, Evreux
	128	Airtech CN-235M-200 [62-IK]	AA ET 01.062 *Vercours*, Evreux
	129	Airtech CN-235M-200 [62-IL]	AA ET 01.062 *Vercours*, Evreux

Serial	Type (code/other identity)	Owner/operator, location or fate	Notes
37	Airtech CN-235M-200 [62-IN]	AA ET 01.062 *Vercours*, Evreux	
41	Airtech CN-235M-200 [62-IO]	AA ET 00.058 *Antilles*, Fort-de-France	
52	Airtech CN-235M-200 [62-IP]	AA ET 01.062 *Vercours*, Evreux	
56	Airtech CN-235M-200 [62-IQ]	AA ET 01.062 *Vercours*, Evreux	
58	Airtech CN-235M-200 [62-IR]	AA ET 01.062 *Vercours*, Evreux	
60	Airtech CN-235M-200 [62-IS]	AA ET 01.062 *Vercours*, Evreux	
65	Airtech CN-235M-200 [62-IT]	AA ET 01.062 *Vercours*, Evreux	
93	Airtech CN-235M-300 [62-HA]	AA ET 03.062 *Ventoux*, Evreux	
94	Airtech CN-235M-300 [62-HB]	AA ET 03.062 *Ventoux*, Evreux	
95	Airtech CN-235M-300 [62-HC]	AA ET 03.062 *Ventoux*, Evreux	
96	Airtech CN-235M-300 [62-HD]	AA ET 03.062 *Ventoux*, Evreux	
97	Airtech CN-235M-300 [62-HE]	AA ET 03.062 *Ventoux*, Evreux	
98	Airtech CN-235M-300 [62-HF]	AA ET 03.062 *Ventoux*, Evreux	
99	Airtech CN-235M-300 [62-HG]	AA ET 03.062 *Ventoux*, Evreux	
00	Airtech CN-235M-300 [62-HH]	AA ET 03.062 *Ventoux*, Evreux	
..	Beechcraft King Air 350 (F-WTAP)	AA (on order)	
..	Beechcraft King Air 350	AA (on order)	
70	Boeing C-135FR Stratotanker [31-CA]	AA GRV 02.093 *Bretagne*, Istres	
71	Boeing C-135FR Stratotanker [31-CB]	AA GRV 02.093 *Bretagne*, Istres	
72	Boeing C-135FR Stratotanker [31-CC]	AA GRV 02.093 *Bretagne*, Istres	
74	Boeing C-135FR Stratotanker [31-CE]	AA GRV 02.093 *Bretagne*, Istres	
75	Boeing C-135FR Stratotanker [31-CF]	AA GRV 02.093 *Bretagne*, Istres	
97	Boeing C-135FR Stratotanker [31-CM]$	AA GRV 02.093 *Bretagne*, Istres	
25	Boeing C-135FR Stratotanker [31-CN]	AA GRV 02.093 *Bretagne*, Istres	
74	Boeing KC-135RG Stratotanker [31-CP]	AA GRV 02.093 *Bretagne*, Istres	
35	Boeing C-135FR Stratotanker [93-CG]	AA GRV 02.093 *Bretagne*, Istres	
36	Boeing C-135FR Stratotanker [93-CH]	AA GRV 02.093 *Bretagne*, Istres	
37	Boeing C-135FR Stratotanker [31-CI]	AA GRV 02.093 *Bretagne*, Istres	
38	Boeing C-135FR Stratotanker [31-CJ]	AA GRV 02.093 *Bretagne*, Istres	
39	Boeing C-135FR Stratotanker [93-CK]	AA GRV 02.093 *Bretagne*, Istres	
40	Boeing C-135FR Stratotanker [31-CL]	AA GRV 02.093 *Bretagne*, Istres	
01	Boeing E-3F Sentry [36-CA]	AA EDCA 00.036, Avord	
02	Boeing E-3F Sentry [36-CB]	AA EDCA 00.036, Avord	
03	Boeing E-3F Sentry [36-CC]	AA EDCA 00.036, Avord	
04	Boeing E-3F Sentry [36-CD] $	AA EDCA 00.036, Avord	
77	CASA 212-300 Aviocar (F-ZAEA)	AA DGA EV, Cazaux & Istres	
78	CASA 212-300 Aviocar [MP]	AA DGA EV, Cazaux & Istres	
86	CASA 212-300 Aviocar [MQ]	AA DGA EV, Cazaux & Istres	
20	Cessna 310Q [CL]	AA DGA EV, Cazaux & Istres	
81	Cessna 310Q [BF]	AA DGA EV, Cazaux & Istres	
4	D-BD Alpha Jet E	AA DGA EV, Cazaux & Istres	
7	D-BD Alpha Jet E [705-TU]	AA DGA EV, Cazaux & Istres	
8	D-BD Alpha Jet E	AA DGA EV, Cazaux & Istres	
11	D-BD Alpha Jet E [705-UB]	AA DGA EV, Cazaux & Istres	
12	D-BD Alpha Jet E	AA DGA EV, Cazaux & Istres	
13	D-BD Alpha Jet E [8-MM]	AA EE 03.008 *Côte d'Or*, Cazaux	
17	D-BD Alpha Jet E [705-AA]	AA, stored Châteaudun	
18	D-BD Alpha Jet E [118-AK]	AA CEAM/ECE 01.030 *Côte d'Argent*, Mont-de-Marsan	
20	D-BD Alpha Jet E [705-MS]	AA EAC 00.314, Tours	
22	D-BD Alpha Jet E [8-LS]	AA EE 03.008 *Côte d'Or*, Cazaux	
25	D-BD Alpha Jet E [705-TJ]	AA EAC 00.314, Tours	
26	D-BD Alpha Jet E [705-ND]	AA EAC 00.314, Tours	
28	D-BD Alpha Jet E [705-AB]	AA EAC 00.314, Tours	
29	D-BD Alpha Jet E [102-NB]	AA EE 03.008 *Côte d'Or*, Cazaux	
30	D-BD Alpha Jet E [705-MD]	AA EAC 00.314, Tours	
31	D-BD Alpha Jet E [705-RK]	AA EAC 00.314, Tours	
32	D-BD Alpha Jet E [102-FI]	AA EE 03.008 *Côte d'Or*, Cazaux	
33	D-BD Alpha Jet E [120-FJ]	AA ETO 01.008 *Saintonge*, Cazaux	
35	D-BD Alpha Jet E [705-MA]	AA EAC 00.314, Tours	
37	D-BD Alpha Jet E [705-NL]	AA EAC 00.314, Tours	
38	D-BD Alpha Jet E $	AA ETO 01.008 *Saintonge*, Cazaux	

Notes	Serial	Type (code/other identity)	Owner/operator, location or fate
	E41	D-BD Alpha Jet E [8-RA]	AA EE 03.008 Côte d'Or, Cazaux
	E42	D-BD Alpha Jet E $	AA EAC 00.314, Tours
	E44	D-BD Alpha Jet E [F-UHRE,1]	AA Patrouille de France, Salon de Provence
	E45	D-BD Alpha Jet E [F-TETF]	AA Patrouille de France, Salon de Provence
	E46	D-BD Alpha Jet E [F-UHRF,2]	AA Patrouille de France, Salon de Provence
	E48	D-BD Alpha Jet E [705-MH]	AA EAC 00.314, Tours
	E51	D-BD Alpha Jet E [705-AD]	AA EAC 00.314, Tours
	E53	D-BD Alpha Jet E [102-LI]	AA EE 03.008 Côte d'Or, Cazaux
	E58	D-BD Alpha Jet E [705-TK]	AA EAC 00.314, Tours
	E60	D-BD Alpha Jet E	AA EPNER, Istres
	E67	D-BD Alpha Jet E [705-TB]	AA EAC 00.314, Tours
	E68	D-BD Alpha Jet E [F-TEMO,7]	AA Patrouille de France, Salon de Provence
	E72	D-BD Alpha Jet E [705-LA]	AA EAC 00.314, Tours
	E73	D-BD Alpha Jet E [F-TENE]	AA Patrouille de France, Salon de Provence
	E74	D-BD Alpha Jet E	AA
	E76	D-BD Alpha Jet E [102-RJ]	AA EE 03.008 Côte d'Or, Cazaux
	E79	D-BD Alpha Jet E [F-TENA,5]	AA Patrouille de France, Salon de Provence
	E80	D-BD Alpha Jet E	AA DGA EV, Cazaux & Istres
	E81	D-BD Alpha Jet E [8-FO]	AA ETO 01.008 Saintonge, Cazaux
	E82	D-BD Alpha Jet E [120-LW]	AA ETO 01.008 Saintonge, Cazaux
	E83	D-BD Alpha Jet E [705-TZ]	AA EAC 00.314, Tours
	E85	D-BD Alpha Jet E [F-UGFF]	AA Patrouille de France, Salon de Provence
	E86	D-BD Alpha Jet E [102-FB]	AA EE 03.008 Côte d'Or, Cazaux
	E87	D-BD Alpha Jet E [705-LC]	AA EAC 00.314, Tours
	E88	D-BD Alpha Jet E [F-TELL]	AA Patrouille de France, Salon de Provence
	E89	D-BD Alpha Jet E [120-LX]	AA ETO 01.008 Saintonge, Cazaux
	E90	D-BD Alpha Jet E [8-TH]	AA ETO 01.008 Saintonge, Cazaux
	E93	D-BD Alpha Jet E [8-TX]	AA ETO 01.008 Saintonge, Cazaux
	E94	D-BD Alpha Jet E [705-RH]	AA EAC 00.314, Tours
	E95	D-BD Alpha Jet E [F-TERQ]	AA Patrouille de France, Salon de Provence
	E97	D-BD Alpha Jet E [102-MB]	AA EE 03.008 Côte d'Or, Cazaux
	E98	D-BD Alpha Jet E [705-MF]	AA EAC 00.314, Tours
	E99	D-BD Alpha Jet E [120-AH]	AA ETO 01.008 Saintonge, Cazaux
	E100	D-BD Alpha Jet E $	AA EPNER, Istres
	E101	D-BD Alpha Jet E [120-TT]	AA ETO 01.008 Saintonge, Cazaux
	E102	D-BD Alpha Jet E [120-LM]	AA ETO 01.008 Saintonge, Cazaux
	E104	D-BD Alpha Jet E [705-TG]	AA EAC 00.314, Tours
	E105	D-BD Alpha Jet E [8-FM]	AA EE 03.008 Côte d'Or, Cazaux
	E107	D-BD Alpha Jet E [705-UD]	AA EAC 00.314, Tours
	E108	D-BD Alpha Jet E [8-AF]	AA ETO 01.008 Saintonge, Cazaux
	E109	D-BD Alpha Jet E [120-AG]	AA ETO 01.008 Saintonge, Cazaux
	E110	D-BD Alpha Jet E [705-AH]	AA EAC 00.314, Tours
	E112	D-BD Alpha Jet E [30-AO]	AA CEAM/ECE 01.030 Côte d'Argent, Mont-de-Marsan
	E113	D-BD Alpha Jet E [F-TETD,9]	AA Patrouille de France, Salon de Provence
	E114	D-BD Alpha Jet E [F-TERR,0]	AA Patrouille de France, Salon de Provence
	E115	D-BD Alpha Jet E [705-MR]	AA CEAM/ECE 01.030 Côte d'Argent, Mont-de-Marsan
	E116	D-BD Alpha Jet E [8-FN]	AA ETO 01.008 Saintonge, Cazaux
	E117	D-BD Alpha Jet E [102-AI]	AA EE 03.008 Côte d'Or, Cazaux
	E118	D-BD Alpha Jet E [8-LN]	AA ETO 01.008 Saintonge, Cazaux
	E119	D-BD Alpha Jet E [F-UGFE,3]	AA Patrouille de France, Salon de Provence
	E120	D-BD Alpha Jet E [705-LG]	AA EAC 00.314, Tours
	E123	D-BD Alpha Jet E [8-RM]	AA EE 03.008 Côte d'Or, Cazaux
	E124	D-BD Alpha Jet E [120-RN]	AA ETO 01.008 Saintonge, Cazaux
	E125	D-BD Alpha Jet E [705-LK]	AA EAC 00.314, Tours
	E127	D-BD Alpha Jet E [F-UGFK,6]	AA Patrouille de France, Salon de Provence
	E128	D-BD Alpha Jet E [705-TM]	AA EAC 00.314, Tours
	E129	D-BD Alpha Jet E [705-LP]	AA EAC 00.314, Tours
	E130	D-BD Alpha Jet E [F-TERP]	AA Patrouille de France, Salon de Provence
	E131	D-BD Alpha Jet E [120-RO]	AA ETO 01.008 Saintonge, Cazaux
	E134	D-BD Alpha Jet E [705-RM]	AA EAC 00.314, Tours

Serial	Type (code/other identity)	Owner/operator, location or fate	Notes
E135	D-BD Alpha Jet E [8-RX]	AA EE 03.008 Côte d'Or, Cazaux	
E136	D-BD Alpha Jet E [8-RP]	AA EE 03.008 Côte d'Or, Cazaux	
E137	D-BD Alpha Jet E [705-LJ]	AA EAC 00.314, Tours	
E138	D-BD Alpha Jet E [8-RQ]	AA EE 03.008 Côte d'Or, Cazaux	
E139	D-BD Alpha Jet E [F-UGFC]	AA Patrouille de France, Salon de Provence	
E140	D-BD Alpha Jet E [102-FA]	AA, stored Châteaudun	
E141	D-BD Alpha Jet E [705-NF]	AA EAC 00.314, Tours	
E142	D-BD Alpha Jet E [120-LO]	AA ETO 01.008 Saintonge, Cazaux	
E143	D-BD Alpha Jet E	AA	
E144	D-BD Alpha Jet E [8-AK]	AA ETO 01.008 Saintonge, Cazaux	
E145	D-BD Alpha Jet E	AA	
E146	D-BD Alpha Jet E [F-UHRR]	AA Patrouille de France, Salon de Provence	
E147	D-BD Alpha Jet E [118-LT]	AA CEAM/ECE 01.030 Côte d'Argent, Mont-de-Marsan	
E148	D-BD Alpha Jet E [705-LU]	AA EAC 00.314, Tours	
E149	D-BD Alpha Jet E [705-RS]	AA EAC 00.314, Tours	
E151	D-BD Alpha Jet E [8-FD]	AA EE 03.008 Côte d'Or, Cazaux	
E152	D-BD Alpha Jet E [F-UHRT,8]	AA Patrouille de France, Salon de Provence	
E153	D-BD Alpha Jet E [705-RU]	AA EAC 00.314, Tours	
E154	D-BD Alpha Jet E [120-AL]	AA ETO 01.008 Saintonge, Cazaux	
E156	D-BD Alpha Jet E [30-TI]	AA CEAM/ECE 01.030 Côte d'Argent, Mont-de-Marsan	
E157	D-BD Alpha Jet E [120-UC]	AA ETO 02.008 Nice, Cazaux	
E158	D-BD Alpha Jet E [8-RF]	AA ETO 01.008 Saintonge, Cazaux	
E160	D-BD Alpha Jet E [8-UH]	AA ETO 01.008 Saintonge, Cazaux	
E162	D-BD Alpha Jet E [F-TERJ,4]	AA Patrouille de France, Salon de Provence	
E163	D-BD Alpha Jet E [705-RB]	AA EAC 00.314, Tours	
E164	D-BD Alpha Jet E [120-RV]	AA ETO 01.008 Saintonge, Cazaux	
E165	D-BD Alpha Jet E [8-RE]	AA EE 03.008 Côte d'Or, Cazaux	
E166	D-BD Alpha Jet E [705-RW]	AA EAC 00.314, Tours	
E167	D-BD Alpha Jet E [705-MN]	AA EAC 00.314, Tours	
E168	D-BD Alpha Jet E [102-FP]	AA EE 03.008 Côte d'Or, Cazaux	
E169	D-BD Alpha Jet E [30-RX]	AA CEAM/ECE 01.030 Côte d'Argent, Mont-de-Marsan	
E170	D-BD Alpha Jet E [705-RY]	AA EAC 00.314, Tours	
E171	D-BD Alpha Jet E [705-RZ]	AA EAC 00.314, Tours	
E173	D-BD Alpha Jet E [8-MA]	AA EE 03.008 Côte d'Or, Cazaux	
E176	D-BD Alpha Jet E [120-MB]	AA ETO 01.008 Saintonge, Cazaux	
68	Dassault Falcon 7X (F-RAFA)	AA ET 00.060, Villacoublay	
86	Dassault Falcon 7X (F-RAFB)	AA ET 00.060, Villacoublay	
79	Dassault Falcon 20C [CT]	AA DGA EV, Cazaux & Istres	
104	Dassault Falcon 20C [CW]	AA DGA EV, Cazaux & Istres	
138	Dassault Falcon 20C [CR]	AA, stored Cazaux	
252	Dassault Falcon 20E [CA]	AA DGA EV, Cazaux & Istres	
288	Dassault Falcon 20E [CV]	AA DGA EV, Cazaux & Istres	
342	Dassault Falcon 20F [CU]	AA DGA EV, Cazaux & Istres	
375	Dassault Falcon 20F [CZ]	AA DGA EV, Cazaux & Istres	
02	Dassault Falcon 900 (F-RAFP)	AA ET 00.060, Villacoublay	
004	Dassault Falcon 900 (F-RAFQ)	AA ET 00.060, Villacoublay	
...	Dassault Falcon 900	(on order)	
...	Dassault Falcon 900	(on order)	
...	Dassault Falcon 900	(on order)	
231	Dassault Falcon 2000LX (F-RAFC)	AA ET 00.060, Villacoublay	
237	Dassault Falcon 2000LX (F-RAFD)	AA ET 00.060, Villacoublay	
501	Dassault Mirage 2000B (BX1)	AA DGA EV, Cazaux & Istres	
523	Dassault Mirage 2000B [115-KJ]	AA EC 02.005 Ile de France, Orange	
524	Dassault Mirage 2000B [115-OA]	AA EC 02.005 Ile de France, Orange	
525	Dassault Mirage 2000B [115-AM]	AA EC 02.005 Ile de France, Orange	
527	Dassault Mirage 2000B [115-OR]	AA EC 02.005 Ile de France, Orange	
528	Dassault Mirage 2000B [115-KS]	AA EC 02.005 Ile de France, Orange	
529	Dassault Mirage 2000B [115-OC]	AA EC 02.005 Ile de France, Orange	
530	Dassault Mirage 2000B [115-OL]	AA EC 02.005 Ile de France, Orange	

Notes	Serial	Type (code/other identity)	Owner/operator, location or fate
	01	Dassault Mirage 2000-5F	AA DGA EV, Istres
	2	Dassault Mirage 2000C	AA DGA EV, Istres
	38	Dassault Mirage 2000-5F [116-EI]	AA GC 01.002 Cigognes, Luxeuil
	40	Dassault Mirage 2000-5F [2-EX]	AA GC 01.002 Cigognes, Luxeuil
	41	Dassault Mirage 2000-5F [2-FZ]	AA GC 01.002 Cigognes, Luxeuil
	42	Dassault Mirage 2000-5F [2-EY]	AA GC 01.002 Cigognes, Luxeuil
	43	Dassault Mirage 2000-5F [116-EJ] $	AA GC 01.002 Cigognes, Luxeuil
	44	Dassault Mirage 2000-5F [2-EQ]	AA GC 01.002 Cigognes, Luxeuil
	45	Dassault Mirage 2000-5F [188-EF] $	AA EC 03.011 Corse, Djibouti
	46	Dassault Mirage 2000-5F [2-EN]	AA GC 01.002 Cigognes, Luxeuil
	47	Dassault Mirage 2000-5F [2-EP]	AA GC 01.002 Cigognes, Luxeuil
	48	Dassault Mirage 2000-5F [2-EW]	AA GC 01.002 Cigognes, Luxeuil
	49	Dassault Mirage 2000-5F [116-EA]	AA GC 01.002 Cigognes, Luxeuil
	51	Dassault Mirage 2000-5F [30-AS]	AA CEAM/ECE 01.030 Côte d'Argent, Mont-de-Marsan
	52	Dassault Mirage 2000-5F [2-EH]	AA GC 01.002 Cigognes, Luxeuil
	54	Dassault Mirage 2000-5F [2-EZ]	AA GC 01.002 Cigognes, Luxeuil
	55	Dassault Mirage 2000-5F [2-EU]	AA GC 01.002 Cigognes, Luxeuil
	56	Dassault Mirage 2000-5F [2-EG]	AA GC 01.002 Cigognes, Luxeuil
	57	Dassault Mirage 2000-5F [2-ET]	AA GC 01.002 Cigognes, Luxeuil
	58	Dassault Mirage 2000-5F [2-EL]	AA GC 01.002 Cigognes, Luxeuil
	59	Dassault Mirage 2000-5F [2-EV]	AA GC 01.002 Cigognes, Luxeuil
	61	Dassault Mirage 2000-5F [2-ME]	AA GC 01.002 Cigognes, Luxeuil
	62	Dassault Mirage 2000-5F [2-ED]	AA GC 01.002 Cigognes, Luxeuil
	63	Dassault Mirage 2000-5F [2-EM]	AA GC 01.002 Cigognes, Luxeuil
	64	Dassault Mirage 2000C	AA DGA EV, Istres
	65	Dassault Mirage 2000-5F [2-MG]	AA GC 01.002 Cigognes, Luxeuil
	66	Dassault Mirage 2000-5F [2-EO]	AA GC 01.002 Cigognes, Luxeuil
	67	Dassault Mirage 2000-5F [2-MH]	AA GC 01.002 Cigognes, Luxeuil
	71	Dassault Mirage 2000-5F [116-EE]	AA GC 01.002 Cigognes, Luxeuil
	74	Dassault Mirage 2000-5F [2-MK]	AA GC 01.002 Cigognes, Luxeuil
	77	Dassault Mirage 2000-5F [2-AX]	AA
	78	Dassault Mirage 2000-5F [116-EC]	AA GC 01.002 Cigognes, Luxeuil
	82	Dassault Mirage 2000C [115-YL]	AA EC 02.005 Ile de France, Orange
	83	Dassault Mirage 2000C [115-YC]	AA EC 02.005 Ile de France, Orange
	85	Dassault Mirage 2000C [115-LK]	AA EC 02.005 Ile de France, Orange
	88	Dassault Mirage 2000C [115-KV]	AA EC 02.005 Ile de France, Orange
	93	Dassault Mirage 2000C [115-YA]	AA EC 02.005 Ile de France, Orange
	94	Dassault Mirage 2000C [115-KB]	AA EC 02.005 Ile de France, Orange
	96	Dassault Mirage 2000C [115-KI]	AA EC 02.005 Ile de France, Orange
	99	Dassault Mirage 2000C [115-YB]	AA EC 02.005 Ile de France, Orange
	100	Dassault Mirage 2000C [115-YF]	AA EC 02.005 Ile de France, Orange
	101	Dassault Mirage 2000C [115-KE] $	AA EC 02.005 Ile de France, Orange
	102	Dassault Mirage 2000C [115-KR]	AA EC 02.005 Ile de France, Orange
	104	Dassault Mirage 2000C [115-KG]	AA EC 02.005 Ile de France, Orange
	105	Dassault Mirage 2000C [115-LJ]	AA EC 02.005 Ile de France, Orange
	106	Dassault Mirage 2000C [115-KL]	AA EC 02.005 Ile de France, Orange
	107	Dassault Mirage 2000C [115-YD]	AA EC 02.005 Ile de France, Orange
	108	Dassault Mirage 2000C [115-LC]	AA EC 02.005 Ile de France, Orange
	109	Dassault Mirage 2000C [115-YH]	AA EC 02.005 Ile de France, Orange
	111	Dassault Mirage 2000C [115-KF]	AA EC 02.005 Ile de France, Orange
	113	Dassault Mirage 2000C [115-YO]	AA EC 02.005 Ile de France, Orange
	115	Dassault Mirage 2000C [115-YM]	AA EC 02.005 Ile de France, Orange
	117	Dassault Mirage 2000C [115-LD]	AA EC 02.005 Ile de France, Orange
	118	Dassault Mirage 2000C [115-YG]	AA EC 02.005 Ile de France, Orange
	120	Dassault Mirage 2000C [115-KC]	AA EC 02.005 Ile de France, Orange
	121	Dassault Mirage 2000C [115-KN]	AA EC 02.005 Ile de France, Orange
	122	Dassault Mirage 2000C [115-YE]	AA EC 02.005 Ile de France, Orange
	123	Dassault Mirage 2000C [115-KD]	AA EC 02.005 Ile de France, Orange
	124	Dassault Mirage 2000C [115-YT]	AA EC 02.005 Ile de France, Orange
	601	Dassault Mirage 2000D [133-JG]	AA EC 01.003 Navarre, Nancy
	602	Dassault Mirage 2000D [3-XJ] $	AA EC 03.003 Ardennes, Nancy

Serial	Type (code/other identity)	Owner/operator, location or fate	Notes
03	Dassault Mirage 2000D [3-XL]	AA EC 03.003 *Ardennes*, Nancy	
04	Dassault Mirage 2000D [30-IP]	AA CEAM/ECE 01.030 *Côte d'Argent*, Mont-de-Marsan	
05	Dassault Mirage 2000D [133-LF]	AA EC 02.003 *Champagne*, Nancy	
06	Dassault Mirage 2000D [3-JC]	AA EC 02.003 *Champagne*, Nancy	
07	Dassault Mirage 2000D	AA DGA EV, Istres	
09	Dassault Mirage 2000D [118-IF]	AA CEAM/ECE 01.030 *Côte d'Argent*, Mont-de-Marsan	
10	Dassault Mirage 2000D [133-XX]	AA EC 03.003 *Ardennes*, Nancy	
11	Dassault Mirage 2000D [3-JP]	AA EC 02.003 *Champagne*, Nancy	
13	Dassault Mirage 2000D [133-MO]	AA EC 03.003 *Ardennes*, Nancy	
14	Dassault Mirage 2000D [3-JU]	AA EC 02.003 *Champagne*, Nancy	
15	Dassault Mirage 2000D [3-JY]	AA EC 02.003 *Champagne*, Nancy	
16	Dassault Mirage 2000D [118-XH]	AA CEAM/ECE 01.030 *Côte d'Argent*, Mont-de-Marsan	
17	Dassault Mirage 2000D [3-IS]	AA EC 01.003 *Navarre*, Nancy	
18	Dassault Mirage 2000D [3-XC] $	AA EC 03.003 *Ardennes*, Nancy	
20	Dassault Mirage 2000D [3-IU]	AA EC 01.003 *Navarre*, Nancy	
22	Dassault Mirage 2000D [3-IL]	AA EC 01.003 *Navarre*, Nancy	
23	Dassault Mirage 2000D [133-MP]	AA EC 02.003 *Champagne*, Nancy	
24	Dassault Mirage 2000D [3-IT] $	AA EC 02.003 *Champagne*, Nancy	
25	Dassault Mirage 2000D [3-XG]	AA EC 03.003 *Ardennes*, Nancy	
26	Dassault Mirage 2000D [133-IC]	AA EC 01.003 *Navarre*, Nancy	
27	Dassault Mirage 2000D [30-JO]	AA CEAM/ECE 01.030 *Côte d'Argent*, Mont-de-Marsan	
28	Dassault Mirage 2000D [133-JL]	AA EC 02.003 *Champagne*, Nancy	
29	Dassault Mirage 2000D [3-XO]	AA EC 03.003 *Ardennes*, Nancy	
30	Dassault Mirage 2000D [3-XD] $	AA EC 03.003 *Ardennes*, Nancy	
31	Dassault Mirage 2000D [133-IH]	AA EC 01.003 *Navarre*, Nancy	
32	Dassault Mirage 2000D [133-XE]	AA EC 01.003 *Navarre*, Nancy	
34	Dassault Mirage 2000D [133-JE]	AA EC 01.003 *Navarre*, Nancy	
35	Dassault Mirage 2000D [133-AS]	AA EC 01.003 *Navarre*, Nancy	
36	Dassault Mirage 2000D [133-JV]	AA EC 02.003 *Champagne*, Nancy	
37	Dassault Mirage 2000D [30-XQ]	AA CEAM/ECE 01.030 *Côte d'Argent*, Mont-de-Marsan	
38	Dassault Mirage 2000D [3-IJ]	AA EC 03.003 *Ardennes*, Nancy	
39	Dassault Mirage 2000D [3-JJ]	AA EC 02.003 *Champagne*, Nancy	
40	Dassault Mirage 2000D [3-IN]	AA EC 01.003 *Navarre*, Nancy	
41	Dassault Mirage 2000D [3-JW]	AA EC 02.003 *Champagne*, Nancy	
42	Dassault Mirage 2000D [30-IE]	AA CEAM/ECE 01.030 *Côte d'Argent*, Mont-de-Marsan	
43	Dassault Mirage 2000D [3-JD]	AA EC 02.003 *Champagne*, Nancy	
44	Dassault Mirage 2000D $	AA DGA EV, Istres	
45	Dassault Mirage 2000D [133-XP]	AA EC 03.003 *Ardennes*, Nancy	
46	Dassault Mirage 2000D [3-MQ]	AA EC 01.003 *Navarre*, Nancy	
47	Dassault Mirage 2000D [133-IO]	AA EC 01.003 *Navarre*, Nancy	
48	Dassault Mirage 2000D [3-XT] $	AA EC 03.003 *Ardennes*, Nancy	
49	Dassault Mirage 2000D [3-XY]	AA EC 03.003 *Ardennes*, Nancy	
50	Dassault Mirage 2000D [3-IA]	AA EC 01.003 *Navarre*, Nancy	
52	Dassault Mirage 2000D [3-XN] $	AA EC 03.003 *Ardennes*, Nancy	
53	Dassault Mirage 2000D [3-AU]	AA ETD 04.003 *Argonne*, Nancy	
54	Dassault Mirage 2000D [3-ID]	AA EC 01.003 *Navarre*, Nancy	
55	Dassault Mirage 2000D [133-LH]	AA EC 01.003 *Navarre*, Nancy	
57	Dassault Mirage 2000D [3-JM]	AA EC 03.003 *Ardennes*, Nancy	
58	Dassault Mirage 2000D [3-JN]	AA EC 02.003 *Champagne*, Nancy	
59	Dassault Mirage 2000D [133-XR]	AA EC 03.003 *Ardennes*, Nancy	
60	Dassault Mirage 2000D [3-JF]	AA ETD 04.003 *Argonne*, Nancy	
61	Dassault Mirage 2000D [133-XI]	AA EC 03.003 *Ardennes*, Nancy	
62	Dassault Mirage 2000D [3-XA]	AA EC 03.003 *Ardennes*, Nancy	
64	Dassault Mirage 2000D [133-IW]	AA EC 01.003 *Navarre*, Nancy	
66	Dassault Mirage 2000D [133-IQ]	AA EC 01.003 *Navarre*, Nancy	
67	Dassault Mirage 2000D [133-JZ]	AA EC 02.003 *Champagne*, Nancy	

Notes	Serial	Type (code/other identity)	Owner/operator, location or fate
	668	Dassault Mirage 2000D [3-IG]	AA EC 03.003 *Ardennes*, Nancy
	669	Dassault Mirage 2000D [133-AL]	AA ETD 04.003 *Argonne*, Nancy
	670	Dassault Mirage 2000D [133-XF]	AA EC 03.003 *Ardennes*, Nancy
	671	Dassault Mirage 2000D [3-XK]	AA EC 03.003 *Ardennes*, Nancy
	672	Dassault Mirage 2000D [3-XV]	AA EC 03.003 *Ardennes*, Nancy
	673	Dassault Mirage 2000D	AA DGA EV, Istres
	674	Dassault Mirage 2000D [30-IR]	AA CEAM/ECE 01.030 *Côte d'Argent*, Mont-de-Marsan
	675	Dassault Mirage 2000D [3-JI] $	AA EC 01.003 *Navarre*, Nancy
	676	Dassault Mirage 2000D $	AA DGA EV, Istres
	677	Dassault Mirage 2000D [3-JT]	AA EC 02.003 *Champagne*, Nancy
	678	Dassault Mirage 2000D [133-JB]	AA EC 02.003 *Champagne*, Nancy
	679	Dassault Mirage 2000D [3-JX]	AA EC 01.003 *Navarre*, Nancy
	680	Dassault Mirage 2000D [3-XM]	AA EC 03.003 *Ardennes*, Nancy
	681	Dassault Mirage 2000D [3-AG]	AA EC 01.003 *Navarre*, Nancy
	682	Dassault Mirage 2000D [133-JR]	AA EC 02.003 *Champagne*, Nancy
	683	Dassault Mirage 2000D [3-IV]	AA EC 01.003 *Navarre*, Nancy
	684	Dassault Mirage 2000D	AA
	685	Dassault Mirage 2000D [3-XZ]	AA EC 01.003 *Navarre*, Nancy
	686	Dassault Mirage 2000D [133-JH]	AA EC 02.003 *Champagne*, Nancy
	D02	Dassault Mirage 2000D	AA DGA EV, Istres
	301	Dassault Mirage 2000N	AA DGA EV, Istres
	306	Dassault Mirage 2000N [116-BL]	AA EC 02.004 *La Fayette*, Istres
	316	Dassault Mirage 2000N [116-AU] $	AA EC 02.004 *La Fayette*, Istres
	319	Dassault Mirage 2000N	AA
	333	Dassault Mirage 2000N	AA
	334	Dassault Mirage 2000N	AA DGA EV, Istres
	335	Dassault Mirage 2000N [125-CI]	AA EC 02.004 *La Fayette*, Istres
	338	Dassault Mirage 2000N [125-CG]	AA EC 02.004 *La Fayette*, Istres
	340	Dassault Mirage 2000N [125-AA]	*Withdrawn from use, 2017*
	342	Dassault Mirage 2000N [125-BA]	AA EC 02.004 *La Fayette*, Istres
	345	Dassault Mirage 2000N [125-BU]	AA EC 02.004 *La Fayette*, Istres
	348	Dassault Mirage 2000N [125-AL]	AA EC 02.004 *La Fayette*, Istres
	350	Dassault Mirage 2000N [125-AJ]	AA EC 02.004 *La Fayette*, Istres
	351	Dassault Mirage 2000N [125-AQ]	AA EC 02.004 *La Fayette*, Istres
	354	Dassault Mirage 2000N [125-BJ]	AA EC 02.004 *La Fayette*, Istres
	355	Dassault Mirage 2000N [125-AE]	AA EC 02.004 *La Fayette*, Istres
	356	Dassault Mirage 2000N [125-BX]	AA EC 02.004 *La Fayette*, Istres
	357	Dassault Mirage 2000N [125-CO]	AA EC 02.004 *La Fayette*, Istres
	358	Dassault Mirage 2000N [125-BQ]	AA EC 02.004 *La Fayette*, Istres
	359	Dassault Mirage 2000N [125-AK] $	AA, stored Châteaudun
	360	Dassault Mirage 2000N [125-CB]	*Crashed, Chad, 28 September 2017*
	361	Dassault Mirage 2000N [125-CK]	AA EC 02.004 *La Fayette*, Istres
	362	Dassault Mirage 2000N [125-CU]	AA EC 02.004 *La Fayette*, Istres
	364	Dassault Mirage 2000N [125-BB]	AA EC 02.004 *La Fayette*, Istres
	365	Dassault Mirage 2000N [4-AI]	AA, stored Châteaudun
	366	Dassault Mirage 2000N [125-BC]	AA EC 02.004 *La Fayette*, Istres
	367	Dassault Mirage 2000N [125-AW]	AA EC 02.004 *La Fayette*, Istres
	368	Dassault Mirage 2000N [125-AR]	AA EC 02.004 *La Fayette*, Istres
	369	Dassault Mirage 2000N [125-AG]	AA EC 02.004 *La Fayette*, Istres
	370	Dassault Mirage 2000N [125-CQ]	AA EC 02.004 *La Fayette*, Istres
	371	Dassault Mirage 2000N [125-BD]	AA EC 02.004 *La Fayette*, Istres
	372	Dassault Mirage 2000N [125-CM]	AA EC 02.004 *La Fayette*, Istres
	373	Dassault Mirage 2000N [125-CF]	AA EC 02.004 *La Fayette*, Istres
	374	Dassault Mirage 2000N [125-BS]	AA EC 02.004 *La Fayette*, Istres
	375	Dassault Mirage 2000N [125-CL]	AA EC 02.004 *La Fayette*, Istres
	301	Dassault Rafale B	AA DGA EV, Istres
	302	Dassault Rafale B	AA DGA EV, Istres
	303	Dassault Rafale B [4-EA]	AA ETR 03.004 *Aquitaine*, St Dizier
	304	Dassault Rafale B [4-EB]	AA ETR 03.004 *Aquitaine*, St Dizier
	305	Dassault Rafale B [4-EC]	AA ETR 03.004 *Aquitaine*, St Dizier

Serial	Type (code/other identity)	Owner/operator, location or fate	Notes
306	Dassault Rafale B [30-IB]	AA CEAM/ECE 01.030 Côte d'Argent, Mont-de-Marsan	
307	Dassault Rafale B [30-IA]	AA CEAM/ECE 01.030 Côte d'Argent, Mont-de-Marsan	
308	Dassault Rafale B [4-HA]	AA EC 01.004 Gascogne, St Dizier	
309	Dassault Rafale B [4-HB]	AA EC 01.004 Gascogne, St Dizier	
310	Dassault Rafale B [4-HC]	AA ETR 03.004 Aquitaine, St Dizier	
311	Dassault Rafale B [113-HD]	AA EC 01.004 Gascogne, St Dizier	
312	Dassault Rafale B [4-HF]	AA EC 01.004 Gascogne, St Dizier	
313	Dassault Rafale B [4-HI]	AA ETR 03.004 Aquitaine, St Dizier	
314	Dassault Rafale B [4-HP]	AA EC 01.004 Gascogne, St Dizier	
315	Dassault Rafale B [4-HK]	AA EC 01.004 Gascogne, St Dizier	
317	Dassault Rafale B [4-HO]	AA ETR 03.004 Aquitaine, St Dizier	
318	Dassault Rafale B [30-HM]	AA EC 02.030 Normandie-Niémen, Mont-de-Marsan	
319	Dassault Rafale B [4-HN]	AA EC 01.004 Gascogne, St Dizier	
320	Dassault Rafale B [4-HV]	AA EC 01.004 Gascogne, St Dizier	
321	Dassault Rafale B [4-HQ]	AA EC 03.030 Lorraine, St Dizier	
322	Dassault Rafale B [4-HU]	AA EC 01.004 Gascogne, St Dizier	
323	Dassault Rafale B [30-HT]	AA CEAM/ECE 01.030 Côte d'Argent, Mont-de-Marsan	
324	Dassault Rafale B [30-HW] $	AA CEAM/ECE 01.030 Côte d'Argent, Mont-de-Marsan	
325	Dassault Rafale B [4-HX]	AA ETR 03.004 Aquitaine, St Dizier	
326	Dassault Rafale B [113-HY]	AA EC 01.004 Gascogne, St Dizier	
327	Dassault Rafale B [4-HZ]	AA ETR 03.004 Aquitaine, St Dizier	
328	Dassault Rafale B [4-IC]	AA EC 01.004 Gascogne, St Dizier	
329	Dassault Rafale B [4-ID]	AA ETR 03.004 Aquitaine, St Dizier	
330	Dassault Rafale B [4-IE]	AA EC 01.004 Gascogne, St Dizier	
331	Dassault Rafale B [30-IF]	AA EC 02.030 Normandie-Niémen, Mont-de-Marsan	
332	Dassault Rafale B [4-IG]	AA EC 01.004 Gascogne, St Dizier	
333	Dassault Rafale B [4-IH]	AA EC 01.004 Gascogne, St Dizier	
334	Dassault Rafale B [4-II]	AA ETR 03.004 Aquitaine, St Dizier	
335	Dassault Rafale B [4-IJ]	AA EC 01.004 Gascogne, St Dizier	
336	Dassault Rafale B [4-IK] $	AA EC 01.004 Gascogne, St Dizier	
337	Dassault Rafale B [4-IL]	AA EC 01.004 Gascogne, St Dizier	
338	Dassault Rafale B [4-IO]	AA EC 01.004 Gascogne, St Dizier	
339	Dassault Rafale B [4-FF]	AA ETR 03.004 Aquitaine, St Dizier	
340	Dassault Rafale B [4-FG]	AA EC 01.004 Gascogne, St Dizier	
341	Dassault Rafale B [4-FH]	AA EC 01.004 Gascogne, St Dizier	
342	Dassault Rafale B [4-FI]	AA EC 01.004 Gascogne, St Dizier	
343	Dassault Rafale B [4-FJ]	AA EC 01.004 Gascogne, St Dizier	
344	Dassault Rafale B [4-FK]	AA EC 01.004 Gascogne, St Dizier	
345	Dassault Rafale B [4-FL]	AA EC 01.004 Gascogne, St Dizier	
346	Dassault Rafale B [4-FM]	AA ETR 03.004 Aquitaine, St Dizier	
347	Dassault Rafale B [4-FN]	AA ETR 03.004 Aquitaine, St Dizier	
348	Dassault Rafale B [4-FO]	AA ETR 03.004 Aquitaine, St Dizier	
349	Dassault Rafale B [4-FP] $	AA ETR 03.004 Aquitaine, St Dizier	
350	Dassault Rafale B [113-FQ]	AA ETR 03.004 Aquitaine, St Dizier	
351	Dassault Rafale B [4-FR]	AA EC 02.004 La Fayette, St Dizier	
352	Dassault Rafale B [4-FS]	AA ETR 03.004 Aquitaine, St Dizier	
353	Dassault Rafale B [4-FT]	AA EC 02.004 La Fayette, St Dizier	
354	Dassault Rafale B [4-FU]	AA EC 02.004 La Fayette, St Dizier	
355	Dassault Rafale B [4-FV]	AA EC 02.004 La Fayette, St Dizier	
356	Dassault Rafale B [4-FW]	AA EC 02.004 La Fayette, St Dizier	
357	Dassault Rafale B	AA (on order)	
358	Dassault Rafale B	AA (on order)	
101	Dassault Rafale C	AA DGA EV, Istres	
102	Dassault Rafale C [30-EF]	AA CEAM/ECE 01.030 Côte d'Argent, Mont-de-Marsan	

Notes	Serial	Type (code/other identity)	Owner/operator, location or fate
	103	Dassault Rafale C [30-HR]	AA EC 02.030 *Normandie-Niémen*, Mont-de-Marsan
	104	Dassault Rafale C [113-HH] $	AA EC 03.030 *Lorraine*, St Dizier
	105	Dassault Rafale C [30-HE]	AA EC 03.030 *Lorraine*, St Dizier
	106	Dassault Rafale C [113-HG]	AA EC 03.030 *Lorraine*, St Dizier
	107	Dassault Rafale C [113-HJ] $	AA EC 03.030 *Lorraine*, St Dizier
	108	Dassault Rafale C [113-HS]	AA EC 03.030 *Lorraine*, St Dizier
	109	Dassault Rafale C [30-IM]	AA EC 02.030 *Normandie-Niémen*, Mont-de-Marsan
	110	Dassault Rafale C [30-IN]	AA EC 03.030 *Lorraine*, St Dizier
	111	Dassault Rafale C [30-IP]	AA EC 02.030 *Normandie-Niémen*, Mont-de-Marsan
	112	Dassault Rafale C [30-IQ]	AA EC 02.030 *Normandie-Niémen*, Mont-de-Marsan
	113	Dassault Rafale C [30-IR]	AA EC 02.030 *Normandie-Niémen*, Mont-de-Marsan
	114	Dassault Rafale C [30-IS]	AA EC 02.030 *Normandie-Niémen*, Mont-de-Marsan
	115	Dassault Rafale C [30-IT]	AA EC 03.030 *Lorraine*, St Dizier
	116	Dassault Rafale C [30-IU]	AA EC 02.030 *Normandie-Niémen*, Mont-de-Marsan
	117	Dassault Rafale C [113-IV]	AA EC 03.030 *Lorraine*, St Dizier
	118	Dassault Rafale C [30-IW]	AA EC 02.030 *Normandie-Niémen*, Mont-de-Marsan
	119	Dassault Rafale C [30-IX]	AA EC 03.030 *Lorraine*, St Dizier
	120	Dassault Rafale C [30-IY] $	AA EC 03.030 *Lorraine*, St Dizier
	121	Dassault Rafale C [113-IZ]	AA EC 01.004 *Gascogne*, St Dizier
	122	Dassault Rafale C [4-GA]	AA ETR 03.004 *Aquitaine*, St Dizier
	123	Dassault Rafale C [30-GB]	AA EC 02.030 *Normandie-Niémen*, Mont-de-Marsan
	124	Dassault Rafale C [104-GC]	AA EC 01.007 *Provence*, Al Dhafra, UAE
	125	Dassault Rafale C [30-GD]	AA EC 02.030 *Normandie-Niémen*, Mont-de-Marsan
	126	Dassault Rafale C [30-GE]	AA EC 02.030 *Normandie-Niémen*, Mont-de-Marsan
	127	Dassault Rafale C [30-GF]	AA EC 02.030 *Normandie-Niémen*, Mont-de-Marsan
	128	Dassault Rafale C [30-GG]	AA EC 02.030 *Normandie-Niémen*, Mont-de-Marsan
	129	Dassault Rafale C [30-GH]	AA EC 02.030 *Normandie-Niémen*, Mont-de-Marsan
	130	Dassault Rafale C [104-GI]	AA EC 01.007 *Provence*, Al Dhafra, UAE
	131	Dassault Rafale C [30-GJ]	AA EC 02.030 *Normandie-Niémen*, Mont-de-Marsan
	132	Dassault Rafale C [30-GK]	AA EC 02.030 *Normandie-Niémen*, Mont-de-Marsan
	133	Dassault Rafale C [4-GL] $	AN ETR 03.004 *Aquitaine*, St Dizier
	134	Dassault Rafale C [104-GM]	AA EC 01.007 *Provence*, Al Dhafra, UAE
	135	Dassault Rafale C [30-GN]	AA EC 03.030 *Lorraine*, St Dizier
	136	Dassault Rafale C [104-GO]	AA EC 01.007 *Provence*, Al Dhafra, UAE
	137	Dassault Rafale C [104-GP]	AA EC 01.007 *Provence*, Al Dhafra, UAE
	138	Dassault Rafale C [30-GQ]	AA EC 02.030 *Normandie-Niémen*, Mont-de-Marsan
	139	Dassault Rafale C [30-GR]	AA EC 02.030 *Normandie-Niémen*, Mont-de-Marsan
	140	Dassault Rafale C [30-GS]	AA EC 02.030 *Normandie-Niémen*, Mont-de-Marsan
	141	Dassault Rafale C [30-GT]	AA EC 02.030 *Normandie-Niémen*, Mont-de-Marsan
	142	Dassault Rafale C [4-GU]	AA ETR 03.004 *Aquitaine*, St Dizier
	143	Dassault Rafale C [30-GV] $	AA EC 03.030 *Lorraine*, St Dizier
	144	Dassault Rafale C [30-GW]	AA EC 03.030 *Lorraine*, St Dizier

Serial	Type (code/other identity)	Owner/operator, location or fate	Notes
145	Dassault Rafale C [30-GX]	AA EC 03.030 *Lorraine*, St Dizier	
146	Dassault Rafale C [30-GY]	AA EC 03.030 *Lorraine*, St Dizier	
147	Dassault Rafale C [30-GZ]	AA EC 02.030 *Normandie-Niémen*, Mont-de-Marsan	
148	Dassault Rafale [30-VA] $	AA EC 02.030 *Normandie-Niémen*, Mont-de-Marsan	
149	Dassault Rafale C	AA (on order)	
150	Dassault Rafale C	AA (on order)	
151	Dassault Rafale C	AA (on order)	
152	Dassault Rafale C	AA (on order)	
153	Dassault Rafale C	AA (on order)	
154	Dassault Rafale C	AA (on order)	
155	Dassault Rafale C	AA (on order)	
156	Dassault Rafale C	AA (on order)	
157	Dassault Rafale C	AA (on order)	
158	Dassault Rafale C	AA (on order)	
159	Dassault Rafale C	AA (on order)	
160	Dassault Rafale C	AA (on order)	
292	DHC-6 Twin Otter 200 [F-RACC]	AA GAM 00.056 *Vaucluse*, Evreux	
298	DHC-6 Twin Otter 200 [F-RACD]	AA GAM 00.056 *Vaucluse*, Evreux	
300	DHC-6 Twin Otter 200 [F-RACE]	AA GAM 00.056 *Vaucluse*, Evreux	
730	DHC-6 Twin Otter 300 [F-RACA]	AA ET 03.061 *Poitou*, Orléans	
745	DHC-6 Twin Otter 300 [CV]	AA ET 03.061 *Poitou*, Orléans	
054	Embraer EMB.121AA Xingu [YX]	AA EAT 00.319 *Capitaine Dartigues*, Avord	
064	Embraer EMB.121AA Xingu [YY]	AA EAT 00.319 *Capitaine Dartigues*, Avord	
066	Embraer EMB.121AN Xingu [ZA]	AA EAT 00.319 *Capitaine Dartigues*, Avord	
072	Embraer EMB.121AA Xingu [YA]	AA EAT 00.319 *Capitaine Dartigues*, Avord	
075	Embraer EMB.121AA Xingu [YC]	AA EAT 00.319 *Capitaine Dartigues*, Avord	
078	Embraer EMB.121AA Xingu [YE]	AA EAT 00.319 *Capitaine Dartigues*, Avord	
082	Embraer EMB.121AA Xingu [YG] $	AA EAT 00.319 *Capitaine Dartigues*, Avord	
083	Embraer EMB.121AN Xingu [ZE]	AA EAT 00.319 *Capitaine Dartigues*, Avord	
084	Embraer EMB.121AA Xingu [YH]	AA EAT 00.319 *Capitaine Dartigues*, Avord	
086	Embraer EMB.121AA Xingu [YI]	AA EAT 00.319 *Capitaine Dartigues*, Avord	
089	Embraer EMB.121AA Xingu [YJ]	AA EAT 00.319 *Capitaine Dartigues*, Avord	
090	Embraer EMB.121AN Xingu [ZF]	AA EAT 00.319 *Capitaine Dartigues*, Avord	
091	Embraer EMB.121AA Xingu [YK]	AA EAT 00.319 *Capitaine Dartigues*, Avord	
092	Embraer EMB.121AA Xingu [YL]	AA EAT 00.319 *Capitaine Dartigues*, Avord	
096	Embraer EMB.121AA Xingu [YN]	AA EAT 00.319 *Capitaine Dartigues*, Avord	
098	Embraer EMB.121AA Xingu [YO]	AA EAT 00.319 *Capitaine Dartigues*, Avord	
099	Embraer EMB.121AA Xingu [YP]	AA EAT 00.319 *Capitaine Dartigues*, Avord	
102	Embraer EMB.121AA Xingu [YS]	AA EAT 00.319 *Capitaine Dartigues*, Avord	
103	Embraer EMB.121AA Xingu [YT]	AA EAT 00.319 *Capitaine Dartigues*, Avord	
105	Embraer EMB.121AA Xingu [YU]	AA EAT 00.319 *Capitaine Dartigues*, Avord	
107	Embraer EMB.121AA Xingu [YV]	AA EAT 00.319 *Capitaine Dartigues*, Avord	
108	Embraer EMB.121AA Xingu [YW]	AA EAT 00.319 *Capitaine Dartigues*, Avord	
2233	Eurocopter AS.332L-1 Super Puma [FY]	AA GAM 00.056 *Vaucluse*, Evreux	
2235	Eurocopter AS.332L-1 Super Puma [FZ]	AA EH 03.067 *Parisis*, Villacoublay	
2244	Eurocopter AS.332L-1 Super Puma [PM]	AA EH 01.044 *Solenzara*, Solenzara	
2377	Eurocopter AS.332L-1 Super Puma [FU]	AA EH 03.067 *Parisis*, Villacoublay	
2461	Eurocopter EC.725AP Caracal [SA]	AA EH 01.067 *Pyrénées*, Cazaux	
2549	Eurocopter EC.725AP Caracal [SB]	AA EH 01.067 *Pyrénées*, Cazaux	
2552	Eurocopter EC.725AP Caracal [SE]	AA EH 01.067 *Pyrénées*, Cazaux	
2619	Eurocopter EC.725AP Caracal [SC]	AA EH 05.067 *Alpilles*, Aix-en-Provence	
2626	Eurocopter EC.725AP Caracal [SD]	AA EH 01.067 *Pyrénées*, Cazaux	
2741	Eurocopter EC.225LP Caracal [SY]	AA GAM 00.056 *Vaucluse*, Evreux	
2752	Eurocopter EC.225LP Caracal [SZ]	AA GAM 00.056 *Vaucluse*, Evreux	
2770	Eurocopter EC.725R-2 Caracal [SG]	AA EH 01.067 *Pyrénées*, Cazaux	
2772	Eurocopter EC.725R-2 Caracal [SH]	AA EH 01.067 *Pyrénées*, Cazaux	
2778	Eurocopter EC.725R-2 Caracal [SI]	AA EH 01.067 *Pyrénées*, Cazaux	
2789	Eurocopter EC.725R-2 Caracal [SJ]	AA EH 01.067 *Pyrénées*, Cazaux	
2802	Eurocopter EC.725R-2 Caracal [SK]	AA EH 01.067 *Pyrénées*, Cazaux	
5361	Eurocopter AS.555AN Fennec [UT]	AA EH 05.067 *Alpilles*, Orange	

Notes	Serial	Type (code/other identity)	Owner/operator, location or fate
	5382	Eurocopter AS.555AN Fennec [UV]	AA EH 05.067 *Alpilles*, Orange
	5386	Eurocopter AS.555AN Fennec [UX]	AA EH 05.067 *Alpilles*, Orange
	5387	Eurocopter AS.555AN Fennec [UY]	AA EH 05.067 *Alpilles*, Orange
	5390	Eurocopter AS.555AN Fennec [UZ]	AA EH 03.067 *Parisis*, Villacoublay
	5391	Eurocopter AS.555AN Fennec [VA]	AA EH 05.067 *Alpilles*, Orange
	5392	Eurocopter AS.555AN Fennec [VB]	AA EH 05.067 *Alpilles*, Orange
	5393	Eurocopter AS.555AN Fennec [VC]	AA EH 05.067 *Alpilles*, Orange
	5396	Eurocopter AS.555AN Fennec [VD]	AA EH 05.067 *Alpilles*, Orange
	5397	Eurocopter AS.555AN Fennec [VE]	AA ET 00.068 *Antilles-Guyane*, Cayenne
	5398	Eurocopter AS.555AN Fennec [VF]	AA EH 03.067 *Parisis*, Villacoublay
	5399	Eurocopter AS.555AN Fennec [VG] $	AA
	5400	Eurocopter AS.555AN Fennec [VH]	AA EH 05.067 *Alpilles*, Orange
	5412	Eurocopter AS.555AN Fennec [VI]	AA EH 05.067 *Alpilles*, Orange
	5427	Eurocopter AS.555AN Fennec [VJ]	AA EH 03.067 *Parisis*, Villacoublay
	5430	Eurocopter AS.555AN Fennec [VL]	AA EH 03.067 *Parisis*, Villacoublay
	5431	Eurocopter AS.555AN Fennec [VM] $	AA EH 03.067 *Parisis*, Villacoublay
	5440	Eurocopter AS.555AN Fennec [VN]	AA, stored Creil
	5441	Eurocopter AS.555AN Fennec [VO]	AA EH 03.067 *Parisis*, Villacoublay
	5444	Eurocopter AS.555AN Fennec [VP]	AA EH 03.067 *Parisis*, Villacoublay
	5445	Eurocopter AS.555AN Fennec [VQ]	AA EH 05.067 *Alpilles*, Orange
	5448	Eurocopter AS.555AN Fennec [VR]	AA EH 03.067 *Parisis*, Villacoublay
	5452	Eurocopter AS.555AN Fennec [VS]	AA EH 05.067 *Alpilles*, Orange
	5455	Eurocopter AS.555AN Fennec [VT]	AA EH 03.067 *Parisis*, Villacoublay
	5457	Eurocopter AS.555AN Fennec [VU]	AA ET 00.068 *Antilles-Guyane*, Cayenne
	5458	Eurocopter AS.555AN Fennec [VV]	AA EH 05.067 *Alpilles*, Orange
	5466	Eurocopter AS.555AN Fennec [VW]	AA ET 00.068 *Antilles-Guyane*, Cayenne
	5468	Eurocopter AS.555AN Fennec [VX]	AA EH 03.067 *Parisis*, Villacoublay
	5490	Eurocopter AS.555AN Fennec [VY]	AA EH 05.067 *Alpilles*, Orange
	5506	Eurocopter AS.555AN Fennec [WA]	AA EH 05.067 *Alpilles*, Orange
	5509	Eurocopter AS.555AN Fennec [WB]	AA EH 05.067 *Alpilles*, Orange
	5511	Eurocopter AS.555AN Fennec [WC]	AA EH 03.067 *Parisis*, Villacoublay
	5516	Eurocopter AS.555AN Fennec [WD]	AA EH 03.067 *Parisis*, Villacoublay
	5520	Eurocopter AS.555AN Fennec [WE]	AA EH 03.067 *Parisis*, Villacoublay
	5523	Eurocopter AS.555AN Fennec [WF]	AA EH 05.067 *Alpilles*, Orange
	5526	Eurocopter AS.555AN Fennec [WG]	AA EH 03.067 *Parisis*, Villacoublay
	5530	Eurocopter AS.555AN Fennec [WH]	AA EH 05.067 *Alpilles*, Orange
	5532	Eurocopter AS.555AN Fennec [WI]	AA EH 05.067 *Alpilles*, Orange
	5534	Eurocopter AS.555AN Fennec [WJ]	AA EH 05.067 *Alpilles*, Orange
	5536	Eurocopter AS.555AN Fennec [WK]	AA EH 03.067 *Parisis*, Villacoublay
	5559	Eurocopter AS.555AN Fennec [WL]	AA EH 05.067 *Alpilles*, Orange
	03	Extra EA-330LC [F-TGCH]	AA EVAA, Salon de Provence
	04	Extra EA-330SC [F-TGCI]	AA EVAA, Salon de Provence
	05	Extra EA-330SC [F-TGCJ]	AA EVAA, Salon de Provence
	290	Fokker 100 [F-ZAFT]	AA DGA EV, Istres
	...	Fokker 100 [F-ZAFT]	AA DGA EV, Istres (on order)
	4588	Lockheed C-130H Hercules [61-PM] $	AA ET 02.061 *Franche-Comté*, Orléans
	4589	Lockheed C-130H Hercules [61-PN]	AA ET 02.061 *Franche-Comté*, Orléans
	5114	Lockheed C-130H Hercules [61-PA]	AA ET 02.061 *Franche-Comté*, Orléans
	5116	Lockheed C-130H Hercules [61-PB]	AA ET 02.061 *Franche-Comté*, Orléans
	5119	Lockheed C-130H Hercules [61-PC]	AA ET 02.061 *Franche-Comté*, Orléans
	5140	Lockheed C-130H Hercules [61-PD]	AA ET 02.061 *Franche-Comté*, Orléans
	5142	Lockheed C-130H-30 Hercules [61-PE]	AA ET 02.061 *Franche-Comté*, Orléans
	5144	Lockheed C-130H-30 Hercules [61-PF] $	AA ET 02.061 *Franche-Comté*, Orléans
	5150	Lockheed C-130H-30 Hercules [61-PG]	AA ET 02.061 *Franche-Comté*, Orléans
	5151	Lockheed C-130H-30 Hercules [61-PH]	AA ET 02.061 *Franche-Comté*, Orléans
	5152	Lockheed C-130H-30 Hercules [61-PI]	AA ET 02.061 *Franche-Comté*, Orléans
	5153	Lockheed C-130H-30 Hercules [61-PJ]	AA ET 02.061 *Franche-Comté*, Orléans
	5226	Lockheed C-130H-30 Hercules [61-PK]	AA ET 02.061 *Franche-Comté*, Orléans
	5227	Lockheed C-130H-30 Hercules [61-PL]	AA ET 02.061 *Franche-Comté*, Orléans
	5836	Lockheed C-130J Hercules II [61-PO]	AA ET 02.061 *Franche-Comté*, Orléans
	....	Lockheed C-130J Hercules II	AA (on order)
	....	Lockheed KC-130J Hercules II	AA (on order)

Serial	Type (code/other identity)	Owner/operator, location or fate	Notes
...	Lockheed KC-130J Hercules II	AA (on order)	
01	Pilatus PC-21 (HB-HVA) [709-FC]	AA (on order)	
02	Pilatus PC-21 (HB-HVB) [709-FD]	AA (on order)	
03	Pilatus PC-21 (HB-HVC) [709-FE]	AA (on order)	
04	Pilatus PC-21 (HB-HVD) [709-FF]	AA (on order)	
05	Pilatus PC-21 (HB-HVE) [709-FG]	AA (on order)	
06	Pilatus PC-21 (HB-HVF) [709-FH]	AA (on order)	
07	Pilatus PC-21 (HB-HVG) [709-FI]	AA (on order)	
08	Pilatus PC-21 (HB-HVH) [709-FJ]	AA (on order)	
09	Pilatus PC-21 (HB-HVI) [709-FK]	AA (on order)	
10	Pilatus PC-21 (HB-HVJ) [709-FL]	AA (on order)	
11	Pilatus PC-21 (HB-HVK) [709-FM]	AA (on order)	
12	Pilatus PC-21 (HB-HVL) [709-FN]	AA (on order)	
13	Pilatus PC-21 (HB-HVM) [709-FO]	AA (on order)	
14	Pilatus PC-21 (HB-HVN) [709-FP]	AA (on order)	
15	Pilatus PC-21 (HB-HVO) [709-FQ]	AA (on order)	
16	Pilatus PC-21 (HB-HVP) [709-FR]	AA (on order)	
17	Pilatus PC-21 (HB-HVQ) [709-FS]	AA (on order)	
7	SOCATA TB-30 Epsilon [315-UF]	AA EPAA 00.315, Cognac	
26	SOCATA TB-30 Epsilon [315-UY]	AA EPAA 00.315, Cognac	
27	SOCATA TB-30 Epsilon [315-UZ]	AA EPAA 00.315, Cognac	
30	SOCATA TB-30 Epsilon [315-VC]	AA EPAA 00.315, Cognac	
64	SOCATA TB-30 Epsilon [315-WG]	AA EPAA 00.315, Cognac	
65	SOCATA TB-30 Epsilon [315-WH]	AA EPAA 00.315, Cognac	
66	SOCATA TB-30 Epsilon [315-WI]	AA EPAA 00.315, Cognac	
67	SOCATA TB-30 Epsilon [315-WJ]	AA EPAA 00.315, Cognac	
69	SOCATA TB-30 Epsilon [F-SEWL]	AA Cartouche Dorée (EPAA 00.315), Cognac	
73	SOCATA TB-30 Epsilon [315-WP]	AA EPAA 00.315, Cognac	
78	SOCATA TB-30 Epsilon [315-WU]	AA EPAA 00.315, Cognac	
82	SOCATA TB-30 Epsilon [315-WY]	AA EPAA 00.315, Cognac	
83	SOCATA TB-30 Epsilon [315-WZ]	AA EPAA 00.315, Cognac	
84	SOCATA TB-30 Epsilon [315-XA]	AA EPAA 00.315, Cognac	
90	SOCATA TB-30 Epsilon [F-SEXG]	AA Cartouche Dorée (EPAA 00.315), Cognac	
91	SOCATA TB-30 Epsilon [315-XH]	AA EPAA 00.315, Cognac	
92	SOCATA TB-30 Epsilon [315-XI]	AA EPAA 00.315, Cognac	
95	SOCATA TB-30 Epsilon [315-XL]	AA EPAA 00.315, Cognac	
96	SOCATA TB-30 Epsilon [315-XM]	AA EPAA 00.315, Cognac	
97	SOCATA TB-30 Epsilon [315-XN]	AA EPAA 00.315, Cognac	
99	SOCATA TB-30 Epsilon [F-SEXP]	AA Cartouche Dorée (EPAA 00.315), Cognac	
101	SOCATA TB-30 Epsilon [315-XR]	AA EPAA 00.315, Cognac	
102	SOCATA TB-30 Epsilon [F-SEXS,2]	AA Cartouche Dorée (EPAA 00.315), Cognac	
103	SOCATA TB-30 Epsilon [315-XT]	AA EPAA 00.315, Cognac	
104	SOCATA TB-30 Epsilon [315-XU]	AA EPAA 00.315, Cognac	
113	SOCATA TB-30 Epsilon [F-SEYD]	AA Cartouche Dorée (EPAA 00.315), Cognac	
116	SOCATA TB-30 Epsilon [F-SEYG]	AA Cartouche Dorée (EPAA 00.315), Cognac	
117	SOCATA TB-30 Epsilon [315-YH]	AA EPAA 00.315, Cognac	
118	SOCATA TB-30 Epsilon [315-YI]	AA EPAA 00.315, Cognac	
121	SOCATA TB-30 Epsilon [315-YL]	AA EPAA 00.315, Cognac	
127	SOCATA TB-30 Epsilon [315-YR]	AA EPAA 00.315, Cognac	
131	SOCATA TB-30 Epsilon [315-YV]	AA EPAA 00.315, Cognac	
133	SOCATA TB-30 Epsilon [315-YX]	AA EPAA 00.315, Cognac	
136	SOCATA TB-30 Epsilon [315-ZA]	AA EPAA 00.315, Cognac	
141	SOCATA TB-30 Epsilon [F-SEZF]	AA Cartouche Dorée (EPAA 00.315), Cognac	
142	SOCATA TB-30 Epsilon [315-ZG]	AA EPAA 00.315, Cognac	
144	SOCATA TB-30 Epsilon [315-ZI]	AA EPAA 00.315, Cognac	
146	SOCATA TB-30 Epsilon [315-ZK]	AA EPAA 00.315, Cognac	
149	SOCATA TB-30 Epsilon [315-ZM]	AA EPAA 00.315, Cognac	
150	SOCATA TB-30 Epsilon [315-ZN]	AA EPAA 00.315, Cognac	
33	SOCATA TBM 700A [XA]	AA ET 00.043 Médoc, Bordeaux	
35	SOCATA TBM 700A [BW]	AA DGA EV, Cazaux & Istres	
77	SOCATA TBM 700A [XD]	AA ET 00.043 Médoc, Bordeaux	
78	SOCATA TBM 700A [XE]	AA CEAM, Mont-de-Marsan	

Notes	Serial	Type (code/other identity)	Owner/operator, location or fate
	80	SOCATA TBM 700A [BY]	AA DGA EV, Cazaux & Istres
	93	SOCATA TBM 700A [XL]	AA ET 00.041 Verdun, Villacoublay
	94	SOCATA TBM 700A [BZ]	AA DGA EV, Cazaux & Istres
	95	SOCATA TBM 700A [XH]	AA CEAM, Mont-de-Marsan
	103	SOCATA TBM 700A [XI]	AA ET 00.041 Verdun, Villacoublay
	104	SOCATA TBM 700A [XJ]	AA ET 00.043 Médoc, Bordeaux
	105	SOCATA TBM 700A [XK] $	AA ET 00.043 Médoc, Bordeaux
	106	SOCATA TBM 700A [BX]	AA DGA EV, Cazaux & Istres
	110	SOCATA TBM 700A [XP]	AA ET 00.041 Verdun, Villacoublay
	111	SOCATA TBM 700A [XM]	AA ET 00.041 Verdun, Villacoublay
	115	SOCATA TBM 700A [BQ]	AA DGA EV, Cazaux & Istres
	117	SOCATA TBM 700A [XN]	AA ET 00.043 Médoc, Bordeaux
	125	SOCATA TBM 700A [XO]	AA ET 00.043 Médoc, Bordeaux
	131	SOCATA TBM 700A [XQ]	AA ET 00.041 Verdun, Villacoublay
	146	SOCATA TBM 700A [XR]	AA ET 00.041 Verdun, Villacoublay
	147	SOCATA TBM 700A [XS]	AA ET 00.041 Verdun, Villacoublay
	R87	Transall C-160R [61-ZE]	Withdrawn from use, 2017
	R89	Transall C-160R [61-ZG] $	Withdrawn from use, 2017
	R90	Transall C-160R [61-ZH]	Withdrawn from use, 2017
	R91	Transall C-160R [61-ZI]	Withdrawn from use, 2017
	R93	Transall C-160R [61-ZK]	AA ET 02.064 Anjou, Evreux
	R94	Transall C-160R [61-ZL]	Withdrawn from use, 2017
	R96	Transall C-160R [61-ZN]	Withdrawn from use, 2017
	R97	Transall C-160R [61-ZA]	AA ET 02.064 Anjou, Evreux
	R158	Transall C-160R [61-ZX]	Withdrawn from use
	R160	Transall C-160R [61-ZZ]	AA ET 02.064 Anjou, Evreux
	R201	Transall C-160R [64-GA]	AA ET 02.064 Anjou, Evreux
	R202	Transall C-160R [64-GB]	AA ET 02.064 Anjou, Evreux
	R203	Transall C-160R [64-GC] $	AA ET 02.064 Anjou, Evreux
	R204	Transall C-160R [64-GD]	Withdrawn from use, October 2016
	R206	Transall C-160R [64-GF]	AA ET 02.064 Anjou, Evreux
	R208	Transall C-160R [64-GH] $	AA ET 02.064 Anjou, Evreux
	R210	Transall C-160R [64-GJ]	AA ET 02.064 Anjou, Evreux
	R212	Transall C-160R [64-GL]	AA ET 02.064 Anjou, Evreux
	R213	Transall C-160R [64-GM]	AA ET 02.064 Anjou, Evreux
	R214	Transall C-160R [64-GN]	AA ET 02.064 Anjou, Evreux
	F216	Transall C-160NG GABRIEL [GT]	AA EEA 00.054 Dunkerque, Evreux
	R217	Transall C-160R [64-GQ]	AA ET 02.064 Anjou, Evreux
	R218	Transall C-160R [64-GR]	AA ET 02.064 Anjou, Evreux
	F221	Transall C-160NG GABRIEL [GS] $	AA EEA 00.054 Dunkerque, Evreux
	R223	Transall C-160R [64-GW]	AA ET 02.064 Anjou, Evreux
	R224	Transall C-160R [64-GX]	AA ET 02.064 Anjou, Evreux
	R225	Transall C-160R [64-GY]	AA ET 02.064 Anjou, Evreux
	R226	Transall C-160R [64-GZ]	AA ET 02.064 Anjou, Evreux
	Aéronautique Navale/Marine (AN)		
	2	Dassault-Breguet Atlantique 2	AN 21 Flottille, Lorient/Lann Bihoué
	3	Dassault-Breguet Atlantique 2	AN 23 Flottille, Lorient/Lann Bihoué
	4	Dassault-Breguet Atlantique 2	AN 23 Flottille, Lorient/Lann Bihoué
	5	Dassault-Breguet Atlantique 2	AN 21 Flottille, Lorient/Lann Bihoué
	9	Dassault-Breguet Atlantique 2	AN 23 Flottille, Lorient/Lann Bihoué
	12	Dassault-Breguet Atlantique 2	AN 21 Flottille, Lorient/Lann Bihoué
	13	Dassault-Breguet Atlantique 2	AN 21 Flottille, Lorient/Lann Bihoué
	14	Dassault-Breguet Atlantique 2	AN 23 Flottille, Lorient/Lann Bihoué
	16	Dassault-Breguet Atlantique 2	AN 21 Flottille, Lorient/Lann Bihoué
	17	Dassault-Breguet Atlantique 2 $	AN 21 Flottille, Lorient/Lann Bihoué
	18	Dassault-Breguet Atlantique 2	AN 21 Flottille, Lorient/Lann Bihoué
	19	Dassault-Breguet Atlantique 2	AN 23 Flottille, Lorient/Lann Bihoué
	20	Dassault-Breguet Atlantique 2	AN 23 Flottille, Lorient/Lann Bihoué
	21	Dassault-Breguet Atlantique 2	AN 21 Flottille, Lorient/Lann Bihoué
	22	Dassault-Breguet Atlantique 2	AN 21 Flottille, Lorient/Lann Bihoué
	23	Dassault-Breguet Atlantique 2	AN 21 Flottille, Lorient/Lann Bihoué
	24	Dassault-Breguet Atlantique 2	AN 21 Flottille, Lorient/Lann Bihoué

Serial	Type (code/other identity)	Owner/operator, location or fate	Notes
26	Dassault-Breguet Atlantique 2	AN 21 Flottille, Lorient/Lann Bihoué	
27	Dassault-Breguet Atlantique 2	AN 21 Flottille, Lorient/Lann Bihoué	
32	Dassault Falcon 10(MER)	AN 57 Escadrille, Landivisiau	
101	Dassault Falcon 10(MER)	AN 57 Escadrille, Landivisiau	
129	Dassault Falcon 10(MER)	AN 57 Escadrille, Landivisiau	
133	Dassault Falcon 10(MER)	AN 57 Escadrille, Landivisiau	
143	Dassault Falcon 10(MER)	AN 57 Escadrille, Landivisiau	
185	Dassault Falcon 10(MER) $	AN 57 Escadrille, Landivisiau	
48	Dassault Falcon 20G Guardian	AN 25 Flottille, Papeete & Tontouta	
65	Dassault Falcon 20G Guardian	AN 25 Flottille, Papeete & Tontouta	
72	Dassault Falcon 20G Guardian	AN 25 Flottille, Papeete & Tontouta	
77	Dassault Falcon 20G Guardian	AN 25 Flottille, Papeete & Tontouta	
80	Dassault Falcon 20G Guardian	AN 25 Flottille, Papeete & Tontouta	
5	Dassault Falcon 50MS SURMAR	AN 24 Flottille, Lorient/Lann Bihoué	
7	Dassault Falcon 50MI SURMAR	AN 24 Flottille, Lorient/Lann Bihoué	
27	Dassault Falcon 50MS SURMAR	AN 24 Flottille, Lorient/Lann Bihoué	
30	Dassault Falcon 50MI SURMAR	AN 24 Flottille, Lorient/Lann Bihoué	
34	Dassault Falcon 50MS SURMAR	AN 24 Flottille, Lorient/Lann Bihoué	
36	Dassault Falcon 50MI SURMAR	AN 24 Flottille, Lorient/Lann Bihoué	
78	Dassault Falcon 50MS SURMAR	AN 24 Flottille, Lorient/Lann Bihoué	
132	Dassault Falcon 50MI SURMAR	AN 24 Flottille, Lorient/Lann Bihoué	
2	Dassault Rafale M	AN 12 Flottille, Landivisiau	
5	Dassault Rafale M	AN 12 Flottille, Landivisiau	
6	Dassault Rafale M	AN 12 Flottille, Landivisiau	
7	Dassault Rafale M	AMD-BA, Istres	
8	Dassault Rafale M	AN 12 Flottille, Landivisiau	
9	Dassault Rafale M	AN 12 Flottille, Landivisiau	
10	Dassault Rafale M	AN 12 Flottille, Landivisiau	
11	Dassault Rafale M	AN 11 Flottille, Landivisiau	
12	Dassault Rafale M	AN ETR 03.004 *Aquitaine*, St Dizier	
13	Dassault Rafale M	AN 11 Flottille, Landivisiau	
14	Dassault Rafale M	AN 11 Flottille, Landivisiau	
15	Dassault Rafale M	AN 12 Flottille, Landivisiau	
16	Dassault Rafale M	AN 12 Flottille, Landivisiau	
17	Dassault Rafale M	AN 12 Flottille, Landivisiau	
19	Dassault Rafale M $	AN 12 Flottille, Landivisiau	
20	Dassault Rafale M	AN 17 Flottille, Landivisiau	
21	Dassault Rafale M	AN 12 Flottille, Landivisiau	
23	Dassault Rafale M	AN 12 Flottille, Landivisiau	
26	Dassault Rafale M	AN 12 Flottille, Landivisiau	
27	Dassault Rafale M $	AN ETR 03.004 *Aquitaine*, St Dizier	
28	Dassault Rafale M	AN ETR 03.004 *Aquitaine*, St Dizier	
29	Dassault Rafale M	AN 12 Flottille, Landivisiau	
30	Dassault Rafale M	AN 12 Flottille, Landivisiau	
31	Dassault Rafale M	AN 11 Flottille, Landivisiau	
32	Dassault Rafale M	AN 11 Flottille, Landivisiau	
33	Dassault Rafale M	AN ETR 03.004 *Aquitaine*, St Dizier	
34	Dassault Rafale M	AN ETR 03.004 *Aquitaine*, St Dizier	
35	Dassault Rafale M	AN 12 Flottille, Landivisiau	
36	Dassault Rafale M $	AN 11 Flottille, Landivisiau	
37	Dassault Rafale M	AN ETR 03.004 *Aquitaine*, St Dizier	
38	Dassault Rafale M	AN 12 Flottille, Landivisiau	
39	Dassault Rafale M	AN 11 Flottille, Landivisiau	
40	Dassault Rafale M	AN 11 Flottille, Landivisiau	
41	Dassault Rafale M	AN	
42	Dassault Rafale M	AN 11 Flottille, Landivisiau	
43	Dassault Rafale M	AN 11 Flottille, Landivisiau	
44	Dassault Rafale M	AN 11 Flottille, Landivisiau	
45	Dassault Rafale M	AN 11 Flottille, Landivisiau	
46	Dassault Rafale M	AN 17 Flottille, Landivisiau	
47	Dassault Rafale M	AN (on order)	
48	Dassault Rafale M	AN (on order)	

Notes	Serial	Type (code/other identity)	Owner/operator, location or fate
	49	Dassault Rafale M	AN (on order)
	50	Dassault Rafale M	AN (on order)
	M01	Dassault Rafale M	Withdrawn from use
	M02	Dassault Rafale M	AN DGA EV, Istres
	65	Embraer EMB.121AN Xingu	AN 28 Flottille, Hyères
	67	Embraer EMB.121AN Xingu $	AN 28 Flottille, Hyères
	68	Embraer EMB.121AN Xingu	AN 28 Flottille, Hyères
	69	Embraer EMB.121AN Xingu	AN 28 Flottille, Hyères
	71	Embraer EMB.121AN Xingu	AN 28 Flottille, Hyères
	74	Embraer EMB.121AN Xingu $	AN 28 Flottille, Hyères
	77	Embraer EMB.121AN Xingu	AN 28 Flottille, Hyères
	81	Embraer EMB.121AN Xingu	AN 24 Flottille, Lorient/Lann Bihoué
	85	Embraer EMB.121AN Xingu	AN 24 Flottille, Lorient/Lann Bihoué
	87	Embraer EMB.121AN Xingu	AN 28 Flottille, Hyères
	17	Eurocopter AS.365N Dauphin	AN 35 Flottille, Hyères
	19	Eurocopter AS.365N Dauphin	AN 35 Flottille, Hyères
	24	Eurocopter AS.365N Dauphin	AN 35 Flottille, Hyères
	57	Eurocopter AS.365N Dauphin	AN 35 Flottille, Hyères
	81	Eurocopter AS.365N Dauphin	AN 35 Flottille, Le Touquet
	91	Eurocopter AS.365N Dauphin	AN 35 Flottille, Hyères
	157	Eurocopter AS.365N Dauphin	AN 35 Flottille, Hyères
	313	Eurocopter SA.365F-1 Dauphin II	AN 35 Flottille, Hyères
	318	Eurocopter SA.365F-1 Dauphin II	AN 35 Flottille, Hyères
	322	Eurocopter SA.365F-1 Dauphin II	AN 35 Flottille, Hyères
	355	Eurocopter AS.565MA Panther	AN 36 Flottille, Hyères
	362	Eurocopter AS.565MA Panther	AN 36 Flottille, Hyères
	403	Eurocopter AS.565MA Panther	AN 36 Flottille, Hyères
	436	Eurocopter AS.565MA Panther	AN 36 Flottille, Hyères
	452	Eurocopter AS.565MA Panther	AN 36 Flottille, Hyères
	453	Eurocopter AS.565MA Panther	AN 36 Flottille, Hyères
	466	Eurocopter AS.565MA Panther	AN 36 Flottille, Hyères
	482	Eurocopter AS.565MA Panther	AN 36 Flottille, Hyères
	486	Eurocopter AS.565MA Panther	AN 36 Flottille, Hyères
	488	Eurocopter AS.565MA Panther	AN 36 Flottille, Hyères
	503	Eurocopter AS.565MA Panther	AN 36 Flottille, Hyères
	505	Eurocopter AS.565MA Panther	AN 36 Flottille, Hyères
	506	Eurocopter AS.565MA Panther	AN 36 Flottille, Hyères
	507	Eurocopter AS.565MA Panther $	AN 36 Flottille, Hyères
	511	Eurocopter AS.565MA Panther	AN 36 Flottille, Hyères
	519	Eurocopter AS.565MA Panther	AN 36 Flottille, Hyères
	522	Eurocopter AS.565MA Panther $	AN 36 Flottille, Hyères
	524	Eurocopter AS.565MA Panther	AN 36 Flottille, Hyères
	542	Eurocopter AS.565MA Panther	AN 36 Flottille, Hyères
	6872	Eurocopter AS.365N-3 Dauphin	AN 35 Flottille, Tahiti
	6928	Eurocopter AS.365N-3 Dauphin	AN 35 Flottille, Tahiti
	1	NH Industries NH.90-NFH Caïman (F-ZWTO)	AN 33 Flottille, Lanvéoc/Poulmic
	2	NH Industries NH.90-NFH Caïman	AN CEPA/10 Escadrille, Hyères
	3	NH Industries NH.90-NFH Caïman	AN 31 Flottille, Hyères
	4	NH Industries NH.90-NFH Caïman	AN 33 Flottille, Lanvéoc/Poulmic
	5	NH Industries NH.90-NFH Caïman	AN 33 Flottille, Lanvéoc/Poulmic
	6	NH Industries NH.90-NFH Caïman	AN 33 Flottille, Lanvéoc/Poulmic
	7	NH Industries NH.90-NFH Caïman	AN 33 Flottille, Lanvéoc/Poulmic
	8	NH Industries NH.90-NFH Caïman	AN 31 Flottille, Hyères
	9	NH Industries NH.90-NFH Caïman	AN 31 Flottille, Hyères
	10	NH Industries NH.90-NFH Caïman	AN 31 Flottille, Hyères
	11	NH Industries NH.90-NFH Caïman	AN 33 Flottille, Lanvéoc/Poulmic
	12	NH Industries NH.90-NFH Caïman	AN 31 Flottille, Hyères
	13	NH Industries NH.90-NFH Caïman	AN 31 Flottille, Hyères
	14	NH Industries NH.90-NFH Caïman	AN 33 Flottille, Lanvéoc/Poulmic
	15	NH Industries NH.90-NFH Caïman	AN CEPA/10 Escadrille, Hyères
	16	NH Industries NH.90-NFH Caïman	AN 31 Flottille, Hyères
	17	NH Industries NH.90-NFH Caïman	AN

Airco DH9 E8894 is registered as G-CDLI and is one of more than eight thousand built. Currently there are seven known survivors and this one is the only one in flyable condition.

Hurricane I R4118 (G-HUPW) is the sole surviving airworthy Battle of Britain Hurricane and is now based at Old Warden.

Spitfire LF IXe MK356 belongs to the Battle of Britain Memorial Flight and is now painted to represent Spitfire EN152 of 92 Sqn, flown by Neville Duke. She is seen here at Biggin Hill heading back to her Coningsby base following repaint. [Photo copyright: Andrew P March]

The Battle of Britain Memorial Flight's Lancaster, PA474, returned to the UK air show circuit in 2017 wearing the code AR-L on its port side, depicting a 460 Sqn (RAAF) machine and the code VN-T on its starboard side, for a 50 Sqn machine from World War II.

e 'QQ' sequence has been allocated to QinetiQ and in 2017 its BAe RJ.70ER finally took up the rks QQ102. Based at Boscombe Down, the QinetiQ fleet is currently undergoing considerable change n several types due to be retired and a smaller, new fleet joining the company with most aircraft now the UK civil register.

44 vintage Auster AOP5 TJ534 is registered at G-AKSY and currently operates from Dunsfold, home the BBC's 'Top Gear' programme.

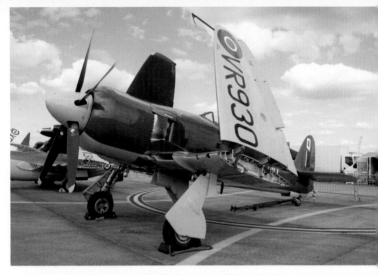

Sea Fury FB11 VR930 belongs to the Royal Navy Historic Flight at Yeovilton and is currently awaiting a engine rebuild before it can fly again. She wears the 110-Q code from her days with 802 NAS when she was delivered in 1948.

WA638 is a modified Meteor T7, used for ejector seat trials and registered as G-JWMA. It is one of a p operated by Martin-Baker from Chalgrove in Oxfordshire.

K585 is a Chipmunk 22, registered as G-BZGA. In 2017 it joined the fleet at Compton Abbas airfield
d visitors can now pay for a flight in it.

e of the delights of the annual air day at Yeovilton is that visitors can often view one of the FAA Museum's
craft on a rare foray outside. In this case it was beautiful Sea Venom FAW22 WW138, coded 227-Z.

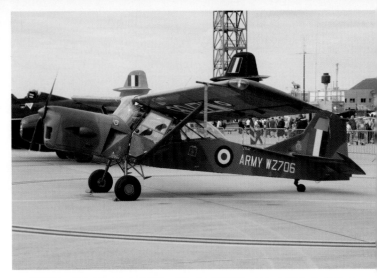

WZ706 is a 1955 vintage Auster AOP9, registered as G-BURR and based at Eggesford in Devon.

Whirlwind HAR10 XJ729 is registered as G-BVGE and based at Chard in Somerset. It is the only examp of its type currently airworthy.

Former Lyneham gate guard Comet C2 XK699 now exists as a nose only outside the Boscombe Down Aviation Collection at Old Sarum. In 2017 it was repainted and is caught here in the sunshine, gleaming nicely.

Lightning F3 XR713 now wears the markings of 56 Squadron on its starboard side, complete with fake identity XR718 while on its port side it wears the markings of 111 Sqn and XR713. Seen here at its Bruntingthorpe base.

Sea King HU5 XV666 is one of two flown by HeliOperations Ltd from the former RN base at Portland in Dorset. With most of the UK Sea King fleet being retired it was a pleasant surprise to see a pair restored to flight, currently for a contract to train German crews.

XW324 is a Jet Provost T5, registered as G-BWSG and based at East Midlands Airport. It wears the code U from its time with no 6 FTS, where it spent most of its service life.

Gazelle HT2 XX436/39-CU is registered as G-ZZLE and is affectionately known as 'Gordon' with the Gazelle Squadron at Hurstbourne Tarrant.

Lynx HAS3S(ICE) XZ246/434-EE wears the colours that it had when it flew from HMS Endurance in the South Atlantic. It is now preserved at the delightful South Yorkshire Aircraft Museum at Doncaster. 2017 was the year when the Navy ended Lynx operations.

41(R) Sqn at Coningsby ended Tornado GR4 operations during 2017 and ZA607/EB-X was one of the last aircraft in the fleet. 2018 sees the last full year of operations with the type with RAF Marham now the sole RAF Tornado base.

ZF378 is a Tucano T1 operated by No 1 FTS at Linton-on-Ouse and specially painted with the code RN-S to celebrate the centenary in 2017 of No 72(R) Sqn.

Lynx HMA8SRU ZF563/312-VL was one of a quartet that did a final flypast around the UK on 17 March 2017. Seen here overflying Compton Abbas, she was minutes away from being grounded forever.

Culdrose based Merlin HM2 ZH857/86-CU of 824 NAS wears its code only on its nose, along with the name 'Tristan', one of the Knights of the Round Table.

Merlin ZJ127/L is very much the shape (and colour) of things to come as the first HC4 conversion. It is operated by Leonardo MW at Yeovil.

Typhoon FGR4 ZJ927 reflects the markings of much of the RAF's Typhoon fleet as 2017 saw the end of 'squadron' codes with aircraft simply having their 'last three' painted on the tail. Other squadron markings also seem to be going out of fashion, perhaps reflecting the constant changes within a fleet which is still seeing new deliveries while older examples are now undergoing Reduction To Produce at Coningsby.

With the familiar background of the Royal International Air Tattoo at Fairford, Hawk T2 ZK021/L of No 4(R) Sqn, part of 4 FTS at Valley gleams under a typical 2017 'Summer' sky!

ZM301 is a Grob Prefect T1 wearing the markings of No 3 FTS, at its Barkston Heath base. 23 of the type are on order with deliveries well under way.

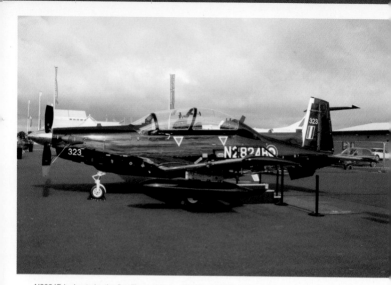

N2824B is due to be the first Texan II for the RAF, as ZM323. It flew to the UK in 2017 to be on display at the Royal International Air Tattoo but then returned to the US for the remainder of the year for further trials.

ZM509 is a Juno HT1, one of 29 due to be in service when the fleet becomes fully operational with the Defence Helicopter Flying School at RAF Shawbury on 1 April 2018, replacing the Squirrel.

ZZ379 is a Wildcat HMA2 operated by 815 NAS from RNAS Yeovilton in Somerset. Another type which wears no distinguishable squadron markings, it appears that the Wildcat fleet will also be bereft of the three digit squadron codes worn by previous Navy helicopters.

With 28 of the fleet being sold to Finland during 2017, the Tutor T1 still soldiers on. The ones based at Yeovilton with 727 NAS also wear Royal Navy badges, as indeed does G-BYXK depicted here.

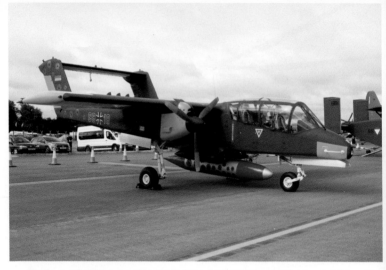

99+18 is an OV-10B Bronco, registered in the UK as G-ONAA but based at Wevelgem in Belgium with the Bronco Demonstration Team.

PT-17 Kaydet N62658 wears 107, the 'last three' of its serial 42-16107 and is based at Hurstbourne Tarrant.

330238/24-A is a Piper L-4H Grasshopper (G-LIVH), based at Yarcombe in Devon.

262 is one of a fleet of eight Pilatus PC-9Ms operated by the Irish Air Corps' Flying Training School at Baldonnel.

BE-35 is a SAAB 105OE operated by the Austrian Air Force's D₂sentrainerstaffel at Linz. The first of these were delivered in 1970.

F-16A MLU FA-132 of the Belgian Air Component wore these special marks in 2017 commemorating the centenary of 1 Smaldeel.

Nose inspection of this L-159A ALCA reveals that it hasn't joined the RAF as AD572/DU-C but does still wear serial 6053 (and, of course, Czech Air Force titles on the nose). The markings reflect the Spitfire of Frantisek Perina of 312 (Czechoslovak) Sqn RAF, the first Czech ace of World War II.

Danish Lynx 90B S-191 was painted in these special markings to commemorate 37 years of service. The type was withdrawn from Danish use in December 2017.

Rafale M 36 of the French Navy was painted in these superb markings for the 2017 Tiger Meet. While the serial certainly wasn't prominent, its operator, 11F, was 'scratched' on the tail in red!

2017 saw significant deliveries of the A400M to the Luftwaffe as the Transall C-160D retires. 54+06 belongs to LTG 62 at Wunstorf.

Tornado IDS(MLU) CSX 7041/6-01 was painted in these superb markings to commemorate 60 years of the Italian Air Force's 311 Gruppo/RSV.

N-175 is an NH.90-NFH of the Dutch Navy (MLD), based at de Kooij. Operated by 860 Sqn, it carries special marks for the centenary of the MLD.

EF-18M Hornet C.15-14/15-01 of Ala 15 of the Spanish Air Force still wears these special markings from the 2016 Tiger Meet.

91471 (59-1471) is a KC-135T Stratotanker here depicted in the markings of the 351st ARS of the 100th ARW at RAF Mildenhall. It left the unit and returned to the US in October 2017.

U-2S 80-1073/BB of the 9th RW based at Beale AFB California appeared in the static display at the Royal International Air Tattoo at Fairford looking decidedly in need of some attention to its paintwork.

The blue and white tail markings reveal that this F-15E Strike Eagle, 91-0327/LN, belongs to the 492nd Fighter Squadron of the 48th Fighter Wing, based at RAF Lakenheath.

91-0418/LN is a F-16CM-50 Fighting Falcon of the 480th Fighter Squadron 'Warhawks' of the 52nd Fighter Wing, based at Spangdahlem in Germany.

Wearing special markings, C-130J-30 Hercules II 08-8602/RS belongs to the 37th Airlift Squadron of the 86th Airlift Wing, based at Ramstein in Germany.

rial	Type (code/other identity)	Owner/operator, location or fate	Notes
	NH Industries NH.90-NFH Caïman	AN 33 Flottille, Lanvéoc/Poulmic	
	NH Industries NH.90-NFH Caïman	AN	
	NH Industries NH.90-NFH Caïman	AN (on order)	
	NH Industries NH.90-NFH Caïman	AN (on order)	
	NH Industries NH.90-NFH Caïman	AN (on order)	
	NH Industries NH.90-NFH Caïman	AN (on order)	
	NH Industries NH.90-NFH Caïman	AN (on order)	
	NH Industries NH.90-NFH Caïman	AN (on order)	
	NH Industries NH.90-NFH Caïman	AN (on order)	
	NH Industries NH.90-NFH Caïman	AN (on order)	
	Northrop Grumman E-2C Hawkeye (165455)	AN 4 Flottille, Lorient/Lann Bihoué	
	Northrop Grumman E-2C Hawkeye (165456)	AN 4 Flottille, Lorient/Lann Bihoué	
	Northrop Grumman E-2C Hawkeye (166417)	AN 4 Flottille, Lorient/Lann Bihoué	
	Northrop Grumman E-2C Hawkeye	AN (on order)	
	Sud Aviation SE.3160 Alouette III	AN 35 Flottille, Hyères	
	Sud Aviation SE.3160 Alouette III	AN 22 Escadrille/ESHE, Lanvéoc/Poulmic	
	Sud Aviation SE.3160 Alouette III	AN 35 Flottille, Hyères	
)	Sud Aviation SA.319B Alouette III	AN 22 Escadrille/ESHE, Lanvéoc/Poulmic	
5	Sud Aviation SA.319B Alouette III	AN 22 Escadrille/ESHE, Lanvéoc/Poulmic	
4	Sud Aviation SA.319B Alouette III	AN 22 Escadrille/ESHE, Lanvéoc/Poulmic	
)	Sud Aviation SA.319B Alouette III	AN 22 Escadrille/ESHE, Lanvéoc/Poulmic	
1	Sud Aviation SA.319B Alouette III	AN 22 Escadrille/ESHE, Lanvéoc/Poulmic	
)	Sud Aviation SE.3160 Alouette III	AN 35 Flottille, Hyères	
7	Sud Aviation SA.319B Alouette III	AN 35 Flottille, Hyères	
4	Sud Aviation SE.3160 Alouette III	AN 22 Escadrille/ESHE, Lanvéoc/Poulmic	
5	Sud Aviation SE.3160 Alouette III	AN 22 Escadrille/ESHE, Lanvéoc/Poulmic	
2	Sud Aviation SA.319B Alouette III	AN 22 Escadrille/ESHE, Lanvéoc/Poulmic	
8	Sud Aviation SA.319B Alouette III	AN 22 Escadrille/ESHE, Lanvéoc/Poulmic	
)	Sud Aviation SE.3160 Alouette III	AN 22 Escadrille/ESHE, Lanvéoc/Poulmic	
2	Sud Aviation SA.319B Alouette III	AN 22 Escadrille/ESHE, Lanvéoc/Poulmic	
8	Sud Aviation SA.319B Alouette III	AN 22 Escadrille/ESHE, Lanvéoc/Poulmic	
1	Sud Aviation SA.319B Alouette III	AN 22 Escadrille/ESHE, Lanvéoc/Poulmic	
7	Sud Aviation SA.319B Alouette III	AN 22 Escadrille/ESHE, Lanvéoc/Poulmic	
3	Sud Aviation SA.319B Alouette III	AN 22 Escadrille/ESHE, Lanvéoc/Poulmic	
4	Sud Aviation SE.3160 Alouette III	AN 22 Escadrille/ESHE, Lanvéoc/Poulmic	
5	Sud Aviation SA.316B Alouette III	AN 22 Escadrille/ESHE, Lanvéoc/Poulmic	
)	Sud Aviation SA.316B Alouette III	AN 22 Escadrille/ESHE, Lanvéoc/Poulmic	
7	Sud Aviation SA.319B Alouette III	AN 22 Escadrille/ESHE, Lanvéoc/Poulmic	
0	Westland Lynx HAS2(FN)	*Withdrawn from use*	
3	Westland Lynx HAS2(FN)	AN 34 Flottille, Lanvéoc/Poulmic	
4	Westland Lynx HAS2(FN)	AN 34 Flottille, Lanvéoc/Poulmic	
5	Westland Lynx HAS2(FN)	AN 34 Flottille, Lanvéoc/Poulmic	
7	Westland Lynx HAS2(FN)	AN 34 Flottille, Lanvéoc/Poulmic	
)	Westland Lynx HAS2(FN)	AN 34 Flottille, Lanvéoc/Poulmic	
4	Westland Lynx HAS2(FN)	*Withdrawn from use*	
2	Westland Lynx HAS2(FN) $	AN 34 Flottille, Lanvéoc/Poulmic	
3	Westland Lynx HAS2(FN)	AN 34 Flottille, Lanvéoc/Poulmic	
5	Westland Lynx HAS2(FN)	AN 34 Flottille, Lanvéoc/Poulmic	
4	Westland Lynx HAS2(FN)	AN 34 Flottille, Lanvéoc/Poulmic	
2	Westland Lynx HAS2(FN)	AN 34 Flottille, Lanvéoc/Poulmic	
3	Westland Lynx HAS2(FN)	*Withdrawn from use*	
4	Westland Lynx HAS2(FN)	AN 34 Flottille, Lanvéoc/Poulmic	
5	Westland Lynx HAS2(FN)	*Withdrawn from use*	
7	Westland Lynx HAS2(FN)	*Withdrawn from use*	
4	Westland Lynx HAS4(FN)	*Withdrawn from use*	
2	Westland Lynx HAS4(FN)	AN 34 Flottille, Lanvéoc/Poulmic	
4	Westland Lynx HAS4(FN)	AN 34 Flottille, Lanvéoc/Poulmic	
5	Westland Lynx HAS4(FN)	AN 34 Flottille, Lanvéoc/Poulmic	
7	Westland Lynx HAS4(FN)	AN 34 Flottille, Lanvéoc/Poulmic	
3	Westland Lynx HAS4(FN)	AN 34 Flottille, Lanvéoc/Poulmic	

Notes	Serial	Type (code/other identity)	Owner/operator, location or fate
	810	Westland Lynx HAS4(FN)	AN 34 Flottille, Lanvéoc/Poulmic
	811	Westland Lynx HAS4(FN)	AN 34 Flottille, Lanvéoc/Poulmic
	813	Westland Lynx HAS4(FN)	*Withdrawn from use*
	814	Westland Lynx HAS4(FN)	AN 34 Flottille, Lanvéoc/Poulmic
Aviation Legére de l'Armée de Terre (ALAT)			
	1005	Aérospatiale SA.330Ba Puma [DCA]	ALAT ESAM, Bourges
	1006	Aérospatiale SA.330Ba Puma [DAA]	*Withdrawn from use, 2016*
	1020	Aérospatiale SA.330Ba Puma [DAB]	ALAT 5 RHC, Pau
	1036	Aérospatiale SA.330Ba Puma [DAC]	ALAT 3 RHC, Etain
	1037	Aérospatiale SA.330Ba Puma [DAD]	ALAT 5 RHC, Pau
	1049	Aérospatiale SA.330Ba Puma [DAE]	ALAT 5 RHC, Pau
	1052	Aérospatiale SA.330Ba Puma [DCB]	ALAT EALAT, Le Luc
	1055	Aérospatiale SA.330Ba Puma [DAF]	ALAT GIH, Cazaux
	1056	Aérospatiale SA.330Ba Puma [DCC]	ALAT GAM/STAT, Valence
	1057	Aérospatiale SA.330Ba Puma [DCD]	ALAT EALAT, Le Luc
	1069	Aérospatiale SA.330Ba Puma [DAG]	ALAT
	1071	Aérospatiale SA.330Ba Puma [DCE]	ALAT EALAT, Le Luc
	1073	Aérospatiale SA.330Ba Puma [DCF]	ALAT EALAT, Le Luc
	1078	Aérospatiale SA.330Ba Puma [DAH]	ALAT 3 RHC, Etain
	1092	Aérospatiale SA.330Ba Puma [DAI]	ALAT
	1093	Aérospatiale SA.330Ba Puma [DCG]	ALAT 3 RHC, Etain
	1100	Aérospatiale SA.330Ba Puma [DAJ]	ALAT 3 RHC, Etain
	1102	Aérospatiale SA.330Ba Puma [DAK]	ALAT
	1107	Aérospatiale SA.330Ba Puma [DAL]	ALAT
	1109	Aérospatiale SA.330Ba Puma [DAM]	ALAT 5 RHC, Pau
	1114	Aérospatiale SA.330Ba Puma [DCH]	ALAT 3 RHC, Etain
	1122	Aérospatiale SA.330Ba Puma [DCI]	ALAT 5 RHC, Pau
	1123	Aérospatiale SA.330Ba Puma [DCJ]	ALAT 5 RHC, Pau
	1128	Aérospatiale SA.330Ba Puma [DAN]	ALAT 3 RHC, Etain
	1130	Aérospatiale SA.330Ba Puma [DCK]	ALAT 5 RHC, Pau
	1135	Aérospatiale SA.330Ba Puma [DCL]	ALAT
	1136	Aérospatiale SA.330Ba Puma [DCM]	ALAT
	1142	Aérospatiale SA.330Ba Puma [DCN]	ALAT EALAT, Le Luc
	1143	Aérospatiale SA.330Ba Puma [DAO]	ALAT
	1145	Aérospatiale SA.330Ba Puma [DCO]	ALAT 3 RHC, Etain
	1149	Aérospatiale SA.330Ba Puma [DAP]	ALAT 5 RHC, Pau
	1150	Aérospatiale SA.330Ba Puma [DCP]	ALAT 3 RHC, Etain
	1155	Aérospatiale SA.330Ba Puma [DCQ]	ALAT 4 RHFS, Pau
	1156	Aérospatiale SA.330Ba Puma [DAQ]	ALAT
	1163	Aérospatiale SA.330Ba Puma [DCR]	ALAT EALAT, Le Luc
	1164	Aérospatiale SA.330Ba Puma [DCS]	ALAT
	1165	Aérospatiale SA.330Ba Puma [DCT]	ALAT
	1171	Aérospatiale SA.330Ba Puma [DCU]	ALAT
	1172	Aérospatiale SA.330Ba Puma [DCV]	ALAT EALAT, Le Luc
	1173	Aérospatiale SA.330Ba Puma [DAR]	ALAT 3 RHC, Etain
	1176	Aérospatiale SA.330Ba Puma [DAS]	ALAT 3 RHC, Etain
	1177	Aérospatiale SA.330Ba Puma [DCW]	ALAT 3 RHC, Etain
	1179	Aérospatiale SA.330Ba Puma [DCX]	ALAT
	1182	Aérospatiale SA.330Ba Puma [DCY]	ALAT
	1186	Aérospatiale SA.330Ba Puma [DCZ]	ALAT 5 RHC, Pau
	1189	Aérospatiale SA.330Ba Puma [DAT]	ALAT 3 RHC, Etain
	1190	Aérospatiale SA.330Ba Puma [DDA]	ALAT 5 RHC, Pau
	1192	Aérospatiale SA.330Ba Puma [DDB]	ALAT
	1196	Aérospatiale SA.330Ba Puma [DDC]	ALAT EALAT, Le Luc
	1197	Aérospatiale SA.330Ba Puma [DAU]	ALAT 5 RHC, Pau
	1198	Aérospatiale SA.330Ba Puma [DDD]	ALAT
	1204	Aérospatiale SA.330Ba Puma [DAV]	ALAT 3 RHC, Etain
	1206	Aérospatiale SA.330Ba Puma [DDE]	ALAT 3 RHC, Etain
	1211	Aérospatiale SA.330Ba Puma [DAW]	ALAT
	1213	Aérospatiale SA.330Ba Puma [DDF]	ALAT
	1214	Aérospatiale SA.330Ba Puma [DAX]	ALAT 3 RHC, Etain
	1217	Aérospatiale SA.330Ba Puma [DAY]	ALAT

ial	Type (code/other identity)	Owner/operator, location or fate	Notes
9	Aérospatiale SA.330Ba Puma [DAZ]	ALAT 3 RHC, Etain	
2	Aérospatiale SA.330Ba Puma [DDG]	ALAT	
3	Aérospatiale SA.330Ba Puma [DDH]	ALAT EALAT, Le Luc	
9	Aérospatiale SA.330Ba Puma [DDJ]	ALAT EALAT, Le Luc	
1	Aérospatiale SA.330Ba Puma [DDK]	ALAT 5 RHC, Pau	
2	Aérospatiale SA.330Ba Puma [DBA]	ALAT 5 RHC, Pau	
5	Aérospatiale SA.330Ba Puma [DDL]	ALAT 5 RHC, Pau	
6	Aérospatiale SA.330Ba Puma [DDM]	ALAT EALAT, Le Luc	
9	Aérospatiale SA.330Ba Puma [DDN]	ALAT 5 RHC, Pau	
3	Aérospatiale SA.330Ba Puma [DBB]	ALAT 5 RHC, Pau	
4	Aérospatiale SA.330Ba Puma [DDO]	ALAT 5 RHC, Pau	
8	Aérospatiale SA.330Ba Puma [DBC]	ALAT 3 RHC, Etain	
2	Aérospatiale SA.330Ba Puma [DDP]	ALAT EALAT, Le Luc	
5	Aérospatiale SA.330Ba Puma [DDQ]	ALAT	
6	Aérospatiale SA.330Ba Puma [DDR]	ALAT GAM/STAT, Valence	
0	Aérospatiale SA.330Ba Puma [DDS]	ALAT EALAT, Le Luc	
2	Aérospatiale SA.330Ba Puma [DBD]	ALAT 5 RHC, Pau	
9	Aérospatiale SA.330Ba Puma [DDT]	ALAT 3 RHC, Etain	
7	Aérospatiale SA.330Ba Puma [DBE]	ALAT	
1	Aérospatiale SA.330Ba Puma [DDU]	ALAT 3 RHC, Etain	
7	Aérospatiale SA.330Ba Puma [DBF]	ALAT	
9	Aérospatiale SA.330Ba Puma [DDV]	ALAT	
8	Aérospatiale SA.330Ba Puma [DBG]	ALAT GAM/STAT, Valence	
7	Aérospatiale SA.330Ba Puma [DDW]	ALAT 3 RHC, Etain	
1	Aérospatiale SA.330Ba Puma [DBH]	ALAT	
7	Aérospatiale SA.330Ba Puma [DBI]	ALAT EALAT, Le Luc	
0	Aérospatiale SA.330Ba Puma [DBJ]	ALAT 3 RHC, Etain	
2	Aérospatiale SA.330Ba Puma [DBK]	ALAT	
9	Aérospatiale SA.330Ba Puma [DBL]	ALAT 3 RHC, Etain	
7	Aérospatiale SA.330Ba Puma [DBM]	ALAT	
2	Aérospatiale SA.330Ba Puma [DBN]	ALAT 5 RHC, Pau	
4	Aérospatiale SA.330Ba Puma [DBO]	ALAT 3 RHC, Etain	
4	Aérospatiale SA.330Ba Puma [DBP]	ALAT 5 RHC, Pau	
2	Aérospatiale SA.330Ba Puma [DDX]	ALAT EALAT, Le Luc	
3	Aérospatiale SA.330Ba Puma [DBQ]	ALAT 3 RHC, Etain	
2	Aérospatiale SA.330Ba Puma [DBR]	ALAT 4 RHFS, Pau	
2	Aérospatiale SA.342M Gazelle [GJA]	ALAT EALAT, Le Luc	
8	Aérospatiale SA.342M Gazelle [GNA]	ALAT EALAT, Le Luc	
9	Aérospatiale SA.342M Gazelle [GAA]	ALAT 1 RHC, Phalsbourg	
6	Aérospatiale SA.342M Gazelle [GAB]	ALAT 4 RHFS, Pau	
7	Aérospatiale SA.342M Gazelle [GJB]	*To Niger, 2017*	
1	Aérospatiale SA.342M Gazelle [GJC]	ALAT EALAT, Le Luc	
2	Aérospatiale SA.342M Gazelle [GAC]	ALAT 1 RHC, Phalsbourg	
3	Aérospatiale SA.342M Gazelle [GNB]	ALAT 1 RHC, Phalsbourg	
9	Aérospatiale SA.342M Gazelle [GJD]	ALAT EALAT, Le Luc	
0	Aérospatiale SA.342M Gazelle [GAD]	ALAT 4 RHFS, Pau	
6	Aérospatiale SA.342M Gazelle [GJF]	ALAT EALAT, Le Luc	
8	Aérospatiale SA.342M Gazelle [GAE]	ALAT 1 RHC, Phalsbourg	
9	Aérospatiale SA.342M Gazelle [GNC]	ALAT EALAT, Le Luc	
7	Aérospatiale SA.342M Gazelle [GMA]	ALAT EALAT, Le Luc	
5	Aérospatiale SA.342M Gazelle [GJH]	ALAT 1 RHC, Phalsbourg	
7	Aérospatiale SA.342M Gazelle [GND]	ALAT GAM/STAT, Valence	
4	Aérospatiale SA.342M Gazelle [GAF]	ALAT 1 RHC, Phalsbourg	
8	Aérospatiale SA.342M Gazelle [GAG]	ALAT 5 RHC, Pau	
9	Aérospatiale SA.342M Gazelle [GAH]	ALAT 5 RHC, Pau	
0	Aérospatiale SA.342M Gazelle [GAI]	ALAT 3 RHC, Etain	
1	Aérospatiale SA.342M Gazelle [GJI]	ALAT EALAT, Le Luc	
2	Aérospatiale SA.342M Gazelle [GNE]	ALAT 1 RHC, Phalsbourg	
3	Aérospatiale SA.342M Gazelle [GNF]	ALAT EALAT, Le Luc	
5	Aérospatiale SA.342M Gazelle [GJJ]	ALAT EALAT, Le Luc	
6	Aérospatiale SA.342M Gazelle [GAJ]	ALAT 5 RHC, Pau	
7	Aérospatiale SA.342M Gazelle [GJK]	ALAT EALAT, Le Luc	

Notes	Serial	Type (code/other identity)	Owner/operator, location or fate
	3858	Aérospatiale SA.342M Gazelle [GNG]	ALAT
	3859	Aérospatiale SA.342M Gazelle [GAK]	ALAT 5 RHC, Pau
	3862	Aérospatiale SA.342M Gazelle [GAL] $	ALAT 1 RHC, Phalsbourg
	3863	Aérospatiale SA.342M Gazelle [GAM]	ALAT 3 RHC, Etain
	3864	Aérospatiale SA.342M Gazelle [GJL]	ALAT
	3865	Aérospatiale SA.342M Gazelle [GAN]	ALAT EALAT, Le Luc
	3866	Aérospatiale SA.342M Gazelle [GNI]	ALAT 1 RHC, Phalsbourg
	3867	Aérospatiale SA.342M Gazelle [GJM]	ALAT EALAT, Le Luc
	3868	Aérospatiale SA.342M Gazelle [GAO]	ALAT 1 RHC, Phalsbourg
	3870	Aérospatiale SA.342M Gazelle [GME]	ALAT
	3896	Aérospatiale SA.342M Gazelle [GNJ]	ALAT
	3911	Aérospatiale SA.342M Gazelle [GAP]	ALAT 1 RHC, Phalsbourg
	3921	Aérospatiale SA.342M Gazelle [GAQ]	ALAT EALAT, Le Luc
	3929	Aérospatiale SA.342M Gazelle [GJN]	ALAT EALAT, Le Luc
	3930	Aérospatiale SA.342M Gazelle [GMF]	ALAT
	3938	Aérospatiale SA.342M Gazelle [GAR]	ALAT EALAT, Le Luc
	3939	Aérospatiale SA.342M Gazelle [GMG]	ALAT
	3947	Aérospatiale SA.342M Gazelle [GAS]	ALAT 5 RHC, Pau
	3948	Aérospatiale SA.342M Gazelle [GAT]	ALAT 1 RHC, Phalsbourg
	3956	Aérospatiale SA.342M Gazelle [GNK]	ALAT
	3957	Aérospatiale SA.342M Gazelle [GAU]	ALAT 5 RHC, Pau
	3964	Aérospatiale SA.342M Gazelle [GAV]	ALAT 3 RHC, Etain
	3965	Aérospatiale SA.342M Gazelle [GJO]	ALAT EALAT, Le Luc
	3992	Aérospatiale SA.342M Gazelle [GNM]	ALAT EALAT, Le Luc
	3996	Aérospatiale SA.342M Gazelle [GAW]	ALAT 5 RHC, Pau
	4008	Aérospatiale SA.342M Gazelle [GNN]	ALAT
	4014	Aérospatiale SA.342M Gazelle [GJP]	ALAT GAM/STAT, Valence
	4018	Aérospatiale SA.342M Gazelle [GAX]	ALAT 3 RHC, Etain
	4019	Aérospatiale SA.342M Gazelle [GAY]	*Crashed Bar-le-Duc, 13 November 2017*
	4020	Aérospatiale SA.342M Gazelle [GAZ]	ALAT 1 RHC, Phalsbourg
	4022	Aérospatiale SA.342M Gazelle [GJQ]	ALAT EALAT, Le Luc
	4023	Aérospatiale SA.342M Gazelle [GMH]	ALAT ESAM, Bourges
	4026	Aérospatiale SA.342M Gazelle [GBA]	ALAT 1 RHC, Phalsbourg
	4032	Aérospatiale SA.342M Gazelle [GNO]	ALAT EALAT, Le Luc
	4034	Aérospatiale SA.342M Gazelle [GBB]	ALAT 1 RHC, Phalsbourg
	4038	Aérospatiale SA.342M Gazelle [GJR]	ALAT EALAT, Le Luc
	4039	Aérospatiale SA.342M Gazelle [GBC]	ALAT 1 RHC, Phalsbourg
	4042	Aérospatiale SA.342M Gazelle [GMB]	ALAT EALAT, Le Luc
	4047	Aérospatiale SA.342M Gazelle [GJS]	ALAT EALAT, Le Luc
	4048	Aérospatiale SA.342M Gazelle [GBD]	ALAT EALAT, Le Luc
	4049	Aérospatiale SA.342M Gazelle [GNP]	ALAT EALAT, Le Luc
	4053	Aérospatiale SA.342M Gazelle [GBE]	ALAT 1 RHC, Phalsbourg
	4059	Aérospatiale SA.342M Gazelle [GBF]	ALAT 1 RHC, Phalsbourg
	4060	Aérospatiale SA.342M Gazelle [GNQ]	ALAT EALAT, Le Luc
	4061	Aérospatiale SA.342M Gazelle [GBG]	ALAT GAM/STAT, Valence
	4065	Aérospatiale SA.342M Gazelle [GNR]	ALAT EALAT, Le Luc
	4066	Aérospatiale SA.342M Gazelle [GBH]	ALAT 3 RHC, Etain
	4067	Aérospatiale SA.342M Gazelle [GJU]	ALAT EALAT, Le Luc
	4071	Aérospatiale SA.342M Gazelle [GNS]	ALAT EHADT, Etain
	4072	Aérospatiale SA.342M Gazelle [GBI]	ALAT 3 RHC, Etain
	4078	Aérospatiale SA.342M Gazelle [GJV]	ALAT EALAT, Le Luc
	4079	Aérospatiale SA.342M Gazelle [GMC]	ALAT EALAT, Le Luc
	4083	Aérospatiale SA.342M Gazelle [GNT]	ALAT EALAT, Le Luc
	4084	Aérospatiale SA.342M Gazelle [GBJ]	ALAT 3 RHC, Etain
	4095	Aérospatiale SA.342M Gazelle [GBL]	ALAT 5 RHC, Pau
	4096	Aérospatiale SA.342M Gazelle [GNU]	ALAT EALAT, Le Luc
	4102	Aérospatiale SA.342M Gazelle [GJW]	ALAT EALAT, Le Luc
	4103	Aérospatiale SA.342M Gazelle [GJX]	ALAT EALAT, Le Luc
	4108	Aérospatiale SA.342M Gazelle [GBM]	ALAT GAM/STAT, Valence
	4109	Aérospatiale SA.342M Gazelle [GBN]	ALAT 5 RHC, Pau
	4114	Aérospatiale SA.342M Gazelle [GBO]	ALAT EALAT, Le Luc
	4115	Aérospatiale SA.342M Gazelle [GBP]	ALAT 5 RHC, Pau

Serial	Type (code/other identity)	Owner/operator, location or fate	Notes
18	Aérospatiale SA.342M Gazelle [GNV]	ALAT EALAT, Le Luc	
19	Aérospatiale SA.342M Gazelle [GBQ]	ALAT 5 RHC, Pau	
20	Aérospatiale SA.342M Gazelle [GBR]	ALAT EALAT, Le Luc	
23	Aérospatiale SA.342M Gazelle [GJY]	ALAT EALAT, Le Luc	
24	Aérospatiale SA.342M Gazelle [GBS]	ALAT 1 RHC, Phalsbourg	
35	Aérospatiale SA.342M Gazelle [GNW]	ALAT	
36	Aérospatiale SA.342M Gazelle [GBT]	ALAT 1 RHC, Phalsbourg	
40	Aérospatiale SA.342M Gazelle [GBU]	ALAT 1 RHC, Phalsbourg	
41	Aérospatiale SA.342M Gazelle [GBV]	ALAT	
42	Aérospatiale SA.342M Gazelle [GBW]	ALAT 5 RHC, Pau	
43	Aérospatiale SA.342M Gazelle [GNX]	ALAT EALAT, Le Luc	
44	Aérospatiale SA.342M Gazelle [GBX]	ALAT 1 RHC, Phalsbourg	
45	Aérospatiale SA.342M Gazelle [GBY] $	ALAT 3 RHC, Etain	
46	Aérospatiale SA.342M Gazelle [GNY]	ALAT EALAT, Le Luc	
51	Aérospatiale SA.342M Gazelle [GBZ]	ALAT 3 RHC, Etain	
55	Aérospatiale SA.342M Gazelle [GCA]	*Crashed Ivory Coast, 4 January 2018*	
59	Aérospatiale SA.342M Gazelle [GNZ]	ALAT EALAT, Le Luc	
60	Aérospatiale SA.342M Gazelle [GCC]	ALAT 1 RHC, Phalsbourg	
61	Aérospatiale SA.342M Gazelle [GCD]	ALAT 1 RHC, Phalsbourg	
62	Aérospatiale SA.342M Gazelle [GCE]	ALAT 5 RHC, Pau	
64	Aérospatiale SA.342M Gazelle [GCF]	ALAT 5 RHC, Pau	
66	Aérospatiale SA.342M Gazelle [GJZ]	ALAT EALAT, Le Luc	
68	Aérospatiale SA.342M Gazelle [GCG]	ALAT 5 RHC, Pau	
71	Aérospatiale SA.342M Gazelle [GMI]	ALAT EALAT, Le Luc	
72	Aérospatiale SA.342M Gazelle [GCH]	*Crashed 9 February 2016, Niger*	
75	Aérospatiale SA.342M Gazelle [GCI]	ALAT 4 RHFS, Pau	
76	Aérospatiale SA.342M Gazelle [GKA]	ALAT EALAT, Le Luc	
77	Aérospatiale SA.342M Gazelle [GKB]	ALAT 1 RHC, Phalsbourg	
78	Aérospatiale SA.342M Gazelle [GOA]	ALAT EALAT, Le Luc	
79	Aérospatiale SA.342M Gazelle [GCJ]	ALAT 3 RHC, Etain	
80	Aérospatiale SA.342M Gazelle [GCK]	ALAT GAM/STAT, Valence	
81	Aérospatiale SA.342M Gazelle [GCL]	ALAT 3 RHC, Etain	
82	Aérospatiale SA.342M Gazelle [GKC]	ALAT EALAT, Le Luc	
83	Aérospatiale SA.342M Gazelle [GOB]	ALAT EALAT, Le Luc	
84	Aérospatiale SA.342M Gazelle [GOC]	ALAT 1 RHC, Phalsbourg	
85	Aérospatiale SA.342M Gazelle [GKD]	ALAT 3 RHC, Etain	
86	Aérospatiale SA.342M Gazelle [GCM]	ALAT 1 RHC, Phalsbourg	
87	Aérospatiale SA.342M Gazelle [GKE]	ALAT EALAT, Le Luc	
89	Aérospatiale SA.342M Gazelle [GCN]	ALAT 4 RHFS, Pau	
90	Aérospatiale SA.342M Gazelle [GMJ]	ALAT EALAT, Le Luc	
91	Aérospatiale SA.342M Gazelle [GCO]	ALAT 4 RHFS, Pau	
92	Aérospatiale SA.342M Gazelle [GOD]	ALAT	
94	Aérospatiale SA.342M Gazelle [GMD]	ALAT EALAT, Le Luc	
95	Aérospatiale SA.342M Gazelle [GCP]	ALAT 3 RHC, Etain	
98	Aérospatiale SA.342M Gazelle [GCQ]	ALAT 3 RHC, Etain	
01	Aérospatiale SA.342M Gazelle [GMK]	ALAT EALAT, Le Luc	
05	Aérospatiale SA.342L-1 Gazelle [GEA]	ALAT 1 RHC, Phalsbourg	
06	Aérospatiale SA.342L-1 Gazelle [GEB]	ALAT EALAT, Le Luc	
07	Aérospatiale SA.342L-1 Gazelle [GEC]	ALAT 3 RHC, Etain	
08	Aérospatiale SA.342L-1 Gazelle [GED]	ALAT GAM/STAT, Valence	
09	Aérospatiale SA.342L-1 Gazelle [GEE]	*Crashed 2 February 2018, Cabasse, France*	
10	Aérospatiale SA.342L-1 Gazelle [GEF]	ALAT 1 RHC, Phalsbourg	
11	Aérospatiale SA.342L-1 Gazelle [GEG]	ALAT 5 RHC, Pau	
12	Aérospatiale SA.342L-1 Gazelle [GEH]	*Crashed 2 February 2018, Cabasse, France*	
14	Aérospatiale SA.342L-1 Gazelle [GEI]	ALAT EALAT, Le Luc	
15	Aérospatiale SA.342L-1 Gazelle [GEJ]	ALAT 5 RHC, Pau	
16	Aérospatiale SA.342L-1 Gazelle [GEK]	ALAT GAM/STAT, Valence	
17	Aérospatiale SA.342L-1 Gazelle [GEL]	ALAT 1 RHC, Phalsbourg	
18	Aérospatiale SA.342L-1 Gazelle [GEM]	ALAT 1 RHC, Phalsbourg	
19	Aérospatiale SA.342L-1 Gazelle [GEN]	ALAT 4 RHFS, Pau	
20	Aérospatiale SA.342L-1 Gazelle [GEO]	ALAT 1 RHC, Phalsbourg	
21	Aérospatiale SA.342L-1 Gazelle [GEP]	ALAT EALAT, Le Luc	

Notes	Serial	Type (code/other identity)	Owner/operator, location or fate
	4222	Aérospatiale SA.342L-1 Gazelle [GEQ]	ALAT EALAT, Le Luc
	4223	Aérospatiale SA.342L-1 Gazelle [GER]	ALAT 3 RHC, Etain
	4224	Aérospatiale SA.342L-1 Gazelle [GES]	ALAT 1 RHC, Phalsbourg
	4225	Aérospatiale SA.342L-1 Gazelle [GET]	ALAT GAM/STAT, Valence
	4226	Aérospatiale SA.342L-1 Gazelle [GEU]	ALAT GAM/STAT, Valence
	4227	Aérospatiale SA.342L-1 Gazelle [GEV]	ALAT 1 RHC, Phalsbourg
	4228	Aérospatiale SA.342L-1 Gazelle [GEW]	ALAT 1 RHC, Phalsbourg
	4229	Aérospatiale SA.342L-1 Gazelle [GEX]	ALAT 4 RHFS, Pau
	4230	Aérospatiale SA.342L-1 Gazelle [GEY]	ALAT GAM/STAT, Valence
	4231	Aérospatiale SA.342L-1 Gazelle [GEZ]	ALAT 5 RHC, Pau
	4232	Aérospatiale SA.342L-1 Gazelle [GFA]	ALAT EALAT, Le Luc
	4233	Aérospatiale SA.342L-1 Gazelle [GFB]	ALAT 3 RHC, Etain
	4234	Aérospatiale SA.342L-1 Gazelle [GFC]	ALAT
	2252	Aérospatiale AS.532UL Cougar [CGA]	ALAT GAM/STAT, Valence
	2266	Aérospatiale AS.532UL Cougar [CGB]	ALAT 5 RHC, Pau
	2267	Aérospatiale AS.532UL Cougar [CGC]	ALAT 4 RHFS, Pau
	2271	Aérospatiale AS.532UL Cougar [CGD]	ALAT 4 RHFS, Pau
	2272	Aérospatiale AS.532UL Cougar [CGE]	ALAT GAM/STAT, Valence
	2273	Aérospatiale AS.532UL Cougar [CGF]	ALAT 1 RHC, Phalsbourg
	2282	Aérospatiale AS.532UL Cougar [CGG]	ALAT
	2285	Aérospatiale AS.532UL Cougar [CGH]	ALAT
	2290	Aérospatiale AS.532UL Cougar [CGI]	ALAT 4 RHFS, Pau
	2293	Aérospatiale AS.532UL Cougar [CGJ]	ALAT 4 RHFS, Pau
	2299	Aérospatiale AS.532UL Cougar [CGK]	ALAT 4 RHFS, Pau
	2300	Aérospatiale AS.532UL Cougar [CGL]	ALAT 1 RHC, Phalsbourg
	2301	Aérospatiale AS.532UL Cougar [CGM]	ALAT 1 RHC, Phalsbourg
	2303	Aérospatiale AS.532UL Cougar [CGN]	ALAT 1 RHC, Phalsbourg
	2316	Aérospatiale AS.532UL Cougar [CGO]	ALAT 4 RHFS, Pau
	2323	Aérospatiale AS.532UL Cougar [CGQ]	ALAT 4 RHFS, Pau
	2324	Aérospatiale AS.532UL Cougar [CGR]	ALAT 4 RHFS, Pau
	2325	Aérospatiale AS.532UL Cougar [CGS]	ALAT
	2327	Aérospatiale AS.532UL Cougar [CGT]	ALAT
	2331	Aérospatiale AS.532UL Cougar [CGU]	ALAT
	2336	Aérospatiale AS.532UL Cougar [CGV]	ALAT 4 RHFS, Pau
	2342	Aérospatiale AS.532UL Cougar [CHA]	ALAT
	2369	Aérospatiale AS.532UL Cougar [CHB]	ALAT
	2375	Aérospatiale AS.532UL Cougar [CHC]	ALAT
	2443	Aérospatiale AS.532UL Cougar [CGW]	ALAT
	2446	Aérospatiale AS.532UL Cougar [CGX]	ALAT 1 RHC, Phalsbourg
	2001	Eurocopter EC.665 Tigre HAP [BHH]	ALAT EFA, Le Luc
	2002	Eurocopter EC.665 Tigre HAP [BHI]	ALAT EFA, Le Luc
	2003	Eurocopter EC.665 Tigre HAP [BHJ]	ALAT 5 RHC, Pau
	2004	Eurocopter EC.665 Tigre HAP [BHK]	ALAT EFA, Le Luc
	2006	Eurocopter EC.665 Tigre HAP [BHL]	ALAT EFA, Le Luc
	2009	Eurocopter EC.665 Tigre HAP [BHB]	ALAT EFA, Le Luc
	2010	Eurocopter EC.665 Tigre HAP [BHA]	ALAT EFA, Le Luc
	2011	Eurocopter EC.665 Tigre HAP [BHM]	ALAT 5 RHC, Pau
	2012	Eurocopter EC.665 Tigre HAP [BHT]	ALAT GAM/STAT, Valence
	2013	Eurocopter EC.665 Tigre HAP [BHC]	ALAT GAM/STAT, Valence
	2015	Eurocopter EC.665 Tigre HAP [BHD]	ALAT 5 RHC, Pau
	2016	Eurocopter EC.665 Tigre HAP [BIA]	Airbus Helicopters, Marseille
	2018	Eurocopter EC.665 Tigre HAP [BHE]	ALAT 5 RHC, Pau
	2019	Eurocopter EC.665 Tigre HAP [BHF]	ALAT 5 RHC, Pau
	2021	Eurocopter EC.665 Tigre HAP [BHN] $	ALAT EFA, Le Luc
	2022	Eurocopter EC.665 Tigre HAP [BHG]	ALAT 5 RHC, Pau
	2023	Eurocopter EC.665 Tigre HAP [BHP]	ALAT 5 RHC, Pau
	2024	Eurocopter EC.665 Tigre HAP [BHO]	ALAT 3 RHC, Etain
	2025	Eurocopter EC.665 Tigre HAP [BHQ]	ALAT 5 RHC, Pau
	2026	Eurocopter EC.665 Tigre HAP [BHR]	ALAT GAM/STAT, Valence
	2027	Eurocopter EC.665 Tigre HAP [BHS]	ALAT 5 RHC, Pau
	2028	Eurocopter EC.665 Tigre HAP [BHU]	ALAT 5 RHC, Pau
	2029	Eurocopter EC.665 Tigre HAP [BHV]	ALAT 5 RHC, Pau

Serial	Type (code/other identity)	Owner/operator, location or fate	Notes
2030	Eurocopter EC.665 Tigre HAP [BHW]	ALAT	
2031	Eurocopter EC.665 Tigre HAP [BHX]	ALAT EFA, Le Luc	
2032	Eurocopter EC.665 Tigre HAP [BHY]	*Withdrawn from use*	
2033	Eurocopter EC.665 Tigre HAP [BHZ]	ALAT 5 RHC, Pau	
2034	Eurocopter EC.665 Tigre HAP [BIB]	ALAT EFA, Le Luc	
2035	Eurocopter EC.665 Tigre HAP [BIC]	ALAT 4 RHFS, Pau	
2036	Eurocopter EC.665 Tigre HAP [BID]	*Withdrawn from use*	
2037	Eurocopter EC.665 Tigre HAP [BIE]	ALAT 5 RHC, Pau	
2038	Eurocopter EC.665 Tigre HAP	Airbus Helicopters, Marseille	
2039	Eurocopter EC.665 Tigre HAP [BIG]	ALAT	
2040	Eurocopter EC.665 Tigre HAP [BIH]	ALAT 5 RHC, Pau	
2041	Eurocopter EC.665 Tigre HAP [BII]	ALAT	
2042	Eurocopter EC.665 Tigre HAP [BIJ]	ALAT 5 RHC, Pau	
2043	Eurocopter EC.665 Tigre HAP [BIK]	ALAT 5 RHC, Pau	
2044	Eurocopter EC.665 Tigre HAP [BIL]	ALAT GAM/STAT, Valence	
2045	Eurocopter EC.665 Tigre HAP [BIM]	ALAT EFA, Le Luc	
2046	Eurocopter EC.665 Tigre HAP [BIN]	ALAT EFA, Le Luc	
2047	Eurocopter EC.665 Tigre HAP [BIO]	ALAT (on order)	
2048	Eurocopter EC.665 Tigre HAP [BIP]	ALAT (on order)	
2049	Eurocopter EC.665 Tigre HAP [BIQ]	ALAT (on order)	
2050	Eurocopter EC.665 Tigre HAP [BIR]	ALAT (on order)	
2051	Eurocopter EC.665 Tigre HAP [BIS]	ALAT (on order)	
2052	Eurocopter EC.665 Tigre HAP [BIT]	ALAT (on order)	
6001	Eurocopter EC.665 Tigre HAD [BJA]	ALAT 1 RHC, Phalsbourg	
6002	Eurocopter EC.665 Tigre HAD [BJB]	ALAT EFA, Le Luc	
6003	Eurocopter EC.665 Tigre HAD [BJC]	ALAT EFA, Le Luc	
6004	Eurocopter EC.665 Tigre HAD [BJD]	ALAT EFA, Le Luc	
6005	Eurocopter EC.665 Tigre HAD [BJE]	ALAT EFA, Le Luc	
6006	Eurocopter EC.665 Tigre HAD [BJF]	ALAT 1 RHC, Phalsbourg	
6007	Eurocopter EC.665 Tigre HAD [BJG]	ALAT EFA, Le Luc	
6008	Eurocopter EC.665 Tigre HAD [BJH]	ALAT	
6009	Eurocopter EC.665 Tigre HAD [BJI]	ALAT 1 RHC, Phalsbourg	
6010	Eurocopter EC.665 Tigre HAD [BJJ]	ALAT	
6011	Eurocopter EC.665 Tigre HAD [BJK]	ALAT	
6012	Eurocopter EC.665 Tigre HAD [BJL]	ALAT 1 RHC, Phalsbourg	
6013	Eurocopter EC.665 Tigre HAD [BJM]	ALAT 1 RHC, Phalsbourg	
6014	Eurocopter EC.665 Tigre HAD [BJN]	ALAT EALAT, Le Luc	
6015	Eurocopter EC.665 Tigre HAD [BJO]	ALAT 1 RHC, Phalsbourg	
6016	Eurocopter EC.665 Tigre HAD [BJP]	ALAT 1 RHC, Phalsbourg	
6017	Eurocopter EC.665 Tigre HAD [BJQ]	ALAT 1 RHC, Phalsbourg	
6018	Eurocopter EC.665 Tigre HAD [BJR]	ALAT	
6019	Eurocopter EC.665 Tigre HAD [BJS]	ALAT	
6020	Eurocopter EC.665 Tigre HAD [BJT]	ALAT 1 RHC, Phalsbourg	
6021	Eurocopter EC.665 Tigre HAD [BJU]	ALAT EALAT, Le Luc	
6022	Eurocopter EC.665 Tigre HAD [BJV]	ALAT (on order)	
6023	Eurocopter EC.665 Tigre HAD [BJW]	ALAT (on order)	
6024	Eurocopter EC.665 Tigre HAD [BJX]	ALAT (on order)	
6025	Eurocopter EC.665 Tigre HAD [BJY]	ALAT (on order)	
6026	Eurocopter EC.665 Tigre HAD	ALAT (on order)	
6027	Eurocopter EC.665 Tigre HAD [BJZ]	ALAT (on order)	
6028	Eurocopter EC.665 Tigre HAD	ALAT (on order)	
6029	Eurocopter EC.665 Tigre HAD	ALAT (on order)	
6030	Eurocopter EC.665 Tigre HAD	ALAT (on order)	
6031	Eurocopter EC.665 Tigre HAD	ALAT (on order)	
2511	Eurocopter EC.725AP Caracal [CAA]	ALAT 4 RHFS, Pau	
2528	Eurocopter EC.725AP Caracal [CAB]	ALAT GIH, Cazaux	
2530	Eurocopter EC.725AP Caracal [CAC]	ALAT 4 RHFS, Pau	
2531	Eurocopter EC.725AP Caracal [CAD]	ALAT 4 RHFS, Pau	
2533	Eurocopter EC.725AP Caracal [CAE]	ALAT 4 RHFS, Pau	
2538	Eurocopter EC.725AP Caracal [CAF]	ALAT GIH, Cazaux	
2540	Eurocopter EC.725AP Caracal [CAG]	ALAT GIH, Cazaux	
2542	Eurocopter EC.725AP Caracal [CAH]	ALAT GIH, Cazaux	

Notes	Serial	Type (code/other identity)	Owner/operator, location or fate
	1239	NH Industries NH.90-TTH Caïman [EAA]	ALAT CFIA NH.90, Le Luc
	1256	NH Industries NH.90-TTH Caïman [EAB]	ALAT GAM/STAT, Valence
	1271	NH Industries NH.90-TTH Caïman [EAC]	ALAT CFIA NH.90, Le Luc
	1273	NH Industries NH.90-TTH Caïman [EAD]	ALAT 1 RHC, Phalsbourg
	1290	NH Industries NH.90-TTH Caïman [EAE]	ALAT CFIA NH.90, Le Luc
	1291	NH Industries NH.90-TTH Caïman [EAF]	ALAT CFIA NH.90, Le Luc
	1292	NH Industries NH.90-TTH Caïman [EAG]	ALAT 1 RHC, Phalsbourg
	1293	NH Industries NH.90-TTH Caïman [EAH]	ALAT CFIA NH.90, Le Luc
	1294	NH Industries NH.90-TTH Caïman [EAI]	ALAT 1 RHC, Phalsbourg
	1295	NH Industries NH.90-TTH Caïman [EAJ]	ALAT 1 RHC, Phalsbourg
	1306	NH Industries NH.90-TTH Caïman [EAK]	ALAT
	1307	NH Industries NH.90-TTH Caïman [EAL]	ALAT 1 RHC, Phalsbourg
	1308	NH Industries NH.90-TTH Caïman [EAM]	ALAT
	1309	NH Industries NH.90-TTH Caïman [EAN]	ALAT
	1310	NH Industries NH.90-TTH Caïman [EAO]	ALAT 1 RHC, Phalsbourg
	1311	NH Industries NH.90-TTH Caïman [EAP]	ALAT 1 RHC, Phalsbourg
	1312	NH Industries NH.90-TTH Caïman [EAQ]	ALAT 1 RHC, Phalsbourg
	1313	NH Industries NH.90-TTH Caïman [EAR]	ALAT 1 RHC, Phalsbourg
	1332	NH Industries NH.90-TTH Caïman [EAS]	ALAT
	1333	NH Industries NH.90-TTH Caïman [EAT]	ALAT
	1334	NH Industries NH.90-TTH Caïman [EAU]	ALAT 1 RHC, Phalsbourg
	1335	NH Industries NH.90-TTH Caïman [EAV]	ALAT 1 RHC, Phalsbourg
	1336	NH Industries NH.90-TTH Caïman [EAW]	ALAT 1 RHC, Phalsbourg
	1337	NH Industries NH.90-TTH Caïman [EAX]	ALAT 1 RHC, Phalsbourg
	1338	NH Industries NH.90-TTH Caïman [EAY]	ALAT
	1386	NH Industries NH.90-TTH Caïman [EAZ]	ALAT
	1390	NH Industries NH.90-TTH Caïman [EBA]	ALAT
	1391	NH Industries NH.90-TTH Caïman [EBB]	ALAT
	....	NH Industries NH.90-TTH Caïman [EBC]	ALAT (on order)
	....	NH Industries NH.90-TTH Caïman [EBD]	ALAT (on order)
	....	NH Industries NH.90-TTH Caïman [EBE]	ALAT (on order)
	....	NH Industries NH.90-TTH Caïman [EBF]	ALAT (on order)
	....	NH Industries NH.90-TTH Caïman [EBG]	ALAT (on order)
	....	NH Industries NH.90-TTH Caïman [EBH]	ALAT (on order)
	....	NH Industries NH.90-TTH Caïman [EBI]	ALAT (on order)
	....	NH Industries NH.90-TTH Caïman [EBJ]	ALAT (on order)
	887	Pilatus PC-6B/B2-H4 Turbo Porter [MCA]	ALAT 1 GSALAT, Montauban
	888	Pilatus PC-6B/B2-H4 Turbo Porter [MCB]	ALAT 1 GSALAT, Montauban
	889	Pilatus PC-6B/B2-H4 Turbo Porter [MCC]	ALAT 1 GSALAT, Montauban
	890	Pilatus PC-6B/B2-H4 Turbo Porter [MCD]	ALAT 1 GSALAT, Montauban
	891	Pilatus PC-6B/B2-H4 Turbo Porter [MCE]	ALAT 1 GSALAT, Montauban
	99	SOCATA TBM 700A [ABO]	ALAT EAAT, Rennes
	100	SOCATA TBM 700A [ABP]	ALAT EAAT, Rennes
	136	SOCATA TBM 700A [ABR]	ALAT EAAT, Rennes
	139	SOCATA TBM 700A [ABS]	ALAT EAAT, Rennes
	156	SOCATA TBM 700B [ABT]	ALAT EAAT, Rennes
	159	SOCATA TBM 700B [ABU]	ALAT EAAT, Rennes
	160	SOCATA TBM 700B [ABV]	ALAT EAAT, Rennes
French Government			
	JBA	Eurocopter EC.145C-1 (9008)	Gendarmerie
	JBC	Eurocopter EC.145C-1 (9018)	Gendarmerie
	JBD	Eurocopter EC.145C-1 (9019)	Gendarmerie
	JBE	Eurocopter EC.145C-1 (9025)	Gendarmerie
	JBF	Eurocopter EC.145C-2 (9035)	Gendarmerie
	JBG	Eurocopter EC.145C-2 (9036)	Gendarmerie
	JBH	Eurocopter EC.145C-2 (9037)	Gendarmerie
	JBI	Eurocopter EC.145C-2 (9127)	Gendarmerie
	JBJ	Eurocopter EC.145C-2 (9140)	Gendarmerie, Briançon
	JBK	Eurocopter EC.145C-2 (9162)	Gendarmerie
	JBM	Eurocopter EC.145C-2 (9113)	Gendarmerie
	JBN	Eurocopter EC.145C-2 (9173)	Gendarmerie
	JBO	Eurocopter EC.145C-2 (9124)	Gendarmerie

Serial	Type (code/other identity)	Owner/operator, location or fate	Notes
BR	Eurocopter EC.145C-2 (9169)	Gendarmerie	
BT	Eurocopter EC.145C-2 (9173)	Gendarmerie	
CA	Aérospatiale AS.350BA Ecureuil (1028)	Gendarmerie, St Nazaire	
CB	Aérospatiale AS.350BA Ecureuil (1574)	Gendarmerie, Bayonne	
CD	Aérospatiale AS.350BA Ecureuil (1576)	Gendarmerie, Hyères	
CE	Aérospatiale AS.350B-2 Ecureuil (1812)	Gendarmerie, Saint-Denis, Réunion	
CF	Aérospatiale AS.350B-2 Ecureuil (1691)	Gendarmerie, Mayotte	
CI	Aérospatiale AS.350B-2 Ecureuil (2222)	Gendarmerie, Pointe-à-Pitre	
CK	Aérospatiale AS.350BA Ecureuil (1953)	Gendarmerie, Egletons	
CL	Aérospatiale AS.350B-2 Ecureuil (1811)	Gendarmerie, Fort-de-France	
CM	Aérospatiale AS.350BA Ecureuil (1952)	Gendarmerie, Rennes	
CN	Aérospatiale AS.350BA Ecureuil (2044)	Gendarmerie, Bordeaux	
CO	Aérospatiale AS.350BA Ecureuil (1917)	Gendarmerie, Metz	
CP	Aérospatiale AS.350BA Ecureuil (2045)	Gendarmerie, stored Orléans	
CQ	Aérospatiale AS.350BA Ecureuil (2057)	Gendarmerie, Dijon	
CR	Aérospatiale AS.350BA Ecureuil (2088)	Gendarmerie, stored Orléans	
CS	Aérospatiale AS.350B-2 Ecureuil (1575)	Gendarmerie, Cayenne	
CT	Aérospatiale AS.350BA Ecureuil (2104)	Gendarmerie, Amiens	
CU	Aérospatiale AS.350BA Ecureuil (2117)	Gendarmerie, Orléans	
CV	Aérospatiale AS.350BA Ecureuil (2118)	Gendarmerie, Orléans	
CW	Aérospatiale AS.350BA Ecureuil (2218)	Gendarmerie, Cazaux	
CX	Aérospatiale AS.350BA Ecureuil (2219)	Gendarmerie, Tours	
CY	Aérospatiale AS.350BA Ecureuil (2221)	Gendarmerie, Limoges	
CZ	Aérospatiale AS.350BA Ecureuil (1467) $	Gendarmerie, Lyon	
DA	Eurocopter EC.135T-2 (0642)	Gendarmerie	
DB	Eurocopter EC.135T-2 (0654)	Gendarmerie	
DC	Eurocopter EC.135T-2 (0717)	Gendarmerie, Lyon	
DD	Eurocopter EC.135T-2 (0727)	Gendarmerie, Lille/Lesquin	
DE	Eurocopter EC.135T-2 (0747)	Gendarmerie	
DF	Eurocopter EC.135T-2 (0757)	Gendarmerie, Brest/Guipavas	
DG	Eurocopter EC.135T-2 (0772)	Gendarmerie	
DH	Eurocopter EC.135T-2 (0787)	Gendarmerie	
DI	Eurocopter EC.135T-2 (0797)	Gendarmerie	
DJ	Eurocopter EC.135T-2 (0806)	Gendarmerie	
DK	Eurocopter EC.135T-2 (0857)	Gendarmerie, Toulouse/Francazal	
DL	Eurocopter EC.135T-2 (0867)	Gendarmerie	
DM	Eurocopter EC.135T-2 (1055)	Gendarmerie	
DN	Eurocopter EC.135T-2 (1058)	Gendarmerie	
DO	Eurocopter EC.135T-2 (1086)	Gendarmerie, Bordeaux/Merignac	
ED	Aérospatiale AS.350B-2 Ecureuil (2096)	Gendarmerie, St Nazaire	
EE	Aérospatiale AS.350B-2 Ecureuil (2423)	Gendarmerie, Nouméa	
EF	Aérospatiale AS.350B-2 Ecureuil (2225)	Gendarmerie, Nouméa	
F-ZBAA	Conair Turbo Firecat [22]	Sécurité Civile, Nîmes/Garons	
F-ZBAB	Cessna F.406 Caravan II (0025)	Douanes Françaises, stored Bordeaux/Merignac	
F-ZBAD	Aérospatiale AS.355F-2 Twin Ecureuil	Douanes Françaises	
F-ZBAP	Conair Turbo Firecat [12]	Sécurité Civile, Nîmes/Garons	
F-ZBAZ	Conair Turbo Firecat [01]	Sécurité Civile, Nîmes/Garons	
F-ZBBB	Cessna F.406 Caravan II (0039)	*Withdrawn from use, February 2017*	
F-ZBBN	Aérospatiale AS.350B-2 Ecureuil	Sécurité Civile, Nîmes/Garons	
F-ZBCE	Cessna F.406 Caravan II (0042)	Douanes Françaises	
F-ZBCF	Cessna F.406 Caravan II (0077)	Douanes Françaises	
F-ZBCG	Cessna F.406 Caravan II (0066)	Douanes Françaises	
F-ZBCH	Cessna F.406 Caravan II (0075)	Douanes Françaises	
F-ZBCI	Cessna F.406 Caravan II (0070)	Douanes Françaises	
F-ZBCJ	Cessna F.406 Caravan II (0074)	Douanes Françaises	
F-ZBCZ	Conair Turbo Firecat [23]	Sécurité Civile, Nîmes/Garons	
F-ZBEA	Aérospatiale AS.350B-2 Ecureuil	Sécurité Civile, Nîmes/Garons	
F-ZBEF	Aérospatiale AS.355F-1 Twin Ecureuil	Douanes Françaises	
F-ZBEG	Canadair CL-415 [39]	Sécurité Civile, Nîmes/Garons	
F-ZBEH	Conair Turbo Firecat [20]	Sécurité Civile, Nîmes/Garons	
F-ZBEK	Aérospatiale AS.355F-1 Twin Ecureuil	Douanes Françaises	
F-ZBEL	Aérospatiale AS.355F-1 Twin Ecureuil	Douanes Françaises	

Notes	Serial	Type (code/other identity)	Owner/operator, location or fate
	F-ZBEP	Cessna F.406 Caravan II (0006)	*Withdrawn from use, February 2017*
	F-ZBES	Cessna F.406 Caravan II (0017)	Douanes Françaises
	F-ZBET	Conair Turbo Firecat [15]	Sécurité Civile, Nîmes/Garons
	F-ZBEU	Canadair CL-415 [42]	Sécurité Civile, Nîmes/Garons
	F-ZBEW	Conair Turbo Firecat [11] $	Sécurité Civile, Nîmes/Garons
	F-ZBEY	Conair Turbo Firecat [07]	Sécurité Civile, Nîmes/Garons
	F-ZBFC	Aérospatiale AS.350B-2 Ecureuil	Sécurité Civile, Nîmes/Garons
	F-ZBFD	Aérospatiale AS.350B-2 Ecureuil	Sécurité Civile, Nîmes/Garons
	F-ZBFJ	Beech Super King Air B200 [98]	Sécurité Civile, Nîmes/Garons
	F-ZBFK	Beech Super King Air B200 [96]	Sécurité Civile, Nîmes/Garons
	F-ZBFN	Canadair CL-415 [33]	Sécurité Civile, Nîmes/Garons
	F-ZBFP	Canadair CL-415 [31]	Sécurité Civile, Nîmes/Garons
	F-ZBFS	Canadair CL-415 [32] $	Sécurité Civile, Nîmes/Garons
	F-ZBFV	Canadair CL-415 [37]	Sécurité Civile, Nîmes/Garons
	F-ZBFW	Canadair CL-415 [38]	Sécurité Civile, Nîmes/Garons
	F-ZBFX	Canadair CL-415 [34]	Sécurité Civile, Nîmes/Garons
	F-ZBFY	Canadair CL-415 [35]	Sécurité Civile, Nîmes/Garons
	F-ZBGA	Cessna F.406 Caravan II (0086)	Douanes Françaises
	F-ZBGD	Cessna F.406 Caravan II (0090)	Douanes Françaises
	F-ZBGE	Cessna F.406 Caravan II (0061)	Douanes Françaises
	F-ZBGF	Eurocopter EC.135T-2	Douanes Françaises
	F-ZBGG	Eurocopter EC.135T-2	Douanes Françaises, Calais
	F-ZBGH	Eurocopter EC.135T-2	Douanes Françaises
	F-ZBGI	Eurocopter EC.135T-2	Douanes Françaises
	F-ZBGJ	Eurocopter EC.135T-2	Douanes Françaises
	F-ZBGK	Hawker Beechcraft King Air B350ER (FL-682)	Douanes Françaises
	F-ZBGL	Hawker Beechcraft King Air B350ER (FL-746)	Douanes Françaises
	F-ZBGM	Hawker Beechcraft King Air B350ER (FL-752)	Douanes Françaises
	F-ZBGN	Hawker Beechcraft King Air B350ER (FL-781)	Douanes Françaises
	F-ZBGO	Hawker Beechcraft King Air B350ER (FL-800)	Douanes Françaises
	F-ZBGP	Hawker Beechcraft King Air B350ER (FL-802)	Douanes Françaises
	F-ZBGQ	Hawker Beechcraft King Air B350ER (FL-777)	Douanes Françaises
	F-ZBGR	Hawker Beechcraft King Air B350ER	Douanes Francaises (on order)
	F-ZBMA	Conair Turbo Firecat [24]	Sécurité Civile, Nîmes/Garons
	F-ZBMB	Beech Super King Air B200 [97]	Sécurité Civile, Nîmes/Garons
	F-ZBMC	de Havilland Canada DHC-8Q-402MR [73] $	Sécurité Civile, Nîmes/Garons
	F-ZBMD	de Havilland Canada DHC-8Q-402MR [74]	Sécurité Civile, Nîmes/Garons
	F-ZBME	Canadair CL-415 [44]	Sécurité Civile, Nîmes/Garons
	F-ZBMF	Canadair CL-415 [45]	Sécurité Civile, Nîmes/Garons
	F-ZBMG	Canadair CL-415 [48]	Sécurité Civile, Nîmes/Garons
	F-ZBPA	Eurocopter EC.145C-1	Sécurité Civile, Perpignan
	F-ZBPD	Eurocopter EC.145C-1	Sécurité Civile, Granville
	F-ZBPE	Eurocopter EC.145C-1	Sécurité Civile, Clermont-Ferrand
	F-ZBPF	Eurocopter EC.145C-1	Sécurité Civile, Cannes/Mandelieu
	F-ZBPG	Eurocopter EC.145C-1	Sécurité Civile, Strasbourg/Entzheim
	F-ZBPH	Eurocopter EC.145C-1	Sécurité Civile, Le Luc
	F-ZBPI	Eurocopter EC.145C-1	Sécurité Civile, Quimper
	F-ZBPJ	Eurocopter EC.145C-1	Sécurité Civile, La Rochelle
	F-ZBPK	Eurocopter EC.145C-1	Sécurité Civile, Ajaccio
	F-ZBPL	Eurocopter EC.145C-1	Sécurité Civile, Le Havre/Octeville
	F-ZBPM	Eurocopter EC.145C-1	Sécurité Civile, Bordeaux/Merignac
	F-ZBPN	Eurocopter EC.145C-1	Sécurité Civile, Courchevel
	F-ZBPO	Eurocopter EC.145C-1	Sécurité Civile, Paris/Issy-les-Molineaux
	F-ZBPP	Eurocopter EC.145C-2	Sécurité Civile, Fort-de-France, Martinique
	F-ZBPQ	Eurocopter EC.145C-2	Sécurité Civile, Chamonix
	F-ZBPS	Eurocopter EC.145C-2	Sécurité Civile, Nîmes/Garons
	F-ZBPT	Eurocopter EC.145C-2	Sécurité Civile, L'Alpe de Huez
	F-ZBPU	Eurocopter EC.145C-2	Sécurité Civile, Lorient
	F-ZBPV	Eurocopter EC.145C-2	Sécurité Civile, Besançon/La Veze
	F-ZBPW	Eurocopter EC.145C-2	Sécurité Civile, Lyon/Bron
	F-ZBPX	Eurocopter EC.145C-2	Sécurité Civile, Paris/Issy-les-Molineaux
	F-ZBPY	Eurocopter EC.145C-2	Sécurité Civile, Montpellier

Serial	Type (code/other identity)	Owner/operator, location or fate	Notes
F-ZBPZ	Eurocopter EC.145C-2	Sécurité Civile, Mende-Brenoux	
F-ZBQA	Eurocopter EC.145C-2	Sécurité Civile, Annecy	
F-ZBQB	Eurocopter EC.145C-2	Sécurité Civile, Nîmes/Garons	
F-ZBQC	Eurocopter EC.145C-2	Sécurité Civile, Strasbourg/Entzheim	
F-ZBQD	Eurocopter EC.145C-2	Sécurité Civile, Le Raizet, Guadeloupe	
F-ZBQE	Eurocopter EC.145C-2	Sécurité Civile, Guyane	
F-ZBQF	Eurocopter EC.145C-2	Sécurité Civile, Marseille/Provence	
F-ZBQG	Eurocopter EC.145C-2	Sécurité Civile, Nîmes/Garons	
F-ZBQH	Eurocopter EC.145C-2	Sécurité Civile, Nîmes/Garons	
F-ZBQI	Eurocopter EC.145C-2	Sécurité Civile, Grenoble/Le Versoud	
F-ZBQJ	Eurocopter EC.145C-2	Sécurité Civile, Bastia	
F-ZBQK	Eurocopter EC.145C-2	Sécurité Civile, Pau	
F-ZBQL	Eurocopter EC.145C-2	Sécurité Civile, Lacanau/le Huga	
Civil operated aircraft in military use			
F-GJDB	Dassault Falcon 20C	AVDEF, Nîmes/Garons	
F-GKCI	Cirrus SR.22	CATS/CFAMI 05.312, Salon de Provence	
F-GPAA	Dassault Falcon 20ECM	AVDEF, Nîmes/Garons	
F-GPAD	Dassault Falcon 20E	AVDEF, Nîmes/Garons	
F-GUKA	Grob G120A-F	CATS/EPAA 00.315, Cognac	
F-GUKB	Grob G120A-F	CATS/EPAA 00.315, Cognac	
F-GUKC	Grob G120A-F	CATS/EPAA 00.315, Cognac	
F-GUKD	Grob G120A-F	CATS/EPAA 00.315, Cognac	
F-GUKE	Grob G120A-F	CATS/EPAA 00.315, Cognac	
F-GUKF	Grob G120A-F	CATS/EPAA 00.315, Cognac	
F-GUKG	Grob G120A-F	CATS/EPAA 00.315, Cognac	
F-GUKH	Grob G120A-F	CATS/EPAA 00.315, Cognac	
F-GUKI	Grob G120A-F	CATS/EPAA 00.315, Cognac	
F-GUKJ	Grob G120A-F	CATS/EPAA 00.315, Cognac	
F-GUKK	Grob G120A-F	CATS/EPAA 00.315, Cognac	
F-GUKL	Grob G120A-F	CATS/EPAA 00.315, Cognac	
F-GUKM	Grob G120A-F	CATS/EPAA 00.315, Cognac	
F-GUKN	Grob G120A-F	CATS/EPAA 00.315, Cognac	
F-GUKO	Grob G120A-F	CATS/EPAA 00.315, Cognac	
F-GUKP	Grob G120A-F	CATS/EPAA 00.315, Cognac	
F-GUKR	Grob G120A-F	CATS/EPAA 00.315, Cognac	
F-GUKS	Grob G120A-F	CATS/EPAA 00.315, Cognac	
F-HAVD	BAE Jetstream 41	AVDEF, Nîmes/Garons	
F-HAVF	BAE Jetstream 41	AVDEF, Nîmes/Garons	
F-HGDU	Cirrus SR.20	CATS/CFAMI 05.312, Salon de Provence	
F-HKCA	Cirrus SR.22	CATS/CFAMI 05.312, Salon de Provence	
F-HKCB	Cirrus SR.20	CATS/CFAMI 05.312, Salon de Provence	
F-HKCC	Cirrus SR.22	CATS/CFAMI 05.312, Salon de Provence	
F-HKCD	Cirrus SR.20	CATS/CFAMI 05.312, Salon de Provence	
F-HKCE	Cirrus SR.20	CATS/CFAMI 05.312, Salon de Provence	
F-HKCF	Cirrus SR.22	CATS/CFAMI 05.312, Salon de Provence	
F-HKCG	Cirrus SR.20	CATS/CFAMI 05.312, Salon de Provence	
F-HKCH	Cirrus SR.20	CATS/CFAMI 05.312, Salon de Provence	
F-HKCI	Cirrus SR.22	CATS/CFAMI 05.312, Salon de Provence	
F-HKCJ	Cirrus SR.20	CATS/CFAMI 05.312, Salon de Provence	
F-HKCK	Cirrus SR.20	CATS/CFAMI 05.312, Salon de Provence	
F-HKCL	Cirrus SR.22	CATS/CFAMI 05.312, Salon de Provence	
F-HKCN	Cirrus SR.20	CATS/CFAMI 05.312, Salon de Provence	
F-HKCO	Cirrus SR.22	CATS/CFAMI 05.312, Salon de Provence	
F-HKCP	Cirrus SR.20	CATS/CFAMI 05.312, Salon de Provence	
F-HKCQ	Cirrus SR.20	CATS/CFAMI 05.312, Salon de Provence	
F-HKCR	Cirrus SR.22	CATS/CFAMI 05.312, Salon de Provence	
F-HKCS	Cirrus SR.22	CATS/CFAMI 05.312, Salon de Provence	
F-HKCT	Cirrus SR.20	CATS/CFAMI 05.312, Salon de Provence	
F-HKCU	Cirrus SR.20	CATS/CFAMI 05.312, Salon de Provence	
F-HKCV	Cirrus SR.20	CATS/CFAMI 05.312, Salon de Provence	
F-HKCX	Cirrus SR.20	CATS/CFAMI 05.312, Salon de Provence	
F-HKCY	Cirrus SR.22	CATS/CFAMI 05.312, Salon de Provence	

Notes	Serial	Type (code/other identity)	Owner/operator, location or fate
	F-HKCZ	Cirrus SR.22	CATS/CFAMI 05.312, Salon de Provence
	GABON		
	TR-KGM	Gulfstream Aerospace G.650ER	Gabonese Government, Libreville
	TR-KPR	Boeing 777-236	Gabonese Government, Libreville
	TR-KSP	Grumman G.1159C Gulfstream IVSP	Gabonese Government, Libreville
	TR-LEX	Dassault Falcon 900EX	Gabonese Government, Libreville

GERMANY

Please note that German serials do not officially include the '+' part in them but aircraft wearing German markings are often painted with a cross in the middle, which is why it is included here.

Luftwaffe, Marineflieger & Heeresfliegertruppe (Heer)

Notes	Serial	Type (code/other identity)	Owner/operator, location or fate
	10+23	Airbus A.310-304	Luftwaffe 1/FBS, Köln-Bonn
	10+24	Airbus A.310-304/MRTT	Luftwaffe 1/FBS, Köln-Bonn
	10+25	Airbus A.310-304/MRTT	Luftwaffe 1/FBS, Köln-Bonn
	10+26	Airbus A.310-304/MRTT	Luftwaffe 1/FBS, Köln-Bonn
	10+27	Airbus A.310-304/MRTT	Luftwaffe 1/FBS, Köln-Bonn
	14+01	Bombardier Global 5000	Luftwaffe 3/FBS, Köln-Bonn
	14+02	Bombardier Global 5000	Luftwaffe 3/FBS, Köln-Bonn
	14+03	Bombardier Global 5000	Luftwaffe 3/FBS, Köln-Bonn
	14+04	Bombardier Global 5000	Luftwaffe 3/FBS, Köln-Bonn
	15+01	Airbus A.319CJ-115X	Luftwaffe 3/FBS, Köln-Bonn
	15+02	Airbus A.319CJ-115X	Luftwaffe 3/FBS, Köln-Bonn
	16+01	Airbus A.340-313X	Luftwaffe 3/FBS, Köln-Bonn
	16+02	Airbus A.340-313X	Luftwaffe 3/FBS, Köln-Bonn
	30+01	Eurofighter EF.2000GT	Luftwaffe TLG 73 *Steinhoff*, Laage
	30+02	Eurofighter EF.2000GT	Luftwaffe TLG 71 *Richthofen*, Wittmund
	30+03	Eurofighter EF.2000GT	Luftwaffe TLG 74 *Molders*, Neuburg/Donau
	30+04	Eurofighter EF.2000GT	Luftwaffe TLG 31 *Boelcke*, Nörvenich
	30+05	Eurofighter EF.2000GT	Luftwaffe TLG 31 *Boelcke*, Nörvenich
	30+06	Eurofighter EF.2000GS	Luftwaffe TLG 74 *Molders*, Neuburg/Donau
	30+07	Eurofighter EF.2000GS	Luftwaffe TLG 74 *Molders*, Neuburg/Donau
	30+09	Eurofighter EF.2000GS	Luftwaffe TLG 31 *Boelcke*, Nörvenich
	30+10	Eurofighter EF.2000GS	Luftwaffe TLG 74 *Molders*, Neuburg/Donau
	30+11	Eurofighter EF.2000GS	Luftwaffe TLG 74 *Molders*, Neuburg/Donau
	30+12	Eurofighter EF.2000GS	Luftwaffe TLG 74 *Molders*, Neuburg/Donau
	30+14	Eurofighter EF.2000GT	Luftwaffe TLG 71 *Richthofen*, Wittmund
	30+15	Eurofighter EF.2000GS	Luftwaffe TLG 74 *Molders*, Neuburg/Donau
	30+17	Eurofighter EF.2000GT	Luftwaffe TLG 73 *Steinhoff*, Laage
	30+20	Eurofighter EF.2000GT	Luftwaffe TLG 73 *Steinhoff*, Laage
	30+22	Eurofighter EF.2000GS	Luftwaffe TLG 74 *Molders*, Neuburg/Donau
	30+23	Eurofighter EF.2000GS	Luftwaffe TLG 74 *Molders*, Neuburg/Donau
	30+24	Eurofighter EF.2000GT	Luftwaffe TLG 73 *Steinhoff*, Laage
	30+25	Eurofighter EF.2000GS	Luftwaffe TLG 74 *Molders*, Neuburg/Donau
	30+26	Eurofighter EF.2000GS $	Luftwaffe TLG 74 *Molders*, Neuburg/Donau
	30+27	Eurofighter EF.2000GT	Luftwaffe TLG 73 *Steinhoff*, Laage
	30+28	Eurofighter EF.2000GS	Luftwaffe TLG 74 *Molders*, Neuburg/Donau
	30+29	Eurofighter EF.2000GS $	Luftwaffe TLG 74 *Molders*, Neuburg/Donau
	30+30	Eurofighter EF.2000GS	Luftwaffe TLG 74 *Molders*, Neuburg/Donau
	30+31	Eurofighter EF.2000GT	Luftwaffe TLG 31 *Boelcke*, Nörvenich
	30+32	Eurofighter EF.2000GS	Luftwaffe TLG 74 *Molders*, Neuburg/Donau
	30+33	Eurofighter EF.2000GS	Luftwaffe TLG 74 *Molders*, Neuburg/Donau
	30+35	Eurofighter EF.2000GT	Luftwaffe TLG 73 *Steinhoff*, Laage
	30+38	Eurofighter EF.2000GT	Luftwaffe TLG 73 *Steinhoff*, Laage
	30+39	Eurofighter EF.2000GS	Luftwaffe TLG 74 *Molders*, Neuburg/Donau
	30+40	Eurofighter EF.2000GS	Luftwaffe TLG 74 *Molders*, Neuburg/Donau
	30+42	Eurofighter EF.2000GT	Luftwaffe TLG 74 *Molders*, Neuburg/Donau
	30+45	Eurofighter EF.2000GS $	Luftwaffe TLG 73 *Steinhoff*, Laage
	30+46	Eurofighter EF.2000GS	Luftwaffe TLG 73 *Steinhoff*, Laage
	30+47	Eurofighter EF.2000GS	Luftwaffe TLG 71 *Richthofen*, Wittmund
	30+48	Eurofighter EF.2000GS $	Luftwaffe TLG 73 *Steinhoff*, Laage
	30+49	Eurofighter EF.2000GS	Luftwaffe TLG 73 *Steinhoff*, Laage

Serial	Type (code/other identity)	Owner/operator, location or fate	Notes
30+50	Eurofighter EF.2000GS	Luftwaffe TLG 73 *Steinhoff*, Laage	
30+51	Eurofighter EF.2000GS	Luftwaffe TLG 73 *Steinhoff*, Laage	
30+52	Eurofighter EF.2000GS	Luftwaffe TLG 31 *Boelcke*, Nörvenich	
30+53	Eurofighter EF.2000GS	Luftwaffe TLG 31 *Boelcke*, Nörvenich	
30+54	Eurofighter EF.2000GT	Luftwaffe TLG 73 *Steinhoff*, Laage	
30+55	Eurofighter EF.2000GS	Luftwaffe TLG 73 *Steinhoff*, Laage	
30+56	Eurofighter EF.2000GS	Luftwaffe TLG 73 *Steinhoff*, Laage	
30+57	Eurofighter EF.2000GS	Luftwaffe TLG 31 *Boelcke*, Nörvenich	
30+58	Eurofighter EF.2000GS	Luftwaffe TLG 31 *Boelcke*, Nörvenich	
30+59	Eurofighter EF.2000GT	Luftwaffe TLG 73 *Steinhoff*, Laage	
30+60	Eurofighter EF.2000GS	Luftwaffe TLG 73 *Steinhoff*, Laage	
30+61	Eurofighter EF.2000GS	Luftwaffe TLG 74 *Molders*, Neuburg/Donau	
30+62	Eurofighter EF.2000GS	Luftwaffe TLG 73 *Steinhoff*, Laage	
30+63	Eurofighter EF.2000GS	Luftwaffe TLG 74 *Molders*, Neuburg/Donau	
30+64	Eurofighter EF.2000GS	Luftwaffe TLG 73 *Steinhoff*, Laage	
30+65	Eurofighter EF.2000GS	Luftwaffe TLG 73 *Steinhoff*, Laage	
30+66	Eurofighter EF.2000GS	Luftwaffe TLG 71 *Richthofen*, Wittmund	
30+67	Eurofighter EF.2000GT	Luftwaffe TLG 73 *Steinhoff*, Laage	
30+68	Eurofighter EF.2000GS $	Luftwaffe TLG 74 *Molders*, Neuburg/Donau	
30+69	Eurofighter EF.2000GS	Luftwaffe TLG 74 *Molders*, Neuburg/Donau	
30+70	Eurofighter EF.2000GS	Luftwaffe TLG 73 *Steinhoff*, Laage	
30+71	Eurofighter EF.2000GT	Luftwaffe TLG 73 *Steinhoff*, Laage	
30+72	Eurofighter EF.2000GS	Luftwaffe TLG 74 *Molders*, Neuburg/Donau	
30+73	Eurofighter EF.2000GS	Luftwaffe TLG 73 *Steinhoff*, Laage	
30+74	Eurofighter EF.2000GS	Luftwaffe TLG 74 *Molders*, Neuburg/Donau	
30+75	Eurofighter EF.2000GS $	Luftwaffe TLG 71 *Richthofen*, Wittmund	
30+76	Eurofighter EF.2000GS	Luftwaffe TLG 74 *Molders*, Neuburg/Donau	
30+77	Eurofighter EF.2000GT	Luftwaffe TLG 73 *Steinhoff*, Laage	
30+78	Eurofighter EF.2000GS	Luftwaffe TLG 71 *Richthofen*, Wittmund	
30+79	Eurofighter EF.2000GS	Luftwaffe TLG 73 *Steinhoff*, Laage	
30+80	Eurofighter EF.2000GS	Luftwaffe TLG 74 *Molders*, Neuburg/Donau	
30+81	Eurofighter EF.2000GS	Luftwaffe TLG 73 *Steinhoff*, Laage	
30+82	Eurofighter EF.2000GS	Luftwaffe TLG 31 *Boelcke*, Nörvenich	
30+83	Eurofighter EF.2000GS	Luftwaffe TLG 31 *Boelcke*, Nörvenich	
30+84	Eurofighter EF.2000GT	Luftwaffe TLG 31 *Boelcke*, Nörvenich	
30+85	Eurofighter EF.2000GS	Luftwaffe TLG 71 *Richthofen*, Wittmund	
30+86	Eurofighter EF.2000GS	Luftwaffe TLG 71 *Richthofen*, Wittmund	
30+87	Eurofighter EF.2000GS $	Luftwaffe TLG 71 *Richthofen*, Wittmund	
30+88	Eurofighter EF.2000GS	Luftwaffe TLG 74 *Molders*, Neuburg/Donau	
30+89	Eurofighter EF.2000GS	Luftwaffe TLG 71 *Richthofen*, Wittmund	
30+90	Eurofighter EF.2000GS $	Luftwaffe TLG 71 *Richthofen*, Wittmund	
30+91	Eurofighter EF.2000GS	Luftwaffe TLG 31 *Boelcke*, Nörvenich	
30+92	Eurofighter EF.2000GS	Luftwaffe TLG 73 *Steinhoff*, Laage	
30+93	Eurofighter EF.2000GS	Luftwaffe TLG 74 *Molders*, Neuburg/Donau	
30+94	Eurofighter EF.2000GS	Luftwaffe TLG 74 *Molders*, Neuburg/Donau	
30+95	Eurofighter EF.2000GT	Luftwaffe TLG 74 *Molders*, Neuburg/Donau	
30+96	Eurofighter EF.2000GS	Luftwaffe TLG 31 *Boelcke*, Nörvenich	
30+97	Eurofighter EF.2000GS	Luftwaffe TLG 31 *Boelcke*, Nörvenich	
30+98	Eurofighter EF.2000GS	Luftwaffe TLG 31 *Boelcke*, Nörvenich	
30+99	Eurofighter EF.2000GT	Luftwaffe TLG 31 *Boelcke*, Nörvenich	
31+00	Eurofighter EF.2000GS $	Luftwaffe TLG 74 *Molders*, Neuburg/Donau	
31+01	Eurofighter EF.2000GS	Luftwaffe TLG 31 *Boelcke*, Nörvenich	
31+02	Eurofighter EF.2000GS	Luftwaffe TLG 74 *Molders*, Neuburg/Donau	
31+03	Eurofighter EF.2000GT	EADS, Manching	
31+04	Eurofighter EF.2000GS	Luftwaffe TLG 71 *Richthofen*, Wittmund	
31+05	Eurofighter EF.2000GS	Luftwaffe TLG 31 *Boelcke*, Nörvenich	
31+06	Eurofighter EF.2000GS $	Luftwaffe TLG 31 *Boelcke*, Nörvenich	
31+07	Eurofighter EF.2000GS	Luftwaffe TLG 71 *Richthofen*, Wittmund	
31+08	Eurofighter EF.2000GS	Luftwaffe TLG 31 *Boelcke*, Nörvenich	
31+09	Eurofighter EF.2000GS	Luftwaffe TLG 31 *Boelcke*, Nörvenich	
31+10	Eurofighter EF.2000GS	Luftwaffe TLG 31 *Boelcke*, Nörvenich	
31+11	Eurofighter EF.2000GS	Luftwaffe TLG 74 *Molders*, Neuburg/Donau	

Notes	Serial	Type (code/other identity)	Owner/operator, location or fate
	31+12	Eurofighter EF.2000GS	Luftwaffe TLG 31 *Boelcke*, Nörvenich
	31+13	Eurofighter EF.2000GT	Luftwaffe TLG 73 *Steinhoff*, Laage
	31+14	Eurofighter EF.2000GS	Luftwaffe TAubZLwSüd, Kaufbeuren
	31+15	Eurofighter EF.2000GS	Luftwaffe TAubZLwSüd, Kaufbeuren
	31+16	Eurofighter EF.2000GS	Luftwaffe TLG 73 *Steinhoff*, Laage
	31+17	Eurofighter EF.2000GS	Luftwaffe TLG 73 *Steinhoff*, Laage
	31+18	Eurofighter EF.2000GS	Luftwaffe TLG 73 *Steinhoff*, Laage
	31+19	Eurofighter EF.2000GS	Luftwaffe TLG 74 *Molders*, Neuburg/Donau
	31+20	Eurofighter EF.2000GS	Luftwaffe TLG 73 *Steinhoff*, Laage
	31+21	Eurofighter EF.2000GS	Luftwaffe TLG 73 *Steinhoff*, Laage
	31+22	Eurofighter EF.2000GS	Luftwaffe TLG 73 *Steinhoff*, Laage
	31+24	Eurofighter EF.2000GT	Luftwaffe TLG 73 *Steinhoff*, Laage
	31+25	Eurofighter EF.2000GT	Luftwaffe TLG 31 *Boelcke*, Nörvenich
	31+26	Eurofighter EF.2000GT	Airbus Defence & Space, Manching
	31+27	Eurofighter EF.2000GT	Luftwaffe
	31+28	Eurofighter EF.2000GT	Luftwaffe
	31+29	Eurofighter EF.2000GS	Luftwaffe TLG 31 *Boelcke*, Nörvenich
	31+30	Eurofighter EF.2000GS	Luftwaffe TLG 31 *Boelcke*, Nörvenich
	31+31	Eurofighter EF.2000GS $	Luftwaffe TLG 31 *Boelcke*, Nörvenich
	31+32	Eurofighter EF.2000GS $	Luftwaffe TLG 31 *Boelcke*, Nörvenich
	31+33	Eurofighter EF.2000GS	Luftwaffe TLG 31 *Boelcke*, Nörvenich
	31+34	Eurofighter EF.2000GS	Luftwaffe TLG 31 *Boelcke*, Nörvenich
	31+35	Eurofighter EF.2000GS	Luftwaffe TLG 31 *Boelcke*, Nörvenich
	31+36	Eurofighter EF.2000GS	Luftwaffe TLG 31 *Boelcke*, Nörvenich
	31+37	Eurofighter EF.2000GS	Luftwaffe TLG 31 *Boelcke*, Nörvenich
	31+38	Eurofighter EF.2000GS	Luftwaffe TLG 31 *Boelcke*, Nörvenich
	31+39	Eurofighter EF.2000GS	Luftwaffe TLG 31 *Boelcke*, Nörvenich
	31+40	Eurofighter EF.2000GS	Luftwaffe TLG 31 *Boelcke*, Nörvenich
	31+41	Eurofighter EF.2000GS	Luftwaffe (on order)
	31+42	Eurofighter EF.2000GS	Luftwaffe (on order)
	31+43	Eurofighter EF.2000GS	Luftwaffe (on order)
	31+44	Eurofighter EF.2000GS	Luftwaffe (on order)
	31+45	Eurofighter EF.2000GS	Luftwaffe (on order)
	31+46	Eurofighter EF.2000GS	Luftwaffe (on order)
	31+47	Eurofighter EF.2000GS	Luftwaffe (on order)
	31+48	Eurofighter EF.2000GS	Luftwaffe (on order)
	31+49	Eurofighter EF.2000GS	Luftwaffe (on order)
	31+50	Eurofighter EF.2000GS	Luftwaffe (on order)
	31+51	Eurofighter EF.2000GS	Luftwaffe (on order)
	31+52	Eurofighter EF.2000GS	Luftwaffe (on order)
	31+53	Eurofighter EF.2000GS	Luftwaffe (on order)
	43+01	Panavia Tornado IDS(T) $	Luftwaffe TLG 33, Büchel
	43+07	Panavia Tornado IDS(T)	Luftwaffe TLG 51 *Immelmann*, Schleswig/Jagel
	43+10	Panavia Tornado IDS(T)	Luftwaffe TLG 33, Büchel
	43+25	Panavia Tornado IDS	Luftwaffe TLG 33, Büchel
	43+29	Panavia Tornado IDS(T)	Luftwaffe TLG 33, Büchel
	43+34	Panavia Tornado IDS	Luftwaffe TAubZLwSüd, Kaufbeuren
	43+38	Panavia Tornado IDS	Luftwaffe TLG 33, Büchel
	43+42	Panavia Tornado IDS(T)	Luftwaffe
	43+45	Panavia Tornado IDS(T)	Luftwaffe TLG 51 *Immelmann*, Schleswig/Jagel
	43+46	Panavia Tornado IDS	Luftwaffe TLG 33, Büchel
	43+48	Panavia Tornado IDS	Luftwaffe TLG 33, Büchel
	43+50	Panavia Tornado IDS	Luftwaffe TLG 33, Büchel
	43+52	Panavia Tornado IDS	Luftwaffe TLG 33, Büchel
	43+54	Panavia Tornado IDS	Luftwaffe TAubZLwSüd, Kaufbeuren
	43+59	Panavia Tornado IDS	Luftwaffe TLG 51 *Immelmann*, Schleswig/Jagel
	43+92	Panavia Tornado IDS(T)	Luftwaffe
	43+94	Panavia Tornado IDS(T)	Luftwaffe
	43+97	Panavia Tornado IDS(T)	Luftwaffe TLG 51 *Immelmann*, Schleswig/Jagel
	43+98	Panavia Tornado IDS	Luftwaffe TLG 33, Büchel
	44+06	Panavia Tornado IDS	Luftwaffe
	44+16	Panavia Tornado IDS(T)	Luftwaffe TLG 33, Büchel

Serial	Type (code/other identity)	Owner/operator, location or fate	Notes
44+17	Panavia Tornado IDS	Luftwaffe TLG 51 *Immelmann*, Schleswig/Jagel	
44+21	Panavia Tornado IDS	Luftwaffe TLG 51 *Immelmann*, Schleswig/Jagel	
44+23	Panavia Tornado IDS	Luftwaffe TLG 33, Büchel	
44+29	Panavia Tornado IDS	Luftwaffe	
44+30	Panavia Tornado IDS	Luftwaffe	
44+33	Panavia Tornado IDS	Luftwaffe TLG 33, Büchel	
44+34	Panavia Tornado IDS	Luftwaffe TLG 33, Büchel	
44+58	Panavia Tornado IDS	Luftwaffe TLG 33, Büchel	
44+61	Panavia Tornado IDS $	Luftwaffe TLG 33, Büchel	
44+64	Panavia Tornado IDS	Luftwaffe TLG 33, Büchel	
44+65	Panavia Tornado IDS	Luftwaffe TLG 33, Büchel	
44+69	Panavia Tornado IDS	Luftwaffe TLG 51 *Immelmann*, Schleswig/Jagel	
44+70	Panavia Tornado IDS	Luftwaffe TLG 33, Büchel	
44+72	Panavia Tornado IDS(T)	Luftwaffe TLG 33, Büchel	
44+73	Panavia Tornado IDS(T)	Luftwaffe WTD 61, Ingolstadt	
44+75	Panavia Tornado IDS(T)	Luftwaffe TLG 51 *Immelmann*, Schleswig/Jagel	
44+78	Panavia Tornado IDS	Luftwaffe TLG 33, Büchel	
44+79	Panavia Tornado IDS	Luftwaffe TLG 33, Büchel	
44+90	Panavia Tornado IDS	Luftwaffe TLG 51 *Immelmann*, Schleswig/Jagel	
45+00	Panavia Tornado IDS	Luftwaffe	
45+08	Panavia Tornado IDS	Luftwaffe	
45+09	Panavia Tornado IDS	Luftwaffe TLG 33, Büchel	
45+13	Panavia Tornado IDS(T)	Luftwaffe TLG 51 *Immelmann*, Schleswig/Jagel	
45+14	Panavia Tornado IDS(T)	Luftwaffe	
45+16	Panavia Tornado IDS(T)	Luftwaffe	
45+19	Panavia Tornado IDS	Luftwaffe TLG 33, Büchel	
45+20	Panavia Tornado IDS	Luftwaffe TLG 33, Büchel	
45+22	Panavia Tornado IDS	Luftwaffe TLG 51 *Immelmann*, Schleswig/Jagel	
45+23	Panavia Tornado IDS	Luftwaffe TLG 33, Büchel	
45+28	Panavia Tornado IDS	Luftwaffe TLG 33, Büchel	
45+35	Panavia Tornado IDS	Luftwaffe	
45+39	Panavia Tornado IDS	Luftwaffe TLG 33, Büchel	
45+50	Panavia Tornado IDS	Luftwaffe TLG 51 *Immelmann*, Schleswig/Jagel	
45+53	Panavia Tornado IDS	Luftwaffe TAubZLwSüd, Kaufbeuren	
45+54	Panavia Tornado IDS	Luftwaffe	
45+57	Panavia Tornado IDS	Luftwaffe TLG 33, Büchel	
45+59	Panavia Tornado IDS	Luftwaffe TLG 51 *Immelmann*, Schleswig/Jagel	
45+60	Panavia Tornado IDS(T)	*Withdrawn from use, 2017*	
45+61	Panavia Tornado IDS(T)	Luftwaffe TLG 51 *Immelmann*, Schleswig/Jagel	
45+64	Panavia Tornado IDS	Luftwaffe TLG 33, Büchel	
45+66	Panavia Tornado IDS	Luftwaffe TLG 33, Büchel	
45+67	Panavia Tornado IDS	Luftwaffe TLG 33, Büchel	
45+68	Panavia Tornado IDS	Luftwaffe TLG 33, Büchel	
45+69	Panavia Tornado IDS	Luftwaffe	
45+70	Panavia Tornado IDS(T)	Luftwaffe TLG 51 *Immelmann*, Schleswig/Jagel	
45+71	Panavia Tornado IDS	Luftwaffe TLG 33, Büchel	
45+72	Panavia Tornado IDS	Luftwaffe	
45+74	Panavia Tornado IDS	Luftwaffe TAubZLwSüd, Kaufbeuren	
45+76	Panavia Tornado IDS	Luftwaffe TLG 33, Büchel	
45+77	Panavia Tornado IDS(T)	Luftwaffe TLG 51 *Immelmann*, Schleswig/Jagel	
45+84	Panavia Tornado IDS	Luftwaffe TLG 33, Büchel	
45+85	Panavia Tornado IDS	Luftwaffe TLG 33, Büchel	
45+88	Panavia Tornado IDS	Luftwaffe TLG 33, Büchel	
45+90	Panavia Tornado IDS	Luftwaffe TLG 33, Büchel	
45+92	Panavia Tornado IDS	Luftwaffe TLG 33, Büchel	
45+93	Panavia Tornado IDS	Luftwaffe TLG 33, Büchel	
45+94	Panavia Tornado IDS	Luftwaffe TLG 33, Büchel	
46+00	Panavia Tornado IDS(T)	Luftwaffe	
46+02	Panavia Tornado IDS	Luftwaffe TLG 33, Büchel	
46+05	Panavia Tornado IDS(T)	Luftwaffe	
46+07	Panavia Tornado IDS(T)	Luftwaffe TLG 33, Büchel	
46+09	Panavia Tornado IDS(T)	Luftwaffe	

Notes	Serial	Type (code/other identity)	Owner/operator, location or fate
	46+10	Panavia Tornado IDS	Luftwaffe TLG 33, Büchel
	46+11	Panavia Tornado IDS	Luftwaffe TLG 33, Büchel
	46+15	Panavia Tornado IDS	Luftwaffe TLG 33, Büchel
	46+18	Panavia Tornado IDS	Luftwaffe TLG 33, Büchel
	46+20	Panavia Tornado IDS	Luftwaffe TLG 51 *Immelmann*, Schleswig/Jagel
	46+21	Panavia Tornado IDS	Luftwaffe TLG 33, Büchel
	46+22	Panavia Tornado IDS	Luftwaffe TLG 33, Büchel
	46+23	Panavia Tornado ECR	Luftwaffe TLG 51 *Immelmann*, Schleswig/Jagel
	46+24	Panavia Tornado ECR	Luftwaffe TLG 51 *Immelmann*, Schleswig/Jagel
	46+25	Panavia Tornado ECR	Luftwaffe TLG 51 *Immelmann*, Schleswig/Jagel
	46+26	Panavia Tornado ECR	Luftwaffe
	46+28	Panavia Tornado ECR $	Luftwaffe TLG 51 *Immelmann*, Schleswig/Jagel
	46+29	Panavia Tornado ECR	Luftwaffe
	46+30	Panavia Tornado ECR	Luftwaffe
	46+32	Panavia Tornado ECR	Luftwaffe TLG 51 *Immelmann*, Schleswig/Jagel
	46+33	Panavia Tornado ECR	Luftwaffe
	46+34	Panavia Tornado ECR	Luftwaffe
	46+35	Panavia Tornado ECR	Luftwaffe TLG 51 *Immelmann*, Schleswig/Jagel
	46+36	Panavia Tornado ECR	Luftwaffe TLG 51 *Immelmann*, Schleswig/Jagel
	46+37	Panavia Tornado ECR	Luftwaffe
	46+38	Panavia Tornado ECR	Luftwaffe WTD 61, Ingolstadt
	46+39	Panavia Tornado ECR	Luftwaffe TAubZLwSüd, Kaufbeuren
	46+40	Panavia Tornado ECR	Luftwaffe TLG 51 *Immelmann*, Schleswig/Jagel
	46+41	Panavia Tornado ECR	Luftwaffe
	46+43	Panavia Tornado ECR	Luftwaffe
	46+44	Panavia Tornado ECR	Luftwaffe TLG 51 *Immelmann*, Schleswig/Jagel
	46+45	Panavia Tornado ECR	Luftwaffe TLG 51 *Immelmann*, Schleswig/Jagel
	46+46	Panavia Tornado ECR	Luftwaffe TLG 51 *Immelmann*, Schleswig/Jagel
	46+48	Panavia Tornado ECR	Luftwaffe TLG 51 *Immelmann*, Schleswig/Jagel
	46+49	Panavia Tornado ECR	Luftwaffe TLG 51 *Immelmann*, Schleswig/Jagel
	46+50	Panavia Tornado ECR	Luftwaffe TLG 51 *Immelmann*, Schleswig/Jagel
	46+51	Panavia Tornado ECR	Luftwaffe TLG 51 *Immelmann*, Schleswig/Jagel
	46+52	Panavia Tornado ECR	Luftwaffe TLG 51 *Immelmann*, Schleswig/Jagel
	46+53	Panavia Tornado ECR	Luftwaffe
	46+54	Panavia Tornado ECR $	Luftwaffe TLG 51 *Immelmann*, Schleswig/Jagel
	46+55	Panavia Tornado ECR	Luftwaffe TLG 51 *Immelmann*, Schleswig/Jagel
	46+56	Panavia Tornado ECR	Luftwaffe TLG 51 *Immelmann*, Schleswig/Jagel
	46+57	Panavia Tornado ECR $	Luftwaffe TLG 51 *Immelmann*, Schleswig/Jagel
	50+08	Transall C-160D	Luftwaffe
	50+09	Transall C-160D	Luftwaffe
	50+10	Transall C-160D	Luftwaffe
	50+17	Transall C-160D	Luftwaffe LTG 63 (4.LwDiv), Hohn
	50+29	Transall C-160D	Luftwaffe
	50+33	Transall C-160D	Luftwaffe LTG 63 (4.LwDiv), Hohn
	50+34	Transall C-160D	*Withdrawn from use at Jever, 2017*
	50+36	Transall C-160D	Luftwaffe LTG 63 (4.LwDiv), Hohn
	50+38	Transall C-160D	Luftwaffe LTG 63 (4.LwDiv), Hohn
	50+40	Transall C-160D	Luftwaffe LTG 63 (4.LwDiv), Hohn
	50+41	Transall C-160D $	Luftwaffe LTG 63 (4.LwDiv), Hohn
	50+42	Transall C-160D	Luftwaffe LTG 63 (4.LwDiv), Hohn
	50+44	Transall C-160D	Luftwaffe
	50+45	Transall C-160D	Luftwaffe
	50+46	Transall C-160D	Luftwaffe
	50+47	Transall C-160D	Luftwaffe
	50+48	Transall C-160D $	Luftwaffe
	50+49	Transall C-160D	Luftwaffe LTG 63 (4.LwDiv), Hohn
	50+51	Transall C-160D	Luftwaffe
	50+53	Transall C-160D	Luftwaffe
	50+54	Transall C-160D	Luftwaffe LTG 63 (4.LwDiv), Hohn
	50+55	Transall C-160D	Luftwaffe LTG 63 (4.LwDiv), Hohn
	50+57	Transall C-160D	Luftwaffe LTG 63 (4.LwDiv), Hohn
	50+58	Transall C-160D	Luftwaffe LTG 63 (4.LwDiv), Hohn

Serial	Type (code/other identity)	Owner/operator, location or fate	Notes
50+59	Transall C-160D	Luftwaffe LTG 63 (4.LwDiv), Hohn	
50+61	Transall C-160D	Luftwaffe LTG 63 (4.LwDiv), Hohn	
50+64	Transall C-160D $	Luftwaffe LTG 63 (4.LwDiv), Hohn	
50+65	Transall C-160D $	Luftwaffe	
50+66	Transall C-160D	Luftwaffe/Airbus, Manching	
50+67	Transall C-160D	Luftwaffe LTG 63 (4.LwDiv), Hohn	
50+69	Transall C-160D	Luftwaffe LTG 63 (4.LwDiv), Hohn	
50+70	Transall C-160D	Luftwaffe	
50+71	Transall C-160D	Luftwaffe LTG 63 (4.LwDiv), Hohn	
50+72	Transall C-160D	Luftwaffe	
50+73	Transall C-160D	Luftwaffe	
50+74	Transall C-160D	Luftwaffe	
50+75	Transall C-160D	Luftwaffe LTG 63 (4.LwDiv), Hohn	
50+76	Transall C-160D	Luftwaffe LTG 63 (4.LwDiv), Hohn	
50+77	Transall C-160D	Luftwaffe LTG 63 (4.LwDiv), Hohn	
50+78	Transall C-160D	Luftwaffe LTG 63 (4.LwDiv), Hohn	
50+79	Transall C-160D	Luftwaffe LTG 63 (4.LwDiv), Hohn	
50+81	Transall C-160D	Luftwaffe LTG 63 (4.LwDiv), Hohn	
50+82	Transall C-160D $	Luftwaffe LTG 63 (4.LwDiv), Hohn	
50+83	Transall C-160D	Luftwaffe	
50+84	Transall C-160D	Luftwaffe	
50+86	Transall C-160D	Luftwaffe WTD 61, Ingolstadt	
50+87	Transall C-160D	Luftwaffe LTG 63 (4.LwDiv), Hohn	
50+88	Transall C-160D	Luftwaffe	
50+89	Transall C-160D	Luftwaffe	
50+91	Transall C-160D	Luftwaffe	
50+92	Transall C-160D	Luftwaffe	
50+93	Transall C-160D $	Luftwaffe LTG 63 (4.LwDiv), Hohn	
50+96	Transall C-160D	Luftwaffe	
50+97	Transall C-160D	Luftwaffe LTG 63 (4.LwDiv), Hohn	
51+01	Transall C-160D $	*Withdrawn from use, January 2018*	
51+03	Transall C-160D	Luftwaffe LTG 63 (4.LwDiv), Hohn	
51+04	Transall C-160D	Luftwaffe LTG 63 (4.LwDiv), Hohn	
51+05	Transall C-160D	Luftwaffe LTG 63 (4.LwDiv), Hohn	
51+06	Transall C-160D	Luftwaffe LTG 63 (4.LwDiv), Hohn	
51+08	Transall C-160D	Luftwaffe WTD 61, Ingolstadt	
51+10	Transall C-160D	Luftwaffe	
51+12	Transall C-160D	Luftwaffe LTG 63 (4.LwDiv), Hohn	
51+13	Transall C-160D	Luftwaffe	
51+14	Transall C-160D	Luftwaffe LTG 63 (4.LwDiv), Hohn	
51+15	Transall C-160D	Luftwaffe	
54+01	Airbus Military A.400M	Luftwaffe LTG 62, Wunstorf	
54+02	Airbus Military A.400M	Luftwaffe LTG 62, Wunstorf	
54+03	Airbus Military A.400M $	Luftwaffe LTG 62, Wunstorf	
54+04	Airbus Military A.400M	Luftwaffe LTG 62, Wunstorf	
54+05	Airbus Military A.400M	Luftwaffe LTG 62, Wunstorf	
54+06	Airbus Military A.400M	Luftwaffe LTG 62, Wunstorf	
54+07	Airbus Military A.400M	Luftwaffe LTG 62, Wunstorf	
54+08	Airbus Military A.400M	Luftwaffe LTG 62, Wunstorf	
54+09	Airbus Military A.400M	Luftwaffe LTG 62, Wunstorf	
54+10	Airbus Military A.400M	Luftwaffe LTG 62, Wunstorf	
54+11	Airbus Military A.400M	Luftwaffe LTG 62, Wunstorf	
54+12	Airbus Military A.400M	Luftwaffe LTG 62, Wunstorf	
54+13	Airbus Military A.400M	Luftwaffe LTG 62, Wunstorf	
54+14	Airbus Military A.400M	Luftwaffe LTG 62, Wunstorf	
54+15	Airbus Military A.400M	Luftwaffe LTG 62, Wunstorf	
54+16	Airbus Military A.400M	Luftwaffe LTG 62, Wunstorf	
54+17	Airbus Military A.400M	Airbus Defence & Space, Seville	
54+18	Airbus Military A.400M	Airbus Defence & Space, Seville	
54+19	Airbus Military A.400M	Luftwaffe (on order)	
54+20	Airbus Military A.400M	Luftwaffe (on order)	
54+21	Airbus Military A.400M	Luftwaffe (on order)	

Notes	Serial	Type (code/other identity)	Owner/operator, location or fate
	54+22	Airbus Military A.400M	Luftwaffe (on order)
	54+23	Airbus Military A.400M	Luftwaffe (on order)
	54+24	Airbus Military A.400M	Luftwaffe (on order)
	54+25	Airbus Military A.400M	Luftwaffe (on order)
	54+26	Airbus Military A.400M	Luftwaffe (on order)
	54+27	Airbus Military A.400M	Luftwaffe (on order)
	54+28	Airbus Military A.400M	Luftwaffe (on order)
	54+29	Airbus Military A.400M	Luftwaffe (on order)
	54+30	Airbus Military A.400M	Luftwaffe (on order)
	57+04	Dornier Do.228LM	Marineflieger MFG 3, Nordholz
	57+05	Dornier Do.228NG	Marineflieger MFG 3, Nordholz
	60+01	Lockheed P-3C CUP Orion $	Marineflieger MFG 3, Nordholz
	60+02	Lockheed P-3C CUP Orion	Marineflieger MFG 3, Nordholz
	60+03	Lockheed P-3C CUP Orion	Marineflieger MFG 3, Nordholz
	60+04	Lockheed P-3C CUP Orion	Marineflieger MFG 3, Nordholz
	60+05	Lockheed P-3C CUP Orion $	Marineflieger MFG 3, Nordholz
	60+06	Lockheed P-3C CUP Orion	Marineflieger MFG 3, Nordholz
	60+07	Lockheed P-3C CUP Orion	Marineflieger MFG 3, Nordholz
	60+08	Lockheed P-3C CUP Orion	Marineflieger MFG 3, Nordholz
	74+01	Eurocopter EC.665 Tiger UHT	Luftwaffe WTD 61, Ingolstadt
	74+02	Eurocopter EC.665 Tiger UHT	Heer KHR 36, Fritzlar
	74+03	Eurocopter EC.665 Tiger UHT	Luftwaffe TsLw 3, Fassberg
	74+05	Eurocopter EC.665 Tiger UHT	Heer IntHubschrAusbZ, Le Luc, France
	74+06	Eurocopter EC.665 Tiger UHT	Heer KHR 36, Fritzlar
	74+07	Eurocopter EC.665 Tiger UHT	Heer IntHubschrAusbZ, Le Luc, France
	74+08	Eurocopter EC.665 Tiger UHT	Luftwaffe TsLw 3, Fassberg
	74+09	Eurocopter EC.665 Tiger UHT	Heer IntHubschrAusbZ, Le Luc, France
	74+10	Eurocopter EC.665 Tiger UHT	Heer KHR 36, Fritzlar
	74+11	Eurocopter EC.665 Tiger UHT	Heer IntHubschrAusbZ, Le Luc, France
	74+13	Eurocopter EC.665 Tiger UHT	Heer IntHubschrAusbZ, Le Luc, France
	74+14	Eurocopter EC.665 Tiger UHT	Heer IntHubschrAusbZ, Le Luc, France
	74+15	Eurocopter EC.665 Tiger UHT	Heer IntHubschrAusbZ, Le Luc, France
	74+16	Eurocopter EC.665 Tiger UHT	Heer KHR 36, Fritzlar
	74+17	Eurocopter EC.665 Tiger UHT	Heer KHR 36, Fritzlar
	74+18	Eurocopter EC.665 Tiger UHT	Heer KHR 36, Fritzlar
	74+19	Eurocopter EC.665 Tiger UHT	Heer KHR 36, Fritzlar
	74+20	Eurocopter EC.665 Tiger UHT	Heer KHR 36, Fritzlar
	74+21	Eurocopter EC.665 Tiger UHT	Heer KHR 36, Fritzlar
	74+22	Eurocopter EC.665 Tiger UHT	Heer KHR 36, Fritzlar
	74+23	Eurocopter EC.665 Tiger UHT	Heer KHR 36, Fritzlar
	74+24	Eurocopter EC.665 Tiger UHT	Heer KHR 36, Fritzlar
	74+25	Eurocopter EC.665 Tiger UHT	Heer KHR 36, Fritzlar
	74+26	Eurocopter EC.665 Tiger UHT	Heer KHR 36, Fritzlar
	74+28	Eurocopter EC.665 Tiger UHT	Heer KHR 36, Fritzlar
	74+29	Eurocopter EC.665 Tiger UHT	Heer KHR 36, Fritzlar
	74+30	Eurocopter EC.665 Tiger UHT	Heer KHR 36, Fritzlar
	74+31	Eurocopter EC.665 Tiger UHT	Heer KHR 36, Fritzlar
	74+32	Eurocopter EC.665 Tiger UHT	Heer KHR 36, Fritzlar
	74+34	Eurocopter EC.665 Tiger UHT	Heer KHR 36, Fritzlar
	74+35	Eurocopter EC.665 Tiger UHT	Heer KHR 36, Fritzlar
	74+36	Eurocopter EC.665 Tiger UHT	Heer KHR 36, Fritzlar
	74+37	Eurocopter EC.665 Tiger UHT	Heer IntHubschrAusbZ, Le Luc, France
	74+38	Eurocopter EC.665 Tiger UHT	Heer KHR 36, Fritzlar
	74+39	Eurocopter EC.665 Tiger UHT	Heer
	74+40	Eurocopter EC.665 Tiger UHT	Heer KHR 36, Fritzlar
	74+41	Eurocopter EC.665 Tiger UHT	Heer
	74+42	Eurocopter EC.665 Tiger UHT	Heer KHR 36, Fritzlar
	74+43	Eurocopter EC.665 Tiger UHT	Heer
	74+44	Eurocopter EC.665 Tiger UHT	Heer
	74+45	Eurocopter EC.665 Tiger UHT	Heer KHR 36, Fritzlar
	74+46	Eurocopter EC.665 Tiger UHT	Heer KHR 36, Fritzlar
	74+47	Eurocopter EC.665 Tiger UHT	Heer KHR 36, Fritzlar

Serial	Type (code/other identity)	Owner/operator, location or fate	Notes
4+48	Eurocopter EC.665 Tiger UHT	Heer KHR 26, Roth	
4+49	Eurocopter EC.665 Tiger UHT	Heer	
4+50	Eurocopter EC.665 Tiger UHT	Heer KHR 36, Fritzlar	
4+51	Eurocopter EC.665 Tiger UHT	Heer IntHubschrAusbZ, Le Luc, France	
4+52	Eurocopter EC.665 Tiger UHT	Heer	
4+53	Eurocopter EC.665 Tiger UHT	Heer KHR 36, Fritzlar	
4+54	Eurocopter EC.665 Tiger UHT	Heer KHR 36, Fritzlar	
4+55	Eurocopter EC.665 Tiger UHT	Heer	
4+56	Eurocopter EC.665 Tiger UHT	Heer	
4+57	Eurocopter EC.665 Tiger UHT	Heer KHR 36, Fritzlar	
4+58	Eurocopter EC.665 Tiger UHT	Heer	
4+59	Eurocopter EC.665 Tiger UHT	Heer	
4+61	Eurocopter EC.665 Tiger UHT	Heer KHR 36, Fritzlar	
4+62	Eurocopter EC.665 Tiger UHT	Airbus Helicopters, Donauwörth	
4+63	Eurocopter EC.665 Tiger UHT	Heer KHR 36, Fritzlar	
4+64	Eurocopter EC.665 Tiger UHT	Heer (on order)	
4+65	Eurocopter EC.665 Tiger UHT	Heer (on order)	
4+66	Eurocopter EC.665 Tiger UHT	Airbus Helicopters, Donauwörth	
4+67	Eurocopter EC.665 Tiger UHT	Airbus Helicopters, Donauwörth	
4+68	Eurocopter EC.665 Tiger UHT	Airbus Helicopters, Donauwörth	
4+69	Eurocopter EC.665 Tiger UHT	Heer (on order)	
4+70	Eurocopter EC.665 Tiger UHT	Heer (on order)	
4+71	Eurocopter EC.665 Tiger UHT	Heer (on order)	
4+72	Eurocopter EC.665 Tiger UHT	Heer (on order)	
4+73	Eurocopter EC.665 Tiger UHT	Heer (on order)	
4+74	Eurocopter EC.665 Tiger UHT	Heer (on order)	
4+75	Eurocopter EC.665 Tiger UHT	Heer (on order)	
4+76	Eurocopter EC.665 Tiger UHT	Heer (on order)	
4+77	Eurocopter EC.665 Tiger UHT	Heer (on order)	
4+78	Eurocopter EC.665 Tiger UHT	Heer (on order)	
4+79	Eurocopter EC.665 Tiger UHT	Heer (on order)	
4+80	Eurocopter EC.665 Tiger UHT	Heer (on order)	
6+01	Airbus Helicopters H.145M	Luftwaffe HSG 64, Laupheim	
6+02	Airbus Helicopters H.145M	Luftwaffe HSG 64, Laupheim	
6+03	Airbus Helicopters H.145M	Luftwaffe HSG 64, Laupheim	
6+04	Airbus Helicopters H.145M	Luftwaffe HSG 64, Laupheim	
6+05	Airbus Helicopters H.145M	Luftwaffe HSG 64, Laupheim	
6+06	Airbus Helicopters H.145M	Luftwaffe HSG 64, Laupheim	
6+07	Airbus Helicopters H.145M	Luftwaffe HSG 64, Laupheim	
6+08	Airbus Helicopters H.145M	Luftwaffe HSG 64, Laupheim	
6+09	Airbus Helicopters H.145M	Luftwaffe HSG 64, Laupheim	
6+10	Airbus Helicopters H.145M	Luftwaffe HSG 64, Laupheim	
6+11	Airbus Helicopters H.145M	Luftwaffe HSG 64, Laupheim	
6+12	Airbus Helicopters H.145M	Luftwaffe HSG 64, Laupheim	
6+13	Airbus Helicopters H.145M	Luftwaffe HSG 64, Laupheim	
6+14	Airbus Helicopters H.145M	Luftwaffe (on order)	
6+15	Airbus Helicopters H.145M	Luftwaffe (on order)	
8+01	NH Industries NH.90-TTH	Heer IntHubschrAusbZ, Bückeburg	
8+02	NH Industries NH.90-TTH	Heer IntHubschrAusbZ, Bückeburg	
8+03	NH Industries NH.90-TTH	Heer IntHubschrAusbZ, Bückeburg	
8+04	NH Industries NH.90-TTH	Luftwaffe TsLw 3, Fassberg	
8+05	NH Industries NH.90-TTH	Luftwaffe TsLw 3, Fassberg	
8+06	NH Industries NH.90-TTH	Heer IntHubschrAusbZ, Bückeburg	
8+07	NH Industries NH.90-TTH	Heer IntHubschrAusbZ, Bückeburg	
8+08	NH Industries NH.90-TTH	Heer IntHubschrAusbZ, Bückeburg	
8+09	NH Industries NH.90-TTH	Heer IntHubschrAusbZ, Bückeburg	
8+10	NH Industries NH.90-TTH	Luftwaffe TsLw 3, Fassberg	
8+11	NH Industries NH.90-TTH	Heer THR 10, Fassberg	
8+12	NH Industries NH.90-TTH	Heer THR 10, Fassberg	
8+13	NH Industries NH.90-TTH	Heer THR 10, Fassberg	
8+14	NH Industries NH.90-TTH	Heer THR 10, Fassberg	
8+15	NH Industries NH.90-TTH	Heer THR 10, Fassberg	

Notes	Serial	Type (code/other identity)	Owner/operator, location or fate
	78+16	NH Industries NH.90-TTH	Airbus Helicopters, Donauwörth
	78+17	NH Industries NH.90-TTH	Heer THR 10, Fassberg
	78+18	NH Industries NH.90-TTH	Heer THR 10, Fassberg
	78+19	NH Industries NH.90-TTH	Heer IntHubschrAusbZ, Bückeburg
	78+20	NH Industries NH.90-TTH	Heer IntHubschrAusbZ, Bückeburg
	78+21	NH Industries NH.90-TTH	Heer IntHubschrAusbZ, Bückeburg
	78+22	NH Industries NH.90-TTH	Heer IntHubschrAusbZ, Bückeburg
	78+23	NH Industries NH.90-TTH	Heer THR 10, Fassberg
	78+24	NH Industries NH.90-TTH	Heer THR 10, Fassberg
	78+25	NH Industries NH.90-TTH	Heer THR 10, Fassberg
	78+26	NH Industries NH.90-TTH	Heer IntHubschrAusbZ, Bückeburg
	78+27	NH Industries NH.90-TTH	Heer IntHubschrAusbZ, Bückeburg
	78+28	NH Industries NH.90-TTH	Heer THR 10, Fassberg
	78+29	NH Industries NH.90-TTH	Heer IntHubschrAusbZ, Bückeburg
	78+30	NH Industries NH.90-TTH	Heer IntHubschrAusbZ, Bückeburg
	78+31	NH Industries NH.90-TTH	Heer THR 10, Fassberg
	78+32	NH Industries NH.90-TTH	Heer IntHubschrAusbZ, Bückeburg
	78+33	NH Industries NH.90-TTH	Heer THR 10, Fassberg
	78+34	NH Industries NH.90-TTH	Heer IntHubschrAusbZ, Bückeburg
	78+35	NH Industries NH.90-TTH	Heer (on order)
	78+36	NH Industries NH.90-TTH	Heer (on order)
	78+37	NH Industries NH.90-TTH	Heer (on order)
	78+38	NH Industries NH.90-TTH	Heer (on order)
	78+39	NH Industries NH.90-TTH	Heer (on order)
	78+40	NH Industries NH.90-TTH	Heer (on order)
	78+41	NH Industries NH.90-TTH	Heer (on order)
	78+42	NH Industries NH.90-TTH	Heer (on order)
	78+43	NH Industries NH.90-TTH	Heer (on order)
	78+44	NH Industries NH.90-TTH	Heer (on order)
	78+45	NH Industries NH.90-TTH	Heer (on order)
	78+46	NH Industries NH.90-TTH	Heer (on order)
	78+47	NH Industries NH.90-TTH	Heer (on order)
	78+48	NH Industries NH.90-TTH	Heer (on order)
	78+49	NH Industries NH.90-TTH	Heer (on order)
	78+50	NH Industries NH.90-TTH	Heer (on order)
	79+01	NH Industries NH.90-TTH	Heer IntHubschrAusbZ, Bückeburg
	79+02	NH Industries NH.90-TTH	Heer IntHubschrAusbZ, Bückeburg
	79+03	NH Industries NH.90-TTH	Heer THR 10, Fassberg
	79+04	NH Industries NH.90-TTH	Heer THR 10, Fassberg
	79+05	NH Industries NH.90-TTH	Heer THR 10, Fassberg
	79+06	NH Industries NH.90-TTH	Heer IntHubschrAusbZ, Bückeburg
	79+07	NH Industries NH.90-TTH	Heer IntHubschrAusbZ, Bückeburg
	79+08	NH Industries NH.90-TTH	Heer IntHubschrAusbZ, Bückeburg
	79+09	NH Industries NH.90-TTH	Heer IntHubschrAusbZ, Bückeburg
	79+10	NH Industries NH.90-TTH	Heer
	79+24	NH Industries NH.90-TTH	Heer THR 10, Fassberg
	79+25	NH Industries NH.90-TTH	Heer
	79+26	NH Industries NH.90-TTH	Luftwaffe TsLw 3, Fassberg
	79+27	NH Industries NH.90-TTH	Heer (on order)
	79+28	NH Industries NH.90-TTH	Heer (on order)
	79+29	NH Industries NH.90-TTH	Heer (on order)
	79+30	NH Industries NH.90-TTH	Heer (on order)
	79+52	NH Industries NH.90-NFH Sea Lion	Marineflieger (on order)
	79+53	NH Industries NH.90-NFH Sea Lion	Marineflieger (on order)
	79+54	NH Industries NH.90-NFH Sea Lion	Marineflieger (on order)
	79+55	NH Industries NH.90-NFH Sea Lion	Marineflieger (on order)
	79+56	NH Industries NH.90-NFH Sea Lion	Marineflieger (on order)
	79+57	NH Industries NH.90-NFH Sea Lion	Marineflieger (on order)
	79+58	NH Industries NH.90-NFH Sea Lion	Marineflieger (on order)
	79+59	NH Industries NH.90-NFH Sea Lion	Marineflieger (on order)
	79+60	NH Industries NH.90-NFH Sea Lion	Marineflieger (on order)
	79+61	NH Industries NH.90-NFH Sea Lion	Marineflieger (on order)

Serial	Type (code/other identity)	Owner/operator, location or fate	Notes
9+62	NH Industries NH.90-NFH Sea Lion	Marineflieger (on order)	
9+63	NH Industries NH.90-NFH Sea Lion	Marineflieger (on order)	
9+64	NH Industries NH.90-NFH Sea Lion	Marineflieger (on order)	
9+65	NH Industries NH.90-NFH Sea Lion	Marineflieger (on order)	
9+66	NH Industries NH.90-NFH Sea Lion	Marineflieger (on order)	
9+67	NH Industries NH.90-NFH Sea Lion	Marineflieger (on order)	
9+68	NH Industries NH.90-NFH Sea Lion	Marineflieger (on order)	
2+01	Eurocopter AS.532U-2 Cougar	Luftwaffe 3/FBS, Berlin-Tegel	
2+02	Eurocopter AS.532U-2 Cougar	Luftwaffe 3/FBS, Berlin-Tegel	
2+03	Eurocopter AS.532U-2 Cougar	Luftwaffe 3/FBS, Berlin-Tegel	
2+51	Eurocopter EC.135P-1	Heer IntHubschrAusbZ, Bückeburg	
2+52	Eurocopter EC.135P-1	Heer IntHubschrAusbZ, Bückeburg	
2+53	Eurocopter EC.135P-1	Heer IntHubschrAusbZ, Bückeburg	
2+54	Eurocopter EC.135P-1	Heer IntHubschrAusbZ, Bückeburg	
2+55	Eurocopter EC.135P-1	Heer IntHubschrAusbZ, Bückeburg	
2+56	Eurocopter EC.135P-1	Heer IntHubschrAusbZ, Bückeburg	
2+57	Eurocopter EC.135P-1	Heer IntHubschrAusbZ, Bückeburg	
2+59	Eurocopter EC.135P-1	Heer IntHubschrAusbZ, Bückeburg	
2+60	Eurocopter EC.135P-1	Heer IntHubschrAusbZ, Bückeburg	
2+61	Eurocopter EC.135P-1	Heer IntHubschrAusbZ, Bückeburg	
2+62	Eurocopter EC.135P-1	Heer IntHubschrAusbZ, Bückeburg	
2+63	Eurocopter EC.135P-1	Heer IntHubschrAusbZ, Bückeburg	
2+64	Eurocopter EC.135P-1	Heer IntHubschrAusbZ, Bückeburg	
2+65	Eurocopter EC.135P-1	Heer IntHubschrAusbZ, Bückeburg	
3+02	Westland Sea Lynx Mk88A	Marineflieger MFG 5, Nordholz	
3+03	Westland Sea Lynx Mk88A	Marineflieger MFG 5, Nordholz	
3+04	Westland Sea Lynx Mk88A	Marineflieger MFG 5, Nordholz	
3+05	Westland Sea Lynx Mk88A	Marineflieger MFG 5, Nordholz	
3+06	Westland Sea Lynx Mk88A	Marineflieger MFG 5, Nordholz	
3+07	Westland Sea Lynx Mk88A	Luftwaffe WTD 61, Ingolstadt	
3+09	Westland Sea Lynx Mk88A	Marineflieger MFG 5, Nordholz	
3+10	Westland Sea Lynx Mk88A	Marineflieger MFG 5, Nordholz	
3+11	Westland Sea Lynx Mk88A $	Marineflieger MFG 5, Nordholz	
3+12	Westland Sea Lynx Mk88A	Marineflieger MFG 5, Nordholz	
3+13	Westland Sea Lynx Mk88A	Marineflieger MFG 5, Nordholz	
3+15	Westland Sea Lynx Mk88A	Marineflieger MFG 5, Nordholz	
3+17	Westland Sea Lynx Mk88A	Marineflieger MFG 5, Nordholz	
3+18	Westland Sea Lynx Mk88A	Marineflieger MFG 5, Nordholz	
3+19	Westland Sea Lynx Mk88A	Marineflieger MFG 5, Nordholz	
3+20	Westland Sea Lynx Mk88A $	Marineflieger MFG 5, Nordholz	
3+21	Westland Sea Lynx Mk88A	Marineflieger MFG 5, Nordholz	
3+22	Westland Sea Lynx Mk88A	Marineflieger MFG 5, Nordholz	
3+23	Westland Sea Lynx Mk88A	Marineflieger MFG 5, Nordholz	
3+24	Westland Sea Lynx Mk88A	Marineflieger MFG 5, Nordholz	
3+25	Westland Sea Lynx Mk88A	Marineflieger MFG 5, Nordholz	
4+05	Sikorsky/VFW CH-53G	Luftwaffe HSG 64, Laupheim & Rheine-Bentlage	
4+09	Sikorsky/VFW CH-53G	Luftwaffe TsLw 3, Fassberg	
4+10	Sikorsky/VFW CH-53G	Luftwaffe TsLw 3, Fassberg	
4+12	Sikorsky/VFW CH-53G	Luftwaffe HSG 64, Laupheim & Rheine-Bentlage	
4+13	Sikorsky/VFW CH-53GA	Luftwaffe HSG 64, Laupheim & Rheine-Bentlage	
4+14	Sikorsky/VFW CH-53GE	Luftwaffe HSG 64, Laupheim & Rheine-Bentlage	
4+15	Sikorsky/VFW CH-53GS	Luftwaffe HSG 64, Laupheim & Rheine-Bentlage	
4+16	Sikorsky/VFW CH-53G	Luftwaffe	
4+18	Sikorsky/VFW CH-53G	Luftwaffe HSG 64, Laupheim & Rheine-Bentlage	
4+19	Sikorsky/VFW CH-53G	Luftwaffe TsLw 3, Fassberg	
4+24	Sikorsky/VFW CH-53GA	Luftwaffe HSG 64, Laupheim & Rheine-Bentlage	
4+25	Sikorsky/VFW CH-53GS	Luftwaffe HSG 64, Laupheim & Rheine-Bentlage	
4+26	Sikorsky/VFW CH-53GE	Luftwaffe WTD 61, Ingolstadt	
4+27	Sikorsky/VFW CH-53G	Luftwaffe	
4+28	Sikorsky/VFW CH-53G	Luftwaffe HSG 64, Laupheim & Rheine-Bentlage	
4+29	Sikorsky/VFW CH-53G	Luftwaffe HSG 64, Laupheim & Rheine-Bentlage	
4+30	Sikorsky/VFW CH-53GS	Luftwaffe HSG 64, Laupheim & Rheine-Bentlage	

Notes	Serial	Type (code/other identity)	Owner/operator, location or fate
	84+31	Sikorsky/VFW CH-53GA	Luftwaffe HSG 64, Laupheim & Rheine-Bentlage
	84+32	Sikorsky/VFW CH-53G	Luftwaffe HSG 64, Laupheim & Rheine-Bentlage
	84+33	Sikorsky/VFW CH-53GA	Luftwaffe HSG 64, Laupheim & Rheine-Bentlage
	84+34	Sikorsky/VFW CH-53G	Luftwaffe HSG 64, Laupheim & Rheine-Bentlage
	84+35	Sikorsky/VFW CH-53G	Luftwaffe HSG 64, Laupheim & Rheine-Bentlage
	84+37	Sikorsky/VFW CH-53GA	Luftwaffe HSG 64, Laupheim & Rheine-Bentlage
	84+38	Sikorsky/VFW CH-53G	Luftwaffe HSG 64, Laupheim & Rheine-Bentlage
	84+39	Sikorsky/VFW CH-53GA	Luftwaffe HSG 64, Laupheim & Rheine-Bentlage
	84+40	Sikorsky/VFW CH-53G	Luftwaffe HSG 64, Laupheim & Rheine-Bentlage
	84+42	Sikorsky/VFW CH-53GS	Luftwaffe HSG 64, Laupheim & Rheine-Bentlage
	84+43	Sikorsky/VFW CH-53G	Luftwaffe HSG 64, Laupheim & Rheine-Bentlage
	84+44	Sikorsky/VFW CH-53G	Luftwaffe HSG 64, Laupheim & Rheine-Bentlage
	84+45	Sikorsky/VFW CH-53GS	Luftwaffe HSG 64, Laupheim & Rheine-Bentlage
	84+46	Sikorsky/VFW CH-53G	Luftwaffe HSG 64, Laupheim & Rheine-Bentlage
	84+47	Sikorsky/VFW CH-53GA	Luftwaffe HSG 64, Laupheim & Rheine-Bentlage
	84+48	Sikorsky/VFW CH-53G	Luftwaffe HSG 64, Laupheim & Rheine-Bentlage
	84+49	Sikorsky/VFW CH-53GA	Luftwaffe HSG 64, Laupheim & Rheine-Bentlage
	84+50	Sikorsky/VFW CH-53GA	Luftwaffe HSG 64, Laupheim & Rheine-Bentlage
	84+51	Sikorsky/VFW CH-53GS	Luftwaffe HSG 64, Laupheim & Rheine-Bentlage
	84+52	Sikorsky/VFW CH-53GS	Luftwaffe HSG 64, Laupheim & Rheine-Bentlage
	84+53	Sikorsky/VFW CH-53GE	Luftwaffe HSG 64, Laupheim & Rheine-Bentlage
	84+54	Sikorsky/VFW CH-53G	Luftwaffe HSG 64, Laupheim & Rheine-Bentlage
	84+55	Sikorsky/VFW CH-53G	Airbus Helicopters, Donauwörth
	84+57	Sikorsky/VFW CH-53G	Luftwaffe HSG 64, Laupheim & Rheine-Bentlage
	84+58	Sikorsky/VFW CH-53G	Luftwaffe HSG 64, Laupheim & Rheine-Bentlage
	84+59	Sikorsky/VFW CH-53GS	Luftwaffe HSG 64, Laupheim & Rheine-Bentlage
	84+60	Sikorsky/VFW CH-53G	Luftwaffe HSG 64, Laupheim & Rheine-Bentlage
	84+62	Sikorsky/VFW CH-53GS	Luftwaffe HSG 64, Laupheim & Rheine-Bentlage
	84+63	Sikorsky/VFW CH-53G	Luftwaffe HSG 64, Laupheim & Rheine-Bentlage
	84+64	Sikorsky/VFW CH-53GS	Luftwaffe HSG 64, Laupheim & Rheine-Bentlage
	84+65	Sikorsky/VFW CH-53G	Luftwaffe HSG 64, Laupheim & Rheine-Bentlage
	84+66	Sikorsky/VFW CH-53GS	Luftwaffe HSG 64, Laupheim & Rheine-Bentlage
	84+67	Sikorsky/VFW CH-53GS	Luftwaffe HSG 64, Laupheim & Rheine-Bentlage
	84+68	Sikorsky/VFW CH-53GS	Luftwaffe HSG 64, Laupheim & Rheine-Bentlage
	84+70	Sikorsky/VFW CH-53GA	Luftwaffe TsLw 3, Fassberg
	84+71	Sikorsky/VFW CH-53G	Luftwaffe HSG 64, Laupheim & Rheine-Bentlage
	84+72	Sikorsky/VFW CH-53G	Luftwaffe HSG 64, Laupheim & Rheine-Bentlage
	84+73	Sikorsky/VFW CH-53GS	Luftwaffe HSG 64, Laupheim & Rheine-Bentlage
	84+74	Sikorsky/VFW CH-53G	Luftwaffe HSG 64, Laupheim & Rheine-Bentlage
	84+75	Sikorsky/VFW CH-53G	Luftwaffe HSG 64, Laupheim & Rheine-Bentlage
	84+76	Sikorsky/VFW CH-53G	Luftwaffe HSG 64, Laupheim & Rheine-Bentlage
	84+77	Sikorsky/VFW CH-53G	Luftwaffe HSG 64, Laupheim & Rheine-Bentlage
	84+78	Sikorsky/VFW CH-53GS	Luftwaffe TsLw 3, Fassberg
	84+79	Sikorsky/VFW CH-53GS	Luftwaffe HSG 64, Laupheim & Rheine-Bentlage
	84+80	Sikorsky/VFW CH-53G	Luftwaffe HSG 64, Laupheim & Rheine-Bentlage
	84+82	Sikorsky/VFW CH-53GE	Luftwaffe HSG 64, Laupheim & Rheine-Bentlage
	84+83	Sikorsky/VFW CH-53G	Luftwaffe TsLw 3, Fassberg
	84+84	Sikorsky/VFW CH-53G	Luftwaffe HSG 64, Laupheim & Rheine-Bentlage
	84+85	Sikorsky/VFW CH-53GS	Luftwaffe HSG 64, Laupheim & Rheine-Bentlage
	84+86	Sikorsky/VFW CH-53GA	Luftwaffe HSG 64, Laupheim & Rheine-Bentlag
	84+87	Sikorsky/VFW CH-53GS	Luftwaffe HSG 64, Laupheim & Rheine-Bentlage
	84+88	Sikorsky/VFW CH-53G	Luftwaffe HSG 64, Laupheim & Rheine-Bentlage
	84+89	Sikorsky/VFW CH-53GA	Luftwaffe HSG 64, Laupheim & Rheine-Bentlage
	84+90	Sikorsky/VFW CH-53G	Luftwaffe HSG 64, Laupheim & Rheine-Bentlage
	84+91	Sikorsky/VFW CH-53GS	Luftwaffe HSG 64, Laupheim & Rheine-Bentlage
	84+92	Sikorsky/VFW CH-53GS	Luftwaffe HSG 64, Laupheim & Rheine-Bentlage
	84+94	Sikorsky/VFW CH-53G	Luftwaffe WTD 61, Ingolstadt
	84+95	Sikorsky/VFW CH-53GA	Luftwaffe HSG 64, Laupheim & Rheine-Bentlage
	84+96	Sikorsky/VFW CH-53GE	Luftwaffe HSG 64, Laupheim & Rheine-Bentlage
	84+97	Sikorsky/VFW CH-53G	Luftwaffe HSG 64, Laupheim & Rheine-Bentlage
	84+98	Sikorsky/VFW CH-53GS	Luftwaffe HSG 64, Laupheim & Rheine-Bentlage
	84+99	Sikorsky/VFW CH-53GA	Luftwaffe HSG 64, Laupheim & Rheine-Bentlage

erial	Type (code/other identity)	Owner/operator, location or fate	Notes
+00	Sikorsky/VFW CH-53GS	Luftwaffe HSG 64, Laupheim & Rheine-Bentlage	
+01	Sikorsky/VFW CH-53GS	Luftwaffe HSG 64, Laupheim & Rheine-Bentlage	
+02	Sikorsky/VFW CH-53G	Luftwaffe HSG 64, Laupheim & Rheine-Bentlage	
+03	Sikorsky/VFW CH-53G	Luftwaffe HSG 64, Laupheim & Rheine-Bentlage	
+04	Sikorsky/VFW CH-53GA	Luftwaffe HSG 64, Laupheim & Rheine-Bentlage	
+05	Sikorsky/VFW CH-53GS	Luftwaffe HSG 64, Laupheim & Rheine-Bentlage	
+06	Sikorsky/VFW CH-53GA	Luftwaffe HSG 64, Laupheim & Rheine-Bentlage	
+07	Sikorsky/VFW CH-53GS	Luftwaffe HSG 64, Laupheim & Rheine-Bentlage	
+08	Sikorsky/VFW CH-53G	Luftwaffe HSG 64, Laupheim & Rheine-Bentlage	
+10	Sikorsky/VFW CH-53GS	Luftwaffe HSG 64, Laupheim & Rheine-Bentlage	
+11	Sikorsky/VFW CH-53G	Luftwaffe HSG 64, Laupheim & Rheine-Bentlage	
+12	Sikorsky/VFW CH-53GS	Luftwaffe HSG 64, Laupheim & Rheine-Bentlage	
+50	Westland Sea King Mk.41	Marineflieger MFG 5, Nordholz	
+51	Westland Sea King Mk.41	Marineflieger MFG 5, Nordholz	
+52	Westland Sea King Mk.41	Marineflieger MFG 5, Nordholz	
+53	Westland Sea King Mk.41	Marineflieger MFG 5, Nordholz	
+54	Westland Sea King Mk.41	Marineflieger MFG 5, Nordholz	
+55	Westland Sea King Mk.41 $	Marineflieger MFG 5, Nordholz	
+56	Westland Sea King Mk.41	Marineflieger MFG 5, Nordholz	
+57	Westland Sea King Mk.41	Marineflieger MFG 5, Nordholz	
+58	Westland Sea King Mk.41 $	Marineflieger MFG 5, Nordholz	
+60	Westland Sea King Mk.41	Marineflieger MFG 5, Nordholz	
+61	Westland Sea King Mk.41	Marineflieger MFG 5, Nordholz	
+62	Westland Sea King Mk.41	Marineflieger MFG 5, Nordholz	
+63	Westland Sea King Mk.41	Marineflieger MFG 5, Nordholz	
+64	Westland Sea King Mk.41 $	Marineflieger MFG 5, Nordholz	
+65	Westland Sea King Mk.41	Marineflieger MFG 5, Nordholz	
+66	Westland Sea King Mk.41	Marineflieger MFG 5, Nordholz	
+67	Westland Sea King Mk.41	Marineflieger MFG 5, Nordholz	
+68	Westland Sea King Mk.41	Marineflieger MFG 5, Nordholz	
+69	Westland Sea King Mk.41	Marineflieger MFG 5, Nordholz	
+70	Westland Sea King Mk.41	Marineflieger MFG 5, Nordholz	
+71	Westland Sea King Mk.41	Marineflieger MFG 5, Nordholz	
+03	Eurofighter EF.2000(T) (IPA3)	Luftwaffe WTD 61, Ingolstadt	
+07	Eurofighter EF.2000 (IPA7)	Luftwaffe WTD 61, Ingolstadt	
+08	Eurofighter EF.2000GT (IPA8)	Airbus Defence & Space, Manching	
+16	Eurocopter EC.665 Tiger UHT	Luftwaffe TsLw 3, Fassberg	
+18	Eurocopter EC.665 Tiger UHT	Airbus Helicopters, Donauwörth	
+50	NH Industries NH.90-TTH	Airbus Helicopters, Donauwörth	
+51	NH Industries NH.90-NFH Sea Lion	Airbus Helicopters, Donauwörth	
+56	NH Industries NH.90-NFH Sea Lion	Airbus Helicopters, Donauwörth	
+59	Panavia Tornado IDS(T)	Luftwaffe WTD 61, Ingolstadt	
+60	Panavia Tornado IDS $	Luftwaffe WTD 61, Ingolstadt	
+77	Panavia Tornado IDS $	Luftwaffe WTD 61, Ingolstadt	
+79	Panavia Tornado ECR	Luftwaffe WTD 61, Ingolstadt	
+90	NH Industries NH.90-TTH	Airbus Helicopters, Donauwörth	
+01	Northrop Grumman RQ-4E Euro Hawk	Luftwaffe WTD 61, Manching	
vil operated aircraft in military use			
HCDL	Eurocopter EC.135P-2+	Marineflieger MFG 5, Nordholz	
HDDL	Eurocopter EC.135P-2+	Marineflieger MFG 5, Nordholz	
HANA			
G-EXE	Dassault Falcon 900EASy	Ghana Air Force VIP Flight, Accra	
REECE			
liniki Polemiki Aeroporía/Hellenic Air Force (HAF)			
1	Lockheed Martin F-16C-52 Fighting Falcon	HAF 335 Mira/116 PM, Áraxos	
2	Lockheed Martin F-16C-52 Fighting Falcon	HAF 335 Mira/116 PM, Áraxos	
3	Lockheed Martin F-16C-52 Fighting Falcon	HAF 335 Mira/116 PM, Áraxos	
4	Lockheed Martin F-16C-52 Fighting Falcon	HAF 335 Mira/116 PM, Áraxos	
5	Lockheed Martin F-16C-52 Fighting Falcon $	HAF 335 Mira/116 PM, Áraxos	
6	Lockheed Martin F-16C-52 Fighting Falcon	HAF 335 Mira/116 PM, Áraxos	

Notes	Serial	Type (code/other identity)	Owner/operator, location or fate
	007	Lockheed Martin F-16C-52 Fighting Falcon	HAF 335 Mira/116 PM, Áraxos
	008	Lockheed Martin F-16C-52 Fighting Falcon	HAF 335 Mira/116 PM, Áraxos
	009	Lockheed Martin F-16C-52 Fighting Falcon	HAF 335 Mira/116 PM, Áraxos
	010	Lockheed Martin F-16C-52 Fighting Falcon	HAF 335 Mira/116 PM, Áraxos
	011	Lockheed Martin F-16C-52 Fighting Falcon	HAF 335 Mira/116 PM, Áraxos
	012	Lockheed Martin F-16C-52 Fighting Falcon	HAF 335 Mira/116 PM, Áraxos
	013	Lockheed Martin F-16C-52 Fighting Falcon	HAF 335 Mira/116 PM, Áraxos
	014	Lockheed Martin F-16C-52 Fighting Falcon	HAF 335 Mira/116 PM, Áraxos
	015	Lockheed Martin F-16C-52 Fighting Falcon	HAF 335 Mira/116 PM, Áraxos
	016	Lockheed Martin F-16C-52 Fighting Falcon	HAF 335 Mira/116 PM, Áraxos
	017	Lockheed Martin F-16C-52 Fighting Falcon	HAF 335 Mira/116 PM, Áraxos
	018	Lockheed Martin F-16C-52 Fighting Falcon	HAF 335 Mira/116 PM, Áraxos
	019	Lockheed Martin F-16C-52 Fighting Falcon	HAF 335 Mira/116 PM, Áraxos
	020	Lockheed Martin F-16C-52 Fighting Falcon	HAF 335 Mira/116 PM, Áraxos
	021	Lockheed Martin F-16D-52 Fighting Falcon	HAF 335 Mira/116 PM, Áraxos
	022	Lockheed Martin F-16D-52 Fighting Falcon	HAF 335 Mira/116 PM, Áraxos
	023	Lockheed Martin F-16D-52 Fighting Falcon	HAF 335 Mira/116 PM, Áraxos
	024	Lockheed Martin F-16D-52 Fighting Falcon	HAF 335 Mira/116 PM, Áraxos
	025	Lockheed Martin F-16D-52 Fighting Falcon	HAF 335 Mira/116 PM, Áraxos
	026	Lockheed Martin F-16D-52 Fighting Falcon	HAF 335 Mira/116 PM, Áraxos
	027	Lockheed Martin F-16D-52 Fighting Falcon	HAF 335 Mira/116 PM, Áraxos
	028	Lockheed Martin F-16D-52 Fighting Falcon	HAF 335 Mira/116 PM, Áraxos
	029	Lockheed Martin F-16D-52 Fighting Falcon	HAF 335 Mira/116 PM, Áraxos
	030	Lockheed Martin F-16D-52 Fighting Falcon	HAF 335 Mira/116 PM, Áraxos
	045	Lockheed Martin F-16C-50 Fighting Falcon	HAF 347 Mira/111 PM, Nea Ankhialos
	046	Lockheed Martin F-16C-50 Fighting Falcon	HAF 341 Mira/111 PM, Nea Ankhialos
	047	Lockheed Martin F-16C-50 Fighting Falcon	HAF 347 Mira/111 PM, Nea Ankhialos
	048	Lockheed Martin F-16C-50 Fighting Falcon	HAF 341 Mira/111 PM, Nea Ankhialos
	049	Lockheed Martin F-16C-50 Fighting Falcon	HAF 347 Mira/111 PM, Nea Ankhialos
	050	Lockheed Martin F-16C-50 Fighting Falcon	HAF 341 Mira/111 PM, Nea Ankhialos
	051	Lockheed Martin F-16C-50 Fighting Falcon	HAF 347 Mira/111 PM, Nea Ankhialos
	052	Lockheed Martin F-16C-50 Fighting Falcon	HAF 341 Mira/111 PM, Nea Ankhialos
	053	Lockheed Martin F-16C-50 Fighting Falcon	HAF 347 Mira/111 PM, Nea Ankhialos
	054	Lockheed Martin F-16C-50 Fighting Falcon	HAF 341 Mira/111 PM, Nea Ankhialos
	055	Lockheed Martin F-16C-50 Fighting Falcon	HAF 347 Mira/111 PM, Nea Ankhialos
	056	Lockheed Martin F-16C-50 Fighting Falcon	HAF 341 Mira/111 PM, Nea Ankhialos
	057	Lockheed Martin F-16C-50 Fighting Falcon	HAF 347 Mira/111 PM, Nea Ankhialos
	058	Lockheed Martin F-16C-50 Fighting Falcon	HAF 341 Mira/111 PM, Nea Ankhialos
	060	Lockheed Martin F-16C-50 Fighting Falcon	HAF 347 Mira/111 PM, Nea Ankhialos
	061	Lockheed Martin F-16C-50 Fighting Falcon	HAF 347 Mira/111 PM, Nea Ankhialos
	062	Lockheed Martin F-16C-50 Fighting Falcon $	HAF 341 Mira/111 PM, Nea Ankhialos
	063	Lockheed Martin F-16C-50 Fighting Falcon	HAF 347 Mira/111 PM, Nea Ankhialos
	064	Lockheed Martin F-16C-50 Fighting Falcon	HAF 341 Mira/111 PM, Nea Ankhialos
	065	Lockheed Martin F-16C-50 Fighting Falcon	HAF 347 Mira/111 PM, Nea Ankhialos
	066	Lockheed Martin F-16C-50 Fighting Falcon	HAF 341 Mira/111 PM, Nea Ankhialos
	067	Lockheed Martin F-16C-50 Fighting Falcon	HAF 347 Mira/111 PM, Nea Ankhialos
	068	Lockheed Martin F-16C-50 Fighting Falcon	HAF 341 Mira/111 PM, Nea Ankhialos
	069	Lockheed Martin F-16C-50 Fighting Falcon	HAF 347 Mira/111 PM, Nea Ankhialos
	070	Lockheed Martin F-16C-50 Fighting Falcon	HAF 341 Mira/111 PM, Nea Ankhialos
	071	Lockheed Martin F-16C-50 Fighting Falcon	HAF 347 Mira/111 PM, Nea Ankhialos
	072	Lockheed Martin F-16C-50 Fighting Falcon	HAF 341 Mira/111 PM, Nea Ankhialos
	073	Lockheed Martin F-16C-50 Fighting Falcon	HAF 347 Mira/111 PM, Nea Ankhialos
	074	Lockheed Martin F-16C-50 Fighting Falcon	HAF 341 Mira/111 PM, Nea Ankhialos
	075	Lockheed Martin F-16C-50 Fighting Falcon	HAF 347 Mira/111 PM, Nea Ankhialos
	076	Lockheed Martin F-16C-50 Fighting Falcon $	HAF 341 Mira/111 PM, Nea Ankhialos
	077	Lockheed Martin F-16D-50 Fighting Falcon	HAF 341 Mira/111 PM, Nea Ankhialos
	078	Lockheed Martin F-16D-50 Fighting Falcon	HAF 347 Mira/111 PM, Nea Ankhialos
	079	Lockheed Martin F-16D-50 Fighting Falcon	HAF 347 Mira/111 PM, Nea Ankhialos
	080	Lockheed Martin F-16D-50 Fighting Falcon	HAF 341 Mira/111 PM, Nea Ankhialos
	081	Lockheed Martin F-16D-50 Fighting Falcon	HAF 347 Mira/111 PM, Nea Ankhialos
	082	Lockheed Martin F-16D-50 Fighting Falcon	HAF 341 Mira/111 PM, Nea Ankhialos
	083	Lockheed Martin F-16D-50 Fighting Falcon	HAF 347 Mira/111 PM, Nea Ankhialos

Serial	Type (code/other identity)	Owner/operator, location or fate	Notes
10	Lockheed Martin F-16C-30 Fighting Falcon	HAF 330 Mira/111 PM, Nea Ankhialos	
11	Lockheed Martin F-16C-30 Fighting Falcon	HAF 330 Mira/111 PM, Nea Ankhialos	
12	Lockheed Martin F-16C-30 Fighting Falcon	HAF	
13	Lockheed Martin F-16C-30 Fighting Falcon	HAF 330 Mira/111 PM, Nea Ankhialos	
14	Lockheed Martin F-16C-30 Fighting Falcon	HAF 330 Mira/111 PM, Nea Ankhialos	
15	Lockheed Martin F-16C-30 Fighting Falcon	HAF 330 Mira/111 PM, Nea Ankhialos	
16	Lockheed Martin F-16C-30 Fighting Falcon	HAF 330 Mira/111 PM, Nea Ankhialos	
17	Lockheed Martin F-16C-30 Fighting Falcon	HAF 330 Mira/111 PM, Nea Ankhialos	
18	Lockheed Martin F-16C-30 Fighting Falcon	HAF	
19	Lockheed Martin F-16C-30 Fighting Falcon	HAF 330 Mira/111 PM, Nea Ankhialos	
20	Lockheed Martin F-16C-30 Fighting Falcon	HAF	
21	Lockheed Martin F-16C-30 Fighting Falcon	HAF 341 Mira/111 PM, Nea Ankhialos	
22	Lockheed Martin F-16C-30 Fighting Falcon	HAF 330 Mira/111 PM, Nea Ankhialos	
24	Lockheed Martin F-16C-30 Fighting Falcon	HAF	
25	Lockheed Martin F-16C-30 Fighting Falcon	HAF 330 Mira/111 PM, Nea Ankhialos	
26	Lockheed Martin F-16C-30 Fighting Falcon	HAF 330 Mira/111 PM, Nea Ankhialos	
27	Lockheed Martin F-16C-30 Fighting Falcon	HAF 330 Mira/111 PM, Nea Ankhialos	
28	Lockheed Martin F-16C-30 Fighting Falcon	HAF 330 Mira/111 PM, Nea Ankhialos	
29	Lockheed Martin F-16C-30 Fighting Falcon	HAF 330 Mira/111 PM, Nea Ankhialos	
30	Lockheed Martin F-16C-30 Fighting Falcon	HAF 330 Mira/111 PM, Nea Ankhialos	
32	Lockheed Martin F-16C-30 Fighting Falcon	HAF	
33	Lockheed Martin F-16C-30 Fighting Falcon	HAF 330 Mira/111 PM, Nea Ankhialos	
34	Lockheed Martin F-16C-30 Fighting Falcon	HAF 330 Mira/111 PM, Nea Ankhialos	
36	Lockheed Martin F-16C-30 Fighting Falcon	HAF 330 Mira/111 PM, Nea Ankhialos	
38	Lockheed Martin F-16C-30 Fighting Falcon	HAF	
39	Lockheed Martin F-16C-30 Fighting Falcon	HAF 330 Mira/111 PM, Nea Ankhialos	
40	Lockheed Martin F-16C-30 Fighting Falcon	HAF 330 Mira/111 PM, Nea Ankhialos	
41	Lockheed Martin F-16C-30 Fighting Falcon	HAF 330 Mira/111 PM, Nea Ankhialos	
43	Lockheed Martin F-16C-30 Fighting Falcon	HAF 330 Mira/111 PM, Nea Ankhialos	
44	Lockheed Martin F-16D-30 Fighting Falcon	HAF 330 Mira/111 PM, Nea Ankhialos	
45	Lockheed Martin F-16D-30 Fighting Falcon	HAF 330 Mira/111 PM, Nea Ankhialos	
46	Lockheed Martin F-16D-30 Fighting Falcon	HAF	
47	Lockheed Martin F-16D-30 Fighting Falcon	HAF 330 Mira/111 PM, Nea Ankhialos	
48	Lockheed Martin F-16D-30 Fighting Falcon	HAF 330 Mira/111 PM, Nea Ankhialos	
49	Lockheed Martin F-16D-30 Fighting Falcon	HAF 330 Mira/111 PM, Nea Ankhialos	
01	Dassault Mirage 2000-BG	HAF 332 MAPK/114 PM, Tanagra	
02	Dassault Mirage 2000-BG	HAF 332 MAPK/114 PM, Tanagra	
10	Dassault Mirage 2000-EG	HAF 332 MAPK/114 PM, Tanagra	
12	Dassault Mirage 2000-EG	HAF 332 MAPK/114 PM, Tanagra	
13	Dassault Mirage 2000-EG	HAF 332 MAPK/114 PM, Tanagra	
15	Dassault Mirage 2000-EG	HAF 332 MAPK/114 PM, Tanagra	
16	Dassault Mirage 2000-EG	HAF 332 MAPK/114 PM, Tanagra	
17	Dassault Mirage 2000-EG	HAF 332 MAPK/114 PM, Tanagra	
18	Dassault Mirage 2000-EG	HAF 332 MAPK/114 PM, Tanagra	
19	Dassault Mirage 2000-EG	HAF 332 MAPK/114 PM, Tanagra	
20	Dassault Mirage 2000-EG	HAF 332 MAPK/114 PM, Tanagra	
21	Dassault Mirage 2000-EG	HAF 332 MAPK/114 PM, Tanagra	
26	Dassault Mirage 2000-EG	HAF 332 MAPK/114 PM, Tanagra	
31	Dassault Mirage 2000-EG	HAF 332 MAPK/114 PM, Tanagra	
32	Dassault Mirage 2000-EG	HAF 332 MAPK/114 PM, Tanagra	
33	Dassault Mirage 2000-EG	HAF 332 MAPK/114 PM, Tanagra	
37	Dassault Mirage 2000-EG	HAF 332 MAPK/114 PM, Tanagra	
39	Dassault Mirage 2000-EG $	Crashed 29 May 2017, Sporades Islands	
41	Dassault Mirage 2000-EG	HAF 332 MAPK/114 PM, Tanagra	
42	Dassault Mirage 2000-EG	HAF 332 MAPK/114 PM, Tanagra	
874	Embraer ERJ.145H AEW&C	HAF 380 Mira/112 PM, Elefsis	
600	Lockheed Martin F-16C-52 Fighting Falcon	HAF 343 Mira/115 PM, Souda	
601	Lockheed Martin F-16C-52 Fighting Falcon	HAF 337 Mira/110 PM, Larissa	
602	Lockheed Martin F-16C-52 Fighting Falcon	HAF 337 Mira/110 PM, Larissa	
603	Lockheed Martin F-16C-52 Fighting Falcon	HAF 343 Mira/115 PM, Souda	
604	Lockheed Martin F-16C-52 Fighting Falcon	HAF 343 Mira/115 PM, Souda	
605	Dassault Mirage 2000-5BG	HAF 331 MAPK/114 PM, Tanagra	

Notes	Serial	Type (code/other identity)	Owner/operator, location or fate
	505	Lockheed Martin F-16C-52 Fighting Falcon $	HAF 343 Mira/115 PM, Souda
	506	Dassault Mirage 2000-5BG	HAF 331 MAPK/114 PM, Tanagra
	506	Lockheed Martin F-16C-52 Fighting Falcon	HAF 340 Mira/115 PM, Souda
	507	Dassault Mirage 2000-5BG	HAF 331 MAPK/114 PM, Tanagra
	507	Lockheed Martin F-16C-52 Fighting Falcon	HAF 337 Mira/110 PM, Larissa
	508	Dassault Mirage 2000-5BG	HAF 331 MAPK/114 PM, Tanagra
	508	Lockheed Martin F-16C-52 Fighting Falcon	HAF 337 Mira/110 PM, Larissa
	509	Dassault Mirage 2000-5BG	HAF 331 MAPK/114 PM, Tanagra
	509	Lockheed Martin F-16C-52 Fighting Falcon	HAF 343 Mira/115 PM, Souda
	510	Lockheed Martin F-16C-52 Fighting Falcon	HAF 343 Mira/115 PM, Souda
	511	Dassault Mirage 2000-5BG	HAF 331 MAPK/114 PM, Tanagra
	511	Lockheed Martin F-16C-52 Fighting Falcon	HAF 343 Mira/115 PM, Souda
	513	Lockheed Martin F-16C-52 Fighting Falcon	HAF 343 Mira/115 PM, Souda
	514	Dassault Mirage 2000-5BG	HAF 331 MAPK/114 PM, Tanagra
	515	Lockheed Martin F-16C-52 Fighting Falcon	HAF 343 Mira/115 PM, Souda
	517	Lockheed Martin F-16C-52 Fighting Falcon	HAF 337 Mira/110 PM, Larissa
	518	Lockheed Martin F-16C-52 Fighting Falcon	HAF 340 Mira/115 PM, Souda
	519	Lockheed Martin F-16C-52 Fighting Falcon	HAF 340 Mira/115 PM, Souda
	520	Lockheed Martin F-16C-52 Fighting Falcon	HAF 343 Mira/115 PM, Souda
	521	Lockheed Martin F-16C-52 Fighting Falcon	HAF 340 Mira/115 PM, Souda
	523	Lockheed Martin F-16C-52 Fighting Falcon $	HAF 340 Mira/115 PM, Souda
	524	Lockheed Martin F-16C-52 Fighting Falcon	HAF 337 Mira/110 PM, Larissa
	525	Lockheed Martin F-16C-52 Fighting Falcon	HAF 340 Mira/115 PM, Souda
	526	Lockheed Martin F-16C-52 Fighting Falcon	HAF 343 Mira/115 PM, Souda
	527	Dassault Mirage 2000-5BG	HAF 331 MAPK/114 PM, Tanagra
	527	Lockheed Martin F-16C-52 Fighting Falcon	HAF 343 Mira/115 PM, Souda
	528	Lockheed Martin F-16C-52 Fighting Falcon	HAF 337 Mira/110 PM, Larissa
	529	Lockheed Martin F-16C-52 Fighting Falcon	HAF 343 Mira/115 PM, Souda
	530	Dassault Mirage 2000-5BG	HAF 331 MAPK/114 PM, Tanagra
	530	Lockheed Martin F-16C-52 Fighting Falcon	HAF 337 Mira/110 PM, Larissa
	531	Lockheed Martin F-16C-52 Fighting Falcon $	HAF 337 Mira/110 PM, Larissa
	532	Lockheed Martin F-16C-52 Fighting Falcon	HAF 337 Mira/110 PM, Larissa
	533	Lockheed Martin F-16C-52 Fighting Falcon	HAF 340 Mira/115 PM, Souda
	534	Dassault Mirage 2000-5BG	HAF 331 MAPK/114 PM, Tanagra
	534	Lockheed Martin F-16C-52 Fighting Falcon	HAF 340 Mira/115 PM, Souda
	535	Dassault Mirage 2000-5BG	HAF 331 MAPK/114 PM, Tanagra
	535	Lockheed Martin F-16C-52 Fighting Falcon	HAF 340 Mira/115 PM, Souda
	536	Dassault Mirage 2000-5BG	HAF 331 MAPK/114 PM, Tanagra
	536	Lockheed Martin F-16C-52 Fighting Falcon	HAF 340 Mira/115 PM, Souda
	537	Lockheed Martin F-16C-52 Fighting Falcon	HAF 340 Mira/115 PM, Souda
	538	Lockheed Martin F-16C-52 Fighting Falcon	HAF 340 Mira/115 PM, Souda
	539	Lockheed Martin F-16C-52 Fighting Falcon	HAF 337 Mira/110 PM, Larissa
	540	Dassault Mirage 2000-5BG	HAF 331 MAPK/114 PM, Tanagra
	543	Dassault Mirage 2000-5BG	HAF 331 MAPK/114 PM, Tanagra
	545	Dassault Mirage 2000-5BG	HAF 331 MAPK/114 PM, Tanagra
	546	Dassault Mirage 2000-5BG	HAF 331 MAPK/114 PM, Tanagra
	547	Dassault Mirage 2000-5BG	HAF 331 MAPK/114 PM, Tanagra
	548	Dassault Mirage 2000-5BG	HAF 331 MAPK/114 PM, Tanagra
	549	Dassault Mirage 2000-5BG	HAF 331 MAPK/114 PM, Tanagra
	550	Dassault Mirage 2000-5BG	HAF 331 MAPK/114 PM, Tanagra
	551	Dassault Mirage 2000-5BG	HAF 331 MAPK/114 PM, Tanagra
	552	Dassault Mirage 2000-5BG	HAF 331 MAPK/114 PM, Tanagra
	553	Dassault Mirage 2000-5BG	HAF 331 MAPK/114 PM, Tanagra
	554	Dassault Mirage 2000-5BG	HAF 331 MAPK/114 PM, Tanagra
	555	Dassault Mirage 2000-5BG	HAF 331 MAPK/114 PM, Tanagra
	600	Lockheed Martin F-16D-52 Fighting Falcon	HAF 337 Mira/110 PM, Larissa
	601	Lockheed Martin F-16D-52 Fighting Falcon	HAF 340 Mira/115 PM, Souda
	602	Lockheed Martin F-16D-52 Fighting Falcon	HAF 340 Mira/115 PM, Souda
	603	Lockheed Martin F-16D-52 Fighting Falcon	HAF 340 Mira/115 PM, Souda
	605	Lockheed Martin F-16D-52 Fighting Falcon	HAF 340 Mira/115 PM, Souda
	606	Lockheed Martin F-16D-52 Fighting Falcon	HAF 337 Mira/110 PM, Larissa
	607	Lockheed Martin F-16D-52 Fighting Falcon	HAF 343 Mira/115 PM, Souda

Serial	Type (code/other identity)	Owner/operator, location or fate	Notes
608	Lockheed Martin F-16D-52 Fighting Falcon	HAF 340 Mira/115 PM, Souda	
609	Lockheed Martin F-16D-52 Fighting Falcon	HAF 337 Mira/110 PM, Larissa	
610	Lockheed Martin F-16D-52 Fighting Falcon	HAF 340 Mira/115 PM, Souda	
611	Lockheed Martin F-16D-52 Fighting Falcon	HAF 337 Mira/110 PM, Larissa	
612	Lockheed Martin F-16D-52 Fighting Falcon	HAF 337 Mira/110 PM, Larissa	
613	Lockheed Martin F-16D-52 Fighting Falcon	HAF 343 Mira/115 PM, Souda	
615	Lockheed Martin F-16D-52 Fighting Falcon	HAF 343 Mira/115 PM, Souda	
616	Lockheed Martin F-16D-52 Fighting Falcon	HAF 343 Mira/115 PM, Souda	
617	Lockheed Martin F-16D-52 Fighting Falcon	HAF 343 Mira/115 PM, Souda	
618	Lockheed Martin F-16D-52 Fighting Falcon	HAF 343 Mira/115 PM, Souda	
619	Lockheed Martin F-16D-52 Fighting Falcon $	HAF 337 Mira/110 PM, Larissa	
671	Embraer ERJ.145H AEW&C	HAF 380 Mira/112 PM, Elefsís	
678	Gulfstream Aerospace Gulfstream V	HAF 352 MMYP/112 PM, Elefsís	
729	Embraer ERJ.145H AEW&C	HAF 380 Mira/112 PM, Elefsís	
741	Lockheed C-130H Hercules (ECM)	HAF 356 MTM/112 PM, Elefsís	
742	Lockheed C-130H Hercules	HAF 356 MTM/112 PM, Elefsís	
743	Lockheed C-130H Hercules	HAF 356 MTM/112 PM, Elefsís	
744	Lockheed C-130H Hercules	HAF 356 MTM/112 PM, Elefsís	
745	Lockheed C-130H Hercules $	HAF 356 MTM/112 PM, Elefsís	
746	Lockheed C-130H Hercules	HAF 356 MTM/112 PM, Elefsís	
747	Lockheed C-130H Hercules (ECM)	HAF 356 MTM/112 PM, Elefsís	
749	Lockheed C-130H Hercules	HAF 356 MTM/112 PM, Elefsís	
751	Lockheed C-130H Hercules	HAF 356 MTM/112 PM, Elefsís	
752	Lockheed C-130H Hercules $	HAF 356 MTM/112 PM, Elefsís	
757	Embraer ERJ.145H AEW&C	HAF 380 Mira/112 PM, Elefsís	
4117	Aeritalia C-27J Spartan	HAF 354 Mira, Elefsís	
4118	Aeritalia C-27J Spartan	HAF 354 Mira, Elefsís	
4120	Aeritalia C-27J Spartan	HAF 354 Mira, Elefsís	
4121	Aeritalia C-27J Spartan	HAF 354 Mira, Elefsís	
4122	Aeritalia C-27J Spartan	HAF 354 Mira, Elefsís	
4123	Aeritalia C-27J Spartan	HAF 354 Mira, Elefsís	
4124	Aeritalia C-27J Spartan	HAF 354 Mira, Elefsís	
4125	Aeritalia C-27J Spartan	HAF 354 Mira, Elefsís	
135L-484	Embraer ERJ.135BJ Legacy	HAF 352 MMYP/112 PM, Elefsís	
145-209	Embraer ERJ.135LR	HAF 352 MMYP/112 PM, Elefsís	

HONDURAS

Fuerza Aérea Hondureña (FAH)/Honduran Air Force

FAH-001	Embraer ERJ.135BJ Legacy 600	FAH, Tegucigalpa	

HUNGARY

Magyar Légierö/Hungarian Air Force

01	Boeing C-17A Globemaster III (08-0001)	NATO SAC, Heavy Airlift Wing, Pápa	
02	Boeing C-17A Globemaster III (08-0002)	NATO SAC, Heavy Airlift Wing, Pápa	
03	Boeing C-17A Globemaster III (08-0003)	NATO SAC, Heavy Airlift Wing, Pápa	
30	SAAB 39C Gripen	Hungarian AF 59 Sz.D.REB, Kecskemét	
31	SAAB 39C Gripen	Hungarian AF 59 Sz.D.REB, Kecskemét	
32	SAAB 39C Gripen	Hungarian AF 59 Sz.D.REB, Kecskemét	
33	SAAB 39C Gripen	Hungarian AF 59 Sz.D.REB, Kecskemét	
34	SAAB 39C Gripen	Hungarian AF 59 Sz.D.REB, Kecskemét	
35	SAAB 39C Gripen	Hungarian AF 59 Sz.D.REB, Kecskemét	
36	SAAB 39C Gripen	Hungarian AF 59 Sz.D.REB, Kecskemét	
37	SAAB 39C Gripen	Hungarian AF 59 Sz.D.REB, Kecskemét	
38	SAAB 39C Gripen	Hungarian AF 59 Sz.D.REB, Kecskemét	
39	SAAB 39C Gripen	Hungarian AF 59 Sz.D.REB, Kecskemét	
40	SAAB 39C Gripen $	Hungarian AF 59 Sz.D.REB, Kecskemét	
41	SAAB 39C Gripen	Hungarian AF 59 Sz.D.REB, Kecskemét	
43	SAAB 39D Gripen	Hungarian AF 59 Sz.D.REB, Kecskemét	
44	SAAB 39D Gripen (39842)	Hungarian AF 59 Sz.D.REB, Kecskemét	
110	Antonov An-26	Hungarian AF 59 Sz.D.REB, Kecskemét	
405	Antonov An-26	Hungarian AF 59 Sz.D.REB, Kecskemét	
406	Antonov An-26	Hungarian AF 59 Sz.D.REB, Kecskemét	

Notes	Serial	Type (code/other identity)	Owner/operator, location or fate
	407	Antonov An-26	Hungarian AF 59 Sz.D.REB, Kecskemét
	603	Antonov An-26	Hungarian AF 59 Sz.D.REB, Kecskemét
	604	Airbus A.319CJ-112 (9H-AGM)	Hungarian AF 59 Sz.D.REB, Kecskemét
	605	Airbus A.319CJ-112 (9H-AGN)	Hungarian AF 59 Sz.D.REB, Kecskemét

INDIA
Bharatiya Vayu Sena/Indian Air Force (IAF)

	CB-8001	Boeing C-17A Globemaster III (11-0101)	IAF 81 Sqn, Hindon AB
	CB-8002	Boeing C-17A Globemaster III (11-0102)	IAF 81 Sqn, Hindon AB
	CB-8003	Boeing C-17A Globemaster III (11-0103)	IAF 81 Sqn, Hindon AB
	CB-8004	Boeing C-17A Globemaster III (11-0104)	IAF 81 Sqn, Hindon AB
	CB-8005	Boeing C-17A Globemaster III (11-0105)	IAF 81 Sqn, Hindon AB
	CB-8006	Boeing C-17A Globemaster III (11-0106)	IAF 81 Sqn, Hindon AB
	CB-8007	Boeing C-17A Globemaster III (11-0107)	IAF 81 Sqn, Hindon AB
	CB-8008	Boeing C-17A Globemaster III (11-0108)	IAF 81 Sqn, Hindon AB
	CB-8009	Boeing C-17A Globemaster III (11-0109)	IAF 81 Sqn, Hindon AB
	CB-8010	Boeing C-17A Globemaster III (11-0110)	IAF 81 Sqn, Hindon AB
	CB-8011	Boeing C-17A Globemaster III (14-0003)	IAF 81 Sqn, Hindon AB
	KC-3801	Lockheed C-130J-30 Hercules II	IAF 77 Sqn, Hindon AB
	KC-3802	Lockheed C-130J-30 Hercules II	IAF 77 Sqn, Hindon AB
	KC-3804	Lockheed C-130J-30 Hercules II	IAF 77 Sqn, Hindon AB
	KC-3805	Lockheed C-130J-30 Hercules II	IAF 77 Sqn, Hindon AB
	KC-3806	Lockheed C-130J-30 Hercules II	IAF 77 Sqn, Hindon AB
	KC-3807	Lockheed C-130J-30 Hercules II	IAF 87 Sqn, Arjan Singh AB
	KC-3808	Lockheed C-130J-30 Hercules II	IAF 87 Sqn, Arjan Singh AB
	KC-3809	Lockheed C-130J-30 Hercules II	IAF 87 Sqn, Arjan Singh AB
	KC-3810	Lockheed C-130J-30 Hercules II	IAF 87 Sqn, Arjan Singh AB
	KC-3811	Lockheed C-130J-30 Hercules II	IAF 87 Sqn, Arjan Singh AB
	KC-3812	Lockheed C-130J-30 Hercules II	IAF 87 Sqn, Arjan Singh AB
	KC-3813	Lockheed C-130J-30 Hercules II	IAF (on order)

INDONESIA
Indonesian Government

	A-001	Boeing 737-8U3	Government of Indonesia, Jakarta

ISRAEL
Heyl ha'Avir/Israeli Air Force

	102	Lockheed C-130H Karnaf	Israeli AF 131 Sqn, Nevatim
	140	Boeing KC-707 Re'em	Israeli AF 120 Sqn, Nevatim
	208	Lockheed C-130E Karnaf	Israeli AF 131 Sqn, Nevatim
	248	Boeing KC-707 Re'em	Israeli AF 120 Sqn, Nevatim
	250	Boeing KC-707 Re'em	Israeli AF 120 Sqn, Nevatim
	260	Boeing KC-707 Re'em	Israeli AF 120 Sqn, Nevatim
	264	Boeing KC-707 Re'em	Israeli AF 120 Sqn, Nevatim
	272	Boeing KC-707 Re'em	Israeli AF 120 Sqn, Nevatim
	275	Boeing KC-707 Re'em	Israeli AF 120 Sqn, Nevatim
	290	Boeing KC-707 Re'em	Israeli AF 120 Sqn, Nevatim
	295	Boeing KC-707 Re'em	Israeli AF 120 Sqn, Nevatim
	305	Lockheed C-130E Karnaf	Israeli AF 131 Sqn, Nevatim
	309	Lockheed C-130E Karnaf	Israeli AF 131 Sqn, Nevatim
	310	Lockheed C-130E Karnaf	Israeli AF 131 Sqn, Nevatim
	314	Lockheed C-130E Karnaf	Israeli AF 131 Sqn, Nevatim
	316	Lockheed C-130E Karnaf	Israeli AF 131 Sqn, Nevatim
	318	Lockheed C-130E Karnaf	Israeli AF 131 Sqn, Nevatim
	420	Lockheed KC-130H Karnaf	Israeli AF 131 Sqn, Nevatim
	427	Lockheed C-130H Karnaf	Israeli AF 131 Sqn, Nevatim
	428	Lockheed C-130H Karnaf	Israeli AF 131 Sqn, Nevatim
	435	Lockheed C-130H Karnaf	Israeli AF 131 Sqn, Nevatim
	436	Lockheed KC-130H Karnaf	Israeli AF 131 Sqn, Nevatim
	522	Lockheed KC-130H Karnaf	Israeli AF 131 Sqn, Nevatim
	545	Lockheed KC-130H Karnaf	Israeli AF 131 Sqn, Nevatim
	661	Lockheed C-130J-30 Shimshon	Israeli AF 103 Sqn, Nevatim

erial	Type (code/other identity)	Owner/operator, location or fate	Notes
62	Lockheed C-130J-30 Shimshon	Israeli AF 103 Sqn, Nevatim	
63	Lockheed C-130J-30 Shimshon	Israeli AF 103 Sqn, Nevatim	
64	Lockheed C-130J-30 Shimshon	(on order)	
65	Lockheed C-130J-30 Shimshon	Israeli AF 103 Sqn, Nevatim	
67	Lockheed C-130J-30 Shimshon	Israeli AF 103 Sqn, Nevatim	
68	Lockheed C-130J-30 Shimshon	Israeli AF 103 Sqn, Nevatim	

ITALY:

Aeronautica Militare Italiana (AMI), Aviazione dell'Esercito, Guardia di Finanza (GdiF) &
Marina Militare Italiana (MMI)

MMX602	Eurofighter F-2000A Typhoon [RS-01]	Alenia, stored Torino/Caselle	
MMX614	Eurofighter TF-2000A Typhoon	Alenia, Torino/Caselle	
CPX616	Aermacchi M-346 Master	Aermacchi, Venegono	
CPX619	Aermacchi M-345HET [1]	Aermacchi, Venegono	
CPX622	Aermacchi M-346A Master	Aermacchi, Venegono	
MM7004	Panavia A-200C Tornado (IDS (MLU)) [6-55]	AMI GEA 6° Stormo, Ghedi	
MM7006	Panavia A-200C Tornado (IDS (MLU)) [6-31] $	AMI GEA 6° Stormo, Ghedi	
MM7007	Panavia A-200A Tornado (IDS) [6-01] $	AMI GEA 6° Stormo, Ghedi	
MM7008	Panavia A-200C Tornado (IDS (MLU)) [50-53]	AMI GEA 6° Stormo, Ghedi	
MM7013	Panavia A-200C Tornado (IDS (MLU)) [6-75]	AMI GEA 6° Stormo, Ghedi	
MM7014	Panavia A-200C Tornado (IDS (MLU)) [6-13]	AMI GEA 6° Stormo, Ghedi	
MM7015	Panavia A-200C Tornado (IDS (MLU)) [6-32]	AMI GEA 6° Stormo, Ghedi	
MM7019	Panavia EA-200B Tornado (ECR) [50-05]	AMI GEA 6° Stormo, Ghedi	
MM7020	Panavia EA-200C Tornado (ECR (MLU)) [6-77]	AMI GEA 6° Stormo, Ghedi	
MM7021	Panavia EA-200B Tornado (ECR) [6-20]	AMI GEA 6° Stormo, Ghedi	
MM7023	Panavia A-200A Tornado (IDS) [6-63]	AMI GEA 6° Stormo, Ghedi	
MM7024	Panavia A-200C Tornado (IDS (MLU)) [6-50]	AMI GEA 6° Stormo, Ghedi	
MM7025	Panavia A-200A Tornado (IDS) [6-05]	AMI GEA 6° Stormo, Ghedi	
MM7026	Panavia A-200C Tornado (IDS (MLU)) [6-35]	AMI GEA 6° Stormo, Ghedi	
MM7029	Panavia A-200A Tornado (IDS) [6-22]	AMI GEA 6° Stormo, Ghedi	
CSX7030	Panavia EA-200C Tornado (ECR (MLU))	Leonardo, Turin	
MM7034	Panavia EA-200B Tornado (ECR)	AMI, stored Gioia del Colle	
MM7035	Panavia A-200C Tornado (IDS (MLU)) [6-27]	AMI GEA 6° Stormo, Ghedi	
MM7036	Panavia EA-200B Tornado (ECR) [6-06]	AMI GEA 6° Stormo, Ghedi	
MM7037	Panavia A-200A Tornado (IDS) [6-16]	AMI GEA 6° Stormo, Ghedi	
MM7038	Panavia A-200C Tornado (IDS (MLU)) [6-37]	AMI GEA 6° Stormo, Ghedi	
MM7039	Panavia EA-200C Tornado (ECR (MLU)) [6-33]	AMI GEA 6° Stormo, Ghedi	
MM7040	Panavia A-200A Tornado (IDS) [6-21]	AMI GEA 6° Stormo, Ghedi	
CSX7041	Panavia A-200C Tornado (IDS (MLU)) [RS-01] $	AMI RSV, Pratica di Mare	
MM7043	Panavia A-200A Tornado (IDS) [6-25]	AMI GEA 6° Stormo, Ghedi	
MM7044	Panavia A-200C Tornado (IDS (MLU))	Leonardo, Turin	
MM7047	Panavia EA-200C Tornado (ECR (MLU)) [6-61]	AMI GEA 6° Stormo, Ghedi	
MM7051	Panavia EA-200B Tornado (ECR) [6-72]	AMI GEA 6° Stormo, Ghedi	
MM7052	Panavia EA-200C Tornado (ECR (MLU)) [6-64]	AMI GEA 6° Stormo, Ghedi	
MM7053	Panavia EA-200B Tornado (ECR (MLU)) [6-101]	AMI GEA 6° Stormo, Ghedi	
MM7054	Panavia EA-200C Tornado (ECR (MLU)) [6-100] $	AMI GEA 6° Stormo, Ghedi	
MM7055	Panavia A-200A Tornado (ECR (MLU)) [6-65]	AMI GEA 6° Stormo, Ghedi	
MM7056	Panavia A-200A Tornado (IDS)	AMI GEA 6° Stormo, Ghedi	
MM7057	Panavia A-200A Tornado (IDS) [6-04]	AMI GEA 6° Stormo, Ghedi	
MM7058	Panavia A-200C Tornado (IDS (MLU)) [6-11]	AMI GEA 6° Stormo, Ghedi	
MM7059	Panavia A-200A Tornado (IDS) [6-66]	AMI GEA 6° Stormo, Ghedi	
MM7062	Panavia EA-200C Tornado (ECR (MLU)) [6-74]	AMI GEA 6° Stormo, Ghedi	
MM7063	Panavia A-200C Tornado (IDS (MLU)) [6-26]	AMI GEA 6° Stormo, Ghedi	
CSX7066	Panavia A-200A Tornado (ECR (MLU))	Leonardo, Turin	
MM7067	Panavia EA-200C Tornado (ECR (MLU))	AMI GEA 6° Stormo, Ghedi	
MM7068	Panavia EA-200B Tornado (ECR) [6-67]	AMI GEA 6° Stormo, Ghedi	
MM7070	Panavia EA-200C Tornado (ECR (MLU)) [6-71]	AMI GEA 6° Stormo, Ghedi	
MM7071	Panavia A-200C Tornado (IDS (MLU)) [6-12]	AMI GEA 6° Stormo, Ghedi	
MM7072	Panavia A-200C Tornado (IDS (MLU)) [6-30]	AMI GEA 6° Stormo, Ghedi	
MM7073	Panavia A-200B Tornado (ECR) [6-34]	AMI GEA 6° Stormo, Ghedi	
MM7075	Panavia A-200A Tornado (IDS) [6-07]	AMI GEA 6° Stormo, Ghedi	
CMX7079	Panavia EA-200B Tornado (ECR)	Alenia, Torino/Caselle	

Notes	Serial	Type (code/other identity)	Owner/operator, location or fate
	MM7081	Panavia EA-200C Tornado (ECR (MLU)) [6-57]	AMI GEA 6° Stormo, Ghedi
	MM7082	Panavia EA-200C Tornado (ECR (MLU)) [6-62]	AMI GEA 6° Stormo, Ghedi
	MM7083	Panavia A-200A Tornado (IDS)	AMI GEA 6° Stormo, Ghedi
	MM7084	Panavia EA-200C Tornado (ECR (MLU)) [6-03]	AMI GEA 6° Stormo, Ghedi
	CMX7085	Panavia A-200A Tornado (IDS) [36-50]	Alenia, Torino/Caselle
	MM7086	Panavia A-200A Tornado (IDS) [6-60]	AMI GEA 6° Stormo, Ghedi
	MM7088	Panavia A-200A Tornado (IDS) [6-10]	AMI GEA 6° Stormo, Ghedi
	MM7114	Aeritalia-EMB A-11B (AMX-ACOL) [51-27]	AMI GEA 51° Stormo, Istrana
	MM7126	Aeritalia-EMB A-11B (AMX-ACOL) [51-61]	AMI GEA 51° Stormo, Istrana
	MM7129	Aeritalia-EMB A-11B (AMX-ACOL) [32-15]	AMI, stored Amendola
	MM7148	Aeritalia-EMB A-11B (AMX-ACOL)	AMI, stored Amendola
	MM7149	Aeritalia-EMB A-11B (AMX-ACOL) [51-26]	AMI GEA 51° Stormo, Istrana
	MM7151	Aeritalia-EMB A-11B (AMX-ACOL) [51-51]	AMI GEA 51° Stormo, Istrana
	MM7159	Aeritalia-EMB A-11A (AMX) [51-10] $	AMI GEA 51° Stormo, Istrana
	MM7160	Aeritalia-EMB A-11B (AMX-ACOL)	AMI, stored Amendola
	MM7161	Aeritalia-EMB A-11B (AMX-ACOL) [51-37]	AMI GEA 51° Stormo, Istrana
	MM7162	Aeritalia-EMB A-11B (AMX-ACOL) [51-33]	AMI GEA 51° Stormo, Istrana
	MM7163	Aeritalia-EMB A-11B (AMX-ACOL) [51-72]	AMI GEA 51° Stormo, Istrana
	MM7164	Aeritalia-EMB A-11B (AMX-ACOL)	AMI
	MM7165	Aeritalia-EMB A-11B (AMX-ACOL) [32-16]	AMI, stored Amendola
	MM7166	Aeritalia-EMB A-11B (AMX-ACOL) [51-32]	AMI GEA 51° Stormo, Istrana
	MM7167	Aeritalia-EMB A-11B (AMX-ACOL) [51-56]	AMI GEA 51° Stormo, Istrana
	MM7168	Aeritalia-EMB A-11B (AMX-ACOL) [51-55]	AMI GEA 51° Stormo, Istrana
	MM7169	Aeritalia-EMB A-11B (AMX-ACOL) [51-66]	AMI GEA 51° Stormo, Istrana
	MM7170	Aeritalia-EMB A-11B (AMX-ACOL) [51-30]	AMI GEA 51° Stormo, Istrana
	MM7171	Aeritalia-EMB A-11B (AMX-ACOL) [51-52]	AMI GEA 51° Stormo, Istrana
	MM7172	Aeritalia-EMB A-11B (AMX-ACOL)	AMI GEA 51° Stormo, Istrana
	MM7173	Aeritalia-EMB A-11B (AMX-ACOL) [51-63]	AMI GEA 51° Stormo, Istrana
	MM7174	Aeritalia-EMB A-11B (AMX-ACOL) [51-60]	AMI GEA 51° Stormo, Istrana
	MM7175	Aeritalia-EMB A-11A (AMX) [51-45]	AMI GEA 51° Stormo, Istrana
	MM7176	Aeritalia-EMB A-11B (AMX-ACOL)	AMI GEA 51° Stormo, Istrana
	MM7177	Aeritalia-EMB A-11B (AMX-ACOL) [51-42]	AMI GEA 51° Stormo, Istrana
	MM7178	Aeritalia-EMB A-11B (AMX-ACOL) [51-43]	AMI GEA 51° Stormo, Istrana
	MM7179	Aeritalia-EMB A-11B (AMX-ACOL) [51-64]	AMI GEA 51° Stormo, Istrana
	MM7180	Aeritalia-EMB A-11B (AMX-ACOL) [51-53]	AMI GEA 51° Stormo, Istrana
	MM7182	Aeritalia-EMB A-11B (AMX-ACOL) [51-62]	AMI GEA 51° Stormo, Istrana
	MM7183	Aeritalia-EMB A-11B (AMX-ACOL) [51-41]	AMI GEA 51° Stormo, Istrana
	MM7184	Aeritalia-EMB A-11B (AMX-ACOL) [51-65]	AMI GEA 51° Stormo, Istrana
	MM7185	Aeritalia-EMB A-11B (AMX-ACOL) [51-36]	AMI GEA 51° Stormo, Istrana
	MM7186	Aeritalia-EMB A-11B (AMX-ACOL) [51-50]	AMI GEA 51° Stormo, Istrana
	MM7189	Aeritalia-EMB A-11B (AMX-ACOL) [51-71]	AMI GEA 51° Stormo, Istrana
	MM7190	Aeritalia-EMB A-11B (AMX-ACOL) [51-57]	AMI GEA 51° Stormo, Istrana
	MM7191	Aeritalia-EMB A-11B (AMX-ACOL) [51-34]	AMI GEA 51° Stormo, Istrana
	MM7192	Aeritalia-EMB A-11B (AMX-ACOL) [51-70]	AMI GEA 51° Stormo, Istrana
	MM7194	Aeritalia-EMB A-11B (AMX-ACOL) [51-67]	AMI GEA 51° Stormo, Istrana
	MM7196	Aeritalia-EMB A-11A (AMX) [51-35]	AMI GEA 51° Stormo, Istrana
	MM7197	Aeritalia-EMB A-11B (AMX-ACOL) [51-46]	AMI GEA 51° Stormo, Istrana
	MM7198	Aeritalia-EMB A-11B (AMX-ACOL) [51-44] $	AMI GEA 51° Stormo, Istrana
	MM7199	McDonnell Douglas AV-8B Harrier II+ [1-03]	MMI Gruppo Aerei Imbarcarti, Taranto/Grottaglie
	MM7200	McDonnell Douglas AV-8B Harrier II+ [1-04]	MMI Gruppo Aerei Imbarcarti, Taranto/Grottaglie
	MM7201	McDonnell Douglas AV-8B Harrier II+ [1-05]	MMI Gruppo Aerei Imbarcarti, Taranto/Grottaglie
	MM7212	McDonnell Douglas AV-8B Harrier II+ [1-06]	MMI Gruppo Aerei Imbarcarti, Taranto/Grottaglie
	MM7213	McDonnell Douglas AV-8B Harrier II+ [1-07]	MMI Gruppo Aerei Imbarcarti, Taranto/Grottaglie
	MM7214	McDonnell Douglas AV-8B Harrier II+ [1-08]	MMI Gruppo Aerei Imbarcarti, Taranto/Grottaglie
	MM7215	McDonnell Douglas AV-8B Harrier II+ [1-09]	MMI Gruppo Aerei Imbarcarti, Taranto/Grottaglie
	MM7217	McDonnell Douglas AV-8B Harrier II+ [1-11]	MMI Gruppo Aerei Imbarcarti, Taranto/Grottaglie
	MM7218	McDonnell Douglas AV-8B Harrier II+ [1-12]	MMI Gruppo Aerei Imbarcarti, Taranto/Grottaglie
	MM7219	McDonnell Douglas AV-8B Harrier II+ [1-13]	MMI Gruppo Aerei Imbarcarti, Taranto/Grottaglie
	MM7220	McDonnell Douglas AV-8B Harrier II+ [1-14]	MMI Gruppo Aerei Imbarcarti, Taranto/Grottaglie
	MM7222	McDonnell Douglas AV-8B Harrier II+ [1-16]	MMI Gruppo Aerei Imbarcarti, Taranto/Grottaglie
	MM7223	McDonnell Douglas AV-8B Harrier II+ [1-18]	MMI Gruppo Aerei Imbarcarti, Taranto/Grottaglie
	MM7224	McDonnell Douglas AV-8B Harrier II+ [1-19] $	MMI Gruppo Aerei Imbarcarti, Taranto/Grottaglie

Serial	Type (code/other identity)	Owner/operator, location or fate	Notes
MM7235	Eurofighter F-2000A Typhoon [4-13]	AMI 904° GEA, Grosseto	
MM7270	Eurofighter F-2000A Typhoon [4-1]	AMI 904° GEA, Grosseto	
MM7271	Eurofighter F-2000A Typhoon [4-15]	AMI 904° GEA, Grosseto	
MM7272	Eurofighter F-2000A Typhoon [4-18]	AMI 904° GEA, Grosseto	
MM7273	Eurofighter F-2000A Typhoon [4-10]	AMI 904° GEA, Grosseto	
MM7274	Eurofighter F-2000A Typhoon [4-4]	AMI 904° GEA, Grosseto	
MM7275	Eurofighter F-2000A Typhoon	AMI RSV, Pratica di Mare	
MM7276	Eurofighter F-2000A Typhoon [36-05]	AMI 936° GEA, Gioia del Colle	
MM7277	Eurofighter F-2000A Typhoon [4-40]	AMI 904° GEA, Grosseto	
MM7278	Eurofighter F-2000A Typhoon [RS-23]	Crashed 24 September 2017, Terracina	
MM7279	Eurofighter F-2000A Typhoon [4-20]	AMI 904° GEA, Grosseto	
MM7280	Eurofighter F-2000A Typhoon [36-30]	AMI 936° GEA, Gioia del Colle	
MM7281	Eurofighter F-2000A Typhoon [4-14]	AMI 904° GEA, Grosseto	
MM7282	Eurofighter F-2000A Typhoon [36-15]	AMI 936° GEA, Gioia del Colle	
MM7284	Eurofighter F-2000A Typhoon [4-12]	AMI 904° GEA, Grosseto	
MM7285	Eurofighter F-2000A Typhoon	AMI 904° GEA, Grosseto	
MM7286	Eurofighter F-2000A Typhoon [36-02]	AMI 936° GEA, Gioia del Colle	
MM7287	Eurofighter F-2000A Typhoon [4-3]	AMI 904° GEA, Grosseto	
MM7288	Eurofighter F-2000A Typhoon [36-42]	AMI 936° GEA, Gioia del Colle	
MM7289	Eurofighter F-2000A Typhoon [4-5]	AMI 904° GEA, Grosseto	
MM7290	Eurofighter F-2000A Typhoon [4-7]	AMI 904° GEA, Grosseto	
MM7291	Eurofighter F-2000A Typhoon [4-11]	AMI 904° GEA, Grosseto	
MM7292	Eurofighter F-2000A Typhoon [36-21]	AMI 936° GEA, Gioia del Colle	
MM7293	Eurofighter F-2000A Typhoon [37-18] $	AMI 18° Gruppo/37° Stormo, Trapani/Birgi	
MM7294	Eurofighter F-2000A Typhoon [4-52]	AMI 904° GEA, Grosseto	
MM7295	Eurofighter F-2000A Typhoon [4-51]	AMI 904° GEA, Grosseto	
MM7296	Eurofighter F-2000A Typhoon [36-22]	AMI 936° GEA, Gioia del Colle	
MM7297	Eurofighter F-2000A Typhoon [36-23]	AMI 936° GEA, Gioia del Colle	
MM7298	Eurofighter F-2000A Typhoon [36-24]	AMI 936° GEA, Gioia del Colle	
MM7299	Eurofighter F-2000A Typhoon [4-41]	AMI 904° GEA, Grosseto	
MM7300	Eurofighter F-2000A Typhoon [4-44]	AMI 904° GEA, Grosseto	
MM7301	Eurofighter F-2000A Typhoon [37-11]	AMI 18° Gruppo/37° Stormo, Trapani/Birgi	
MM7302	Eurofighter F-2000A Typhoon [36-25]	AMI 936° GEA, Gioia del Colle	
MM7303	Eurofighter F-2000A Typhoon [4-2]	AMI 904° GEA, Grosseto	
MM7304	Eurofighter F-2000A Typhoon [4-21]	AMI 904° GEA, Grosseto	
CSX7305	Eurofighter F-2000A Typhoon	AMI RSV, Pratica di Mare	
MM7306	Eurofighter F-2000A Typhoon [4-50]	AMI 904° GEA, Grosseto	
MM7307	Eurofighter F-2000A Typhoon [37-01]	AMI 18° Gruppo/37° Stormo, Trapani/Birgi	
MM7308	Eurofighter F-2000A Typhoon [36-31]	AMI 936° GEA, Gioia del Colle	
MM7309	Eurofighter F-2000A Typhoon [4-22]	AMI 904° GEA, Grosseto	
MM7310	Eurofighter F-2000A Typhoon [36-32]	AMI 936° GEA, Gioia del Colle	
MM7311	Eurofighter F-2000A Typhoon [37-10]	AMI 18° Gruppo/37° Stormo, Trapani/Birgi	
MM7312	Eurofighter F-2000A Typhoon [36-34]	AMI 936° GEA, Gioia del Colle	
MM7313	Eurofighter F-2000A Typhoon [36-35]	AMI 936° GEA, Gioia del Colle	
MM7314	Eurofighter F-2000A Typhoon [36-37]	AMI 936° GEA, Gioia del Colle	
MM7315	Eurofighter F-2000A Typhoon [36-46]	AMI 936° GEA, Gioia del Colle	
MM7316	Eurofighter F-2000A Typhoon [37-07]	AMI 18° Gruppo/37° Stormo, Trapani/Birgi	
MM7317	Eurofighter F-2000A Typhoon [4-43]	AMI 904° GEA, Grosseto	
MM7318	Eurofighter F-2000A Typhoon [36-12] $	AMI 936° GEA, Gioia del Colle	
MM7319	Eurofighter F-2000A Typhoon [36-45]	AMI 936° GEA, Gioia del Colle	
MM7320	Eurofighter F-2000A Typhoon [4-45]	AMI 904° GEA, Grosseto	
MM7321	Eurofighter F-2000A Typhoon [37-12]	AMI 18° Gruppo/37° Stormo, Trapani/Birgi	
MM7322	Eurofighter F-2000A Typhoon [36-40]	AMI 936° GEA, Gioia del Colle	
MM7323	Eurofighter F-2000A Typhoon [4-6]	AMI 904° GEA, Grosseto	
MM7324	Eurofighter F-2000A Typhoon [36-41]	AMI 936° GEA, Gioia del Colle	
MM7325	Eurofighter F-2000A Typhoon [36-44]	AMI 936° GEA, Gioia del Colle	
MM7326	Eurofighter F-2000A Typhoon [4-46] $	AMI 904° GEA, Grosseto	
MM7327	Eurofighter F-2000A Typhoon [4-47]	AMI 904° GEA, Grosseto	
MM7328	Eurofighter F-2000A Typhoon [37-14]	AMI 18° Gruppo/37° Stormo, Trapani/Birgi	
MM7329	Eurofighter F-2000A Typhoon [37-15]	AMI 18° Gruppo/37° Stormo, Trapani/Birgi	
MM7330	Eurofighter F-2000A Typhoon [37-21]	AMI 18° Gruppo/37° Stormo, Trapani/Birgi	
MM7331	Eurofighter F-2000A Typhoon [37-16]	AMI 18° Gruppo/37° Stormo, Trapani/Birgi	

Notes	Serial	Type (code/other identity)	Owner/operator, location or fate
	MM7332	Lockheed Martin F-35A Lightning II [32-01]	AMI 62nd FS/56th FW, Luke AFB, AZ, USA
	MM7333	Lockheed Martin F-35A Lightning II [32-02]	AMI 62nd FS/56th FW, Luke AFB, AZ, USA
	MM7334	Lockheed Martin F-35A Lightning II [32-03]	AMI 62nd FS/56th FW, Luke AFB, AZ, USA
	MM7335	Lockheed Martin F-35A Lightning II [32-04]	AMI 62nd FS/56th FW, Luke AFB, AZ, USA
	MM7336	Lockheed Martin F-35A Lightning II [32-05]	AMI 13° Gruppo/32° Stormo, Cameri
	MM7337	Lockheed Martin F-35A Lightning II [32-13]	AMI 13° Gruppo/32° Stormo, Cameri
	MM7338	Eurofighter F-2000A Typhoon [4-60]	AMI 904° GEA, Grosseto
	MM7339	Eurofighter F-2000A Typhoon [4-61]	AMI 904° GEA, Grosseto
	MM7340	Eurofighter F-2000A Typhoon [4-9] $	AMI 904° GEA, Grosseto
	MM7341	Eurofighter F-2000A Typhoon [36-10] $	AMI 936° GEA, Gioia del Colle
	MM7342	Eurofighter F-2000A Typhoon [36-51]	AMI 936° GEA, Gioia del Colle
	MM7343	Eurofighter F-2000A Typhoon [36-52]	AMI 936° GEA, Gioia del Colle
	CSX7344	Eurofighter F-2000A Typhoon	AMI
	MM7345	Eurofighter F-2000A Typhoon [37-45]	AMI 18° Gruppo/37° Stormo, Trapani/Birgi
	MM7346	Eurofighter F-2000A Typhoon [37-37]	AMI 18° Gruppo/37° Stormo, Trapani/Birgi
	MM7347	Eurofighter F-2000A Typhoon [36-53]	AMI 936° GEA, Gioia del Colle
	MM7348	Eurofighter F-2000A Typhoon [37-24]	AMI 18° Gruppo/37° Stormo, Trapani/Birgi
	MM7349	Eurofighter F-2000A Typhoon	AMI 936° GEA, Gioia del Colle
	CSX7350	Eurofighter F-2000A Typhoon	Leonardo, Turin
	CSX7351	Eurofighter F-2000A Typhoon	Leonardo, Turin
	MM7352	Eurofighter F-2000A Typhoon	AMI (on order)
	MM7353	Eurofighter F-2000A Typhoon	AMI (on order)
	MM7354	Eurofighter F-2000A Typhoon	AMI (on order)
	MM7355	Eurofighter F-2000A Typhoon	AMI (on order)
	MM7356	Eurofighter F-2000A Typhoon	AMI (on order)
	MM7357	Lockheed Martin F-35A Lightning II [32-07] $	AMI 13° Gruppo/32° Stormo, Cameri
	MM7358	Lockheed Martin F-35A Lightning II [32-08]	AMI 13° Gruppo/32° Stormo, Cameri
	MM7359	Lockheed Martin F-35A Lightning II [32-09]	AMI 13° Gruppo/32° Stormo, Cameri
	MM7451	Lockheed Martin F-35B Lightning II [4-01]	MMI FACO, Cameri
	MM40115	Breguet P-1150A (Br.1150) Atlantic [41-77] $	*Withdrawn from use*
	MM40118	Breguet P-1150A (Br.1150) Atlantic [41-03] $	*Withdrawn from use, November 2017*
	MM40122	Breguet P-1150A (Br.1150) Atlantic [41-07]	*Withdrawn from use, 2017*
	MM40125	Breguet P-1150A (Br.1150) Atlantic [41-12]	*Withdrawn from use, June 2017*
	MM54456	Aermacchi T-339A (MB339A) [61-10]	AMI, stored Lecce
	MM54457	Aermacchi T-339A (MB339A(MLU)) [61-11]	AMI 61° Stormo, Lecce
	MM54458	Aermacchi T-339A (MB339A(MLU)) [61-12]	AMI 61° Stormo, Lecce
	MM54465	Aermacchi T-339A (MB339A(MLU)) [61-21]	AMI 61° Stormo, Lecce
	MM54468	Aermacchi T-339A (MB339A(MLU)) [61-24]	AMI 61° Stormo, Lecce
	MM54473	Aermacchi AT-339A (MB339PAN)	AMI *Frecce Tricolori* (313° Gruppo), Rivolto
	MM54477	Aermacchi AT-339A (MB339PAN)	AMI *Frecce Tricolori* (313° Gruppo), Rivolto
	MM54479	Aermacchi AT-339A (MB339PAN)	AMI 632ª SC/32° Stormo, Amendola
	MM54480	Aermacchi AT-339A (MB339PAN)	AMI *Frecce Tricolori* (313° Gruppo), Rivolto
	MM54482	Aermacchi AT-339A (MB339PAN)	AMI *Frecce Tricolori* (313° Gruppo), Rivolto
	MM54487	Aermacchi AT-339A (MB339PAN)	AMI *Frecce Tricolori* (313° Gruppo), Rivolto
	MM54488	Aermacchi T-339A (MB339A(MLU)) [61-32]	AMI 61° Stormo, Lecce
	MM54492	Aermacchi T-339A (MB339A(MLU)) [61-36]	AMI 61° Stormo, Lecce
	MM54493	Aermacchi T-339A (MB339A(MLU)) [61-37]	AMI 61° Stormo, Lecce
	MM54496	Aermacchi T-339A (MB339A(MLU)) [61-42]	AMI 61° Stormo, Lecce
	MM54499	Aermacchi T-339A (MB339A(MLU)) [61-45]	AMI 61° Stormo, Lecce
	MM54500	Aermacchi AT-339A (MB339PAN)	AMI *Frecce Tricolori* (313° Gruppo), Rivolto
	MM54504	Aermacchi T-339A (MB339A(MLU)) [61-52]	AMI 61° Stormo, Lecce
	MM54505	Aermacchi AT-339A (MB339PAN) [5]	AMI *Frecce Tricolori* (313° Gruppo), Rivolto
	MM54507	Aermacchi T-339A (MB339A(MLU)) [61-55]	AMI 61° Stormo, Lecce
	MM54509	Aermacchi T-339A (MB339A(MLU)) [61-57]	AMI 61° Stormo, Lecce
	MM54510	Aermacchi AT-339A (MB339PAN) [12]	AMI *Frecce Tricolori* (313° Gruppo), Rivolto
	MM54511	Aermacchi T-339A (MB339A(MLU)) [61-61]	AMI 61° Stormo, Lecce
	MM54512	Aermacchi T-339A (MB339A(MLU)) [61-62]	AMI 61° Stormo, Lecce
	MM54514	Aermacchi AT-339A (MB339PAN) [0]	AMI *Frecce Tricolori* (313° Gruppo), Rivolto
	MM54515	Aermacchi T-339A (MB339A(MLU)) [61-65]	AMI 61° Stormo, Lecce
	MM54516	Aermacchi T-339A (MB339A(MLU)) [61-66]	AMI 61° Stormo, Lecce
	MM54517	Aermacchi AT-339A (MB339PAN) [2]	AMI *Frecce Tricolori* (313° Gruppo), Rivolto
	MM54518	Aermacchi AT-339A (MB339PAN) [5]	AMI *Frecce Tricolori* (313° Gruppo), Rivolto

rial	Type (code/other identity)	Owner/operator, location or fate	Notes
154533	Aermacchi T-339A (MB339A(MLU)) [61-72]	AMI 61° Stormo, Lecce	
154534	Aermacchi AT-339A (MB339PAN) [6]	AMI Frecce Tricolori (313° Gruppo), Rivolto	
154535	Aermacchi T-339A (MB339A(MLU)) [61-74]	AMI 61° Stormo, Lecce	
154538	Aermacchi AT-339A (MB339PAN) [1]	AMI Frecce Tricolori (313° Gruppo), Rivolto	
154539	Aermacchi AT-339A (MB339PAN) [11]	AMI Frecce Tricolori (313° Gruppo), Rivolto	
154542	Aermacchi AT-339A (MB339PAN)	Preserved at Rivolto, 2017	
154547	Aermacchi AT-339A (MB339PAN)	AMI Frecce Tricolori (313° Gruppo), Rivolto	
154548	Aermacchi T-339A (MB339A(MLU)) [61-106]	AMI 61° Stormo, Lecce	
154549	Aermacchi T-339A (MB339A(MLU)) [61-107]	AMI 61° Stormo, Lecce	
154551	Aermacchi AT-339A (MB339PAN) [1]	AMI Frecce Tricolori (313° Gruppo), Rivolto	
155002	Panavia TA-200A Tornado (IDS Trainer) [6-52] $	AMI GEA 6° Stormo, Ghedi	
155003	Panavia TA-200A Tornado (IDS Trainer)	AMI	
155004	Panavia TA-200A Tornado (IDS Trainer) [6-53]	AMI GEA 6° Stormo, Ghedi	
155006	Panavia TA-200C Tornado (IDS Trainer (MLU)) [6-15]	AMI GEA 6° Stormo, Ghedi	
155007	Panavia TA-200A Tornado (IDS Trainer) [6-51]	AMI GEA 6° Stormo, Ghedi	
155008	Panavia TA-200A Tornado (IDS Trainer) [6-45]	AMI GEA 6° Stormo, Ghedi	
155009	Panavia TA-200A Tornado (IDS Trainer) [6-44]	AMI GEA 6° Stormo, Ghedi	
155010	Panavia TA-200A Tornado (IDS Trainer) [6-42]	AMI GEA 6° Stormo, Ghedi	
155029	Aeritalia-EMB TA-11A (AMX-T) [32-50] $]	AMI GEA 51° Stormo, Istrana	
155030	Aeritalia-EMB TA-11A (AMX-T) [32-41]	AMI GEA 51° Stormo, Istrana	
155032	McDonnell Douglas TAV-8B Harrier II+ [1-01]	MMI Gruppo Aerei Imbarcati, Taranto/Grottaglie	
155033	McDonnell Douglas TAV-8B Harrier II+ [1-02]	MMI, stored Taranto/Grottaglie	
X55034	Aeritalia-EMB TA-11B (AMX-T-ACOL) [RS-18]	AMI RSV, Pratica di Mare	
155036	Aeritalia-EMB TA-11A (AMX-T) [32-51]	AMI GEA 51° Stormo, Istrana	
155037	Aeritalia-EMB TA-11A (AMX-T) [51-80]	AMI GEA 51° Stormo, Istrana	
155042	Aeritalia-EMB TA-11A (AMX-T) [32-56]	AMI GEA 51° Stormo, Istrana	
155043	Aeritalia-EMB TA-11A (AMX-T) [51-21]	AMI GEA 51° Stormo, Istrana	
155044	Aeritalia-EMB TA-11A (AMX-T) [51-82]	AMI GEA 51° Stormo, Istrana	
155046	Aeritalia-EMB TA-11A (AMX-T) [32-47]	AMI GEA 51° Stormo, Istrana	
155047	Aeritalia-EMB TA-11A (AMX-T) [32-53]	AMI GEA 51° Stormo, Istrana	
155049	Aeritalia-EMB TA-11A (AMX-T) [51-83]	AMI GEA 51° Stormo, Istrana	
155051	Aeritalia-EMB TA-11A (AMX-T) [51-84]	AMI GEA 51° Stormo, Istrana	
155052	Aermacchi AT-339A (MB339PAN) [4]	AMI Frecce Tricolori (313° Gruppo), Rivolto	
155053	Aermacchi AT-339A (MB339PAN) [7]	AMI Frecce Tricolori (313° Gruppo), Rivolto	
155054	Aermacchi AT-339A (MB339PAN) [9]	AMI Frecce Tricolori (313° Gruppo), Rivolto	
155055	Aermacchi AT-339A (MB339PAN)	AMI Frecce Tricolori (313° Gruppo), Rivolto	
155058	Aermacchi AT-339A (MB339PAN) [3]	AMI Frecce Tricolori (313° Gruppo), Rivolto	
155059	Aermacchi AT-339A (MB339PAN) [8]	AMI Frecce Tricolori (313° Gruppo), Rivolto	
155062	Aermacchi FT-339 (MB339CD) [61-126]	AMI 61° Stormo, Lecce	
155063	Aermacchi FT-339 (MB339CD) [61-127]	AMI 61° Stormo, Lecce	
155064	Aermacchi FT-339 (MB339CD) [61-130]	AMI 61° Stormo, Lecce	
155065	Aermacchi FT-339 (MB339CD) [61-131]	AMI 61° Stormo, Lecce	
155066	Aermacchi FT-339 (MB339CD) [61-132]	AMI 632ª SC/32° Stormo, Amendola	
155067	Aermacchi FT-339 (MB339CD) [61-133]	AMI 61° Stormo, Lecce	
155068	Aermacchi FT-339 (MB339CD) [RS-33]	AMI RSV, Pratica di Mare	
155069	Aermacchi FT-339 (MB339CD) [61-135]	AMI 61° Stormo, Lecce	
155070	Aermacchi FT-339 (MB339CD) [61-136]	AMI 61° Stormo, Lecce	
155072	Aermacchi FT-339 (MB339CD) [61-140]	AMI 61° Stormo, Lecce	
155073	Aermacchi FT-339 (MB339CD) [61-141]	AMI 61° Stormo, Lecce	
155074	Aermacchi FT-339 (MB339CD) [36-06]	AMI 12° Gruppo/36° Stormo, Gioia del Colle	
155075	Aermacchi FT-339 (MB339CD) [61-143]	AMI 61° Stormo, Lecce	
155076	Aermacchi FT-339 (MB339CD) [61-144]	AMI 61° Stormo, Lecce	
155077	Aermacchi FT-339 (MB339CD) [61-145]	AMI 61° Stormo, Lecce	
155078	Aermacchi FT-339 (MB339CD) [61-146]	AMI 61° Stormo, Lecce	
155079	Aermacchi FT-339 (MB339CD) [61-147]	AMI 61° Stormo, Lecce	
155080	Aermacchi FT-339 (MB339CD) [61-150]	AMI 61° Stormo, Lecce	
155081	Aermacchi FT-339 (MB339CD) [61-151]	AMI 61° Stormo, Lecce	
155082	Aermacchi FT-339 (MB339CD) [61-152]	AMI 61° Stormo, Lecce	
155084	Aermacchi FT-339 (MB339CD) [61-154]	AMI 61° Stormo, Lecce	
155085	Aermacchi FT-339 (MB339CD) [61-155]	AMI 61° Stormo, Lecce	
155086	Aermacchi FT-339 (MB339CD) [61-156]	AMI 61° Stormo, Lecce	
155087	Aermacchi FT-339 (MB339CD) [61-167]	AMI 61° Stormo, Lecce	

Notes	Serial	Type (code/other identity)	Owner/operator, location or fate
	MM55088	Aermacchi FT-339 (MB339CD) [61-160]	AMI 61° Stormo, Lecce
	MM55089	Aermacchi FT-339 (MB339CD) [32-161]	AMI 632ª SC/32° Stormo, Amendola
	MM55090	Aermacchi FT-339 (MB339CD) [61-162]	AMI 61° Stormo, Lecce
	MM55091	Aermacchi FT-339 (MB339CD) [RS-32]	AMI RSV, Pratica di Mare
	MM55092	Eurofighter TF-2000A Typhoon [36-62]	AMI 936° GEA, Gioia del Colle
	MM55093	Eurofighter TF-2000A Typhoon [4-31]	AMI 904° GEA, Grosseto
	MM55094	Eurofighter TF-2000A Typhoon [36-60]	AMI 904° GEA, Grosseto
	MM55095	Eurofighter TF-2000A Typhoon [4-23]	AMI 904° GEA, Grosseto
	MM55096	Eurofighter TF-2000A Typhoon [4-30]	AMI 904° GEA, Grosseto
	MM55097	Eurofighter TF-2000A Typhoon [4-27]	AMI 904° GEA, Grosseto
	MM55128	Eurofighter TF-2000A Typhoon [4-26]	AMI 904° GEA, Grosseto
	MM55129	Eurofighter TF-2000A Typhoon [4-32]	AMI 904° GEA, Grosseto
	MM55130	Eurofighter TF-2000A Typhoon [4-33]	AMI 904° GEA, Grosseto
	MM55131	Eurofighter TF-2000A Typhoon [37-30]	AMI 18° Gruppo/37° Stormo, Trapani/Birgi
	MM55132	Eurofighter TF-2000A Typhoon [4-35]	AMI RSV, Pratica di Mare
	MM55133	Eurofighter TF-2000A Typhoon [37-33]	AMI 18° Gruppo/37° Stormo, Trapani/Birgi
	MM55144	Aermacchi T-346A Master [61-02]	AMI 61° Stormo, Lecce
	MM55145	Aermacchi T-346A Master [61-03]	AMI 61° Stormo, Lecce
	MT55152	Aermacchi M-346FT [61-11]	Leonardo, Turin
	MM55153	Aermacchi T-346A Master [61-05]	AMI 61° Stormo, Lecce
	MM55154	Aermacchi T-346A Master [61-01]	AMI 61° Stormo, Lecce
	MM55155	Aermacchi T-346A Master [61-04]	AMI 61° Stormo, Lecce
	MM55168	Eurofighter TF-2000A Typhoon [4-37]	AMI 904° GEA, Grosseto
	CSX55169	Eurofighter TF-2000A Typhoon	Leonardo, Turin
	MM55213	Aermacchi T-346A Master [61-06]	AMI 61° Stormo, Lecce
	MM55214	Aermacchi T-346A Master [61-07]	AMI 61° Stormo, Lecce
	MM55215	Aermacchi T-346A Master [61-10]	AMI 61° Stormo, Lecce
	MM55216	Aermacchi T-346A Master [61-12]	AMI 61° Stormo, Lecce
	MT55217	Aermacchi T-346A Master	Leonardo, Turin
	MM55218	Aermacchi T-346A Master [61-14]	AMI 61° Stormo, Lecce
	MT55219	Aermacchi T-346A Master [61-20]	AMI 61° Stormo, Lecce
	MT55220	Aermacchi T-346A Master [61-16]	AMI 61° Stormo, Lecce
	MM55221	Aermacchi T-346A Master [61-15]	AMI 61° Stormo, Lecce
	MT55222	Aermacchi T-346A Master [61-21]	AMI 61° Stormo, Lecce
	MT55223	Aermacchi T-346A Master [61-22]	AMI 61° Stormo, Lecce
	MT55224	Aermacchi T-346A Master [61-23]	AMI 61° Stormo, Lecce
	MM62026	Dassault VC-50A (Falcon 50)	AMI 93° Gruppo/31° Stormo, Roma-Ciampino
	MM62029	Dassault VC-50A (Falcon 50)	AMI 93° Gruppo/31° Stormo, Roma-Ciampino
	CSX62127	Aeritalia MC-27J Pretorian	Alenia, Turin
	MM62156	Dornier UC-228 (Do.228-212) [E.I.101]	Esercito 28° Gruppo Squadroni, Viterbo
	MM62157	Dornier UC-228 (Do.228-212) [E.I.102]	Esercito 28° Gruppo Squadroni, Viterbo
	MM62158	Dornier UC-228 (Do.228-212) [E.I.103]	Esercito 28° Gruppo Squadroni, Viterbo
	MM62159	Piaggio VC-180A (P-180AM) Avanti	AMI RSV, Pratica di Mare
	MM62160	Piaggio RC-180A (P-180RM) Avanti	AMI 71° Gruppo/14° Stormo, Pratica di Mare
	MM62161	Piaggio VC-180A (P-180AM) Avanti	AMI RSV, Pratica di Mare
	MM62162	Piaggio RC-180A (P-180RM) Avanti	AMI 71° Gruppo/14° Stormo, Pratica di Mare
	MM62163	Piaggio RC-180A (P-180RM) Avanti	AMI 71° Gruppo/14° Stormo, Pratica di Mare
	MM62164	Piaggio RC-180A (P-180RM) Avanti	AMI 71° Gruppo/14° Stormo, Pratica di Mare
	MM62165	Aérospatiale P-42A (ATR.42-400MP) [GF-13]	GdiF GEA, Pratica di Mare
	MM62166	Aérospatiale P-42A (ATR.42-400MP) [GF-14]	GdiF GEA, Pratica di Mare
	MM62167	Piaggio VC-180A (P-180AM) Avanti	Esercito 28° Gruppo Sqd Det, Roma/Ciampino
	MM62168	Piaggio VC-180A (P-180AM) Avanti	Esercito 28° Gruppo Sqd Det, Roma/Ciampino
	MM62169	Piaggio VC-180A (P-180AM) Avanti	Esercito 28° Gruppo Sqd Det, Roma/Ciampino
	MM62170	Aérospatiale P-42A (ATR.42-400MP) [10-01]	Guardia Costiera 3° Nucleo, Pescara
	MM62171	Dassault VC-900A (Falcon 900EX) \$	AMI 93° Gruppo/31° Stormo, Roma-Ciampino
	MM62172	Dassault VC-900A (Falcon 900EX)	*To I-TARH, March 2017*
	MM62174	Airbus VC-319A (A.319CJ-115X)	AMI 306° Gruppo/31° Stormo, Roma-Ciampino
	MM62175	Lockheed C-130J Hercules II [46-40]	AMI, stored Pisa
	MM62177	Lockheed C-130J Hercules II [46-42]	AMI 46ª Brigata Aerea, Pisa
	MM62178	Lockheed C-130J Hercules II [46-43]	AMI 46ª Brigata Aerea, Pisa
	MM62179	Lockheed C-130J Hercules II [46-44]	AMI 46ª Brigata Aerea, Pisa
	MM62180	Lockheed C-130J Hercules II [46-45]	AMI 46ª Brigata Aerea, Pisa

rial	Type (code/other identity)	Owner/operator, location or fate	Notes
162181	Lockheed KC-130J Hercules II [46-46]	AMI 46ª Brigata Aerea, Pisa	
162182	Lockheed C-130J Hercules II [46-47]	AMI, stored Pisa	
162183	Lockheed KC-130J Hercules II [46-48]	AMI 46ª Brigata Aerea, Pisa	
162184	Lockheed KC-130J Hercules II [46-49]	AMI, stored Pisa	
162185	Lockheed C-130J Hercules II [46-50]	AMI 46ª Brigata Aerea, Pisa	
162186	Lockheed C-130J Hercules II [46-51]	AMI 46ª Brigata Aerea, Pisa	
162187	Lockheed C-130J-30 Hercules II [46-53]	AMI 46ª Brigata Aerea, Pisa	
162188	Lockheed C-130J-30 Hercules II [46-54]	AMI 46ª Brigata Aerea, Pisa	
162189	Lockheed C-130J-30 Hercules II [46-55]	AMI 46ª Brigata Aerea, Pisa	
162190	Lockheed C-130J-30 Hercules II [46-56]	AMI 46ª Brigata Aerea, Pisa	
162191	Lockheed C-130J-30 Hercules II [46-57]	AMI, stored Pisa	
162192	Lockheed C-130J-30 Hercules II [46-58]	AMI, stored Pisa	
162193	Lockheed C-130J-30 Hercules II [46-59]	AMI 46ª Brigata Aerea, Pisa	
162194	Lockheed C-130J-30 Hercules II [46-60]	AMI 46ª Brigata Aerea, Pisa	
162195	Lockheed C-130J-30 Hercules II [46-61]	AMI 46ª Brigata Aerea, Pisa	
162196	Lockheed C-130J-30 Hercules II [46-62]	AMI 46ª Brigata Aerea, Pisa	
162199	Piaggio VC-180A (P-180AM) Avanti	AMI CAE Multicrew, Pratica di Mare	
162200	Piaggio VC-180A (P-180AM) Avanti	AMI 71º Gruppo/14º Stormo, Pratica di Mare	
162201	Piaggio VC-180A (P-180AM) Avanti	AMI CAE Multicrew, Pratica di Mare	
162202	Piaggio VC-180A (P-180AM) Avanti	AMI 71º Gruppo/14º Stormo, Pratica di Mare	
162203	Piaggio VC-180A (P-180AM) Avanti	AMI CAE Multicrew, Pratica di Mare	
162204	Piaggio VC-180A (P-180AM) Avanti	AMI 71º Gruppo/14º Stormo, Pratica di Mare	
162205	Piaggio VC-180A (P-180AM) Avanti	AMI CAE Multicrew, Pratica di Mare	
162206	Piaggio VC-180A (P-180AM) Avanti	AMI CAE Multicrew, Pratica di Mare	
162207	Piaggio VC-180A (P-180AM) Avanti	AMI CAE Multicrew, Pratica di Mare	
162208	Aérospatiale P-42A (ATR.42-400MP) [10-02]	Guardia Costiera 2º Nucleo, Catania	
162209	Airbus VC-319A (A.319CJ-115X)	AMI 306º Gruppo/31º Stormo, Roma-Ciampino	
162210	Dassault VC-900A (Falcon 900EX)	AMI 93º Gruppo/31º Stormo, Roma-Ciampino	
162211	Piaggio VC-180A (P-180AM) Avanti [9-02]	MMI 9ª Brigata Aerea, Pratica di Mare	
162212	Piaggio VC-180A (P-180AM) Avanti [9-01]	MMI 9ª Brigata Aerea, Pratica di Mare	
162213	Piaggio VC-180A (P-180AM) Avanti [9-03]	MMI 9ª Brigata Aerea, Pratica di Mare	
162214	Aeritalia C-27J Spartan [46-84]	AMI, stored Pisa	
162215	Aeritalia C-27J Spartan [46-80]	AMI 98º Gruppo/46ª Brigata Aerea, Pisa	
162217	Aeritalia C-27J Spartan [46-81]	AMI, stored Pisa	
162218	Aeritalia C-27J Spartan [46-82]	AMI 98º Gruppo/46ª Brigata Aerea, Pisa	
X62219	Aeritalia C-27J Spartan [RS-50]	AMI RSV, Pratica di Mare	
162220	Aeritalia MC-27J Pretorian [46-83]	AMI 98º Gruppo/46ª Brigata Aerea, Pisa	
162221	Aeritalia EC-27J JEDI [46-85]	AMI 98º Gruppo/46ª Brigata Aerea, Pisa	
162222	Aeritalia C-27J Spartan [46-86]	AMI 98º Gruppo/46ª Brigata Aerea, Pisa	
162223	Aeritalia C-27J Spartan [46-88]	AMI 98º Gruppo/46ª Brigata Aerea, Pisa	
162224	Aeritalia EC-27J JEDI [46-89]	AMI 98º Gruppo/46ª Brigata Aerea, Pisa	
162225	Aeritalia C-27J Spartan [46-90]	AMI 98º Gruppo/46ª Brigata Aerea, Pisa	
162226	Boeing KC-767A (767-2EYER) [14-01] $	AMI 8º Gruppo/14º Stormo, Pratica di Mare	
162227	Boeing KC-767A (767-2EYER) [14-02]	AMI 8º Gruppo/14º Stormo, Pratica di Mare	
162228	Boeing KC-767A (767-2EYER) [14-03]	AMI 8º Gruppo/14º Stormo, Pratica di Mare	
162229	Boeing KC-767A (767-2EYER) [14-04]	AMI 8º Gruppo/14º Stormo, Pratica di Mare	
162230	Aérospatiale P-42A (ATR.42-400MP) [GF-15]	GdiF GEA, Pratica di Mare	
162243	Airbus VC-319A (A.319CJ-115X)	AMI 306º Gruppo/31º Stormo, Roma-Ciampino	
162244	Dassault VC-900B (Falcon 900EX EASy)	AMI 93º Gruppo/31º Stormo, Roma-Ciampino	
162245	Dassault VC-900B (Falcon 900EX EASy)	AMI 93º Gruppo/31º Stormo, Roma-Ciampino	
162248	Piaggio VC-180A (P-180AM) Avanti [GF-18]	GdiF GEA, Pratica di Mare	
162249	Piaggio VC-180B (P-180AM) Avanti II [GF-19]	GdiF GEA, Pratica di Mare	
162250	Aeritalia C-27J Spartan [46-91]	AMI 98º Gruppo/46ª Brigata Aerea, Pisa	
162251	Aérospatiale P-42A (ATR.42-400MP) [GF-16]	GdiF GEA, Pratica di Mare	
162270	Aérospatiale P-42B (ATR.42-500MP) [10-03]	Guardia Costiera 2º Nucleo, Catania	
X62279	Aérospatiale P-72A (ATR.72-600MP) [41-01]	Alenia	
X62280	Aérospatiale P-72A (ATR.72-600MP) [41-02]	Alenia	
162281	Aérospatiale P-72A (ATR.72-600MP) [41-04]	AMI 88º Gruppo/41º Stormo, Catania	
X62282	Aérospatiale P-72A (ATR.72-600MP) [41-05]	(on order)	
162286	Piaggio VC-180A (P-180AM) Avanti	AMI 93º Gruppo/31º Stormo, Roma-Ciampino	
162287	Piaggio VC-180A (P-180AM) Avanti	AMI 93º Gruppo/31º Stormo, Roma-Ciampino	
162293	Gulfstream Aerospace E-550A (N849GA) [14-11]	AMI 71º Gruppo/14º Stormo, Pratica di Mare	

Notes	Serial	Type (code/other identity)	Owner/operator, location or fate
	MM62298	Aérospatiale P-72A (ATR.72-600MP) [41-03]	AMI (on order)
	MM62300	Beechcraft King Air 350ER	AMI 71° Gruppo/14° Stormo, Pratica di Mare
	MM62303	Gulfstream Aerospace E-550A (N554GA) [14-12]	AMI 71° Gruppo/14° Stormo, Pratica di Mare
	MM81480	AgustaWestland SH-101A (EH-101 Mk110 ASW) [2-01]	MMI 3° Grupelicot, Catania
	MM81481	AgustaWestland SH-101A (EH-101 Mk110 ASW) [2-02]	MMI 3° Grupelicot, Catania
	MM81482	AgustaWestland SH-101A (EH-101 Mk110 ASW) [2-03]	MMI 3° Grupelicot, Catania
	MM81483	AgustaWestland SH-101A (EH-101 Mk110 ASW) [2-04]	MMI 3° Grupelicot, Catania
	MM81484	AgustaWestland SH-101A (EH-101 Mk110 ASW) [2-05]	MMI 3° Grupelicot, Catania
	MM81485	AgustaWestland SH-101A (EH-101 Mk110 ASW) [2-06]	MMI 3° Grupelicot, Catania
	MM81486	AgustaWestland SH-101A (EH-101 Mk110 ASW) [2-07]	MMI 3° Grupelicot, Catania
	MM81487	AgustaWestland SH-101A (EH-101 Mk110 ASW) [2-08]	MMI 3° Grupelicot, Catania
	MM81488	AgustaWestland EH-101A (EH-101 Mk112 AEW) [2-09]	MMI 1° Grupelicot, La Spezia/Luni
	MM81489	AgustaWestland EH-101A (EH-101 Mk112 AEW) [2-10]	MMI 3° Grupelicot, Catania
	MM81490	AgustaWestland EH-101A (EH-101 Mk112 AEW) [2-11]	MMI 3° Grupelicot, Catania
	MM81491	AgustaWestland EH-101A (EH-101 Mk112 AEW) [2-12]	MMI 1° Grupelicot, La Spezia/Luni
	MM81492	AgustaWestland UH-101A (EH-101 Mk410 UTY) [2-13]	MMI 1° Grupelicot, La Spezia/Luni
	MM81493	AgustaWestland UH-101A (EH-101 Mk410 UTY) [2-14]	MMI 1° Grupelicot, La Spezia/Luni
	MM81494	AgustaWestland UH-101A (EH-101 Mk410 UTY) [2-15]	MMI 1° Grupelicot, La Spezia/Luni
	MM81495	AgustaWestland UH-101A (EH-101 Mk410 UTY) [2-16]	MMI 1° Grupelicot, La Spezia/Luni
	MM81633	AgustaWestland UH-101A (EH-101 Mk410 UTY) [2-18]	MMI 1° Grupelicot, La Spezia/Luni
	MM81634	AgustaWestland UH-101A (EH-101 Mk410 UTY) [2-19]	MMI 1° Grupelicot, La Spezia/Luni
	MM81635	AgustaWestland UH-101A (EH-101 Mk410 UTY) [2-20]	MMI 1° Grupelicot, La Spezia/Luni
	MM81636	AgustaWestland UH-101A (EH-101 Mk410 UTY) [2-21]	MMI 1° Grupelicot, La Spezia/Luni
	MM81719	AgustaWestland SH-101A (EH-101 Mk110 ASW) [2-22]	MMI 1° Grupelicot, La Spezia/Luni
	MM81726	AgustaWestland SH-101A (EH-101 Mk110 ASW) [2-23]	MMI 1° Grupelicot, La Spezia/Luni
	MM81796	AgustaWestland HH-139A [15-40]	AMI 83° Gruppo SAR/15° Stormo, Cervia
	MM81797	AgustaWestland HH-139A [15-41]	AMI 84° Centro SAR/15° Stormo, Gioia del Coll
	MM81798	AgustaWestland HH-139A [15-42]	AMI 83° Gruppo SAR/15° Stormo, Cervia
	MM81799	AgustaWestland HH-139A [15-43]	AMI 81° Centro/15° Stormo, Cervia
	MM81800	AgustaWestland HH-139A [15-44]	AMI 82° Centro SAR/15° Stormo, Trapani/Birgi
	MM81801	AgustaWestland HH-139A [15-45]	AMI 85° Centro SAR/15° Stormo, Gioia del Col
	MM81802	AgustaWestland HH-139A [15-46]	AMI 85° Centro SAR/15° Stormo, Gioia del Coll
	MM81803	AgustaWestland HH-139A [15-47]	AMI 81° Centro/15° Stormo, Cervia
	MM81804	AgustaWestland HH-139A [15-48]	AMI 83° Gruppo SAR/15° Stormo, Cervia
	MM81805	AgustaWestland HH-139A [15-49]	AMI 82° Centro SAR/15° Stormo, Trapani/Birgi
	MM81806	AgustaWestland VH-139A	AMI 93° Gruppo/31° Stormo, Roma-Ciampino
	MM81807	AgustaWestland VH-139A	AMI 93° Gruppo/31° Stormo, Roma-Ciampino
	MM81811	AgustaWestland VH-139A	AMI 93° Gruppo/31° Stormo, Roma-Ciampino
	MM81812	AgustaWestland VH-139A	AMI 93° Gruppo/31° Stormo, Roma-Ciampino
	MM81822	AgustaWestland HH-139A [15-50]	AMI 85° Centro SAR/15° Stormo, Gioia del Co
	MM81823	AgustaWestland HH-139A [15-51]	AMI 81° Centro/15° Stormo, Cervia
	MM81824	AgustaWestland HH-139A [15-52]	AMI 85° Centro SAR/15° Stormo, Gioia del Col
	CSX81848	AgustaWestland AW149 [1-49]	Leonardo
	MM81864	AgustaWestland HH-101A Caesar [15-01]	AMI 85° Centro SAR/15° Stormo, Pratica di Ma
	MM81865	AgustaWestland HH-101A Caesar [15-02]	AMI 81° Centro/15° Stormo, Cervia
	MM81866	AgustaWestland HH-101A Caesar [15-03]	AMI 85° Centro SAR/15° Stormo, Pratica di Ma
	MM81867	AgustaWestland HH-101A Caesar [15-04]	AMI 81° Centro/15° Stormo, Cervia
	MM81868	AgustaWestland HH-101A Caesar [15-05]	AMI 81° Centro/15° Stormo, Cervia
	MM81869	AgustaWestland HH-101A Caesar [15-06]	AMI 81° Centro/15° Stormo, Cervia
	CSX81890	AgustaWestland AW149	Leonardo
	MM81...	AgustaWestland HH-101A Caesar	AMI (on order)
	MM81...	AgustaWestland HH-101A Caesar	AMI (on order)
	MM81...	AgustaWestland HH-101A Caesar	AMI (on order)
	MM81...	AgustaWestland HH-101A Caesar	AMI (on order)
	MM81...	AgustaWestland HH-101A Caesar	AMI (on order)
	MM81...	AgustaWestland HH-101A Caesar	AMI (on order)

Italian Government

	I-CAEX	Dassault Falcon 900	Italian Government/Soc. CAI, Roma/Ciampino
	I-DIES	Dassault Falcon 900	Italian Government/Soc. CAI, Roma/Ciampino
	I-TALY	Airbus A.340-541 (A6-EHA)	AMI 306° Gruppo/31° Stormo, Roma-Ciampino
	I-TARH	Dassault Falcon 900EX (MM62172)	Italian Government/Soc. CAI, Roma/Ciampino

Serial	Type (code/other identity)	Owner/operator, location or fate	Notes
IVORY COAST			
TU-VAD	Grumman G.1159C Gulfstream IV	Ivory Coast Government, Abidjan	
TU-VAE	Gulfstream Aerospace G.550	Ivory Coast Government, Abidjan	
TU-VAF	Grumman G.1159A Gulfstream III	Ivory Coast Government, Abidjan	
TU-VAS	Airbus A.319CJ-133	Ivory Coast Government, Abidjan	
JAPAN			
Japan Air Self Defence Force (JASDF)			
87-3604	Boeing KC-767J	JASDF 404th Hikotai, Nagoya	
10-1101	Boeing 747-47C	JASDF 701st Flight Sqn, Chitose	
20-1102	Boeing 747-47C	JASDF 701st Flight Sqn, Chitose	
07-3601	Boeing KC-767J	JASDF 404th Hikotai, Nagoya	
07-3602	Boeing KC-767J	JASDF 404th Hikotai, Nagoya	
87-3603	Boeing KC-767J	JASDF 404th Hikotai, Nagoya	
....	Boeing 777-3SB(ER) (N509BJ)	JASDF, on order	
...	Boeing 777-3SB(ER) (N511BJ)	JASDF, on order	
JORDAN			
Al Quwwat al Jawwiya al Malakiya al Urduniya/Jordanian Air Force			
344	Lockheed C-130H Hercules	Jordanian AF 3 Sqn, Amman/Marka	
345	Lockheed C-130H Hercules $	Jordanian AF 3 Sqn, Amman/Marka	
346	Lockheed C-130H Hercules	Jordanian AF 3 Sqn, Amman/Marka	
347	Lockheed C-130H Hercules	Jordanian AF 3 Sqn, Amman/Marka	
350	Ilyushin Il-76MF (JY-JIC)	Jordanian AF 3 Sqn, Amman/Marka	
351	Ilyushin Il-76MF (JY-JID)	Jordanian AF 3 Sqn, Amman/Marka	
2-RFA	Extra EA-300LP	Jordanian AF *Royal Jordanian Falcons*, Amman	
2-RFB	Extra EA-300LP	Jordanian AF *Royal Jordanian Falcons*, Amman	
2-RFC	Extra EA-300LP	Jordanian AF *Royal Jordanian Falcons*, Amman	
2-RFD	Extra EA-300LP	Jordanian AF *Royal Jordanian Falcons*, Amman	
2-RFE	Extra EA-300LP	Jordanian AF *Royal Jordanian Falcons*, Amman	
2-R..	Extra EA-330LX	Jordanian AF (on order)	
2-R..	Extra EA-330LX	Jordanian AF (on order)	
2-R..	Extra EA-330LX	Jordanian AF (on order)	
2-R..	Extra EA-330LX	Jordanian AF (on order)	
2-R..	Extra EA-330LX	Jordanian AF (on order)	
Jordanian Government			
JY-BDD	Airbus A.318-112	Jordanian Government, Amman	
JY-BMZ	Gulfstream Aerospace G.650	Jordanian Government, Amman	
JY-BNZ	Gulfstream Aerospace G.650ER	Jordanian Government, Amman	
KAZAKHSTAN			
r	CASA C-295M	Kazakstan ADF 18th Air Transport Sqn, Almaty	
r	CASA C-295M	Kazakstan ADF 18th Air Transport Sqn, Almaty	
r	CASA C-295M	Kazakstan ADF 18th Air Transport Sqn, Almaty	
r	CASA C-295M	Kazakstan ADF 18th Air Transport Sqn, Almaty	
r	CASA C-295M	Kazakstan ADF 18th Air Transport Sqn, Almaty	
r	CASA C-295M	Kazakstan ADF (on order)	
r	CASA C-295M	Kazakstan ADF (on order)	
r	Antonov An-72	Kazakstan ADF 18th Air Transport Sqn, Almaty	
r	Antonov An-72	Kazakstan ADF 18th Air Transport Sqn, Almaty	
UP-A3001	Airbus A.330-223	Government of Kazakhstan, Almaty	
UP-B5701	Boeing 757-2M6	Government of Kazakhstan, Almaty	
UP-T5401	Tupolev Tu-154M	Government of Kazakhstan, Almaty	
KENYA			
AF 308	Fokker 70ER	Kenyan Government, Nairobi	
KUWAIT			
Al Quwwat al Jawwiya al Kuwaitiya/Kuwaiti Air Force			
AF 323	Lockheed L100-30 Hercules	Kuwaiti AF 41 Sqn, Kuwait International	
AF 324	Lockheed L100-30 Hercules	Kuwaiti AF 41 Sqn, Kuwait International	
AF 325	Lockheed L100-30 Hercules	Kuwaiti AF 41 Sqn, Kuwait International	

Notes	Serial	Type (code/other identity)	Owner/operator, location or fate
	KAF 326	Lockheed KC-130J Hercules II	Kuwaiti AF 41 Sqn, Kuwait International
	KAF 327	Lockheed KC-130J Hercules II	Kuwaiti AF 41 Sqn, Kuwait International
	KAF 328	Lockheed KC-130J Hercules II	Kuwaiti AF 41 Sqn, Kuwait International
	KAF 342	Boeing C-17A Globemaster III (13-0001)	Kuwaiti AF 41 Sqn, Kuwait International
	KAF 343	Boeing C-17A Globemaster III (13-0002)	Kuwaiti AF 41 Sqn, Kuwait International
	Kuwaiti Government		
	9K-AKD	Airbus A.320-212	Kuwaiti Government, Safat
	9K-GAA	Boeing 747-8JK	Kuwaiti Government, Safat
	9K-GBA	Airbus A.340-542	Kuwaiti Government, Safat
	9K-GBB	Airbus A.340-542	Kuwaiti Government, Safat
	9K-GCC	Boeing 737-9BQER	Kuwaiti Government, Safat
	9K-GEA	Airbus A.319CJ-115X	Kuwaiti Government, Safat
	9K-GFA	Gulfstream Aerospace G.550	Kuwaiti Government, Safat
	9K-GGA	Gulfstream Aerospace G.650	Kuwaiti Government, Safat
	9K-GGB	Gulfstream Aerospace G.650	Kuwaiti Government, Safat
	9K-GGC	Gulfstream Aerospace G.650	Kuwaiti Government, Safat
	9K-GGD	Gulfstream Aerospace G.650	Kuwaiti Government, Safat
	KYRGYZSTAN		
	EX-00001	Tupolev Tu-154M	Government of Kyrgyzstan, Bishkek
	LITHUANIA		
	Karines Oro Pajegos (KOP)		
	01 bl	LET 410UVP Turbolet	KOP Transporto Esk, Siauliai/Zokniai
	02 bl	Mil Mi-8T	*Withdrawn from use*
	03 bl	Antonov An-26RV	*Withdrawn from use*
	04 bl	Antonov An-26RV	*Withdrawn from use*
	05 bl	Antonov An-26RV	*Withdrawn from use*
	06 bl	Aeritalia C-27J Spartan	KOP Transporto Esk, Siauliai/Zokniai
	07 bl	Aeritalia C-27J Spartan	KOP Transporto Esk, Siauliai/Zokniai
	08 bl	Aeritalia C-27J Spartan	KOP Transporto Esk, Siauliai/Zokniai
	09 bl	Mil Mi-8T	*Re-registered as 26 bl*
	10 w	Mil Mi-8T	*Re-registered as 25 bl*
	21 w	Mil Mi-8MTV-1	KOP Sraigtasparniu Esk, Panevezys/Pajuostis
	22 bl	Mil Mi-8T	KOP Sraigtasparniu Esk, Panevezys/Pajuostis
	25 bl	Mil Mi-8T (10 bl)	KOP Sraigtasparniu Esk, Panevezys/Pajuostis
	26 bl	Mil Mi-8T (09 bl)	KOP Sraigtasparniu Esk, Panevezys/Pajuostis
	28 bl	Mil Mi-8T	KOP Sraigtasparniu Esk, Panevezys/Pajuostis
	LUXEMBOURG		
	NATO		
	LX-N90442	Boeing E-3A Sentry	NATO NAEW&CF, Geilenkirchen, Germany
	LX-N90443	Boeing E-3A Sentry $	NATO NAEW&CF, Geilenkirchen, Germany $
	LX-N90444	Boeing E-3A Sentry	NATO NAEW&CF, Geilenkirchen, Germany
	LX-N90445	Boeing E-3A Sentry	NATO NAEW&CF, Geilenkirchen, Germany
	LX-N90446	Boeing E-3A Sentry	NATO NAEW&CF, Geilenkirchen, Germany
	LX-N90447	Boeing E-3A Sentry	NATO NAEW&CF, Geilenkirchen, Germany
	LX-N90448	Boeing E-3A Sentry	NATO NAEW&CF, Geilenkirchen, Germany
	LX-N90450	Boeing E-3A Sentry $	NATO NAEW&CF, Geilenkirchen, Germany
	LX-N90451	Boeing E-3A Sentry	NATO NAEW&CF, Geilenkirchen, Germany
	LX-N90452	Boeing E-3A Sentry	NATO NAEW&CF, Geilenkirchen, Germany
	LX-N90453	Boeing E-3A Sentry	Boeing, Renton, USA (on upgrade)
	LX-N90454	Boeing E-3A Sentry	Airbus, Manching, Germany (on upgrade)
	LX-N90455	Boeing E-3A Sentry	*To AMARG, December 2017*
	LX-N90456	Boeing E-3A Sentry	NATO NAEW&CF, Geilenkirchen, Germany
	LX-N90458	Boeing E-3A Sentry $	NATO NAEW&CF, Geilenkirchen, Germany
	LX-N90459	Boeing E-3A Sentry	NATO NAEW&CF, Geilenkirchen, Germany
	OO-TFA	Boeing 757-28A	NATO, Geilenkirchen, Germany
	MACEDONIA		
	Z3-MKD	Bombardier Lear 60	Macedonian Government, Skopje

rial	Type (code/other identity)	Owner/operator, location or fate	Notes

ALI

| -PRM | Boeing 737-7DW | Government of Mali, Bamako | |

ALAYSIA

ntera Udara Diraja Malaysia/Royal Malaysian Air Force (RMAF)

0-01	Lockheed C-130T Hercules	RMAF 20 Sqn, Subang	
0-02	Lockheed C-130H Hercules	RMAF 20 Sqn, Subang	
0-03	Lockheed C-130H Hercules	RMAF 14 Sqn, Labuan	
0-04	Lockheed C-130H-30 Hercules	RMAF 20 Sqn, Subang	
0-05	Lockheed C-130H-30 Hercules	RMAF 14 Sqn, Labuan	
0-06	Lockheed C-130H-30 Hercules	RMAF 14 Sqn, Labuan	
0-07	Lockheed C-130T Hercules	RMAF 20 Sqn, Subang	
0-08	Lockheed C-130H(MP) Hercules	RMAF 20 Sqn, Subang	
0-09	Lockheed C-130H(MP) Hercules	RMAF 20 Sqn, Subang	
0-10	Lockheed C-130H-30 Hercules	RMAF 20 Sqn, Subang	
0-11	Lockheed C-130H-30 Hercules	RMAF 20 Sqn, Subang	
0-12	Lockheed C-130H-30 Hercules	RMAF 20 Sqn, Subang	
0-14	Lockheed C-130H-30 Hercules	RMAF 14 Sqn, Labuan	
0-15	Lockheed C-130H-30 Hercules	RMAF 20 Sqn, Subang	
0-16	Lockheed C-130H-30 Hercules	RMAF 20 Sqn, Subang	
7-01	Dassault Falcon 900	RMAF 2 Sqn, Simpang	
8-02	Bombardier BD.700-1A10 Global Express	RMAF 2 Sqn, Simpang	
63-01	Boeing 737-7H6	RMAF 2 Sqn, Simpang	
4-01	Airbus Military A.400M	RMAF 22 Sqn, Subang	
54-02	Airbus Military A.400M	RMAF 22 Sqn, Subang	
54-03	Airbus Military A.400M	RMAF 22 Sqn, Subang	
54-04	Airbus Military A.400M	RMAF 22 Sqn, Subang	
I-NAA	Airbus A.319CJ-115X	RMAF, Subang	
I-NAB	Airbus A.320CJ-214 (M37-07)	RMAF, Subang	

ALTA

| I-AFK | Bombardier Learjet 60 | Government of Malta, Luqa | |

EXICO

erza Aérea Mexicana (FAM)/Mexican Air Force

| -01 | Boeing 787-8 (XC-MEX) | FAM 8° Grupo Aéreo, Mexico City | |
| 7-02 | Boeing 757-225 (XC-UJM) | FAM 8° Grupo Aéreo, Mexico City | |

mada de Mexico/Mexican Navy

IX-1201	Gulfstream Aerospace G.550	Armada PRIESCAERTRANS, Mexico City	
IX-1207	Gulfstream Aerospace G.550	*To ANX-1201, 2017*	
C-LMF	Gulfstream Aerospace G.450	Armada PRIESCAERTRANS, Mexico City	

OROCCO

Quwwat al Jawwiya al Malakiya Marakishiya/Force Aérienne Royaume Marocaine/Royal Moroccan Air Force MAF) & Moroccan Government

I-ABP	CAP-232 (28) [6]	RMAF *Marche Verte*, Marrakech/Ménara	
I-ABQ	CAP-232 (29) [5]	RMAF *Marche Verte*, Marrakech/Ménara	
I-ABR	CAP-232 (31) [2]	RMAF *Marche Verte*, Marrakech/Ménara	
I-ABS	CAP-232 (36)	RMAF *Marche Verte*, Marrakech/Ménara	
I-ABT	CAP-232 (37) [1]	RMAF *Marche Verte*, Marrakech/Ménara	
N-ABU	CAP-232 (41) [3]	RMAF *Marche Verte*, Marrakech/Ménara	
I-ABV	CAP-232 (42) [4]	RMAF *Marche Verte*, Marrakech/Ménara	
I-ABW	CAP-232 (43) [8]	RMAF *Marche Verte*, Marrakech/Ménara	
N-ABX	CAP-232 (44) [7]	RMAF *Marche Verte*, Marrakech/Ménara	
I-AMA	Airtech CN.235M-100 (023)	RMAF Escadrille de Transport 3, Kenitra	
I-AMB	Airtech CN.235M-100 (024)	RMAF Escadrille de Transport 3, Kenitra	
N-AMC	Airtech CN.235M-100 (025)	RMAF Escadrille de Transport 3, Kenitra	
N-AMD	Airtech CN.235M-100 (026)	RMAF Escadrille de Transport 3, Kenitra	
I-AME	Airtech CN.235M-100 (027)	RMAF Escadrille de Transport 3, Kenitra	
N-AMF	Airtech CN.235M-100 (028)	RMAF Escadrille de Transport 3, Kenitra	
IA-MG	Airtech CN.235M-100 (031)	RMAF Escadrille de Transport 3, Kenitra	
I-AMJ	Cessna 560XLS Citation Excel	Government of Morocco, Rabat	

Notes	Serial	Type (code/other identity)	Owner/operator, location or fate
	CN-AMK	Cessna 560XLS Citation Excel	Government of Morocco, Rabat
	CN-AMN	Aeritalia C-27J Spartan	RMAF Escadrille de Transport 3, Kenitra
	CN-AMO	Aeritalia C-27J Spartan	RMAF Escadrille de Transport 3, Kenitra
	CN-AMP	Aeritalia C-27J Spartan	RMAF Escadrille de Transport 3, Kenitra
	CN-AMQ	Aeritalia C-27J Spartan	RMAF Escadrille de Transport 3, Kenitra
	CN-AMR	Gulfstream Aerospace G.550	Government of Morocco, Rabat
	CN-AMS	Gulfstream Aerospace G.550	Government of Morocco, Rabat
	CN-ANL	Grumman G.1159 Gulfstream IITT	Government of Morocco, Rabat
	CN-ANO	Dassault Falcon 50	Government of Morocco, Rabat
	CN-ANU	Grumman G.1159A Gulfstream III	Government of Morocco, Rabat
	CNA-NV	Cessna 560 Citation V	Government of Morocco, Rabat
	CNA-NW	Cessna 560 Citation V	Government of Morocco, Rabat
	CN-AOA	Lockheed C-130H Hercules (4535)	RMAF Escadrille de Transport 3, Kenitra
	CN-AOC	Lockheed C-130H Hercules (4551)	RMAF Escadrille de Transport 3, Kenitra
	CN-AOD	Lockheed C-130H Hercules (4575)	RMAF Escadrille de Transport 3, Kenitra
	CN-AOE	Lockheed C-130H Hercules (4581)	RMAF Escadrille de Transport 3, Kenitra
	CNA-OF	Lockheed C-130H Hercules (4583)	RMAF Escadrille de Transport 3, Kenitra
	CN-AOG	Lockheed C-130H Hercules (4713)	RMAF Escadrille de Transport 3, Kenitra
	CN-AOI	Lockheed C-130H Hercules (4733)	RMAF Escadrille de Transport 3, Kenitra
	CNA-OJ	Lockheed C-130H Hercules (4738)	RMAF Escadrille de Transport 3, Kenitra
	CNA-OK	Lockheed C-130H Hercules (4739)	RMAF Escadrille de Transport 3, Kenitra
	CN-AOL	Lockheed C-130H Hercules (4742)	RMAF Escadrille de Transport 3, Kenitra
	CN-AOM	Lockheed C-130H Hercules (4875)	RMAF Escadrille de Transport 3, Kenitra
	CN-AON	Lockheed C-130H Hercules (4876)	RMAF Escadrille de Transport 3, Kenitra
	CNA-OO	Lockheed EC-130H Hercules (4877)	RMAF Escadron Electronique, Kenitra
	CN-AOP	Lockheed C-130H Hercules (4888)	RMAF Escadrille de Transport 3, Kenitra
	CN-AOR	Lockheed KC-130H Hercules (4907)	RMAF Escadrille de Transport 3, Kenitra
	CNA-OS	Lockheed KC-130H Hercules (4909)	RMAF Escadrille de Transport 3, Kenitra
	CNA-SM	BAE RJ100	Government of Morocco, Rabat
	CN-MBH	Boeing 747-48E	*Sold as A6-DAW, November 2017*
	CN-MVI	Boeing 737-8KB	Government of Morocco, Rabat

NAMIBIA

	V5-GON	Dassault Falcon 7X	Government of Namibia, Eros
	V5-NAM	Dassault Falcon 900B	Government of Namibia, Eros

NETHERLANDS
Koninklijke Luchtmacht (KLu)

	D-101	Boeing-Vertol CH-47D Chinook	KLu 298 Sqn, Gilze-Rijen
	D-102	Boeing-Vertol CH-47D Chinook	KLu 298 Sqn, Gilze-Rijen
	D-103	Boeing-Vertol CH-47D Chinook	KLu 298 Sqn, Gilze-Rijen
	D-106	Boeing-Vertol CH-47D Chinook	KLu 298 Sqn, Gilze-Rijen
	D-661	Boeing-Vertol CH-47D Chinook	KLu 298 Sqn, Gilze-Rijen
	D-662	Boeing-Vertol CH-47D Chinook	KLu 298 Sqn, Gilze-Rijen
	D-663	Boeing-Vertol CH-47D Chinook	KLu 298 Sqn, Gilze-Rijen
	D-664	Boeing-Vertol CH-47D Chinook	KLu 298 Sqn, Gilze-Rijen
	D-665	Boeing-Vertol CH-47D Chinook	KLu 298 Sqn, Gilze-Rijen
	D-666	Boeing-Vertol CH-47D Chinook	KLu 298 Sqn, Gilze-Rijen
	D-667	Boeing-Vertol CH-47D Chinook	KLu 298 Sqn, Gilze-Rijen
	D-890	Boeing-Vertol CH-47F Chinook	KLu 298 Sqn, Gilze-Rijen
	D-891	Boeing-Vertol CH-47F Chinook	KLu 302 Sqn, Fort Hood, Texas, USA
	D-892	Boeing-Vertol CH-47F Chinook	KLu 298 Sqn, Gilze-Rijen
	D-893	Boeing-Vertol CH-47F Chinook	KLu 302 Sqn, Fort Hood, Texas, USA
	D-894	Boeing-Vertol CH-47F Chinook	KLu 302 Sqn, Fort Hood, Texas, USA
	D-895	Boeing-Vertol CH-47F Chinook	KLu 302 Sqn, Fort Hood, Texas, USA
	F-001	Lockheed Martin F-35A Lightning II [OT]	KLu 323 Sqn, Edwards AFB California, USA
	F-002	Lockheed Martin F-35A Lightning II [OT]	KLu 323 Sqn, Edwards AFB California, USA
	G-273	Lockheed C-130H-30 Hercules	KLu 336 Sqn, Eindhoven
	G-275	Lockheed C-130H-30 Hercules	KLu 336 Sqn, Eindhoven
	G-781	Lockheed C-130H Hercules	KLu 336 Sqn, Eindhoven
	G-988	Lockheed C-130H Hercules	KLu 336 Sqn, Eindhoven
	J-001	Fokker (GD) F-16AM Fighting Falcon [AZ]	KLu 148th FS/162th FW, Tucson IAP, Arizona, US

Serial	Type (code/other identity)	Owner/operator, location or fate	Notes
J-002	Fokker (GD) F-16AM Fighting Falcon $	KLu 322 Sqn, Leeuwarden	
J-003	Fokker (GD) F-16AM Fighting Falcon	KLu 313 Sqn, Volkel	
J-004	Fokker (GD) F-16AM Fighting Falcon [AZ]	KLu 148th FS/162th FW, Tucson IAP, Arizona, USA	
J-005	Fokker (GD) F-16AM Fighting Falcon	KLu 313 Sqn, Volkel	
J-006	Fokker (GD) F-16AM Fighting Falcon $	KLu 322 Sqn, Leeuwarden	
J-008	Fokker (GD) F-16AM Fighting Falcon $	KLu 313 Sqn, Volkel	
J-009	Fokker (GD) F-16AM Fighting Falcon	KLu 322 Sqn, Leeuwarden	
J-010	Fokker (GD) F-16AM Fighting Falcon [AZ]	KLu 148th FS/162th FW, Tucson IAP, Arizona, USA	
J-011	Fokker (GD) F-16AM Fighting Falcon [AZ]	KLu 148th FS/162th FW, Tucson IAP, Arizona, USA	
J-013	Fokker (GD) F-16AM Fighting Falcon	KLu 312 Sqn/313 Sqn, Volkel	
J-014	Fokker (GD) F-16AM Fighting Falcon	KLu 313 Sqn, Volkel	
J-015	Fokker (GD) F-16AM Fighting Falcon	KLu 313 Sqn, Volkel	
J-016	Fokker (GD) F-16AM Fighting Falcon	KLu 313 Sqn, Volkel	
J-017	Fokker (GD) F-16AM Fighting Falcon	KLu 322 Sqn, Leeuwarden	
J-018	Fokker (GD) F-16AM Fighting Falcon [AZ]	KLu 148th FS/162th FW, Tucson IAP, Arizona, USA	
J-019	Fokker (GD) F-16AM Fighting Falcon [AZ]	KLu 148th FS/162th FW, Tucson IAP, Arizona, USA	
J-020	Fokker (GD) F-16AM Fighting Falcon	KLu 312 Sqn, Volkel	
J-021	Fokker (GD) F-16AM Fighting Falcon	KLu 322 Sqn, Leeuwarden	
J-055	Fokker (GD) F-16AM Fighting Falcon	KLu 313 Sqn, Volkel	
J-057	Fokker (GD) F-16AM Fighting Falcon	*To Jordan as 249, 14 December 2017*	
J-060	Fokker (GD) F-16AM Fighting Falcon	KLu 322 Sqn, Leeuwarden	
J-061	Fokker (GD) F-16AM Fighting Falcon	KLu 322 Sqn, Leeuwarden	
J-062	Fokker (GD) F-16AM Fighting Falcon	KLu 313 Sqn, Volkel	
J-063	Fokker (GD) F-16AM Fighting Falcon	KLu 313 Sqn, Volkel	
J-064	Fokker (GD) F-16BM Fighting Falcon [AZ]	KLu 148th FS/162th FW, Tucson IAP, Arizona, USA	
J-065	Fokker (GD) F-16BM Fighting Falcon	KLu 322 Sqn, Leeuwarden	
J-066	Fokker (GD) F-16BM Fighting Falcon	KLu Test Flt, Leeuwarden	
J-067	Fokker (GD) F-16BM Fighting Falcon [AZ]	KLu 148th FS/162th FW, Tucson IAP, Arizona, USA	
J-135	Fokker (GD) F-16AM Fighting Falcon	KLu 322 Sqn, Leeuwarden	
J-136	Fokker (GD) F-16AM Fighting Falcon	KLu 313 Sqn, Volkel	
J-142	Fokker (GD) F-16AM Fighting Falcon	KLu 322 Sqn, Leeuwarden	
J-144	Fokker (GD) F-16AM Fighting Falcon	KLu 312 Sqn/313 Sqn, Volkel	
J-145	Fokker (GD) F-16AM Fighting Falcon	*To Jordan as 248, 25 October 2017*	
J-146	Fokker (GD) F-16AM Fighting Falcon	KLu 322 Sqn, Leeuwarden	
J-193	Fokker (GD) F-16AM Fighting Falcon	*To Jordan as 246, 14 December 2017*	
J-196	Fokker (GD) F-16AM Fighting Falcon $	KLu 313 Sqn, Volkel	
J-197	Fokker (GD) F-16AM Fighting Falcon	KLu 312 Sqn/313 Sqn, Volkel	
J-199	Fokker (GD) F-16AM Fighting Falcon	*To Jordan as 247, 25 October 2017*	
J-201	Fokker (GD) F-16AM Fighting Falcon	KLu 322 Sqn, Leeuwarden	
J-202	Fokker (GD) F-16AM Fighting Falcon	KLu, stored Volkel	
J-208	Fokker (GD) F-16BM Fighting Falcon	*To Jordan as 237, 29 November 2017*	
J-209	Fokker (GD) F-16BM Fighting Falcon [AZ]	KLu 148th FS/162th FW, Tucson IAP, Arizona, USA	
J-210	Fokker (GD) F-16BM Fighting Falcon [AZ]	KLu 148th FS/162th FW, Tucson IAP, Arizona, USA	
J-362	Fokker (GD) F-16AM Fighting Falcon	KLu 322 Sqn, Leeuwarden	
J-366	Fokker (GD) F-16AM Fighting Falcon [AZ]	KLu 148th FS/162th FW, Tucson IAP, Arizona, USA	
J-367	Fokker (GD) F-16AM Fighting Falcon	KLu 322 Sqn, Leeuwarden	
J-368	Fokker (GD) F-16BM Fighting Falcon	KLu 313 Sqn, Volkel	
J-369	Fokker (GD) F-16BM Fighting Falcon [AZ]	KLu 148th FS/162th FW, Tucson IAP, Arizona, USA	
J-508	Fokker (GD) F-16AM Fighting Falcon	KLu 313 Sqn, Volkel	
J-509	Fokker (GD) F-16AM Fighting Falcon	KLu 322 Sqn, Leeuwarden	
J-510	Fokker (GD) F-16AM Fighting Falcon	*To Jordan as 250, 29 November 2017*	
J-511	Fokker (GD) F-16AM Fighting Falcon	KLu 322 Sqn, Leeuwarden	
J-512	Fokker (GD) F-16AM Fighting Falcon	KLu 313 Sqn, Volkel	
J-513	Fokker (GD) F-16AM Fighting Falcon	KLu 323 Sqn, Volkel	
J-514	Fokker (GD) F-16AM Fighting Falcon	KLu 313 Sqn, Volkel	
J-515	Fokker (GD) F-16AM Fighting Falcon	KLu 312 Sqn/313 Sqn, Volkel	
J-516	Fokker (GD) F-16AM Fighting Falcon	KLu 322 Sqn, Leeuwarden	
J-616	Fokker (GD) F-16AM Fighting Falcon	KLu 312 Sqn, Volkel	
J-623	Fokker (GD) F-16AM Fighting Falcon	*To Jordan as 238, 29 November 2017*	
J-624	Fokker (GD) F-16AM Fighting Falcon	KLu 322 Sqn, Leeuwarden	
J-628	Fokker (GD) F-16AM Fighting Falcon	KLu 322 Sqn, Leeuwarden	
J-630	Fokker (GD) F-16AM Fighting Falcon	KLu 312 Sqn/313 Sqn, Volkel	

Notes	Serial	Type (code/other identity)	Owner/operator, location or fate
	J-631	Fokker (GD) F-16AM Fighting Falcon $	KLu 322 Sqn, Leeuwarden
	J-632	Fokker (GD) F-16AM Fighting Falcon	KLu 322 Sqn, Leeuwarden
	J-635	Fokker (GD) F-16AM Fighting Falcon	KLu 312 Sqn, Volkel
	J-637	Fokker (GD) F-16AM Fighting Falcon	*To Jordan as 239, 29 November 2017*
	J-638	Fokker (GD) F-16AM Fighting Falcon	*To Jordan as 240, 25 October 2017*
	J-641	Fokker (GD) F-16AM Fighting Falcon	KLu 312 Sqn, Volkel
	J-642	Fokker (GD) F-16AM Fighting Falcon	KLu 322 Sqn, Leeuwarden
	J-643	Fokker (GD) F-16AM Fighting Falcon	KLu 313 Sqn, Volkel
	J-644	Fokker (GD) F-16AM Fighting Falcon	KLu 312 Sqn/313 Sqn, Volkel
	J-646	Fokker (GD) F-16AM Fighting Falcon	KLu 313 Sqn, Volkel
	J-647	Fokker (GD) F-16AM Fighting Falcon	KLu, stored Volkel
	J-866	Fokker (GD) F-16AM Fighting Falcon	KLu 312 Sqn, Volkel
	J-868	Fokker (GD) F-16AM Fighting Falcon	*To Jordan as 241, 29 November 2017*
	J-870	Fokker (GD) F-16AM Fighting Falcon	*To Jordan as 242, 14 December 2017*
	J-871	Fokker (GD) F-16AM Fighting Falcon	KLu 322 Sqn, Leeuwarden
	J-872	Fokker (GD) F-16AM Fighting Falcon	*To Jordan as 243, 25 October 2017*
	J-873	Fokker (GD) F-16AM Fighting Falcon	*To Jordan as 244, 25 October 2017*
	J-876	Fokker (GD) F-16AM Fighting Falcon	*To Jordan as 245, 29 November 2017*
	J-877	Fokker (GD) F-16AM Fighting Falcon	KLu Leeuwarden, WLT
	J-879	Fokker (GD) F-16AM Fighting Falcon	KLu 322 Sqn, Leeuwarden
	J-881	Fokker (GD) F-16AM Fighting Falcon	KLu 322 Sqn, Leeuwarden
	J-882	Fokker (GD) F-16BM Fighting Falcon	KLu 322 Sqn, Leeuwarden
	J-884	Fokker (GD) F-16BM Fighting Falcon	*To Jordan as 236, 25 October 2017*
	L-01	Pilatus PC-7 Turbo Trainer	KLu 131 EMVO Sqn, Woensdrecht
	L-02	Pilatus PC-7 Turbo Trainer $	Pilatus, Stans, Switzerland (upgrade)
	L-03	Pilatus PC-7 Turbo Trainer	KLu 131 EMVO Sqn, Woensdrecht
	L-04	Pilatus PC-7 Turbo Trainer	KLu 131 EMVO Sqn, Woensdrecht
	L-05	Pilatus PC-7 Turbo Trainer	KLu 131 EMVO Sqn, Woensdrecht
	L-06	Pilatus PC-7 Turbo Trainer	KLu 131 EMVO Sqn, Woensdrecht
	L-07	Pilatus PC-7 Turbo Trainer	Pilatus, Stans, Switzerland (upgrade)
	L-08	Pilatus PC-7 Turbo Trainer	KLu 131 EMVO Sqn, Woensdrecht
	L-09	Pilatus PC-7 Turbo Trainer	KLu 131 EMVO Sqn, Woensdrecht
	L-10	Pilatus PC-7 Turbo Trainer	KLu 131 EMVO Sqn, Woensdrecht
	L-11	Pilatus PC-7 Turbo Trainer	Pilatus, Stans, Switzerland (upgrade)
	L-12	Pilatus PC-7 Turbo Trainer	Pilatus, Stans, Switzerland (upgrade)
	L-13	Pilatus PC-7 Turbo Trainer	Pilatus, Stans, Switzerland (upgrade)
	N-088	NH Industries NH.90-NFH	KLu 860 Sqn, De Kooij
	N-102	NH Industries NH.90-NFH	KLu 860 Sqn, De Kooij
	N-110	NH Industries NH.90-NFH	KLu 860 Sqn, De Kooij
	N-164	NH Industries NH.90-NFH	KLu 860 Sqn, De Kooij
	N-175	NH Industries NH.90-NFH $	KLu 860 Sqn, De Kooij
	N-195	NH Industries NH.90-NFH	KLu 860 Sqn, De Kooij
	N-227	NH Industries NH.90-NFH	KLu 860 Sqn, De Kooij
	N-228	NH Industries NH.90-NFH	KLu 860 Sqn, De Kooij
	N-233	NH Industries NH.90-NFH	KLu 860 Sqn, De Kooij
	N-234	NH Industries NH.90-NFH	KLu 860 Sqn, De Kooij
	N-258	NH Industries NH.90-NFH	KLu 860 Sqn, De Kooij
	N-277	NH Industries NH.90-NFH	KLu 860 Sqn, De Kooij
	N-316	NH Industries NH.90-NFH	KLu 860 Sqn, De Kooij
	N-317	NH Industries NH.90-NFH	KLu 860 Sqn, De Kooij
	N-318	NH Industries NH.90-NFH	KLu 860 Sqn, De Kooij
	N-319	NH Industries NH.90-NFH	KLu 860 Sqn, De Kooij
	N-324	NH Industries NH.90-NFH	KLu 860 Sqn, De Kooij
	N-325	NH Industries NH.90-NFH	KLu 860 Sqn, De Kooij
	N-326	NH Industries NH.90-NFH	KLu 860 Sqn, De Kooij
	N-327	NH Industries NH.90-NFH	KLu 860 Sqn, De Kooij
	Q-01	MDH AH-64D Apache Longbow	KLu 301 Sqn, Gilze-Rijen
	Q-02	MDH AH-64D Apache Longbow	KLu 302 Sqn, Fort Hood, Texas, USA
	Q-03	MDH AH-64D Apache Longbow	KLu 302 Sqn, Fort Hood, Texas, USA
	Q-04	MDH AH-64D Apache Longbow	KLu 301 Sqn, Gilze-Rijen
	Q-05	MDH AH-64D Apache Longbow	KLu 301 Sqn, Gilze-Rijen
	Q-06	MDH AH-64D Apache Longbow	KLu 302 Sqn, Fort Hood, Texas, USA

Serial	Type (code/other identity)	Owner/operator, location or fate	Notes
Q-07	MDH AH-64D Apache Longbow	KLu 302 Sqn, Fort Hood, Texas, USA	
Q-08	MDH AH-64D Apache Longbow	KLu 301 Sqn, Gilze-Rijen	
Q-09	MDH AH-64D Apache Longbow	KLu 301 Sqn, Gilze-Rijen	
Q-10	MDH AH-64D Apache Longbow	KLu 301 Sqn, Gilze-Rijen	
Q-11	MDH AH-64D Apache Longbow	KLu 302 Sqn, Fort Hood, Texas, USA	
Q-12	MDH AH-64D Apache Longbow	KLu 302 Sqn, Fort Hood, Texas, USA	
Q-13	MDH AH-64D Apache Longbow	KLu 301 Sqn, Gilze-Rijen	
Q-14	MDH AH-64D Apache Longbow	KLu 301 Sqn, Gilze-Rijen	
Q-16	MDH AH-64D Apache Longbow	KLu 301 Sqn, Gilze-Rijen	
Q-17	MDH AH-64D Apache Longbow	KLu 301 Sqn, Gilze-Rijen	
Q-18	MDH AH-64D Apache Longbow	KLu 301 Sqn, Gilze-Rijen	
Q-19	MDH AH-64D Apache Longbow	KLu 301 Sqn, Gilze-Rijen	
Q-21	MDH AH-64D Apache Longbow	KLu 301 Sqn, Gilze-Rijen	
Q-22	MDH AH-64D Apache Longbow	KLu 301 Sqn, Gilze-Rijen	
Q-23	MDH AH-64D Apache Longbow	KLu 301 Sqn, Gilze-Rijen	
Q-24	MDH AH-64D Apache Longbow	KLu 301 Sqn, Gilze-Rijen	
Q-25	MDH AH-64D Apache Longbow	KLu 301 Sqn, Gilze-Rijen	
Q-26	MDH AH-64D Apache Longbow	KLu 301 Sqn, Gilze-Rijen	
Q-27	MDH AH-64D Apache Longbow	KLu 302 Sqn, Fort Hood, Texas, USA	
Q-28	MDH AH-64D Apache Longbow	KLu 302 Sqn, Fort Hood, Texas, USA	
Q-29	MDH AH-64D Apache Longbow	KLu 301 Sqn, Gilze-Rijen	
Q-30	MDH AH-64D Apache Longbow	KLu 301 Sqn, Gilze-Rijen	
S-419	Eurocopter AS.532U-2 Cougar	KLu 300 Sqn, Gilze-Rijen	
S-440	Eurocopter AS.532U-2 Cougar	KLu 300 Sqn, Gilze-Rijen	
S-441	Eurocopter AS.532U-2 Cougar	KLu 300 Sqn, Gilze-Rijen	
S-442	Eurocopter AS.532U-2 Cougar	KLu 300 Sqn, Gilze-Rijen	
S-444	Eurocopter AS.532U-2 Cougar	KLu 300 Sqn, Gilze-Rijen	
S-445	Eurocopter AS.532U-2 Cougar	KLu 300 Sqn, Gilze-Rijen	
S-447	Eurocopter AS.532U-2 Cougar	KLu 300 Sqn, Gilze-Rijen	
S-453	Eurocopter AS.532U-2 Cougar	KLu 300 Sqn, Gilze-Rijen	
S-454	Eurocopter AS.532U-2 Cougar	KLu 300 Sqn, Gilze-Rijen	
S-456	Eurocopter AS.532U-2 Cougar	KLu 300 Sqn, Gilze-Rijen	
S-457	Eurocopter AS.532U-2 Cougar	KLu, Woensdrecht (wfu)	
S-458	Eurocopter AS.532U-2 Cougar	KLu 300 Sqn, Gilze-Rijen	
S-459	Eurocopter AS.532U-2 Cougar	KLu 300 Sqn, Gilze-Rijen	
T-235	McDonnell Douglas KDC-10	KLu 334 Sqn, Eindhoven	
T-264	McDonnell Douglas KDC-10	KLu 334 Sqn, Eindhoven	
T-...	Airbus A.330-243 MRTT (KC-30)	KLu/MMF (or oder)	
T-...	Airbus A.330-243 MRTT (KC-30)	KLu/MMF (or oder)	
T-...	Airbus A.330-243 MRTT (KC-30)	KLu/MMF (or oder)	
T-...	Airbus A.330-243 MRTT (KC-30)	KLu/MMF (or oder)	
T-...	Airbus A.330-243 MRTT (KC-30)	KLu/MMF (or oder)	
T-...	Airbus A.330-243 MRTT (KC-30)	KLu/MMF (or oder)	
T-...	Airbus A.330-243 MRTT (KC-30)	KLu/MMF (or oder)	
T-...	Airbus A.330-243 MRTT (KC-30)	KLu/MMF (or oder)	
V-11	Grumman G.1159C Gulfstream IV	KLu 334 Sqn, Eindhoven	

Kustwacht & Netherlands Government

PH-CGC	Dornier Do.228-212	Kustwacht, Amsterdam/Schiphol	
PH-CGN	Dornier Do.228-212	Kustwacht, Amsterdam/Schiphol	
PH-KBX	Fokker 70	Dutch Royal Flight, Amsterdam/Schiphol	

NEW ZEALAND
Royal New Zealand Air Force (RNZAF)

NZ4201	Lockheed P-3K2 Orion	RNZAF 5 Sqn, Whenuapai	
NZ4202	Lockheed P-3K2 Orion	RNZAF 5 Sqn, Whenuapai	
NZ4203	Lockheed P-3K2 Orion	RNZAF 5 Sqn, Whenuapai	
NZ4204	Lockheed P-3K2 Orion	RNZAF 5 Sqn, Whenuapai	
NZ4205	Lockheed P-3K2 Orion	RNZAF 5 Sqn, Whenuapai	
NZ4206	Lockheed P-3K2 Orion	RNZAF 5 Sqn, Whenuapai	
NZ7001	Lockheed C-130H(NZ) Hercules $	RNZAF 40 Sqn, Whenuapai	
NZ7002	Lockheed C-130H(NZ) Hercules	RNZAF 40 Sqn, Whenuapai	
NZ7003	Lockheed C-130H(NZ) Hercules	RNZAF 40 Sqn, Whenuapai	

Notes	Serial	Type (code/other identity)	Owner/operator, location or fate
	NZ7004	Lockheed C-130H(NZ) Hercules	RNZAF 40 Sqn, Whenuapai
	NZ7005	Lockheed C-130H(NZ) Hercules	RNZAF 40 Sqn, Whenuapai
	NZ7571	Boeing 757-2K2	RNZAF 40 Sqn, Whenuapai
	NZ7572	Boeing 757-2K2	RNZAF 40 Sqn, Whenuapai
	NIGER		
	5U-BAG	Boeing 737-2N9C	Withdrawn from use, 2017
	5U-GRN	Boeing 737-75U	Government of Niger, Niamey
	NIGERIA		
	Nigerian Air Force (NAF)		
	NAF-910	Lockheed C-130H Hercules	NAF 301 HAG, Ikeja
	NAF-912	Lockheed C-130H Hercules	NAF 301 HAG, Ikeja
	NAF-913	Lockheed C-130H Hercules	NAF 301 HAG, Ikeja
	NAF-917	Lockheed C-130H-30 Hercules	NAF 301 HAG, Ikeja
	NAF-918	Lockheed C-130H-30 Hercules	NAF 301 HAG, Ikeja
	NAF-961	Dassault Falcon 900	NAF 307 HAG, Minna
	Nigerian Government		
	5N-FGS	Gulfstream Aerospace Gulfstream V	Federal Government of Nigeria, Abuja
	5N-FGT	Boeing 737-7N6 [001]	Federal Government of Nigeria, Abuja
	5N-FGU	Dassault Falcon 7X	Federal Government of Nigeria, Abuja
	5N-FGV	Dassault Falcon 7X	Federal Government of Nigeria, Abuja
	5N-FGW	Gulfstream Aerospace G.550	Federal Government of Nigeria, Abuja
	5N-FGX	Hawker 4000 Horizon	Federal Government of Nigeria, Abuja
	NORWAY		
	Luftforsvaret/Royal Norwegian Air Force (RNoAF)		
	013	NH Industries NH.90-NFH	RNoAF (on order)
	027	NH Industries NH.90-NFH	RNoAF (on order)
	041	Dassault Falcon 20 ECM	RNoAF 717 Skv, Gardermoen
	049	NH Industries NH.90-NFH	RNoAF 337 Skv, Bardufoss
	053	Dassault Falcon 20 ECM	RNoAF 717 Skv, Gardermoen
	057	NH Industries NH.90-NFH	RNoAF 337 Skv, Bardufoss
	058	NH Industries NH.90-NFH	RNoAF 337 Skv, Bardufoss
	060	Westland Sea King Mk.43	RNoAF 330 Skv Bodø/Banak/Ørland & Sola
	062	Westland Sea King Mk.43	RNoAF 330 Skv Bodø/Banak/Ørland & Sola
	066	Westland Sea King Mk.43	RNoAF 330 Skv Bodø/Banak/Ørland & Sola
	069	Westland Sea King Mk.43	RNoAF 330 Skv Bodø/Banak/Ørland & Sola
	070	Westland Sea King Mk.43	RNoAF 330 Skv Bodø/Banak/Ørland & Sola
	071	Westland Sea King Mk.43B	RNoAF 330 Skv Bodø/Banak/Ørland & Sola
	072	Westland Sea King Mk.43	RNoAF 330 Skv Bodø/Banak/Ørland & Sola
	073	Westland Sea King Mk.43	RNoAF 330 Skv Bodø/Banak/Ørland & Sola
	074	Westland Sea King Mk.43	RNoAF 330 Skv Bodø/Banak/Ørland & Sola
	087	NH Industries NH.90-NFH	RNoAF 337 Skv, Bardufoss
	0125	Dassault Falcon 20 ECM	Withdrawn from use, 14 December 2017
	139	Bell 412HP	RNoAF 339 Skv, Bardufoss
	140	Bell 412HP	RNoAF 339 Skv, Bardufoss
	141	Bell 412HP	RNoAF 339 Skv, Bardufoss
	142	Bell 412HP	RNoAF 339 Skv, Bardufoss
	143	Bell 412HP	RNoAF 339 Skv, Bardufoss
	144	Bell 412HP	RNoAF 339 Skv, Bardufoss
	145	Bell 412HP	RNoAF 339 Skv, Bardufoss
	146	Bell 412HP	RNoAF 339 Skv, Bardufoss
	147	Bell 412HP	RNoAF 339 Skv, Bardufoss
	148	Bell 412HP	RNoAF 339 Skv, Bardufoss
	149	Bell 412HP	RNoAF 339 Skv, Bardufoss
	161	Bell 412HP	RNoAF 339 Skv, Bardufoss
	162	Bell 412HP	RNoAF 339 Skv, Bardufoss
	163	Bell 412HP	RNoAF 339 Skv, Bardufoss
	164	Bell 412HP	RNoAF 339 Skv, Bardufoss
	165	Bell 412HP	RNoAF 339 Skv, Bardufoss
	166	Bell 412HP	RNoAF 339 Skv, Bardufoss

Serial	Type (code/other identity)	Owner/operator, location or fate	Notes
167	Bell 412HP	RNoAF 339 Skv, Bardufoss	
171	NH Industries NH.90-NFH	RNoAF 337 Skv, Bardufoss	
189	Westland Sea King Mk.43A	RNoAF 330 Skv Bodø/Banak/Ørland & Sola	
194	Bell 412SP	RNoAF 339 Skv, Bardufoss	
217	NH Industries NH.90-NFH	RNoAF (on order)	
0262	AgustaWestland AW101 Mk.612	RNoAF (on order)	
0264	AgustaWestland AW101 Mk.612	RNoAF (on order)	
0265	AgustaWestland AW101 Mk.612	RNoAF 330 Skv Sola	
0268	AgustaWestland AW101 Mk.612	*Crashed Sola, 24 November 2017*	
0270	AgustaWestland AW101 Mk.612	RNoAF (on order)	
272	Fokker (GD) F-16A MLU Fighting Falcon $	RNoAF FLO 331 Skv, Bodø/338 Skv, Ørland	
273	Fokker (GD) F-16A MLU Fighting Falcon	RNoAF FLO 331 Skv, Bodø/338 Skv, Ørland	
0273	AgustaWestland AW101 Mk.612	RNoAF (on order)	
275	Fokker (GD) F-16A MLU Fighting Falcon	RNoAF FLO 331 Skv, Bodø/338 Skv, Ørland	
0275	AgustaWestland AW101 Mk.612	RNoAF (on order)	
276	Fokker (GD) F-16A MLU Fighting Falcon	RNoAF FLO 331 Skv, Bodø/338 Skv, Ørland	
0276	AgustaWestland AW101 Mk.612	RNoAF (on order)	
277	Fokker (GD) F-16A MLU Fighting Falcon	RNoAF FLO 331 Skv, Bodø/338 Skv, Ørland	
0277	AgustaWestland AW101 Mk.612	RNoAF (on order)	
0278	AgustaWestland AW101 Mk.612	RNoAF (on order)	
279	Fokker (GD) F-16A MLU Fighting Falcon	RNoAF FLO 331 Skv, Bodø/338 Skv, Ørland	
0279	AgustaWestland AW101 Mk.612	RNoAF (on order)	
0280	AgustaWestland AW101 Mk.612	RNoAF (on order)	
281	Fokker (GD) F-16A MLU Fighting Falcon	RNoAF FLO 331 Skv, Bodø/338 Skv, Ørland	
0281	AgustaWestland AW101 Mk.612	RNoAF (on order)	
282	Fokker (GD) F-16A MLU Fighting Falcon	RNoAF FLO 331 Skv, Bodø/338 Skv, Ørland	
0282	AgustaWestland AW101 Mk.612	RNoAF (on order)	
0283	AgustaWestland AW101 Mk.612	RNoAF (on order)	
284	Fokker (GD) F-16A MLU Fighting Falcon	RNoAF FLO 331 Skv, Bodø/338 Skv, Ørland	
0284	AgustaWestland AW101 Mk.612	RNoAF (on order)	
285	Fokker (GD) F-16A MLU Fighting Falcon	RNoAF FLO 331 Skv, Bodø/338 Skv, Ørland	
286	Fokker (GD) F-16A MLU Fighting Falcon	RNoAF FLO 331 Skv, Bodø/338 Skv, Ørland	
288	Fokker (GD) F-16A MLU Fighting Falcon	RNoAF FLO 331 Skv, Bodø/338 Skv, Ørland	
289	Fokker (GD) F-16A MLU Fighting Falcon	RNoAF FLO 331 Skv, Bodø/338 Skv, Ørland	
291	Fokker (GD) F-16A MLU Fighting Falcon	RNoAF FLO 331 Skv, Bodø/338 Skv, Ørland	
292	Fokker (GD) F-16A MLU Fighting Falcon	RNoAF FLO 331 Skv, Bodø/338 Skv, Ørland	
293	Fokker (GD) F-16A MLU Fighting Falcon	RNoAF FLO 331 Skv, Bodø/338 Skv, Ørland	
295	Fokker (GD) F-16A MLU Fighting Falcon	RNoAF FLO 331 Skv, Bodø/338 Skv, Ørland	
297	Fokker (GD) F-16A MLU Fighting Falcon	RNoAF FLO 331 Skv, Bodø/338 Skv, Ørland	
298	Fokker (GD) F-16A MLU Fighting Falcon $	RNoAF FLO 331 Skv, Bodø/338 Skv, Ørland	
299	Fokker (GD) F-16A MLU Fighting Falcon	RNoAF FLO 331 Skv, Bodø/338 Skv, Ørland	
302	Fokker (GD) F-16B MLU Fighting Falcon	RNoAF FLO 331 Skv, Bodø/338 Skv, Ørland	
304	Fokker (GD) F-16B MLU Fighting Falcon	RNoAF FLO 331 Skv, Bodø/338 Skv, Ørland	
305	Fokker (GD) F-16B MLU Fighting Falcon	RNoAF FLO 331 Skv, Bodø/338 Skv, Ørland	
306	Fokker (GD) F-16B MLU Fighting Falcon	RNoAF FLO 331 Skv, Bodø/338 Skv, Ørland	
322	Westland Sea King Mk.43B	RNoAF 330 Skv Bodø/Banak/Ørland & Sola	
329	Westland Sea King Mk.43B	RNoAF 330 Skv Bodø/Banak/Ørland & Sola	
330	Westland Sea King Mk.43B	RNoAF 330 Skv Bodø/Banak/Ørland & Sola	
658	Fokker (GD) F-16A MLU Fighting Falcon	RNoAF FLO 331 Skv, Bodø/338 Skv, Ørland	
659	Fokker (GD) F-16A MLU Fighting Falcon	RNoAF FLO 331 Skv, Bodø/338 Skv, Ørland	
660	Fokker (GD) F-16A MLU Fighting Falcon	RNoAF FLO 331 Skv, Bodø/338 Skv, Ørland	
661	Fokker (GD) F-16A MLU Fighting Falcon	RNoAF FLO 331 Skv, Bodø/338 Skv, Ørland	
662	Fokker (GD) F-16A MLU Fighting Falcon	RNoAF FLO 331 Skv, Bodø/338 Skv, Ørland	
663	Fokker (GD) F-16A MLU Fighting Falcon	RNoAF FLO 331 Skv, Bodø/338 Skv, Ørland	
664	Fokker (GD) F-16A MLU Fighting Falcon $	RNoAF FLO 331 Skv, Bodø/338 Skv, Ørland	
665	Fokker (GD) F-16A MLU Fighting Falcon	RNoAF FLO 331 Skv, Bodø/338 Skv, Ørland	
666	Fokker (GD) F-16A MLU Fighting Falcon	RNoAF/USAF 416th FTS/412th TW, Edwards AFB, USA	
667	Fokker (GD) F-16A MLU Fighting Falcon	RNoAF FLO 331 Skv, Bodø/338 Skv, Ørland	
668	Fokker (GD) F-16A MLU Fighting Falcon	RNoAF FLO 331 Skv, Bodø/338 Skv, Ørland	
670	Fokker (GD) F-16A MLU Fighting Falcon	RNoAF FLO 331 Skv, Bodø/338 Skv, Ørland	
671	Fokker (GD) F-16A MLU Fighting Falcon $	RNoAF FLO 331 Skv, Bodø/338 Skv, Ørland	

Notes	Serial	Type (code/other identity)	Owner/operator, location or fate
	672	Fokker (GD) F-16A MLU Fighting Falcon	RNoAF FLO 331 Skv, Bodø/338 Skv, Ørland
	673	Fokker (GD) F-16A MLU Fighting Falcon	RNoAF FLO 331 Skv, Bodø/338 Skv, Ørland
	674	Fokker (GD) F-16A MLU Fighting Falcon	RNoAF FLO 331 Skv, Bodø/338 Skv, Ørland
	675	Fokker (GD) F-16A MLU Fighting Falcon	RNoAF FLO 331 Skv, Bodø/338 Skv, Ørland
	677	Fokker (GD) F-16A MLU Fighting Falcon	RNoAF FLO 331 Skv, Bodø/338 Skv, Ørland
	678	Fokker (GD) F-16A MLU Fighting Falcon	RNoAF FLO 331 Skv, Bodø/338 Skv, Ørland
	680	Fokker (GD) F-16A MLU Fighting Falcon	RNoAF FLO 331 Skv, Bodø/338 Skv, Ørland
	681	Fokker (GD) F-16A MLU Fighting Falcon	RNoAF FLO 331 Skv, Bodø/338 Skv, Ørland
	682	Fokker (GD) F-16A MLU Fighting Falcon	RNoAF FLO 331 Skv, Bodø/338 Skv, Ørland
	683	Fokker (GD) F-16A MLU Fighting Falcon	RNoAF FLO 331 Skv, Bodø/338 Skv, Ørland
	686	Fokker (GD) F-16A MLU Fighting Falcon $	RNoAF FLO 331 Skv, Bodø/338 Skv, Ørland
	687	Fokker (GD) F-16A MLU Fighting Falcon	RNoAF FLO 331 Skv, Bodø/338 Skv, Ørland
	688	Fokker (GD) F-16A MLU Fighting Falcon	RNoAF FLO 331 Skv, Bodø/338 Skv, Ørland
	689	Fokker (GD) F-16B MLU Fighting Falcon	RNoAF FLO 331 Skv, Bodø/338 Skv, Ørland
	690	Fokker (GD) F-16B MLU Fighting Falcon	*Withdrawn from use, March 2017*
	691	Fokker (GD) F-16B MLU Fighting Falcon	RNoAF FLO 331 Skv, Bodø/338 Skv, Ørland
	692	Fokker (GD) F-16B MLU Fighting Falcon $	RNoAF FLO 331 Skv, Bodø/338 Skv, Ørland
	693	Fokker (GD) F-16B MLU Fighting Falcon	RNoAF FLO 331 Skv, Bodø/338 Skv, Ørland
	711	GD F-16B MLU Fighting Falcon	RNoAF FLO 331 Skv, Bodø/338 Skv, Ørland
	1216	NH Industries NH.90-NFH (ASW)	RNoAF 337 Skv, Bardufoss
	3296	Lockheed P-3C UIP Orion	RNoAF 333 Skv, Andøya
	3297	Lockheed P-3C UIP Orion	RNoAF 333 Skv, Andøya
	3298	Lockheed P-3C UIP Orion	RNoAF 333 Skv, Andøya
	3299	Lockheed P-3C UIP Orion	RNoAF 333 Skv, Andøya
	4576	Lockheed P-3N Orion	RNoAF 333 Skv, Andøya
	5087	Lockheed Martin F-35A Lightning II	RNoAF 62nd FS/56th FW, Luke AFB, AZ, USA
	5088	Lockheed Martin F-35A Lightning II	RNoAF 62nd FS/56th FW, Luke AFB, AZ, USA
	5110	Lockheed Martin F-35A Lightning II	RNoAF 62nd FS/56th FW, Luke AFB, AZ, USA
	5111	Lockheed Martin F-35A Lightning II	RNoAF 62nd FS/56th FW, Luke AFB, AZ, USA
	5145	Lockheed Martin F-35A Lightning II	RNoAF 62nd FS/56th FW, Luke AFB, AZ, USA
	5146	Lockheed Martin F-35A Lightning II	RNoAF 62nd FS/56th FW, Luke AFB, AZ, USA
	5147	Lockheed Martin F-35A Lightning II	RNoAF 62nd FS/56th FW, Luke AFB, AZ, USA
	5148	Lockheed Martin F-35A Lightning II	RNoAF, NDMA Ørland (for FLO/338 Skv)
	5149	Lockheed Martin F-35A Lightning II	RNoAF, NDMA Ørland (for FLO/338 Skv)
	5150	Lockheed Martin F-35A Lightning II	RNoAF, NDMA Ørland (for FLO/338 Skv)
	5205	Lockheed Martin F-35A Lightning II	RNoAF 62nd FS/56th FW, Luke AFB, AZ, USA
	5601	Lockheed C-130J-30 Hercules II	RNoAF 335 Skv, Gardermoen
	5607	Lockheed C-130J-30 Hercules II	RNoAF 335 Skv, Gardermoen
	5629	Lockheed C-130J-30 Hercules II	RNoAF 335 Skv, Gardermoen
	5699	Lockheed C-130J-30 Hercules II	RNoAF 335 Skv, Gardermoen
	6603	Lockheed P-3N Orion	RNoAF 333 Skv, Andøya
	...	NH Industries NH.90-NFH	RNoAF (on order)
	...	NH Industries NH.90-NFH	RNoAF (on order)
	...	NH Industries NH.90-NFH	RNoAF (on order)
	...	NH Industries NH.90-NFH	RNoAF (on order)
	OMAN		
	Royal Air Force of Oman (RAFO)		
	501	Lockheed C-130H Hercules	RAFO 16 Sqn, Al Musana
	502	Lockheed C-130H Hercules	RAFO 16 Sqn, Al Musana
	503	Lockheed C-130H Hercules	RAFO 16 Sqn, Al Musana
	505	Lockheed C-130J Hercules II	RAFO 16 Sqn, Al Musana
	506	Lockheed C-130J Hercules II	RAFO 16 Sqn, Al Musana
	507	Lockheed C-130J-30 Hercules II	RAFO (on order)
	508	Lockheed C-130J-30 Hercules II	RAFO (on order)
	525	Lockheed C-130J-30 Hercules II	RAFO Royal Flt, Seeb
	554	Airbus A.320-214X	RAFO 4 Sqn, Seeb
	555	Airbus A.320-214X	RAFO 4 Sqn, Seeb
	556	Airbus A.320-214X	RAFO 4 Sqn, Seeb
	557	Grumman G.1159C Gulfstream IV	RAFO 4 Sqn, Seeb
	558	Grumman G.1159C Gulfstream IV	RAFO 4 Sqn, Seeb
	901	CASA C-295M	RAFO 5 Sqn, Salalah

Serial	Type (code/other identity)	Owner/operator, location or fate	Notes
902	CASA C-295M	RAFO 5 Sqn, Salalah	
903	CASA C-295M	RAFO 5 Sqn, Salalah	
904	CASA C-295M	RAFO 5 Sqn, Salalah	
905	CASA C-295M	RAFO (on order)	
906	CASA C-295M	RAFO (on order)	
907	CASA C-295M	RAFO (on order)	
908	CASA C-295M	RAFO (on order)	
909	CASA C-295M	RAFO (on order)	
910	CASA C-295MPA Persuader	RAFO 2 Sqn, Al Musana	
911	CASA C-295MPA Persuader	RAFO 2 Sqn, Al Musana	
912	CASA C-295MPA Persuader	RAFO 2 Sqn, Al Musana	
913	CASA C-295MPA Persuader	RAFO 2 Sqn, Al Musana	
914	CASA C-295MPA Persuader	RAFO (on order)	
915	CASA C-295MPA Persuader	RAFO (on order)	
916	CASA C-295MPA Persuader	RAFO (on order)	
Omani Government			
A4O-AA	Airbus A.320-233	Government of Oman, Seeb	
A4O-AJ	Airbus A.319-115CJ	Government of Oman, Seeb	
A4O-AD	Gulfstream Aerospace G.550	Government of Oman, Seeb	
A4O-AE	Gulfstream Aerospace G.550	Government of Oman, Seeb	
A4O-SO	Boeing 747SP-27	Government of Oman, Seeb	
A4O-HMS	Boeing 747-8H0	Government of Oman, Seeb	
A4O-OMN	Boeing 747-430	Government of Oman, Seeb	
PAKISTAN			
Pakistan Air Force (PAF)/Pakistani Army			
4119	Lockheed C-130E Hercules [119]	PAF 21 Sqn, Karachi	
4144	Lockheed L.100 Hercules [144]	PAF 6 Sqn, Islamabad	
4148	Lockheed C-130E Hercules [148]	PAF 6 Sqn, Islamabad	
4153	Lockheed C-130E Hercules [153] $	PAF 21 Sqn, Karachi	
4159	Lockheed C-130E Hercules [159]	PAF 21 Sqn, Karachi	
4171	Lockheed C-130E Hercules [171]	PAF 6 Sqn, Islamabad	
4177	Lockheed C-130E Hercules [177]	PAF 6 Sqn, Islamabad	
4178	Lockheed C-130E Hercules [178]	PAF 21 Sqn, Karachi	
4180	Lockheed C-130E Hercules [180]	PAF 6 Sqn, Islamabad	
4189	Lockheed C-130E Hercules [189]	PAF 6 Sqn, Islamabad	
4270	Gulfstream Aerospace G.450	Pakistani Army, Rawalpindi	
4282	Lockheed C-130E Hercules [282]	PAF 6 Sqn, Islamabad	
EYE77	Bombardier Challenger 605	Pakistani Army, Rawalpindi	
J-754	Cessna 560 Citation VI	PAF 12 VIP Communications Sqn, Islamabad	
J-755	Gulfstream Aerospace G.1159C Gulfstream IV-SP	PAF 12 VIP Communications Sqn, Islamabad	
J-756	Gulfstream Aerospace G.450	PAF 12 VIP Communications Sqn, Islamabad	
POLAND			
Siły Powietrzne (SP)/Polish Air Force & Lotnictwo Marynarki Wojennej (LMW)/Polish Navy			
0001	Gulfstream Aerospace G.550 (N547GA)	SP 1.BLTr, Warszawa	
0002	Gulfstream Aerospace G.550 (N554GD)	SP 1.BLTr, Warszawa	
011	CASA C-295M	SP 13.eltr/8.BLTr, Kraków/Balice	
012	CASA C-295M $	SP 13.eltr/8.BLTr, Kraków/Balice	
013	CASA C-295M	SP 13.eltr/8.BLTr, Kraków/Balice	
014	CASA C-295M	SP 13.eltr/8.BLTr, Kraków/Balice	
015	CASA C-295M	SP 13.eltr/8.BLTr, Kraków/Balice	
15	Mikoyan MiG-29UB $	SP 1.elt/23.BLT, Minsk/Mazowiecki	
016	CASA C-295M	SP 13.eltr/8.BLTr, Kraków/Balice	
016	PZL 130TC-I Orlik	SP 2.OSzL/42.BLSz, Radom	
017	CASA C-295M	SP 13.eltr/8.BLTr, Kraków/Balice	
018	CASA C-295M	SP 13.eltr/8.BLTr, Kraków/Balice	
020	CASA C-295M	SP 13.eltr/8.BLTr, Kraków/Balice	
021	CASA C-295M	SP 13.eltr/8.BLTr, Kraków/Balice	
022	CASA C-295M	SP 13.eltr/8.BLTr, Kraków/Balice	
023	CASA C-295M	SP 13.eltr/8.BLTr, Kraków/Balice	
024	CASA C-295M	SP 13.eltr/8.BLTr, Kraków/Balice	

Notes	Serial	Type (code/other identity)	Owner/operator, location or fate
	025	CASA C-295M	SP 13.eltr/8.BLTr, Kraków/Balice
	026	CASA C-295M	SP 13.eltr/8.BLTr, Kraków/Balice
	027	CASA C-295M	SP 13.eltr/8.BLTr, Kraków/Balice
	28	Mikoyan MiG-29UB	SP 1.elt/23.BLT, Minsk/Mazowiecki
	029	PZL 130TC-II Orlik	SP 2.OSzL/42.BLSz, Radom
	030	PZL 130TC-II Orlik	SP 2.OSzL/42.BLSz, Radom
	031	PZL 130TC-II Orlik	SP 2.OSzL/42.BLSz, Radom
	032	PZL 130TC-II Orlik	SP 2.OSzL/42.BLSz, Radom
	037	PZL 130TC-II Orlik	SP 2.OSzL/42.BLSz, Radom
	38	Mikoyan MiG-29A	SP 1.elt/23.BLT, Minsk/Mazowiecki
	038	PZL 130TC-II Orlik	SP 2.OSzL/42.BLSz, Radom
	40	Mikoyan MiG-29A	SP 1.elt/23.BLT, Minsk/Mazowiecki
	040	PZL 130TC-II Orlik	SP 2.OSzL/42.BLSz, Radom
	041	PZL 130TC-II Orlik	SP 2.OSzL/42.BLSz, Radom
	42	Mikoyan MiG-29UB	SP 1.elt/23.BLT, Minsk/Mazowiecki
	042	PZL 130TC-II Orlik	SP 2.OSzL/42.BLSz, Radom
	043	PZL 130TC-II Orlik	SP 2.OSzL/42.BLSz, Radom
	045	PZL 130TC-I Orlik	SP 2.OSzL/42.BLSz, Radom
	047	PZL 130TC-II Orlik	SP 2.OSzL/42.BLSz, Radom
	048	PZL 130TC-II Orlik	SP 2.OSzL/42.BLSz, Radom
	049	PZL 130TC-I Orlik	SP 2.OSzL/42.BLSz, Radom
	050	PZL 130TC-II Orlik	SP 2.OSzL/42.BLSz, Radom
	051	PZL 130TC-II Orlik	SP 2.OSzL/42.BLSz, Radom
	052	PZL 130TC-II Orlik	SP 2.OSzL/42.BLSz, Radom
	54	Mikoyan MiG-29A	SP 1.elt/23.BLT, Minsk/Mazowiecki
	56	Mikoyan MiG-29A	SP 1.elt/23.BLT, Minsk/Mazowiecki
	59	Mikoyan MiG-29A	SP 1.elt/23.BLT, Minsk/Mazowiecki
	64	Mikoyan MiG-29UB	SP
	65	Mikoyan MiG-29A	SP 41.elt/22.BLT, Malbork
	66	Mikoyan MiG-29A	SP 41.elt/22.BLT, Malbork
	67	Mikoyan MiG-29A	*Crashed Mazowiecki, 18 December 2017*
	70	Mikoyan MiG-29A	SP 41.elt/22.BLT, Malbork
	83	Mikoyan MiG-29A	SP 1.elt/23.BLT, Minsk/Mazowiecki
	89	Mikoyan MiG-29A	SP 1.elt/23.BLT, Minsk/Mazowiecki
	92	Mikoyan MiG-29A	SP 41.elt/22.BLT, Malbork
	105	Mikoyan MiG-29A	SP 1.elt/23.BLT, Minsk/Mazowiecki
	108	Mikoyan MiG-29A	SP 1.elt/23.BLT, Minsk/Mazowiecki
	0110	Boeing 737-800 (N893BA)	SP 1.BLTr, Warszawa
	111	Mikoyan MiG-29A	SP 1.elt/23.BLT, Minsk/Mazowiecki
	114	Mikoyan MiG-29A	SP 1.elt/23.BLT, Minsk/Mazowiecki
	115	Mikoyan MiG-29A	SP 1.elt/23.BLT, Minsk/Mazowiecki
	0204	PZL M28B-TD Bryza	SP 1.OSzL/41.BLSz, Deblin
	0205	PZL M28B-TD Bryza	SP 1.OSzL/41.BLSz, Deblin
	0206	PZL M28B-TD Bryza	SP 14.eltr/33.BLTr, Powidz
	0207	PZL M28B-TD Bryza	SP 13.eltr/8.BLTr, Kraków/Balice
	0208	PZL M28B-TD Bryza	SP 14.eltr/33.BLTr, Powidz
	0209	PZL M28B-TD Bryza	SP 14.eltr/33.BLTr, Powidz
	0210	PZL M28B-TD Bryza	SP 14.eltr/33.BLTr, Powidz
	0211	PZL M28B-TD Bryza	SP 14.eltr/33.BLTr, Powidz
	0212	PZL M28B-TD Bryza	SP 13.eltr/8.BLTr, Kraków/Balice
	0213	PZL M28B/PT Bryza	SP 13.eltr/8.BLTr, Kraków/Balice
	0214	PZL M28B/PT Bryza	SP 13.eltr/8.BLTr, Kraków/Balice
	0215	PZL M28B/PT Bryza	SP 13.eltr/8.BLTr, Kraków/Balice
	0216	PZL M28B/PT Bryza	SP 13.eltr/8.BLTr, Kraków/Balice
	0217	PZL M28B/PT Bryza	SP 13.eltr/8.BLTr, Kraków/Balice
	0218	PZL M28B/PT Bryza	SP 13.eltr/8.BLTr, Kraków/Balice
	0219	PZL M28B/PT Bryza	SP 13.eltr/8.BLTr, Kraków/Balice
	0220	PZL M28B/PT Bryza	SP 13.eltr/8.BLTr, Kraków/Balice
	0221	PZL M28B/PT Bryza	SP 13.eltr/8.BLTr, Kraków/Balice
	0222	PZL M28B/PT Bryza	SP 13.eltr/8.BLTr, Kraków/Balice
	0223	PZL M28B/PT Bryza	SP 13.eltr/8.BLTr, Kraków/Balice
	0224	PZL M28B/PT Bryza	SP 13.eltr/8.BLTr, Kraków/Balice

Serial	Type (code/other identity)	Owner/operator, location or fate	Notes
0225	PZL M28B/PT Bryza	SP 13.eltr/8.BLTr, Kraków/Balice	
305	Sukhoi Su-22UM-3K	SP 8.elt/21.BLT, Swidwin	
308	Sukhoi Su-22UM-3K	SP 40.elt/21.BLT, Swidwin	
310	Sukhoi Su-22UM-3K	SP 40.elt/21.BLT, Swidwin	
0404	PZL M28B-1E Bryza	LMW 30.el/44.BLMW, Cewice/Siemirowice	
0405	PZL M28B-1E Bryza	LMW 30.el/44.BLMW, Cewice/Siemirowice	
508	Sukhoi Su-22UM-3K	SP 8.elt/21.BLT, Swidwin	
509	Sukhoi Su-22UM-3K	SP 40.elt/21.BLT, Swidwin	
707	Sukhoi Su-22UM-3K	SP 8.elt/21.BLT, Swidwin	
0723	PZL M28B-TD Bryza	LMW 28.el/43.BLMW, Gydnia/Babie Doly	
0810	PZL M28B-1RM Bryza	LMW 30.el/44.BLMW, Cewice/Siemirowice	
1001	Mil Mi-14PL	LMW 29.el/44.BLMW, Darlowo	
1002	Mil Mi-14PL	LMW 29.el/44.BLMW, Darlowo	
1003	Mil Mi-14PL	LMW 29.el/44.BLMW, Darlowo	
1003	PZL M28B-TD Bryza	LMW 28.el/43.BLMW, Gydnia/Babie Doly	
1005	Mil Mi-14PL	LMW 29.el/44.BLMW, Darlowo	
1006	PZL M28B-1R Bryza	LMW 30.el/44.BLMW, Cewice/Siemirowice	
1007	Mil Mi-14PL	LMW 29.el/44.BLMW, Darlowo	
1008	Mil Mi-14PL	LMW 29.el/44.BLMW, Darlowo	
1008	PZL M28B-1R Bryza	LMW 30.el/44.BLMW, Cewice/Siemirowice	
1009	Mil Mi-14PL	LMW 29.el/44.BLMW, Darlowo	
1010	Mil Mi-14PL	LMW 29.el/44.BLMW, Darlowo	
1011	Mil Mi-14PL	LMW 29.el/44.BLMW, Darlowo	
1012	Mil Mi-14PL/R	LMW 29.el/44.BLMW, Darlowo	
1017	PZL M28B-1R Bryza $	LMW 30.el/44.BLMW, Cewice/Siemirowice	
1022	PZL M28B-1R Bryza	LMW 30.el/44.BLMW, Cewice/Siemirowice	
1114	PZL M28B-1R Bryza	LMW 30.el/44.BLMW, Cewice/Siemirowice	
1115	PZL M28B-1R Bryza	LMW 30.el/44.BLMW, Cewice/Siemirowice	
1116	PZL M28B-1R Bryza	LMW 30.el/44.BLMW, Cewice/Siemirowice	
1117	PZL M28B-1 Bryza	LMW 28.el/43.BLMW, Gydnia/Babie Doly	
1118	PZL M28B-1 Bryza	LMW 28.el/43.BLMW, Gydnia/Babie Doly	
1501	Lockheed C-130E Hercules	SP 14.eltr/33.BLTr, Powidz	
1502	Lockheed C-130E Hercules	SP 14.eltr/33.BLTr, Powidz	
1503	Lockheed C-130E Hercules	SP 14.eltr/33.BLTr, Powidz	
1504	Lockheed C-130E Hercules	SP 14.eltr/33.BLTr, Powidz	
1505	Lockheed C-130E Hercules	SP 14.eltr/33.BLTr, Powidz	
3201	Sukhoi Su-22M-4	SP 8.elt/21.BLT, Swidwin	
3304	Sukhoi Su-22M-4	SP 8.elt/21.BLT, Swidwin	
3612	Sukhoi Su-22M-4	SP 40.elt/21.BLT, Swidwin	
3713	Sukhoi Su-22M-4 $	SP 40.elt/21.BLT, Swidwin	
3715	Sukhoi Su-22M-4	SP 40.elt/21.BLT, Swidwin	
3816	Sukhoi Su-22M-4	SP 40.elt/21.BLT, Swidwin	
3817	Sukhoi Su-22M-4	SP 40.elt/21.BLT, Swidwin	
3819	Sukhoi Su-22M-4	SP 8.elt/21.BLT, Swidwin	
3920	Sukhoi Su-22M-4	SP 40.elt/21.BLT, Swidwin	
4040	Lockheed Martin F-16C-52 Fighting Falcon	SP/USAF 416th FTS/412th TW, Edwards AFB, USA	
4041	Lockheed Martin F-16C-52 Fighting Falcon	SP 6.elt/31.BLT, Poznan/Krzesiny	
4042	Lockheed Martin F-16C-52 Fighting Falcon	SP 3.elt/31.BLT, Poznan/Krzesiny	
4043	Lockheed Martin F-16C-52 Fighting Falcon	SP 3.elt/31.BLT, Poznan/Krzesiny	
4044	Lockheed Martin F-16C-52 Fighting Falcon	SP 3.elt/31.BLT, Poznan/Krzesiny	
4045	Lockheed Martin F-16C-52 Fighting Falcon	SP 3.elt/31.BLT, Poznan/Krzesiny	
4046	Lockheed Martin F-16C-52 Fighting Falcon	SP 3.elt/31.BLT, Poznan/Krzesiny	
4047	Lockheed Martin F-16C-52 Fighting Falcon	SP 3.elt/31.BLT, Poznan/Krzesiny	
4048	Lockheed Martin F-16C-52 Fighting Falcon	SP 3.elt/31.BLT, Poznan/Krzesiny	
4049	Lockheed Martin F-16C-52 Fighting Falcon	SP 3.elt/31.BLT, Poznan/Krzesiny	
4050	Lockheed Martin F-16C-52 Fighting Falcon	SP 3.elt/31.BLT, Poznan/Krzesiny	
4051	Lockheed Martin F-16C-52 Fighting Falcon	SP 3.elt/31.BLT, Poznan/Krzesiny	
4052	Lockheed Martin F-16C-52 Fighting Falcon $	SP 6.elt/31.BLT, Poznan/Krzesiny	
4053	Lockheed Martin F-16C-52 Fighting Falcon	SP 6.elt/31.BLT, Poznan/Krzesiny	
4054	Lockheed Martin F-16C-52 Fighting Falcon	SP 6.elt/31.BLT, Poznan/Krzesiny	
4055	Lockheed Martin F-16C-52 Fighting Falcon $	SP 6.elt/31.BLT, Poznan/Krzesiny	
4056	Lockheed Martin F-16C-52 Fighting Falcon $	SP 6.elt/31.BLT, Poznan/Krzesiny	

Notes	Serial	Type (code/other identity)	Owner/operator, location or fate
	4057	Lockheed Martin F-16C-52 Fighting Falcon	SP 6.elt/31.BLT, Poznan/Krzesiny
	4058	Lockheed Martin F-16C-52 Fighting Falcon	SP 6.elt/31.BLT, Poznan/Krzesiny
	4059	Lockheed Martin F-16C-52 Fighting Falcon	SP 6.elt/31.BLT, Poznan/Krzesiny
	4060	Lockheed Martin F-16C-52 Fighting Falcon	SP 6.elt/31.BLT, Poznan/Krzesiny
	4061	Lockheed Martin F-16C-52 Fighting Falcon	SP 6.elt/31.BLT, Poznan/Krzesiny
	4062	Lockheed Martin F-16C-52 Fighting Falcon $	SP 6.elt/31.BLT, Poznan/Krzesiny
	4063	Lockheed Martin F-16C-52 Fighting Falcon	SP 10.elt/32.BLT, Lask
	4064	Lockheed Martin F-16C-52 Fighting Falcon	SP 10.elt/32.BLT, Lask
	4065	Lockheed Martin F-16C-52 Fighting Falcon	SP 10.elt/32.BLT, Lask
	4066	Lockheed Martin F-16C-52 Fighting Falcon	SP 10.elt/32.BLT, Lask
	4067	Lockheed Martin F-16C-52 Fighting Falcon	SP 10.elt/32.BLT, Lask
	4068	Lockheed Martin F-16C-52 Fighting Falcon	SP 10.elt/32.BLT, Lask
	4069	Lockheed Martin F-16C-52 Fighting Falcon	SP 10.elt/32.BLT, Lask
	4070	Lockheed Martin F-16C-52 Fighting Falcon	SP 10.elt/32.BLT, Lask
	4071	Lockheed Martin F-16C-52 Fighting Falcon	SP 10.elt/32.BLT, Lask
	4072	Lockheed Martin F-16C-52 Fighting Falcon	SP 10.elt/32.BLT, Lask
	4073	Lockheed Martin F-16C-52 Fighting Falcon	SP 10.elt/32.BLT, Lask
	4074	Lockheed Martin F-16C-52 Fighting Falcon	SP 10.elt/32.BLT, Lask
	4075	Lockheed Martin F-16C-52 Fighting Falcon	SP 10.elt/32.BLT, Lask
	4076	Lockheed Martin F-16D-52 Fighting Falcon	SP 3.elt/31.BLT, Poznan/Krzesiny
	4077	Lockheed Martin F-16D-52 Fighting Falcon	SP 3.elt/31.BLT, Poznan/Krzesiny
	4078	Lockheed Martin F-16D-52 Fighting Falcon	SP 3.elt/31.BLT, Poznan/Krzesiny
	4079	Lockheed Martin F-16D-52 Fighting Falcon	SP 3.elt/31.BLT, Poznan/Krzesiny
	4080	Lockheed Martin F-16D-52 Fighting Falcon	SP 3.elt/31.BLT, Poznan/Krzesiny
	4081	Lockheed Martin F-16D-52 Fighting Falcon	SP 3.elt/31.BLT, Poznan/Krzesiny
	4082	Lockheed Martin F-16D-52 Fighting Falcon $	SP 6.elt/31.BLT, Poznan/Krzesiny
	4083	Lockheed Martin F-16D-52 Fighting Falcon $	SP 6.elt/31.BLT, Poznan/Krzesiny
	4084	Lockheed Martin F-16D-52 Fighting Falcon $	SP 6.elt/31.BLT, Poznan/Krzesiny
	4085	Lockheed Martin F-16D-52 Fighting Falcon	SP 10.elt/32.BLT, Lask
	4086	Lockheed Martin F-16D-52 Fighting Falcon	SP 10.elt/32.BLT, Lask
	4087	Lockheed Martin F-16D-52 Fighting Falcon	SP 10.elt/32.BLT, Lask
	4101	Mikoyan MiG-29A	SP 41.elt/22.BLT, Malbork
	4103	Mikoyan MiG-29A	SP 41.elt/22.BLT, Malbork
	4104	Mikoyan MiG-29A	SP 41.elt/22.BLT, Malbork
	4105	Mikoyan MiG-29A	SP 1.elt/23.BLT, Minsk/Mazowiecki
	4110	Mikoyan MiG-29UB	SP 41.elt/22.BLT, Malbork
	4113	Mikoyan MiG-29A	SP 41.elt/22.BLT, Malbork
	4116	Mikoyan MiG-29A	SP 41.elt/22.BLT, Malbork
	4120	Mikoyan MiG-29A	SP 41.elt/22.BLT, Malbork
	4121	Mikoyan MiG-29A	SP 41.elt/22.BLT, Malbork
	4122	Mikoyan MiG-29A	SP 41.elt/22.BLT, Malbork
	4123	Mikoyan MiG-29UB	SP 41.elt/22.BLT, Malbork
	7411	Sukhoi Su-22M-4	*Withdrawn from use, April 2014*
	7412	Sukhoi Su-22M-4	*Withdrawn from use, June 2014*
	7701	Aermacchi M-346 Master (CSX55209)	SP 1.OSzL/41.BLSz, Deblin
	7702	Aermacchi M-346 Master (CSX55210)	SP 1.OSzL/41.BLSz, Deblin
	7703	Aermacchi M-346 Master (CSX55211)	SP 1.OSzL/41.BLSz, Deblin
	7704	Aermacchi M-346 Master	SP 1.OSzL/41.BLSz, Deblin
	7705	Aermacchi M-346 Master (MM55225)	SP 1.OSzL/41.BLSz, Deblin
	7706	Aermacchi M-346 Master (MM55226)	SP 1.OSzL/41.BLSz, Deblin
	7707	Aermacchi M-346 Master (MT55227)	SP 1.OSzL/41.BLSz, Deblin
	7708	Aermacchi M-346 Master	SP 1.OSzL/41.BLSz, Deblin
	8101	Sukhoi Su-22M-4	SP 40.elt/21.BLT, Swidwin
	8102	Sukhoi Su-22M-4	*Withdrawn from use, August 2014*
	8103	Sukhoi Su-22M-4	*Withdrawn from use, March 2015*
	8205	Sukhoi Su-22M-4	SP 40.elt/21.BLT, Swidwin
	8308	Sukhoi Su-22M-4 $	*Withdrawn from use, June 2014*
	8309	Sukhoi Su-22M-4	SP 40.elt/21.BLT, Swidwin
	8310	Sukhoi Su-22M-4	*Withdrawn from use, March 2015*
	8715	Sukhoi Su-22M-4	*Withdrawn from use, July 2015*
	8816	Sukhoi Su-22M-4	*Withdrawn from use, August 2015*
	8818	Sukhoi Su-22M-4 $	*Withdrawn from use, October 2013*

Serial	Type (code/other identity)	Owner/operator, location or fate	Notes
919	Sukhoi Su-22M-4 $	*Withdrawn from use, May 2014*	
920	Sukhoi Su-22M-4	*Withdrawn from use, May 2014*	
102	Sukhoi Su-22M-4 $	*Withdrawn from use, June 2015*	
615	Sukhoi Su-22M-4	*Withdrawn from use, August 2015*	
616	Sukhoi Su-22M-4	*Withdrawn from use, August 2015*	
..	Boeing 737-800	SP (on order)	
.	Boeing 737-800	SP (on order)	
Straz Graniczna (Polish Border Guard)			
SN-50YG	PZL M28-05 Skytruck	Straz Graniczna, Gdansk/Rebiechowo	
SN-60YG	PZL M28-05 Skytruck	Straz Graniczna, Gdansk/Rebiechowo	
Polish Government			
SP-LIG	Embraer EMB.175-200LR	Polish Government, Warszawa	
SP-LIH	Embraer EMB.175-200LR	Polish Government, Warszawa	
PORTUGAL			
Força Aérea Portuguesa (FAP)/Marinha			
1401	Aérospatiale TB-30 Epsilon	FAP Esq 101, Sintra	
1402	Aérospatiale TB-30 Epsilon	FAP Esq 101, Sintra	
1403	Aérospatiale TB-30 Epsilon	FAP Esq 101, Sintra	
1404	Aérospatiale TB-30 Epsilon	FAP Esq 101, Sintra	
1405	Aérospatiale TB-30 Epsilon $	FAP Esq 101, Sintra	
1406	Aérospatiale TB-30 Epsilon	FAP Esq 101, Sintra	
1407	Aérospatiale TB-30 Epsilon	FAP Esq 101, Sintra	
1409	Aérospatiale TB-30 Epsilon	FAP Esq 101, Sintra	
1410	Aérospatiale TB-30 Epsilon $	FAP Esq 101, Sintra	
1411	Aérospatiale TB-30 Epsilon	FAP Esq 101, Sintra	
1413	Aérospatiale TB-30 Epsilon	FAP Esq 101, Sintra	
1414	Aérospatiale TB-30 Epsilon	FAP Esq 101, Sintra	
1415	Aérospatiale TB-30 Epsilon	FAP Esq 101, Sintra	
1416	Aérospatiale TB-30 Epsilon $	FAP Esq 101, Sintra	
1417	Aérospatiale TB-30 Epsilon	FAP Esq 101, Sintra	
1418	Aérospatiale TB-30 Epsilon	FAP Esq 101, Sintra	
4807	Lockheed P-3C CUP+ Orion	FAP Esq 601, Beja	
4808	Lockheed P-3C CUP+ Orion $	FAP Esq 601, Beja	
4809	Lockheed P-3C CUP+ Orion	FAP Esq 601, Beja	
4810	Lockheed P-3C CUP+ Orion	FAP, stored Beja	
4811	Lockheed P-3C CUP+ Orion	FAP Esq 601, Beja	
5101	Lockheed Martin F-16A MLU Fighting Falcon	FAP Esq 201/Esq 301, Monte Real	
5102	Lockheed Martin F-16A MLU Fighting Falcon	FAP Esq 201/Esq 301, Monte Real	
5103	Lockheed Martin F-16A MLU Fighting Falcon	FAP Esq 201/Esq 301, Monte Real	
5104	Lockheed Martin F-16A MLU Fighting Falcon	FAP Esq 201/Esq 301, Monte Real	
5105	Lockheed Martin F-16A MLU Fighting Falcon	FAP Esq 201/Esq 301, Monte Real	
5106	Lockheed Martin F-16A MLU Fighting Falcon $	FAP Esq 201/Esq 301, Monte Real	
5107	Lockheed Martin F-16A MLU Fighting Falcon	FAP Esq 201/Esq 301, Monte Real	
5108	Lockheed Martin F-16A MLU Fighting Falcon	FAP Esq 201/Esq 301, Monte Real	
5109	Lockheed Martin F-16A MLU Fighting Falcon	FAP Esq 201/Esq 301, Monte Real	
5110	Lockheed Martin F-16A MLU Fighting Falcon	FAP Esq 201/Esq 301, Monte Real	
5112	Lockheed Martin F-16A MLU Fighting Falcon	FAP Esq 201/Esq 301, Monte Real	
5113	Lockheed Martin F-16A MLU Fighting Falcon	FAP Esq 201/Esq 301, Monte Real	
5114	Lockheed Martin F-16A MLU Fighting Falcon	FAP Esq 201/Esq 301, Monte Real	
5115	Lockheed Martin F-16A MLU Fighting Falcon	FAP Esq 201/Esq 301, Monte Real	
5116	Lockheed Martin F-16A MLU Fighting Falcon	FAP Esq 201/Esq 301, Monte Real	
5117	Lockheed Martin F-16A MLU Fighting Falcon	FAP Esq 201/Esq 301, Monte Real	
5118	Lockheed Martin F-16B MLU Fighting Falcon	FAP Esq 201/Esq 301, Monte Real	
5119	Lockheed Martin F-16B MLU Fighting Falcon	FAP Esq 201/Esq 301, Monte Real	
5120	Lockheed Martin F-16B MLU Fighting Falcon	FAP Esq 201/Esq 301, Monte Real	
5122	Lockheed Martin F-16A MLU Fighting Falcon	FAP Esq 201/Esq 301, Monte Real	
5131	Lockheed Martin F-16A MLU Fighting Falcon	FAP Esq 201/Esq 301, Monte Real	
5132	Lockheed Martin F-16A MLU Fighting Falcon	FAP Esq 201/Esq 301, Monte Real	
5133	Lockheed Martin F-16A MLU Fighting Falcon	FAP Esq 201/Esq 301, Monte Real	
5134	Lockheed Martin F-16A MLU Fighting Falcon	FAP Esq 201/Esq 301, Monte Real	
5135	Lockheed Martin F-16A MLU Fighting Falcon	FAP Esq 201/Esq 301, Monte Real	

Notes	Serial	Type (code/other identity)	Owner/operator, location or fate
	15136	Lockheed Martin F-16A MLU Fighting Falcon	FAP Esq 201/Esq 301, Monte Real
	15141	Lockheed Martin F-16A MLU Fighting Falcon	FAP Esq 201/Esq 301, Monte Real
	15202	D-BD Alpha Jet A	*Withdrawn from use, January 2018*
	15206	D-BD Alpha Jet A	*Withdrawn from use, January 2018*
	15208	D-BD Alpha Jet A	*Withdrawn from use, January 2018*
	15211	D-BD Alpha Jet A $	*Withdrawn from use, January 2018*
	15220	D-BD Alpha Jet A	*Withdrawn from use, January 2018*
	15226	D-BD Alpha Jet A	*Withdrawn from use, January 2018*
	15227	D-BD Alpha Jet A	*Withdrawn from use, January 2018*
	15230	D-BD Alpha Jet A	*Withdrawn from use, January 2018*
	15236	D-BD Alpha Jet A	*Withdrawn from use, January 2018*
	15250	D-BD Alpha Jet A	*Withdrawn from use, January 2018*
	16701	CASA C-295M	FAP Esq 502, Lisbon/Montijo & Lajes
	16702	CASA C-295M	FAP Esq 502, Lisbon/Montijo & Lajes
	16703	CASA C-295M	FAP Esq 502, Lisbon/Montijo & Lajes
	16704	CASA C-295M	FAP Esq 502, Lisbon/Montijo & Lajes
	16705	CASA C-295M $	FAP Esq 502, Lisbon/Montijo & Lajes
	16706	CASA C-295M	FAP Esq 502, Lisbon/Montijo & Lajes
	16707	CASA C-295M	FAP Esq 502, Lisbon/Montijo & Lajes
	16708	CASA C-295MPA	FAP Esq 502, Lisbon/Montijo & Lajes
	16709	CASA C-295MPA	FAP Esq 502, Lisbon/Montijo & Lajes
	16710	CASA C-295MPA	FAP Esq 502, Lisbon/Montijo & Lajes
	16711	CASA C-295MPA	FAP Esq 502, Lisbon/Montijo & Lajes
	16712	CASA C-295MPA	FAP Esq 502, Lisbon/Montijo & Lajes
	16801	Lockheed C-130H-30 Hercules	FAP Esq 501, Lisbon/Montijo
	16802	Lockheed C-130H-30 Hercules	FAP Esq 501, Lisbon/Montijo
	16803	Lockheed C-130H Hercules $	FAP Esq 501, Lisbon/Montijo
	16805	Lockheed C-130H Hercules	FAP Esq 501, Lisbon/Montijo
	16806	Lockheed C-130H-30 Hercules	FAP Esq 501, Lisbon/Montijo
	17401	Dassault Falcon 50	FAP Esq 504, Lisbon/Montijo
	17402	Dassault Falcon 50	FAP Esq 504, Lisbon/Montijo
	17403	Dassault Falcon 50	FAP Esq 504, Lisbon/Montijo
	19201	Westland Super Lynx Mk.95	Marinha Esq de Helicopteros, Lisbon/Montijo
	19202	Westland Super Lynx Mk.95	Marinha Esq de Helicopteros, Lisbon/Montijo
	19203	Westland Super Lynx Mk.95	Marinha Esq de Helicopteros, Lisbon/Montijo
	19204	Westland Super Lynx Mk.95	Leonardo MW, Yeovil, UK (update)
	19205	Westland Super Lynx Mk.95	Marinha Esq de Helicopteros, Lisbon/Montijo
	19601	EHI EH-101 Mk.514	FAP Esq 751, Lisbon/Montijo
	19602	EHI EH-101 Mk.514	FAP Esq 751, Lisbon/Montijo
	19603	EHI EH-101 Mk.514	FAP Esq 751, Lisbon/Montijo
	19604	EHI EH-101 Mk.514	FAP Esq 751, Lisbon/Montijo
	19605	EHI EH-101 Mk.514	FAP Esq 751, Lisbon/Montijo
	19606	EHI EH-101 Mk.514	FAP Esq 751, Lisbon/Montijo
	19607	EHI EH-101 Mk.515	FAP Esq 751, Lisbon/Montijo
	19608	EHI EH-101 Mk.515	FAP Esq 751, Lisbon/Montijo
	19609	EHI EH-101 Mk.516	FAP Esq 751, Lisbon/Montijo
	19610	EHI EH-101 Mk.516	FAP Esq 751, Lisbon/Montijo
	19611	EHI EH-101 Mk.516	FAP Esq 751, Lisbon/Montijo
	19612	EHI EH-101 Mk.516	FAP Esq 751, Lisbon/Montijo

QATAR

Qatar Emiri Air Force (QEAF)

Notes	Serial	Type (code/other identity)	Owner/operator, location or fate
	211	Lockheed C-130J-30 Hercules II (08-0211) [MAH]	QEAF 12 Transport Sqn, Al-Udeid
	212	Lockheed C-130J-30 Hercules II (08-0212) [MAI]	QEAF 12 Transport Sqn, Al-Udeid
	213	Lockheed C-130J-30 Hercules II (08-0213) [MAJ]	QEAF 12 Transport Sqn, Al-Udeid
	214	Lockheed C-130J-30 Hercules II (08-0214) [MAK]	QEAF 12 Transport Sqn, Al-Udeid
	MAA	Boeing C-17A Globemaster III (08-0201)	QEAF 12 Transport Sqn, Al-Udeid
	MAB	Boeing C-17A Globemaster III (08-0202)	QEAF 12 Transport Sqn, Al-Udeid
	MAC	Boeing C-17A Globemaster III (12-0203)	QEAF 12 Transport Sqn, Al-Udeid
	MAE	Boeing C-17A Globemaster III (12-0204)	QEAF 12 Transport Sqn, Al-Udeid
	MAM	Boeing C-17A Globemaster III (14-0005)	QEAF 12 Transport Sqn, Al-Udeid
	MAN	Boeing C-17A Globemaster III (14-0006)	QEAF 12 Transport Sqn, Al-Udeid

Serial	Type (code/other identity)	Owner/operator, location or fate	Notes
MAO	Boeing C-17A Globemaster III (14-0009)	QEAF 12 Transport Sqn, Al-Udeid	
MAP	Boeing C-17A Globemaster III (14-0010)	QEAF 12 Transport Sqn, Al-Udeid	
Qatari Government			
A7-AAG	Airbus A.320-232	Qatari Amiri Flight, Doha	
A7-AAH	Airbus A.340-313X	Qatari Amiri Flight, Doha	
A7-AAM	Bombardier Global Express	Qatari Amiri Flight/Qatar Airways, Doha	
A7-AFE	Airbus A.310-308	Qatari Amiri Flight, Doha	
A7-HBJ	Boeing 747-8KB	Qatari Amiri Flight, Doha	
A7-HHE	Boeing 747-8KJ	Qatari Amiri Flight, Doha	
A7-HHF	Boeing 747-8Z5	Qatari Amiri Flight, Doha	
A7-HHH	Airbus A.340-541	Qatari Amiri Flight, Doha	
A7-HHJ	Airbus A.319CJ-133	Qatari Amiri Flight, Doha	
A7-HHK	Airbus A.340-211	Qatari Amiri Flight, Doha	
A7-HHM	Airbus A.330-203	Qatari Amiri Flight, Doha	
A7-HJJ	Airbus A.330-202	Qatari Amiri Flight, Doha	
A7-HSJ	Airbus A.320-232	Qatari Amiri Flight, Doha	
A7-MBK	Airbus A.320-232CJ	Qatari Amiri Flight, Doha	
A7-MED	Airbus A.319CJ-133	Qatari Amiri Flight, Doha	
A7-MHH	Airbus A.319CJ-115	Qatari Amiri Flight, Doha	
ROMANIA			
Fortele Aeriene Romania (FAR)			
2701	Alenia C-27J Spartan	FAR Escadrila 902, Bucharest/Otopeni	
2702	Alenia C-27J Spartan	FAR Escadrila 902, Bucharest/Otopeni	
703	Alenia C-27J Spartan	FAR Escadrila 902, Bucharest/Otopeni	
2704	Alenia C-27J Spartan	FAR Escadrila 902, Bucharest/Otopeni	
2705	Alenia C-27J Spartan	FAR Escadrila 902, Bucharest/Otopeni	
706	Alenia C-27J Spartan	FAR Escadrila 902, Bucharest/Otopeni	
707	Alenia C-27J Spartan	FAR Escadrila 902, Bucharest/Otopeni	
6930	Lockheed C-130B Hercules	FAR Escadrila 901, Bucharest/Otopeni	
6166	Lockheed C-130H Hercules	FAR Escadrila 901, Bucharest/Otopeni	
6191	Lockheed C-130H Hercules	FAR Escadrila 901, Bucharest/Otopeni	
RUSSIA			
Voenno-Vozdushniye Sily Rossioki Federatsii (VVS) (Russian Air Force)/Russian Government			
95 w	Sukhoi Su-27P(LL) (36911037511)	VVS, Gromov Research Institute, Zhukhovsky	
97 w	Sukhoi Su-30LL (79371010102)	VVS, Gromov Research Institute, Zhukhovsky	
698 w	Sukhoi Su-27P(LL) (36911037820)	VVS, Gromov Research Institute, Zhukhovsky	
RA-09007	Dassault Falcon 7X	Rossiya Special Flight Det, Moscow/Vnukovo	
RA-26226	Antonov An-30	VVS (Open Skies), Moscow/Kubinka	
RA-30078	Antonov An-30	VVS (Open Skies), Moscow/Kubinka	
RA-64053	Tupolev Tu-204-300	Rossiya Special Flight Det, Moscow/Vnukovo	
RA-64057	Tupolev Tu-204-300	Rossiya Special Flight Det, Moscow/Vnukovo	
RA-64058	Tupolev Tu-204-300	Rossiya Special Flight Det, Moscow/Vnukovo	
RA-64059	Tupolev Tu-204-300	Rossiya Special Flight Det, Moscow/Vnukovo	
RA-64504	Tupolev Tu-214	Rossiya Special Flight Det, Moscow/Vnukovo	
RA-64505	Tupolev Tu-214	Rossiya Special Flight Det, Moscow/Vnukovo	
RA-64506	Tupolev Tu-214	Rossiya Special Flight Det, Moscow/Vnukovo	
RA-64515	Tupolev Tu-214SR	Rossiya Special Flight Det, Moscow/Vnukovo	
RA-64516	Tupolev Tu-214SR	Rossiya Special Flight Det, Moscow/Vnukovo	
RA-64517	Tupolev Tu-214PU	Rossiya Special Flight Det, Moscow/Vnukovo	
RA-64520	Tupolev Tu-214PU	Rossiya Special Flight Det, Moscow/Vnukovo	
RA-64521	Tupolev Tu-214	Rossiya Special Flight Det, Ulyanovsk	
RA-64522	Tupolev Tu-214SUS	Rossiya Special Flight Det, Moscow/Vnukovo	
RA-64524	Tupolev Tu-214SUS	Rossiya Special Flight Det, Moscow/Vnukovo	
RA-64526	Tupolev Tu-214SR	Rossiya Special Flight Det, Moscow/Vnukovo	
RA-64527	Tupolev Tu-214SR	Rossiya Special Flight Det, Moscow/Vnukovo	
RA-64528	Tupolev Tu-214SR	Rossiya Special Flight Det, Moscow/Vnukovo	
RA-65904	Tupolev Tu-134AK-3	Rossiya Special Flight Det, Moscow/Vnukovo	
RA-65905	Tupolev Tu-134AK-3	Rossiya Special Flight Det, Moscow/Vnukovo	
RA-65911	Tupolev Tu-134AK-3	Rossiya Special Flight Det, Moscow/Vnukovo	
RA-73026	Airbus A.319-115CJ	Rossiya Special Flight Det, Moscow/Vnukovo	

Notes	Serial	Type (code/other identity)	Owner/operator, location or fate
	RA-73026	Airbus A.319-115CJ	Rossiya Special Flight Det, Moscow/Vnukovo
	RA-82011	Antonov An-124	VVS 224th Transport Regiment, Seshcha/Bryans
	RA-82021	Antonov An-124	VVS 224th Transport Regiment, Seshcha/Bryans
	RA-82023	Antonov An-124	VVS 224th Transport Regiment, Seshcha/Bryans
	RA-82025	Antonov An-124	VVS 224th Transport Regiment, Seshcha/Bryans
	RA-82028	Antonov An-124	VVS 224th Transport Regiment, Seshcha/Bryans
	RA-82030	Antonov An-124	VVS 224th Transport Regiment, Seshcha/Bryans
	RA-82032	Antonov An-124	VVS 224th Transport Regiment, Seshcha/Bryans
	RA-82035	Antonov An-124	VVS 224th Transport Regiment, Seshcha/Bryans
	RA-82036	Antonov An-124	VVS 224th Transport Regiment, Seshcha/Bryans
	RA-82038	Antonov An-124	VVS 224th Transport Regiment, Seshcha/Bryans
	RA-82039	Antonov An-124	VVS 224th Transport Regiment, Seshcha/Bryans
	RA-82040	Antonov An-124	VVS 224th Transport Regiment, Seshcha/Bryans
	RA-82041	Antonov An-124	VVS 224th Transport Regiment, Seshcha/Bryans
	RA-85041	Tupolev Tu-154M	VVS 6991 AvB, Chalovskiy
	RA-85155	Tupolev Tu-154M	VVS 8 oae, Chalovskiy
	RA-85629	Tupolev Tu-154M	*Scrapped*
	RA-85631	Tupolev Tu-154M	*Scrapped*
	RA-85659	Tupolev Tu-154M	*Scrapped*
	RA-85843	Tupolev Tu-154M	*Withdrawn from use*
	RA-86466	Ilyushin Il-62M	*Scrapped*
	RA-86467	Ilyushin Il-62M	*Scrapped*
	RA-86468	Ilyushin Il-62M	*Scrapped*
	RA-86536	Ilyushin Il-62M	*Scrapped*
	RA-86540	Ilyushin Il-62M	*Withdrawn from use*
	RA-86710	Ilyushin Il-62M	*Scrapped*
	RA-86712	Ilyushin Il-62M	*Withdrawn from use*
	RA-96012	Ilyushin Il-96-300PU	Rossiya Special Flight Det, Moscow/Vnukovo
	RA-96016	Ilyushin Il-96-300PU	Rossiya Special Flight Det, Moscow/Vnukovo
	RA-96017	Ilyushin Il-96-300S	Rossiya Special Flight Det, Moscow/Vnukovo
	RA-96018	Ilyushin Il-96-300	Rossiya Special Flight Det, Moscow/Vnukovo
	RA-96019	Ilyushin Il-96-300	Rossiya Special Flight Det, Moscow/Vnukovo
	RA-96020	Ilyushin Il-96-300PU	Rossiya Special Flight Det, Moscow/Vnukovo
	RA-96021	Ilyushin Il-96-300PU	Rossiya Special Flight Det, Moscow/Vnukovo
	RA-96022	Ilyushin Il-96-300PU	Rossiya Special Flight Det, Moscow/Vnukovo
	RA-96023	Ilyushin Il-96-300	Rossiya Special Flight Det, Moscow/Vnukovo
	RA-96102	Ilyushin Il-96-400T	Rossiya Special Flight Det, Moscow/Vnukovo
	RA-96104	Ilyushin Il-96-400T	Rossiya Special Flight Det, Moscow/Vnukovo
	RF-36052	Antonov An-30B (87 bk)	VVS (Open Skies), Moscow/Kubinka
	RF-64519	Tupolev Tu-214ON	VVS (Open Skies), Moscow/Kubinka
	RF-85655	Tupolev Tu-154M-LK1	VVS (Open Skies), Moscow/Kubinka

SAUDI ARABIA

Al Quwwat al Jawwiya as Sa'udiya/Royal Saudi Air Force (RSAF) & Saudi Government

Notes	Serial	Type (code/other identity)	Owner/operator, location or fate
	111	Lockheed VC-130H Hercules	RSAF 1 Sqn, Riyadh
	112	Lockheed VC-130H Hercules	RSAF 1 Sqn, Riyadh
	464	Lockheed C-130H Hercules	RSAF 4 Sqn, Jeddah
	465	Lockheed C-130H Hercules	RSAF 4 Sqn, Jeddah
	466	Lockheed C-130H Hercules	RSAF 4 Sqn, Jeddah
	467	Lockheed C-130H Hercules	RSAF 4 Sqn, Jeddah
	468	Lockheed C-130H Hercules	RSAF 4 Sqn, Jeddah
	472	Lockheed C-130H Hercules	RSAF 4 Sqn, Jeddah
	473	Lockheed C-130H Hercules	RSAF 4 Sqn, Jeddah
	474	Lockheed C-130H Hercules	RSAF 4 Sqn, Jeddah
	475	Lockheed C-130H Hercules	RSAF 4 Sqn, Jeddah
	477	Lockheed C-130H Hercules	RSAF 4 Sqn, Jeddah
	478	Lockheed C-130H Hercules	RSAF 4 Sqn, Jeddah
	482	Lockheed C-130H Hercules	RSAF 4 Sqn, Jeddah
	483	Lockheed C-130H Hercules	RSAF 4 Sqn, Jeddah
	484	Lockheed C-130H Hercules	RSAF 4 Sqn, Jeddah
	485	Lockheed C-130H Hercules	RSAF 4 Sqn, Jeddah
	486	Lockheed C-130H Hercules	RSAF 4 Sqn, Jeddah

Serial	Type (code/other identity)	Owner/operator, location or fate	Notes
01	Lockheed C-130H Hercules	RSAF 4 Sqn, Jeddah	
02	Lockheed C-130H Hercules	RSAF 16 Sqn, Jeddah	
04	Lockheed C-130H Hercules	RSAF 16 Sqn, Jeddah	
05	Lockheed C-130H Hercules	RSAF 16 Sqn, Jeddah	
15	Lockheed C-130H Hercules	RSAF 16 Sqn, Jeddah	
22	Lockheed C-130H-30 Hercules	RSAF 16 Sqn, Jeddah	
23	Lockheed C-130H Hercules	RSAF 16 Sqn, Jeddah	
24	Lockheed C-130H Hercules	RSAF 16 Sqn, Jeddah	
25	Lockheed C-130H Hercules	RSAF 16 Sqn, Jeddah	
26	Lockheed C-130H Hercules	RSAF 16 Sqn, Jeddah	
27	Lockheed C-130H Hercules	RSAF 16 Sqn, Jeddah	
28	Lockheed C-130H Hercules	RSAF 16 Sqn, Jeddah	
29	Lockheed C-130H Hercules	RSAF 16 Sqn, Jeddah	
30	Lockheed C-130H-30 Hercules	RSAF 16 Sqn, Jeddah	
31	Lockheed C-130H-30 Hercules	RSAF 16 Sqn, Jeddah	
32	Lockheed L.100-30 Hercules	RSAF 16 Sqn, Jeddah	
01	Boeing E-3A Sentry	RSAF 18 Sqn, Al Kharj	
02	Boeing E-3A Sentry	RSAF 18 Sqn, Al Kharj	
03	Boeing E-3A Sentry	RSAF 18 Sqn, Al Kharj	
04	Boeing E-3A Sentry	RSAF 18 Sqn, Al Kharj	
05	Boeing E-3A Sentry	RSAF 18 Sqn, Al Kharj	
01	Boeing RE-3A Sentry	RSAF 19 Sqn, Al Kharj	
02	Boeing RE-3A Sentry	RSAF 19 Sqn, Al Kharj	
01	Boeing KE-3A Sentry (1811)	RSAF 23 Sqn, Al Kharj	
02	Boeing KE-3A Sentry (1812)	RSAF 23 Sqn, Al Kharj	
03	Boeing KE-3A Sentry (1813)	RSAF 23 Sqn, Al Kharj	
04	Boeing KE-3A Sentry (1814)	RSAF 23 Sqn, Al Kharj	
05	Boeing KE-3A Sentry (1815)	RSAF 23 Sqn, Al Kharj	
06	Boeing KE-3A Sentry (1816)	RSAF 23 Sqn, Al Kharj	
07	Boeing KE-3A Sentry (1818)	RSAF 23 Sqn, Al Kharj	
01	Airbus A.330-203 MRTT	RSAF 24 Sqn, Al Kharj	
02	Airbus A.330-203 MRTT	RSAF 24 Sqn, Al Kharj	
03	Airbus A.330-203 MRTT	RSAF 24 Sqn, Al Kharj	
04	Airbus A.330-203 MRTT	RSAF 24 Sqn, Al Kharj	
05	Airbus A.330-203 MRTT	RSAF 24 Sqn, Al Kharj	
06	Airbus A.330-203 MRTT	RSAF 24 Sqn, Al Kharj	
01	Lockheed KC-130H Hercules	RSAF 32 Sqn, Al Kharj	
02	Lockheed KC-130H Hercules	RSAF 32 Sqn, Al Kharj	
03	Lockheed KC-130H Hercules	RSAF 32 Sqn, Al Kharj	
04	Lockheed KC-130H Hercules	RSAF 32 Sqn, Al Kharj	
05	Lockheed KC-130H Hercules	RSAF 32 Sqn, Al Kharj	
06	Lockheed KC-130H Hercules	RSAF 32 Sqn, Al Kharj	
07	Lockheed KC-130H Hercules	RSAF 32 Sqn, Al Kharj	
08	Lockheed KC-130J Hercules II	RSAF 32 Sqn, Al Kharj	
09	Lockheed KC-130J Hercules II	RSAF 32 Sqn, Al Kharj	
05	BAe Hawk 65A	RSAF 88 Sqn, *Saudi Hawks*, Tabuk	
06	BAe Hawk 65A	RSAF 88 Sqn, *Saudi Hawks*, Tabuk	
07	BAe Hawk 65	RSAF 88 Sqn, *Saudi Hawks*, Tabuk	
08	BAe Hawk 65	RSAF 88 Sqn, *Saudi Hawks*, Tabuk	
10	BAe Hawk 65	RSAF 88 Sqn, *Saudi Hawks*, Tabuk	
11	BAe Hawk 65A	RSAF 88 Sqn, *Saudi Hawks*, Tabuk	
12	BAe Hawk 65A	RSAF 88 Sqn, *Saudi Hawks*, Tabuk	
13	BAe Hawk 65	RSAF 88 Sqn, *Saudi Hawks*, Tabuk	
14	BAe Hawk 65	RSAF 88 Sqn, *Saudi Hawks*, Tabuk	
16	BAe Hawk 65	RSAF 88 Sqn, *Saudi Hawks*, Tabuk	
17	BAe Hawk 65	RSAF 88 Sqn, *Saudi Hawks*, Tabuk	
18	BAe Hawk 65A	RSAF 88 Sqn, *Saudi Hawks*, Tabuk	
20	BAe Hawk 65	RSAF 88 Sqn, *Saudi Hawks*, Tabuk	
21	BAe Hawk 65	RSAF 88 Sqn, *Saudi Hawks*, Tabuk	
Z-101	Boeing 737-7DP	RSAF 1 Sqn, Riyadh	
Z-102	Boeing 737-8DP	RSAF 1 Sqn, Riyadh	
Z-103	Grumman G.1159C Gulfstream IV	RSAF 1 Sqn, Riyadh	

Notes	Serial	Type (code/other identity)	Owner/operator, location or fate
	HZ-105	BAe 125-800	RSAF 1 Sqn, Riyadh
	HZ-109	BAe 125-800B	RSAF 1 Sqn, Riyadh
	HZ-110	BAe 125-800B	RSAF 1 Sqn, Riyadh
	HZ-117	Lockheed L.100-30 Hercules	RSAF 1 Sqn, Riyadh
	HZ-124	Airbus A.340-211	RSAF 1 Sqn, Riyadh
	HZ-128	Lockheed L.100-30 Hercules	RSAF 1 Sqn, Riyadh
	HZ-129	Lockheed L.100-30 Hercules	RSAF 1 Sqn, Riyadh
	HZ-130	BAe 125-800B	RSAF 1 Sqn, Riyadh
	HZ-132	Lockheed L.100-30 Hercules	RSAF 1 Sqn, Riyadh
	HZ-133	Cessna 550 Citation II	RSAF 1 Sqn, Riyadh
	HZ-134	Cessna 550 Citation II	RSAF 1 Sqn, Riyadh
	HZ-135	Cessna 550 Citation II	RSAF 1 Sqn, Riyadh
	HZ-136	Cessna 550 Citation II	RSAF 1 Sqn, Riyadh
	HZ-AFN	Grumman G.1159A Gulfstream III	Saudi Special Flight Services, Jeddah
	HZ-AFR	Grumman G.1159A Gulfstream III	Saudi Special Flight Services, Jeddah
	HZ-AFT	Dassault Falcon 900	Saudi Special Flight Services, Jeddah
	HZ-AFU	Grumman G.1159C Gulfstream IV	*Sold as N431TL, May 2017*
	HZ-AFV	Grumman G.1159C Gulfstream IV	*Sold as N435TF, May 2017*
	HZ-AFW	Grumman G.1159C Gulfstream IV	*Withdrawn from use*
	HZ-AFX	Grumman G.1159C Gulfstream IV	*Sold as N143PK, May 2017*
	HZ-AFY	Grumman G.1159C Gulfstream IV	*Sold as N166JM, May 2017*
	HZ-AFZ	Dassault Falcon 900	Saudi Special Flight Services, Jeddah
	HZ-AIF	Boeing 747SP-68	*Withdrawn from use*
	HZ-AS99	Airbus A.318-112CJ	Saudi Royal Flight, Jeddah
	HZ-HM1	Boeing 747-468	Saudi Royal Flight, Jeddah
	HZ-HM1A	Boeing 747-3G1	Saudi Royal Flight, Jeddah
	HZ-HM1B	Boeing 747SP-68	Saudi Royal Flight, Jeddah
	HZ-HM1C	Boeing 747SP-68	Saudi Royal Flight, Jeddah
	HZ-HMED	Boeing 757-23A	Saudi Royal Flight, Riyadh
	HZ-HMS2	Airbus A.340-213X	RSAF, Riyadh
	HZ-MFL	Grumman G.1159C Gulfstream IV	*Sold as N428BC, May 2017*
	HZ-MS1A	Bombardier Lear 60	Saudi Armed Forces Medical Services, Riyadh
	HZ-MS1B	Bombardier Lear 60	Saudi Armed Forces Medical Services, Riyadh
	HZ-MS02	Lockheed C-130H Hercules	Saudi Armed Forces Medical Services, Riyadh
	HZ-MS4	Grumman G.1159C Gulfstream IV-SP	Saudi Armed Forces Medical Services, Riyadh
	HZ-MS4A	Gulfstream Aerospace G.450	Saudi Armed Forces Medical Services, Riyadh
	HZ-MS4B	Gulfstream Aerospace G.450	Saudi Armed Forces Medical Services, Riyadh
	HZ-MS4C	Gulfstream Aerospace G.450	Saudi Armed Forces Medical Services, Riyadh
	HZ-MS5A	Gulfstream Aerospace Gulfstream V	Saudi Armed Forces Medical Services, Riyadh
	HZ-MS5B	Gulfstream Aerospace Gulfstream V	Saudi Armed Forces Medical Services, Riyadh
	HZ-MS06	Lockheed L.100-30 Hercules	Saudi Armed Forces Medical Services, Riyadh
	HZ-MS07	Lockheed C-130H Hercules	Saudi Armed Forces Medical Services, Riyadh
	HZ-MS09	Lockheed L.100-30 Hercules	Saudi Armed Forces Medical Services, Riyadh

SENEGAL

| | 6V-ONE | Airbus A.319CJ-115X | Government of Senegal, Dakar |

SERBIA

| | YU-BNA | Dassault Falcon 50 | Government of Serbia, Belgrade |

SINGAPORE
Republic of Singapore Air Force (RSAF)

	720	Lockheed KC-130B Hercules	RSAF 122 Sqn, Paya Labar
	721	Lockheed KC-130B Hercules	RSAF 122 Sqn, Paya Labar
	724	Lockheed KC-130B Hercules	RSAF 122 Sqn, Paya Labar
	725	Lockheed KC-130B Hercules	RSAF 122 Sqn, Paya Labar
	730	Lockheed C-130H Hercules	RSAF 122 Sqn, Paya Labar
	731	Lockheed KC-130H Hercules	RSAF 122 Sqn, Paya Labar
	732	Lockheed C-130H Hercules	RSAF 122 Sqn, Paya Labar
	733	Lockheed C-130H Hercules	RSAF 122 Sqn, Paya Labar
	734	Lockheed KC-130H Hercules	RSAF 122 Sqn, Paya Labar
	735	Lockheed C-130H Hercules	RSAF 122 Sqn, Paya Labar

Serial	Type (code/other identity)	Owner/operator, location or fate	Notes
750	Boeing KC-135R Stratotanker	RSAF 112 Sqn, Changi	
751	Boeing KC-135R Stratotanker	RSAF 112 Sqn, Changi	
752	Boeing KC-135R Stratotanker	RSAF 112 Sqn, Changi	
753	Boeing KC-135R Stratotanker	RSAF 112 Sqn, Changi	
760	Airbus A.330-203 MRTT (EC-333)	RSAF 112 Sqn, Changi (on order)	
761	Airbus A.330-203 MRTT (EC-332)	RSAF 112 Sqn, Changi (on order)	
762	Airbus A.330-203 MRTT	RSAF 112 Sqn, Changi (on order)	
763	Airbus A.330-203 MRTT	RSAF 112 Sqn, Changi (on order)	
764	Airbus A.330-203 MRTT	RSAF 112 Sqn, Changi (on order)	

SLOVAKIA
Slovenské Vojenske Letectvo (SVL)

Serial	Type (code/other identity)	Owner/operator, location or fate	Notes
0619	Mikoyan MiG-29AS	SVL 1.Blt/Zmiešané Letecké Kridlo, Sliač	
0807	Mil Mi-17	SVL 2.Dvlt/Vrtulnikové Letcecké Kridlo, Prešov	
0808	Mil Mi-17	SVL 2.Dvlt/Vrtulnikové Letcecké Kridlo, Prešov	
0820	Mil Mi-17	SVL 2.Dvlt/Vrtulnikové Letcecké Kridlo, Prešov	
0821	Mil Mi-17	SVL 2.Dvlt/Vrtulnikové Letcecké Kridlo, Prešov	
0823	Mil Mi-17M	SVL 2.Dvlt/Vrtulnikové Letcecké Kridlo, Prešov	
0824	Mil Mi-17	SVL 2.Dvlt/Vrtulnikové Letcecké Kridlo, Prešov	
0826	Mil Mi-17	SVL 2.Dvlt/Vrtulnikové Letcecké Kridlo, Prešov	
0841	Mil Mi-17	SVL 2.Dvlt/Vrtulnikové Letcecké Kridlo, Prešov	
0844	Mil Mi-17	SVL 2.Dvlt/Vrtulnikové Letcecké Kridlo, Prešov	
0845	Mil Mi-17	SVL 2.Dvlt/Vrtulnikové Letcecké Kridlo, Prešov	
0846	Mil Mi-17	SVL 2.Dvlt/Vrtulnikové Letcecké Kridlo, Prešov	
0847	Mil Mi-17	SVL 2.Dvlt/Vrtulnikové Letcecké Kridlo, Prešov	
0921	Mikoyan MiG-29AS	SVL 1.Blt/Zmiešané Letecké Kridlo, Sliač	
1133	LET L-410T Turbolet	SVL 2 Dopravná Roj/Dopravniho Kridlo, Malacky	
1303	Mikoyan MiG-29UBS $	SVL 1.Blt/Zmiešané Letecké Kridlo, Sliač	
1521	LET L-410FG Turbolet	SVL 2 Dopravná Roj/Dopravniho Kridlo, Malacky	
1931	Aeritalia C-27J Spartan (CSX62302)	SVL	
1962	Aeritalia C-27J Spartan	SVL (on order)	
2123	Mikoyan MiG-29AS	SVL 1.Blt/Zmiešané Letecké Kridlo, Sliač	
2311	LET L-410UVP Turbolet	SVL 2 Dopravná Roj/Dopravniho Kridlo, Malacky	
2421	LET L-410UVP Turbolet	SVL 2 Dopravná Roj/Dopravniho Kridlo, Malacky	
2718	LET L-401UVP-E Turbolet	SVL 2 Dopravná Roj/Dopravniho Kridlo, Malacky	
2721	LET L-401UVP-E Turbolet	SVL 2 Dopravná Roj/Dopravniho Kridlo, Malacky	
2818	LET L-401UVP-20 Turbolet	SVL 2 Dopravná Roj/Dopravniho Kridlo, Malacky	
2901	LET L-401UVP-20 Turbolet	SVL 2 Dopravná Roj/Dopravniho Kridlo, Malacky	
3208	Antonov An-26	Withdrawn from use	
3709	Mikoyan MiG-29AS	SVL 1.Blt/Zmiešané Letecké Kridlo, Sliač	
3911	Mikoyan MiG-29AS	SVL 1.Blt/Zmiešané Letecké Kridlo, Sliač	
4701	Aero L-39ZAM Albatros	SVL 2.vlt/Zmiešané Letecké Kridlo, Sliač	
4703	Aero L-39ZAM Albatros	SVL 2.vlt/Zmiešané Letecké Kridlo, Sliač	
4707	Aero L-39ZAM Albatros	SVL 2.vlt/Zmiešané Letecké Kridlo, Sliač	
4711	Aero L-39ZAM Albatros	SVL 2.vlt/Zmiešané Letecké Kridlo, Sliač	
5252	Aero L-39CM Albatros	SVL 2.vlt/Zmiešané Letecké Kridlo, Sliač	
5253	Aero L-39CM Albatros	SVL 2.vlt/Zmiešané Letecké Kridlo, Sliač	
5301	Aero L-39CM Albatros $	SVL 2.vlt/Zmiešané Letecké Kridlo, Sliač	
5302	Aero L-39CM Albatros	SVL 2.vlt/Zmiešané Letecké Kridlo, Sliač	
5304	Mikoyan MiG-29UBS $	SVL 1.Blt/Zmiešané Letecké Kridlo, Sliač	
6124	Mikoyan MiG-29AS	SVL 1.Blt/Zmiešané Letecké Kridlo, Sliač	
6526	Mikoyan MiG-29AS	SVL 1.Blt/Zmiešané Letecké Kridlo, Sliač	
6627	Mikoyan MiG-29AS	SVL 1.Blt/Zmiešané Letecké Kridlo, Sliač	
6728	Mikoyan MiG-29AS	SVL 1.Blt/Zmiešané Letecké Kridlo, Sliač	
7639	Sikorsky UH-60M Black Hawk	SVL 2.Dvlt/Vrtulnikové Letecké Kridlo, Prešov	
7640	Sikorsky UH-60M Black Hawk	SVL 2.Dvlt/Vrtulnikové Letecké Kridlo, Prešov	
...	Sikorsky UH-60M Black Hawk	SVL (on order)	
...	Sikorsky UH-60M Black Hawk	SVL (on order)	
...	Sikorsky UH-60M Black Hawk	SVL (on order)	
...	Sikorsky UH-60M Black Hawk	SVL (on order)	
...	Sikorsky UH-60M Black Hawk	SVL (on order)	
...	Sikorsky UH-60M Black Hawk	SVL (on order)	

Notes	Serial	Type (code/other identity)	Owner/operator, location or fate
	....	Sikorsky UH-60M Black Hawk	SVL (on order)
	Slovak Government		
	OM-BYA	Airbus A.319-115	Slovak Government, Bratislava/Ivanka
	OM-BYB	Fokker 100	Slovak Government, Bratislava/Ivanka
	OM-BYC	Fokker 100	Slovak Government, Bratislava/Ivanka
	OM-BYE	Yakovlev Yak-40	*Withdrawn from use, 2016*
	OM-BYK	Airbus A.319-115XCJ	Slovak Government, Bratislava/Ivanka
	OM-BYL	Yakovlev Yak-40	*Withdrawn from use*
	OM-BYO	Tupolev Tu-154M	*Withdrawn from use, August 2017*

SLOVENIA
Slovenska Vojska (SV)/Slovenian Armed Forces

Notes	Serial	Type (code/other identity)	Owner/operator, location or fate
	L1-01	Dassault Falcon 2000EX	Government of Slovenia, Ljubljana
	L4-01	LET 410UVP-E Turbolet	SV 107.Letalska Baza, Cerklje ob Krki
	L9-61	Pilatus PC-9M	SV Letalska Šola, Cerklje ob Krki
	L9-62	Pilatus PC-9M	SV Letalska Šola, Cerklje ob Krki
	L9-63	Pilatus PC-9M	SV Letalska Šola, Cerklje ob Krki
	L9-64	Pilatus PC-9M	SV Letalska Šola, Cerklje ob Krki
	L9-65	Pilatus PC-9M	SV Letalska Šola, Cerklje ob Krki
	L9-66	Pilatus PC-9M	SV Letalska Šola, Cerklje ob Krki
	L9-67	Pilatus PC-9M	SV Letalska Šola, Cerklje ob Krki
	L9-68	Pilatus PC-9M	SV Letalska Šola, Cerklje ob Krki
	L9-69	Pilatus PC-9M	SV Letalska Šola, Cerklje ob Krki

SOUTH AFRICA
Suid Afrikaanse Lugmag/South African Air Force (SAAF)

Notes	Serial	Type (code/other identity)	Owner/operator, location or fate
	401	Lockheed C-130BZ Hercules	SAAF 28 Sqn, Waterkloof
	402	Lockheed C-130BZ Hercules	SAAF 28 Sqn, Waterkloof
	403	Lockheed C-130BZ Hercules	SAAF 28 Sqn, Waterkloof
	404	Lockheed C-130BZ Hercules	SAAF 28 Sqn, Waterkloof
	405	Lockheed C-130BZ Hercules $	SAAF 28 Sqn, Waterkloof
	406	Lockheed C-130BZ Hercules	SAAF 28 Sqn, Waterkloof
	409	Lockheed C-130BZ Hercules	SAAF 28 Sqn, Waterkloof
	ZS-NAN	Dassault Falcon 900	SAAF 21 Sqn, Waterkloof
	ZS-RSA	Boeing 737-7ED	SAAF 21 Sqn, Waterkloof

SOUTH KOREA
Han Guk Gong Gun/Republic of Korea Air Force

Notes	Serial	Type (code/other identity)	Owner/operator, location or fate
	10001	Boeing 747-4B5	RoKAF 296 Sqn/35 Combined Group, Seoul AB

SPAIN
Arma Aérea de l'Armada Española, Ejército del Aire (EdA)/Spanish Air Force & Guardia Civil

Notes	Serial	Type (code/other identity)	Owner/operator, location or fate
	CE.15-01	McDonnell Douglas EF-18BM Hornet [15-70] $	EdA 151 Esc/152 Esc/153 Esc/Ala 15, Zaragoza
	CE.15-2	McDonnell Douglas EF-18BM Hornet [15-71]	EdA 151 Esc/152 Esc/153 Esc/Ala 15, Zaragoza
	CE.15-03	McDonnell Douglas EF-18BM Hornet [15-72]	EdA 151 Esc/152 Esc/153 Esc/Ala 15, Zaragoza
	CE.15-04	McDonnell Douglas EF-18BM Hornet [15-73]	EdA 151 Esc/152 Esc/153 Esc/Ala 15, Zaragoza
	CE.15-5	McDonnell Douglas EF-18BM Hornet [15-74]	EdA 151 Esc/152 Esc/153 Esc/Ala 15, Zaragoza
	CE.15-06	McDonnell Douglas EF-18BM Hornet [15-75]	EdA 151 Esc/152 Esc/153 Esc/Ala 15, Zaragoza
	CE.15-07	McDonnell Douglas EF-18BM Hornet [15-76]	EdA 151 Esc/152 Esc/153 Esc/Ala 15, Zaragoza
	CE.15-08	McDonnell Douglas EF-18BM Hornet [12-71]	EdA 121 Esc/122 Esc/Ala 12, Madrid/Torrejón
	CE.15-09	McDonnell Douglas EF-18BM Hornet [15-77]	EdA 151 Esc/152 Esc/153 Esc/Ala 15, Zaragoza
	CE.15-10	McDonnell Douglas EF-18BM Hornet [12-73] $	EdA 121 Esc/122 Esc/Ala 12, Madrid/Torrejón
	CE.15-11	McDonnell Douglas EF-18BM Hornet [12-74]	EdA 121 Esc/122 Esc/Ala 12, Madrid/Torrejón
	CE.15-12	McDonnell Douglas EF-18BM Hornet [12-75]	EdA 121 Esc/122 Esc/Ala 12, Madrid/Torrejón
	C.15-13	McDonnell Douglas EF-18M Hornet [12-01]	EdA 121 Esc/122 Esc/Ala 12, Madrid/Torrejón
	C.15-14	McDonnell Douglas EF-18M Hornet [15-01] $	EdA 151 Esc/152 Esc/153 Esc/Ala 15, Zaragoza
	C.15-15	McDonnell Douglas EF-18M Hornet [15-02]	EdA 151 Esc/152 Esc/153 Esc/Ala 15, Zaragoza
	C.15-16	McDonnell Douglas EF-18M Hornet [15-03]	EdA 151 Esc/152 Esc/153 Esc/Ala 15, Zaragoza
	C.15-18	McDonnell Douglas EF-18M Hornet [15-05]	EdA 151 Esc/152 Esc/153 Esc/Ala 15, Zaragoza
	C.15-20	McDonnell Douglas EF-18M Hornet [15-07]	EdA 151 Esc/152 Esc/153 Esc/Ala 15, Zaragoza
	C.15-21	McDonnell Douglas EF-18M Hornet [15-08]	EdA 151 Esc/152 Esc/153 Esc/Ala 15, Zaragoza
	C.15-22	McDonnell Douglas EF-18M Hornet [15-09]	EdA 151 Esc/152 Esc/153 Esc/Ala 15, Zaragoza

Serial	Type (code/other identity)	Owner/operator, location or fate	Notes
C.15-23	McDonnell Douglas EF-18M Hornet [15-10]	EdA 151 Esc/152 Esc/153 Esc/Ala 15, Zaragoza	
C.15-24	McDonnell Douglas EF-18M Hornet [15-11]	EdA 151 Esc/152 Esc/153 Esc/Ala 15, Zaragoza	
C.15-25	McDonnell Douglas EF-18M Hornet [15-12]	EdA 151 Esc/152 Esc/153 Esc/Ala 15, Zaragoza	
C.15-26	McDonnell Douglas EF-18M Hornet [15-13] $	EdA 151 Esc/152 Esc/153 Esc/Ala 15, Zaragoza	
C.15-27	McDonnell Douglas EF-18M Hornet [15-14]	EdA 151 Esc/152 Esc/153 Esc/Ala 15, Zaragoza	
C.15-28	McDonnell Douglas EF-18M Hornet [15-15]	EdA 151 Esc/152 Esc/153 Esc/Ala 15, Zaragoza	
C.15-29	McDonnell Douglas EF-18M Hornet [15-16]	EdA 151 Esc/152 Esc/153 Esc/Ala 15, Zaragoza	
C.15-30	McDonnell Douglas EF-18M Hornet [15-17]	EdA 151 Esc/152 Esc/153 Esc/Ala 15, Zaragoza	
C.15-31	McDonnell Douglas EF-18M Hornet [15-18]	EdA 151 Esc/152 Esc/153 Esc/Ala 15, Zaragoza	
C.15-32	McDonnell Douglas EF-18M Hornet [15-19]	EdA 151 Esc/152 Esc/153 Esc/Ala 15, Zaragoza	
C.15-33	McDonnell Douglas EF-18M Hornet [15-20]	EdA 151 Esc/152 Esc/153 Esc/Ala 15, Zaragoza	
C.15-34	McDonnell Douglas EF-18M Hornet [12-50] $	EdA 121 Esc/122 Esc/Ala 12, Madrid/Torrejón	
C.15-35	McDonnell Douglas EF-18M Hornet [15-22]	EdA 151 Esc/152 Esc/153 Esc/Ala 15, Zaragoza	
C.15-36	McDonnell Douglas EF-18M Hornet [15-23]	EdA 151 Esc/152 Esc/153 Esc/Ala 15, Zaragoza	
C.15-37	McDonnell Douglas EF-18M Hornet [15-24]	EdA 151 Esc/152 Esc/153 Esc/Ala 15, Zaragoza	
C.15-38	McDonnell Douglas EF-18M Hornet [15-25]	EdA 151 Esc/152 Esc/153 Esc/Ala 15, Zaragoza	
C.15-39	McDonnell Douglas EF-18M Hornet [15-26]	EdA 151 Esc/152 Esc/153 Esc/Ala 15, Zaragoza	
C.15-40	McDonnell Douglas EF-18M Hornet [15-27]	EdA 151 Esc/152 Esc/153 Esc/Ala 15, Zaragoza	
C.15-41	McDonnell Douglas EF-18M Hornet [15-28] $	EdA 151 Esc/152 Esc/153 Esc/Ala 15, Zaragoza	
C.15-43	McDonnell Douglas EF-18M Hornet [15-30]	EdA 151 Esc/152 Esc/153 Esc/Ala 15, Zaragoza	
C.15-44	McDonnell Douglas EF-18M Hornet [12-02]	EdA 121 Esc/122 Esc/Ala 12, Madrid/Torrejón	
C.15-45	McDonnell Douglas EF-18M Hornet [12-03]	EdA 121 Esc/122 Esc/Ala 12, Madrid/Torrejón	
C.15-46	McDonnell Douglas EF-18M Hornet [12-04]	EdA 121 Esc/122 Esc/Ala 12, Madrid/Torrejón	
C.15-47	McDonnell Douglas EF-18M Hornet [15-31]	EdA 151 Esc/152 Esc/153 Esc/Ala 15, Zaragoza	
C.15-48	McDonnell Douglas EF-18M Hornet [12-06]	EdA 121 Esc/122 Esc/Ala 12, Madrid/Torrejón	
C.15-49	McDonnell Douglas EF-18M Hornet [12-07]	EdA 121 Esc/122 Esc/Ala 12, Madrid/Torrejón	
C.15-50	McDonnell Douglas EF-18M Hornet [12-08]	EdA 121 Esc/122 Esc/Ala 12, Madrid/Torrejón	
C.15-51	McDonnell Douglas EF-18M Hornet [12-09]	EdA 121 Esc/122 Esc/Ala 12, Madrid/Torrejón	
C.15-52	McDonnell Douglas EF-18M Hornet [12-10]	*Crashed 17 October 2017, Torrejón*	
C.15-53	McDonnell Douglas EF-18M Hornet [12-11]	EdA 121 Esc/122 Esc/Ala 12, Madrid/Torrejón	
C.15-54	McDonnell Douglas EF-18M Hornet [12-12]	EdA 121 Esc/122 Esc/Ala 12, Madrid/Torrejón	
C.15-55	McDonnell Douglas EF-18M Hornet [12-13]	EdA 121 Esc/122 Esc/Ala 12, Madrid/Torrejón	
C.15-56	McDonnell Douglas EF-18M Hornet [12-14]	EdA 121 Esc/122 Esc/Ala 12, Madrid/Torrejón	
C.15-57	McDonnell Douglas EF-18M Hornet [12-15]	EdA 121 Esc/122 Esc/Ala 12, Madrid/Torrejón	
C.15-59	McDonnell Douglas EF-18M Hornet [12-17]	EdA 121 Esc/122 Esc/Ala 12, Madrid/Torrejón	
C.15-60	McDonnell Douglas EF-18M Hornet [12-18]	EdA 121 Esc/122 Esc/Ala 12, Madrid/Torrejón	
C.15-61	McDonnell Douglas EF-18M Hornet [12-19]	EdA 121 Esc/122 Esc/Ala 12, Madrid/Torrejón	
C.15-62	McDonnell Douglas EF-18M Hornet [12-20]	EdA 121 Esc/122 Esc/Ala 12, Madrid/Torrejón	
C.15-64	McDonnell Douglas EF-18M Hornet [15-34]	EdA 151 Esc/152 Esc/153 Esc/Ala 15, Zaragoza	
C.15-65	McDonnell Douglas EF-18M Hornet [12-23]	EdA 121 Esc/122 Esc/Ala 12, Madrid/Torrejón	
C.15-66	McDonnell Douglas EF-18M Hornet [12-24]	EdA 121 Esc/122 Esc/Ala 12, Madrid/Torrejón	
C.15-67	McDonnell Douglas EF-18M Hornet [15-33]	EdA 151 Esc/152 Esc/153 Esc/Ala 15, Zaragoza	
C.15-68	McDonnell Douglas EF-18M Hornet [12-26] $	EdA 121 Esc/122 Esc/Ala 12, Madrid/Torrejón	
C.15-69	McDonnell Douglas EF-18M Hornet [12-27]	EdA 121 Esc/122 Esc/Ala 12, Madrid/Torrejón	
C.15-70	McDonnell Douglas EF-18M Hornet [12-28]	EdA 121 Esc/122 Esc/Ala 12, Madrid/Torrejón	
C.15-72	McDonnell Douglas EF-18M Hornet [12-30]	EdA 121 Esc/122 Esc/Ala 12, Madrid/Torrejón	
C.15-73	McDonnell Douglas F/A-18A+ Hornet [46-01] $	EdA 462 Esc/Ala 46, Gran Canaria	
C.15-75	McDonnell Douglas F/A-18A+ Hornet [46-03]	EdA 462 Esc/Ala 46, Gran Canaria	
C.15-77	McDonnell Douglas F/A-18A+ Hornet [46-05]	EdA 462 Esc/Ala 46, Gran Canaria	
C.15-79	McDonnell Douglas F/A-18A+ Hornet [46-07]	EdA 462 Esc/Ala 46, Gran Canaria	
C.15-80	McDonnell Douglas F/A-18A+ Hornet [46-08]	EdA 462 Esc/Ala 46, Gran Canaria	
C.15-81	McDonnell Douglas F/A-18A+ Hornet [46-09]	EdA 462 Esc/Ala 46, Gran Canaria	
C.15-82	McDonnell Douglas F/A-18A+ Hornet [46-10]	EdA 462 Esc/Ala 46, Gran Canaria	
C.15-83	McDonnell Douglas F/A-18A+ Hornet [46-11]	EdA 462 Esc/Ala 46, Gran Canaria	
C.15-84	McDonnell Douglas F/A-18A+ Hornet [46-12]	EdA 462 Esc/Ala 46, Gran Canaria	
C.15-85	McDonnell Douglas F/A-18A+ Hornet [46-13]	EdA 462 Esc/Ala 46, Gran Canaria	
C.15-86	McDonnell Douglas F/A-18A+ Hornet [46-14]	EdA 462 Esc/Ala 46, Gran Canaria	
C.15-87	McDonnell Douglas F/A-18A+ Hornet [46-15]	EdA 462 Esc/Ala 46, Gran Canaria	
C.15-88	McDonnell Douglas F/A-18A+ Hornet [46-16] $	EdA 462 Esc/Ala 46, Gran Canaria	
C.15-89	McDonnell Douglas F/A-18A+ Hornet [46-17]	EdA 462 Esc/Ala 46, Gran Canaria	
C.15-90	McDonnell Douglas F/A-18A+ Hornet [46-18]	EdA 462 Esc/Ala 46, Gran Canaria	
C.15-92	McDonnell Douglas F/A-18A+ Hornet [46-20]	EdA 462 Esc/Ala 46, Gran Canaria	

Notes	Serial	Type (code/other identity)	Owner/operator, location or fate
	C.15-93	McDonnell Douglas F/A-18A+ Hornet [46-21]	EdA 462 Esc/Ala 46, Gran Canaria
	C.15-94	McDonnell Douglas F/A-18A+ Hornet [46-22]	EdA 462 Esc/Ala 46, Gran Canaria
	C.15-95	McDonnell Douglas F/A-18A+ Hornet [46-23]	EdA 462 Esc/Ala 46, Gran Canaria
	C.15-96	McDonnell Douglas F/A-18A+ Hornet [46-24]	EdA 462 Esc/Ala 46, Gran Canaria
	CE.16-01	Eurofighter EF.2000(T) Tifón [11-70]	EdA 111 Esc/113 Esc/Ala 11, Sevilla/Morón
	CE.16-02	Eurofighter EF.2000(T) Tifón [11-71]	EdA 111 Esc/113 Esc/Ala 11, Sevilla/Morón
	CE.16-03	Eurofighter EF.2000(T) Tifón [11-72]	EdA 111 Esc/113 Esc/Ala 11, Sevilla/Morón
	CE.16-04	Eurofighter EF.2000(T) Tifón [11-73]	EdA 111 Esc/113 Esc/Ala 11, Sevilla/Morón
	CE.16-05	Eurofighter EF.2000(T) Tifón [11-74]	EdA 111 Esc/113 Esc/Ala 11, Sevilla/Morón
	CE.16-06	Eurofighter EF.2000(T) Tifón [11-75]	EdA 111 Esc/113 Esc/Ala 11, Sevilla/Morón
	CE.16-07	Eurofighter EF.2000(T) Tifón [11-76]	EdA 111 Esc/113 Esc/Ala 11, Sevilla/Morón
	CE.16-09	Eurofighter EF.2000(T) Tifón [11-78]	EdA 111 Esc/113 Esc/Ala 11, Sevilla/Morón
	CE.16-10	Eurofighter EF.2000(T) Tifón [11-79]	EdA 111 Esc/113 Esc/Ala 11, Sevilla/Morón
	CE.16-11	Eurofighter EF.2000(T) Tifón [14-70]	EdA 142 Esc/Ala 14, Albacete/Los Llanos
	CE.16-12	Eurofighter EF.2000(T) Tifón (CE.16-10000) [14-71]	EdA 142 Esc/Ala 14, Albacete/Los Llanos
	CE.16-13	Eurofighter EF.2000(T) Tifón (10005) [11-80]	EdA 111 Esc/113 Esc/Ala 11, Sevilla/Morón
	CE.16-14	Eurofighter EF.2000(T) Tifón (10015) [11-81]	EdA 111 Esc/113 Esc/Ala 11, Sevilla/Morón
	C.16-20	Eurofighter EF.2000 Tifón [11-91]	EdA 111 Esc/113 Esc/Ala 11, Sevilla/Morón
	C.16-21	Eurofighter EF.2000 Tifón [11-01]	EdA 111 Esc/113 Esc/Ala 11, Sevilla/Morón
	C.16-22	Eurofighter EF.2000 Tifón [11-02]	EdA 111 Esc/113 Esc/Ala 11, Sevilla/Morón
	C.16-23	Eurofighter EF.2000 Tifón [11-03]	EdA 111 Esc/113 Esc/Ala 11, Sevilla/Morón
	C.16-24	Eurofighter EF.2000 Tifón [11-04]	EdA 111 Esc/113 Esc/Ala 11, Sevilla/Morón
	C.16-25	Eurofighter EF.2000 Tifón [11-05]	EdA 111 Esc/113 Esc/Ala 11, Sevilla/Morón
	C.16-26	Eurofighter EF.2000 Tifón [11-06]	EdA 111 Esc/113 Esc/Ala 11, Sevilla/Morón
	C.16-27	Eurofighter EF.2000 Tifón [11-07]	EdA 111 Esc/113 Esc/Ala 11, Sevilla/Morón
	C.16-28	Eurofighter EF.2000 Tifón [11-08]	EdA 111 Esc/113 Esc/Ala 11, Sevilla/Morón
	C.16-29	Eurofighter EF.2000 Tifón [11-09]	EdA 111 Esc/113 Esc/Ala 11, Sevilla/Morón
	C.16-30	Eurofighter EF.2000 Tifón [11-10]	EdA 111 Esc/113 Esc/Ala 11, Sevilla/Morón
	C.16-31	Eurofighter EF.2000 Tifón [14-01]	EdA 142 Esc/Ala 14, Albacete/Los Llanos
	C.16-32	Eurofighter EF.2000 Tifón [11-11]	EdA 111 Esc/113 Esc/Ala 11, Sevilla/Morón
	C.16-33	Eurofighter EF.2000 Tifón [11-12]	EdA 111 Esc/113 Esc/Ala 11, Sevilla/Morón
	C.16-35	Eurofighter EF.2000 Tifón [11-14]	EdA 111 Esc/113 Esc/Ala 11, Sevilla/Morón
	C.16-36	Eurofighter EF.2000 Tifón [14-03] $	EdA 142 Esc/Ala 14, Albacete/Los Llanos
	C.16-37	Eurofighter EF.2000 Tifón [14-04]	EdA 142 Esc/Ala 14, Albacete/Los Llanos
	C.16-38	Eurofighter EF.2000 Tifón [14-05]	EdA 142 Esc/Ala 14, Albacete/Los Llanos
	C.16-39	Eurofighter EF.2000 Tifón [14-06] $	EdA 142 Esc/Ala 14, Albacete/Los Llanos
	C.16-40	Eurofighter EF.2000 Tifón [11-16]	EdA 111 Esc/113 Esc/Ala 11, Sevilla/Morón
	C.16-41	Eurofighter EF.2000 Tifón [14-07]	EdA 142 Esc/Ala 14, Albacete/Los Llanos
	C.16-42	Eurofighter EF.2000 Tifón [14-08] $	EdA 142 Esc/Ala 14, Albacete/Los Llanos
	C.16-43	Eurofighter EF.2000 Tifón [11-19]	EdA 111 Esc/113 Esc/Ala 11, Sevilla/Morón
	C.16-44	Eurofighter EF.2000 Tifón [14-09]	EdA 142 Esc/Ala 14, Albacete/Los Llanos
	C.16-45	Eurofighter EF.2000 Tifón [14-10]	EdA 142 Esc/Ala 14, Albacete/Los Llanos
	C.16-46	Eurofighter EF.2000 Tifón [11-20]	EdA 111 Esc/113 Esc/Ala 11, Sevilla/Morón
	C.16-47	Eurofighter EF.2000 Tifón [14-11]	EdA 142 Esc/Ala 14, Albacete/Los Llanos
	C.16-48	Eurofighter EF.2000 Tifón [14-12]	EdA 142 Esc/Ala 14, Albacete/Los Llanos
	C.16-49	Eurofighter EF.2000 Tifón [14-13]	EdA 142 Esc/Ala 14, Albacete/Los Llanos
	C.16-50	Eurofighter EF.2000 Tifón [14-14]	EdA 142 Esc/Ala 14, Albacete/Los Llanos
	C.16-51	Eurofighter EF.2000 Tifón [11-21]	EdA 111 Esc/113 Esc/Ala 11, Sevilla/Morón
	C.16-52	Eurofighter EF.2000 Tifón (C.16-10001) [11-22]	EdA 111 Esc/113 Esc/Ala 11, Sevilla/Morón
	C.16-53	Eurofighter EF.2000 Tifón (C.16-10002) [11-23]	EdA 111 Esc/113 Esc/Ala 11, Sevilla/Morón
	C.16-54	Eurofighter EF.2000 Tifón (C.16-10003) [11-24]	EdA 111 Esc/113 Esc/Ala 11, Sevilla/Morón
	C.16-55	Eurofighter EF.2000 Tifón (C.16-10004) [11-25]	EdA 111 Esc/113 Esc/Ala 11, Sevilla/Morón
	C.16-56	Eurofighter EF.2000 Tifón (10007)	EdA 142 Esc/Ala 14, Albacete/Los Llanos
	C.16-57	Eurofighter EF.2000 Tifón (10012) [11-27]	EdA 111 Esc/113 Esc/Ala 11, Sevilla/Morón
	C.16-58	Eurofighter EF.2000 Tifón (10019)	EdA 142 Esc/Ala 14, Albacete/Los Llanos
	C.16-59	Eurofighter EF.2000 Tifón (10020)	EdA 142 Esc/Ala 14, Albacete/Los Llanos
	C.16-60	Eurofighter EF.2000 Tifón (10040)	EdA 142 Esc/Ala 14, Albacete/Los Llanos
	C.16-61	Eurofighter EF.2000 Tifón (10046)	EdA 142 Esc/Ala 14, Albacete/Los Llanos
	C.16-62	Eurofighter EF.2000 Tifón (10047)	EdA 142 Esc/Ala 14, Albacete/Los Llanos
	C.16-63	Eurofighter EF.2000 Tifón (10048) [11-28]	EdA 111 Esc/113 Esc/Ala 11, Sevilla/Morón
	C.16-64	Eurofighter EF.2000 Tifón (10053)	EdA 142 Esc/Ala 14, Albacete/Los Llanos
	C.16-65	Eurofighter EF.2000 Tifón (10054)	EdA 142 Esc/Ala 14, Albacete/Los Llanos

Serial	Type (code/other identity)	Owner/operator, location or fate	Notes
C.16-66	Eurofighter EF.2000 Tifón (10064)	EdA 142 Esc/Ala 14, Albacete/Los Llanos	
C.16-67	Eurofighter EF.2000 Tifón (10090)	EdA 142 Esc/Ala 14, Albacete/Los Llanos	
C.16-68	Eurofighter EF.2000 Tifón (10091)	EdA 142 Esc/Ala 14, Albacete/Los Llanos	
C.16-69	Eurofighter EF.2000 Tifón (10092)	EdA 142 Esc/Ala 14, Albacete/Los Llanos	
C.16-70	Eurofighter EF.2000 Tifón	*Crashed 12 October 2017, Albacete*	
C.16-71	Eurofighter EF.2000 Tifón (10146)	EdA	
C.16-72	Eurofighter EF.2000 Tifón (10147)	EdA 142 Esc/Ala 14, Albacete/Los Llanos	
C.16-73	Eurofighter EF.2000 Tifón (10155)	EdA 142 Esc/Ala 14, Albacete/Los Llanos	
C.16-74	Eurofighter EF.2000 Tifón (10202)	EdA 142 Esc/Ala 14, Albacete/Los Llanos	
C.16-75	Eurofighter EF.2000 Tifón	EdA (on order)	
C.16-76	Eurofighter EF.2000 Tifón	EdA (on order)	
D.4-01	Airtech CN.235M-100(MPA) [T.19B-12]	EdA 801 Esc/Ala 49, Palma/Son San Juan	
D.4-02	Airtech CN.235M-100(MPA) [T.19B-09]	EdA 801 Esc/Ala 49, Palma/Son San Juan	
D.4-03	Airtech CN.235M-100(MPA) [T.19B-10]	EdA 801 Esc/Ala 49, Palma/Son San Juan	
D.4-04	Airtech CN.235M-100(MPA) [T.19B-08]	EdA 802 Esc/Ala 46, Gran Canaria	
D.4-05	Airtech CN.235M-100(MPA) [T.19B-06]	EdA 801 Esc/Ala 49, Palma/Son San Juan	
D.4-06	Airtech CN.235M-100(MPA) [T.19B-05]	EdA 801 Esc/Ala 49, Palma/Son San Juan	
D.4-07	Airtech CN.235M-100(MPA) [T.19B-15]	EdA 803 Esc/Ala 48, Madrid/Getafe	
D.4-08	Airtech CN.235M-100(MPA) [T.19B-14]	EdA 802 Esc/Ala 46, Gran Canaria	
E.25-05	CASA 101EB Aviojet [79-05]	EdA 793 Esc/794 Esc/AGA, Murcia/San Javier	
E.25-06	CASA 101EB Aviojet [79-06,3]	*EdA Patrulla Aguila/AGA, Murcia/San Javier*	
E.25-08	CASA 101EB Aviojet [79-08]	EdA 793 Esc/794 Esc/AGA, Murcia/San Javier	
E.25-09	CASA 101EB Aviojet [79-09]	EdA 793 Esc/794 Esc/AGA, Murcia/San Javier	
E.25-10	CASA 101EB Aviojet [79-20]	*Preserved at San Javier, 2010*	
E.25-11	CASA 101EB Aviojet [79-11]	EdA 793 Esc/794 Esc/AGA, Murcia/San Javier	
E.25-12	CASA 101EB Aviojet [79-12]	EdA 793 Esc/794 Esc/AGA, Murcia/San Javier	
E.25-13	CASA 101EB Aviojet [79-13,5]	*EdA Patrulla Aguila/AGA, Murcia/San Javier*	
E.25-14	CASA 101EB Aviojet [79-14]	EdA 793 Esc/794 Esc/AGA, Murcia/San Javier	
E.25-15	CASA 101EB Aviojet [79-15]	EdA 793 Esc/794 Esc/AGA, Murcia/San Javier	
E.25-16	CASA 101EB Aviojet [79-16]	EdA 793 Esc/794 Esc/AGA, Murcia/San Javier	
E.25-17	CASA 101EB Aviojet [74-40]	EdA 741 Esc/GEM, Salamanca/Matacán	
E.25-18	CASA 101EB Aviojet [74-42] $	EdA 741 Esc/GEM, Salamanca/Matacán	
E.25-19	CASA 101EB Aviojet [79-19]	EdA 793 Esc/794 Esc/AGA, Murcia/San Javier	
E.25-20	CASA 101EB Aviojet [79-20]	EdA 793 Esc/794 Esc/AGA, Murcia/San Javier	
E.25-21	CASA 101EB Aviojet [79-21,7]	EdA Patrulla Aguila/AGA, Murcia/San Javier	
E.25-22	CASA 101EB Aviojet [79-22]	EdA 793 Esc/794 Esc/AGA, Murcia/San Javier	
E.25-23	CASA 101EB Aviojet [79-23]	EdA 793 Esc/794 Esc/AGA, Murcia/San Javier	
E.25-24	CASA 101EB Aviojet [79-24]	EdA 793 Esc/794 Esc/AGA, Murcia/San Javier	
E.25-25	CASA 101EB Aviojet [79-25]	EdA 793 Esc/794 Esc/AGA, Murcia/San Javier	
E.25-26	CASA 101EB Aviojet [79-26]	EdA 793 Esc/794 Esc/AGA, Murcia/San Javier	
E.25-27	CASA 101EB Aviojet [79-27]	EdA 793 Esc/794 Esc/AGA, Murcia/San Javier	
E.25-28	CASA 101EB Aviojet [79-28]	EdA 793 Esc/794 Esc/AGA, Murcia/San Javier	
E.25-29	CASA 101EB Aviojet [74-45]	EdA 741 Esc/GEM, Salamanca/Matacán	
E.25-31	CASA 101EB Aviojet [79-31]	EdA 793 Esc/794 Esc/AGA, Murcia/San Javier	
E.25-33	CASA 101EB Aviojet [74-02]	EdA 741 Esc/GEM, Salamanca/Matacán	
E.25-34	CASA 101EB Aviojet [74-44]	EdA 741 Esc/GEM, Salamanca/Matacán	
E.25-35	CASA 101EB Aviojet [54-20] $	EdA 541 Esc/CLAEX/Grupo 54, Madrid/Torrejón	
E.25-37	CASA 101EB Aviojet [79-37]	EdA 793 Esc/794 Esc/AGA, Murcia/San Javier	
E.25-38	CASA 101EB Aviojet [79-38,4]	*EdA Patrulla Aguila/AGA, Murcia/San Javier*	
E.25-40	CASA 101EB Aviojet [79-40]	EdA 793 Esc/794 Esc/AGA, Murcia/San Javier	
E.25-41	CASA 101EB Aviojet [74-41]	EdA 741 Esc/GEM, Salamanca/Matacán	
E.25-43	CASA 101EB Aviojet [74-43]	EdA 741 Esc/GEM, Salamanca/Matacán	
E.25-44	CASA 101EB Aviojet [79-44]	EdA 793 Esc/794 Esc/AGA, Murcia/San Javier	
E.25-46	CASA 101EB Aviojet [79-46]	EdA 793 Esc/794 Esc/AGA, Murcia/San Javier	
E.25-50	CASA 101EB Aviojet [79-33]	EdA 793 Esc/794 Esc/AGA, Murcia/San Javier	
E.25-51	CASA 101EB Aviojet [74-07]	EdA 741 Esc/GEM, Salamanca/Matacán	
E.25-52	CASA 101EB Aviojet [79-34]	EdA 793 Esc/794 Esc/AGA, Murcia/San Javier	
E.25-53	CASA 101EB Aviojet [74-09]	EdA 741 Esc/GEM, Salamanca/Matacán	
E.25-54	CASA 101EB Aviojet [79-35]	EdA 793 Esc/794 Esc/AGA, Murcia/San Javier	
E.25-55	CASA 101EB Aviojet [54-21]	EdA 541 Esc/CLAEX/Grupo 54, Madrid/Torrejón	
E.25-56	CASA 101EB Aviojet [74-11]	EdA 741 Esc/GEM, Salamanca/Matacán	
E.25-57	CASA 101EB Aviojet [74-12]	EdA 741 Esc/GEM, Salamanca/Matacán	

Notes	Serial	Type (code/other identity)	Owner/operator, location or fate
	E.25-59	CASA 101EB Aviojet [74-13]	EdA 741 Esc/GEM, Salamanca/Matacán
	E.25-61	CASA 101EB Aviojet [54-22]	EdA 541 Esc/CLAEX/Grupo 54, Madrid/Torrejón
	E.25-62	CASA 101EB Aviojet [79-17,1]	EdA Patrulla Aguila/AGA, Murcia/San Javier
	E.25-63	CASA 101EB Aviojet [74-17]	EdA 741 Esc/GEM, Salamanca/Matacán
	E.25-65	CASA 101EB Aviojet [79-95]	EdA 793 Esc/794 Esc/AGA, Murcia/San Javier
	E.25-66	CASA 101EB Aviojet [74-20]	EdA 741 Esc/GEM, Salamanca/Matacán
	E.25-67	CASA 101EB Aviojet [74-21]	EdA 741 Esc/GEM, Salamanca/Matacán
	E.25-68	CASA 101EB Aviojet [74-22]	EdA 741 Esc/GEM, Salamanca/Matacán
	E.25-69	CASA 101EB Aviojet [79-97,8]	EdA Patrulla Aguila/AGA, Murcia/San Javier
	E.25-71	CASA 101EB Aviojet [74-25]	EdA 741 Esc/GEM, Salamanca/Matacán
	E.25-72	CASA 101EB Aviojet [74-26]	EdA 741 Esc/GEM, Salamanca/Matacán
	E.25-73	CASA 101EB Aviojet [79-98]	EdA 793 Esc/794 Esc/AGA, Murcia/San Javier
	E.25-74	CASA 101EB Aviojet [74-28]	EdA 741 Esc/GEM, Salamanca/Matacán
	E.25-76	CASA 101EB Aviojet [74-30]	EdA 741 Esc/GEM, Salamanca/Matacán
	E.25-78	CASA 101EB Aviojet [79-02,6]	EdA Patrulla Aguila/AGA, Murcia/San Javier
	E.25-79	CASA 101EB Aviojet [79-39]	EdA 793 Esc/794 Esc/AGA, Murcia/San Javier
	E.25-80	CASA 101EB Aviojet [79-03]	EdA 793 Esc/794 Esc/AGA, Murcia/San Javier
	E.25-81	CASA 101EB Aviojet [74-34]	EdA 741 Esc/GEM, Salamanca/Matacán
	E.25-83	CASA 101EB Aviojet [74-35]	EdA 741 Esc/GEM, Salamanca/Matacán
	E.25-84	CASA 101EB Aviojet [79-04]	EdA 793 Esc/794 Esc/AGA, Murcia/San Javier
	E.25-86	CASA 101EB Aviojet [79-32]	EdA 793 Esc/794 Esc/AGA, Murcia/San Javier
	E.25-87	CASA 101EB Aviojet [79-29]	EdA 793 Esc/794 Esc/AGA, Murcia/San Javier
	E.25-88	CASA 101EB Aviojet [74-39]	EdA 741 Esc/GEM, Salamanca/Matacán
	HS.23-01	Sikorsky SH-60B Seahawk [01-1001]	Armada 10 Esc, Rota
	HS.23-02	Sikorsky SH-60B Seahawk [01-1002]	Armada 10 Esc, Rota
	HS.23-03	Sikorsky SH-60B Seahawk [01-1003]	Armada 10 Esc, Rota
	HS.23-04	Sikorsky SH-60B Seahawk [01-1004]	Armada 10 Esc, Rota
	HS.23-05	Sikorsky SH-60B Seahawk [01-1005]	Armada 10 Esc, Rota
	HS.23-06	Sikorsky SH-60B Seahawk [01-1006]	Armada 10 Esc, Rota
	HS.23-07	Sikorsky SH-60B Seahawk [01-1007]	Armada 10 Esc, Rota
	HS.23-08	Sikorsky SH-60B Seahawk [01-1008]	Armada 10 Esc, Rota
	HS.23-09	Sikorsky SH-60B Seahawk [01-1009]	Armada 10 Esc, Rota
	HS.23-10	Sikorsky SH-60B Seahawk [01-1010]	Armada 10 Esc, Rota
	HS.23-11	Sikorsky SH-60B Seahawk [01-1011]	Armada 10 Esc, Rota
	HS.23-12	Sikorsky SH-60B Seahawk [01-1012]	Armada 10 Esc, Rota
	HS.25-1	Eurocopter EC.120B Colibri [78-20]	EdA Patrulla Aspa/Ala 78, Granada/Armilla
	HS.25-2	Eurocopter EC.120B Colibri [78-21]	EdA Patrulla Aspa/Ala 78, Granada/Armilla
	HS.25-3	Eurocopter EC.120B Colibri [78-22]	EdA Patrulla Aspa/Ala 78, Granada/Armilla
	HS.25-4	Eurocopter EC.120B Colibri [78-23]	EdA Patrulla Aspa/Ala 78, Granada/Armilla
	HS.25-5	Eurocopter EC.120B Colibri [78-24]	EdA Patrulla Aspa/Ala 78, Granada/Armilla
	HS.25-6	Eurocopter EC.120B Colibri [78-25]	EdA Patrulla Aspa/Ala 78, Granada/Armilla
	HS.25-7	Eurocopter EC.120B Colibri [78-26]	EdA Patrulla Aspa/Ala 78, Granada/Armilla
	HS.25-8	Eurocopter EC.120B Colibri [78-27]	EdA Patrulla Aspa/Ala 78, Granada/Armilla
	HS.25-9	Eurocopter EC.120B Colibri [78-28]	EdA Patrulla Aspa/Ala 78, Granada/Armilla
	HS.25-10	Eurocopter EC.120B Colibri [78-29]	EdA 782 Esc/Ala 78, Granada/Armilla
	HS.25-11	Eurocopter EC.120B Colibri [78-30]	EdA 782 Esc/Ala 78, Granada/Armilla
	HS.25-12	Eurocopter EC.120B Colibri [78-31]	EdA Patrulla Aspa/Ala 78, Granada/Armilla
	HS.25-13	Eurocopter EC.120B Colibri [78-32]	EdA Patrulla Aspa/Ala 78, Granada/Armilla
	HS.25-14	Eurocopter EC.120B Colibri [78-33]	EdA Patrulla Aspa/Ala 78, Granada/Armilla
	HS.25-15	Eurocopter EC.120B Colibri [78-34]	EdA Patrulla Aspa/Ala 78, Granada/Armilla
	P.3A-01	Lockheed P-3A Orion [22-21]	Withdrawn from use, 2017
	P.3M-08	Lockheed P-3M Orion [22-31]	EdA 221 Esc/Grupo 22, Sevilla/Morón
	P.3M-09	Lockheed P-3M Orion [22-32]	EdA 221 Esc/Grupo 22, Sevilla/Morón
	P.3M-12	Lockheed P-3M Orion [22-35]	EdA 221 Esc/Grupo 22, Sevilla/Morón
	TL.10-01	Lockheed C-130H-30 Hercules [31-01]	EdA 311 Esc/312 Esc/Ala 31, Zaragoza
	T.10-03	Lockheed C-130H Hercules [31-03]	EdA 311 Esc/312 Esc/Ala 31, Zaragoza
	T.10-04	Lockheed C-130H Hercules [31-04]	EdA, stored Sevilla/Morón
	TK.10-05	Lockheed KC-130H Hercules [31-50]	EdA 311 Esc/312 Esc/Ala 31, Zaragoza
	TK.10-06	Lockheed KC-130H Hercules [31-51]	EdA 311 Esc/312 Esc/Ala 31, Zaragoza
	TK.10-07	Lockheed KC-130H Hercules [31-52]	EdA 311 Esc/312 Esc/Ala 31, Zaragoza
	T.10-08	Lockheed C-130H Hercules [31-05]	EdA 311 Esc/312 Esc/Ala 31, Zaragoza
	T.10-09	Lockheed C-130H Hercules [31-06]	EdA 311 Esc/312 Esc/Ala 31, Zaragoza

Serial	Type (code/other identity)	Owner/operator, location or fate	Notes
T.10-10	Lockheed C-130H Hercules [31-07]	EdA 311 Esc/312 Esc/Ala 31, Zaragoza	
TK.10-11	Lockheed KC-130H Hercules [31-53]	EdA 311 Esc/312 Esc/Ala 31, Zaragoza	
TK.10-12	Lockheed KC-130H Hercules [31-54]	EdA 311 Esc/312 Esc/Ala 31, Zaragoza	
TM.11-2	Dassault Falcon 20D [47-22]	*Withdrawn from use, January 2018*	
TM.11-3	Dassault Falcon 20D [47-23]	EdA 472 Esc/Grupo Mixto 47, Madrid/Torrejón	
TM.11-4	Dassault Falcon 20E [47-24]	EdA 472 Esc/Grupo Mixto 47, Madrid/Torrejón	
T.12B-13	CASA 212A Aviocar [72-01]	EdA 721 Esc/Ala 72, Murcia/Alcantarilla	
T.12B-49	CASA 212A Aviocar [72-07]	EdA 721 Esc/Ala 72, Murcia/Alcantarilla	
T.12B-55	CASA 212A Aviocar [72-08]	EdA 721 Esc/Ala 72, Murcia/Alcantarilla	
T.12B-62	CASA 212A Aviocar [72-18]	EdA 721 Esc/Ala 72, Murcia/Alcantarilla	
T.12B-63	CASA 212A Aviocar [72-14]	EdA 721 Esc/Ala 72, Murcia/Alcantarilla	
T.12B-65	CASA 212A Aviocar [72-11]	EdA 721 Esc/Ala 72, Murcia/Alcantarilla	
T.12B-67	CASA 212A Aviocar [72-12]	EdA 721 Esc/Ala 72, Murcia/Alcantarilla	
T.12B-70	CASA 212A Aviocar [72-17]	EdA 721 Esc/Ala 72, Murcia/Alcantarilla	
T.12B-71	CASA 212A Aviocar [72-10]	EdA 721 Esc/Ala 72, Murcia/Alcantarilla	
TM.12D-72	CASA 212-200ECM Aviocar [47-12]	EdA 472 Esc/Grupo Mixto 47, Madrid/Torrejón	
T.12D-75	CASA 212-200 Aviocar [47-14]	EdA 472 Esc/Grupo Mixto 47, Madrid/Torrejón	
TR.12D-76	CASA 212-200 Aviocar [72-21]	EdA 721 Esc/Ala 72, Murcia/Alcantarilla	
TR.12D-77	CASA 212-200 Aviocar [72-22]	EdA 721 Esc/Ala 72, Murcia/Alcantarilla	
TR.12D-79	CASA 212-200 Aviocar [72-23]	EdA 721 Esc/Ala 72, Murcia/Alcantarilla	
TR.12D-81	CASA 212-200 Aviocar [72-24]	EdA 721 Esc/Ala 72, Murcia/Alcantarilla	
T.18-1	Dassault Falcon 900 [45-40]	EdA 451 Esc/Grupo 45, Madrid/Torrejón	
T.18-2	Dassault Falcon 900 [45-41]	EdA 451 Esc/Grupo 45, Madrid/Torrejón	
T.18-3	Dassault Falcon 900B [45-42]	EdA 451 Esc/Grupo 45, Madrid/Torrejón	
T.18-4	Dassault Falcon 900B [45-43]	EdA 451 Esc/Grupo 45, Madrid/Torrejón	
T.18-5	Dassault Falcon 900B [45-44]	EdA 451 Esc/Grupo 45, Madrid/Torrejón	
T.19A-01	Airtech CN.235M-10 [403-01]	EdA 403 Esc, Madrid/Getafe	
T.19A-02	Airtech CN.235M-10 [403-02]	EdA 403 Esc, Madrid/Getafe	
T.19B-07	Airtech CN.235M-100 [74-07]	EdA 744 Esc/GEM, Salamanca/Matacán	
T.19B-11	Airtech CN.235M-100 [74-13]	EdA 744 Esc/GEM, Salamanca/Matacán	
T.19B-13	Airtech CN.235M-100 [74-13]	EdA 744 Esc/GEM, Salamanca/Matacán	
T.19B-16	Airtech CN.235M-100 [74-16]	EdA 744 Esc/GEM, Salamanca/Matacán	
T.19B-17	Airtech CN.235M-100 [74-17]	EdA 744 Esc/GEM, Salamanca/Matacán	
T.19B-18	Airtech CN.235M-100 [74-18]	EdA 744 Esc/GEM, Salamanca/Matacán	
T.19B-19	Airtech CN.235M-100 [74-19]	EdA 744 Esc/GEM, Salamanca/Matacán	
T.19B-20	Airtech CN.235M-100 [74-20]	EdA 744 Esc/GEM, Salamanca/Matacán	
T.19B-21	Airtech CN.235M VIGMA [09-501]	Guardia Civil Servicio Aéreo, Gran Canaria	
T.19B-22	Airtech CN.235M VIGMA [09-502]	Guardia Civil Servicio Aéreo, Gran Canaria	
TR.20-01	Cessna 560 Citation VI [403-11]	EdA 403 Esc, Madrid/Getafe	
TR.20-02	Cessna 560 Citation VI [403-12]	EdA 403 Esc, Madrid/Getafe	
TR.20-03	Cessna 560 Citation VI [403-21]	EdA 403 Esc, Madrid/Getafe	
T.21-01	CASA C-295M [35-39]	EdA 353 Esc/Ala 35, Madrid/Getafe	
T.21-02	CASA C-295M [35-40]	EdA 353 Esc/Ala 35, Madrid/Getafe	
T.21-03	CASA C-295M [35-41]	EdA 353 Esc/Ala 35, Madrid/Getafe	
T.21-04	CASA C-295M [35-42]	EdA 353 Esc/Ala 35, Madrid/Getafe	
T.21-05	CASA C-295M [35-43]	EdA 353 Esc/Ala 35, Madrid/Getafe	
T.21-06	CASA C-295M [35-44]	EdA 353 Esc/Ala 35, Madrid/Getafe	
T.21-07	CASA C-295M [35-45]	EdA 353 Esc/Ala 35, Madrid/Getafe	
T.21-08	CASA C-295M [35-46]	EdA 353 Esc/Ala 35, Madrid/Getafe	
T.21-09	CASA C-295M [35-47]	EdA 353 Esc/Ala 35, Madrid/Getafe	
T.21-10	CASA C-295M [35-48]	EdA 353 Esc/Ala 35, Madrid/Getafe	
T.21-11	CASA C-295M [35-49]	EdA 353 Esc/Ala 35, Madrid/Getafe	
T.21-12	CASA C-295M [35-50]	EdA 353 Esc/Ala 35, Madrid/Getafe	
T.21-13	CASA C-295M [35-51]	EdA 353 Esc/Ala 35, Madrid/Getafe	
T.22-1	Airbus A.310-304 [45-50]	EdA 451 Esc/Grupo 45, Madrid/Torrejón	
T.22-2	Airbus A.310-304 [45-51]	EdA 451 Esc/Grupo 45, Madrid/Torrejón	
T.23-01	Airbus Military A.400M (10074) [31-21]	EdA 311 Esc/312 Esc/Ala 31, Zaragoza	
TK.23-02	Airbus Military A.400M (10075) [31-61]	EdA (on order)	
TK.23-03	Airbus Military A.400M (10076) [31-62]	EdA (on order)	
T.23-04	Airbus Military A.400M	EdA (on order)	
T.23-05	Airbus Military A.400M	EdA (on order)	
T.23-06	Airbus Military A.400M	EdA (on order)	

Notes	Serial	Type (code/other identity)	Owner/operator, location or fate
	T.23-07	Airbus Military A.400M	EdA (on order)
	U.20-1	Cessna 550 Citation II [01-405]	Armada 4 Esc, Rota
	U.20-2	Cessna 550 Citation II [01-406]	Armada 4 Esc, Rota
	U.20-3	Cessna 550 Citation II [01-407]	Armada 4 Esc, Rota
	U.21-01	Cessna 650 Citation VII [01-408]	Armada 4 Esc, Rota
	VA.1A-15	McDonnell Douglas EAV-8B Matador [01-903]	*Withdrawn from use*
	VA.1A-19	McDonnell Douglas EAV-8B Matador [01-907]	*Withdrawn from use*
	VA.1A-20	McDonnell Douglas EAV-8B Matador [01-909]	*Withdrawn from use*
	VA.1A-22	McDonnell Douglas EAV-8B Matador [01-911]	*Withdrawn from use*
	VA.1B-24	McDonnell Douglas EAV-8B+ Matador [01-914]	Armada 9 Esc, Rota
	VA.1B-25	McDonnell Douglas EAV-8B+ Matador [01-915]	Armada 9 Esc, Rota
	VA.1B-26	McDonnell Douglas EAV-8B+ Matador [01-916]	Armada 9 Esc, Rota
	VA.1B-27	McDonnell Douglas EAV-8B+ Matador [01-917]	Armada 9 Esc, Rota
	VA.1B-28	McDonnell Douglas EAV-8B+ Matador [01-918]	Armada 9 Esc, Rota
	VA.1B-29	McDonnell Douglas EAV-8B+ Matador [01-919]	Armada 9 Esc, Rota
	VA.1B-30	McDonnell Douglas EAV-8B+ Matador [01-920]	Armada 9 Esc, Rota
	VA.1B-33	McDonnell Douglas TAV-8B Matador [01-922]	Armada 9 Esc, Rota
	VA.1B-35	McDonnell Douglas EAV-8B+ Matador [01-923]	Armada 9 Esc, Rota
	VA.1B-36	McDonnell Douglas EAV-8B+ Matador [01-924]	Armada 9 Esc, Rota
	VA.1B-37	McDonnell Douglas EAV-8B+ Matador [01-925]	Armada 9 Esc, Rota
	VA.1B-38	McDonnell Douglas EAV-8B+ Matador [01-926]	Armada 9 Esc, Rota
	VA.1B-39	McDonnell Douglas EAV-8B+ Matador [01-927]	Armada 9 Esc, Rota

SUDAN

	ST-PSA	Dassault Falcon 900B	Sudanese Government, Khartoum
	ST-PSR	Dassault Falcon 50	Sudanese Government, Khartoum

SWEDEN

Försvarsmakten/Swedish Armed Forces: Försvarsmaktens Helikopterflottilj (Hkpflj)/Armed Forces Helicopter Wing & Svenska Flygvapnet/Swedish Air Force

	39-6	SAAB JAS 39C Gripen [6]	SAAB, Linköping/Malmen
	39-7	SAAB JAS 39NG Gripen	SAAB, Linköping/Malmen
	39-8	SAAB JAS 39E Gripen	SAAB, Linköping/Malmen
	39-9	SAAB JAS 39E Gripen	SAAB, Linköping/Malmen
	39-10	SAAB JAS 39E Gripen	SAAB, Linköping/Malmen
	39208	SAAB JAS 39C Gripen [208]	Flygvapnet Flottiljer 17, Ronneby/Kallinge
	39209	SAAB JAS 39C Gripen [209]	Flygvapnet Flottiljer 7, Såtenäs
	39210	SAAB JAS 39C Gripen [210]	Flygvapnet Flottiljer 21, Luleå/Kallax
	39211	SAAB JAS 39C Gripen [211]	Flygvapnet Flottiljer 7, Såtenäs
	39212	SAAB JAS 39C Gripen [212]	Flygvapnet Flottiljer 17, Ronneby/Kallinge
	39213	SAAB JAS 39C Gripen [213]	Flygvapnet Flottiljer 7, Såtenäs
	39214	SAAB JAS 39C Gripen [214]	Flygvapnet Flottiljer 7, Såtenäs
	39215	SAAB JAS 39C Gripen [215]	Flygvapnet Flottiljer 7, Såtenäs
	39216	SAAB JAS 39C Gripen [216]	Flygvapnet Flottiljer 17, Ronneby/Kallinge
	39217	SAAB JAS 39C Gripen [217]	Flygvapnet Flottiljer 7, Såtenäs
	39218	SAAB JAS 39C Gripen [218]	Flygvapnet Flottiljer 21, Luleå/Kallax
	39219	SAAB JAS 39C Gripen [219]	Flygvapnet Flottiljer 21, Luleå/Kallax
	39220	SAAB JAS 39C Gripen [220]	Flygvapnet Flottiljer 7, Såtenäs
	39221	SAAB JAS 39C Gripen [221]	Flygvapnet Flottiljer 17, Ronneby/Kallinge
	39222	SAAB JAS 39C Gripen [222]	Flygvapnet Flottiljer 17, Ronneby/Kallinge
	39223	SAAB JAS 39C Gripen [223]	Flygvapnet Flottiljer 21, Luleå/Kallax
	39224	SAAB JAS 39C Gripen [224]	Flygvapnet Flottiljer 17, Ronneby/Kallinge
	39225	SAAB JAS 39C Gripen [225]	Flygvapnet Flottiljer 7, Såtenäs
	39226	SAAB JAS 39C Gripen [226]	Flygvapnet Flottiljer 7, Såtenäs
	39227	SAAB JAS 39C Gripen [227]	Flygvapnet Flottiljer 7, Såtenäs
	39228	SAAB JAS 39C Gripen [228]	Flygvapnet Flottiljer 17, Ronneby/Kallinge
	39229	SAAB JAS 39C Gripen [229]	Flygvapnet Flottiljer 21, Luleå/Kallax
	39230	SAAB JAS 39C Gripen [230]	Flygvapnet Flottiljer 21, Luleå/Kallax
	39231	SAAB JAS 39C Gripen [231]	Flygvapnet Flottiljer 7, Såtenäs
	39232	SAAB JAS 39C Gripen [232]	Flygvapnet Flottiljer 21, Luleå/Kallax
	39233	SAAB JAS 39C Gripen [233]	Flygvapnet Flottiljer 21, Luleå/Kallax
	39246	SAAB JAS 39C Gripen [246]	Flygvapnet Flottiljer 21, Luleå/Kallax

rial	Type (code/other identity)	Owner/operator, location or fate	Notes
247	SAAB JAS 39C Gripen [247]	Flygvapnet Flottiljer 17, Ronneby/Kallinge	
248	SAAB JAS 39C Gripen [248]	Flygvapnet Flottiljer 21, Luleå/Kallax	
249	SAAB JAS 39C Gripen [249]	Flygvapnet Flottiljer 17, Ronneby/Kallinge	
250	SAAB JAS 39C Gripen [250]	Flygvapnet FC, Linköping/Malmen	
251	SAAB JAS 39C Gripen [251]	Flygvapnet FC, Linköping/Malmen	
252	SAAB JAS 39C Gripen [252]	Flygvapnet Flottiljer 17, Ronneby/Kallinge	
253	SAAB JAS 39C Gripen [253]	Flygvapnet Flottiljer 7, Såtenäs	
254	SAAB JAS 39C Gripen [254]	Flygvapnet Flottiljer 17, Ronneby/Kallinge	
255	SAAB JAS 39C Gripen [255]	Flygvapnet Flottiljer 17, Ronneby/Kallinge	
256	SAAB JAS 39C Gripen [256]	Flygvapnet Flottiljer 17, Ronneby/Kallinge	
257	SAAB JAS 39C Gripen [257]	Flygvapnet Flottiljer 21, Luleå/Kallax	
258	SAAB JAS 39C Gripen [258]	Flygvapnet Flottiljer 21, Luleå/Kallax	
260	SAAB JAS 39C Gripen [260]	Flygvapnet Flottiljer 21, Luleå/Kallax	
261	SAAB JAS 39C Gripen [261]	Flygvapnet Flottiljer 21, Luleå/Kallax	
262	SAAB JAS 39C Gripen [262]	SAAB, Linköping/Malmen	
263	SAAB JAS 39C Gripen [263]	Flygvapnet Flottiljer 21, Luleå/Kallax	
264	SAAB JAS 39C Gripen [264]	Flygvapnet Flottiljer 17, Ronneby/Kallinge	
265	SAAB JAS 39C Gripen [265]	Flygvapnet Flottiljer 21, Luleå/Kallax	
266	SAAB JAS 39C Gripen [266]	Flygvapnet Flottiljer 7, Såtenäs	
267	SAAB JAS 39C Gripen [267]	Flygvapnet Flottiljer 21, Luleå/Kallax	
268	SAAB JAS 39C Gripen [268]	Flygvapnet Flottiljer 7, Såtenäs	
269	SAAB JAS 39C Gripen [269]	Flygvapnet Flottiljer 17, Ronneby/Kallinge	
270	SAAB JAS 39C Gripen [270]	Flygvapnet Flottiljer 7, Såtenäs	
271	SAAB JAS 39C Gripen [271]	Flygvapnet Flottiljer 21, Luleå/Kallax	
272	SAAB JAS 39C Gripen [272]	Flygvapnet Flottiljer 7, Såtenäs	
273	SAAB JAS 39C Gripen [273]	Flygvapnet Flottiljer 17, Ronneby/Kallinge	
274	SAAB JAS 39C Gripen [274]	Flygvapnet Flottiljer 21, Luleå/Kallax	
275	SAAB JAS 39C Gripen [275]	Flygvapnet Flottiljer 7, Såtenäs	
276	SAAB JAS 39C Gripen [276]	Flygvapnet Flottiljer 21, Luleå/Kallax	
277	SAAB JAS 39C Gripen [277]	Flygvapnet Flottiljer 7, Såtenäs	
278	SAAB JAS 39C Gripen [278]	Flygvapnet Flottiljer 7, Såtenäs	
279	SAAB JAS 39C Gripen [279]	Flygvapnet Flottiljer 21, Luleå/Kallax	
280	SAAB JAS 39C Gripen [280]	Flygvapnet Flottiljer 21, Luleå/Kallax	
281	SAAB JAS 39C Gripen [281]	Flygvapnet Flottiljer 17, Ronneby/Kallinge	
282	SAAB JAS 39C Gripen [282]	Flygvapnet Flottiljer 17, Ronneby/Kallinge	
283	SAAB JAS 39C Gripen [283]	Flygvapnet Flottiljer 21, Luleå/Kallax	
284	SAAB JAS 39C Gripen [284]	Flygvapnet Flottiljer 17, Ronneby/Kallinge	
285	SAAB JAS 39C Gripen [285]	Flygvapnet Flottiljer 21, Luleå/Kallax	
286	SAAB JAS 39C Gripen [286]	Flygvapnet Flottiljer 21, Luleå/Kallax	
287	SAAB JAS 39C Gripen [287]	Flygvapnet Flottiljer 17, Ronneby/Kallinge	
288	SAAB JAS 39C Gripen [288]	Flygvapnet Flottiljer 21, Luleå/Kallax	
289	SAAB JAS 39C Gripen [289]	Flygvapnet Flottiljer 17, Ronneby/Kallinge	
290	SAAB JAS 39C Gripen [290]	Flygvapnet Flottiljer 21, Luleå/Kallax	
291	SAAB JAS 39C Gripen [291]	Flygvapnet Flottiljer 21, Luleå/Kallax	
292	SAAB JAS 39C Gripen [292]	Flygvapnet Flottiljer 17, Ronneby/Kallinge	
293	SAAB JAS 39C Gripen [293]	Flygvapnet Flottiljer 7, Såtenäs	
294	SAAB JAS 39C Gripen [294]	Flygvapnet Flottiljer 17, Ronneby/Kallinge	
815	SAAB JAS 39D Gripen [815]	Flygvapnet Flottiljer 7, Såtenäs	
816	SAAB JAS 39D Gripen [816]	Flygvapnet Flottiljer 7, Såtenäs	
817	SAAB JAS 39D Gripen [817]	Flygvapnet Flottiljer 21, Luleå/Kallax	
818	SAAB JAS 39D Gripen	*To South Africa as 3901*	
821	SAAB JAS 39D Gripen [821]	Flygvapnet Flottiljer 7, Såtenäs	
822	SAAB JAS 39D Gripen [822]	Flygvapnet Flottiljer 21, Luleå/Kallax	
823	SAAB JAS 39D Gripen [823]	Flygvapnet Flottiljer 21, Luleå/Kallax	
824	SAAB JAS 39D Gripen [824]	Flygvapnet Flottiljer 21, Luleå/Kallax	
825	SAAB JAS 39D Gripen [825]	Flygvapnet Flottiljer 7, Såtenäs	
826	SAAB JAS 39D Gripen [826]	Flygvapnet Flottiljer 17, Ronneby/Kallinge	
827	SAAB JAS 39D Gripen [827]	Flygvapnet Flottiljer 7, Såtenäs	
829	SAAB JAS 39D Gripen [829]	Flygvapnet Flottiljer 17, Ronneby/Kallinge	
830	SAAB JAS 39D Gripen [830]	SAAB, Linköping/Malmen	
831	SAAB JAS 39D Gripen [831]	Flygvapnet Flottiljer 17, Ronneby/Kallinge	
832	SAAB JAS 39D Gripen [832]	SAAB, Linköping/Malmen	

Notes	Serial	Type (code/other identity)	Owner/operator, location or fate
	39833	SAAB JAS 39D Gripen [833]	Flygvapnet Flottiljer 21, Luleå/Kallax
	39834	SAAB JAS 39D Gripen [834]	Flygvapnet Flottiljer 7, Såtenäs
	39835	SAAB JAS 39D Gripen [835]	Flygvapnet Flottiljer 7, Såtenäs
	39836	SAAB JAS 39D Gripen [836]	Flygvapnet Flottiljer 17, Ronneby/Kallinge
	39837	SAAB JAS 39D Gripen [837]	SAAB, Linköping/Malmen
	39838	SAAB JAS 39D Gripen [838]	Flygvapnet Flottiljer 21, Luleå/Kallax
	39839	SAAB JAS 39D Gripen [839]	Flygvapnet Flottiljer 7, Såtenäs
	39840	SAAB JAS 39D Gripen [840]	Flygvapnet Flottiljer 17, Ronneby/Kallinge
	39841	SAAB JAS 39D Gripen [841]	Flygvapnet Flottiljer 7, Såtenäs
	84004	Lockheed C-130H Hercules (Tp.84) [844]	Flygvapnet TSFE, Såtenäs
	84005	Lockheed C-130H Hercules (Tp.84) [845]	Flygvapnet TSFE, Såtenäs
	84006	Lockheed C-130H Hercules (Tp.84) [846]	Flygvapnet TSFE, Såtenäs
	84007	Lockheed C-130H Hercules (Tp.84) [847]	Flygvapnet TSFE, Såtenäs
	84008	Lockheed C-130H Hercules (Tp.84) [848]	Flygvapnet TSFE, Såtenäs
	86001	Rockwell Sabreliner-40 (Tp.86) [861]	Flygvapnet FC, Linköping/Malmen
	100001	SAAB SF.340 (OS.100) [001]	Flygvapnet TSFE, Linköping/Malmen
	100003	SAAB SF.340AEW&C (S.100D Argus) [003]	Flygvapnet TSFE, Linköping/Malmen
	100004	SAAB SF.340AEW&C (S.100D Argus) [004]	Flygvapnet TSFE, Linköping/Malmen
	100008	SAAB SF.340 (Tp.100C) [008]	Flygvapnet TSFE, Linköping/Malmen
	102001	Grumman G.1159C Gulfstream IV (Tp.102A) [021]	*Withdrawn from use, August 2017*
	102002	Grumman G.1159C Gulfstream IV (S.102B Korpen)[022]	Flygvapnet TSFE, Linköping/Malmen
	102003	Grumman G.1159C Gulfstream IV (S.102B Korpen)[023]	Flygvapnet TSFE, Linköping/Malmen
	102004	Grumman G.1159C Gulfstream IV-SP (Tp.102C) [024]	Flygvapnet TSFE, Linköping/Malmen
	102005	Gulfstream Aerospace G.550 (Tp.102D) [025]	Flygvapnet TSFE, Linköping/Malmen
	141041	NH Industries NH.90-TTH (Hkp.14A) [41]	Airbus Helicopters, Marignane, France
	141046	NH Industries NH.90-TTH (Hkp.14A) [46]	Hkpflj 1.HkpSkv, Luleå/Kallax
	141047	NH Industries NH.90-TTH (Hkp.14A) [47]	Hkpflj 1.HkpSkv, Luleå/Kallax
	142042	NH Industries NH.90-TTH (Hkp.14B) [42]	Hkpflj 3.HkpSkv, Ronneby/Kallinge
	142043	NH Industries NH.90-TTH (Hkp.14B) [43]	Hkpflj 3.HkpSkv, Ronneby/Kallinge
	142044	NH Industries NH.90-TTH (Hkp.14B) [44]	Hkpflj 3.HkpSkv, Ronneby/Kallinge
	142045	NH Industries NH.90-TTH (Hkp.14B) [45]	Hkpflj 1.HkpSkv, Luleå/Kallax
	144048	NH Industries NH.90-TTH (Hkp.14D) [48]	Hkpflj 1.HkpSkv, Luleå/Kallax
	144049	NH Industries NH.90-TTH (Hkp.14D) [49]	Hkpflj 1.HkpSkv, Luleå/Kallax
	144050	NH Industries NH.90-TTH (Hkp.14D) [50]	Hkpflj 1.HkpSkv, Luleå/Kallax
	144051	NH Industries NH.90-TTH (Hkp.14D) [51]	Hkpflj 1.HkpSkv, Luleå/Kallax
	144052	NH Industries NH.90-TTH (Hkp.14D) [52]	Hkpflj 1.HkpSkv, Luleå/Kallax
	144053	NH Industries NH.90-TTH (Hkp.14D) [53]	Hkpflj 1.HkpSkv, Luleå/Kallax
	144054	NH Industries NH.90-TTH (Hkp.14D) [54]	Hkpflj 3.HkpSkv, Ronneby/Kallinge
	142055	NH Industries NH.90-SAR (Hkp.14B) [55]	Hkpflj 3.HkpSkv, Ronneby/Kallin
	146056	NH Industries NH.90-SAR (Hkp.14F) [56]	Hkpflj 3.HkpSkv, Ronneby/Kallinge
	146057	NH Industries NH.90-SAR (Hkp.14F) [57]	Hkpflj (on order)
	146058	NH Industries NH.90-SAR (Hkp.14F) [58]	Hkpflj (on order)
	146059	NH Industries NH.90-SAR (Hkp.14F) [59]	Hkpflj (on order)
	151751	Agusta A109LUH Power (Hkp.15A) [21]	Hkpflj 2.HkpSkv, Linköping/Malmen
	151752	Agusta A109LUH Power (Hkp.15A) [22]	Hkpflj 2.HkpSkv, Linköping/Malmen
	151753	Agusta A109LUH Power (Hkp.15A) [23]	Hkpflj 2.HkpSkv, Linköping/Malmen
	151754	Agusta A109LUH Power (Hkp.15A) [24]	Hkpflj 2.HkpSkv, Linköping/Malmen
	151755	Agusta A109LUH Power (Hkp.15A) [25]	Hkpflj 2.HkpSkv, Linköping/Malmen
	151756	Agusta A109LUH Power (Hkp.15A) [26]	Hkpflj 2.HkpSkv, Linköping/Malmen
	151757	Agusta A109LUH Power (Hkp.15A) [27]	Hkpflj 2.HkpSkv, Linköping/Malmen
	151758	Agusta A109LUH Power (Hkp.15A) [28]	Hkpflj 2.HkpSkv, Linköping/Malmen
	151759	Agusta A109LUH Power (Hkp.15A) [29]	Hkpflj 2.HkpSkv, Linköping/Malmen
	152760	Agusta A109LUH Power (Hkp.15B) [30]	Hkpflj 3.HkpSkv, Ronneby/Kallinge
	151761	Agusta A109LUH Power (Hkp.15A) [31]	Hkpflj 2.HkpSkv, Linköping/Malmen
	151762	Agusta A109LUH Power (Hkp.15A) [32]	Hkpflj 2.HkpSkv, Linköping/Malmen
	152763	Agusta A109LUH Power (Hkp.15B) [33]	Hkpflj 3.HkpSkv, Ronneby/Kallinge
	151764	Agusta A109LUH Power (Hkp.15A) [34]	Hkpflj 2.HkpSkv, Linköping/Malmen
	152765	Agusta A109LUH Power (Hkp.15B) [35]	Hkpflj 3.HkpSkv, Ronneby/Kallinge
	152766	Agusta A109LUH Power (Hkp.15B) [36]	Hkpflj 3.HkpSkv, Ronneby/Kallinge
	152767	Agusta A109LUH Power (Hkp.15B) [37]	Hkpflj 3.HkpSkv, Ronneby/Kallinge
	152768	Agusta A109LUH Power (Hkp.15B) [38]	Hkpflj 3.HkpSkv, Ronneby/Kallinge
	152769	Agusta A109LUH Power (Hkp.15B) [39]	Hkpflj 3.HkpSkv, Ronneby/Kallinge

Serial	Type (code/other identity)	Owner/operator, location or fate	Notes
152770	Agusta A109LUH Power (Hkp.15B) [40]	Hkpflj 3.HkpSkv, Ronneby/Kallinge	
161226	Sikorsky UH-60M Black Hawk (Hkp.16A) [01]	Hkpflj 2.HkpSkv, Linköping/Malmen	
161227	Sikorsky UH-60M Black Hawk (Hkp.16A) [02]	Hkpflj 2.HkpSkv, Linköping/Malmen	
161228	Sikorsky UH-60M Black Hawk (Hkp.16A) [03]	Hkpflj 2.HkpSkv, Linköping/Malmen	
161229	Sikorsky UH-60M Black Hawk (Hkp.16A) [04]	Hkpflj 2.HkpSkv, Linköping/Malmen	
161230	Sikorsky UH-60M Black Hawk (Hkp.16A) [05]	Hkpflj 2.HkpSkv, Linköping/Malmen	
161231	Sikorsky UH-60M Black Hawk (Hkp.16A) [06]	Hkpflj 2.HkpSkv, Linköping/Malmen	
161232	Sikorsky UH-60M Black Hawk (Hkp.16A) [07]	Hkpflj 2.HkpSkv, Linköping/Malmen	
161233	Sikorsky UH-60M Black Hawk (Hkp.16A) [08]	Hkpflj 2.HkpSkv, Linköping/Malmen	
161234	Sikorsky UH-60M Black Hawk (Hkp.16A) [09]	Hkpflj 2.HkpSkv, Linköping/Malmen	
161235	Sikorsky UH-60M Black Hawk (Hkp.16A) [10]	Hkpflj 2.HkpSkv, Linköping/Malmen	
161236	Sikorsky UH-60M Black Hawk (Hkp.16A) [11]	Hkpflj 2.HkpSkv, Linköping/Malmen	
161237	Sikorsky UH-60M Black Hawk (Hkp.16A) [12]	Hkpflj 2.HkpSkv, Linköping/Malmen	
161238	Sikorsky UH-60M Black Hawk (Hkp.16A) [13]	Hkpflj 2.HkpSkv, Linköping/Malmen	
161239	Sikorsky UH-60M Black Hawk (Hkp.16A) [14]	Hkpflj 2.HkpSkv, Linköping/Malmen	
161240	Sikorsky UH-60M Black Hawk (Hkp.16A) [15]	Hkpflj 2.HkpSkv, Linköping/Malmen	

Kustbevakning/Swedish Coast Guard

Serial	Type (code/other identity)	Owner/operator, location or fate	Notes
SE-MAA	Bombardier DHC-8Q-311 [501]	Kustbevakning, Nykoping	
SE-MAB	Bombardier DHC-8Q-311 [502]	Kustbevakning, Nykoping	
SE-MAC	Bombardier DHC-8Q-311 [503]	Kustbevakning, Nykoping	

SWITZERLAND

Schweizer Luftwaffe/Swiss Air Force

(Most aircraft are pooled centrally. Some carry unit badges but these rarely indicate actual operators.)

Serial	Type (code/other identity)	Owner/operator, location or fate	Notes
A-101	Pilatus PC-21	Swiss AF Pilotenschule, Emmen	
A-102	Pilatus PC-21	Swiss AF Pilotenschule, Emmen	
A-103	Pilatus PC-21	Swiss AF Pilotenschule, Emmen	
A-104	Pilatus PC-21	Swiss AF Pilotenschule, Emmen	
A-105	Pilatus PC-21	Swiss AF Pilotenschule, Emmen	
A-106	Pilatus PC-21	Swiss AF Pilotenschule, Emmen	
A-107	Pilatus PC-21	Swiss AF Pilotenschule, Emmen	
A-108	Pilatus PC-21	Swiss AF Pilotenschule, Emmen	
A-912	Pilatus NCPC-7 Turbo Trainer	Swiss AF Instrumentenflugstaffel 14, Emmen	
A-913	Pilatus NCPC-7 Turbo Trainer	Swiss AF Instrumentenflugstaffel 14, Emmen	
A-914	Pilatus NCPC-7 Turbo Trainer	Swiss AF Instrumentenflugstaffel 14, Emmen	
A-915	Pilatus NCPC-7 Turbo Trainer	Swiss AF Instrumentenflugstaffel 14, Emmen	
A-916	Pilatus NCPC-7 Turbo Trainer	Swiss AF Instrumentenflugstaffel 14, Emmen	
A-917	Pilatus NCPC-7 Turbo Trainer	Swiss AF Instrumentenflugstaffel 14, Emmen	
A-918	Pilatus NCPC-7 Turbo Trainer	Swiss AF Instrumentenflugstaffel 14, Emmen	
A-919	Pilatus NCPC-7 Turbo Trainer	Swiss AF Instrumentenflugstaffel 14, Emmen	
A-922	Pilatus NCPC-7 Turbo Trainer	Swiss AF Instrumentenflugstaffel 14, Emmen	
A-923	Pilatus NCPC-7 Turbo Trainer	Swiss AF Instrumentenflugstaffel 14, Emmen	
A-924	Pilatus NCPC-7 Turbo Trainer	Swiss AF Instrumentenflugstaffel 14, Emmen	
A-925	Pilatus NCPC-7 Turbo Trainer	Swiss AF Instrumentenflugstaffel 14, Emmen	
A-926	Pilatus NCPC-7 Turbo Trainer	Swiss AF Instrumentenflugstaffel 14, Emmen	
A-927	Pilatus NCPC-7 Turbo Trainer	Swiss AF Instrumentenflugstaffel 14, Emmen	
A-928	Pilatus NCPC-7 Turbo Trainer	Swiss AF Instrumentenflugstaffel 14, Emmen	
A-929	Pilatus NCPC-7 Turbo Trainer	Swiss AF Instrumentenflugstaffel 14, Emmen	
A-930	Pilatus NCPC-7 Turbo Trainer	Swiss AF Instrumentenflugstaffel 14, Emmen	
A-931	Pilatus NCPC-7 Turbo Trainer	Swiss AF Instrumentenflugstaffel 14, Emmen	
A-932	Pilatus NCPC-7 Turbo Trainer	Swiss AF Instrumentenflugstaffel 14, Emmen	
A-933	Pilatus NCPC-7 Turbo Trainer	Swiss AF Instrumentenflugstaffel 14, Emmen	
A-934	Pilatus NCPC-7 Turbo Trainer	Swiss AF Instrumentenflugstaffel 14, Emmen	
A-935	Pilatus NCPC-7 Turbo Trainer	Swiss AF Instrumentenflugstaffel 14, Emmen	
A-936	Pilatus NCPC-7 Turbo Trainer	Swiss AF Instrumentenflugstaffel 14, Emmen	
A-937	Pilatus NCPC-7 Turbo Trainer	*Crashed 12 September 2017, Schreckhorn*	
A-938	Pilatus NCPC-7 Turbo Trainer	Swiss AF Instrumentenflugstaffel 14, Emmen	
A-939	Pilatus NCPC-7 Turbo Trainer	Swiss AF Instrumentenflugstaffel 14, Emmen	
A-940	Pilatus NCPC-7 Turbo Trainer	Swiss AF Instrumentenflugstaffel 14, Emmen	
A-941	Pilatus NCPC-7 Turbo Trainer	Swiss AF Instrumentenflugstaffel 14, Emmen	
C-405	Pilatus PC-9	Swiss AF Zielflugstaffel 12, Emmen	
C-406	Pilatus PC-9	Swiss AF Zielflugstaffel 12, Emmen	

Notes	Serial	Type (code/other identity)	Owner/operator, location or fate
	C-407	Pilatus PC-9	Swiss AF Zielflugstaffel 12, Emmen
	C-408	Pilatus PC-9	Swiss AF Zielflugstaffel 12, Emmen
	C-409	Pilatus PC-9	Swiss AF Zielflugstaffel 12, Emmen
	C-410	Pilatus PC-9	Swiss AF Zielflugstaffel 12, Emmen
	C-411	Pilatus PC-9	Swiss AF Zielflugstaffel 12, Emmen
	C-412	Pilatus PC-9	Swiss AF Zielflugstaffel 12, Emmen
	J-3005	Northrop F-5E Tiger II	Swiss AF FlSt 6 & 19, Payerne
	J-3015	Northrop F-5E Tiger II	Swiss AF FlSt 6 & 19, Payerne
	J-3030	Northrop F-5E Tiger II	Swiss AF FlSt 6 & 19, Payerne
	J-3033	Northrop F-5E Tiger II $	Swiss AF FlSt 6 & 19, Payerne
	J-3036	Northrop F-5E Tiger II $	Swiss AF, stored Sion
	J-3038	Northrop F-5E Tiger II $	Swiss AF FlSt 6 & 19, Payerne
	J-3041	Northrop F-5E Tiger II	Swiss AF, stored Sion
	J-3044	Northrop F-5E Tiger II	Swiss AF, stored Emmen
	J-3056	Northrop F-5E Tiger II	Swiss AF, stored Emmen
	J-3062	Northrop F-5E Tiger II	Swiss AF, stored Sion
	J-3063	Northrop F-5E Tiger II	Swiss AF FlSt 6 & 19, Payerne
	J-3065	Northrop F-5E Tiger II	Swiss AF FlSt 6 & 19, Payerne
	J-3067	Northrop F-5E Tiger II	Swiss AF FlSt 6 & 19, Payerne
	J-3068	Northrop F-5E Tiger II	Swiss AF FlSt 6 & 19, Payerne
	J-3069	Northrop F-5E Tiger II	Swiss AF FlSt 6 & 19, Payerne
	J-3070	Northrop F-5E Tiger II	Swiss AF FlSt 6 & 19, Payerne
	J-3072	Northrop F-5E Tiger II	Swiss AF FlSt 6 & 19, Payerne
	J-3073	Northrop F-5E Tiger II $	Swiss AF FlSt 6 & 19, Payerne
	J-3074	Northrop F-5E Tiger II $	Swiss AF FlSt 6 & 19, Payerne
	J-3076	Northrop F-5E Tiger II	Swiss AF FlSt 6 & 19, Payerne
	J-3077	Northrop F-5E Tiger II	Swiss AF FlSt 6 & 19, Payerne
	J-3079	Northrop F-5E Tiger II	Swiss AF, stored Sion
	J-3080	Northrop F-5E Tiger II	RUAG, Emmen
	J-3081	Northrop F-5E Tiger II	Swiss AF *Patrouille Suisse*, Emmen
	J-3082	Northrop F-5E Tiger II	Swiss AF *Patrouille Suisse*, Emmen
	J-3083	Northrop F-5E Tiger II	Swiss AF *Patrouille Suisse*, Emmen
	J-3084	Northrop F-5E Tiger II	Swiss AF *Patrouille Suisse*, Emmen
	J-3085	Northrop F-5E Tiger II	Swiss AF *Patrouille Suisse*, Emmen
	J-3087	Northrop F-5E Tiger II	Swiss AF *Patrouille Suisse*, Emmen
	J-3088	Northrop F-5E Tiger II	Swiss AF *Patrouille Suisse*, Emmen
	J-3089	Northrop F-5E Tiger II	Swiss AF *Patrouille Suisse*, Emmen
	J-3090	Northrop F-5E Tiger II	Swiss AF *Patrouille Suisse*, Emmen
	J-3091	Northrop F-5E Tiger II	Swiss AF *Patrouille Suisse*, Emmen
	J-3092	Northrop F-5E Tiger II	Swiss AF FlSt 6 & 19, Payerne
	J-3093	Northrop F-5E Tiger II	Swiss AF FlSt 6 & 19, Payerne
	J-3094	Northrop F-5E Tiger II	Swiss AF, stored Payerne
	J-3095	Northrop F-5E Tiger II	Swiss AF FlSt 6 & 19, Payerne
	J-3097	Northrop F-5E Tiger II	Swiss AF FlSt 6 & 19, Payerne
	J-3201	Northrop F-5F Tiger II	Swiss AF, stored Emmen
	J-3202	Northrop F-5F Tiger II	*Preserved at Dübendorf, 2017*
	J-3203	Northrop F-5F Tiger II	Swiss AF FlSt 6 & 19, Payerne
	J-3204	Northrop F-5F Tiger II	Swiss AF FlSt 6 & 19, Payerne
	J-3206	Northrop F-5F Tiger II	Swiss AF, stored Emmen
	J-3210	Northrop F-5F Tiger II	Swiss AF FlSt 6 & 19, Payerne
	J-3211	Northrop F-5F Tiger II	Swiss AF FlSt 6 & 19, Payerne
	J-3212	Northrop F-5F Tiger II	Swiss AF FlSt 6 & 19, Payerne
	J-5001	McDonnell Douglas F/A-18C Hornet	Swiss AF FlSt 11, Meiringen/FlSt 17 & 18 Payer
	J-5002	McDonnell Douglas F/A-18C Hornet	Swiss AF FlSt 11, Meiringen/FlSt 17 & 18 Payer
	J-5003	McDonnell Douglas F/A-18C Hornet	Swiss AF FlSt 11, Meiringen/FlSt 17 & 18 Payer
	J-5004	McDonnell Douglas F/A-18C Hornet	Swiss AF FlSt 11, Meiringen/FlSt 17 & 18 Payer
	J-5005	McDonnell Douglas F/A-18C Hornet	Swiss AF FlSt 11, Meiringen/FlSt 17 & 18 Payer
	J-5006	McDonnell Douglas F/A-18C Hornet	Swiss AF FlSt 11, Meiringen/FlSt 17 & 18 Payer
	J-5007	McDonnell Douglas F/A-18C Hornet	Swiss AF FlSt 11, Meiringen/FlSt 17 & 18 Payer
	J-5008	McDonnell Douglas F/A-18C Hornet	Swiss AF FlSt 11, Meiringen/FlSt 17 & 18 Payer
	J-5009	McDonnell Douglas F/A-18C Hornet	Swiss AF FlSt 11, Meiringen/FlSt 17 & 18 Payer
	J-5010	McDonnell Douglas F/A-18C Hornet	Swiss AF FlSt 11, Meiringen/FlSt 17 & 18 Payer

Serial	Type (code/other identity)	Owner/operator, location or fate	Notes
J-5011	McDonnell Douglas F/A-18C Hornet $	Swiss AF FlSt 11, Meiringen/FlSt 17 & 18 Payerne	
J-5012	McDonnell Douglas F/A-18C Hornet	Swiss AF FlSt 11, Meiringen/FlSt 17 & 18 Payerne	
J-5013	McDonnell Douglas F/A-18C Hornet	Swiss AF FlSt 11, Meiringen/FlSt 17 & 18 Payerne	
J-5014	McDonnell Douglas F/A-18C Hornet $	Swiss AF FlSt 11, Meiringen/FlSt 17 & 18 Payerne	
J-5015	McDonnell Douglas F/A-18C Hornet	Swiss AF FlSt 11, Meiringen/FlSt 17 & 18 Payerne	
J-5016	McDonnell Douglas F/A-18C Hornet	Swiss AF FlSt 11, Meiringen/FlSt 17 & 18 Payerne	
J-5017	McDonnell Douglas F/A-18C Hornet $	Swiss AF FlSt 11, Meiringen/FlSt 17 & 18 Payerne	
J-5018	McDonnell Douglas F/A-18C Hornet $	Swiss AF FlSt 11, Meiringen/FlSt 17 & 18 Payerne	
J-5019	McDonnell Douglas F/A-18C Hornet	Swiss AF FlSt 11, Meiringen/FlSt 17 & 18 Payerne	
J-5020	McDonnell Douglas F/A-18C Hornet	Swiss AF FlSt 11, Meiringen/FlSt 17 & 18 Payerne	
J-5021	McDonnell Douglas F/A-18C Hornet	Swiss AF FlSt 11, Meiringen/FlSt 17 & 18 Payerne	
J-5023	McDonnell Douglas F/A-18C Hornet	Swiss AF FlSt 11, Meiringen/FlSt 17 & 18 Payerne	
J-5024	McDonnell Douglas F/A-18C Hornet	Swiss AF FlSt 11, Meiringen/FlSt 17 & 18 Payerne	
J-5025	McDonnell Douglas F/A-18C Hornet	Swiss AF FlSt 11, Meiringen/FlSt 17 & 18 Payerne	
J-5026	McDonnell Douglas F/A-18C Hornet	Swiss AF FlSt 11, Meiringen/FlSt 17 & 18 Payerne	
J-5232	McDonnell Douglas F/A-18D Hornet	Swiss AF FlSt 11, Meiringen/FlSt 17 & 18 Payerne	
J-5233	McDonnell Douglas F/A-18D Hornet	Swiss AF FlSt 11, Meiringen/FlSt 17 & 18 Payerne	
J-5234	McDonnell Douglas F/A-18D Hornet	Swiss AF FlSt 11, Meiringen/FlSt 17 & 18 Payerne	
J-5236	McDonnell Douglas F/A-18D Hornet	Swiss AF FlSt 11, Meiringen/FlSt 17 & 18 Payerne	
J-5238	McDonnell Douglas F/A-18D Hornet	Swiss AF FlSt 11, Meiringen/FlSt 17 & 18 Payerne	
N711	Aurora Flight Services Centaur OPA	Armasuisse, Emmen	
T-311	Aérospatiale AS.332M-1 Super Puma (TH 89)	Swiss AF LtSt 6 & 8, Alpnach/ LtSt 3 & 4, Dübendorf/LtSt 1 & 5, Payerne	
T-312	Aérospatiale AS.332M-1 Super Puma (TH 89)	Swiss AF LtSt 6 & 8, Alpnach/ LtSt 3 & 4, Dübendorf/LtSt 1 & 5, Payerne	
T-313	Aérospatiale AS.332M-1 Super Puma (TH 89)	Swiss AF LtSt 6 & 8, Alpnach/ LtSt 3 & 4, Dübendorf/LtSt 1 & 5, Payerne	
T-314	Aérospatiale AS.332M-1 Super Puma (TH 89)	Swiss AF LtSt 6 & 8, Alpnach/ LtSt 3 & 4, Dübendorf/LtSt 1 & 5, Payerne	
T-315	Aérospatiale AS.332M-1 Super Puma (TH 89)	Swiss AF LtSt 6 & 8, Alpnach/ LtSt 3 & 4, Dübendorf/LtSt 1 & 5, Payerne	
T-316	Aérospatiale AS.332M-1 Super Puma (TH 89) $	Swiss AF LtSt 6 & 8, Alpnach/ LtSt 3 & 4, Dübendorf/LtSt 1 & 5, Payerne	
T-317	Aérospatiale AS.332M-1 Super Puma (TH 89)	Swiss AF LtSt 6 & 8, Alpnach/ LtSt 3 & 4, Dübendorf/LtSt 1 & 5, Payerne	
T-318	Aérospatiale AS.332M-1 Super Puma (TH 89)	Swiss AF LtSt 6 & 8, Alpnach/ LtSt 3 & 4, Dübendorf/LtSt 1 & 5, Payerne	
T-319	Aérospatiale AS.332M-1 Super Puma (TH 89)	Swiss AF LtSt 6 & 8, Alpnach/ LtSt 3 & 4, Dübendorf/LtSt 1 & 5, Payerne	
T-320	Aérospatiale AS.332M-1 Super Puma (TH 89)	Swiss AF LtSt 6 & 8, Alpnach/ LtSt 3 & 4, Dübendorf/LtSt 1 & 5, Payerne	
T-321	Aérospatiale AS.332M-1 Super Puma (TH 89)	Swiss AF LtSt 6 & 8, Alpnach/ LtSt 3 & 4, Dübendorf/LtSt 1 & 5, Payerne	
T-322	Aérospatiale AS.332M-1 Super Puma (TH 89)	Swiss AF LtSt 6 & 8, Alpnach/ LtSt 3 & 4, Dübendorf/LtSt 1 & 5, Payerne	
T-323	Aérospatiale AS.332M-1 Super Puma (TH 89)	Swiss AF LtSt 6 & 8, Alpnach/ LtSt 3 & 4, Dübendorf/LtSt 1 & 5, Payerne	
T-324	Aérospatiale AS.332M-1 Super Puma (TH 89)	Swiss AF LtSt 6 & 8, Alpnach/ LtSt 3 & 4, Dübendorf/LtSt 1 & 5, Payerne	
T-325	Aérospatiale AS.332M-1 Super Puma (TH 89)	Swiss AF LtSt 6 & 8, Alpnach/ LtSt 3 & 4, Dübendorf/LtSt 1 & 5, Payerne	
T-331	Aérospatiale AS.532UL Super Puma (TH 98)	Swiss AF LtSt 6 & 8, Alpnach/ LtSt 3 & 4, Dübendorf/LtSt 1 & 5, Payerne	
T-332	Aérospatiale AS.532UL Super Puma (TH 98)	Swiss AF LtSt 6 & 8, Alpnach/ LtSt 3 & 4, Dübendorf/LtSt 1 & 5, Payerne	
T-333	Aérospatiale AS.532UL Super Puma (TH 98)	Swiss AF LtSt 6 & 8, Alpnach/ LtSt 3 & 4, Dübendorf/LtSt 1 & 5, Payerne	
T-334	Aérospatiale AS.532UL Super Puma (TH 98)	Swiss AF LtSt 6 & 8, Alpnach/ LtSt 3 & 4, Dübendorf/LtSt 1 & 5, Payerne	
T-335	Aérospatiale AS.532UL Super Puma (TH 98)	Swiss AF LtSt 6 & 8, Alpnach/ LtSt 3 & 4, Dübendorf/LtSt 1 & 5, Payerne	

Notes	Serial	Type (code/other identity)	Owner/operator, location or fate
	T-336	Aérospatiale AS.532UL Super Puma (TH 98)	Swiss AF LtSt 6 & 8, Alpnach/ LtSt 3 & 4, Dübendorf/LtSt 1 & 5, Payerne
	T-337	Aérospatiale AS.532UL Super Puma (TH 98)	Swiss AF LtSt 6 & 8, Alpnach/ LtSt 3 & 4, Dübendorf/LtSt 1 & 5, Payerne
	T-339	Aérospatiale AS.532UL Super Puma (TH 98)	Swiss AF LtSt 6 & 8, Alpnach/ LtSt 3 & 4, Dübendorf/LtSt 1 & 5, Payerne
	T-340	Aérospatiale AS.532UL Super Puma (TH 98)	Swiss AF LtSt 6 & 8, Alpnach/ LtSt 3 & 4, Dübendorf/LtSt 1 & 5, Payerne
	T-342	Aérospatiale AS.532UL Super Puma (TH 98)	Swiss AF LtSt 6 & 8, Alpnach/ LtSt 3 & 4, Dübendorf/LtSt 1 & 5, Payerne
	T-351	Eurocopter EC.135P-2	Swiss AF LTDB, Dübendorf
	T-352	Eurocopter EC.135P-2	Swiss AF LTDB, Dübendorf
	T-353	Eurocopter EC.635P-2	Swiss AF LtSt 6 & 8, Alpnach/ LtSt 3 & 4, Dübendorf/LtSt 1 & 5, Payerne
	T-354	Eurocopter EC.635P-2	Swiss AF LtSt 6 & 8, Alpnach/ LtSt 3 & 4, Dübendorf/LtSt 1 & 5, Payerne
	T-355	Eurocopter EC.635P-2	Swiss AF LtSt 6 & 8, Alpnach/ LtSt 3 & 4, Dübendorf/LtSt 1 & 5, Payerne
	T-356	Eurocopter EC.635P-2	Swiss AF LtSt 6 & 8, Alpnach/ LtSt 3 & 4, Dübendorf/LtSt 1 & 5, Payerne
	T-357	Eurocopter EC.635P-2	Swiss AF LtSt 6 & 8, Alpnach/ LtSt 3 & 4, Dübendorf/LtSt 1 & 5, Payerne
	T-358	Eurocopter EC.635P-2	Swiss AF LtSt 6 & 8, Alpnach/ LtSt 3 & 4, Dübendorf/LtSt 1 & 5, Payerne
	T-359	Eurocopter EC.635P-2	Swiss AF LtSt 6 & 8, Alpnach/ LtSt 3 & 4, Dübendorf/LtSt 1 & 5, Payerne
	T-360	Eurocopter EC.635P-2	Swiss AF LtSt 6 & 8, Alpnach/ LtSt 3 & 4, Dübendorf/LtSt 1 & 5, Payerne
	T-361	Eurocopter EC.635P-2	Swiss AF LtSt 6 & 8, Alpnach/ LtSt 3 & 4, Dübendorf/LtSt 1 & 5, Payerne
	T-362	Eurocopter EC.635P-2	Swiss AF LtSt 6 & 8, Alpnach/ LtSt 3 & 4, Dübendorf/LtSt 1 & 5, Payerne
	T-363	Eurocopter EC.635P-2	Swiss AF LtSt 6 & 8, Alpnach/ LtSt 3 & 4, Dübendorf/LtSt 1 & 5, Payerne
	T-364	Eurocopter EC.635P-2	Swiss AF LtSt 6 & 8, Alpnach/ LtSt 3 & 4, Dübendorf/LtSt 1 & 5, Payerne
	T-365	Eurocopter EC.635P-2	Swiss AF LtSt 6 & 8, Alpnach/ LtSt 3 & 4, Dübendorf/LtSt 1 & 5, Payerne
	T-366	Eurocopter EC.635P-2	Swiss AF LtSt 6 & 8, Alpnach/ LtSt 3 & 4, Dübendorf/LtSt 1 & 5, Payerne
	T-367	Eurocopter EC.635P-2	Swiss AF LtSt 6 & 8, Alpnach/ LtSt 3 & 4, Dübendorf/LtSt 1 & 5, Payerne
	T-368	Eurocopter EC.635P-2	Swiss AF LtSt 6 & 8, Alpnach/ LtSt 3 & 4, Dübendorf/LtSt 1 & 5, Payerne
	T-369	Eurocopter EC.635P-2	Swiss AF LtSt 6 & 8, Alpnach/ LtSt 3 & 4, Dübendorf/LtSt 1 & 5, Payerne
	T-370	Eurocopter EC.635P-2	Swiss AF LtSt 6 & 8, Alpnach/ LtSt 3 & 4, Dübendorf/LtSt 1 & 5, Payerne
	T-721	Beech King Air 350C	Swiss AF LTDB, Dübendorf
	T-729	Beech 1900D	Swiss AF LTDB, Dübendorf
	T-784	Cessna 560XL Citation Excel	Swiss AF LTDB, Bern/Belp
	T-785	Dassault Falcon 900EX EASy II	Swiss AF LTDB, Bern/Belp
	V-612	Pilatus PC.6B/B2-H2 Turbo Porter	Swiss AF LtSt 7, Emmen
	V-613	Pilatus PC.6B/B2-H2 Turbo Porter	Swiss AF LtSt 7, Emmen
	V-614	Pilatus PC.6B/B2-H2 Turbo Porter	Swiss AF LtSt 7, Emmen
	V-616	Pilatus PC.6B/B2-H2 Turbo Porter	Swiss AF LtSt 7, Emmen
	V-617	Pilatus PC.6B/B2-H2 Turbo Porter	Swiss AF LtSt 7, Emmen
	V-618	Pilatus PC.6B/B2-H2 Turbo Porter	Swiss AF LtSt 7, Emmen
	V-619	Pilatus PC.6B/B2-H2 Turbo Porter	Swiss AF LtSt 7, Emmen
	V-620	Pilatus PC.6B/B2-H2 Turbo Porter	Swiss AF LtSt 7, Emmen
	V-622	Pilatus PC.6B/B2-H2 Turbo Porter $	Swiss AF LtSt 7, Emmen
	V-623	Pilatus PC.6B/B2-H2 Turbo Porter	Swiss AF LtSt 7, Emmen

Serial	Type (code/other identity)	Owner/operator, location or fate	Notes
J-631	Pilatus PC.6B/B2-H2 Turbo Porter	Swiss AF LtSt 7, Emmen	
J-632	Pilatus PC.6B/B2-H2 Turbo Porter	Swiss AF LtSt 7, Emmen	
J-633	Pilatus PC.6B/B2-H2 Turbo Porter	Swiss AF LtSt 7, Emmen	
J-634	Pilatus PC.6B/B2-H2 Turbo Porter	Swiss AF LtSt 7, Emmen	
J-635	Pilatus PC.6B/B2-H2 Turbo Porter	Swiss AF LtSt 7, Emmen	

Swiss Government

HB-FOG	Pilatus PC-12/45	Armasuisse, Emmen	

SYRIA

K-ASC	Dassault Falcon 900	Government of Syria, Damascus	

TANZANIA

H-ONE	Gulfstream Aerospace G.550	Tanzanian Government, Dar-es-Salaam	

THAILAND

HS-CMV	Boeing 737-4Z6 (L11Kh.MWK-01/38) [11-111, 90401]	Royal Flight, Bangkok	
HS-HMK	Boeing 737-8Z6 (L11K.WPR-03/59) [99-904, 90410]	*Withdrawn from use, September 2017*	
HS-HRH	Boeing 737-448 (L11Kh.MWK-02/47) [99-999, 90409]	Royal Flight, Bangkok	
HS-MVS	Boeing 737-8Z6 (L11Kh2-1/50) [99-904, 90411]	Royal Flight, Bangkok	
HS-TYR	Airbus A.319CJ-133 (B.L15-1/47) [60202]	Royal Thai AF 6 Wing, Don Muang	
HS-TYS	Boeing 737-8Z6 (L11Kh2-1/50) [55-555]	*Repainted as HS-MVS, July 2017*	
HS-TYT	Airbus A.320CJ-214 (L15K-1/58) [60203]	Royal Thai AF 6 Wing, Don Muang	
HS-TYU	Boeing 737-8Z6 (L11Kh2-2/59) [60205]	*Repainted as HS-HMK, February 2017*	
HS-TYV	Airbus A.340-541 (L19-1/59) [60204]	Royal Thai AF 6 Wing, Don Muang	
18-1/59	Sukhoi SSJ100-95LR Superjet [60317]	Royal Thai AF 6 Wing, Don Muang	
18-2/59	Sukhoi SSJ100-95LR Superjet [60318]	Royal Thai AF 6 Wing, Don Muang	

TUNISIA

Tunisian Air Force/Al Quwwat al-Jawwiya al-Jamahiriyah At'Tunisia & Tunisian Government

21012	Lockheed C-130H Hercules (TS-MTB)	Tunisian AF 21 Sqn, Bizerte/Sidi Ahmed	
21121	Lockheed C-130J-30 Hercules II (TS-MTK)	Tunisian AF 21 Sqn, Bizerte/Sidi Ahmed	
21122	Lockheed C-130J-30 Hercules II (TS-MTL)	Tunisian AF 21 Sqn, Bizerte/Sidi Ahmed	
S-IOO	Boeing 737-7HJ	Government of Tunisia, Tunis	

TURKEY

Türk Hava Kuvvetleri (THK)/Turkish Air Force & Turkish Government

4	Cessna 650 Citation VII	THK 212 Filo/11 HUAÜK, Ankara/Etimesgut	
04	Canadair NF-5A-2000 Freedom Fighter	THK 134 Filo, *Turkish Stars*/3 AJEÜ, Konya	
23	Canadair NF-5A-2000 Freedom Fighter	THK 134 Filo, *Turkish Stars*/3 AJEÜ, Konya	
25	Canadair NF-5A-2000 Freedom Fighter	THK 134 Filo, *Turkish Stars*/3 AJEÜ, Konya	
27	Canadair NF-5A-2000 Freedom Fighter	THK 134 Filo, *Turkish Stars*/3 AJEÜ, Konya	
32	Canadair NF-5A-2000 Freedom Fighter	THK 134 Filo, *Turkish Stars*/3 AJEÜ, Konya	
36	Canadair NF-5A-2000 Freedom Fighter	THK 134 Filo, *Turkish Stars*/3 AJEÜ, Konya	
39	Canadair NF-5A-2000 Freedom Fighter	THK 134 Filo, *Turkish Stars*/3 AJEÜ, Konya	
46	Canadair NF-5A-2000 Freedom Fighter [7]	THK 134 Filo, *Turkish Stars*/3 AJEÜ, Konya	
48	Canadair NF-5A-2000 Freedom Fighter [5]	THK 134 Filo, *Turkish Stars*/3 AJEÜ, Konya	
49	Canadair NF-5A-2000 Freedom Fighter [6]	THK 134 Filo, *Turkish Stars*/3 AJEÜ, Konya	
52	Canadair NF-5A-2000 Freedom Fighter [2]	THK 134 Filo, *Turkish Stars*/3 AJEÜ, Konya	
58	Canadair NF-5A-2000 Freedom Fighter [3]	THK 134 Filo, *Turkish Stars*/3 AJEÜ, Konya	
66	Canadair NF-5A-2000 Freedom Fighter	THK 134 Filo, *Turkish Stars*/3 AJEÜ, Konya	
72	Canadair NF-5A-2000 Freedom Fighter	THK 134 Filo, *Turkish Stars*/3 AJEÜ, Konya	
01	Canadair NF-5B-2000 Freedom Fighter [4]	THK 134 Filo, *Turkish Stars*/3 AJEÜ, Konya	
05	Canadair NF-5B-2000 Freedom Fighter	THK 134 Filo, *Turkish Stars*/3 AJEÜ, Konya	
09	Canadair NF-5B-2000 Freedom Fighter	THK 134 Filo, *Turkish Stars*/3 AJEÜ, Konya	
13	Canadair NF-5B-2000 Freedom Fighter	THK 134 Filo, *Turkish Stars*/3 AJEÜ, Konya	
20	Canadair NF-5B-2000 Freedom Fighter	THK 134 Filo, *Turkish Stars*/3 AJEÜ, Konya	
21	Canadair NF-5B-2000 Freedom Fighter	THK 134 Filo, *Turkish Stars*/3 AJEÜ, Konya	
26	Canadair NF-5B-2000 Freedom Fighter [1]	THK 134 Filo, *Turkish Stars*/3 AJEÜ, Konya	
2609	Boeing KC-135R Stratotanker	THK 101 Filo/10 TÜK, Incirlik	
0110	Boeing KC-135R Stratotanker	THK 101 Filo/10 TÜK, Incirlik	
0325	Boeing KC-135R Stratotanker	THK 101 Filo/10 TÜK, Incirlik	
0326	Boeing KC-135R Stratotanker	THK 101 Filo/10 TÜK, Incirlik	

Notes	Serial	Type (code/other identity)	Owner/operator, location or fate
	62-3539	Boeing KC-135R Stratotanker	THK 101 Filo/10 TÜK, Incirlik
	62-3563	Boeing KC-135R Stratotanker	THK 101 Filo/10 TÜK, Incirlik
	62-3567	Boeing KC-135R Stratotanker	THK 101 Filo/10 TÜK, Incirlik
	63-3186	Lockheed C-130E Hercules (63-13186)	THK 222 Filo/12 HUAÜ, Erkilet
	63-13187	Lockheed C-130E Hercules $	THK 222 Filo/12 HUAÜ, Erkilet
	63-3188	Lockheed C-130E Hercules (63-13188)	THK 222 Filo/12 HUAÜ, Erkilet
	63-13189	Lockheed C-130E Hercules $	THK 222 Filo/12 HUAÜ, Erkilet
	65-0451	Lockheed C-130E Hercules	THK 222 Filo/12 HUAÜ, Erkilet
	67-0455	Lockheed C-130E Hercules	THK 222 Filo/12 HUAÜ, Erkilet
	68-020	Transall C-160D	THK 221 Filo/12 HUAÜ, Erkilet
	68-023	Transall C-160D	THK 221 Filo/12 HUAÜ, Erkilet
	68-01606	Lockheed C-130E Hercules	THK 222 Filo/12 HUAÜ, Erkilet
	68-01608	Lockheed C-130E Hercules	THK 222 Filo/12 HUAÜ, Erkilet
	68-01609	Lockheed C-130E Hercules	THK 222 Filo/12 HUAÜ, Erkilet
	69-019	Transall C-160D	THK 221 Filo/12 HUAÜ, Erkilet
	69-021	Transall C-160D	THK 221 Filo/12 HUAÜ, Erkilet
	69-024	Transall C-160D	THK 221 Filo/12 HUAÜ, Erkilet
	69-026	Transall C-160D	THK 221 Filo/12 HUAÜ, Erkilet
	69-027	Transall C-160D	THK 221 Filo/12 HUAÜ, Erkilet
	69-029	Transall C-160D	THK 221 Filo/12 HUAÜ, Erkilet
	69-031	Transall C-160D	THK 221 Filo/12 HUAÜ, Erkilet
	69-032	Transall C-160D	THK 221 Filo/12 HUAÜ, Erkilet
	69-033	Transall C-160D $	THK 221 Filo/12 HUAÜ, Erkilet
	69-034	Transall C-160D	THK 221 Filo/12 HUAÜ, Erkilet
	69-036	Transall C-160D	THK 221 Filo/12 HUAÜ, Erkilet
	69-040	Transall C-160D $	THK 221 Filo/12 HUAÜ, Erkilet
	70-01610	Lockheed C-130E Hercules	THK 222 Filo/12 HUAÜ, Erkilet
	70-1947	Lockheed C-130E Hercules	THK 222 Filo/12 HUAÜ, Erkilet
	71-01468	Lockheed C-130E Hercules	THK 222 Filo/12 HUAÜ, Erkilet
	73-0991	Lockheed C-130E Hercules $	THK 222 Filo/12 HUAÜ, Erkilet
	86-0066	TUSAS (GD) F-16C-30 Fighting Falcon	THK 132 Filo/3 AJEÜ, Konya
	86-0068	TUSAS (GD) F-16C-30 Fighting Falcon	THK 132 Filo/3 AJEÜ, Konya
	86-0069	TUSAS (GD) F-16C-30 Fighting Falcon	THK 132 Filo/3 AJEÜ, Konya
	86-0070	TUSAS (GD) F-16C-30 Fighting Falcon	THK 152 Filo/5 AJÜ, Merzifon
	86-0071	TUSAS (GD) F-16C-30 Fighting Falcon	THK 152 Filo/5 AJÜ, Merzifon
	86-0072	TUSAS (GD) F-16C-30 Fighting Falcon	THK 152 Filo/5 AJÜ, Merzifon
	86-0192	TUSAS (GD) F-16D-30 Fighting Falcon	THK 132 Filo/3 AJEÜ, Konya
	86-0193	TUSAS (GD) F-16D-30 Fighting Falcon	THK 132 Filo/3 AJEÜ, Konya
	86-0194	TUSAS (GD) F-16D-30 Fighting Falcon	THK 132 Filo/3 AJEÜ, Konya
	86-0195	TUSAS (GD) F-16D-30 Fighting Falcon	THK 132 Filo/3 AJEÜ, Konya
	86-0196	TUSAS (GD) F-16D-30 Fighting Falcon	THK 132 Filo/3 AJEÜ, Konya
	87-0002	TUSAS (GD) F-16D-30 Fighting Falcon	THK 113 Filo/1 AJÜ, Eskisehir
	87-0003	TUSAS (GD) F-16D-30 Fighting Falcon	THK 401 Filo/1 AJÜ, Eskisehir
	87-0009	TUSAS (GD) F-16C-30 Fighting Falcon	THK 113 Filo/1 AJÜ, Eskisehir
	87-0010	TUSAS (GD) F-16C-30 Fighting Falcon	THK 132 Filo/3 AJEÜ, Konya
	87-0011	TUSAS (GD) F-16C-30 Fighting Falcon	THK 132 Filo/3 AJEÜ, Konya
	87-0013	TUSAS (GD) F-16C-30 Fighting Falcon	THK 152 Filo/5 AJÜ, Merzifon
	87-0014	TUSAS (GD) F-16C-30 Fighting Falcon	THK 113 Filo/1 AJÜ, Eskisehir
	87-0015	TUSAS (GD) F-16C-30 Fighting Falcon	THK 113 Filo/1 AJÜ, Eskisehir
	87-0016	TUSAS (GD) F-16C-30 Fighting Falcon	THK 132 Filo/3 AJEÜ, Konya
	87-0017	TUSAS (GD) F-16C-30 Fighting Falcon	THK 152 Filo/5 AJÜ, Merzifon
	87-0018	TUSAS (GD) F-16C-30 Fighting Falcon	THK 152 Filo/5 AJÜ, Merzifon
	87-0019	TUSAS (GD) F-16C-30 Fighting Falcon	THK 132 Filo/3 AJEÜ, Konya
	87-0020	TUSAS (GD) F-16C-30 Fighting Falcon	THK 152 Filo/5 AJÜ, Merzifon
	87-0021	TUSAS (GD) F-16C-30 Fighting Falcon	THK 132 Filo/3 AJEÜ, Konya
	88-0013	TUSAS (GD) F-16D-30 Fighting Falcon	THK 152 Filo/5 AJÜ, Merzifon
	88-0014	TUSAS (GD) F-16D-40 Fighting Falcon	THK 192 Filo/9 AJÜ, Balikesir
	88-0015	TUSAS (GD) F-16D-40 Fighting Falcon	THK 191 Filo/9 AJÜ, Balikesir
	88-0019	TUSAS (GD) F-16C-30 Fighting Falcon	THK 132 Filo/3 AJEÜ, Konya
	88-0020	TUSAS (GD) F-16C-30 Fighting Falcon	THK 132 Filo/3 AJEÜ, Konya
	88-0021	TUSAS (GD) F-16C-30 Fighting Falcon	THK 152 Filo/5 AJÜ, Merzifon
	88-0024	TUSAS (GD) F-16C-30 Fighting Falcon	THK 152 Filo/5 AJÜ, Merzifon

Serial	Type (code/other identity)	Owner/operator, location or fate	Notes
88-0025	TUSAS (GD) F-16C-30 Fighting Falcon	THK 152 Filo/5 AJÜ, Merzifon	
88-0026	TUSAS (GD) F-16C-30 Fighting Falcon	THK 152 Filo/5 AJÜ, Merzifon	
88-0027	TUSAS (GD) F-16C-30 Fighting Falcon	THK 152 Filo/5 AJÜ, Merzifon	
88-0028	TUSAS (GD) F-16C-30 Fighting Falcon	THK 191 Filo/9 AJÜ, Balikesir	
88-0029	TUSAS (GD) F-16C-30 Fighting Falcon $	THK 132 Filo/3 AJEÜ, Konya	
88-0030	TUSAS (GD) F-16C-30 Fighting Falcon	THK 152 Filo/5 AJÜ, Merzifon	
88-0031	TUSAS (GD) F-16C-30 Fighting Falcon	THK 401 Filo/1 AJÜ, Eskisehir	
88-0032	TUSAS (GD) F-16C-30 Fighting Falcon $	THK 132 Filo/3 AJEÜ, Konya	
88-0033	TUSAS (GD) F-16C-40 Fighting Falcon	THK 152 Filo/5 AJÜ, Merzifon	
88-0034	TUSAS (GD) F-16C-40 Fighting Falcon	THK 191 Filo/9 AJÜ, Balikesir	
88-0035	TUSAS (GD) F-16C-40 Fighting Falcon	THK 152 Filo/5 AJÜ, Merzifon	
88-0036	TUSAS (GD) F-16C-40 Fighting Falcon	THK 191 Filo/9 AJÜ, Balikesir	
88-0037	TUSAS (GD) F-16C-40 Fighting Falcon	THK 182 Filo/8 AJÜ, Diyarbakir	
89-0022	TUSAS (GD) F-16C-40 Fighting Falcon	THK	
89-0023	TUSAS (GD) F-16C-40 Fighting Falcon	THK 192 Filo/9 AJÜ, Balikesir	
89-0024	TUSAS (GD) F-16C-40 Fighting Falcon	THK 192 Filo/9 AJÜ, Balikesir	
89-0025	TUSAS (GD) F-16C-40 Fighting Falcon	THK 191 Filo/9 AJÜ, Balikesir	
89-0026	TUSAS (GD) F-16C-40 Fighting Falcon	THK	
89-0027	TUSAS (GD) F-16C-40 Fighting Falcon	THK	
89-0028	TUSAS (GD) F-16C-40 Fighting Falcon	THK	
89-0030	TUSAS (GD) F-16C-40 Fighting Falcon	THK	
89-0031	TUSAS (GD) F-16C-40 Fighting Falcon	THK	
89-0034	TUSAS (GD) F-16C-40 Fighting Falcon	THK	
89-0035	TUSAS (GD) F-16C-40 Fighting Falcon	THK 152 Filo/5 AJÜ, Merzifon	
89-0036	TUSAS (GD) F-16C-40 Fighting Falcon	THK	
89-0037	TUSAS (GD) F-16C-40 Fighting Falcon	THK	
89-0038	TUSAS (GD) F-16C-40 Fighting Falcon	THK	
89-0039	TUSAS (GD) F-16C-40 Fighting Falcon	THK 152 Filo/5 AJÜ, Merzifon	
89-0040	TUSAS (GD) F-16C-40 Fighting Falcon	THK 192 Filo/9 AJÜ, Balikesir	
89-0041	TUSAS (GD) F-16C-40 Fighting Falcon	THK 152 Filo/5 AJÜ, Merzifon	
89-0042	TUSAS (GD) F-16D-40 Fighting Falcon	THK 191 Filo/9 AJÜ, Balikesir	
89-0043	TUSAS (GD) F-16D-40 Fighting Falcon	THK 192 Filo/9 AJÜ, Balikesir	
89-0044	TUSAS (GD) F-16D-40 Fighting Falcon	THK 132 Filo/3 AJEÜ, Konya	
89-0045	TUSAS (GD) F-16C-40 Fighting Falcon	THK 152 Filo/5 AJÜ, Merzifon	
90-0004	TUSAS (GD) F-16C-40 Fighting Falcon	THK 152 Filo/5 AJÜ, Merzifon	
90-0005	TUSAS (GD) F-16C-40 Fighting Falcon	THK 191 Filo/9 AJÜ, Balikesir	
90-0006	TUSAS (GD) F-16C-40 Fighting Falcon	THK 182 Filo/8 AJÜ, Diyarbakir	
90-0007	TUSAS (GD) F-16C-40 Fighting Falcon	THK	
90-0008	TUSAS (GD) F-16C-40 Fighting Falcon	THK	
90-0009	TUSAS (GD) F-16C-40 Fighting Falcon	THK	
90-0010	TUSAS (GD) F-16C-40 Fighting Falcon	THK	
90-0011	TUSAS (GD) F-16C-40 Fighting Falcon $	THK	
90-0012	TUSAS (GD) F-16C-40 Fighting Falcon	THK 191 Filo/9 AJÜ, Balikesir	
90-0013	TUSAS (GD) F-16C-40 Fighting Falcon	THK 182 Filo/8 AJÜ, Diyarbakir	
90-0014	TUSAS (GD) F-16C-40 Fighting Falcon $	THK	
90-0016	TUSAS (GD) F-16C-40 Fighting Falcon	THK 182 Filo/8 AJÜ, Diyarbakir	
90-0017	TUSAS (GD) F-16C-40 Fighting Falcon	THK 191 Filo/9 AJÜ, Balikesir	
90-0018	TUSAS (GD) F-16C-40 Fighting Falcon	THK 191 Filo/9 AJÜ, Balikesir	
90-0019	TUSAS (GD) F-16C-40 Fighting Falcon	THK	
90-0020	TUSAS (GD) F-16C-40 Fighting Falcon	THK	
90-0021	TUSAS (GD) F-16C-40 Fighting Falcon	THK	
90-0022	TUSAS (GD) F-16D-40 Fighting Falcon	THK 182 Filo/8 AJÜ, Diyarbakir	
90-0023	TUSAS (GD) F-16D-40 Fighting Falcon	THK 152 Filo/5 AJÜ, Merzifon	
90-0024	TUSAS (GD) F-16D-40 Fighting Falcon	THK 182 Filo/8 AJÜ, Diyarbakir	
91-003	Grumman G.1159C Gulfstream IV	THK 212 Filo/11 HUAÜK, Ankara/Etimesgut	
91-0001	TUSAS (GD) F-16C-40 Fighting Falcon	THK	
91-0002	TUSAS (GD) F-16C-40 Fighting Falcon	THK 401 Filo/1 AJÜ, Eskisehir	
91-0003	TUSAS (GD) F-16C-40 Fighting Falcon	THK 182 Filo/8 AJÜ, Diyarbakir	
91-0004	TUSAS (GD) F-16C-40 Fighting Falcon	THK	
91-0005	TUSAS (GD) F-16C-40 Fighting Falcon	THK 182 Filo/8 AJÜ, Diyarbakir	
91-0006	TUSAS (GD) F-16C-40 Fighting Falcon	THK	
91-0007	TUSAS (GD) F-16C-40 Fighting Falcon	THK	

Notes	Serial	Type (code/other identity)	Owner/operator, location or fate
	91-0008	TUSAS (GD) F-16C-40 Fighting Falcon	THK 192 Filo/9 AJÜ, Balikesir
	91-0010	TUSAS (GD) F-16C-40 Fighting Falcon	THK
	91-0011	TUSAS (GD) F-16C-40 Fighting Falcon $	THK
	91-0012	TUSAS (GD) F-16C-40 Fighting Falcon	THK
	91-0013	TUSAS (GD) F-16C-40 Fighting Falcon	THK 192 Filo/9 AJÜ, Balikesir
	91-0014	TUSAS (GD) F-16C-40 Fighting Falcon	THK
	91-0015	TUSAS (GD) F-16C-40 Fighting Falcon	THK 401 Filo/1 AJÜ, Eskisehir
	91-0016	TUSAS (GD) F-16C-40 Fighting Falcon	THK 182 Filo/8 AJÜ, Diyarbakir
	91-0017	TUSAS (GD) F-16C-40 Fighting Falcon	THK 182 Filo/8 AJÜ, Diyarbakir
	91-0018	TUSAS (GD) F-16C-40 Fighting Falcon	THK 191 Filo/9 AJÜ, Balikesir
	91-0020	TUSAS (GD) F-16C-40 Fighting Falcon	THK
	91-0022	TUSAS (GD) F-16D-40 Fighting Falcon	THK 191 Filo/9 AJÜ, Balikesir
	91-0024	TUSAS (GD) F-16D-40 Fighting Falcon	THK
	92-0001	TUSAS (GD) F-16C-40 Fighting Falcon	THK 182 Filo/8 AJÜ, Diyarbakir
	92-0002	TUSAS (GD) F-16C-40 Fighting Falcon	THK 182 Filo/8 AJÜ, Diyarbakir
	92-0003	TUSAS (GD) F-16C-40 Fighting Falcon	THK 191 Filo/9 AJÜ, Balikesir
	92-0004	TUSAS (GD) F-16C-40 Fighting Falcon	THK
	92-0005	TUSAS (GD) F-16C-40 Fighting Falcon	THK 192 Filo/9 AJÜ, Balikesir
	92-0006	TUSAS (GD) F-16C-40 Fighting Falcon	THK 182 Filo/8 AJÜ, Diyarbakir
	92-0007	TUSAS (GD) F-16C-40 Fighting Falcon	THK 192 Filo/9 AJÜ, Balikesir
	92-0008	TUSAS (GD) F-16C-40 Fighting Falcon	THK 152 Filo/5 AJÜ, Merzifon
	92-0009	TUSAS (GD) F-16C-40 Fighting Falcon	THK 191 Filo/9 AJÜ, Balikesir
	92-0010	TUSAS (GD) F-16C-40 Fighting Falcon	THK 191 Filo/9 AJÜ, Balikesir
	92-0011	TUSAS (GD) F-16C-40 Fighting Falcon	THK 182 Filo/8 AJÜ, Diyarbakir
	92-0012	TUSAS (GD) F-16C-40 Fighting Falcon	THK 182 Filo/8 AJÜ, Diyarbakir
	92-0013	TUSAS (GD) F-16C-40 Fighting Falcon	THK
	92-0014	TUSAS (GD) F-16C-40 Fighting Falcon $	THK 192 Filo/9 AJÜ, Balikesir
	92-0015	TUSAS (GD) F-16C-40 Fighting Falcon	THK
	92-0016	TUSAS (GD) F-16C-40 Fighting Falcon	THK
	92-0017	TUSAS (GD) F-16C-40 Fighting Falcon	THK 152 Filo/5 AJÜ, Merzifon
	92-0018	TUSAS (GD) F-16C-40 Fighting Falcon	THK
	92-0019	TUSAS (GD) F-16C-40 Fighting Falcon	THK 181 Filo/8 AJÜ, Diyarbakir
	92-0020	TUSAS (GD) F-16C-40 Fighting Falcon	THK 181 Filo/8 AJÜ, Diyarbakir
	92-0021	TUSAS (GD) F-16C-40 Fighting Falcon	THK 191 Filo/9 AJÜ, Balikesir
	92-0022	TUSAS (GD) F-16D-40 Fighting Falcon	THK
	92-0023	TUSAS (GD) F-16D-40 Fighting Falcon	THK
	92-0024	TUSAS (GD) F-16D-40 Fighting Falcon	THK 191 Filo/9 AJÜ, Balikesir
	93-005	Cessna 650 Citation VII	THK 212 Filo/11 HUAÜK, Ankara/Etimesgut
	93-0001	TUSAS (GD) F-16C-40 Fighting Falcon	THK 401 Filo/1 AJÜ, Eskisehir
	93-0003	TUSAS (GD) F-16C-40 Fighting Falcon	THK 192 Filo/9 AJÜ, Balikesir
	93-0004	TUSAS (GD) F-16C-40 Fighting Falcon	THK 181 Filo/8 AJÜ, Diyarbakir
	93-0005	TUSAS (GD) F-16C-40 Fighting Falcon	THK 181 Filo/8 AJÜ, Diyarbakir
	93-0006	TUSAS (GD) F-16C-40 Fighting Falcon	THK 181 Filo/8 AJÜ, Diyarbakir
	93-0007	TUSAS (GD) F-16C-40 Fighting Falcon	THK 182 Filo/8 AJÜ, Diyarbakir
	93-0008	TUSAS (GD) F-16C-40 Fighting Falcon	THK 181 Filo/8 AJÜ, Diyarbakir
	93-0009	TUSAS (GD) F-16C-40 Fighting Falcon	THK 182 Filo/8 AJÜ, Diyarbakir
	93-0010	TUSAS (GD) F-16C-40 Fighting Falcon	THK 132 Filo/3 AJEÜ, Konya
	93-0011	TUSAS (GD) F-16C-40 Fighting Falcon	THK 181 Filo/8 AJÜ, Diyarbakir
	93-0012	TUSAS (GD) F-16C-40 Fighting Falcon	THK 181 Filo/8 AJÜ, Diyarbakir
	93-0013	TUSAS (GD) F-16C-40 Fighting Falcon	THK 181 Filo/8 AJÜ, Diyarbakir
	93-0658	TUSAS (GD) F-16C-50 Fighting Falcon	THK 132 Filo/3 AJEÜ, Konya
	93-0659	TUSAS (GD) F-16C-50 Fighting Falcon	THK 191 Filo/9 AJÜ, Balikesir
	93-0660	TUSAS (GD) F-16C-50 Fighting Falcon	THK 152 Filo/5 AJÜ, Merzifon
	93-0661	TUSAS (GD) F-16C-50 Fighting Falcon	THK 132 Filo/3 AJEÜ, Konya
	93-0663	TUSAS (GD) F-16C-50 Fighting Falcon	THK 401 Filo/1 AJÜ, Eskisehir
	93-0664	TUSAS (GD) F-16C-50 Fighting Falcon	THK 132 Filo/3 AJEÜ, Konya
	93-0665	TUSAS (GD) F-16C-50 Fighting Falcon	THK 191 Filo/9 AJÜ, Balikesir
	93-0667	TUSAS (GD) F-16C-50 Fighting Falcon	THK 151 Filo/5 AJÜ, Merzifon
	93-0668	TUSAS (GD) F-16C-50 Fighting Falcon	THK
	93-0669	TUSAS (GD) F-16C-50 Fighting Falcon	THK 151 Filo/5 AJÜ, Merzifon
	93-0670	TUSAS (GD) F-16C-50 Fighting Falcon	THK 191 Filo/9 AJÜ, Balikesir
	93-0671	TUSAS (GD) F-16C-50 Fighting Falcon	THK

Serial	Type (code/other identity)	Owner/operator, location or fate	Notes
93-0672	TUSAS (GD) F-16C-50 Fighting Falcon	THK 132 Filo/3 AJEÜ, Konya	
93-0673	TUSAS (GD) F-16C-50 Fighting Falcon	THK 132 Filo/3 AJEÜ, Konya	
93-0674	TUSAS (GD) F-16C-50 Fighting Falcon	THK 132 Filo/3 AJEÜ, Konya	
93-0675	TUSAS (GD) F-16C-50 Fighting Falcon	THK 191 Filo/9 AJÜ, Balikesir	
93-0676	TUSAS (GD) F-16C-50 Fighting Falcon	THK 192 Filo/9 AJÜ, Balikesir	
93-0677	TUSAS (GD) F-16C-50 Fighting Falcon $	THK 141 Filo/4 AJÜ, Akinci	
93-0678	TUSAS (GD) F-16C-50 Fighting Falcon	THK 152 Filo/5 AJÜ, Merzifon	
93-0679	TUSAS (GD) F-16C-50 Fighting Falcon	THK 192 Filo/9 AJÜ, Balikesir	
93-0680	TUSAS (GD) F-16C-50 Fighting Falcon $	THK 192 Filo/9 AJÜ, Balikesir	
93-0681	TUSAS (GD) F-16C-50 Fighting Falcon	THK 192 Filo/9 AJÜ, Balikesir	
93-0682	TUSAS (GD) F-16C-50 Fighting Falcon $	THK 192 Filo/9 AJÜ, Balikesir	
93-0683	TUSAS (GD) F-16C-50 Fighting Falcon	THK 192 Filo/9 AJÜ, Balikesir	
93-0684	TUSAS (GD) F-16C-50 Fighting Falcon	THK	
93-0685	TUSAS (GD) F-16C-50 Fighting Falcon	THK	
93-0687	TUSAS (GD) F-16C-50 Fighting Falcon	THK 132 Filo/3 AJEÜ, Konya	
93-0688	TUSAS (GD) F-16C-50 Fighting Falcon	THK 151 Filo/5 AJÜ, Merzifon	
93-0689	TUSAS (GD) F-16C-50 Fighting Falcon	THK 192 Filo/9 AJÜ, Balikesir	
93-0690	TUSAS (GD) F-16C-50 Fighting Falcon	THK 141 Filo/4 AJÜ, Akinci	
93-0691	TUSAS (GD) F-16D-50 Fighting Falcon $	THK 192 Filo/9 AJÜ, Balikesir	
93-0692	TUSAS (GD) F-16D-50 Fighting Falcon	THK 151 Filo/5 AJÜ, Merzifon	
93-0693	TUSAS (GD) F-16D-50 Fighting Falcon	THK 152 Filo/5 AJÜ, Merzifon	
93-0694	TUSAS (GD) F-16D-50 Fighting Falcon	THK 151 Filo/5 AJÜ, Merzifon	
93-0695	TUSAS (GD) F-16D-50 Fighting Falcon	THK 141 Filo/4 AJÜ, Akinci	
93-0696	TUSAS (GD) F-16D-50 Fighting Falcon $	THK 151 Filo/5 AJÜ, Merzifon	
94-0071	TUSAS (GD) F-16C-50 Fighting Falcon	THK 192 Filo/9 AJÜ, Balikesir	
94-0072	TUSAS (GD) F-16C-50 Fighting Falcon	THK 151 Filo/5 AJÜ, Merzifon	
94-0073	TUSAS (GD) F-16C-50 Fighting Falcon	THK 151 Filo/5 AJÜ, Merzifon	
94-0074	TUSAS (GD) F-16C-50 Fighting Falcon	THK 191 Filo/9 AJÜ, Balikesir	
94-0075	TUSAS (GD) F-16C-50 Fighting Falcon	THK 151 Filo/5 AJÜ, Merzifon	
94-0076	TUSAS (GD) F-16C-50 Fighting Falcon	THK 151 Filo/5 AJÜ, Merzifon	
94-0077	TUSAS (GD) F-16C-50 Fighting Falcon	THK 141 Filo/4 AJÜ, Akinci	
94-0078	TUSAS (GD) F-16C-50 Fighting Falcon	THK 151 Filo/5 AJÜ, Merzifon	
94-0079	TUSAS (GD) F-16C-50 Fighting Falcon	THK 191 Filo/9 AJÜ, Balikesir	
94-0080	TUSAS (GD) F-16C-50 Fighting Falcon	THK 191 Filo/9 AJÜ, Balikesir	
94-0082	TUSAS (GD) F-16C-50 Fighting Falcon	THK 151 Filo/5 AJÜ, Merzifon	
94-0083	TUSAS (GD) F-16C-50 Fighting Falcon	THK 151 Filo/5 AJÜ, Merzifon	
94-0084	TUSAS (GD) F-16C-50 Fighting Falcon	THK 141 Filo/4 AJÜ, Akinci	
94-0085	TUSAS (GD) F-16C-50 Fighting Falcon	THK 191 Filo/9 AJÜ, Balikesir	
94-0086	TUSAS (GD) F-16C-50 Fighting Falcon	THK 191 Filo/9 AJÜ, Balikesir	
94-0088	TUSAS (GD) F-16C-50 Fighting Falcon	THK 151 Filo/5 AJÜ, Merzifon	
94-0089	TUSAS (GD) F-16C-50 Fighting Falcon	THK 152 Filo/5 AJÜ, Merzifon	
94-0090	TUSAS (GD) F-16C-50 Fighting Falcon $	THK 192 Filo/9 AJÜ, Balikesir	
94-0091	TUSAS (GD) F-16C-50 Fighting Falcon	THK 132 Filo/3 AJEÜ, Konya	
94-0092	TUSAS (GD) F-16C-50 Fighting Falcon	THK 132 Filo/3 AJEÜ, Konya	
94-0093	TUSAS (GD) F-16C-50 Fighting Falcon	THK 141 Filo/4 AJÜ, Akinci	
94-0094	TUSAS (GD) F-16C-50 Fighting Falcon	THK 141 Filo/4 AJÜ, Akinci	
94-0095	TUSAS (GD) F-16C-50 Fighting Falcon	THK 192 Filo/9 AJÜ, Balikesir	
94-0096	TUSAS (GD) F-16C-50 Fighting Falcon	THK 141 Filo/4 AJÜ, Akinci	
94-0105	TUSAS (GD) F-16D-50 Fighting Falcon	THK 141 Filo/4 AJÜ, Akinci	
94-0106	TUSAS (GD) F-16D-50 Fighting Falcon	THK 401 Filo/1 AJÜ, Eskisehir	
94-0108	TUSAS (GD) F-16D-50 Fighting Falcon	THK 191 Filo/9 AJÜ, Balikesir	
94-0109	TUSAS (GD) F-16D-50 Fighting Falcon	THK 132 Filo/3 AJEÜ, Konya	
94-0110	TUSAS (GD) F-16D-50 Fighting Falcon	THK 401 Filo/1 AJÜ, Eskisehir	
94-1557	TUSAS (GD) F-16D-50 Fighting Falcon	THK 152 Filo/5 AJÜ, Merzifon	
94-1558	TUSAS (GD) F-16D-50 Fighting Falcon	THK 132 Filo/3 AJEÜ, Konya	
94-1559	TUSAS (GD) F-16D-50 Fighting Falcon	THK 152 Filo/5 AJÜ, Merzifon	
94-1560	TUSAS (GD) F-16D-50 Fighting Falcon	THK 192 Filo/9 AJÜ, Balikesir	
94-1561	TUSAS (GD) F-16D-50 Fighting Falcon	THK 192 Filo/9 AJÜ, Balikesir	
94-1562	TUSAS (GD) F-16D-50 Fighting Falcon	THK 192 Filo/9 AJÜ, Balikesir	
94-1563	TUSAS (GD) F-16D-50 Fighting Falcon	THK 192 Filo/9 AJÜ, Balikesir	
94-1564	TUSAS (GD) F-16D-50 Fighting Falcon	THK 192 Filo/9 AJÜ, Balikesir	
07-1001	TUSAS (GD) F-16C-50 Fighting Falcon	THK	

Notes	Serial	Type (code/other identity)	Owner/operator, location or fate
	07-1002	TUSAS (GD) F-16C-50 Fighting Falcon	THK 181 Filo/8 AJÜ, Diyarbakir
	07-1003	TUSAS (GD) F-16C-50 Fighting Falcon	THK 181 Filo/8 AJÜ, Diyarbakir
	07-1004	TUSAS (GD) F-16C-50 Fighting Falcon	THK
	07-1005	TUSAS (GD) F-16C-50 Fighting Falcon	THK 181 Filo/8 AJÜ, Diyarbakir
	07-1006	TUSAS (GD) F-16C-50 Fighting Falcon	THK 181 Filo/8 AJÜ, Diyarbakir
	07-1007	TUSAS (GD) F-16C-50 Fighting Falcon	THK
	07-1008	TUSAS (GD) F-16C-50 Fighting Falcon	THK
	07-1009	TUSAS (GD) F-16C-50 Fighting Falcon	THK 152 Filo/5 AJÜ, Merzifon
	07-1010	TUSAS (GD) F-16C-50 Fighting Falcon	THK 152 Filo/5 AJÜ, Merzifon
	07-1011	TUSAS (GD) F-16C-50 Fighting Falcon	THK
	07-1012	TUSAS (GD) F-16C-50 Fighting Falcon	THK
	07-1013	TUSAS (GD) F-16C-50 Fighting Falcon	THK 181 Filo/8 AJÜ, Diyarbakir
	07-1014	TUSAS (GD) F-16C-50 Fighting Falcon	THK
	07-1015	TUSAS (GD) F-16D-50 Fighting Falcon	THK
	07-1016	TUSAS (GD) F-16D-50 Fighting Falcon	THK 181 Filo/8 AJÜ, Diyarbakir
	07-1017	TUSAS (GD) F-16D-50 Fighting Falcon	THK 181 Filo/8 AJÜ, Diyarbakir
	07-1018	TUSAS (GD) F-16D-50 Fighting Falcon	THK 181 Filo/8 AJÜ, Diyarbakir
	07-1019	TUSAS (GD) F-16D-50 Fighting Falcon	THK
	07-1020	TUSAS (GD) F-16D-50 Fighting Falcon	THK 182 Filo/8 AJÜ, Diyarbakir
	07-1021	TUSAS (GD) F-16D-50 Fighting Falcon	THK 181 Filo/8 AJÜ, Diyarbakir
	07-1022	TUSAS (GD) F-16D-50 Fighting Falcon	THK 181 Filo/8 AJÜ, Diyarbakir
	07-1023	TUSAS (GD) F-16D-50 Fighting Falcon	THK 152 Filo/5 AJÜ, Merzifon
	07-1024	TUSAS (GD) F-16D-50 Fighting Falcon	THK 181 Filo/8 AJÜ, Diyarbakir
	07-1025	TUSAS (GD) F-16D-50 Fighting Falcon	THK 181 Filo/8 AJÜ, Diyarbakir
	07-1026	TUSAS (GD) F-16D-50 Fighting Falcon	THK 181 Filo/8 AJÜ, Diyarbakir
	07-1027	TUSAS (GD) F-16D-50 Fighting Falcon	THK
	07-1028	TUSAS (GD) F-16D-50 Fighting Falcon	THK
	07-1029	TUSAS (GD) F-16D-50 Fighting Falcon	THK
	07-1030	TUSAS (GD) F-16D-50 Fighting Falcon	THK
	09-001	Gulfstream Aerospace G.550	THK 212 Filo/11 HUAÜK, Ankara/Etimesgut
	13-001	Boeing 737-7FS AEW&C (E-7T)	THK 131 Filo/3 AJEÜ, Konya
	13-002	Boeing 737-7FS AEW&C (E-7T)	THK 131 Filo/3 AJEÜ, Konya
	13-003	Boeing 737-7FS AEW&C (E-7T)	THK 131 Filo/3 AJEÜ, Konya
	13-0009	Airbus Military A.400M	THK 221 Filo/12 HUAÜ, Erkilet
	13-004	Boeing 737-7FS AEW&C (E-7T)	THK 131 Filo/3 AJEÜ, Konya
	14-0013	Airbus Military A.400M	THK 221 Filo/12 HUAÜ, Erkilet
	14-0028	Airbus Military A.400M	THK 221 Filo/12 HUAÜ, Erkilet
	15-0051	Airbus Military A.400M	THK 221 Filo/12 HUAÜ, Erkilet
	16-0055	Airbus Military A.400M	THK 221 Filo/12 HUAÜ, Erkilet
	1.-....	Airbus Military A.400M	THK (on order)
	1.-....	Airbus Military A.400M	THK (on order)
	1.-....	Airbus Military A.400M	THK (on order)
	1.-....	Airbus Military A.400M	THK (on order)
	TC-ANA	Airbus A.319CJ-115X	Turkish Government, Istanbul/Ataturk
	TC-CAN	Airbus A.340-541 (TC-TRK)	Turkish Government, Istanbul/Ataturk
	TC-CBK	Gulfstream Aerospace G.550	THK 212 Filo/11 HUAÜK, Ankara/Etimesgut
	TC-DAP	Gulfstream Aerospace G.550	Turkish Government, Ankara
	TC-GVA	Gulfstream Aerospace G.550 (TC-ATA)	Turkish Government, Ankara
	TC-GVB	Gulfstream Aerospace G.450 (TC-GAP)	Turkish Government, Ankara
	TC-IST	Airbus A.319CJ-133	Turkish Government, Istanbul/Ataturk
	TC-TRK	Airbus A.340-541	*Repainted as TC-CAN, April 2017*
	TC-TUR	Airbus A.330-243	Turkish Government, Istanbul/Ataturk

TURKMENISTAN

	Serial	Type	Owner/operator
	EZ-A010	Boeing 757-23A	*Withdrawn from use*
	EZ-A777	Boeing 777-22KLR	Government of Turkmenistan, Ashkhabad
	EZ-B021	BAe 1000B	Government of Turkmenistan, Ashkhabad
	EZ-B024	Canadair Challenger 870CS	Government of Turkmenistan, Ashkhabad

UGANDA

	Serial	Type	Owner/operator
	5X-UGF	Gulfstream Aerospace G.550	Government of Uganda, Entebbe

Serial	Type (code/other identity)	Owner/operator, location or fate	Notes
UKRAINE			
Ukrainian Air Force			
81 y	Antonov An-30	Ukrainian AF 15 Tr AB, Kiev/Boryspil	
76321	Ilyushin Il-76MD	Ukrainian AF 25 Tr AB, Melitopol	
76322	Ilyushin Il-76MD	Ukrainian AF 25 Tr AB, Melitopol	
76323	Ilyushin Il-76MD	Ukrainian AF 25 Tr AB, Melitopol	
76413	Ilyushin Il-76MD	Ukrainian AF 25 Tr AB, Melitopol	
76423	Ilyushin Il-76MD	Ukrainian AF 25 Tr AB, Melitopol	
76531	Ilyushin Il-76MD	Ukrainian AF 25 Tr AB, Melitopol	
76559	Ilyushin Il-76MD	Ukrainian AF 25 Tr AB, Melitopol	
76564	Ilyushin Il-76MD	Ukrainian AF 25 Tr AB, Melitopol	
76566	Ilyushin Il-76MD	Ukrainian AF 25 Tr AB, Melitopol	
76585	Ilyushin Il-76MD	Ukrainian AF 25 Tr AB, Melitopol	
76631	Ilyushin Il-76MD	Ukrainian AF 25 Tr AB, Melitopol	
76637	Ilyushin Il-76MD	Ukrainian AF 25 Tr AB, Melitopol	
76645	Ilyushin Il-76MD	Ukrainian AF 25 Tr AB, Melitopol	
76647	Ilyushin Il-76MD	Ukrainian AF 25 Tr AB, Melitopol	
76654	Ilyushin Il-76MD	Ukrainian AF 25 Tr AB, Melitopol	
76660	Ilyushin Il-76MD	Ukrainian AF 25 Tr AB, Melitopol	
76661	Ilyushin Il-76MD	Ukrainian AF 25 Tr AB, Melitopol	
76680	Ilyushin Il-76MD	Ukrainian AF 25 Tr AB, Melitopol	
76683	Ilyushin Il-76MD	Ukrainian AF 25 Tr AB, Melitopol	
76697	Ilyushin Il-76MD	Ukrainian AF 25 Tr AB, Melitopol	
76698	Ilyushin Il-76MD	Ukrainian AF 25 Tr AB, Melitopol	
76699	Ilyushin Il-76MD	Ukrainian AF 25 Tr AB, Melitopol	
76732	Ilyushin Il-76MD	Ukrainian AF 25 Tr AB, Melitopol	
78820	Ilyushin Il-76MD	Ukrainian AF 25 Tr AB, Melitopol	
86915	Ilyushin Il-76MD	Ukrainian AF 25 Tr AB, Melitopol	
86922	Ilyushin Il-76MD	Ukrainian AF 25 Tr AB, Melitopol	
Government of Ukraine			
UR-86527	Ilyushin Il-62M	*Withdrawn from use*	
UR-86528	Ilyushin Il-62M	*Withdrawn from use*	
UR-ABA	Airbus A.319CJ-115X	Government of Ukraine, Kiev/Boryspil	
UNITED ARAB EMIRATES			
United Arab Emirates Air Force (UAEAF)			
311	Lockheed C-130H-30 Hercules (A6-QFY)	UAEAF 4 Sqn/Transport Wing, Abu Dhabi/Bateen	
312	Lockheed C-130H-30 Hercules	UAEAF 4 Sqn/Transport Wing, Abu Dhabi/Bateen	
430	Aermacchi MB339NAT	UAEAF *Al Fursan*, Al Ain	
431	Aermacchi MB339NAT	UAEAF *Al Fursan*, Al Ain	
432	Aermacchi MB339NAT	UAEAF *Al Fursan*, Al Ain	
433	Aermacchi MB339NAT	UAEAF *Al Fursan*, Al Ain	
434	Aermacchi MB339NAT	UAEAF *Al Fursan*, Al Ain	
435	Aermacchi MB339NAT	UAEAF *Al Fursan*, Al Ain	
436	Aermacchi MB339NAT	UAEAF *Al Fursan*, Al Ain	
437	Aermacchi MB339NAT	UAEAF *Al Fursan*, Al Ain	
438	Aermacchi MB339NAT	UAEAF *Al Fursan*, Al Ain	
439	Aermacchi MB339NAT	UAEAF *Al Fursan*, Al Ain	
440	Aermacchi MB339NAT	UAEAF *Al Fursan*, Al Ain	
441	Aermacchi MB339NAT	UAEAF *Al Fursan*, Al Ain	
442	Aermacchi MB339NAT	UAEAF *Al Fursan*, Al Ain	
1211	Lockheed C-130H Hercules	UAEAF 4 Sqn/Transport Wing, Abu Dhabi/Bateen	
1212	Lockheed C-130H Hercules	UAEAF 4 Sqn/Transport Wing, Abu Dhabi/Bateen	
1213	Lockheed C-130H Hercules	UAEAF 4 Sqn/Transport Wing, Abu Dhabi/Bateen	
1214	Lockheed C-130H Hercules	UAEAF 4 Sqn/Transport Wing, Abu Dhabi/Bateen	
1215	Lockheed L.100-30 Hercules	UAEAF 4 Sqn/Transport Wing, Abu Dhabi/Bateen	
1216	Lockheed L.100-30 Hercules	UAEAF 4 Sqn/Transport Wing, Abu Dhabi/Bateen	
1217	Lockheed L.100-30 Hercules	UAEAF 4 Sqn/Transport Wing, Abu Dhabi/Bateen	
1223	Boeing C-17A Globemaster III (10-0401)	UAEAF Heavy Transport Sqn, Abu Dhabi/Bateen	
1224	Boeing C-17A Globemaster III (10-0402)	UAEAF Heavy Transport Sqn, Abu Dhabi/Bateen	
1225	Boeing C-17A Globemaster III (10-0403)	UAEAF Heavy Transport Sqn, Abu Dhabi/Bateen	
1226	Boeing C-17A Globemaster III (10-0404)	UAEAF Heavy Transport Sqn, Abu Dhabi/Bateen	

Notes	Serial	Type (code/other identity)	Owner/operator, location or fate
	1227	Boeing C-17A Globemaster III (10-0405)	UAEAF Heavy Transport Sqn, Abu Dhabi/Bateen
	1228	Boeing C-17A Globemaster III (10-0406)	UAEAF Heavy Transport Sqn, Abu Dhabi/Bateen
	1229	Boeing C-17A Globemaster III (14-0007)	UAEAF Heavy Transport Sqn, Abu Dhabi/Bateen
	1230	Boeing C-17A Globemaster III (14-0008)	UAEAF Heavy Transport Sqn, Abu Dhabi/Bateen
	1300	Airbus A.330-243 MRTT (EC-339)	UAEAF MRTT Sqn, Al Ain
	1301	Airbus A.330-243 MRTT (EC-334)	UAEAF MRTT Sqn, Al Ain
	1302	Airbus A.330-243 MRTT (EC-332)	UAEAF MRTT Sqn, Al Ain
	1303	Airbus A.330-243 MRTT	UAEAF (on order)
	1326	Bombardier Global 6000	UAEAF (on order)
	1327	Bombardier Global 6000	UAEAF (on order)

UAE Government

Notes	Serial	Type (code/other identity)	Owner/operator, location or fate
	A6-ALN	Boeing 777-2ANER	Amiri Flight, Abu Dhabi
	A6-AUH	Boeing 737-8EX	Amiri Flight, Abu Dhabi
	A6-COM	Boeing 747-433	Dubai Air Wing
	A6-DAW	Boeing 747-48E	Dubai Air Wing
	A6-DFR	Boeing 737-7BC	Amiri Flight, Abu Dhabi
	A6-DLM	Airbus A.320-232	Amiri Flight, Abu Dhabi
	A6-FZZ	Boeing 737-8KN	Dubai Air Wing
	A6-GGP	Boeing 747-412F	Dubai Air Wing
	A6-HEH	Boeing 737-8AJ	Dubai Air Wing
	A6-HHH	Gulfstream Aerospace G.400	Dubai Air Wing
	A6-HMS	Airbus A.320-232	Dubai Air Wing
	A6-HRM	Boeing 747-422	Dubai Air Wing
	A6-HRS	Boeing 737-7F0	Dubai Air Wing
	A6-MMM	Boeing 747-422	Dubai Air Wing
	A6-MRM	Boeing 737-8EC	Dubai Air Wing
	A6-MRS	Boeing 737-8EO	Dubai Air Wing
	A6-PFA	Boeing 747-8Z5	Amiri Flight, Abu Dhabi
	A6-PFC	Boeing 787-8	Amiri Flight, Abu Dhabi
	A6-PFE	Boeing 787-9	Amiri Flight, Abu Dhabi
	A6-RJ1	BAE RJ.85	Dubai Air Wing
	A6-RJ2	BAE RJ.85	Dubai Air Wing
	A6-SHJ	Airbus A.320CJ-232X	Ruler of Sharjah Air Wing
	A6-SIL	Boeing 777-35RER	Amiri Flight, Abu Dhabi
	A6-YAS	Boeing 747-4F6	Amiri Flight, Abu Dhabi
	DU-141	AgustaWestland AW.139	Dubai Air Wing, Fairoaks, UK (Summer)
	DU-142	AgustaWestland AW.139	Dubai Air Wing, Fairoaks, UK (Summer)

A very close look above the cockpit reveals the serial, 276, of this French Navy Lynx operated by 34 F at LanvÈoc/Poulmic.

This section lists the codes worn by some overseas air forces and, alongside, the serial of the aircraft currently wearing this code. This list will be updated occasionally and those with Internet access can download the latest version via the 'Military Aircraft Markings' Web Site, www.militaryaircraftmarkings.co.uk and via the MAM2009 Yahoo! Group.

FRANCE
FRENCH AIR FORCE
D-BD Alpha Jet

Code	Serial	Code	Serial	Code	Serial	Code	Serial
0 [PDF]	E114	120-RN	E124	F-UGFE	E119	3-XG	625
1 [PDF]	E44	120-RO	E131	F-UHRE	E44	3-XJ	602
2 [PDF]	E46	120-RV	E164	F-UHRF	E46	3-XK	671
3 [PDF]	E119	120-TT	E101	F-UHRR	E146	3-XL	603
4 [PDF]	E162	120-UC	E157	F-UHRT	E152	3-XM	680
5 [PDF]	E79	705-AB	E28			3-XN	652
6 [PDF]	E127	705-AD	E51	**Dassault Mirage 2000**		3-XO	629
7 [PDF]	E68	705-AH	E110	2-AX	77	3-XT	648
8 [PDF]	E152	705-LA	E72	2-ED	62	3-XV	672
9 [PDF]	E113	705-LC	E87	2-EG	56	3-XY	649
3-AF	E108	705-LG	E120	2-EH	52	3-XZ	685
8-AK	E144	705-LJ	E137	2-EJ	43	30-AS	51
8-FD	E151	705-LK	E125	2-EL	58	30-IE	642
8-FM	E105	705-LP	E129	2-EM	63	30-IP	604
8-FN	E116	705-LU	E148	2-EN	46	30-IR	674
8-FO	E81	705-MA	E35	2-EO	66	30-JO	627
8-LN	E118	705-MD	E30	2-EP	47	30-XQ	637
3-LS	E22	705-MF	E98	2-EQ	44	115-AM	525
8-MA	E173	705-MH	E48	2-ET	57	115-KB	94
8-MM	E13	705-MN	E167	2-EU	55	115-KC	120
8-RA	E41	705-MR	E115	2-EV	59	115-KD	123
8-RE	E165	705-MS	E20	2-EW	48	115-KE	101
8-RF	E158	705-ND	E26	2-EX	40	115-KF	111
8-RM	E123	705-NF	E141	2-EY	42	115-KG	104
8-RP	E136	705-NL	E37	2-EZ	54	115-KI	96
8-RQ	E138	705-NP	E155	2-FZ	41	115-KJ	523
8-RX	E135	705-RB	E163	2-ME	61	115-KL	106
8-TH	E90	705-RH	E94	2-MG	65	115-KN	121
8-TX	E93	705-RK	E31	2-MH	67	115-KR	102
8-UH	E160	705-RM	E134	2-MK	74	115-KS	528
30-AO	E112	705-RS	E149	3-AG	681	115-KV	88
30-RX	E169	705-RT	E152	3-AU	653	115-LB	87
30-TI	E156	705-RU	E153	3-IA	650	115-LC	108
102-AI	E117	705-RW	E166	3-ID	654	115-LD	117
102-FA	E140	705-RY	E170	3-IG	668	115-LE	79
102-FB	E86	705-RZ	E171	3-IJ	638	115-LJ	105
102-FI	E32	705-TA	E42	3-IL	622	115-LK	85
102-FP	E168	705-TB	E67	3-IN	640	115-OA	524
102-LI	E53	705-TG	E104	3-IS	617	115-OC	529
102-MB	E97	705-TJ	E25	3-IT	624	115-OL	530
102-NA	E79	705-TK	E58	3-IU	620	115-OR	527
102-NB	E29	705-TM	E138	3-IV	683	115-YA	93
102-RJ	E76	705-TU	E7	3-JC	606	115-YB	99
118-AK	E18	705-TZ	E83	3-JD	643	115-YC	85
118-FE	E119	705-UB	E11	3-JF	660	115-YD	107
118-LT	E147	705-UD	E107	3-JI	675	115-YE	122
120-AG	E109	F-TELL	E88	3-JJ	639	115-YF	100
120-AH	E99	F-TEMO	E68	3-JM	657	115-YG	118
120-AL	E154	F-TENE	E73	3-JN	658	115-YH	109
120-FJ	E33	F-TERI	E117	3-JP	611	115-YL	82
120-FM	E105	F-TERJ	E162	3-JT	677	115-YM	115
120-LM	E102	F-TERK	E31	3-JU	614	115-YO	113
120-LO	E142	F-TERN	E46	3-JW	641	115-YT	124
120-LW	E82	F-TERP	E130	3-JX	679	116-AU	316
120-LX	E89	F-TERQ	E95	3-JY	615	116-BL	306
120-MB	E176	F-TERR	E114	3-MQ	646	116-EA	49
		F-TETD	E113	3-XA	662	116-EC	78
		F-TETF	E45	3-XC	618	116-EE	71
		F-UGFC	E139	3-XD	630	116-EI	38

Code	No.	Code	No.	Code	No.	Code	No.
116-ER	68	4-FH	341	30-HR	103	DAB	1020
118-EB	76	4-FI	342	30-HT	323	DAC	1036
118-IF	609	4-FJ	343	30-HW	324	DAD	1037
118-JK	612	4-FK	344	30-IA	307	DAE	1049
118-KQ	112	4-FL	345	30-IB	306	DAF	1055
118-XH	616	4-FM	346	30-IF	331	DAG	1069
125-AE	355	4-FN	347	30-IM	109	DAH	1078
125-AL	348	4-FO	348	30-IN	110	DAI	1092
125-AK	359	4-FP	349	30-IP	112	DAJ	1100
125-AQ	351	4-FR	351	30-IQ	112	DAK	1102
125-AR	368	4-FS	352	30-IR	113	DAL	1107
125-BA	342	4-FT	353	30-IS	114	DAM	1109
125-BB	364	4-FU	354	30-IT	115	DAN	1128
125-BC	366	4-FV	355	30-IU	116	DAO	1143
125-BD	371	4-FW	356	30-IW	118	DAP	1149
125-BJ	354	4-GA	122	30-IX	119	DAQ	1156
125-BQ	358	4-GL	133	30-IY	120	DAR	1173
125-BS	374	4-GU	142	30-VA	148	DAS	1176
125-BU	345	4-HA	308	104-GC	124	DAT	1189
125-BX	356	4-HB	309	104-GI	130	DAU	1197
125-CF	373	4-HC	310	104-GM	134	DAV	1204
125-CG	338	4-HF	312	104-GO	136	DAW	1211
125-CI	335	4-HI	313	104-GP	137	DAX	1214
125-CL	375	4-HK	315	104-HR	103	DAY	1217
125-CM	372	4-HN	319	113-FQ	350	DAZ	1219
125-CO	357	4-HO	317	113-GC	124	DBA	1232
125-CQ	370	4-HP	314	113-HD	311	DBB	1243
125-CU	362	4-HQ	321	113-HG	106	DBC	1248
133-AL	669	4-HU	322	113-HJ	107	DBD	1262
133-AS	635	4-HV	320	113-HS	108	DBE	1277
133-IC	626	4-HX	325	113-HY	326	DBF	1417
133-IH	631	4-HZ	327	113-IV	117	DBG	1438
133-IO	647	4-IC	328	113-IZ	121	DBH	1451
133-IQ	666	4-ID	329	118-FQ	350	DBI	1507
133-IW	664	4-IE	330	118-FR	351	DBJ	1510
133-JB	678	4-IG	332	118-GP	137	DBK	1512
133-JE	634	4-IH	333	118-IR	113	DBL	1519
133-JG	601	4-II	334			DBM	1617
133-JH	686	4-IJ	335	**Pilatus PC-21**		DBN	1632
133-JL	628	4-IK	336	(NB: So far none have been		DBO	1634
133-JR	682	4-IL	337	seen with a hyphen in the		DBP	1654
133-JV	636	4-IO	338	code)		DBQ	1663
133-JZ	667	30-EF	102	709 FC	01	DBR	5682
133-LF	605	30-GB	123	709 FD	02	DCA	1005
133-LH	655	30-GD	125	709 FE	03	DCB	1052
133-MO	613	30-GE	126	709 FF	04	DCC	1056
133-MP	623	30-GF	127	709 FG	05	DCD	1057
133-XE	632	30-GG	128	709 FH	06	DCE	1071
133-XF	670	30-GH	129	709 FI	07	DCF	1073
133-XI	661	30-GJ	131	709 FJ	08	DCG	1093
133-XP	645	30-GK	132	709 FK	09	DCH	1114
133-XR	659	30-GN	135	709 FL	10	DCI	1122
133-XX	610	30-GQ	138	709 FM	11	DCJ	1122
188-EF	45	30-GR	139	709 FN	12	DCK	1130
188-XJ	602	30-GS	140	709 FO	13	DCL	1135
188-YR	91	30-GT	141	709 FP	14	DCM	1136
		30-GV	143	709 FQ	15	DCN	1142
Dassault Rafale		30-GW	144	709 FR	16	DCO	1145
4-EA	303	30-GX	145	709 FS	17	DCP	1150
4-EB	304	30-GY	146			DCQ	1155
4-EC	305	30-GZ	147	**FRENCH ARMY**		DCR	1163
4-FF	339	30-HE	105	**SA.330 Puma**		DCS	1164
4-FG	340	30-HM	318	DAA	1006	DCT	1165

Code	Value
DCU	1171
DCV	1172
DCW	1177
DCX	1179
DCY	1182
DCZ	1186
DDA	1190
DDB	1192
DDC	1196
DDD	1198
DDE	1206
DDF	1213
DDG	1222
DDH	1223
DDI	1228
DDJ	1229
DDK	1231
DDL	1235
DDM	1236
DDN	1239
DDO	1244
DDP	1252
DDQ	1255
DDR	1256
DDS	1260
DDT	1269
DDU	1411
DDV	1419
DDW	1447
DDX	1662

SA.342 Gazelle

Code	Value
GAA	3459
GAB	3476
GAC	3512
GAD	3530
GAE	3548
GAF	3664
GAG	3848
GAH	3849
GAI	3850
GAJ	3856
GAK	3859
GAL	3862
GAM	3863
GAN	3865
GAO	3868
GAP	3911
GAQ	3921
GAR	3938
GAS	3947
GAT	3948
GAU	3957
GAV	3964
GAW	3996
GAX	4018
GAY	4019
GAZ	4020
GBA	4026
GBB	4034
GBC	4039
GBD	4048
GBE	4053
GBF	4059
GBG	4061
GBH	4066
GBI	4072
GBJ	4084
GBL	4095
GBM	4108
GBN	4109
GBO	4114
GBP	4115
GBQ	4119
GBR	4120
GBS	4124
GBT	4136
GBU	4140
GBV	4141
GBW	4142
GBX	4144
GBY	4145
GBZ	4151
GCA	4155
GCC	4160
GCD	4161
GCE	4162
GCF	4164
GCG	4168
GCH	4172
GCI	4175
GCJ	4179
GCK	4180
GCL	4181
GCM	4186
GCN	4189
GCO	4191
GCP	4195
GCQ	4198
GEA	4204
GEB	4206
GEC	4207
GED	4208
GEF	4210
GEG	4211
GEI	4214
GEJ	4215
GEK	4216
GEL	4217
GEM	4218
GEN	4219
GEO	4220
GEP	4221
GEQ	4222
GER	4223
GES	4224
GET	4225
GEU	4226
GEV	4227
GEW	4228
GEX	4229
GEY	4230
GEZ	4231
GFA	4231
GFB	4233
GFC	4234
GJA	1732
GJC	3511
GJD	3529
GJF	3546
GJH	3615
GJI	3851
GJJ	3855
GJK	3857
GJL	3864
GJM	3867
GJN	3929
GJO	3965
GJP	4014
GJQ	4022
GJR	4038
GJS	4047
GJU	4067
GJV	4078
GJW	4102
GJX	4103
GJY	4123
GJZ	4166
GKA	4176
GKB	4177
GKC	4182
GKD	4185
GKE	4187
GMA	3567
GMB	4042
GMC	4079
GMD	4194
GME	3870
GMF	3930
GMG	3939
GMH	4023
GMI	4171
GMJ	4190
GMK	4201
GNA	3458
GNB	3513
GNC	3549
GND	3617
GNE	3852
GNF	3853
GNG	3858
GNI	3866
GNJ	3896
GNK	3956
GNM	3992
GNN	4008
GNO	4032
GNP	4049
GNQ	4060
GNR	4065
GNS	4071
GNT	4083
GNU	4096
GNV	4118
GNW	4135
GNX	4143
GNY	4146
GNZ	4159
GOA	4178
GOB	4183
GOC	4184
GOD	4192

AS.532UL/EC.725AP Cougar

Code	Value
CAA	2611
CAB	2628
CAC	2630
CAD	2631
CAE	2633
CAF	2638
CAG	2640
CAH	2642
CGA	2252
CGB	2266
CGC	2267
CGD	2271
CGE	2272
CGF	2273
CGG	2282
CGH	2285
CGI	2290
CGJ	2292
CGK	2299
CGL	2300
CGM	2301
CGN	2303
CGO	2316
CGQ	2323
CGR	2324
CGS	2325
CGT	2327
CGU	2331
CGV	2336
CGW	2443
CGX	2446
CHA	2342
CHB	2369
CHC	2375

EC.665 Tigre

Code	Value
BHA	2010
BHB	2009
BHC	2013
BHD	2015
BHE	2018
BHF	2019
BHG	2022
BHH	2001
BHI	2002
BHJ	2003
BHK	2004
BHL	2006
BHM	2011
BHN	2021
BHO	2024
BHP	2023
BHQ	2025
BHR	2026
BHS	2027
BHT	2012
BHU	2028
BHV	2029

Code	Serial
BHW	2030
BHX	2031
BHX	
BHZ	2033
BIA	2016
BIB	2034
BIC	2035
BIE	2037
BIG	2039
BIH	2040
BII	2041
BIJ	2042
BIK	2043
BIL	2044
BIM	2045
BIN	2046
BIO	2047
BIP	2048
BIQ	2049
BIR	2050
BIS	2051
BIT	2052
BJA	6001
BJB	6002
BJC	6003
BJD	6004
BJE	6005
BJF	6006
BJG	6007
BJH	6008
BJI	6009
BJJ	6010
BJK	6011
BJL	6012
BJM	6013
BJN	6014
BJO	6015
BJP	6016
BJQ	6017
BJR	6018
BJS	6019
BJT	6020
BJU	6021
BJV	6022
BJW	6023
BJX	6024
BJY	6025
BJZ	6027

NH.90-TTH

Code	Serial
EAA	1239
EAB	1256
EAC	1271
EAD	1273
EAE	1290
EAF	1291
EAG	1292
EAH	1293
EAI	1294
EAJ	1295
EAK	1306
EAL	1307
EAM	1308
EAN	1309
EAO	1310
EAP	1311
EAQ	1312
EAR	1313
EAS	1332
EAT	1333
EAU	1334
EAV	1335
EAW	1336
EAX	1337
EAY	1338
EAZ	1386
EBA	1390
EBB	1391

ITALY

Aeritalia-EMB AMX

Code	Serial
32-41	MM55030
32-47	MM55046
32-50	MM55029
32-51	MM55036
32-53	MM55047
32-56	MM55042
51-10	MM7159
51-21	MM55043
51-26	MM7149
51-27	MM7114
51-30	MM7170
51-32	MM7166
51-33	MM7162
51-34	MM7191
51-35	MM7196
51-36	MM7185
51-37	MM7161
51-41	MM7183
51-42	MM7177
51-43	MM7178
51-44	MM7198
51-45	MM7175
51-46	MM7197
51-50	MM7186
51-51	MM7151
51-52	MM7171
51-53	MM7180
51-55	MM7168
51-56	MM7167
51-57	MM7190
51-60	MM7174
51-61	MM7126
51-62	MM7182
51-63	MM7173
51-64	MM7179
51-65	MM7184
51-66	MM7169
51-67	MM7194
51-70	MM7192
51-71	MM7189
51-72	MM7163
51-80	MM55037
51-82	MM55044
51-83	MM55049
51-84	MM55051
RS-14	MM7177
RS-18	MM55034

Aermacchi MB339

Code	Serial
1 [FT]	MM54551
2 [FT]	MM54517
3 [FT]	MM55058
4 [FT]	MM55052
5 [FT]	MM54505
6 [FT]	MM54534
7 [FT]	MM55053
8 [FT]	MM55059
9 [FT]	MM55054
10 [FT]	MM54500
11 [FT]	MM54539
12 [FT]	MM54510
32-161	MM55089
36-06	MM55074
61-11	MM54457
61-12	MM54458
61-15	MM55054
61-20	MM55055
61-21	MM54465
61-24	MM54468
61-26	MM55059
61-32	MM54488
61-36	MM54492
61-37	MM54493
61-42	MM54496
61-45	MM54499
61-52	MM54504
61-55	MM54507
61-57	MM54509
61-60	MM54510
61-61	MM54511
61-62	MM54512
61-64	MM54514
61-65	MM54515
61-66	MM54516
61-70	MM54518
61-72	MM54533
61-74	MM54535
61-106	MM54548
61-107	MM54549
61-126	MM55062
61-127	MM55063
61-130	MM55064
61-131	MM55065
61-132	MM55066
61-133	MM55067
61-135	MM55069
61-136	MM55070
61-140	MM55072
61-141	MM55073
61-143	MM55075
61-144	MM55076
61-145	MM55077
61-146	MM55078
61-147	MM55079
61-150	MM55080
61-151	MM55081
61-152	MM55082
61-154	MM55084
61-155	MM55085
61-156	MM55086
61-157	MM55087
61-160	MM55088
61-162	MM55090
RS-32	MM55091
RS-33	MM55068

Aermacchi T-346A Master

Code	Serial
61-01	MM55154
61-02	MM55144
61-03	MM55145
61-04	MM55155
61-05	MM55153
61-06	MM55213
61-07	MM55214
61-10	MM55215
61-11	MT55152
61-12	MM55216
61-14	MM55218
61-15	MM55221
61-16	MM55220

Eurofighter Typhoon

Code	Serial
4-1	MM7270
4-2	MM7303
4-3	MM7287
4-4	MM7274
4-5	MM7289
4-6	MM7323
4-7	MM7290
4-9	MM7340
4-11	MM7291
4-12	MM7284
4-13	MM7235
4-14	MM7281
4-15	MM7271
4-18	MM7272
4-20	MM7279
4-21	MM7304
4-22	MM7309
4-23	MM55095
4-24	MM55097
4-26	MM55128
4-30	MM55096
4-31	MM55093
4-32	MM55129
4-33	MM55130
4-35	MM55132
4-37	MM55168
4-40	MM7277
4-41	MM7299
4-44	MM7300
4-45	MM7320
4-46	MM7326
4-47	MM7327
4-50	MM7306
4-51	MM7295
4-52	MM7294
4-60	MM7338
4-61	MM7339
36-02	MM7286
36-05	MM7276

Code	Type	Code	Type	Code	Type	Code	Type
36-10	MM7341	6-07	MM7075	74-17	E.25-63	72-11	T.12B-65
36-12	MM7318	6-10	MM7088	74-20	E.25-66	72-12	T.12B-67
36-15	MM7282	6-11	MM7058	74-21	E.25-67	72-14	T.12B-63
36-21	MM7292	6-12	MM7071	74-22	E.25-68	72-15	T.12B-69
36-22	MM7296	6-13	MM7014	74-25	E.25-71	72-17	T.12B-70
36-23	MM7297	6-15	MM55006	74-26	E.25-72	72-18	T.12B-62
36-24	MM7298	6-16	MM7037	74-28	E.25-74	72-21	TR.12D-76
36-25	MM7302	6-20	MM7021	74-30	E.25-76	72-22	TR.12D-77
36-30	MM7280	6-21	MM7040	74-34	E.25-81	72-23	TR.12D-79
36-31	MM7308	6-22	MM7029	74-35	E.25-83	72-24	TR.12D-81
36-32	MM7310	6-25	MM7043	74-39	E.25-88		
36-34	MM7312	6-26	MM7063	74-40	E.25-17	**Eurofighter Tifón**	
36-35	MM7313	6-27	MM7035	74-41	E.25-41	11-01	C.16-21
36-37	MM7314	6-30	MM7072	74-42	E.25-18	11-02	C.16-22
36-40	MM7322	6-31	MM7006	74-43	E.25-43	11-03	C.16-23
36-41	MM7324	6-32	MM7015	74-44	E.25-34	11-04	C.16-24
36-42	MM7288	6-33	MM7039	74-45	E.25-29	11-05	C.16-25
36-44	MM7325	6-34	MM7073	79-02	E.25-78	11-06	C.16-26
36-46	MM7315	6-35	MM7026	79-03	E.25-80	11-07	C.16-27
36-50	MM7341	6-37	MM7038	79-04	E.25-84	11-08	C.16-28
36-51	MM7342	6-42	MM55010	79-05	E.25-05	11-09	C.16-29
36-52	MM7343	6-44	MM55009	79-06	E.25-06	11-10	C.16-30
36-53	MM7347	6-45	MM55008	79-08	E.25-08	11-11	C.16-32
36-60	MM55094	6-50	MM7024	79-09	E.25-09	11-12	C.16-33
36-62	MM55092	6-51	MM55007	79-11	E.25-11	11-14	C.16-35
37-01	MM7307	6-52	MM55001	79-12	E.25-12	11-16	C.16-40
37-05	MM7319	6-53	MM55004	79-13	E.25-13	11-19	C.16-43
37-07	MM7316	6-55	MM7004	79-14	E.25-14	11-20	C.16-46
37-10	MM7311	6-57	MM7081	79-15	E.25-15	11-21	C.16-51
37-11	MM7301	6-60	MM7086	79-16	E.25-16	11-22	C.16-52
37-12	MM7321	6-61	MM7047	79-17	E.25-62	11-23	C.16-53
37-14	MM7328	6-62	MM7082	79-20	E.25-20	11-24	C.16-54
37-15	MM7329	6-63	MM7023	79-21	E.25-21	11-25	C.16-55
37-16	MM7331	6-64	MM7052	79-22	E.25-22	11-27	C.16-57
37-18	MM7293	6-65	MM7055	79-23	E.25-23	11-70	CE.16-01
37-21	MM7330	6-66	MM7059	79-24	E.25-24	11-71	CE.16-02
37-24	MM7348	6-67	MM7068	79-25	E.25-25	11-72	CE.16-03
37-30	MM55131	6-71	MM7070	79-27	E.25-27	11-73	CE.16-04
37-33	MM55133	6-72	MM7051	79-28	E.25-28	11-74	CE.16-05
37-37	MM7346	6-74	MM7062	79-29	E.25-87	11-75	CE.16-06
37-45	MM7345	6-75	MM7013	79-31	E.25-31	11-76	CE.16-07
RMV-01	MMX603	6-77	MM7020	79-32	E.25-86	11-78	CE.16-09
RS-01	MMX602	6-100	MM7054	79-33	E.25-50	11-79	CE.16-10
		36-50	CSX7085	79-34	E.25-52	11-80	CE.16-13
Lockheed Martin F-35A/		50-01	MM7021	79-35	E.25-54	11-81	CE.16-14
F-35B Lightning II		50-04	MM7030	79-37	E.25-37	11-91	C.16-20
4-01	MM7451	50-05	MM7019	79-38	E.25-38	14-01	C.16-31
32-01	MM7332	50-53	MM7008	79-39	E.25-79	14-03	C.16-36
32-02	MM7333	50-57	MM7067	79-40	E.25-40	14-04	C.16-37
32-03	MM7334	RS-01	CSX7041	79-44	E.25-44	14-05	C.16-38
32-04	MM7335	RS-05	CSX7047	79-46	E.25-46	14-06	C.16-39
32-05	MM7336			79-49	E.25-49	14-07	C.16-41
32-07	MM7357	**SPAIN**		79-95	E.25-65	14-08	C.16-42
32-08	MM7358	**CASA 101EB Aviojet**		79-97	E.25-69	14-09	C.16-44
32-09	MM7359	54-20	E.25-35	79-98	E.25-73	14-10	C.16-45
32-13	MM7337	54-21	E.25-55			14-11	C.16-47
		54-22	E.25-61	**CASA 212 Aviocar**		14-12	C.16-48
Panavia Tornado		74-02	E.25-33	47-12	TM.12D-72	14-13	C.16-49
-01	MM7007	74-07	E.25-51	47-14	T.12D-75	14-14	C.16-50
-03	MM7084	74-09	E.25-53	72-01	T.12B-13	14-70	CE.16-11
-04	MM7057	74-11	E.25-56	72-07	T.12B-49	14-71	CE.16-12
-05	MM7025	74-12	E.25-57	72-08	T.12B-55		
-06	MM7036	74-13	E.25-59	72-09	T.12B-66		

US MILITARY AIRCRAFT MARKINGS

All USAF and US Army aircraft have been allocated a fiscal year (FY) number since 1921. Individual aircraft are given a serial according to the fiscal year in which they are ordered. The numbers commence at 0001 and are prefixed with the year of allocation. For example F-15C Eagle 84-0001 was the first aircraft ordered in 1984. The fiscal year (FY) serial is carried on the technical data block which is usually stencilled on the left-hand side of the aircraft just below the cockpit. The number displayed on the fin is a corruption of the FY serial. Most tactical aircraft carry the fiscal year in small figures followed by the last three or four digits of the serial in large figures. Large transport and tanker aircraft such as C-130s and KC-135s sometimes display a five-figure number commencing with the last digit of the appropriate fiscal year and four figures of the production number. An example of this is Boeing KC-135R Stratotanker 58-0128 which displays 80128 on its fin.

US Army serials have been allocated in a similar way to USAF serials although in recent years an additional zero has been added so that all US Army serials now have the two-figure fiscal year part followed by five digits. This means that, for example C-20E 70140 is officially 87-00140 although as yet this has not led to any alterations to serials painted on aircraft.

USN and USMC serials follow a straightforward numerical sequence which commenced, for the present series, with the allocation of 00001 to an SB2C Helldiver by the Bureau of Aeronautics in 1940. Numbers in the 168000 series are presently being issued. They are usually carried in full on the rear fuselage of the aircraft.

US Coast Guard serials began with the allocation of the serial 1 to a Loening OL-5 in 1927.

UK-BASED USAF AIRCRAFT

The following aircraft are normally based in the UK. They are listed in numerical order of type with individual aircraft in serial number order, as depicted on the aircraft. The number in brackets is either the alternative presentation of the five-figure number commencing with the last digit of the fiscal year, or the fiscal year where a five-figure serial is presented on the aircraft. Where it is possible to identify the allocation of aircraft to individual squadrons by means of colours carried on fin or cockpit edge, this is also provided.

Notes	Serial	Type (code/other identity)	Owner/operator, location or fate
	McDonnell Douglas F-15C Eagle/F-15D Eagle/F-15E Strike Eagle		
	84-0001	McD F-15C Eagle [LN] *bk/y*	USAF 493rd FS/48th FW, Lakenheath
	84-0010	McD F-15C Eagle [LN] *bk/y*	USAF 493rd FS/48th FW, Lakenheath
	84-0015	McD F-15C Eagle [LN] *bk/y*	USAF 493rd FS/48th FW, Lakenheath
	84-0019	McD F-15C Eagle [LN] *bk/y*	USAF 493rd FS/48th FW, Lakenheath
	84-0027	McD F-15C Eagle [LN] *bk/y* [493 FS]	USAF 493rd FS/48th FW, Lakenheath
	84-0044	McD F-15D Eagle [LN] *bk/y*	USAF 493rd FS/48th FW, Lakenheath
	84-0046	McD F-15D Eagle [LN] *bk/y*	USAF 493rd FS/48th FW, Lakenheath
	86-0154	McD F-15C Eagle [LN] *bk/y*	USAF 493rd FS/48th FW, Lakenheath
	86-0156	McD F-15C Eagle [LN] *bk/y*	USAF 493rd FS/48th FW, Lakenheath
	86-0159	McD F-15C Eagle [LN] *bk/y*	USAF 493rd FS/48th FW, Lakenheath
	86-0160	McD F-15C Eagle [LN] *bk/y*	USAF 493rd FS/48th FW, Lakenheath
	86-0163	McD F-15C Eagle [LN] *bk/y*	USAF 493rd FS/48th FW, Lakenheath
	86-0164	McD F-15C Eagle [LN] *bk/y*	USAF 493rd FS/48th FW, Lakenheath
	86-0165	McD F-15C Eagle [LN] *bk/y*	USAF 493rd FS/48th FW, Lakenheath
	86-0166	McD F-15C Eagle [LN] *bk/y*	USAF 493rd FS/48th FW, Lakenheath
	86-0171	McD F-15C Eagle [LN] *bk/y*	USAF 493rd FS/48th FW, Lakenheath
	86-0172	McD F-15C Eagle [LN] *bk/y*	USAF 493rd FS/48th FW, Lakenheath
	86-0174	McD F-15C Eagle [LN] *bk/y*	USAF 493rd FS/48th FW, Lakenheath
	86-0175	McD F-15C Eagle [LN] *bk/y*	USAF 493rd FS/48th FW, Lakenheath
	86-0176	McD F-15C Eagle [LN] *bk/y*	USAF 493rd FS/48th FW, Lakenheath
	86-0178	McD F-15C Eagle [LN] *bk/y*	USAF 493rd FS/48th FW, Lakenheath
	91-0301	McD F-15E Strike Eagle [LN]	USAF 492nd FS/48th FW, Lakenheath
	91-0302	McD F-15E Strike Eagle [LN] *bl/w*	USAF 492nd FS/48th FW, Lakenheath
	91-0303	McD F-15E Strike Eagle [LN] *bl/w*	USAF 492nd FS/48th FW, Lakenheath
	91-0306	McD F-15E Strike Eagle [LN] *bl/w*	USAF 492nd FS/48th FW, Lakenheath
	91-0307	McD F-15E Strike Eagle [LN] *bl/w*	USAF 492nd FS/48th FW, Lakenheath
	91-0308	McD F-15E Strike Eagle [LN] *bl/w*	USAF 492nd FS/48th FW, Lakenheath
	91-0309	McD F-15E Strike Eagle [LN] *r/w*	USAF 494th FS/48th FW, Lakenheath
	91-0310	McD F-15E Strike Eagle [LN] *r/w*	USAF 494th FS/48th FW, Lakenheath
	91-0311	McD F-15E Strike Eagle [LN] *m* [48 FW]	USAF 494th FS/48th FW, Lakenheath
	91-0312	McD F-15E Strike Eagle [LN] *bl/w*	USAF 492nd FS/48th FW, Lakenheath
	91-0313	McD F-15E Strike Eagle [LN] *r/w*	USAF 494th FS/48th FW, Lakenheath
	91-0314	McD F-15E Strike Eagle [LN] *r/w* [494 FS]	USAF 494th FS/48th FW, Lakenheath
	91-0315	McD F-15E Strike Eagle [LN] *bl/w*	USAF 492nd FS/48th FW, Lakenheath
	91-0316	McD F-15E Strike Eagle [LN] *bl/w*	USAF 492nd FS/48th FW, Lakenheath

Serial	Type (code/other identity)	Owner/operator, location or fate	Notes
91-0317	McD F-15E Strike Eagle [LN] bl/w	USAF 492nd FS/48th FW, Lakenheath	
91-0318	McD F-15E Strike Eagle [LN] m [48 OG]	USAF 494th FS/48th FW, Lakenheath	
91-0320	McD F-15E Strike Eagle [LN] r/w [494 FS]	Returned to the US, 28 January 2018	
91-0321	McD F-15E Strike Eagle [LN] bl/w	USAF 492nd FS/48th FW, Lakenheath	
91-0324	McD F-15E Strike Eagle [LN] r/w	USAF 494th FS/48th FW, Lakenheath	
91-0326	McD F-15E Strike Eagle [LN] r/w	USAF 494th FS/48th FW, Lakenheath	
91-0327	McD F-15E Strike Eagle [LN] bl/w	USAF 492nd FS/48th FW, Lakenheath	
91-0329	McD F-15E Strike Eagle [LN] r/w	USAF 494th FS/48th FW, Lakenheath	
91-0331	McD F-15E Strike Eagle [LN] bl/w	USAF 492nd FS/48th FW, Lakenheath	
91-0332	McD F-15E Strike Eagle [LN] bl/w	USAF 492nd FS/48th FW, Lakenheath	
91-0334	McD F-15E Strike Eagle [LN] r/w	USAF 494th FS/48th FW, Lakenheath	
91-0335	McD F-15E Strike Eagle [LN] r/w	USAF 494th FS/48th FW, Lakenheath	
91-0602	McD F-15E Strike Eagle [LN] r/w	USAF 494th FS/48th FW, Lakenheath	
91-0603	McD F-15E Strike Eagle [LN] r/w	USAF 494th FS/48th FW, Lakenheath	
91-0604	McD F-15E Strike Eagle [LN] r/w	USAF 494th FS/48th FW, Lakenheath	
91-0605	McD F-15E Strike Eagle [LN] bl/w	USAF 492nd FS/48th FW, Lakenheath	
92-0364	McD F-15E Strike Eagle [LN] r/w	USAF 494th FS/48th FW, Lakenheath	
96-0201	McD F-15E Strike Eagle [LN] r/w	USAF 494th FS/48th FW, Lakenheath	
96-0202	McD F-15E Strike Eagle [LN] bl/w	USAF 492nd FS/48th FW, Lakenheath	
96-0204	McD F-15E Strike Eagle [LN] r/w	USAF 494th FS/48th FW, Lakenheath	
96-0205	McD F-15E Strike Eagle [LN] bl/w	USAF 492nd FS/48th FW, Lakenheath	
97-0218	McD F-15E Strike Eagle [LN] bl/w	USAF 492nd FS/48th FW, Lakenheath	
97-0219	McD F-15E Strike Eagle [LN] bl/w	USAF 492nd FS/48th FW, Lakenheath	
97-0220	McD F-15E Strike Eagle [LN] bl/w	USAF 492nd FS/48th FW, Lakenheath	
97-0221	McD F-15E Strike Eagle [LN] bl/w [492 FS]	USAF 492nd FS/48th FW, Lakenheath	
97-0222	McD F-15E Strike Eagle [LN] r/w	USAF 492nd FS/48th FW, Lakenheath	
98-0131	McD F-15E Strike Eagle [LN] bl/w	USAF 492nd FS/48th FW, Lakenheath	
98-0132	McD F-15E Strike Eagle [LN] r/w	Returned to the USA, 20 January 2017	
98-0133	McD F-15E Strike Eagle [LN] bl/w	USAF 492nd FS/48th FW, Lakenheath	
98-0134	McD F-15E Strike Eagle [LN] bl/w	USAF 492nd FS/48th FW, Lakenheath	
98-0135	McD F-15E Strike Eagle [LN] bl/w	USAF 492nd FS/48th FW, Lakenheath	
00-3000	McD F-15E Strike Eagle [LN] r/w	USAF 494th FS/48th FW, Lakenheath	
00-3001	McD F-15E Strike Eagle [LN] r/w	USAF 494th FS/48th FW, Lakenheath	
00-3002	McD F-15E Strike Eagle [LN] r/w	USAF 494th FS/48th FW, Lakenheath	
00-3003	McD F-15E Strike Eagle [LN]	USAF 494th FS/48th FW, Lakenheath	
00-3004	McD F-15E Strike Eagle [LN]	USAF 494th FS/48th FW, Lakenheath	
01-2000	McD F-15E Strike Eagle [LN] r/w	USAF 494th FS/48th FW, Lakenheath	
01-2001	McD F-15E Strike Eagle [LN] r/w	USAF 494th FS/48th FW, Lakenheath	
01-2002	McD F-15E Strike Eagle [LN] r/w	USAF 494th FS/48th FW, Lakenheath	
01-2003	McD F-15E Strike Eagle [LN] r/w	USAF 494th FS/48th FW, Lakenheath	
01-2004	McD F-15E Strike Eagle [LN] r/w	USAF 494th FS/48th FW, Lakenheath	

Bell-Boeing CV-22B Osprey

0033	Bell-Boeing CV-22B Osprey (07-0033)	USAF 7th SOS/352nd SOW, Mildenhall	
0050	Bell-Boeing CV-22B Osprey (08-0050)	USAF 7th SOS/352nd SOW, Mildenhall	
0051	Bell-Boeing CV-22B Osprey (08-0051)	USAF 7th SOS/352nd SOW, Mildenhall	
0057	Bell-Boeing CV-22B Osprey (11-0057)	USAF 7th SOS/352nd SOW, Mildenhall	
0058	Bell-Boeing CV-22B Osprey (11-0058)	USAF 7th SOS/352nd SOW, Mildenhall	
0061	Bell-Boeing CV-22B Osprey (11-0061)	USAF 7th SOS/352nd SOW, Mildenhall	
0063	Bell-Boeing CV-22B Osprey (12-0063)	USAF 7th SOS/352nd SOW, Mildenhall	
0064	Bell-Boeing CV-22B Osprey (12-0064)	USAF 7th SOS/352nd SOW, Mildenhall	
0065	Bell-Boeing CV-22B Osprey (12-0065)	USAF 7th SOS/352nd SOW, Mildenhall	

Sikorsky HH-60G Pave Hawk

Note: 56th RQS is expected to complete its move to Aviano by June 2018

26205	Sikorsky HH-60G Pave Hawk (89-26205) [LN]	USAF 56th RQS/48th FW, RAF Lakenheath	
26353	Sikorsky HH-60G Pave Hawk (91-26353) [LN]	USAF 56th RQS/48th FW, RAF Lakenheath	

Lockheed MC-130J Commando II

5714	Lockheed MC-130J Commando II (10-5714)	USAF 67th SOS/352nd SOW, RAF Mildenhall	
5731	Lockheed MC-130J Commando II (11-5731)	USAF 67th SOS/352nd SOW, RAF Mildenhall	
5733	Lockheed MC-130J Commando II (11-5733)	Returned to the USA, 22 May 2017	

Notes	Serial	Type (code/other identity)	Owner/operator, location or fate
	15737	Lockheed MC-130J Commando II (11-5737)	USAF 67th SOS/352nd SOW, RAF Mildenhall
	25757	Lockheed MC-130J Commando II (12-5757)	USAF 67th SOS/352nd SOW, RAF Mildenhall
	25759	Lockheed MC-130J Commando II (12-5759)	USAF 67th SOS/352nd SOW, RAF Mildenhall
	25760	Lockheed MC-130J Commando II (12-5760)	USAF 67th SOS/352nd SOW, RAF Mildenhall
	35778	Lockheed MC-130J Commando II (13-5778)	USAF 67th SOS/352nd SOW, RAF Mildenhall
	35786	Lockheed MC-130J Commando II (13-5786)	USAF 67th SOS/352nd SOW, RAF Mildenhall
		Boeing KC-135R Stratotanker/Boeing KC-135T Stratotanker	
	00324	Boeing KC-135R Stratotanker (60-0324) [D] r/w/bl	USAF 351st ARS/100th ARW, RAF Mildenhall
	00333	Boeing KC-135R Stratotanker (60-0333) [D] r/w/bl	USAF 351st ARS/100th ARW, RAF Mildenhall
	10267	Boeing KC-135R Stratotanker (61-0267) [D] r/w/bl	*Returned to the USA, 26 July 2017*
	10288	Boeing KC-135R Stratotanker (61-0288) [D] r/w/bl	USAF 351st ARS/100th ARW, RAF Mildenhall
	10299	Boeing KC-135R Stratotanker (61-0299) [D] r/w/bl	USAF 351st ARS/100th ARW, RAF Mildenhall
	10321	Boeing KC-135R Stratotanker (61-0321) [D] r/w/bl	USAF 351st ARS/100th ARW, RAF Mildenhall
	23559	Boeing KC-135R Stratotanker (62-3559) [D] r/w/bl	USAF 351st ARS/100th ARW, RAF Mildenhall
	37999	Boeing KC-135R Stratotanker (63-7999) [D] r/w/bl	USAF 351st ARS/100th ARW, RAF Mildenhall
	38021	Boeing KC-135R Stratotanker (63-8021) [D] r/w/bl	*Returned to the USA, 6 March 2017*
	38871	Boeing KC-135R Stratotanker (63-8871) [D] r/w/bl	USAF 351st ARS/100th ARW, RAF Mildenhall
	38884	Boeing KC-135R Stratotanker (63-8884) [D] r/w/bl	*Returned to the USA, 9 June 2017*
	71493	Boeing KC-135R Stratotanker (57-1493) [D] r/w/bl	USAF 351st ARS/100th ARW, RAF Mildenhall
	72605	Boeing KC-135R Stratotanker (57-2605) [D] r/w/bl	USAF 351st ARS/100th ARW, RAF Mildenhall
	80001	Boeing KC-135T Stratotanker (58-0001) [D] r/w/bl	USAF 351st ARS/100th ARW, RAF Mildenhall
	80069	Boeing KC-135T Stratotanker (58-0069) [D] r/w/bl	*Returned to the USA, 10 January 2018*
	80094	Boeing KC-135T Stratotanker (58-0094) [D] r/w/bl	USAF 351st ARS/100th ARW, RAF Mildenhall
	80100	Boeing KC-135R Stratotanker (58-0100) [D] r/w/bl	USAF 351st ARS/100th ARW, RAF Mildenhall
	80118	Boeing KC-135R Stratotanker (58-0118) [D] r/w/bl	*Returned to the USA, 12 December 2017*
	91471	Boeing KC-135T Stratotanker (59-1471) [D] r/w/bl	*Returned to the USA, 18 October 2017*
	91511	Boeing KC-135R Stratotanker (59-1511) [D] r/w/bl	USAF 351st ARS/100th ARW, RAF Mildenhall
	91513	Boeing KC-135T Stratotanker (59-1513) [D] r/w/bl	USAF 351st ARS/100th ARW, RAF Mildenhall

84-0027/LN is a F-15C Eagle wearing special markings for the 493rd Fighter Squadron of the 48th Fighter Wing, based at RAF Lakenheath.

These aircraft are normally based in Western Europe with the USAFE. They are shown in numerical order of type designation, with individual aircraft in serial number order as carried on the aircraft. Fiscal year (FY) details are also provided if necessary. The unit allocation and operating bases are given for most aircraft.

Serial	Type (code/other identity)	Owner/operator, location or fate	Notes
Beech C-12 Super King Air			
30497	Beech C-12D Super King Air (83-0497)	USAF US Embassy Flight, Taszár, Hungary	
63239	Beech C-12C Super King Air (76-3239)	USAF US Embassy Flight, Taszár, Hungary	
Lockheed (GD) F-16CM/F-16DM Fighting Falcon			
87-0350	Lockheed (GD) F-16CM-40 Fighting Falcon [AV] gn/y	USAF 555th FS/31st FW, Aviano, Italy	
87-0351	Lockheed (GD) F-16CM-40 Fighting Falcon [AV] gn/y	USAF 555th FS/31st FW, Aviano, Italy	
87-0355	Lockheed (GD) F-16CM-40 Fighting Falcon [AV] pr/w	USAF 510th FS/31st FW, Aviano, Italy	
87-0359	Lockheed (GD) F-16CM-40 Fighting Falcon [AV] gn/y	USAF 555th FS/31st FW, Aviano, Italy	
88-0413	Lockheed (GD) F-16CM-40 Fighting Falcon [AV] pr/w	USAF 510th FS/31st FW, Aviano, Italy	
88-0425	Lockheed (GD) F-16CM-40 Fighting Falcon [AV] gn/y	USAF 555th FS/31st FW, Aviano, Italy	
88-0435	Lockheed (GD) F-16CM-40 Fighting Falcon [AV] gn/y	USAF 555th FS/31st FW, Aviano, Italy	
88-0443	Lockheed (GD) F-16CM-40 Fighting Falcon [AV] pr/w	USAF 510th FS/31st FW, Aviano, Italy	
88-0444	Lockheed (GD) F-16CM-40 Fighting Falcon [AV] pr/w	USAF 510th FS/31st FW, Aviano, Italy	
88-0446	Lockheed (GD) F-16CM-40 Fighting Falcon [AV] gn/y	USAF 555th FS/31st FW, Aviano, Italy	
88-0462	Lockheed (GD) F-16CM-40 Fighting Falcon [AV] pr/w	USAF 510th FS/31st FW, Aviano, Italy	
88-0491	Lockheed (GD) F-16CM-40 Fighting Falcon [AV] pr/w	USAF 510th FS/31st FW, Aviano, Italy	
88-0516	Lockheed (GD) F-16CM-40 Fighting Falcon [AV] pr/w	USAF 510th FS/31st FW, Aviano, Italy	
88-0521	Lockheed (GD) F-16CM-40 Fighting Falcon [AV] pr/w	USAF 510th FS/31st FW, Aviano, Italy	
88-0525	Lockheed (GD) F-16CM-40 Fighting Falcon [AV] pr/w	USAF 510th FS/31st FW, Aviano, Italy	
88-0526	Lockheed (GD) F-16CM-40 Fighting Falcon [AV] gn/y	USAF 555th FS/31st FW, Aviano, Italy	
88-0532	Lockheed (GD) F-16CM-40 Fighting Falcon [AV] gn/y	USAF 555th FS/31st FW, Aviano, Italy	
88-0535	Lockheed (GD) F-16CM-40 Fighting Falcon [AV] gn/y	USAF 555th FS/31st FW, Aviano, Italy	
88-0541	Lockheed (GD) F-16CM-40 Fighting Falcon [AV] pr/w	USAF 510th FS/31st FW, Aviano, Italy	
89-2001	Lockheed (GD) F-16CM-40 Fighting Falcon [AV] m [31 FW]	USAF 31st FW, Aviano, Italy	
89-2008	Lockheed (GD) F-16CM-40 Fighting Falcon [AV] pr/w	USAF 510th FS/31st FW, Aviano, Italy	
89-2009	Lockheed (GD) F-16CM-40 Fighting Falcon [AV] pr/w	USAF 510th FS/31st FW, Aviano, Italy	
89-2011	Lockheed (GD) F-16CM-40 Fighting Falcon [AV] pr/w	USAF 510th FS/31st FW, Aviano, Italy	
89-2016	Lockheed (GD) F-16CM-40 Fighting Falcon [AV] gn/y	USAF 555th FS/31st FW, Aviano, Italy	
89-2018	Lockheed (GD) F-16CM-40 Fighting Falcon [AV] gn/y	USAF 555th FS/31st FW, Aviano, Italy	
89-2023	Lockheed (GD) F-16CM-40 Fighting Falcon [AV] gn/y	USAF 555th FS/31st FW, Aviano, Italy	
89-2024	Lockheed (GD) F-16CM-40 Fighting Falcon [AV] gn/y	USAF 555th FS/31st FW, Aviano, Italy	
89-2026	Lockheed (GD) F-16CM-40 Fighting Falcon [AV] pr/w	USAF 510th FS/31st FW, Aviano, Italy	
89-2029	Lockheed (GD) F-16CM-40 Fighting Falcon [AV] pr/w	USAF 510th FS/31st FW, Aviano, Italy	
89-2030	Lockheed (GD) F-16CM-40 Fighting Falcon [AV] pr/w [510 FS]	USAF 510th FS/31st FW, Aviano, Italy	
89-2035	Lockheed (GD) F-16CM-40 Fighting Falcon [AV] gn/y [555 FS]	USAF 555th FS/31st FW, Aviano, Italy	
89-2038	Lockheed (GD) F-16CM-40 Fighting Falcon [AV] pr/w	USAF 510th FS/31st FW, Aviano, Italy	
89-2039	Lockheed (GD) F-16CM-40 Fighting Falcon [AV] gn/y	USAF 555th FS/31st FW, Aviano, Italy	
89-2041	Lockheed (GD) F-16CM-40 Fighting Falcon [AV] gn/y	USAF 555th FS/31st FW, Aviano, Italy	
89-2044	Lockheed (GD) F-16CM-40 Fighting Falcon [AV] gn/y	USAF 555th FS/31st FW, Aviano, Italy	
89-2046	Lockheed (GD) F-16CM-40 Fighting Falcon [AV] pr/w	USAF 510th FS/31st FW, Aviano, Italy	
89-2047	Lockheed (GD) F-16CM-40 Fighting Falcon [AV] pr/w	USAF 510th FS/31st FW, Aviano, Italy	
89-2049	Lockheed (GD) F-16CM-40 Fighting Falcon [AV] pr/w [USAFE]	USAF 510th FS/31st FW, Aviano, Italy	
89-2057	Lockheed (GD) F-16CM-40 Fighting Falcon [AV] pr/w	USAF 510th FS/31st FW, Aviano, Italy	
89-2068	Lockheed (GD) F-16CM-40 Fighting Falcon [AV] gn/y	USAF 555th FS/31st FW, Aviano, Italy	
89-2096	Lockheed (GD) F-16CM-40 Fighting Falcon [AV] pr/w	USAF 510th FS/31st FW, Aviano, Italy	
89-2102	Lockheed (GD) F-16CM-40 Fighting Falcon [AV] pr/w	USAF 510th FS/31st FW, Aviano, Italy	
89-2118	Lockheed (GD) F-16CM-40 Fighting Falcon [AV] gn/y	USAF 555th FS/31st FW, Aviano, Italy	
89-2137	Lockheed (GD) F-16CM-40 Fighting Falcon [AV] pr/w [31 OG]	USAF 510th FS/31st FW, Aviano, Italy	
89-2152	Lockheed (GD) F-16CM-40 Fighting Falcon [AV] gn/y	USAF 555th FS/31st FW, Aviano, Italy	
89-2178	Lockheed (GD) F-16DM-40 Fighting Falcon [AV] gn/y	USAF 555th FS/31st FW, Aviano, Italy	
90-0709	Lockheed (GD) F-16CM-40 Fighting Falcon [AV] pr/w	USAF 510th FS/31st FW, Aviano, Italy	
90-0772	Lockheed (GD) F-16CM-40 Fighting Falcon [AV] gn/y	USAF 555th FS/31st FW, Aviano, Italy	

Notes	Serial	Type (code/other identity)	Owner/operator, location or fate
	90-0773	Lockheed (GD) F-16CM-40 Fighting Falcon [AV] *gn/y*	USAF 555th FS/31st FW, Aviano, Italy
	90-0777	Lockheed (GD) F-16DM-40 Fighting Falcon [AV] *pr/w*	USAF 510th FS/31st FW, Aviano, Italy
	90-0795	Lockheed (GD) F-16CM-40 Fighting Falcon [AV] *gn/y*	USAF 555th FS/31st FW, Aviano, Italy
	90-0796	Lockheed (GD) F-16DM-40 Fighting Falcon [AV] *gn/y*	USAF 555th FS/31st FW, Aviano, Italy
	90-0800	Lockheed (GD) F-16DM-40 Fighting Falcon [AV] *gn/y*	USAF 555th FS/31st FW, Aviano, Italy
	90-0813	Lockheed (GD) F-16CM-50 Fighting Falcon [SP] *r/w*	USAF 480th FS/52nd FW, Spangdahlem, Germany
	90-0818	Lockheed (GD) F-16CM-50 Fighting Falcon [SP] *r/w*	USAF 480th FS/52nd FW, Spangdahlem, Germany
	90-0827	Lockheed (GD) F-16CM-50 Fighting Falcon [SP] *r/w*	USAF 480th FS/52nd FW, Spangdahlem, Germany
	90-0828	Lockheed (GD) F-16CM-50 Fighting Falcon [SP] *r/w*	USAF 480th FS/52nd FW, Spangdahlem, Germany
	90-0829	Lockheed (GD) F-16CM-50 Fighting Falcon [SP] *r/w* [52 OG]	USAF 480th FS/52nd FW, Spangdahlem, Germany
	90-0833	Lockheed (GD) F-16CM-50 Fighting Falcon [SP] *r/w*	USAF 480th FS/52nd FW, Spangdahlem, Germany
	91-0338	Lockheed (GD) F-16CM-50 Fighting Falcon [SP] *r/w*	USAF 480th FS/52nd FW, Spangdahlem, Germany
	91-0340	Lockheed (GD) F-16CM-50 Fighting Falcon [SP] *r/w*	USAF 480th FS/52nd FW, Spangdahlem, Germany
	91-0342	Lockheed (GD) F-16CM-50 Fighting Falcon [SP] *r/w*	USAF 480th FS/52nd FW, Spangdahlem, Germany
	91-0343	Lockheed (GD) F-16CM-50 Fighting Falcon [SP] *r/w*	USAF 480th FS/52nd FW, Spangdahlem, Germany
	91-0344	Lockheed (GD) F-16CM-50 Fighting Falcon [SP] *r/w*	USAF 480th FS/52nd FW, Spangdahlem, Germany
	91-0351	Lockheed (GD) F-16CM-50 Fighting Falcon [SP] *r/w*	USAF 480th FS/52nd FW, Spangdahlem, Germany
	91-0352	Lockheed (GD) F-16CM-50 Fighting Falcon [SP] *m* [52 FW]	USAF 480th FS/52nd FW, Spangdahlem, Germany
	91-0358	Lockheed (GD) F-16CM-50 Fighting Falcon [SP] *r/w*	USAF 480th FS/52nd FW, Spangdahlem, Germany
	91-0360	Lockheed (GD) F-16CM-50 Fighting Falcon [SP] *r/w*	USAF 480th FS/52nd FW, Spangdahlem, Germany
	91-0361	Lockheed (GD) F-16CM-50 Fighting Falcon [SP] *r/w*	USAF 480th FS/52nd FW, Spangdahlem, Germany
	91-0368	Lockheed (GD) F-16CM-50 Fighting Falcon [SP]	USAF 480th FS/52nd FW, Spangdahlem, Germany
	91-0402	Lockheed (GD) F-16CM-50 Fighting Falcon [SP] *r/w*	USAF 480th FS/52nd FW, Spangdahlem, Germany
	91-0403	Lockheed (GD) F-16CM-50 Fighting Falcon [SP] *r/w*	USAF 480th FS/52nd FW, Spangdahlem, Germany
	91-0407	Lockheed (GD) F-16CM-50 Fighting Falcon [SP] *r/w*	USAF 480th FS/52nd FW, Spangdahlem, Germany
	91-0412	Lockheed (GD) F-16CM-50 Fighting Falcon [SP] *r/w*	USAF 480th FS/52nd FW, Spangdahlem, Germany
	91-0416	Lockheed (GD) F-16CM-50 Fighting Falcon [SP] *r/w*	USAF 480th FS/52nd FW, Spangdahlem, Germany
	91-0417	Lockheed (GD) F-16CM-50 Fighting Falcon [SP] *r/w*	USAF 480th FS/52nd FW, Spangdahlem, Germany
	91-0418	Lockheed (GD) F-16CM-50 Fighting Falcon [SP] *r/w*	USAF 480th FS/52nd FW, Spangdahlem, Germany
	91-0472	Lockheed (GD) F-16DM-50 Fighting Falcon [SP] *r/w*	USAF 480th FS/52nd FW, Spangdahlem, Germany
	91-0481	Lockheed (GD) F-16DM-50 Fighting Falcon [SP] *r/w*	USAF 480th FS/52nd FW, Spangdahlem, Germany
	92-3918	Lockheed (GD) F-16CM-50 Fighting Falcon [SP] *r/w*	USAF 480th FS/52nd FW, Spangdahlem, Germany
	96-0080	Lockheed (GD) F-16CM-50 Fighting Falcon [SP] *r/w* [480 FS]	USAF 480th FS/52nd FW, Spangdahlem, Germany

Serial	Type (code/other identity)	Owner/operator, location or fate	Notes
96-0083	Lockheed (GD) F-16CM-50 Fighting Falcon [SP] r/w	USAF 480th FS/52nd FW, Spangdahlem, Germany	

Grumman C-20H Gulfstream IV

00300	Grumman C-20H Gulfstream IV (90-0300)	*Returned to the USA, 28 August 2017*	
20375	Grumman C-20H Gulfstream IV (92-0375)	*Sold as N108EW, October 2017*	

Gates C-21A

40083	Gates C-21A (84-0083)	USAF 76th AS/86th AW, Ramstein, Germany	
40085	Gates C-21A (84-0085)	USAF 76th AS/86th AW, Ramstein, Germany	
40087	Gates C-21A (84-0087)	USAF 76th AS/86th AW, Ramstein, Germany	
40096	Gates C-21A (84-0096)	USAF 76th AS/86th AW, Ramstein, Germany	
40126	Gates C-21A (84-0126)	USAF 76th AS/86th AW, Ramstein, Germany	

Gulfstream Aerospace C-37A Gulfstream V

10076	Gulfstream Aerospace C-37A Gulfstream V (01-0076)	USAF 309th AS/86th AW, Chièvres, Belgium	
90402	Gulfstream Aerospace C-37A Gulfstream V (99-0402)	USAF 309th AS/86th AW, Chièvres, Belgium	

Boeing C-40B

20042	Boeing C-40B (02-0042)	USAF 76th AS/86th AW, Ramstein, Germany	

Sikorsky HH-60G Pave Hawk

26206	Sikorsky HH-60G Pave Hawk (89-26206) [LN]	USAF 56th RQS/31st FW, Aviano, Italy	
26208	Sikorsky HH-60G Pave Hawk (89-26208) [LN]	USAF 56th RQS/31st FW, Aviano, Italy	
26212	Sikorsky HH-60G Pave Hawk (89-26212) [LN]	USAF 56th RQS/31st FW, Aviano, Italy	

Lockheed C-130J-30 Hercules II

15736	Lockheed C-130J-30 Hercules II (11-5736)[RS] bl/w	USAF 37th AS/86th AW, Ramstein, Germany	
43142	Lockheed C-130J-30 Hercules II (04-3142)[RS] bl/w	USAF 37th AS/86th AW, Ramstein, Germany	
55822	Lockheed C-130J-30 Hercules II (15-5822)[RS] bl/w	USAF 37th AS/86th AW, Ramstein, Germany	
55831	Lockheed C-130J-30 Hercules II (15-5831)[RS] bl/w	USAF 37th AS/86th AW, Ramstein, Germany	
65840	Lockheed C-130J-30 Hercules II (16-5840)[RS] bl/w	USAF 37th AS/86th AW, Ramstein, Germany	
68610	Lockheed C-130J-30 Hercules II (06-8610)[RS] bl/w	USAF 37th AS/86th AW, Ramstein, Germany	
68611	Lockheed C-130J-30 Hercules II (06-8611)[RS] bl/w	USAF 37th AS/86th AW, Ramstein, Germany	
68612	Lockheed C-130J-30 Hercules II (06-8612)[RS] bl/w	USAF 37th AS/86th AW, Ramstein, Germany	
78608	Lockheed C-130J-30 Hercules II (07-8608)[RS] bl/w	USAF 37th AS/86th AW, Ramstein, Germany	
78609	Lockheed C-130J-30 Hercules II (07-8609)[RS] bl/w	USAF 37th AS/86th AW, Ramstein, Germany	
78613	Lockheed C-130J-30 Hercules II (07-8613)[RS] bl/w	USAF 37th AS/86th AW, Ramstein, Germany	
78614	Lockheed C-130J-30 Hercules II (07-8614)[RS] bl/w	USAF 37th AS/86th AW, Ramstein, Germany	
88601	Lockheed C-130J-30 Hercules II (08-8601)[RS] bl/w [86 AW]	USAF 37th AS/86th AW, Ramstein, Germany	
88602	Lockheed C-130J-30 Hercules II (08-8602)[RS] bl/w [86 OG]	USAF 37th AS/86th AW, Ramstein, Germany	
88603	Lockheed C-130J-30 Hercules II (08-8603)[RS] bl/w [37 AS]	USAF 37th AS/86th AW, Ramstein, Germany	
88604	Lockheed C-130J-30 Hercules II (08-8604)[RS] bl/w	*Transferred to 374th AW, September 2017*	
88605	Lockheed C-130J-30 Hercules II (08-8605)[RS] bl/w	*Transferred to 374th AW, October 2017*	
88607	Lockheed C-130J-30 Hercules II (08-8607)[RS] bl/w	USAF 37th AS/86th AW, Ramstein, Germany	

Notes	Serial	Type (code/other identity)	Owner/operator, location or fate
	Fairchild C-26D		
	900528	Fairchild C-26D	USN NAF Sigonella, Italy
	900530	Fairchild C-26D	USN NAF Sigonella, Italy
	900531	Fairchild C-26D	USN NAF Naples, Italy
	910502	Fairchild C-26D	USN NAF Naples, Italy

EUROPEAN-BASED US ARMY AIRCRAFT

Notes	Serial	Type (code/other identity)	Owner/operator, location or fate
	Beech C-12 Huron		
	40156	Beech C-12U-3 Huron (84-00156)	US Army E/1-214th AVN, Wiesbaden, Germany
	40157	Beech C-12U-3 Huron (84-00157)	US Army E/1-214th AVN, Wiesbaden, Germany
	40160	Beech C-12U-3 Huron (84-00160)	US Army E/1-214th AVN, Wiesbaden, Germany
	40162	Beech C-12U-3 Huron (84-00162)	US Army E/1-214th AVN, Wiesbaden, Germany
	40165	Beech C-12U-3 Huron (84-00165)	US Army E/1-214th AVN, Wiesbaden, Germany
	40173	Beech C-12U-3 Huron (84-00173)	US Army E/1-214th AVN, Wiesbaden, Germany
	Cessna UC-35A Citation V		
	50123	Cessna UC-35A Citation V (95-00123)	US Army E/1-214th AVN, Wiesbaden, Germany
	70102	Cessna UC-35A Citation V (97-00102)	US Army E/1-214th AVN, Wiesbaden, Germany
	70105	Cessna UC-35A Citation V (97-00105)	US Army E/1-214th AVN, Wiesbaden, Germany
	90102	Cessna UC-35A Citation V (99-00102)	US Army E/1-214th AVN, Wiesbaden, Germany
	Boeing-Vertol CH-47F Chinook		
	13-08132	Boeing-Vertol CH-47F Chinook	US Army H/1-214th AVN, Ansbach, Germany
	13-08133	Boeing-Vertol CH-47F Chinook	US Army H/1-214th AVN, Ansbach, Germany
	13-08134	Boeing-Vertol CH-47F Chinook	US Army H/1-214th AVN, Ansbach, Germany
	13-08135	Boeing-Vertol CH-47F Chinook	US Army H/1-214th AVN, Ansbach, Germany
	13-08432	Boeing-Vertol CH-47F Chinook	US Army H/1-214th AVN, Ansbach, Germany
	13-08434	Boeing-Vertol CH-47F Chinook	US Army H/1-214th AVN, Ansbach, Germany
	13-08435	Boeing-Vertol CH-47F Chinook	US Army H/1-214th AVN, Ansbach, Germany
	13-08436	Boeing-Vertol CH-47F Chinook	US Army H/1-214th AVN, Ansbach, Germany
	13-08437	Boeing-Vertol CH-47F Chinook	US Army H/1-214th AVN, Ansbach, Germany
	Sikorsky H-60 Black Hawk		
	23936	Sikorsky UH-60A+ Black Hawk (84-23936)	US Army C/1-214th AVN, Grafenwöhr, Germany
	24397	Sikorsky UH-60A+ Black Hawk (85-24397)	US Army C/1-214th AVN, Grafenwöhr, Germany
	24437	Sikorsky UH-60A+ Black Hawk (85-24437)	US Army C/1-214th AVN, Grafenwöhr, Germany
	24446	Sikorsky UH-60A+ Black Hawk (85-24446)	US Army C/1-214th AVN, Grafenwöhr, Germany
	24538	Sikorsky UH-60A Black Hawk (86-24538)	US Army A/1-214th AVN, Wiesbaden, Germany
	24583	Sikorsky UH-60A Black Hawk (87-24583)	US Army A/1-214th AVN, Wiesbaden, Germany
	24584	Sikorsky UH-60A Black Hawk (87-24584)	US Army A/1-214th AVN, Wiesbaden, Germany
	24589	Sikorsky UH-60A Black Hawk (87-24589)	US Army A/1-214th AVN, Wiesbaden, Germany
	24614	Sikorsky UH-60A+ Black Hawk (87-24614)	US Army C/1-214th AVN, Grafenwöhr, Germany
	24642	Sikorsky UH-60A Black Hawk (87-24642)	US Army A/1-214th AVN, Wiesbaden, Germany
	24643	Sikorsky UH-60A Black Hawk (87-24643)	US Army A/1-214th AVN, Wiesbaden, Germany
	26004	Sikorsky UH-60A+ Black Hawk (87-26004)	US Army C/1-214th AVN, Grafenwöhr, Germany
	26027	Sikorsky UH-60A Black Hawk (88-26027)	US Army A/1-214th AVN, Wiesbaden, Germany
	26071	Sikorsky UH-60A Black Hawk (88-26071)	US Army A/1-214th AVN, Wiesbaden, Germany
	26142	Sikorsky UH-60A Black Hawk (89-26142)	*Returned to the US, November 2017*
	26163	Sikorsky UH-60A+ Black Hawk (89-26163)	US Army C/1-214th AVN, Grafenwöhr, Germany
	26165	Sikorsky UH-60A Black Hawk (89-26165)	*Returned to the US, November 2017*
	26485	Sikorsky UH-60L Black Hawk (93-26485)	US Army A/1-214th AVN, Wiesbaden, Germany

Serial	Type (code/other identity)	Owner/operator, location or fate	Notes
MDH AH-64D Apache			
05316	MDH AH-64D Apache (02-05316)	US Army 1-3rd AVN, Ansbach, Germany	
05321	MDH AH-64D Apache (02-05321)	US Army 1-3rd AVN, Ansbach, Germany	
05327	MDH AH-64D Apache (02-05327)	US Army 1-3rd AVN, Ansbach, Germany	
05381	MDH AH-64D Apache (03-05381)	US Army 1-3rd AVN, Ansbach, Germany	
05384	MDH AH-64D Apache (03-05384)	US Army 1-3rd AVN, Ansbach, Germany	
05419	MDH AH-64D Apache (04-05419)	US Army 1-3rd AVN, Ansbach, Germany	
05426	MDH AH-64D Apache (04-05426)	US Army 1-3rd AVN, Ansbach, Germany	
05429	MDH AH-64D Apache (04-05429)	US Army 1-3rd AVN, Ansbach, Germany	
05431	MDH AH-64D Apache (04-05431)	US Army 1-3rd AVN, Ansbach, Germany	
05437	MDH AH-64D Apache (04-05437)	US Army 1-3rd AVN, Ansbach, Germany	
05439	MDH AH-64D Apache (04-05439)	US Army 1-3rd AVN, Ansbach, Germany	
05444	MDH AH-64D Apache (04-05444)	US Army 1-3rd AVN, Ansbach, Germany	
05453	MDH AH-64D Apache (04-05453)	US Army 1-3rd AVN, Ansbach, Germany	
05467	MDH AH-64D Apache (04-05467)	US Army 1-3rd AVN, Ansbach, Germany	
05535	MDH AH-64D Apache (07-05535)	US Army 1-3rd AVN, Ansbach, Germany	
05543	MDH AH-64D Apache (08-05543)	US Army 1-3rd AVN, Ansbach, Germany	
05550	MDH AH-64D Apache (08-05550)	US Army 1-3rd AVN, Ansbach, Germany	
05580	MDH AH-64D Apache (09-05580)	US Army 1-3rd AVN, Ansbach, Germany	
05581	MDH AH-64D Apache (09-05581)	US Army 1-3rd AVN, Ansbach, Germany	
05587	MDH AH-64D Apache (09-05587)	US Army 1-3rd AVN, Ansbach, Germany	
05589	MDH AH-64D Apache (09-05589)	US Army 1-3rd AVN, Ansbach, Germany	
05620	MDH AH-64D Apache (10-05620)	US Army 1-3rd AVN, Ansbach, Germany	
07010	MDH AH-64D Apache (05-07010)	US Army 1-3rd AVN, Ansbach, Germany	
07014	MDH AH-64D Apache (06-07014)	US Army 1-3rd AVN, Ansbach, Germany	
Eurocopter UH-72A Lakota			
72029	Eurocopter UH-72A Lakota (07-72029)	*Transferred to the USA, April 2017*	
72097	Eurocopter UH-72A Lakota (09-72097)	US Army JMRC, Hohenfels	
72098	Eurocopter UH-72A Lakota (09-72098)	US Army JMRC, Hohenfels	
72100	Eurocopter UH-72A Lakota (09-72100)	US Army JMRC, Hohenfels	
72105	Eurocopter UH-72A Lakota (09-72105)	US Army JMRC, Hohenfels	
72106	Eurocopter UH-72A Lakota (09-72106)	US Army JMRC, Hohenfels	
72107	Eurocopter UH-72A Lakota (09-72107)	US Army JMRC, Hohenfels	
72108	Eurocopter UH-72A Lakota (09-72108)	US Army JMRC, Hohenfels	

The following aircraft are normally based in the USA but are likely to be seen visiting the UK from time to time. The presentation is in numerical order of the type, commencing with the B-**1B** and concluding with the C-**135**. The aircraft are listed in numerical progression by the serial actually carried externally. Fiscal year information is provided, together with details of mark variations and in some cases operating units. Where base-code letter information is carried on the aircrafts' tails, this is detailed with the squadron/base data; for example the 7th Wing's B-1B 60105 carries the letters DY on its tail, thus identifying the Wing's home base as Dyess AFB, Texas.

Notes	Serial	Type (code/other identity)	Owner/operator, location or fate
	Rockwell B-1B Lancer		
	50059	Rockwell B-1B Lancer (85-0059) [DY] bk/w $	USAF 9th BS/7th BW, Dyess AFB, TX
	50060	Rockwell B-1B Lancer (85-0060) [EL] bk/r	USAF 34th BS/28th BW, Ellsworth AFB, SD
	50061	Rockwell B-1B Lancer (85-0061) [DY] bl/w	USAF 28th BS/7th BW, Dyess AFB, TX
	50064	Rockwell B-1B Lancer (85-0064) [DY] bl/w	USAF 28th BS/7th BW, Dyess AFB, TX
	50066	Rockwell B-1B Lancer (85-0066) [EL] bk/y $	USAF 37th BS/28th BW, Ellsworth AFB, SD
	50068	Rockwell B-1B Lancer (85-0068) [ED]	USAF 419th FLTS/412th TW, Edwards AFB
	50069	Rockwell B-1B Lancer (85-0069) [EL] bk/w	USAF 28th BW, Ellsworth AFB, SD
	50072	Rockwell B-1B Lancer (85-0072) [EL] bk/r	USAF 34th BS/28th BW, Ellsworth AFB, SD
	50073	Rockwell B-1B Lancer (85-0073) [DY] bk/w [7 OG]	USAF 9th BS/7th BW, Dyess AFB, TX
	50074	Rockwell B-1B Lancer (85-0074) [DY] bk/w	USAF 9th BS/7th BW, Dyess AFB, TX
	50075	Rockwell B-1B Lancer (85-0075) [ED]	USAF 419th FLTS/412th TW, Edwards AFB
	50077	Rockwell B-1B Lancer (85-0077) [WA] y/bk [77 WPS]	USAF 77th WPS/57th Wg, Dyess AFB, TX
	50079	Rockwell B-1B Lancer (85-0079) [EL] bk/r	USAF 34th BS/28th BW, Ellsworth AFB, SD
	50080	Rockwell B-1B Lancer (85-0080) [DY] bk/w	USAF 9th BS/7th BW, Dyess AFB, TX
	50081	Rockwell B-1B Lancer (85-0081) [EL] bk/r	USAF 34th BS/28th BW, Ellsworth AFB, SD
	50083	Rockwell B-1B Lancer (85-0083) [EL] bk/r	USAF 34th BS/28th BW, Ellsworth AFB, SD
	50084	Rockwell B-1B Lancer (85-0084) [EL] bk/r	USAF 34th BS/28th BW, Ellsworth AFB, SD
	50085	Rockwell B-1B Lancer (85-0085) [EL] bk/y	USAF 37th BS/28th BW, Ellsworth AFB, SD
	50087	Rockwell B-1B Lancer (85-0087) [DY] bk/w	USAF 98th BS/7th BW, Dyess AFB, TX
	50088	Rockwell B-1B Lancer (85-0088) [DY] bl/w	USAF 28th BS/7th BW, Dyess AFB, TX
	50089	Rockwell B-1B Lancer (85-0089) [DY] r/y [489 BG]	USAF 28th BS/7th BW, Dyess AFB, TX
	50090	Rockwell B-1B Lancer (85-0090) [DY] bl/w	USAF 28th BS/7th BW, Dyess AFB, TX
	60094	Rockwell B-1B Lancer (86-0094) [EL] bk/y $	USAF 37th BS/28th BW, Ellsworth AFB, SD
	60095	Rockwell B-1B Lancer (86-0095) [EL] bk/r	USAF 34th BS/28th BW, Ellsworth AFB, SD
	60097	Rockwell B-1B Lancer (86-0097) [EL] bk/y	USAF 37th BS/28th BW, Ellsworth AFB, SD
	60098	Rockwell B-1B Lancer (86-0098) [DY] bk/w	USAF 9th BS/7th BW, Dyess AFB, TX
	60099	Rockwell B-1B Lancer (86-0099) [EL] bk/y $	USAF 37th BS/28th BW, Ellsworth AFB, SD
	60101	Rockwell B-1B Lancer (86-0101) [DY] bl/w	USAF 28th BS/7th BW, Dyess AFB, TX
	60102	Rockwell B-1B Lancer (86-0102) [EL] bk/y	USAF 37th BS/28th BW, Ellsworth AFB, SD
	60103	Rockwell B-1B Lancer (86-0103) [DY] bl/w	USAF 28th BS/7th BW, Dyess AFB, TX
	60104	Rockwell B-1B Lancer (86-0104) [EL] bk/y	USAF 37th BS/28th BW, Ellsworth AFB, SD
	60105	Rockwell B-1B Lancer (86-0105) [DY] bl/w	USAF 28th BS/7th BW, Dyess AFB, TX
	60107	Rockwell B-1B Lancer (86-0107) [DY] bk/w	USAF 9th BS/7th BW, Dyess AFB, TX
	60108	Rockwell B-1B Lancer (86-0108) [EL] bk/y	USAF 37th BS/28th BW, Ellsworth AFB, SD
	60109	Rockwell B-1B Lancer (86-0109) [DY] bl/w	USAF 289th BS/7th BW, Dyess AFB, TX
	60110	Rockwell B-1B Lancer (86-0110) [DY] bl/w	USAF 28th BS/7th BW, Dyess AFB, TX
	60111	Rockwell B-1B Lancer (86-0111) [EL] bk/r	USAF 34th BS/28th BW, Ellsworth AFB, SD
	60112	Rockwell B-1B Lancer (86-0112) [DY] bl/w	USAF 28th BS/7th BW, Dyess AFB, TX
	60113	Rockwell B-1B Lancer (86-0113) [EL] bk/y	USAF 37th BS/28th BW, Ellsworth AFB, SD
	60115	Rockwell B-1B Lancer (86-0115) [EL] bk/r	USAF 34th BS/28th BW, Ellsworth AFB, SD
	60117	Rockwell B-1B Lancer (86-0117) [DY] bk/w	USAF 9th BS/7th BW, Dyess AFB, TX
	60118	Rockwell B-1B Lancer (86-0118) [EL] bk/y	USAF 37th BS/28th BW, Ellsworth AFB, SD
	60119	Rockwell B-1B Lancer (86-0119) [DY] bl/w	USAF 28th BS/7th BW, Dyess AFB, TX
	60120	Rockwell B-1B Lancer (86-0120) [EL] bk/y	USAF 37th BS/28th BW, Ellsworth AFB, SD
	60121	Rockwell B-1B Lancer (86-0121) [EL] bk/y	USAF 37th BS/28th BW, Ellsworth AFB, SD
	60122	Rockwell B-1B Lancer (86-0122) [OT] bk/gy [337 TES]	USAF 337th TES/53rd Wg, Dyess AFB, TX
	60123	Rockwell B-1B Lancer (86-0123) [DY] bl/w	USAF 28th BS/7th BW, Dyess AFB, TX
	60124	Rockwell B-1B Lancer (86-0124) [DY] bk/w	USAF 9th BS/7th BW, Dyess AFB, TX
	60125	Rockwell B-1B Lancer (86-0125) [DY] bk/w	USAF 9th BS/7th BW, Dyess AFB, TX
	60126	Rockwell B-1B Lancer (86-0126) [DY] bl/w	USAF 28th BS/7th BW, Dyess AFB, TX
	60127	Rockwell B-1B Lancer (86-0127) [DY] bk/w	USAF 9th BS/7th BW, Dyess AFB, TX
	60129	Rockwell B-1B Lancer (86-0129) [EL] bk/y	USAF 37th BS/28th BW, Ellsworth AFB, SD
	60132	Rockwell B-1B Lancer (86-0132) [DY] bl/w	USAF 28th BS/7th BW, Dyess AFB, TX

Serial	Type (code/other identity)	Owner/operator, location or fate	Notes
60133	Rockwell B-1B Lancer (86-0133) [DY] *bl/w*	USAF 28th BS/7th BW, Dyess AFB, TX	
60134	Rockwell B-1B Lancer (86-0134) [EL] *bk/r*	USAF 34th BS/28th BW, Ellsworth AFB, SD	
60135	Rockwell B-1B Lancer (86-0135) [DY] *bl/w*	USAF 28th BS/7th BW, Dyess AFB, TX	
60136	Rockwell B-1B Lancer (86-0136) [DY] *bl/w*	USAF 28th BS/7th BW, Dyess AFB, TX	
60138	Rockwell B-1B Lancer (86-0138) [DY] *y/bk*	USAF 7th BW, Dyess AFB, TX	
60139	Rockwell B-1B Lancer (86-0139) [EL] *bl/y* [34 BS]	USAF 34th BS/28th BW, Ellsworth AFB, SD	
60140	Rockwell B-1B Lancer (86-0140) [DY] *bl/w*	USAF 28th BS/7th BW, Dyess AFB, TX	

Northrop B-2 Spirit
(Names are given where known. Each begins *Spirit of ...*)

Serial	Type (code/other identity)	Owner/operator, location or fate	Notes
00040	Northrop B-2 Spirit (90-0040) [WM] *Alaska*	USAF 509th BW, Whiteman AFB, MO	
00041	Northrop B-2 Spirit (90-0041) [WM] *Hawaii*	USAF 509th BW, Whiteman AFB, MO	
20700	Northrop B-2 Spirit (92-0700) [WM] *Florida*	USAF 509th BW, Whiteman AFB, MO	
21066	Northrop B-2 Spirit (82-1066) [WM] *America*	USAF 509th BW, Whiteman AFB, MO	
21067	Northrop B-2 Spirit (82-1067) [WM] *Arizona*	USAF 509th BW, Whiteman AFB, MO	
21068	Northrop B-2 Spirit (82-1068) [WM] *New York*	USAF 509th BW, Whiteman AFB, MO	
21069	Northrop B-2 Spirit (82-1069) [WM] *Indiana*	USAF 509th BW, Whiteman AFB, MO	
21070	Northrop B-2 Spirit (82-1070) [WM] *Ohio*	USAF 509th BW, Whiteman AFB, MO	
21071	Northrop B-2 Spirit (82-1071) [WM] *Mississippi*	USAF 509th BW, Whiteman AFB, MO	
31085	Northrop B-2 Spirit (93-1085) [ED] *Oklahoma*	USAF 419th FLTS/412th TW, Edwards AFB,CA	
31086	Northrop B-2 Spirit (93-1086) [WM] *Kitty Hawk*	USAF 509th BW, Whiteman AFB, MO	
31087	Northrop B-2 Spirit (93-1087) [WM] *Pennsylvania*	USAF 509th BW, Whiteman AFB, MO	
31088	Northrop B-2 Spirit (93-1088) [WM] *Louisiana*	USAF 509th BW, Whiteman AFB, MO	
80328	Northrop B-2 Spirit (88-0328) [WM] *Texas*	USAF 509th BW, Whiteman AFB, MO	
80329	Northrop B-2 Spirit (88-0329) [WM] *Missouri*	USAF 509th BW, Whiteman AFB, MO	
80330	Northrop B-2 Spirit (88-0330) [WM] *California*	USAF 509th BW, Whiteman AFB, MO	
80331	Northrop B-2 Spirit (88-0331) [WM] *South Carolina*	USAF 509th BW, Whiteman AFB, MO	
80332	Northrop B-2 Spirit (88-0332) [WM] *Washington*	USAF 509th BW, Whiteman AFB, MO	
90128	Northrop B-2 Spirit (89-0128) [WM] *Nebraska*	USAF 509th BW, Whiteman AFB, MO	
90129	Northrop B-2 Spirit (89-0129) [WM] *Georgia*	USAF 509th BW, Whiteman AFB, MO	

Lockheed U-2

Serial	Type (code/other identity)	Owner/operator, location or fate	Notes
68-10329	Lockheed U-2S [BB]	USAF 9th RW, Beale AFB, CA	
68-10331	Lockheed U-2S [BB]	USAF 9th RW, Beale AFB, CA	
68-10336	Lockheed U-2S [BB]	USAF 9th RW, Beale AFB, CA	
68-10337	Lockheed U-2S [BB] [9 OG]	USAF 9th RW, Beale AFB, CA	
80-1064	Lockheed TU-2S [BB]	USAF 9th RW, Beale AFB, CA	
80-1065	Lockheed TU-2S [BB]	USAF 9th RW, Beale AFB, CA	
80-1066	Lockheed U-2S [BB]	USAF 9th RW, Beale AFB, CA	
80-1067	Lockheed U-2S [BB]	USAF 9th RW, Beale AFB, CA	
80-1069	Lockheed U-2S [BB]	USAF 9th RW, Beale AFB, CA	
80-1070	Lockheed U-2S	USAF WR-ALC, Robins AFB, GA	
80-1071	Lockheed U-2S [BB]	USAF 9th RW, Beale AFB, CA	
80-1073	Lockheed U-2S [BB]	USAF 9th RW, Beale AFB, CA	
80-1074	Lockheed U-2S [BB]	USAF 9th RW, Beale AFB, CA	
80-1076	Lockheed U-2S [BB]	USAF 9th RW, Beale AFB, CA	
80-1077	Lockheed U-2S [BB]	USAF 9th RW, Beale AFB, CA	
80-1078	Lockheed TU-2S [BB]	USAF 9th RW, Beale AFB, CA	
80-1079	Lockheed U-2S [BB]	USAF 9th RW, Beale AFB, CA	
80-1080	Lockheed U-2S [BB]	USAF 9th RW, Beale AFB, CA	
80-1081	Lockheed U-2S [BB]	USAF 9th RW, Beale AFB, CA	
80-1083	Lockheed U-2S [BB]	USAF 9th RW, Beale AFB, CA	
80-1084	Lockheed U-2S [BB]	USAF 9th RW, Beale AFB, CA	
80-1085	Lockheed U-2S [BB]	USAF 9th RW, Beale AFB, CA	
80-1086	Lockheed U-2S [BB]	USAF 9th RW, Beale AFB, CA	
80-1087	Lockheed U-2S [BB]	USAF 9th RW, Beale AFB, CA	
80-1089	Lockheed U-2S [BB]	USAF 9th RW, Beale AFB, CA	
80-1090	Lockheed U-2S [BB]	USAF 9th RW, Beale AFB, CA	
80-1091	Lockheed TU-2S [BB]	USAF 9th RW, Beale AFB, CA	
80-1092	Lockheed U-2S [BB]	USAF 9th RW, Beale AFB, CA	
80-1093	Lockheed U-2S [BB]	USAF 9th RW, Beale AFB, CA	
80-1094	Lockheed U-2S [BB]	USAF 9th RW, Beale AFB, CA	

Notes	Serial	Type (code/other identity)	Owner/operator, location or fate
	80-1096	Lockheed U-2S [BB]	USAF 9th RW, Beale AFB, CA
	80-1099	Lockheed U-2S [BB]	USAF 9th RW, Beale AFB, CA
	Boeing E-3 Sentry		
	00137	Boeing E-3B(mod) Sentry (80-0137) [OK] w	USAF 552nd ACW, Tinker AFB, OK
	00138	Boeing E-3G Sentry (80-0138) [OK] w	USAF 552nd ACW, Tinker AFB, OK
	00139	Boeing E-3C Sentry (80-0139) [OK] w	USAF 552nd ACW, Tinker AFB, OK
	10004	Boeing E-3C Sentry (81-0004) [OK] w	USAF 552nd ACW, Tinker AFB, OK
	10005	Boeing E-3G Sentry (81-0005) [OK] w	USAF 552nd ACW, Tinker AFB, OK
	11407	Boeing E-3B Sentry (71-1407) [ZZ] or	USAF 961st ACS/18th Wg, Kadena AB, Japan
	11408	Boeing E-3B Sentry (71-1408) [ZZ] or	USAF 961st ACS/18th Wg, Kadena AB, Japan
	20006	Boeing E-3C Sentry (82-0006) [OK]	USAF 552nd ACW, Tinker AFB, OK
	20007	Boeing E-3G Sentry (82-0007)	Boeing, Seattle, WA
	30009	Boeing E-3C Sentry (83-0009) [OK]	USAF 552nd ACW, Tinker AFB, OK
	31675	Boeing E-3G Sentry (73-1675) [OK] w	USAF 552nd ACW, Tinker AFB, OK
	50556	Boeing E-3B Sentry (75-0556) [OK] w	USAF 552nd ACW, Tinker AFB, OK
	50557	Boeing E-3B Sentry (75-0557) [OK] r	USAF 552nd ACW, Tinker AFB, OK
	50558	Boeing E-3B Sentry (75-0558) [OK]	USAF 552nd ACW, Tinker AFB, OK
	50559	Boeing E-3B Sentry (75-0559) [OK] r	USAF 552nd ACW, Tinker AFB, OK
	50560	Boeing E-3B Sentry (75-0560) [AK] gn	USAF 3rd Wg, Elmendorf, AK
	61604	Boeing E-3G Sentry (76-1604) [OK] w	USAF 552nd ACW, Tinker AFB, OK
	61605	Boeing E-3G Sentry (76-1605) [OK] r/w	USAF 552nd ACW, Tinker AFB, OK
	61606	Boeing E-3B Sentry (76-1606) [OK] w	USAF 552nd ACW, Tinker AFB, OK
	61607	Boeing E-3G Sentry (76-1607) [OK] w	USAF 552nd ACW, Tinker AFB, OK
	70351	Boeing E-3G Sentry (77-0351) [OK] w	USAF 552nd ACW, Tinker AFB, OK
	70352	Boeing E-3B Sentry (77-0352) [OK] w	USAF 552nd ACW, Tinker AFB, OK
	70353	Boeing E-3B Sentry (77-0353) [OK] r	USAF 552nd ACW, Tinker AFB, OK
	70355	Boeing E-3B Sentry (77-0355) [ZZ] or	USAF 961st ACS/18th Wg, Kadena AB, Japan
	70356	Boeing E-3B Sentry (77-0356) [OK] w	USAF 552nd ACW, Tinker AFB, OK
	80576	Boeing E-3G Sentry (78-0576) [OK] w	USAF 552nd ACW, Tinker AFB, OK
	80577	Boeing E-3B Sentry (78-0577) [OK] r	USAF 552nd ACW, Tinker AFB, OK
	80578	Boeing E-3B Sentry (78-0578) [OK] w	USAF 552nd ACW, Tinker AFB, OK
	90001	Boeing E-3G Sentry (79-0001) [OK] w	USAF 552nd ACW, Tinker AFB, OK
	90002	Boeing E-3B Sentry (79-0002) [OK] w	USAF 552nd ACW, Tinker AFB, OK
	90003	Boeing E-3B Sentry (79-0003) [OK] m	USAF 552nd ACW, Tinker AFB, OK
	Boeing E-4B		
	31676	Boeing E-4B (73-1676)	USAF 1st ACCS/595th CACG, Offutt AFB, NE
	31677	Boeing E-4B (73-1677)	USAF 1st ACCS/595th CACG, Offutt AFB, NE
	40787	Boeing E-4B (74-0787)	USAF 1st ACCS/595th CACG, Offutt AFB, NE
	50125	Boeing E-4B (75-0125)	USAF 1st ACCS/595th CACG, Offutt AFB, NE
	Lockheed C-5 Galaxy/C-5M Super Galaxy		
	00448	Lockheed C-5A Galaxy (70-0448) bl/r	*To AMARG, June 2017*
	00451	Lockheed C-5A Galaxy (70-0451) bl/r	*Withdrawn from use, July 2017*
	00456	Lockheed C-5A Galaxy (70-0456) bl/r	*To AMARG, March 2017*
	00461	Lockheed C-5A Galaxy (70-0461) bl/r	*To AMARG, September 2017*
	31285	Lockheed C-5M Super Galaxy (83-1285) bl/y	USAF 9th AS/436th AW, Dover AFB, DE
	40060	Lockheed C-5M Super Galaxy (84-0060) w/bk	USAF 22nd AS/60th AMW, Travis AFB, CA
	40061	Lockheed C-5M Super Galaxy (84-0061) bl/y	USAF 9th AS/436th AW, Dover AFB, DE
	40062	Lockheed C-5M Super Galaxy (84-0062) w/bk	USAF 22nd AS/60th AMW, Travis AFB, CA
	50001	Lockheed C-5M Super Galaxy (85-0001) bl/y	USAF 9th AS/436th AW, Dover AFB, DE
	50002	Lockheed C-5M Super Galaxy (85-0002) bl/y	USAF 9th AS/436th AW, Dover AFB, DE
	50003	Lockheed C-5M Super Galaxy (85-0003) bl/y	USAF 9th AS/436th AW, Dover AFB, DE
	50004	Lockheed C-5M Super Galaxy (85-0004) bl/y	USAF 9th AS/436th AW, Dover AFB, DE
	50005	Lockheed C-5M Super Galaxy (85-0005) bl/y	USAF 9th AS/436th AW, Dover AFB, DE
	50006	Lockheed C-5M Super Galaxy (85-0006)	USAF 68th AS/433rd AW Kelly AFB, TX
	50007	Lockheed C-5M Super Galaxy (85-0007) bl/y	USAF 9th AS/436th AW, Dover AFB, DE
	50008	Lockheed C-5M Super Galaxy (85-0008) bl/y	USAF 9th AS/436th AW, Dover AFB, DE
	50009	Lockheed C-5M Super Galaxy (85-0009)	USAF 68th AS/433rd AW Kelly AFB, TX
	50010	Lockheed C-5M Super Galaxy (85-0010) w/bk	USAF 22nd AS/60th AMW, Travis AFB, CA
	60011	Lockheed C-5M Super Galaxy (86-0011) w/bk	USAF 22nd AS/60th AMW, Travis AFB, CA

Serial	Type (code/other identity)	Owner/operator, location or fate	Notes
60012	Lockheed C-5M Super Galaxy (86-0012) *bl/r*	USAF 337th AS/439th AW, Westover ARB, MA	
60013	Lockheed C-5M Super Galaxy (86-0013) *bl/y*	USAF 9th AS/436th AW, Dover AFB, DE	
60014	Lockheed C-5M Super Galaxy (86-0014)	LMTAS, Marietta, GA	
60015	Lockheed C-5M Super Galaxy (86-0015) *w/bk*	USAF 22nd AS/60th AMW, Travis AFB, CA	
60016	Lockheed C-5M Super Galaxy (86-0016) *w/bk*	USAF 22nd AS/60th AMW, Travis AFB, CA	
60017	Lockheed C-5M Super Galaxy (86-0017) *bl/y*	USAF 9th AS/436th AW, Dover AFB, DE	
60018	Lockheed C-5M Super Galaxy (86-0018)	LMTAS, Marietta, GA	
60019	Lockheed C-5M Super Galaxy (86-0019)	USAF 68th AS/433rd AW Kelly AFB, TX	
60020	Lockheed C-5M Super Galaxy (86-0020) *bl/y*	USAF 9th AS/436th AW, Dover AFB, DE	
60021	Lockheed C-5M Super Galaxy (86-0021)	LMTAS, Marietta, GA	
60022	Lockheed C-5M Super Galaxy (86-0022) *w/bk*	USAF 22nd AS/60th AMW, Travis AFB, CA	
60023	Lockheed C-5M Super Galaxy (86-0023)	USAF 68th AS/433rd AW Kelly AFB, TX	
60024	Lockheed C-5M Super Galaxy (86-0024) *w/bk*	USAF 22nd AS/60th AMW, Travis AFB, CA	
60025	Lockheed C-5M Super Galaxy (86-0025) *bl/y*	USAF 9th AS/436th AW, Dover AFB, DE	
60026	Lockheed C-5M Super Galaxy (86-0026)	USAF 68th AS/433rd AW Kelly AFB, TX	
70027	Lockheed C-5M Super Galaxy (87-0027)	USAF 68th AS/433rd AW Kelly AFB, TX	
70028	Lockheed C-5M Super Galaxy (87-0028) *w/bk*	USAF 22nd AS/60th AMW, Travis AFB, CA	
70029	Lockheed C-5M Super Galaxy (87-0029) *w/bk*	USAF 22nd AS/60th AMW, Travis AFB, CA	
70030	Lockheed C-5M Super Galaxy (87-0030) *w/bk*	USAF 22nd AS/60th AMW, Travis AFB, CA	
70031	Lockheed C-5M Super Galaxy (87-0031)	LMTAS, Marietta, GA	
70032	Lockheed C-5M Super Galaxy (87-0032) *w/bk*	USAF 22nd AS/60th AMW, Travis AFB, CA	
70033	Lockheed C-5M Super Galaxy (87-0033)	LMTAS, Marietta, GA	
70034	Lockheed C-5M Super Galaxy (87-0034) *w/bk*	USAF 22nd AS/60th AMW, Travis AFB, CA	
70035	Lockheed C-5M Super Galaxy (87-0035) *bl/y*	USAF 9th AS/436th AW, Dover AFB, DE	
70036	Lockheed C-5M Super Galaxy (87-0036) *bl/y*	USAF 9th AS/436th AW, Dover AFB, DE	
70037	Lockheed C-5M Super Galaxy (87-0037)	LMTAS, Marietta, GA	
70038	Lockheed C-5M Super Galaxy (87-0038)	USAF 68th AS/433rd AW Kelly AFB, TX	
70039	Lockheed C-5M Super Galaxy (87-0039) *bl/r*	USAF 337th AS/439th AW, Westover ARB, MA	
70040	Lockheed C-5M Super Galaxy (87-0040) *bl/y*	USAF 9th AS/436th AW, Dover AFB, DE	
70041	Lockheed C-5M Super Galaxy (87-0041)	LMTAS, Marietta, GA	
70042	Lockheed C-5M Super Galaxy (87-0042) *w/bk*	USAF 22nd AS/60th AMW, Travis AFB, CA	
70043	Lockheed C-5M Super Galaxy (87-0043)	LMTAS, Marietta, GA	
70044	Lockheed C-5M Super Galaxy (87-0044) *w/bk*	USAF 22nd AS/60th AMW, Travis AFB, CA	
70045	Lockheed C-5M Super Galaxy (87-0045) *bl/y*	USAF 9th AS/436th AW, Dover AFB, DE	
80213	Lockheed C-5M Super Galaxy (68-0213) *w/bk*	USAF 22nd AS/60th AMW, Travis AFB, CA	
80216	Lockheed C-5M Super Galaxy (68-0216)	LMTAS, Marietta, GA	
90020	Lockheed C-5A Galaxy (69-0020) *bl/r*	*To AMARG, July 2017*	
90024	Lockheed C-5M Super Galaxy (69-0024) *bl/y*	USAF 9th AS/436th AW, Dover AFB, DE	

Boeing E-8C J-STARS

Serial	Type (code/other identity)	Owner/operator, location or fate	Notes
02000	Boeing E-8C J-STARS (00-2000) [GA] *r/bk*	USAF 116th ACW GA ANG, Robins AFB	
12005	Boeing E-8C J-STARS (01-2005) [GA] *r/bk*	USAF 116th ACW GA ANG, Robins AFB	
29111	Boeing E-8C J-STARS (02-9111) [GA] *r/bk*	USAF 116th ACW GA ANG, Robins AFB	
23289	Boeing E-8C J-STARS (02-3289) [GA] *r/bk*	USAF 116th ACW GA ANG, Robins AFB	
23290	Boeing E-8C J-STARS (02-3290) [GA] *r/bk*	USAF 116th ACW GA ANG, Robins AFB	
31097	Boeing E-8C J-STARS (93-1097) [GA] *r/bk*	USAF 116th ACW GA ANG, Robins AFB	
40284	Boeing E-8C J-STARS (94-0284) [GA] *r/bk*	USAF 116th ACW GA ANG, Robins AFB	
40285	Boeing E-8C J-STARS (94-0285) [GA] *r/bk*	USAF 116th ACW GA ANG, Robins AFB	
50121	Boeing E-8C J-STARS (95-0121) [GA] *r/bk*	USAF 116th ACW GA ANG, Robins AFB	
50122	Boeing E-8C J-STARS (95-0122) [GA] *r/bk*	USAF 116th ACW GA ANG, Robins AFB	
60042	Boeing E-8C J-STARS (96-0042) [GA] *r/bk*	USAF 116th ACW GA ANG, Robins AFB	
60043	Boeing E-8C J-STARS (96-0043) [GA] *r/bk*	USAF 116th ACW GA ANG, Robins AFB	
70100	Boeing E-8C J-STARS (97-0100) [GA] *r/bk*	USAF 116th ACW GA ANG, Robins AFB	
70200	Boeing E-8C J-STARS (97-0200) [GA] *r/bk*	USAF 116th ACW GA ANG, Robins AFB	
70201	Boeing E-8C J-STARS (97-0201) [GA] *r/bk*	USAF 116th ACW GA ANG, Robins AFB	
90006	Boeing E-8C J-STARS (99-0006) [GA] *r/bk*	USAF 116th ACW GA ANG, Robins AFB	

McDonnell Douglas KC-10A Extender

Serial	Type (code/other identity)	Owner/operator, location or fate	Notes
20191	McDonnell Douglas KC-10A Extender (82-0191) *w/bk*	USAF 60th AMW, Travis AFB, CA	
20192	McDonnell Douglas KC-10A Extender (82-0192) *w/bk*	USAF 60th AMW, Travis AFB, CA	
20193	McDonnell Douglas KC-10A Extender (82-0193) *w/bk*	USAF 60th AMW, Travis AFB, CA	
30075	McDonnell Douglas KC-10A Extender (83-0075) *w/bk*	USAF 60th AMW, Travis AFB, CA	

Notes	Serial	Type (code/other identity)	Owner/operator, location or fate
	30076	McDonnell Douglas KC-10A Extender (83-0076) *w/bk*	USAF 60th AMW, Travis AFB, CA
	30077	McDonnell Douglas KC-10A Extender (83-0077) *w/bk*	USAF 60th AMW, Travis AFB, CA
	30078	McDonnell Douglas KC-10A Extender (83-0078) *w/bk*	USAF 60th AMW, Travis AFB, CA
	30079	McDonnell Douglas KC-10A Extender (83-0079) *bl*	USAF 305th AMW, McGuire AFB, NJ
	30080	McDonnell Douglas KC-10A Extender (83-0080) *w/bk*	USAF 60th AMW, Travis AFB, CA
	30081	McDonnell Douglas KC-10A Extender (83-0081) *bl*	USAF 305th AMW, McGuire AFB, NJ
	30082	McDonnell Douglas KC-10A Extender (83-0082) *bl*	USAF 305th AMW, McGuire AFB, NJ
	40185	McDonnell Douglas KC-10A Extender (84-0185) *w/bk*	USAF 60th AMW, Travis AFB, CA
	40186	McDonnell Douglas KC-10A Extender (84-0186) *bl*	USAF 305th AMW, McGuire AFB, NJ
	40187	McDonnell Douglas KC-10A Extender (84-0187) *w/bk*	USAF 60th AMW, Travis AFB, CA
	40188	McDonnell Douglas KC-10A Extender (84-0188) *bl*	USAF 305th AMW, McGuire AFB, NJ
	40189	McDonnell Douglas KC-10A Extender (84-0189) *bl*	USAF 305th AMW, McGuire AFB, NJ
	40190	McDonnell Douglas KC-10A Extender (84-0190) *bl*	USAF 305th AMW, McGuire AFB, NJ
	40191	McDonnell Douglas KC-10A Extender (84-0191) *w/bk*	USAF 60th AMW, Travis AFB, CA
	40192	McDonnell Douglas KC-10A Extender (84-0192) *bl*	USAF 305th AMW, McGuire AFB, NJ
	50027	McDonnell Douglas KC-10A Extender (85-0027) *bl*	USAF 305th AMW, McGuire AFB, NJ
	50028	McDonnell Douglas KC-10A Extender (85-0028) *bl*	USAF 305th AMW, McGuire AFB, NJ
	50029	McDonnell Douglas KC-10A Extender (85-0029) *w/bk*	USAF 60th AMW, Travis AFB, CA
	50030	McDonnell Douglas KC-10A Extender (85-0030) *bl*	USAF 305th AMW, McGuire AFB, NJ
	50031	McDonnell Douglas KC-10A Extender (85-0031) *bl*	USAF 305th AMW, McGuire AFB, NJ
	50032	McDonnell Douglas KC-10A Extender (85-0032) *bl*	USAF 305th AMW, McGuire AFB, NJ
	50033	McDonnell Douglas KC-10A Extender (85-0033) *w/bk*	USAF 60th AMW, Travis AFB, CA
	50034	McDonnell Douglas KC-10A Extender (85-0034) *bl*	USAF 305th AMW, McGuire AFB, NJ
	60027	McDonnell Douglas KC-10A Extender (86-0027) *bl*	USAF 305th AMW, McGuire AFB, NJ
	60028	McDonnell Douglas KC-10A Extender (86-0028) *bl*	USAF 305th AMW, McGuire AFB, NJ
	60029	McDonnell Douglas KC-10A Extender (86-0029) *w/bk*	USAF 60th AMW, Travis AFB, CA
	60030	McDonnell Douglas KC-10A Extender (86-0030) *bl*	USAF 305th AMW, McGuire AFB, NJ
	60031	McDonnell Douglas KC-10A Extender (86-0031) *w/bk*	USAF 60th AMW, Travis AFB, CA
	60032	McDonnell Douglas KC-10A Extender (86-0032) *bl*	USAF 305th AMW, McGuire AFB, NJ
	60033	McDonnell Douglas KC-10A Extender (86-0033) *w/bk*	USAF 60th AMW, Travis AFB, CA
	60034	McDonnell Douglas KC-10A Extender (86-0034) *w/bk*	USAF 60th AMW, Travis AFB, CA
	60035	McDonnell Douglas KC-10A Extender (86-0035) *bl*	USAF 305th AMW, McGuire AFB, NJ
	60036	McDonnell Douglas KC-10A Extender (86-0036) *bl*	USAF 305th AMW, McGuire AFB, NJ
	60037	McDonnell Douglas KC-10A Extender (86-0037) *w/bk*	USAF 60th AMW, Travis AFB, CA
	60038	McDonnell Douglas KC-10A Extender (86-0038) *w/bk*	USAF 60th AMW, Travis AFB, CA
	70117	McDonnell Douglas KC-10A Extender (87-0117) *w/bk*	USAF 60th AMW, Travis AFB, CA
	70118	McDonnell Douglas KC-10A Extender (87-0118) *bl*	USAF 305th AMW, McGuire AFB, NJ
	70119	McDonnell Douglas KC-10A Extender (87-0119) *w/bk*	USAF 60th AMW, Travis AFB, CA
	70120	McDonnell Douglas KC-10A Extender (87-0120) *bl*	USAF 305th AMW, McGuire AFB, NJ
	70121	McDonnell Douglas KC-10A Extender (87-0121) *bl*	USAF 305th AMW, McGuire AFB, NJ
	70122	McDonnell Douglas KC-10A Extender (87-0122) *bl*	USAF 305th AMW, McGuire AFB, NJ
	70123	McDonnell Douglas KC-10A Extender (87-0123) *w/bk*	USAF 60th AMW, Travis AFB, CA
	70124	McDonnell Douglas KC-10A Extender (87-0124) *bl*	USAF 305th AMW, McGuire AFB, NJ
	90433	McDonnell Douglas KC-10A Extender (79-0433) *bl*	USAF 305th AMW, McGuire AFB, NJ
	90434	McDonnell Douglas KC-10A Extender (79-0434) *bl*	USAF 305th AMW, McGuire AFB, NJ
	91710	McDonnell Douglas KC-10A Extender (79-1710) *bl*	USAF 305th AMW, McGuire AFB, NJ
	91711	McDonnell Douglas KC-10A Extender (79-1711) *bl*	USAF 305th AMW, McGuire AFB, NJ
	91712	McDonnell Douglas KC-10A Extender (79-1712) *bl*	USAF 305th AMW, McGuire AFB, NJ
	91713	McDonnell Douglas KC-10A Extender (79-1713) *w/bk*	USAF 60th AMW, Travis AFB, CA
	91946	McDonnell Douglas KC-10A Extender (79-1946) *w/bk*	USAF 60th AMW, Travis AFB, CA
	91947	McDonnell Douglas KC-10A Extender (79-1947) *bl*	USAF 305th AMW, McGuire AFB, NJ
	91948	McDonnell Douglas KC-10A Extender (79-1948) *w/bk*	USAF 60th AMW, Travis AFB, CA
	91949	McDonnell Douglas KC-10A Extender (79-1949) *bl*	USAF 305th AMW, McGuire AFB, NJ
	91950	McDonnell Douglas KC-10A Extender (79-1950) *w/bk*	USAF 60th AMW, Travis AFB, CA
	91951	McDonnell Douglas KC-10A Extender (79-1951) *w/bk*	USAF 60th AMW, Travis AFB, CA
		Bombardier E-11A Global Express	
	19001	Bombardier E-11A Global Express (11-9001)	USAF 430th EECS/653rd ELSW, Hanscom MA
	19355	Bombardier E-11A Global Express (11-9355)	USAF 430th EECS/653rd ELSW, Hanscom MA
	19358	Bombardier E-11A Global Express (11-9358)	USAF 430th EECS/653rd ELSW, Hanscom MA
	29506	Bombardier E-11A Global Express (12-9506)	USAF 430th EECS/653rd ELSW, Hanscom MA

Serial	Type (code/other identity)	Owner/operator, location or fate	Notes
Boeing C-17A Globemaster III			
00171	Boeing C-17A Globemaster III (00-0171) [AK] w/bk	USAF 517th AS/3rd Wg, Elmendorf AFB, AK	
00172	Boeing C-17A Globemaster III (00-0172) y/bl	USAF 437th AW, Charleston AFB, SC	
00174	Boeing C-17A Globemaster III (00-0174) [AK] w/bk	USAF 517th AS/3rd Wg, Elmendorf AFB, AK	
00175	Boeing C-17A Globemaster III (00-0175) bl	USAF 6th AS/305th AMW, McGuire AFB, NJ	
00176	Boeing C-17A Globemaster III (00-0176) r/w	USAF 155th AS/164th AW, Memphis, TN ANG	
00177	Boeing C-17A Globemaster III (00-0177) bl	USAF 137th AS/105th AW, Stewart AFB, NY ANG	
00178	Boeing C-17A Globemaster III (00-0178) r/w	USAF 89th AS/445th AW AFRC, Wright-Patterson AFB, OH	
00179	Boeing C-17A Globemaster III (00-0179) r/y	USAF 58th AS/97th AMW, Altus AFB, OK	
00180	Boeing C-17A Globemaster III (00-0180) gn	USAF 62nd AW, McChord AFB, WA	
00181	Boeing C-17A Globemaster III (00-0181) r/w	USAF 167th AS/167th AW, Martinsburg, WV ANG	
00182	Boeing C-17A Globemaster III (00-0182) r/w	USAF 167th AS/167th AW, Martinsburg, WV ANG	
00183	Boeing C-17A Globemaster III (00-0183) gn	USAF 62nd AW, McChord AFB, WA	
00184	Boeing C-17A Globemaster III (00-0184) gn	USAF 62nd AW, McChord AFB, WA	
00185	Boeing C-17A Globemaster III (00-0185) [AK] w/bk	USAF 517th AS/3rd Wg, Elmendorf AFB, AK	
00213	Boeing C-17A Globemaster III (10-0213) y/bl	USAF 437th AW, Charleston AFB, SC	
00214	Boeing C-17A Globemaster III (10-0214) y/bl	USAF 437th AW, Charleston AFB, SC	
00215	Boeing C-17A Globemaster III (10-0215) y/bl	USAF 437th AW, Charleston AFB, SC	
00216	Boeing C-17A Globemaster III (10-0216) gn	USAF 62nd AW, McChord AFB, WA	
00217	Boeing C-17A Globemaster III (10-0217) gn	USAF 62nd AW, McChord AFB, WA	
00218	Boeing C-17A Globemaster III (10-0218) gn	USAF 62nd AW, McChord AFB, WA	
00219	Boeing C-17A Globemaster III (10-0219) gn	USAF 62nd AW, McChord AFB, WA	
00220	Boeing C-17A Globemaster III (10-0220) gn	USAF 62nd AW, McChord AFB, WA	
00221	Boeing C-17A Globemaster III (10-0221) y/bl	USAF 437th AW, Charleston AFB, SC	
00222	Boeing C-17A Globemaster III (10-0222) y/bl	USAF 437th AW, Charleston AFB, SC	
00223	Boeing C-17A Globemaster III (10-0223) y/bl	USAF 437th AW, Charleston AFB, SC	
00532	Boeing C-17A Globemaster III (90-0532) gn	USAF 62nd AW, McChord AFB, WA	
00533	Boeing C-17A Globemaster III (90-0533) [HH] r/y	USAF 535th AS/15th Wg, Hickam AFB, HI	
00534	Boeing C-17A Globemaster III (90-0534) bl	USAF 437th AW, Charleston AFB, SC	
00535	Boeing C-17A Globemaster III (90-0535) r/w	USAF 89th AS/445th AW AFRC, Wright-Patterson AFB, OH	
10186	Boeing C-17A Globemaster III (01-0186) bl/y	USAF 3rd AS/436th AW, Dover AFB, DE	
10187	Boeing C-17A Globemaster III (01-0187) gn	USAF 62nd AW, McChord AFB, WA	
10188	Boeing C-17A Globemaster III (01-0188) bl	USAF 137th AS/105th AW, Stewart AFB, NY ANG	
10189	Boeing C-17A Globemaster III (01-0189) r/w	USAF 155th AS/164th AW, Memphis, TN ANG	
10190	Boeing C-17A Globemaster III (01-0190) r/y	USAF 58th AS/97th AMW, Altus AFB, OK	
10191	Boeing C-17A Globemaster III (01-0191) bl/y	USAF 3rd AS/436th AW, Dover AFB, DE	
10192	Boeing C-17A Globemaster III (01-0192) bl	USAF 137th AS/105th AW, Stewart AFB, NY ANG	
10193	Boeing C-17A Globemaster III (01-0193) y/bl	USAF 437th AW, Charleston AFB, SC	
10194	Boeing C-17A Globemaster III (01-0194) r/w	USAF 89th AS/445th AW AFRC, Wright-Patterson AFB, OH	
10195	Boeing C-17A Globemaster III (01-0195) r/y	USAF 58th AS/97th AMW, Altus AFB, OK	
10196	Boeing C-17A Globemaster III (01-0196) r/w	USAF 167th AS/167th AW, Martinsburg, WV ANG	
10197	Boeing C-17A Globemaster III (01-0197) y/bl	USAF 437th AW, Charleston AFB, SC	
21098	Boeing C-17A Globemaster III (02-1098) bl	USAF 6th AS/305th AMW, McGuire AFB, NJ	
21099	Boeing C-17A Globemaster III (02-1099) y/bl	USAF 437th AW, Charleston AFB, SC	
21100	Boeing C-17A Globemaster III (02-1100) r/w	USAF 155th AS/164th AW, Memphis, TN ANG	
21101	Boeing C-17A Globemaster III (02-1101) y/bl	USAF 437th AW, Charleston AFB, SC	
21102	Boeing C-17A Globemaster III (02-1102) r/y	USAF 58th AS/97th AMW, Altus AFB, OK	
21103	Boeing C-17A Globemaster III (02-1103) gn	USAF 62nd AW, McChord AFB, WA	
21104	Boeing C-17A Globemaster III (02-1104) r/y [97 OG]	USAF 58th AS/97th AMW, Altus AFB, OK	
21105	Boeing C-17A Globemaster III (02-1105) gn	USAF 62nd AW, McChord AFB, WA	
21106	Boeing C-17A Globemaster III (02-1106) gn	USAF 62nd AW, McChord AFB, WA	
21107	Boeing C-17A Globemaster III (02-1107) gn	USAF 62nd AW, McChord AFB, WA	
21108	Boeing C-17A Globemaster III (02-1108) gn	USAF 62nd AW, McChord AFB, WA	
21109	Boeing C-17A Globemaster III (02-1109) gn	USAF 62nd AW, McChord AFB, WA	
21110	Boeing C-17A Globemaster III (02-1110) r/w	USAF 155th AS/164th AW, Memphis, TN ANG	
21111	Boeing C-17A Globemaster III (02-1111) gn	USAF 62nd AW, McChord AFB, WA	
21112	Boeing C-17A Globemaster III (02-1112) bl/gd	USAF 183rd AS/172nd AW, Jackson Int'l Airport, MS ANG	
23291	Boeing C-17A Globemaster III (92-3291) r/w	USAF 155th AS/164th AW, Memphis, TN ANG	

Notes	Serial	Type (code/other identity)	Owner/operator, location or fate
	23292	Boeing C-17A Globemaster III (92-3292) y/bl	USAF 437th AW, Charleston AFB, SC
	23293	Boeing C-17A Globemaster III (92-3293) y/bl	USAF 437th AW, Charleston AFB, SC
	23294	Boeing C-17A Globemaster III (92-3294) gn	USAF 62nd AW, McChord AFB, WA
	30599	Boeing C-17A Globemaster III (93-0599) [AK] w/bk	USAF 517th AS/3rd Wg, Elmendorf AFB, AK
	30600	Boeing C-17A Globemaster III (93-0600) r/w	USAF 155th AS/164th AW, Memphis, TN ANG
	30601	Boeing C-17A Globemaster III (93-0601) gn	USAF 62nd AW, McChord AFB, WA
	30602	Boeing C-17A Globemaster III (93-0602) y/bl	USAF 437th AW, Charleston AFB, SC
	30603	Boeing C-17A Globemaster III (93-0603) r/w	USAF 89th AS/445th AW AFRC, Wright-Patterson AFB, OH
	30604	Boeing C-17A Globemaster III (93-0604) r/w	USAF 89th AS/445th AW AFRC, Wright-Patterson AFB, OH
	33113	Boeing C-17A Globemaster III (03-3113) bl/gd	USAF 183rd AS/172nd AW, Jackson Int'l Airport, MS ANG
	33114	Boeing C-17A Globemaster III (03-3114) bl/gd	USAF 183rd AS/172nd AW, Jackson Int'l Airport, MS ANG
	33115	Boeing C-17A Globemaster III (03-3115) bl/gd	USAF 183rd AS/172nd AW, Jackson Int'l Airport, MS ANG
	33116	Boeing C-17A Globemaster III (03-3116) bl/gd	USAF 183rd AS/172nd AW, Jackson Int'l Airport, MS ANG
	33117	Boeing C-17A Globemaster III (03-3117) bl/gd	USAF 183rd AS/172nd AW, Jackson Int'l Airport, MS ANG
	33118	Boeing C-17A Globemaster III (03-3118) bl/gd	USAF 183rd AS/172nd AW, Jackson Int'l Airport, MS ANG
	33119	Boeing C-17A Globemaster III (03-3119) bl/gd	USAF 183rd AS/172nd AW, Jackson Int'l Airport, MS ANG
	33120	Boeing C-17A Globemaster III (03-3120) gn	USAF 62nd AW, McChord AFB, WA
	33121	Boeing C-17A Globemaster III (03-3121) [ED]	USAF 418th FLTS/412th TW, Edwards AFB, CA
	33122	Boeing C-17A Globemaster III (03-3122) y/bl	USAF 437th AW, Charleston AFB, SC
	33123	Boeing C-17A Globemaster III (03-3123) r/w	USAF 167th AS/167th AW, Martinsburg, WV ANG
	33124	Boeing C-17A Globemaster III (03-3124) y/bl	USAF 437th AW, Charleston AFB, SC
	33125	Boeing C-17A Globemaster III (03-3125) bl	USAF 6th AS/305th AMW, McGuire AFB, NJ
	33126	Boeing C-17A Globemaster III (03-3126) bl	USAF 6th AS/305th AMW, McGuire AFB, NJ
	33127	Boeing C-17A Globemaster III (03-3127) gn	USAF 62nd AW, McChord AFB, WA
	40065	Boeing C-17A Globemaster III (94-0065) r/w	USAF 155th AS/164th AW, Memphis, TN ANG
	40066	Boeing C-17A Globemaster III (94-0066) gn	USAF 62nd AW, McChord AFB, WA
	40067	Boeing C-17A Globemaster III (94-0067) bl	USAF 137th AS/105th AW, Stewart AFB, NY ANG
	40068	Boeing C-17A Globemaster III (94-0068) or/y	USAF 729th AS/452nd AMW AFRC, March ARB, CA
	40069	Boeing C-17A Globemaster III (94-0069) r/w	USAF 167th AS/167th AW, Martinsburg, WV ANG
	40070	Boeing C-17A Globemaster III (94-0070) r/w	USAF 167th AS/167th AW, Martinsburg, WV ANG
	44128	Boeing C-17A Globemaster III (04-4128) bl	USAF 6th AS/305th AMW, McGuire AFB, NJ
	44129	Boeing C-17A Globemaster III (04-4129) r/y	USAF 58th AS/97th AMW, Altus AFB, OK
	44130	Boeing C-17A Globemaster III (04-4130) bl	USAF 6th AS/305th AMW, McGuire AFB, NJ
	44131	Boeing C-17A Globemaster III (04-4131) bl	USAF 6th AS/305th AMW, McGuire AFB, NJ
	44132	Boeing C-17A Globemaster III (04-4132) bl	USAF 6th AS/305th AMW, McGuire AFB, NJ
	44133	Boeing C-17A Globemaster III (04-4133) bl	USAF 6th AS/305th AMW, McGuire AFB, NJ
	44134	Boeing C-17A Globemaster III (04-4134) bl	USAF 6th AS/305th AMW, McGuire AFB, NJ
	44135	Boeing C-17A Globemaster III (04-4135) y/bl	USAF 437th AW, Charleston AFB, SC
	44136	Boeing C-17A Globemaster III (04-4136) bl	USAF 6th AS/305th AMW, McGuire AFB, NJ
	44137	Boeing C-17A Globemaster III (04-4137) bl	USAF 6th AS/305th AMW, McGuire AFB, NJ
	44138	Boeing C-17A Globemaster III (04-4138) or/y	USAF 729th AS/452nd AMW AFRC, March ARB, CA
	50102	Boeing C-17A Globemaster III (95-0102) y/bl	USAF 437th AW, Charleston AFB, SC
	50103	Boeing C-17A Globemaster III (95-0103) gn	USAF 62nd AW, McChord AFB, WA
	50104	Boeing C-17A Globemaster III (95-0104) r/w	USAF 155th AS/164th AW, Memphis, TN ANG
	50105	Boeing C-17A Globemaster III (95-0105) bl	USAF 137th AS/105th AW, Stewart AFB, NY ANG
	50106	Boeing C-17A Globemaster III (95-0106) gn	USAF 62nd AW, McChord AFB, WA
	50107	Boeing C-17A Globemaster III (95-0107) y/bl	USAF 437th AW, Charleston AFB, SC
	55139	Boeing C-17A Globemaster III (05-5139) or/y	USAF 729th AS/452nd AMW AFRC, March ARB, CA
	55140	Boeing C-17A Globemaster III (05-5140) or/y	USAF 729th AS/452nd AMW AFRC, March ARB, CA

Serial	Type (code/other identity)	Owner/operator, location or fate	Notes
55141	Boeing C-17A Globemaster III (05-5141) *or/y*	USAF 729th AS/452nd AMW AFRC, March ARB, CA	
55142	Boeing C-17A Globemaster III (05-5142) *or/y*	USAF 729th AS/452nd AMW AFRC, March ARB, CA	
55143	Boeing C-17A Globemaster III (05-5143) *r/w*	USAF 89th AS/445th AW AFRC, Wright-Patterson AFB, OH	
55144	Boeing C-17A Globemaster III (05-5144) *or/y*	USAF 729th AS/452nd AMW AFRC, March ARB, CA	
55145	Boeing C-17A Globemaster III (05-5145) *or/y*	USAF 729th AS/452nd AMW AFRC, March ARB, CA	
55146	Boeing C-17A Globemaster III (05-5146) [HH] *r/y*	USAF 535th AS/15th Wg, Hickam AFB, HI	
55147	Boeing C-17A Globemaster III (05-5147) [HH] *r/y*	USAF 535th AS/15th Wg, Hickam AFB, HI	
55148	Boeing C-17A Globemaster III (05-5148) [HH] *r/y*	USAF 535th AS/15th Wg, Hickam AFB, HI	
55149	Boeing C-17A Globemaster III (05-5149) [HH] *r/y*	USAF 535th AS/15th Wg, Hickam AFB, HI	
55150	Boeing C-17A Globemaster III (05-5150) [HH] *r/y*	USAF 535th AS/15th Wg, Hickam AFB, HI	
55151	Boeing C-17A Globemaster III (05-5151) [HH] *r/y*	USAF 535th AS/15th Wg, Hickam AFB, HI	
55152	Boeing C-17A Globemaster III (05-5152) [HH] *r/y*	USAF 535th AS/15th Wg, Hickam AFB, HI	
55153	Boeing C-17A Globemaster III (05-5153) [HH] *r/y]*	USAF 535th AS/15th Wg, Hickam AFB, HI	
60001	Boeing C-17A Globemaster III (96-0001) *gn*	USAF 62nd AW, McChord AFB, WA	
60002	Boeing C-17A Globemaster III (96-0002) *y/bl*	USAF 437th AW, Charleston AFB, SC	
60003	Boeing C-17A Globemaster III (96-0003) *gn*	USAF 62nd AW, McChord AFB, WA	
60004	Boeing C-17A Globemaster III (96-0004) *gn*	USAF 62nd AW, McChord AFB, WA	
60005	Boeing C-17A Globemaster III (96-0005) *bl*	USAF 137th AS/105th AW, Stewart AFB, NY ANG	
60006	Boeing C-17A Globemaster III (96-0006) *r/w*	USAF 167th AS/167th AW, Martinsburg, WV ANG	
60007	Boeing C-17A Globemaster III (96-0007) *bl/gd*	USAF 183rd AS/172nd AW, Jackson Int'l Airport, MS ANG	
60008	Boeing C-17A Globemaster III (96-0008) *r/y*	USAF 58th AS/97th AMW, Altus AFB, OK	
66154	Boeing C-17A Globemaster III (06-6154) *w/bk*	USAF 21st AS/60th AMW, Travis AFB, CA	
66155	Boeing C-17A Globemaster III (06-6155) *w/bk*	USAF 21st AS/60th AMW, Travis AFB, CA	
66156	Boeing C-17A Globemaster III (06-6156) *w/bk*	USAF 21st AS/60th AMW, Travis AFB, CA	
66157	Boeing C-17A Globemaster III (06-6157) *w/bk*	USAF 21st AS/60th AMW, Travis AFB, CA	
66158	Boeing C-17A Globemaster III (06-6158) *w/bk*	USAF 21st AS/60th AMW, Travis AFB, CA	
66159	Boeing C-17A Globemaster III (06-6159) *w/bk*	USAF 21st AS/60th AMW, Travis AFB, CA	
66160	Boeing C-17A Globemaster III (06-6160) *w/bk*	USAF 21st AS/60th AMW, Travis AFB, CA	
66161	Boeing C-17A Globemaster III (06-6161) *w/bk*	USAF 21st AS/60th AMW, Travis AFB, CA	
66162	Boeing C-17A Globemaster III (06-6162) *w/bk*	USAF 21st AS/60th AMW, Travis AFB, CA	
66163	Boeing C-17A Globemaster III (06-6163) *w/bk*	USAF 21st AS/60th AMW, Travis AFB, CA	
66164	Boeing C-17A Globemaster III (06-6164) *w/bk*	USAF 21st AS/60th AMW, Travis AFB, CA	
66165	Boeing C-17A Globemaster III (06-6165) *bl/y*	USAF 3rd AS/436th AW, Dover AFB, DE	
66166	Boeing C-17A Globemaster III (06-6166) *bl/y*	USAF 3rd AS/436th AW, Dover AFB, DE	
66167	Boeing C-17A Globemaster III (06-6167) *bl/y*	USAF 3rd AS/436th AW, Dover AFB, DE	
66168	Boeing C-17A Globemaster III (06-6168) *bl/y*	USAF 3rd AS/436th AW, Dover AFB, DE	
70041	Boeing C-17A Globemaster III (97-0041) *y/bl*	USAF 437th AW, Charleston AFB, SC	
70042	Boeing C-17A Globemaster III (97-0042) *r/w*	USAF 155th AS/164th AW, Memphis, TN ANG	
70043	Boeing C-17A Globemaster III (97-0043) *or/y*	USAF 729th AS/452nd AMW AFRC, March ARB, CA	
70044	Boeing C-17A Globemaster III (97-0044) *r/w*	USAF 89th AS/445th AW AFRC, Wright-Patterson AFB, OH	
70045	Boeing C-17A Globemaster III (97-0045) *bl*	USAF 137th AS/105th AW, Stewart AFB, NY ANG	
70046	Boeing C-17A Globemaster III (97-0046) *y/bl*	USAF 437th AW, Charleston AFB, SC	
70047	Boeing C-17A Globemaster III (97-0047) *y/bl*	USAF 437th AW, Charleston AFB, SC	
70048	Boeing C-17A Globemaster III (97-0048) *r/w*	USAF 89th AS/445th AW AFRC, Wright-Patterson AFB, OH	
77169	Boeing C-17A Globemaster III (07-7169) *bl/y*	USAF 3rd AS/436th AW, Dover AFB, DE	
7170	Boeing C-17A Globemaster III (07-7170) *bl/y*	USAF 3rd AS/436th AW, Dover AFB, DE	
7171	Boeing C-17A Globemaster III (07-7171) *bl*	USAF 6th AS/305th AMW, McGuire AFB, NJ	
7172	Boeing C-17A Globemaster III (07-7172) *w/bk*	USAF 21st AS/60th AMW, Travis AFB, CA	
7173	Boeing C-17A Globemaster III (07-7173) *bl/y*	USAF 3rd AS/436th AW, Dover AFB, DE	
7174	Boeing C-17A Globemaster III (07-7174) *bl/y*	USAF 3rd AS/436th AW, Dover AFB, DE	
7175	Boeing C-17A Globemaster III (07-7175) *bl/y*	USAF 3rd AS/436th AW, Dover AFB, DE	
7176	Boeing C-17A Globemaster III (07-7176) *bl/y*	USAF 3rd AS/436th AW, Dover AFB, DE	
7177	Boeing C-17A Globemaster III (07-7177) *bl/y*	USAF 3rd AS/436th AW, Dover AFB, DE	

Notes	Serial	Type (code/other identity)	Owner/operator, location or fate
	77178	Boeing C-17A Globemaster III (07-7178) *bl*	USAF 6th AS/305th AMW, McGuire AFB, NJ
	77179	Boeing C-17A Globemaster III (07-7179) *w/bk*	USAF 21st AS/60th AMW, Travis AFB, CA
	77180	Boeing C-17A Globemaster III (07-7180) *y/bl*	USAF 437th AW, Charleston AFB, SC
	77181	Boeing C-17A Globemaster III (07-7181) *y/bl*	USAF 437th AW, Charleston AFB, SC
	77182	Boeing C-17A Globemaster III (07-7182) *y/bl*	USAF 437th AW, Charleston AFB, SC
	77183	Boeing C-17A Globemaster III (07-7183) *y/bl*	USAF 437th AW, Charleston AFB, SC
	77184	Boeing C-17A Globemaster III (07-7184) *y/bl*	USAF 437th AW, Charleston AFB, SC
	77185	Boeing C-17A Globemaster III (07-7185) *y/bl*	USAF 437th AW, Charleston AFB, SC
	77186	Boeing C-17A Globemaster III (07-7186) *y/bl*	USAF 437th AW, Charleston AFB, SC
	77187	Boeing C-17A Globemaster III (07-7187) *y/bl*	USAF 437th AW, Charleston AFB, SC
	77188	Boeing C-17A Globemaster III (07-7188) *y/bl*	USAF 437th AW, Charleston AFB, SC
	77189	Boeing C-17A Globemaster III (07-7189) *y/bl*	USAF 437th AW, Charleston AFB, SC
	80049	Boeing C-17A Globemaster III (98-0049) *r/y*	USAF 58th AS/97th AMW, Altus AFB, OK
	80050	Boeing C-17A Globemaster III (98-0050) *r/y*	USAF 58th AS/97th AMW, Altus AFB, OK
	80051	Boeing C-17A Globemaster III (98-0051) [AK] *w/bk*	USAF 517th AS/3rd Wg, Elmendorf AFB, AK
	80052	Boeing C-17A Globemaster III (98-0052) *gn*	USAF 62nd AW, McChord AFB, WA
	80053	Boeing C-17A Globemaster III (98-0053) *gn*	USAF 62nd AW, McChord AFB, WA
	80054	Boeing C-17A Globemaster III (98-0054) *r/w*	USAF 155th AS/164th AW, Memphis, TN ANG
	80055	Boeing C-17A Globemaster III (98-0055) *r/y $*	USAF 58th AS/97th AMW, Altus AFB, OK
	80056	Boeing C-17A Globemaster III (98-0056) [AK] *w/bk*	USAF 517th AS/3rd Wg, Elmendorf AFB, AK
	80057	Boeing C-17A Globemaster III (98-0057) *bl*	USAF 137th AS/105th AW, Stewart AFB, NY ANG
	80265	Boeing C-17A Globemaster III (88-0265) *gn*	USAF 62nd AW, McChord AFB, WA
	80266	Boeing C-17A Globemaster III (88-0266) *y/bl*	USAF 437th AW, Charleston AFB, SC
	88190	Boeing C-17A Globemaster III (08-8190) *y/bl*	USAF 437th AW, Charleston AFB, SC
	88191	Boeing C-17A Globemaster III (08-8191) *y/bl*	USAF 437th AW, Charleston AFB, SC
	88192	Boeing C-17A Globemaster III (08-8192) *gn*	USAF 62nd AW, McChord AFB, WA
	88193	Boeing C-17A Globemaster III (08-8193) *gn*	USAF 62nd AW, McChord AFB, WA
	88194	Boeing C-17A Globemaster III (08-8194) *gn*	USAF 62nd AW, McChord AFB, WA
	88195	Boeing C-17A Globemaster III (08-8195) *gn*	USAF 62nd AW, McChord AFB, WA
	88196	Boeing C-17A Globemaster III (08-8196) *gn*	USAF 62nd AW, McChord AFB, WA
	88197	Boeing C-17A Globemaster III (08-8197) *gn*	USAF 62nd AW, McChord AFB, WA
	88198	Boeing C-17A Globemaster III (08-8198) *y/bl*	USAF 437th AW, Charleston AFB, SC
	88199	Boeing C-17A Globemaster III (08-8199) *gn*	USAF 62nd AW, McChord AFB, WA
	88200	Boeing C-17A Globemaster III (08-8200) *gn*	USAF 62nd AW, McChord AFB, WA
	88201	Boeing C-17A Globemaster III (08-8201) *gn*	USAF 62nd AW, McChord AFB, WA
	88202	Boeing C-17A Globemaster III (08-8202) *gn*	USAF 62nd AW, McChord AFB, WA
	88203	Boeing C-17A Globemaster III (08-8203) *gn*	USAF 62nd AW, McChord AFB, WA
	88204	Boeing C-17A Globemaster III (08-8204) *y/bl*	USAF 437th AW, Charleston AFB, SC
	90058	Boeing C-17A Globemaster III (99-0058) *gn*	USAF 62nd AW, McChord AFB, WA
	90059	Boeing C-17A Globemaster III (99-0059) *gn*	USAF 62nd AW, McChord AFB, WA
	90060	Boeing C-17A Globemaster III (99-0060) *gn*	USAF 62nd AW, McChord AFB, WA
	90061	Boeing C-17A Globemaster III (99-0061) *r/y*	USAF 58th AS/97th AMW, Altus AFB, OK
	90062	Boeing C-17A Globemaster III (99-0062) *y/bl*	USAF 437th AW, Charleston AFB, SC
	90063	Boeing C-17A Globemaster III (99-0063) *r/y*	USAF 58th AS/97th AMW, Altus AFB, OK
	90064	Boeing C-17A Globemaster III (99-0064) *r/y*	USAF 58th AS/97th AMW, Altus AFB, OK
	90165	Boeing C-17A Globemaster III (99-0165) *r/w*	USAF 89th AS/445th AW AFRC, Wright-Patterson AFB, OH
	90166	Boeing C-17A Globemaster III (99-0166) *gn*	USAF 62nd AW, McChord AFB, WA
	90167	Boeing C-17A Globemaster III (99-0167) [AK] *w/bk*	USAF 517th AS/3rd Wg, Elmendorf AFB, AK
	90168	Boeing C-17A Globemaster III (99-0168) [AK] *w/bk*	USAF 517th AS/3rd Wg, Elmendorf AFB, AK
	90169	Boeing C-17A Globemaster III (99-0169) *y/bl*	USAF 437th AW, Charleston AFB, SC
	90170	Boeing C-17A Globemaster III (99-0170) [AK] *w/bk*	USAF 517th AS/3rd Wg, Elmendorf AFB, AK
	91189	Boeing C-17A Globemaster III (89-1189) *y/bl*	USAF 437th AW, Charleston AFB, SC
	91190	Boeing C-17A Globemaster III (89-1190) *r/w*	USAF 167th AS/167th AW, Martinsburg, WV ANG
	91191	Boeing C-17A Globemaster III (89-1191) *bl*	USAF 137th AS/105th AW, Stewart AFB, NY ANG
	91192	Boeing C-17A Globemaster III (89-1192) *y/bl*	USAF 437th AW, Charleston AFB, SC
	99205	Boeing C-17A Globemaster III (09-9205) *y/bl*	USAF 437th AW, Charleston AFB, SC
	99206	Boeing C-17A Globemaster III (09-9206) *y/bl*	USAF 437th AW, Charleston AFB, SC
	99207	Boeing C-17A Globemaster III (09-9207) *y/bl*	USAF 437th AW, Charleston AFB, SC
	99208	Boeing C-17A Globemaster III (09-9208) *y/bl*	USAF 437th AW, Charleston AFB, SC
	99209	Boeing C-17A Globemaster III (09-9209) *gn*	USAF 62nd AW, McChord AFB, WA
	99210	Boeing C-17A Globemaster III (09-9210) *gn*	USAF 62nd AW, McChord AFB, WA

Serial	Type (code/other identity)	Owner/operator, location or fate	Notes
9211	Boeing C-17A Globemaster III (09-9211) *gn*	USAF 62nd AW, McChord AFB, WA	
9212	Boeing C-17A Globemaster III (09-9212) *y/bl*	USAF 437th AW, Charleston AFB, SC	
	Grumman C-20 Gulfstream III/IV		
0108	Grumman C-20F Gulfstream IV (91-00108)	US Army OSAC/PAT, Andrews AFB, MD	
0201	Grumman C-20B Gulfstream III (86-0201)	*Withdrawn from use, 2017*	
0203	Grumman C-20B Gulfstream III (86-0203)	*Withdrawn from use, September 2017*	
0204	Grumman C-20B Gulfstream III (86-0204)	*Withdrawn from use, September 2017*	
0206	Grumman C-20B Gulfstream III (86-0206)	*To AMARG, August 2017*	
	Lockheed Martin F-22A Raptor		
1-4004	Lockheed Martin F-22A Raptor [ED]	USAF 411th FLTS/412th TW, Edwards AFB, CA	
1-4006	Lockheed Martin F-22A Raptor	USAF	
1-4007	Lockheed Martin F-22A Raptor [ED] [412 TW]	USAF 411th FLTS/412th TW, Edwards AFB, CA	
1-4009	Lockheed Martin F-22A Raptor [ED]	USAF 411th FLTS/412th TW, Edwards AFB, CA	
9-4010	Lockheed Martin F-22A Raptor [OT] [422 TES]	USAF 422nd TES/53rd Wg, Nellis AFB, NV	
9-4011	Lockheed Martin F-22A Raptor [WA]	USAF 433rd WPS/57th Wg, Nellis AFB, NV	
0-4012	Lockheed Martin F-22A Raptor [TY]	USAF 43rd FS/325th FW, Tyndall AFB, FL	
0-4015	Lockheed Martin F-22A Raptor [TY]	USAF 43rd FS/325th FW, Tyndall AFB, FL	
0-4016	Lockheed Martin F-22A Raptor [TY]	USAF 43rd FS/325th FW, Tyndall AFB, FL	
0-4017	Lockheed Martin F-22A Raptor [TY]	USAF 43rd FS/325th FW, Tyndall AFB, FL	
1-4018	Lockheed Martin F-22A Raptor [TY]	USAF 43rd FS/325th FW, Tyndall AFB, FL	
1-4019	Lockheed Martin F-22A Raptor [TY]	USAF 43rd FS/325th FW, Tyndall AFB, FL	
1-4020	Lockheed Martin F-22A Raptor [TY]	USAF 43rd FS/325th FW, Tyndall AFB, FL	
1-4021	Lockheed Martin F-22A Raptor [TY]	USAF 43rd FS/325th FW, Tyndall AFB, FL	
1-4022	Lockheed Martin F-22A Raptor [TY]	USAF 43rd FS/325th FW, Tyndall AFB, FL	
1-4023	Lockheed Martin F-22A Raptor [TY]	USAF 43rd FS/325th FW, Tyndall AFB, FL	
1-4024	Lockheed Martin F-22A Raptor [TY]	USAF 43rd FS/325th FW, Tyndall AFB, FL	
1-4025	Lockheed Martin F-22A Raptor [TY]	USAF 43rd FS/325th FW, Tyndall AFB, FL	
1-4026	Lockheed Martin F-22A Raptor [TY]	USAF 43rd FS/325th FW, Tyndall AFB, FL	
1-4027	Lockheed Martin F-22A Raptor [TY]	USAF 43rd FS/325th FW, Tyndall AFB, FL	
2-4028	Lockheed Martin F-22A Raptor [TY]	USAF 43rd FS/325th FW, Tyndall AFB, FL	
2-4029	Lockheed Martin F-22A Raptor [TY]	USAF 43rd FS/325th FW, Tyndall AFB, FL	
2-4030	Lockheed Martin F-22A Raptor [TY]	USAF 43rd FS/325th FW, Tyndall AFB, FL	
2-4031	Lockheed Martin F-22A Raptor [TY]	USAF 43rd FS/325th FW, Tyndall AFB, FL	
2-4032	Lockheed Martin F-22A Raptor [TY]	USAF 43rd FS/325th FW, Tyndall AFB, FL	
2-4033	Lockheed Martin F-22A Raptor [TY]	USAF 43rd FS/325th FW, Tyndall AFB, FL	
2-4034	Lockheed Martin F-22A Raptor [TY]	USAF 43rd FS/325th FW, Tyndall AFB, FL	
2-4035	Lockheed Martin F-22A Raptor [TY] [325 OG]	USAF 43rd FS/325th FW, Tyndall AFB, FL	
2-4036	Lockheed Martin F-22A Raptor [TY]	USAF 43rd FS/325th FW, Tyndall AFB, FL	
2-4037	Lockheed Martin F-22A Raptor	USAF	
2-4038	Lockheed Martin F-22A Raptor [TY]	USAF 43rd FS/325th FW, Tyndall AFB, FL	
2-4039	Lockheed Martin F-22A Raptor [TY]	USAF 43rd FS/325th FW, Tyndall AFB, FL	
2-4040	Lockheed Martin F-22A Raptor [TY] [325 FW]	USAF 43rd FS/325th FW, Tyndall AFB, FL	
3-4041	Lockheed Martin F-22A Raptor [TY]	USAF 43rd FS/325th FW, Tyndall AFB, FL	
3-4042	Lockheed Martin F-22A Raptor [TY]	USAF 43rd FS/325th FW, Tyndall AFB, FL	
3-4043	Lockheed Martin F-22A Raptor [TY] [43 FS]	USAF 43rd FS/325th FW, Tyndall AFB, FL	
3-4044	Lockheed Martin F-22A Raptor [TY]	USAF 43rd FS/325th FW, Tyndall AFB, FL	
3-4045	Lockheed Martin F-22A Raptor [HH]	USAF 199th FS/154th Wg, Hickam AFB, HI ANG	
3-4046	Lockheed Martin F-22A Raptor [HH]	USAF 199th FS/154th Wg, Hickam AFB, HI ANG	
3-4047	Lockheed Martin F-22A Raptor [HH]	USAF 199th FS/154th Wg, Hickam AFB, HI ANG	
3-4048	Lockheed Martin F-22A Raptor [HH]	USAF 199th FS/154th Wg, Hickam AFB, HI ANG	
3-4049	Lockheed Martin F-22A Raptor [HH]	USAF 199th FS/154th Wg, Hickam AFB, HI ANG	
3-4050	Lockheed Martin F-22A Raptor [HH]	USAF 199th FS/154th Wg, Hickam AFB, HI ANG	
3-4051	Lockheed Martin F-22A Raptor [HH]	USAF 199th FS/154th Wg, Hickam AFB, HI ANG	
3-4052	Lockheed Martin F-22A Raptor [TY]	USAF 95th FS/325th FW, Tyndall AFB, FL	
3-4053	Lockheed Martin F-22A Raptor [HH]	USAF 199th FS/154th Wg, Hickam AFB, HI ANG	
3-4054	Lockheed Martin F-22A Raptor [HH] [154 Wg]	USAF 199th FS/154th Wg, Hickam AFB, HI ANG	
3-4055	Lockheed Martin F-22A Raptor [HH]	USAF 199th FS/154th Wg, Hickam AFB, HI ANG	
3-4056	Lockheed Martin F-22A Raptor [HH]	USAF 199th FS/154th Wg, Hickam AFB, HI ANG	
3-4057	Lockheed Martin F-22A Raptor [HH]	USAF 199th FS/154th Wg, Hickam AFB, HI ANG	
3-4058	Lockheed Martin F-22A Raptor [HH]	USAF 199th FS/154th Wg, Hickam AFB, HI ANG	

Notes	Serial	Type (code/other identity)	Owner/operator, location or fate
	03-4059	Lockheed Martin F-22A Raptor [HH]	USAF 199th FS/154th Wg, Hickam AFB, HI ANG
	03-4060	Lockheed Martin F-22A Raptor [HH]	USAF 199th FS/154th Wg, Hickam AFB, HI ANG
	03-4061	Lockheed Martin F-22A Raptor [HH]	USAF 199th FS/154th Wg, Hickam AFB, HI ANG
	04-4062	Lockheed Martin F-22A Raptor [HH]	USAF 199th FS/154th Wg, Hickam AFB, HI ANG
	04-4063	Lockheed Martin F-22A Raptor [HH]	USAF 199th FS/154th Wg, Hickam AFB, HI ANG
	04-4064	Lockheed Martin F-22A Raptor [HH]	USAF 199th FS/154th Wg, Hickam AFB, HI ANG
	04-4065	Lockheed Martin F-22A Raptor [FF]	USAF 94th FS/1st FW, Langley AFB, VA
	04-4066	Lockheed Martin F-22A Raptor [OT]	USAF 422nd TES/53rd Wg, Nellis AFB, NV
	04-4067	Lockheed Martin F-22A Raptor [FF]	USAF 94th FS/1st FW, Langley AFB, VA
	04-4068	Lockheed Martin F-22A Raptor [OT]	USAF 422nd TES/53rd Wg, Nellis AFB, NV
	04-4069	Lockheed Martin F-22A Raptor [OT]	USAF 422nd TES/53rd Wg, Nellis AFB, NV
	04-4070	Lockheed Martin F-22A Raptor [FF]	USAF 94th FS/1st FW, Langley AFB, VA
	04-4071	Lockheed Martin F-22A Raptor [WA]	USAF 433rd WPS/57th Wg, Nellis AFB, NV
	04-4072	Lockheed Martin F-22A Raptor [TY]	USAF 95th FS/325th FW, Tyndall AFB, FL
	04-4073	Lockheed Martin F-22A Raptor [FF]	USAF 27th FS/1st FW, Langley AFB, VA
	04-4074	Lockheed Martin F-22A Raptor [AK]	USAF 90th FS/3rd Wg, Elmendorf AFB, AK
	04-4075	Lockheed Martin F-22A Raptor [AK]	USAF 90th FS/3rd Wg, Elmendorf AFB, AK
	04-4076	Lockheed Martin F-22A Raptor [TY]	USAF 95th FS/325th FW, Tyndall AFB, FL
	04-4077	Lockheed Martin F-22A Raptor [AK]	USAF 525th FS/3rd Wg, Elmendorf AFB, AK
	04-4078	Lockheed Martin F-22A Raptor [TY]	USAF 95th FS/325th FW, Tyndall AFB, FL
	04-4079	Lockheed Martin F-22A Raptor [TY]	USAF 95th FS/325th FW, Tyndall AFB, FL
	04-4080	Lockheed Martin F-22A Raptor [TY]	USAF 95th FS/325th FW, Tyndall AFB, FL
	04-4082	Lockheed Martin F-22A Raptor [FF] [149 FS]	USAF 149th FS/192nd FW/1st FW, Langley AFB, VA ANG
	04-4083	Lockheed Martin F-22A Raptor [TY] [301 FS]	USAF 301st FS/44th FG AFRES/325th FW, Tyndall AFB, FL
	05-4081	Lockheed Martin F-22A Raptor (04-4081) [TY]	USAF 95th FS/325th FW, Tyndall AFB, FL
	05-4084	Lockheed Martin F-22A Raptor [TY]	USAF 95th FS/325th FW, Tyndall AFB, FL
	05-4085	Lockheed Martin F-22A Raptor [FF]	USAF 94th FS/1st FW, Langley AFB, VA
	05-4086	Lockheed Martin F-22A Raptor [TY]	USAF 95th FS/325th FW, Tyndall AFB, FL
	05-4087	Lockheed Martin F-22A Raptor [AK]	USAF 90th FS/3rd Wg, Elmendorf AFB, AK
	05-4088	Lockheed Martin F-22A Raptor [TY]	USAF 95th FS/325th FW, Tyndall AFB, FL
	05-4089	Lockheed Martin F-22A Raptor [TY]	USAF 95th FS/325th FW, Tyndall AFB, FL
	05-4090	Lockheed Martin F-22A Raptor [AK]	USAF 90th FS/3rd Wg, Elmendorf AFB, AK
	05-4091	Lockheed Martin F-22A Raptor [TY]	USAF 95th FS/325th FW, Tyndall AFB, FL
	05-4092	Lockheed Martin F-22A Raptor [AK]	USAF 525th FS/3rd Wg, Elmendorf AFB, AK
	05-4093	Lockheed Martin F-22A Raptor [TY]	USAF 95th FS/325th FW, Tyndall AFB, FL
	05-4094	Lockheed Martin F-22A Raptor [TY]	USAF 95th FS/325th FW, Tyndall AFB, FL
	05-4095	Lockheed Martin F-22A Raptor [TY] [95 FS]	USAF 95th FS/325th FW, Tyndall AFB, FL
	05-4096	Lockheed Martin F-22A Raptor [WA]	USAF 433rd WPS/57th Wg, Nellis AFB, NV
	05-4097	Lockheed Martin F-22A Raptor [TY]	USAF 95th FS/325th FW, Tyndall AFB, FL
	05-4098	Lockheed Martin F-22A Raptor [TY]	USAF 95th FS/325th FW, Tyndall AFB, FL
	05-4099	Lockheed Martin F-22A Raptor [TY]	USAF 95th FS/325th FW, Tyndall AFB, FL
	05-4100	Lockheed Martin F-22A Raptor [TY]	USAF 95th FS/325th FW, Tyndall AFB, FL
	05-4101	Lockheed Martin F-22A Raptor [TY]	USAF 95th FS/325th FW, Tyndall AFB, FL
	05-4102	Lockheed Martin F-22A Raptor [AK] [302 FS]	USAF 302nd FS/477th FG AFRES/3rd Wg, Elmendorf AFB, AK
	05-4103	Lockheed Martin F-22A Raptor [AK] [3 Wg]	USAF 90th FS/3rd Wg, Elmendorf AFB, AK
	05-4104	Lockheed Martin F-22A Raptor [TY]	USAF 95th FS/325th FW, Tyndall AFB, FL
	05-4105	Lockheed Martin F-22A Raptor [TY] [44 FG]	USAF 95th FS/325th FW, Tyndall AFB, FL
	05-4106	Lockheed Martin F-22A Raptor [TY]	USAF 95th FS/325th FW, Tyndall AFB, FL
	05-4107	Lockheed Martin F-22A Raptor [TY]	USAF 95th FS/325th FW, Tyndall AFB, FL
	06-4108	Lockheed Martin F-22A Raptor [AK]	USAF 525th FS/3rd Wg, Elmendorf AFB, AK
	06-4109	Lockheed Martin F-22A Raptor [WA]	USAF 433rd WPS/57th Wg, Nellis AFB, NV
	06-4110	Lockheed Martin F-22A Raptor [AK] [11 AF]	USAF 525th FS/3rd Wg, Elmendorf AFB, AK
	06-4111	Lockheed Martin F-22A Raptor [OT]	USAF 422nd TES/53rd Wg, Nellis AFB, NV
	06-4112	Lockheed Martin F-22A Raptor [AK]	USAF 525th FS/3rd Wg, Elmendorf AFB, AK
	06-4113	Lockheed Martin F-22A Raptor [AK] [3 OG]	USAF 525th FS/3rd Wg, Elmendorf AFB, AK
	06-4114	Lockheed Martin F-22A Raptor [AK]	USAF 525th FS/3rd Wg, Elmendorf AFB, AK
	06-4115	Lockheed Martin F-22A Raptor [AK] [525 FS]	USAF 525th FS/3rd Wg, Elmendorf AFB, AK
	06-4116	Lockheed Martin F-22A Raptor [WA] [433 WPS]	USAF 433rd WPS/57th Wg, Nellis AFB, NV
	06-4117	Lockheed Martin F-22A Raptor [AK]	USAF 525th FS/3rd Wg, Elmendorf AFB, AK

Serial	Type (code/other identity)	Owner/operator, location or fate	Notes
06-4118	Lockheed Martin F-22A Raptor [AK]	USAF 525th FS/3rd Wg, Elmendorf AFB, AK	
06-4119	Lockheed Martin F-22A Raptor [AK]	USAF 525th FS/3rd Wg, Elmendorf AFB, AK	
06-4120	Lockheed Martin F-22A Raptor [OT]	USAF 422nd TES/53rd Wg, Nellis AFB, NV	
06-4121	Lockheed Martin F-22A Raptor [AK]	USAF 525th FS/3rd Wg, Elmendorf AFB, AK	
06-4122	Lockheed Martin F-22A Raptor [AK]	USAF 525th FS/3rd Wg, Elmendorf AFB, AK	
06-4123	Lockheed Martin F-22A Raptor [AK]	USAF 525th FS/3rd Wg, Elmendorf AFB, AK	
06-4124	Lockheed Martin F-22A Raptor [OT]	USAF 422nd TES/53rd Wg, Nellis AFB, NV	
06-4126	Lockheed Martin F-22A Raptor [AK]	USAF 525th FS/3rd Wg, Elmendorf AFB, AK	
06-4127	Lockheed Martin F-22A Raptor [AK]	USAF 525th FS/3rd Wg, Elmendorf AFB, AK	
06-4128	Lockheed Martin F-22A Raptor [OT]	USAF 422nd TES/53rd Wg, Nellis AFB, NV	
06-4129	Lockheed Martin F-22A Raptor [AK]	USAF 525th FS/3rd Wg, Elmendorf AFB, AK	
06-4130	Lockheed Martin F-22A Raptor [AK]	USAF 525th FS/3rd Wg, Elmendorf AFB, AK	
07-4131	Lockheed Martin F-22A Raptor [AK]	USAF 525th FS/3rd Wg, Elmendorf AFB, AK	
07-4132	Lockheed Martin F-22A Raptor [ED] [411 FLTS]	USAF 411th FLTS/412th TW, Edwards AFB, CA	
07-4133	Lockheed Martin F-22A Raptor [AK]	USAF 525th FS/3rd Wg, Elmendorf AFB, AK	
07-4134	Lockheed Martin F-22A Raptor [AK]	USAF 525th FS/3rd Wg, Elmendorf AFB, AK	
07-4135	Lockheed Martin F-22A Raptor [AK]	USAF 90th FS/3rd Wg, Elmendorf AFB, AK	
07-4136	Lockheed Martin F-22A Raptor [AK]	USAF 90th FS/3rd Wg, Elmendorf AFB, AK	
07-4137	Lockheed Martin F-22A Raptor [AK]	USAF 90th FS/3rd Wg, Elmendorf AFB, AK	
07-4138	Lockheed Martin F-22A Raptor [AK]	USAF 90th FS/3rd Wg, Elmendorf AFB, AK	
07-4139	Lockheed Martin F-22A Raptor [AK]	USAF 90th FS/3rd Wg, Elmendorf AFB, AK	
07-4140	Lockheed Martin F-22A Raptor [AK]	USAF 90th FS/3rd Wg, Elmendorf AFB, AK	
07-4141	Lockheed Martin F-22A Raptor [AK]	USAF 90th FS/3rd Wg, Elmendorf AFB, AK	
07-4142	Lockheed Martin F-22A Raptor [AK]	USAF 90th FS/3rd Wg, Elmendorf AFB, AK	
07-4143	Lockheed Martin F-22A Raptor [AK]	USAF 90th FS/3rd Wg, Elmendorf AFB, AK	
07-4144	Lockheed Martin F-22A Raptor [AK]	USAF 90th FS/3rd Wg, Elmendorf AFB, AK	
07-4145	Lockheed Martin F-22A Raptor [AK]	USAF 90th FS/3rd Wg, Elmendorf AFB, AK	
07-4146	Lockheed Martin F-22A Raptor [AK]	USAF 90th FS/3rd Wg, Elmendorf AFB, AK	
07-4147	Lockheed Martin F-22A Raptor [AK]	USAF 90th FS/3rd Wg, Elmendorf AFB, AK	
07-4148	Lockheed Martin F-22A Raptor [AK]	USAF 90th FS/3rd Wg, Elmendorf AFB, AK	
07-4149	Lockheed Martin F-22A Raptor [AK]	USAF 90th FS/3rd Wg, Elmendorf AFB, AK	
07-4150	Lockheed Martin F-22A Raptor [AK]	USAF 90th FS/3rd Wg, Elmendorf AFB, AK	
07-4151	Lockheed Martin F-22A Raptor [AK]	USAF 90th FS/3rd Wg, Elmendorf AFB, AK	
08-4152	Lockheed Martin F-22A Raptor [FF]	USAF 94th FS/1st FW, Langley AFB, VA	
08-4153	Lockheed Martin F-22A Raptor [FF]	USAF 27th FS/1st FW, Langley AFB, VA	
08-4154	Lockheed Martin F-22A Raptor [FF]	USAF 94th FS/1st FW, Langley AFB, VA	
08-4155	Lockheed Martin F-22A Raptor [FF]	USAF 27th FS/1st FW, Langley AFB, VA	
08-4156	Lockheed Martin F-22A Raptor [FF]	USAF 94th FS/1st FW, Langley AFB, VA	
08-4157	Lockheed Martin F-22A Raptor [FF]	USAF 27th FS/1st FW, Langley AFB, VA	
08-4158	Lockheed Martin F-22A Raptor [FF]	USAF 27th FS/1st FW, Langley AFB, VA	
08-4159	Lockheed Martin F-22A Raptor [FF]	USAF 27th FS/1st FW, Langley AFB, VA	
08-4160	Lockheed Martin F-22A Raptor [FF]	USAF 27th FS/1st FW, Langley AFB, VA	
08-4161	Lockheed Martin F-22A Raptor [FF]	USAF 27th FS/1st FW, Langley AFB, VA	
08-4162	Lockheed Martin F-22A Raptor [FF] [1 FW]	USAF 94th FS/1st FW, Langley AFB, VA	
08-4163	Lockheed Martin F-22A Raptor [FF]	USAF 27th FS/1st FW, Langley AFB, VA	
08-4164	Lockheed Martin F-22A Raptor [FF]	USAF 94th FS/1st FW, Langley AFB, VA	
08-4165	Lockheed Martin F-22A Raptor [FF]	USAF 27th FS/1st FW, Langley AFB, VA	
08-4166	Lockheed Martin F-22A Raptor [FF]	USAF 94th FS/1st FW, Langley AFB, VA	
08-4167	Lockheed Martin F-22A Raptor [FF]	USAF 27th FS/1st FW, Langley AFB, VA	
08-4168	Lockheed Martin F-22A Raptor [FF]	USAF 94th FS/1st FW, Langley AFB, VA	
08-4169	Lockheed Martin F-22A Raptor [FF]	USAF 27th FS/1st FW, Langley AFB, VA	
08-4170	Lockheed Martin F-22A Raptor [FF]	USAF 27th FS/1st FW, Langley AFB, VA	
08-4171	Lockheed Martin F-22A Raptor [FF]	USAF 27th FS/1st FW, Langley AFB, VA	
09-4172	Lockheed Martin F-22A Raptor [FF] [27 FS]	USAF 27th FS/1st FW, Langley AFB, VA	
09-4173	Lockheed Martin F-22A Raptor [FF]	USAF 27th FS/1st FW, Langley AFB, VA	
09-4174	Lockheed Martin F-22A Raptor [FF]	USAF 27th FS/1st FW, Langley AFB, VA	
09-4175	Lockheed Martin F-22A Raptor [FF]	USAF 94th FS/1st FW, Langley AFB, VA	
09-4176	Lockheed Martin F-22A Raptor [FF]	USAF 27th FS/1st FW, Langley AFB, VA	
09-4177	Lockheed Martin F-22A Raptor [FF]	USAF 27th FS/1st FW, Langley AFB, VA	
09-4178	Lockheed Martin F-22A Raptor [FF]	USAF 27th FS/1st FW, Langley AFB, VA	
09-4179	Lockheed Martin F-22A Raptor [FF]	USAF 94th FS/1st FW, Langley AFB, VA	
09-4180	Lockheed Martin F-22A Raptor [FF]	USAF 27th FS/1st FW, Langley AFB, VA	

Notes	Serial	Type (code/other identity)	Owner/operator, location or fate
	09-4181	Lockheed Martin F-22A Raptor [FF]	USAF 94th FS/1st FW, Langley AFB, VA
	09-4182	Lockheed Martin F-22A Raptor [FF]	USAF 27th FS/1st FW, Langley AFB, VA
	09-4183	Lockheed Martin F-22A Raptor [FF]	USAF 94th FS/1st FW, Langley AFB, VA
	09-4184	Lockheed Martin F-22A Raptor [FF]	USAF 27th FS/1st FW, Langley AFB, VA
	09-4185	Lockheed Martin F-22A Raptor [FF] [1 OG]	USAF 27th FS/1st FW, Langley AFB, VA
	09-4186	Lockheed Martin F-22A Raptor [FF]	USAF 27th FS/1st FW, Langley AFB, VA
	09-4187	Lockheed Martin F-22A Raptor [FF]	USAF 94th FS/1st FW, Langley AFB, VA
	09-4188	Lockheed Martin F-22A Raptor [OT]	USAF 422nd TES/53rd Wg, Nellis AFB, NV
	09-4189	Lockheed Martin F-22A Raptor [FF]	USAF 27th FS/1st FW, Langley AFB, VA
	09-4190	Lockheed Martin F-22A Raptor [AK]	USAF 90th FS/3rd Wg, Elmendorf AFB, AK
	09-4191	Lockheed Martin F-22A Raptor [FF]	USAF 94th FS/1st FW, Langley AFB, VA
	10-4192	Lockheed Martin F-22A Raptor [FF] [192 FW]	USAF 149th FS/192nd FW/1st FW, Langley AFB, VA ANG
	10-4193	Lockheed Martin F-22A Raptor [AK] [3 Wg]	USAF 525th FS/3rd Wg, Elmendorf AFB, AK
	10-4194	Lockheed Martin F-22A Raptor [FF] [94 FS]	USAF 94th FS/1st FW, Langley AFB, VA
	10-4195	Lockheed Martin F-22A Raptor [AK] [525 FS]	USAF 525th FS/3rd Wg, Elmendorf AFB, AK
	Boeing VC-25A/VC-25B		
	28000	Boeing VC-25A (82-8000)	USAF PAS/89th AW, Andrews AFB, MD
	29000	Boeing VC-25A (92-9000)	USAF PAS/89th AW, Andrews AFB, MD
	N894BA	Boeing VC-25B	USAF (on order)
	N895BA	Boeing VC-25B	USAF (on order)
	Pilatus U-28A		
	10415	Pilatus U-28A (N415PB/01-0415)	USAF 318th SOS/27th SOW, Cannon AFB, NM
	40688	Pilatus U-28A (N707KH/04-0688)	USAF 318th SOS/27th SOW, Cannon AFB, NM
	50409	Pilatus U-28A (N922RG/05-0409)	USAF 319th SOS/1st SOW, Hurlburt Field, FL
	50419	Pilatus U-28A (N419WA/05-0419)	USAF 319th SOS/1st SOW, Hurlburt Field, FL
	50424	Pilatus U-28A (N424PB/05-0424)	USAF 318th SOS/27th SOW, Cannon AFB, NM
	50446	Pilatus U-28A (N131JN/05-0446)	USAF 318th SOS/27th SOW, Cannon AFB, NM
	50447	Pilatus U-28A (N447PC/05-0447)	USAF 319th SOS/1st SOW, Hurlburt Field, FL
	50482	Pilatus U-28A (N482WA/05-0482)	USAF 319th SOS/1st SOW, Hurlburt Field, FL
	50556	Pilatus U-28A (N556HL/05-0556)	USAF 319th SOS/1st SOW, Hurlburt Field, FL
	50573	Pilatus U-28A (N666GT/05-0573)	USAF 319th SOS/1st SOW, Hurlburt Field, FL
	50597	Pilatus U-28A (N597CH/05-0597)	USAF 318th SOS/27th SOW, Cannon AFB, NM
	60692	Pilatus U-28A (N692BC/06-0692)	USAF 318th SOS/27th SOW, Cannon AFB, NM
	60740	Pilatus U-28A (N740AF/06-0740)	USAF 318th SOS/27th SOW, Cannon AFB, NM
	70488	Pilatus U-28A (N56EZ/07-0488)	USAF 319th SOS/1st SOW, Hurlburt Field, FL
	70691	Pilatus U-28A (N691PC/07-0691)	USAF 319th SOS/1st SOW, Hurlburt Field, FL
	70711	Pilatus U-28A (N711PN/07-0711)	USAF 319th SOS/1st SOW, Hurlburt Field, FL
	70712	Pilatus U-28A (N609TW/07-0712)	USAF 319th SOS/1st SOW, Hurlburt Field, FL
	70777	Pilatus U-28A (N72DZ/07-0777)	USAF 318th SOS/27th SOW, Cannon AFB, NM
	70779	Pilatus U-28A (N779PC/07-0779)	USAF 319th SOS/1st SOW, Hurlburt Field, FL
	70793	Pilatus U-28A (N96MV/07-0793)	USAF 319th SOS/1st SOW, Hurlburt Field, FL
	70808	Pilatus U-28A (N531MP/07-0808)	USAF 318th SOS/27th SOW, Cannon AFB, NM
	70821	Pilatus U-28A (N821PE/07-0821)	USAF 319th SOS/1st SOW, Hurlburt Field, FL
	70829	Pilatus U-28A (N829PE/07-0829)	USAF 319th SOS/1st SOW, Hurlburt Field, FL
	70838	Pilatus U-28A (N838PE/07-0838)	USAF 319th SOS/1st SOW, Hurlburt Field, FL
	70840	Pilatus U-28A (N840PE/07-0840)	USAF 319th SOS/1st SOW, Hurlburt Field, FL
	80519	Pilatus U-28A (N519PC/08-0519)	USAF 319th SOS/1st SOW, Hurlburt Field, FL
	80581	Pilatus U-28A (N581PC/08-0581)	USAF 319th SOS/1st SOW, Hurlburt Field, FL
	80646	Pilatus U-28A (N875RJ/08-0646)	USAF 319th SOS/1st SOW, Hurlburt Field, FL
	80700	Pilatus U-28A (N600KP/08-0700)	USAF 319th SOS/1st SOW, Hurlburt Field, FL
	80718	Pilatus U-28A (N824BK/08-0718)	USAF 319th SOS/1st SOW, Hurlburt Field, FL
	80724	Pilatus U-28A (N624TS/08-0724)	*Crashed 14 March 2017, Clovis NM*
	80790	Pilatus U-28A (N757ED/08-0790)	USAF 319th SOS/1st SOW, Hurlburt Field, FL
	80809	Pilatus U-28A (N36EG/08-0809)	USAF 319th SOS/1st SOW, Hurlburt Field, FL
	80822	Pilatus U-28A (N822BM/08-0822)	USAF 319th SOS/1st SOW, Hurlburt Field, FL
	80835	Pilatus U-28A (N100MS/08-0835)	USAF 318th SOS/27th SOW, Cannon AFB, NM
	80850	Pilatus U-28A (N850CB/08-0850)	USAF 319th SOS/1st SOW, Hurlburt Field, FL

Serial	Type (code/other identity)	Owner/operator, location or fate	Notes

Boeing C-32

* Please note that there is evidence to suggest that the serials 25001, 86001, 86006 and 96143 are used by more than one airframe.

Serial	Type (code/other identity)	Owner/operator, location or fate	Notes
09001	Boeing C-32B (00-9001)	USAF 150th SOS/108th Wg, McGuire AFB, NJ	
24452	Boeing C-32B (02-4452)	USAF 150th SOS/108th Wg, McGuire AFB, NJ	
25001	Boeing C-32B (N226G or N610G/02-5001)*	USAF 486th FLTS/46th TW, Eglin AFB, FL	
80001	Boeing C-32A (98-0001)	USAF 1st AS/89th AW, Andrews AFB, MD	
80002	Boeing C-32A (98-0002)	USAF 1st AS/89th AW, Andrews AFB, MD	
86006	Boeing C-32B (N226G or N610G/98-6006)*	USAF 486th FLTS/46th TW, Eglin AFB, FL	
90003	Boeing C-32A (99-0003)	USAF 1st AS/89th AW, Andrews AFB, MD	
90004	Boeing C-32A (99-0004)	USAF 1st AS/89th AW, Andrews AFB, MD	
90015	Boeing C-32A (09-0015)	USAF 1st AS/89th AW, Andrews AFB, MD	
90016	Boeing C-32A (09-0016)	USAF 1st AS/89th AW, Andrews AFB, MD	
90017	Boeing C-32A (09-0017)	USAF 1st AS/89th AW, Andrews AFB, MD	
96143	Boeing C-32B (N226G or N610G/99-6143)*	USAF 486th FLTS/46th TW, Eglin AFB, FL	

Gulfstream Aerospace C-37 Gulfstream V

Serial	Type (code/other identity)	Owner/operator, location or fate	Notes
1778	Gulfstream Aerospace C-37A Gulfstream V (04-01778)	US Army OSAC/PAT, Andrews AFB, MD	
1863	Gulfstream Aerospace C-37A Gulfstream V (02-01863)	US Army OSAC/PAT, Andrews AFB, MD	
1944	Gulfstream Aerospace C-37A Gulfstream V (97-01944)	US Army OSAC/PAT, Andrews AFB, MD	
10028	Gulfstream Aerospace C-37A Gulfstream V (01-0028)	USAF 310th AS/6th AMW, MacDill AFB, FL	
10029	Gulfstream Aerospace C-37A Gulfstream V (01-0029)	USAF 310th AS/6th AMW, MacDill AFB, FL	
10030	Gulfstream Aerospace C-37A Gulfstream V (01-0030)	USAF 310th AS/6th AMW, MacDill AFB, FL	
10065	Gulfstream Aerospace C-37A Gulfstream V (01-0065)	USAF 65th AS/15th Wg, Hickam AFB, HI	
10550	Gulfstream Aerospace C-37B Gulfstream V (11-0550)	USAF 99th AS/89th AW, Andrews AFB, MD	
60500	Gulfstream Aerospace C-37B Gulfstream V (06-0500)	USAF 99th AS/89th AW, Andrews AFB, MD	
70400	Gulfstream Aerospace C-37A Gulfstream V (97-0400)	USAF 99th AS/89th AW, Andrews AFB, MD	
70401	Gulfstream Aerospace C-37A Gulfstream V (97-0401)	USAF 99th AS/89th AW, Andrews AFB, MD	
90404	Gulfstream Aerospace C-37A Gulfstream V (99-0404)	USAF 99th AS/89th AW, Andrews AFB, MD	
90525	Gulfstream Aerospace C-37B Gulfstream V (09-0525)	USAF 99th AS/89th AW, Andrews AFB, MD	

Boeing C-40

Serial	Type (code/other identity)	Owner/operator, location or fate	Notes
10015	Boeing C-40B (N378BJ/01-0015)	USAF 65th AS/15th Wg, Hickam AFB, HI	
10040	Boeing C-40B (N371BJ/01-0040)	USAF 1st AS/89th AW, Andrews AFB, MD	
10041	Boeing C-40B (N374BC/01-0041)	USAF 1st AS/89th AW, Andrews AFB, MD	
20201	Boeing C-40C (N752BC/02-0201)	USAF 201st AS/113th FW DC ANG, Andrews AFB, MD	
20202	Boeing C-40C (N754BC/02-0202)	USAF 201st AS/113th FW DC ANG, Andrews AFB, MD	
20203	Boeing C-40C (N236BA/02-0203)	USAF 201st AS/113th FW DC ANG, Andrews AFB, MD	
50730	Boeing C-40C (N365BJ/05-0730)	USAF 73rd AS/932nd AW AFRC, Scott AFB, IL	
50932	Boeing C-40C (N366BJ/05-0932)	USAF 73rd AS/932nd AW AFRC, Scott AFB, IL	
54613	Boeing C-40C (N368BJ/05-4613)	USAF 73rd AS/932nd AW AFRC, Scott AFB, IL	
90540	Boeing C-40C (N736JS/09-0540)	USAF 73rd AS/932nd AW AFRC, Scott AFB, IL	

Boeing 767-2C/KC-46A Pegasus

Serial	Type (code/other identity)	Owner/operator, location or fate	Notes
46001	Boeing 767-2LKC (N461FT/11-46001)	USAF 418th FLTS, 412th TW, Edwards AFB, CA	
46002	Boeing KC-46A Pegasus (N462KC/11-46002)	Boeing, Everett, for USAF	
46003	Boeing 767-2LKC (N463FT/11-46003)	Boeing, Everett, for USAF	
46004	Boeing KC-46A Pegasus (N464KC/11-46004)	Boeing, Everett, for USAF	
46005	Boeing KC-46A Pegasus (N842BA/16-46005)	Boeing, Everett, for USAF	
46006	Boeing 767-2LKC (N884BA/16-46006)	Boeing, Everett, for USAF	
46007	Boeing KC-46A Pegasus (15-46007)	USAF (on order)	
46008	Boeing KC-46A Pegasus (15-46008)	USAF (on order)	
46009	Boeing KC-46A Pegasus (N50217/15-46009)	USAF (on order)	
46010	Boeing KC-46A Pegasus (15-46010)	USAF (on order)	
46011	Boeing KC-46A Pegasus (15-46011)	USAF (on order)	
46012	Boeing KC-46A Pegasus (16-46012)	USAF (on order)	
46013	Boeing KC-46A Pegasus (16-46013)	USAF (on order)	
46014	Boeing KC-46A Pegasus (16-46014)	USAF (on order)	
46015	Boeing KC-46A Pegasus (16-46015)	USAF (on order)	

Notes	Serial	Type (code/other identity)	Owner/operator, location or fate
	46016	Boeing KC-46A Pegasus (16-46016)	USAF (on order)
	46017	Boeing KC-46A Pegasus (16-46017)	USAF (on order)
	46018	Boeing KC-46A Pegasus (16-46018)	USAF (on order)
	46019	Boeing KC-46A Pegasus (16-46019)	USAF (on order)
	46020	Boeing KC-46A Pegasus (16-46020)	USAF (on order)
	46021	Boeing KC-46A Pegasus (16-46021)	USAF (on order)
	46022	Boeing KC-46A Pegasus (16-46022)	USAF (on order)
	46023	Boeing KC-46A Pegasus (16-46023)	USAF (on order)
	46024	Boeing KC-46A Pegasus (17-46024)	USAF (on order)
	46025	Boeing KC-46A Pegasus (17-46025)	USAF (on order)
	46026	Boeing KC-46A Pegasus (17-46026)	USAF (on order)
	46027	Boeing KC-46A Pegasus (17-46027)	USAF (on order)
	46028	Boeing KC-46A Pegasus (17-46028)	USAF (on order)
	46029	Boeing KC-46A Pegasus (17-46029)	USAF (on order)
	46030	Boeing KC-46A Pegasus (1.-46030)	USAF (on order)
	46031	Boeing KC-46A Pegasus (1.-46031)	USAF (on order)
	46032	Boeing KC-46A Pegasus (1.-46032)	USAF (on order)
	46033	Boeing KC-46A Pegasus (1.-46033)	USAF (on order)
	46034	Boeing KC-46A Pegasus (1.-46034)	USAF (on order)

Boeing B-52H Stratofortress

Notes	Serial	Type (code/other identity)	Owner/operator, location or fate
	00001	Boeing B-52H Stratofortress (60-0001) [LA] r	USAF 96th BS/2nd BW, Barksdale AFB, LA
	00002	Boeing B-52H Stratofortress (60-0002) [LA] gn [2 BW]	USAF 96th BS/2nd BW, Barksdale AFB, LA
	00003	Boeing B-52H Stratofortress (60-0003) [BD] or/bl	USAF 93rd BS/307th BW AFRC, Barksdale AFB, LA
	00004	Boeing B-52H Stratofortress (60-0004) [MT] r/y	USAF 23rd BS/5th BW, Minot AFB, ND
	00005	Boeing B-52H Stratofortress (60-0005) [MT] r/y $	USAF 23rd BS/5th BW, Minot AFB, ND
	00007	Boeing B-52H Stratofortress (60-0007) [MT] r/y	USAF 23rd BS/5th BW, Minot AFB, ND
	00008	Boeing B-52H Stratofortress (60-0008) [LA] bl [8th AF]	USAF 20th BS/2nd BW, Barksdale AFB, LA
	00009	Boeing B-52H Stratofortress (60-0009) [MT] y/bk $	USAF 69th BS/5th BW, Minot AFB, ND
	00011	Boeing B-52H Stratofortress (60-0011) [BD] or/bl [11 BS]	USAF 93rd BS/307th BW AFRC, Barksdale AFB, LA
	00012	Boeing B-52H Stratofortress (60-0012) [MT] y/bk	USAF 69th BS/5th BW, Minot AFB, ND
	00013	Boeing B-52H Stratofortress (60-0013) [LA] bl	USAF 20th BS/2nd BW, Barksdale AFB, LA
	00015	Boeing B-52H Stratofortress (60-0015) [BD] or/bl	USAF 93rd BS/307th BW AFRC, Barksdale AFB, LA
	00017	Boeing B-52H Stratofortress (60-0017) [MT] y/bk	USAF 69th BS/5th BW, Minot AFB, ND
	00018	Boeing B-52H Stratofortress (60-0018) [MT] y/bk	USAF 69th BS/5th BW, Minot AFB, ND
	00021	Boeing B-52H Stratofortress (60-0021) [LA] r	USAF 96th BS/2nd BW, Barksdale AFB, LA
	00022	Boeing B-52H Stratofortress (60-0022) [LA] r	USAF 96th BS/2nd BW, Barksdale AFB, LA
	00023	Boeing B-52H Stratofortress (60-0023) [BD] or/bl	USAF 93rd BS/307th BW AFRC, Barksdale AFB, LA
	00024	Boeing B-52H Stratofortress (60-0024) [LA] bl	USAF 20th BS/2nd BW, Barksdale AFB, LA
	00025	Boeing B-52H Stratofortress (60-0025) [LA] bl	USAF 20th BS/2nd BW, Barksdale AFB, LA
	00026	Boeing B-52H Stratofortress (60-0026) [MT] r/y	USAF 23rd BS/5th BW, Minot AFB, ND
	00028	Boeing B-52H Stratofortress (60-0028) [LA] r	USAF 96th BS/2nd BW, Barksdale AFB, LA
	00029	Boeing B-52H Stratofortress (60-0029) [BD] or/bl [93 BS]	USAF 93rd BS/307th BW AFRC, Barksdale AFB, LA
	00031	Boeing B-52H Stratofortress (60-0031) [OT] or/w	USAF 49th TES/53rd TEG, Barksdale AFB, LA
	00032	Boeing B-52H Stratofortress (60-0032) [LA] r	USAF 96th BS/2nd BW, Barksdale AFB, LA
	00033	Boeing B-52H Stratofortress (60-0033) [MT] r/y	USAF 23rd BS/5th BW, Minot AFB, ND
	00035	Boeing B-52H Stratofortress (60-0035) [BD] or/bl	USAF 93rd BS/307th BW AFRC, Barksdale AFB, LA
	00036	Boeing B-52H Stratofortress (60-0036) [ED]	USAF 419th FLTS/412th TW, Edwards AFB, CA
	00037	Boeing B-52H Stratofortress (60-0037) [MT] r/y	USAF 23rd BS/5th BW, Minot AFB, ND
	00038	Boeing B-52H Stratofortress (60-0038) [BD] or/bl	USAF 93rd BS/307th BW AFRC, Barksdale AFB, LA
	00041	Boeing B-52H Stratofortress (60-0041) [BD] or/bl	USAF 93rd BS/307th BW AFRC, Barksdale AFB, LA

US-BASED USAF AIRCRAFT — B-52

Serial	Type (code/other identity)	Owner/operator, location or fate	Notes
00042	Boeing B-52H Stratofortress (60-0042) [BD] or/bl	USAF 93rd BS/307th BW AFRC, Barksdale AFB, LA	
00044	Boeing B-52H Stratofortress (60-0044) [MT] r/y	USAF 23rd BS/5th BW, Minot AFB, ND	
00045	Boeing B-52H Stratofortress (60-0045) [BD] or/bl [307 BG]	USAF 93rd BS/307th BW AFRC, Barksdale AFB, LA	
00048	Boeing B-52H Stratofortress (60-0048) [LA] bl	USAF 20th BS/2nd BW, Barksdale AFB, LA	
00050	Boeing B-52H Stratofortress (60-0050) [ED]	USAF 419th FLTS/412th TW, Edwards AFB, CA	
00051	Boeing B-52H Stratofortress (60-0051) [OT] or/w [49 TES]	USAF 49th TES/53rd TEG, Barksdale AFB, LA	
00052	Boeing B-52H Stratofortress (60-0052) [LA] r	USAF 96th BS/2nd BW, Barksdale AFB, LA	
00054	Boeing B-52H Stratofortress (60-0054) [LA] bl	USAF 20th BS/2nd BW, Barksdale AFB, LA	
00055	Boeing B-52H Stratofortress (60-0055) [MT] r/y	USAF 23rd BS/5th BW, Minot AFB, ND	
00056	Boeing B-52H Stratofortress (60-0056) [MT] r/y	USAF 23rd BS/5th BW, Minot AFB, ND	
00057	Boeing B-52H Stratofortress (60-0057) [BD] or/bl $	USAF 93rd BS/307th BW AFRC, Barksdale AFB, LA	
00058	Boeing B-52H Stratofortress (60-0058) [LA] bl	USAF 20th BS/2nd BW, Barksdale AFB, LA	
00059	Boeing B-52H Stratofortress (60-0059) [LA] r [96 BS]	USAF 96th BS/2nd BW, Barksdale AFB, LA	
00060	Boeing B-52H Stratofortress (60-0060) [MT] r/y	USAF 23rd BS/5th BW, Minot AFB, ND	
00061	Boeing B-52H Stratofortress (60-0061) [BD] or/bl [307 BW]	USAF 93rd BS/307th BW AFRC, Barksdale AFB, LA	
00062	Boeing B-52H Stratofortress (60-0062) [LA] r	USAF 96th BS/2nd BW, Barksdale AFB, LA	
10001	Boeing B-52H Stratofortress (61-0001) [MT] y/bk	USAF 69th BS/5th BW, Minot AFB, ND	
10002	Boeing B-52H Stratofortress (61-0002) [LA] bl	USAF 20th BS/2nd BW, Barksdale AFB, LA	
10003	Boeing B-52H Stratofortress (61-0003) [MT] y/bk	USAF 69th BS/5th BW, Minot AFB, ND	
10004	Boeing B-52H Stratofortress (61-0004) [LA] bl	USAF 20th BS/2nd BW, Barksdale AFB, LA	
10005	Boeing B-52H Stratofortress (61-0005) [MT] y/bk	USAF 69th BS/5th BW, Minot AFB, ND	
10006	Boeing B-52H Stratofortress (61-0006) [LA] r	USAF 96th BS/2nd BW, Barksdale AFB, LA	
10007	Boeing B-52H Stratofortress (61-0007) [MT] y/bk	USAF 69th BS/5th BW, Minot AFB, ND	
10008	Boeing B-52H Stratofortress (61-0008) [BD] or/bl	USAF 93rd BS/307th BW AFRC, Barksdale AFB, LA	
10010	Boeing B-52H Stratofortress (61-0010) [LA] bl [434 BS]	USAF 20th BS/2nd BW, Barksdale AFB, LA	
10011	Boeing B-52H Stratofortress (61-0011) [BD] or/bl	USAF 93rd BS/307th BW AFRC, Barksdale AFB, LA	
10012	Boeing B-52H Stratofortress (61-0012) [LA] r	USAF 96th BS/2nd BW, Barksdale AFB, LA	
10013	Boeing B-52H Stratofortress (61-0013) [LA] bl	USAF 20th BS/2nd BW, Barksdale AFB, LA	
10014	Boeing B-52H Stratofortress (61-0014) [MT] y/bk	USAF 69th BS/5th BW, Minot AFB, ND	
10015	Boeing B-52H Stratofortress (61-0015) [LA] r	USAF 96th BS/2nd BW, Barksdale AFB, LA	
10016	Boeing B-52H Stratofortress (61-0016) [LA] r	USAF 96th BS/2nd BW, Barksdale AFB, LA	
10017	Boeing B-52H Stratofortress (61-0017) [BD] or/bl	USAF 93rd BS/307th BW AFRC, Barksdale AFB, LA	
10018	Boeing B-52H Stratofortress (61-0018) [MT] y/bk	USAF 69th BS/5th BW, Minot AFB, ND	
10019	Boeing B-52H Stratofortress (61-0019) [LA] r	USAF 96th BS/2nd BW, Barksdale AFB, LA	
10020	Boeing B-52H Stratofortress (61-0020) [LA] bl [20 BS]	USAF 20th BS/2nd BW, Barksdale AFB, LA	
10021	Boeing B-52H Stratofortress (61-0021) [BD] or/bl	USAF 93rd BS/307th BW AFRC, Barksdale AFB, LA	
10028	Boeing B-52H Stratofortress (61-0028) [OT] y/w [49 TES]	USAF 49th TES/53rd TEG, Barksdale AFB, LA	
10029	Boeing B-52H Stratofortress (61-0029) [BD] or/bl [93 BS]	USAF 93rd BS/307th BW AFRC, Barksdale AFB, LA	
10031	Boeing B-52H Stratofortress (61-0031) [BD] or/bl	USAF 93rd BS/307th BW AFRC, Barksdale AFB, LA	
10032	Boeing B-52H Stratofortress (61-0032) [MT] r/y	USAF 23rd BS/5th BW, Minot AFB, ND	
10034	Boeing B-52H Stratofortress (61-0034) [MT] r/y	USAF 23rd BS/5th BW, Minot AFB, ND	
10035	Boeing B-52H Stratofortress (61-0035) [MT] r/y	USAF 23rd BS/5th BW, Minot AFB, ND	
10036	Boeing B-52H Stratofortress (61-0036) [LA] r	USAF 96th BS/2nd BW, Barksdale AFB, LA	
10038	Boeing B-52H Stratofortress (61-0038) [BD] or/bl	USAF 93rd BS/307th BW AFRC, Barksdale AFB, LA	
10039	Boeing B-52H Stratofortress (61-0039) [MT] y/bky	USAF 69th BS/5th BW, Minot AFB, ND	
10040	Boeing B-52H Stratofortress (61-0040) [MT] r/y	USAF 23rd BS/5th BW, Minot AFB, ND	

267

Notes	Serial	Type (code/other identity)	Owner/operator, location or fate
	Lockheed C-130		
	00162	Lockheed MC-130H Combat Talon II (90-0162)	USAF 1st SOS/353rd SOG, Kadena AB, Japan
	00164	Lockheed AC-130U Spooky (90-0164)	USAF 4th SOS/1st SOW, Hurlburt Field, FL
	00165	Lockheed AC-130U Spooky (90-0165)	USAF 4th SOS/1st SOW, Hurlburt Field, FL
	00166	Lockheed AC-130U Spooky (90-0166)	USAF 4th SOS/1st SOW, Hurlburt Field, FL
	00167	Lockheed AC-130U Spooky (90-0167)	USAF 4th SOS/1st SOW, Hurlburt Field, FL
	00322	Lockheed C-130H Hercules (80-0322) *y/bk*	USAF 118th AS/103rd AW, Bradley ANGB, CT ANG
	00324	Lockheed C-130H Hercules (80-0324)	USAF 186th AS/120th AW, Great Falls, MT ANG
	00326	Lockheed C-130H Hercules (80-0326) *y/bk*	USAF 118th AS/103rd AW, Bradley ANGB, CT ANG
	01057	Lockheed C-130H Hercules (90-1057) *bl*	USAF 142nd AS/166th AW, New Castle County, DE ANG
	01058	Lockheed AC-130W Stinger II (90-1058)	USAF 16th SOS/27th SOW, Cannon AFB, NM
	01791	Lockheed C-130H Hercules (90-1791)	USAF 180th AS/139th AW, Rosencrans Memorial, MO ANG
	01792	Lockheed C-130H Hercules (90-1792)	USAF 180th AS/139th AW, Rosencrans Memorial, MO ANG
	01793	Lockheed C-130H Hercules (90-1793)	USAF 180th AS/139th AW, Rosencrans Memorial, MO ANG
	01794	Lockheed C-130H Hercules (90-1794)	USAF 180th AS/139th AW, Rosencrans Memorial, MO ANG
	01795	Lockheed C-130H Hercules (90-1795)	USAF 180th AS/139th AW, Rosencrans Memorial, MO ANG
	01796	Lockheed C-130H Hercules (90-1796)	USAF 180th AS/139th AW, Rosencrans Memorial, MO ANG
	01797	Lockheed C-130H Hercules (90-1797) *r/bk*	USAF 158th AS/165th AW, Savannah, GA ANG
	01798	Lockheed C-130H Hercules (90-1798)	USAF 180th AS/139th AW, Rosencrans Memorial, MO ANG
	01934	Lockheed EC-130J Commando Solo III (00-1934)	USAF 193rd SOS/193rd SOW, Harrisburg, PA ANG
	02103	Lockheed HC-130N Combat King (90-2103)	USAF 211th RQS/176th Wg, Elmendorf AFB, AK ANG
	05700	Lockheed C-130J-30 Hercules II (10-5700) *r*	USAF 39th AS/317th AW, Dyess AFB, TX
	05701	Lockheed C-130J-30 Hercules II (10-5701) *r*	USAF 39th AS/317th AW, Dyess AFB, TX
	05714	Lockheed MC-130J Commando II (10-5714)	USAF 67th SOS/352nd SOG, RAF Mildenhall, UK
	05716	Lockheed HC-130J Combat King II (10-5716) [FT]	USAF 79th RQS/563rd RQG, Davis-Monthan AFB, AZ
	05717	Lockheed HC-130J Combat King II (10-5717) [FT]	USAF 79th RQS/563rd RQG, Davis-Monthan AFB, AZ
	05728	Lockheed C-130J-30 Hercules II (10-5728) *y*	USAF 48th AS/314th AW, Little Rock AFB, AR
	05771	Lockheed C-130J-30 Hercules II (10-5771) *w/bk*	USAF 61st AS/19th AW Little Rock AFB, AR
	09107	Lockheed C-130H Hercules (90-9107) *bl/r*	USAF 757th AS/910th AW AFRC, Youngstown ARS, OH
	09108	Lockheed C-130H Hercules (90-9108) *bl/r*	USAF 757th AS/910th AW AFRC, Youngstown ARS, OH
	10626	Lockheed C-130H Hercules (81-0626) *r*	USAF 164th AS/179th AW, Mansfield, OH ANG
	10627	Lockheed C-130H Hercules (81-0627)	*To AMARG, June 2017*
	10628	Lockheed C-130H Hercules (81-0628)	*To AMARG, September 2017*
	10629	Lockheed C-130H Hercules (81-0629) *r*	USAF 164th AS/179th AW, Mansfield, OH ANG
	10630	Lockheed C-130H Hercules (81-0630)	*To AMARG, June 2017*
	10631	Lockheed C-130H Hercules (81-0631)	*To AMARG, September 2017*
	11231	Lockheed C-130H Hercules (91-1231)	USAF 165th AS/123rd AW, Standiford Field, KY ANG
	11232	Lockheed C-130H Hercules (91-1232)	USAF 165th AS/123rd AW, Standiford Field, KY ANG
	11233	Lockheed C-130H Hercules (91-1233)	USAF 165th AS/123rd AW, Standiford Field, KY ANG
	11234	Lockheed C-130H Hercules (91-1234)	USAF 165th AS/123rd AW, Standiford Field, KY ANG
	11235	Lockheed C-130H Hercules (91-1235)	USAF 165th AS/123rd AW, Standiford Field, KY ANG

Serial	Type (code/other identity)	Owner/operator, location or fate	Notes
11236	Lockheed C-130H Hercules (91-1236)	USAF 165th AS/123rd AW, Standiford Field, KY ANG	
11237	Lockheed C-130H Hercules (91-1237)	USAF 165th AS/123rd AW, Standiford Field, KY ANG	
11238	Lockheed C-130H Hercules (91-1238)	USAF 165th AS/123rd AW, Standiford Field, KY ANG	
11239	Lockheed C-130H Hercules (91-1239)	*To AMARG, July 2017*	
11461	Lockheed C-130J-30 Hercules II (01-1461) *gn*	USAF 115th AS/146th AW, Channel Island ANGS, CA ANG	
11462	Lockheed C-130J-30 Hercules II (01-1462) *gn*	USAF 115th AS/146th AW, Channel Island ANGS, CA ANG	
11651	Lockheed C-130H Hercules (91-1651)	*To AMARG, December 2017*	
11652	Lockheed C-130H Hercules (91-1652)	USAF 180th AS/139th AW, Rosencrans Memorial, MO ANG	
11653	Lockheed C-130H Hercules (91-1653)	USAF 180th AS/139th AW, Rosencrans Memorial, MO ANG	
11935	Lockheed EC-130J Commando Solo III (01-1935)	USAF 193rd SOS/193rd SOW, Harrisburg, PA ANG	
14852	Lockheed HC-130P Combat King (64-14852)	*To AMARG, March 2017*	
14862	Lockheed EC-130H Compass Call (64-14862)	USAF 43rd ECS/55th ECG, Davis-Monthan AFB, AZ	
14866	Lockheed C-130H Hercules (64-14866)	USAF 198th AS/156th AW, San Juan, PR ANG	
15719	Lockheed HC-130J Combat King II (11-5719) [FT]	USAF 79th RQS/563rd RQG, Davis-Monthan AFB, AZ	
15725	Lockheed HC-130J Combat King II (11-5725) [FT]	USAF 71st RQS/347th RG, Moody AFB, GA	
15727	Lockheed HC-130J Combat King II (11-5727) [FT]	USAF 71st RQS/347th RG, Moody AFB, GA	
15729	Lockheed AC-130J Ghostrider (11-5729)	USAF 1st SOG Det.2, Hurlburt Field, FL	
15731	Lockheed MC-130J Commando II (11-5731)	USAF 67th SOS/352nd SOG, RAF Mildenhall, UK	
15732	Lockheed C-130J-30 Hercules II (11-5732) *y*	USAF 48th AS/314th AW, Little Rock AFB, AR	
15733	Lockheed MC-130J Commando II (11-5733)	USAF	
15734	Lockheed C-130J-30 Hercules II (11-5734) [YJ] *r*	USAF 36th AS/374th AW, Yokota AB, Japan	
15735	Lockheed MC-130J Commando II (11-5735)	USAF 522nd SOS/27th SOW, Cannon AFB, NM	
15736	Lockheed C-130J-30 Hercules II (11-5736) [RS] *bl/w*	USAF 37th AS/86th AW, Ramstein AB, Germany	
15737	Lockheed MC-130J Commando II (11-5737)	USAF 67th SOS/352nd SOG, RAF Mildenhall, UK	
15738	Lockheed C-130J-30 Hercules II (11-5738) *w/bk*	USAF 61st AS/19th AW Little Rock AFB, AR	
15740	Lockheed C-130J-30 Hercules II (11-5740) *w/bk*	USAF 61st AS/19th AW Little Rock AFB, AR	
15745	Lockheed C-130J-30 Hercules II (11-5745) *w/bk*	USAF 41st AS/19th AW Little Rock AFB, AR	
15748	Lockheed C-130J-30 Hercules II (11-5748) *w/bk*	USAF 61st AS/19th AW Little Rock AFB, AR	
15752	Lockheed C-130J-30 Hercules II (11-5752) *w/bk*	USAF 61st AS/19th AW Little Rock AFB, AR	
15765	Lockheed HC-130J Combat King II (11-5765) [FT]	USAF 71st RQS/347th RG, Moody AFB, GA	
19141	Lockheed C-130H Hercules (91-9141) *bl/w*	USAF 357th AS/908th AW AFRC, Maxwell AFB, AL	
19142	Lockheed C-130H Hercules (91-9142) *bl/w*	USAF 357th AS/908th AW AFRC, Maxwell AFB, AL	
19143	Lockheed C-130H Hercules (91-9143) *bl/w*	USAF 357th AS/908th AW AFRC, Maxwell AFB, AL	
9144	Lockheed C-130H Hercules (91-9144) *bl/y*	USAF 328th AS/914th AW AFRC, Niagara Falls, NY	
0054	Lockheed C-130H Hercules (82-0054)	*Withdrawn from use, 2017*	
0055	Lockheed C-130H Hercules (82-0055) *r*	USAF 164th AS/179th AW, Mansfield, OH ANG	
0056	Lockheed C-130H Hercules (82-0056)	USAF 16th SOS/27th SOW, Cannon AFB, NM	
0057	Lockheed C-130H Hercules (82-0057)	*To AMARG, June 2017*	
0059	Lockheed C-130H Hercules (82-0059)	*To AMARG, September 2017*	
0060	Lockheed C-130H Hercules (82-0060)	*To AMARG, March 2017*	
0061	Lockheed C-130H Hercules (82-0061)	USAF	
0253	Lockheed AC-130U Spooky (92-0253)	USAF 4th SOS/1st SOW, Hurlburt Field, FL	
0314	Lockheed C-130J-30 Hercules II (02-0314) *y $*	USAF 48th AS/314th AW, Little Rock AFB, AR	
0547	Lockheed C-130H Hercules (92-0547) *bl/w*	USAF 192nd AS/152nd AW, Reno, NV ANG	
0548	Lockheed C-130H Hercules (92-0548) *r/bk*	USAF 158th AS/165th AW, Savannah, GA ANG	
0549	Lockheed C-130H Hercules (92-0549) *bl/w*	USAF 192nd AS/152nd AW, Reno, NV ANG	
550	Lockheed C-130H Hercules (92-0550) *bl*	USAF 700th AS/94th AW AFRC, Dobbins ARB, GA	

Notes	Serial	Type (code/other identity)	Owner/operator, location or fate
	20551	Lockheed C-130H Hercules (92-0551) bl	USAF 700th AS/94th AW AFRC, Dobbins ARB, GA
	20552	Lockheed C-130H Hercules (92-0552) bl	USAF 700th AS/94th AW AFRC, Dobbins ARB, GA
	20553	Lockheed C-130H Hercules (92-0553) bl/w	USAF 181st AS/136th AW, NAS Dallas, TX ANG
	20554	Lockheed C-130H Hercules (92-0554) bl/w	USAF 192nd AS/152nd AW, Reno, NV ANG
	21094	Lockheed LC-130H Hercules (92-1094)	USAF 139th AS/109th AW, Schenectady, NY ANG
	21095	Lockheed LC-130H Hercules (92-1095)	USAF 139th AS/109th AW, Schenectady, NY ANG
	21434	Lockheed C-130J-30 Hercules II (02-1434) r	USAF 143rd AS/143rd AW, Quonset, RI ANG
	21451	Lockheed C-130H Hercules (92-1451) or/bk	USAF 169th AS/182nd AW, Peoria, IL ANG
	21452	Lockheed C-130H Hercules (92-1452) or/bk	USAF 169th AS/182nd AW, Peoria, IL ANG
	21453	Lockheed C-130H-3 Hercules (92-1453) bl/w	USAF 181st AS/136th AW, NAS Dallas, TX ANG
	21454	Lockheed C-130H-3 Hercules (92-1454) bl/w	USAF 181st AS/136th AW, NAS Dallas, TX ANG
	21463	Lockheed C-130J Hercules II (02-1463) gn	USAF 115th AS/146th AW, Channel Island ANGS, CA ANG
	21464	Lockheed C-130J Hercules II (02-1464) gn	USAF 115th AS/146th AW, Channel Island ANGS, CA ANG
	21531	Lockheed C-130H-3 Hercules (92-1531) y/bk	USAF 187th AS/153rd AW, Cheyenne, WY ANG
	21532	Lockheed C-130H-3 Hercules (92-1532) y/bk	USAF 187th AS/153rd AW, Cheyenne, WY ANG
	21533	Lockheed C-130H-3 Hercules (92-1533) y/bk	USAF 187th AS/153rd AW, Cheyenne, WY ANG
	21534	Lockheed C-130H-3 Hercules (92-1534) y/bk	USAF 187th AS/153rd AW, Cheyenne, WY ANG
	21535	Lockheed C-130H-3 Hercules (92-1535) y/bk	USAF 187th AS/153rd AW, Cheyenne, WY ANG
	21536	Lockheed C-130H-3 Hercules (92-1536) y/bk	USAF 187th AS/153rd AW, Cheyenne, WY ANG
	21537	Lockheed C-130H-3 Hercules (92-1537) y/bk	USAF 187th AS/153rd AW, Cheyenne, WY ANG
	21538	Lockheed C-130H-3 Hercules (92-1538) y/bk	USAF 187th AS/153rd AW, Cheyenne, WY ANG
	22104	Lockheed HC-130N Combat King (92-2104)	USAF 211th RQS/176th Wg, Elmendorf AFB, AK ANG
	23021	Lockheed C-130H Hercules (92-3021) bl/w	USAF 357th AS/908th AW AFRC, Maxwell AFB, AL
	23022	Lockheed C-130H Hercules (92-3022) bl/y	USAF 328th AS/914th AW AFRC, Niagara Falls, NY
	23023	Lockheed C-130H Hercules (92-3023) bl/r	USAF 757th AS/910th AW AFRC, Youngstown ARS, OH
	23024	Lockheed C-130H Hercules (92-3024) bl/r	USAF 757th AS/910th AW AFRC, Youngstown ARS, OH
	23281	Lockheed C-130H-3 Hercules (92-3281) pr/w	USAF 96th AS/934th AW AFRC, Minneapolis/ St Paul, MN
	23282	Lockheed C-130H-3 Hercules (92-3282) pr/w	USAF 96th AS/934th AW AFRC, Minneapolis/ St Paul, MN
	23283	Lockheed C-130H-3 Hercules (92-3283) pr/w	USAF 96th AS/934th AW AFRC, Minneapolis/ St Paul, MN
	23284	Lockheed C-130H-3 Hercules (92-3284) pr/w	USAF 96th AS/934th AW AFRC, Minneapolis/ St Paul, MN
	23285	Lockheed C-130H-3 Hercules (92-3285) pr/w	USAF 96th AS/934th AW AFRC, Minneapolis/ St Paul, MN
	23286	Lockheed C-130H-3 Hercules (92-3286) pr/w	USAF 96th AS/934th AW AFRC, Minneapolis/ St Paul, MN
	23287	Lockheed C-130H-3 Hercules (92-3287) pr/w	USAF 96th AS/934th AW AFRC, Minneapolis/ St Paul, MN
	23288	Lockheed C-130H-3 Hercules (92-3288) pr/w	USAF 96th AS/934th AW AFRC, Minneapolis/ St Paul, MN
	25753	Lockheed AC-130J Ghostrider (12-5753)	USAF 1st SOG Det.2, Hurlburt Field, FL
	25754	Lockheed AC-130J Ghostrider (12-5754)	LMTAS, Marietta, GA
	25755	Lockheed HC-130J Combat King II (12-5755)	USAF 415th SOS/58th SOW, Kirtland AFB, NM
	25756	Lockheed C-130J-30 Hercules II (12-5756) w/bk	USAF 61st AS/19th AW Little Rock AFB, AR
	25757	Lockheed MC-130J Commando II (12-5757)	USAF 67th SOS/352nd SOG, RAF Mildenhall, UK
	25759	Lockheed MC-130J Commando II (12-5759)	USAF 67th SOS/352nd SOG, RAF Mildenhall, UK
	25760	Lockheed MC-130J Commando II (12-5760)	USAF 67th SOS/352nd SOG, RAF Mildenhall, UK
	25761	Lockheed MC-130J Commando II (12-5761)	USAF 17th SOS/353rd SOG, Kadena AB, Japan
	25762	Lockheed MC-130J Commando II (12-5762)	USAF 17th SOS/353rd SOG, Kadena AB, Japan
	25763	Lockheed MC-130J Commando II (12-5763)	USAF 17th SOS/353rd SOG, Kadena AB, Japan
	25768	Lockheed HC-130J Combat King II (12-5768) [FT]	USAF 71st RQS/347th RG, Moody AFB, GA
	25769	Lockheed HC-130J Combat King II (12-5769) [FT]	USAF 71st RQS/347th RG, Moody AFB, GA
	25772	Lockheed AC-130J Ghostrider (12-5772)	USAF 1st SOG Det.2, Hurlburt Field, FL
	25773	Lockheed HC-130J Combat King II (12-5773) [FT]	USAF 71st RQS/347th RG, Moody AFB, GA

Serial	Type (code/other identity)	Owner/operator, location or fate	Notes
28155	Lockheed C-130J-30 Hercules II (02-8155) r	USAF 815th AS/403rd AW AFRC, Keesler AFB, MO	
30487	Lockheed C-130H Hercules (83-0487)	USAF 139th AS/109th AW, Schenectady, NY ANG	
30489	Lockheed C-130H Hercules (83-0489)	USAF 139th AS/109th AW, Schenectady, NY ANG	
30490	Lockheed LC-130H Hercules (83-0490)	USAF 139th AS/109th AW, Schenectady, NY ANG	
30491	Lockheed LC-130H Hercules (83-0491)	USAF 139th AS/109th AW, Schenectady, NY ANG	
30492	Lockheed LC-130H Hercules (83-0492)	USAF 139th AS/109th AW, Schenectady, NY ANG	
30493	Lockheed LC-130H Hercules (83-0493)	USAF 139th AS/109th AW, Schenectady, NY ANG	
31036	Lockheed C-130H Hercules (93-1036) bl	USAF 700th AS/94th AW AFRC, Dobbins ARB, GA	
31037	Lockheed C-130H Hercules (93-1037) bl	USAF 700th AS/94th AW AFRC, Dobbins ARB, GA	
31038	Lockheed C-130H Hercules (93-1038) bl	USAF 700th AS/94th AW AFRC, Dobbins ARB, GA	
31039	Lockheed C-130H Hercules (93-1039) bl	USAF 700th AS/94th AW AFRC, Dobbins ARB, GA	
31040	Lockheed C-130H Hercules (93-1040) bl	USAF 700th AS/94th AW AFRC, Dobbins ARB, GA	
31041	Lockheed C-130H Hercules (93-1041) bl	USAF 700th AS/94th AW AFRC, Dobbins ARB, GA	
31096	Lockheed LC-130H Hercules (93-1096)	USAF 139th AS/109th AW, Schenectady, NY ANG	
31455	Lockheed C-130H-3 Hercules (93-1455) bl/w	USAF 181st AS/136th AW, NAS Dallas, TX ANG	
31456	Lockheed C-130H-3 Hercules (93-1456) bl/w	USAF 181st AS/136th AW, NAS Dallas, TX ANG	
31457	Lockheed C-130H-3 Hercules (93-1457) bl/w	USAF 181st AS/136th AW, NAS Dallas, TX ANG	
31459	Lockheed C-130H-3 Hercules (93-1459) bl/w	USAF 181st AS/136th AW, NAS Dallas, TX ANG	
31561	Lockheed C-130H-3 Hercules (93-1561) r/bk	USAF 158th AS/165th AW, Savannah, GA ANG	
31562	Lockheed C-130H-3 Hercules (93-1562) r/bk	USAF 158th AS/165th AW, Savannah, GA ANG	
31563	Lockheed C-130H-3 Hercules (93-1563) r/bk	USAF 158th AS/165th AW, Savannah, GA ANG	
31580	Lockheed EC-130H Compass Call (73-1580)	USAF 43rd ECS/55th ECG, Davis-Monthan AFB, AZ	
31581	Lockheed EC-130H Compass Call (73-1581) $	USAF 43rd ECS/55th ECG, Davis-Monthan AFB, AZ	
31583	Lockheed EC-130H Compass Call (73-1583) r	USAF 43rd ECS/55th ECG, Davis-Monthan AFB, AZ	
31584	Lockheed EC-130H Compass Call (73-1584)	USAF 43rd ECS/55th ECG, Davis-Monthan AFB, AZ	
31585	Lockheed EC-130H Compass Call (73-1585)	USAF 43rd ECS/55th ECG, Davis-Monthan AFB, AZ	
31586	Lockheed EC-130H Compass Call (73-1586) bl	USAF 41st ECS/55th ECG, Davis-Monthan AFB, AZ	
31587	Lockheed EC-130H Compass Call (73-1587)	USAF 43rd ECS/55th ECG, Davis-Monthan AFB, AZ	
31588	Lockheed EC-130H Compass Call (73-1588)	USAF 43rd ECS/55th ECG, Davis-Monthan AFB, AZ	
31590	Lockheed EC-130H Compass Call (73-1590)	USAF 43rd ECS/55th ECG, Davis-Monthan AFB, AZ	
31592	Lockheed EC-130H Compass Call (73-1592) bl	USAF 41st ECS/55th ECG, Davis-Monthan AFB, AZ	
31594	Lockheed EC-130H Compass Call (73-1594)	USAF 41st ECS/55th ECG, Davis-Monthan AFB, AZ	
31595	Lockheed EC-130H Compass Call (73-1595)	USAF 43rd ECS/55th ECG, Davis-Monthan AFB, AZ	
2041	Lockheed C-130H-3 Hercules (93-2041) or/bk	USAF 169th AS/182nd AW, Peoria, IL ANG	
2042	Lockheed C-130H-3 Hercules (93-2042) or/bk	USAF 169th AS/182nd AW, Peoria, IL ANG	
2105	Lockheed HC-130N Combat King (93-2105)	USAF 39th RQS/920th RQW AFRC, Patrick AFB, FL	
2106	Lockheed HC-130N Combat King (93-2106)	USAF 39th RQS/920th RQW AFRC, Patrick AFB, FL	
3300	Lockheed LC-130H Hercules (73-3300)	USAF 139th AS/109th AW, Schenectady, NY ANG	
5770	Lockheed MC-130J Commando II (13-5770)	USAF 522nd SOS/27th SOW, Cannon AFB, NM	
5775	Lockheed MC-130J Commando II (13-5775)	USAF 17th SOS/353rd SOG, Kadena AB, Japan	
5776	Lockheed MC-130J Commando II (13-5776)	USAF 17th SOS/353rd SOG, Kadena AB, Japan	

Notes	Serial	Type (code/other identity)	Owner/operator, location or fate
	35777	Lockheed MC-130J Commando II (13-5777)	USAF 17th SOS/353rd SOG, Kadena AB, Japan
	35778	Lockheed MC-130J Commando II (13-5778)	USAF 67th SOS/352nd SOG, RAF Mildenhall, UK
	35782	Lockheed HC-130J Combat King II (13-5782) [FT]	USAF 71st RQS/347th RG, Moody AFB, GA
	35783	Lockheed AC-130J Ghostrider (13-5783)	USAF 1st SOG Det.2, Hurlburt Field, FL
	35784	Lockheed HC-130J Combat King II (13-5784) [FT]	USAF 71st RQS/347th RG, Moody AFB, GA
	35785	Lockheed HC-130J Combat King II (13-5785) [FT]	USAF 71st RQS/347th RG, Moody AFB, GA
	35786	Lockheed MC-130J Commando II (13-5786)	USAF 67th SOS/352nd SOG, RAF Mildenhall, UK
	35790	Lockheed HC-130J Combat King II (13-5790) [FT]	USAF 71st RQS/347th RG, Moody AFB, GA
	37311	Lockheed C-130H-3 Hercules (93-7311) bl/w	USAF 192nd AS/152nd AW, Reno, NV ANG
	37312	Lockheed C-130H-3 Hercules (93-7312) or/bk	USAF 169th AS/182nd AW, Peoria, IL ANG
	37313	Lockheed C-130H-3 Hercules (93-7313) bl/w	USAF 192nd AS/152nd AW, Reno, NV ANG
	37314	Lockheed C-130H-3 Hercules (93-7314) bl/w	USAF 192nd AS/152nd AW, Reno, NV ANG
	38154	Lockheed C-130J-30 Hercules II (03-8154) r	USAF 815th AS/403rd AW AFRC, Keesler AFB, MO
	40204	Lockheed C-130H Hercules (84-0204)	To AMARG, August 2017
	40205	Lockheed C-130H Hercules (84-0205)	To AMARG, August 2017
	40206	Lockheed C-130H Hercules (84-0206) bl	USAF 142nd AS/166th AW, New Castle County, DE ANG
	40207	Lockheed C-130H Hercules (84-0207) bl	USAF 142nd AS/166th AW, New Castle County, DE ANG
	40208	Lockheed C-130H Hercules (84-0208) bl	USAF 142nd AS/166th AW, New Castle County, DE ANG
	40209	Lockheed C-130H Hercules (84-0209) bl	USAF 142nd AS/166th AW, New Castle County, DE ANG
	40210	Lockheed C-130H Hercules (84-0210) bl	USAF 142nd AS/166th AW, New Castle County, DE ANG
	40212	Lockheed C-130H Hercules (84-0212) bl	USAF 142nd AS/166th AW, New Castle County, DE ANG
	40213	Lockheed C-130H Hercules (84-0213) bl	USAF 142nd AS/166th AW, New Castle County, DE ANG
	40476	Lockheed MC-130H Combat Talon II (84-0476)	USAF 15th SOS/1st SOW, Hurlburt Field, FL
	41659	Lockheed C-130H Hercules (74-1659) r	USAF 164th AS/179th AW, Mansfield, OH ANG
	41660	Lockheed C-130H Hercules (74-1660) r	USAF 164th AS/179th AW, Mansfield, OH ANG
	41661	Lockheed C-130H Hercules (74-1661)	USAF 186th AS/120th AW, Great Falls, MT ANG
	41663	Lockheed C-130H Hercules (74-1663)	USAF
	41664	Lockheed C-130H Hercules (74-1664) y/bk	USAF 118th AS/103rd AW, Bradley ANGB, CT ANG
	41666	Lockheed C-130H Hercules (74-1666)	USAF
	41669	Lockheed C-130H Hercules (74-1669) y/bk	USAF 118th AS/103rd AW, Bradley ANGB, CT ANG
	41670	Lockheed C-130H Hercules (74-1670)	USAF 186th AS/120th AW, Great Falls, MT ANG
	41671	Lockheed C-130H Hercules (74-1671)	USAF 186th AS/120th AW, Great Falls, MT ANG
	41674	Lockheed C-130H Hercules (74-1674)	USAF
	41679	Lockheed C-130H Hercules (74-1679)	USAF 186th AS/120th AW, Great Falls, MT ANG
	41680	Lockheed C-130H Hercules (74-1680) y/bk	USAF 118th AS/103rd AW, Bradley ANGB, CT ANG
	41682	Lockheed C-130H Hercules (74-1682)	USAF
	41685	Lockheed C-130H Hercules (74-1685)	USAF
	41687	Lockheed C-130H Hercules (74-1687) y/bk	USAF 118th AS/103rd AW, Bradley ANGB, CT ANG
	41688	Lockheed C-130H Hercules (74-1688)	USAF 186th AS/120th AW, Great Falls, MT ANG
	41691	Lockheed C-130H Hercules (74-1691)	USAF 186th AS/120th AW, Great Falls, MT ANG
	41692	Lockheed C-130H Hercules (74-1692)	USAF
	42061	Lockheed C-130H Hercules (74-2061) r	USAF 164th AS/179th AW, Mansfield, OH ANG
	42065	Lockheed C-130H Hercules (74-2065)	USAF
	42067	Lockheed C-130H Hercules (74-2067)	USAF
	42069	Lockheed C-130H Hercules (74-2069) y/bk	USAF 118th AS/103rd AW, Bradley ANGB, CT ANG
	42132	Lockheed C-130H Hercules (74-2132)	USAF
	42134	Lockheed C-130H Hercules (74-2134) y/bk	USAF 118th AS/103rd AW, Bradley ANGB, CT ANG
	43142	Lockheed C-130J-30 Hercules II (04-3142)	USAF 37th AS/86th AW, Ramstein AB, Germany
	43143	Lockheed C-130J-30 Hercules II (04-3143) w/bk	USAF 41st AS/19th AW Little Rock AFB, AR
	45787	Lockheed AC-130J Ghostrider (14-5787)	USAF 1st SOG Det.2, Hurlburt Field, FL
	45788	Lockheed C-130J-30 Hercules II (14-5788) w/bk	USAF 61st AS/19th AW Little Rock AFB, AR
	45789	Lockheed MC-130J Commando II (14-5789)	USAF 15th SOS/1st SOW, Hurlburt Field, FL
	45791	Lockheed C-130J-30 Hercules II (14-5791) w/bk	USAF 61st AS/19th AW Little Rock AFB, AR
	45793	Lockheed MC-130J Commando II (14-5793)	USAF 9th SOS/27th SOW, Cannon AFB, NM
	45795	Lockheed MC-130J Commando II (14-5795)	USAF 9th SOS/27th SOW, Cannon AFB, NM

Serial	Type (code/other identity)	Owner/operator, location or fate	Notes
45796	Lockheed C-130J-30 Hercules II (14-5796) w/bk	USAF 61st AS/19th AW Little Rock AFB, AR	
45797	Lockheed AC-130J Ghostrider (14-5797)	USAF 1st SOG Det.2, Hurlburt Field, FL	
45800	Lockheed MC-130J Commando II (14-5800)	USAF 9th SOS/27th SOW, Cannon AFB, NM	
45802	Lockheed C-130J-30 Hercules II (14-5802) y	USAF 48th AS/314th AW, Little Rock AFB, AR	
45803	Lockheed AC-130J Ghostrider (14-5803)	USAF 1st SOG Det.2, Hurlburt Field, FL	
45804	Lockheed C-130J-30 Hercules II (14-5804) y	USAF 48th AS/314th AW, Little Rock AFB, AR	
45805	Lockheed MC-130J Commando II (14-5805)	USAF 9th SOS/27th SOW, Cannon AFB, NM	
45807	Lockheed C-130J-30 Hercules II (14-5807) [YJ] r [374 AW]	USAF 36th AS/374th AW, Yokota AB, Japan	
45809	Lockheed AC-130J Ghostrider (14-5809)	USAF 1st SOG Det.2, Hurlburt Field, FL	
45815	Lockheed HC-130J Combat King II (14-5815) [AK]	USAF 211th RQS/176th Wg, Elmendorf AFB, AK ANG	
46701	Lockheed C-130H-3 Hercules (94-6701) or/bk	USAF 169th AS/182nd AW, Peoria, IL ANG	
46702	Lockheed C-130H-3 Hercules (94-6702) or/bk	USAF 169th AS/182nd AW, Peoria, IL ANG	
46703	Lockheed C-130H-3 Hercules (94-6703) or/bk	USAF 169th AS/182nd AW, Peoria, IL ANG	
46704	Lockheed C-130H-3 Hercules (94-6704)	To AMARG, August 2017	
46705	Lockheed C-130H-3 Hercules (94-6705) r/bk	USAF 158th AS/165th AW, Savannah, GA ANG	
46706	Lockheed C-130H-3 Hercules (94-6706) r/bk	USAF 158th AS/165th AW, Savannah, GA ANG	
46707	Lockheed C-130H-3 Hercules (94-6707) r/bk	USAF 158th AS/165th AW, Savannah, GA ANG	
46708	Lockheed C-130H-3 Hercules (94-6708) r/bk	USAF 158th AS/165th AW, Savannah, GA ANG	
47310	Lockheed C-130H-3 Hercules (94-7310) pr/w	USAF 731st AS/302nd AW AFRC, Peterson AFB, CO	
47315	Lockheed C-130H-3 Hercules (94-7315) pr/w	USAF 731st AS/302nd AW AFRC, Peterson AFB, CO	
47316	Lockheed C-130H-3 Hercules (94-7316) pr/w	USAF 731st AS/302nd AW AFRC, Peterson AFB, CO	
47317	Lockheed C-130H-3 Hercules (94-7317) pr/w	USAF 731st AS/302nd AW AFRC, Peterson AFB, CO	
47318	Lockheed C-130H-3 Hercules (94-7318) pr/w	USAF 731st AS/302nd AW AFRC, Peterson AFB, CO	
47319	Lockheed C-130H-3 Hercules (94-7319) pr/w	USAF 731st AS/302nd AW AFRC, Peterson AFB, CO	
47320	Lockheed C-130H-3 Hercules (94-7320) pr/w	USAF 731st AS/302nd AW AFRC, Peterson AFB, CO	
47321	Lockheed C-130H-3 Hercules (94-7321) r/bk	USAF 158th AS/165th AW, Savannah, GA ANG	
48151	Lockheed C-130J Hercules II (94-8151) r	USAF 815th AS/403rd AW AFRC, Keesler AFB, MO	
48152	Lockheed C-130J Hercules II (94-8152) r	USAF 815th AS/403rd AW AFRC, Keesler AFB, MO	
48153	Lockheed C-130J-30 Hercules II (04-8153) r	USAF 815th AS/403rd AW AFRC, Keesler AFB, MO	
50011	Lockheed MC-130H Combat Talon II (85-0011)	USAF 15th SOS/1st SOW, Hurlburt Field, FL	
50035	Lockheed C-130H Hercules (85-0035)	To AMARG, September 2017	
50036	Lockheed C-130H Hercules (85-0036)	To AMARG, May 2017	
50037	Lockheed C-130H Hercules (85-0037)	To AMARG, September 2017	
50038	Lockheed C-130H Hercules (85-0038)	To AMARG, February 2017	
50039	Lockheed C-130H Hercules (85-0039)	To AMARG, July 2017	
50040	Lockheed C-130H Hercules (85-0040)	To AMARG, July 2017	
50041	Lockheed C-130H Hercules (85-0041)	To AMARG, July 2017	
50042	Lockheed C-130H Hercules (85-0042)	To AMARG, July 2017	
50963	Lockheed C-130H Hercules (65-0963)	USAF 198th AS/156th AW, San Juan, PR ANG	
50966	Lockheed C-130H Hercules (65-0966)	USAF 198th AS/156th AW, San Juan, PR ANG	
50967	Lockheed EC-130H Compass Call (65-0967)	L-3 Communications, Waco, TX	
50968	Lockheed C-130H Hercules (65-0968)	USAF 198th AS/156th AW, San Juan, PR ANG	
50974	Lockheed HC-130P Combat King (65-0974)	USAF 102nd RQS/106th RQW, Suffolk Field, NY ANG	
50978	Lockheed HC-130P Combat King (65-0978)	USAF 102nd RQS/106th RQW, Suffolk Field, NY ANG	
50980	Lockheed WC-130H Hercules (65-0980)	USAF 198th AS/156th AW, San Juan, PR ANG	
50984	Lockheed WC-130H Hercules (65-0984)	USAF 198th AS/156th AW, San Juan, PR ANG	
50985	Lockheed WC-130H Hercules (65-0985)	USAF 198th AS/156th AW, San Juan, PR ANG	
50989	Lockheed EC-130H Compass Call (65-0989) r	USAF 43rd ECS/55th ECG, Davis-Monthan AFB, AZ	
51001	Lockheed C-130H Hercules (95-1001) pr/bk	USAF 109th AS/133rd AW, Minneapolis, MN ANG	
51002	Lockheed C-130H Hercules (95-1002) pr/bk	USAF 109th AS/133rd AW, Minneapolis, MN ANG	

Notes	Serial	Type (code/other identity)	Owner/operator, location or fate
	51361	Lockheed C-130H Hercules (85-1361)	*Withdrawn from use, February 2018*
	51362	Lockheed C-130H Hercules (85-1362)	*To AMARG, September 2017*
	51363	Lockheed C-130H Hercules (85-1363) *bl/w*	USAF 181st AS/136th AW, NAS Dallas, TX ANG
	51364	Lockheed C-130H Hercules (85-1364) *bl/w*	USAF 181st AS/136th AW, NAS Dallas, TX ANG
	51365	Lockheed C-130H Hercules (85-1365) *bl/w*	USAF 181st AS/136th AW, NAS Dallas, TX ANG
	51366	Lockheed C-130H Hercules (85-1366) *bl/w*	USAF 181st AS/136th AW, NAS Dallas, TX ANG
	51367	Lockheed C-130H Hercules (85-1367) *bl/w*	USAF 181st AS/136th AW, NAS Dallas, TX ANG
	51368	Lockheed C-130H Hercules (85-1368)	*To AMARG, October 2017*
	51435	Lockheed C-130J-30 Hercules II (05-1435) *r*	USAF 143rd AS/143rd AW, Quonset, RI ANG
	51436	Lockheed C-130J-30 Hercules II (05-1436) *r*	USAF 143rd AS/143rd AW, Quonset, RI ANG
	51465	Lockheed C-130J-30 Hercules II (05-1465) *gn*	USAF 115th AS/146th AW, Channel Island ANGS, CA ANG
	51466	Lockheed C-130J-30 Hercules II (05-1466) *gn*	USAF 115th AS/146th AW, Channel Island ANGS, CA ANG
	53145	Lockheed C-130J-30 Hercules II (05-3145) *w/bk*	USAF 53rd AS/19th AW Little Rock AFB, AR
	53146	Lockheed C-130J-30 Hercules II (05-3146) *y*	USAF 48th AS/314th AW, Little Rock AFB, AR
	53147	Lockheed C-130J-30 Hercules II (05-3147) *gn*	USAF 41st AS/19th AW Little Rock AFB, AR
	55810	Lockheed C-130J-30 Hercules II (15-5810) [YJ] *r* [374 OG]	USAF 36th AS/374th AW, Yokota AB, Japan
	55811	Lockheed AC-130J Ghostrider (15-5811)	USAF 1st SOG Det.2, Hurlburt Field, FL
	55813	Lockheed C-130J-30 Hercules II (15-5813) [YJ] *r* [36 AS]	USAF 36th AS/374th AW, Yokota AB, Japan
	55817	Lockheed C-130J-30 Hercules II (15-5817) [YJ] *r*	USAF 36th AS/374th AW, Yokota AB, Japan
	55822	Lockheed C-130J-30 Hercules II (15-5822) [RS] *bl/w*	USAF 37th AS/86th AW, Ramstein AB, Germany
	55825	Lockheed MC-130J Commando II (15-5825)	USAF 15th SOS/1st SOW, Hurlburt Field, FL
	55826	Lockheed C-130J-30 Hercules II (15-5826)	USAF 40th AS/317th AW, Dyess AFB, TX
	55827	Lockheed HC-130J Combat King II (15-5827) [AK]	USAF 211th RQS/176th Wg, Elmendorf AFB, AK ANG
	55828	Lockheed C-130J-30 Hercules II (15-5828) *w/bk*	USAF 61st AS/19th AW Little Rock AFB, AR
	55829	Lockheed HC-130J Combat King II (15-5829) [AK]	USAF 211th RQS/176th Wg, Elmendorf AFB, AK ANG
	55831	Lockheed C-130J-30 Hercules II (15-5831) [RS] *bl/w*	USAF 37th AS/86th AW, Ramstein AB, Germany
	55833	Lockheed C-130J-30 Hercules II (15-5833) [YJ] *r* [5 AF]	USAF 36th AS/374th AW, Yokota AB, Japan
	56709	Lockheed C-130H-3 Hercules (95-6709)	USAF
	56710	Lockheed C-130H-3 Hercules (95-6710) *pr/y*	USAF 130th AS/130th AW, Yeager Int'l, Charleston, WV ANG
	56711	Lockheed C-130H-3 Hercules (95-6711) *pr/y*	USAF 130th AS/130th AW, Yeager Int'l, Charleston, WV ANG
	56712	Lockheed C-130H-3 Hercules (95-6712) *pr/y*	USAF 130th AS/130th AW, Yeager Int'l, Charleston, WV ANG
	58152	Lockheed C-130J-30 Hercules II (05-8152) *r*	USAF 815th AS/403rd AW AFRC, Keesler AFB, M•
	58156	Lockheed C-130J-30 Hercules II (05-8156) *r*	USAF 815th AS/403rd AW AFRC, Keesler AFB, M•
	58157	Lockheed C-130J-30 Hercules II (05-8157) *r*	USAF 815th AS/403rd AW AFRC, Keesler AFB, M•
	58158	Lockheed C-130J-30 Hercules II (05-8158) *r*	USAF 815th AS/403rd AW AFRC, Keesler AFB, M•
	60212	Lockheed MC-130P Combat Shadow (66-0212) *bl*	USAF 130th RQS/129th RQW, Moffett Field CA ANG
	60216	Lockheed MC-130P Combat Shadow (66-0216) *bl*	USAF 130th RQS/129th RQW, Moffett Field CA ANG
	60219	Lockheed MC-130P Combat Shadow (66-0219) *bl*	USAF 130th RQS/129th RQW, Moffett Field CA ANG
	60221	Lockheed HC-130P Combat King (66-0221)	*To AMARG, March 2017*
	60222	Lockheed HC-130P Combat King (66-0222)	USAF 102nd RQS/106th RQW, Suffolk Field, NY ANG
	60223	Lockheed MC-130P Combat Shadow (66-0223) *bl*	USAF 130th RQS/129th RQW, Moffett Field CA ANG
	60410	Lockheed C-130H Hercules (86-0410)	USAF
	60411	Lockheed C-130H Hercules (86-0411)	USAF
	60413	Lockheed C-130H Hercules (86-0413)	*To AMARG, March 2017*
	60414	Lockheed C-130H Hercules (86-0414)	USAF

Serial	Type (code/other identity)	Owner/operator, location or fate	Notes
60415	Lockheed C-130H Hercules (86-0415)	*To AMARG, January 2017*	
60418	Lockheed C-130H Hercules (86-0418)	USAF	
60419	Lockheed C-130H Hercules (86-0419) *r*	USAF 154th TS/189th AW, Little Rock, AR ANG	
61003	Lockheed C-130H Hercules (96-1003) *pr/bk*	USAF 109th AS/133rd AW, Minneapolis, MN ANG	
61004	Lockheed C-130H Hercules (96-1004) *pr/bk*	USAF 109th AS/133rd AW, Minneapolis, MN ANG	
61005	Lockheed C-130H Hercules (96-1005) *pr/bk*	USAF 109th AS/133rd AW, Minneapolis, MN ANG	
61006	Lockheed C-130H Hercules (96-1006) *pr/bk*	USAF 109th AS/133rd AW, Minneapolis, MN ANG	
61007	Lockheed C-130H Hercules (96-1007) *pr/bk*	USAF 109th AS/133rd AW, Minneapolis, MN ANG	
61008	Lockheed C-130H Hercules (96-1008) *pr/bk*	USAF 109th AS/133rd AW, Minneapolis, MN ANG	
61391	Lockheed C-130H Hercules (86-1391) *r*	USAF 154th TS/189th AW, Little Rock, AR ANG	
61395	Lockheed C-130H Hercules (86-1395)	*To AMARG, January 2018*	
61437	Lockheed C-130J-30 Hercules II (06-1437) *r*	USAF 143rd AS/143rd AW, Quonset, RI ANG	
61438	Lockheed C-130J-30 Hercules II (06-1438) *r*	USAF 143rd AS/143rd AW, Quonset, RI ANG	
61467	Lockheed C-130J-30 Hercules II (06-1467) *gn*	USAF 115th AS/146th AW, Channel Island ANGS, CA ANG	
61699	Lockheed MC-130H Combat Talon II (86-1699)	USAF 15th SOS/1st SOW, Hurlburt Field, FL	
63171	Lockheed C-130J-30 Hercules II (06-3171) *bl*	USAF 40th AS/317th AW, Dyess AFB, TX	
63301	Lockheed LC-130H Hercules (76-3301)	USAF 139th AS/109th AW, Schenectady, NY ANG	
63302	Lockheed LC-130H Hercules (76-3302)	USAF 139th AS/109th AW, Schenectady, NY ANG	
64631	Lockheed C-130J-30 Hercules II (06-4631) *w/bk*	USAF 41st AS/19th AW Little Rock AFB, AR	
64632	Lockheed C-130J-30 Hercules II (06-4632) *y/bk*	USAF 41st AS/19th AW Little Rock AFB, AR	
64633	Lockheed C-130J-30 Hercules II (06-4633) [YJ] *r*	USAF 36th AS/374th AW, Yokota AB, Japan	
64634	Lockheed C-130J-30 Hercules II (06-4634) *w/bk*	USAF 41st AS/19th AW Little Rock AFB, AR	
65300	Lockheed WC-130J Hercules II (96-5300)	USAF 53rd WRS/403rd AW AFRC, Keesler AFB, MO	
65301	Lockheed WC-130J Hercules II (96-5301)	USAF 53rd WRS/403rd AW AFRC, Keesler AFB, MO	
65302	Lockheed WC-130J Hercules II (96-5302)	USAF 53rd WRS/403rd AW AFRC, Keesler AFB, MO	
65832	Lockheed AC-130J Ghostrider (16-5832)	LMTAS, Marietta, GA	
65834	Lockheed C-130J-30 Hercules II (16-5834)	USAF 40th AS/317th AW, Dyess AFB, TX	
65836	Lockheed AC-130J Ghostrider (16-5836)	LMTAS, Marietta, GA	
65840	Lockheed C-130J-30 Hercules II (16-5840) [RS] *bl/w*	USAF 37th AS/86th AW, Ramstein AB, Germany	
65842	Lockheed AC-130J Ghostrider (16-5842)	LMTAS, Marietta, GA	
65844	Lockheed AC-130J Ghostrider (16-5844)	LMTAS, Marietta, GA	
65846	Lockheed HC-130J Combat King II (16-5846)	LMTAS, Marietta, GA	
67322	Lockheed C-130H-3 Hercules (96-7322) *pr/y*	USAF 130th AS/130th AW, Yeager Int'l, Charleston, WV ANG	
67323	Lockheed C-130H-3 Hercules (96-7323) *pr/y*	USAF 130th AS/130th AW, Yeager Int'l, Charleston, WV ANG	
67324	Lockheed C-130H-3 Hercules (96-7324) *pr/y*	USAF 130th AS/130th AW, Yeager Int'l, Charleston, WV ANG	
7325	Lockheed C-130H-3 Hercules (96-7325) *pr/w*	USAF 731st AS/302nd AW AFRC, Peterson AFB, CO	
8153	Lockheed EC-130J Commando Solo III (96-8153)	USAF 193rd SOS/193rd SOW, Harrisburg, PA ANG	
8154	Lockheed EC-130J Commando Solo III (96-8154)	USAF 193rd SOS/193rd SOW, Harrisburg, PA ANG	
8159	Lockheed C-130J Hercules II (06-8159) *r*	USAF 815th AS/403rd AW AFRC, Keesler AFB, MO	
8610	Lockheed C-130J-30 Hercules II (06-8610) [RS] *bl/w*	USAF 37th AS/86th AW, Ramstein AB, Germany	
8611	Lockheed C-130J-30 Hercules II (06-8611) [RS] *bl/w*	USAF 37th AS/86th AW, Ramstein AB, Germany	
8612	Lockheed C-130J-30 Hercules II (06-8612) [RS] *bl/w*	USAF 37th AS/86th AW, Ramstein AB, Germany	
023	Lockheed MC-130H Combat Talon II (87-0023)	USAF 15th SOS/1st SOW, Hurlburt Field, FL	
0024	Lockheed MC-130H Combat Talon II (87-0024)	USAF 15th SOS/1st SOW, Hurlburt Field, FL	
125	Lockheed MC-130H Combat Talon II (87-0125)	USAF 15th SOS/1st SOW, Hurlburt Field, FL	
126	Lockheed MC-130H Combat Talon II (87-0126)	USAF 15th SOS/1st SOW, Hurlburt Field, FL	
128	Lockheed AC-130U Spooky (87-0128)	USAF 4th SOS/1st SOW, Hurlburt Field, FL	
351	Lockheed C-130J Hercules II (97-1351) *y*	USAF 48th AS/314th AW, Little Rock AFB, AR	

Notes	Serial	Type (code/other identity)	Owner/operator, location or fate
	71352	Lockheed C-130J Hercules II (97-1352) *y*	USAF 48th AS/314th AW, Little Rock AFB, AR
	71353	Lockheed C-130J Hercules II (97-1353) *y*	USAF 48th AS/314th AW, Little Rock AFB, AR
	71354	Lockheed C-130J Hercules II (97-1354) *y*	USAF 48th AS/314th AW, Little Rock AFB, AR
	71468	Lockheed C-130J-30 Hercules II (07-1468) *gn*	USAF 115th AS/146th AW, Channel Island ANGS, CA ANG
	71931	Lockheed EC-130J Commando Solo III (97-1931)	USAF 193rd SOS/193rd SOW, Harrisburg, PA ANG
	73170	Lockheed C-130J-30 Hercules II (07-3170) *bl*	USAF 40th AS/317th AW, Dyess AFB, TX
	74635	Lockheed C-130J-30 Hercules II (07-4635) *w/bk*	USAF 41st AS/19th AW Little Rock AFB, AR
	74636	Lockheed C-130J-30 Hercules II (07-4636) *w/bk*	USAF 41st AS/19th AW Little Rock AFB, AR
	74637	Lockheed C-130J-30 Hercules II (07-4637) *w/bk*	USAF 41st AS/19th AW Little Rock AFB, AR
	74638	Lockheed C-130J-30 Hercules II (07-4638) *w/bk*	USAF 41st AS/19th AW Little Rock AFB, AR
	74639	Lockheed C-130J-30 Hercules II (07-4639) *w/bk*	USAF 41st AS/19th AW Little Rock AFB, AR
	75303	Lockheed WC-130J Hercules II (97-5303)	USAF 53rd WRS/403rd AW AFRC, Keesler AFB, MO
	75304	Lockheed WC-130J Hercules II (97-5304)	USAF 53rd WRS/403rd AW AFRC, Keesler AFB, MO
	75305	Lockheed WC-130J Hercules II (97-5305)	USAF 53rd WRS/403rd AW AFRC, Keesler AFB, MO
	75306	Lockheed WC-130J Hercules II (97-5306)	USAF 53rd WRS/403rd AW AFRC, Keesler AFB, MO
	76310	Lockheed C-130J-30 Hercules II (07-46310) *w/bk*	USAF 41st AS/19th AW Little Rock AFB, AR
	76311	Lockheed C-130J-30 Hercules II (07-46311) *w/bk*	USAF 41st AS/19th AW Little Rock AFB, AR
	76312	Lockheed C-130J-30 Hercules II (07-46312) *w/bk*	USAF 41st AS/19th AW Little Rock AFB, AR
	78608	Lockheed C-130J-30 Hercules II (07-8608) [RS] *bl/w*	USAF 37th AS/86th AW, Ramstein AB, Germany
	78609	Lockheed C-130J-30 Hercules II (07-8609) [RS] *bl/w*	USAF 37th AS/86th AW, Ramstein AB, Germany
	78613	Lockheed C-130J-30 Hercules II (07-8613) [RS] *bl/w*	USAF 37th AS/86th AW, Ramstein AB, Germany
	78614	Lockheed C-130J-30 Hercules II (07-8614) [RS] *bl/w*	USAF 37th AS/86th AW, Ramstein AB, Germany
	79281	Lockheed C-130H Hercules (87-9281) *bl/y*	USAF 328th AS/914th AW AFRC, Niagara Falls, NY
	79282	Lockheed C-130H Hercules (87-9282) *bl/y*	USAF 328th AS/914th AW AFRC, Niagara Falls, NY
	79283	Lockheed C-130H Hercules (87-9283) *pr/w*	USAF 96th AS/934th AW AFRC, Minneapolis/ St Paul, MN
	79285	Lockheed C-130H Hercules (87-9285) *bl/y*	USAF 328th AS/914th AW AFRC, Niagara Falls, NY
	79286	Lockheed AC-130W Stinger II (87-9286)	USAF 16th SOS/27th SOW, Cannon AFB, NM
	79287	Lockheed C-130H Hercules (87-9287) *bk/y*	USAF 758th AS/911th AW AFRC, Pittsburgh ARS, PA
	79288	Lockheed AC-130W Stinger II (87-9288)	USAF 16th SOS/27th SOW, Cannon AFB, NM
	80191	Lockheed MC-130H Combat Talon II (88-0191)	USAF 1st SOS/353rd SOG, Kadena AB, Japan
	80193	Lockheed MC-130H Combat Talon II (88-0193)	USAF 15th SOS/1st SOW, Hurlburt Field, FL
	80194	Lockheed MC-130H Combat Talon II (88-0194)	USAF 15th SOS/1st SOW, Hurlburt Field, FL
	80195	Lockheed MC-130H Combat Talon II (88-0195)	USAF 15th SOS/1st SOW, Hurlburt Field, FL
	80264	Lockheed MC-130H Combat Talon II (88-0264)	USAF 15th SOS/1st SOW, Hurlburt Field, FL
	80809	Lockheed C-130H Hercules (78-0809)	*To AMARG, September 2015*
	81301	Lockheed AC-130W Stinger II (88-1301)	USAF 16th SOS/27th SOW, Cannon AFB, NM
	81302	Lockheed AC-130W Stinger II (88-1302)	USAF 16th SOS/27th SOW, Cannon AFB, NM
	81303	Lockheed AC-130W Stinger II (88-1303)	USAF 16th SOS/27th SOW, Cannon AFB, NM
	81304	Lockheed AC-130W Stinger II (88-1304)	USAF 16th SOS/27th SOW, Cannon AFB, NM
	81305	Lockheed AC-130W Stinger II (88-1305)	USAF 16th SOS/27th SOW, Cannon AFB, NM
	81306	Lockheed AC-130W Stinger II (88-1306)	USAF 16th SOS/27th SOW, Cannon AFB, NM
	81307	Lockheed AC-130W Stinger II (88-1307)	USAF 16th SOS/27th SOW, Cannon AFB, NM
	81308	Lockheed AC-130W Stinger II (88-1308)	USAF 16th SOS/27th SOW, Cannon AFB, NM
	81355	Lockheed C-130J Hercules II (98-1355) *y*	USAF 48th AS/314th AW, Little Rock AFB, AR
	81356	Lockheed C-130J Hercules II (98-1356) *y*	USAF 48th AS/314th AW, Little Rock AFB, AR
	81357	Lockheed C-130J Hercules II (98-1357) *y*	USAF 48th AS/314th AW, Little Rock AFB, AR
	81358	Lockheed C-130J Hercules II (98-1358) *y*	USAF 48th AS/314th AW, Little Rock AFB, AR
	81803	Lockheed MC-130H Combat Talon II (88-1803)	USAF 1st SOS/353rd SOG, Kadena AB, Japan
	81932	Lockheed EC-130J Commando Solo III (98-1932)	USAF 193rd SOS/193rd SOW, Harrisburg, PA ANG

Serial	Type (code/other identity)	Owner/operator, location or fate	Notes
82101	Lockheed HC-130N Combat King (88-2101)	USAF 102nd RQS/106th RQW, Suffolk Field, NY ANG	
82102	Lockheed HC-130P Combat King (88-2102)	USAF 102nd RQS/106th RQW, Suffolk Field, NY ANG	
83172	Lockheed C-130J-30 Hercules II (08-3172) *bl*	USAF 40th AS/317th AW, Dyess AFB, TX	
83173	Lockheed C-130J-30 Hercules II (08-3173) *bl*	USAF 40th AS/317th AW, Dyess AFB, TX	
83175	Lockheed C-130J-30 Hercules II (08-3175) *bl*	USAF 40th AS/317th AW, Dyess AFB, TX	
83176	Lockheed C-130J-30 Hercules II (08-3176) *bl*	USAF 40th AS/317th AW, Dyess AFB, TX	
83177	Lockheed C-130J-30 Hercules II (08-3177) [YJ] *r*	USAF 36th AS/374th AW, Yokota AB, Japan	
83178	Lockheed C-130J-30 Hercules II (08-3178) *bl*	USAF 40th AS/317th AW, Dyess AFB, TX	
83179	Lockheed C-130J-30 Hercules II (08-3179) *bl*	USAF 40th AS/317th AW, Dyess AFB, TX	
84401	Lockheed C-130H Hercules (88-4401) *bk/y*	USAF 758th AS/911th AW AFRC, Pittsburgh ARS, PA	
84402	Lockheed C-130H Hercules (88-4402) *r*	USAF 154th TS/189th AW, Little Rock, AR ANG	
84403	Lockheed C-130H Hercules (88-4403) *r*	USAF 154th TS/189th AW, Little Rock, AR ANG	
84405	Lockheed C-130H Hercules (88-4405)	USAF	
84406	Lockheed C-130H Hercules (88-4406)	USAF	
85307	Lockheed WC-130J Hercules II (98-5307)	USAF 53rd WRS/403rd AW AFRC, Keesler AFB, MO	
85308	Lockheed WC-130J Hercules II (98-5308)	USAF 53rd WRS/403rd AW AFRC, Keesler AFB, MO	
85675	Lockheed C-130J-30 Hercules II (08-5675) *bl*	USAF 40th AS/317th AW, Dyess AFB, TX	
85678	Lockheed C-130J-30 Hercules II (08-5678) *bl*	USAF 40th AS/317th AW, Dyess AFB, TX	
85679	Lockheed C-130J-30 Hercules II (08-5679) *bl*	USAF 40th AS/317th AW, Dyess AFB, TX	
85683	Lockheed C-130J-30 Hercules II (08-5683) *r*	USAF 39th AS/317th AW, Dyess AFB, TX	
85684	Lockheed C-130J-30 Hercules II (08-5684) *r*	USAF 39th AS/317th AW, Dyess AFB, TX	
85685	Lockheed C-130J-30 Hercules II (08-5685) *r*	USAF 39th AS/317th AW, Dyess AFB, TX	
85686	Lockheed C-130J-30 Hercules II (08-5686) *r*	USAF 39th AS/317th AW, Dyess AFB, TX	
85691	Lockheed C-130J-30 Hercules II (08-5691) *r*	USAF 39th AS/317th AW, Dyess AFB, TX	
85692	Lockheed C-130J-30 Hercules II (08-5692) [YJ] *r*	USAF 36th AS/374th AW, Yokota AB, Japan	
85693	Lockheed C-130J-30 Hercules II (08-5693) *r*	USAF 39th AS/317th AW, Dyess AFB, TX	
85697	Lockheed MC-130J Commando II (08-5697)	USAF 522nd SOS/27th SOW, Cannon AFB, NM	
85705	Lockheed C-130J-30 Hercules II (08-5705) *r*	USAF 39th AS/317th AW, Dyess AFB, TX	
85712	Lockheed C-130J-30 Hercules II (08-5712) *r*	USAF 39th AS/317th AW, Dyess AFB, TX	
85715	Lockheed C-130J-30 Hercules II (08-5715) *r*	USAF 39th AS/317th AW, Dyess AFB, TX	
85724	Lockheed C-130J-30 Hercules II (08-5724) *r*	USAF 39th AS/317th AW, Dyess AFB, TX	
85726	Lockheed C-130J-30 Hercules II (08-5726) *r*	USAF 39th AS/317th AW, Dyess AFB, TX	
86201	Lockheed MC-130J Commando II (08-6201)	USAF 522nd SOS/27th SOW, Cannon AFB, NM	
86202	Lockheed MC-130J Commando II (08-6202)	USAF 522nd SOS/27th SOW, Cannon AFB, NM	
86203	Lockheed MC-130J Commando II (08-6203) [58 OG]	USAF 415th SOS/58th SOW, Kirtland AFB, NM	
86204	Lockheed MC-130J Commando II (08-6204)	USAF 522nd SOS/27th SOW, Cannon AFB, NM	
86205	Lockheed MC-130J Commando II (08-6205)	USAF 415th SOS/58th SOW, Kirtland AFB, NM	
86206	Lockheed MC-130J Commando II (08-6206)	USAF 415th SOS/58th SOW, Kirtland AFB, NM	
88601	Lockheed C-130J-30 Hercules II (08-8601) [RS] *bl/w* $	USAF 37th AS/86th AW, Ramstein AB, Germany	
88602	Lockheed C-130J-30 Hercules II (08-8602) [RS] *bl/w* $	USAF 37th AS/86th AW, Ramstein AB, Germany	
88603	Lockheed C-130J-30 Hercules II (08-8603) [RS] *bl/w* $	USAF 37th AS/86th AW, Ramstein AB, Germany	
88604	Lockheed C-130J-30 Hercules II (08-8604) [YJ] *r*	USAF 36th AS/374th AW, Yokota AB, Japan	
88605	Lockheed C-130J-30 Hercules II (08-8605) [YJ] *r*	USAF 36th AS/374th AW, Yokota AB, Japan	
88606	Lockheed C-130J-30 Hercules II (08-8606) *w/bk*	USAF 41st AS/19th AW Little Rock AFB, AR	
88607	Lockheed C-130J-30 Hercules II (08-8607) [RS] *bl/w*	USAF 37th AS/86th AW, Ramstein AB, Germany	
90108	Lockheed HC-130J Combat King II (09-0108) [OT]	USAF 85th TES/53rd Wg, Eglin AFB, FL	
90109	Lockheed HC-130J Combat King II (09-0109)	USAF 415th SOS/58th SOW, Kirtland AFB, NM	
90280	Lockheed MC-130H Combat Talon II (89-0280)	USAF 1st SOS/353rd SOG, Kadena AB, Japan	
90282	Lockheed MC-130H Combat Talon II (89-0282)	USAF 15th SOS/1st SOW, Hurlburt Field, FL	
90283	Lockheed MC-130H Combat Talon II (89-0283)	USAF 1st SOS/353rd SOG, Kadena AB, Japan	
90473	Lockheed C-130H Hercules (79-0473)	*To AMARG, August 2015*	
90475	Lockheed C-130H Hercules (79-0475)	*To AMARG, October 2017*	

Notes	Serial	Type (code/other identity)	Owner/operator, location or fate
	90476	Lockheed C-130H Hercules (79-0476)	*To AMARG, August 2017*
	90479	Lockheed C-130H Hercules (79-0479)	*To AMARG, September 2017*
	90480	Lockheed C-130H Hercules (79-0480)	*To AMARG, December 2017*
	90509	Lockheed AC-130U Spooky (89-0509)	USAF 4th SOS/1st SOW, Hurlburt Field, FL
	90510	Lockheed AC-130U Spooky (89-0510)	USAF 4th SOS/1st SOW, Hurlburt Field, FL
	90511	Lockheed AC-130U Spooky (89-0511)	USAF 4th SOS/1st SOW, Hurlburt Field, FL
	90512	Lockheed AC-130U Spooky (89-0512)	USAF 4th SOS/1st SOW, Hurlburt Field, FL
	90513	Lockheed AC-130U Spooky (89-0513)	USAF 4th SOS/1st SOW, Hurlburt Field, FL
	90514	Lockheed AC-130U Spooky (89-0514)	*To AMARG, October 2017*
	91051	Lockheed AC-130W Stinger II (89-1051)	USAF 16th SOS/27th SOW, Cannon AFB, NM
	91052	Lockheed AC-130U Spooky (89-1052)	USAF 4th SOS/1st SOW, Hurlburt Field, FL
	91053	Lockheed AC-130U Spooky (89-1053)	USAF 4th SOS/1st SOW, Hurlburt Field, FL
	91054	Lockheed AC-130U Spooky (89-1054)	USAF 4th SOS/1st SOW, Hurlburt Field, FL
	91055	Lockheed C-130H Hercules (89-1055) *bl/w*	USAF 357th AS/908th AW AFRC, Maxwell AFB, AL
	91056	Lockheed AC-130U Spooky (89-1056)	USAF 4th SOS/1st SOW, Hurlburt Field, FL
	91181	Lockheed C-130H Hercules (89-1181) *r/bk*	USAF 158th AS/165th AW, Savannah, GA ANG
	91182	Lockheed C-130H Hercules (89-1182)	USAF
	91183	Lockheed C-130H Hercules (89-1183)	USAF
	91184	Lockheed C-130H Hercules (89-1184)	USAF
	91185	Lockheed C-130H Hercules (89-1185)	USAF
	91186	Lockheed C-130H Hercules (89-1186) *bl/y*	USAF 328th AS/914th AW AFRC, Niagara Falls, NY
	91187	Lockheed C-130H Hercules (89-1187) *bl/w*	USAF 357th AS/908th AW AFRC, Maxwell AFB, AL
	91188	Lockheed C-130H Hercules (89-1188) *bl/w*	USAF 357th AS/908th AW AFRC, Maxwell AFB, AL
	91431	Lockheed C-130J-30 Hercules II (99-1431) *r*	USAF 143rd AS/143rd AW, Quonset, RI ANG
	91432	Lockheed C-130J-30 Hercules II (99-1432) *r*	USAF 143rd AS/143rd AW, Quonset, RI ANG
	91433	Lockheed C-130J-30 Hercules II (99-1433) *r*	USAF 143rd AS/143rd AW, Quonset, RI ANG
	91933	Lockheed EC-130J Commando Solo III (99-1933)	USAF 193rd SOS/193rd SOW, Harrisburg, PA ANG
	95309	Lockheed WC-130J Hercules II (99-5309)	USAF 53rd WRS/403rd AW AFRC, Keesler AFB, MO
	95706	Lockheed HC-130J Combat King II (09-5706)	USAF 415th SOS/58th SOW, Kirtland AFB, NM
	95707	Lockheed HC-130J Combat King II (09-5707) [FT]	USAF 79th RQS/563rd RQG, Davis-Monthan AFB, AZ
	95708	Lockheed HC-130J Combat King II (09-5708) [FT]	USAF 79th RQS/563rd RQG, Davis-Monthan AFB, AZ
	95709	Lockheed HC-130J Combat King II (09-5709) [FT]	USAF 79th RQS/563rd RQG, Davis-Monthan AFB, AZ
	95711	Lockheed MC-130J Commando II (09-5711)	USAF 522nd SOS/27th SOW, Cannon AFB, NM
	95713	Lockheed MC-130J Commando II (09-5713)	USAF 522nd SOS/27th SOW, Cannon AFB, NM
	95829	Lockheed HC-130N Combat King (69-5829)	USAF 39th RQS/920th RQW AFRC, Patrick AFB, FL
	95830	Lockheed HC-130N Combat King (69-5830)	*To AMARG, August 2017*
	95833	Lockheed HC-130N Combat King (69-5833)	*To AMARG, July 2017*
	96207	Lockheed MC-130J Commando II (09-6207)	USAF 415th SOS/58th SOW, Kirtland AFB, NM
	96208	Lockheed MC-130J Commando II (09-6208)	USAF 522nd SOS/27th SOW, Cannon AFB, NM
	96209	Lockheed MC-130J Commando II (09-6209) [58 SOW]	USAF 415th SOS/58th SOW, Kirtland AFB, NM
	96210	Lockheed MC-130J Commando II (09-6210)	USAF 522nd SOS/27th SOW, Cannon AFB, NM
	99101	Lockheed C-130H Hercules (89-9101)	*To AMARG, July 2017*
	99102	Lockheed C-130H Hercules (89-9102) *r/bk*	USAF 158th AS/165th AW, Savannah, GA ANG
	99103	Lockheed C-130H Hercules (89-9103) *bl/r*	USAF 757th AS/910th AW AFRC, Youngstown ARS, OH
	99104	Lockheed C-130H Hercules (89-9104) *bl/r*	USAF 757th AS/910th AW AFRC, Youngstown ARS, OH
	99105	Lockheed C-130H Hercules (89-9105) *bl/r*	USAF 757th AS/910th AW AFRC, Youngstown ARS, OH
	99106	Lockheed C-130H Hercules (89-9106) *bl/r*	USAF 757th AS/910th AW AFRC, Youngstown ARS, OH
Boeing C-135			
	00313	Boeing KC-135R Stratotanker (60-0313)	USAF 22nd ARW, McConnell AFB, KS

Serial	Type (code/other identity)	Owner/operator, location or fate	Notes
00314	Boeing KC-135R Stratotanker (60-0314) *r/w*	USAF 74th ARS/434th ARW AFRC, Grissom AFB, IN	
00315	Boeing KC-135R Stratotanker (60-0315) *w/bl*	USAF 126th ARS/128th ARW, Mitchell Field, WI ANG	
00316	Boeing KC-135R Stratotanker (60-0316) *bl/bk*	USAF 191st ARS/151st ARW, Salt Lake City, UT ANG	
00318	Boeing KC-135R Stratotanker (60-0318)	USAF 314th ARS/940th ARW, Beale AFB, CA	
00320	Boeing KC-135R Stratotanker (60-0320) *y/bl*	USAF 91st ARS/6th AMW, MacDill AFB, FL	
00322	Boeing KC-135R Stratotanker (60-0322) *bl*	USAF 72nd ARS/434th ARW AFRC, Grissom AFB, IN	
00323	Boeing KC-135R Stratotanker (60-0323) [HH] *y/bk*	USAF 203rd ARS/15th Wg, Hickam AFB, HI ANG	
00324	Boeing KC-135R Stratotanker (60-0324) [D] *r/w/bl*	USAF 351st ARS/100th ARW, RAF Mildenhall, UK	
00328	Boeing KC-135R Stratotanker (60-0328) [ZZ] *or/bk*	USAF 909th ARS/18th Wg, Kadena AB, Japan	
00329	Boeing KC-135R Stratotanker (60-0329) [HH] *y/bk*	USAF 203rd ARS/15th Wg, Hickam AFB, HI ANG	
00331	Boeing KC-135R Stratotanker (60-0331)	USAF 314th ARS/940th ARW, Beale AFB, CA	
00332	Boeing KC-135R Stratotanker (60-0332) [AK] *bl/y*	USAF 168th ARS/168th ARW, Eielson AFB, AK ANG	
00333	Boeing KC-135R Stratotanker (60-0333) [D] *r/w/bl*	USAF 351st ARS/100th ARW, RAF Mildenhall, UK	
00334	Boeing KC-135R Stratotanker (60-0334) [AK] *bl/y*	USAF 168th ARS/168th ARW, Eielson AFB, AK ANG	
00335	Boeing KC-135T Stratotanker (60-0335)	USAF 22nd ARW, McConnell AFB, KS	
00336	Boeing KC-135T Stratotanker (60-0336)	USAF 22nd ARW, McConnell AFB, KS	
00337	Boeing KC-135T Stratotanker (60-0337)	USAF 22nd ARW, McConnell AFB, KS	
00339	Boeing KC-135T Stratotanker (60-0339)	USAF 92nd ARW, Fairchild AFB, WA	
00341	Boeing KC-135R Stratotanker (60-0341)	USAF 153rd ARS/186th AW, Meridian, MS ANG	
00342	Boeing KC-135T Stratotanker (60-0342)	USAF 92nd ARW, Fairchild AFB, WA	
00343	Boeing KC-135T Stratotanker (60-0343)	USAF 22nd ARW, McConnell AFB, KS	
00344	Boeing KC-135T Stratotanker (60-0344)	USAF 22nd ARW, McConnell AFB, KS	
00345	Boeing KC-135T Stratotanker (60-0345) *bk/y*	USAF 171st ARS/127th Wg, Selfridge ANGB, MI ANG	
00346	Boeing KC-135T Stratotanker (60-0346) *bk/y*	USAF 171st ARS/127th Wg, Selfridge ANGB, MI ANG	
00347	Boeing KC-135R Stratotanker (60-0347) *r/w*	USAF 166th ARS/121st ARW, Rickenbacker ANGB, OH ANG	
00348	Boeing KC-135R Stratotanker (60-0348) *y/r*	USAF 54th ARS/97th AMW, Altus AFB, OK	
00349	Boeing KC-135R Stratotanker (60-0349) *gn/y*	USAF 77th ARS/916th ARW AFRC, Seymour Johnson AFB, NC	
00350	Boeing KC-135R Stratotanker (60-0350) *y/r*	USAF 54th ARS/97th AMW, Altus AFB, OK	
00351	Boeing KC-135R Stratotanker (60-0351) *y/r*	USAF 54th ARS/97th AMW, Altus AFB, OK	
00353	Boeing KC-135R Stratotanker (60-0353) *y/bl*	USAF 91st ARS/6th AMW, MacDill AFB, FL	
00355	Boeing KC-135R Stratotanker (60-0355)	USAF 22nd ARW, McConnell AFB, KS	
00356	Boeing KC-135R(RT) Stratotanker (60-0356)	USAF 22nd ARW, McConnell AFB, KS	
00357	Boeing KC-135R(RT) Stratotanker (60-0357)	USAF 22nd ARW, McConnell AFB, KS	
00358	Boeing KC-135R Stratotanker (60-0358) *w/bl*	USAF 108th ARS/126th ARW, Scott AFB, IL ANG	
00359	Boeing KC-135R Stratotanker (60-0359) *r/w*	USAF 74th ARS/434th ARW AFRC, Grissom AFB, IN	
00360	Boeing KC-135R Stratotanker (60-0360) [ZZ] *or/bk*	USAF 909th ARS/18th Wg, Kadena AB, Japan	
00362	Boeing KC-135R(RT) Stratotanker (60-0362)	USAF 22nd ARW, McConnell AFB, KS	
00363	Boeing KC-135R Stratotanker (60-0363) *bl*	USAF 72nd ARS/434th ARW AFRC, Grissom AFB, IN	
00364	Boeing KC-135R Stratotanker (60-0364) *r/w*	USAF 74th ARS/434th ARW AFRC, Grissom AFB, IN	
00365	Boeing KC-135R Stratotanker (60-0365) *bl/y*	USAF 117th ARS/190th ARW, Forbes Field, KS ANG	
00366	Boeing KC-135R Stratotanker (60-0366) *r*	USAF 141st ARS/108th ARW, McGuire AFB, NJ ANG	
00367	Boeing KC-135R Stratotanker (60-0367) *r/w*	USAF 166th ARS/121st ARW, Rickenbacker ANGB, OH ANG	
0264	Boeing KC-135R Stratotanker (61-0264) *r/w*	USAF 166th ARS/121st ARW, Rickenbacker ANGB, OH ANG	
0266	Boeing KC-135R Stratotanker (61-0266) *bl/y*	USAF 117th ARS/190th ARW, Forbes Field, KS ANG	

Notes	Serial	Type (code/other identity)	Owner/operator, location or fate
	10267	Boeing KC-135R Stratotanker (61-0267)	USAF
	10272	Boeing KC-135R Stratotanker (61-0272) r/w	USAF 74th ARS/434th ARW AFRC, Grissom AFB, IN
	10275	Boeing KC-135R Stratotanker (61-0275) bl/bk	USAF 191st ARS/151st ARW, Salt Lake City, UT ANG
	10276	Boeing KC-135R Stratotanker (61-0276) r/w	USAF 173rd ARS/155th ARW, Lincoln, NE ANG
	10277	Boeing KC-135R Stratotanker (61-0277) bl/y	USAF 117th ARS/190th ARW, Forbes Field, KS ANG
	10280	Boeing KC-135R Stratotanker (61-0280) or/y	USAF 336th ARS/452nd AMW AFRC, March ARB, CA
	10284	Boeing KC-135R Stratotanker (61-0284)	USAF 197th ARS/161st ARW, Phoenix, AZ ANG
	10288	Boeing KC-135R Stratotanker (61-0288) [D] r/w/bl	USAF 351st ARS/100th ARW, RAF Mildenhall, UK
	10290	Boeing KC-135R Stratotanker (61-0290) [HH] y/bk	USAF 203rd ARS/15th Wg, Hickam AFB, HI ANG
	10292	Boeing KC-135R Stratotanker (61-0292)	USAF 22nd ARW, McConnell AFB, KS
	10293	Boeing KC-135R(RT) Stratotanker (61-0293)	USAF 22nd ARW, McConnell AFB, KS
	10294	Boeing KC-135R Stratotanker (61-0294) gn/y	USAF 77th ARS/916th ARW AFRC, Seymour Johnson AFB, NC
	10295	Boeing KC-135R Stratotanker (61-0295)	USAF 22nd ARW, McConnell AFB, KS
	10298	Boeing KC-135R Stratotanker (61-0298) w/bl	USAF 126th ARS/128th ARW, Mitchell Field, WI ANG
	10299	Boeing KC-135R Stratotanker (61-0299) [D] r/w/bl	USAF 351st ARS/100th ARW, RAF Mildenhall, UK
	10300	Boeing KC-135R Stratotanker (61-0300) w/bl	USAF 108th ARS/126th ARW, Scott AFB, IL ANG
	10305	Boeing KC-135R Stratotanker (61-0305)	USAF 22nd ARW, McConnell AFB, KS
	10307	Boeing KC-135R Stratotanker (61-0307) y/bk	USAF 756th ARS/459th ARW AFRC, Andrews AFB, MD
	10308	Boeing KC-135R Stratotanker (61-0308)	USAF 22nd ARW, McConnell AFB, KS
	10309	Boeing KC-135R Stratotanker (61-0309) w/bl	USAF 126th ARS/128th ARW, Mitchell Field, WI ANG
	10310	Boeing KC-135R Stratotanker (61-0310) bl	USAF 133rd ARS/157th ARW, Pease ANGB, NH ANG
	10311	Boeing KC-135R Stratotanker (61-0311)	USAF 22nd ARW, McConnell AFB, KS
	10313	Boeing KC-135R Stratotanker (61-0313) gn/y	USAF 77th ARS/916th ARW AFRC, Seymour Johnson AFB, NC
	10314	Boeing KC-135R Stratotanker (61-0314) y/bl	USAF 91st ARS/6th AMW, MacDill AFB, FL
	10315	Boeing KC-135R Stratotanker (61-0315) y/bl	USAF 91st ARS/6th AMW, MacDill AFB, FL
	10317	Boeing KC-135R Stratotanker (61-0317) bl/y	USAF 117th ARS/190th ARW, Forbes Field, KS ANG
	10318	Boeing KC-135R Stratotanker (61-0318) w/r	USAF 106th ARS/117th ARW, Birmingham, AL ANG
	10320	Boeing KC-135R Stratotanker (61-0320) [ED]	USAF 445th FLTS/412th TW, Edwards AFB, CA
	10321	Boeing KC-135R Stratotanker (61-0321) [D] r/w/bl	USAF 351st ARS/100th ARW, RAF Mildenhall, UK
	10323	Boeing KC-135R Stratotanker (61-0323)	USAF 314th ARS/940th ARW, Beale AFB, CA
	10324	Boeing KC-135R Stratotanker (61-0324) or/y	USAF 336th ARS/452nd AMW AFRC, March ARB, CA
	12662	Boeing RC-135S Cobra Ball (61-2662) [OF] bk	USAF 45th RS/55th Wg, Offutt AFB, NE
	12663	Boeing RC-135S Cobra Ball (61-2663) [OF] bk	USAF 45th RS/55th Wg, Offutt AFB, NE
	12666	Boeing NC-135W (61-2666)	USAF 645th Materiel Sqn, Greenville, TX
	12667	Boeing WC-135W Constant Phoenix (61-2667) [OF] bk	USAF 45th RS/55th Wg, Offutt AFB, NE
	12670	Boeing OC-135B Open Skies (61-2670) [OF] bk	USAF 45th RS/55th Wg, Offutt AFB, NE
	12672	Boeing OC-135B Open Skies (61-2672) [OF] bk	USAF 45th RS/55th Wg, Offutt AFB, NE
	14828	Boeing KC-135R Stratotanker (64-14828) bl/bk	USAF 191st ARS/151st ARW, Salt Lake City, UT ANG
	14829	Boeing KC-135R Stratotanker (64-14829)	USAF 197th ARS/161st ARW, Phoenix, AZ ANG
	14830	Boeing KC-135R Stratotanker (64-14830)	USAF
	14831	Boeing KC-135R Stratotanker (64-14831)	USAF 197th ARS/161st ARW, Phoenix, AZ ANG
	14832	Boeing KC-135R Stratotanker (64-14832) w/or	USAF 151st ARS/134th ARW, Knoxville, TN ANG
	14834	Boeing KC-135R Stratotanker (64-14834) r/w	USAF 74th ARS/434th ARW AFRC, Grissom AFB, IN
	14835	Boeing KC-135R Stratotanker (64-14835) or/y	USAF 336th ARS/452nd AMW AFRC, March ARB, CA
	14836	Boeing KC-135R Stratotanker (64-14836) bl	USAF 133rd ARS/157th ARW, Pease ANGB, NH ANG

Serial	Type (code/other identity)	Owner/operator, location or fate	Notes
14837	Boeing KC-135R Stratotanker (64-14837) y/bl	USAF 91st ARS/6th AMW, MacDill AFB, FL	
14839	Boeing KC-135R Stratotanker (64-14839) w/bl	USAF 108th ARS/126th ARW, Scott AFB, IL ANG	
14840	Boeing KC-135R Stratotanker (64-14840) r/w	USAF 166th ARS/121st ARW, Rickenbacker ANGB, OH ANG	
14841	Boeing RC-135V Rivet Joint (64-14841) [OF] gn	USAF 38th RS/55th Wg, Offutt AFB, NE	
14842	Boeing RC-135V Rivet Joint (64-14842) gn	USAF 38th RS/55th Wg, Offutt AFB, NE	
14843	Boeing RC-135V Rivet Joint (64-14843) gn	USAF 38th RS/55th Wg, Offutt AFB, NE	
14844	Boeing RC-135V Rivet Joint (64-14844) gn	USAF 38th RS/55th Wg, Offutt AFB, NE	
14845	Boeing RC-135V Rivet Joint (64-14845) [OF] gn	USAF 38th RS/55th Wg, Offutt AFB, NE	
14846	Boeing RC-135V Rivet Joint (64-14846) gn	USAF 38th RS/55th Wg, Offutt AFB, NE	
14847	Boeing RC-135U Combat Sent (64-14847) [OF] bk	USAF 45th RS/55th Wg, Offutt AFB, NE	
14848	Boeing RC-135V Rivet Joint (64-14848) gn	USAF 343rd RS/55th Wg, Offutt AFB, NE	
14849	Boeing RC-135U Combat Sent (64-14849) [OF] bk	USAF 45th RS/55th Wg, Offutt AFB, NE	
23498	Boeing KC-135R Stratotanker (62-3498) [ZZ] or/bk	USAF 909th ARS/18th Wg, Kadena AB, Japan	
23499	Boeing KC-135R Stratotanker (62-3499)	USAF 92nd ARW, Fairchild AFB, WA	
23500	Boeing KC-135R Stratotanker (62-3500) bl	USAF 133rd ARS/157th ARW, Pease ANGB, NH ANG	
23502	Boeing KC-135R Stratotanker (62-3502) y/bl	USAF 91st ARS/6th AMW, MacDill AFB, FL	
23503	Boeing KC-135R Stratotanker (62-3503) bl/y	USAF 465th ARS/507th ARW AFRC, Tinker AFB, OK	
23505	Boeing KC-135R Stratotanker (62-3505) y/bl	USAF 91st ARS/6th AMW, MacDill AFB, FL	
23506	Boeing KC-135R Stratotanker (62-3506) bl	USAF 133rd ARS/157th ARW, Pease ANGB, NH ANG	
23507	Boeing KC-135R Stratotanker (62-3507) [ZZ] or/bk	USAF 909th ARS/18th Wg, Kadena AB, Japan	
23508	Boeing KC-135R Stratotanker (62-3508) r $	USAF 141st ARS/108th ARW, McGuire AFB, NJ ANG	
23509	Boeing KC-135R Stratotanker (62-3509) gn/y	USAF 77th ARS/916th ARW AFRC, Seymour Johnson AFB, NC	
23510	Boeing KC-135R Stratotanker (62-3510) r/w	USAF 74th ARS/434th ARW AFRC, Grissom AFB, IN	
23511	Boeing KC-135R Stratotanker (62-3511) r/w	USAF 166th ARS/121st ARW, Rickenbacker ANGB, OH ANG	
23512	Boeing KC-135R Stratotanker (62-3512) w/bl	USAF 126th ARS/128th ARW, Mitchell Field, WI ANG	
23513	Boeing KC-135R Stratotanker (62-3513) w/gn	USAF 132nd ARS/101st ARW, Bangor, MN ANG	
23514	Boeing KC-135R Stratotanker (62-3514) r	USAF 141st ARS/108th ARW, McGuire AFB, NJ ANG	
23515	Boeing KC-135R Stratotanker (62-3515) bl	USAF 133rd ARS/157th ARW, Pease ANGB, NH ANG	
23516	Boeing KC-135R Stratotanker (62-3516) $	USAF 197th ARS/161st ARW, Phoenix, AZ ANG	
23517	Boeing KC-135R Stratotanker (62-3517) y/bl	USAF 91st ARS/6th AMW, MacDill AFB, FL	
23518	Boeing KC-135R Stratotanker (62-3518) bl	USAF 72nd ARS/434th ARW AFRC, Grissom AFB, IN	
23519	Boeing KC-135R Stratotanker (62-3519)	USAF 22nd ARW, McConnell AFB, KS	
23521	Boeing KC-135R Stratotanker (62-3521) bl	USAF 72nd ARS/434th ARW AFRC, Grissom AFB, IN	
23523	Boeing KC-135R Stratotanker (62-3523)	USAF 22nd ARW, McConnell AFB, KS	
23524	Boeing KC-135R Stratotanker (62-3524) [AK] bl/y	USAF 168th ARS/168th ARW, Eielson AFB, AK ANG	
23526	Boeing KC-135R Stratotanker (62-3526) r/w	USAF 173rd ARS/155th ARW, Lincoln, NE ANG	
23528	Boeing KC-135R Stratotanker (62-3528) gn/y	USAF 77th ARS/916th ARW AFRC, Seymour Johnson AFB, NC	
23529	Boeing KC-135R Stratotanker (62-3529)	USAF 314th ARS/940th ARW, Beale AFB, CA	
23530	Boeing KC-135R Stratotanker (62-3530) bl	USAF 72nd ARS/434th ARW AFRC, Grissom AFB, IN	
23531	Boeing KC-135R Stratotanker (62-3531) r/w	USAF 166th ARS/121st ARW, Rickenbacker ANGB, OH ANG	
23533	Boeing KC-135R Stratotanker (62-3533)	USAF 328th ARS/914th ARW AFRC, Niagara Falls NY	
23534	Boeing KC-135R Stratotanker (62-3534)	USAF 22nd ARW, McConnell AFB, KS	
23537	Boeing KC-135R Stratotanker (62-3537) bl/y	USAF 465th ARS/507th ARW AFRC, Tinker AFB, OK	

Notes	Serial	Type (code/other identity)	Owner/operator, location or fate
	23538	Boeing KC-135R Stratotanker (62-3538) *y/bl*	USAF 91st ARS/6th AMW, MacDill AFB, FL
	23540	Boeing KC-135R Stratotanker (62-3540) *y/r*	USAF 54th ARS/97th AMW, Altus AFB, OK
	23541	Boeing KC-135R Stratotanker (62-3541)	USAF 92nd ARW, Fairchild AFB, WA
	23542	Boeing KC-135R Stratotanker (62-3542) *gn/y*	USAF 77th ARS/916th ARW AFRC, Seymour Johnson AFB, NC
	23543	Boeing KC-135R Stratotanker (62-3543) *y/bk*	USAF 756th ARS/459th ARW AFRC, Andrews AFB, MD
	23544	Boeing KC-135R Stratotanker (62-3544) *r*	USAF 141st ARS/108th ARW, McGuire AFB, NJ ANG
	23545	Boeing KC-135R Stratotanker (62-3545)	USAF 22nd ARW, McConnell AFB, KS
	23547	Boeing KC-135R Stratotanker (62-3547) *bl/y*	USAF 117th ARS/190th ARW, Forbes Field, KS ANG
	23549	Boeing KC-135R Stratotanker (62-3549) *y/r*	USAF 54th ARS/97th AMW, Altus AFB, OK
	23550	Boeing KC-135R Stratotanker (62-3550)	USAF 197th ARS/161st ARW, Phoenix, AZ ANG
	23551	Boeing KC-135R Stratotanker (62-3551)	USAF 92nd ARW, Fairchild AFB, WA
	23552	Boeing KC-135R Stratotanker (62-3552) [ZZ] *or/bk*	USAF 909th ARS/18th Wg, Kadena AB, Japan
	23553	Boeing KC-135R Stratotanker (62-3553) [ZZ] *or/bk*	USAF 909th ARS/18th Wg, Kadena AB, Japan
	23554	Boeing KC-135R Stratotanker (62-3554)	USAF 22nd ARW, McConnell AFB, KS
	23556	Boeing KC-135R Stratotanker (62-3556) *y/bk*	USAF 756th ARS/459th ARW AFRC, Andrews AFB, MD
	23557	Boeing KC-135R Stratotanker (62-3557)	USAF 328th ARS/914th ARW AFRC, Niagara Falls NY
	23558	Boeing KC-135R Stratotanker (62-3558) *or/y*	USAF 336th ARS/452nd AMW AFRC, March ARB, CA
	23559	Boeing KC-135R Stratotanker (62-3559) [D] *r/w/bl*	USAF 351st ARS/100th ARW, RAF Mildenhall, UK
	23561	Boeing KC-135R Stratotanker (62-3561) [ZZ] *or/bk*	USAF 909th ARS/18th Wg, Kadena AB, Japan
	23562	Boeing KC-135R Stratotanker (62-3562) [ZZ] *or/bk*	USAF 909th ARS/18th Wg, Kadena AB, Japan
	23564	Boeing KC-135R Stratotanker (62-3564)	USAF 22nd ARW, McConnell AFB, KS
	23565	Boeing KC-135R Stratotanker (62-3565)	USAF 92nd ARW, Fairchild AFB, WA
	23566	Boeing KC-135R Stratotanker (62-3566) *y/bk*	USAF 174th ARS/185th ARW, Sioux City, IA ANG
	23568	Boeing KC-135R Stratotanker (62-3568)	USAF 22nd ARW, McConnell AFB, KS
	23569	Boeing KC-135R Stratotanker (62-3569)	USAF 22nd ARW, McConnell AFB, KS
	23571	Boeing KC-135R Stratotanker (62-3571) [AK] *bl/y*	USAF 168th ARS/168th ARW, Eielson AFB, AK ANG
	23572	Boeing KC-135R Stratotanker (62-3572) *bl/y*	USAF 117th ARS/190th ARW, Forbes Field, KS ANG
	23573	Boeing KC-135R Stratotanker (62-3573) *y/bl*	USAF 91st ARS/6th AMW, MacDill AFB, FL
	23575	Boeing KC-135R Stratotanker (62-3575)	USAF 22nd ARW, McConnell AFB, KS
	23576	Boeing KC-135R Stratotanker (62-3576) *bl*	USAF 133rd ARS/157th ARW, Pease ANGB, NH ANG
	23577	Boeing KC-135R Stratotanker (62-3577) *gn/y*	USAF 77th ARS/916th ARW AFRC, Seymour Johnson AFB, NC
	23578	Boeing KC-135R Stratotanker (62-3578) *r*	USAF 141st ARS/108th ARW, McGuire AFB, NJ ANG
	23580	Boeing KC-135R Stratotanker (62-3580) *gn/y*	USAF 77th ARS/916th ARW AFRC, Seymour Johnson AFB, NC
	23582	Boeing WC-135C Constant Phoenix (62-3582) [OF] *bk*	USAF 45th RS/55th Wg, Offutt AFB, NE
	24125	Boeing RC-135W Rivet Joint (62-4125) *gn*	USAF 38th RS/55th Wg, Offutt AFB, NE
	24126	Boeing RC-135W Rivet Joint (62-4126) *gn*	USAF 38th RS/55th Wg, Offutt AFB, NE
	24127	Boeing TC-135W (62-4127) *gn*	USAF 38th RS/55th Wg, Offutt AFB, NE
	24128	Boeing RC-135S Cobra Ball (62-4128) [OF] *bk*	USAF 45th RS/55th Wg, Offutt AFB, NE
	24129	Boeing TC-135W (62-4129) *gn*	USAF 38th RS/55th Wg, Offutt AFB, NE
	24130	Boeing RC-135W Rivet Joint (62-4130) *gn*	USAF 38th RS/55th Wg, Offutt AFB, NE
	24131	Boeing RC-135W Rivet Joint (62-4131) [OF] *bl*	USAF 343rd RS/55th Wg, Offutt AFB, NE
	24132	Boeing RC-135W Rivet Joint (62-4132) *gn*	USAF 38th RS/55th Wg, Offutt AFB, NE
	24133	Boeing TC-135W (62-4133) *gn*	USAF 38th RS/55th Wg, Offutt AFB, NE
	24134	Boeing RC-135W Rivet Joint (62-4134) *bl*	USAF 343rd RS/55th Wg, Offutt AFB, NE
	24135	Boeing RC-135W Rivet Joint (62-4135) *gn*	USAF 38th RS/55th Wg, Offutt AFB, NE
	24138	Boeing RC-135W Rivet Joint (62-4138) *bl*	USAF 343rd RS/55th Wg, Offutt AFB, NE
	24139	Boeing RC-135W Rivet Joint (62-4139) *gn*	USAF 38th RS/55th Wg, Offutt AFB, NE
	37976	Boeing KC-135R Stratotanker (63-7976) *y/r*	USAF 54th ARS/97th AMW, Altus AFB, OK
	37977	Boeing KC-135R Stratotanker (63-7977) [ZZ] *or/bk*	USAF 909th ARS/18th Wg, Kadena AB, Japan

Serial	Type (code/other identity)	Owner/operator, location or fate	Notes
37978	Boeing KC-135R Stratotanker (63-7978)	USAF 22nd ARW, McConnell AFB, KS	
37979	Boeing KC-135R Stratotanker (63-7979) y/bl	USAF 91st ARS/6th AMW, MacDill AFB, FL	
37980	Boeing KC-135R Stratotanker (63-7980) [ED]	USAF 418th FLTS/412th TW, Edwards AFB, CA	
37981	Boeing KC-135R Stratotanker (63-7981) w/bl	USAF 108th ARS/126th ARW, Scott AFB, IL ANG	
37982	Boeing KC-135R Stratotanker (63-7982)	USAF 92nd ARW, Fairchild AFB, WA	
37984	Boeing KC-135R Stratotanker (63-7984) w/r	USAF 106th ARS/117th ARW, Birmingham, AL ANG	
37985	Boeing KC-135R Stratotanker (63-7985) bl/y	USAF 465th ARS/507th ARW AFRC, Tinker AFB, OK	
37987	Boeing KC-135R Stratotanker (63-7987) [ZZ] or/bk	USAF 909th ARS/18th Wg, Kadena AB, Japan	
37988	Boeing KC-135R Stratotanker (63-7988) r/w	USAF 173rd ARS/155th ARW, Lincoln, NE ANG	
37991	Boeing KC-135R Stratotanker (63-7991) r/w	USAF 173rd ARS/155th ARW, Lincoln, NE ANG	
37992	Boeing KC-135R Stratotanker (63-7992)	USAF 153rd ARS/186th AW, Meridian, MS ANG	
37993	Boeing KC-135R Stratotanker (63-7993) m	USAF 166th ARS/121st ARW, Rickenbacker ANGB, OH ANG	
37995	Boeing KC-135R Stratotanker (63-7995)	USAF 22nd ARW, McConnell AFB, KS	
37996	Boeing KC-135R Stratotanker (63-7996) bl	USAF 72nd ARS/434th ARW AFRC, Grissom AFB, IN	
37997	Boeing KC-135R Stratotanker (63-7997) [ZZ] or/bk	USAF 909th ARS/18th Wg, Kadena AB, Japan	
37999	Boeing KC-135R Stratotanker (63-7999) [D] r/w/bl	USAF 351st ARS/100th ARW, RAF Mildenhall, UK	
38000	Boeing KC-135R Stratotanker (63-8000)	USAF 92nd ARW, Fairchild AFB, WA	
38002	Boeing KC-135R Stratotanker (63-8002)	USAF 22nd ARW, McConnell AFB, KS	
38003	Boeing KC-135R Stratotanker (63-8003) r	USAF 141st ARS/108th ARW, McGuire AFB, NJ ANG	
38004	Boeing KC-135R Stratotanker (63-8004) bl/y	USAF 117th ARS/190th ARW, Forbes Field, KS ANG	
38006	Boeing KC-135R Stratotanker (63-8006) y/r	USAF 54th ARS/97th AMW, Altus AFB, OK	
38007	Boeing KC-135R Stratotanker (63-8007) w/r	USAF 106th ARS/117th ARW, Birmingham, AL ANG	
38008	Boeing KC-135R Stratotanker (63-8008)	USAF 92nd ARW, Fairchild AFB, WA	
38011	Boeing KC-135R Stratotanker (63-8011) y/bl	USAF 91st ARS/6th AMW, MacDill AFB, FL	
38012	Boeing KC-135R Stratotanker (63-8012) bl/y	USAF 465th ARS/507th ARW AFRC, Tinker AFB, OK	
38013	Boeing KC-135R Stratotanker (63-8013) r/w	USAF 166th ARS/121st ARW, Rickenbacker ANGB, OH ANG	
38014	Boeing KC-135R Stratotanker (63-8014) gn/y	USAF 77th ARS/916th ARW AFRC, Seymour Johnson AFB, NC	
38015	Boeing KC-135R Stratotanker (63-8015) [AK] bl/y	USAF 168th ARS/168th ARW, Eielson AFB, AK ANG	
38017	Boeing KC-135R Stratotanker (63-8017) y/bl	USAF 91st ARS/6th AMW, MacDill AFB, FL	
38018	Boeing KC-135R Stratotanker (63-8018) r/w	USAF 173rd ARS/155th ARW, Lincoln, NE ANG	
38019	Boeing KC-135R Stratotanker (63-8019)	USAF 22nd ARW, McConnell AFB, KS	
38020	Boeing KC-135R Stratotanker (63-8020) [ZZ] or/bk [909 ARS]	USAF 909th ARS/18th Wg, Kadena AB, Japan	
38021	Boeing KC-135R Stratotanker (63-8021)	USAF 92nd ARW, Fairchild AFB, WA	
38022	Boeing KC-135R Stratotanker (63-8022) [ZZ] or/bk	USAF 909th ARS/18th Wg, Kadena AB, Japan	
38023	Boeing KC-135R Stratotanker (63-8023) w/bl	USAF 126th ARS/128th ARW, Mitchell Field, WI ANG	
38024	Boeing KC-135R Stratotanker (63-8024) or/y	USAF 336th ARS/452nd AMW AFRC, March ARB, CA	
38025	Boeing KC-135R Stratotanker (63-8025)	USAF 22nd ARW, McConnell AFB, KS	
38026	Boeing KC-135R Stratotanker (63-8026) bl/bk	USAF 191st ARS/151st ARW, Salt Lake City, UT ANG	
38027	Boeing KC-135R Stratotanker (63-8027)	USAF 22nd ARW, McConnell AFB, KS	
38028	Boeing KC-135R Stratotanker (63-8028) [AK] bl/y	USAF 168th ARS/168th ARW, Eielson AFB, AK ANG	
38029	Boeing KC-135R Stratotanker (63-8029) r	USAF 141st ARS/108th ARW, McGuire AFB, NJ ANG	
38030	Boeing KC-135R Stratotanker (63-8030) [HH] y/bk	USAF 203rd ARS/15th Wg, Hickam AFB, HI ANG	
38031	Boeing KC-135R Stratotanker (63-8031)	USAF 22nd ARW, McConnell AFB, KS	
38032	Boeing KC-135R Stratotanker (63-8032) bl	USAF 72nd ARS/434th ARW AFRC, Grissom AFB, IN	

Notes	Serial	Type (code/other identity)	Owner/operator, location or fate
	38033	Boeing KC-135R Stratotanker (63-8033) y/bl	USAF 91st ARS/6th AMW, MacDill AFB, FL
	38034	Boeing KC-135R Stratotanker (63-8034) [ZZ] or/bk	USAF 909th ARS/18th Wg, Kadena AB, Japan
	38035	Boeing KC-135R Stratotanker (63-8035) w/r	USAF 106th ARS/117th ARW, Birmingham, AL ANG
	38036	Boeing KC-135R Stratotanker (63-8036)	USAF 197th ARS/161st ARW, Phoenix, AZ ANG
	38038	Boeing KC-135R Stratotanker (63-8038) [HH] y/bk	USAF 203rd ARS/15th Wg, Hickam AFB, HI ANG
	38039	Boeing KC-135R Stratotanker (63-8039) bl/y	USAF 465th ARS/507th ARW AFRC, Tinker AFB, OK
	38040	Boeing KC-135R Stratotanker (63-8040) r	USAF 141st ARS/108th ARW, McGuire AFB, NJ ANG
	38041	Boeing KC-135R Stratotanker (63-8041) bl	USAF 72nd ARS/434th ARW AFRC, Grissom AFB, IN
	38043	Boeing KC-135R Stratotanker (63-8043) [AK] bl/y	USAF 168th ARS/168th ARW, Eielson AFB, AK ANG
	38044	Boeing KC-135R Stratotanker (63-8044)	USAF 328th ARS/914th ARW AFRC, Niagara Falls NY
	38045	Boeing KC-135R Stratotanker (63-8045) y/bl	USAF 91st ARS/6th AMW, MacDill AFB, FL
	38871	Boeing KC-135R Stratotanker (63-8871) [D] r/w/bl	USAF 351st ARS/100th ARW, RAF Mildenhall, UK
	38872	Boeing KC-135R Stratotanker (63-8872) w/gn	USAF 132nd ARS/101st ARW, Bangor, MN ANG
	38873	Boeing KC-135R Stratotanker (63-8873) w/gn	USAF 132nd ARS/101st ARW, Bangor, MN ANG
	38874	Boeing KC-135R Stratotanker (63-8874) y/bl	USAF 91st ARS/6th AMW, MacDill AFB, FL
	38875	Boeing KC-135R Stratotanker (63-8875) bl/y	USAF 117th ARS/190th ARW, Forbes Field, KS ANG
	38876	Boeing KC-135R Stratotanker (63-8876) [AK] bl/y	USAF 168th ARS/168th ARW, Eielson AFB, AK ANG
	38878	Boeing KC-135R Stratotanker (63-8878) y/r	USAF 54th ARS/97th AMW, Altus AFB, OK
	38879	Boeing KC-135R Stratotanker (63-8879)	USAF 314th ARS/940th ARW, Beale AFB, CA
	38880	Boeing KC-135R Stratotanker (63-8880) [HH] y/bk	USAF 203rd ARS/15th Wg, Hickam AFB, HI ANG
	38881	Boeing KC-135R Stratotanker (63-8881) bl/bk	USAF 191st ARS/151st ARW, Salt Lake City, UT ANG
	38883	Boeing KC-135R Stratotanker (63-8883)	USAF 22nd ARW, McConnell AFB, KS
	38884	Boeing KC-135R Stratotanker (63-8884)	USAF
	38885	Boeing KC-135R Stratotanker (63-8885)	USAF 92nd ARW, Fairchild AFB, WA
	38887	Boeing KC-135R Stratotanker (63-8887)	USAF 22nd ARW, McConnell AFB, KS
	38888	Boeing KC-135R Stratotanker (63-8888) y/r	USAF 54th ARS/97th AMW, Altus AFB, OK
	39792	Boeing RC-135V Rivet Joint (63-9792) gn $	USAF 38th RS/55th Wg, Offutt AFB, NE
	71419	Boeing KC-135R Stratotanker (57-1419) bl	USAF 133rd ARS/157th ARW, Pease ANGB, NH ANG
	71427	Boeing KC-135R Stratotanker (57-1427) bl/y	USAF 117th ARS/190th ARW, Forbes Field, KS ANG
	71428	Boeing KC-135R Stratotanker (57-1428) w/or	USAF 151st ARS/134th ARW, Knoxville, TN ANG
	71430	Boeing KC-135R Stratotanker (57-1430) bl	USAF 133rd ARS/157th ARW, Pease ANGB, NH ANG
	71432	Boeing KC-135R Stratotanker (57-1432) bl/bk	USAF 191st ARS/151st ARW, Salt Lake City, UT ANG
	71435	Boeing KC-135R Stratotanker (57-1435) bl/bk	USAF 191st ARS/151st ARW, Salt Lake City, UT ANG
	71436	Boeing KC-135R Stratotanker (57-1436) w/or	USAF 151st ARS/134th ARW, Knoxville, TN ANG
	71437	Boeing KC-135R Stratotanker (57-1437) gn/y	USAF 77th ARS/916th ARW AFRC, Seymour Johnson AFB, NC
	71438	Boeing KC-135R Stratotanker (57-1438) or/y	USAF 336th ARS/452nd AMW AFRC, March ARB, CA
	71439	Boeing KC-135R Stratotanker (57-1439) y/bl	USAF 91st ARS/6th AMW, MacDill AFB, FL
	71440	Boeing KC-135R Stratotanker (57-1440)	USAF 92nd ARW, Fairchild AFB, WA
	71441	Boeing KC-135R Stratotanker (57-1441) y/bk	USAF 174th ARS/185th ARW, Sioux City, IA ANG
	71451	Boeing KC-135R Stratotanker (57-1451) w/or	USAF 151st ARS/134th ARW, Knoxville, TN ANG
	71453	Boeing KC-135R Stratotanker (57-1453) w/r	USAF 106th ARS/117th ARW, Birmingham, AL ANG
	71454	Boeing KC-135R Stratotanker (57-1454) [ZZ] or/bk	USAF 909th ARS/18th Wg, Kadena AB, Japan
	71456	Boeing KC-135R Stratotanker (57-1456) gn/y	USAF 77th ARS/916th ARW AFRC, Seymour Johnson AFB, NC

Serial	Type (code/other identity)	Owner/operator, location or fate	Notes
71459	Boeing KC-135R Stratotanker (57-1459) *or/y*	USAF 336th ARS/452nd AMW AFRC, March ARB, CA	
71461	Boeing KC-135R Stratotanker (57-1461) *r/w*	USAF 173rd ARS/155th ARW, Lincoln, NE ANG	
71462	Boeing KC-135R Stratotanker (57-1462)	USAF 153rd ARS/186th AW, Meridian, MS ANG	
71468	Boeing KC-135R Stratotanker (57-1468) *or/y*	USAF 336th ARS/452nd AMW AFRC, March ARB, CA	
71469	Boeing KC-135R Stratotanker (57-1469) $	USAF 197th ARS/161st ARW, Phoenix, AZ ANG	
71472	Boeing KC-135R Stratotanker (57-1472) *bl*	USAF 72nd ARS/434th ARW AFRC, Grissom AFB, IN	
71473	Boeing KC-135R Stratotanker (57-1473) *w/r*	USAF 106th ARS/117th ARW, Birmingham, AL ANG	
71474	Boeing KC-135R Stratotanker (57-1474)	USAF 22nd ARW, McConnell AFB, KS	
71479	Boeing KC-135R Stratotanker (57-1479) *y/bk*	USAF 756th ARS/459th ARW AFRC, Andrews AFB, MD	
71483	Boeing KC-135R Stratotanker (57-1483)	USAF 92nd ARW, Fairchild AFB, WA	
71486	Boeing KC-135R Stratotanker (57-1486)	USAF 153rd ARS/186th AW, Meridian, MS ANG	
71487	Boeing KC-135R Stratotanker (57-1487) *y/bk*	USAF 756th ARS/459th ARW AFRC, Andrews AFB, MD	
71488	Boeing KC-135R Stratotanker (57-1488) *y/r*	USAF 54th ARS/97th AMW, Altus AFB, OK	
71493	Boeing KC-135R Stratotanker (57-1493) [D] *r/w/bl*	USAF 351st ARS/100th ARW, RAF Mildenhall, UK	
71499	Boeing KC-135R Stratotanker (57-1499) *bl/bk*	USAF 191st ARS/151st ARW, Salt Lake City, UT ANG	
71502	Boeing KC-135R Stratotanker (57-1502) [ZZ] *or/bk*	USAF 909th ARS/18th Wg, Kadena AB, Japan	
71506	Boeing KC-135R Stratotanker (57-1506) *y/r*	USAF 54th ARS/97th AMW, Altus AFB, OK	
71508	Boeing KC-135R Stratotanker (57-1508) [HH] *y/bk*	USAF 203rd ARS/15th Wg, Hickam AFB, HI ANG	
71512	Boeing KC-135R Stratotanker (57-1512) *y/bk*	USAF 756th ARS/459th ARW AFRC, Andrews AFB, MD	
71514	Boeing KC-135R Stratotanker (57-1514) *w/bl*	USAF 126th ARS/128th ARW, Mitchell Field, WI ANG	
72597	Boeing KC-135R Stratotanker (57-2597) *w/or*	USAF 151st ARS/134th ARW, Knoxville, TN ANG	
72598	Boeing KC-135R Stratotanker (57-2598) *or/y*	USAF 336th ARS/452nd AMW AFRC, March ARB, CA	
72599	Boeing KC-135R Stratotanker (57-2599) *gn/y*	USAF 77th ARS/916th ARW AFRC, Seymour Johnson AFB, NC	
72603	Boeing KC-135R Stratotanker (57-2603) *or/y*	USAF 336th ARS/452nd AMW AFRC, March ARB, CA	
72605	Boeing KC-135R Stratotanker (57-2605) [D] *r/w/bl*	USAF 351st ARS/100th ARW, RAF Mildenhall, UK	
72606	Boeing KC-135R Stratotanker (57-2606) *bl/bk*	USAF 174th ARS/185th ARW, Sioux City, IA ANG	
80001	Boeing KC-135R Stratotanker (58-0001) [D] *r/w/bl*	USAF 351st ARS/100th ARW, RAF Mildenhall, UK	
80004	Boeing KC-135R Stratotanker (58-0004) *w/r*	USAF 106th ARS/117th ARW, Birmingham, AL ANG	
80009	Boeing KC-135R Stratotanker (58-0009) *w/bl*	USAF 126th ARS/128th ARW, Mitchell Field, WI ANG	
80010	Boeing KC-135R Stratotanker (58-0010) *r*	USAF 141st ARS/108th ARW, McGuire AFB, NJ ANG	
80011	Boeing KC-135R(RT) Stratotanker (58-0011)	USAF 22nd ARW, McConnell AFB, KS	
80015	Boeing KC-135R Stratotanker (58-0015) *bl/y*	USAF 465th ARS/507th ARW AFRC, Tinker AFB, OK	
80016	Boeing KC-135R Stratotanker (58-0016)	USAF 92nd ARW, Fairchild AFB, WA	
80018	Boeing KC-135R(RT) Stratotanker (58-0018)	USAF 22nd ARW, McConnell AFB, KS	
80021	Boeing KC-135R Stratotanker (58-0021) *w/gn*	USAF 132nd ARS/101st ARW, Bangor, MN ANG	
80023	Boeing KC-135R Stratotanker (58-0023) *bl*	USAF 133rd ARS/157th ARW, Pease ANGB, NH ANG	
80027	Boeing KC-135R Stratotanker (58-0027) *bl/bk*	USAF 191st ARS/151st ARW, Salt Lake City, UT ANG	
80030	Boeing KC-135R Stratotanker (58-0030) *w/gn*	USAF 132nd ARS/101st ARW, Bangor, MN ANG	
80034	Boeing KC-135R Stratotanker (58-0034) *y/bl*	USAF 91st ARS/6th AMW, MacDill AFB, FL	
80035	Boeing KC-135R Stratotanker (58-0035)	USAF 92nd ARW, Fairchild AFB, WA	
80036	Boeing KC-135R Stratotanker (58-0036) *y/r*	USAF 54th ARS/97th AMW, Altus AFB, OK	
80038	Boeing KC-135R Stratotanker (58-0038) *gn/y*	USAF 77th ARS/916th ARW AFRC, Seymour Johnson AFB, NC	
80042	Boeing KC-135T Stratotanker (58-0042)	USAF 22nd ARW, McConnell AFB, KS	

Notes	Serial	Type (code/other identity)	Owner/operator, location or fate
	80045	Boeing KC-135T Stratotanker (58-0045)	USAF 171st ARW, Greater Pittsburgh, PA ANG
	80046	Boeing KC-135T Stratotanker (58-0046)	USAF 22nd ARW, McConnell AFB, KS
	80047	Boeing KC-135T Stratotanker (58-0047)	USAF 22nd ARW, McConnell AFB, KS
	80049	Boeing KC-135T Stratotanker (58-0049) bk/y	USAF 171st ARS/127th Wg, Selfridge ANGB, MI ANG
	80050	Boeing KC-135T Stratotanker (58-0050)	USAF 92nd ARW, Fairchild AFB, WA
	80051	Boeing KC-135R Stratotanker (58-0051) bl/y	USAF 465th ARS/507th ARW AFRC, Tinker AFB, OK
	80052	Boeing KC-135R Stratotanker (58-0052) or/y	USAF 336th ARS/452nd AMW AFRC, March ARB, CA
	80054	Boeing KC-135T Stratotanker (58-0054) y/bk	USAF 171st ARW, Greater Pittsburgh, PA ANG
	80055	Boeing KC-135R Stratotanker (58-0055) y/bl	USAF 91st ARS/6th AMW, MacDill AFB, FL
	80056	Boeing KC-135R Stratotanker (58-0056) [HH] y/bk	USAF 203rd ARS/15th Wg, Hickam AFB, HI ANG
	80057	Boeing KC-135R Stratotanker (58-0057) y/bk	USAF 174th ARS/185th ARW, Sioux City, IA ANG
	80058	Boeing KC-135R Stratotanker (58-0058) bl/y	USAF 465th ARS/507th ARW AFRC, Tinker AFB, OK
	80059	Boeing KC-135R Stratotanker (58-0059) bl/y	USAF 117th ARS/190th ARW, Forbes Field, KS ANG
	80060	Boeing KC-135T Stratotanker (58-0060) y/bk	USAF 171st ARW, Greater Pittsburgh, PA ANG
	80061	Boeing KC-135T Stratotanker (58-0061)	USAF 22nd ARW, McConnell AFB, KS
	80062	Boeing KC-135T Stratotanker (58-0062) bk/y	USAF 171st ARS/127th Wg, Selfridge ANGB, MI ANG
	80063	Boeing KC-135R Stratotanker (58-0063) bl	USAF 133rd ARS/157th ARW, Pease ANGB, NH ANG
	80065	Boeing KC-135T Stratotanker (58-0065)	USAF 22nd ARW, McConnell AFB, KS
	80066	Boeing KC-135R Stratotanker (58-0066) bl	USAF 133rd ARS/157th ARW, Pease ANGB, NH ANG
	80067	Boeing KC-135R Stratotanker (58-0067) y/bk	USAF 174th ARS/185th ARW, Sioux City, IA ANG
	80069	Boeing KC-135R Stratotanker (58-0069)	USAF
	80071	Boeing KC-135T Stratotanker (58-0071)	USAF 22nd ARW, McConnell AFB, KS
	80072	Boeing KC-135T Stratotanker (58-0072) y/bk	USAF 171st ARW, Greater Pittsburgh, PA ANG
	80073	Boeing KC-135R Stratotanker (58-0073) w/r	USAF 106th ARS/117th ARW, Birmingham, AL ANG
	80074	Boeing KC-135T Stratotanker (58-0074) y/bk	USAF 171st ARW, Greater Pittsburgh, PA ANG
	80075	Boeing KC-135R Stratotanker (58-0075) y/bk	USAF 756th ARS/459th ARW AFRC, Andrews AFB, MD
	80076	Boeing KC-135R Stratotanker (58-0076) r/w	USAF 74th ARS/434th ARW AFRC, Grissom AFB, IN
	80077	Boeing KC-135T Stratotanker (58-0077) y/bk	USAF 171st ARW, Greater Pittsburgh, PA ANG
	80079	Boeing KC-135R Stratotanker (58-0079)	USAF 153rd ARS/186th AW, Meridian, MS ANG
	80083	Boeing KC-135R Stratotanker (58-0083) r/w	USAF 166th ARS/121st ARW, Rickenbacker ANGB, OH ANG
	80084	Boeing KC-135T Stratotanker (58-0084) y/bk	USAF 171st ARW, Greater Pittsburgh, PA ANG
	80085	Boeing KC-135R Stratotanker (58-0085) or/y	USAF 336th ARS/452nd AMW AFRC, March ARB, CA
	80086	Boeing KC-135T Stratotanker (58-0086)	USAF 92nd ARW, Fairchild AFB, WA
	80088	Boeing KC-135T Stratotanker (58-0088) bk/y	USAF 171st ARS/127th Wg, Selfridge ANGB, MI ANG
	80089	Boeing KC-135R Stratotanker (58-0089) y/bl	USAF 91st ARS/6th AMW, MacDill AFB, FL
	80092	Boeing KC-135T Stratotanker (58-0092)	USAF 22nd ARW, McConnell AFB, KS
	80093	Boeing KC-135R Stratotanker (58-0093) [ZZ] or/bk	USAF 909th ARS/18th Wg, Kadena AB, Japan
	80094	Boeing KC-135T Stratotanker (58-0094) [D] r/w/bl	USAF 351st ARS/100th ARW, RAF Mildenhall, UK
	80095	Boeing KC-135T Stratotanker (58-0095)	USAF 92nd ARW, Fairchild AFB, WA
	80098	Boeing KC-135R Stratotanker (58-0098) w/gn	USAF 132nd ARS/101st ARW, Bangor, MN ANG
	80099	Boeing KC-135T Stratotanker (58-0099) y/bk	USAF 171st ARW, Greater Pittsburgh, PA ANG
	80100	Boeing KC-135R Stratotanker (58-0100) [D] r/w/bl	USAF 351st ARS/100th ARW, RAF Mildenhall, UK
	80102	Boeing KC-135R Stratotanker (58-0102) bl/y	USAF 465th ARS/507th ARW AFRC, Tinker AFB, OK
	80103	Boeing KC-135T Stratotanker (58-0103)	USAF 92nd ARW, Fairchild AFB, WA
	80104	Boeing KC-135R Stratotanker (58-0104) w/bl	USAF 108th ARS/126th ARW, Scott AFB, IL ANG
	80106	Boeing KC-135R Stratotanker (58-0106) w/r	USAF 106th ARS/117th ARW, Birmingham, AL ANG

Serial	Type (code/other identity)	Owner/operator, location or fate	Notes
80107	Boeing KC-135R Stratotanker (58-0107) w/gn	USAF 132nd ARS/101st ARW, Bangor, MN ANG	
80109	Boeing KC-135R Stratotanker (58-0109) y/bk	USAF 174th ARS/185th ARW, Sioux City, IA ANG	
80112	Boeing KC-135T Stratotanker (58-0112) y/bk	USAF 171st ARW, Greater Pittsburgh, PA ANG	
80113	Boeing KC-135R Stratotanker (58-0113) y/r	USAF 54th ARS/97th AMW, Altus AFB, OK	
80117	Boeing KC-135T Stratotanker (58-0117) y/bk	USAF 171st ARW, Greater Pittsburgh, PA ANG	
80118	Boeing KC-135R Stratotanker (58-0118) [D]	USAF	
80119	Boeing KC-135R Stratotanker (58-0119) w/or	USAF 151st ARS/134th ARW, Knoxville, TN ANG	
80120	Boeing KC-135R Stratotanker (58-0120)	USAF 153rd ARS/186th AW, Meridian, MS ANG	
80121	Boeing KC-135R Stratotanker (58-0121) bl/y	USAF 465th ARS/507th ARW AFRC, Tinker AFB, OK	
80122	Boeing KC-135R Stratotanker (58-0122) bl/y	USAF 117th ARS/190th ARW, Forbes Field, KS ANG	
80123	Boeing KC-135R Stratotanker (58-0123)	USAF 22nd ARW, McConnell AFB, KS	
80124	Boeing KC-135R(RT) Stratotanker (58-0124)	USAF 22nd ARW, McConnell AFB, KS	
80125	Boeing KC-135R Stratotanker (58-0125)	USAF 22nd ARW, McConnell AFB, KS	
80126	Boeing KC-135R(RT) Stratotanker (58-0126)	USAF 22nd ARW, McConnell AFB, KS	
80128	Boeing KC-135R Stratotanker (58-0128) [ZZ] or/bk	USAF 909th ARS/18th Wg, Kadena AB, Japan	
80129	Boeing KC-135T Stratotanker (58-0129) bk/y	USAF 171st ARS/127th Wg, Selfridge ANGB, MI ANG	
91444	Boeing KC-135R Stratotanker (59-1444) r/w	USAF 166th ARS/121st ARW, Rickenbacker ANGB, OH ANG	
91446	Boeing KC-135R Stratotanker (59-1446) w/gn	USAF 132nd ARS/101st ARW, Bangor, MN ANG	
91448	Boeing KC-135R Stratotanker (59-1448)	USAF 153rd ARS/186th AW, Meridian, MS ANG	
91450	Boeing KC-135R Stratotanker (59-1450)	USAF 197th ARS/161st ARW, Phoenix, AZ ANG	
91453	Boeing KC-135R Stratotanker (59-1453)	USAF 153rd ARS/186th AW, Meridian, MS ANG	
91455	Boeing KC-135R Stratotanker (59-1455) [HH] y/bk	USAF 203rd ARS/15th Wg, Hickam AFB, HI ANG	
91458	Boeing KC-135R Stratotanker (59-1458) r/w	USAF 166th ARS/121st ARW, Rickenbacker ANGB, OH ANG	
91459	Boeing KC-135R Stratotanker (59-1459)	USAF 22nd ARW, McConnell AFB, KS	
91460	Boeing KC-135T Stratotanker (59-1460) y/bk	USAF 171st ARW, Greater Pittsburgh, PA ANG	
91461	Boeing KC-135R Stratotanker (59-1461) w/bl	USAF 126th ARS/128th ARW, Mitchell Field, WI ANG	
91462	Boeing KC-135T Stratotanker (59-1462)	USAF 22nd ARW, McConnell AFB, KS	
91463	Boeing KC-135R Stratotanker (59-1463) r/w	USAF 173rd ARS/155th ARW, Lincoln, NE ANG	
91464	Boeing KC-135T Stratotanker (59-1464)	USAF 92nd ARW, Fairchild AFB, WA	
91466	Boeing KC-135R Stratotanker (59-1466) w/bl	USAF 108th ARS/126th ARW, Scott AFB, IL ANG	
91467	Boeing KC-135T Stratotanker (59-1467) y/bk	USAF 171st ARW, Greater Pittsburgh, PA ANG	
91468	Boeing KC-135T Stratotanker (59-1468) y/bk	USAF 171st ARW, Greater Pittsburgh, PA ANG	
91469	Boeing KC-135R Stratotanker (59-1469) y/bk	USAF 756th ARS/459th ARW AFRC, Andrews AFB, MD	
91470	Boeing KC-135T Stratotanker (59-1470)	USAF 92nd ARW, Fairchild AFB, WA	
91471	Boeing KC-135T Stratotanker (59-1471)	USAF	
91472	Boeing KC-135R Stratotanker (59-1472)	USAF 314th ARS/940th ARW, Beale AFB, CA	
91474	Boeing KC-135T Stratotanker (59-1474) bk/y	USAF 171st ARS/127th Wg, Selfridge ANGB, MI ANG	
91475	Boeing KC-135R Stratotanker (59-1475) [ZZ] or/bk	USAF 909th ARS/18th Wg, Kadena AB, Japan	
91476	Boeing KC-135R Stratotanker (59-1476)	USAF 92nd ARW, Fairchild AFB, WA	
91478	Boeing KC-135R Stratotanker (59-1478) w/or	USAF 151st ARS/134th ARW, Knoxville, TN ANG	
91480	Boeing KC-135T Stratotanker (59-1480) y/bl	USAF 91st ARS/6th AMW, MacDill AFB, FL	
91482	Boeing KC-135R Stratotanker (59-1482) or/y	USAF 336th ARS/452nd AMW AFRC, March ARB, CA	
91483	Boeing KC-135R Stratotanker (59-1483) r/w	USAF 166th ARS/121st ARW, Rickenbacker ANGB, OH ANG	
91486	Boeing KC-135R Stratotanker (59-1486)	USAF 92nd ARW, Fairchild AFB, WA	
91488	Boeing KC-135R Stratotanker (59-1488) w/gn	USAF 132nd ARS/101st ARW, Bangor, MN ANG	
91490	Boeing KC-135T Stratotanker (59-1490) y/bk	USAF 171st ARW, Greater Pittsburgh, PA ANG	
91492	Boeing KC-135R Stratotanker (59-1492)	USAF 22nd ARW, McConnell AFB, KS	
91495	Boeing KC-135R Stratotanker (59-1495) r/w	USAF 173rd ARS/155th ARW, Lincoln, NE ANG	
91498	Boeing KC-135R Stratotanker (59-1498) w/gn	USAF 132nd ARS/101st ARW, Bangor, MN ANG	
1499	Boeing KC-135R Stratotanker (59-1499) [HH] y/bk	USAF 203rd ARS/15th Wg, Hickam AFB, HI ANG	
1500	Boeing KC-135R Stratotanker (59-1500) w/bl	USAF 108th ARS/126th ARW, Scott AFB, IL ANG	
1501	Boeing KC-135R Stratotanker (59-1501) y/bl	USAF 91st ARS/6th AMW, MacDill AFB, FL	

Notes	Serial	Type (code/other identity)	Owner/operator, location or fate
	91502	Boeing KC-135R Stratotanker (59-1502)	USAF 22nd ARW, McConnell AFB, KS
	91504	Boeing KC-135T Stratotanker (59-1504) y/bk	USAF 171st ARW, Greater Pittsburgh, PA ANG
	91505	Boeing KC-135R Stratotanker (59-1505) w/or	USAF 151st ARS/134th ARW, Knoxville, TN ANG
	91506	Boeing KC-135R Stratotanker (59-1506) y/bk	USAF 174th ARS/185th ARW, Sioux City, IA ANG
	91507	Boeing KC-135R Stratotanker (59-1507) bl/y	USAF 117th ARS/190th ARW, Forbes Field, KS ANG
	91508	Boeing KC-135R Stratotanker (59-1508)	USAF 92nd ARW, Fairchild AFB, WA
	91509	Boeing KC-135R Stratotanker (59-1509) w/or	USAF 151st ARS/134th ARW, Knoxville, TN ANG
	91510	Boeing KC-135T Stratotanker (59-1510) y/bl	USAF 91st ARS/6th AMW, MacDill AFB, FL
	91511	Boeing KC-135R Stratotanker (59-1511) [D] r/w/bl	USAF 351st ARS/100th ARW, RAF Mildenhall, UK
	91512	Boeing KC-135T Stratotanker (59-1512) bk/y	USAF 171st ARS/127th Wg, Selfridge ANGB, MI ANG
	91513	Boeing KC-135T Stratotanker (59-1513) [D] r/w/bl	USAF 351st ARS/100th ARW, RAF Mildenhall, UK
	91515	Boeing KC-135R Stratotanker (59-1515)	USAF 92nd ARW, Fairchild AFB, WA
	91516	Boeing KC-135R Stratotanker (59-1516) w/bl	USAF 126th ARS/128th ARW, Mitchell Field, WI ANG
	91517	Boeing KC-135R Stratotanker (59-1517) w/or	USAF 151st ARS/134th ARW, Knoxville, TN ANG
	91519	Boeing KC-135R Stratotanker (59-1519) y/bk	USAF 174th ARS/185th ARW, Sioux City, IA ANG
	91520	Boeing KC-135T Stratotanker (59-1520)	USAF 92nd ARW, Fairchild AFB, WA
	91521	Boeing KC-135R Stratotanker (59-1521) [AK] bl/y	USAF 168th ARS/168th ARW, Eielson AFB, AK ANG
	91522	Boeing KC-135R Stratotanker (59-1522) w/bl	USAF 108th ARS/126th ARW, Scott AFB, IL ANG
	91523	Boeing KC-135T Stratotanker (59-1523) y/bk	USAF 171st ARW, Greater Pittsburgh, PA ANG

PZL-Mielec C-145A Combat Coyote

	Serial	Type (code/other identity)	Owner/operator, location or fate
	20331	PZL-Mielec C-145A Combat Coyote (N331MF/12-0331)	USAF 6th SOS/919th SOW, Duke Field, FL
	20335	PZL-Mielec C-145A Combat Coyote (N335RH/12-0335)	USAF 6th SOS/919th SOW, Duke Field, FL
	20336	PZL-Mielec C-145A Combat Coyote (N336MJ/12-0336)	USAF 6th SOS/919th SOW, Duke Field, FL
	20337	PZL-Mielec C-145A Combat Coyote (N337GU/12-0337)	USAF 6th SOS/919th SOW, Duke Field, FL
	20338	PZL-Mielec C-145A Combat Coyote (N338CH/12-0338)	USAF 6th SOS/919th SOW, Duke Field, FL

Dornier C-146A Wolfhound

	Serial	Type (code/other identity)	Owner/operator, location or fate
	03026	Dornier C-146A Wolfhound (N929EF/10-3026)	USAF 524th SOS/27th SOW, Cannon AFB, NM
	03068	Dornier C-146A Wolfhound (N565EF/10-3068)	USAF 524th SOS/27th SOW, Cannon AFB, NM
	03077	Dornier C-146A Wolfhound (N577EF/10-3077)	USAF 524th SOS/27th SOW, Cannon AFB, NM
	13016	Dornier C-146A Wolfhound (N941EF/11-3016)	USAF 524th SOS/27th SOW, Cannon AFB, NM
	13031	Dornier C-146A Wolfhound (N975EF/11-3031)	USAF 524th SOS/27th SOW, Cannon AFB, NM
	13075	Dornier C-146A Wolfhound (N953EF/11-3075)	USAF 524th SOS/27th SOW, Cannon AFB, NM
	13097	Dornier C-146A Wolfhound (N307EF/11-3097)	USAF 524th SOS/27th SOW, Cannon AFB, NM
	13104	Dornier C-146A Wolfhound (N907EF/11-3104)	USAF 524th SOS/27th SOW, Cannon AFB, NM
	23040	Dornier C-146A Wolfhound (N340LS/12-3040)	USAF 859th SOS/919th SOW, Duke Field, FL
	23047	Dornier C-146A Wolfhound (N347EF/12-3047)	USAF 524th SOS/27th SOW, Cannon AFB, NM
	23050	Dornier C-146A Wolfhound (N355EF/12-3050)	USAF 524th SOS/27th SOW, Cannon AFB, NM
	23060	Dornier C-146A Wolfhound (N360EF/12-3060)	USAF 524th SOS/27th SOW, Cannon AFB, NM
	23085	Dornier C-146A Wolfhound (N385EF/12-3085)	USAF 49th SOS/919th SOW, Duke Field, FL
	53058	Dornier C-146A Wolfhound (N570EF/95-3058)	USAF 524th SOS/27th SOW, Cannon AFB, NM
	53086	Dornier C-146A Wolfhound (N328ST/15-3086)	USAF 859th SOS/919th SOW, Duke Field, FL
	63020	Dornier C-146A Wolfhound (N524AW/16-3020)	USAF 524th SOS/27th SOW, Cannon AFB, NM
	63025	Dornier C-146A Wolfhound (N250BG/16-3025)	USAF 859th SOS/919th SOW, Duke Field, FL
	73091	Dornier C-146A Wolfhound (N391EF/97-3091)	USAF 524th SOS/27th SOW, Cannon AFB, NM
	73093	Dornier C-146A Wolfhound (N545EF/97-3093)	USAF 859th SOS/919th SOW, Duke Field, FL
	93106	Dornier C-146A Wolfhound (N525EF/99-3106)	USAF 524th SOS/27th SOW, Cannon AFB, NM

Serial	Type (code/other identity)	Owner/operator, location or fate	Notes
150521	Lockheed NP-3D Orion [521]	USN VX-30, NAS Point Mugu, CA	
153442	Lockheed NP-3D Orion [357]	To AMARG, June 2017	
156511	Lockheed EP-3E ARIES II [511]	USN VQ-1, NAS Whidbey Island, WA	
156515	Lockheed P-3C CDU Orion [LL-515]	Withdrawn from use, September 2017	
156517	Lockheed EP-3E ARIES II [517]	USN VQ-1, NAS Whidbey Island, WA	
156528	Lockheed EP-3E ARIES II [528]	USN VQ-1, NAS Whidbey Island, WA	
156529	Lockheed EP-3E ARIES II [529]	USN VQ-1, NAS Whidbey Island, WA	
157316	Lockheed EP-3E ARIES II [316]	USN VQ-1, NAS Whidbey Island, WA	
157318	Lockheed EP-3E ARIES II [318]	USN VQ-1, NAS Whidbey Island, WA	
157325	Lockheed EP-3E ARIES II [325]	USN VQ-1, NAS Whidbey Island, WA	
157326	Lockheed EP-3E ARIES II [326]	USN VQ-1, NAS Whidbey Island, WA	
158210	Lockheed P-3C AIP+ Orion [PJ-210]	USN VP-69, NAS Whidbey Island, WA	
158215	Lockheed P-3C AIP Orion [215]	USN VP-1, NAS Whidbey Island, WA	
158222	Lockheed P-3C AIP+ Orion [222]	USN	
158224	Lockheed P-3C AIP+ Orion [224]	USN	
158225	Lockheed P-3C AIP Orion [225]	USN VP-30, NAS Jacksonville, FL	
158227	Lockheed NP-3D Orion [300]	To AMARG, November 2017	
158563	Lockheed P-3C AIP+ Orion [PD-563]	To AMARG, May 2017	
158564	Lockheed P-3C AIP+ Orion [564]	USN	
158567	Lockheed P-3C AIP+ Orion [PD-567]	USN VP-9, NAS Whidbey Island, WA	
158570	Lockheed P-3C-IIIR Orion [RL-570]	USN VXS-1, Patuxent River, MD	
158574	Lockheed P-3C-IIIR Orion	USN NASC-FS, Point Mugu, CA	
158912	Lockheed NP-3C Orion [RL-912]	USN VXS-1, Patuxent River, MD	
158914	Lockheed P-3C-IIIR Orion [914]	To AMARG, June 2017	
158922	Lockheed P-3C AIP Orion [922]	USN VP-9, NAS Whidbey Island, WA	
158934	Lockheed P-3C AIP+ Orion [934]	USN VP-40, NAS Whidbey Island, WA	
159326	Lockheed P-3C AIP+ Orion [RC-326]	USN VP-46, NAS Whidbey Island, WA	
159504	Lockheed P-3CSPA Orion	USN VPU-2, NAS Whidbey Island, WA	
159887	Lockheed EP-3E ARIES II [887]	USN VQ-1, NAS Whidbey Island, WA	
159893	Lockheed EP-3E ARIES II [893]	USN VQ-1, NAS Whidbey Island, WA	
159894	Lockheed P-3C AIP+ Orion [RC-894]	To AMARG, December 2017	
160287	Lockheed P-3C AIP+ Orion [287]	USN	
160290	Lockheed P-3CSPA Orion [LL-290]	USN VP-30, NAS Jacksonville, FL	
160292	Lockheed P-3CSPA Orion [292]	USN VPU-2, NAS Whidbey Island, WA	
160293	Lockheed P-3C BMUO Orion	USN NASC-FS, Point Mugu, CA	
160610	Lockheed P-3C AIP+ Orion [YD-610]	USN	
160627	Lockheed KC-130R Hercules [627]	USN VX-20, Patuxent River, MD	
160764	Lockheed EP-3E ARIES II [764]	USN VQ-1, NAS Whidbey Island, WA	
161012	Lockheed P-3C AIP+ Orion [012]	USN	
161121	Lockheed P-3C BMUP+ Orion [121]	USN VP-62, NAS Jacksonville, FL	
161122	Lockheed P-3CSPA Orion [226]	USN VPU-2, NAS Whidbey Island, WA	
161126	Lockheed P-3C BMUP+ Orion [126]	To AMARG, June 2017	
161127	Lockheed P-3C BMUP Orion [127]	USN VP-69, NAS Whidbey Island, WA	
161129	Lockheed P-3C BMUP Orion [129]	USN VXS-1, Patuxent River, MD	
161132	Lockheed P-3C BMUP+ Orion [132]	USN VP-46, NAS Whidbey Island, WA	
161333	Lockheed P-3C AIP+ Orion [333]	USN VP-62, NAS Jacksonville, FL	
161337	Lockheed P-3C-II½ Orion [337]	USN	
161339	Lockheed P-3C BMUP Orion [RC-339]	USN VP-46, NAS Whidbey Island, WA	
161404	Lockheed P-3C BMUP+ Orion [YB-404]	USN VP-1, NAS Whidbey Island, WA	
161405	Lockheed P-3C BMUP+ Orion [405]	USN VP-69, NAS Whidbey Island, WA	
161406	Lockheed P-3C AIP+ Orion [PD-406]	USN VP-9, NAS Whidbey Island, WA	
161407	Lockheed P-3C AIP+ Orion [407]	USN	
161408	Lockheed P-3C BMUP+ Orion [408]	USN VP-1, NAS Whidbey Island, WA	
161410	Lockheed EP-3E ARIES II [410]	USN VQ-1, NAS Whidbey Island, WA	
161411	Lockheed P-3C BMUP+ Orion [411]	USN VP-69, NAS Whidbey Island, WA	
161412	Lockheed P-3C BMUP+ Orion [306]	To AMARG, September 2017	
161413	Lockheed P-3C AIP+ Orion [413]	USN	
161414	Lockheed P-3C BMUP+ Orion [RC-414]	USN VP-46, NAS Whidbey Island, WA	
161415	Lockheed P-3C BMUP+ Orion [415]	USN VP-62, NAS Jacksonville, FL	
161529	McDD C-9B Skytrain II	Withdrawn from use, July 2017	
161530	McDD C-9B Skytrain II	Withdrawn from use, July 2017	
161586	Lockheed P-3C BMUP+ Orion [QE-586]	USN VP-40, NAS Whidbey Island, WA	

Notes	Serial	Type (code/other identity)	Owner/operator, location or fate
	161587	Lockheed P-3C BMUP+ Orion [587]	USN VP-1, NAS Whidbey Island, WA
	161588	Lockheed P-3C BMUP+ Orion [588]	USN VP-46, NAS Whidbey Island, WA
	161589	Lockheed P-3C BMUP+ Orion [589]	USN VP-40, NAS Whidbey Island, WA
	161590	Lockheed P-3C BMUP+ Orion [590]	USN VP-30, NAS Jacksonville, FL
	161593	Lockheed P-3C BMUP+ Orion [593]	USN VP-46, NAS Whidbey Island, WA
	161594	Lockheed P-3C AIP+ Orion [594]	USN VP-9, NAS Whidbey Island, WA
	161596	Lockheed P-3C BMUP+ Orion [596]	USN VP-40, NAS Whidbey Island, WA
	161764	Lockheed P-3C AIP+ Orion [764]	*To AMARG, September 2017*
	161766	Lockheed P-3C AIP Orion [RC-766]	USN VP-46, NAS Whidbey Island, WA
	162308	Lockheed KC-130T Hercules [308]	USN VX-20, Patuxent River, MD
	162309	Lockheed KC-130T Hercules [406]	USN VX-30, NAS Point Mugu, CA
	162310	Lockheed KC-130T Hercules [309]	USN VX-20, Patuxent River, MD
	162311	Lockheed KC-130T Hercules [405]	USN VX-30, NAS Point Mugu, CA
	162316	Lockheed P-3C AIP+ Orion [316]	USN VP-69, NAS Whidbey Island, WA
	162317	Lockheed P-3C AIP+ Orion [317]	USN VP-30, NAS Jacksonville, FL
	162318	Lockheed P-3C AIP+ Orion [RC-318]	USN VP-46, NAS Whidbey Island, WA
	162770	Lockheed P-3C AIP+ Orion [770]	USN VP-30, NAS Jacksonville, FL
	162771	Lockheed P-3C AIP+ Orion [771]	USN
	162772	Lockheed P-3C AIP+ Orion [772]	USN VP-40, NAS Whidbey Island, WA
	162773	Lockheed P-3C AIP+ Orion [773]	USN
	162775	Lockheed P-3C AIP+ Orion [PD-775]	*To AMARG, August 2017*
	162776	Lockheed P-3C AIP+ Orion [776]	USN VP-40, NAS Whidbey Island, WA
	162777	Lockheed P-3C AIP+ Orion [777]	USN VP-40, NAS Whidbey Island, WA
	162778	Lockheed P-3C AIP+ Orion [PD-778]	USN VP-9, NAS Whidbey Island, WA
	162782	Boeing E-6B Mercury	USN VQ-3/SCW-1, Tinker AFB, OK
	162783	Boeing E-6B Mercury	USN VQ-3/SCW-1, Tinker AFB, OK
	162784	Boeing E-6B Mercury	USN VQ-4/SCW-1, Tinker AFB, OK
	162998	Lockheed P-3C AIP+ Orion [RC-998]	USN VP-46, NAS Whidbey Island, WA
	162999	Lockheed P-3C AIP+ Orion [RC-999]	USN VP-46, NAS Whidbey Island, WA
	163000	Lockheed P-3C AIP+ Orion [000]	USN VP-30, NAS Jacksonville, FL
	163001	Lockheed P-3C AIP+ Orion [001]	USN
	163004	Lockheed P-3C AIP+ Orion [004]	USN VP-69, NAS Whidbey Island, WA
	163023	Lockheed KC-130T Hercules [404]	USN VX-30, NAS Point Mugu, CA
	163290	Lockheed P-3C AIP+ Orion [LL-290]	USN VP-30, NAS Jacksonville, FL
	163291	Lockheed P-3C AIP+ Orion [291]	USN VP-1, NAS Whidbey Island, WA
	163293	Lockheed P-3C AIP+ Orion [PD-293]	USN VP-9, NAS Whidbey Island, WA
	163294	Lockheed P-3C AIP+ Orion [303]	USN VX-30, NAS Point Mugu, CA
	163295	Lockheed P-3C AIP+ Orion [295]	USN VP-1, NAS Whidbey Island, WA
	163310	Lockheed KC-130T Hercules [3310]	USN VX-20, Patuxent River, MD
	163311	Lockheed KC-130T Hercules [RU-311]	USN VR-55, NAS Point Mugu, CA
	163591	Lockheed KC-130T Hercules [RU-591]	USN VR-55, NAS Point Mugu, CA
	163592	Lockheed KC-130T Hercules [NY-592]	*To AMARG, January 2017*
	163691	Grumman C-20D Gulfstream III	USN VR-1, NAF Washington, MD
	163692	Grumman C-20D Gulfstream III	USN VR-1, NAF Washington, MD
	163918	Boeing E-6B Mercury	USN VQ-3/SCW-1, Tinker AFB, OK
	163919	Boeing E-6B Mercury	USN VQ-3/SCW-1, Tinker AFB, OK
	163920	Boeing E-6B Mercury	USN VQ-3/SCW-1, Tinker AFB, OK
	164105	Lockheed KC-130T Hercules [NY-105]	USMC VMGR-452, Stewart Field, NY
	164106	Lockheed KC-130T Hercules [RU-106]	USN VR-55, NAS Point Mugu, CA
	164180	Lockheed KC-130T Hercules [NY-180]	USMC VMGR-452, Stewart Field, NY
	164181	Lockheed KC-130T Hercules [NY-181]	USMC VMGR-452, Stewart Field, NY
	164386	Boeing E-6B Mercury	USN VQ-4/SCW-1, Tinker AFB, OK
	164387	Boeing E-6B Mercury	USN VQ-3/SCW-1, Tinker AFB, OK
	164388	Boeing E-6B Mercury	USN VQ-4/SCW-1, Tinker AFB, OK
	164404	Boeing E-6B Mercury	USN VQ-4/SCW-1, Tinker AFB, OK
	164405	Boeing E-6B Mercury	USN VQ-4/SCW-1, Tinker AFB, OK
	164406	Boeing E-6B Mercury	USN VQ-3/SCW-1, Tinker AFB, OK
	164407	Boeing E-6B Mercury	USN VQ-4/SCW-1, Tinker AFB, OK
	164408	Boeing E-6B Mercury	USN VQ-4/SCW-1, Tinker AFB, OK
	164409	Boeing E-6B Mercury	USN VQ-4/SCW-1, Tinker AFB, OK
	164410	Boeing E-6B Mercury	USN VQ-4/SCW-1, Tinker AFB, OK
	164441	Lockheed KC-130T Hercules [NY-441]	USMC VMGR-452, Stewart Field, NY

Serial	Type (code/other identity)	Owner/operator, location or fate	Notes
164442	Lockheed KC-130T Hercules [NY-442]	USMC VMGR-452, Stewart Field, NY	
164597	Lockheed KC-130T-30 Hercules [RU-597]	USN VR-55, NAS Point Mugu, CA	
164598	Lockheed KC-130T-30 Hercules [RU-598]	USN VR-55, NAS Point Mugu, CA	
164762	Lockheed C-130T Hercules [CW-762]	USN VR-54, NAS New Orleans, LA	
164763	Lockheed C-130T Hercules	USN *Blue Angels*, Pensacola NAS, FL	
164993	Lockheed C-130T Hercules [BD-993]	USN VR-64, NAS Willow Grove, PA	
164994	Lockheed C-130T Hercules [CW-994]	USN VR-54, NAS New Orleans, LA	
164995	Lockheed C-130T Hercules [CW-995]	USN VR-54, NAS New Orleans, LA	
164996	Lockheed C-130T Hercules [BD-996]	USN VR-64, NAS Willow Grove, PA	
164997	Lockheed C-130T Hercules [AX-997]	USN VR-53, NAF Washington, MD	
164998	Lockheed C-130T Hercules [AX-998]	USN VR-53, NAF Washington, MD	
164999	Lockheed KC-130T Hercules [NY-999]	USMC VMGR-452, Stewart Field, NY	
165000	Lockheed KC-130T Hercules [NY-000]	*Crashed 10 July 2017, Itta Bena, MS*	
165093	Grumman C-20G Gulfstream IV	USN VR-51, MCBH Kaneohe Bay, Hawaii	
165094	Grumman C-20G Gulfstream IV	USN VR-51, MCBH Kaneohe Bay, Hawaii	
165151	Grumman C-20G Gulfstream IV	USN CFLSW Det., Sigonella, Italy	
165152	Grumman C-20G Gulfstream IV	USN VR-51, MCBH Kaneohe Bay, Hawaii	
165153	Grumman C-20G Gulfstream IV	USMC VMR-Det, MCBH Kaneohe Bay, HI	
165158	Lockheed C-130T Hercules [CW-158]	USN VR-54, NAS New Orleans, LA	
165159	Lockheed C-130T Hercules [CW-159]	USN VR-54, NAS New Orleans, LA	
165160	Lockheed C-130T Hercules [JW-160]	USN VR-62, NAS Jacksonville, FL	
165161	Lockheed C-130T Hercules [BD-161]	USN VR-64, NAS Willow Grove, PA	
165162	Lockheed KC-130T Hercules [NY-162]	USMC VMGR-452, Stewart Field, NY	
165163	Lockheed KC-130T Hercules [NY-163]	USMC VMGR-452, Stewart Field, NY	
165313	Lockheed C-130T Hercules [JW-313]	USN VR-62, NAS Jacksonville, FL	
165314	Lockheed C-130T Hercules [JW-314]	USN VR-62, NAS Jacksonville, FL	
165315	Lockheed KC-130T Hercules [NY-315]	USMC VMGR-452, Stewart Field, NY	
165316	Lockheed KC-130T Hercules [NY-316]	USMC VMGR-452, Stewart Field, NY	
165348	Lockheed C-130T Hercules [JW-348]	USN VR-62, NAS Jacksonville, FL	
165349	Lockheed C-130T Hercules [JW-349]	USN VR-62, NAS Jacksonville, FL	
165350	Lockheed C-130T Hercules [350]	USN VX-20, Patuxent River, MD	
165351	Lockheed C-130T Hercules [AX-351]	USN VR-53, NAF Washington, MD	
165352	Lockheed KC-130T Hercules [NY-352]	USMC VMGR-452, Stewart Field, NY	
165353	Lockheed KC-130T Hercules [NY-353]	USMC VMGR-452, Stewart Field, NY	
165378	Lockheed C-130T Hercules [RU-378]	USN VR-55, NAS Point Mugu, CA	
165379	Lockheed C-130T Hercules [BD-379]	USN VR-64, NAS Willow Grove, PA	
165735	Lockheed KC-130J Hercules II [QB-735]	USMC VMGR-352, Miramar MCAS, CA	
165736	Lockheed KC-130J Hercules II [QB-736]	USMC VMGR-352, Miramar MCAS, CA	
165737	Lockheed KC-130J Hercules II [QB-737]	USMC VMGR-352, Miramar MCAS, CA	
165738	Lockheed KC-130J Hercules II [BH-738]	USMC VMGR-252, Cherry Point MCAS, NC	
165739	Lockheed KC-130J Hercules II [QH-739]	USMC VMGR-234, Fort Worth JRB, TX	
165740	Cessna UC-35C Citation V [EZ]	USMC MWHS-4, NAS New Orleans, LA	
165741	Cessna UC-35C Citation V [EZ]	USMC MWHS-4, NAS New Orleans, LA	
165809	Lockheed KC-130J Hercules II [BH-809]	USMC VMGR-252, Cherry Point MCAS, NC	
165810	Lockheed KC-130J Hercules II [BH-810]	USMC VMGR-252, Cherry Point MCAS, NC	
165829	Boeing C-40A Clipper [829]	USN VR-58, NAS Jacksonville, FL	
165830	Boeing C-40A Clipper [830]	USN VR-59, Fort Worth JRB, TX	
165831	Boeing C-40A Clipper [831]	USN VR-59, Fort Worth JRB, TX	
165832	Boeing C-40A Clipper [832]	USN VR-61, Fort Worth JRB, TX	
165833	Boeing C-40A Clipper [833]	USN VR-59, Fort Worth JRB, TX	
165834	Boeing C-40A Clipper [834]	USN VR-58, NAS Jacksonville, FL	
165835	Boeing C-40A Clipper [835]	USN VR-57, NAS North Island, CA	
165836	Boeing C-40A Clipper [836]	USN VR-57, NAS North Island, CA	
165939	Cessna UC-35D Citation V	USMC MWHS-1, Futenma MCAS, Japan	
165957	Lockheed KC-130J Hercules II [QD-957] $	USMC VMGR-152, Iwakuni MCAS, Japan	
166374	Cessna UC-35D Citation V	USMC VMR-2, NAF Washington, MD	
166375	Gulfstream Aerospace C-37A Gulfstream V [365]	USN CFLSW Det, MCBH Kaneohe Bay, HI	
166376	Gulfstream Aerospace C-37B Gulfstream V [376]	USN VR-1, NAF Washington, MD	
166377	Gulfstream Aerospace C-37B Gulfstream V [377]	USN VR-1, NAF Washington, MD	
166378	Gulfstream Aerospace C-37B Gulfstream V [378]	USN VR-1, NAF Washington, MD	
166380	Lockheed KC-130J Hercules II [BH-380]	USMC VMGR-252, Cherry Point MCAS, NC	
166381	Lockheed KC-130J Hercules II [381]	USN VX-20, Patuxent River, MD	

Notes	Serial	Type (code/other identity)	Owner/operator, location or fate
	166382	Lockheed KC-130J Hercules II [QB-382]	USMC VMGR-352, Miramar MCAS, CA
	166472	Lockheed KC-130J Hercules II [BH-472]	USMC VMGR-252, Cherry Point MCAS, NC
	166473	Lockheed KC-130J Hercules II [QH-473]	USMC VMGR-234, Fort Worth JRB, TX
	166474	Cessna UC-35D Citation V	USMC MAW-4, Miramar MCAS, CA
	166500	Cessna UC-35D Citation V	USMC MAW-4, Miramar MCAS, CA
	166511	Lockheed KC-130J Hercules II [511]	USN VX-20, Patuxent River, MD
	166512	Lockheed KC-130J Hercules II [QH-512]	USMC VMGR-234, Fort Worth JRB, TX
	166513	Lockheed KC-130J Hercules II [BH-513]	USMC VMGR-252, Cherry Point MCAS, NC
	166514	Lockheed KC-130J Hercules II [BH-514]	USMC VMGR-252, Cherry Point MCAS, NC
	166693	Boeing C-40A Clipper [693]	USN VR-57, NAS North Island, CA
	166694	Boeing C-40A Clipper [694]	USN VR-56, NAS Oceana, VA
	166695	Boeing C-40A Clipper [695]	USN VR-56, NAS Oceana, VA
	166696	Boeing C-40A Clipper [696]	USN VR-56, NAS Oceana, VA
	166712	Cessna UC-35D Citation V	USMC MWHS-1, Futenma MCAS, Japan
	166713	Cessna UC-35D Citation V	USMC MWHS-1, Futenma MCAS, Japan
	166714	Cessna UC-35D Citation V [VM]	USMC VMR-2, NAF Washington, MD
	166715	Cessna UC-35D Citation V	USMC MAW-4, Miramar MCAS, CA
	166762	Lockheed KC-130J Hercules II [QB-762]	USMC VMGR-352, Miramar MCAS, CA
	166763	Lockheed KC-130J Hercules II [QD-763]	USMC VMGR-152, Iwakuni MCAS, Japan
	166764	Lockheed KC-130J Hercules II [BH-764]	USMC VMGR-252, Cherry Point MCAS, NC
	166765	Lockheed KC-130J Hercules II [QB-765]	USMC VMGR-352, Miramar MCAS, CA
	166766	Cessna UC-35D Citation V	USMC MWHS-1, Futenma MCAS, Japan
	166767	Cessna UC-35D Citation V [VM]	USMC VMR-2, NAF Washington, MD
	167108	Lockheed KC-130J Hercules II [QB-108]	USMC VMGR-352, Miramar MCAS, CA
	167109	Lockheed KC-130J Hercules II [QD-109]	USN VX-20, Patuxent River, MD
	167110	Lockheed KC-130J Hercules II [QB-110]	USMC VMGR-352, Miramar MCAS, CA
	167111	Lockheed KC-130J Hercules II [QH-111]	USMC VMGR-234, Fort Worth JRB, TX
	167112	Lockheed KC-130J Hercules II [BH-112]	USMC VMGR-252, Cherry Point MCAS, NC
	167923	Lockheed KC-130J Hercules II [QD-923]	USMC VMGR-152, Iwakuni MCAS, Japan
	167924	Lockheed KC-130J Hercules II [QD-924]	USMC VMGR-352, Miramar MCAS, CA
	167925	Lockheed KC-130J Hercules II [QD-925]	USMC VMGR-152, Iwakuni MCAS, Japan
	167926	Lockheed KC-130J Hercules II [QD-926]	USMC VMGR-152, Iwakuni MCAS, Japan
	167927	Lockheed KC-130J Hercules II [QD-927]	USMC VMGR-152, Iwakuni MCAS, Japan
	167951	Boeing P-8A Poseidon [951]	USN VX-20, Patuxent River, MD
	167952	Boeing P-8A Poseidon [JA-952]	USN VX-1, NAS Patuxent River, MD
	167953	Boeing P-8A Poseidon [953]	USN VX-20, Patuxent River, MD
	167954	Boeing P-8A Poseidon	Boeing, Renton, WA
	167955	Boeing P-8A Poseidon [JA-955]	USN VX-1, NAS Patuxent River, MD
	167956	Boeing P-8A Poseidon [JA-956]	USN VX-1, NAS Patuxent River, MD
	167981	Lockheed KC-130J Hercules II [QD-981]	USMC VMGR-152, Iwakuni MCAS, Japan
	167982	Lockheed KC-130J Hercules II [QD-982]	USMC VMGR-152, Iwakuni MCAS, Japan
	167983	Lockheed KC-130J Hercules II [QD-983]	USMC VMGR-152, Iwakuni MCAS, Japan
	167984	Lockheed KC-130J Hercules II [QB-984]	USMC VMGR-352, Miramar MCAS, CA
	167985	Lockheed KC-130J Hercules II [QB-985]	USMC VMGR-352, Miramar MCAS, CA
	168065	Lockheed KC-130J Hercules II [QD-065]	USMC VMGR-152, Iwakuni MCAS, Japan
	168066	Lockheed KC-130J Hercules II [QD-066]	USMC VMGR-152, Iwakuni MCAS, Japan
	168067	Lockheed KC-130J Hercules II [QB-067]	USMC VMGR-352, Miramar MCAS, CA
	168068	Lockheed KC-130J Hercules II [QB-068]	USMC VMGR-352, Miramar MCAS, CA
	168069	Lockheed KC-130J Hercules II [BH-069]	USMC VMGR-252, Cherry Point MCAS, NC
	168070	Lockheed KC-130J Hercules II [BH-070]	USMC VMGR-252, Cherry Point MCAS, NC
	168071	Lockheed KC-130J Hercules II [BH-071]	USMC VMGR-252, Cherry Point MCAS, NC
	168072	Lockheed KC-130J Hercules II [QB-072]	USMC VMGR-352, Miramar MCAS, CA
	168073	Lockheed KC-130J Hercules II [QH-073]	USMC VMGR-234, Fort Worth JRB, TX
	168074	Lockheed KC-130J Hercules II [QD-074]	USMC VMGR-152, Iwakuni MCAS, Japan
	168075	Lockheed KC-130J Hercules II [QD-075]	USMC VMGR-152, Iwakuni MCAS, Japan
	168428	Boeing P-8A Poseidon [LF-428]	USN VP-16, NAS Jacksonville, FL
	168429	Boeing P-8A Poseidon [429]	USN VP-30, NAS Jacksonville, FL
	168430	Boeing P-8A Poseidon [LK-430]	USN VP-26, NAS Jacksonville, FL
	168431	Boeing P-8A Poseidon [LK-431]	USN VP-26, NAS Jacksonville, FL
	168432	Boeing P-8A Poseidon [LA-432]	USN VP-5, NAS Jacksonville, FL
	168433	Boeing P-8A Poseidon [LD-433]	USN VP-10, NAS Jacksonville, FL
	168434	Boeing P-8A Poseidon [LN-434]	USN VP-45, NAS Jacksonville, FL

Serial	Type (code/other identity)	Owner/operator, location or fate	Notes
168435	Boeing P-8A Poseidon [435]	USN VP-30, NAS Jacksonville, FL	
168436	Boeing P-8A Poseidon [LA-436]	USN VP-5, NAS Jacksonville, FL	
168437	Boeing P-8A Poseidon [LA-437]	USN VP-5, NAS Jacksonville, FL	
168438	Boeing P-8A Poseidon [LA-438]	USN VP-5, NAS Jacksonville, FL	
168439	Boeing P-8A Poseidon [LD-439]	USN VP-10, NAS Jacksonville, FL	
168440	Boeing P-8A Poseidon [440]	USN VP-16, NAS Jacksonville, FL	
168754	Boeing P-8A Poseidon [LC-754]	USN VP-8, NAS Jacksonville, FL	
168755	Boeing P-8A Poseidon [755]	USN VP-4, NAS Whidbey Island, WA	
168756	Boeing P-8A Poseidon [756]	USN VP-26, NAS Jacksonville, FL	
168757	Boeing P-8A Poseidon [757]	USN VP-26, NAS Jacksonville, FL	
168758	Boeing P-8A Poseidon [LC-758]	USN VP-8, NAS Jacksonville, FL	
168759	Boeing P-8A Poseidon [LC-759]	USN VP-8, NAS Jacksonville, FL	
168760	Boeing P-8A Poseidon [LC-760]	USN VP-8, NAS Jacksonville, FL	
168761	Boeing P-8A Poseidon [LN-761]	USN VP-45, NAS Jacksonville, FL	
168762	Boeing P-8A Poseidon [762]	USN VP-16, NAS Jacksonville, FL	
168763	Boeing P-8A Poseidon [LD-763]	USN VP-10, NAS Jacksonville, FL	
168764	Boeing P-8A Poseidon [LD-764]	USN VP-10, NAS Jacksonville, FL	
168848	Boeing P-8A Poseidon [LK-848]	USN VP-26, NAS Jacksonville, FL	
168849	Boeing P-8A Poseidon [849]	USN VP-10, NAS Jacksonville, FL	
168850	Boeing P-8A Poseidon [850]	USN VP-4, NAS Whidbey Island, WA	
168851	Boeing P-8A Poseidon [851]	USN VP-26, NAS Jacksonville, FL	
168852	Boeing P-8A Poseidon [852]	USN VP-45, NAS Jacksonville, FL	
168853	Boeing P-8A Poseidon [LF-853]	USN VP-16, NAS Jacksonville, FL	
168854	Boeing P-8A Poseidon [LC-854]	USN VP-8, NAS Jacksonville, FL	
168855	Boeing P-8A Poseidon [855]	USN VP-45, NAS Jacksonville, FL	
168856	Boeing P-8A Poseidon [856]	USN VP-30, NAS Jacksonville, FL	
168857	Boeing P-8A Poseidon [LK-857]	USN VP-26, NAS Jacksonville, FL	
168858	Boeing P-8A Poseidon [LD-858]	USN VP-10, NAS Jacksonville, FL	
168859	Boeing P-8A Poseidon [859]	USN VP-45, NAS Jacksonville, FL	
168860	Boeing P-8A Poseidon [860]	USN VP-45, NAS Jacksonville, FL	
168980	Boeing C-40A Clipper [980]	USN VR-61, Fort Worth JRB, TX	
168981	Boeing C-40A Clipper [981]	USN VR-61, Fort Worth JRB, TX	
168996	Boeing P-8A Poseidon [996]	USN VP-30, NAS Jacksonville, FL	
168997	Boeing P-8A Poseidon [LC-997]	USN VP-8, NAS Whidbey Island, WA	
168998	Boeing P-8A Poseidon [LA-998]	USN VP-5, NAS Jacksonville, FL	
168999	Boeing P-8A Poseidon [999]	USN VP-30, NAS Jacksonville, FL	
169000	Boeing P-8A Poseidon [000]	USN VP-30, NAS Jacksonville, FL	
169001	Boeing P-8A Poseidon [LA-001]	USN VP-5, NAS Jacksonville, FL	
169002	Boeing P-8A Poseidon [002]	USN VP-30, NAS Jacksonville, FL	
169003	Boeing P-8A Poseidon [LA-003]	USN VP-5, NAS Jacksonville, FL	
169004	Boeing P-8A Poseidon [004]	USN VP-30, NAS Jacksonville, FL	
169005	Boeing P-8A Poseidon [LC-005]	USN VP-8, NAS Jacksonville, FL	
169006	Boeing P-8A Poseidon [006]	USN VP-30, NAS Jacksonville, FL	
169007	Boeing P-8A Poseidon [LC-007]	USN VP-8, NAS Jacksonville, FL	
169008	Boeing P-8A Poseidon [008]	USN VP-4, NAS Whidbey Island, WA	
169009	Boeing P-8A Poseidon [YD-009]	USN VP-4, NAS Whidbey Island, WA	
169010	Boeing P-8A Poseidon [LL-010]	USN VP-30, NAS Jacksonville, FL	
169011	Boeing P-8A Poseidon [011]	USN VP-5, NAS Jacksonville, FL	
169018	Lockheed KC-130J Hercules II [QH-018]	USMC VMGR-234, Fort Worth JRB, TX	
169036	Boeing C-40A Clipper [036]	USN VR-61, Fort Worth JRB, TX	
169225	Lockheed KC-130J Hercules II [BH-225]	USMC VMGR-252, Cherry Point MCAS, NC	
169226	Lockheed KC-130J Hercules II [QB-226]	USMC VMGR-352, Miramar MCAS, CA	
169227	Lockheed KC-130J Hercules II [QD-227]	USMC VMGR-152, Iwakuni MCAS, Japan	
169228	Lockheed KC-130J Hercules II [QH-228]	USMC VMGR-234, Fort Worth JRB, TX	
169229	Lockheed KC-130J Hercules II [QH-229]	USMC VMGR-234, Fort Worth JRB, TX	
169324	Boeing P-8A Poseidon [324]	USN VP-30, NAS Jacksonville, FL	
169325	Boeing P-8A Poseidon [325]	USN VP-47, NAS Whidbey Island, WA	
169326	Boeing P-8A Poseidon [326]	USN VP-4, NAS Whidbey Island, WA	
169327	Boeing P-8A Poseidon [327]	USN VP-47, NAS Whidbey Island, WA	
169328	Boeing P-8A Poseidon [328]	USN VP-4, NAS Whidbey Island, WA	
169329	Boeing P-8A Poseidon [329]	USN VP-30, NAS Jacksonville, FL	
169330	Boeing P-8A Poseidon [330]	USN VP-30, NAS Jacksonville, FL	

Notes	Serial	Type (code/other identity)	Owner/operator, location or fate
	169331	Boeing P-8A Poseidon [331]	USN VP-47, NAS Whidbey Island, WA
	169332	Boeing P-8A Poseidon [332]	USN VP-30, NAS Jacksonville, FL
	169333	Boeing P-8A Poseidon [333]	USN VX-1/VX-20, NAS Patuxent River, MD
	169334	Boeing P-8A Poseidon [334]	USN VP-30, NAS Jacksonville, FL
	169335	Boeing P-8A Poseidon [335]	USN VP-30, NAS Jacksonville, FL
	169339	Boeing P-8A Poseidon [339]	USN (on order)
	169340	Boeing P-8A Poseidon [340]	USN (on order)
	169341	Boeing P-8A Poseidon [341]	USN (on order)
	169...	Boeing P-8A Poseidon	USN (on order)
	169...	Boeing P-8A Poseidon	USN (on order)
	169...	Boeing C-40A Clipper	USN (on order)
	169...	Boeing C-40A Clipper	USN (on order)

Wearing no titles, no insignia and just 5829 on the tail, casual observers might not realise that this is C-40A Clipper 165829 of VR-58 of the US Navy, based at NAS Jacksonville in Florida.

US-BASED US COAST GUARD AIRCRAFT

Serial	Type (code/other identity)	Owner/operator, location or fate	Notes
01	Gulfstream Aerospace C-37A Gulfstream V (N527GA)	USCG, Commandants Flt, Washington DC	
02	Gulfstream Aerospace C-37A Gulfstream V	Sold as N888HE, April 2017	
02	Gulfstream Aerospace C-37B Gulfstream V (N640W)	USCG, Commandants Flt, Washington DC	
1503	Lockheed HC-130H Hercules	USCG, USCGS Clearwater, FL	
1701	Lockheed HC-130H Hercules	USCG, USCGS Sacramento, CA	
1702	Lockheed HC-130H Hercules	USCG, USCGS Sacramento, CA	
1703	Lockheed HC-130H Hercules	USCG, USCGS Sacramento, CA	
1704	Lockheed HC-130H Hercules	USCG, USCGS Clearwater, FL	
1706	Lockheed HC-130H Hercules	USCG, USCGS Clearwater, FL	
1707	Lockheed HC-130H Hercules	USCG, USCGS Barbers Point, HI	
1709	Lockheed HC-130H Hercules	USCG, USCGS Sacramento, CA	
1711	Lockheed HC-130H Hercules	USCG, USCGS Clearwater, FL	
1712	Lockheed HC-130H Hercules	USCG, USCGS Kodiak, AK	
1715	Lockheed HC-130H Hercules	USCG, USCGS Clearwater, FL	
1716	Lockheed HC-130H Hercules	USCG, USCGS Barbers Point, HI	
1718	Lockheed HC-130H Hercules	USCG, USCGS Clearwater, FL	
1720	Lockheed HC-130H Hercules	USCG, USCGS Elizabeth City, NC	
1790	Lockheed HC-130H Hercules	USCG, USCGS Barbers Point, HI	
2001	Lockheed HC-130J Hercules II	USCG, USCGS Elizabeth City, NC	
2002	Lockheed HC-130J Hercules II	USCG, USCGS Elizabeth City, NC	
2003	Lockheed HC-130J Hercules II	USCG, USCGS Elizabeth City, NC	
2004	Lockheed HC-130J Hercules II	USCG, USCGS Elizabeth City, NC	
2005	Lockheed HC-130J Hercules II	USCG, USCGS Elizabeth City, NC	
2006	Lockheed HC-130J Hercules II	USCG, USCGS Elizabeth City, NC	
2007	Lockheed HC-130J Hercules II	USCG, USCGS Elizabeth City, NC	
2008	Lockheed HC-130J Hercules II	USCG, USCGS Elizabeth City, NC	
2009	Lockheed HC-130J Hercules II	USCG, USCGS Elizabeth City, NC	
2010	Lockheed HC-130J Hercules II	USCG, USCGS Elizabeth City, NC	

Aircraft in US Government or Military Service with Civil Registrations

Serial	Type (code/other identity)	Owner/operator, location or fate	Notes
N85	Canadair CL.601 Challenger	Federal Aviation Administration, Oklahoma City, OK	
N86	Canadair CL.601 Challenger	Federal Aviation Administration, Oklahoma City, OK	
N87	Canadair CL.601 Challenger	Federal Aviation Administration, Oklahoma City, OK	
N88	Canadair CL.604 Challenger	Federal Aviation Administration, Oklahoma City, OK	
N89	Canadair CL.605 Challenger	Federal Aviation Administration, Oklahoma City, OK	
N90	Canadair CL.605 Challenger	Federal Aviation Administration, Oklahoma City, OK	

The list below is not intended to be a complete list of military aviation sites on the Internet. The sites listed cover Museums, Locations, Air Forces, Companies and Organisations that are mentioned elsewhere in 'Military Aircraft Markings'. Sites listed are in English or contain sufficient English to be reasonably easily understood. Each site address was correct at the time of going to press. Additions are welcome, via the usual address found at the front of the book, or via e-mail to admin@aviation-links.co.uk. An up to date copy of this list is to be found at The 'Military Aircraft Markings' Web Site, http://www.militaryaircraftmarkings.co.uk/.

Name of Site	Web Address All prefixed 'http://')
MILITARY SITES-UK	
No 1 Sqn	www.raf.mod.uk/organisation/1squadron.cfm
No 2 Sqn	www.raf.mod.uk/organisation/2squadron.cfm
No 3 Sqn	www.raf.mod.uk/organisation/3squadron.cfm
No 4 Sqn	www.raf.mod.uk/organisation/4squadron.cfm
No 5 Sqn	www.raf.mod.uk/organisation/5squadron.cfm
No 6 Sqn	www.raf.mod.uk/organisation/6squadron.cfm
No 7 Sqn	www.raf.mod.uk/organisation/7squadron.cfm
No 8 Sqn	www.viiisquadron.co.uk//
No 9 Sqn	www.raf.mod.uk/organisation/9squadron.cfm
No 10 Sqn	www.raf.mod.uk/organisation/10squadron.cfm
No 11 Sqn	www.raf.mod.uk/organisation/11squadron.cfm
No 12 Sqn	www.raf.mod.uk/organisation/12squadron.cfm
No 14 Sqn	www.raf.mod.uk/organisation/14squadron.cfm
No 15 Sqn	www.raf.mod.uk/organisation/15squadron.cfm
No 16 Sqn	www.raf.mod.uk/organisation/16squadron.cfm
No 17 Sqn	www.raf.mod.uk/organisation/17squadron.cfm
No 18 Sqn	www.raf.mod.uk/organisation/18squadron.cfm
No 24 Sqn	www.raf.mod.uk/organisation/24squadron.cfm
No 27 Sqn	www.raf.mod.uk/organisation/27squadron.cfm
No 28 Sqn	www.raf.mod.uk/organisation/28squadron.cfm
No 29 Sqn	www.raf.mod.uk/organisation/29squadron.cfm
No 30 Sqn	www.raf.mod.uk/organisation/30squadron.cfm
No 31 Sqn	www.raf.mod.uk/organisation/31squadron.cfm
No 32(The Royal) Sqn	www.raf.mod.uk/organisation/32squadron.cfm
No 33 Sqn	www.raf.mod.uk/organisation/33squadron.cfm
No 39 Sqn	www.raf.mod.uk/organisation/39squadron.cfm
No 41 Sqn	www.raf.mod.uk/organisation/41squadron.cfm
No 45 Sqn	www.raf.mod.uk/organisation/45squadron.cfm
No 47 Sqn	www.raf.mod.uk/organisation/47squadron.cfm
No 51 Sqn	www.raf.mod.uk/organisation/51squadron.cfm
No 54 Sqn	www.raf.mod.uk/organisation/54squadron.cfm
No 55 Sqn	www.raf.mod.uk/organisation/55squadron.cfm
No 56 Sqn	www.raf.mod.uk/organisation/56squadron.cfm
No 60 Sqn	www.raf.mod.uk/organisation/60squadron.cfm
No 70 Sqn	www.raf.mod.uk/organisation/70squadron.cfm
No 72 Sqn	www.raf.mod.uk/organisation/72squadron.cfm
No 84 Sqn	www.raf.mod.uk/organisation/84squadron.cfm
No 99 Sqn	www.raf.mod.uk/organisation/99squadron.cfm
No 100 Sqn	www.raf.mod.uk/organisation/100squadron.cfm
No 101 Sqn	www.raf.mod.uk/organisation/101squadron.cfm
No 202 Sqn	www.raf.mod.uk/organisation/202squadron.cfm
No 230 Sqn	www.raf.mod.uk/organisation/230squadron.cfm
No 617 Sqn	www.raf.mod.uk/organisation/617squadron.cfm
No 703 NAS	www.royalnavy.mod.uk/our-organisation/the-fighting-arms/fleet-air-arm/support-and-training/703-naval-air-squadronng
No 705 NAS	www.royalnavy.mod.uk/our-organisation/the-fighting-arms/fleet-air-arm/support-and-training/705-naval-air-squadron
No 727 NAS	www.royalnavy.mod.uk/our-organisation/the-fighting-arms/fleet-air-arm/support-and-training/727-naval-air-squadron
No 736 NAS	www.royalnavy.mod.uk/our-organisation/the-fighting-arms/fleet-air-arm/hawk-jets/736-naval-air-squadron
No 750 NAS	www.royalnavy.mod.uk/our-organisation/the-fighting-arms/fleet-air-arm/support-and-training/750-naval-air-squadron

Name of Site	Web Address All prefixed 'http://')
No 809 NAS	www.royalnavy.mod.uk/our-organisation/the-fighting-arms/fleet-air-arm/future-aircraft/809-naval-air-squadron
No 814 NAS	www.royalnavy.mod.uk/our-organisation/the-fighting-arms/fleet-air-arm/helicopter-squadrons/merlin-mk2/814-naval-air-squadron
No 815 NAS	www.royalnavy.mod.uk/our-organisation/the-fighting-arms/fleet-air-arm/helicopter-squadrons/wildcat/815-naval-air-squadron
No 820 NAS	www.royalnavy.mod.uk/our-organisation/the-fighting-arms/fleet-air-arm/helicopter-squadrons/merlin-mk2/820-naval-air-squadron
No 824 NAS	www.royalnavy.mod.uk/our-organisation/the-fighting-arms/fleet-air-arm/helicopter-squadrons/merlin-mk2/824-naval-air-squadron
No 825 NAS	www.royalnavy.mod.uk/our-organisation/the-fighting-arms/fleet-air-arm/helicopter-squadrons/wildcat/825-naval-air-squadron
No 829 NAS	www.royalnavy.mod.uk/our-organisation/the-fighting-arms/fleet-air-arm/helicopter-squadrons/merlin-mk2/829-naval-air-squadron
No 845 NAS	www.royalnavy.mod.uk/our-organisation/the-fighting-arms/fleet-air-arm/helicopter-squadrons/merlin-mk-3/845-naval-air-squadron
No 846 NAS	www.royalnavy.mod.uk/our-organisation/the-fighting-arms/fleet-air-arm/helicopter-squadrons/merlin-mk-3/846-naval-air-squadron
No 847 NAS	www.royalnavy.mod.uk/our-organisation/the-fighting-arms/fleet-air-arm/helicopter-squadrons/wildcat/847-naval-air-squadron
No 849 NAS	www.royalnavy.mod.uk/our-organisation/the-fighting-arms/fleet-air-arm/helicopter-squadrons/sea-king-asac-mk7/849-naval-air-squadron
The Army Air Corps	www.army.mod.uk/aviation/default.aspx
Fleet Air Arm	www.royalnavy.mod.uk/our-organisation/the-fighting-arms/fleet-air-arm
Ministry of Defence	www.mod.uk/
QinetiQ	www.qinetiq.com/
RAF Benson	www.raf.mod.uk/rafbenson/
RAF Brize Norton	www.raf.mod.uk/rafbrizenorton/
RAF Coningsby	www.raf.mod.uk/rafconingsby/
Coningsby Aviation Site (unofficial)	milky01.co.uk/
RAF Cosford	www.raf.mod.uk/rafcosford/
RAF Linton-on-Ouse	www.raf.mod.uk/raflintononouse/
RAF Lossiemouth	www.raf.mod.uk/raflossiemouth/
RAF Marham	www.raf.mod.uk/rafmarham/
RAF Northolt	www.raf.mod.uk/rafnortholt/
RAF Odiham	www.raf.mod.uk/rafodiham/
RAF Shawbury	www.raf.mod.uk/rafshawbury/
RAF Valley	www.raf.mod.uk/rafvalley/
RAF Waddington	www.raf.mod.uk/rafwaddington/
RAF Wittering	www.raf.mod.uk/rafwittering/
Red Arrows	www.raf.mod.uk/reds/
Royal Air Force	www.raf.mod.uk/
Royal Air Force Reserves	www.raf.mod.uk/rafreserves/
University Air Squadrons	www.raf.mod.uk/universityairsquadrons/findasquadron/
MILITARY SITES-US	
Air Combat Command	www.acc.af.mil/
Air Force Reserve Command	www.afrc.af.mil/
Air National Guard	www.ang.af.mil/
Aviano Air Base	www.aviano.af.mil/
Liberty Wing Home Page (48th FW)	www.lakenheath.af.mil/
NASA	www.nasa.gov/
Mildenhall	www.mildenhall.af.mil/
Ramstein Air Base	www.ramstein.af.mil/
Spangdahlem Air Base	www.spangdahlem.af.mil/
USAF	www.af.mil/
USAF Europe	www.usafe.af.mil/
USAF World Wide Web Sites	www.af.mil/publicwebsites/index.asp
US Army	www.army.mil/
US Marine Corps	www.marines.mil/
US Navy	www.navy.mil/
US Navy Patrol Squadrons (unofficial)	www.vpnavy.com/

Name of Site	Web Address All prefixed 'http://'
MILITARY SITES-ELSEWHERE	
Armée de l'Air	www.defense.gouv.fr/air/
Aeronautica Militare	www.aeronautica.difesa.it
Austrian Armed Forces (in German)	www.bmlv.gv.at/
Finnish Defence Force	www.puolustusvoimat.fi/en/
Forca Aerea Portuguesa	www.emfa.pt/
German Marine	www.deutschemarine.de/
Greek Air Force	www.haf.gr/en/
Irish Air Corps	www.military.ie/air-corps
Luftforsvaret	www.mil.no/
Luftwaffe	www.luftwaffe.de/
NATO	www.nato.int/
Royal Australian Air Force	www.airforce.gov.au/
Royal Canadian Air Force	www.airforce.forces.gc.ca/
Royal Danish Air Force (in Danish)	forsvaret.dk/
Royal Netherlands AF	www.defensie.nl/luchtmacht
Royal New Zealand AF	www.airforce.mil.nz/
Singapore Air Force	www.mindef.gov.sg/rsaf/
South African AF Site (unofficial)	www.saairforce.co.za/
Swedish Air Force	www.forsvarsmakten.se/sv/Forband-och-formagor/Flygvapnet/
Turkish Air Force	www.hvkk.tsk.tr/en-us/
AIRCRAFT & AERO ENGINE MANUFACTURERS	
Airbus Defence & Space	airbusdefenceandspace.com/
Airbus Group	www.airbusgroup.com/
BAE Systems	www.baesystems.com/
Beechcraft	www.beechcraft.com/
Bell Helicopter Textron	www.bellhelicopter.textron.com/
Boeing	www.boeing.com/
Bombardier	www.bombardier.com/
Britten-Norman	www.britten-norman.com/
Dassault	www.dassault-aviation.com/
Embraer	www.embraer.com/
General Electric	www.ge.com/
Grob Aircraft AG	grob-aircraft.com/en/
Gulfstream Aerospace	www.gulfstream.com/
Kaman Aerospace	www.kaman.com/
Leonardo	www.leonardocompany.com/
Lockheed Martin	www.lockheedmartin.com/
Rolls-Royce	www.rolls-royce.com/
Sikorsky	www.sikorsky.com/
UK AVIATION MUSEUMS	
Boscombe Down Aviation Collection, Old Sarum	www.boscombedownaviationcollection.co.uk/
Bournemouth Aviation Museum	www.aviation-museum.co.uk/
Brooklands Museum	www.brooklandsmuseum.com/
City of Norwich Aviation Museum	www.cnam.org.uk/
de Havilland Aircraft Museum	www.dehavillandmuseum.co.uk/
Dumfries & Galloway Aviation Museum	www.dumfriesaviationmuseum.com/
Fleet Air Arm Museum	www.fleetairarm.com/
Gatwick Aviation Museum	www.gatwick-aviation-museum.co.uk/
IWM, Duxford	www.iwm.org.uk/visits/iwm-duxford
Imperial War Museum, Duxford (unofficial)	www.axtd59.dsl.pipex.com/
The Jet Age Museum	www.jetagemuseum.org/
Lincs Aviation Heritage Centre	www.lincsaviation.co.uk/
Midland Air Museum	www.midlandairmuseum.co.uk/
Museum of Army Flying	www.armyflying.com/
Museum of Berkshire Aviation	www.museumofberkshireaviation.co.uk/
Museum of Science & Industry, Manchester	mosi.org.uk/
National Museum of Flight, East Fortune	www.nms.ac.uk/our_museums/museum_of_flight.aspx
Newark Air Museum	www.newarkairmuseum.org/
North East Aircraft Museum	www.nelsam.org.uk/NEAM/NEAM.htm

Name of Site	Web Address All prefixed 'http://')
RAF Museum, Cosford & Hendon	www.rafmuseum.org.uk/
Science Museum, South Kensington	www.sciencemuseum.org.uk/
South Yorkshire Aircraft Museum	www.southyorkshireaircraftmuseum.org.uk/
Yorkshire Air Museum, Elvington	www.yorkshireairmuseum.org/

AVIATION SOCIETIES

Air Britain	www.air-britain.com/
Air Yorkshire	www.airyorkshire.org.uk/
British Aircraft Preservation Council	www.bapc.org.uk/
LAAS International	www.laasdata.com/
Military Aviation Review	militaryaviationreview.com/
Royal Aeronautical Society	aerosociety.com/
Scramble (Dutch Aviation Society)	www.scramble.nl/
Solent Aviation Society	www.solent-aviation-society.co.uk/
Spitfire Society	www.spitfiresociety.com/
The Aviation Society Manchester	www.tasmanchester.com/
Ulster Aviation Society	www.ulsteraviationsociety.org/
Wolverhampton Aviation Group	www.wolverhamptonaviationgroup.co.uk/

OPERATORS OF HISTORIC AIRCRAFT

The Aircraft Restoration Company	www.arc-duxford.co.uk/
Battle of Britain Memorial Flight	www.raf.mod.uk/bbmf/
The Catalina Society	www.catalina.org.uk/
Hangar 11 Collection	www.hangar11.co.uk/
Horizon Aircraft Services	www.horizonaircraft.co.uk/
Navy Wings	www.navywings.org.uk/
The Fighter Collection	www.fighter-collection.com/
The Real Aeroplane Company	www.realaero.com/
The Shuttleworth Collection	www.shuttleworth.org/

SITES RELATING TO SPECIFIC TYPES OF MILITARY AIRCRAFT

The 655 Maintenance & Preservation Society	www.xm655.com/
B-24 Liberator	www.b24bestweb.com/
C-130 Hercules	www.c-130hercules.net/
EE Canberra	www.bywat.co.uk/
English Electric Lightning - Vertical Reality	www.aviation-picture-hangar.co.uk/Lightning.html
The Eurofighter site	www.eurofighter.com/
The ex FRADU Canberra Site	www.fradu-canberras.co.uk/
The ex FRADU Hunter Site	www.fradu-hunters.co.uk/
F-4 Phantom II Society	www.f4phantom.com/
F-15E.info: Strike Eagle	www.f-15e.info/
F-16: The Complete Reference	www.f-16.net/
The Gripen	www.gripen.com/
Jet Provost Heaven	www.jetprovosts.com
K5083 - Home Page (Hawker Hurricane)	www.k5083.mistral.co.uk/
Lockheed SR-71 Blackbird	www.wvi.com/~lelandh/sr-71~1.htm
The MiG-21 Page	www.topedge.com/panels/aircraft/sites/kraft/mig.htm
P-3 Orion Research Group	www.p3orion.nl/
Thunder & Lightnings (Postwar British Aircraft)	www.thunder-and-lightnings.co.uk/
UK Apache Resource Centre	www.ukapache.com/

Name of Site	Web Address All prefixed 'http://'
MISCELLANEOUS	
Aerodata Software Ltd.	www.aerodata.org/
AeroResource	www.aeroresource.co.uk/
The AirNet Web Site	www.aviation-links.co.uk/
Aviation Databases	www.aviationdatabases.com/
Delta Reflex	www.deltareflex.com/forum
Demobbed - Out of Service British Military Aircraft	demobbed.org.uk/
Euro Demobbed	www.eurodemobbed.org.uk/
Fighter Control	fightercontrol.co.uk/
Freebird Aviation Database	www.freebirddb.com/
Iconic Aircraft	www.iconicaircraft.co.uk/
Joseph F. Baugher's US Military Serials Site	www.joebaugher.com/
The 'Military Aircraft Markings' Web Site	www.militaryaircraftmarkings.co.uk/
Pacific Aviation Database Organisation	www.gfiapac.com/
PlaneBaseNG	www.planebase.biz/
Thunder & Lightnings: Airfield Viewing Guides	www.thunder-and-lightnings.co.uk/spotting/
UK Airshow Review	www.airshows.co.uk/
UK Military Aircraft Serials Resource Centre	www.ukserials.com/

Merlin HC3A ZK001/AF is one of half a dozen ex Danish machines now used by the Royal Navy, distinguished by having a different nose radome.

01-2000/LN is a F-15E Strike Eagle wearing the red and white tail markings of the 494th Fighter Squadron of the 48th Fighter Wing, based at RAF Lakenheath.

Serial	Type	Operator	
Serial	Type	Operator	

Serial	Type	Operator

Serial	Type	Operator

Reg	Type	Owner or Operator

BRITISH MILITARY AIRCRAFT MARKINGS

LB314	Taylorcraft Plus D (OY-DSZ)	South Yorkshire Aircraft Museum, Doncaster

AIRCRAFT IN UK MILITARY SERVICE WITH CIVIL REGISTRATIONS

G-BYUE	Grob G.115E Tutor T1	Babcock/Cambridge UAS/East Midlands Universities AS/ University of London AS/No 115 Sqn, Wittering

HISTORIC AIRCRAFT IN OVERSEAS MARKINGS

RUSSIA (& FORMER SOVIET UNION)

10 r	Yakovlev Yak-50 (801810/G-BTZB)	*Repainted as 18 r, 2018*
18 r	Yakovlev Yak-50 (801810/G-BTZB)	Privately owned, Henstridge

USA

464005	NA P-51D Mustang (44-64005/N51CK) [E9-Z]	Privately owned, Sywell
479878	Piper L-4H Grasshopper (44-79878/G-BEUI) [MF]	Privately owned, Yarcombe, Devon

OVERSEAS MILITARY MARKINGS

BELGIUM

G-17	MDH MD.902 Explorer	FAB Federal Police (on order)

NORWAY

352	NH Industries NH.90-ASW	RNoAF 334 Skv, Haakonsvern
5206	Lockheed Martin F-35A Lightning II	RNoAF (on order)
5207	Lockheed Martin F-35A Lightning II	RNoAF (on order)
5208	Lockheed Martin F-35A Lightning II	RNoAF (on order)
5209	Lockheed Martin F-35A Lightning II	RNoAF (on order)
5210	Lockheed Martin F-35A Lightning II	RNoAF (on order)

SAUDI ARABIA

8819	BAe Hawk 65	RSAF 88 Sqn, Saudi Hawks, Tabuk

SPAIN

HT.23-13	Sikorsky SH-60F Seahawk (10013) [01-1014]	Armada 10 Esc, Rota
HT.23-14	Sikorsky SH-60F Seahawk (10014) [01-1015]	Armada 10 Esc, Rota
HT.23-15	Sikorsky SH-60F Seahawk	Armada (on order)
HT.23-16	Sikorsky SH-60F Seahawk	Armada (on order)
HT.23-17	Sikorsky SH-60F Seahawk	Armada (on order)
HT.23-18	Sikorsky SH-60F Seahawk	Armada (on order)

US-BASED USAF AIRCRAFT

65835	Lockheed AC-130J Ghostrider (16-5835)	USAF 1st SOG Det.2, Hurlburt Field, FL
65843	Lockheed C-130J-30 Hercules II (16-5843) [YJ] r	USAF 36th AS/374th AW, Yokota AB, Japan
79281	Lockheed C-130H Hercules (87-9281) *bk/y*	USAF 758th AS/911th AW AFRC, Pittsburgh ARS, PA
79283	Lockheed C-130H Hercules (87-9283) *bk/y*	USAF 758th AS/911th AW AFRC, Pittsburgh ARS, PA
79285	Lockheed C-130H Hercules (87-9285) *bk/y*	USAF 758th AS/911th AW AFRC, Pittsburgh ARS, PA